Collins
ITALIAN
DICTIONARY
POCKET EDITION

Published by Collins
An imprint of HarperCollins Publishers
Westerhill Road
Bishopbriggs
Glasgow G64 2QT

Eighth Edition 2017

10 9 8 7 6 5 4 3 2 1

© HarperCollins Publishers 1996, 1999,
2002, 2008, 2010, 2013, 2017

ISBN 978-0-00-818364-6

Collins® is a registered trademark of
HarperCollins Publishers Limited

collinsdictionary.com

Typeset by Davidson Publishing
Solutions, Glasgow

Printed in Italy by Grafica Veneta S.p.A.

If you would like to comment on any
aspect of this book, please contact us
at the given address or online.
E-mail: dictionaries@harpercollins.co.uk
facebook.com/collinsdictionary
@collinsdict

Acknowledgements

We would like to thank those authors
and publishers who kindly gave
permission for copyright material to
be used in the Collins Corpus. We
would also like to thank Times
Newspapers Ltd for providing
valuable data.

INDICE

CONTENTS

I MARCHI REGISTRATI
I termini che a nostro parere costituiscono un marchio registrato sono stati designati come tali. In ogni caso, né la presenza né l'assenza di tale designazione implicano alcuna valutazione del loro reale stato giuridico.

NOTE ON TRADEMARKS
Entered words that we have reason to believe constitute trademarks have been designated as such. However, neither the presence nor the absence of such designation should be regarded as affecting the legal status of any trademark.

EDITOR/
DIRETTORE DEL PROGETTO
Maree Airlie

CONTRIBUTORS/
COLLABORATORI
Mirella Alessio
Gabriella Bacchelli
Katya Browne
Michela Clari
Janice McNeillie

FOR THE PUBLISHER/
PER L'EDITORE
Gerry Breslin
Helen Newstead
Sheena Shanks

BASED ON THE FIRST EDITION BY/
BASATO SULLA PRIMA EDIZIONE A CURA DI
Catherine E. Love
P.L. Rossi
D.M. Chaplin
F. Villa
E. Bilucaglia

INTRODUZIONE

Vi ringraziamo di aver scelto il dizionario inglese Collins e ci auguriamo che si riveli uno strumento utile e piacevole da usare nello studio, in vacanza e sul lavoro.

In questa introduzione troverete alcuni suggerimenti per aiutarvi a trarre il massimo beneficio dal vostro nuovo dizionario, ricco non solo per il suo ampio lemmario ma anche per il gran numero di informazioni contenute in ciascuna voce.

All'inizio del dizionario troverete l'elenco delle abbreviazioni usate nel testo e una guida alla pronuncia.Troverete inoltre un utile elenco delle forme dei verbi irregolari inglesi e italiani, seguito da una sezione finale con i numeri, l'ora e la data.

COME USARE IL DIZIONARIO COLLINS
Per imparare ad usare in modo efficace il dizionario è importante comprendere la funzione delle differenziazioni tipografiche, dei simboli e delle abbreviazioni usati nel testo. Vi forniamo pertanto qui di seguito alcuni chiarimenti in merito a tali convenzioni.

I LEMMI
Sono le parole in **colore** elencate in ordine alfabetico. Il primo e l'ultimo lemma di ciascuna pagina appaiono al margine superiore.

Dove opportuno, informazioni sull'ambito d'uso o il livello di formalità di certe parole vengono fornite tra parentesi in corsivo e spesso in forma abbreviata dopo l'indicazione della categoria grammaticale (es. (*Comm*), (*col*)).

In certi casi più parole con radice comune sono raggruppate sotto lo stesso lemma. Tali parole appaiono in neretto ma in un carattere leggermente ridotto (es. **acceptance**).

Esempi d'uso del lemma sono a loro volta in neretto ma in un carattere diverso dal lemma (es. **cold** [kəʊld] **to be ~**).

LA TRASCRIZIONE FONETICA
La trascrizione fonetica che illustra la corretta pronuncia del lemma è tra parentesi quadre e segue immediatamente il lemma (es. **knee** [niː]). L'elenco dei simboli fonetici è alle pagine xiii–xiv.

LE TRADUZIONI

Le traduzioni sono in carattere tondo e, quando il lemma ha più di un significato, le traduzioni sono separate da un punto e virgola. Spesso diverse traduzioni di un lemma sono introdotte da una o più parole in corsivo tra parentesi tonde: la loro funzione è di chiarire a quale significato del lemma si riferisce la traduzione. Possono essere sinonimi, indicazioni di ambito d'uso o di registro del lemma (es. **party** *(Pol)*, *(team)*, *(celebration)*; **laid-back** *(col)* ecc.).

LE 'PAROLE CHIAVE'

Un trattamento particolare è stato riservato a quelle parole che, per frequenza d'uso o complessità, necessitano una strutturazione più chiara ed esauriente (es. **da, di, avere** in italiano, **at, to, be, this** in inglese). Frecce e numeri vi guidano attraverso le varie distinzioni grammaticali e di significato; ulteriori informazioni sono fornite in corsivo tra parentesi.

INFORMAZIONI GRAMMATICALI

Le parti del discorso (noun, adjective ecc.) sono espresse da abbreviazioni convenzionali in corsivo *(n, adj* ecc.) e seguono la trascrizione fonetica del lemma.

Eventuali ulteriori informazioni grammaticali, come ad esempio le forme di un verbo irregolare o il plurale irregolare di un sostantivo, precedono tra parentesi la parte del discorso (es. **give** *(pt* **gave**, *pp* **given**) *vt*; **man** [...] *(pl* **men**) *n*).

INTRODUCTION

We are delighted that you have decided to buy this Collins Italian dictionary and hope you will enjoy and benefit from using it at school, at home, on holiday or at work.

This introduction gives you a few tips on how to get the most out of your dictionary – not simply from its comprehensive wordlist but also from the information provided in each entry. This will help you to read and understand modern Italian, as well as communicate and express yourself in the language.

The dictionary begins by listing the abbreviations used in the text and illustrating the sounds shown by the phonetic symbols. You will also find Italian and English verb tables, followed by a section on numbers and time expressions.

USING YOUR COLLINS DICTIONARY

A wealth of information is presented in the dictionary, using various typefaces, sizes of type, symbols, abbreviations and brackets. The various conventions and symbols used are explained in the following sections.

HEADWORDS

The words you look up in a dictionary – 'headwords' – are listed alphabetically. They are printed in **colour** for rapid identification. The two headwords appearing at the top of each page indicate the first and last word dealt with on the page in question.

Information about the usage or form of certain headwords is given in brackets after the part of speech. This usually appears in abbreviated form and in italics (e.g.*(fam)*, *(Comm)*).

Where appropriate, words related to headwords are grouped in the same entry (e.g. **illustrare, illustrazione**) in a slightly smaller bold type than the headword.

Common expressions in which the headword appears are shown in a different bold roman type (e.g. **freddo, -a aver ~**).

PHONETIC SPELLINGS

Where the phonetic spelling of headwords (indicating their pronunciation) is given, it will appear in square brackets immediately after the headword (e.g. **calza** ['kaltsa]). A list of these symbols is given on pages xiii–xiv.

TRANSLATIONS

Headword translations are given in ordinary type and, where more than one meaning or usage exists, these are separated by a semicolon. You will often find other words in italics in brackets before the translations. These offer suggested contexts in which the headword might appear (e.g. **duro** (*pietra*) or (*lavoro*)) or provide synonyms (e.g. **duro** (*ostinato*)).

KEYWORDS

Special status is given to certain Italian and English words which are considered as 'key' words in each language. They may, for example, occur very frequently or have several types of usage (e.g. **da**, **di**, **avere** in Italian, **at**, **to**, **be**, **this** in English). A combination of arrows and numbers helps you to distinguish different parts of speech and different meanings. Further helpful information is provided in brackets and italics.

GRAMMATICAL INFORMATION

Parts of speech are given in abbreviated form in italics after the phonetic spellings of headwords (e.g. *vt*, *av*, *cong*).

Genders of Italian nouns are indicated as follows: *sm* for a masculine and *sf* for a feminine noun. Feminine and irregular plural forms of nouns are also shown (e.g. **uovo**, (*pl f* **uova**); **dottore**, **-essa**).

Feminine adjective endings are given, as are plural forms (e.g. **opaco**, **-a**, **-chi**, **-che**).

ABBREVIAZIONI   ABBREVIATIONS

abbreviazione	*abbr*	abbreviation
aggettivo	*adj*	adjective
amministrazione	*Admin*	administration
avverbio	*adv*	adverb
aeronautica, viaggi aerei	*Aer*	flying, air travel
aggettivo	*ag*	adjective
agricoltura	*Agr*	agriculture
amministrazione	*Amm*	administration
anatomia	*Anat*	anatomy
architettura	*Archit*	architecture
articolo determinativo	*art def*	definite article
articolo indeterminativo	*art indef*	indefinite article
attributivo	*attrib*	attributive
ausiliare	*aus, aux*	auxiliary
Australia	*Aust*	Australia
automobile	*Aut*	motor car and motoring
avverbio	*av*	adverb
aeronautica, viaggi aerei	*Aviat*	flying, air travel
biologia	*Biol*	biology
botanica	*Bot*	botany
inglese britannico	*BRIT*	British English
consonante	C	consonant
chimica	*Chim, Chem*	chemistry
familiare (! da evitare)	*col(!)*	colloquial usage (! particularly offensive)
commercio, finanza	*Comm*	commerce, finance
comparativo	*compar*	comparative
informatica	*Comput*	computing
congiunzione	*cong, conj*	conjunction
edilizia	*Constr*	building
sostantivo usato come aggettivo, ma mai con funzione predicativa	*cpd*	compound element: noun used as adjective and which cannot follow the noun it qualifies

cucina	*Cuc, Culin*	cookery
davanti a	*dav*	before
articolo determinativo	*def art*	definite article
determinativo; articolo, aggettivo dimostrativo o indefinito	*det*	determiner; article, demonstrative
diminutivo	*dimin*	diminutive
diritto	*Dir*	law
economia	*Econ*	economics
edilizia	*Edil*	building
elettricità, elettronica	*Elettr, Elec*	electricity, electronics
esclamazione	*escl, excl*	exclamation
femminile	*f*	feminine
familiare (! da evitare)	*fam(!)*	colloquial usage (! particularly offensive)
ferrovia	*Ferr*	railways
senso figurato	*fig*	figurative use
fisiologia	*Fisiol*	physiology
fotografia	*Fot*	photography
verbo inglese la cui particella è inseparabile dal verbo	*fus*	(phrasal verb) where the particle cannot be separated from the main verb
nella maggior parte dei sensi; generalmente	*gen*	in most or all senses; generally
geografia, geologia	*Geo*	geography, geology
geometria	*Geom*	geometry
storia, storico	*Hist*	history, historical
impersonale	*impers*	impersonal
articolo indeterminativo	*indef art*	indefinite article
infinito	*infin*	infinitive
informatica	*Inform*	computing
insegnamento, sistema scolastico e universitario	*Ins*	schooling, schools and universities

invariabile	*inv*	invariable
irregolare	*irreg*	irregular
grammatica, linguistica	*Ling*	grammar, linguistics
maschile	*m*	masculine
matematica	*Mat(h)*	mathematics
termine medico, medicina	*Med*	medical term, medicine
il tempo, meteorologia	*Meteor*	the weather, meteorology
maschile o femminile	*m/f*	masculine or feminine
esercito, linguaggio militare	*Mil*	military matters
musica	*Mus*	music
sostantivo	*n*	noun
nautica	*Naut*	sailing, navigation
numerale (aggettivo, sostantivo)	*num*	numeral adjective or noun
Nuova Zelanda	*NZ*	New Zealand
	o.s.	oneself
peggiorativo	*peg, pej*	derogatory, pejorative
fotografia	*Phot*	photography
fisiologia	*Physiol*	physiology
plurale	*pl*	plural
politica	*Pol*	politics
participio passato	*pp*	past participle
preposizione	*prep*	preposition
pronome	*pron*	pronoun
psicologia, psichiatria	*Psic, Psych*	psychology, psychiatry
tempo passato	*pt*	past tense
qualcosa	*qc*	
qualcuno	*qn*	
religione, liturgia	*Rel*	religions, church service
sostantivo	*s*	noun
	sb	somebody

ABBREVIAZIONI / ABBREVIATIONS

insegnamento, sistema scolastico e universitario	Scol	schooling, schools and universities
singolare	sg	singular
soggetto (grammaticale)	sog	(grammatical) subject
	sth	something
congiuntivo	sub	subjunctive
soggetto (grammaticale)	subj	(grammatical) subject
superlativo	superl	superlative
termine tecnico, technology	Tecn, Tech	technical term, tecnologia
telecomunicazioni	Tel	telecommunications
tipografia	Tip	typography, printing
televisione	TV	television
tipografia	Typ	typography, printing
università	Univ	university
inglese americano	US	American English
vocale	V	vowel
verbo	vb	verb
verbo o gruppo verbale con funzione intransitiva	vi	verb or phrasal verb used intransitively
verbo pronominale o riflessivo	vpr	pronominal or reflexive verb
verbo o gruppo verbale con funzione transitiva	vt	verb or phrasal verb used transitively
zoologia	Zool	zoology
marchio registrato	®	registered trademark
introduce un'equivalenza culturale	≈	introduces a cultural equivalent

TRASCRIZIONE FONETICA

CONSONANTI		CONSONANTS
p, b, t, d, k, g sono seguite da un'aspirazione in inglese.		p, b, t, d, k, g are not aspirated in Italian.
padre	p	puppy
bambino	b	baby
tutto	t	tent
dado	d	daddy
cane che	k	cork kiss chord
gola ghiro	g	gag guess
sano	s	so rice kiss
svago esame	z	cousin buzz
scena	ʃ	sheep sugar
	ʒ	pleasure beige
pece lanciare	tʃ	church
giro gioco	dʒ	judge general
afa faro	f	farm raffle
vero bravo	v	very rev
	θ	thin maths
	ð	that other
letto ala	l	little ball
gli	ʎ	million
rete arco	r	rat rare
ramo madre	m	mummy comb
no fumante	n	no ran
gnomo	ɲ	canyon
	ŋ	singing bank
	h	hat reheat
buio piacere	j	yet
uomo guaio	w	wall bewail
	x	loch

VARI		MISCELLANEOUS
per l'inglese: la 'r' finale viene pronunciata se seguita da una vocale	r	
precede la sillaba accentata	ˈ	precedes the stressed syllable

PHONETIC TRANSCRIPTION

VOCALI	VOWELS
La messa in equivalenza di certi suoni indica solo una rassomiglianza approssimativa.	The pairing of some vowel sounds only indicates approximate equivalence.

vino idea	i iː	heel bead
	ɪ	hit pity
stella edera	e	
epoca eccetto	ɛ	set tent
mamma amore	a æ	bat apple
	ɑː	after car calm
	ã	fiancé
	ʌ	fun cousin
müsli	y	
	ə	over above
	əː	urn fern work
rosa occhio	ɔ	wash pot
	ɔː	born cork
ponte ognuno	o	
föhn	ø	
utile zucca	u	full soot
	uː	boon lewd

DITTONGHI		DIPHTHONGS
	ɪə	beer tier
	ɛə	tear fair there
	eɪ	date plaice day
	aɪ	life buy cry
	au	owl foul now
	əu	low no
	ɔɪ	boil boy oily
	uə	poor tour

ITALIAN PRONUNCIATION

VOWELS

Where the vowel **e** or the vowel **o** appears in a stressed syllable it can be either open [ɛ],[ɔ] or closed [e],[o]. As the open or closed pronunciation of these vowels is subject to regional variation, the distinction is of little importance to the user of this dictionary. Phonetic transcription for headwords containing these vowels will therefore only appear where other pronunciation difficulties are present.

CONSONANTS

c before 'e' or 'i' is pronounced like the '*tch*' in match.

ch is pronounced like the '*k*' in 'kit'.

g before 'e' or 'i' is pronounced like the '*j*' in 'jet'.

gh is pronounced like the '*g*' in 'get'.

gl before 'e' or 'i' is normally pronounced like the '*lli*' in 'million', and in a few cases only like the '*gl*' in 'glove'.

gn is pronounced like the '*ny*' in 'canyon'

sc before 'e' or 'i' is pronounced '*sh*'.

z is pronounced like the '*ts*' in 'stetson', or like the '*d's*' in 'bird's-eye'.

Headwords containing the above consonants and consonantal groups have been given full phonetic transcription in this dictionary.

NB All double written consonants in Italian are fully sounded: e.g. the *tt* in 'tutto' is pronounced as in 'hat trick'.

ITALIAN VERB FORMS

a Gerund **b** Past participle **c** Present **d** Imperfect **e** Past historic **f** Future
g Conditional **h** Present subjunctive **i** Imperfect subjunctive **j** Imperative

1 **abbattere e** abbattei, abbattesti
   (*doesn't have alternative forms* -etti,
   -ette, -ettero)
2 **accendere b** acceso **e** accesi,
   accendesti
3 **accludere b** accluso **e** acclusi,
   accludesti
4 **accorgersi b** accorto **e** mi
   accorsi, ti accorgesti
5 **aggiungere b** aggiunto
   e aggiunsi, aggiungesti
6 **andare c** vado, vai, va, andiamo,
   andate, vanno **f** andrò *etc.*
   h vada **j** va'!, vada!, andate!,
   vadano!
7 **apparire b** apparso **c** appaio,
   appari *or* apparisci, appare *or*
   apparisce, appaiono *or*
   appariscono **e** apparvi *or*
   apparsi, apparisti, apparve *or*
   appari *or* apparse, apparvero *or*
   apparirono *or* apparsero
   h appaia *or* apparisca
8 **appendere b** appeso **e** appesi,
   appendesti
9 **aprire b** aperto **c** apro **e** aprii,
   apristi **h** apra
10 **ardere b** arso **e** arsi, ardesti
11 **assistere b** assistito **e** assistei *or*
   assistetti, assistesti
12 **assumere b** assunto **e** assunsi,
   assumesti
13 **AVERE c** ho, hai, ha, abbiamo,
   avete, hanno **e** ebbi, avesti,
   ebbe, avemmo, aveste, ebbero
   f avrò *etc.* **h** abbia *etc.* **j** abbi!,
   abbia!, abbiate!, abbiano!
14 **baciare** *when the ending begins*
   with -e, *the* i *is dropped* → bacerò
   (*not* bacierò)

15 **bagnare c** bagniamo, bagniate
   h bagniamo, bagniate (*not*
   bagnamo, bagnate)
16 **bere a** bevendo **b** bevuto **c** bevo
   etc. **d** bevevo *etc.* **e** bevvi *or*
   bevetti, bevesti **f** berrò *etc.*
   h beva *etc.* **i** bevessi *etc.*
17 **bollire c** bollo *or* bollisco, bolli *or*
   bollisci *etc.*
18 **cadere e** caddi, cadesti **f** cadrò
   etc.
19 **cambiare** *drops the* i *of the root if*
   the ending starts with i (cambi,
   cambino *not* cambii, cambiino
   (*cf.* inviare)
20 **caricare** *when* c *in the root is*
   followed by -i *or* -e *an* h *should be*
   inserted (*i.e.* carichi, carichiamo,
   caricherò)
21 **chiedere b** chiesto **e** chiesi,
   chiedesti
22 **chiudere b** chiuso **e** chiusi,
   chiudesti
23 **cogliere b** colto **c** colgo,
   colgono **e** colsi, cogliesti **h** colga
24 **compiere b** compiuto **e** compii,
   compisti
25 **confondere b** confuso
   e confusi, confondesti
26 **conoscere b** conosciuto
   e conobbi, conoscesti
27 **consigliare** *when the ending*
   begins with -i, *the* i *of the root is*
   dropped → consigli (*not* consiglii)
28 **correre b** corso **e** corsi, corresti
29 **CREDERE a** credendo **b** creduto
   c credo, credi, crede, crediamo,
   credete, credono **d** credevo,
   credevi, credeva, credevamo,
   credevate, credevano **e** credei *or*

credetti, credesti, credé *or* credette, credemmo, credeste, crederono *or* credettero **f** crederò, crederai, crederà, crederemo, crederete, crederanno **g** crederei, crederesti, crederebbe, crederemmo, credereste, crederebbero **h** creda, creda, creda, crediamo, crediate, credano **i** credessi, credessi, credesse, credessimo, credeste, credessero **j** credi!, creda!, credete!, credano!

30 **crescere c** cresciuto **e** crebbi, crescesti

31 **cucire** *when c or g in the root is followed by -o or -a an i should be inserted* (i.e. cucio, cucia)

32 **cuocere b** cotto **c** cuocio, cuociamo, cuociono **e** cossi, cocesti

33 **dare b** do, dai, dà, diamo, date, danno **e** diedi *or* detti, desti **f** darò *etc.* **h** dia *etc.* **i** dessi *etc.* **j** da'!, dai!, date!, diano!

34 **decidere b** deciso **e** decisi, decidesti

35 **deludere b** deluso **e** delusi, deludesti

36 **difendere b** difeso **e** difesi, difendesti

37 **dipingere b** dipinto **e** dipinsi, dipingesti

38 **dire a** dicendo **b** detto **c** dico, dici, dice, diciamo, dite, dicono **d** dicevo *etc.* **e** dissi, dicesti **f** dirò *etc.* **h** dica, diciamo, diciate, dicano **i** dicessi *etc.* **j** di'!, dica!, dite!, dicano!

39 **dirigere b** diretto **e** diressi, dirigesti

40 **discutere b** discusso **e** discussi, discutesti

41 **disfare** *like* fare *but* **c** disfo, disfi

etc. **f** disferò, disferai *etc.* **i** disfi, disfi *etc.* (*regular forms*)

42 **distinguere b** distinto **e** distinsi, distinguesti

43 **dividere b** diviso **e** divisi, dividesti

44 **dolere c** dolgo, duoli, duole, dolgono **e** dolsi, dolesti **f** dorrò *etc.* **h** dolga

45 **DORMIRE a** dormendo **b** dormito **c** dormo, dormi, dorme, dormiamo, dormite, dormono **d** dormivo, dormivi, dormiva, dormivamo, dormivate, dormivano **e** dormii, dormisti, dormì, dormimmo, dormiste, dormirono **f** dormirò, dormirai, dormirà, dormiremo, dormirete, dormiranno **g** dormirei, dormiresti, dormirebbe, dormiremmo, dormireste, dormirebbero **h** dorma, dorma, dorma, dormiamo, dormiate, dormano **i** dormissi, dormissi, dormisse, dormissimo, dormiste, dormissero **j** dormi!, dorma!, dormite!, dormano!

46 **dovere c** devo *or* debbo, devi, deve, dobbiamo, dovete, devono *or* debbono **f** dovrò *etc.* **h** debba, dobbiamo, dobbiate, devano *or* debbano

47 **esigere b** esatto (*not common*) **e** esigei *or* esigetti, esigesti

48 **espellere b** espulso **e** espulsi, espellesti

49 **esplodere b** esploso **e** esplosi, esplodesti

50 **esprimere b** espresso **e** espressi, esprimesti

51 **ESSERE b** stato **c** sono, sei, è, siamo, siete, sono **d** ero, eri, era, eravamo, eravate, erano **e** fui, fosti, fu, fummo, foste, furono

f sarò *etc.* **h** sia *etc.* **i** fossi, fossi, fosse, fossimo, foste, fossero **j** sii!, sia!, siate!, siano!

52 evadere b evaso **e** evasi, evadesti

53 fare a facendo **b** fatto **c** faccio, fai, fa, facciamo, fate, fanno **d** facevo *etc.* **e** feci, facesti **f** farò *etc.* **h** faccia *etc.* **i** facessi *etc.* **j** fa'!, faccia!, fate!, facciano!

54 fingere b finto **e** finsi, fingesti

55 FINIRE a finendo **b** finito **c** finisco, finisci, finisce, finiamo, finite, finiscono **d** finivo, finivi, finiva, finivamo, finivate, finivano **e** finii, finisti, finì, finimmo, finiste, finirono **f** finirò, finirai, finirà, finiremo, finirete, finiranno **g** finirei, finiresti, finirebbe, finiremmo, finireste, finirebbero **h** finisca, finisca, finisca, finiamo, finiate, finiscano **i** finissi, finissi, finisse, finissimo, finiste, finissero **j** finisci!, finisca!, finite!, finiscano!

56 friggere b fritto **e** frissi, friggesti

57 giacere b giaciuto **e** giacqui, giacesti

58 godere f godrò, godrai *etc.* **g** godrei, godresti *etc.*

59 immergere b immerso **e** immersi, immergesti

60 inviare c (tu) invii **f** (essi) inviino

61 leggere b letto **e** lessi, leggesti

62 mangiare *when the ending begins with -e, the i is dropped* → mangerò (*not* mangierò)

63 mettere b messo **e** misi, mettesti

64 mordere b morso **e** morsi, mordesti

65 morire b morto **c** muoio, muori, muore, moriamo, morite, muoiono **f** morirò *or* morrò *etc.* **h** muoia

66 muovere b mosso **e** mossi, muovesti

67 nascere b nato **e** nacqui, nascesti

68 nascondere b nascosto **e** nascosi, nascondesti

69 nuocere b nuociuto **c** nuoccio, nuoci, nuoce, nociamo *or* nuociamo, nuocete, nuocciono **d** nuocevo *etc.* **e** nocqui, nuocesti **f** nuocerò *etc.* **g** nuoccia

70 offrire b offerto **c** offro **e** offersi *or* offrii, offristi **h** offra

71 parere b parso **c** paio, paiamo, paiono **e** parvi *or* parsi, paresti **f** parrò *etc.* **h** paia, paiamo, paiate, paiano

72 PARLARE a parlando **b** parlato **c** parlo, parli, parla, parliamo, parlate, parlano **d** parlavo, parlavi, parlava, parlavamo, parlavate, parlavano **e** parlai, parlasti, parlò, parlammo, parlaste, parlarono **f** parlerò, parlerai, parlerà, parleremo, parlerete, parleranno **g** parlerei, parleresti, parlerebbe, parleremmo, parlereste, parlerebbero **h** parli, parli, parli, parliamo, parliate, parlino **i** parlassi, parlassi, parlasse, parlassimo, parlaste, parlassero **j** parla!, parli!, parlate!, parlino!

73 perdere b perso *or* perduto **e** persi, perdesti

74 piacere b piaciuto **c** piaccio, piacciamo, piacciono **e** piacqui, piacesti **h** piaccia *etc.*

75 piangere b pianto **e** piansi, piangesti

76 piovere b piovuto **e** piovve

77 porre a ponendo **b** posto **c** pongo, poni, pone, poniamo, ponete, pongono **d** ponevo *etc.* **e** posi, ponesti **f** porrò *etc.*

h ponga, poniamo, poniate, pongano **i** ponessi *etc.*

78 **potere c** posso, puoi, può, possiamo, potete, possono **f** potrò *etc.* **h** possa, possiamo, possiate, possano

79 **prefiggersi b** prefisso **e** mi prefissi, ti prefiggesti

80 **pregare** *when* g *in the root is followed by* -i *or* -e *an* h *should be inserted* (*i.e.* preghi, preghiamo, pregherò)

81 **prendere b** preso **e** presi, prendesti

82 **prevedere** *like* vedere *but* **f** prevederò, prevederai *etc.* **g** prevederei *etc.*

83 **proteggere b** protetto **e** protessi, proteggesti

84 **pungere b** punto **e** punsi, pungesti

85 **radere b** raso **e** rasi, radesti

86 **redimere b** redento **e** redensi, redimesti

87 **reggere b** retto **e** ressi, reggesti

88 **rendere b** reso **e** resi, rendesti

89 **ridere b** riso **e** risi, ridesti

90 **ridurre a** riducendo **b** ridotto **c** riduco *etc.* **d** riducevo *etc.* **e** ridussi, riducesti **f** ridurrò *etc.* **h** riduca *etc.* **i** riducessi *etc.*

91 **riempire a** riempiendo **c** riempio, riempi, riempie, riempiono

92 **riflettere b** riflettuto *or* riflesso

93 **rimanere b** rimasto **c** rimango, rimangono **e** rimasi, rimanesti **f** rimarrò *etc.* **h** rimanga

94 **risolvere b** risolto **e** risolsi, risolvesti

95 **rispondere b** risposto **e** risposi, rispondesti

96 **rivolgere b** rivolto **e** rivolsi, rivolgesti

97 **rompere b** rotto **e** ruppi, rompesti

98 **salire c** salgo, sali, salgono **h** salga

99 **sapere c** so, sai, sa, sappiamo, sapete, sanno **e** seppi, sapesti **f** saprò *etc.* **h** sappia *etc.* **j** sappi!, sappia!, sappiate!, sappiano!

100 **scegliere b** scelto **c** scelgo, scegli, sceglie, scegliamo, scegliete, scelgono **e** scelsi, scegliesti **h** scelga, scegliamo, scegliate, scelgano **j** scegli!, scelga!, scegliamo!, scegliete!, scelgano!

101 **scendere b** sceso **e** scesi, scendesti

102 **scindere b** scisso **e** scissi, scindesti

103 **sciogliere b** sciolto **c** sciolgo, sciogli, scioglie, sciogliamo, sciogliete, sciolgono **e** sciolsi, sciogliesti **h** sciolga, sciogliamo, sciogliate, sciolgano **j** sciogli!, sciolga!, sciogliamo!, sciogliete!, sciolgano!

104 **sconfiggere b** sconfitto **e** sconfissi, sconfiggesti

105 **scrivere b** scritto **e** scrissi, scrivesti

106 **scuotere b** scosso **e** scossi, scuotesti

107 **sedere c** siedo, siedi, siede, siedono **h** sieda

108 **solere b** solito **e** soglio, suoli, suole, sogliamo, solete, sogliono **h** soglia (*regular imperfect, gerund, past participle; no other verb forms*)

109 **sorgere b** sorto **e** sorse, sorsero

110 **spandere b** spanto **e** spansi, spandesti

111 **spargere b** sorto **e** sorse, sorsero

112 **sparire e** sparii, sparisti

113 spegnere b spento c spengo, spengono e spensi, spegnesti h spenga

114 spingere b spinto e spinsi, spingesti

115 sporgere b sporto e sporsi, sporgesti

116 stare b stato c sto, stai, sta, stiamo, state, stanno e stetti, stesti f starò *etc.* h stia *etc.* i stessi *etc.* j sta'!, stia!, state!, stiano!

117 stringere b stretto e strinsi, stringesti

118 succedere b successo e successi, succedesti

119 tacere b taciuto c taccio, tacciono e tacqui, tacesti h taccia

120 tendere b teso e tesi, tendesti

121 tenere c tengo, tieni, tiene, tengono e tenni, tenesti f terrò *etc.* h tenga

122 togliere b tolto c tolgo, togli, toglie, togliamo, togliete, tolgono e tolsi, togliesti h tolga j togli!, tolga!, togliamo!, togliete!, tolgano!

123 trarre a traendo b tratto c traggo, trai, trae, traiamo, traete, traggono d traevo *etc.* e trassi, traesti f trarrò *etc.* h tragga i traessi *etc.*

124 udire c odo, odi, ode, odono h oda

125 uscire c esco, esci, esce, escono h esca

126 valere b valso c valgo, valgono e valsi, valesti f varrò *etc.* h valga

127 vedere b visto *or* veduto e vidi, vedesti f vedrò *etc.*

128 venire b venuto c vengo, vieni, viene, vengono e venni, venisti f verrò *etc.* h venga

129 vincere b vinto e vinsi, vincesti

130 vivere b vissuto e vissi, vivesti

131 volere c voglio, vuoi, vuole, vogliamo, volete, vogliono e volli, volesti f vorrò *etc.* h voglia *etc.* j *not common*

VERBI INGLESI

PRESENT	PAST TENSE	PAST PARTICIPLE	PRESENT	PAST TENSE	PAST PARTICIPLE
arise	arose	arisen	feed	fed	fed
awake	awoke	awoken	feel	felt	felt
be (am, is, are; being)	was, were	been	fight	fought	fought
			find	found	found
bear	bore	born(e)	flee	fled	fled
beat	beat	beaten	fling	flung	flung
become	became	become	fly	flew	flown
begin	began	begun	forbid	forbade	forbidden
bend	bent	bent	forecast	forecast	forecast
bet	bet, betted	bet, betted	forget	forgot	forgotten
			forgive	forgave	forgiven
bid (at auction, cards)	bid	bid	forsake	forsook	forsaken
bid (say)	bade	bidden	freeze	froze	frozen
bind	bound	bound	get	got	got, (US) gotten
bite	bit	bitten			
bleed	bled	bled	give	gave	given
blow	blew	blown	go (goes)	went	gone
break	broke	broken	grind	ground	ground
breed	bred	bred	grow	grew	grown
bring	brought	brought	hang	hung	hung
build	built	built	hang (execute)	hanged	hanged
burn	burnt, burned	burnt, burned	have (has; having)	had	had
burst	burst	burst	hear	heard	heard
buy	bought	bought	hide	hid	hidden
can	could	(been able)	hit	hit	hit
cast	cast	cast	hold	held	held
catch	caught	caught	hurt	hurt	hurt
choose	chose	chosen	keep	kept	kept
cling	clung	clung	kneel	knelt, kneeled	knelt, kneeled
come	came	come			
cost	cost	cost	know	knew	known
cost (work out price of)	costed	costed	lay	laid	laid
			lead	led	led
creep	crept	crept	lean	leant, leaned	leant, leaned
cut	cut	cut			
deal	dealt	dealt	leap	leapt, leaped	leapt, leaped
dig	dug	dug			
do (does)	did	done	learn	learnt, learned	learnt, learned
draw	drew	drawn			
dream	dreamed, dreamt	dreamed, dreamt	leave	left	left
			lend	lent	lent
drink	drank	drunk	let	let	let
drive	drove	driven	lie (lying)	lay	lain
dwell	dwelt	dwelt	light	lit, lighted	lit, lighted
eat	ate	eaten			
fall	fell	fallen	lose	lost	lost
			make	made	made

PRESENT	PAST TENSE	PAST PARTICIPLE	PRESENT	PAST TENSE	PAST PARTICIPLE
may	might	—	spell	spelt, spelled	spelt, spelled
mean	meant	meant			
meet	met	met	spend	spent	spent
mistake	mistook	mistaken	spill	spilt, spilled	spilt, spilled
mow	mowed	mown, mowed			
			spin	spun	spun
must	(had to)	(had to)	spit	spat	spat
pay	paid	paid	split	split	split
put	put	put	spoil	spoiled, spoilt	spoiled, spoilt
quit	quit, quitted	quit, quitted			
			spread	spread	spread
read	read	read	spring	sprang	sprung
rid	rid	rid	stand	stood	stood
ride	rode	ridden	steal	stole	stolen
ring	rang	rung	stick	stuck	stuck
rise	rose	risen	sting	stung	stung
run	ran	run	stink	stank	stunk
saw	sawed	sawed, sawn	stride	strode	stridden
			strike	struck	struck, stricken
say	said	said			
see	saw	seen	strive	strove	striven
seek	sought	sought	swear	swore	sworn
sell	sold	sold	sweep	swept	swept
send	sent	sent	swell	swelled	swollen, swelled
sew	sewed	sewn			
shake	shook	shaken	swim	swam	swum
shear	sheared	shorn, sheared	swing	swung	swung
			take	took	taken
shed	shed	shed	teach	taught	taught
shine	shone	shone	tear	tore	torn
shoot	shot	shot	tell	told	told
show	showed	shown	think	thought	thought
shrink	shrank	shrunk	throw	threw	thrown
shut	shut	shut	thrust	thrust	thrust
sing	sang	sung	tread	trod	trodden
sink	sank	sunk	wake	woke, waked	woken, waked
sit	sat	sat			
slay	slew	slain	wear	wore	worn
sleep	slept	slept	weave	wove, weaved	woven, weaved
slide	slid	slid			
sling	slung	slung	wed	wedded, wed	wedded, wed
slit	slit	slit			
smell	smelt, smelled	smelt, smelled	weep	wept	wept
			win	won	won
sow	sowed	sown, sowed	wind	wound	wound
			wring	wrung	wrung
speak	spoke	spoken	write	wrote	written
speed	sped, speeded	sped, speeded			

I NUMERI		NUMBERS
uno(a)	1	one
due	2	two
tre	3	three
quattro	4	four
cinque	5	five
sei	6	six
sette	7	seven
otto	8	eight
nove	9	nine
dieci	10	ten
undici	11	eleven
dodici	12	twelve
tredici	13	thirteen
quattordici	14	fourteen
quindici	15	fifteen
sedici	16	sixteen
diciassette	17	seventeen
diciotto	18	eighteen
diciannove	19	nineteen
venti	20	twenty
ventuno	21	twenty-one
ventidue	22	twenty-two
ventitré	23	twenty-three
ventotto	28	twenty-eight
trenta	30	thirty
quaranta	40	forty
cinquanta	50	fifty
sessanta	60	sixty
settanta	70	seventy
ottanta	80	eighty
novanta	90	ninety
cento	100	a hundred
cento uno, centouno	101	a hundred and one
duecento	200	two hundred
mille	1 000	a thousand
milleduecentodue	1 202	one thousand two hundred and two
cinquemila	5000	five thousand
un milione	1 000 000	a million

I NUMERI	NUMBERS
primo(a)	first, 1st
secondo(a)	second, 2nd
terzo(a)	third, 3rd
quarto(a)	fourth, 4th
quinto(a)	fifth, 5th
sesto(a)	sixth, 6th
settimo(a)	seventh
ottavo(a)	eighth
nono(a)	ninth
decimo(a)	tenth
undicesimo(a)	eleventh
dodicesimo(a)	twelfth
tredicesimo(a)	thirteenth
quattordicesimo(a)	fourteenth
quindicesimo(a)	fifteenth
sedicesimo(a)	sixteenth
diciassettesimo(a)	seventeenth
diciottesimo(a)	eighteenth
diciannovesimo(a)	nineteenth
ventesimo(a)	twentieth
ventunesimo(a)	twenty-first
ventiduesimo(a)	twenty-second
ventitreesimo(a)	twenty-third
ventottesimo(a)	twenty-eighth
trentesimo(a)	thirtieth
centesimo(a)	hundredth
centunesimo(a)	hundred-and-first
millesimo(a)	thousandth
milionesimo(a)	millionth

ESEMPI	EXAMPLES
abita al numero dieci	he lives at number 10
si trova nel capitolo sette, a pagina sette	it's in chapter 7, on page 7
abita al terzo piano	he lives on the 3rd floor
arrivò quarto	he came in 4th
scala uno a venticinquemila	scale 1:25,000

L'ORA

che ora è?, che ore sono?

è ..., sono ...

mezzanotte
l'una (di notte)

le tre del mattino

l'una e cinque
l'una e dieci
l'una e un quarto, l'una e quindici

l'una e venticinque

l'una e mezzo *or* mezza, l'una e
  trenta
le due meno venticinque, l'una
  e trentacinque
le due meno venti, l'una e
  quaranta
le due meno un quarto, l'una e
  tre quarti
le due meno dieci, l'una e cinquanta
le dodici, mezzogiorno

l'una, le tredici

le sette (di sera), le diciannove

a che ora?

a mezzanotte
all'una, alle tredici
fra venti minuti
venti minuti fa

THE TIME

what time is it?

it's ...

midnight
one o'clock (in the
  morning), one (a.m.)
three o'clock (in the
  morning), three (a.m.)
five past one
ten past one
a quarter past one,
  one fifteen
twenty-five past one,
  one twenty-five
half past one, one thirty

twenty-five to two,
  one thirty-five
twenty to two, one forty

a quarter to two, one
  forty-five
ten to two, one fifty
twelve o'clock, midday,
  noon
one o'clock (in the
  afternoon), one (p.m.)
seven o'clock (in the
  evening), seven (p.m.)

at what time?

at midnight
at one o'clock
in twenty minutes
twenty minutes ago

LA DATA

oggi
ogni giorno, tutti i giorni
ieri
stamattina
domani notte; domani sera
l'altroieri notte; l'altroieri sera
l'altroieri
ieri notte; ieri sera
due giorni/sei anni fa
domani pomeriggio
dopodomani
tutti i giovedì, di *or* il giovedì

ci va di *or* il venerdì
'chiuso il mercoledì'
dal lunedì al venerdì
per giovedì, entro giovedì
un sabato di marzo
tra una settimana
martedì a otto
questa/la prossima/la scorsa
   settimana
tra due settimane, tra quindici
   giorni
lunedì a quindici
il primo/l'ultimo venerdì del mese

il mese prossimo
l'anno scorso
il primo giugno
il 18 agosto

nel 2016
quanti ne abbiamo oggi?

oggi è il 15

2016 – duemilasedici

DATES

today
every day
yesterday
this morning
tomorrow night
the night before last
the day before yesterday
last night
two days/six years ago
tomorrow afternoon
the day after tomorrow
every Thursday, on
   Thursdays
he goes on Fridays
'closed on Wednesdays'
from Monday to Friday
by Thursday
one Saturday in March
in a week's time
a week next *or* on Tuesday
this/next/last week

in two weeks *or* a fortnight

two weeks on Monday
the first/last Friday of the
   month
next month
last year
the 1st of June, June first
on 18th August (*BRIT*) *or*
   August 18 (*US*)
in 2016
what's the date? *or* what
   date is it today?
today's date is the 15th *or*
   today is the 15th
2016 – two thousand and
   sixteen

a

A *abbr* (= *autostrada*) ≈ M (*BRIT*)

a (*a* + *il* = **al**, *a* + *lo* = **allo**, *a* + *l'* = **all'**, *a* + *la* = **alla**, *a* + *i* = **ai**, *a* + *gli* = **agli**, *a* + *le* = **alle**) *prep* **1** (*stato in luogo*) at; (: *in*) in; **essere alla stazione** to be at the station; **essere a casa/a scuola/a Roma** to be at home/at school/in Rome; **è a 10 km da qui** it's 10 km from here, it's 10 km away
2 (*moto a luogo*) to; **andare a casa/a scuola/alla stazione** to go home/to school/to the station
3 (*tempo*) at; (*epoca, stagione*) in; **alle cinque** at five (o'clock); **a mezzanotte/Natale** at midnight/Christmas; **al mattino** in the morning; **a maggio/primavera** in May/spring; **a cinquant'anni** at fifty (years of age); **a domani!** see you tomorrow!

4 (*complemento di termine*) to; **dare qc a qn** to give sb sth
5 (*mezzo, modo*) with, by; **a piedi/cavallo** on foot/horseback; **fatto a mano** made by hand, handmade; **una barca a motore** a motorboat; **a uno a uno** one by one; **all'italiana** the Italian way, in the Italian fashion
6 (*rapporto*) a, per; (: *con prezzi*) at; **prendo 2000 euro al mese** I get 2000 euro a *o* per month; **pagato a ore** paid by the hour; **vendere qc a 2 euro il chilo** to sell sth at 2 euros a *o* per kilo

abbagli'ante [abbaʎ'ʎante] *ag* dazzling; **abbaglianti** *smpl* (*Aut*): **accendere gli abbaglianti** to put one's headlights on full (*BRIT*) *o* high (*US*) beam
abbagli'are [abbaʎ'ʎare] /27/ *vt* to dazzle; (*illudere*) to delude
abbai'are /19/ *vi* to bark
abbando'nare /72/ *vt* to leave, abandon, desert; (*trascurare*) to neglect; (*rinunciare a*) to abandon, give up; **abbandonarsi** *vpr* to let o.s. go; **abbandonarsi a** (*ricordi, vizio*) to give o.s. up to
abbas'sare /72/ *vt* to lower; (*radio*) to turn down; **abbassarsi** *vpr* (*chinarsi*) to stoop; (*livello, sole*) to go down; (*fig: umiliarsi*) to demean o.s.; **~ i fari** (*Aut*) to dip (*BRIT*) *o* dim (*US*) one's lights
ab'basso *escl*: **~ il re!** down with the king!
abbas'tanza [abbas'tantsa] *av* (*a sufficienza*) enough; (*alquanto*) quite, rather, fairly; **non è ~ furbo** he's not shrewd enough; **un vino ~ dolce** quite a sweet wine; **averne ~ di qn/qc** to have had enough of sb/sth
ab'battere /1/ *vt* (*muro, casa, ostacolo*) to knock down; (*albero*) to fell; (: *vento*) to bring down; (*bestie da macello*) to slaughter; (*cane, cavallo*) to destroy, put down; (*selvaggina, aereo*) to shoot down; (*fig: malattia,

disgrazia) to lay low; **abbattersi** vpr (avvilirsi) to lose heart; **abbat'tuto, -a** ag (fig) depressed

abba'zia [abbat'tsia] sf abbey

'abbia vb vedi **avere**

abbi'ente ag well-to-do, well-off; **abbienti** smpl: **gli abbienti** the well-to-do

abbiglia'mento [abbiλλa'mento] sm dress no pl; (indumenti) clothes pl; (industria) clothing industry

abbi'nare /72/ vt: ~ **(con** o **a)** to combine (with)

abboc'care /20/ vi (pesce) to bite; (tubi) to join; ~ **(all'amo)** (fig) to swallow the bait

abbona'mento sm subscription; (alle ferrovie ecc) season ticket; **fare l'~ (a)** to take out a subscription (to)

abbo'nare /72/ vt to deduct; **abbonarsi** vpr: **abbonarsi a un giornale** to take out a subscription to a newspaper; **abbonarsi al teatro/ alle ferrovie** to take out a season ticket for the theatre/the train

abbon'dante ag abundant, plentiful; (giacca) roomy

abbon'danza [abbon'dantsa] sf abundance; plenty

abbor'dabile ag (persona) approachable; (prezzo) reasonable

abbotto'nare /72/ vt to button up, do up

abbracci'are [abbrat'tʃare] /14/ vt to embrace; (persona) to hug, embrace; (professione) to take up; (contenere) to include; **abbracciarsi** vpr to hug o embrace (one another); **ab'braccio** sm hug, embrace

abbrevi'are /19/ vt to shorten; (parola) to abbreviate

abbreviazi'one [abbrevjat'tsjone] sf abbreviation

abbron'zante [abbron'dzante] ag tanning, sun cpd

abbron'zare [abbron'dzare] /72/ vt to tan; **abbronzarsi** vpr to tan, get a tan

abbron'zato, -a [abbron'dzato] ag (sun)tanned

abbrusto'lire /55/ vt (pane) to toast; (caffè) to roast; **abbrustolirsi** vpr to toast; (fig, al sole) to soak up the sun

abbuf'farsi /72/ vpr (fam): ~ **(di qc)** to stuff o.s. (with sth)

abdi'care /20/ vi to abdicate; ~ **a** to give up, renounce

a'bete sm fir (tree); ~ **rosso** spruce

'abile ag (idoneo): ~ **(a qc/a fare qc)** fit (for sth/to do sth); (capace) able; (astuto) clever; (accorto) skilful; ~ **al servizio militare** fit for military service; **abilità** sf inv ability; cleverness; skill

a'bisso sm abyss, gulf

abi'tante smf inhabitant

abi'tare /72/ vt to live in, dwell in ▷ vi: ~ **in campagna/a Roma** to live in the country/in Rome; **dove abita?** where do you live?; **abitazi'one** sf residence; house

'abito sm dress no pl; (da uomo) suit; (da donna) dress; (abitudine, disposizione, Rel) habit; **abiti** smpl (vestiti) clothes; **in ~ da sera** in evening dress

abitu'ale ag usual, habitual; (cliente) regular

abitual'mente av usually, normally

abitu'are /72/ vt: ~ **qn a** to get sb used o accustomed to; **abituarsi a** to get used to, accustom o.s. to

abitudi'nario, -a ag of fixed habits ▷ sm/f creature of habit

abi'tudine sf habit; **aver l'~ di fare qc** to be in the habit of doing sth; **d'~** usually; **per ~** from o out of habit

abo'lire /55/ vt to abolish; (Dir) to repeal

abor'tire /55/ vi (Med) to miscarry, have a miscarriage; (: deliberatamente) to have an abortion; (fig) to miscarry, fail; **a'borto** sm miscarriage; abortion

ABS [abi'ɛsse] sigla m (= Anti-Blockier System) ABS = **anti-lock braking system**

'abside *sf* apse

abu'sare /72/ *vi*: **~ di** to abuse, misuse; (*approfittare, violare*) to take advantage of; **~ dell'alcool/dei cibi** to drink/eat to excess

abu'sivo, -a *ag* unauthorized, unlawful; **(occupante) ~** (*di una casa*) squatter

Attenzione! In inglese esiste la parola *abusive*, che però vuol dire *ingiurioso*.

a.C. *abbr* (= *avanti Cristo*) BC

a'cacia, -cie [a'katʃa] *sf* (*Bot*) acacia

ac'cadde *vb vedi* accadere

acca'demia *sf* (*società*) learned society; (*scuola: d'arte, militare*) academy

acca'dere /18/ *vb impers* to happen, occur

accal'dato *ag* hot

accalo'rarsi /61/ *vpr* (*fig*) to get excited

accampa'mento *sm* camp

accam'pare /72/ *vt* to encamp; **accamparsi** *vpr* to camp

acca'nirsi /55/ *vpr* (*infierire*) to rage; (*ostinarsi*) to persist; **acca'nito, -a** *ag* (*odio, gelosia*) fierce, bitter; (*lavoratore*) assiduous; (*giocatore, fumatore*) inveterate

ac'canto *av* near, nearby; **~ a** *prep* near, beside, close to

accanto'nare /72/ *vt* (*problema*) to shelve; (*somma*) to set aside

accappa'toio *sm* bathrobe

accarez'zare [akkaret'tsare] /72/ *vt* to caress, stroke, fondle; (*fig*) to toy with

acca'sarsi /27/ *vpr* to set up house; to get married

accasci'arsi [akkaʃ'ʃarsi] /14/ *vpr* to collapse; (*fig*) to lose heart

accat'tone, -a *sm/f* beggar

accaval'lare /72/ *vt* (*gambe*) to cross

acce'care [attʃe'kare] /20/ *vt* to blind ▷ *vi* to go blind

ac'cedere [at'tʃɛdere] /29/ *vi*: **~ a** to enter; (*richiesta*) to grant, accede to

accele'rare [attʃele'rare] /72/ *vt* to speed up ▷ *vi* (*Aut*) to accelerate; **~ il passo** to quicken one's pace; **accelera'tore** *sm* (*Aut*) accelerator

ac'cendere [at'tʃɛndere] /2/ *vt* (*fuoco, sigaretta*) to light; (*luce, televisione*) to put o switch o turn on; (*Aut: motore*) to switch on; (*Comm: conto*) to open; (*fig: suscitare*) to inflame, stir up; **accen'dino, accendi'sigaro** *sm* (cigarette) lighter

accen'nare [attʃen'nare] /72/ *vt* (*Mus*) to pick out the notes of; to hum ▷ *vi*: **~ a** (*fig*) (*alludere a*) to hint at; (*far atto di*) to make as if; **~ un saluto** (*con la mano*) to make as if to wave; (*col capo*) to half nod; **accenna a piovere** it looks as if it's going to rain

ac'cenno [at'tʃenno] *sm* (*cenno*) sign; nod; (*allusione*) hint

accensi'one [attʃen'sjone] *sf* (*vedi accendere*) lighting; switching on; opening; (*Aut*) ignition

ac'cento [at'tʃɛnto] *sm* accent; (*Fonetica, fig*) stress; (*inflessione*) tone (of voice)

accentu'are [attʃentu'are] /72/ *vt* to stress, emphasize; **accentuarsi** *vpr* to become more noticeable

accerchi'are [attʃer'kjare] /19/ *vt* to surround, encircle

accerta'mento [attʃerta'mento] *sm* check; assessment

accer'tare [attʃer'tare] /72/ *vt* to ascertain; (*verificare*) to check; (*reddito*) to assess; **accertarsi** *vpr*: **accertarsi (di qc/che)** to make sure (of sth/that)

ac'ceso, -a [at'tʃeso] *pp di* **accendere** ▷ *ag* lit; on; open; (*colore*) bright

acces'sibile [attʃes'sibile] *ag* (*luogo*) accessible; (*persona*) approachable; (*prezzo*) reasonable

ac'cesso [at'tʃɛsso] *sm* (*anche Inform*) access; (*Med*) attack, fit; (*impulso violento*) fit, outburst

acces'sorio, -a [attʃes'sɔrjo] *ag* secondary; **accessori** *smpl* accessories

ac'cetta [at'tʃetta] *sf* hatchet

accet'tabile [attʃet'tabile] *ag* acceptable

accet'tare [attʃet'tare] /72/ *vt* to accept; **~ di fare qc** to agree to do sth; **accettazi'one** *sf* acceptance; (*locale di servizio pubblico*) reception; **accettazione bagagli** (*Aer*) check-in (desk)

acchiap'pare [akkjap'pare] /72/ *vt* to catch

acciaie'ria [attʃaje'ria] *sf* steelworks *sg*

acci'aio [at'tʃajo] *sm* steel

acciden'tato, -a [attʃiden'tato] *ag* (*terreno ecc*) uneven

accigli'ato, -a [attʃiʎ'ʎato] *ag* frowning

ac'cingersi [at'tʃindʒersi] /54/ *vpr*: **~ a fare** to be about to do

acciuffare [attʃuf'fare] /72/ *vt* to seize, catch

acci'uga, -ghe [at'tʃuga] *sf* anchovy

ac'cludere /3/ *vt* to enclose

accocco'larsi /72/ *vpr* to crouch

accogli'ente [akkoʎ'ʎɛnte] *ag* welcoming, friendly

ac'cogliere /23/ *vt* (*ricevere*) to receive; (*dare il benvenuto*) to welcome; (*approvare*) to agree to, accept; (*contenere*) to hold, accommodate

ac'colgo *ecc vb vedi* **accogliere**

ac'colsi *ecc vb vedi* **accogliere**

accoltel'lare /72/ *vt* to knife, stab

accomoda'mento *sm* agreement, settlement

accomo'dante *ag* accommodating

accomo'dare /72/ *vt* to repair; **accomodarsi** *vpr* (*sedersi*) to sit down; (*fig: risolversi: situazione*) to work out; **si accomodi!** (*venga avanti*) come in!; (*si sieda*) take a seat!

accompagna'mento [akkompaɲɲa'mento] *sm* (*Mus*) accompaniment

accompa'gnare [akkompaɲ'ɲare] /15/ *vt* to accompany, come *o* go with; (*Mus*) to accompany; (*unire*) to couple; **~ la porta** to close the door gently

accompagna'tore, -'trice *sm/f* companion; **~ turistico** courier

acconcia'tura [akkontʃa'tura] *sf* hairstyle

accondiscen'dente [akkondiʃʃen'dɛnte] *ag* affable

acconsen'tire /17/ *vi*: **~ (a)** to agree *o* consent (to)

acconten'tare /72/ *vt* to satisfy; **accontentarsi** *vpr*: **accontentarsi di** to be satisfied with, content o.s. with

ac'conto *sm* part payment; **pagare una somma in ~** to pay a sum of money as a deposit

acco'rato, -a *ag* heartfelt

accorci'are [akkor'tʃare] /14/ *vt* to shorten; **accorciarsi** *vpr* to become shorter

accor'dare /72/ *vt* to reconcile; (*colori*) to match; (*Mus*) to tune; (*Ling*): **~ qc con qc** to make sth agree with sth; (*Dir*) to grant; **accordarsi** *vpr* to agree, come to an agreement; (*colori*) to match

ac'cordo *sm* agreement; (*armonia*) harmony; (*Mus*) chord; **essere d'~** to agree; **andare d'~** to get on well together; **d'~!** all right!, agreed!; **~ commerciale** trade agreement

ac'corgersi [ak'kɔrdʒersi] /4/ *vpr*: **~ di** to notice; (*fig*) to realize

ac'correre /28/ *vi* to run up

ac'corto, -a *pp di* **accorgersi** ▷ *ag* shrewd; **stare ~** to be on one's guard

accos'tare /72/ *vt* (*avvicinarsi a*) to approach; (*socchiudere: imposte*) to half-close; (: *porta*) to leave ajar ▷ *vi*: (*Naut*) to come alongside; **accostarsi** *vpr*: **accostarsi a** to draw near, approach; (*idee politiche*) to come to agree with; **~ qc a** (*avvicinare*) to bring sth near to, put sth near to

accredi'tare /72/ vt (notizia) to confirm the truth of; (Comm) to credit; (diplomatico) to accredit

ac'credito sm (Comm: atto) crediting; (: effetto) credit

accucci'arsi [akkut'tʃarsi] /14/ vpr (cane) to lie down

accu'dire /55/ vi: **~ a** to attend to

accumu'lare /72/ vt to accumulate; **accumularsi** vpr to accumulate; (Finanza) to accrue

accu'rato, -a ag (diligente) careful; (preciso) accurate

ac'cusa sf accusation; (Dir) charge; **la pubblica ~** the prosecution

accu'sare /72/ vt: **~ qn di qc** to accuse sb of sth; (Dir) to charge sb with sth; **~ ricevuta di** (Comm) to acknowledge receipt of

accusa'tore, -'trice sm/f accuser ▷ sm (Dir) prosecutor

a'cerbo, -a [a'tʃerbo] ag bitter; (frutta) sour, unripe; (persona) immature

'acero ['atʃero] sm maple

a'cerrimo, -a [a'tʃerrimo] ag very fierce

a'ceto [a'tʃeto] sm vinegar

ace'tone [atʃe'tone] sm nail varnish remover

'A.C.I. ['atʃi] sigla m (= Automobile Club d'Italia) ≈ AA (BRIT)

'acido, -a ['atʃido] ag (sapore) acid, sour; (Chim) acid ▷ sm (Chim) acid

'acino ['atʃino] sm berry; **~ d'uva** grape

'acne sf acne

'acqua sf water; (pioggia) rain; **acque** sfpl (di mare, fiume ecc) waters; **fare ~** (Naut) to leak, take in water; **~ in bocca!** mum's the word!; **~ corrente** running water; **~ dolce** fresh water; **~ minerale** mineral water; **~ potabile** drinking water; **~ salata** o **salmastra** salt water; **~ tonica** tonic water

a'cquaio sm sink

acqua'ragia [akkwa'radʒa] sf turpentine

a'cquario sm aquarium; **A~** Aquarius

acquas'cooter [akkwas'cuter] sm inv Jet Ski®

a'cquatico, -a, -ci, -che ag aquatic; (sport, sci) water cpd

acqua'vite sf brandy

acquaz'zone [akkwat'tsone] sm cloudburst, heavy shower

acque'dotto sm aqueduct; waterworks pl, water system

acque'rello sm watercolour

acqui'rente smf purchaser, buyer

acquis'tare /72/ vt to purchase, buy; (fig) to gain; **a'cquisto** sm purchase; **fare acquisti** to go shopping

acquo'lina sf: **far venire l'~ in bocca a qn** to make sb's mouth water

a'crobata, -i, -e sm/f acrobat

a'culeo sm (Zool) sting; (Bot) prickle

a'cume sm acumen, perspicacity

a'custico, -a, -ci, -che ag acoustic ▷ sf (scienza) acoustics sg; (di una sala) acoustics pl: **apparecchio ~** hearing aid; **cornetto ~** ear trumpet

a'cuto, -a ag (appuntito) sharp, pointed; (suono, voce) shrill, piercing; (Mat, Ling, Med) acute; (Mus) high-pitched; (fig: dolore, desiderio) intense; (: perspicace) acute, keen

a'dagio [a'dadʒo] av slowly ▷ sm (Mus) adagio; (proverbio) adage, saying

adatta'mento sm adaptation

adat'tare /72/ vt to adapt; (sistemare) to fit; **adattarsi** vpr: **adattarsi (a)** (ambiente, tempi) to adapt (to); (essere adatto) to be suitable (for)

a'datto, -a ag: **~ (a)** suitable (for), right (for)

addebi'tare /72/ vt: **~ qc a qn** to debit sb with sth

ad'debito sm (Comm) debit

adden'tare /72/ vt to bite into

adden'trarsi /72/ vpr: **~ in** to penetrate, go into

addestra'mento sm training

addes'trare /72/ vt to train

ad'detto, -a ag: ~ **a** (persona) assigned to; (oggetto) intended for ▷ sm employee; (funzionario) attaché; ~ **commerciale/stampa** commercial/press attaché; **gli addetti ai lavori** authorized personnel; (fig) those in the know

ad'dio sm, escl goodbye, farewell

addirit'tura av (veramente) really, absolutely; (perfino) even; (direttamente) directly, right away

addi'tare /72/ vt to point out; (fig) to expose

addi'tivo sm additive

addizi'one sf addition

addob'bare /72/ vt to decorate; **ad'dobbo** sm decoration

addolo'rare /72/ vt to pain, grieve; **addolorarsi** vpr: **addolorarsi (per)** to be distressed (by)

addolo'rato, -a ag distressed, upset; **l'Addolorata** (Rel) Our Lady of Sorrows

ad'dome sm abdomen

addomesti'care /20/ vt to tame

addomi'nale ag abdominal; **(muscoli) addominali** stomach muscles

addormen'tare /72/ vt to put to sleep; **addormentarsi** vpr to fall asleep, go to sleep

ad'dosso av on; ~ **a** (sopra) on; (molto vicino) right next to; **mettersi ~ il cappotto** to put one's coat on; **stare ~ a qn** (fig) to breathe down sb's neck; **dare ~ a qn** (fig) to attack sb

adegu'are /72/ vt: ~ **qc a** to adjust sth to; **adeguarsi** vpr to adapt

adegu'ato, -a ag adequate; (conveniente) suitable; (equo) fair

a'dempiere /24/ vt to fulfil, carry out

ade'rente ag adhesive; (vestito) close-fitting ▷ smf follower

ade'rire /55/ vi (stare attaccato) to adhere, stick; ~ **a** to adhere to, stick to; (fig: società, partito) to join; (opinione) to support; (richiesta) to agree to

adesi'one sf adhesion; (fig) agreement, acceptance; **ade'sivo, -a** ag, sm adhesive

a'desso av (ora) now; (or ora, poco fa) just now; (tra poco) any moment now

adia'cente [adja'tʃɛnte] ag adjacent

adi'bire /55/ vt (usare): ~ **qc a** to turn sth into

adole'scente [adoleʃʃɛnte] ag, smf adolescent

adope'rare /72/ vt to use

ado'rare /72/ vt to adore; (Rel) to adore, worship

adot'tare /72/ vt to adopt; (decisione, provvedimenti) to pass; **adot'tivo, -a** ag (genitori) adoptive; (figlio, patria) adopted; **adozi'one** sf adoption; **adozione a distanza** child sponsorship

adri'atico, -a, -ci, -che ag Adriatic ▷ sm: **l'A~, il mare A~** the Adriatic, the Adriatic Sea

ADSL sigla m ADSL = **asymmetric digital subscriber line**

adu'lare /72/ vt to flatter

a'dultero, -a ag adulterous ▷ sm/f adulterer (adulteress)

a'dulto, -a ag adult; (fig) mature ▷ sm adult, grown-up

a'ereo, -a ag air cpd; (radice) aerial ▷ sm aerial; (aeroplano) plane; ~ **da caccia** fighter (plane); ~ **di linea** airliner; ~ **a reazione** jet (plane); **ae'robica** sf aerobics sg; **aero'nautica** sf (scienza) aeronautics sg: **aeronautica militare** air force

aero'porto sm airport

aero'sol sm inv aerosol

'afa sf sultriness

affabile ag affable

affaccen'dato, -a [affattʃen'dato] ag (persona) busy

affacci'arsi [affat'tʃarsi] /14/ vpr: ~ **(a)** to appear (at)

affa'mato, -a ag starving; (fig): ~ **(di)** eager (for)

affan'noso, -a ag (respiro) difficult; (fig) troubled, anxious

affare *sm* (*faccenda*) matter, affair; (*Comm*) piece of business, (business) deal; (*occasione*) bargain; (*Dir*) case; (*fam: cosa*) thing; **affari** *smpl* (*Comm*) business *sg*: **ministro degli Affari Esteri** Foreign Secretary (BRIT), Secretary of State (US)

affascinante [affaʃʃi'nante] *ag* fascinating

affascinare [affaʃʃi'nare] /72/ *vt* to bewitch; (*fig*) to charm, fascinate

affaticare /20/ *vt* to tire; **affaticarsi** *vpr* (*durar fatica*) to tire o.s. out; **affaticato, -a** *ag* tired

affatto *av* completely; **non ... ~** not ... at all; **niente ~** not at all

affermare /72/ *vt* (*dichiarare*) to maintain, affirm; **affermarsi** *vpr* to assert o.s., make one's name known; **affermato, -a** *ag* established, well-known; **affermazione** *sf* affirmation, assertion; (*successo*) achievement

afferrare /72/ *vt* to seize, grasp; (*fig: idea*) to grasp; **afferrarsi** *vpr*: **afferrarsi a** to cling to

affettare /72/ *vt* (*tagliare a fette*) to slice; (*ostentare*) to affect

affettatrice [affetta'tritʃe] *sf* meat slicer

affettivo, -a *ag* emotional, affective

affetto *sm* affection; **affettuoso, -a** *ag* affectionate

affezionarsi [affettsjo'narsi] /72/ *vpr*: **~ a** to grow fond of

affezionato, -a [affettsjo'nato] *ag*: **~ a qn/qc** fond of sb/sth; (*attaccato*) attached to sb/sth

affiatato, -a *ag*: **essere affiatati** to work well together o get on

affibbiare /19/ *vt* (*fig: dare*) to give

affidabile *ag* reliable

affidamento *sm* (*Dir: di bambino*) custody; (*fiducia*): **fare ~ su qn** to rely on sb; **non dà nessun ~** he's not to be trusted

affidare /72/ *vt*: **~ qc o qn a qn** to entrust sth o sb to sb; **affidarsi** *vpr*: **affidarsi a** to place one's trust in

affilare /72/ *vt* to sharpen

affilato, -a *ag* (*gen*) sharp; (*volto, naso*) thin

affinché [affin'ke] *cong* in order that, so that

affittare /72/ *vt* (*dare in affitto*) to let, rent (out); (*prendere in affitto*) to rent; **affitto** *sm* rent; (*contratto*) lease

affliggere [af'fliddʒere] /104/ *vt* to torment; **affliggersi** *vpr* to grieve

afflissi *ecc vb vedi* **affliggere**

afflosciarsi [affloʃ'ʃarsi] /14/ *vpr* to go limp

affluente *sm* tributary

affogare /80/ *vt, vi* to drown

affollare /72/ *vt*, **affollarsi** *vpr* to crowd; **affollato, -a** *ag* crowded

affondare /72/ *vt* to sink

affrancare /20/ *vt* to free, liberate; (*Amm*) to redeem; (*lettera*) to stamp; (: *meccanicamente*) to frank (BRIT), meter (US)

affresco, -schi *sm* fresco

affrettare /72/ *vt* to quicken; **affrettarsi** *vpr* to hurry; **affrettarsi a fare qc** to hurry o hasten to do sth

affrettato, -a *ag* (*veloce: passo, ritmo*) quick, fast; (*frettoloso: decisione*) hurried, hasty; (: *lavoro*) rushed

affrontare /72/ *vt* (*pericolo ecc*) to face; (*nemico*) to confront; **affrontarsi** *vpr* (*reciproco*) to confront each other

affumicato, -a *ag* (*prosciutto, aringa ecc*) smoked

affusolato, -a *ag* tapering

Afghanistan *sm*: **l'~** Afghanistan

afoso, -a *ag* sultry, close

Africa *sf*: **l'~** Africa; **africano, -a** *ag*, *sm/f* African

agenda [a'dʒɛnda] *sf* diary

> Attenzione! In inglese esiste la parola *agenda*, che però vuol dire *ordine del giorno*.

agente [a'dʒɛnte] *sm* agent; **~ di cambio** stockbroker; **~ di polizia** police officer; **~ segreto** secret agent; **agenzia** *sf* agency;

(*succursale*) branch; **agenzia di collocamento** employment agency; **agenzia immobiliare** estate agent's (office) (BRIT), real estate office (US); **agenzia di stampa** press agency; **agenzia viaggi** travel agency

agevo'lare [adʒevo'lare] /72/ vt to facilitate, make easy

agevolazi'one [adʒevolat'tsjone] sf (*facilitazione economica*) facility; **~ di pagamento** payment on easy terms; **agevolazioni creditizie** credit facilities; **agevolazioni fiscali** tax concessions

a'gevole [a'dʒevole] ag easy; (*strada*) smooth

agganci'are [aggan'tʃare] /14/ vt to hook up; (Ferr) to couple

ag'geggio [ad'dʒeddʒo] sm gadget, contraption

agget'tivo [addʒet'tivo] sm adjective

agghiacci'ante [aggjat'tʃante] ag chilling

aggior'nare [addʒor'nare] /72/ vt (*opera, manuale*) to bring up-to-date; (*seduta ecc*) to postpone; **aggiornarsi** vpr to bring (o keep) o.s. up-to-date; **aggior'nato, -a** ag up-to-date

aggi'rare [addʒi'rare] /72/ vt to go round; (*fig: ingannare*) to trick; **aggirarsi** vpr to wander about; **il prezzo s'aggira sul milione** the price is around the million mark

aggi'ungere [ad'dʒundʒere] /5/ vt to add; (*Inform*): **grazie per avermi aggiunto (come amico)** thanks for the add

aggi'unsi ecc [ad'dʒunsi] vb vedi **aggiungere**

aggius'tare [addʒus'tare] /72/ vt (*accomodare*) to mend, repair; (*riassettare*) to adjust; (*fig: lite*) to settle

aggrap'parsi /72/ vpr: **~ a** to cling to

aggra'vare /72/ vt (*aumentare*) to increase; (*appesantire: anche fig*) to weigh down, make heavy; (*pena*) to make worse; **aggravarsi** vpr to worsen, become worse

aggre'dire /55/ vt to attack, assault

aggressi'one sf aggression; (*atto*) attack, assault

aggres'sivo, -a ag aggressive

aggres'sore sm aggressor, attacker

aggrot'tare /72/ vt: **~ le sopracciglia** to frown

aggrovigli'are /27/ vt to tangle; **aggrovigliarsi** vpr (fig) to become complicated

aggu'ato sm trap; (*imboscata*) ambush; **tendere un ~ a qn** to set a trap for sb

agguer'rito, -a ag fierce

agi'ato, -a [a'dʒato] ag (vita) easy; (*persona*) well-off, well-to-do

'agile ['adʒile] ag agile, nimble

'agio ['adʒo] sm ease, comfort; **agi** smpl comforts; **mettersi a proprio ~** to make o.s. at home o comfortable; **dare ~ a qn di fare qc** to give sb the chance of doing sth

a'gire [a'dʒire] /55/ vi to act; (*esercitare un'azione*) to take effect; (*Tecn*) to work, function; **~ contro qn** (*Dir*) to take action against sb

agi'tare [adʒi'tare] /72/ vt (*bottiglia*) to shake; (*mano, fazzoletto*) to wave; (*fig: turbare*) to disturb; (*: incitare*) to stir (up); (*: dibattere*) to discuss; **agitarsi** vpr (*mare*) to be rough; (*malato, dormitore*) to toss and turn; (*bambino*) to fidget; (*emozionarsi*) to get upset; (*Pol*) to agitate; **agi'tato, -a** ag rough; restless; fidgety; upset, perturbed

'aglio ['aʎʎo] sm garlic

a'gnello [aɲ'ɲɛllo] sm lamb

'ago (pl **aghi**) sm needle

ago'nistico, -a, -ci, -che ag athletic; (fig) competitive

agopun'tura sf acupuncture

a'gosto sm August

a'grario, -a ag agrarian, agricultural; (*riforma*) land cpd

a'gricolo, -a ag agricultural, farm cpd; **agricol'tore** sm farmer; **agricol'tura** sf agriculture, farming

agri'foglio [agri'fɔʎʎo] *sm* holly
agritu'rismo *sm* farm holidays *pl*
agro'dolce *ag* bittersweet; (*salsa*) sweet and sour
a'grume *sm* (*spesso al pl: pianta*) citrus; (: *frutto*) citrus fruit
a'guzzo, -a [a'guttso] *ag* sharp
'ahi *escl* (*dolore*) ouch!
'Aia *sf*: **L'~** The Hague
AIDS ['aids] *abbr m, abbr f* AIDS
airbag *sm inv* air bag
ai'rone *sm* heron
aiu'ola *sf* flower bed
aiu'tante *smf* assistant ▷ *sm* (*Mil*) adjutant; (*Naut*) master-at-arms; **~ di campo** aide-de-camp
aiu'tare /72/ *vt* to help; **~ qn (a fare)** to help sb (to do); **aiutarsi** *vpr* to help each other; **~ qn in qc/a fare qc** to help sb with sth/to do sth; **può aiutarmi?** can you help me?
ai'uto *sm* help, assistance, aid; (*aiutante*) assistant; **venire in ~ di qn** to come to sb's aid; **~ chirurgo** assistant surgeon
'ala (*pl* **ali**) *sf* wing; **fare ~** to fall back, make way; **~ destra/sinistra** (*Sport*) right/left wing
ala'bastro *sm* alabaster
a'lano *sm* Great Dane
'alba *sf* dawn
alba'nese *ag, smf, sm* Albanian
Alba'nia *sf*: **l'~** Albania
albe'rato, -a *ag* (*viale, piazza*) lined with trees, tree-lined
al'bergo, -ghi *sm* hotel; **~ della gioventù** youth hostel
'albero *sm* tree; (*Naut*) mast; (*Tecn*) shaft; **~ genealogico** family tree; **~ a gomiti** crankshaft; **~ maestro** mainmast; **~ di Natale** Christmas tree; **~ di trasmissione** transmission shaft
albi'cocca, -che *sf* apricot
'album *sm* album; **~ da disegno** sketch book
al'bume *sm* albumen
'alce ['altʃe] *sm* elk

'alcol *sm inv* = alcool
al'colico, -a, -ci, -che *ag* alcoholic ▷ *sm* alcoholic drink
alcoliz'zato, -a [alkolid'dzato] *sm/f* alcoholic
'alcool *sm inv* alcohol
al'cuno, -a *det* (*dav sm*: **alcun** + C, V, **alcuno** + s impura, gn, pn, ps, x, z; *dav sf*: **alcuna** + C, **alcun'** + V: *nessuno*): **non … ~** no, not any; **alcuni, e** *det pl, pron pl* some, a few; **non c'è alcuna fretta** there's no hurry, there isn't any hurry; **senza alcun riguardo** without any consideration
alfa'betico, -a, -ci, -che *ag* alphabetical
alfa'beto *sm* alphabet
'alga, -ghe *sf* seaweed *no pl*, alga
'algebra ['aldʒebra] *sf* algebra
Alge'ria [aldʒe'ria] *sf*: **l'~** Algeria; **alge'rino, -a** *ag, sm/f* Algerian
ali'ante *sm* (*Aer*) glider
'alibi *sm inv* alibi
a'lice [a'litʃe] *sf* anchovy
ali'eno, -a *ag* (*avverso*): **~ (da)** opposed (to), averse (to) ▷ *sm/f* alien
alimen'tare /72/ *vt* to feed; (*Tecn*) to feed, supply; (*fig*) to sustain ▷ *ag* food *cpd*; **alimentari** *smpl* foodstuffs; (*anche*: **negozio di alimentari**) grocer's shop; **alimentazi'one** *sf* feeding; supplying; sustaining; (*cibi*) diet
a'liquota *sf* share; **~ d'imposta** tax rate
alis'cafo *sm* hydrofoil
'alito *sm* breath
all. *abbr* (= *allegato*) encl.
allaccia'mento [allattʃa'mento] *sm* (*Tecn*) connection
allacci'are [allat'tʃare] /14/ *vt* (*scarpe*) to tie, lace (up); (*cintura*) to do up, fasten; (*luce, gas*) to connect; (*amicizia*) to form
allaccia'tura [allattʃa'tura] *sf* fastening
alla'gare /80/ *vt*, **alla'garsi** *vpr* to flood

allar'gare /80/ *vt* to widen; (*vestito*) to let out; (*aprire*) to open; (*fig: dilatare*) to extend; **allargarsi** *vpr* (*gen*) to widen; (*scarpe, pantaloni*) to stretch; (*fig: problema, fenomeno*) to spread

allar'mare /72/ *vt* to alarm

al'larme *sm* alarm; **~ aereo** air-raid warning

allat'tare /72/ *vt* to (breast-)feed

alle'anza [alle'antsa] *sf* alliance

alle'arsi /72/ *vpr* to form an alliance; **alle'ato, -a** *ag* allied ▷ *sm/f* ally

alle'gare /80/ *vt* (*accludere*) to enclose; (*Dir: citare*) to cite, adduce; (*denti*) to set on edge; **alle'gato, -a** *ag* enclosed ▷ *sm* enclosure; (*di e-mail*) attachment; **in allegato** enclosed

allegge'rire [alledddʒe'rire] /55/ *vt* to lighten, make lighter; (*fig: lavoro, tasse*) to reduce

alle'gria *sf* gaiety, cheerfulness

al'legro, -a *ag* cheerful, merry; (*un po' brillo*) merry, tipsy; (*vivace: colore*) bright ▷ *sm* (*Mus*) allegro

allena'mento *sm* training

alle'nare /72/ *vt*, **alle'narsi** *vpr* to train; **allena'tore** *sm* (*Sport*) trainer, coach

allen'tare /72/ *vt* to slacken; (*disciplina*) to relax; **allentarsi** *vpr* to become slack; (*ingranaggio*) to work loose

aller'gia, -'gie [aller'dʒia] *sf* allergy; **al'lergico, -a, -ci, -che** [al'lɛrdʒiko] *ag* allergic

alles'tire /55/ *vt* (*cena*) to prepare; (*esercito, nave*) to equip, fit out; (*spettacolo*) to stage

allet'tante *ag* attractive, alluring

alle'vare /72/ *vt* (*animale*) to breed, rear; (*bambino*) to bring up

allevi'are /19/ *vt* to alleviate

alli'bito, -a *ag* pale; disconcerted; astounded

alli'evo *sm* pupil; (*apprendista*) apprentice; **~ ufficiale** cadet

alliga'tore *sm* alligator

alline'are /72/ *vt* (*persone, cose*) to line up; (*Tip*) to align; (*fig: economia, salari*) to adjust, align; **allinearsi** *vpr* to line up; (*fig: a idee*): **allinearsi a** to come into line with

al'lodola *sf* (sky)lark

alloggi'are [allod'dʒare] /62/ *vt* to accommodate ▷ *vi* to live; **al'loggio** *sm* lodging, accommodation (BRIT), accommodations (US)

allonta'nare /72/ *vt* to send away, send off; (*impiegato*) to dismiss; (*pericolo*) to avert, remove; (*estraniare*) to alienate; **allontanarsi** *vpr*: **allontanarsi (da)** to go away (from); (*estraniarsi*) to become estranged (from)

al'lora *av* (*in quel momento*) then ▷ *cong* (*in questo caso*) well then; (*dunque*) well then, so; **la gente d'~** people then o in those days; **da ~ in poi** from then on

al'loro *sm* laurel

'alluce ['allutʃe] *sm* big toe

alluci'nante [allutʃi'nante] *ag* awful; (*fam*) amazing

allucinazi'one [allutʃinat'tsjone] *sf* hallucination

al'ludere /35/ *vi*: **~ a** to allude to, hint at

allu'minio *sm* aluminium (BRIT), aluminum (US)

allun'gare /80/ *vt* to lengthen; (*distendere*) to prolong, extend; (*diluire*) to water down; **allungarsi** *vpr* to lengthen; (*ragazzo*) to stretch, grow taller; (*sdraiarsi*) to lie down, stretch out

al'lusi *ecc vb vedi* **alludere**

allusi'one *sf* hint, allusion

alluvi'one *sf* flood

al'meno *av* at least ▷ *cong*: **(se) ~** if only; **(se) ~ piovesse!** if only it would rain!

a'logeno, -a [a'lɔdʒeno] *ag*: **lampada alogena** halogen lamp

a'lone *sm* halo

'Alpi *sfpl*: **le ~** the Alps

alpi'nismo *sm* mountaineering, climbing; **alpi'nista, -i, -e** *sm/f* mountaineer, climber

al'pino, -a *ag* Alpine; mountain *cpd*; **alpini** *smpl* (*Mil*) Italian Alpine troops

alt *escl* halt!, stop!

alta'lena *sf* (*a funi*) swing; (*in bilico*) seesaw

al'tare *sm* altar

alter'nare /72/ *vt*, **alter'narsi** *vpr* to alternate; **alterna'tivo, -a** *ag* alternative

al'terno, -a *ag* alternate; **a giorni alterni** on alternate days, every other day

al'tero, -a *ag* proud

al'tezza [al'tettsa] *sf* height; (*di tessuto*) width, breadth; (*di acqua, pozzo*) depth; (*di suono*) pitch; (*Geo*) latitude; (*titolo*) highness; (*fig: nobiltà*) greatness; **essere all'~ di** to be on a level with; (*fig*) to be up to o equal to

al'ticcio, -a, -ci, -ce [al'tittʃo] *ag* tipsy

alti'tudine *sf* altitude

'alto, -a *ag* high; (*persona*) tall; (*tessuto*) wide, broad; (*sonno, acque*) deep; (*suono*) high(-pitched); (*Geo*) upper; (: *settentrionale*) northern ▷ *sm* top (part) ▷ *av* high; (*parlare*) aloud, loudly; **il palazzo è ~ 20 metri** the building is 20 metres high; **ad alta voce** aloud; **a notte alta** in the dead of night; **in ~** up, upwards; at the top; **dall'~ in** o **al basso** up and down; **degli alti e bassi** (*fig*) ups and downs; **alta fedeltà** high fidelity, hi-fi; **alta finanza/società** high finance/society; **alta moda** haute couture; **alta definizione** (*TV*) high definition; **alta velocità** (*Ferr*) high speed rail system

altopar'lante *sm* loudspeaker

altopi'ano (*pl* **altipiani**) *sm* upland plain, plateau

altret'tanto, -a *ag, pron* as much; (*pl*) as many ▷ *av* equally; **tanti**

auguri! — grazie, ~ all the best! — thank you, the same to you

altri'menti *av* otherwise

PAROLA CHIAVE

'altro, -a *det* **1** (*diverso*) other, different; **questa è un'altra cosa** that's another o a different thing

2 (*supplementare*) other; **prendi un altro cioccolatino** have another chocolate; **hai avuto altre notizie?** have you had any more o any other news?

3 (*nel tempo*): **l'altro giorno** the other day; **l'altr'anno** last year; **l'altro ieri** the day before yesterday; **domani l'altro** the day after tomorrow; **quest'altro mese** next month

4: **d'altra parte** on the other hand

▶ *pron* **1** (*persona, cosa diversa o supplementare*): **un altro, un'altra** another (one); **lo farà un altro** someone else will do it; **altri, e** others; **gli altri** (*la gente*) others, other people; **l'uno e l'altro** both (of them); **aiutarsi l'un l'altro** to help one another; **da un giorno all'altro** from day to day; (*nel giro di 24 ore*) from one day to the next; (*da un momento all'altro*) any day now

2 (*sostantivato: solo maschile*) something else; (: *in espressioni interrogative*) anything else; **non ho altro da dire** I have nothing else o I don't have anything else to say; **più che altro** above all; **se non altro** at least; **tra l'altro** among other things; **ci mancherebbe altro!** that's all we need!; **non faccio altro che lavorare** I do nothing but work; **contento? — altro che!** are you pleased? — I certainly am!; *vedi anche* **senza; noialtri; voialtri; tutto**

al'trove *av* elsewhere, somewhere else

altru'ista, -i, -e *ag* altruistic

a'lunno, -a sm/f pupil

alve'are sm hive

al'zare [al'tsare] /72/ vt to raise, lift; (issare) to hoist; (costruire) to build, erect; **alzarsi** vpr to rise; (dal letto) to get up; (crescere) to grow tall (o taller); **~ le spalle** to shrug one's shoulders; **alzarsi in piedi** to stand up, get to one's feet

a'maca, -che sf hammock

amalga'mare /72/ vt, **amalga'marsi** vpr to amalgamate

a'mante ag: **~ di** (musica ecc) fond of ▷ smf lover (mistress)

a'mare /72/ vt to love; (amico, musica, sport) to like; **amarsi** vpr to love each other

amareggi'ato, -a [amared'dʒato] ag upset, saddened

ama'rena sf sour black cherry

ama'rezza [ama'rettsa] sf bitterness

a'maro, -a ag bitter ▷ sm bitterness; (liquore) bitters pl

amaz'zonico, -a, -ci, -che [amad'dzɔniko] ag Amazonian; Amazon cpd

ambasci'ata [ambaʃ'ʃata] sf embassy; (messaggio) message; **ambascia'tore, -'trice** sm/f ambassador (ambassadress)

ambe'due ag inv: **~ i ragazzi** both boys ▷ pron inv both

ambienta'lista, -i, -e ag environmental ▷ sm/f environmentalist

ambien'tare /72/ vt to acclimatize; (romanzo, film) to set; **ambientarsi** vpr to get used to one's surroundings

ambi'ente sm environment; (fig: insieme di persone) milieu; (stanza) room

am'biguo, -a ag ambiguous

ambizi'one [ambit'tsjone] sf ambition; **ambizi'oso, -a** ag ambitious

'ambo ag inv both ▷ sm (al gioco) double

'ambra sf amber; **~ grigia** ambergris

ambu'lante ag itinerant ▷ sm peddler

ambu'lanza [ambu'lantsa] sf ambulance; **chiamate un ~** call an ambulance

ambula'torio sm (studio medico) surgery

A'merica sf: **l'~** America; **l'~ latina** Latin America; **ameri'cano, -a** ag, sm/f American

ami'anto sm asbestos

ami'chevole [ami'kevole] ag friendly

ami'cizia [ami'tʃittsja] sf friendship; **amicizie** sfpl (amici) friends

a'mico, -a, -ci, -che sm/f friend; (amante) boyfriend (girlfriend); **~ del cuore** o **intimo** bosom friend; **aggiungere come ~** (Internet) to friend

'amido sm starch

ammac'care /20/ vt (pentola) to dent; (persona) to bruise; **ammacca'tura** sf dent; bruise

ammaes'trare /72/ vt (animale) to train

ammai'nare /72/ vt to lower, haul down

amma'larsi /72/ vpr to fall ill; **amma'lato, -a** ag ill, sick ▷ sm/f sick person; (paziente) patient

ammanet'tare /72/ vt to handcuff

ammas'sare /72/ vt (ammucchiare) to amass; (raccogliere) to gather together; **ammassarsi** vpr to pile up; to gather

ammat'tire /55/ vi to go mad

ammaz'zare [ammat'tsare] /72/ vt to kill; **ammazzarsi** vpr (uccidersi) to kill o.s.; (rimanere ucciso) to be killed; **ammazzarsi di lavoro** to work o.s. to death

am'mettere /63/ vt to admit; (riconoscere: fatto) to acknowledge, admit; (permettere) to allow, accept; (supporre) to suppose

amminis'trare /72/ vt to run, manage; (Rel, Dir) to

administer; **amministra'tore** sm administrator; (di condominio) flats manager; **amministratore delegato** managing director; **amministrazi'one** sf management; administration

ammi'raglio [ammi'raλλo] sm admiral

ammi'rare /72/ vt to admire; **ammirazi'one** sf admiration

am'misi ecc vb vedi **ammettere**

ammobili'ato, -a ag furnished

am'mollo sm: **lasciare in ~** to leave to soak

ammo'niaca sf ammonia

ammo'nire /55/ vt (avvertire) to warn; (rimproverare) to admonish; (Dir) to caution

ammonizi'one [ammonit'tsjone] sf (monito: anche Sport) warning; (rimprovero) reprimand; (Dir) caution

ammon'tare /72/ vi: **~ a** to amount to ▷ sm (total) amount

ammorbi'dente sm fabric softener

ammorbi'dire /55/ vt to soften

ammortizza'tore [ammortiddza'tore] sm (Aut, Tecn) shock absorber

ammucchi'are [ammuk'kjare] /19/ vt to pile up, accumulate

ammuf'fire /55/ vi to go mouldy (BRIT) o moldy (US)

ammuto'lire /55/ vi to be struck dumb

amne'sia sf amnesia

amnis'tia sf amnesty

'amo sm (Pesca) hook; (fig) bait

a'more sm love; **amori** smpl love affairs; **il tuo bambino è un ~** your baby's a darling; **fare l'~** o **all'~** to make love; **per ~** o **per forza** by hook or by crook; **amor proprio** self-esteem, pride

amo'roso, -a ag (affettuoso) loving, affectionate; (: d'amore: sguardo) amorous; (: poesia, relazione) love cpd

'ampio, -a ag wide, broad; (spazioso) spacious; (abbondante: vestito)

loose; (: gonna) full; (: spiegazione) ample, full

am'plesso sm intercourse

ampli'are /19/ vt (ingrandire) to enlarge; (allargare) to widen; **ampliarsi** vpr to grow, increase

amplifica'tore sm (Tecn, Mus) amplifier

ampu'tare /72/ vt (Med) to amputate

A.N. sigla f (Pol) = **Alleanza Nazionale**

anabbagli'ante [anabbaλ'λante] ag (Aut) dipped; **anabbaglianti** smpl dipped or dimmed headlights

anaboliz'zante sm anabolic steroid

anal'colico, -a, -ci, -che ag non-alcoholic ▷ sm soft drink

analfa'beta, -i, -e ag, smf illiterate

anal'gesico, -a, -ci, -che [anal'dʒeziko] ag, sm analgesic

a'nalisi sf inv analysis; (Med: esame) test; **~ del sangue** blood test

analiz'zare [analid'dzare] /72/ vt to analyse; (Med) to test

a'nalogo, -a, -ghi, -ghe ag analogous

'ananas sm inv pineapple

anar'chia [anar'kia] sf anarchy; **a'narchico, -a, -ci, -che** ag anarchic(al) ▷ sm/f anarchist

anarco-insurreziona'lista ag anarcho-revolutionary

'A.N.A.S. sigla f (= Azienda Nazionale Autonoma delle Strade) national roads department

anato'mia sf anatomy

'anatra sf duck

'anca, -che sf (Anat) hip

'anche ['anke] cong (inoltre, pure) also, too; (perfino) even; **vengo anch'io!** I'm coming too!; **~ se** even if

an'cora av still; (di nuovo) again; (di più) some more; (persino): **~ più forte** even stronger; **non ~** not yet; **~ una volta** once more, once again; **~ un po'** a little more; (di tempo) a little longer

an'dare /6/ sm: **a lungo ~** in the long run ▷ vi to go; (essere adatto) to suit; **il suo comportamento non mi va** (*piace*) I don't like the way he behaves; **ti va di ~ al cinema?** do you feel like going to the cinema?; **~ a cavallo** to ride; **~ in macchina/aereo** to go by car/plane; **~ a fare qc** to go and do sth; **~ a pescare/sciare** to go fishing/skiing; **andarsene** to go away; **questa camicia va lavata** this shirt needs a wash *o* should be washed; **~ a male** to go bad; **come va?** (*lavoro, progetto*) how are things?; **come va? — bene, grazie!** how are you? — fine, thanks!; **va fatto entro oggi** it's got to be done today; **ne va della nostra vita** our lives are at stake; **an'data** *sf* going; (*viaggio*) outward journey; **biglietto di sola andata** single (BRIT) *o* one-way ticket; **biglietto di andata e ritorno** return (BRIT) *o* round-trip (US) ticket

andrò *ecc vb vedi* **andare**

a'neddoto *sm* anecdote

a'nello *sm* ring; (*di catena*) link; **anelli** *smpl* (*Ginnastica*) rings

a'nemico, -a, -ci, -che *ag* anaemic

aneste'sia *sf* anaesthesia

anfeta'mina *sf* amphetamine

'angelo ['andʒelo] *sm* angel; **~ custode** guardian angel

anghe'ria [ange'ria] *sf* vexation

angli'cano, -a *ag* Anglican

anglo'sassone *ag* Anglo-Saxon

'angolo *sm* corner; (*Mat*) angle; **~ cottura** (*di appartamento ecc*) cooking area

an'goscia, -sce [an'goʃʃa] *sf* deep anxiety, anguish *no pl*

angu'illa *sf* eel

an'guria *sf* watermelon

'anice ['anitʃe] *sm* (*Cuc*) aniseed; (*Bot*) anise

'anima *sf* soul; (*abitante*) inhabitant; **~ gemella** soul mate; **non c'era ~ viva** there wasn't a living soul

ani'male *sm, ag* animal; **~ domestico** pet

anna'cquare /72/ *vt* to water down, dilute

annaffi'are /19/ *vt* to water; **annaffia'toio** *sm* watering can

an'nata *sf* year; (*importo annuo*) annual amount; **vino d'~** vintage wine

anne'gare /80/ *vt, vi* to drown

anne'rire /55/ *vt* to blacken ▷ *vi* to become black

annien'tare /72/ *vt* to annihilate, destroy

anniver'sario *sm* anniversary; **~ di matrimonio** wedding anniversary

'anno *sm* year; **quanti anni hai? — ho 40 anni** how old are you? — I'm 40 (years old)

anno'dare /72/ *vt* to knot, tie; (*fig: rapporto*) to form

annoi'are /19/ *vt* to bore; **annoiarsi** *vpr* to be bored

> Attenzione! In inglese esiste il verbo *to annoy*, che però vuol dire *dare fastidio a*.

anno'tare /72/ *vt* (*registrare*) to note, note down; (*commentare*) to annotate

annu'ale *ag* annual

annu'ire /55/ *vi* to nod; (*acconsentire*) to agree

annul'lare /72/ *vt* to annihilate, destroy; (*contratto, francobollo*) to cancel; (*matrimonio*) to annul; (*sentenza*) to quash; (*risultati*) to declare void

annunci'are [annun'tʃare] /14/ *vt* to announce; (*dar segni rivelatori*) to herald

an'nuncio [an'nuntʃo] *sm* announcement; (*fig*) sign; **~ pubblicitario** advertisement; **annunci economici** classified advertisements, small ads; **annunci mortuari** (*colonna*) obituary column

'annuo, -a *ag* annual, yearly

annu'sare /72/ *vt* to sniff, smell; **~ tabacco** to take snuff

a'nomalo, -a *ag* anomalous

a'nonimo, -a *ag* anonymous ▷ *sm* (*autore*) anonymous writer (*o* painter *ecc*); **società anonima** (*Comm*) joint stock company

anores'sia *sf* anorexia

ano'ressico, -a, -ci, -che *ag* anorexic

anor'male *ag* abnormal ▷ *smf* subnormal person

'ANSA *sigla f* (= *Agenzia Nazionale Stampa Associata*) national press agency

'ansia *sf* anxiety

ansi'mare /72/ *vi* to pant

ansi'oso, -a *ag* anxious

'anta *sf* (*di finestra*) shutter; (*di armadio*) door

An'tartide *sf*: **l'~** Antarctica

an'tenna *sf* (*Radio, TV*) aerial; (*Zool*) antenna, feeler; (*Naut*) yard; **~ parabolica** satellite dish

ante'prima *sf* preview; **~ di stampa** (*Inform*) print preview

anteri'ore *ag* (*ruota, zampa*) front *cpd*; (*fatti*) previous, preceding

antiade'rente *ag* non-stick

antibi'otico, -a, -ci, -che *ag, sm* antibiotic

anti'camera *sf* anteroom; **fare ~** to be kept waiting

antici'pare [antitʃi'pare] /72/ *vt* (*consegna, visita*) to bring forward, anticipate; (*somma di denaro*) to pay in advance; (*notizia*) to disclose ▷ *vi* to be ahead of time; **an'ticipo** *sm* anticipation; (*di denaro*) advance; **in anticipo** early, in advance

an'tico, -a, -chi, -che *ag* (*quadro, mobili*) antique; (*dell'antichità*) ancient; **all'antica** old-fashioned

anticoncezio'nale [antikontʃettsjo'nale] *sm* contraceptive

anticonfor'mista, -i, -e *ag, smf* nonconformist

anti'corpo *sm* antibody

antidolo'rifico, -ci *sm* painkiller

anti'doping *sm inv, ag inv* drug testing; **test ~** drugs (*BRIT*) o drug (*US*) test

an'tifona *sf* (*Mus, Rel*) antiphon; **capire l'~** (*fig*) to take the hint

anti'forfora *ag inv* anti-dandruff

anti'furto *sm* anti-theft device

anti'gelo [anti'dʒɛlo] *ag inv* antifreeze *cpd* ▷ *sm* (*per motore*) antifreeze; (*per cristalli*) de-icer

antiglobalizza'zione [antiglobaliddza'tsjone] *ag* anti-globalization

An'tille *sfpl*: **le ~** the West Indies

antin'cendio [antin'tʃendjo] *ag inv* fire *cpd*

anti'nebbia *sm inv* (*anche*: **faro ~**) (*Aut*) fog lamp

antin'fiammatorio, -a *ag, sm* anti-inflammatory

antio'rario *ag*: **in senso ~** anticlockwise

anti'pasto *sm* hors d'œuvre

antipa'tia *sf* antipathy, dislike; **anti'patico, -a, -ci, -che** *ag* unpleasant, disagreeable

antipro'iettile *ag inv* bulletproof

antiquari'ato *sm* antique trade; **un pezzo d'~** an antique; **anti'quario** *sm* antique dealer; **anti'quato, -a** *ag* antiquated, old-fashioned

anti'rughe [anti'ruge] *ag inv* (*crema, prodotto*) anti-wrinkle

antitraspi'rante *ag* antiperspirant

anti'vipera *ag inv*: **siero ~** remedy for snake bites

antivi'rale *ag* antiviral

anti'virus [anti'virus] *sm inv* antivirus software *no pl*

antolo'gia, -'gie [antolo'dʒia] *sf* anthology

anu'lare *ag* ring *cpd* ▷ *sm* ring finger

'anzi ['antsi] *av* (*invece*) on the contrary; (*o meglio*) or rather, or better still

anzi'ano, -a [an'tsjano] *ag* old; (*Amm*) senior ▷ *sm/f* old person; senior member

anziché [antsi'ke] *cong* rather than

a'patico, -a, -ci, -che *ag* apathetic

'ape *sf* bee

aperi'tivo *sm* apéritif

aperta'mente *av* openly

a

a'perto, -a pp di **aprire** ▷ ag open ▷ sm: **all'~** in the open (air)

aper'tura sf opening; (ampiezza) width; (Fot) aperture; **~ alare** wing span; **~ mentale** open-mindedness

ap'nea sf: **immergersi in ~** to dive without breathing apparatus

a'postrofo sm apostrophe

ap'paio ecc vb vedi **apparire**

ap'palto sm (Comm) contract; **dare/prendere in ~ un lavoro** to let out/undertake a job on contract

appan'nare /72/ vt (vetro) to mist; **appannarsi** vpr to mist over; to grow dim

apparecchi'are [apparek'kjare] /19/ vt to prepare; (tavola) to set ▷ vi to set the table

appa'recchio [appa'rekkjo] sm piece of apparatus, device; (aeroplano) aircraft inv; **~ acustico** hearing aid; **~ televisivo/telefonico** television set/telephone

appa'rente ag apparent

appa'rire /7/ vi to appear; (sembrare) to seem, appear

apparta'mento sm flat (BRIT), apartment (US)

appar'tarsi /72/ vpr to withdraw

apparte'nere /121/ vi: **~ a** to belong to

ap'parvi ecc vb vedi **apparire**

appassio'nare /72/ vt to thrill; (commuovere) to move; **appassionarsi** vpr: **appassionarsi a qc** to take a great interest in sth; **appassio'nato, -a** ag passionate; (entusiasta): **appassionato (di)** keen (on)

appas'sire /55/ vi to wither; **appas'sito, -a** ag dead

ap'pello sm roll-call; (implorazione, Dir) appeal; **fare ~ a** to appeal to

ap'pena av (a stento) hardly, scarcely; (solamente, da poco) just ▷ cong as soon as; **(non) ~ furono arrivati …** as soon as they had arrived …; **~ … che** o **quando** no sooner … than

ap'pendere /8/ vt to hang (up)

appen'dice [appen'ditʃe] sf appendix; **romanzo d'~** popular serial; **appendi'cite** sf appendicitis

Appen'nini smpl: **gli ~** the Apennines

appesan'tire /55/ vt to make heavy; **appesantirsi** vpr to grow stout

appe'tito sm appetite

appic'care /20/ vt: **~ il fuoco a** to set fire to, set on fire

appicci'care [appittʃi'kare] /20/ vt to stick; **appicciicarsi** vpr to stick; (fig: persona) to cling

appiso'larsi /72/ vpr to doze off

applau'dire /45/ vt, vi to applaud; **ap'plauso** sm applause no pl

appli'care /20/ vt to apply; (regolamento) to enforce; **applicarsi** vpr to apply o.s.; **applicazi'one** sf application; **applicazione per il cellulare** mobile app

appoggi'are [appod'dʒare] /62/ vt (fig: sostenere) to support; **~ qc a qc** (mettere contro) to lean o rest sth against sth; **appoggiarsi** vpr: **appoggiarsi a** to lean against; (fig) to rely upon; **ap'poggio** sm support

apposita'mente av (apposta) on purpose; (specialmente) specially

ap'posito, -a ag appropriate

ap'posta av on purpose, deliberately

appos'tarsi /72/ vpr to lie in wait

ap'prendere /81/ vt (imparare) to learn; **appren'dista, -i, -e** sm/f apprentice

apprensi'one sf apprehension

apprez'zare [appret'tsare] /72/ vt to appreciate

appro'dare /72/ vi (Naut) to land; (fig): **non ~ a nulla** to come to nothing

approfit'tare /72/ vi: **~ di** (situazione) to make the most of; (persona) to take advantage of

approfon'dire /55/ vt to deepen; (fig) to study in depth

appropri'ato, -a ag appropriate

approssima'tivo, -a ag approximate, rough; (impreciso) inexact, imprecise

appro'vare /72/ vt (condotta, azione) to approve of; (candidato) to pass; (progetto di legge) to approve

appunta'mento sm appointment; (amoroso) date; **darsi ~** to arrange to meet (one another); **ho un ~ con...** I have an appointment with ...; **vorrei prendere un ~** I'd like to make an appointment

ap'punto sm note; (rimprovero) reproach ▷ av (proprio) exactly, just; **per l'~!, ~!** exactly!

apribot'tiglie [apribot'tiʎʎe] sm inv bottleopener

a'prile sm April

a'prire /9/ vt to open; (via, cadavere) to open up; (gas, luce, acqua) to turn on ▷ vi to open; **aprirsi** vpr to open; **aprirsi a qn** to confide in sb, open one's heart to sb

apris'catole sm inv tin (BRIT) o can opener

APT sigla f (= Azienda di Promozione) ≈ tourist board

aquagym [akwa'dʒim] sf aquarobics

'aquila sf (Zool) eagle; (fig) genius

aqui'lone sm (giocattolo) kite; (vento) North wind

A/R abbr (= andata e ritorno) (biglietto) return (ticket) (BRIT), round-trip ticket (US)

A'rabia Sau'dita sf: **l'~** Saudi Arabia

'arabo, -a ag, sm/f Arab ▷ sm (Ling) Arabic

a'rachide [a'rakide] sf peanut

ara'gosta sf crayfish; spiny lobster

a'rancia, -ce [a'rantʃa] sf orange; **aranci'ata** sf orangeade; **aranci'one** ag inv: **(color) arancione** bright orange

a'rare /72/ vt to plough (BRIT), plow (US)

a'ratro sm plough (BRIT), plow (US)

a'razzo [a'rattso] sm tapestry

arbi'trare /72/ vt (Sport) to referee; to umpire; (Dir) to arbitrate

arbi'trario, -a ag arbitrary

'arbitro sm arbiter, judge; (Dir) arbitrator; (Sport) referee; (: Tennis, Cricket) umpire

ar'busto sm shrub

archeolo'gia [arkeolo'dʒia] sf arch(a)eology; **arche'ologo, -a, -gi, -ghe** sm/f arch(a)eologist

architet'tare [arkitet'tare] /72/ vt (fig: ideare) to devise; (: macchinare) to plan, concoct

archi'tetto [arki'tetto] sm architect; **architet'tura** [arkitet'tura] sf architecture

ar'chivio [ar'kivjo] sm archives pl; (Inform) file

'arco sm (arma, Mus) bow; (Archit) arch; (Mat) arc

arcoba'leno sm rainbow

arcu'ato, -a ag curved, bent

'ardere /10/ vt, vi to burn

ar'desia sf slate

'area sf area; (Edil) land, ground; **~ di rigore** (Sport) penalty area; **~ di servizio** (Aut) service area

a'rena sf arena; (per corride) bullring; (sabbia) sand

are'narsi /72/ vpr to run aground

argente'ria [ardʒente'ria] sf silverware, silver

Argen'tina [ardʒen'tina] sf: **l'~** Argentina; **argen'tino, -a** ag, sm/f Argentinian

ar'gento [ar'dʒento] sm silver; **~ vivo** quicksilver

ar'gilla [ar'dʒilla] sf clay

'argine ['ardʒine] sm embankment, bank; (diga) dyke, dike

argo'mento sm argument; (motivo) motive; (materia, tema) subject

'aria sf air; (espressione, aspetto) air, look; (Mus: melodia) tune; (: di opera) aria; **all'~ aperta** in the open (air); **mandare all'~ qc** to ruin o upset sth

'arido, -a ag arid

arieggi'are [arjed'dʒare] /72/ vt (cambiare aria) to air; (imitare) to imitate

ari'ete sm ram; (Mil) battering ram; **A~** Aries

a'ringa, -ghe sf herring inv

arit'metica sf arithmetic

'arma, -i sf weapon, arm; (parte dell'esercito) arm; **alle armi!** to arms!; **chiamare alle armi** to call up (BRIT), draft (US); **sotto le armi** in the army (o forces); **~ atomica/nucleare** atomic/nuclear weapon; **~ da fuoco** firearm; **armi di distruzione de massa** weapons of mass destruction

arma'dietto sm (di medicinali) medicine cabinet; (in palestra ecc) locker; (in cucina) (kitchen) cupboard

ar'madio sm cupboard; (per abiti) wardrobe; **~ a muro** built-in cupboard

ar'mato, -a ag: **~ (di)** (anche fig) armed (with) ⊳ sf (Mil) army; (Naut) fleet; **rapina a mano armata** armed robbery

arma'tura sf (struttura di sostegno) framework; (impalcatura) scaffolding; (Storia) armour no pl, suit of armour

armis'tizio [armis'tittsjo] sm armistice

armo'nia sf harmony

ar'nese sm tool, implement; (oggetto indeterminato) thing, contraption; **male in ~** (malvestito) badly dressed; (di salute malferma) in poor health; (di condizioni economiche) down-at-heel

'arnia sf hive

a'roma, -i sm aroma; fragrance; **aromi** smpl (Cuc) herbs and spices; **aromatera'pia** sf aromatherapy

'arpa sf (Mus) harp

arrabbi'are /19/ vi (cane) to be affected with rabies; **arrabbiarsi** vpr (essere preso dall'ira) to get angry, fly into a rage; **arrabbi'ato, -a** ag rabid, with rabies; (persona) furious, angry

arrampi'carsi /20/ vpr to climb (up)

arran'giare [arran'dʒare] /62/ vt to arrange; **arrangiarsi** vpr to manage, do the best one can

arreda'mento sm (studio) interior design; (mobili ecc) furnishings pl

arre'dare /72/ vt to furnish

ar'rendersi /88/ vpr to surrender

arres'tare /72/ vt (fermare) to stop, halt; (catturare) to arrest; **arrestarsi** vpr (fermarsi) to stop; **ar'resto** sm (cessazione) stopping; (fermata) stop; (cattura, Med) arrest; **subire un arresto** to come to a stop o standstill; **mettere agli arresti** to place under arrest; **arresti domiciliari** house arrest sg

arre'trare /72/ vt, vi to withdraw; **arre'trato, -a** ag (lavoro) behind schedule; (paese, bambino) backward; (numero di giornale) back cpd; **arretrati** smpl arrears

arric'chire [arrik'kire] /55/ vt to enrich; **arricchirsi** vpr to become rich

arri'vare /72/ vi to arrive; (accadere) to happen, occur; **~ a** (livello, grado ecc) to reach; **lui arriva a Roma alle 7** he gets to o arrives at Rome at 7; **non ci arrivo** I can't reach it; (fig: non capisco) I can't understand it

arrive'derci [arrive'dertʃi] escl goodbye!

arri'vista, -i, -e sm/f go-getter

ar'rivo sm arrival; (Sport) finish, finishing line

arro'gante ag arrogant

arros'sire /55/ vi (per vergogna, timidezza) to blush; (per gioia) to flush

arros'tire /55/ vt to roast; (pane) to toast; (ai ferri) to grill

ar'rosto sm, ag inv roast

arroto'lare /72/ vt to roll up

arroton'dare /72/ vt (forma, oggetto) to round; (stipendio) to add to; (somma) to round off

arruggi'nito, -a [arruddʒin'nito] ag rusty

'arsi vb vedi **ardere**

'arte sf art; (abilità) skill

ar'teria sf artery; **~ stradale** main road

'artico, -a, -ci, -che ag Arctic

articolazi'one [artikolat'tsjone] *sf*
(*Anat, Tecn*) joint

ar'ticolo *sm* article; **~ di fondo**
(*Stampa*) leader, leading article

artifici'ale [artifi'tʃale] *ag* artificial

artigia'nato [artidʒa'nato] *sm*
craftsmanship; craftsmen *pl*

artigi'ano, -a [arti'dʒano] *sm/f*
craftsman/woman

ar'tista, -i, -e *sm/f* artist; **un lavoro
da ~** (*fig*) a professional piece of work;
ar'tistico, -a, -ci, -che *ag* artistic

ar'trite *sf* (*Med*) arthritis

a'scella [aʃʃɛlla] *sf* (*Anat*) armpit

ascen'dente [aʃʃen'dɛnte] *sm*
ancestor; (*fig*) ascendancy; (*Astr*)
ascendant

ascen'sore [aʃʃen'sore] *sm* lift

a'scesso [aʃʃɛsso] *sm* (*Med*) abscess

asciugaca'pelli [aʃʃugaka'pelli] *sm*
hair dryer

asciuga'mano [aʃʃuga'mano] *sm*
towel

asciu'gare [aʃʃu'gare] /80/ *vt* to dry;
asciugarsi *vpr* to dry o.s.; (*diventare
asciutto*) to dry

asci'utto, -a [aʃʃutto] *ag* dry;
(*fig: magro*) lean; (: *burbero*) curt;
restare a bocca asciutta (*fig*) to be
disappointed

ascol'tare /72/ *vt* to listen to

as'falto *sm* asphalt

'Asia *sf* **l'~** Asia; **asi'atico, -a, -ci, -che**
ag, sm/f Asiatic, Asian

a'silo *sm* refuge, sanctuary; **~
(d'infanzia)** nursery(-school); **~ nido**
crèche; **~ politico** political asylum

'asino *sm* donkey, ass

ASL *sigla f* (= *Azienda Sanitaria Locale*)
local health centre

'asma *sf* asthma

as'parago, -gi *sm* asparagus *no pl*

aspet'tare /72/ *vt* to wait for; (*anche
Comm*) to await; (*aspettarsi*) to expect
▷ *vi* to wait

as'petto *sm* (*apparenza*) aspect,
appearance, look; (*punto di vista*)
point of view; **di bell'~** good-looking

aspira'polvere *sm inv* vacuum
cleaner

aspi'rare /72/ *vt* (*respirare*) to breathe
in, inhale; (*apparecchi*) to suck (up)
▷ *vi*: **~ a** to aspire to

aspi'rina *sf* aspirin

'aspro, -a *ag* (*sapore*) sour, tart; (*odore*)
acrid, pungent; (*voce, clima, fig*)
harsh; (*superficie*) rough; (*paesaggio*)
rugged

assaggi'are [assad'dʒare] /62/ *vt* to
taste; **assag'gini** [assad'dʒini] *smpl*
(*Cuc*) selection of first courses

as'sai *av* (*molto*) a lot, much; (: *con ag*)
very; (*a sufficienza*) enough ▷ *ag inv*
(*quantità*) a lot of, much; (*numero*) a lot
of, many; **~ contento** very pleased

as'salgo *ecc vb vedi* **assalire**

assa'lire /98/ *vt* to attack, assail

assal'tare /72/ *vt* (*Mil*) to storm;
(*banca*) to raid; (*treno, diligenza*) to
hold up

as'salto *sm* attack, assault

assassi'nare /72/ *vt* to murder;
(*Pol*) to assassinate; (*fig*) to ruin;
assas'sino, -a *ag* murderous ▷ *sm/f*
murderer; assassin

'asse *sm* (*Tecn*) axle; (*Mat*) axis ▷ *sf*
board; **~ da stiro** ironing board

assedi'are /19/ *vt* to besiege

asse'gnare [assen'ɲare] /15/ *vt* to
assign, allot; (*premio*) to award

as'segno [as'seɲɲo] *sm* allowance;
(*anche:* **~ bancario**) cheque (BRIT),
check (US); **contro ~** cash on
delivery; **~ circolare** bank draft; **~
di malattia** *o* **di invalidità** sick pay/
disability benefit; **~ sbarrato** crossed
cheque; **~ di viaggio** travel(l)er's
cheque; **~ a vuoto** dud cheque;
assegni familiari ≈ child benefit *sg*

assem'blea *sf* assembly

assen'tarsi /72/ *vpr* to go out;
as'sente *ag* absent; (*fig*) faraway,
vacant; **as'senza** *sf* absence

asse'tato, -a *ag* thirsty, parched

assicu'rare /72/ *vt* (*accertare*) to
ensure; (*infondere certezza*) to assure;

(*fermare, legare*) to make fast, secure; (*fare un contratto di assicurazione*) to insure; **assicurarsi** *vpr*: **assicurarsi (di)** (*accertarsi*) to make sure (of); **assicurarsi (contro)** (*il furto ecc*) to insure o.s. (against); **assicurazi'one** *sf* assurance; insurance

assi'eme *av* (*insieme*) together ▷ *prep*: **~ a** (together) with

assil'lare /72/ *vt* to pester, torment

assis'tente *smf* assistant; **~ sociale** social worker; **~ di volo** (*Aer*) steward (stewardess); **assis'tenza** *sf* assistance; **assistenza ospedaliera** free hospital treatment; **assistenza sanitaria** health service; **assistenza sociale** welfare services *pl*; **as'sistere** /11/ *vt* (*aiutare*) to assist, help; (*curare*) to treat ▷ *vi*: **assistere (a qc)** (*essere presente*) to be present (at sth), attend (sth)

'**asso** *sm* ace; **piantare qn in ~** to leave sb in the lurch

associ'are [asso'tʃare] /14/ *vt* to associate; **associarsi** *vpr* to enter into partnership; **associarsi a** to become a member of, join; (*dolori, gioie*) to share in; **~ qn alle carceri** to take sb to prison

associazi'one [assotʃat'tsjone] *sf* association; (*Comm*) association, society; **~ a o per delinquere** (*Dir*) criminal association

as'solsi *ecc vb vedi* **assolvere**

assoluta'mente *av* absolutely

asso'luto, -a *ag* absolute

assoluzi'one [assolut'tsjone] *sf* (*Dir*) acquittal; (*Rel*) absolution

as'solvere /94/ *vt* (*Dir*) to acquit; (*Rel*) to absolve; (*adempiere*) to carry out, perform

assomigli'are [assomiʎ'ʎare] /27/ *vi*: **~ a** to resemble, look like; **assomigliarsi** *vpr* to look alike; (*nel carattere*) to be alike

asson'nato, -a *ag* sleepy

asso'pirsi /55/ *vpr* to doze off

assor'bente *ag* absorbent ▷ *sm*: **~ igienico/esterno** sanitary towel; **~ interno** tampon

assor'bire /17/ *vt* to absorb

assor'dare /72/ *vt* to deafen

assorti'mento *sm* assortment; **assor'tito, -a** *ag* assorted; (*colori*) matched, matching

assuefazi'one [assuefat'tsjone] *sf* (*Med*) addiction

as'sumere /12/ *vt* (*impiegato*) to take on, engage; (*responsabilità*) to assume, take upon o.s.; (*contegno, espressione*) to assume, put on; (*droga*) to consume

as'sunsi *ecc vb vedi* **assumere**

assurdità *sf inv* absurdity; **dire delle ~** to talk nonsense; **as'surdo, -a** *ag* absurd

'**asta** *sf* pole; (*modo di vendita*) auction

as'temio, -a *ag* teetotal ▷ *sm/f* teetotaller

> Attenzione! In inglese esiste la parola *abstemious*, che però vuol dire *moderato*.

aste'nersi /121/ *vpr*: **~ (da)** to abstain (from), refrain (from); (*Pol*) to abstain (from)

aste'risco, -schi *sm* asterisk

'**astice** ['astitʃe] *sm* lobster

astig'matico, -a, -ci, -che *ag* astigmatic

asti'nenza [asti'nɛntsa] *sf* abstinence; **essere in crisi di ~** to suffer from withdrawal symptoms

as'tratto, -a *ag* abstract

'**astro...** *prefisso* astro; **astrolo'gia** [astrolo'dʒia] *sf* astrology; **astro'nauta, -i, -e** *sm/f* astronaut; **astro'nave** *sf* space ship; **astrono'mia** *sf* astronomy; **astro'nomico, -a, -ci, -che** *ag* astronomic(al)

as'tuccio [as'tuttʃo] *sm* case, box, holder

as'tuto, -a *ag* astute, cunning, shrewd

A'tene *sf* Athens

'ateo, -a ag, sm/f atheist
at'lante sm atlas
at'lantico, -a, -ci, -che ag Atlantic
▷ sm: **l'A~, l'Oceano A~** the Atlantic, the Atlantic Ocean
at'leta, -i, -e sm/f athlete; **at'letica** sf athletics sg: **atletica leggera** track and field events pl: **atletica pesante** weightlifting and wrestling
atmos'fera sf atmosphere
a'tomico, -a, -ci, -che ag atomic; (nucleare) atomic, atom cpd, nuclear
'atomo sm atom
'atrio sm entrance hall, lobby
a'troce [a'trotʃe] ag (che provoca orrore) dreadful; (terribile) atrocious
attac'cante smf (Sport) forward
attacca'panni sm hook, peg; (mobile) hall stand
attac'care /20/ vt (unire) to attach; (cucire) to sew on; (far aderire) to stick (on); (appendere) to hang (up); (assalire: anche fig) to attack; (iniziare) to begin, start; (fig: contagiare) to pass on ▷ vi to stick, adhere; **attaccarsi** vpr to stick, adhere; (trasmettersi per contagio) to be contagious; (afferrarsi): **attaccarsi (a)** to cling (to); (fig: affezionarsi): **attaccarsi (a)** to become attached (to); **~ discorso** to start a conversation; **at'tacco, -chi** sm (azione offensiva: anche fig) attack; (Med) attack, fit; (Sci) binding; (Elettr) socket
atteggia'mento [atteddʒa'mento] sm attitude
at'tendere /120/ vt to wait for, await ▷ vi: **~ a** to attend to
atten'dibile ag (scusa, storia) credible; (fonte, testimone, notizia) reliable
atten'tato sm attack; **~ alla vita di qn** attempt on sb's life
attenta'tore, -'trice sm/f bomber; **~ suicida** suicide bomber
at'tento, -a ag attentive; (accurato) careful, thorough ▷ escl be careful!; **stare ~ a qc** to pay attention to

sth; **attenzi'one** [atten'tsjone] sf attention ▷ escl watch out!, be careful!; **attenzioni** sfpl (premure) attentions; **fare attenzione a** to watch out for; **coprire qn di attenzioni** to lavish attention on sb
atter'raggio [atter'raddʒo] sm landing
atter'rare /72/ vt to bring down ▷ vi to land
at'tesa sf waiting; (tempo trascorso aspettando) wait; **essere in ~ di qc** to be waiting for sth
at'tesi ecc vb vedi **attendere**
at'teso, -a pp di **attendere**
'attico, -ci sm attic
attil'lato, -a ag (vestito) close-fitting
'attimo sm moment; **in un ~** in a moment
atti'rare /72/ vt to attract
atti'tudine sf (disposizione) aptitude; (atteggiamento) attitude
attività sf inv activity; (Comm) assets pl
at'tivo, -a ag active; (Comm) profit-making, credit cpd ▷ sm (Comm) assets pl: **in ~** in credit
'atto sm act; (azione, gesto) action, act, deed; (Dir: documento) deed, document; **atti** smpl (di congressi ecc) proceedings; **mettere in ~** to put into action; **fare ~ di fare qc** to make as if to do sth; **~ di nascita/morte** birth/death certificate
at'tore, -'trice sm/f actor (actress)
at'torno av round, around, about ▷ prep: **~ a** round, around, about
attrac'care /20/ vt, vi (Naut) to dock, berth
at'tracco, -chi sm (Naut) docking; (: luogo) berth
at'trae ecc vb vedi **attrarre**
attra'ente ag attractive
at'traggo ecc vb vedi **attrarre**
at'trarre /123/ vt to attract
at'trassi ecc vb vedi **attrarre**
attraver'sare /72/ vt to cross; (città, bosco, fig: periodo) to go through; (fiume) to run through

attra'verso prep through; (da una
parte all'altra) across
attrazi'one [attrat'tsjone] sf
attraction
attrezza'tura sf equipment no pl;
rigging
at'trezzo sm tool, instrument; (Sport)
piece of equipment
at'trice [at'tritʃe] sf vedi **attore**
attu'ale ag (presente) present; (di
attualità) topical
> Attenzione! In inglese esiste la
> parola actual, che però vuol dire
> effettivo.
attualità sf inv topicality;
(avvenimento) current event;
attual'mente av at the moment,
at present
> Attenzione! In inglese esiste
> la parola actually, che però
> vuol dire effettivamente oppure
> veramente.
attu'are /72/ vt to carry out; **attuarsi**
vpr to be realized
attu'tire /55/ vt to deaden, reduce
'audio sm (TV, Radio, Cine) sound
audiovi'sivo, -a ag audiovisual
audizi'one [audit'tsjone] sf hearing;
(Mus) audition
augu'rare /72/ vt to wish; **augurarsi**
qc to hope for sth
au'gurio sm (good) wish; **auguri**
smpl best wishes; **fare gli auguri**
a qn to give sb one's best wishes;
tanti auguri! best wishes!; (per
compleanno) happy birthday!
'aula sf (scolastica) classroom;
(universitaria) lecture theatre; (di
edificio pubblico) hall
aumen'tare /72/ vt, vi to increase; ~
di peso (persona) to put on weight; **la
produzione è aumentata del 50%**
production has increased by 50%;
au'mento sm increase
au'rora sf dawn
ausili'are ag, sm, smf auxiliary
Aus'tralia sf: l'~ Australia;
australi'ano, -a ag, sm/f Australian

'Austria sf: l'~ Austria; **aus'triaco, -a,
-ci, -che** ag, sm/f Austrian
au'tentico, -a, -ci, -che ag
authentic, genuine
au'tista, -i sm driver
'auto sf inv car
autoabbron'zante ag self-tanning
autoade'sivo, -a ag self-adhesive
> sm sticker
autobio'grafico, -a, -ci, -che ag
autobiographic(al)
'autobus sm inv bus
auto'carro sm lorry (BRIT), truck
autocertificazi'one
[autotʃertifikat'tsjone] sf self-
declaration
autodistrut'tivo, -a ag self-
destructive
auto'gol sm inv own goal
au'tografo, -a ag, sm autograph
auto'grill® sm inv motorway café
auto'matico, -a, -ci, -che ag
automatic > sm (bottone) snap
fastener; (fucile) automatic
auto'mobile sf (motor) car;
automobi'lista, -i, -e sm/f
motorist
autono'leggio [autono'leddʒo]
sm car hire
autono'mia sf autonomy; (di
volo) range; **au'tonomo, -a** ag
autonomous; independent
autop'sia sf post-mortem
(examination), autopsy
auto'radio sf inv (apparecchio) car
radio; (autoveicolo) radio car
au'tore, -'trice sm/f author
autoreg'gente [autored'dʒente]
ag: **calze autoreggenti** hold ups
auto'revole ag authoritative;
(persona) influential
autoricari'cabile ag: **scheda ~**
top-up card
autori'messa sf garage
autorità sf inv authority
autoriz'zare [autorid'dzare] /72/ vt
(permettere) to authorize; (giustificare)
to allow, sanction

autos'contro *sm* dodgem car (BRIT), bumper car (US)

autoscu'ola *sf* driving school

autos'tima *sf* self-esteem

autos'top *sm* hitchhiking; **autostop'pista, -i, -e** *sm/f* hitchhiker

autos'trada *sf* motorway (BRIT), highway (US); **~ informatica** information superhighway

- **AUTOSTRADE**
-
- You have to pay to use Italian
- motorways. They are indicated
- by an "A" followed by a number on
- a green sign. The speed limit on
- Italian motorways is 130 kph.

auto'velox® *sm inv* (police) speed camera

autovet'tura *sf* (motor) car

au'tunno *sm* autumn

avam'braccio [avam'brattʃo] (*pl f* **avambraccia**) *sm* forearm

avangu'ardia *sf* vanguard

a'vanti *av* (*stato in luogo*) in front; (*moto: andare, venire*) forward; (*tempo: prima*) before ▷ *prep* (*luogo*): **~ a** before, in front of; (*tempo*): **~ Cristo** before Christ ▷ *escl* (*entrate*) come (*o go*) in!; (*Mil*) forward!; (*coraggio*) come on! ▷ *sm inv* (*Sport*) forward; **~ e indietro** backwards and forwards; **andare ~** to go forward; (*continuare*) to go on; (*precedere*) to go (on) ahead; (*orologio*) to be fast; **essere ~ negli studi** to be well advanced with one's studies

avan'zare [avan'tsare] /72/ *vt* (*spostare in avanti*) to move forward, advance; (*domanda*) to put forward; (*promuovere*) to promote; (*essere creditore*): **~ qc da qn** to be owed sth by sb ▷ *vi* (*andare avanti*) to move forward, advance; (*progredire*) to make progress; (*essere d'avanzo*) to be left, remain

ava'ria *sf* (*guasto*) damage; (: *meccanico*) breakdown

a'varo, -a *ag* avaricious, miserly ▷ *sm* miser

PAROLA CHIAVE

a'vere /13/ *sm* (Comm) credit; **gli averi** (*ricchezze*) wealth *sg*

▶ *vt* **1** (*possedere*) to have; **ha due bambini/una bella casa** she has (got) two children/a lovely house; **ha i capelli lunghi** he has (got) long hair; **non ho da mangiare/bere** I've (got) nothing to eat/drink, I don't have anything to eat/drink

2 (*indossare*) to wear, have on; **aveva una maglietta rossa** he was wearing *o* he had on a red T-shirt; **ha gli occhiali** he wears *o* has glasses

3 (*ricevere*) to get; **hai avuto l'assegno?** did you get *o* have you had the cheque?

4 (*età, dimensione*) to be; **ha 9 anni** he is 9 (years old); **la stanza ha 3 metri di lunghezza** the room is 3 metres in length; *vedi* **fame; paura; sonno** *ecc*

5 (*tempo*): **quanti ne abbiamo oggi?** what's the date today?; **ne hai per molto?** will you be long?

6 (*fraseologia*): **avercela con qn** to be angry with sb; **cos'hai?** what's wrong *o* what's the matter (with you)?; **non ha niente a che vedere** *o* **fare con me** it's got nothing to do with me

▶ *vb aus* **1** to have; **aver bevuto/ mangiato** to have drunk/eaten

2 (+ *da* + *infinito*): **avere da fare qc** to have to do sth; **non hai che da chiederlo** you only have to ask him

aviazi'one [avjat'tsjone] *sf* aviation; (Mil) air force

'avido, -a *ag* eager; (*peg*) greedy

avo'cado *sm* avocado

a'vorio *sm* ivory

Avv. *abbr* = **avvocato**

avvantaggi'are [avvantad'dʒare] /62/ vt to favour; **avvantaggiarsi** vpr: **avvantaggiarsi negli affari/sui concorrenti** to get ahead in business/of one's competitors

avvele'nare /72/ vt to poison

av'vengo ecc vb vedi **avvenire**

avveni'mento sm event

avve'nire /128/ vi, vb impers to happen, occur ▷ sm future

av'venni ecc vb vedi **avvenire**

avven'tato, -a ag rash, reckless

avven'tura sf adventure; (amorosa) affair

avventu'rarsi /72/ vpr to venture

avventu'roso, -a ag adventurous

avve'rarsi /72/ vpr to come true

av'verbio sm adverb

avverrò ecc vb vedi **avvenire**

avver'sario, -a ag opposing ▷ sm opponent, adversary

avver'tenza [avver'tɛntsa] sf (ammonimento) warning; (cautela) care; (premessa) foreword; **avvertenze** sfpl (istruzioni per l'uso) instructions

avverti'mento sm warning

avver'tire /45/ vt (avvisare) to warn; (rendere consapevole) to inform, notify; (percepire) to feel

avvi'are /60/ vt (mettere sul cammino) to direct; (impresa, trattative) to begin, start; (motore) to start; **avviarsi** vpr to set off, set out

avvici'nare [avvitʃi'nare] /72/ vt to bring near; (trattare con: persona) to approach; **avvicinarsi** vpr: **avvicinarsi (a qn/qc)** to approach (sb/sth), draw near (to sb/sth)

avvi'lito, -a ag discouraged

avvin'cente [avvin'tʃɛnte] ag enthralling

avvi'sare /72/ vt (far sapere) to inform; (mettere in guardia) to warn; **av'viso** sm warning; (annuncio) announcement; (affisso) notice; (inserzione pubblicitaria) advertisement; **a mio avviso** in my opinion; **avviso di chiamata** (servizio) call waiting; (segnale) call waiting signal; **avviso di garanzia** (Dir) notification (of impending investigation and of the right to name a defence laywer)

> Attenzione! In inglese esiste la parola advice, che però vuol dire consiglio.

avvis'tare /72/ vt to sight

avvi'tare /72/ vt to screw down (o in)

avvo'cato, -'essa sm/f (Dir) barrister (BRIT), lawyer; (fig) defender, advocate

av'volgere [av'vɔldʒere] /96/ vt to roll up; (avviluppare) to wrap up; **avvolgersi** vpr (avvilupparsi) to wrap o.s. up; **avvol'gibile** sm roller blind (BRIT), blind

av'volsi ecc vb vedi **avvolgere**

avvol'toio sm vulture

aza'lea [addza'lɛa] sf azalea

azi'enda [ad'dzjɛnda] sf business, firm, concern; **~ agricola** farm

azi'one [at'tsjone] sf action; (Comm) share

a'zoto [ad'dzɔto] sm nitrogen

azzar'dare [addzar'dare] /72/ vt (soldi, vita) to risk, hazard; (domanda, ipotesi) to hazard, venture; **azzardarsi** vpr: **azzardarsi a fare** to dare (to) do

az'zardo [ad'dzardo] sm risk

azzec'care [attsek'kare] /20/ vt (risposta, pronostico) to get right

azzuf'farsi [attsuf'farsi] /72/ vpr to come to blows

az'zurro, -a [ad'dzurro] ag blue ▷ sm (colore) blue; **gli azzurri** (Sport) the Italian national team

'bacca, -che *sf* berry

baccalà *sm* dried salted cod; *(fig: peg)* dummy

bac'chetta [bak'ketta] *sf (verga)* stick, rod; *(di direttore d'orchestra)* baton; *(di tamburo)* drumstick; **~ magica** magic wand

ba'checa, -che [ba'kɛka] *sf (mobile)* showcase, display case; *(Università, in ufficio)* notice board *(BRIT)*, bulletin board *(US)*

baci'are [ba'tʃare] /14/ *vt* to kiss; **baciarsi** *vpr* to kiss (one another)

baci'nella [batʃi'nɛlla] *sf* basin

ba'cino [ba'tʃino] *sm* basin; *(Mineralogia)* field, bed; *(Anat)* pelvis; *(Naut)* dock; **~ d'utenza** catchment area

'bacio ['batʃo] *sm* kiss

'baco, -chi *sm* worm; **~ da seta** silkworm

ba'dante *smf* care worker

ba'dare /72/ *vi (fare attenzione)* to take care, be careful; **~ a** *(occuparsi di)* to look after, take care of; *(dar ascolto)* to pay attention to; **bada ai fatti tuoi!** mind your own business!

'baffi *smpl* moustache *sg*; *(di animale)* whiskers; **leccarsi i ~** to lick one's lips; **ridere sotto i ~** to laugh up one's sleeve

bagagli'aio [bagaʎ'ʎajo] *sm* luggage van *(BRIT)* o car *(US)*; *(Aut)* boot *(BRIT)*, trunk *(US)*

ba'gaglio [ba'gaʎʎo] *sm* luggage *no pl*, baggage *no pl*; **fare/disfare i bagagli** to pack/unpack; **~ a mano** hand luggage

bagli'ore [baʎ'ʎore] *sm* flash, dazzling light; **un ~ di speranza** a (sudden) ray of hope

ba'gnante [baɲ'ɲante] *smf* bather

ba'gnare [baɲ'ɲare] /15/ *vt* to wet; *(inzuppare)* to soak; *(innaffiare)* to water; *(fiume)* to flow through; *(: mare)* to wash, bathe; **bagnarsi** *vpr* to get wet; *(al mare)* to go swimming o bathing; *(in vasca)* to have a bath

ba'gnato, -a [baɲ'ɲato] *ag* wet

ba'gnino [baɲ'ɲino] *sm* lifeguard

'bagno ['baɲɲo] *sm* bath; *(locale)* bathroom; *(toilette)* toilet; **bagni** *smpl (stabilimento)* baths; **fare il ~** to have a bath; *(nel mare)* to go swimming o bathing; **fare il ~ a qn** to give sb a bath; **mettere a ~** to soak

bagnoma'ria [baɲɲoma'ria] *sm*: **cuocere a ~** to cook in a double saucepan *(BRIT)* o double boiler *(US)*

bagnoschi'uma [baɲɲoskj'uma] *sm inv* bubble bath

'baia *sf* bay

balbet'tare /72/ *vi* to stutter, stammer; *(bimbo)* to babble ▷ *vt* to stammer out

bal'canico, -a, -ci, -che *ag* Balkan

bal'cone *sm* balcony

'babbo *sm (fam)* dad, daddy; **B-Natale** Father Christmas

baby'sitter ['beibisitər] *sm inv, f inv* baby-sitter

bal'doria sf: **fare ~** to have a riotous time

ba'lena sf whale

ba'leno sm flash of lightning; **in un ~** in a flash

bal'lare /72/ vt, vi to dance

balle'rina sf dancer; ballet dancer; (scarpa) ballet shoe

balle'rino sm dancer; ballet dancer

bal'letto sm ballet

'ballo sm dance; (azione) dancing no pl; **essere in ~** (fig: persona) to be involved; (: cosa) to be at stake

balne'are ag seaside cpd; (stagione) bathing

'balsamo sm (aroma) balsam; (lenimento, fig) balm; (per capelli) conditioner

bal'zare [bal'tsare] /72/ vi to bounce; (lanciarsi) to jump, leap; **'balzo** sm bounce; jump, leap; (del terreno) crag

bam'bina sf vedi **bambino**

bam'bino, -a sm/f child

'bambola sf doll

bambù sm bamboo

ba'nale ag banal, commonplace

ba'nana sf banana

'banca, -che sf bank; **~ (di) dati** data bank

banca'rella sf stall

banca'rotta sf bankruptcy; **fare ~** to go bankrupt

ban'chetto [ban'ketto] sm banquet

banchi'ere [ban'kjɛre] sm banker

ban'china [ban'kina] sf (di porto) quay; (per pedoni, ciclisti) path; (di stazione) platform; **~ cedevole** (Aut) soft verge (BRIT), soft shoulder (US)

'banco, -chi sm bench; (di negozio) counter; (di mercato) stall; (di officina) (work)bench; (Geo, banca) bank; **~ di corallo** coral reef; **~ degli imputati** dock; **~ di prova** (fig) testing ground; **~ dei testimoni** witness box (BRIT) o stand (US); **~ dei pegni** pawnshop; **~ di nebbia** bank of fog

'Bancomat® sm inv automated banking; (tessera) cash card; (sportello automatico) cashpoint

banco'nota sf banknote

'banda sf band; (di stoffa) band, stripe; (lato, parte) side; **~ larga** broadband

bandi'era sf flag, banner

ban'dito sm outlaw, bandit

'bando sm proclamation; (esilio) exile, banishment; **~ alle ciance!** that's enough talk!; **~ di concorso** announcement of a competition

bar sm inv bar

'bara sf coffin

ba'racca, -che sf shed, hut; (peg) hovel; **mandare avanti la ~** to keep things going

ba'rare /72/ vi to cheat

ba'ratro sm abyss

ba'ratto sm barter

ba'rattolo sm (di latta) tin; (di vetro) jar; (di coccio) pot

'barba sf beard; **farsi la ~** to shave; **farla in ~ a qn** (fig) to do sth to sb's face; **servire qn di ~ e capelli** (fig) to teach sb a lesson; **che ~!** what a bore!

barbabi'etola sf beetroot (BRIT), beet (US); **~ da zucchero** sugar beet

barbi'ere sm barber

bar'bone sm (cane) poodle; (vagabondo) tramp

'barca, -che sf boat; **~ a motore** motorboat; **~ a remi** rowing boat; **~ a vela** sailing boat (BRIT), sailboat (US)

barcol'lare /72/ vi to stagger

ba'rella sf (lettiga) stretcher

ba'rile sm barrel, cask

ba'rista, -i, -e sm/f barman (barmaid); (proprietario) bar owner

ba'rocco, -a, -chi, -che ag, sm baroque

ba'rometro sm barometer

ba'rone sm baron; **baro'nessa** sf baroness

'barra sf bar; (Naut) helm; (linea grafica) line, stroke

bar'rare /72/ vt to bar

barri'care /20/ *vt* to barricade;
barricarsi *vpr* to barricade o.s.
barri'era *sf* barrier; (*Geo*) reef
ba'ruffa *sf* scuffle
barzel'letta [bardzel'letta] *sf* joke,
funny story
ba'sare /72/ *vt* to base, found;
basarsi *vpr*: **basarsi su** (*fatti, prove*)
to be based o founded on; (*persona*) to
base one's arguments on
'basco, -a, -schi, -sche *ag* Basque
▷ *sm* (*copricapo*) beret
'base *sf* base; (*fig: fondamento*) basis;
(*Pol*) rank and file; **di ~** basic; **in ~ a**
on the basis of, according to; **a ~ di
caffè** coffee-based
'baseball ['beisbo:l] *sm* baseball
ba'silica, -che *sf* basilica
ba'silico *sm* basil
'basket ['basket] *sm* basketball
bas'sista, -i, -e *sm/f* bass player
'basso, -a *ag* low; (*di statura*) short;
(*meridionale*) southern ▷ *sm* bottom,
lower part; (*Mus*) bass; **la bassa
Italia** southern Italy
bassorili'evo *sm* bas-relief
bas'sotto, -a *ag* squat ▷ *sm* (*cane*)
dachshund
'basta *escl* (that's) enough!, that
will do!
bas'tardo, -a *ag* (*animale, pianta*)
hybrid, crossbreed; (*persona*)
illegitimate, bastard (*peg*) ▷ *sm/f*
illegitimate child, bastard (*peg*)
bas'tare /72/ *vi, vb impers* to be
enough, be sufficient; **~ a qn** to be
enough for sb; **basta chiedere** o **che
chieda a un vigile** you have only to
o need only ask a policeman; **basta
così, grazie** that's enough, thanks
basto'nare /72/ *vt* to beat, thrash
baston'cino [baston'tʃino] *sm* (*Sci*)
ski pole; **bastoncini di pesce** fish
fingers
bas'tone *sm* stick; **~ da passeggio**
walking stick
bat'taglia [bat'taʎʎa] *sf* battle;
fight

bat'tello *sm* boat
bat'tente *sm* (*imposta: di porta*) wing,
flap; (: *di finestra*) shutter; (*batacchio:
di porta*) knocker; (: *di orologio*)
hammer; **chiudere i battenti** (*fig*) to
shut up shop
'battere /1/ *vt* to beat; (*grano*) to
thresh; (*percorrere*) to scour ▷ *vi*
(*bussare*) to knock; (*pioggia, sole*) to
beat down; (*cuore*) to beat; (*Tennis*)
to serve; (*urtare*): **~ contro** to hit o
strike against; **battersi** *vpr* to fight;
~ le mani to clap; **~ i piedi** to stamp
one's feet; **~ a macchina** to type; **~
bandiera italiana** to fly the Italian
flag; **~ in testa** (*Aut*) to knock; **in
un batter d'occhio** in the twinkling
of an eye
batte'ria *sf* battery; (*Mus*) drums *pl*
bat'terio *sm* bacterium
batte'rista, -i, -e *sm/f* drummer
bat'tesimo *sm* (*rito*) baptism;
christening
battez'zare [batted'dzare] /72/ *vt* to
baptize; to christen
batti'panni *sm inv* carpet-beater
battis'trada *sm inv* (*di pneumatico*)
tread; (*di gara*) pacemaker
'battito *sm* beat, throb; **~ cardiaco**
heartbeat
bat'tuta *sf* blow; (*di macchina da
scrivere*) stroke; (*Mus*) bar; beat; (*Teat*)
cue; (*frase spiritosa*) witty remark; (*di
caccia*) beating; (*Polizia*) combing,
scouring; (*Tennis*) service
ba'tuffolo *sm* wad
ba'ule *sm* trunk; (*Aut*) boot (*BRIT*),
trunk (*US*)
'bava *sf* (*di animale*) slaver, slobber; (*di
lumaca*) slime; (*di vento*) breath
bava'glino [bavaʎ'ʎino] *sm* bib
ba'vaglio [ba'vaʎʎo] *sm* gag
'bavero *sm* collar
ba'zar [bad'dzar] *sm inv* bazaar
BCE *sigla f* (= *Banca centrale europea*)
ECB
be'ato, -a *ag* blessed; (*fig*) happy;
~ te! lucky you!

b

bec'care /20/ vt to peck; (fig: raffreddore) to catch; **beccarsi** vpr (fig) to squabble; **beccarsi qc** to catch sth

beccherò ecc [bekke'rɔ] vb vedi **beccare**

'**becco, -chi** sm beak, bill; (di caffettiera ecc) spout; lip

Be'fana sf old woman who, according to legend, brings children their presents at the Epiphany; (Epifania) Epiphany; **befana** hag, witch

⊕ **BEFANA**

Marking the end of the traditional 12 days of Christmas on 6 January, the Befana, or the feast of the Epiphany, is a national holiday in Italy. It is named after the old woman who, legend has it, comes down the chimney the night before, bringing gifts to children who have been good during the year and leaving lumps of coal for those who have not.

beffardo, -a ag scornful, mocking

'**begli** ['beʎʎi], '**bei** ag vedi **bello**

beige [bɛʒ] ag inv beige

bel ag vedi **bello**

be'lare /72/ vi to bleat

'**belga, -gi, -ghe** ag, smf Belgian

'**Belgio** ['bɛldʒo] sm: **il ~** Belgium

'**bella** sf (Sport) decider; vedi **bello**

bel'lezza [bel'lettsa] sf beauty

PAROLA CHIAVE

'**bello, -a** (ag: dav sm **bel** + C, **bell'** + V, **bello** + s impura, gn, pn, ps, x, z, pl **bei** + C, **begli** + s impura ecc o V) ag **1** (oggetto, donna, paesaggio) beautiful, lovely; (uomo) handsome; (tempo) beautiful, fine, lovely; **le belle arti** fine arts

2 (quantità): **una bella cifra** a considerable sum of money; **un bel niente** absolutely nothing

3 (rafforzativo): **è una truffa bella e buona!** it's a real fraud!; **è bell'e finito** it's already finished

▶ sm **1** (bellezza) beauty; (: tempo) fine weather

2: **adesso viene il bello** now comes the best bit; **sul più bello** at the crucial point; **cosa fai di bello?** are you doing anything interesting?

▶ av: **fa bello** the weather is fine, it's fine

'**belva** sf wild animal

belve'dere sm inv panoramic viewpoint

benché [ben'ke] cong although

'**benda** sf bandage; (per gli occhi) blindfold; **ben'dare** /72/ vt to bandage; to blindfold

'**bene** av well; (completamente, affatto): **è ben difficile** it's very difficult ▷ ag inv: **gente ~** well-to-do people ▷ sm good; **beni** smpl (averi) property sg, estate sg: **io sto ~/poco ~** I'm well/not very well; **va ~** all right; **volere un ~ dell'anima a qn** to love sb very much; **un uomo per ~** a respectable man; **fare ~** to do the right thing; **fare ~ a** (salute) to be good for; **fare del ~ a qn** to do sb a good turn; **beni di consumo** consumer goods

bene'detto, -a pp di **benedire** ▷ ag blessed, holy

bene'dire /38/ vt to bless; to consecrate

benedu'cato, -a ag well-mannered

benefi'cenza [benefi'tʃɛntsa] sf charity

bene'ficio [bene'fitʃo] sm benefit; **con ~ d'inventario** (fig) with reservations

be'nessere sm well-being

benes'tante ag well-to-do

be'nigno, -a [be'niɲɲo] ag kind, kindly; (critica ecc) favourable; (Med) benign

benve'nuto, -a ag, sm welcome; **dare il ~ a qn** to welcome sb

ben'zina [ben'dzina] *sf* petrol (BRIT), gas (US); **fare ~** to get petrol *o* gas; **rimanere senza ~** to run out of petrol *o* gas; **~ verde** unleaded petrol; **benzi'naio** *sm* petrol (BRIT) *o* gas (US) pump attendant

'bere /16/ *vt* to drink; **darla a ~ a qn** (*fig*) to fool sb

ber'lina *sf* (*Aut*) saloon (car) (BRIT), sedan (US)

Ber'lino *sf* Berlin

ber'muda *smpl* (*calzoncini*) Bermuda shorts

ber'noccolo *sm* bump; (*inclinazione*) flair

ber'retto *sm* cap

berrò *ecc vb vedi* **bere**

ber'saglio [ber'saʎʎo] *sm* target

bescia'mella [beʃʃa'mɛlla] *sf* béchamel sauce

bes'temmia *sf* curse; (*Rel*) blasphemy; **bestemmi'are** /19/ *vi* to curse, to blaspheme ▷ *vt* to curse, swear at; to blaspheme

'bestia *sf* animal; **andare in ~** (*fig*) to fly into a rage; **besti'ale** *ag* beastly; animal *cpd*; (*fam*): **fa un freddo bestiale** it's bitterly cold; **besti'ame** *sm* livestock; (*bovino*) cattle *pl*

be'tulla *sf* birch

be'vanda *sf* drink, beverage

'bevo *ecc vb vedi* **bere**

be'vuto, -a *pp di* **bere**

'bevvi *ecc vb vedi* **bere**

bianche'ria [bjanke'ria] *sf* linen; **~ intima** underwear; **~ da donna** ladies' underwear, lingerie; **~ femminile** lingerie

bi'anco, -a, -chi, -che *ag* white; (*non scritto*) blank ▷ *sm* white; (*intonaco*) whitewash ▷ *sm/f* white, white man (woman); **in ~** (*foglio, assegno*) blank; **in ~ e nero** (*TV, Fot*) black and white; **mangiare in ~** to follow a bland diet; **pesce in ~** boiled fish; **andare in ~** (*non riuscire*) to fail; **notte bianca** *o* **in ~** sleepless night; **~ dell'uovo** egg-white

biasi'mare /72/ *vt* to disapprove of, censure

'Bibbia *sf* (*anche fig*) Bible

bibe'ron *sm inv* feeding bottle

'bibita *sf* (soft) drink

biblio'teca, -che *sf* library; (*mobile*) bookcase

bicarbo'nato *sm*: **~ (di sodio)** bicarbonate (of soda)

bicchi'ere [bik'kjɛre] *sm* glass

bici'cletta [bitʃi'kletta] *sf* bicycle; **andare in ~** to cycle

bidè *sm inv* bidet

bi'dello, -a *sm/f* (*Ins*) janitor

bi'done *sm* drum, can; (*anche*: **~ dell'immondizia**) (dust)bin; (*fam*: *truffa*) swindle; **fare un ~ a qn** (*fam*) to let sb down; to cheat sb

bien'nale *ag* biennial

bifami'liare *ag* (*villa, casetta*) semi-detached

bifor'carsi /20/ *vpr* to fork

bigiotte'ria [bidʒotte'ria] *sf* costume jewellery (BRIT) *o* jewelry (US); (*negozio*) jeweller's (shop) (BRIT) *o* jewelry store (US: *selling only costume jewellery*)

bigliet'taio, -a *sm/f* (*nei treni*) ticket inspector; (*in autobus ecc*) conductor

bigliette'ria [biʎʎette'ria] *sf* (*di stazione*) ticket office; booking office; (*di teatro*) box office

bigli'etto [biʎ'ʎetto] *sm* (*per viaggi, spettacoli ecc*) ticket; (*cartoncino*) card; **~ di banca** (bank)note; (*anche:* **~ d'auguri/da visita**) greetings/ visiting card; **~ di andata e ritorno** return (*BRIT*) *o* round-trip (*US*) ticket; **~ di sola andata** single (ticket); **~ elettronico** e-ticket

bignè [biɲ'ɲɛ] *sm inv* cream puff

bigo'dino *sm* roller, curler

bi'gotto, -a *ag* over-pious ▷ *sm/f* church fiend

bi'kini *sm inv* bikini

bi'lancia, -ce [bi'lantʃa] *sf* (*pesa*) scales *pl*; (*: di precisione*) balance; **B~** Libra; **~ commerciale/dei pagamenti** balance of trade/ payments

bi'lancio [bi'lantʃo] *sm* (*Comm*) balance (sheet); (*statale*) budget; **fare il ~ di** (*fig*) to assess; **~ consuntivo** (final) balance; **~ preventivo** budget

biliar'dino *sm* pinball

bili'ardo *sm* billiards *sg*; (*tavolo*) billiard table

bi'lingue *ag* bilingual

bilo'cale *sm* two-room flat (*BRIT*) *o* apartment (*US*)

'bimbo, -a *sm/f* little boy (girl)

bi'nario, -a *ag* (*sistema*) binary ▷ *sm* (*railway*) track *o* line; (*piattaforma*) platform; **~ morto** dead-end track

bi'nocolo *sm* binoculars *pl*

bio... *prefisso* bio; **biocarbu'rante** *sm* biofuel; **biodegra'dabile** *ag* biodegradable; **biodi'namico, -a, -ci, -che** *ag* biodynamic; **biogra'fia** *sf* biography; **biolo'gia** *sf* biology

bio'logico, -a, -ci, -che *ag* (*scienze, fenomeni ecc*) biological; (*agricoltura, prodotti*) organic; **guerra biologica** biological warfare

bi'ondo, -a *ag* blond, fair

biotecnolo'gia [biotecnolo'dʒia] *sf* biotechnology

bipo'lare *ag* bipolar

biri'chino, -a [biri'kino] *ag* mischievous ▷ *sm/f* scamp, little rascal

bi'rillo *sm* skittle (*BRIT*), pin (*US*)

'biro® *sf inv* biro®

'birra *sf* beer; **~ chiara/scura** lager/ stout; **a tutta ~** (*fig*) at top speed; **birre'ria** *sf* ≈ bierkeller

bis *escl, sm inv* encore

bis'betico, -a, -ci, -che *ag* ill-tempered, crabby

bisbigli'are [bizbiʎ'ʎare] /27/ *vt, vi* to whisper

'bisca, -sche *sf* gambling house

'biscia, -sce [biʃʃa] *sf* snake; **~ d'acqua** water snake

biscot'tato, -a *ag* crisp; **fette biscottate** rusks

bis'cotto *sm* biscuit

bisessu'ale *ag, smf* bisexual

bises'tile *ag*: **anno ~** leap year

bis'nonno, -a *sm/f* great grandfather/grandmother

biso'gnare [bizoɲ'ɲare] /15/ *vb impers*: **bisogna che tu parta/lo faccia** you'll have to go/do it; **bisogna parlargli** we'll (*o* I'll) have to talk to him

bi'sogno [bi'zoɲɲo] *sm* need; **ha ~ di qualcosa?** do you need anything?

bis'tecca, -che *sf* steak, beefsteak

bisticci'are [bistit'tʃare] /14/ *vi* to quarrel, bicker; **bisticciarsi** *vpr* to quarrel, bicker

'bisturi *sm inv* scalpel

'bivio *sm* fork; (*fig*) dilemma

biz'zarro, -a [bid'dzarro] *ag* bizarre, strange

blate'rare /72/ *vi* to chatter

blin'dato, -a *ag* armoured

bloc'care /20/ *vt* to block; (*isolare*) to isolate, cut off; (*porto*) to blockade; (*prezzi, beni*) to freeze; (*meccanismo*) to jam; **bloccarsi** *vpr* (*motore*) to stall; (*freni, porta*) to jam, stick; (*ascensore*) to get stuck, stop

blocche'rò *ecc* [blokke'rɔ] *vb vedi* **bloccare**

bloc'chetto [blok'ketto] *sm* notebook; (*di biglietti*) book

'blocco, -chi *sm* block; (*Mil*) blockade; (*dei fitti*) restriction; (*quadernetto*) pad; (fig: unione) coalition; (il bloccare) blocking; isolating, cutting-off; blockading; freezing; jamming; **in ~** (nell'insieme) as a whole; (Comm) in bulk; **~ cardiaco** cardiac arrest; **~ stradale** road block

blog [blog] sm inv blog

bloggare /80/ vi to blog

blogo'sfera sf blogosphere

blu ag inv, sm inv dark blue

'blusa sf (camiciotto) smock; (camicetta) blouse

'boa sm inv (Zool) boa constrictor; (sciarpa) feather boa ▷ sf buoy

bo'ato sm rumble, roar

bob [bɔb] sm inv bobsleigh

'bocca, -che sf mouth; **in ~ al lupo!** good luck!

boc'caccia, -ce [bok'kattʃa] sf (malalingua) gossip; **fare le boccacce** to pull faces

boc'cale sm jug; **~ da birra** tankard

boc'cetta [bot'tʃetta] sf small bottle

'boccia, -ce ['bottʃa] sf bottle; (da vino) decanter, carafe; (palla di legno, metallo) bowl; **gioco delle bocce** bowls sg

bocci'are [bot'tʃare] /14/ vt (proposta, progetto) to reject; (Ins) to fail; (Bocce) to hit

bocci'olo [bot'tʃɔlo] sm bud

boc'cone sm mouthful, morsel

boicot'tare /72/ vt to boycott

'bolla sf bubble; (Med) blister; **~ di consegna** (Comm) delivery note; **~ papale** papal bull

bol'lente ag boiling; boiling hot

bol'letta sf bill; (ricevuta) receipt; **essere in ~** to be hard up

bollet'tino sm bulletin; (Comm) note; **~ meteorologico** weather forecast; **~ di spedizione** consignment note

bolli'cina [bolli'tʃina] sf bubble

bol'lire /17/ vt, vi to boil

bolli'tore sm boiler; (Cuc: per acqua) kettle

'bollo sm stamp; **~ per patente** driving licence tax; **~ postale** postmark

'bomba sf bomb; **~ atomica** atom bomb; **~ a mano** hand grenade; **~ ad orologeria** time bomb

bombarda'mento sm bombardment; bombing

bombar'dare /72/ vt to bombard; (da aereo) to bomb

'bombola sf cylinder

bombo'letta sf spray can

bomboni'era sf box of sweets (as souvenir at weddings, first communions etc)

bo'nifico, -ci sm (riduzione, abbuono) discount; (versamento a terzi) credit transfer

bontà sf goodness; (cortesia) kindness; **aver la ~ di fare qc** to be good o kind enough to do sth

borbot'tare /72/ vi to mumble

'borchia ['borkja] sf stud

bor'deaux [bor'do] ag inv, sm inv maroon

'bordo sm (Naut) ship's side; (orlo) edge; (striscia di guarnizione) border, trim; **a ~ di** (nave, aereo) aboard, on board; (macchina) in

bor'ghese [bor'geze] ag (spesso peg) middle-class; bourgeois; **abito ~** civilian dress

'borgo, -ghi sm (paesino) village; (quartiere) district; (sobborgo) suburb

boro'talco sm talcum powder

bor'raccia, -ce [bor'rattʃa] sf canteen, water-bottle

'borsa sf bag; (anche: **~ da signora**) handbag; (Econ): **la B~ (valori)** the Stock Exchange; **~ dell'acqua calda** hot-water bottle; **~ nera** black market; **~ della spesa** shopping bag; **~ di studio** grant; **borsel'lino** sm purse; **bor'setta** sf handbag

'bosco, -schi sm wood

bos'niaco, -a, -ci, -che ag, sm/f Bosnian

'Bosnia-Erze'govina ['bɔsnja erdze'govina] sf: **la ~** Bosnia-Herzegovina

Bot, bot *sigla m inv* (= *buono ordinario del Tesoro*) short-term Treasury bond

bo'tanico, -a, -ci, -che *ag* botanical ▷ *sm* botanist ▷ *sf* botany

'**botola** *sf* trap door

'**botta** *sf* blow; (*rumore*) bang

'**botte** *sf* barrel, cask

bot'tega, -ghe *sf* shop; (*officina*) workshop

bot'tiglia [bot'tiʎʎa] *sf* bottle; **bottiglie'ria** *sf* wine shop

bot'tino *sm* (*di guerra*) booty; (*di rapina, furto*) loot

'**botto** *sm* bang; crash; **di ~** suddenly

bot'tone *sm* button; **attaccare (un) ~ a qn** to buttonhole sb

bo'vino, -a *ag* bovine; **bovini** *smpl* cattle

box [bɔks] *sm inv* (*per cavalli*) horsebox; (*per macchina*) lock-up; (*per macchina da corsa*) pit; (*per bambini*) playpen

boxe [bɔks] *sf* boxing

'**boxer** ['bɔkser] *sm inv* (*cane*) boxer ▷ *smpl* (*mutande*): **un paio di ~** a pair of boxer shorts

BR *sigla fpl* = **Brigate Rosse**

brac'cetto [brat'tʃetto] *sm*: **a ~** arm in arm

braccia'letto [brattʃa'letto] *sm* bracelet, bangle

bracci'ata [brat'tʃata] *sf* (*nel nuoto*) stroke

'**braccio** ['brattʃo] *sm* (*pl f* **braccia**) (*Anat*) arm; (*pl m* **bracci**) (*di gru, fiume*) arm; (*di edificio*) wing; **~ di mare** sound; **bracci'olo** *sm* (*appoggio*) arm

'**bracco, -chi** *sm* hound

'**brace** ['bratʃe] *sf* embers *pl*

braci'ola [bra'tʃola] *sf* (*Cuc*) chop

'**branca, -che** *sf* branch

'**branchia** ['brankja] *sf* (*Zool*) gill

'**branco, -chi** *sm* (*di cani, lupi*) pack; (*di uccelli, pecore*) flock; (*peg: di persone*) gang, pack

bran'dina *sf* camp bed (BRIT), cot (US)

'**brano** *sm* piece; (*di libro*) passage

Bra'sile *sm*: **il ~** Brazil; **brasili'ano, -a** *ag, sm/f* Brazilian

'**bravo, -a** *ag* (*abile*) clever, capable, skilful; (*buono*) good, honest; (: *bambino*) good; (*coraggioso*) brave; **~!** well done!; (*al teatro*) bravo!

bra'vura *sf* cleverness, skill

Bre'tagna [bre'taɲɲa] *sf*: **la ~** Brittany

bre'tella *sf* (*Aut*) link; **bretelle** *sfpl* (*di calzoni*) braces

bret(t)one *ag, smf* Breton

'**breve** *ag* brief, short; **in ~** in short

brevet'tare /72/ *vt* to patent

bre'vetto *sm* patent; **~ di pilotaggio** pilot's licence (BRIT) o license (US)

'**bricco, -chi** *sm* jug; **~ del caffè** coffeepot

'**briciola** ['britʃola] *sf* crumb

'**briciolo** ['britʃolo] *sm* (*fig*) bit

'**briga, -ghe** *sf* (*fastidio*) trouble, bother; **pigliarsi la ~ di fare qc** to take the trouble to do sth

bri'gata *sf* (*Mil*) brigade; (*gruppo*) group, party; **le Brigate Rosse** (*Pol*) the Red Brigades

'**briglia** ['briʎʎa] *sf* rein; **a ~ sciolta** at full gallop; (*fig*) at full speed

bril'lante *ag* bright; (*anche fig*) brilliant; (*che luccica*) shining ▷ *sm* diamond

bril'lare /72/ *vi* to shine; (*mina*) to blow up ▷ *vt* (*mina*) to set off

'**brillo, -a** *ag* merry, tipsy

'**brina** *sf* hoarfrost

brin'dare /72/ *vi*: **~ a qn/qc** to drink to o toast sb/sth

'**brindisi** *sm inv* toast

bri'oche [bri'ɔʃ] *sf inv* brioche (bun)

bri'tannico, -a, -ci, -che *ag* British

'**brivido** *sm* shiver; (*di ribrezzo*) shudder; (*di febbre*) thrill

brizzo'lato, -a [brittso'lato] *ag* (*persona*) going grey; (*barba, capelli*) greying

'**brocca, -che** *sf* jug

'**broccoli** *smpl* broccoli *sg*

'**brodo** *sm* broth; (*per cucinare*) stock; ~ **ristretto** consommé

bron'chite [bron'kite] *sf* (*Med*) bronchitis

bronto'lare /72/ *vi* to grumble; (*tuono, stomaco*) to rumble

'**bronzo** ['brondzo] *sm* bronze

'**browser** ['brauzer] *sm inv* (*Inform*) browser

brucia'pelo [brutʃa'pelo]: **a ~** *av* point-blank

bruci'are [bru'tʃare] /14/ *vt* to burn; (*scottare*) to scald ▷ *vi* to burn; **bruciarsi** *vpr* to burn o.s.; (*fallire*) to ruin one's chances; ~ **le tappe** *o* **i tempi** (*fig*) to shoot ahead; **bruciarsi la carriera** to put an end to one's career

'**bruco, -chi** *sm* grub; (*di farfalla*) caterpillar

'**brufolo** *sm* pimple, spot

'**brullo, -a** *ag* bare, bleak

'**bruno, -a** *ag* brown, dark; (*persona*) dark(-haired)

'**brusco, -a, -schi, -sche** *ag* (*sapore*) sharp; (*modi, persona*) brusque, abrupt; (*movimento*) abrupt, sudden

bru'sio *sm* buzz, buzzing

bru'tale *ag* brutal

'**brutto, -a** *ag* ugly; (*cattivo*) bad; (*malattia, strada, affare*) nasty, bad; ~ **tempo** bad weather

Bru'xelles [bry'sɛl] *sf* Brussels

BSE [biesse'e] *sigla f* BSE

'**buca, -che** *sf* hole; (*avvallamento*) hollow; ~ **delle lettere** letterbox

buca'neve *sm inv* snowdrop

bu'care /20/ *vt* (*forare*) to make a hole (*o* holes) in; (*pungere*) to pierce; (*biglietto*) to punch; **bucarsi** *vpr* (*con eroina*) to mainline; ~ **una gomma** to have a puncture

bu'cato *sm* (*operazione*) washing; (*panni*) wash, washing

'**buccia, -ce** ['buttʃa] *sf* skin, peel

bucherò *ecc* [buke'rɔ] *vb vedi* **bucare**

'**buco, -chi** *sm* hole

bud'dismo *sm* Buddhism

bu'dino *sm* pudding

'**bue** *sm* ox; (*anche:* **carne di ~**) beef

bu'fera *sf* storm

'**buffo, -a** *ag* funny; (*Teat*) comic

bu'gia, -gie [bu'dʒia] *sf* lie; **dire una ~** to tell a lie; **bugi'ardo, -a** *ag* lying, deceitful ▷ *sm/f* liar

'**buio, -a** *ag* dark ▷ *sm* dark, darkness

'**bulbo** *sm* (*Bot*) bulb; ~ **oculare** eyeball

Bulga'ria *sf*: **la ~** Bulgaria; '**bulgaro, -a** *ag, sm/f, sm* Bulgarian

buli'mia *sf* bulimia; **bu'limico, -a, -ci, -che** *ag* bulimic

bullismo [bul'lizmo] *sm* bullying

bul'lone *sm* bolt

buona'notte *escl* good night! ▷ *sf*: **dare la ~ a** to say good night to

buona'sera *escl* good evening!

buongi'orno [bwon'dʒorno] *escl* good morning (*o* afternoon)!

buongus'taio, -a *sm/f* gourmet

○ **PAROLA CHIAVE**

bu'ono, -a (*ag: dav sm* **buon** + C o V, **buono** + *s impura, gn, pn, ps, z; dav sf* **buon'** + V) *ag* **1** (*gen*) good; **un buon pranzo/ristorante** a good lunch/restaurant; **(stai) buono!** behave!

2 (*benevolo*): **buono (con)** good (to), kind (to)

3 (*giusto, valido*) right; **al momento buono** at the right moment

4 (*adatto*): **buono a/da** fit for/to; **essere buono a nulla** to be no good *o* use at anything

5 (*auguri*): **buon anno!** happy New Year!; **buon appetito!** enjoy your meal!; **buon compleanno!** happy birthday!; **buon divertimento!** have a nice time!; **buona fortuna!** good luck!; **buon riposo!** sleep well!; **buon viaggio!** bon voyage!, have a good trip!

6: a buon mercato cheap; **di buon'ora** early; **buon senso** common sense; **alla buona** *ag* simple

▶ *av* in a simple way, without any fuss
▶ *sm* **1** (*bontà*) goodness, good
2 (*Comm*) voucher, coupon; **buono di cassa** cash voucher; **buono di consegna** delivery note; **buono del Tesoro** Treasury bill

buon'senso *sm* = **buon senso**
burat'tino *sm* puppet
'burbero, -a *ag* surly, gruff
buro'cratico, -a, -ci, -che *ag* bureaucratic
burocra'zia [burokrat'tsia] *sf* bureaucracy
bur'rasca, -sche *sf* storm
'burro *sm* butter
bur'rone *sm* ravine
bus'sare /72/ *vi* to knock
'bussola *sf* compass
'busta *sf* (*da lettera*) envelope; (*astuccio*) case; **in ~ aperta/chiusa** in an unsealed/sealed envelope; **~ paga** pay packet
busta'rella *sf* bribe, backhander
bus'tina *sf* (*piccola busta*) envelope; (*di cibi, farmaci*) sachet; (*Mil*) forage cap; **~ di tè** tea bag
'busto *sm* bust; (*indumento*) corset, girdle; **a mezzo ~** (*fotografia, ritratto*) half-length
but'tare /72/ *vt* to throw; (*anche:* **~ via**) to throw away; **buttarsi** *vpr* (*saltare*) to jump; **~ giù** (*scritto*) to scribble down; (*cibo*) to gulp down; (*edificio*) to pull down, demolish; (*pasta, verdura*) to put into boiling water; **buttarsi dalla finestra** to jump out of the window
byte ['bait] *sm inv* byte

ca'bina *sf* (*di nave*) cabin; (*da spiaggia*) beach hut; (*di autocarro, treno*) cab; (*di aereo*) cockpit; (*di ascensore*) cage; **~ di pilotaggio** cockpit; **~ telefonica** callbox, (tele)phone box *o* booth
cabi'nato *sm* cabin cruiser
ca'cao *sm* cocoa
'caccia ['kattʃa] *sf* hunting; (*con fucile*) shooting; (*inseguimento*) chase; (*cacciagione*) game ▷ *sm inv* (*aereo*) fighter; (*nave*) destroyer; **~ grossa** big-game hunting; **~ all'uomo** manhunt
cacci'are [kat'tʃare] /14/ *vt* to hunt; (*mandar via*) to chase away; (*ficcare*) to shove, stick ▷ *vi* to hunt; **cacciarsi** *vpr*: **~ fuori qc** to whip *o* pull sth out; **~ un urlo** to let out a yell; **dove s'è cacciata la mia borsa?** where has my bag got to?; **cacciarsi nei guai** to get into trouble; **caccia'tore** *sm* hunter; **cacciatore di frodo** poacher

caccia'vite [kattʃa'vite] *sm inv* screwdriver

'cactus *sm inv* cactus

ca'davere *sm* (dead) body, corpse

'caddi *ecc vb vedi* **cadere**

ca'denza [ka'dɛntsa] *sf* cadence; (*andamento ritmico*) rhythm; (*Mus*) cadenza

ca'dere /18/ *vi* to fall; (*denti, capelli*) to fall out; (*tetto*) to fall in; **questa gonna cade bene** this skirt hangs well; **lasciar ~** (*anche fig*) to drop; **~ dal sonno** to be falling asleep on one's feet; **~ dalle nuvole** (*fig*) to be taken aback

cadrò *ecc vb vedi* **cadere**

ca'duta *sf* fall; **la ~ dei capelli** hair loss

caffè *sm inv* coffee; (*locale*) café; **~ corretto** coffee with liqueur; **~ in grani** coffee beans; **~ macchiato** coffee with a dash of milk; **~ macinato** ground coffee

caffel'latte *sm inv* white coffee

caffetti'era *sf* coffeepot

'cagna ['kaɲɲa] *sf* (*Zool, peg*) bitch

CAI *sigla m* = **Club Alpino Italiano**

cala'brone *sm* hornet

cala'maro *sm* squid

cala'mita *sf* magnet

calamità *sf inv* calamity, disaster

ca'lare /72/ *vt* (*far discendere*) to lower; (*Maglia*) to decrease ▷ *vi* (*discendere*) to go down (*o come*) down; (*tramontare*) to set, go down; **~ di peso** to lose weight

cal'cagno [kal'kaɲɲo] *sm* heel

cal'care /20/ *sm* (*incrostazione*) (lime)scale

'calce ['kaltʃe] *sm*: **in ~** at the foot of the page ▷ *sf* lime; **~ viva** quicklime

cal'cetto [kal'tʃetto] *sm* (*calcio-balilla*) table football; (*calcio a cinque*) five-a-side (football)

calci'are [kal'tʃare] /14/ *vt, vi* to kick; **calcia'tore** *sm* footballer

'calcio ['kaltʃo] *sm* (*pedata*) kick; (*sport*) football, soccer; (*di pistola, fucile*) butt; (*Chim*) calcium; **~ d'angolo** (*Sport*) corner (kick); **~ di punizione** (*Sport*) free kick; **~ di rigore** penalty

calco'lare /72/ *vt* to calculate, work out, reckon; (*ponderare*) to weigh (up); **calcola'tore, -'trice** *ag* calculating ▷ *sm* calculator; (*fig*) calculating person ▷ *sf*: **calcolatore elettronico** computer; **calcola'trice** *sf* calculator

'calcolo *sm* (*anche Mat*) calculation; (*infinitesimale ecc*) calculus; (*Med*) stone; **fare i propri calcoli** (*fig*) to weigh the pros and cons; **per ~** out of self-interest

cal'daia *sf* boiler

'caldo, -a *ag* warm; (*molto caldo*) hot; (*fig: appassionato*) keen; hearty ▷ *sm* heat; **ho ~** I'm warm; I'm hot; **fa ~** it's warm; it's hot

caleidos'copio *sm* kaleidoscope

calen'dario *sm* calendar

'calibro *sm* (*di arma*) calibre, bore; (*Tecn*) callipers *pl*; (*fig*) calibre; **di grosso ~** (*fig*) prominent

'calice ['kalitʃe] *sm* goblet; (*Rel*) chalice

Cali'fornia *sf* California; **californi'ano, -a** *ag* Californian

calligra'fia *sf* (*scrittura*) handwriting; (*arte*) calligraphy

'callo *sm* callus; (*ai piedi*) corn

'calma *sf* calm

cal'mante *sm* tranquillizer

cal'mare /72/ *vt* to calm; (*lenire*) to soothe; **calmarsi** *vpr* to grow calm, calm down; (*vento*) to abate; (*dolori*) to ease

'calmo, -a *ag* calm, quiet

'calo *sm* (*Comm: di prezzi*) fall; (*: di volume*) shrinkage; (*: di peso*) loss

ca'lore *sm* warmth; (*intenso*) heat; **essere in ~** (*Zool*) to be on heat

calo'ria *sf* calorie

calo'rifero *sm* radiator

calo'roso, -a *ag* warm

calpes'tare /72/ *vt* to tread on, trample on; **"è vietato ~ l'erba"** "keep off the grass"

ca'lunnia *sf* slander; (*scritta*) libel

cal'vizie [kal'vittsje] *sf* baldness

'calvo, -a *ag* bald

'calza ['kaltsa] *sf* (*da donna*) stocking; (*da uomo*) sock; **fare la ~** to knit; **calze di nailon** nylons, (nylon) stockings

calza'maglia [kaltsa'maʎʎa] *sf* tights *pl*; (*per danza, ginnastica*) leotard

calzet'tone [kaltset'tone] *sm* heavy knee-length sock

cal'zino [kal'tsino] *sm* sock

calzo'laio [kaltso'lajo] *sm* shoemaker; (*che ripara scarpe*) cobbler

calzon'cini [kaltson'tʃini] *smpl* shorts; **~ da bagno** (swimming) trunks

cal'zone [kal'tsone] *sm* trouser leg; (*Cuc*) savoury turnover made with pizza dough; **calzoni** *smpl* (*pantaloni*) trousers (*BRIT*), pants (*US*)

camale'onte *sm* chameleon

cambia'mento *sm* change; **cambiamenti climatici** climate change *sg*

cambi'are /19/ *vt* to change; (*modificare*) to alter, change; (*barattare*) **~ (qc con qn/qc)** to exchange (sth with sb/for sth) ▷ *vi* to change, alter; **cambiarsi** *vpr* (*variare abito*) to change; **~ casa** to move (house); **~ idea** to change one's mind; **~ treno** to change trains

cambiava'lute *sm inv* exchange office

'cambio *sm* change; (*modifica*) alteration, change; (*scambio, Comm*) exchange; (*corso dei cambi*) rate of exchange); (*Tecn, Aut*) gears *pl*: **in ~ di** in exchange for; **dare il ~ a qn** to take over from sb

'camera *sf* room; (*anche:* **~ da letto**) bedroom; (*Pol*) chamber, house; **~ ardente** mortuary chapel; **~ d'aria** inner tube; (*di pallone*) bladder; **C~ di Commercio** Chamber of Commerce; **C~ dei Deputati** Chamber of Deputies, ≈ House of Commons (*BRIT*), ≈ House of Representatives (*US*); **~ a gas** gas chamber; **~ a un letto/a due letti/matrimoniale** single/twin-bedded/double room; **~ oscura** (*Fot*) dark room

> Attenzione! In inglese esiste la parola *camera*, che però significa *macchina fotografica*.

came'rata, -i, -e *sm/f* companion, mate ▷ *sf* dormitory

cameri'era *sf* (*domestica*) maid; (*che serve a tavola*) waitress; (*che fa le camere*) chambermaid

cameri'ere *sm* (*man*)servant; (*di ristorante*) waiter

came'rino *sm* (*Teat*) dressing room

'camice ['kamitʃe] *sm* (*Rel*) alb; (*per medici ecc*) white coat

cami'cetta [kami'tʃetta] *sf* blouse

ca'micia, -cie [ka'mitʃa] *sf* (*da uomo*) shirt; (*da donna*) blouse; **~ di forza** straitjacket; **~ da notte** (*da donna*) nightdress; (*da uomo*) nightshirt

cami'netto *sm* hearth, fireplace

ca'mino *sm* chimney; (*focolare*) fireplace, hearth

'camion *sm inv* lorry (*BRIT*), truck (*US*)

camio'nista, -i *sm* lorry driver (*BRIT*), truck driver (*US*)

cam'mello *sm* (*Zool*) camel; (*tessuto*) camel hair

cammi'nare /72/ *vi* to walk; (*funzionare*) to work, go

cam'mino *sm* walk; (*sentiero*) path; (*itinerario, direzione, tragitto*) way; **mettersi in ~** to set *o* start off

camo'milla *sf* camomile; (*infuso*) camomile tea

ca'moscio [ka'moʃʃo] *sm* chamois; **di ~** (*scarpe, borsa*) suede *cpd*

cam'pagna [kam'paɲɲa] *sf* country, countryside; (*Pol, Comm, Mil*) campaign; **in ~** in the country; **andare in ~** to go to the country; **fare una ~** to campaign; **~ pubblicitaria** advertising campaign

cam'pana *sf* bell; (*anche*: **~ di vetro**) bell jar; **~ (per la raccolta del vetro)** bottle bank; **campa'nello** *sm* (*all'uscio, da tavola*) bell

campa'nile *sm* bell tower, belfry

cam'peggio *sm* camping; (*terreno*) camp site; **fare (del) ~** to go camping

camper ['kamper] *sm inv* motor caravan (BRIT), motor home (US)

campio'nario, -a *ag*: **fiera campionaria** trade fair ▷ *sm* collection of samples

campio'nato *sm* championship

campi'one, -'essa *sm/f* (*Sport*) champion ▷ *sm* (*Comm*) sample

'campo *sm* field; (*Mil*) field; (*: accampamento*) camp; (*spazio delimitato: sportivo ecc*) ground; field; (*di quadro*) background; **i campi** (*campagna*) the countryside; **~ da aviazione** airfield; **~ di battaglia** (*Mil, fig*) battlefield; **~ di concentramento** concentration camp; **~ di golf** golf course; **~ profughi** refugee camp; **~ sportivo** sports ground; **~ da tennis** tennis court; **~ visivo** field of vision

'Canada *sm*: **il ~** Canada; **cana'dese** *ag, smf* Canadian ▷ *sf* (*anche*: **tenda canadese**) ridge tent

ca'naglia [ka'naʎʎa] *sf* rabble, mob; (*persona*) scoundrel, rogue

ca'nale *sm* (*anche fig*) channel; (*artificiale*) canal

'canapa *sf* hemp; **~ indiana** (*droga*) cannabis

cana'rino *sm* canary

cancel'lare [kantʃel'lare] /72/ *vt* (*con la gomma*) to rub out, erase; (*con la penna*) to strike out; (*annullare*) to annul, cancel; (*disdire*) to cancel

cancelle'ria [kantʃelle'ria] *sf* chancery; (*quanto necessario per scrivere*) stationery

can'cello [kan'tʃɛllo] *sm* gate

'cancro *sm* (*Med*) cancer; **C~** Cancer

candeg'gina [kanded'dʒina] *sf* bleach

can'dela *sf* candle; **~ (di accensione)** (*Aut*) spark(ing) plug

cande'labro *sm* candelabra

candeli'ere *sm* candlestick

candi'dare /72/ *vt* to present as candidate; **candidarsi** *vpr* to present o.s. as candidate

candi'dato, -a *sm/f* candidate; (*aspirante a una carica*) applicant

'candido, -a *ag* white as snow; (*puro*) pure; (*sincero*) sincere, candid

can'dito, -a *ag* candied

'cane *sm* dog; (*di pistola, fucile*) cock; **fa un freddo ~** it's bitterly cold; **non c'era un ~** there wasn't a soul; **~ da caccia** hunting dog; **~ da guardia** guard dog; **~ lupo** alsatian; **~ pastore** sheepdog

ca'nestro *sm* basket

can'guro *sm* kangaroo

ca'nile *sm* kennel; (*di allevamento*) kennels *pl*: **~ municipale** dog pound

'canna *sf* (*pianta*) reed; (*: indica, da zucchero*) cane; (*bastone*) stick, cane; (*di fucile*) barrel; (*di organo*) pipe; (*fam: Droga*) joint; **~ fumaria** chimney flue; **~ da pesca** (fishing) rod; **~ da zucchero** sugar cane

cannel'loni *smpl* pasta tubes stuffed with sauce and baked

cannocchi'ale [kannok'kjale] *sm* telescope

can'none *sm* (*Mil*) gun; (*: Storia*) cannon; (*tubo*) pipe, tube; (*piega*) box pleat; (*fig*) ace

can'nuccia, -ce [kan'nuttʃa] *sf* (drinking) straw

ca'noa *sf* canoe

ca'none *sm* canon, criterion; (*mensile, annuo*) rent; fee

canot'taggio [kanot'taddʒo] *sm* rowing

canotti'era *sf* vest

ca'notto sm small boat, dinghy; canoe

can'tante smf singer

can'tare /72/ vt, vi to sing; **cantau'tore, -'trice** sm/f singer-composer

canti'ere sm (Edil) (building) site; (anche: **~ navale**) shipyard

can'tina sf cellar; (bottega) wine shop; **~ sociale** cooperative winegrowers' association

> Attenzione! In inglese esiste la parola canteen, che però significa mensa.

'canto sm song; (arte) singing; (Rel) chant; chanting; (Poesia) poem, lyric; (parte di una poesia) canto; (parte, lato): **da un ~** on the one hand; **d'altro ~** on the other hand

canzo'nare [kantso'nare] /72/ vt to tease

can'zone [kan'tsone] sf song; (Poesia) canzone

'caos sm inv chaos; **ca'otico, -a, -ci, -che** ag chaotic

CAP sigla m = **codice di avviamento postale**

ca'pace [ka'patʃe] ag able, capable; (ampio, vasto) large, capacious; **sei ~ di farlo?** can you o are you able to do it?; **capacità** sf inv ability; (Dir, di recipiente) capacity

ca'panna sf hut

capan'none sm (Agr) barn; (fabbricato industriale) (factory) shed

ca'parbio, -a ag stubborn

ca'parra sf deposit, down payment

ca'pello sm hair; **capelli** smpl (capigliatura) hair sg

ca'pezzolo [ka'pettsolo] sm nipple

ca'pire /55/ vt to understand

capi'tale ag (mortale) capital; (fondamentale) main cpd, chief cpd ▷ sf (città) capital ▷ sm (Econ) capital

capi'tano sm captain

capi'tare /72/ vi (giungere casualmente) to happen to go, find o.s.; (accadere) to happen; (presentarsi: cosa) to turn up, present itself ▷ vb impers to happen; **mi è capitato un guaio** I've had a spot of trouble

capi'tello sm (Archit) capital

ca'pitolo sm chapter

capi'tombolo sm headlong fall, tumble

'capo sm head; (persona) head, leader; (: in ufficio) head, boss; (: in tribù) chief; (di tavolo, scale) head, top; (di filo) end; (Geo) cape; **andare a ~** to start a new paragraph; **da ~** over again; **~ di bestiame** head inv of cattle; **~ di vestiario** item of clothing; **Capo'danno** sm New Year; **capo'giro** sm dizziness no pl; **capola'voro, -i** sm masterpiece; **capo'linea** (pl **capilinea**) sm terminus; **capostazi'one** (pl **capistazione**) sm station master; **capo'tavola** (mpl **capitavola**, fpl **capotavola**) smf (persona) head of the table; **sedere a capotavola** to sit at the head of the table; **capo'volgere** /96/ vt to overturn; (fig) to reverse; **capovolgersi** vpr to overturn; (barca) to capsize; (fig) to be reversed

'cappa sf (mantello) cape, cloak; (del camino) hood

cap'pella sf (Rel) chapel

cap'pello sm hat

'cappero sm caper

cap'pone sm capon

cap'potto sm (over)coat

cappuc'cino [kapput'tʃino] sm (frate) Capuchin monk; (bevanda) cappuccino

cap'puccio [kap'puttʃo] sm (copricapo) hood; (della biro) cap

'capra sf (she-)goat

ca'priccio [ka'prittʃo] sm caprice, whim; (bizza) tantrum; **fare i capricci** to be very naughty; **capricci'oso, -a** ag capricious, whimsical; naughty

Capri'corno sm Capricorn

capri'ola sf somersault

capri'olo sm roe deer
'capro sm: **~ espiatorio** scapegoat
ca'prone sm billy-goat
'capsula sf capsule; (di arma, per bottiglie) cap
cap'tare /72/ vt (Radio, TV) to pick up; (cattivarsi) to gain, win
carabini'ere sm member of Italian military police force

§ **CARABINIERI**

Originally part of the armed forces, the Carabinieri are police who now have civil as well as military duties, such as maintaining public order. They include paratroop units and mounted divisions and report to either the Minister of the Interior or the Minister of Defence, depending on the function they are performing.

ca'raffa sf carafe
Ca'raibi smpl: **il mar dei ~** the Caribbean (Sea)
cara'mella sf sweet
ca'rattere sm character; (caratteristica) characteristic, trait; **avere un buon ~** to be good-natured; **~ jolly** wild card; **caratte'ristico, -a, -ci, -che** ag characteristic ▷ sf characteristic, trait
car'bone sm coal
carbu'rante sm (motor) fuel
carbura'tore sm carburettor
carce'rato, -a [kartʃe'rato] sm/f prisoner
'carcere ['kartʃere] sm prison; (pena) imprisonment
carci'ofo [kar'tʃɔfo] sm artichoke
cardel'lino sm goldfinch
car'diaco, -a, -ci, -che ag cardiac, heart cpd
cardi'nale ag, sm cardinal
'cardine sm hinge
'cardo sm thistle

ca'rente ag: **~ di** lacking in
cares'tia sf famine; (penuria) scarcity, dearth
ca'rezza [ka'rettsa] sf caress
'carica sf vedi **carico**
caricabatte'ria sm inv (Elettr) battery charger
cari'care /20/ vt (merce) to load; (orologio) to wind up; (batteria, Mil) to charge; (Inform) to load
'carico, -a, -chi, -che ag (fucile) loaded; (orologio) wound up; (batteria) charged; (colore) deep; (caffè, tè) strong; **~ di** (che porta un peso) loaded o laden with ▷ sm (il caricare) loading; (ciò che si carica) load; (fig: peso) burden, weight; **persona a ~** dependent; **essere a ~ di qn** (spese ecc) to be charged to sb
'carie sf (dentaria) decay
ca'rino, -a ag (grazioso) lovely, pretty, nice; (simpatico) nice
carità sf charity; **per ~!** (escl di rifiuto) good heavens, no!
carnagi'one [karna'dʒone] sf complexion
'carne sf flesh; (bovina, ovina ecc) meat; **~ di manzo/maiale/pecora** beef/pork/mutton; **~ in scatola** tinned o canned meat; **~ tritata** o **macinata** mince (BRIT), hamburger meat (US), minced (BRIT) o ground (US) meat
carne'vale sm carnival; **C~**; see note **"Carnevale"**

§ **CARNEVALE**

Carnevale is the name given to the period between Epiphany (6 January) and the beginning of Lent, when people throw parties, put on processions with spectacular floats, build bonfires in the "piazze" and dress up in fabulous costumes and masks. Building to a peak just before Lent, Carnevale culminates in the festivities of Martedì grasso (Shrove Tuesday).

'caro, -a ag (amato) dear; (costoso) dear, expensive; **è troppo ~** it's too expensive

ca'rogna [ka'roɲɲa] sf carrion; (fig: fam) swine

ca'rota sf carrot

caro'vana sf caravan

car'poni av on all fours

car'rabile ag suitable for vehicles; **"passo ~"** "keep clear"

carreggi'ata [karred'dʒata] sf carriageway (BRIT), roadway

car'rello sm trolley; (Aer) undercarriage; (Cine) dolly; (di macchina da scrivere) carriage

carri'era sf career; **fare ~** to get on; **a gran ~** at full speed

carri'ola sf wheelbarrow

'carro sm cart, wagon; **~ armato** tank; **~ attrezzi** (Aut) breakdown van

car'rozza [kar'rɔttsa] sf carriage, coach

carrozze'ria [karrottse'ria] sf body, coachwork (BRIT); (officina) coachbuilder's workshop (BRIT), body shop

carroz'zina [karrot'tsina] sf pram (BRIT), baby carriage (US)

'carta sf paper; (al ristorante) menu; (Geo) map; plan; (documento) card; (costituzione) charter; **carte** sfpl (documenti) papers, documents; **alla ~** (al ristorante) à la carte; **~ assegni** bank card; **~ assorbente** blotting paper; **~ bollata** o **da bollo** official stamped paper; **~ (da gioco)** playing card; **~ di credito** credit card; **~ fedeltà** loyalty card; **~ (geografica)** map; **~ d'identità** identity card; **~ igienica** toilet paper; **~ d'imbarco** (Aer, Naut) boarding card; **~ da lettere** writing paper; **~ libera** (Amm) unstamped paper; **~ stradale** road map; **~ da pacchi** wrapping paper; **~ da parati** wallpaper; **~ verde** (Aut) green card; **~ vetrata** sandpaper; **~ da visita** visiting card

car'taccia, -ce [kar'tattʃa] sf waste paper

carta'pesta sf papier-mâché

car'tella sf (scheda) card; (custodia: di cartone, Inform) folder; (: di uomo d'affari ecc) briefcase; (: di scolaro) schoolbag, satchel; **~ clinica** (Med) case sheet

cartel'lino sm (etichetta) label; (su porta) notice; (scheda) card; **timbrare il ~** (all'entrata) to clock in; (all'uscita) to clock out; **~ di presenza** clock card, timecard

car'tello sm sign; (pubblicitario) poster; (stradale) sign, signpost; (in dimostrazioni) placard; (Econ) cartel; **~ stradale** sign; **cartel'lone** sm (della tombola) scoring frame; (Teat) playbill; **tenere il cartellone** (spettacolo) to have a long run; **cartellone pubblicitario** advertising poster

car'tina sf (Aut, Geo) map

car'toccio [kar'tottʃo] sm paper bag

cartolarizzazi'one [kartolaridza'tsjone] sf securitization

cartole'ria sf stationer's (shop)

carto'lina sf postcard; **~ postale** ready-stamped postcard

car'tone sm cardboard; (Arte) cartoon; **cartoni animati** (Cine) cartoons

car'tuccia, -ce [kar'tuttʃa] sf cartridge

'casa sf house; (specialmente la propria casa) home; (Comm) firm, house; **essere a ~** to be at home; **vado a ~ mia/tua** I'm going home/to your house; **vino della ~** house wine; **~ di cura** nursing home; **~ editrice** publishing house; **C~ delle Libertà** centre-right coalition; **~ di riposo** (old people's) home, care home; **~ dello studente** student hostel; **case popolari** ≈ council houses (o flats) (BRIT), ≈ public housing units (US)

ca'sacca, -che sf military coat; (di fantino) blouse

casa'lingo, -a, -ghi, -ghe *ag* household, domestic; *(fatto a casa)* home-made; *(semplice)* homely; *(amante della casa)* home-loving ▷ *sf* housewife

cas'care /20/ *vi* to fall; **cas'cata** *sf* fall; *(d'acqua)* cascade, waterfall

cascherò *ecc* [kaske'rɔ] *vb vedi* **cascare**

'**casco** *(pl* **caschi)** *sm* helmet; *(del parrucchiere)* hair-dryer; *(di banane)* bunch; **~ blu** *(Mil)* blue helmet (UN soldier)

casei'ficio [kazei'fitʃo] *sm* creamery

ca'sella *sf* pigeonhole; **~ email** mailbox; **~ postale** post office box

ca'sello *sm (di autostrada)* tollgate

ca'serma *sf* barracks

ca'sino *sm (fam: confusione)* row, racket; *(casa di prostituzione)* brothel

casinò *sm inv* casino

'**caso** *sm* chance; *(fatto, vicenda)* event, incident; *(possibilità)* possibility; *(Med, Ling)* case; **a ~** at random; **per ~** by chance, by accident; **in ogni ~, in tutti i casi** in any case, at any rate; **al ~** should the opportunity arise; **nel ~ che** in case; **~ mai** if by chance; **~ limite** borderline case

caso'lare *sm* cottage

'**caspita** *escl (di sorpresa)* good heavens!; *(di impazienza)* for goodness' sake!

'**cassa** *sf* case, crate, box; *(bara)* coffin; *(mobile)* chest; *(involucro: di orologio ecc)* case; *(macchina)* cash register, till; *(luogo di pagamento)* cash desk, checkout (counter); *(fondo)* fund; *(istituto bancario)* bank; **~ automatica prelievi** automatic telling machine, cash dispenser; **~ continua** night safe; **mettere in ~ integrazione** ≈ to lay off; **~ mutua** *o* **malattia** health insurance scheme; **~ di risparmio** savings bank; **~ toracica** *(Anat)* chest

cassa'forte *(pl* **casseforti)** *sf* safe

cassa'panca *(pl* **cassapanche** *o* **cassepanche)** *sf* settle

casseru'ola, casse'rola *sf* saucepan

cas'setta *sf* box; *(per registratore)* cassette; *(Cine, Teat)* box-office takings *pl*: **film di ~** box-office draw; **~ delle lettere** letterbox; **~ di sicurezza** strongbox

cas'setto *sm* drawer

cassi'ere, -a *sm/f* cashier; *(di banca)* teller

casso'netto *sm* wheelie-bin

cas'tagna [kas'taɲɲa] *sf* chestnut

cas'tagno [kas'taɲɲo] *sm* chestnut (tree)

cas'tano, -a *ag* chestnut (brown)

cas'tello *sm* castle; *(Tecn)* scaffolding

casti'gare /80/ *vt* to punish; **cas'tigo, -ghi** *sm* punishment; **mettere/essere in castigo** to punish/be punished

cas'toro *sm* beaver

casu'ale *ag* chance *cpd*; *(Inform)* random *cpd*

cataliz'zatore [kataliddza'tore] *sm (anche fig)* catalyst; *(Aut)* catalytic converter

ca'talogo, -ghi *sm* catalogue

catarifran'gente [katarifran'dʒɛnte] *sm (Aut)* reflector

ca'tarro *sm* catarrh

ca'tastrofe *sf* catastrophe, disaster; **catastro'fista, -i, -e** *ag, smf* doommonger

catego'ria *sf* category

ca'tena *sf* chain; **~ di montaggio** assembly line; **catene da neve** *(Aut)* snow chains; **cate'nina** *sf (gioiello)* (thin) chain

cate'ratta *sf* cataract; *(chiusa)* sluice gate

ca'tino *sm* basin

ca'trame *sm* tar

'**cattedra** *sf* teacher's desk; *(di università)* chair

catte'drale *sf* cathedral

catti'veria *sf* wickedness, malice; *(di bambino)* naughtiness; *(azione)* spiteful act; *(parole)* malicious o spiteful remark

cat'tivo, -a *ag* bad; *(malvagio)* bad, wicked; *(turbolento: bambino)* bad, naughty; (: *mare*) rough; *(odore, sapore)* nasty, bad

cat'tolico, -a, -ci, -che *ag, sm/f* (Roman) Catholic

cattu'rare /72/ *vt* to capture

'causa *sf* cause; *(Dir)* lawsuit, case, action; **a ~ di, per ~ di** because of; **fare** o **muovere ~ a qn** to take legal action against sb

cau'sare /72/ *vt* to cause

cau'tela *sf* caution, prudence

'cauto, -a *ag* cautious, prudent

cauzi'one [kaut'tsjone] *sf* security; *(Dir)* bail

'cava *sf* quarry

caval'care /20/ *vt* (*cavallo*) to ride; *(muro)* to sit astride; *(ponte)* to span; **caval'cata** *sf* ride; *(gruppo di persone)* riding party

cavalca'via *sm inv* flyover

cavalci'oni [kaval'tʃoni]: **a ~ di** *prep* astride

cavali'ere *sm* rider; *(feudale, titolo)* knight; *(soldato)* cavalryman; *(al ballo)* partner

caval'letta *sf* grasshopper

caval'letto *sm* (*Fot*) tripod; *(da pittore)* easel

ca'vallo *sm* horse; *(Scacchi)* knight; *(Aut: anche: ~ vapore)* horsepower; *(dei pantaloni)* crotch; **a ~** on horseback; **a ~ di** astride, straddling; **~ di battaglia** *(fig)* hobbyhorse; **~ da corsa** racehorse; **~ a dondolo** rocking horse

ca'vare /72/ *vt* (*togliere*) to draw out, extract, take out; (: *giacca, scarpe*) to take off; (: *fame, sete, voglia*) to satisfy; **cavarsela** to get away with it; to manage, get on all right

cava'tappi *sm inv* corkscrew

ca'verna *sf* cave

'cavia *sf* guinea pig

cavi'ale *sm* caviar

ca'viglia [ka'viʎʎa] *sf* ankle

'cavo, -a *ag* hollow ▷ *sm* (*Anat*) cavity; *(grossa corda)* rope, cable; *(Elettr, Tel)* cable

cavo'letto *sm*: **~ di Bruxelles** Brussels sprout

cavolfi'ore *sm* cauliflower

'cavolo *sm* cabbage; **non m'importa un ~** *(fam)* I don't give a hoot

'cazzo ['kattso] *sm* (*fam!: pene*) prick (!); **non gliene importa un ~** *(fig: fam!)* he doesn't give a damn about it; **fatti i cazzi tuoi** *(fig: fam!)* mind your own damn business

C.C.D. *sigla m* (= *Centro Cristiano Democratico*) party originating from Democrazia Cristiana

C.D. *sm inv* (= *compact disc*) CD; *(lettore)* CD player

CD-Rom [tʃidi'rɔm] *sigla m inv* CD-Rom

C.d.U. *sigla m* (= *Cristiano Democratici Uniti*) United Christian Democrats *(Italian centre-right political party)*

ce [tʃe] *pron, av vedi* **ci**

Ce'cenia [tʃe'tʃenja] *sf* Chechnya; **ce'ceno, -a** *ag, sm/f* Chechen

'ceco, -a, -chi, -che ['tʃɛko] *ag, sm/f, sm* Czech; **la Repubblica Ceca** the Czech Republic

'cedere ['tʃɛdere] /29/ *vt* (*concedere: posto*) to give up; *(Dir)* to transfer, make over ▷ *vi* (*cadere*) to give way, subside; **~ (a)** to surrender (to), yield (to), give in (to)

'cedola ['tʃɛdola] *sf* (*Comm*) coupon; voucher

'ceffo ['tʃɛffo] *sm* (*peg*) ugly mug

cef'fone [tʃef'fone] *sm* slap, smack

cele'brare [tʃele'brare] /72/ *vt* to celebrate

'celebre ['tʃɛlebre] *ag* famous, celebrated

ce'leste [tʃe'lɛste] *ag* celestial; heavenly; *(colore)* sky-blue

'celibe ['tʃɛlibe] *ag* single, unmarried

'cella ['tʃɛlla] *sf* cell; **~ frigorifera** cold store

'cellula ['tʃɛllula] *sf* (*Biol, Elettr, Pol*) cell; **cellu'lare** *sm* cellphone

cellu'lite [tʃellu'lite] *sf* cellulite

cemen'tare [tʃemen'tare] /72/ *vt* (*anche fig*) to cement

ce'mento [tʃe'mento] *sm* cement; **~ armato** reinforced concrete

'cena ['tʃena] *sf* dinner; (*leggera*) supper

ce'nare [tʃe'nare] /72/ *vi* to dine, have dinner

'cenere ['tʃenere] *sf* ash

'cenno ['tʃenno] *sm* (*segno*) sign, signal; (*gesto*) gesture; (*col capo*) nod; (*con la mano*) wave; (*allusione*) hint, mention; (*breve esposizione*) short account; **far ~ di sì/no** to nod (one's head)/shake one's head

censi'mento [tʃensi'mento] *sm* census

cen'sura [tʃen'sura] *sf* censorship; censor's office; (*fig*) censure

cente'nario, -a [tʃente'narjo] *ag* (*che ha cento anni*) hundred-year-old; (*che ricorre ogni cento anni*) centennial, centenary *cpd* ▷ *sm/f* centenarian ▷ *sm* centenary

cen'tesimo, -a [tʃen'tɛzimo] *ag, sm* hundredth; (*di euro, dollaro*) cent

cen'tigrado, -a [tʃen'tigrado] *ag* centigrade; **20 gradi centigradi** 20 degrees centigrade

cen'timetro [tʃen'timetro] *sm* centimetre

centi'naio [tʃenti'najo] (*pl f* **centinaia**) *sm*: **un ~ (di)** a hundred; about a hundred

'cento ['tʃɛnto] *num* a hundred, one hundred

cento'mila [tʃento'mila] *num* a o one hundred thousand; **te l'ho detto ~ volte** (*fig*) I've told you a thousand times

cen'trale [tʃen'trale] *ag* central ▷ *sf*: **~ elettrica** electric power station; **~ eolica** wind farm; **~ telefonica** (telephone) exchange; **centrali'nista** *smf* operator; **centra'lino** *sm* (telephone) exchange; (*di albergo ecc*) switchboard; **centraliz'zato, -a** [tʃentralid'dzato] *ag* central

cen'trare [tʃen'trare] /72/ *vt* to hit the centre (BRIT) o center (US) of; (*Tecn*) to centre

cen'trifuga [tʃen'trifuga] *sf* spin-dryer

'centro ['tʃɛntro] *sm* centre; **~ civico** civic centre; **~ commerciale** shopping centre; (*città*) commercial centre; **~ di permanenza temporanea** reception centre

centro'destra [tʃentro'dɛstra] *sm* (*Pol*) centre right

centrosi'nistra [tʃentrosi'nistra] *sm* (*Pol*) centre left

'ceppo ['tʃeppo] *sm* (*di albero*) stump; (*pezzo di legno*) log

'cera ['tʃera] *sf* wax; (*aspetto*) appearance

ce'ramica (*pl* **ceramiche**) [tʃe'ramika] *sf* ceramic; (*Arte*) ceramics *sg*

cerbi'atto [tʃer'bjatto] *sm* (*Zool*) fawn

cercaper'sone [tʃerkaper'sone] *sm inv* bleeper

cer'care [tʃer'kare] /20/ *vt* to look for, search for ▷ *vi*: **~ di fare qc** to try to do sth

cercherò *ecc* [tʃerke'rɔ] *vb vedi* **cercare**

'cerchia ['tʃerkja] *sf* circle

cer'chietto [tʃer'kjetto] *sm* (*per capelli*) hairband

'cerchio ['tʃerkjo] *sm* circle; (*giocattolo, di botte*) hoop

cere'ale [tʃere'ale] *sm* cereal

ceri'monia [tʃeri'mɔnja] *sf* ceremony

ce'rino [tʃe'rino] *sm* wax match

'cernia ['tʃɛrnja] *sf* (*Zool*) stone bass

cerni'era [tʃer'njɛra] *sf* hinge;
~ lampo zip (fastener) (BRIT),
zipper (US)

'cero ['tʃero] *sm* (church) candle

ce'rotto [tʃe'rɔtto] *sm* sticking
plaster

certa'mente [tʃerta'mente] *av*
certainly

certifi'cato [tʃertifi'kato] *sm*
certificate; **~ medico/di nascita/
di morte** medical/birth/death
certificate

PAROLA CHIAVE

'certo, -a ['tʃɛrto] *ag* (*sicuro*): **certo
(di/che)** certain *o* sure (of/that)
▶ *det* **1** (*tale*) certain; **un certo
signor Smith** a (certain) Mr Smith
2 (*qualche: con valore intensivo*)
some; **dopo un certo tempo** after
some time; **un fatto di una certa
importanza** a matter of some
importance; **di una certa età** past
one's prime, not so young
▶ *pron*: **certi, e** (*pl*) some
▶ *av* (*certamente*) certainly; (*senz'altro*)
of course; **di certo** certainly; **no (di)
certo!, certo che no!** certainly not!;
sì certo yes indeed, certainly

cer'vello [tʃer'vɛllo] (*pl* **cervelli**)
sm (Anat) (*pl f* **cervella**) brain ;
~ elettronico computer

'cervo, -a ['tʃɛrvo] *sm/f* stag (hind)
▶ *sm* deer; **~ volante** stag beetle

ces'puglio [tʃes'puʎʎo] *sm* bush

ces'sare [tʃes'sare] /72/ *vi, vt* to stop,
cease; **~ di fare qc** to stop doing sth

ces'tino [tʃes'tino] *sm* basket; (*per
la carta straccia*) wastepaper basket;
(*Inform*) recycle bin; **~ da viaggio**
(*Ferr*) packed lunch (*o* dinner)

'cesto ['tʃesto] *sm* basket

'ceto ['tʃɛto] *sm* (social) class

cetrio'lino [tʃetrio'lino] *sm* gherkin

cetri'olo [tʃetri'ɔlo] *sm* cucumber

Cfr. *abbr* (= confronta) cf

C.G.I.L. *sigla f* (= Confederazione
Generale Italiana del Lavoro) trades
union organization

chat'line [tʃæt'laɛn] *sf inv* chat room

chat'tare [tʃat'tare] /72/ *vi* (online) to
chat; **chat'tata** [tʃat'tata] *sf* chat

PAROLA CHIAVE

che [ke] *pron* **1** (*relativo: persona:
soggetto*) who; (: *oggetto*) whom,
that; (: *cosa, animale*) which, that;
il ragazzo che è venuto the boy
who came; **l'uomo che io vedo** the
man (whom) I see; **il libro che è sul
tavolo** the book which *o* that is on
the table; **il libro che vedi** the book
(which *o* that) you see; **la sera che ti
ho visto** the evening I saw you
2 (*interrogativo, esclamativo*) what;
che (cosa) fai? what are you doing?;
a che (cosa) pensi? what are you
thinking about?; **non sa che (cosa)
fare** he doesn't know what to do; **ma
che dici!** what are you saying!
3 (*indefinito*): **quell'uomo ha un
che di losco** there's something
suspicious about that man; **un
certo non so che** an indefinable
something
▶ *det* **1** (*interrogativo: tra tanti*) what;
(: *tra pochi*) which; **che tipo di film
preferisci?** what sort of film do
you prefer?; **che vestito ti vuoi
mettere?** what (*o* which) dress do
you want to put on?
2 (*esclamativo: seguito da aggettivo*)
how; (: *seguito da sostantivo*) what;
che buono! how delicious!; **che bel
vestito!** what a lovely dress!
▶ *cong* **1** (*con proposizioni subordinate*)
that; **credo che verrà** I think he'll
come; **voglio che tu studi** I want
you to study; **so che tu c'eri** I know
(that) you were there; **non che
sia sbagliato, ma ...** not that it's
wrong, but ...
2 (*finale*) so that; **vieni qua, che**

ti veda come here, so (that) I can see you

3 (*temporale*): **arrivai che eri già partito** you had already left when I arrived; **sono anni che non lo vedo** I haven't seen him for years

4 (*in frasi imperative, concessive*): **che venga pure!** let him come by all means!; **che tu sia benedetto!** may God bless you!

5 (*comparativo: con più, meno*) than; *vedi anche* **più; meno; così** *ecc*

chemiotera'pia [kemjotera'pia] *sf* chemotherapy

chero'sene [kero'zɛne] *sm* kerosene

PAROLA CHIAVE

chi [ki] *pron* **1** (*interrogativo: soggetto*) who; (: *oggetto*) who, whom; **chi è?** who is it?; **di chi è questo libro?** whose book is this?; **con chi parli?** who are you talking to?; **a chi pensi?** who are you thinking about?; **chi di voi?** which of you?; **non so a chi rivolgermi** I don't know who to ask

2 (*relativo*) whoever, anyone who; **dillo a chi vuoi** tell whoever you like

3 (*indefinito*): **chi ... chi ...** some ... others ...; **chi dice una cosa, chi dice un'altra** some say one thing, others say another

chiacchie'rare [kjakkje'rare] /72/ *vi* to chat; (*discorrere futilmente*) to chatter; (*far pettegolezzi*) to gossip; **chiacchiere** *sfpl*: **fare due** *o* **quattro chiacchiere** to have a chat

chia'mare [kja'mare] /72/ *vt* to call; (*rivolgersi a qn*) to call (in), send for; **chiamarsi** *vpr* (*aver nome*) to be called; **come ti chiami?** what's your name?; **mi chiamo Paolo** my name is Paolo, I'm called Paolo; **~ alle armi** to call up; **~ in giudizio** to summon; **chia'mata** *sf* (*Tel*) call; (*Mil*) call-up

chia'rezza [kja'rettsa] *sf* clearness; clarity

chia'rire [kja'rire] /55/ *vt* to make clear; (*fig: spiegare*) to clear up, explain

chi'aro, -a ['kjaro] *ag* clear; (*luminoso*) clear, bright; (*colore*) pale, light

chi'asso ['kjasso] *sm* uproar, row

chi'ave ['kjave] *sf* key ▷ *ag inv* key *cpd*; **~ d'accensione** (*Aut*) ignition key; **~ inglese** monkey wrench; **~ di volta** keystone; **~ USB** (*Inform*) USB key

chia'vetta [kja'vetta] *sf* (*Inform*) dongle

chi'azza ['kjattsa] *sf* stain, splash

chicco, -chi ['kikko] *sm* grain; (*di caffè*) bean; **~ d'uva** grape

chi'edere ['kjɛdere] /21/ *vt* (*per sapere*) to ask; (*per avere*) to ask for ▷ *vi*: **~ di qn** to ask after sb; (*al telefono*) to ask for *o* want sb; **chiedersi** *vpr*: **chiedersi (se)** to wonder (whether); **~ qc a qn** to ask sb sth; to ask sb for sth

chi'esa ['kjɛza] *sf* church

chi'esi *ecc* ['kjɛzi] *vb vedi* **chiedere**

chi'glia ['kiʎʎa] *sf* keel

chilo ['kilo] *sm* kilo; **chilo'grammo** *sm* kilogram(me); **chi'lometro** *sm* kilometre

chimico, -a, -ci, -che ['kimiko] *ag* chemical ▷ *sm/f* chemist

chi'nare [ki'nare] /72/ *vt* to lower, bend; **chinarsi** *vpr* to stoop, bend

chi'occiola ['kjottʃola] *sf* snail; (*di indirizzo e-mail*) at (symbol); **scala a ~** spiral staircase

chi'odo ['kjɔdo] *sm* nail; (*fig*) obsession; **~ di garofano** (*Cuc*) clove

chi'osco, -schi ['kjɔsko] *sm* kiosk, stall

chi'ostro ['kjɔstro] *sm* cloister

chiro'mante [kiro'mante] *smf* palmist

chirur'gia [kirur'dʒia] *sf* surgery; **~ estetica** cosmetic surgery; **chi'rurgo, -ghi** *o* **-gi** *sm* surgeon

chissà [kis'sa] *av* who knows, I wonder

chi'tarra [ki'tarra] sf guitar

chitar'rista, -i, -e [kitar'rista] sm/f
guitarist, guitar player

chi'udere ['kjudere] /22/ vt to close,
shut; (luce, acqua) to put off, turn off;
(definitivamente: fabbrica) to close
down, shut down; (strada) to close;
(recingere) to enclose; (porre termine
a) to end ▷ vi to close, shut; to close
down, shut down, to end; **chiudersi**
vpr to shut, close; (ritirarsi: anche fig)
to shut o.s. away; (ferita) to close up

chi'unque [ki'unkwe] pron (relativo)
whoever; (indefinito) anyone,
anybody; **~ sia** whoever it is

'chiusi ecc ['kjusi] vb vedi **chiudere**

chi'uso, -a ['kjuso] pp di **chiudere**
▷ sf (di corso d'acqua) sluice, lock;
(recinto) enclosure; (di discorso ecc)
conclusion, ending; **chiu'sura** sf
closing; shutting; closing o shutting
down; enclosing; putting o turning
off; ending; (dispositivo) catch;
fastening; fastener; **chiusura
lampo**® zip (fastener) (BRIT),
zipper (US)

PAROLA CHIAVE

ci [tʃi] (dav lo, la, li, le, ne diventa
ce) pron **1** (personale: complemento
oggetto) us; (: a noi, complemento di
termine) (to) us; (: riflessivo) ourselves;
(: reciproco) each other, one another;
(: impersonale): **ci si veste** we get
dressed; **che c'ha visti** he's seen us;
non ci ha dato niente he gave
us nothing; **ci vestiamo** we get
dressed; **ci amiamo** we love one
another o each other
2 (dimostrativo, di ciò, su ciò, in ciò ecc)
about (o on o of) it; **non so cosa
farci** I don't know what to do about
it; **che c'entro io?** what have I got
to do with it?
▶ av (qui) here; (lì) there; (moto
attraverso luogo): **ci passa sopra
un ponte** a bridge passes over it;

non ci passa più nessuno nobody
comes this way any more; **esserci**
vedi **essere**

C.I. abbr = **carta d'identità**

cia'batta [tʃa'batta] sf slipper; (pane)
ciabatta

ciam'bella [tʃam'bɛlla] sf (Cuc)
ring-shaped cake; (salvagente)
rubber ring

ci'ao ['tʃao] escl (all'arrivo) hello!; (alla
partenza) cheerio! (BRIT), bye!

cias'cuno, -a [tʃas'kuno] (dav sm:
ciascun + C, V, **ciascuno** + s impura,
gn, pn, ps, x, z; dav sf: **ciascuna** + C,
ciascun' + V) det every, each; (ogni)
every ▷ pron each (one); (tutti)
everyone, everybody

ci'barie [tʃi'barje] sfpl foodstuffs

cibernauta, -i, -e [tʃiber'nauta]
sm/f Internet surfer

ciberspazio [tʃiber'spattsjo] sm
cyberspace

'cibo ['tʃibo] sm food

ci'cala [tʃi'kala] sf cicada

cica'trice [tʃika'tritʃe] sf scar

'cicca, -che ['tʃikka] sf cigarette
end

'ciccia ['tʃittʃa] sf (fam) fat

cicci'one, -a [tʃit'tʃone] sm/f (fam)
fatty

cicla'mino [tʃikla'mino] sm
cyclamen

ci'clismo [tʃi'klizmo] sm cycling;
ci'clista, -i, -e sm/f cyclist

'ciclo ['tʃiklo] sm cycle; (di malattia)
course

ciclomo'tore [tʃiklomo'tore] sm
moped

ci'clone [tʃi'klone] sm cyclone

ci'cogna [tʃi'koɲɲa] sf stork

ci'eco, -a, -chi, -che [tʃɛko] ag blind
▷ sm/f blind man/woman

ci'elo ['tʃɛlo] sm sky; (Rel) heaven

'cifra ['tʃifra] sf (numero) figure,
numeral; (somma di denaro) sum,
figure; (monogramma) monogram,
initials pl; (codice) code, cipher

'**ciglio** ['tʃiʎʎo] *sm* (*margine*) edge, verge; (*pl*(*f*) **ciglia**: *delle palpebre*) (eye) lash; (eye)lid; (*sopracciglio*) eyebrow

'**cigno** ['tʃiɲɲo] *sm* swan

cigo'lare [tʃigo'lare] /72/ *vi* to squeak, creak

'**Cile** ['tʃile] *sm*: **il ~** Chile; **ci'leno, -a** [tʃi'lɛno] *ag, sm/f* Chilean

cili'egia, -gie *o* **-ge** [tʃi'ljɛdʒa] *sf* cherry

cilie'gina [tʃilje'dʒina] *sf* glacé cherry

cilin'drata [tʃilin'drata] *sf* (*Aut*) (cubic) capacity; **una macchina di grossa ~** a big-engined car

ci'lindro [tʃi'lindro] *sm* cylinder; (*cappello*) top hat

'**cima** ['tʃima] *sf* (*sommità*) top; (*di monte*) top, summit; (*estremità*) end; **in ~ a** at the top of; **da ~ a fondo** from top to bottom; (*fig*) from beginning to end

'**cimice** ['tʃimitʃe] *sf* (*Zool*) bug; (*puntina*) drawing pin (*BRIT*), thumbtack (*US*)

cimini'era [tʃimi'njɛra] *sf* chimney; (*di nave*) funnel

cimi'tero [tʃimi'tɛro] *sm* cemetery

'**Cina** ['tʃina] *sf*: **la ~** China

cin'cin, cin cin [tʃin'tʃin] *escl* cheers!

'**cinema** ['tʃinema] *sm inv* cinema

ci'nese [tʃi'nese] *ag, smf, sm* Chinese *inv*

'**cinghia** ['tʃingja] *sf* strap; (*cintura, Tecn*) belt

cinghi'ale [tʃin'gjale] *sm* wild boar

cinguet'tare [tʃingwet'tare] /72/ *vi* to twitter

'**cinico, -a, -ci, -che** ['tʃiniko] *ag* cynical ▷ *sm/f* cynic

cin'quanta [tʃin'kwanta] *num* fifty; **cinquan'tesimo, -a** *num* fiftieth

cinquan'tina [tʃinkwan'tina] *sf* (*serie*): **una ~ (di)** about fifty; (*età*): **essere sulla ~** to be about fifty

'**cinque** ['tʃinkwe] *num* five; **avere ~ anni** to be five (years old); **il ~ dicembre 2008** the fifth of

December 2008; **alle ~** (*ora*) at five (o'clock)

cinque'cento [tʃinkwe'tʃɛnto] *num* five hundred ▷ *sm*: **il C~** the sixteenth century

cin'tura [tʃin'tura] *sf* belt; **~ di salvataggio** lifebelt (*BRIT*), life preserver (*US*); **~ di sicurezza** (*Aut, Aer*) safety *o* seat belt

cintu'rino [tʃintu'rino] *sm* strap; **~ dell'orologio** watch strap

ciò [tʃɔ] *pron* this; that; **~ che** what; **~ nonostante** *o* **nondimeno** nevertheless, in spite of that

ci'occa, -che ['tʃɔkka] *sf* (*di capelli*) lock

ciocco'lata [tʃokko'lata] *sf* chocolate; (*bevanda*) (hot) chocolate; **cioccola'tino** *sm* chocolate

cio'è [tʃo'ɛ] *av* that is (to say)

ci'otola ['tʃɔtola] *sf* bowl

ci'ottolo ['tʃɔttolo] *sm* pebble; (*di strada*) cobble(stone)

ci'polla [tʃi'polla] *sf* onion; (*di tulipano ecc*) bulb

cipol'lina [tʃipol'lina] *sf*: **cipolline sottaceto** pickled onions

ci'presso [tʃi'prɛsso] *sm* cypress (tree)

'**cipria** ['tʃiprja] *sf* (face) powder

'**Cipro** ['tʃipro] *sf* Cyprus

'**circa** ['tʃirka] *av* about, roughly ▷ *prep* about, concerning; **a mezzogiorno ~** about midday

'**circo, -chi** ['tʃirko] *sm* circus

circo'lare [tʃirko'lare] /72/ *vi* to circulate; (*Aut*) to drive (along), move (along) ▷ *ag* circular ▷ *sf* (*Amm*) circular; (*di autobus*) circle (line); **circolazi'one** *sf* circulation; (*Aut*): **la circolazione** (the) traffic

'**circolo** ['tʃirkolo] *sm* circle

circon'dare [tʃirkon'dare] /72/ *vt* to surround; **circondarsi** *vpr*: **circondarsi di** to surround o.s. with

circonvallazi'one [tʃirkonvallat'tsjone] *sf* ring road

(BRIT), beltway (US); (per evitare una città) by-pass

circos'petto, -a [tʃirkos'pɛtto] *ag* circumspect, cautious

circos'tante [tʃirkos'tante] *ag* surrounding, neighbouring

circos'tanza [tʃirkos'tantsa] *sf* circumstance; (occasione) occasion

cir'cuito [tʃir'kuito] *sm* circuit

C.I.S.L. *sigla f* (= Confederazione Italiana Sindacati Lavoratori) trades union organization

cis'terna [tʃis'tɛrna] *sf* tank, cistern

'cisti ['tʃisti] *sf inv* cyst

cis'tite [tʃis'tite] *sf* cystitis

ci'tare [tʃi'tare] /72/ *vt* (Dir) to summon; (autore) to quote; (a esempio, modello) to cite

ci'tofono [tʃi'tofono] *sm* entry phone; (in uffici) intercom

città [tʃit'ta] *sf inv* town; (importante) city; **~ universitaria** university campus

cittadi'nanza [tʃittadi'nantsa] *sf* citizens *pl*; (Dir) citizenship

citta'dino, -a [tʃitta'dino] *ag* town *cpd*; city *cpd* ▷ *sm/f* (di uno Stato) citizen; (abitante di città) town dweller, city dweller

ci'uccio ['tʃuttʃo] *sm* (fam) comforter, dummy (BRIT), pacifier (US)

ci'uffo ['tʃuffo] *sm* tuft

ci'vetta [tʃi'vetta] *sf* (Zool) owl; (fig: donna) coquette, flirt ▷ *ag inv*: **auto/ nave ~** decoy car/ship

'civico, -a, -ci, -che ['tʃiviko] *ag* civic; (museo) municipal, town *cpd*; city *cpd*

ci'vile [tʃi'vile] *ag* civil; (non militare) civilian; (nazione) civilized ▷ *sm* civilian

civiltà [tʃivil'ta] *sf* civilization; (cortesia) courtesy

'clacson *sm inv* (Aut) horn

clandes'tino, -a *ag* clandestine; (Pol) underground, clandestine; (immigrato) illegal ▷ *sm/f* stowaway;

(anche: **immigrato ~**) illegal immigrant

'classe *sf* class; **di ~** (fig) with class; of excellent quality; **~ operaia** working class; **~ turistica** (Aer) economy class

'classico, -a, -ci, -che *ag* classical; (tradizionale: moda) classic(al) ▷ *sm* classic; classical author

clas'sifica, -che *sf* classification; (Sport) placings *pl*

classifi'care /20/ *vt* to classify; (candidato, compito) to grade; **classificarsi** *vpr* to be placed

'clausola *sf* (Dir) clause

clavi'cembalo [klavi'tʃembalo] *sm* harpsichord

cla'vicola *sf* (Anat) collarbone

clic'care /20/ *vi* (Inform): **~ su** to click on

cli'ente *smf* customer, client

'clima, -i *sm* climate; **climatizza'tore** *sm* air conditioner

'clinico, -a, -ci, -che *ag* clinical ▷ *sf* (scienza) clinical medicine; (casa di cura) clinic, nursing home; (settore d'ospedale) clinic

clo'nare /72/ *vt* to clone; **clona'zione** [klonat'tsjone] *sf* cloning

'cloro *sm* chlorine

club *sm inv* club

cm *abbr* (= centimetro) cm

c.m. *abbr* (= corrente mese) inst.

coalizi'one [koalit'tsjone] *sf* coalition

'COBAS *sigla mpl* (= Comitati di base) independent trades unions

'coca *sf* (bibita) Coke; (droga) cocaine

coca'ina *sf* cocaine

cocci'nella [kottʃi'nɛlla] *sf* ladybird (BRIT), ladybug (US)

cocci'uto, -a [kot'tʃuto] *ag* stubborn, pigheaded

'cocco, -chi *sm* (pianta) coconut palm; (frutto): **noce di ~** coconut ▷ *sm/f* (fam) darling

cocco'drillo *sm* crocodile

cocco'lare /72/ *vt* to cuddle, fondle

cocerò *ecc* [kotʃe'rɔ] *vb vedi* **cuocere**

co'comero sm watermelon

'coda sf tail; (fila di persone, auto) queue (BRIT), line (US); (di abiti) train; con la ~ dell'occhio out of the corner of one's eye; mettersi in ~ to queue (up) (BRIT), line up (US); to join the queue o line; ~ di cavallo (acconciatura) ponytail

co'dardo, -a ag cowardly ▷ sm/f coward

'codice ['kɔditʃe] sm code; ~ di avviamento postale postcode (BRIT), zip code (US); ~ a barre bar code; ~ civile civil code; ~ fiscale tax code; ~ penale penal code; ~ segreto (di tessera magnetica) PIN (number); ~ della strada highway code

coe'rente ag coherent

coe'taneo, -a ag, sm/f contemporary

'cofano sm (Aut) bonnet (BRIT), hood (US); (forziere) chest

'cogliere ['kɔʎʎere] /23/ vt (fiore, frutto) to pick, gather; (sorprendere) to catch, surprise; (bersaglio) to hit; (fig: momento opportuno ecc) to grasp, seize, take; (: capire) to grasp; ~ sul fatto o in flagrante/alla sprovvista to catch red-handed/unprepared

co'gnato, -a [koɲˈɲato] sm/f brother-in-law/sister-in-law

co'gnome [koɲˈɲome] sm surname

coinci'denza [kointʃiˈdɛntsa] sf coincidence; (Ferr, Aer, di autobus) connection

coin'cidere [koinˈtʃidere] /34/ vi to coincide

coin'volgere [koinˈvɔldʒere] /96/ vt: ~ in to involve in

cola'pasta sm inv colander

co'lare /72/ vt (liquido) to strain; (pasta) to drain; (oro fuso) to pour ▷ vi, vi (sudore) to drip; (botte) to leak; (cera) to melt; ~ a picco vt (nave) to sink

colazi'one [kolatˈtsjone] sf breakfast; lunch; fare ~ to have breakfast (o lunch)

co'lera sm (Med) cholera

'colgo ecc vb vedi cogliere

'colica sf (Med) colic

co'lino sm strainer

'colla prep + det vedi con ▷ sf glue; (di farina) paste

collabo'rare /72/ vi to collaborate; ~ a to collaborate on; (giornale) to contribute to; collabora'tore, -'trice sm/f collaborator; (di giornale, rivista) contributor; collaboratore esterno freelance; collaboratrice familiare home help

col'lana sf necklace; (collezione) collection, series

col'lant [kɔˈlã] sm inv tights pl

col'lare sm collar

col'lasso sm (Med) collapse

collau'dare /72/ vt to test, try out

col'lega, -ghi, -ghe sm/f colleague

collega'mento sm connection; (Mil) liaison

colle'gare /80/ vt to connect, join, link; collegarsi vpr (Radio, TV) to link up; collegarsi con (Tel) to get through to

col'legio [kolˈlɛdʒo] sm college; (convitto) boarding school; ~ elettorale (Pol) constituency

'collera sf anger

col'lerico, -a, -ci, -che ag quick-tempered, irascible

col'letta sf collection

col'letto sm collar

collezio'nare [kollettsjoˈnare] /72/ vt to collect

collezi'one [kolletˈtsjone] sf collection

col'lina sf hill

col'lirio sm eyewash

'collo prep + det vedi con ▷ sm neck; (di abito) neck, collar; (pacco) parcel; ~ del piede instep

colloca'mento sm (impiego) employment; (disposizione) placing, arrangement

collo'care /20/ vt (libri, mobili) to place; (Comm: merce) to find a market for

collocazi'one [kollokat'tsjone] sf placing; (di libro) classification

col'loquio sm conversation, talk; (ufficiale, per un lavoro) interview; (Ins) preliminary oral exam

col'mare /72/ vt: ~ **di** (anche fig) to fill with; (dare in abbondanza) to load o overwhelm with

co'lombo, -a sm/f dove; pigeon

co'lonia sf colony; (per bambini) holiday camp; **(acqua di) ~** (eau de) cologne

co'lonna sf column; ~ **sonora** (Cine) sound track; ~ **vertebrale** spine, spinal column

colon'nello sm colonel

colo'rante sm colouring

colo'rare /72/ vt to colour; (disegno) to colour in

co'lore sm colour; **a colori** in colour, colour cpd; **farne di tutti i colori** to get up to all sorts of mischief

colo'rito, -a ag coloured; (viso) rosy, pink; (linguaggio) colourful ▷ sm (tinta) colour; (carnagione) complexion

'colpa sf fault; (biasimo) blame; (colpevolezza) guilt; (azione colpevole) offence; (peccato) sin; **di chi è la ~?** whose fault is it?; **è ~ sua** it's his fault; **per ~ di** through, owing to; **col'pevole** ag guilty

col'pire /55/ vt to hit, strike; (fig) to strike; **rimanere colpito da qc** to be amazed o struck by sth

'colpo sm (urto) knock; (fig: affettivo) blow, shock; (: aggressivo) blow; (di pistola) shot; (Med) stroke; (furto) raid; **di ~** suddenly; **fare ~** to make a strong impression; **il motore perde colpi** the engine is misfiring; ~ **d'aria** chill; ~ **in banca** bank job o raid; ~ **basso** (Pugilato, fig) punch below the belt; ~ **di fulmine** love at first sight; ~ **di grazia** coup de grâce; ~ **di scena** (Teat) coup de théâtre; (fig) dramatic turn of events; ~ **di sole** sunstroke; **colpi di sole** (nei capelli) highlights; ~ **di Stato** coup d'état; ~ **di telefono** phone call; ~ **di testa** (sudden) impulse o whim; ~ **di vento** gust (of wind)

'colsi ecc vb vedi **cogliere**

coltel'lata sf stab

col'tello sm knife; ~ **a serramanico** clasp knife

colti'vare /72/ vt to cultivate; (verdura) to grow, cultivate

'colto, -a pp di **cogliere** ▷ ag (istruito) cultured, educated

'coma sm inv coma

comanda'mento sm (Rel) commandment

coman'dante sm (Mil) commander, commandant; (di reggimento) commanding officer; (Naut, Aer) captain

coman'dare /72/ vi to be in command ▷ vt to command; (imporre) to order, command; ~ **a qn di fare** to order sb to do

combaci'are [komba'tʃare] /14/ vi to meet; (fig: coincidere) to coincide

com'battere /1/ vt, vi to fight

combi'nare /72/ vt to combine; (organizzare) to arrange; (fam: fare) to make, cause; **combinazi'one** sf combination; (caso fortuito) coincidence; **per combinazione** by chance

combus'tibile ag combustible ▷ sm fuel

PAROLA CHIAVE

'come av **1** (alla maniera di) like; **ti comporti come lui** you behave like him o like he does; **bianco come la neve** (as) white as snow; **come se** as if, as though

2 (*in qualità di*) as a; **lavora come autista** he works as a driver **3** (*interrogativo*) how; **come ti chiami?** what's your name?; **come sta?** how are you?; **com'è il tuo amico?** what is your friend like?; **come?** (*prego?*) pardon?, sorry?; **come mai?** how come?; **come mai non ci hai avvertiti?** how come you didn't warn us? **4** (*esclamativo*): **come sei bravo!** how clever you are!; **come mi dispiace!** I'm terribly sorry! ▶cong **1** (*in che modo*) how; **mi ha spiegato come l'ha conosciuto** he told me how he met him **2** (*correlativo*) as; (*con comparativi di maggioranza*) than; **non è bravo come pensavo** he isn't as clever as I thought; **è meglio di come pensassi** it's better than I thought **3** (*appena che, quando*) as soon as; **come arrivò, iniziò a lavorare** as soon as he arrived, he set to work; *vedi anche* **così; tanto**

'comico, -a, -ci, -che *ag* (*Teat*) comic; (*buffo*) comical ▷ *sm* (*attore*) comedian, comic actor
cominci'are [komin'tʃare] /14/ *vt, vi* to begin, start; **~ a fare/col fare** to begin to do/by doing
comi'tato *sm* committee
comi'tiva *sf* party, group
co'mizio [ko'mittsjo] *sm* (*Pol*) meeting, assembly
com'media *sf* comedy; (*opera teatrale*) play; (: *che fa ridere*) comedy; (*fig*) playacting *no pl*
commemo'rare /72/ *vt* to commemorate
commen'tare /72/ *vt* to comment on; (*testo*) to annotate; (*Radio, TV*) to give a commentary on
commerci'ale [kommer'tʃale] *ag* commercial, trading; (*peg*) commercial
commercia'lista, -i, -e [kommertʃa'lista] *sm/f* (*laureato*)

graduate in economics and commerce; (*consulente*) business consultant
commerci'ante [kommer'tʃante] *smf* trader, dealer; (*negoziante*) shopkeeper
commerci'are [kommer'tʃare] /14/ *vi*: **~ in** to deal o trade in ▷ *vt* to deal o trade in
com'mercio [kom'mɛrtʃo] *sm* trade, commerce; **essere in ~** (*prodotto*) to be on the market o on sale; **essere nel ~** (*persona*) to be in business; **~ all'ingrosso/al dettaglio** wholesale/retail trade
com'messo, -a *pp di* **commettere** ▷ *sm/f* shop assistant (BRIT), sales clerk (US) ▷ *sm* (*impiegato*) clerk; **~ viaggiatore** commercial traveller
commes'tibile *ag* edible
com'mettere /63/ *vt* to commit
com'misi *ecc vb vedi* **commettere**
commissari'ato *sm* (*Amm*) commissionership; (: *sede*) commissioner's office; (: *di polizia*) police station
commis'sario *sm* commissioner; (*di pubblica sicurezza*) ≈ (police) superintendent (BRIT), ≈ (police) captain (US); (*Sport*) steward; (*membro di commissione*) member of a committee o board
commissi'one *sf* (*incarico*) errand; (*comitato, percentuale*) commission; (*Comm: ordinazione*) order; **commissioni** *sfpl* (*acquisti*) shopping *sg*: **~ d'esame** examining board; **commissioni bancarie** bank charges
com'mosso, -a *pp di* **commuovere**
commo'vente *ag* moving
commozi'one [kommot'tsjone] *sf* emotion, deep feeling; **~ cerebrale** (*Med*) concussion
commu'overe /66/ *vt* to move, affect; **commuoversi** *vpr* to be moved
como'dino *sm* bedside table

comodità sf inv comfort; convenience

'comodo, -a ag comfortable; (facile) easy; (conveniente) convenient; (utile) useful, handy ▷ sm comfort; convenience; **con ~** at one's convenience o leisure; **fare il proprio ~** to do as one pleases; **far ~** to be useful o handy

compa'gnia [kompaɲ'nia] sf company; (gruppo) gathering

com'pagno, -a [kom'paɲɲo] sm/f (di classe, gioco) companion; (Pol) comrade

com'paio ecc vb vedi **comparire**

compa'rare /72/ vt to compare

compara'tivo, -a ag, sm comparative

compa'rire /7/ vi to appear

com'parvi ecc vb vedi **comparire**

compassi'one sf compassion, pity; **avere ~ di qn** to feel sorry for sb, pity sb

com'passo sm (pair of) compasses pl; callipers pl

compa'tibile ag (scusabile) excusable; (conciliabile, Inform) compatible

compa'tire /55/ vt (aver compassione di) to sympathize with, feel sorry for; (scusare) to make allowances for

com'patto, -a ag compact; (roccia) solid; (folla) dense; (fig: gruppo, partito) united

compen'sare /72/ vt (equilibrare) to compensate for, make up for; **~ qn di** (rimunerare) to pay o remunerate sb for; (risarcire) to pay compensation to sb for; (fig: fatiche, dolori) to reward sb for; **com'penso** sm compensation; payment, remuneration; reward; **in compenso** (d'altra parte) on the other hand

compe'rare /72/ vt = **comprare**

'compere sfpl: **fare ~** to do the shopping

compe'tente ag competent; (mancia) apt, suitable

com'petere /45/ vi to compete, vie; (Dir: spettare): **~ a** to lie within the competence of; **competizi'one** sf competition

compi'angere [kom'pjandʒere] /75/ vt to sympathize with, feel sorry for

'compiere /24/ vt (concludere) to finish, complete; (adempiere) to carry out, fulfil; **compiersi** vpr (avverarsi) to be fulfilled, come true; **~ gli anni** to have one's birthday

compi'lare /72/ vt to compile; (modulo) to complete, fill in (BRIT), fill out (US)

'compito sm (incarico) task, duty; (dovere) duty; (Ins) exercise; (: a casa) piece of homework; **fare i compiti** to do one's homework

comple'anno sm birthday

complessità sf complexity

comples'sivo, -a ag (globale) comprehensive, overall; (totale: cifra) total

com'plesso, -a ag complex ▷ sm (Psic, Edil) complex; (Mus: corale) ensemble; (: orchestrina) band; (: di musica pop) group; **in** o **nel ~** on the whole; **~ alberghiero** hotel complex; **~ edilizio** building complex; **~ vitaminico** vitamin complex

completa'mente av completely

comple'tare /72/ vt to complete

com'pleto, -a ag complete; (teatro, autobus) full ▷ sm suit; **al ~** full; **~ da sci** ski suit

compli'care /20/ vt to complicate; **complicarsi** vpr to become complicated

'complice ['komplitʃe] smf accomplice

complicità [komplitʃi'ta] sf inv complicity; **un sorriso/uno sguardo di ~** a knowing smile/look

complimen'tarsi /72/ vpr: **~ con** to congratulate

compli'mento sm compliment; **complimenti** smpl (cortesia eccessiva) ceremony sg; (ossequi) regards, compliments; **complimenti!** congratulations!; **senza complimenti!** don't stand on ceremony!; make yourself at home!; help yourself!

complot'tare /72/ vi to plot, conspire

com'plotto sm plot, conspiracy

com'pone ecc vb vedi **comporre**

compo'nente smf member ▷ sm component

com'pongo ecc vb vedi **comporre**

componi'mento sm (Dir) settlement; (Ins) composition; (poetico, teatrale) work

com'porre /77/ vt (musica, testo) to compose; (mettere in ordine) to arrange; (Dir: lite) to settle; (Tip) to set; (Tel) to dial; **comporsi** vpr: **comporsi di** to consist of, be composed of

comporta'mento sm behaviour

compor'tare /72/ vt (implicare) to involve; **comportarsi** vpr to behave

com'posi ecc vb vedi **comporre**

composi'tore, -'trice sm/f composer; (Tip) compositor, typesetter

com'posto, -a pp di **comporre** ▷ ag (persona) composed, self-possessed; (: decoroso) dignified; (formato da più elementi) compound cpd ▷ sm compound

com'prare /72/ vt to buy

com'prendere /81/ vt (contenere) to comprise, consist of; (capire) to understand

compren'sibile ag understandable

comprensi'one sf understanding

compren'sivo, -a ag (prezzo): **~ di** inclusive of; (indulgente) understanding

> Attenzione! In inglese esiste la parola comprehensive, che però in genere significa completo.

com'preso, -a pp di **comprendere** ▷ ag (incluso) included

com'pressa sf vedi **compresso**

com'presso, -a pp di **comprimere** ▷ sf (Med: garza) compress; (: pastiglia) tablet

com'primere /50/ vt (premere) to press; (Fisica) to compress; (fig) to repress

compro'messo, -a pp di **compromettere** ▷ sm compromise

compro'mettere /63/ vt to compromise; **compromettersi** vpr to compromise o.s.

com'puter sm inv computer

comu'nale ag municipal, town cpd; **consiglio/palazzo ~** town council/hall

Co'mune sm (Amm) town council; (sede) town hall

co'mune ag common; (consueto) common, everyday; (di livello medio) average; (ordinario) ordinary ▷ sf (di persone) commune; **fuori del ~** out of the ordinary; **avere in ~** to have in common, share; **mettere in ~** to share

comuni'care /20/ vt (notizia) to pass on, convey; (malattia) to pass on; (ansia ecc) to communicate; (trasmettere: calore ecc) to transmit, communicate; (Rel) to administer communion to ▷ vi to communicate

comuni'cato sm communiqué; **~ stampa** press release

comunicazi'one [komunikat'tsjone] sf communication; (annuncio) announcement; (Tel): **~ (telefonica)** (telephone) call; **dare la ~ a qn** to put sb through; **ottenere la ~** to get through

comuni'one sf communion; **~ dei beni** (Dir) joint ownership of property

comu'nismo sm communism

comunità sf inv community; **C~ Economica Europea** European Economic Community

co'munque cong however, no matter how ▷ av (in ogni modo) in any case; (tuttavia) however, nevertheless

con *prep (nei seguenti casi* **con** *può fondersi con l'articolo definito,* con + il = **col**, con + la = **colla**, con + gli = **cogli**, con + i = **coi**, con + le = **colle**) with; **partire col treno** to leave by train; **~ mio grande stupore** to my great astonishment; **~ tutto ciò** for all that

con'cedere [kon'tʃɛdere] /29/ *vt (accordare)* to grant; *(ammettere)* to admit, concede; **concedersi qc** to treat o.s. to sth, allow o.s. sth

concen'trare [kontʃen'trare] /72/ *vt,* **concen'trarsi** *vpr* to concentrate

concentrazi'one *sf* concentration

conce'pire [kontʃe'pire] /55/ *vt (bambino)* to conceive; *(progetto, idea)* to conceive (of); *(metodo, piano)* to devise

con'certo [kon'tʃɛrto] *sm (Mus)* concert; *(: componimento)* concerto

con'cessi *ecc* [kon'tʃɛssi] *vb vedi* **concedere**

con'cetto [kon'tʃɛtto] *sm (pensiero, idea)* concept; *(opinione)* opinion

concezi'one [kontʃet'tsjone] *sf* conception

con'chiglia [kon'kiʎʎa] *sf* shell

conci'are [kon'tʃare] /14/ *vt (pelli)* to tan; *(tabacco)* to cure; *(fig: ridurre in cattivo stato)* to beat up; **conciarsi** *vpr (sporcarsi)* to get in a mess; *(vestirsi male)* to dress badly

concili'are [kontʃi'ljare] /19/ *vt* to reconcile; *(contravvenzione)* to pay on the spot; *(sonno)* to be conducive to, induce; **conciliarsi qc** to gain o win sth (for o.s.); **conciliarsi qn** to win sb over; **conciliarsi con** to be reconciled with

con'cime [kon'tʃime] *sm* manure; *(chimico)* fertilizer

con'ciso, -a [kon'tʃizo] *ag* concise, succinct

concitta'dino, -a [kontʃitta'dino] *sm/f* fellow citizen

con'cludere /3/ *vt* to conclude; *(portare a compimento)* to conclude, finish, bring to an end; *(operare positivamente)* to achieve ▷ *vi (essere convincente)* to be conclusive; **concludersi** *vpr* to come to an end, close

concor'dare /72/ *vt (prezzo)* to agree on; *(Ling)* to make agree ▷ *vi* to agree

con'corde *ag (d'accordo)* in agreement; *(simultaneo)* simultaneous

concor'rente *ag* competing; *(Mat)* concurrent ▷ *smf* competitor; *(Ins)* candidate; **concor'renza** *sf* competition

concorrenzi'ale [konkorren'tsjale] *ag* competitive

con'correre /28/ *vi:* **~ (in)** *(Mat)* to converge o meet (in); **~ (a)** *(competere)* to compete (for); *(Ins: a una cattedra)* to apply (for); *(partecipare: a un'impresa)* to take part (in), contribute (to); **con'corso, -a** *pp di* **concorrere** ▷ *sm* competition; *(esame)* competitive examination; **concorso di colpa** *(Dir)* contributory negligence

con'creto, -a *ag* concrete

con'danna *sf* condemnation; sentence; conviction

condan'nare /72/ *vt (disapprovare)* to condemn; *(Dir)* **~ a** to sentence to; **~ per** to convict of

conden'sare /72/ *vt* to condense

condi'mento *sm* seasoning; dressing

con'dire /55/ *vt* to season; *(insalata)* to dress

condi'videre /43/ *vt* to share

condizio'nale [kondittsjo'nale] *ag* conditional ▷ *sm (Ling)* conditional ▷ *sf (Dir)* suspended sentence

condizio'nare [kondittsjo'nare] /72/ *vt* to condition; **ad aria condizionata** air-conditioned; **condiziona'tore** *sm* air conditioner

condizi'one [kondit'tsjone] *sf* condition

condogli'anze [kondoʎ'ʎantse] *sfpl* condolences

condo'minio *sm* joint ownership; (*edificio*) jointly-owned building

con'dotta *sf vedi* **condotto**

con'dotto, -a *pp di* **condurre** ▷ *sf* (*modo di comportarsi*) conduct, behaviour; (*di un affare ecc*) handling; (*di acqua*) piping; (*incarico sanitario*) country medical practice controlled by a local authority

condu'cente [kondu'tʃɛnte] *sm* driver

con'duco *ecc vb vedi* **condurre**

con'durre /90/ *vt* to conduct; (*azienda*) to manage; (*accompagnare: bambino*) to take; (*automobile*) to drive; (*trasportare: acqua, gas*) to convey, conduct; (*fig*) to lead ▷ *vi* to lead

con'dussi *ecc vb vedi* **condurre**

confe'renza [konfe'rɛntsa] *sf* (*discorso*) lecture; (*riunione*) conference; **~ stampa** press conference

con'ferma *sf* confirmation

confer'mare /72/ *vt* to confirm

confes'sare /72/ *vt*, **confes'sarsi** *vpr* to confess; **andare a confessarsi** (*Rel*) to go to confession

con'fetto *sm* sugared almond; (*Med*) pill

> Attenzione! In inglese esiste la parola *confetti*, che però significa *coriandoli*.

confet'tura *sf* (*gen*) jam; (*di arance*) marmalade

confezio'nare [konfettsjo'nare] /72/ *vt* (*vestito*) to make (up); (*merci, pacchi*) to package

confezi'one [konfet'tsjone] *sf* (*di abiti: da uomo*) tailoring; (*: da donna*) dressmaking; (*imballaggio*) packaging; **~ regalo** gift pack; **confezioni per signora** ladies' wear *no pl*; **confezioni da uomo** menswear *no pl*

confic'care /20/ *vt*: **~ qc in** to hammer o drive sth into; **conficcarsi** *vpr* to stick

confi'dare /72/ *vi*: **~ in** to confide in, rely on ▷ *vt* to confide; **confidarsi con qn** to confide in sb

configu'rare /72/ *vt* (*Inform*) to set

configurazi'one [konfigurat'tsjone] *sf* configuration; (*Inform*) setting

confi'nare /72/ *vi*: **~ con** to border on ▷ *vt* (*Pol*) to intern; (*fig*) to confine

CONFIN'DUSTRIA *sigla f* (= *Confederazione Generale dell'Industria Italiana*) employers' association ≈ CBI (*BRIT*)

con'fine *sm* boundary; (*di paese*) border, frontier

confis'care /20/ *vt* to confiscate

con'flitto *sm* conflict; **~ d'interessi** conflict of interests

conflu'enza [konflu'ɛntsa] *sf* (*di fiumi*) confluence; (*di strade*) junction

con'fondere /25/ *vt* to mix up, confuse; (*imbarazzare*) to embarrass; **confondersi** *vpr* (*mescolarsi*) to mingle; (*turbarsi*) to be confused; (*sbagliare*) to get mixed up

confor'tare /72/ *vt* to comfort, console

confron'tare /72/ *vt* to compare

con'fronto *sm* comparison; **in o a ~ di** in comparison with, compared to; **nei miei** (*o tuoi ecc*) **confronti** towards me (*o you ecc*)

con'fusi *ecc vb vedi* **confondere**

confusi'one *sf* confusion; (*imbarazzo*) embarrassment; **far ~** (*chiasso*) to make a racket

con'fuso, -a *pp di* **confondere** ▷ *ag* (*vedi* confondere) confused; embarrassed

conge'dare [kondʒe'dare] /72/ *vt* to dismiss; (*Mil*) to demobilize; **congedarsi** *vpr* to take one's leave

con'gegno *sm* device, mechanism

conge'lare [kondʒe'lare] /72/ *vt* to freeze; **congela'tore** *sm* freezer

congesti'one [kondʒes'tjone] *sf* congestion

conget'tura [kondʒet'tura] *sf* conjecture

con'giungere [kon'dʒundʒere] /5/ *vt*, **con'giungersi** *vpr* to join (together)

congiunti'vite [kondʒunti'vite] *sf* conjunctivitis

congiun'tivo [kondʒun'tivo] *sm* (*Ling*) subjunctive

congi'unto, -a [kon'dʒunto] *pp di* **congiungere** ▷ *ag* (*unito*) joined ▷ *sm/f* relative

congiunzi'one [kondʒun'tsjone] *sf* (*Ling*) conjunction

congi'ura [kon'dʒura] *sf* conspiracy

congratu'larsi /72/ *vpr*: **~ con qn per qc** to congratulate sb on sth

congratulazi'oni [kongratulat'tsjoni] *sfpl* congratulations

con'gresso *sm* congress

C.O.N.I. *sigla m* (= *Comitato Olimpico Nazionale Italiano*) Italian Olympic Games Committee

coni'are /19/ *vt* to mint, coin; (*fig*) to coin

co'niglio [ko'niʎʎo] *sm* rabbit

coniu'gare /80/ *vt* (*Ling*) to conjugate; **coniugarsi** *vpr* to get married

'coniuge ['kɔnjudʒe] *smf* spouse

connazio'nale [konnattsjo'nale] *smf* fellow-countryman/woman

connessi'one *sf* connection

con'nettere /63/ *vt* to connect, join ▷ *vi* (*fig*) to think straight

'cono *sm* cone; **~ gelato** ice-cream cone

co'nobbi *ecc vb vedi* **conoscere**

cono'scente [konoʃʃɛnte] *smf* acquaintance

cono'scenza [konoʃʃɛntsa] *sf* (*il sapere*) knowledge *no pl*; (*persona*) acquaintance; (*facoltà sensoriale*) consciousness *no pl*; **perdere ~** to lose consciousness

co'noscere [ko'noʃʃere] /26/ *vt* to know; **ci siamo conosciuti a Firenze** we (first) met in Florence; **conoscersi** *vpr* to know o.s.; (*reciproco*) to know each other; (*incontrarsi*) to meet; **~ qn di vista** to know sb by sight; **farsi ~** (*fig*) to make a name for o.s.; **conosci'uto, -a** *pp di* **conoscere** ▷ *ag* well-known

con'quista *sf* conquest

conquis'tare /72/ *vt* to conquer; (*fig*) to gain, win

consa'pevole *ag*: **~ di** aware of

'conscio, -a, -sci, -sce ['kɔnʃo] *ag*: **~ di** aware o conscious of

consecu'tivo, -a *ag* consecutive; (*successivo: giorno*) following, next

con'segna [kon'seɲɲa] *sf* delivery; (*merce consegnata*) consignment; (*custodia*) care, custody; (*Mil: ordine*) orders *pl*; (: *punizione*) confinement to barracks; **dare qc in ~ a qn** to entrust sth to sb; **pagamento alla ~** cash on delivery

conse'gnare [konseɲ'ɲare] /15/ *vt* to deliver; (*affidare*) to entrust, hand over; (*Mil*) to confine to barracks

consegu'enza [konse'gwɛntsa] *sf* consequence; **per o di ~** consequently

con'senso *sm* approval, consent; **~ informato** informed consent

consen'tire /45/ *vi*: **~ a** to consent o agree to ▷ *vt* to allow, permit

con'serva *sf* (*Cuc*) preserve; **~ di frutta** jam; **~ di pomodoro** tomato purée

conser'vante *sm* (*per alimenti*) preservative

conser'vare /72/ *vt* (*Cuc*) to preserve; (*custodire*) to keep; (: *dalla distruzione ecc*) to preserve, conserve

conserva'tore, -'trice *sm/f* (*Pol*) conservative

conserva'torio *sm* (*di musica*) conservatory

conservazi'one [konservat'tsjone] *sf* preservation; conservation

conside'rare /72/ vt to consider; (*reputare*) to consider, regard; **considerarsi** vpr to consider o.s.

consigli'are [konsiʎˈʎare] /27/ vt (*persona*) to advise; (*metodo, azione*) to recommend, advise, suggest; **con'siglio** sm (*suggerimento*) advice no pl, piece of advice; (*assemblea*) council; **consiglio d'amministrazione** board; **Consiglio d'Europa** Council of Europe; **il Consiglio dei Ministri** (*Pol*) ≈ the Cabinet

consis'tente ag thick; solid; (*fig*) sound, valid

con'sistere /11/ vi: ~ **in** to consist of

conso'lare /72/ ag consular ▷ vt (*confortare*) to console, comfort; (*rallegrare*) to cheer up; **consolarsi** vpr to be comforted; to cheer up

conso'lato sm consulate

consolazi'one [konsolatˈtsjone] sf consolation, comfort

'console sm consul

conso'nante sf consonant

'consono, -a ag: ~ **a** consistent with, consonant with

con'sorte smf consort

consta'tare /72/ vt to establish, verify

consu'eto, -a ag habitual, usual

consu'lente smf consultant

consul'tare /72/ vt to consult; **consultarsi** vpr: **consultarsi con qn** to seek the advice of sb

consul'torio sm: ~ **familiare** family planning clinic

consu'mare /72/ vt (*logorare: abiti, scarpe*) to wear out; (*usare*) to consume, use up; (*mangiare, bere*) to consume; (*Dir*) to consummate; **consumarsi** vpr to wear out; to be used up; (*anche fig*) to be consumed; (*combustibile*) to burn out

con'tabile ag accounts cpd, accounting ▷ smf accountant

contachi'lometri [kontakiˈlɔmetri] sm inv ≈ mileometer

conta'dino, -a sm/f countryman/woman; farm worker; (*peg*) peasant

contagi'are [kontaˈdʒare] /62/ vt to infect

contagi'oso, -a ag infectious; contagious

conta'gocce [kontaˈɡottʃe] sm inv (*Med*) dropper

contami'nare /72/ vt to contaminate

con'tante sm cash; **pagare in contanti** to pay cash; **non ho contanti** I haven't got any cash

con'tare /72/ vt to count; (*considerare*) to consider ▷ vi to count, be of importance; ~ **su qn** to count o rely on sb; ~ **di fare qc** to intend to do sth; **conta'tore** sm meter

contat'tare /72/ vt to contact

con'tatto sm contact

'conte sm count

conteggi'are [kontedˈdʒare] /62/ vt to charge, put on the bill

con'tegno [konˈteɲɲo] sm (*comportamento*) behaviour; (*atteggiamento*) attitude; **darsi un ~** to act nonchalant; (*ricomporsi*) to pull o.s. together

contemporanea'mente av simultaneously; at the same time

contempo'raneo, -a ag, sm/f contemporary

conten'dente smf opponent, adversary

con'tenere /121/ vt to contain; **conteni'tore** sm container

conten'tezza [kontenˈtettsa] sf contentment

con'tento, -a ag pleased, glad; ~ **di** pleased with

conte'nuto sm contents pl; (*argomento*) content

con'tessa sf countess

contes'tare /72/ vt (*Dir*) to notify; (*fig*) to dispute

con'testo sm context

continen'tale ag, smf continental

conti'nente *ag* continent ▷ *sm* (*Geo*) continent; (: *terra ferma*) mainland

contin'gente [kontin'dʒɛnte] *ag* contingent ▷ *sm* (*Comm*) quota; (*Mil*) contingent

continua'mente *av* (*senza interruzione*) continuously, nonstop; (*ripetutamente*) continually

continu'are /72/ *vt* to continue (with), go on with ▷ *vi* to continue, go on; **~ a fare qc** to go on *o* continue doing sth

continuità *sf* continuity

con'tinuo, -a *ag* (*numerazione*) continuous; (*pioggia*) continual, constant; (*Elettr: corrente*) direct; **di ~** continually

'conto *sm* (*calcolo*) calculation; (*Comm, Econ*) account; (*di ristorante, albergo*) bill; (*fig: stima*) consideration, esteem; **fare i conti con qn** to settle one's account with sb; **fare ~ su qn** to count *o* rely on sb; **rendere ~ a qn di qc** to be accountable to sb for sth; **tener ~ di qn/qc** to take sb/sth into account; **per ~ di** on behalf of; **per ~ mio** as far as I'm concerned; **a conti fatti, in fin dei conti** all things considered; **~ corrente** current account; **~ alla rovescia** countdown

con'torno *sm* (*linea*) outline, contour; (*ornamento*) border; (*Cuc*) vegetables *pl*

contrabbandi'ere, -a *sm/f* smuggler

contrab'bando *sm* smuggling, contraband; **merce di ~** contraband, smuggled goods *pl*

contrab'basso *sm* (*Mus*) (double) bass

contraccambi'are /19/ *vt* (*favore ecc*) to return

contraccet'tivo, -a [kontrattʃet'tivo] *ag, sm* contraceptive

contrac'colpo *sm* rebound; (*di arma da fuoco*) recoil; (*fig*) repercussion

contrad'dire /38/ *vt* to contradict; **contraddirsi** *vpr* to contradict o.s.; (*uso reciproco: persone*) to contradict each other *o* one another; (: *testimonianze ecc*) to be contradictory

contraf'fare /41/ *vt* (*persona*) to mimic; (*alterare: voce*) to disguise; (: *firma*) to forge, counterfeit

contraria'mente *av*: **~ a** contrary to

contrari'are /19/ *vt* (*contrastare*) to thwart, oppose; (*irritare*) to annoy, bother

con'trario, -a *ag* opposite; (*sfavorevole*) unfavourable ▷ *sm* opposite; **essere ~ a qc** (*persona*) to be against sth; **al ~** on the contrary; **in caso ~** otherwise; **avere qualcosa in ~** to have some objection

contrasse'gnare [kontrassen'ɲare] /15/ *vt* to mark

contras'tare /72/ *vt* (*avversare*) to oppose; (*impedire*) to bar; (*negare: diritto*) to contest, dispute ▷ *vi*: **~ (con)** (*essere in disaccordo*) to contrast (with); (*lottare*) to struggle (with)

contrat'tacco *sm* counterattack

contrat'tare /72/ *vt, vi* to negotiate

contrat'tempo *sm* hitch

con'tratto, -a *pp di* **contrarre** ▷ *sm* contract

contravvenzi'one *sf* contravention; (*ammenda*) fine

contrazi'one [kontrat'tsjone] *sf* contraction; (*di prezzi ecc*) reduction

contribu'ente *smf* taxpayer; ratepayer (BRIT), property tax payer (US)

contribu'ire /55/ *vi* to contribute

'contro *prep* against; **~ di me/ lui** against me/him; **pastiglie ~ la tosse** throat lozenges; **~ pagamento** (*Comm*) on payment; **controfi'gura** *sf* (*Cine*) double

control'lare /72/ *vt* (*accertare*) to check; (*sorvegliare*) to watch, control; (*tenere nel proprio potere, fig: dominare*) to control; **controllarsi** vpr to control o.s.; **con'trollo** sm check; watch; control; **controllo delle nascite** birth control; **control'lore** sm (Ferr, Aut) (ticket) inspector

contro'luce [kontro'lutʃe] sf inv (Fot) backlit shot ▷ av: **(in) ~** against the light; (fotografare) into the light

contro'mano av: **guidare ~** to drive on the wrong side of the road; (in un senso unico) to drive the wrong way up a one-way street

controprodu'cente [kontroprodu'tʃɛnte] ag counterproductive

contro'senso sm (contraddizione) contradiction in terms; (assurdità) nonsense

controspio'naggio [kontrospio'naddʒo] sm counterespionage

contro'versia sf controversy; (Dir) dispute

contro'verso, -a ag controversial

contro'voglia [kontro'vɔʎʎa] av unwillingly

contusi'one sf (Med) bruise

convale'scente [konvaleʃʃɛnte] ag, smf convalescent

convali'dare /72/ vt (Amm) to validate; (fig: sospetto, dubbio) to confirm

con'vegno [kon'veɲɲo] sm (incontro) meeting; (congresso) convention, congress; (luogo) meeting place

conve'nevoli smpl civilities

conveni'ente ag suitable; (vantaggioso) profitable; (: prezzo) cheap

Attenzione! In inglese esiste la parola convenient, che però significa comodo.

conve'nire /128/ vi (riunirsi) to gather, assemble; (concordare) to agree; (tornare utile) to be worthwhile ▷ vb impers: **conviene fare questo** it

is advisable to do this; **conviene andarsene** we should go; **ne convengo** I agree

con'vento sm (di frati) monastery; (di suore) convent

convenzio'nale [konventsjo'nale] ag conventional

convenzi'one [konven'tsjone] sf (Dir) agreement; (nella società) convention

conver'sare /72/ vi to have a conversation, converse

conversazi'one [konversat'tsjone] sf conversation; **fare ~** to chat, have a chat

conversi'one sf conversion; **~ ad U** (Aut) U-turn

conver'tire /45/ vt (trasformare) to change; (Inform, Pol, Rel) to convert; **convertirsi** vpr: **convertirsi (a)** to be converted (to)

con'vesso, -a ag convex

convin'cente [konvin'tʃɛnte] ag convincing

con'vincere [kon'vintʃere] /129/ vt to convince; **convincersi** vpr: **convincersi (di qc)** to convince o.s. (of sth); **~ qn di qc** to convince sb of sth; **~ qn a fare qc** to persuade sb to do sth

convi'vente smf common-law husband/wife

con'vivere /130/ vi to live together

convo'care /20/ vt to call, convene; (Dir) to summon

convulsi'one sf convulsion

coope'rare /72/ vi: **~ (a)** to cooperate (in); **coopera'tiva** sf cooperative

coordi'nare /72/ vt to coordinate

co'perchio [ko'pɛrkjo] sm cover; (di pentola) lid

co'perta sf cover; (di lana) blanket; (da viaggio) rug; (Naut) deck

coper'tina sf (Stampa) cover, jacket

co'perto, -a pp di **coprire** ▷ ag covered; (cielo) overcast ▷ sm place setting; (posto a tavola) place; (al *ristorante*) cover charge; **~ di** covered in *o* with

coper'tone *sm* (*Aut*) rubber tyre

coper'tura *sf* (*anche Econ, Mil*) cover; (*di edificio*) roofing

'**copia** *sf* copy; **brutta/bella ~** rough/final copy

copi'are /19/ *vt* to copy

copincol'lare /72/ *vt* to copy and paste

copin'collo *sm* copy and paste

copi'one *sm* (*Cine, Teat*) script

'**coppa** *sf* (*bicchiere*) goblet; (*per frutta, gelato*) dish; (*trofeo*) cup, trophy; **~ dell'olio** oil sump (*BRIT*) *o* pan (*US*)

'**coppia** *sf* (*di persone*) couple; (*di animali, Sport*) pair

coprifu'oco, -chi *sm* curfew

copri'letto *sm* bedspread

copripiu'mino *sm inv* duvet cover

co'prire /9/ *vt* to cover; (*occupare: carica, posto*) to hold; **coprirsi** *vpr* (*cielo*) to cloud over; (*vestirsi*) to wrap up, cover up; (*Econ*) to cover o.s.; **coprirsi di** (*macchie, muffa*) to become covered in

coque [kɔk] *sf*: **uovo alla ~** boiled egg

co'raggio [koˈraddʒo] *sm* courage, bravery; **~!** (*forza!*) come on!; (*animo!*) cheer up!

co'rallo *sm* coral

Co'rano *sm* (*Rel*) Koran

co'razza [koˈrattsa] *sf* armour; (*di animali*) carapace, shell; (*Mil*) armour(-plating)

'**corda** *sf* cord; (*fune*) rope; (*spago, Mus*) string; **dare ~ a qn** to let sb have his (*o* her) way; **tenere sulla ~ qn** to keep sb on tenterhooks; **tagliare la ~** to slip away, sneak off; **corde vocali** vocal cords

cordi'ale *ag* cordial, warm ▷ *sm* (*bevanda*) cordial

'**cordless** [ˈkɔːdlɪs] *sm inv* cordless phone

cor'done *sm* cord, string; (*linea: di polizia*) cordon; **~ ombelicale** umbilical cord

Co'rea *sf*: **la ~** Korea

coreogra'fia *sf* choreography

cori'andolo *sm* (*Bot*) coriander; **coriandoli** *smpl* confetti *no pl*

cor'nacchia [korˈnakkja] *sf* crow

corna'musa *sf* bagpipes *pl*

cor'netta *sf* (*Mus*) cornet; (*Tel*) receiver

cor'netto *sm* (*Cuc*) croissant; (*gelato*) cone

cor'nice [korˈnitʃe] *sf* frame; (*fig*) background, setting

cornici'one [korniˈtʃone] *sm* (*di edificio*) ledge; (*Archit*) cornice

'**corno** *sm* (*Zool*) (*pl f* **corna**) horn; (*Mus*) (*pl m* **corni**) horn; **fare le corna a qn** to be unfaithful to sb

Corno'vaglia [kornoˈvaʎʎa] *sf*: **la ~** Cornwall

cor'nuto, -a *ag* (*con corna*) horned; (*fam!: marito*) cuckolded ▷ *sm* (*fam!*) cuckold; (: *insulto*) bastard (!)

'**coro** *sm* chorus; (*Rel*) choir

co'rona *sf* crown; (*di fiori*) wreath

'**corpo** *sm* body; (*militare, diplomatico*) corps *inv*; **prendere ~** to take shape; **a ~ a ~** hand-to-hand; **~ di ballo** corps de ballet; **~ insegnante** teaching staff

corpora'tura *sf* build, physique

cor'reggere [korˈreddʒere] /87/ *vt* to correct; (*compiti*) to correct, mark

cor'rente *ag* (*fiume*) flowing; (*acqua del rubinetto*) running; (*moneta, prezzo*) current; (*comune*) everyday ▷ *sm*: **essere al ~ (di)** to be well-informed (about) ▷ *sf* (*movimento di liquido*) current, stream; (*spiffero*) draught; (*Elettr, Meteor*) current; (*fig*) trend, tendency; **la vostra lettera del 5 ~ mese** (*in lettere commerciali*) in your letter of the 5th inst.; **~ alternata (c.a.)** alternating current (AC); **~ continua (c.c.)** direct current (DC); **corrente'mente** *av* commonly; **parlare una lingua correntemente** to speak a language fluently

'correre /28/ *vi* to run; *(precipitarsi)* to rush; *(partecipare a una gara)* to race, run; *(fig: diffondersi)* to go round ▷ *vt* *(Sport: gara)* to compete in; *(rischio)* to run; *(pericolo)* to face; **~ dietro a qn** to run after sb; **corre voce che ...** it is rumoured that ...

cor'ressi *ecc vb vedi* **correggere**

correzi'one [korret'tsjone] *sf* correction; marking; **~ di bozze** proofreading

corri'doio *sm* corridor; *(in aereo, al cinema)* aisle

corri'dore *sm* (Sport) runner; (: *su veicolo)* racer

corri'era *sf* coach (BRIT), bus

corri'ere *sm* (diplomatico, di guerra, postale) courier; *(spedizioniere)* carrier

corri'mano *sm* handrail

corrispon'dente *ag* corresponding ▷ *smf* correspondent

corrispon'denza [korrispon'dɛntsa] *sf* correspondence

corris'pondere /95/ *vi (equivalere):* **~ (a)** to correspond (to) ▷ *vt (stipendio)* to pay; *(fig: amore)* to return

cor'rodere /49/ *vt* to corrode

cor'rompere /97/ *vt* to corrupt; *(comprare)* to bribe

cor'roso, -a *pp di* **corrodere**

cor'rotto, -a *pp di* **corrompere** ▷ *ag* corrupt

corru'gare /80/ *vt* to wrinkle; **~ la fronte** to knit one's brows

cor'ruppi *ecc vb vedi* **corrompere**

corruzi'one [korrut'tsjone] *sf* corruption; bribery

'corsa *sf* running *no pl*; *(gara)* race; *(di autobus, taxi)* journey, trip; **fare una ~** to run, dash; *(Sport)* to run a race; **~ campestre** cross-country race

'corsi *ecc vb vedi* **correre**

cor'sia *sf* (Aut, Sport) lane; *(di ospedale)* ward

'Corsica *sf:* **la ~** Corsica

cor'sivo *sm* cursive (writing); *(Tip)* italics *pl*

'corso, -a *pp di* **correre** ▷ *sm* course; *(strada cittadina)* main street; *(di unità monetaria)* circulation; *(di titoli, valori)* rate, price; **in ~** in progress, under way; *(annata)* current; **~ d'acqua** river; stream; *(artificiale)* waterway; **~ d'aggiornamento** refresher course; **~ serale** evening class

'corte *sf* (court)yard; *(Dir, regale)* court; **fare la ~ a qn** to court sb; **~ marziale** court-martial

cor'teccia, -ce [kor'tettʃa] *sf* bark

corteggi'are [korted'dʒare] /62/ *vt* to court

cor'teo *sm* procession

cor'tese *ag* courteous; **corte'sia** *sf* courtesy; **per cortesia, dov'è ...?** excuse me, please, where is ...?

cor'tile *sm* (court)yard

cor'tina *sf* curtain; *(anche fig)* screen

'corto, -a *ag* short; **essere a ~ di qc** to be short of sth; **~ circuito** short-circuit

'corvo *sm* raven

'cosa *sf* thing; *(faccenda)* affair, matter, business *no pl*; **(che) ~?** what?; **(che) cos'è?** what is it?; **a ~ pensi?** what are you thinking about?

'coscia, -sce ['kɔʃʃa] *sf* thigh; **~ di pollo** (Cuc) chicken leg

cosci'ente [koʃʃɛnte] *ag* conscious; **~ di** conscious o aware of

PAROLA CHIAVE

così *av* **1** *(in questo modo)* like this, (in) this way; *(in tal modo)* so; **le cose stanno così** this is the way things stand; **non ho detto così!** I didn't say that!; **come stai? — (e) così** how are you? — so-so; **e così via** and so on; **per così dire** so to speak; **così sia** amen

2 *(tanto)* so; **così lontano** so far away; **un ragazzo così intelligente** such an intelligent boy

▶ *ag inv (tale):* **non ho mai visto un film così** I've never seen such a film

▶ *cong* **1** (*perciò*) so, therefore
2: così ... come as ... as; **non è così bravo come te** he's not as good as you; **così ... che** so ... that

cosid'detto, -a *ag* so-called

cos'metico, -a, -ci, -che *ag, sm* cosmetic

cos'pargere [kos'pardʒere] /111/ *vt*: **~ di** to sprinkle with

cos'picuo, -a *ag* considerable, large

cospi'rare /72/ *vi* to conspire

'cossi *ecc vb vedi* **cuocere**

'costa *sf* (*tra terra e mare*) coast(line); (*litorale*) shore; (*Anat*) rib; **la C~ Azzurra** the French Riviera

cos'tante *ag* constant; (*persona*) steadfast ▷ *sf* constant

cos'tare /72/ *vi, vt* to cost; **~ caro** to be expensive, cost a lot

cos'tata *sf* (*Cuc*) large chop

costeggi'are [kosted'dʒare] /62/ *vt* to be close to; to run alongside

costi'ero, -a *ag* coastal, coast *cpd*

costitu'ire /55/ *vt* (*comitato, gruppo*) to set up, form; (*elementi, parti: comporre*) to make up, constitute; (*: rappresentare*) to constitute; (*Dir*) to appoint; **costituirsi** *vpr*: **costituirsi (alla polizia)** to give o.s. up (to the police)

costituzi'one [kostitut'tsjone] *sf* setting up; building up; constitution

'costo *sm* cost; **a ogni** *o* **qualunque ~, a tutti i costi** at all costs

'costola *sf* (*Anat*) rib

cos'toso, -a *ag* expensive, costly

cos'tringere [kos'trindʒere] /117/ *vt*: **~ qn a fare qc** to force sb to do sth

costru'ire /55/ *vt* to construct, build; **costruzi'one** *sf* construction, building

cos'tume *sm* (*uso*) custom; (*foggia di vestire, indumento*) costume; **~ da bagno** bathing *o* swimming costume (*BRIT*), swimsuit; (*da uomo*) bathing *o* swimming trunks *pl*

co'tenna *sf* bacon rind

coto'letta *sf* (*di maiale, montone*) chop; (*di vitello, agnello*) cutlet

co'tone *sm* cotton; **~ idrofilo** cotton wool (*BRIT*), absorbent cotton (*US*)

'cotta *sf* (*fam: innamoramento*) crush

'cottimo *sm*: **lavorare a ~** to do piecework

'cotto, -a *pp di* **cuocere** ▷ *ag* cooked; (*fam: innamorato*) head-over-heels in love; **ben ~** (*carne*) well done

cot'tura *sf* cooking; (*in forno*) baking; (*in umido*) stewing

co'vare /72/ *vt* to hatch; (*fig: malattia*) to be sickening for; (*: odio, rancore*) to nurse ▷ *vi* (*fuoco, fig*) to smoulder

'covo *sm* den

co'vone *sm* sheaf

'cozza ['kɔttsa] *sf* mussel

coz'zare [kot'tsare] /72/ *vi*: **~ contro** to bang into, collide with

CPT *sigla m inv* = **Centro di Permanenza Temporanea**

crac'care /20/ *vt* (*Inform*) to crack

'crampo *sm* cramp; **ho un ~ alla gamba** I've got cramp in my leg

'cranio *sm* skull

cra'tere *sm* crater

cra'vatta *sf* tie

cre'are /72/ *vt* to create

'crebbi *ecc vb vedi* **crescere**

cre'dente *smf* (*Rel*) believer

cre'denza [kre'dɛntsa] *sf* belief; (*armadio*) sideboard

'credere /29/ *vt* to believe ▷ *vi*: **~ in, ~ a** to believe in; **~ qn onesto** to believe sb (to be) honest; **~ che** to believe *o* think that; **credersi furbo** to think one is clever

'credito *sm* (*anche Comm*) credit; (*reputazione*) esteem, repute; **comprare a ~** to buy on credit

'crema *sf* cream; (*con uova, zucchero ecc*) custard; **~ pasticciera** confectioner's custard; **~ solare** sun cream

cre'mare /72/ *vt* to cremate

'crepa *sf* crack

cre'paccio [kre'pattʃo] *sm* large crack, fissure; (*di ghiacciaio*) crevasse

crepacu'ore *sm* broken heart

cre'pare /72/ *vi* (*fam: morire*) to snuff it (BRIT), kick the bucket; **~ dalle risa** to split one's sides laughing

crêpe [krεp] *sf inv* pancake

cre'puscolo *sm* twilight, dusk

'crescere ['krεʃʃere] /30/ *vi* to grow ▷ *vt* (*figli*) to raise

'cresima *sf* (*Rel*) confirmation

'crespo, -a *ag* (*capelli*) frizzy; (*tessuto*) puckered ▷ *sm* crêpe

'cresta *sf* crest; (*di polli, uccelli*) crest, comb

'creta *sf* chalk; (*argilla*) clay

creti'nata *sf* (*fam*): **dire/fare una ~** to say/do a stupid thing

cre'tino, -a *ag* stupid ▷ *sm/f* idiot, fool

CRI *sigla f* = **Croce Rossa Italiana**

cric *sm inv* (*Tecn*) jack

cri'ceto [kri'tʃeto] *sm* hamster

crimi'nale *ag, smf* criminal

criminalità *sf* crime; **~ organizzata** organized crime

'crimine *sm* (*Dir*) crime

crip'tare /72/ *vt* (*TV: programma*) to encrypt

crisan'temo *sm* chrysanthemum

'crisi *sf inv* crisis; (*Med*) attack, fit; **~ di nervi** attack o fit of nerves

cris'tallo *sm* crystal; **cristalli liquidi** liquid crystals

cristia'nesimo *sm* Christianity

cristi'ano, -a *ag, sm/f* Christian

'cristo *sm*: **C~** Christ

cri'terio *sm* criterion; (*buon senso*) (common) sense

'critica, -che *sf vedi* **critico**

criti'care /20/ *vt* to criticize

'critico, -a, -ci, -che *ag* critical ▷ *sm* critic ▷ *sf* criticism; **la critica** (*attività*) criticism; (*persone*) the critics *pl*

cro'ato, -a *ag, sm/f* Croatian, Croat

Cro'azia [kro'attsja] *sf* Croatia

croc'cante *ag* crisp, crunchy

'croce ['krotʃe] *sf* cross; **in ~** (*di traverso*) crosswise; (*fig*) on tenterhooks; **la C~ Rossa** the Red Cross

croci'ato, -a [kro'tʃato] *ag* cross-shaped ▷ *sf* crusade

croci'era [kro'tʃεra] *sf* (*viaggio*) cruise; (*Archit*) transept

crol'lare /72/ *vi* to collapse; **'crollo** *sm* collapse; (*di prezzi*) slump, sudden fall; **crollo in Borsa** slump in prices on the Stock Exchange

cro'mato, -a *ag* chromium-plated

'cromo *sm* chrome, chromium

'cronaca, -che *sf* (*Stampa*) news *sg*; (: *rubrica*) column; (*TV, Radio*) commentary; **fatto o episodio di ~** news item; **~ nera** crime news *sg*; crime column

'cronico, -a, -ci, -che *ag* chronic

cro'nista, -i *sm* (*Stampa*) reporter

cro'nometro *sm* chronometer; (*a scatto*) stopwatch

'crosta *sf* crust

cros'tacei [kros'tatʃei] *smpl* shellfish

cros'tata *sf* (*Cuc*) tart

cros'tino *sm* (*Cuc*) croûton; (: *da antipasto*) canapé

cruci'ale [kru'tʃale] *ag* crucial

cruci'verba *sm inv* crossword (puzzle)

cru'dele *ag* cruel

'crudo, -a *ag* (*non cotto*) raw; (*aspro*) harsh, severe

cru'miro *sm* (*peg*) blackleg (BRIT), scab

'crusca *sf* bran

crus'cotto *sm* (*Aut*) dashboard

CSI *sigla f* (= *Comunità di Stati Indipendenti*) CIS

CSM [tʃiεsse'εmme] *sigla m* (= *consiglio superiore della magistratura*) Magistrates' Board of Supervisors

'Cuba *sf* Cuba; **cu'bano, -a** *ag, sm/f* Cuban

cu'betto *sm*: **~ di ghiaccio** ice cube

'cubico, -a, -ci, -che *ag* cubic

cu'bista, -i, -e *ag* (*Arte*) Cubist ▷ *sf* podium dancer *dancer who performs on stage in a club*

'cubo, -a *ag* cubic ▷ *sm* cube; **elevare al ~** (*Mat*) to cube

cuc'cagna [kuk'kaɲɲa] *sf*: **paese della ~** land of plenty; **albero della ~** greasy pole (*fig*)

cuc'cetta [kut'tʃetta] *sf* (*Ferr*) couchette; (*Naut*) berth

cucchiai'ata [kukkja'jata] *sf* spoonful

cucchia'ino [kukkja'ino] *sm* teaspoon; coffee spoon

cucchi'aio [kuk'kjajo] *sm* spoon

'cuccia, -ce ['kuttʃa] *sf* dog's bed; **a ~!** down!

'cucciolo ['kuttʃolo] *sm* cub; (*di cane*) puppy

cu'cina [ku'tʃina] *sf* (*locale*) kitchen; (*arte culinaria*) cooking, cookery; (*le vivande*) food, cooking; (*apparecchio*) cooker; **~ componibile** fitted kitchen; **cuci'nare**/72/ *vt* to cook

cu'cire [ku'tʃire] /31/ *vt* to sew, stitch; **cuci'trice** *sf* stapler

cucù cuckoo

'cuffia *sf* bonnet, cap; (*da infermiera*) cap; (*da bagno*) (bathing) cap; (*per ascoltare*) headphones *pl*, headset

cu'gino, -a [ku'dʒino] *sm/f* cousin

PAROLA CHIAVE

'cui *pron* **1**(*nei complementi indiretti: persona*) whom; (: *oggetto, animale*) which; **la persona/le persone a cui accennavi** the person/people you were referring to *o* to whom you were referring; **i libri di cui parlavo** the books I was talking about *o* about which I was talking; **il quartiere in cui vivo** the district where I live; **la ragione per cui** the reason why **2**(*inserito tra articolo e sostantivo*) whose; **la donna i cui figli sono scomparsi** the woman whose children have disappeared; **il**

signore, dal cui figlio ho avuto il libro the man from whose son I got the book

culi'naria *sf* cookery

'culla *sf* cradle

cul'lare/72/ *vt* to rock

'culmine *sm* top, summit

'culo *sm* (*fam !*) arse (*BRIT !*), ass (*US !*); (*fig: fortuna*): **aver ~** to have the luck of the devil

'culto *sm* (*religione*) religion; (*adorazione*) worship, adoration; (*venerazione: anche fig*) cult

cul'tura *sf* culture; (*conoscenza*) education, learning; **cultu'rale** *ag* cultural

cultu'rismo *sm* body-building

cumula'tivo, -a *ag* cumulative; (*prezzo*) inclusive; (*biglietto*) group *cpd*

'cumulo *sm* (*mucchio*) pile, heap; (*Meteor*) cumulus

cu'netta *sf* (*scolo*) gutter; (*avvallamento*) dip

cu'ocere ['kwɔtʃere] /32/ *vt* (*alimenti*) to cook; (*mattoni ecc*) to fire ▷ *vi* to cook; **~ al forno** (*pane*) to bake; (*arrosto*) to roast; **cu'oco, -a, -chi, -che** *sm/f* cook; (*di ristorante*) chef

cu'oio *sm* leather; **~ capelluto** scalp

cu'ore *sm* heart; **cuori** *smpl* (*Carte*) hearts; **avere buon ~** to be kind-hearted; **stare a ~ a qn** to be important to sb

'cupo, -a *ag* dark; (*suono*) dull; (*fig*) gloomy, dismal

'cupola *sf* dome; (*più piccola*) cupola

'cura *sf* care; (*Med: trattamento*) (course of) treatment; **aver ~ di** (*occuparsi di*) to look after; **a ~ di** (*libro*) edited by; **~ dimagrante** diet

cu'rare /72/ *vt* (*malato, malattia*) to treat; (: *guarire*) to cure; (*aver cura di*) to take care of; (*testo*) to edit; **curarsi** *vpr* to take care of o.s.; (*Med*) to follow a course of treatment; **curarsi di** to pay attention to

curio'sare /72/ vi to look round, wander round; (tra libri) to browse; **~ nei negozi** to look o wander round the shops

curiosità sf inv curiosity; (cosa rara) curio, curiosity

curi'oso, -a ag curious; **essere ~ di** to be curious about

cur'sore sm (Inform) cursor

'curva sf curve; (stradale) bend, curve

cur'vare /72/ vt to bend ▷ vi (veicolo) to take a bend; (strada) to bend, curve; **curvarsi** vpr to bend; (legno) to warp

'curvo, -a ag curved; (piegato) bent

cusci'netto [kuʃʃi'netto] sm pad; (Tecn) bearing ▷ ag inv: **stato ~** buffer state; **~ a sfere** ball bearing

cu'scino [kuʃ'ʃino] sm cushion; (guanciale) pillow

cus'tode smf keeper, custodian

cus'todia sf care; (Dir) custody; (astuccio) case, holder

custo'dire /55/ vt (conservare) to keep; (assistere) to look after, take care of; (fare la guardia) to guard

C.V. abbr (= cavallo vapore) h.p.

cyberca'ffè [tʃiberka'fe] sm inv cybercafé

cyber'nauta, -i, -e sm/f Internet surfer

cyber'spazio sm cyberspace

d

○ **PAROLA CHIAVE**

da (da + il = **dal**, da + lo = **dallo**, da + l' = **dall'**, da + la = **dalla**, da + i = **dai**, da + gli = **dagli**, da + le = **dalle**) prep
1 (agente) by; **dipinto da un grande artista** painted by a great artist
2 (causa) with; **tremare dalla paura** to tremble with fear
3 (stato in luogo) at; **abito da lui** I'm living at his house o with him; **sono dal giornalaio** I'm at the newsagent's; **era da Francesco** she was at Francesco's (house)
4 (moto a luogo) to; (moto per luogo) through; **vado da Pietro/dal giornalaio** I'm going to Pietro's (house)/to the newsagent's; **sono passati dalla finestra** they came in through the window
5 (provenienza, allontanamento) from; **arrivare/partire da Milano** to

arrive/depart from Milan; **scendere dal treno/dalla macchina** to get off the train/out of the car; **si trova a 5 km da qui** it's 5 km from here
6 (*tempo: durata*) for; (: *a partire da: nel passato*) since; (: *nel futuro*) from; **vivo qui da un anno** I've been living here for a year; **è dalle 3 che ti aspetto** I've been waiting for you since 3 (o'clock). **da oggi in poi** from today onwards; **da bambino** as a child, when I (*o lei ecc*) was a child
7 (*modo, maniera*) like; **comportarsi da uomo** to behave like a man; **l'ho fatto da me** I did it (by) myself
8 (*descrittivo*): **una macchina da corsa** a racing car; **una ragazza dai capelli biondi** a girl with blonde hair; **un vestito da 100 euro** a 100 euro dress

dà *vb vedi* **dare**
dac'capo *av* (*di nuovo*) (once) again; (*dal principio*) all over again, from the beginning
'dado *sm* (*da gioco*) dice *o* die; (*Cuc*) stock cube (BRIT), bouillon cube (US); (*Tecn*) (screw) nut; **dadi** *smpl* (*gioco of*) dice; **giocare a dadi** to play dice
'daino *sm* (fallow) deer *inv*; (*pelle*) buckskin
dal'tonico, -a, -ci, -che *ag* colour-blind
'dama *sf* lady; (*nei balli*) partner; (*gioco*) draughts *sg* (BRIT), checkers *sg* (US)
damigi'ana [dami'dʒana] *sf* demijohn
da'nese *ag* Danish ▷ *smf* Dane ▷ *sm* (*Ling*) Danish; **Dani'marca** *sf*: **la Danimarca** Denmark
dannazi'one [dannat'tsjone] *sf* damnation
danneggi'are [danned'dʒare] /62/ *vt* to damage; (*rovinare*) to spoil; (*nuocere*) to harm
'danno *sm* damage; (*a persona*) harm, injury; **danni** *smpl* (*Dir*) damages;

dan'noso, -a *ag*: **dannoso (a** *o* **per)** harmful (to), bad (for)
Da'nubio *sm*: **il ~** the Danube
'danza ['dantsa] *sf*: **la ~** dancing; **una ~** a dance; **dan'zare** /72/ *vt, vi* to dance
dap'pertutto *av* everywhere
dap'prima *av* at first
'dare /33/ *sm* (*Comm*) debit ▷ *vt* to give; (*produrre: frutti, suono*) to produce ▷ *vi* (*guardare*): **~ su** to look (out) onto; **darsi** *vpr*: **darsi a** to dedicate o.s. to; **~ da mangiare a qn** to give sb something to eat; **~ per certo qc** to consider sth certain; **~ per morto qn** to give sb up for dead; **darsi al bere** to take to drink; **darsi al commercio** to go into business; **darsi per vinto** to give in
'data *sf* date; **~ di nascita** date of birth; **~ di scadenza** expiry date; **~ limite d'utilizzo** *o* **di consumo** (*Comm*) best-before date
'dato, -a *ag* (*stabilito*) given ▷ *sm* datum; **dati** *smpl* data *pl*: **~ che** given that; **è un ~ di fatto** it's a fact; **dati sensibili** sense data
da'tore, -'trice *sm/f*: **~ di lavoro** employer
'dattero *sm* date (*Bot*)
dattilogra'fia *sf* typing
datti'lografo, -a *sm/f* typist
da'vanti *av* in front; (*dirimpetto*) opposite ▷ *ag inv* front ▷ *sm* front; **~ a** in front of; (*dirimpetto a*) facing, opposite; (*in presenza di*) before, in front of
davan'zale [davan'tsale] *sm* windowsill
dav'vero *av* really, indeed
d.C. *abbr* (= *dopo Cristo*) A.D.
'dea *sf* goddess
'debbo *ecc vb vedi* **dovere**
'debito, -a *ag* due, proper ▷ *sm* debt; (*Comm: dare*) debit; **a tempo ~** at the right time
'debole *ag* weak, feeble; (*suono*) faint; (*luce*) dim ▷ *sm* weakness; **debo'lezza** *sf* weakness

debut'tare /72/ *vi* to make one's début

deca'denza [deka'dɛntsa] *sf* decline; (*Dir*) loss, forfeiture

decaffei'nato, -a *ag* decaffeinated

decapi'tare /72/ *vt* to decapitate, behead

decappot'tabile *ag, sf* convertible

de'cennio [de'tʃɛnnjo] *sm* decade

de'cente [de'tʃɛnte] *ag* decent, respectable, proper; (*accettabile*) satisfactory, decent

de'cesso [de'tʃɛsso] *sm* death

de'cidere [de'tʃidere] /34/ *vt*: ~ **qc** to decide on sth; (*questione, lite*) to settle sth; **decidersi** *vpr*: **decidersi (a fare)** to decide (to do), make up one's mind (to do); ~ **di fare/che** to decide to do/that; ~ **di qc** (*cosa*) to determine sth

deci'frare [detʃi'frare] /72/ *vt* to decode, (*fig*) to decipher, make out

deci'male [detʃi'male] *ag* decimal

'decimo, -a ['dɛtʃimo] *num* tenth

de'cina [de'tʃina] *sf* ten; (*circa dieci*): **una ~ (di)** about ten

de'cisi *ecc* [de'tʃizi] *vb vedi* **decidere**

decisi'one [detʃi'zjone] *sf* decision; **prendere una ~** to make a decision

deci'sivo, -a [detʃi'zivo] *ag* (*gen*) decisive; (*fattore*) deciding

de'ciso, -a [de'tʃizo] *pp di* **decidere**

decli'nare /72/ *vi* (*pendio*) to slope down; (*fig: diminuire*) to decline ▷ *vt* to decline

declinazi'one *sf* (*Ling*) declension

de'clino *sm* decline

decodifica'tore *sm* (*Tel*) decoder

decol'lare /72/ *vi* (*Aer*) to take off; **de'collo** *sm* take-off

deco'rare /72/ *vt* to decorate; **decorazi'one** *sf* decoration

de'creto *sm* decree; ~ **legge** decree with the force of law

'dedica *sf* dedication

dedi'care /20/ *vt* to dedicate; **dedicarsi** *vpr*: **dedicarsi a** to devote o.s. to

dedicherò *ecc* [dedike'rɔ] *vb vedi* **dedicare**

'dedito, -a *ag*: ~ **a** (*studio ecc*) dedicated o devoted to; (*vizio*) addicted to

de'duco *ecc vb vedi* **dedurre**

de'durre /90/ *vt* (*concludere*) to deduce; (*defalcare*) to deduct

de'dussi *ecc vb vedi* **dedurre**

defici'ente [defi'tʃɛnte] *ag* (*insufficiente*) insufficient; ~ **di** (*mancante*) deficient in ▷ *smf* (*peg: cretino*) idiot

'deficit ['dɛfitʃit] *sm inv* (*Econ*) deficit

defi'nire /55/ *vt* to define; (*risolvere*) to settle; **defini'tivo, -a** *ag* definitive, final ▷ *sf*: **in definitiva** (*dopotutto*) when all is said and done; (*dunque*) hence; **definizi'one** *sf* definition; (*di disputa, vertenza*) settlement

defor'mare /72/ *vt* (*alterare*) to put out of shape; (*corpo*) to deform; (*pensiero, fatto*) to distort; **deformarsi** *vpr* to lose its shape

de'forme *ag* deformed; disfigured

de'funto, -a *ag* late *cpd* ▷ *sm/f* deceased

degene'rare [dedʒene'rare] /72/ *vi* to degenerate

de'gente [de'dʒɛnte] *smf* (*ricoverato in ospedale*) in-patient

deglu'tire /55/ *vt* to swallow

de'gnare [deɲ'ɲare] /15/ *vt*: ~ **qn della propria presenza** to honour sb with one's presence; **degnarsi** *vpr*: **degnarsi di fare qc** to deign o condescend to do sth

'degno, -a *ag* dignified; ~ **di** worthy of; ~ **di lode** praiseworthy

de'grado *sm*: ~ **urbano** urban decline

'delega, -ghe *sf* (*procura*) proxy

dele'terio, -a *ag* damaging; (*per salute ecc*) harmful

del'fino *sm* (*Zool*) dolphin; (*Storia*) dauphin; (*fig*) probable successor

deli'cato, -a *ag* delicate; (*salute*) delicate, frail; (*fig: gentile*) thoughtful, considerate; (: *che dimostra tatto*) tactful

delin'quente *smf* criminal, delinquent; **~ abituale** regular offender, habitual offender; **delin'quenza** *sf* criminality, delinquency; **delinquenza minorile** juvenile delinquency

deli'rare /72/ *vi* to be delirious, rave; (*fig*) to rave

de'lirio *sm* delirium; (*ragionamento insensato*) raving; (*fig*): **andare/ mandare in ~** to go/send into a frenzy

de'litto *sm* crime

delizi'oso, -a [delit'tsjoso] *ag* delightful; (*cibi*) delicious

delta'plano *sm* hang-glider; **volo col ~** hang-gliding

delu'dente *ag* disappointing

de'ludere /35/ *vt* to disappoint; **delusi'one** *sf* disappointment; **de'luso, -a** *pp di* **deludere**

'demmo *vb vedi* **dare**

demo'cratico, -a, -ci, -che *ag* democratic

democra'zia [demokrat'tsia] *sf* democracy

demo'lire /55/ *vt* to demolish

de'monio *sm* demon, devil; **il D~** the Devil

de'naro *sm* money

densità *sf inv* density

'denso, -a *ag* thick, dense

den'tale *ag* dental

'dente *sm* tooth; (*di forchetta*) prong; **al ~** (*Cuc: pasta*) al dente; **denti del giudizio** wisdom teeth; **denti da latte** milk teeth; **denti'era** *sf* (set of) false teeth *pl*

denti'fricio [denti'fritʃo] *sm* toothpaste

den'tista, -i, -e *sm/f* dentist

'dentro *av* inside; (*in casa*) indoors; (*fig: nell'intimo*) inwardly ▷ *prep*: **~ (a)** in; **piegato in ~** folded over; **qui/ là ~** in here/there; **~ di sé** (*pensare, brontolare*) to oneself

de'nuncia, -ce o **-cie** [de'nuntʃa] *sf* denunciation; declaration; **~ del reddito** (*income*) tax return

denunci'are [denun'tʃare] /14/ *vt* to denounce; (*dichiarare*) to declare; **~ qn/qc (alla polizia)** to report sb/sth to the police

denu'trito, -a *ag* undernourished

denutrizi'one [denutrit'tsjone] *sf* malnutrition

deodo'rante *sm* deodorant

depe'rire /55/ *vi* to waste away

depi'larsi /72/ *vpr*: **~ (le gambe)** (*con rasoio*) to shave (one's legs); (*con ceretta*) to wax (one's legs)

depila'torio, -a *ag* hair-removing *cpd*, depilatory

dépli'ant [depli'ã] *sm inv* leaflet; (*opuscolo*) brochure

deplo'revole *ag* deplorable

de'pone, de'pongo *ecc vb vedi* **deporre**

de'porre /77/ *vt* (*depositare*) to put down; (*rimuovere: da una carica*) to remove; (: *re*) to depose; (*Dir*) to testify

depor'tare /72/ *vt* to deport

de'posi *ecc vb vedi* **deporre**

deposi'tare /72/ *vt* (*gen, Geo, Econ*) to deposit; (*lasciare*) to leave; (*merci*) to store; **depositarsi** *vpr* (*sabbia, polvere*) to settle

de'posito *sm* deposit; (*luogo*) warehouse; depot; (: *Mil*) depot; **~ bagagli** left-luggage office

deposizi'one [depozit'tsjone] *sf* deposition; (*da una carica*) removal

depra'vato, -a *ag* depraved ▷ *sm/f* degenerate

depre'dare /72/ *vt* to rob, plunder

depressi'one *sf* depression

de'presso, -a *pp di* **deprimere** ▷ *ag* depressed

deprez'zare [depret'tsare] /72/ *vt* (*Econ*) to depreciate

depri'mente *ag* depressing

de'primere /50/ *vt* to depress

depu'rare /72/ *vt* to purify

depu'tato, -a sm/f (Pol) deputy, ≈ Member of Parliament (BRIT), ≈ Congressman/woman (US)

deragli'are [deraʎ'ʎare] /27/ vi to be derailed; **far ~** to derail

de'ridere /89/ vt to mock, deride

de'risi ecc vb vedi **deridere**

de'riva sf (Naut, Aer) drift; **andare alla ~** (anche fig) to drift

deri'vare /72/ vi: **~ da** to derive from ▷ vt to derive; (corso d'acqua) to divert

derma'tologo, -a, -gi, -ghe sm/f dermatologist

deru'bare /72/ vt to rob

des'crivere /105/ vt to describe; **descrizi'one** sf description

de'serto, -a ag deserted ▷ sm (Geo) desert; **isola deserta** desert island

deside'rare /72/ vt to want, wish for; (sessualmente) to desire; **~ fare/ che qn faccia** to want o wish to do/sb to do; **desidera fare una passeggiata?** would you like to go for a walk?

desi'derio sm wish; (più intenso, carnale) desire

deside'roso, -a ag: **~ di** longing o eager for

desi'nenza [dezi'nɛntsa] sf (Ling) ending, inflexion

de'sistere /11/ vi: **~ da** to give up, desist from

'desktop ['dɛsktop] sm inv (Inform) desktop

deso'lato, -a ag (paesaggio) desolate; (persona: spiacente) sorry

'dessi ecc vb vedi **dare**

'deste ecc vb vedi **dare**

desti'nare /72/ vt to destine; (assegnare) to appoint, assign; (indirizzare) to address; **~ qc a qn** to intend to give sth to sb, intend sb to have sth; **destina'tario, -a** sm/f (di lettera) addressee

destinazi'one [destinat'tsjone] sf destination; (uso) purpose

des'tino sm destiny, fate

destitu'ire /55/ vt to dismiss, remove

'destra sf vedi **destro**

destreggi'arsi [destred'dʒarsi] /62/ vpr to manoeuvre (BRIT), maneuver (US)

des'trezza [des'trettsa] sf skill, dexterity

'destro, -a ag right, right-hand ▷ sf (mano) right hand; (parte) right (side); (Pol): **la destra** the right; **a destra** (essere) on the right; (andare) to the right

dete'nuto, -a sm/f prisoner

deter'gente [deter'dʒɛnte] ag (crema, latte) cleansing ▷ sm cleanser

> Attenzione! In inglese esiste la parola detergent, che però significa detersivo.

determi'nare /72/ vt to determine

determina'tivo, -a ag determining; **articolo ~** (Ling) definite article

determi'nato, -a ag (gen) certain; (particolare) specific; (risoluto) determined, resolute

deter'sivo sm detergent

detes'tare /72/ vt to detest, hate

de'trae, de'traggo ecc vb vedi **detrarre**

de'trarre /123/ vt: **~ (da)** to deduct (from), take away (from)

de'trassi ecc vb vedi **detrarre**

'detta sf: **a ~ di** according to

det'taglio [det'taʎʎo] sm detail; (Comm): **il ~** retail; **al ~** (Comm) retail; separately

det'tare /72/ vt to dictate; **~ legge** (fig) to lay down the law; **det'tato** sm dictation

'detto, -a pp di **dire** ▷ ag (soprannominato) called, known as; (già nominato) above-mentioned ▷ sm saying; **~ fatto** no sooner said than done

devas'tare /72/ vt to devastate; (fig) to ravage

devi'are /19/ vi: **~ (da)** to turn off (from) ▷ vt to divert; **deviazi'one** sf (anche Aut) diversion

'devo ecc vb vedi **dovere**

de'volvere /94/ vt (Dir) to transfer, devolve

de'voto, -a ag (Rel) devout, pious; (affezionato) devoted

devozi'one [devot'tsjone] sf devoutness; (anche Rel) devotion

dezip'pare [dedzip'pare] /72/ vt (Inform) to unzip

PAROLA CHIAVE

di (di + il = **del**, di + lo = **dello**, di + l' = **dell'**, di + la = **della**, di + i = **dei**, di + gli = **degli**, di + le = **delle**) prep 1 (possesso, specificazione) of; (composto da, scritto da) by; **la macchina di Paolo/di mio fratello** Paolo's/my brother's car; **un amico di mio fratello** a friend of my brother's, one of my brother's friends; **un quadro di Botticelli** a painting by Botticelli

2 (caratterizzazione, misura) of; **una casa di mattoni** a brick house, a house made of bricks; **un orologio d'oro** a gold watch; **un bimbo di 3 anni** a child of 3, a 3-year-old child

3 (causa, mezzo, modo) with; **tremare di paura** to tremble with fear; **morire di cancro** to die of cancer; **spalmare di burro** to spread with butter

4 (argomento) about, of; **discutere di sport** to talk about sport

5 (luogo, provenienza) from; out of; **essere di Roma** to be from Rome; **uscire di casa** to come out of o leave the house

6 (tempo) in; **d'estate/d'inverno** in (the) summer/winter; **di notte** by night, at night; **di mattina/sera** in the morning/evening; **di lunedì** on Mondays

▶ det (una certa quantità di) some; (: negativo) any; (interrogativo) any; some; **del pane** (some) bread; **delle caramelle** (some) sweets; **degli amici miei** some friends of mine; **vuoi del vino?** do you want some o any wine?

dia'bete sm diabetes sg

dia'betico, -a, -ci, -che ag, sm/f diabetic

dia'framma, -i sm (divisione) screen; (Anat, Fot: contraccettivo) diaphragm

di'agnosi [di'aɲɲozi] sf diagnosis sg

diago'nale ag, sf diagonal

dia'gramma, -i sm diagram

di'aletto sm dialect

di'alisi sf dialysis sg

di'alogo, -ghi sm dialogue

dia'mante sm diamond

di'ametro sm diameter

diaposi'tiva sf transparency, slide

di'ario sm diary

diar'rea sf diarrhoea

di'avolo sm devil

di'battito sm debate, discussion

'dice ['ditʃe] vb vedi **dire**

di'cembre [di'tʃembre] sm December

dice'ria [ditʃe'ria] sf rumour, piece of gossip

dichia'rare [dikja'rare] /72/ vt to declare; **dichiararsi** vpr to declare o.s.; (innamorato) to declare one's love; **dichiararsi vinto** to admit defeat; **dichiarazi'one** sf declaration; **dichiarazione dei redditi** statement of income; (modulo) tax return

dician'nove [ditʃan'nove] num nineteen

dicias'sette [ditʃas'sette] num seventeen

dici'otto [di'tʃɔtto] num eighteen

dici'tura [ditʃi'tura] sf words pl, wording

'dico ecc vb vedi **dire**

didasca'lia sf (di illustrazione) caption; (Cine) subtitle; (Teat) stage directions pl

di'dattico, -a, -ci, -che ag didactic; (metodo, programma) teaching; (libro) educational

di'eci ['djɛtʃi] num ten

di'edi ecc vb vedi **dare**

'diesel ['di:zəl] sm inv diesel engine

dies'sino, -a *sm/f* member of the DS political party

di'eta *sf* diet; **essere a ~** to be on a diet

di'etro *av* behind; (*in fondo*) at the back ▷ *prep* behind; (*tempo: dopo*) after ▷ *sm* back, rear ▷ *ag inv* back *cpd*; **le zampe di ~** the hind legs; **~ richiesta** on demand; (*scritta*) on application

di'fendere /36/ *vt* to defend; **difendersi** *vpr* (*cavarsela*) to get by; **difendersi da/contro** to defend o.s. from/against; **difendersi dal freddo** to protect o.s. from the cold; **difen'sore, -a** *sm/f* defender; **avvocato difensore** counsel for the defence (*BRIT*) o defense (*US*); **di'fesa** *sf vedi* **difeso**

di'fesi *ecc vb vedi* **difendere**

di'fetto *sm* (*mancanza*): **~ di** lack of; shortage of; (*di fabbricazione*) fault, flaw, defect; (*morale*) fault, failing, defect; (*fisico*) defect; **far ~** to be lacking; **in ~** at fault; in the wrong; **difet'toso, -a** *ag* defective, faulty

diffe'rente *ag* different

diffe'renza [diffe'rɛntsa] *sf* difference; **a ~ di** unlike

diffe'rire /55/ *vt* to postpone, defer ▷ *vi* to be different

diffe'rita *sf*: **in ~** (*trasmettere*) prerecorded

diffi'cile [dif'fitʃile] *ag* difficult; (*persona*) hard to please, difficult (to please); (*poco probabile*): **è ~ che sia libero** it is unlikely that he'll be free ▷ *sm* difficult part; difficulty; **difficoltà** *sf inv* difficulty

diffi'dente *ag* suspicious, distrustful

diffi'denza *sf* suspicion, distrust

dif'fondere /25/ *vt* (*luce, calore*) to diffuse; (*notizie*) to spread, circulate; **diffondersi** *vpr* to spread

diffusi *ecc vb vedi* **diffondere**

diffu'so, -a *pp di* **diffondere** ▷ *ag* (*fenomeno, notizia, malattia ecc*) widespread

'diga, -ghe *sf* dam; (*portuale*) breakwater

dige'rente [didʒe'rɛnte] *ag* (*apparato*) digestive

dige'rire [didʒe'rire] /55/ *vt* to digest; **digesti'one** *sf* digestion; **diges'tivo, -a** *ag* digestive ▷ *sm* (*after-dinner*) liqueur

digi'tale [didʒi'tale] *ag* digital; (*delle dita*) finger *cpd*, digital ▷ *sf* (*Bot*) foxglove

digi'tare [didʒi'tare] /72/ *vt* (*dati*) to key (in)

digiu'nare [didʒu'nare] /72/ *vi* to starve o.s.; (*Rel*) to fast; **digi'uno, -a** *ag*: **essere digiuno** not to have eaten ▷ *sm* fast; **a digiuno** on an empty stomach

dignità [diɲɲi'ta] *sf inv* dignity

'DIGOS *sigla f* (= *Divisione Investigazioni Generali e Operazioni Speciali*) police department dealing with political security

digri'gnare [digriɲ'ɲare] /15/ *vt*: **~ i denti** to grind one's teeth

dilapi'dare /72/ *vt* to squander, waste

dila'tare /72/ *vt* to dilate; (*gas*) to cause to expand; (*passaggio, cavità*) to open (up); **dilatarsi** *vpr* to dilate; (*Fisica*) to expand

dilazio'nare [dilattsjo'nare] /72/ *vt* to delay, defer

di'lemma, -i *sm* dilemma

dilet'tante *smf* dilettante; (*anche Sport*) amateur

dili'gente [dili'dʒɛnte] *ag* (*scrupoloso*) diligent; (*accurato*) careful, accurate

dilu'ire /55/ *vt* to dilute

dilun'garsi /80/ *vpr* (*fig*): **~ su** to talk at length on o about

diluvi'are /19/ *vb impers* to pour (down)

di'luvio *sm* downpour; (*inondazione, fig*) flood

dima'grante *ag* slimming *cpd*

dima'grire /55/ *vi* to get thinner, lose weight

dime'nare /72/ vt to wave, shake; **dimenarsi** vpr to toss and turn; (fig) to struggle; **~ la coda** (cane) to wag its tail

dimensi'one sf dimension; (grandezza) size

dimenti'canza [dimenti'kantsa] sf forgetfulness; (errore) oversight, slip; **per ~** inadvertently

dimenti'care /20/ vt to forget; **dimenticarsi** vpr: **dimenticarsi di qc** to forget sth

dimesti'chezza [dimesti'kettsa] sf familiarity

di'mettere /63/ vt: **~ qn da** to dismiss sb from; (dall'ospedale) to discharge sb from; **dimettersi** vpr: **dimettersi (da)** to resign (from)

dimez'zare [dimed'dzare] /72/ vt to halve

diminu'ire /55/ vt to reduce, diminish; (prezzi) to bring down, reduce ▷ vi to decrease, diminish; (rumore) to die down, die away; (prezzi) to fall, go down

diminu'tivo, -a ag, sm diminutive

diminuzi'one [diminut'tsjone] sf decreasing, diminishing

di'misi ecc vb vedi **dimettere**

dimissi'oni sfpl resignation sg: **dare** o **presentare le ~** to resign, hand in one's resignation

dimos'trare /72/ vt to demonstrate, show; (provare) to prove, demonstrate; **dimostrarsi** vpr: **dimostrarsi molto abile** to show o.s. o prove to be very clever; **dimostra 30 anni** he looks about 30 (years old); **dimostrazi'one** sf demonstration; proof

di'namico, -a, -ci, -che ag dynamic ▷ sf dynamics sg

dina'mite sf dynamite

'dinamo sf inv dynamo

dino'sauro sm dinosaur

din'torno av round; **dintorni** smpl outskirts; **nei dintorni di** in the vicinity o neighbourhood of

'dio (pl **dei**) sm god; **D~** God; **gli dei** the gods; **D~ m~!** my God!

diparti'mento sm department

dipen'dente ag dependent ▷ smf employee; **~ statale** state employee

di'pendere /8/ vi: **~ da** to depend on; (finanziariamente) to be dependent on; (derivare) to come from, be due to

di'pesi ecc vb vedi **dipendere**

di'pingere [di'pindʒere] /37/ vt to paint

di'pinsi ecc vb vedi **dipingere**

di'pinto, -a pp di **dipingere** ▷ sm painting

di'ploma, -i sm diploma

diplo'matico, -a, -ci, -che ag diplomatic ▷ sm diplomat

diploma'zia [diplomat'tsia] sf diplomacy

di'porto sm: **imbarcazione da ~** pleasure craft

dira'dare /72/ vt to thin (out); (visite) to reduce, make less frequent; **diradarsi** vpr to disperse; (nebbia) to clear (up)

'dire /38/ vt to say; (segreto, fatto) to tell; **~ qc a qn** to tell sb sth; **~ a qn di fare qc** to tell sb to do sth; **~ di si/no** to say yes/no; **si dice che ...** they say that ...; **si direbbe che ...** it looks (o sounds) as though ...; **dica, signora?** (in un negozio) yes, Madam, can I help you?

di'ressi ecc vb vedi **dirigere**

di'retta sf: **in ~** (trasmettere) live; **un incontro di calcio in ~** a live football match

di'retto, -a pp di **dirigere** ▷ ag direct ▷ sm (Ferr) through train

diret'tore, -'trice sm/f (di azienda) director, manager(manageress); (di scuola elementare) head (teacher) (BRIT), principal (US); **~ d'orchestra** conductor; **~ vendite** sales director o manager; **direzi'one** sf board of directors; management; (senso: anche fig) direction; **in direzione di** in the direction of, towards

diri'gente [diri'dʒɛnte] *smf* executive; (*Pol*) leader ▷ *ag*: **classe ~** ruling class; **di'rigere** /39/ *vt* to direct; (*impresa*) to run, manage; (*Mus*) to conduct; **dirigersi** *vpr*: **dirigersi verso** *o* **a** to make *o* head for

dirim'petto *av* opposite; **~ a** opposite, facing

di'ritto, -a *ag* straight; (*onesto*) straight, upright ▷ *av* straight, directly ▷ *sm* right side; (*Tennis*) forehand; (*Maglia*) plain stitch; (*prerogativa*) right; (*leggi, scienza*): **il ~** law; **diritti** *smpl* (*tasse*) duty *sg*: **stare ~** to stand up straight; **aver ~ a qc** to be entitled to sth; **andare ~** to go straight on; **diritti (d'autore)** royalties

dirotta'mento *sm*: **~ (aereo)** hijack

dirot'tare /72/ *vt* (*nave, aereo*) to change the course of; (*aereo: sotto minaccia*) to hijack; (*traffico*) to divert ▷ *vi* (*nave, aereo*) to change course; **dirotta'tore, -'trice** *sm/f* hijacker

di'rotto, -a *ag* (*pioggia*) torrential; (*pianto*) unrestrained; **piovere a ~** to pour; **piangere a ~** to cry one's heart out

di'rupo *sm* crag, precipice

di'sabile *smf* person with a disability ▷ *ag* disabled; **i disabili** people with disabilities

disabi'tato, -a *ag* uninhabited

disabitu'arsi /72/ *vpr*: **~ a** to get out of the habit of

disac'cordo *sm* disagreement

disadat'tato, -a *ag* (*Psic*) maladjusted

disa'dorno, -a *ag* plain, unadorned

disagi'ato, -a [diza'dʒato] *ag* poor, needy; (*vita*) hard

di'sagio [di'zadʒo] *sm* discomfort; (*disturbo*) inconvenience; (*fig: imbarazzo*) embarrassment; **essere a ~** to be ill at ease

disappro'vare /72/ *vt* to disapprove of; **disapprovazi'one** *sf* disapproval

disap'punto *sm* disappointment

disar'mare /72/ *vt, vi* to disarm; **di'sarmo** *sm* (*Mil*) disarmament

di'sastro *sm* disaster

disas'troso, -a *ag* disastrous

disat'tento, -a *ag* inattentive; **disattenzi'one** *sf* carelessness, lack of attention

disavven'tura *sf* misadventure, mishap

dis'capito *sm*: **a ~ di** to the detriment of

dis'carica, -che *sf* (*di rifiuti*) rubbish tip *o* dump

di'scendere [diʃʃɛndere] /101/ *vt* to go (*o* come) down ▷ *vi* to go (*o* come) down; (*strada*) to go down; (*smontare*) to get off; **~ da** (*famiglia*) to be descended from; **~ dalla macchina/ dal treno** to get out of the car/out of *o* off the train; **~ da cavallo** to dismount, get off one's horse

di'scesa [diʃʃesa] *sf* descent; (*pendio*) slope; **in ~** (*strada*) downhill *cpd*, sloping; **~ libera** (*Sci*) downhill (race)

disci'plina [diʃʃi'plina] *sf* discipline

'disco, -schi *sm* disc; (*Sport*) discus; (*fonografico*) record; (*Inform*) disk; **~ orario** (*Aut*) parking disc; **~ rigido** (*Inform*) hard disk; **~ volante** flying saucer

disco'grafico, -a, -ci, -che *ag* record *cpd*, recording *cpd* ▷ *sm* record producer; **casa discografica** record(ing) company

dis'correre /28/ *vi*: **~ (di)** to talk (about)

dis'corso, -a *pp di* **discorrere** ▷ *sm* speech; (*conversazione*) conversation, talk

disco'teca, -che *sf* (*raccolta*) record library; (*luogo di ballo*) disco(theque)

dis'count [dis'kaunt] *sm inv* (*supermercato*) cut-price supermarket

discre'panza [diskre'pantsa] *sf* discrepancy

dis'creto, -a *ag* discreet; (*abbastanza buono*) reasonable, fair

discriminazi'one [diskriminat'tsjone] *sf* discrimination

dis'cussi *ecc vb vedi* **discutere**

discussi'one *sf* discussion; (*litigio*) argument; **fuori ~** out of the question

dis'cutere /40/ *vt* to discuss, debate; (*contestare*) to question ▷ *vi* (*litigare*) to argue; (*conversare*): **~ (di)** to discuss

dis'detto, -a *pp di* **disdire** ▷ *sf* (*di prenotazione ecc*) cancellation; (*sfortuna*) bad luck

dis'dire /38/ *vt* (*prenotazione*) to cancel; **~ un contratto d'affitto** (*Dir*) to give notice (to quit)

dise'gnare [disen'nare] /15/ *vt* to draw; (*progettare*) to design; (*fig*) to outline; **disegna'tore, -'trice** *sm/f* designer

di'segno [di'zenno] *sm* drawing; (*su stoffa ecc*) design; (*fig: schema*) outline; **~ di legge** (*Dir*) bill

diser'bante *sm* weedkiller

diser'tare /72/ *vt, vi* to desert

dis'fare /41/ *vt* to undo; (*valigie*) to unpack; (*meccanismo*) to take to pieces; (*neve*) to melt; **disfarsi** *vpr* to come undone; (*neve*) to melt; **~ il letto** to strip the bed; **disfarsi di qn** (*liberarsi*) to get rid of sb; **dis'fatto, -a** *pp di* **disfare**

dis'gelo [diz'dʒɛlo] *sm* thaw

dis'grazia [diz'grattsja] *sf* (*sventura*) misfortune; (*incidente*) accident, mishap

disgu'ido *sm* hitch; **~ postale** error in postal delivery

disgu'stare /72/ *vt* to disgust

dis'gusto *sm* disgust; **disgus'toso, -a** *ag* disgusting

disidra'tare /72/ *vt* to dehydrate

disimpa'rare /72/ *vt* to forget

disinfet'tante *ag, sm* disinfectant

disinfet'tare /72/ *vt* to disinfect

disini'bito, -a *ag* uninhibited

disinstal'lare /72/ *vt* (*software*) to uninstall

disinte'grare /72/ *vt, vi* to disintegrate; **disintegrarsi** *vpr* to disintegrate

disinteres'sarsi /72/ *vpr*: **~ di** to take no interest in; **disinte'resse** *sm* indifference; (*generosità*) unselfishness

disintossi'care /20/ *vt* (*alcolizzato, drogato*) to treat for alcoholism (*o* drug addiction); **disintossicarsi** *vpr* to clear out one's system; (*alcolizzato, drogato*) to be treated for alcoholism (*o* drug addiction); **disintossicazione** *sf* detox

disin'volto, -a *ag* casual, free and easy

dismi'sura *sf* excess; **a ~** to excess, excessively

disoccu'pato, -a *ag* unemployed ▷ *sm/f* unemployed person; **disoccupazi'one** *sf* unemployment

diso'nesto, -a *ag* dishonest

disordi'nato, -a *ag* untidy; (*privo di misura*) irregular, wild; **di'sordine** *sm* (*confusione*) disorder, confusion; (*sregolatezza*) debauchery; **disordini** *smpl* (*Pol: ecc*) disorder *sg*; (*tumulti*) riots

disorien'tare /72/ *vt* to disorientate

disorien'tato, -a *ag* disorientated

'dispari *ag inv* odd, uneven

dis'parte: **in ~** *av* (*da lato*) aside, apart; **tenersi** *o* **starsene in ~** to keep to o.s., hold aloof

dispendi'oso, -a *ag* expensive

dis'pensa *sf* pantry, larder; (*mobile*) sideboard; (*Dir*) exemption; (*Rel*) dispensation; (*fascicolo*) number, issue

dispe'rato, -a *ag* (*persona*) in despair; (*caso, tentativo*) desperate

disperazi'one *sf* despair

dis'perdere /73/ *vt* (*disseminare*) to disperse; (*Mil*) to scatter, rout; (*fig: consumare*) to waste, squander; **disperdersi** *vpr* to disperse; to scatter; **dis'perso, -a** *pp di* **disperdere** ▷ *sm/f* missing person

dis'petto sm spite no pl, spitefulness no pl; **fare un ~ a qn** to play a (nasty) trick on sb; **a ~ di** in spite of; **dispet'toso, -a** ag spiteful

dispia'cere [dispja'tʃere] /74/ sm (rammarico) regret, sorrow; (dolore) grief ▷ vi: **~ a** to displease ▷ vb impers: **mi dispiace (che)** I am sorry (that); **le dispiace se…?** do you mind if …?; **dispiaceri** smpl (preoccupazioni) troubles, worries

dis'pone, dis'pongo ecc vb vedi **disporre**

dispo'nibile ag available

dis'porre /77/ vt (sistemare) to arrange; (preparare) to prepare; (Dir) to order; (persuadere): **~ qn a** to incline o dispose sb towards ▷ vi (decidere) to decide; (usufruire): **~ di** to use, have at one's disposal; (essere dotato): **~ di** to have

dis'posi ecc vb vedi **disporre**

disposi'tivo sm (meccanismo) device

disposizi'one [dispozit'tsjone] sf arrangement, layout; (stato d'animo) mood; (tendenza) bent, inclination; (comando) order; (Dir) provision, regulation; **a ~ di qn** at sb's disposal

dis'posto, -a pp di **disporre**

disprez'zare [dispret'tsare] /72/ vt to despise

dis'prezzo [dis'prettso] sm contempt

'disputa sf dispute, quarrel

dispu'tare /72/ vt (contendere) to dispute, contest; (gara) to take part in ▷ vi to quarrel; **~ di** to discuss; **disputarsi qc** to fight for sth

'disse vb vedi **dire**

dissente'ria sf dysentery

dissen'tire /45/ vi: **~ (da)** to disagree (with)

disse'tante ag refreshing

'dissi vb vedi **dire**

dissimu'lare /72/ vt (fingere) to dissemble; (nascondere) to conceal

dissi'pare /72/ vt to dissipate; (scialacquare) to squander, waste

dissu'adere /88/ vt: **~ qn da** to dissuade sb from

dissua'sore sm: **~ di velocità** (Aut) speed bump

distac'care /20/ vt to detach, separate; (Sport) to leave behind; **distaccarsi** vpr to be detached; (fig) to stand out; **distaccarsi da** (fig) (allontanarsi) to grow away from

dis'tacco, -chi sm (separazione) separation; (fig: indifferenza) detachment; (Sport): **vincere con un ~ di …** to win by a distance of …

dis'tante av far away ▷ ag: **essere ~ (da)** to be a long way (from)

dis'tanza [dis'tantsa] sf distance

distanzi'are [distan'tsjare] /19/ vt to space out, place at intervals; (Sport) to outdistance; (fig: superare) to outstrip, surpass

dis'tare /72/ vi: **distiamo pochi chilometri da Roma** we are only a few kilometres (away) from Rome; **quanto dista il centro da qui?** how far is the town centre?

dis'tendere /120/ vt (coperta) to spread out; (gambe) to stretch (out); (mettere a giacere) to lay; (rilassare: muscoli, nervi) to relax; **distendersi** vpr (rilassarsi) to relax; (sdraiarsi) to lie down

dis'teso, -a pp di **distendere** ▷ sf expanse, stretch

distil'lare /72/ vt to distil

distille'ria sf distillery

dis'tinguere /42/ vt to distinguish; **distinguersi** vpr (essere riconoscibile) to be distinguished; (emergere) to stand out, be conspicuous, distinguish o.s.

dis'tinta sf (nota) note; (elenco) list; **~ di versamento** pay-in slip

distin'tivo, -a ag distinctive; distinguishing ▷ sm badge

dis'tinto, -a pp di **distinguere** ▷ ag (dignitoso ed elegante) distinguished; **distinti saluti** (in lettera) yours faithfully

distinzi'one [distin'tsjone] *sf* distinction

dis'togliere [dis'tɔʎʎere] /122/ *vt*: **~ da** to take away from; (*fig*) to dissuade from

distorsi'one *sf* (*Med*) sprain; (*Fisica, Ottica*) distortion

dis'trarre /123/ *vt* to distract; (*divertire*) to entertain, amuse; **distrarsi** *vpr* (*non fare attenzione*) to be distracted, let one's mind wander; (*svagarsi*) to amuse o enjoy o.s.; **dis'tratto, -a** *pp di* **distrarre** ▷ *ag* absent-minded; (*disattento*) inattentive; **distrazi'one** *sf* absent-mindedness; inattention; (*svago*) distraction, entertainment

dis'tretto *sm* district

distribu'ire /55/ *vt* to distribute; (*Carte*) to deal (out); (*posta*) to deliver; (*lavoro*) to allocate, assign; (*ripartire*) to share out; **distribu'tore** *sm* (*di benzina*) petrol (*BRIT*) o gas (*US*) pump; (*Aut, Elettr*) distributor; (*automatico*) vending machine

distri'care /20/ *vt* to disentangle, unravel; **districarsi** *vpr* (*tirarsi fuori*) **districarsi da** to get out of, disentangle o.s. from

dis'truggere [dis'truddʒere] /83/ *vt* to destroy; **distruzi'one** *sf* destruction

distur'bare /72/ *vt* to disturb, trouble; (*sonno, lezioni*) to disturb, interrupt; **disturbarsi** *vpr* to put o.s. out; **dis'turbo** *sm* trouble, bother, inconvenience; (*indisposizione*) (slight) disorder, ailment

disubbidi'ente *ag* disobedient; **disubbi'dire** /55/ *vi*: **disubbidire (a qn)** to disobey (sb)

disu'mano, -a *ag* inhuman

di'tale *sm* thimble

'dito (*pl f* **dita**) *sm* finger; (*misura*) finger, finger's breadth; **~ (del piede)** toe

'ditta *sf* firm, business

ditta'tore *sm* dictator

ditta'tura *sf* dictatorship

dit'tongo, -ghi *sm* diphthong

di'urno, -a *ag* day *cpd*, daytime *cpd*

'diva *sf vedi* **divo**

di'vano *sm* sofa; (*senza schienale*) divan; **~ letto** bed settee, sofa bed

divari'care /20/ *vt* to open wide

di'vario *sm* difference

dive'nire /128/ *vi* = **diventare**

diven'tare /72/ *vi* to become; **~ famoso/professore** to become famous/a teacher

diversifi'care /20/ *vt* to diversify, vary; to differentiate; **diversificarsi** *vpr*: **diversificarsi (per)** to differ (in)

diversità *sf inv* difference, diversity; (*varietà*) variety

diver'sivo *sm* diversion, distraction

di'verso, -a *ag* (*differente*): **~ (da)** different (from); **diversi, e** *det pl*, *pron pl* several, various; (*Comm*) sundry; several people, many (people)

diver'tente *ag* amusing

diverti'mento *sm* amusement, pleasure; (*passatempo*) pastime, recreation

diver'tire /45/ *vt* to amuse, entertain; **divertirsi** *vpr* to amuse o enjoy o.s.

di'videre /43/ *vt* (*anche Mat*) to divide; (*distribuire, ripartire*) to divide (up), split (up); **dividersi** *vpr* (*persone*) to separate; (*ramificarsi*) to fork

divi'eto *sm* prohibition; **"~ di sosta"** (*Aut*) "no waiting"

divinco'larsi /72/ *vpr* to wriggle, writhe

di'vino, -a *ag* divine

di'visa *sf* (*Mil*: *ecc*) uniform; (*Comm*) foreign currency

di'visi *ecc vb vedi* **dividere**

divisi'one *sf* division

'divo, -a *sm/f* star

divo'rare /72/ *vt* to devour

divorzi'are [divor'tsjare] /19/ *vi*: **~ (da qn)** to divorce (sb)

di'vorzio [di'vɔrtsjo] *sm* divorce

divul'gare /80/ vt to divulge, disclose; (rendere comprensibile) to popularize

dizio'nario sm dictionary

DJ [di'dʒei] sigla m, sigla f (= Disc Jockey) DJ

do sm (Mus) C; (: solfeggiando la scala) do(h)

dobbi'amo vb vedi **dovere**

D.O.C. [dɔk] sigla (= denominazione di origine controllata) label guaranteeing the quality of wine

'doccia, -ce ['dottʃa] sf (bagno) shower; **fare la ~** to have a shower

docciaschi'uma [dottʃas'kjuma] sm inv shower gel

do'cente [do'tʃɛnte] ag teaching ⊳ smf teacher; (di università) lecturer

'docile ['dɔtʃile] ag docile

documen'tare /72/ vt to document; **documentarsi** vpr: **documentarsi (su)** to gather information o material (about)

documen'tario, -a sm documentary

docu'mento sm document; **documenti** smpl (d'identità ecc) papers

dodi'cesimo, -a [dodi'tʃɛzimo] num twelfth

'dodici ['doditʃi] num twelve

do'gana sf (ufficio) customs pl; (tassa) (customs) duty; **passare la ~** to go through customs; **dogani'ere** sm customs officer

'doglie ['dɔʎʎe] sfpl (Med) labour sg (BRIT), labour pains

'dolce ['dɔltʃe] ag sweet; (carattere, persona) gentle, mild; (fig: mite: clima) mild; (non ripido: pendio) gentle ⊳ sm (sapore dolce) sweetness, sweet taste; (Cuc: portata) sweet, dessert; (: torta) cake; **dolcifi'cante** sm sweetener

do'lere /44/ vi to be sore

'dollaro sm dollar

Dolo'miti sfpl: **le ~** the Dolomites

do'lore sm (fisico) pain; (morale) sorrow, grief; **dolo'roso, -a** ag painful; sorrowful, sad

'dolsi ecc vb vedi **dolere**

do'manda sf (interrogazione) question; (richiesta) demand; (: cortese) request; (Dir: richiesta scritta) application; (Econ): **la ~** demand; **fare una ~ a qn** to ask sb a question; **fare ~ (per un lavoro)** to apply (for a job)

doman'dare /72/ vt (per avere) to ask for; (per sapere) to ask; (esigere) to demand; **domandarsi** vpr to wonder; to ask o.s.; **~ qc a qn** to ask sb for sth; to ask sb sth

do'mani av tomorrow ⊳ sm: **il ~** (il futuro) the future; (il giorno successivo) the next day; **~ l'altro** the day after tomorrow

do'mare /72/ vt to tame

doma'tore, -'trice sm/f (gen) tamer; **~ di cavalli** horsebreaker; **~ di leoni** lion tamer

domat'tina av tomorrow morning

do'menica, -che sf Sunday; **di** o **la ~** on Sundays

do'mestico, -a, -ci, -che ag domestic ⊳ sm/f servant, domestic

domi'cilio [domi'tʃiljo] sm (Dir) domicile, place of residence

domi'nare /72/ vt to dominate; (fig: sentimenti) to control, master ⊳ vi to be in the dominant position

do'nare /72/ vt to give, present; (per beneficenza ecc) to donate ⊳ vi (fig): **~ a** to suit, become; **~ sangue** to give blood; **dona'tore, -'trice** sm/f donor; **donatore di sangue/di organi** blood/organ donor

dondo'lare /72/ vt (cullare) to rock; **dondolarsi** vpr to swing, sway; **'dondolo** sm: **sedia/cavallo a dondolo** rocking chair/horse

'donna sf woman; **~ di casa** housewife; home-loving woman; **~ di servizio** maid

donnai'olo sm ladykiller

'donnola sf weasel

'dono sm gift

'doping sm doping

'dopo av (tempo) afterwards; (: più tardi) later; (luogo) after, next ▷ prep after ▷ cong (temporale): **~ aver studiato** after having studied ▷ ag inv: **il giorno ~** the following day; **~ mangiato va a dormire** after having eaten o after a meal he goes for a sleep; **un anno ~** a year later; **~ di me/lui** after me/him; **~, a ~!** see you later!

dopo'barba sm inv after-shave

dopodo'mani av the day after tomorrow

doposcì [dopoʃʃi] sm inv après-ski outfit

dopo'sole sm inv: **(lozione/crema) ~** aftersun (lotion/cream)

dopo'tutto av (tutto considerato) after all

doppi'aggio [dop'pjaddʒo] sm (Cine) dubbing

doppi'are /19/ vt (Naut) to round; (Sport) to lap; (Cine) to dub

'doppio, -a ag double; (fig: falso) double-dealing, deceitful ▷ sm (quantità): **il ~ (di)** twice as much (o many), double the amount (o number) of; (Sport) doubles pl ▷ av double

doppi'one sm duplicate (copy)

doppio'petto sm double-breasted jacket

dormicchi'are [dormik'kjare] /19/ vi to doze

dormigli'one, -a [dormiʎ'ʎone] sm/f sleepyhead

dor'mire /45/ vi to sleep; **andare a ~** to go to bed; **dor'mita** sf: **farsi una dormita** to have a good sleep

dormi'torio sm dormitory

dormi'veglia [dormi'veʎʎa] sm drowsiness

'dorso sm back; (di montagna) ridge, crest; (di libro) spine; **a ~ di cavallo** on horseback

do'sare /72/ vt to measure out; (Med) to dose

'dose sf quantity, amount; (Med) dose

do'tato, -a ag: **~ di** (attrezzature) equipped with; (bellezza, intelligenza) endowed with; **un uomo ~** a gifted man

'dote sf (di sposa) dowry; (assegnata a un ente) endowment; (fig) gift, talent

Dott. abbr (= dottore) Dr

dotto'rato sm degree; **~ di ricerca** doctorate, doctor's degree

dot'tore, -'essa sm/f doctor

- DOTTORE

- In Italy, anyone who has a degree in any subject can use the title dottore. Thus a person who is addressed as dottore is not necessarily a doctor of medicine.

dot'trina sf doctrine

Dott.ssa abbr (= dottoressa) Dr

'dove av (gen) where; (in cui) where, in which; (dovunque) wherever ▷ cong (mentre, laddove) whereas; **~ sei?/vai?** where are you?/are you going?; **dimmi dov'è** tell me where it is; **di dov'è?** where are you from?; **per ~ si passa?** which way should we go?; **la città ~ abito** the town where o in which I live; **siediti ~ vuoi** sit wherever you like

do'vere /46/ sm (obbligo) duty ▷ vt (essere debitore): **~ qc (a qn)** to owe (sb) sth ▷ vi (seguito dall'infinito, obbligo) to have to; **devo partire domani** (intenzione) I'm (due) to leave tomorrow; **dev'essere tardi** (probabilità) it must be late; **lui deve farlo** he has to do it, he must do it; **quanto le devo?** how much do I owe you?; **è dovuto partire** he had to leave; **ha dovuto pagare** he had to pay; **rivolgersi a chi di ~** to apply to the appropriate authority o person; **come si deve** (bene) properly; **una persona come si deve** a respectable person

dove'roso, -a ag (right and) proper

dovrò *ecc vb vedi* **dovere**

do'vunque *av* (*in qualunque luogo*) wherever; (*dappertutto*) everywhere; **~ io vada** wherever I go

do'vuto, -a *ag* (*causato*): **~ a** due to

doz'zina [dod'dzina] *sf* dozen; **una ~ di uova** a dozen eggs

dozzi'nale [doddzi'nale] *ag* cheap, second-rate

'drago, -ghi *sm* dragon

'dramma, -i *sm* drama; **dram'matico, -a, -ci, -che** *ag* dramatic

'drastico, -a, -ci, -che *ag* drastic

'dritto, -a *ag, av* = **diritto**

'droga, -ghe *sf* (*sostanza aromatica*) spice; (*stupefacente*) drug; **droghe pesanti/leggere** hard/soft drugs

dro'gare /80/ *vt* to drug; **drogarsi** *vpr* to take drugs

dro'gato, -a *sm/f* drug addict

droghe'ria [droge'ria] *sf* grocer's (shop) (BRIT), grocery (store) (US)

drome'dario *sm* dromedary

DS [di'ɛsse] *smpl* (= *Democratici di Sinistra*) Democrats of the Left (*Italian left-wing party*)

'dubbio, -a *ag* (*incerto*) doubtful, dubious; (*ambiguo*) dubious ▷ *sm* (*incertezza*) doubt; **avere il ~ che** to be afraid that, suspect that; **mettere in ~ qc** to question sth

dubi'tare /72/ *vi*: **~ di** to doubt; (*risultato*) to be doubtful of

Du'blino *sf* Dublin

'duca, -chi *sm* duke

du'chessa [du'kessa] *sf* duchess

'due *num* two

due'cento [due'tʃɛnto] *num* two hundred ▷ *sm*: **il D~** the thirteenth century

due'pezzi [due'pɛttsi] *sm* (*costume da bagno*) two-piece swimsuit; (*abito femminile*) two-piece suit

'dunque *cong* (*perciò*) so, therefore; (*riprendendo il discorso*) well (then) ▷ *sm inv*: **venire al ~** to come to the point

du'omo *sm* cathedral

> Attenzione! In inglese esiste la parola *dome*, che però significa *cupola*.

dupli'cato *sm* duplicate

'duplice ['duplitʃe] *ag* double, twofold; **in ~ copia** in duplicate

du'rante *prep* during

du'rare /72/ *vi* to last; **~ fatica a** to have difficulty in

du'rezza [du'rettsa] *sf* hardness; stubbornness; harshness; toughness

'duro, -a *ag* (*pietra, lavoro, materasso, problema*) hard; (*persona: ostinato*) stubborn, obstinate; (: *severo*) harsh, hard; (*voce*) harsh; (*carne*) tough ▷ *sm/f* hardness; (*difficoltà*) hard part; (*persona*) tough one ▷ *av*: **tener ~** to stand firm, hold out; **~ d'orecchi** hard of hearing

DVD [divu'di] *sm inv* DVD; (*lettore*) DVD player

d

E abbr (= est) E

e (dav V spesso **ed**) cong and; **e lui?** what about him?; **e compralo!** well buy it then!

è vb vedi **essere**

eb'bene cong well (then)

'ebbi ecc vb vedi **avere**

e'braico, -a, -ci, -che ag Hebrew, Hebraic ▷ sm (Ling) Hebrew

e'breo, -a ag Jewish ▷ sm/f Jewish person, Jew

EC abbr (= Eurocity) fast train connecting Western European cities

ecc. abbr (= eccetera) etc

eccel'lente [ettʃel'lɛnte] ag excellent

ec'centrico, -a, -ci, -che [et'tʃɛntriko] ag eccentric

ecces'sivo, -a [ettʃes'sivo] ag excessive

ec'cesso [et'tʃɛsso] sm excess; **all'~** (gentile, generoso) to excess, excessively; **~ di velocità** (Aut) speeding

ec'cetera [et'tʃɛtera] av et cetera, and so on

ec'cetto [et'tʃɛtto] prep except, with the exception of; **~ che** except, other than; **~ che (non)** unless

eccezio'nale [ettʃettsjo'nale] ag exceptional

eccezi'one [ettʃet'tsjone] sf exception; (Dir) objection; **a ~ di** with the exception of, except for; **d'~** exceptional

ecci'tare [ettʃi'tare] /72/ vt (curiosità, interesse) to excite, arouse; (folla) to incite; **eccitarsi** vpr to get excited; (sessualmente) to become aroused

'ecco av (per dimostrare): **~ il treno!** here's o here comes the train!; (dav pronome): **eccomi!** here I am!; **eccone uno!** here's one (of them)!; (dav pp): **~ fatto!** there, that's it done!

ec'come av rather; **ti piace? — ~!** do you like it? — I'll say! o and how! o rather! (BRIT)

e'clisse sf eclipse

'eco (pl m **echi**) sm o f echo

ecogra'fia sf (Med) ultrasound

ecolo'gia [ekolod'dʒia] sf ecology

eco'logico, -a, -ci, -che [eko'lɔdʒiko] ag ecological

eco'mafia sf mafia involved in crimes related to the environment, in particular the illegal disposal of waste

econo'mia sf economy; (scienza) economics sg; (risparmio, azione) saving; **fare ~** to economize, make economies; **eco'nomico, -a, -ci, -che** ag economic; (poco costoso) economical

'ecstasy ['ɛkstasi] sf inv ecstasy

'edera sf ivy

e'dicola sf newspaper kiosk o stand (US)

edi'ficio [edi'fitʃo] sm building

e'dile ag building cpd

Edim'burgo sf Edinburgh

edi'tore, -'trice ag publishing cpd ▷ sm/f publisher

Attenzione! In inglese esiste la parola *editor*, che però significa *redattore*.

edizi'one [edit'tsjone] *sf* edition; (*tiratura*) printing; **~ straordinaria** special edition

edu'care /20/ *vt* to educate; (*gusto, mente*) to train; **~ qn a fare** to train sb to do; **edu'cato, -a** *ag* polite, well-mannered; **educazi'one** *sf* education; (*familiare*) upbringing; (*comportamento*) (good) manners *pl*: **educazione fisica** (*Ins*) physical training o education

educherò *ecc* [eduke'rɔ] *vb vedi* **educare**

effemi'nato, -a *ag* effeminate

efferve'scente [effervef'fente] *ag* effervescent

effet'tivo, -a *ag* (*reale*) real, actual; (*impiegato, professore*) permanent; (*Mil*) regular ▷ *sm* (*Mil*) strength; (*di patrimonio ecc*) sum total

ef'fetto *sm* effect; (*Comm: cambiale*) bill; (*fig: impressione*) impression; **in effetti** in fact, actually; **effetti personali** personal effects, personal belongings; **~ serra** greenhouse effect

effi'cace [effi'katʃe] *ag* effective

effici'ente [effi'tʃɛnte] *ag* efficient

E'geo [e'dʒɛo] *sm*: **l'~, il mare ~** the Aegean (Sea)

E'gitto [e'dʒitto] *sm*: **l'~** Egypt; **egizi'ano, -a** [edʒit'tsjano] *ag, sm/f* Egyptian

'egli ['eʎʎi] *pron* he; **~ stesso** he himself

ego'ismo *sm* selfishness, egoism; **ego'ista, -i, -e** *ag* selfish, egoistic ▷ *sm/f* egoist

Egr. *abbr* = **egregio**

e'gregio, -a, -gi, -gie [e'grɛdʒo] *ag* (*nelle lettere*): **E~ Signore** Dear Sir

E.I. *abbr* = **Esercito Italiano**

elabo'rare /72/ *vt* (*progetto*) to work out, elaborate; (*dati*) to process

elasticiz'zato, -a [elastitʃid'dzato] *ag* stretch *cpd*

e'lastico, -a, -ci, -che *ag* elastic; (*fig: andatura*) springy; (: *decisione, vedute*) flexible ▷ *sm* (*gommino*) rubber band; (*per il cucito*) elastic *no pl*

ele'fante *sm* elephant

ele'gante *ag* elegant

e'leggere [e'lɛddʒere] /61/ *vt* to elect

elemen'tare *ag* elementary; **le (scuole) elementari** *sfpl* primary (*BRIT*) o grade (*US*) school

ele'mento *sm* element; (*parte componente*) element, component, part; **elementi** *smpl* (*della scienza ecc*) elements, rudiments

ele'mosina *sf* charity, alms *pl*: **chiedere l'~** to beg

elen'care /20/ *vt* to list

elencherò *ecc* [elenke'rɔ] *vb vedi* **elencare**

e'lenco, -chi *sm* list; **~ telefonico** telephone directory

e'lessi *ecc vb vedi* **eleggere**

eletto'rale *ag* electoral, election *cpd*

elet'tore, -'trice *sm/f* voter, elector

elet'trauto *sm inv* workshop for car electrical repairs; (*tecnico*) car electrician

elettri'cista, -i [elettri'tʃista] *sm* electrician

elettricità [elettritʃi'ta] *sf* electricity

e'lettrico, -a, -ci, -che *ag* electric(al)

elettriz'zante [elettrid'dzante] *ag* (*fig*) electrifying, thrilling

elettriz'zare [elettrid'dzare] /72/ *vt* to electrify; **elettrizzarsi** *vpr* to become charged with electricity

e'lettro... *prefisso*: **elettrodo'mestico, -a, -ci, -che** *ag*: **apparecchi elettrodomestici** domestic (electrical) appliances; **elet'tronico, -a, -ci, -che** *ag* electronic

elezi'one [elet'tsjone] *sf* election; **elezioni** *sfpl* (*Pol*) election(s)

'elica, -che *sf* propeller

eli'cottero sm helicopter

elimi'nare /72/ vt to eliminate

elisoc'corso sm helicopter ambulance

el'metto sm helmet

elogi'are [elo'dʒare] /62/ vt to praise

elo'quente ag eloquent

e'ludere /35/ vt to evade

e'lusi ecc vb vedi **eludere**

e-'mail [e'meil] sf inv (messaggio, sistema) e-mail ▷ ag inv email; **indirizzo ~** email address

emargi'nato, -a [emardʒi'nato] sm/f outcast; **emarginazione** [emardʒinat'tsjone] sf marginalization

embri'one sm embryo

emenda'mento sm amendment

emer'genza [emer'dʒɛntsa] sf emergency; **in caso di ~** in an emergency

e'mergere [e'mɛrdʒere] /59/ vi to emerge; (sommergibile) to surface; (fig: distinguersi) to stand out

e'mersi ecc vb vedi **emergere**

e'mettere /63/ vt (suono, luce) to give out, emit; (onde radio) to send out; (assegno, francobollo, ordine) to issue

emi'crania sf migraine

emi'grare /72/ vi to emigrate

emis'fero sm hemisphere; **~ boreale/australe** northern/ southern hemisphere

e'misi ecc vb vedi **emettere**

emit'tente ag (banca) issuing; (Radio) broadcasting, transmitting ▷ sf (Radio) transmitter

emorra'gia, -'gie [emorra'dʒia] sf haemorrhage

emor'roidi sfpl haemorrhoids pl (BRIT), hemorrhoids pl (US)

emo'tivo, -a ag emotional

emozio'nante [emottsjo'nante] ag exciting, thrilling

emozio'nare [emottsjo'nare] /72/ vt (appassionare) to excite; (commuovere) to move; (agitare) to make nervous; **emozionarsi** vpr to be

excited; to be moved; to be nervous; **emozionato, -a** [emottsjo'nato] ag (commosso) moved; (agitato) nervous; (elettrizzato) excited

emozi'one [emot'tsjone] sf emotion; (agitazione) excitement

enciclope'dia [entʃiklope'dia] sf encyclop(a)edia

endove'noso, -a ag (Med) intravenous

'E.N.E.L. sigla m (= Ente Nazionale per l'Energia Elettrica) national electricity company

ener'getico, -a, -ci, -che [ener'dʒɛtiko] ag (risorse, crisi) energy cpd; (sostanza, alimento) energy-giving

ener'gia, -'gie [ener'dʒia] sf (Fisica) energy; (fig) energy, strength, vigour; **~ eolica** wind power; **~ solare** solar energy, solar power; **e'nergico, -a, -ci, -che** [e'nɛrdʒiko] ag energetic, vigorous

'enfasi sf emphasis; (peg) bombast, pomposity

en'nesimo, -a ag (Mat, fig) nth; **per l'ennesima volta** for the umpteenth time

e'norme ag enormous, huge

'ente sm (istituzione) body, board, corporation; (Filosofia) being; **~ pubblico** public body; **~ di ricerca** research organization

en'trambi, -e pron pl both (of them) ▷ ag pl: **~ i ragazzi** both boys, both of the boys

en'trare /72/ vi to enter, go (o come) in; **~ in** (luogo) to enter, go (o come) into; (trovar posto, poter stare) to fit into; (essere ammesso a: club ecc) to join, become a member of; **~ in automobile** to get into the car; **far ~ qn** (visitatore ecc) to show sb in; **questo non c'entra** (fig) that's got nothing to do with it; **en'trata** sf entrance, entry; **dov'è l'entrata?** where's the entrance?; **entrate** sfpl (Comm) receipts, takings; (Econ) income sg '**entro** prep (temporale) within

entusias'mare /72/ vt to excite, fill with enthusiasm; **entusiasmarsi** vpr: **entusiasmarsi (per qc/qn)** to become enthusiastic (about sth/sb); **entusi'asmo** sm enthusiasm; **entusi'asta, -i, -e** ag enthusiastic ▷ sm/f enthusiast

e'olico, -a, -chi, -che ag wind; **energia eolica** wind power

epa'tite sf hepatitis

epide'mia sf epidemic

Epifa'nia sf Epiphany

epiles'sia sf epilepsy

epi'lettico, -a, -ci, -che ag, sm/f epileptic

epi'sodio sm episode

'**epoca, -che** sf (periodo storico) age, era; (tempo) time; (Geo) age

ep'pure cong and yet, nevertheless

EPT sigla m (= Ente Provinciale per il Turismo) district tourist bureau

equa'tore sm equator

equazi'one [ekwat'tsjone] sf (Mat) equation

e'questre ag equestrian

equi'librio sm balance, equilibrium; **perdere l'~** to lose one's balance

e'quino, -a ag horse cpd, equine

equipaggia'mento [ekwipaddʒa'mento] sm (operazione: di nave) equipping, fitting out; (: di spedizione, esercito) equipping, kitting out; (attrezzatura) equipment

equipaggi'are [ekwipad'dʒare] /62/ vt (di persone) to man; (di mezzi) to equip; **equipaggiarsi** vpr to equip o.s.; **equi'paggio** sm crew

equitazi'one [ekwitat'tsjone] sf (horse-) riding

equiva'lente ag, sm equivalent

e'quivoco, -a, -ci, -che ag equivocal, ambiguous; (sospetto) dubious ▷ sm misunderstanding; **a scanso di equivoci** to avoid any misunderstanding; **giocare sull'~** to equivocate

'**equo, -a** ag fair, just

'**era** ecc vb vedi **essere**

'**erba** sf grass; **in ~** (fig) budding; **erbe aromatiche** herbs; **~ medica** lucerne; **er'baccia, -ce** sf weed

erboriste'ria sf (scienza) study of medicinal herbs; (negozio) herbalist's (shop)

e'rede smf heir(-ess); **eredità** sf (Dir) inheritance; (Biol) heredity; **lasciare qc in eredità a qn** to leave o bequeath sth to sb; **eredi'tare** /72/ vt to inherit; **eredi'tario, -a** ag hereditary

ere'mita, -i sm hermit

er'gastolo sm (Dir: pena) life imprisonment

'**erica** sf heather

er'metico, -a, -ci, -che ag hermetic

'**ernia** sf (Med) hernia

'**ero** vb vedi **essere**

e'roe sm hero

ero'gare /80/ vt (somme) to distribute; (gas, servizi) to supply

e'roico, -a, -ci, -che ag heroic

ero'ina sf heroine; (droga) heroin

erosi'one sf erosion

e'rotico, -a, -ci, -che ag erotic

er'rato, -a ag wrong

er'rore sm error, mistake; (morale) error; **per ~** by mistake; **ci dev'essere un ~** there must be some mistake; **~ giudiziario** miscarriage of justice

eruzi'one [erut'tsjone] sf eruption

esacer'bare [ezatʃer'bare] /72/ vt to exacerbate

esage'rare [ezadʒe'rare] /72/ vt to exaggerate ▷ vi to exaggerate; (eccedere) to go too far

esal'tare /72/ vt to exalt; (entusiasmare) to excite, stir

e'same sm examination; (Ins) exam, examination; **fare un ~ di coscienza** to search one's conscience; **~ di guida** driving test; **~ del sangue** blood test

esami'nare /72/ vt to examine

esaspe'rare /72/ vt to exasperate; (situazione) to exacerbate

esatta'mente *av* exactly; accurately, precisely

esat'tezza [ezat'tettsa] *sf* exactitude, accuracy, precision

e'satto, -a *pp di* **esigere** ▷ *ag* (*calcolo, ora*) correct, right, exact; (*preciso*) accurate, precise; (*puntuale*) punctual

esau'dire /55/ *vt* to grant, fulfil

esauri'ente *ag* exhaustive

esauri'mento *sm* exhaustion; ~ **nervoso** nervous breakdown

esau'rire /55/ *vt* (*stancare*) to exhaust, wear out; (*provviste, miniera*) to exhaust; **esaurirsi** *vpr* to exhaust o.s., wear o.s. out; (*provviste*) to run out; **esau'rito, -a** *ag* exhausted; (*merci*) sold out; **registrare il tutto esaurito** (*Teat*) to have a full house; **e'sausto, -a** *ag* exhausted

'esca (*pl* **esche**) *sf* bait

'esce ['εʃʃe] *vb vedi* **uscire**

eschi'mese [eski'mese] *ag, smf* Eskimo

'esci ['εʃʃi] *vb vedi* **uscire**

escla'mare /72/ *vi* to exclaim, cry out

esclama'tivo, -a *ag:* **punto ~** exclamation mark

esclamazi'one [esklamat'tsjone] *sf* exclamation

es'cludere /3/ *vt* to exclude

es'clusi *ecc vb vedi* **escludere**

esclusi'one *sf* exclusion; **a ~ di, fatta ~ per** except (for), apart from; **senza ~ (alcuna)** without exception; **procedere per ~** to follow a process of elimination; **senza ~ di colpi** (*fig*) with no holds barred; **~ sociale** social exclusion

esclu'siva *sf vedi* **esclusivo**

esclusiva'mente *av* exclusively, solely

esclu'sivo, -a *ag* exclusive ▷ *sf* (*Dir, Comm*) exclusive o sole rights *pl*

es'cluso, -a *pp di* **escludere**

'esco *vb vedi* **uscire**

escogi'tare [eskodʒi'tare] /72/ *vt* to devise, think up

'escono *vb vedi* **uscire**

escursi'one *sf* (*gita*) excursion, trip; (: *a piedi*) hike, walk; (*Meteor*): ~ **termica** temperature range

esecuzi'one [ezekut'tsjone] *sf* execution, carrying out; (*Mus*) performance; ~ **capitale** execution

esegu'ire /45/ *vt* to carry out, execute; (*Mus*) to perform, execute

e'sempio *sm* example; **per ~** for example, for instance; **fare un ~** to give an example; **esem'plare** *ag* exemplary ▷ *sm* example; (*copia*) copy

eserci'tare [ezertʃi'tare] /72/ *vt* (*professione*) to practise (*BRIT*), practice (*US*); (*allenare: corpo, mente*) to exercise, train; (*diritto*) to exercise; (*influenza, pressione*) to exert; **esercitarsi** *vpr* to practise; **esercitarsi nella guida** to practise one's driving

e'sercito [e'zɛrtʃito] *sm* army

eser'cizio [ezer'tʃittsjo] *sm* practice; exercising; (*fisico: di matematica*) exercise; (*Econ*): ~ **finanziario** financial year; **in ~** (*medico ecc*) practising (*BRIT*), practicing (*US*)

esi'bire /55/ *vt* to exhibit, display; (*documenti*) to produce, present; **esibirsi** *vpr* (*attore*) to perform; (*fig*) to show off; **esibizi'one** *sf* exhibition; (*di documento*) presentation; (*spettacolo*) show, performance

esi'gente [ezi'dʒɛnte] *ag* demanding

e'sigere [e'zidʒere] /47/ *vt* (*pretendere*) to demand; (*richiedere*) to demand, require; (*imposte*) to collect

'esile *ag* (*persona*) slender, slim; (*stelo*) thin; (*voce*) faint

esili'are /19/ *vt* to exile; **e'silio** *sm* exile

esis'tenza [ezis'tɛntsa] *sf* existence

e'sistere /11/ *vi* to exist

esi'tare /72/ *vi* to hesitate

'esito *sm* result, outcome

'esodo *sm* exodus

esone'rare /72/ *vt*: ~ **qn da** to exempt sb from

e'sordio *sm* debut

esor'tare /72/ vt: **~ qn a fare** to urge sb to do

e'sotico, -a, -ci, -che ag exotic

es'pandere /110/ vt to expand; (confini) to extend; (influenza) to extend, spread; **espandersi** vpr to expand; **espansi'one** sf expansion; **espansione di memoria** (Inform) memory upgrade; **espan'sivo, -a** ag expansive, communicative

espatri'are /19/ vi to leave one's country

espedi'ente sm expedient

es'pellere /48/ vt to expel

esperi'enza [espe'rjɛntsa] sf experience

esperi'mento sm experiment

es'perto, -a ag, sm/f expert

espi'rare /72/ vt, vi to breathe out

es'plicito, -a [es'plitʃito] ag explicit

es'plodere /49/ vi (anche fig) to explode ▷ vt to fire

esplo'rare /72/ vt to explore

esplosi'one sf explosion

es'pone ecc vb vedi **esporre**

es'pongo, es'poni ecc vb vedi **esporre**

es'porre /77/ vt (merci) to display; (quadro) to exhibit, show; (fatti, idee) to explain, set out; (porre in pericolo, Fot) to expose; **esporsi** vpr: **esporsi a** (sole, pericolo) to expose o.s. to; (critiche) to lay o.s. open to

espor'tare /72/ vt to export

es'pose ecc vb vedi **esporre**

esposizi'one [espozit'tsjone] sf displaying; exhibiting; setting out; (anche Fot) exposure; (mostra) exhibition; (narrazione) explanation, exposition

es'posto, -a pp di **esporre** ▷ ag: **~ a nord** facing north ▷ sm (Amm) statement, account; (: petizione) petition

espressi'one sf expression

espres'sivo, -a ag expressive

es'presso, -a pp di **esprimere** ▷ ag express ▷ sm (lettera) express letter;

(anche: **treno ~**) express train; (anche: **caffè ~**) espresso

es'primere /50/ vt to express; **esprimersi** vpr to express o.s.

es'pulsi ecc vb vedi **espellere**

espulsi'one sf expulsion

es'senza [es'sɛntsa] sf essence; **essenzi'ale** ag essential ▷ sm: **l'essenziale** the main o most important thing

PAROLA CHIAVE

'essere /51/ sm being; **essere umano** human being

▷ vb copulativo **1** (con attributo, sostantivo) to be; **sei giovane/ simpatico** you are o you're young/ nice; **è medico** he is o he's a doctor

2 (+ di: appartenere) to be; **di chi è la penna?** whose pen is it?; **è di Carla** it is o it's Carla's, it belongs to Carla

3 (+ di: provenire) to be; **è di Venezia** he is o he's from Venice

4 (data, ora): **è il 15 agosto** it is o it's the 15th of August; **è lunedì** it is o it's Monday; **che ora è?, che ore sono?** what time is it?; **è l'una** it is o it's one o'clock; **sono le due** it is o it's two o'clock

5 (costare): **quant'è?** how much is it?; **sono 20 euro** it's 20 euros

▷ vb aus **1** (attivo): **essere arrivato/ venuto** to have arrived/come; **è già partita** she has already left

2 (passivo) to be; **essere fatto da** to be made by; **è stata uccisa** she has been killed

3 (riflessivo): **si sono lavati** they washed, they got washed

4 (+ da + infinito): **è da farsi subito** it must be done o is to be done immediately

▷ vi **1** (esistere, trovarsi) to be; **sono a casa** I'm at home; **essere in piedi/ seduto** to be standing/sitting

2: esserci: c'è there is; **ci sono** there are; **che c'è?** what's the matter?,

what is it?; **ci sono!** (*ho capito*) I get it!
▶ *vb impers*: **è tardi/Pasqua** it's late/
Easter; **è possibile che venga** he
may come; **è così** that's the way it is

'essi *pron mpl vedi* **esso**
'esso, -a *pron* it; (*riferito a persona:
soggetto*) he (she); (: *complemento*)
him (her)
est *sm* east
es'tate *sf* summer
esteri'ore *ag* outward, external
es'terno, -a *ag* (*porta, muro*) outer,
outside; (*scala*) outside; (*alunno,
impressione*) external ▷ *sm* outside,
exterior ▷ *sm/f* (*allievo*) day pupil;
esterni *smpl* (*Cine*) location shots;
"per uso ~" "for external use only";
all'~ outside
'estero, -a *ag* foreign ▷ *sm*: **all'~**
abroad
es'teso, -a *pp di* **estendere** ▷ *ag*
extensive, large; **scrivere per ~** to
write in full
es'tetico, -a, -ci, -che *ag* aesthetic
▷ *sf* (*disciplina*) aesthetics *sg*; (*bellezza*)
attractiveness; **este'tista, -i, -e** *sm/f*
beautician
es'tinguere /42/ *vt* to extinguish, put
out; (*debito*) to pay off; **estinguersi**
vpr to go out; (*specie*) to become
extinct
es'tinsi *ecc vb vedi* **estinguere**
estin'tore *sm* (*fire*) extinguisher
estinzi'one *sf* putting out; (*di specie*)
extinction
estir'pare /72/ *vt* (*pianta*) to uproot,
pull up; (*fig: vizio*) to eradicate
es'tivo, -a *ag* summer *cpd*
es'torcere [es'tɔrtʃere] /106/ *vt*: **~ qc
(a qn)** to extort sth (from sb)
estradizi'one [estradit'tsjone] *sf*
extradition
es'trae, es'traggo *ecc vb vedi*
estrarre
es'traneo, -a *ag* foreign ▷ *sm/f*
stranger; **rimanere ~ a qc** to take
no part in sth

es'trarre /123/ *vt* to extract; (*minerali*)
to mine; (*sorteggiare*) to draw
es'trassi *ecc vb vedi* **estrarre**
estrema'mente *av* extremely
estre'mista, -i, -e *sm/f* extremist
estremità *sf inv* extremity, end ▷ *sfpl*
(*Anat*) extremities
es'tremo, -a *ag* extreme; (*ultimo: ora,
tentativo*) final, last ▷ *sm* extreme; (*di
pazienza, forza*) limit, end; **estremi**
smpl (*Amm: dati essenziali*) details,
particulars; **l'E~ Oriente** the Far
East
estro'verso, -a *ag*, *sm* extrovert
età *sf inv* age; **all'~ di 8 anni** at the
age of 8, at 8 years of age; **ha la mia
~** he (*o* she) is the same age as me *o* as
I am; **raggiungere la maggiore ~** to
come of age; **essere in ~ minore** to
be under age
'etere *sm* ether
eternità *sf* eternity
e'terno, -a *ag* eternal
etero'geneo, -a [etero'dʒɛneo] *ag*
heterogeneous
eterosessu'ale *ag*, *smf*
heterosexual
'etica *sf vedi* **etico**
eti'chetta [eti'ketta] *sf* label;
(*cerimoniale*): **l'~** etiquette
'etico, -a, -ci, -che *ag* ethical ▷ *sf*
ethics *sg*
eti'lometro *sm* Breathalyzer®
etimolo'gia, -'gie [etimolo'dʒia] *sf*
etymology
Eti'opia *sf*: **l'~** Ethiopia
'etnico, -a, -ci, -che *ag* ethnic
e'trusco, -a, -schi, -sche *ag*, *smf*
Etruscan
'ettaro *sm* hectare (10,000 m²)
'etto *abbr m* (= *ettogrammo*) 100 grams
'euro *sm inv* (*divisa*) euro
Eu'ropa *sf*: **l'~** Europe
europarlamen'tare *smf* Member of
the European Parliament, MEP
euro'peo, -a *ag*, *sm/f* European
eutana'sia *sf* euthanasia
evacu'are /72/ *vt* to evacuate

e'vadere /52/ *vi* (*fuggire*): **~ da** to escape from ▷ *vt* (*sbrigare*) to deal with, dispatch; (*tasse*) to evade

evapo'rare /72/ *vi* to evaporate

e'vasi *ecc vb vedi* **evadere**

evasi'one *sf* (*vedi evadere*) escape; dispatch; **~ fiscale** tax evasion

eva'sivo, -a *ag* evasive

e'vaso, -a *pp di* **evadere** ▷ *sm* escapee

e'vento *sm* event

eventu'ale *ag* possible

Attenzione! In inglese esiste la parola *eventual*, che però significa *finale*.

eventual'mente *av* if necessary

Attenzione! In inglese esiste la parola *eventually*, che però significa *alla fine*.

evi'dente *ag* evident, obvious

evidente'mente *av* evidently; (*palesemente*) obviously, evidently

evi'tare /72/ *vt* to avoid; **~ di fare** to avoid doing; **~ qc a qn** to spare sb sth

evoluzi'one [evolut'tsjone] *sf* evolution

e'volversi /94/ *vpr* to evolve

ev'viva *escl* hurrah!; **~ il re!** long live the king!, hurrah for the king!

ex *prefisso* ex-, former

'extra *ag inv* first-rate; top-quality ▷ *sm inv* extra; **extracomuni'tario, -a** *ag* non-EU ▷ *sm/f* non-EU citizen (*often referred to non-European immigrant*)

extrater'restre *ag, smf* extraterrestrial

f

fa *vb vedi* **fare** ▷ *sm inv* (*Mus*) F; (: *solfeggiando la scala*) fa ▷ *av*: **10 anni fa** 10 years ago

'fabbrica *sf* factory; **fabbri'care** /20/ *vt* to build; (*produrre*) to manufacture, make; (*fig*) to fabricate, invent

Attenzione! In inglese esiste la parola *fabric*, che però significa *stoffa*.

fac'cenda [fat't∫ɛnda] *sf* matter, affair; (*cosa da fare*) task, chore

fac'chino [fak'kino] *sm* porter

'faccia, -ce ['fatt∫a] *sf* face; (*di moneta, medaglia*) side; **~ a ~** face to face

facci'ata [fat't∫ata] *sf* façade; (*di pagina*) side

fac'cina [fat't∫ina] *sf* (*Inform*) emoticon

'faccio *ecc* ['fatt∫o] *vb vedi* **fare**

fa'cessi *ecc* [fa't∫essi] *vb vedi* **fare**

fa'cevo *ecc* [fa't∫evo] *vb vedi* **fare**

'facile ['fatʃile] *ag* easy; *(disposto)*: **~ a**
inclined to, prone to; *(probabile)*: **è ~**
che piova it's likely to rain

facoltà *sf inv* faculty; *(autorità)* power

facolta'tivo, -a *ag* optional; *(fermata
d'autobus)* request *cpd*

'faggio ['faddʒo] *sm* beech

fagi'ano [fa'dʒano] *sm* pheasant

fagio'lino [fadʒo'lino] *sm* French
(BRIT) o string bean

fagi'olo [fa'dʒɔlo] *sm* bean

'fai *vb vedi* **fare**

'fai-da-'te *sm inv* DIY, do-it-yourself

'falce ['faltʃe] *sf* scythe; **falci'are** /14/
vt to cut; *(fig)* to mow down

falcia'trice [faltʃa'tritʃe] *sf (per fieno)*
reaping machine; *(per erba)* mowing
machine

'falco, -chi *sm* hawk

'falda *sf* layer, stratum; *(di cappello)*
brim; *(di cappotto)* tails *pl*; *(di monte)*
lower slope; *(di tetto)* pitch

fale'gname [faleɲ'ɲame] *sm* joiner

falli'mento *sm* failure; bankruptcy

fal'lire /55/ *vi (Dir)* to go bankrupt;
(non riuscire): **~ (in)** to fail (in) ▷ *vt*
(colpo, bersaglio) to miss

'fallo *sm* error, mistake; *(imperfezione)*
defect, flaw; *(Sport)* foul; fault; **senza
~** without fail

falò *sm inv* bonfire

falsifi'care /20/ *vt* to forge; *(monete)*
to forge, counterfeit

'falso, -a *ag* false; *(errato)* wrong;
(falsificato) forged; fake; *(: oro, gioielli)*
imitation *cpd* ▷ *sm* forgery; **giurare il
~** to commit perjury

'fama *sf* fame; *(reputazione)*
reputation, name

'fame *sf* hunger; **aver ~** to be hungry

fa'miglia [fa'miʎʎa] *sf* family

famili'are *ag (della famiglia)* family
cpd; *(ben noto)* familiar; *(rapporti,
atmosfera)* friendly; *(Ling)* informal,
colloquial ▷ *smf* relative, relation

fa'moso, -a *ag* famous, well-known

fa'nale *sm (Aut)* light, lamp (BRIT); *(luce
stradale, Naut)* light; *(di faro)* beacon

fa'natico, -a, -ci, -che *ag* fanatical;
(del teatro, calcio ecc): **~ di** o **per**
mad o crazy about ▷ *sm/f* fanatic;
(tifoso) fan

'fango, -ghi *sm* mud

'fanno *vb vedi* **fare**

fannul'lone, -a *sm/f* idler, loafer

fantasci'enza [fantaʃ'ʃɛntsa] *sf*
science fiction

fanta'sia *sf* fantasy, imagination;
(capriccio) whim, caprice ▷ *ag inv*:
vestito ~ patterned dress

fan'tasma, -i *sm* ghost, phantom

fan'tastico, -a, -ci, -che *ag*
fantastic; *(potenza, ingegno)*
imaginative

fan'tino *sm* jockey

fara'butto *sm* crook

fard *sm inv* blusher

PAROLA CHIAVE

'fare /53/ *sm* **1** *(modo di fare)*: **con fare
distratto** absent-mindedly; **ha un
fare simpatico** he has a pleasant
manner

2: **sul far del giorno/della notte** at
daybreak/nightfall

▷ *vt* **1** *(fabbricare, creare)* to make;
(: casa) to build; *(: assegno)* to make
out; **fare un pasto/una promessa/
un film** to make a meal/promise/a
film; **fare rumore** to make a noise

2 *(effettuare: lavoro, attività, studi)* to
do; *(: sport)* to play; **cosa fa?** *(adesso)*
what are you doing?; *(di professione)*
what do you do?; **fare psicologia/
italiano** *(Ins)* to do psychology/
Italian; **fare un viaggio** to go on a
trip o journey; **fare una passeggiata**
to go for a walk; **fare la spesa** to do
the shopping

3 *(funzione)* to be; *(Teat)* to play, be;
fare il medico to be a doctor; **fare il
malato** *(fingere)* to act the invalid

4 *(suscitare: sentimenti)*: **fare paura
a qn** to frighten sb; **(non) fa niente**
(non importa) it doesn't matter

5 (*ammontare*): **3 più 3 fa 6** 3 and 3 are 0 make 6; **fanno 6 euro** that's 6 euros; **Roma fa oltre 2.000.000 di abitanti** Rome has over 2,000,000 inhabitants; **che ora fai?** what time do you make it?

6 (+ *infinito*): **far fare qc a qn** (*obbligare*) to make sb do sth; (*permettere*) to let sb do sth; **fammi vedere** let me see; **far partire il motore** to start (up) the engine; **far riparare la macchina/costruire una casa** to get 0 have the car repaired 0 a house built

7: farsi: farsi una gonna to make o.s. a skirt; **farsi un nome** to make a name for o.s.; **farsi la permanente** to get a perm; **farsi tagliare i capelli** to get one's hair cut; **farsi operare** to have an operation

8 (*fraseologia*): **farcela** to succeed, manage; **non ce la faccio più** I can't go on; **ce la faremo** we'll make it; **me l'hanno fatta!** (*imbrogliare*) I've been done!; **lo facevo più giovane** I thought he was younger; **fare sì/no con la testa** to nod/shake one's head ▶ *vi* **1** (*agire*) to act, do; **fate come volete** do as you like; **fare presto** to be quick; **fare da** to act as; **non c'è niente da fare** it's no use; **saperci fare con qn/qc** to know how to deal with sb/sth; **faccia pure!** go ahead! **2** (*dire*) to say; **"davvero?" fece** "really?" he said

3: fare per (*essere adatto*) to be suitable for; **fare per fare qc** to be about to do sth; **fece per andarsene** he made as if to leave

4: farsi: si fa così you do it like this, this is the way it's done; **non si fa così!** (*rimprovero*) that's no way to behave!; **la festa non si fa** the party is off

5: fare a gara con qn to compete with sb; **fare a pugni** to come to blows; **fare in tempo a fare** to be in time to do

▶ *vb impers*: **fa bel tempo** the weather is fine; **fa caldo/freddo** it's hot/cold; **fa notte** it's getting dark ▶ *vpr* **1** (*diventare*) to become; **farsi prete** to become a priest; **farsi grande/vecchio** to grow tall/old **2** (*spostarsi*): **farsi avanti/indietro** to move forward/back **3** (*fam: drogarsi*) to be a junkie

far'falla *sf* butterfly

fa'rina *sf* flour

farma'cia, -'cie [farma'tʃia] *sf* pharmacy; (*negozio*) chemist's (shop) (BRIT), pharmacy; **farma'cista, -i, -e** [farma'tʃista] *sm/f* chemist (BRIT), pharmacist

'farmaco, -ci 0 **-chi** *sm* drug, medicine

'faro *sm* (*Naut*) lighthouse; (*Aer*) beacon; (*Aut*) headlight

'fascia, -sce ['faʃʃa] *sf* band, strip; (*Med*) bandage; (*di sindaco, ufficiale*) sash; (*parte di territorio*) strip, belt; (*di contribuenti ecc*) group, band; **essere in fasce** (*anche fig*) to be in one's infancy; **~ oraria** time band

fasci'are [faʃʃare] /14/ *vt* to bind; (*Med*) to bandage

fa'scicolo [faʃʃikolo] *sm* (*di documenti*) file, dossier; (*di rivista*) issue, number; (*opuscolo*) booklet, pamphlet

'fascino ['faʃʃino] *sm* charm, fascination

fa'scismo [faʃʃizmo] *sm* fascism

'fase *sf* phase; (*Tecn*) stroke; **essere fuori ~** (*motore*) to be rough

fa'stidio *sm* bother, trouble; **dare ~ a qn** to bother 0 annoy sb; **sento ~ allo stomaco** my stomach's upset; **avere fastidi con la polizia** to have trouble 0 bother with the police; **fastidi'oso, -a** *ag* annoying, tiresome; (*schifiltoso*) fastidious

> Attenzione! In inglese esiste la parola *fastidious*, che però significa *pignolo*.

'fata *sf* fairy

fa'tale *ag* fatal; (*inevitabile*) inevitable; (*fig*) irresistible

fa'tica, -che *sf* hard work, toil; (*sforzo*) effort; (*di metalli*) fatigue; **a ~** with difficulty; **fare ~ a fare qc** to find it difficult to do sth; **fati'coso, -a** *ag* tiring, exhausting; (*lavoro*) laborious

'fatto, -a *pp di* **fare** ▷ *ag*: **un uomo ~** a grown man ▷ *sm* fact; (*azione*) deed; (*avvenimento*) event, occurrence; (*di romanzo, film*) action, story; **~ a mano/in casa** hand-/home-made; **cogliere qn sul ~** to catch sb red-handed; **il ~ sta *o* è che** the fact remains or is that; **in ~ di** as for, as far as ... is concerned; **coppia/unione di ~** long-standing relationship

fat'tore *sm* (*Agr*) farm manager; (*Mat: elemento costitutivo*) factor; **~ di protezione** (*di lozione solare*) factor

fatto'ria *sf* farm; (*casa*) farmhouse

> Attenzione! In inglese esiste la parola *factory*, che però significa *fabbrica*.

fatto'rino *sm* errand boy; (*di ufficio*) office boy; (*d'albergo*) porter

fat'tura *sf* (*Comm*) invoice; (*di abito*) tailoring; (*malia*) spell

fattu'rato *sm* (*Comm*) turnover

'fauna *sf* fauna

'fava *sf* broad bean

'favola *sf* (*fiaba*) fairy tale; (*d'intento morale*) fable; (*fandonia*) yarn; **favo'loso, -a** *ag* fabulous; (*incredibile*) incredible

fa'vore *sm* favour; **per ~** please; **fare un ~ a qn** to do sb a favour; **favo'rire** /55/ *vt* to favour; (*il commercio, l'industria, le arti*) to promote, encourage; **vuole favorire?** won't you help yourself?; **favorisca in salotto** please come into the sitting room

fax *sm inv* fax; **mandare qc via ~** to fax sth

fazzo'letto [fattso'letto] *sm* handkerchief; (*per la testa*) (head) scarf; **~ di carta** tissue

feb'braio *sm* February

'febbre *sf* fever; **aver la ~** to have a high temperature; **~ da fieno** hay fever

'feci *ecc* ['fɛtʃi] *vb vedi* **fare**

fecondazi'one [fekondat'tsjone] *sf* fertilization; **~ artificiale** artificial insemination; **fe'condo, -a** *ag* fertile

'fede *sf* (*credenza*) belief, faith; (*Rel*) faith; (*fiducia*) faith, trust; (*fedeltà*) loyalty; (*anello*) wedding ring; (*attestato*) certificate; **aver ~ in qn** to have faith in sb; **in buona/cattiva ~** in good/bad faith; **"in ~"** (*Dir*) "in witness whereof"; **fe'dele** *ag*: **fedele (a)** faithful (to) ▷ *smf* follower; **i fedeli** (*Rel*) the faithful

'federa *sf* pillowslip, pillowcase

fede'rale *ag* federal

'fegato *sm* liver; (*fig*) guts *pl*, nerve

'felce ['feltʃe] *sf* fern

fe'lice [fe'litʃe] *ag* happy; (*fortunato*) lucky; **felicità** *sf* happiness

felici'tarsi [felitʃi'tarsi] /72/ *vpr* (*congratularsi*): **~ con qn per qc** to congratulate sb on sth

fe'lino, -a *ag, sm* feline

'felpa *sf* sweatshirt

'femmina *sf* (*Zool, Tecn*) female; (*figlia*) girl, daughter; (*spesso peg*) woman; **femmi'nile** *ag* feminine; (*sesso*) female; (*lavoro, giornale*) woman's, women's; (*moda*) women's ▷ *sm* (*Ling*) feminine

'femore *sm* thighbone, femur

fe'nomeno *sm* phenomenon

feri'ale *ag*: **giorno ~** weekday

'ferie *sfpl* holidays (BRIT), vacation *sg* (US); **andare in ~** to go on holiday *o* vacation

fe'rire /55/ *vt* to injure; (*deliberatamente: Mil: ecc*) to wound; (*colpire*) to hurt; **ferirsi** *vpr* to hurt o.s., injure o.s.; **fe'rito, -a** *sm/f* wounded *o* injured man/woman ▷ *sf* injury; wound

fer'maglio [fer'maʎʎo] *sm* clasp; (*per documenti*) clip

fer'mare /72/ vt to stop, halt; (Polizia) to detain, hold ▷ vi to stop; **fermarsi** vpr to stop, halt; **fermarsi a fare qc** to stop to do sth

fer'mata sf stop; **~ dell'autobus** bus stop

fer'menti smpl: **~ lattici** probiotic bacteria

fer'mezza [fer'mettsa] sf (fig) firmness, steadfastness

'fermo, -a ag still, motionless; (veicolo) stationary; (orologio) not working; (saldo: anche fig) firm; (voce, mano) steady ▷ escl stop!; keep still! ▷ sm (chiusura) catch, lock; (Dir): **~ di polizia** police detention

fe'roce [fe'rɔtʃe] ag (animale) fierce, ferocious; (persona) cruel, fierce; (fame, dolore) raging; **le bestie feroci** wild animals

ferra'gosto sm (festa) feast of the Assumption; (periodo) August holidays pl (BRIT) o vacation (US)

- **FERRAGOSTO**
-
- Ferragosto, 15 August, is a national
- holiday. Marking the feast of
- the Assumption, its origins are
- religious but in recent years it
- has simply become the most
- important public holiday of the
- summer season. Most people
- take some extra time off work and
- head out of town to the holiday
- resorts. Consequently, most of
- industry and commerce grinds to
- a standstill.

ferra'menta sfpl: **negozio di ~** ironmonger's (BRIT), hardware shop o store (US)

'ferro sm iron; **una bistecca ai ferri** a grilled steak; **~ battuto** wrought iron; **~ di cavallo** horseshoe; **~ da stiro** iron; **ferri da calza** knitting needles

ferro'via sf railway (BRIT), railroad (US); **ferrovi'ario, -a** ag railway cpd (BRIT), railroad cpd (US); **ferrovi'ere** sm railwayman (BRIT), railroad man (US)

'fertile ag fertile

'fesso, -a pp di **fendere** ▷ ag (fam: sciocco) crazy, cracked

fes'sura sf crack, split; (per gettone, moneta) slot

'festa sf (religiosa) feast; (pubblica) holiday; (compleanno) birthday; (onomastico) name day; (ricevimento) celebration, party; **far ~** to have a holiday; (far baldoria) to live it up; **far ~ a qn** to give sb a warm welcome

festeggi'are [fested'dʒare] /62/ vt to celebrate; (persona) to have a celebration for

fes'tivo, -a ag (atmosfera) festive; **giorno ~** holiday

'feto sm foetus (BRIT), fetus (US)

'fetta sf slice

fettuc'cine [fettut'tʃine] sfpl (Cuc) ribbon-shaped pasta

FF.SS. abbr = **Ferrovie dello Stato**

FI sigla = **Firenze** ▷ abbr (= Forza Italia) Italian centre-right political party

fi'aba sf fairy tale

fi'acca sf weariness; (svogliatezza) listlessness

fi'acco, -a, -chi, -che ag (stanco) tired, weary; (svogliato) listless; (debole) weak; (mercato) slack

fi'accola sf torch

fi'ala sf phial

fi'amma sf flame

fiam'mante ag (colore) flaming; **nuovo ~** brand new

fiam'mifero sm match

fiam'mingo, -a, -ghi, -ghe ag Flemish ▷ sm/f Fleming ▷ sm (Ling) Flemish; **i Fiamminghi** the Flemish

fi'anco, -chi sm side; (Mil) flank; **di ~** sideways, from the side; **a ~ a ~** side by side

fi'asco, -schi sm flask; (fig) fiasco; **fare ~** to fail

fia'tare /72/ vi (fig: parlare): **senza ~** without saying a word

fi'ato sm breath; (resistenza) stamina; **avere il ~ grosso** to be out of breath; **prendere ~** to catch one's breath

'fibbia sf buckle

'fibra sf fibre; (fig) constitution

fic'care /20/ vt to push, thrust, drive; **ficcarsi** vpr (andare a finire) to get to

ficcherò ecc [fikke'rɔ] vb vedi **ficcare**

'fico, -chi sm (pianta) fig tree; (frutto) fig; **~ d'India** prickly pear; **~ secco** dried fig

fiction ['fikʃon] sf inv TV drama
Attenzione! In inglese esiste la parola fiction, che però significa narrativa oppure finzione.

fidanza'mento [fidantsa'mento] sm engagement

fidan'zarsi [fidan'tsarsi] /72/ vpr to get engaged; **fidan'zato, -a** sm/f fiancé (fiancée)

fi'darsi /72/ vpr: **~ di** to trust; **fi'dato, -a** ag reliable, trustworthy

fi'ducia [fi'dutʃa] sf confidence, trust; **incarico di ~** position of trust, responsible position; **persona di ~** reliable person

fie'nile sm barn; hayloft

fi'eno sm hay

fi'era sf fair

fi'ero, -a ag proud; (audace) bold

'fifa sf (fam): **aver ~** to have the jitters

fig. abbr (= figura) fig.

'figlia ['fiʎʎa] sf daughter

figli'astro, -a [fiʎ'ʎastro] sm/f stepson/daughter

'figlio ['fiʎʎo] sm son; (senza distinzione di sesso) child; **~ di papà** spoilt, wealthy young man; **~ unico** only child

fi'gura sf figure; (forma, aspetto esterno) form, shape; (illustrazione) picture, illustration; **far ~** to look smart; **fare una brutta ~** to make a bad impression

figu'rare vi to appear ▷ vt: **figurarsi qc** to imagine sth; **figurarsi** vr: **figurati!** imagine that!; **ti do noia?**

— ma figurati! am I disturbing you? — not at all!

figu'rina sf figurine; (cartoncino) picture card

'fila sf row, line; (coda) queue; (serie) series, string; **di ~** in succession; **fare la ~** to queue; **in ~ indiana** in single file

fi'lare /72/ vt to spin ▷ vi (baco, ragno) to spin; (formaggio fuso) to go stringy; (discorso) to hang together; (fam: amoreggiare) to go steady; (muoversi a forte velocità) to go at full speed; **~ diritto** (fig) to toe the line; **~ via** to dash off

filas'trocca, -che sf nursery rhyme

filate'lia sf philately, stamp collecting

fi'letto sm (di vite) thread; (di carne) fillet

fili'ale ag filial ▷ sf (di impresa) branch

film sm inv film

'filo sm (anche fig) thread; (filato) yarn; (metallico) wire; (di lama, rasoio) edge; **con un ~ di voce** in a whisper; **per ~ e per segno** in detail; **~ d'erba** blade of grass; **~ interdentale** dental floss; **~ di perle** string of pearls; **~ spinato** barbed wire

fi'lone sm (di minerali) seam, vein; (pane) ≈ Vienna loaf; (fig) trend

filoso'fia sf philosophy; **fi'losofo, -a** sm/f philosopher

fil'trare /72/ vt, vi to filter

'filtro sm filter; **~ dell'olio** (Aut) oil filter

fi'nale ag final ▷ sm (di libro, film) end, ending; (Mus) finale ▷ sf (Sport) final; **final'mente** av finally, at last

fi'nanza [fi'nantsa] sf finance; **finanze** sfpl (di individuo, Stato) finances

finché [fin'ke] cong (per tutto il tempo che) as long as; (fino al momento in cui) until; **aspetta ~ io (non) sia ritornato** wait until I get back

'fine ag (lamina, carta) thin; (capelli, polvere) fine; (vista, udito) keen, sharp; (persona: raffinata) refined,

distinguished; (*osservazione*) subtle
▷ *sf* end ▷ *sm* aim, purpose; (*esito*)
result, outcome; **in** *o* **alla ~** in the
end, finally; **secondo ~** ulterior
motive

fi'nestra *sf* window; **fines'trino** *sm*
window

'fingere ['find3ere] /54/ *vt* to feign;
(*supporre*) to imagine, suppose;
fingersi *vpr*: **fingersi ubriaco/
pazzo** to pretend to be drunk/crazy;
~ di fare to pretend to do

fi'nire /55/ *vt* to finish ▷ *vi* to finish,
end; **~ di fare** (*compiere*) to finish
doing; (*smettere*) to stop doing; **~ in
galera** to end up *o* finish up in prison

finlan'dese *ag* Finnish ▷ *smf* Finn
▷ *sm* (*Ling*) Finnish; **Fin'landia** *sf*: **la
Finlandia** Finland

'fino, -a *ag* (*capelli, seta*) fine; (*oro*)
pure; (*fig: acuto*) shrewd ▷ *av* (*spesso
troncato in fin*: *pure, anche*) even ▷ *prep*
(*spesso troncato in fin*): **fin quando?**
till when?; **fin qui** as far as here; **~ a**
(*tempo*) until, till; (*luogo*) as far as, (up)
to; **fin da domani** from tomorrow
onwards; **fin da ieri** since yesterday;
fin dalla nascita from *o* since birth

fi'nocchio [fi'nɔkkjo] *sm* fennel;
(*fam, peg: omosessuale*) queer (!)

fi'nora *av* up till now

'finsi *ecc vb vedi* **fingere**

'finto, -a *pp di* **fingere** ▷ *ag* false;
(*fiori*) artificial ▷ *sf* pretence

finzi'one [fin'tsjone] *sf* pretence
, sham

fi'occo, -chi *sm* (*di nastro*) bow; (*di
stoffa, lana*) flock; (*di neve*) flake;
(*Naut*) jib; **coi fiocchi** (*fig*) first-rate;
fiocchi di avena oatflakes; **fiocchi
di granoturco** cornflakes

fi'ocina ['fjɔtʃina] *sf* harpoon

fi'oco, -a, -chi, -che *ag* faint, dim

fi'onda *sf* catapult

fio'raio, -a *sm/f* florist

fi'ore *sm* flower; **fiori** *smpl* (*Carte*)
clubs; **a fior d'acqua** on the surface
of the water; **aver i nervi a fior di**
pelle to be on edge; **fior di latte**
cream; **fiori di campo** wild flowers

fioren'tino, -a *ag* Florentine

fio'retto *sm* (*Scherma*) foil

fio'rire /55/ *vi* (*rosa*) to flower; (*albero*)
to blossom; (*fig*) to flourish

Fi'renze [fi'rɛntse] *sf* Florence

'firma *sf* signature

> Attenzione! In inglese esiste la
> parola **firm**, che però significa
> **ditta**.

fir'mare /72/ *vt* to sign; **un abito
firmato** a designer suit

fisar'monica, -che *sf* accordion

fis'cale *ag* fiscal, tax *cpd*; **medico ~**
doctor employed by Social Security to
verify cases of sick leave

fischi'are [fis'kjare] /19/ *vi* to whistle
▷ *vt* to whistle; (*attore*) to boo, hiss;
fischi'etto *sm* (*strumento*) whistle;
'fischio *sm* whistle

'fisco *sm* tax authorities *pl*, ≈ Inland
Revenue (BRIT), ≈ Internal Revenue
Service (US)

'fisica *sf vedi* **fisico**

'fisico, -a, -ci, -che *ag* physical
▷ *sm/f* physicist ▷ *sm* physique

fisiotera'pia *sf* physiotherapy;
fisiotera'pista *smf* physiotherapist

fis'sare /72/ *vt* to fix, fasten; (*guardare
intensamente*) to stare at; (*data,
condizioni*) to fix, establish, set;
(*prenotare*) to book; **fissarsi** *vpr*:
fissarsi su (*sguardo, attenzione*)
to focus on; (*fig: idea*) to become
obsessed with

'fisso, -a *ag* fixed; (*stipendio, impiego*)
regular ▷ *av*: **guardare ~ qn/qc** to
stare at sb/sth; **telefono ~** landline

'fitta *sf vedi* **fitto**

fit'tizio, -a *ag* fictitious, imaginary

'fitto, -a *ag* thick, dense; (*pioggia*)
heavy ▷ *sm* depths *pl*, middle; (*affitto,
pigione*) rent ▷ *sf* sharp pain; **una
fitta al cuore** (*fig*) a pang of grief;
nel ~ del bosco in the heart *o* depths
of the wood

fi'ume *sm* river

fiutare | 94

fiu'tare /72/ vt to smell, sniff; (animale) to scent; (fig: inganno) to get wind of, smell; **~ tabacco** to take snuff; **~ cocaina** to snort cocaine

fla'grante ag: **cogliere qn in ~** to catch sb red-handed

fla'nella sf flannel

flash [flaʃ] sm inv (Fot) flash; (giornalistico) newsflash

'flauto sm flute

fles'sibile ag pliable; (fig: che si adatta) flexible

flessibili'tà sf (anche fig) flexibility

flessi'one sf (gen) bending; (Ginnastica: a terra) sit-up; (: in piedi) forward bend; (: sulle gambe) knee-bend; (diminuzione) slight drop, slight fall; (Ling) inflection; **fare una ~** to bend; **una ~ economica** a downward trend in the economy

'flettere /92/ vt to bend

'flipper sm inv pinball machine

F.lli abbr (= fratelli) Bros

'flora sf flora

'florido, -a ag flourishing; (fig) glowing with health

'floscio, -a, -sci, -sce ['floʃʃo] ag (cappello) floppy, soft; (muscoli) flabby

'flotta sf fleet

'fluido, -a ag, sm fluid

flu'oro sm fluorine

'flusso sm flow; (Fisica, Med) flux; **~ e riflusso** ebb and flow

fluvi'ale ag river cpd, fluvial

FMI sigla m (= Fondo Monetario Internazionale) IMF

'foca, -che sf (Zool) seal

fo'caccia, -ce [fo'kattʃa] sf kind of pizza; (dolce) bun

'foce ['fotʃe] sf (Geo) mouth

foco'laio sm (Med) centre (BRIT) o center (US) of infection; (fig) hotbed

foco'lare sm hearth, fireside; (Tecn) furnace

'fodera sf (di vestito) lining; (di libro, poltrona) cover

'fodero sm (di spada) scabbard; (di pugnale) sheath; (di pistola) holster

'foga sf enthusiasm, ardour

'foglia ['fɔʎʎa] sf leaf; **~ d'argento/ d'oro** silver/gold leaf

'foglio ['fɔʎʎo] sm (di carta) sheet (of paper); (di metallo) sheet; **~ di calcolo** (Inform) spreadsheet; **~ rosa** (Aut) provisional licence; **~ di via** (Dir) expulsion order; **~ volante** pamphlet

'fogna ['foɲɲa] sf drain, sewer

föhn [føːn] sm inv hair-dryer

folksono'mia sf (Inform) folksonomy

'folla sf crowd, throng

'folle ag mad, insane; (Tecn) idle; **in ~** (Aut) in neutral

fol'lia sf folly, foolishness; foolish act; (pazzia) madness, lunacy

'folto, -a ag thick

fon sm inv = **föhn**

fondamen'tale ag fundamental, basic

fonda'mento sm foundation; **fondamenta** sfpl (Edil) foundations

fon'dare /72/ vt to found; (fig: dar base): **~ qc su** to base sth on

fon'dente ag: **cioccolato ~** plain o dark chocolate

'fondere /25/ vt (neve) to melt; (metallo) to fuse, melt; (fig: colori) to merge, blend; (: imprese, gruppi) to merge ▷ vi to melt; **fondersi** vpr to melt; (fig: partiti, correnti) to unite, merge

'fondo, -a ag deep ▷ sm (di recipiente, pozzo) bottom; (di stanza) back; (quantità di liquido che resta, deposito) dregs pl; (sfondo) background; (unità immobiliare) property, estate; (somma di denaro) fund; (Sport) long-distance race; **fondi** smpl (denaro) funds; **a notte fonda** at dead of night; **in ~ a** at the bottom of; at the back of; (strada) at the end of; **in ~** (fig) after all, all things considered; **andare fino in ~ a** (fig) to examine thoroughly; **andare a ~** (nave) to sink; **conoscere a ~** to know inside out; **dar ~ a** (provviste, soldi) to use up; **a ~ perduto** (Comm) without security; **~ comune di investimento** investment trust; **fondi di caffè** coffee grounds; **fondi di magazzino** old o unsold stock sg

fondo'tinta sm inv (cosmetico) foundation

fo'netica sf phonetics sg

fon'tana sf fountain

'fonte sf spring, source; (fig) source ▷ sm: **~ battesimale** (Rel) font; **~ energetica** source of energy

fo'raggio [fo'raddʒo] sm fodder, forage

fo'rare /72/ vt to pierce, make a hole in; (pallone) to burst; (biglietto) to punch; **~ una gomma** to burst a tyre (BRIT) o tire (US)

'forbici ['forbitʃi] sfpl scissors

'forca sf (Agr) fork, pitchfork; (patibolo) gallows sg

for'chetta [for'ketta] sf fork

for'cina [for'tʃina] sf hairpin

fo'resta sf forest

foresti'ero, -a ag foreign ▷ sm/f foreigner

'forfora sf dandruff

'forma sf form; (aspetto esteriore) form, shape; (Dir: procedura) procedure; (per calzature) last; (stampo da cucina) mould; **mantenersi in ~** to keep fit

formag'gino [formad'dʒino] sm processed cheese

for'maggio [for'maddʒo] sm cheese

for'male ag formal

for'mare /72/ vt to form, shape, make; (numero di telefono) to dial; (fig: carattere) to form, mould; **formarsi** vpr to form, take shape; **for'mato** sm format, size; **formazi'one** sf formation; (fig: educazione) training; **formazione continua** continuing education; **formazione permanente** lifelong learning; **formazione professionale** vocational training

for'mica¹, -che sf ant

formica²® ['formika] sf (materiale) Formica®

formi'dabile ag powerful, formidable; (straordinario) remarkable

'formula sf formula; **~ di cortesia** (nelle lettere) letter ending

formu'lare /72/ vt to formulate; to express

for'naio sm baker

for'nello sm (elettrico, a gas) ring; (di pipa) bowl

for'nire /55/ vt: **~ qn di qc, ~ qc a qn** to provide o supply sb with sth, supply sth to sb

'forno sm (di cucina) oven; (panetteria) bakery; (Tecn: per calce ecc) kiln; (: per metalli) furnace; **~ a microonde** microwave oven

'foro sm (buco) hole; (Storia) forum; (tribunale) (law) court

'forse av perhaps, maybe; (circa) about; **essere in ~** to be in doubt

'forte ag strong; (suono) loud; (spesa) considerable, great; (passione, dolore) great, deep ▷ av strongly; (velocemente) fast; (a voce alta) loud(ly); (violentemente) hard ▷ sm (edificio) fort; (specialità) forte, strong point; **essere ~ in qc** to be good at sth

for'tezza [for'tettsa] sf (morale) strength; (luogo fortificato) fortress

for'tuito, -a ag fortuitous, chance cpd

for'tuna sf (destino) fortune, luck; (buona sorte) success, fortune; (eredità, averi) fortune; **per ~** luckily, fortunately; **di ~** makeshift, improvised; **atterraggio di ~** emergency landing; **fortu'nato, -a** ag lucky, fortunate; (coronato da successo) successful

'forza ['fortsa] sf strength; (potere) power; (Fisica) force ▷ escl come on!; **forze** sfpl (fisiche) strength sg; (Mil) forces; **per ~** against one's will; (naturalmente) of course; **a viva ~** by force; **a ~ di** by dint of; **per causa di ~ maggiore** due to circumstances beyond one's control; **la ~ pubblica** the police *pl*: **forze dell'ordine** the forces of law and order; **~ di pace** peacekeeping force; **le forze armate** the armed forces; **F~ Italia** moderate right-wing party

for'zare [for'tsare] /72/ *vt* to force; **~ qn a fare** to force sb to do

for'zista, -i, -e [for'tsista] *ag* of Forza Italia ▷ *sm/f* member (*o* supporter) of Forza Italia

fos'chia [fos'kia] *sf* mist, haze

fosco, -a, -schi, -sche *ag* dark, gloomy

'fosforo *sm* phosphorous

'fossa *sf* pit; (*di cimitero*) grave; **~ biologica** septic tank

fos'sato *sm* ditch; (*di fortezza*) moat

fos'setta *sf* dimple

'fossi *ecc vb vedi* **essere**

'fossile *ag*, *sm* fossil (*cpd*)

'fosso *sm* ditch; (*Mil*) trench

'foste *ecc vb vedi* **essere**

'foto *sf inv* photo ▷ *prefisso*: **~ ricordo** souvenir photo; **~ tessera** passport(-type) photo; **foto'camera** *sf*: **fotocamera digitale** digital camera; **foto'copia** *sf* photocopy; **fotocopi'are** /19/ *vt* to photocopy; **fotocopia'trice** [fotokopja'tritʃe] *sf* photocopier; **fotofo'nino** *sm* camera phone; **fotogra'fare** /72/ *vt* to photograph; **fotogra'fia** *sf* (*procedimento*) photography; (*immagine*) photograph; **fare una fotografia** to take a photograph; **una fotografia a colori/in bianco e nero** a colour/black and white photograph; **foto'grafico, -a, -ci, -che** *ag* photographic; **macchina fotografica** camera; **fo'tografo, -a** *sm/f* photographer; **foto'romanzo** *sm* romantic picture story; **fotovol'taico, -a, -ci, -che** *ag* photovoltaic; **pannelli fotovoltaici** solar panels

fou'lard [fu'lar] *sm inv* scarf

fra *prep* = **tra**

'fradicio, -a, -ci, -ce ['fraditʃo] *ag* (*molto bagnato*) soaking (wet); **ubriaco ~** blind drunk

'fragile ['fradʒile] *ag* fragile; (*fig*: *salute*) delicate

'fragola *sf* strawberry

fra'grante *ag* fragrant

frain'tendere /120/ *vt* to misunderstand

fram'mento *sm* fragment

'frana *sf* landslide; (*fig*: *persona*): **essere una ~** to be useless

fran'cese [fran'tʃeze] *ag* French ▷ *smf* Frenchman/woman ▷ *sm* (*Ling*) French; **i Francesi** the French

'Francia ['frantʃa] *sf*: **la ~** France

'franco, -a, -chi, -che *ag* (*Comm*) free; (*sincero*) frank, open, sincere ▷ *sm* (*moneta*) franc; **farla franca** (*fig*) to get off scot-free; **~ di dogana** duty-free; **prezzo ~ fabbrica** ex-works price

franco'bollo *sm* (postage) stamp

'frangia, -ge ['frandʒa] *sf* fringe

frappé *sm* milk shake

'frase *sf* (*Ling*) sentence; (*locuzione, espressione, Mus*) phrase; **~ fatta** set phrase

'frassino *sm* ash (tree)

frastagli'ato, -a [frastaʎ'ʎato] *ag* (*costa*) indented, jagged

frastor'nare /72/ *vt* to daze; (*confondere*) to bewilder

frastu'ono *sm* hubbub, din

'frate *sm* friar, monk

fratel'lastro *sm* stepbrother; (*con genitore in comune*) half brother

fra'tello *sm* brother; **fratelli** *smpl* brothers; (*nel senso di fratelli e sorelle*) brothers and sisters

fra'terno, -a *ag* fraternal, brotherly

frat'tempo *sm*: **nel ~** in the meantime, meanwhile

frat'tura *sf* fracture; (*fig*) split, break

frazi'one [frat'tsjone] *sf* fraction; (*anche*: **~ di comune**) hamlet

'freccia, -ce ['frettʃa] *sf* arrow; **~ di direzione** (*Aut*) indicator

fred'dezza [fred'dettsa] sf coldness

'freddo, -a ag, sm cold; **fa ~** it's cold; **aver ~** to be cold; **a ~** (fig) deliberately; **freddo'loso, -a** ag sensitive to the cold

fre'gare /80/ vt to rub; (fam: truffare) to take in, cheat; (: rubare) to swipe, pinch; **fregarsene** (fam!): **chi se ne frega?** who gives a damn (about it?)

fregherò ecc [frege'rɔ] vb vedi **fregare**

fre'nare /72/ vt (veicolo) to slow down; (cavallo) to rein in; (lacrime) to restrain, hold back ▷ vi to brake; **frenarsi** vpr (fig) to restrain o.s., control o.s.

'freno sm brake; (morso) bit; **tenere a ~** to restrain; **~ a disco** disc brake; **~ a mano** handbrake

frequen'tare /72/ vt (scuola, corso) to attend; (locale, bar) to go to, frequent; (persone) to see (often); **frequen'tato, -a** ag (locale) busy; **fre'quente** ag frequent; **di frequente** frequently

fres'chezza [fres'kettsa] sf freshness; **'fresco, -a, -schi, -sche** ag fresh; (temperatura) cool; (notizia) recent, fresh ▷ sm: **godere il fresco** to enjoy the cool air; **stare fresco** (fig) to be in for it; **mettere al fresco** to put in a cool place

'fretta sf hurry, haste; **in ~** in a hurry; **in ~ e furia** in a mad rush; **aver ~** to be in a hurry

'friggere ['friddʒere] /56/ vt to fry ▷ vi (olio ecc) to sizzle

'frigido, -a ['fridʒido] ag (Med) frigid

'frigo, -ghi sm fridge

frigo'bar sm inv minibar

frigo'rifero, -a ag refrigerating ▷ sm refrigerator

fringu'ello sm chaffinch

'frissi ecc vb vedi **friggere**

frit'tata sf omelet(te); **fare una ~** (fig) to make a mess of things

frit'tella sf (Cuc) fritter

'fritto, -a pp di **friggere** ▷ ag fried ▷ sm fried food; **~ misto** mixed fry

frit'tura sf: **~ di pesce** mixed fried fish

'frivolo, -a ag frivolous

frizi'one [frit'tsjone] sf friction; (di pelle) rub, rub-down; (Aut) clutch

friz'zante [frid'dzante] ag (anche fig) sparkling

fro'dare /72/ vt to defraud, cheat

'frode sf fraud; **~ fiscale** tax evasion

'fronda sf (leafy) branch; (di partito politico) internal opposition; **fronde** sfpl (di albero) foliage sg

fron'tale ag frontal; (scontro) head-on

'fronte sf (Anat) forehead; (di edificio) front, façade ▷ sm (Mil, Pol, Meteor) front; **a ~, di ~** facing, opposite; **di ~ a** (posizione) opposite, facing, in front of; (a paragone di) compared with

fronti'era sf border, frontier

'frottola sf fib

fru'gare /80/ vi to rummage ▷ vt to search

frugherò ecc [fruge'rɔ] vb vedi **frugare**

frul'lare /72/ vt (Cuc) to whisk ▷ vi (uccelli) to flutter; **frul'lato** sm milk shake; fruit drink; **frulla'tore** sm electric mixer

fru'mento sm wheat

fru'scio [fruʃʃio] sm rustle; rustling; (di acque) murmur

'frusta sf whip; (Cuc) whisk

frus'tare /72/ vt to whip

frus'trato, -a ag frustrated

'frutta sf fruit; (portata) dessert; **~ candita/secca** candied/dried fruit

frut'tare /72/ vi to bear dividends, give a return

frut'teto sm orchard

frutti'vendolo, -a sm/f greengrocer (BRIT), produce dealer (US)

'frutto sm fruit; (fig: risultato) result(s); (Econ: interesse) interest; (: reddito) income; **frutti di mare** seafood sg: **frutti di bosco** berries

FS abbr (= Ferrovie dello Stato) Italian railways

fu *vb vedi* **essere** ▷ *ag inv*: **il fu Paolo Bianchi** the late Paolo Bianchi

fuci'lare [futʃi'lare] /72/ *vt* to shoot

fu'cile [fu'tʃile] *sm* rifle, gun; (*da caccia*) shotgun, gun

'fucsia *sf* fuchsia

'fuga, -ghe *sf* escape, flight; (*di gas, liquidi*) leak; (*Mus*) fugue; **~ di cervelli** brain drain

fug'gire [fud'dʒire] /31/ *vi* to flee, run away; (*fig: passar veloce*) to fly ▷ *vt* to avoid

'fui *vb vedi* **essere**

fu'liggine [fu'liddʒine] *sf* soot

'fulmine *sm* bolt of lightning; **fulmini** *smpl* lightning *sg*

fu'mare /72/ *vi* to smoke; (*emettere vapore*) to steam ▷ *vt* to smoke; **fuma'tore, -'trice** *sm/f* smoker

fu'metto *sm* comic strip; **giornale a fumetti** comic

'fummo *vb vedi* **essere**

'fumo *sm* smoke; (*vapore*) steam; (*il fumare tabacco*) smoking; **fumi** *smpl* (*industriali ecc*) fumes; **vendere ~** to deceive, cheat; **i fumi dell'alcool** the after-effects of drink; **~ passivo** passive smoking; **fu'moso, -a** *ag* smoky; (*fig*) muddled

'fune *sf* rope, cord; (*più grossa*) cable

'funebre *ag* (*rito*) funeral; (*aspetto*) gloomy, funereal

fune'rale *sm* funeral

'fungere ['fundʒere] /5/ *vi*: **~ da** to act as

'fungo, -ghi *sm* fungus; (*commestibile*) mushroom; **~ velenoso** toadstool

funico'lare *sf* funicular railway

funi'via *sf* cable railway

'funsi *ecc vb vedi* **fungere**

funzio'nare [funtsjo'nare] /72/ *vi* to work, function; (*fungere*): **~ da** to act as

funzio'nario [funtsjo'narjo] *sm* official; **~ statale** civil servant

funzi'one [fun'tsjone] *sf* function; (*carica*) post, position; (*Rel*) service; **in ~** (*meccanismo*) in operation; **in ~ di** (*come*) as; **fare la ~ di qn** (*farne le veci*) to take sb's place

fu'oco, -chi *sm* fire; (*fornello*) ring; (*Fot, Fisica*) focus; **dare ~ a qc** to set fire to sth; **far ~** (*sparare*) to fire; **al ~!** fire!; **~ d'artificio** firework

fuorché [fwor'ke] *cong, prep* except

fu'ori *av* outside; (*all'aperto*) outdoors, outside; (*fuori di casa, Sport*) out; (*esclamativo*) get out! ▷ *prep*: **~ (di)** out of, outside ▷ *sm* outside; **lasciar ~ qc/qn** to leave sth/sb out; **far ~ qn** (*fam*) to kill sb, do sb in; **essere ~ di sé** to be beside oneself; **~ luogo** (*inopportuno*) out of place, uncalled for; **~ mano** out of the way, remote; **~ pericolo** out of danger; **~ uso** old-fashioned; obsolete; **fuorigi'oco** *sm* offside; **fuoris'trada** *sm* (*Aut*) cross-country vehicle

'furbo, -a *ag* clever, smart; (*peg*) cunning

fu'rente *ag*: **~ (contro)** furious (with)

fur'fante *sm* rascal, scoundrel

fur'gone *sm* van

'furia *sf* (*ira*) fury, rage; (*fig: impeto*) fury, violence; (: *fretta*) rush; **a ~ di** by dint of; **andare su tutte le furie** to fly into a rage; **furi'bondo, -a** *ag* furious

furi'oso, -a *ag* furious

'furono *vb vedi* **essere**

fur'tivo, -a *ag* furtive

'furto *sm* theft; **~ con scasso** burglary

'fusa *sfpl*: **fare le ~** to purr

fu'seaux *smpl* leggings

'fusi *ecc vb vedi* **fondere**

fu'sibile *sm* (*Elettr*) fuse

fusi'one *sf* (*di metalli*) fusion, melting; (*colata*) casting; (*Comm*) merger; (*fig*) merging

'fuso, -a *pp di* **fondere** ▷ *sm* (*Filatura*) spindle; **~ orario** time zone

fus'tino *sm* (*di detersivo*) tub

'fusto *sm* stem; (*Anat, di albero*) trunk; (*recipiente*) drum, can

fu'turo, -a *ag, sm* future

g

G8 [dʒi'otto] sm (= Gruppo degli Otto) G8

G20 [dʒi'venti] sm (= Gruppo dei Venti) G20

'gabbia sf cage; (da imballaggio) crate; **~ dell'ascensore** lift (BRIT) o elevator (US) shaft; **~ toracica** (Anat) rib cage

gabbi'ano sm (sea)gull

gabi'netto sm (Med: ecc) consulting room; (Pol) ministry; (di decenza) toilet, lavatory; (Ins: di fisica ecc) laboratory

gaffe [gaf] sf inv blunder, boob

ga'lante ag gallant, courteous; (avventura, poesia) amorous

ga'lassia sf galaxy

ga'lera sf (Naut) galley; (prigione) prison

'galla sf: **a ~** afloat; **venire a ~** to surface, come to the surface; (fig: verità) to come out

galleggi'are [galled'dʒare] /62/ vi to float

galle'ria sf (traforo) tunnel; (Archit, d'arte) gallery; (Teat) circle; (strada coperta con negozi) arcade

'Galles sm: **il ~** Wales; **gal'lese** ag Welsh ▷ smf Welshman/woman ▷ sm (Ling) Welsh; **i Gallesi** the Welsh

gal'lina sf hen

'gallo sm cock

galop'pare /72/ vi to gallop

ga'loppo sm gallop; **al** o **di ~** at a gallop

'gamba sf leg; (asta: di lettera) stem; **in ~** (in buona salute) well; (bravo, sveglio) bright, smart; **prendere qc sotto ~** (fig) to treat sth too lightly

gambe'retto sm shrimp

'gambero sm (di acqua dolce) crayfish; (di mare) prawn

'gambo sm stem; (di frutta) stalk

'gamma sf (Mus) scale; (di colori, fig) range

'gancio ['gantʃo] sm hook

'gara sf competition; (Sport) competition; contest; match; (: corsa) race; **fare a ~** to compete, vie

ga'rage [ga'raʒ] sm inv garage

garan'tire /55/ vt to guarantee; (debito) to stand surety for; (dare per certo) to assure

garan'zia [garan'tsia] sf guarantee; (pegno) security

gar'bato, -a ag courteous, polite

gareggi'are [gared'dʒare] /62/ vi to compete

garga'rismo sm gargle; **fare i gargarismi** to gargle

ga'rofano sm carnation; **chiodo di ~** clove

'garza ['gardza] sf (per bende) gauze

gar'zone [gar'dzone] sm (di negozio) boy

gas sm inv gas; **a tutto ~** at full speed; **dare ~** (Aut) to accelerate

ga'solio sm diesel (oil)

ga's(s)ato, -a ag fizzy

gast'rite sf gastritis

gastrono'mia sf gastronomy

'gatta sf cat, she-cat

gat'tino sm kitten

'gatto sm cat, tomcat; **~ delle nevi** (Aut, Sci) snowcat; **~ selvatico** wildcat

'gazza ['gaddza] sf magpie

gel [dʒɛl] sm inv gel

ge'lare [dʒe'lare] /72/ vt, vi, vb impers to freeze

gelate'ria [dʒelate'ria] sf ice-cream shop

gela'tina [dʒela'tina] sf gelatine; **~ esplosiva** gelignite; **~ di frutta** fruit jelly

ge'lato, -a [dʒe'lato] ag frozen ▷ sm ice cream

'gelido, -a ['dʒɛlido] ag icy, ice-cold

'gelo ['dʒɛlo] sm (temperatura) intense cold; (brina) frost; (fig) chill

gelo'sia [dʒelo'sia] sf jealousy

ge'loso, -a [dʒe'loso] ag jealous

'gelso ['dʒɛlso] sm mulberry (tree)

gelso'mino [dʒelso'mino] sm jasmine

ge'mello, -a [dʒe'mɛllo] ag, sm/f twin; **gemelli** smpl (di camicia) cufflinks; **Gemelli** Gemini sg

'gemere ['dʒɛmere] /29/ vi to moan, groan; (cigolare) to creak

'gemma ['dʒɛmma] sf (Bot) bud; (pietra preziosa) gem

gene'rale [dʒene'rale] ag, sm general; **in ~** (per sommi capi) in general terms; (di solito) usually, in general

gene'rare [dʒene'rare] /72/ vt (dar vita) to give birth to; (produrre) to produce; (causare) to arouse; (Tecn) to produce, generate; **generazi'one** sf generation

'genere ['dʒɛnere] sm kind, type, sort; (Biol) genus; (merce) article, product; (Ling) gender; (Arte, Letteratura) genre; **in ~** generally, as a rule; **il ~ umano** mankind; **generi alimentari** foodstuffs

ge'nerico, -a, -ci, -che [dʒe'nɛriko] ag generic; (vago) vague, imprecise

'genero ['dʒɛnero] sm son-in-law

gene'roso, -a [dʒene'roso] ag generous

ge'netico, -a, -ci, -che [dʒe'nɛtiko] ag genetic ▷ sf genetics sg

gen'giva [dʒen'dʒiva] sf (Anat) gum

geni'ale [dʒe'njale] ag (persona) of genius; (idea) ingenious, brilliant

'genio ['dʒɛnjo] sm genius; **andare a ~ a qn** to be to sb's liking, appeal to sb

geni'tore [dʒeni'tore] sm parent, father o mother; **genitori** smpl parents

gen'naio [dʒen'najo] sm January

ge'noma [dʒe'nɔma] sm genome

'Genova ['dʒɛnova] sf Genoa

'gente ['dʒɛnte] sf people pl

gen'tile [dʒen'tile] ag (persona, atto) kind; (: garbato) courteous, polite; (nelle lettere): **G~ Signore** Dear Sir; **G~ Signor Fernando Villa** (sulla busta) Mr Fernando Villa

genu'ino, -a [dʒenu'ino] ag (prodotto) natural; (persona, sentimento) genuine, sincere

geogra'fia [dʒeogra'fia] sf geography

geolo'gia [dʒeolo'dʒia] sf geology

ge'ometra, -i, -e [dʒe'ɔmetra] smf (professionista) surveyor

geome'tria [dʒeome'tria] sf geometry

ge'ranio [dʒe'ranjo] sm geranium

gerar'chia [dʒerar'kia] sf hierarchy

'gergo, -ghi ['dʒɛrgo] sm jargon; slang

geria'tria [dʒerja'tria] sf geriatrics sg

Ger'mania [dʒer'manja] sf: **la ~** Germany; **la ~ occidentale/ orientale** West/East Germany

'germe ['dʒɛrme] sm germ; (fig) seed

germogli'are [dʒermoʎ'ʎare] /27/ vi to sprout; (germinare) to germinate

gero'glifico, -ci [dʒero'glifiko] sm hieroglyphic

ge'rundio [dʒe'rundjo] sm gerund

'gesso ['dʒɛsso] sm chalk; (Scultura, Med, Edil) plaster; (statua) plaster figure; (minerale) gypsum

gesti'one [dʒes'tjone] *sf* management

ges'tire [dʒes'tire] /55/ *vt* to run, manage

'**gesto** ['dʒɛsto] *sm* gesture

Gesù [dʒe'zu] *sm* Jesus

gesu'ita, -i [dʒezu'ita] *sm* Jesuit

get'tare [dʒet'tare] /72/ *vt* to throw; *(anche:* ~ **via)** to throw away *o* out; *(Scultura)* to cast; *(Edil)* to lay; *(acqua)* to spout; *(grido)* to utter; **gettarsi** *vpr*: **gettarsi in** *(fiume)* to flow into; ~ **uno sguardo su** to take a quick look at

'**getto** ['dʒɛtto] *sm (di gas, liquido, Aer)* jet; **a** ~ **continuo** uninterruptedly; **di** ~ *(fig)* straight off, in one go

get'tone [dʒet'tone] *sm* token; *(per giochi)* counter; (: *roulette ecc)* chip; ~ **telefonico** telephone token

ghiacci'aio [gjat'tʃajo] *sm* glacier

ghiacci'ato, -a *ag* frozen; *(bevanda)* ice-cold

ghi'accio ['gjattʃo] *sm* ice

ghiacci'olo [gjat'tʃɔlo] *sm* icicle; *(tipo di gelato)* ice lolly *(BRIT)*, popsicle *(US)*

ghi'aia ['gjaja] *sf* gravel

ghi'anda ['gjanda] *sf (Bot)* acorn

ghi'andola ['gjandola] *sf* gland

ghi'otto, -a ['gjotto] *ag* greedy; *(cibo)* delicious, appetizing

ghir'landa [gir'landa] *sf* garland, wreath

'**ghiro** ['giro] *sm* dormouse

'**ghisa** ['giza] *sf* cast iron

già [dʒa] *av* already; *(ex, in precedenza)* formerly ▷ *escl* of course!, yes indeed!

gi'acca, -che ['dʒakka] *sf* jacket; ~ **a vento** windcheater *(BRIT)*, windbreaker *(US)*

giacché [dʒak'ke] *cong* since, as

giac'cone [dʒak'kone] *sm* heavy jacket

gia'cere [dʒa'tʃere] /57/ *vi* to lie

gi'ada ['dʒada] *sf* jade

giagu'aro [dʒa'gwaro] *sm* jaguar

gi'allo ['dʒallo] *ag* yellow; *(carnagione)* sallow ▷ *sm* yellow; *(anche:* **romanzo** ~) detective novel; *(anche:* **film** ~) detective film; ~ **dell'uovo** yolk

Gia'maica [dʒa'maika] *sf*: **la** ~ Jamaica

Giap'pone [dʒap'pone] *sm*: **il** ~ Japan; **giappo'nese** *ag, smf, sm* Japanese *inv*

giardi'naggio [dʒardi'naddʒo] *sm* gardening

giardini'ere, -a [dʒardi'njɛre] *sm/f* gardener

giar'dino [dʒar'dino] *sm* garden; ~ **d'infanzia** nursery school; ~ **pubblico** public gardens *pl*, (public) park; ~ **zoologico** zoo

giavel'lotto [dʒavel'lɔtto] *sm* javelin

'**giga** *sm inv (Inform)* gig

giga'byte [dʒiga'bait] *sm inv* gigabyte

gi'gante, -'essa [dʒi'gante] *sm/f* giant ▷ *ag* giant, gigantic; *(Comm)* giant-size

'**giglio** ['dʒiʎʎo] *sm* lily

gilè [dʒi'lɛ] *sm inv* waistcoat

gin [dʒin] *sm inv* gin

gine'cologo, -a, -gi, -ghe [dʒine'kɔlogo] *sm/f* gynaecologist

gi'nepro [dʒi'nepro] *sm* juniper

gi'nestra [dʒi'nɛstra] *sf (Bot)* broom

Gi'nevra [dʒi'nevra] *sf* Geneva

gin'nastica [dʒin'nastika] *sf* gymnastics *sg*; *(esercizio fisico)* keep-fit exercises *pl*; *(Ins)* physical education

gi'nocchio [dʒi'nɔkkjo] *(pl f* **ginocchia)** *sm* knee; **stare in** ~ to kneel, be on one's knees; **mettersi in** ~ to kneel (down)

gio'care [dʒo'kare] /20/ *vt* to play; *(scommettere)* to stake, wager, bet; *(ingannare)* to take in ▷ *vi* to play; *(a roulette ecc)* to gamble; *(fig)* to play a part, be important; ~ **a** *(gioco, sport)* to play; *(cavalli)* to bet on; **giocarsi la carriera** to put one's career at risk; **gioca'tore, -'trice** *sm/f* player; gambler

gio'cattolo [dʒo'kattolo] *sm* toy

giocherò ecc [dʒoke'rɔ] vb vedi **giocare**

gi'oco, -chi ['dʒɔko] sm game; (divertimento, Tecn) play; (al casinò) gambling; (Carte) hand; (insieme di pezzi ecc necessari per un gioco) set; **per ~** for fun; **fare il doppio ~ con qn** to double-cross sb; **~ d'azzardo** game of chance; **~ degli scacchi** chess set; **i Giochi Olimpici** the Olympic Games

giocoli'ere [dʒoko'ljɛre] sm juggler

gi'oia ['dʒɔja] sf joy, delight; (pietra preziosa) jewel, precious stone

gioielle'ria [dʒojelle'ria] sf jeweller's (BRIT) o jeweler's (US) craft; (negozio) jewel(l)er's (shop)

gioielli'ere, -a [dʒojel'ljɛre] sm/f jeweller

gioi'ello [dʒo'jɛllo] sm jewel, piece of jewellery (BRIT) o jewelry (US); **gioielli** smpl (anelli, collane ecc) jewellery sg; **i miei gioielli** my jewels o jewellery; **i gioielli della Corona** the crown jewels

Gior'dania [dʒor'danja] sf: **la ~** Jordan

giorna'laio, -a [dʒorna'lajo] sm/f newsagent (BRIT), newsdealer (US)

gior'nale [dʒor'nale] sm (news) paper; (diario) journal, diary; (Comm) journal; **~ di bordo** (Naut) ship's log; **~ radio** news radio news sg

giornali'ero, -a [dʒorna'ljɛro] ag daily; (che varia: umore) changeable ▷ sm day labourer (BRIT) o laborer (US)

giorna'lismo [dʒorna'lizmo] sm journalism

giorna'lista, -i, -e [dʒorna'lista] smf journalist

gior'nata [dʒor'nata] sf day; **~ lavorativa** working day

gi'orno ['dʒorno] sm day; (opposto alla notte) day, daytime; (luce del giorno) daylight; **al ~** per day; **di ~** by day; **al ~ d'oggi** nowadays

gi'ostra ['dʒɔstra] sf (per bimbi) merry-go-round; (torneo storico) joust

gi'ovane ['dʒovane] ag young; (aspetto) youthful ▷ sm youth; (far bene) young man ▷ sf girl, young woman; **i giovani** young people

gio'vare [dʒo'vare] /72/ vi: **~ a** (essere utile) to be useful to ▷ (far bene) to be good for ▷ vb impers (essere bene, utile) to be useful; **giovarsi** vpr: **giovarsi di qc** to make use of sth

giovedì [dʒove'di] sm inv Thursday; **di** o **il ~** on Thursdays

gioventù [dʒoven'tu] sf (periodo) youth; (i giovani) young people pl, youth

gip [dʒip] sigla m inv (= giudice per le indagini preliminari) judge for preliminary enquiries

gira'dischi [dʒira'diski] sm inv record player

gi'raffa [dʒi'raffa] sf giraffe

gi'rare [dʒi'rare] /72/ vt (far ruotare) to turn; (percorrere, visitare) to go round; (Cine) to shoot; (: come regista) to make; (Comm) to endorse ▷ vi to turn; (più veloce) to spin; (andare in giro) to wander, go around; **girarsi** vpr to turn; **~ attorno a** to go round; to revolve round; **far ~ la testa a qn** to make sb dizzy; (fig) to turn sb's head

girar'rosto [dʒirar'rɔsto] sm (Cuc) spit

gira'sole [dʒira'sole] sm sunflower

gi'revole [dʒi'revole] ag revolving, turning

gi'rino [dʒi'rino] sm tadpole

giro ['dʒiro] sm (circuito, cerchio) circle; (di chiave, manovella) turn; (viaggio) tour, excursion; (passeggiata) stroll, walk; (in macchina) drive; (in bicicletta) ride; (Sport: della pista) lap; (di denaro) circulation; (Carte) hand; (Tecn) revolution; **fare un ~** to go for a walk (o a drive o a ride); **andare in ~** to go about, walk around; **prendere in ~ qn** (fig) to take sb for a ride; **a stretto ~ di posta** by return of post; **nel ~ di un mese** in a month's time; **essere nel ~** (fig) to belong to a circle (of friends); **~ d'affari** (Comm) turnover; **~ di parole** circumlocution; **~ di prova** (Aut) test drive; **~ turistico** sightseeing tour; **giro'collo** sm: **a girocollo** crewneck cpd

gironzo'lare [dʒirondzo'lare] /72/ vi to stroll about

'**gita** ['dʒita] sf excursion, trip; **fare una ~** to go for a trip, go on an outing

gi'tano, -a [dʒi'tano] sm/f gipsy

giù [dʒu] av down; (dabbasso) downstairs; **in ~** downwards, down; **~ di lì** (pressappoco) thereabouts; **bambini dai 6 anni in ~** children aged 6 and under; **~ per: cadere ~ per le scale** to fall down the stairs; **essere ~** (fig: di salute) to be run down; (: di spirito) to be depressed

giub'botto [dʒub'bɔtto] sm jerkin; **~ antiproiettile** bulletproof vest; **~ salvagente** life jacket

giudi'care [dʒudi'kare] /20/ vt to judge; (accusato) to try; (lite) to arbitrate in; **~ qn/qc bello** to consider sb/sth (to be) beautiful

gi'udice ['dʒuditʃe] sm judge; **~ conciliatore** justice of the peace; **~ istruttore** examining (BRIT) committing (US) magistrate; **~ popolare** member of a jury

giu'dizio [dʒu'dittsjo] sm judgment; (opinione) opinion; (Dir) judgment, sentence; (: processo) trial; (: verdetto) verdict; **aver ~** to be wise o prudent; **citare in ~** to summons

gi'ugno ['dʒuɲɲo] sm June

gi'ungere ['dʒundʒere] /5/ vi to arrive ▷ vt (mani ecc) to join; **~ a** to arrive at, reach

gi'ungla ['dʒungla] sf jungle

gi'unsi ecc ['dʒunsi] vb vedi giungere

giura'mento [dʒura'mento] sm oath; **~ falso** perjury

giu'rare [dʒu'rare] /72/ vt to swear ▷ vi to swear, take an oath

giu'ria [dʒu'ria] sf jury

giu'ridico, -a, -ci, -che [dʒu'ridiko] ag legal

giustifi'care [dʒustifi'kare] /20/ vt to justify; **giustificazi'one** sf justification; (Ins) (note of) excuse

gius'tizia [dʒus'tittsja] sf justice; **giustizi'are** /19/ vt to execute, put to death

gi'usto, -a [dʒusto] ag (equo) fair, just; (vero) true, correct; (adatto) right, suitable; (preciso) exact, correct ▷ av (esattamente) exactly, precisely; (per l'appunto, appena) just; **arrivare ~** to arrive just in time; **ho ~ bisogno di te** you're just the person I need

glaci'ale [gla'tʃale] ag glacial

gli [ʎi] det mpl (davV, s impura, gn, pn, ps, x, z) the ▷ pron (a lui) to him; (a esso) to it; (in coppia con lo, la, li, le, ne, a lui, a lei, a loro ecc): **~ele do** I'm giving them to him (o her o them); vedi anche **il**

glo'bale ag overall

'globo sm globe

'globulo sm (Anat): **~ rosso/bianco** red/white corpuscle

glocalizzazi'one [glokaliddza'tsjone] sf glocalization

'gloria sf glory

'gnocchi ['ɲɔkki] smpl (Cuc) small dumplings made of semolina pasta or potato

'gobba sf (Anat) hump; (protuberanza) bump

'gobbo, -a ag hunchbacked; (ricurvo) round-shouldered ▷ sm/f hunchback

'goccia, -ce ['gɔttʃa] sf drop; **goccio'lare** /72/ vi, vt to drip

go'dere /58/ vi: **~ (di)** (compiacersi) to be delighted (at), rejoice (at); **~ di** (trarre vantaggio) to benefit from ▷ vt to enjoy; **godersi la vita** to enjoy life; **godersela** to have a good time, enjoy o.s.

godrò ecc vb vedi godere

'goffo, -a ag clumsy, awkward

gol [gɔl] sm inv (Sport); = **goal**

'gola sf (Anat) throat; (golosità) gluttony, greed; (di camino) flue; (di monte) gorge; **fare ~** (anche fig) to tempt

golf sm inv (Sport) golf; (maglia) cardigan

'golfo sm gulf

go'loso, -a ag greedy

gomi'tata sf: **dare una ~ a qn** to elbow sb; **farsi avanti a (forza o furia di) gomitate** to elbow one's way through; **fare a gomitate per qc** to fight to get sth

'gomito sm elbow; (di strada ecc) sharp bend

go'mitolo sm ball

'gomma sf rubber; (per cancellare) rubber, eraser; (di veicolo) tyre (BRIT), tire (US); **~ da masticare** chewing gum; **~ a terra** flat tyre; **gom'mone** sm rubber dinghy

gonfi'are /19/ vt (pallone) to blow up, inflate; (dilatare, ingrossare) to swell; (fig: notizia) to exaggerate; **gonfiarsi** vpr to swell; (fiume) to rise; **'gonfio, -a** ag swollen; (stomaco) bloated; (vela) full; **gonfi'ore** sm swelling

'gonna sf skirt; **~ pantalone** culottes pl

goo'glare [gu'glare] /72/ vt (Inform) to google

'gorgo, -ghi sm whirlpool

gorgogli'are [gorgoʎ'ʎare] /27/ vi to gurgle

go'rilla sm inv gorilla; (guardia del corpo) bodyguard

'gotico, -a, -ci, -che ag, sm Gothic

'gotta sf gout

gover'nare /72/ vt (stato) to govern, rule; (pilotare, guidare) to steer; (bestiame) to tend, look after

go'verno sm government

GPL [dʒipi'elle] sigla m (= Gas di Petrolio Liquefatto) LPG

GPS [dʒipi'esse] sigla m GPS

graci'dare [gratʃi'dare] /72/ vi to croak

'gracile ['gratʃile] ag frail, delicate

gradazi'one [gradat'tsjone] sf (sfumatura) gradation; **~ alcolica** alcoholic content, strength

gra'devole ag pleasant, agreeable

gradi'nata sf flight of steps; (in teatro, stadio) tiers pl

gra'dino sm step; (Alpinismo) foothold

gra'dire /55/ vt (accettare con piacere) to accept; (desiderare) to wish, like; **gradisce una tazza di tè?** would you like a cup of tea?

'grado sm (Mat, Fisica: ecc) degree; (stadio) degree, level; (Mil, sociale) rank; **essere in ~ di fare** to be in a position to do

gradu'ale ag gradual

graf'fetta sf paper clip

graffi'are /19/ vt to scratch; **graffiarsi** vpr to get scratched; (con unghie) to scratch o.s.

'graffio sm scratch

gra'fia sf spelling; (scrittura) handwriting

'grafico, -a, -ci, -che ag graphic ▷ sm graph; (persona) graphic designer

gram'matica, -che sf grammar

'grammo sm gram(me)

'grana sf (granello, di minerali, corpi spezzati) grain; (fam: seccatura) trouble; (: soldi) cash ▷ sm inv cheese similar to Parmesan

gra'naio sm granary, barn

gra'nata sf (proiettile) grenade

Gran Bre'tagna [granbre'taɲɲa] sf: **la ~** Great Britain

'granchio ['grankjo] sm crab; (fig) blunder; **prendere un ~** (fig) to blunder

'grande (qualche volta **gran** + C, **grand'** + V) ag (grosso, largo, vasto) big, large; (alto) tall; (lungo) long; (in sensi astratti) great ▷ smf (persona adulta) adult, grown-up; (chi ha ingegno e potenza) great man/woman; **fare le cose in ~** to do things in style; **una gran bella donna** a very beautiful woman; **non**

è una gran cosa o **un gran che** it's nothing special; **non ne so gran che** I don't know very much about it

gran'dezza [gran'dettsa] *sf* (*dimensione*) size; magnitude; (*fig*) greatness; **in ~ naturale** lifesize

grandi'nare /72/ *vb impers* to hail

'**grandine** *sf* hail

gra'nello *sm* (*di cereali, uva*) seed; (*di frutta*) pip; (*di sabbia, sale ecc*) grain

gra'nito *sm* granite

'**grano** *sm* (*in quasi tutti i sensi*) grain; (*frumento*) wheat; (*di rosario, collana*) bead; **~ di pepe** peppercorn

gran'turco *sm* maize

'**grappa** *sf* rough, strong brandy

'**grappolo** *sm* bunch, cluster

gras'setto *sm* (*Tip*) bold (type)

'**grasso, -a** *ag* fat; (*cibo*) fatty; (*pelle*) greasy; (*terreno*) rich; (*fig: guadagno, annata*) plentiful ▷ *sm* (*di persona, animale*) fat; (*sostanza che unge*) grease

'**grata** *sf* grating

gra'ticola *sf* grill

'**gratis** *av* free, for nothing

grati'tudine *sf* gratitude

'**grato, -a** *ag* grateful; (*gradito*) pleasant, agreeable

gratta'capo *sm* worry, headache

gratta'cielo [gratta'tʃɛlo] *sm* skyscraper

gratta e 'sosta *sm inv* scratch card used to pay for parking

gratta e 'vinci [grattae'vintʃi] *sm* (*lotteria*) lottery; (*biglietto*) scratchcard

grat'tare /72/ *vt* (*pelle*) to scratch; (*raschiare*) to scrape; (*pane, formaggio, carote*) to grate; (*fam: rubare*) to pinch ▷ *vi* (*stridere*) to grate; (*Aut*) to grind; **grattarsi** *vpr* to scratch o.s.; **grattarsi la pancia** (*fig*) to twiddle one's thumbs

grat'tugia [grat'tudʒa], **-gie** *sf* grater; **grattugi'are** /62/ *vt* to grate; **pane grattugiato** breadcrumbs *pl*

gra'tuito, -a *ag* free; (*fig*) gratuitous

'**grave** *ag* (*danno, pericolo, peccato ecc*) grave, serious; (*responsabilità*) heavy, grave; (*contegno*) grave, solemn; (*voce, suono*) deep, low-pitched; (*Ling*): **accento ~** grave accent; **un malato ~** a person who is seriously ill

grave'mente *av* (*ammalato, ferito*) seriously

gravi'danza [gravi'dantsa] *sf* pregnancy

gravità *sf* seriousness; (*anche Fisica*) gravity

gra'voso, -a *ag* heavy, onerous

'**grazia** ['grattsja] *sf* grace; (*favore*) favour; (*Dir*) pardon

'**grazie** ['grattsje] *escl* thank you!; **~ mille!** o **tante!** o **infinite!** thank you very much!; **~ a** thanks to

grazi'oso, -a [grat'tsjoso] *ag* charming, delightful; (*gentile*) gracious

'**Grecia** ['grɛtʃa] *sf*: **la ~** Greece; '**greco, -a, -ci, -che** *ag, sm/f, sm* Greek

'**gregge** ['greddʒe] (*pl f* **greggi**) *sm* flock

'**greggio, -a, -gi, -ge** ['greddʒo] *ag* raw, unrefined; (*diamante*) rough, uncut; (*tessuto*) unbleached

grembi'ule *sm* apron; (*sopravveste*) overall

'**grembo** *sm* lap; (*ventre della madre*) womb

'**grezzo, -a** ['greddzo] *ag* = **greggio**

gri'dare /72/ *vi* (*per chiamare*) to shout, cry (out); (*strillare*) to scream, yell ▷ *vt* to shout (out), yell (out); **~ aiuto** to cry o shout for help

'**grido** (*pl f* **grida**) *sm* shout, cry; scream, yell; (*di animale*) (*pl m* **gridi**) cry; **di ~** famous

'**grigio** ['gridʒo], **-a, -gi, -gie** *ag, sm* grey

'**griglia** ['griʎʎa] *sf* (*per arrostire*) grill; (*Elettr*) grid; (*inferriata*) grating; **alla ~** (*Cuc*) grilled

gril'letto *sm* trigger

'grillo sm (Zool) cricket; (fig) whim

'grinta sf grim expression; (Sport) fighting spirit

gris'sino sm bread-stick

Groen'landia sf: **la ~** Greenland

gron'daia sf gutter

gron'dare /72/ vi to pour; (essere bagnato): **~ di** to be dripping with ▷ vt to drip with

'groppa sf (di animale) back, rump; (fam: dell'uomo) back, shoulders pl

gros'sezza [gros'settsa] sf size; thickness

gros'sista, -i, -e smf (Comm) wholesaler

'grosso, -a ag big, large; (di spessore) thick; (grossolano: anche fig) coarse; (grave, insopportabile) serious, great; (tempo, mare) rough ▷ sm: **il ~ di** the bulk of; **un pezzo ~** (fig) a VIP, a bigwig; **farla grossa** to do something very stupid; **dirle grosse** to tell tall stories (BRIT) o tales (US); **sbagliarsi di ~** to be completely wrong

'grotta sf cave; grotto

grot'tesco, -a, -schi, -sche ag grotesque

gro'viglio [gro'viʎʎo] sm tangle; (fig) muddle

gru sf inv crane

'gruccia, -ce ['gruttʃa] sf (per camminare) crutch; (per abiti) coat-hanger

'grumo sm (di sangue) clot; (di farina ecc) lump

'gruppo sm group; **~ sanguigno** blood group

GSM sigla m (= Global System for Mobile Communication) GSM

guada'gnare [gwadaɲ'ɲare] /15/ vt (ottenere) to gain; (soldi, stipendio) to earn; (vincere) to win; (raggiungere) to reach

gua'dagno [gwa'daɲɲo] sm earnings pl; (Comm) profit; (vantaggio, utile) advantage, gain; **~ lordo/netto** gross/net earnings pl

gu'ado sm ford; **passare a ~** to ford

gu'ai escl: **~ a te** (o **lui** ecc)! woe betide you (o him ecc)!

gu'aio sm trouble, mishap; (inconveniente) trouble, snag

gua'ire /55/ vi to whine, yelp

gu'ancia, -ce ['gwantʃa] sf cheek

guanci'ale [gwan'tʃale] sm pillow

gu'anto sm glove

guarda'linee sm inv (Sport) linesman

guar'dare /72/ vt (con lo sguardo: osservare) to look at; (: film, televisione) to watch; (custodire) to look after, take care of ▷ vi to look; (badare): **~ a** to pay attention to; (luoghi: esser orientato): **~ a** to face; **guardarsi** vpr to look at o.s.; **guardarsi da** (astenersi) to refrain from; (stare in guardia) to beware of; **guardarsi dal fare** to take care not to do; **guarda di non sbagliare** try not to make a mistake; **~ a vista qn** to keep a close watch on sb

guarda'roba sm inv wardrobe; (locale) cloakroom

gu'ardia sf (individuo, corpo) guard; (sorveglianza) watch; **fare la ~ a qc/qn** to guard sth/sb; **stare in ~** (fig) to be on one's guard; **il medico di ~** the doctor on call; **~ carceraria** (prison) warder (BRIT) o guard (US); **~ del corpo** bodyguard; **~ di finanza** (corpo) customs pl; (persona) customs officer; **~ medica** emergency doctor service

● **GUARDIA DI FINANZA**
●
● The Guardia di Finanza is a
● military body which deals with
● infringements of the laws
● governing income tax and
● monopolies. It reports to the
● Ministers of Finance, Justice or
● Agriculture, depending on the
● function it is performing.

guardi'ano, -a *sm/f (di carcere)*
warder; *(di villa ecc)* caretaker; *(di
museo)* custodian; *(di zoo)* keeper;
~ notturno night watchman

guarigi'one [gwari'dʒone] *sf*
recovery

gua'rire /55/ *vt (persona, malattia)* to
cure; *(ferita)* to heal ▷ *vi* to recover, be
cured; to heal (up)

guar'nire /55/ *vt (ornare: abiti)* to
trim; *(Cuc)* to garnish

guasta'feste *smf inv* spoilsport

guas'tare /72/ *vt* to spoil; **guastarsi**
vpr (cibo) to go bad; *(meccanismo)* to
break down; *(tempo)* to change for
the worse

gu'asto, -a *ag (non funzionante)*
broken; (: *telefono ecc)* out of order;
(andato a male) bad, rotten; (: *dente)*
decayed, bad; *(fig: corrotto)* depraved
▷ *sm* breakdown; *(avaria)* failure; **~ al
motore** engine failure

gu'erra *sf* war; *(tecnica: atomica,
chimica ecc)* warfare; **fare la ~ (a)**
to wage war (against); **~ mondiale**
world war; **~ preventiva** preventive
war

'gufo *sm* owl

gu'ida *sf (persona)* guide; *(libro)*
guide(book); *(comando, direzione)*
guidance, direction; *(Aut)* driving;
(tappeto: di tenda, cassetto) runner;
~ a destra/sinistra *(Aut)* right-/left-
hand drive; **~ telefonica** telephone
directory; **~ turistica** tourist guide

gui'dare /72/ *vt* to guide; *(squadra,
rivolta)* to lead; *(auto)* to drive; *(aereo,
nave)* to pilot; **sa ~?** can you drive?;
guida'tore, -'trice *sm/f (conducente)*
driver

guin'zaglio [gwin'tsaʎʎo] *sm*
leash, lead

'guscio ['guʃʃo] *sm* shell

gus'tare /72/ *vt (cibi)* to taste;
(: *assaporare con piacere)* to enjoy,
savour; *(fig)* to enjoy, appreciate ▷ *vi*:
~ a to please; **non mi gusta affatto** I
don't like it at all

'gusto *sm* taste; *(sapore)* taste, flavour
(BRIT), flavor (US); *(godimento)*
enjoyment; **al ~ di fragola**
strawberry-flavoured; **mangiare
di ~** to eat heartily; **prenderci ~: ci
ha preso ~** he's acquired a taste for
it, he's got to like it; **gus'toso, -a** *ag*
tasty; *(fig)* agreeable

g

Ha'waii [a'vai] *sf pl*: **le ~** Hawaii *sg*
help [ɛlp] *sm inv* (*Inform*) help
'herpes ['ɛrpes] *sm* (*Med*) herpes *sg*:
  ~ zoster shingles *sg*
'hi-fi ['haifai] *sm inv*, *ag inv* hi-fi
ho [ɔ] *vb vedi* **avere**
'hobby ['hɔbi] *sm inv* hobby
'hockey ['hɔki] *sm* hockey; **~ su**
  ghiaccio ice hockey
'home page ['houm'pɛidʒ] *sf inv*
  home page
'Hong Kong ['ɔkɔg] *sf* Hong Kong
'hostess ['houstis] *sf inv* air hostess
  (*BRIT*) o stewardess
'hot dog ['hɔtdɔg] *sm inv* hot dog
ho'tel *sm inv* hotel
'humour ['jumor] *sm inv* (sense of)
  humour
'humus *sm* humus
'husky ['aski] *sm inv* (*cane*) husky

H, h ['akka] *sf o m inv* (*lettera*) H, h
  ▷ *abbr* (= *ora*) hr; (= *etto, altezza*) h; **H**
  come hotel ≈ H for Harry (*BRIT*), H
  for How (*US*)
ha, hai [a, ai] *vb vedi* **avere**
ha'cker ['haker] *sm inv* hacker
hall [hɔːl] *sf inv* hall, foyer
ham'burger [am'burger] *sm inv*
  (*carne*) hamburger; (*panino*) burger
'handicap ['handikap] *sm inv*
  handicap; **handicap'pato, -a** *ag*
  disabled ▷ *sm/f* person with a
  disability
'hanno ['anno] *vb vedi* **avere**
hard dis'count [ardis'kaunt] *sm inv*
  discount supermarket
hard 'disk [ar'disk] *sm inv* hard disk
'hardware ['ardwer] *sm inv*
  hardware
ha'scisc, hascisch [aʃʃiʃ] *sm*
  hashish
'hashtag ['aʃteg] *sm inv* (*su Twitter*)
  hashtag

i *det mpl* the

'ibrido, -a *ag, sm* hybrid

IC *abbr* (= Intercity) Intercity

'ICI ['itʃi] *sigla f* (= Imposta Comunale sugli Immobili) ≈ Council Tax

i'cona *sf* (Rel, Inform, fig) icon

i'dea *sf* idea; (opinione) opinion, view; (ideale) ideal; **dare l'~ di** to seem, look like; **neanche** o **neppure per ~!** certainly not!; **~ fissa** obsession

ide'ale *ag, sm* ideal

ide'are /72/ *vt* (immaginare) to think up, conceive; (progettare) to plan

i'dentico, -a, -ci, -che *ag* identical

identifi'care /20/ *vt* to identify; **identificarsi** *vpr*: **identificarsi (con)** to identify o.s. (with)

identità *sf inv* identity

ideolo'gia, -'gie [ideolo'dʒia] *sf* ideology

idio'matico, -a, -ci, -che *ag* idiomatic; **frase idiomatica** idiom

idi'ota, -i, -e *ag* idiotic ▷ *smf* idiot

'idolo *sm* idol

idoneità *sf* suitability

i'doneo, -a *ag*: **~ a** suitable for, fit for; (Mil) fit for; (qualificato) qualified for

i'drante *sm* hydrant

idra'tante *ag* moisturizing ▷ *sm* moisturizer

i'draulico, -a, -ci, -che *ag* hydraulic ▷ *sm* plumber

idroe'lettrico, -a, -ci, -che *ag* hydroelectric

i'drofilo, -a *ag*: **cotone ~** cotton wool (BRIT), absorbent cotton (US)

i'drogeno [i'drɔdʒeno] *sm* hydrogen

idrovo'lante *sm* seaplane

i'ena *sf* hyena

i'eri *av, sm* yesterday; **il giornale di ~** yesterday's paper; **~ l'altro** the day before yesterday; **~ sera** yesterday evening

igi'ene [i'dʒɛne] *sf* hygiene; **~ pubblica** public health; **igi'enico, -a, -ci, -che** *ag* hygienic; (salubre) healthy

i'gnaro, -a [iɲ'ɲaro] *ag*: **~ di** unaware of, ignorant of

i'gnobile [iɲ'ɲɔbile] *ag* despicable, vile

igno'rante [iɲɲo'rante] *ag* ignorant

igno'rare [iɲɲo'rare] /72/ *vt* (non sapere, conoscere) to be ignorant o unaware of, not to know; (fingere di non vedere, sentire) to ignore

i'gnoto, -a [iɲ'ɲɔto] *ag* unknown

○ **PAROLA CHIAVE**

il (pl(m) **i**; diventa **lo** (pl **gli**) davanti a s impura, gn, pn, ps, x, z; f **la** (pl **le**)) *det m*
1 the; **il libro/lo studente/l'acqua** the book/the student/the water; **gli scolari** the pupils
2 (astrazione): **il coraggio/l'amore/ la giovinezza** courage/love/youth
3 (tempo): **il mattino/la sera** in the morning/evening; **il venerdì** (abitualmente) on Fridays; (quel giorno) on (the) Friday; **la settimana prossima** next week

i

4 (*distributivo*) a, an; **2 euro il chilo/paio** 2 euros a o per kilo/pair
5 (*partitivo*) some, any; **hai messo lo zucchero?** have you added sugar?; **hai comprato il latte?** did you buy (some o any) milk?
6 (*possesso*): **aprire gli occhi** to open one's eyes; **rompersi la gamba** to break one's leg; **avere i capelli neri/il naso rosso** to have dark hair/a red nose
7 (*con nomi propri*): **il Petrarca** Petrarch; **il Presidente Bush** President Bush; **dov'è la Francesca?** where's Francesca?
8 (*con nomi geografici*): **il Tevere** the Tiber; **l'Italia** Italy; **il Regno Unito** the United Kingdom; **l'Everest** Everest

ille'gale *ag* illegal
illeg'gibile [illed'dʒibile] *ag* illegible
ille'gittimo, -a [ille'dʒittimo] *ag* illegitimate
il'leso, -a *ag* unhurt, unharmed
illimi'tato, -a *ag* boundless; unlimited
ill.mo *abbr* = **illustrissimo**
il'ludere /35/ *vt* to deceive, delude; **illudersi** *vpr* to deceive o.s., delude o.s.
illumi'nare /72/ *vt* to light up, illuminate; (*fig*) to enlighten; **illuminarsi** *vpr* to light up; **~ a giorno** to floodlight; **illuminazi'one** *sf* lighting; illumination; floodlighting; (*fig*) flash of inspiration
il'lusi *ecc vb vedi* **illudere**
illusi'one *sf* illusion; **farsi delle illusioni** to delude o.s.; **~ ottica** optical illusion
il'luso, -a *pp di* **illudere**
illus'trare /72/ *vt* to illustrate; **illustrazi'one** *sf* illustration
il'lustre *ag* eminent, renowned; **illus'trissimo, -a** *ag* (*negli indirizzi*) very revered
i'mam [i'mam] *sm inv* imam

imbal'laggio [imbal'laddʒo] *sm* packing *no pl*
imbal'lare /72/ *vt* to pack; (*Aut*) to race
imbalsa'mare /72/ *vt* to embalm
imbambo'lato, -a *ag* (*sguardo, espressione*) vacant, blank
imbaraz'zante [imbarat'tsante] *ag* embarrassing, awkward
imbaraz'zare [imbarat'tsare] /72/ *vt* (*mettere a disagio*) to embarrass; (*ostacolare: movimenti*) to hamper
imbaraz'zato, -a [imbarat'tsato] *ag* embarrassed; **avere lo stomaco ~** to have an upset stomach
imba'razzo [imba'rattso] *sm* (*disagio*) embarrassment; (*perplessità*) puzzlement, bewilderment; **~ di stomaco** indigestion
imbar'care /20/ *vt* (*passeggeri*) to embark; (*merci*) to load; **imbarcarsi** *vpr*: **imbarcarsi su** to board; **imbarcarsi per l'America** to sail for America; **imbarcarsi in** (*fig: affare*) to embark on
imbarcazi'one [imbarkat'tsjone] *sf* (*small*) boat, (*small*) craft *inv*; **~ di salvataggio** lifeboat
im'barco, -chi *sm* embarkation; loading; boarding; (*banchina*) landing stage
imbas'tire /55/ *vt* (*cucire*) to tack; (*fig: abbozzare*) to sketch, outline
im'battersi /72/ *vpr*: **~ in** (*incontrare*) to bump o run into
imbat'tibile *ag* unbeatable, invincible
imbavagli'are [imbavaʎ'ʎare] /27/ *vt* to gag
imbe'cille [imbe'tʃille] *ag* idiotic ▷ *smf* idiot; (*Med*) imbecile
imbian'care /20/ *vt* to whiten; (*muro*) to whitewash ▷ *vi* to become o turn white
imbian'chino [imbjan'kino] *sm* (*house*) painter, painter and decorator
imboc'care /20/ *vt* (*bambino*) to feed; (*entrare: strada*) to enter, turn into

imbocca'tura sf mouth; (di strada, porto) entrance; (Mus, del morso) mouthpiece

imbos'cata sf ambush

imbottigli'are [imbottiʎ'ʎare] /27/ vt to bottle; (Naut) to blockade; (Mil) to hem in; **imbottigliarsi** vpr to be stuck in a traffic jam

imbot'tire /55/ vt to stuff; (giacca) to pad; **imbottirsi** vpr (rimpinzarsi): **imbottirsi di** to stuff o.s. with; **imbot'tito, -a** ag stuffed; (giacca) padded; **panino imbottito** filled roll

imbra'nato, -a ag clumsy, awkward ▷ sm/f clumsy person

imbrogli'are [imbroʎ'ʎare] /27/ vt to mix up; (fig: raggirare) to deceive, cheat; (: confondere) to confuse, mix up; **imbrogli'one, -a** sm/f cheat, swindler

imbronci'ato, -a ag sulky

imbu'care /20/ vt to post

imbur'rare /72/ vt to butter

im'buto sm funnel

imi'tare /72/ vt to imitate; (riprodurre) to copy; (assomigliare) to look like

immagazzi'nare [immagaddzi'nare] /72/ vt to store

immagi'nare [immadʒi'nare] /72/ vt to imagine; (supporre) to suppose; (inventare) to invent; **s'immagini!** don't mention it!, not at all!; **immaginazi'one** sf imagination; (cosa immaginata) fancy

im'magine [im'madʒine] sf image; (rappresentazione grafica, mentale) picture

imman'cabile ag certain; unfailing

im'mane ag (smisurato) huge; (spaventoso, inumano) terrible

immangi'abile [imman'dʒabile] ag inedible

immatrico'lare /72/ vt to register; **immatricolarsi** vpr (Ins) to matriculate, enrol

imma'turo, -a ag (frutto) unripe; (persona) immature; (prematuro) premature

immedesi'marsi /72/ vpr: ~ **in** to identify with

immediata'mente av immediately, at once

immedi'ato, -a ag immediate

im'menso, -a ag immense

im'mergere [im'mɛrdʒere] /59/ vt to immerse, plunge; **immergersi** vpr to plunge; (sommergibile) to dive, submerge; (dedicarsi a): **immergersi in** to immerse o.s. in

immeri'tato, -a ag undeserved

immersi'one sf immersion; (di sommergibile) submersion, dive; (di palombaro) dive

im'mettere /63/ vt: ~ **(in)** to introduce (into); ~ **dati in un computer** to enter data on a computer

immi'grato, -a sm/f immigrant

immi'nente ag imminent

immischi'are [immis'kjare] /19/ vt: ~ **qn in** to involve sb in; **immischiarsi** vpr: **immischiarsi in** to interfere o meddle in

im'mobile ag motionless, still; **immobili'are** ag (Dir) property cpd

immon'dizia [immon'dittsja] sf dirt, filth; (spesso al pl: spazzatura, rifiuti) rubbish no pl, refuse no pl

immo'rale ag immoral

immor'tale ag immortal

im'mune ag (esente) exempt; (Med, Dir) immune

immu'tabile ag immutable; unchanging

impacchet'tare [impakket'tare] /72/ vt to pack up

impacci'ato, -a ag awkward, clumsy; (imbarazzato) embarrassed

im'pacco, -chi sm (Med) compress

impadro'nirsi /55/ vpr: ~ **di** to seize, take possession of; (fig: apprendere a fondo) to master

impa'gabile ag priceless

impa'lato, -a ag (fig) stiff as a board

impalca'tura sf scaffolding

impalli'dire /55/ vi to turn pale; (fig) to fade

impa'nato, -a *ag* (*Cuc*) coated in breadcrumbs

impanta'narsi /72/ *vpr* to sink (in the mud); (*fig*) to get bogged down

impappi'narsi /72/ *vpr* to stammer, falter

impa'rare /72/ *vt* to learn

impar'tire /55/ *vt* to bestow, give

imparzi'ale [impar'tsjale] *ag* impartial, unbiased

impas'sibile *ag* impassive

impas'tare /72/ *vt* (*pasta*) to knead

impastic'carsi /2o/ *vpr* to pop pills

im'pasto *sm* (*l'impastare: di pane*) kneading; (: *di cemento*) mixing; (*pasta*) dough; (*anche fig*) mixture

im'patto *sm* impact

impau'rire /55/ *vt* to scare, frighten ▷ *vi* (*anche*: **impaurirsi**) to become scared o frightened

impazi'ente [impat'tsjɛnte] *ag* impatient

impaz'zata [impat'tsata] *sf*: **all'~** (*precipitosamente*) at breakneck speed

impaz'zire [impat'tsire] /55/ *vi* to go mad; **~ per qn/qc** to be crazy about sb/sth

impec'cabile *ag* impeccable

impedi'mento *sm* obstacle, hindrance

impe'dire /55/ *vt* (*vietare*): **~ a qn di fare** to prevent sb from doing; (*ostruire*) to obstruct; (*impacciare*) to hamper, hinder

impe'gnare [impeɲ'ɲare] /15/ *vt* (*obbligare*) to oblige; **impegnarsi** *vpr* (*vincolarsi*): **impegnarsi a fare** to undertake to do; (*mettersi risolutamente*): **impegnarsi in qc** to devote o.s. to sth; **impegnarsi con qn** (*accordarsi*) to come to an agreement with sb

impegna'tivo, -a *ag* binding; (*lavoro*) demanding, exacting

impe'gnato, -a *ag* (*occupato*) busy; (*fig: romanzo, autore*) committed, engagé

im'pegno [im'peɲɲo] *sm* (*obbligo*) obligation; (*promessa*) promise, pledge; (*zelo*) diligence, zeal; (*compito: d'autore*) commitment

impel'lente *ag* pressing, urgent

impen'narsi /72/ *vpr* (*cavallo*) to rear up; (*Aer*) to go into a climb; (*fig*) to bridle

impensie'rire /55/ *vt* to worry; **impensierirsi** *vpr* to worry

impera'tivo, -a *ag*, *sm* imperative

impera'tore, -'trice *sm/f* emperor (empress)

imperdo'nabile *ag* unforgivable, unpardonable

imper'fetto, -a *ag* imperfect ▷ *sm* (*Ling*) imperfect (tense)

imperi'ale *ag* imperial

imperi'oso, -a *ag* (*persona*) imperious; (*motivo, esigenza*) urgent, pressing

imper'meabile *ag* waterproof ▷ *sm* raincoat

im'pero *sm* empire; (*forza, autorità*) rule, control

imperso'nale *ag* impersonal

imperso'nare /72/ *vt* to personify; (*Teat*) to play, act (the part of)

imper'territo, -a *ag* unperturbed, undaunted; impassive

imperti'nente *ag* impertinent

'impeto *sm* (*moto, forza*) force, impetus; (*assalto*) onslaught; (*fig: impulso*) impulse; (: *slancio*) transport; **con ~** energetically; vehemently

impet'tito, -a *ag* stiff, erect

impetu'oso, -a *ag* (*vento*) strong, raging; (*persona*) impetuous

impi'anto *sm* (*installazione*) installation; (*apparecchiature*) plant; (*sistema*) system; **~ elettrico** wiring; **~ di riscaldamento** heating system; **~ sportivo** sports complex; **impianti di risalita** (*Sci*) ski lifts

impic'care /2o/ *vt* to hang; **impiccarsi** *vpr* to hang o.s.

impicci'are [impit'tʃare] /14/ *vt* to hinder; **impicciarsi** *vpr* (*immischiarsi*):

impicciarsi (in) to meddle (in), interfere (in); **impicciati degli affari tuoi!** mind your own business!

impicci'one, -a [impit't͡ʃone] *sm/f* busybody

impie'gare /80/ *vt* (*usare*) to use, employ; (*spendere: denaro, tempo*) to spend; (*investire*) to invest; **impie'gato, -a** *sm/f* employee

impi'ego, -ghi *sm* (*uso*) use; (*occupazione*) employment; (*posto di lavoro*) (regular) job, post; (*Econ*) investment

impieto'sire /55/ *vt* to move to pity; **impietosirsi** *vpr* to be moved to pity

impigli'are [impiʎ'ʎare] /27/ *vt* to catch; **impigliarsi** *vpr* to get caught up *o* entangled

impi'grire /55/ *vt* to make lazy ▷ *vi* (*anche*: **impigrirsi**) to grow lazy

impli'care /20/ *vt* to imply; (*coinvolgere*) to involve; **implicarsi** *vpr*: **implicarsi (in)** to become involved (in)

im'plicito, -a [im'plit͡ʃito] *ag* implicit

implo'rare /72/ *vt* to implore; (*pietà ecc*) to beg for

impolve'rare /72/ *vt* to cover with dust; **impolverarsi** *vpr* to get dusty

im'pone *ecc vb vedi* **imporre**

impo'nente *ag* imposing, impressive

im'pongo *ecc vb vedi* **imporre**

impo'nibile *ag* taxable ▷ *sm* taxable income

impopo'lare *ag* unpopular

im'porre /77/ *vt* to impose; (*costringere*) to force, make; (*far valere*) to impose, enforce; **imporsi** *vpr* (*persona*) to assert o.s.; (*cosa: rendersi necessario*) to become necessary; (*aver successo: moda, attore*) to become popular; **~ a qn di fare** to force sb to do, make sb do

impor'tante *ag* important; **impor'tanza** *sf* importance; **dare importanza a qc** to attach importance to sth; **darsi importanza** to give o.s. airs

impor'tare /72/ *vt* (*introdurre dall'estero*) to import ▷ *vi* to matter, be important ▷ *vb impers* (*essere necessario*) to be necessary; (*interessare*) to matter; **non importa!** it doesn't matter!; **non me ne importa!** I don't care!

im'porto *sm* (*total*) amount

importu'nare /72/ *vt* to bother

im'posi *ecc vb vedi* **imporre**

imposizi'one [impozit'tsjone] *sf* imposition; (*ordine*) order, command; (*onere, imposta*) tax

imposses'sarsi /72/ *vpr*: **~ di** to seize, take possession of

impos'sibile *ag* impossible; **fare l'~** to do one's utmost, do all one can

im'posta *sf* (*di finestra*) shutter; (*tassa*) tax; **~ sul reddito** income tax; **~ sul valore aggiunto** value added tax (*BRIT*), sales tax (*US*)

impos'tare /72/ *vt* (*imbucare*) to post; (*resoconto, rapporto*) to plan; (*problema*) to set out; (*avviare*) to begin, start off; **~ la voce** (*Mus*) to pitch one's voice

impostazi'one [impostat'tsjone] *sf* (*di lettera*) posting (*BRIT*), mailing (*US*); (*di problema, questione*) formulation, statement; (*di lavoro*) organization, planning; (*di attività*) setting up; (*Mus: di voce*) pitch; **impostazioni** *sfpl* (*di computer*) settings

impo'tente *ag* weak, powerless; (*anche Med*) impotent

imprati'cabile *ag* (*strada*) impassable; (*campo da gioco*) unplayable

impre'care /20/ *vi* to curse, swear; **~ contro** to hurl abuse at

imprecazi'one [imprekat'tsjone] *sf* abuse, curse

impre'gnare [impreɲ'ɲare] /15/ *vt*: **~ (di)** (*imbevere*) to soak *o* impregnate (with); (*riempire*) to fill (with)

imprendi'tore *sm* (*industriale*) entrepreneur; (*appaltatore*) contractor; **piccolo ~** small businessman

im'presa sf (iniziativa) enterprise; (azione) exploit; (azienda) firm, concern

impressio'nante ag impressive; upsetting

impressio'nare /72/ vt to impress; (turbare) to upset; (Fot) to expose; **impressionarsi** vpr to be easily upset

impressi'one sf impression; (fig: sensazione) sensation, feeling; (stampa) printing; **fare ~** (colpire) to impress; (turbare) to frighten, upset; **fare buona/cattiva ~ a** to make a good/bad impression on

impreve'dibile ag unforeseeable; (persona) unpredictable

impre'visto, -a ag unexpected, unforeseen ▷ sm unforeseen event; **salvo imprevisti** unless anything unexpected happens

imprigio'nare [impridʒo'nare] /72/ vt to imprison

impro'babile ag improbable, unlikely

im'pronta sf imprint, impression, sign; (di piede, mano) print; (fig) mark, stamp; **~ di carbonio** carbon footprint; **~ digitale** fingerprint

improvvisa'mente av suddenly; unexpectedly

improvvi'sare /72/ vt to improvise

improv'viso, -a ag (imprevisto) unexpected; (subitaneo) sudden; **all'~** unexpectedly; suddenly

impru'dente ag unwise, rash

impu'gnare [impuɲ'ɲare] /15/ vt to grasp, grip; (Dir) to contest

impul'sivo, -a ag impulsive

im'pulso sm impulse

impun'tarsi /72/ vpr to stop dead, refuse to budge; (fig) to be obstinate

impu'tato, -a sm/f (Dir) accused, defendant

PAROLA CHIAVE

in (in + il = **nel**, in + lo = **nello**, in + l' = **nell'**, in + la = **nella**, in + i = **nei**, in + gli = **negli**, in + le = **nelle**) prep **1** (stato in luogo) in; **vivere in Italia/città** to live in Italy/town; **essere in casa/ ufficio** to be at home/the office; **se fossi in te** if I were you

2 (moto a luogo) to; (: dentro) into; **andare in Germania/città** to go to Germany/town; **andare in ufficio** to go to the office; **entrare in macchina/casa** to get into the car/ go into the house

3 (tempo) in; **nel 1989** in 1989; **in giugno/estate** in June/summer

4 (modo, maniera) in; **in silenzio** in silence; **in abito da sera** in evening dress; **in guerra** at war; **in vacanza** on holiday; **Maria Bianchi in Rossi** Maria Rossi née Bianchi

5 (mezzo) by; **viaggiare in autobus/ treno** to travel by bus/train

6 (materia) made of; **in marmo** made of marble, marble cpd; **una collana in oro** a gold necklace

7 (misura) in; **siamo in quattro** there are four of us; **in tutto** in all

8 (fine): **dare in dono** to give as a gift; **spende tutto in alcool** he spends all his money on drink; **in onore di** in honour of

inabi'tabile ag uninhabitable

inacces'sibile [inattʃes'sibile] ag (luogo) inaccessible; (persona) unapproachable

inaccet'tabile [inattʃet'tabile] ag unacceptable

ina'datto, -a ag: **~ (a)** unsuitable o unfit (for)

inadegu'ato, -a ag inadequate

inaffi'dabile ag unreliable

inami'dato, -a ag starched

inar'care /20/ vt (schiena) to arch; (sopracciglia) to raise

inaspet'tato, -a ag unexpected

inas'prire /55/ vt (disciplina) to tighten up, make harsher; (carattere) to embitter; **inasprirsi** vpr to become harsher; to become bitter; to become worse

inattac'cabile *ag (anche fig)* unassailable; *(alibi)* cast-iron

inatten'dibile *ag* unreliable

inat'teso, -a *ag* unexpected

inattu'abile *ag* impracticable

inau'dito, -a *ag* unheard of

inaugu'rare /72/ *vt* to inaugurate, open; *(monumento)* to unveil

inaugurazi'one [inaugurat'tsjone] *sf* inauguration; unveiling

incal'lito, -a *ag* calloused; *(fig)* hardened, inveterate; (: *insensibile)* hard

incande'scente [inkandeʃʃɛnte] *ag* incandescent, white-hot

incan'tare /72/ *vt* to enchant, bewitch; **incantarsi** *vpr (rimanere intontito)* to be spellbound; to be in a daze; *(meccanismo: bloccarsi)* to jam; **incan'tevole** *ag* charming, enchanting

in'canto *sm* spell, charm, enchantment; *(asta)* auction; **come per ~** as if by magic; **mettere all'~** to put up for auction

inca'pace [inka'patʃe] *ag* incapable

incarce'rare [inkartʃe'rare] /72/ *vt* to imprison

incari'care /20/ *vt*: **~ qn di fare** to give sb the responsibility of doing; **incaricarsi** *vpr*: **incaricarsi di** to take care o charge of

in'carico, -chi *sm* task, job

incarta'mento *sm* dossier, file

incar'tare /72/ *vt* to wrap (in paper)

incas'sare /72/ *vt (merce)* to pack (in cases); *(gemma: incastonare)* to set; *(Econ: riscuotere)* to collect; *(Pugilato: colpi)* to take, stand up to; **in'casso** *sm* cashing, encashment; *(introito)* takings *pl*

incas'trare /72/ *vt* to fit in, insert; *(fig: intrappolare)* to catch; **incastrarsi** *vpr (combaciare)* to fit together; *(restare bloccato)* to become stuck

incate'nare /72/ *vt* to chain up

in'cauto, -a *ag* imprudent, rash

inca'vato, -a *ag* hollow; *(occhi)* sunken

incendi'are [intʃen'djare] /19/ *vt* to set fire to; **incendiarsi** *vpr* to catch fire, burst into flames

in'cendio [in'tʃɛndjo] *sm* fire

inceneri'tore [intʃeneri'tore] *sm* incinerator

in'censo [in'tʃɛnso] *sm* incense

incensu'rato, -a [intʃensu'rato] *ag* *(Dir)*: **essere ~** to have a clean record

incenti'vare [intʃenti'vare] /72/ *vt (produzione, vendite)* to boost; *(persona)* to motivate

incen'tivo [intʃen'tivo] *sm* incentive

incep'pare [intʃep'pare] /72/ *vt* to obstruct; **incepparsi** *vpr* to jam

incer'tezza [intʃer'tettsa] *sf* uncertainty

in'certo, -a [in'tʃɛrto] *ag* uncertain; *(irresoluto)* undecided, hesitating ▷ *sm* uncertainty

in'cetta [in'tʃetta] *sf* buying up; **fare ~ di qc** to buy up sth

inchi'esta [in'kjɛsta] *sf* investigation, inquiry

inchi'nare [inki'nare] /72/ *vt* to bow; **inchinarsi** *vpr* to bend down; *(per riverenza)* to bow; (: *donna)* to curtsy

inchio'dare [inkjo'dare] /72/ *vt* to nail (down); **~ la macchina** *(Aut)* to jam on the brakes

inchi'ostro [in'kjɔstro] *sm* ink; **~ simpatico** invisible ink

inciam'pare [intʃam'pare] /72/ *vi* to trip, stumble

inci'dente [intʃi'dɛnte] *sm* accident; **~ automobilistico** *o* **d'auto** car accident; **~ diplomatico** diplomatic incident

in'cidere [in'tʃidere] /34/ *vi*: **~ su** to bear upon, affect ▷ *vt (tagliare incavando)* to cut into; *(Arte)* to engrave; to etch; *(canzone)* to record

in'cinta [in'tʃinta] *ag f* pregnant

incipri'are [intʃi'prjare] /19/ vt to powder; **incipriarsi** vpr to powder one's face

in'circa [in'tʃirka] av: **all'~** more or less, very nearly

in'cisi ecc [in'tʃizi] vb vedi **incidere**

incisi'one [intʃi'zjone] sf cut; (disegno) engraving; etching; (registrazione) recording; (Med) incision

in'ciso, -a [in'tʃizo] pp di **incidere** ▷ sm: **per ~** incidentally, by the way

inci'tare [intʃi'tare] /72/ vt to incite

inci'vile [intʃi'vile] ag uncivilized; (villano) impolite

incl. abbr (= incluso) encl.

incli'nare /72/ vt to tilt; **inclinarsi** vpr (barca) to list; (aereo) to bank

in'cludere /3/ vt to include; (accludere) to enclose; **in'cluso, -a** pp di **includere** ▷ ag included; enclosed

incoe'rente ag incoherent; (contraddittorio) inconsistent

in'cognito, -a [in'kɔɲɲito] ag unknown ▷ sm: **in ~** incognito ▷ sf (Mat, fig) unknown quantity

incol'lare /72/ vt to glue, gum; (unire con colla) to stick together

inco'lore ag colourless

incol'pare /72/ vt: **~ qn di** to charge sb with

in'colto, -a ag (terreno) uncultivated; (trascurato: capelli) neglected; (persona) uneducated

in'colume ag safe and sound, unhurt

incom'benza [inkom'bɛntsa] sf duty, task

in'combere /29/ vi (sovrastare minacciando): **~ su** to threaten, hang over

incominci'are [inkomin'tʃare] /14/ vi, vt to begin, start

incompe'tente ag incompetent

incompi'uto, -a ag unfinished, incomplete

incom'pleto, -a ag incomplete

incompren'sibile ag incomprehensible

inconce'pibile [inkontʃe'pibile] ag inconceivable

inconcili'abile [inkontʃi'ljabile] ag irreconcilable

inconclu'dente ag inconclusive; (persona) ineffectual

incondizio'nato, -a [inkondittsjo'nato] ag unconditional

inconfon'dibile ag unmistakable

inconsa'pevole ag: **~ di** unaware of, ignorant of

in'conscio, -a, -sci, -sce [in'kɔnʃo] ag unconscious ▷ sm (Psic): **l'~** the unconscious

inconsis'tente ag insubstantial; (dubbio) unfounded

inconsu'eto, -a ag unusual

incon'trare /72/ vt to meet; (difficoltà) to meet with; **incontrarsi** vpr to meet

in'contro av: **~ a** (verso) towards ▷ sm meeting; (Sport) match; meeting; **~ di calcio** football match

inconveni'ente sm drawback, snag

incoraggia'mento [inkoraddʒa'mento] sm encouragement

incoraggi'are [inkorad'dʒare] /62/ vt to encourage

incornici'are [inkorni'tʃare] /14/ vt to frame

incoro'nare /72/ vt to crown

in'correre /28/ vi: **~ in** to meet with, run into

incosci'ente [inkoʃ'ʃente] ag (inconscio) unconscious; (irresponsabile) reckless, thoughtless

incre'dibile ag incredible, unbelievable

in'credulo, -a ag incredulous, disbelieving

incremen'tare /72/ vt to increase; (dar sviluppo a) to promote

incre'mento sm (sviluppo) development; (aumento numerico) increase, growth

incresci'oso, -a [inkreʃʃoso] *ag*
(*incidente ecc*) regrettable
incrimi'nare /72/ *vt* (*Dir*) to charge
incri'nare /72/ *vt* (*fig:
rapporti, amicizia*) to cause to
deteriorate; **incrinarsi** *vpr* to crack;
to deteriorate
incroci'are [inkro'tʃare] /14/ *vt* to
cross; (*incontrare*) to meet ▷ *vi* (*Naut,
Aer*) to cruise; **incrociarsi** *vpr* (*strade*)
to cross, intersect; (*persone, veicoli*)
to pass each other; **~ le braccia/
le gambe** to fold one's arms/cross
one's legs
in'crocio [in'krotʃo] *sm* (*anche Ferr*)
crossing; (*di strade*) crossroads
incuba'trice [inkuba'tritʃe] *sf*
incubator
'incubo *sm* nightmare
incu'rabile *ag* incurable
incu'rante *ag*: **~ (di)** heedless (of),
careless (of)
incurio'sire /55/ *vt* to make curious;
incuriosirsi *vpr* to become curious
incursi'one *sf* raid
incur'vare /72/ *vt* to bend, curve;
incurvarsi *vpr* to bend, curve
incusto'dito, -a *ag* unguarded,
unattended
in'cutere /40/ *vt*: **~ timore/rispetto
a qn** to strike fear into sb/command
sb's respect
'indaco *sm* indigo
indaffa'rato, -a *ag* busy
inda'gare /80/ *vt* to investigate
in'dagine [in'dadʒine] *sf*
investigation, inquiry; (*ricerca*)
research, study; **~ di mercato**
market survey
indebi'tare /72/ *vt*: **~ qn** to get sb
into debt; **indebitarsi** *vpr* to run *o*
get into debt
indebo'lire /55/ *vt, vi* (*anche:
indebolirsi*) to weaken
inde'cente [inde'tʃɛnte] *ag*
indecent
inde'ciso, -a [inde'tʃizo] *ag*
indecisive; (*irresoluto*) undecided

indefi'nito, -a *ag* (*anche Ling*)
indefinite; (*impreciso, non determinato*)
undefined
in'degno, -a [in'deɲɲo] *ag* (*atto*)
shameful; (*persona*) unworthy
indemoni'ato, -a *ag* possessed (by
the devil)
in'denne *ag* unhurt, uninjured
indenniz'zare [indennid'dzare]
/72/ *vt* to compensate
indetermina'tivo, -a *ag* (*Ling*)
indefinite
'India *sf*: **l'~** India; **indi'ano, -a** *ag*
Indian ▷ *sm/f* (*d'India*) Indian;
(*d'America*) Native American,
(*American*) Indian
indi'care /20/ *vt* (*mostrare*) to show,
indicate; (*: col dito*) to point to,
point out; (*consigliare*) to suggest,
recommend; **indica'tivo, -a** *ag*
indicative ▷ *sm* (*Ling*) indicative
(*mood*); **indicazi'one** *sf* indication;
(*informazione*) piece of information
'indice ['inditʃe] *sm* (*Anat: dito*) index
finger, forefinger; (*fig*) sign; (*nei libri*)
index; **~ di gradimento** (*Radio, TV*)
popularity rating
indicherò *ecc* [indike'rɔ] *vb vedi*
indicare
indi'cibile [indi'tʃibile] *ag*
inexpressible
indietreggi'are [indjetred'dʒare]
/62/ *vi* to draw back, retreat
indi'etro *av* back; (*guardare*) behind,
back; (*andare, cadere: anche:* **all'~**)
backwards; **rimanere ~** to be left
behind; **essere ~** (*col lavoro*) to
be behind; (*orologio*) to be slow;
rimandare qc ~ to send sth back
indi'feso, -a *ag* (*città, confine*)
undefended; (*persona*) defenceless
indiffe'rente *ag* indifferent
in'digeno, -a [in'didʒeno] *ag*
indigenous, native ▷ *sm/f* native
indigesti'one [indidʒes'tjone] *sf*
indigestion
indi'gesto, -a [indi'dʒɛsto] *ag*
indigestible

indi'gnare [indiɲˈɲare] /15/ vt to fill with indignation; **indignarsi** vpr to be (o get) indignant

indimenti'cabile ag unforgettable

indipen'dente ag independent

in'dire /38/ vt (concorso) to announce; (elezioni) to call

indi'retto, -a ag indirect

indiriz'zare [indirit'tsare] /72/ vt (dirigere) to direct; (mandare) to send; (lettera) to address

indi'rizzo [indi'rittso] sm address; (direzione) direction; (avvio) trend, course

indis'creto, -a ag indiscreet

indis'cusso, -a ag unquestioned

indispen'sabile ag indispensable, essential

indispet'tire /55/ vt to irritate, annoy ▷ vi (anche: **indispettirsi**) to get irritated o annoyed

individu'ale ag individual

individu'are /72/ vt (dar forma distinta a) to characterize; (determinare) to locate; (riconoscere) to single out

indi'viduo sm individual

indizi'ato, -a ag suspected ▷ sm/f suspect

in'dizio [in'dittsjo] sm (segno) sign, indication; (Polizia) clue; (Dir) piece of evidence

'indole sf nature, character

indolen'zito, -a [indolen'tsito] ag stiff, aching; (intorpidito) numb

indo'lore ag painless

indo'mani sm: **l'~** the next day, the following day

Indo'nesia sf: **l'~** Indonesia

indos'sare /72/ vt (mettere indosso) to put on; (avere indosso) to have on; **indossa'tore, -'trice** sm/f model

indottri'nare /72/ vt to indoctrinate

indovi'nare /72/ vt (scoprire) to guess; (immaginare) to imagine, guess; (il futuro) to foretell; **indovi'nello** sm riddle

indubbia'mente av undoubtedly

in'dubbio, -a ag certain, undoubted

in'duco ecc vb vedi **indurre**

indugi'are [indu'dʒare] /62/ vi to take one's time, delay

in'dugio [in'dudʒo] sm (ritardo) delay; **senza ~** without delay

indul'gente [indul'dʒɛnte] ag indulgent; (giudice) lenient

indu'mento sm article of clothing, garment

indu'rire /55/ vt to harden ▷ vi (anche: **indurirsi**) to harden, become hard

in'durre /90/ vt: **~ qn a fare qc** to induce o persuade sb to do sth; **~ qn in errore** to mislead sb

in'dussi ecc vb vedi **indurre**

in'dustria sf industry; **industri'ale** ag industrial ▷ sm industrialist

inecce'pibile [inettʃe'pibile] ag unexceptionable

i'nedito, -a ag unpublished

ine'rente ag: **~ a** concerning, regarding

i'nerme ag unarmed, defenceless

inerpi'carsi /72/ vpr: **~ (su)** to clamber (up)

i'nerte ag inert; (inattivo) indolent, sluggish

ine'satto, -a ag (impreciso) inexact; (erroneo) incorrect; (Amm: non riscosso) uncollected

inesis'tente ag non-existent

inesperi'enza [inespe'rjɛntsa] sf inexperience

ines'perto, -a ag inexperienced

inevi'tabile ag inevitable

i'nezia [i'nɛttsja] sf trifle, thing of no importance

infagot'tare /72/ vt to bundle up, wrap up; **infagottarsi** vpr to wrap up

infal'libile ag infallible

infa'mante ag defamatory

in'fame ag infamous; (fig: cosa, compito) awful, dreadful

infan'gare /80/ vt to cover with mud; (fig: nome, reputazione) to sully; **infangarsi** vpr to get covered in mud; to be sullied

infan'tile *ag* child *cpd*; childlike; (*adulto, azione*) childish; **letteratura ~** children's books *pl*

in'fanzia [in'fantsja] *sf* childhood; (*bambini*) children *pl*: **prima ~** babyhood, infancy

infari'nare /72/ *vt* to cover with (*o* sprinkle with *o* dip in) flour; **infarina'tura** *sf* (*fig*) smattering

in'farto *sm* (*Med*): **~ (cardiaco)** coronary

infasti'dire /55/ *vt* to annoy, irritate; **infastidirsi** *vpr* to get annoyed *o* irritated

infati'cabile *ag* tireless, untiring

in'fatti *cong* as a matter of fact, actually
> Attenzione! In inglese esiste l'espressione *in fact*, che però vuol dire *in effetti*.

infatu'arsi /72/ *vpr*: **~ di** *o* **per** to become infatuated with, fall for

infe'dele *ag* unfaithful

infe'lice [infe'litfe] *ag* unhappy; (*sfortunato*) unlucky; (*inopportuno*) inopportune, ill-timed; (*mal riuscito: lavoro*) bad, poor

inferi'ore *ag* lower; (*per intelligenza, qualità*) inferior ▷ *smf* inferior; **~ a** (*numero, quantità*) less *o* smaller than; (*meno buono*) inferior to; **~ alla media** below average; **inferiorità** *sf* inferiority

inferme'ria *sf* infirmary; (*di scuola, nave*) sick bay

infermi'ere, -a *smf* nurse

infermità *sf inv* illness; infirmity; **~ mentale** mental illness; (*Dir*) insanity

in'fermo, -a *ag* (*ammalato*) ill; (*debole*) infirm

infer'nale *ag* infernal; (*proposito, complotto*) diabolical

in'ferno *sm* hell

inferri'ata *sf* grating

infes'tare /72/ *vt* to infest

infet'tare /72/ *vt* to infect; **infettarsi** *vpr* to become infected; **infezi'one** *sf* infection

infiam'mabile *ag* inflammable

infiam'mare /72/ *vt* to set alight; (*fig, Med*) to inflame; **infiammarsi** *vpr* to catch fire; (*Med*) to become inflamed; **infiammazi'one** *sf* (*Med*) inflammation

infie'rire /55/ *vi*: **~ su** (*fisicamente*) to attack furiously; (*verbalmente*) to rage at

infi'lare /72/ *vt* (*ago*) to thread; (*mettere: chiave*) to insert; (: *vestito*) to slip *o* put on; (*strada*) to turn into, take; **infilarsi** *vpr*: **infilarsi in** to slip into; (*indossare*) to slip on; **~ un anello al dito** to slip a ring on one's finger; **~ l'uscio** to slip in; to slip out

infil'trarsi /72/ *vpr* to penetrate, seep through; (*Mil*) to infiltrate

infil'zare [infil'tsare] /72/ *vt* (*infilare*) to string together; (*trafiggere*) to pierce

'infimo, -a *ag* lowest

in'fine *av* finally; (*insomma*) in short

infinità *sf* infinity; (*in quantità*): **un'~ di** an infinite number of

infi'nito, -a *ag* infinite; (*Ling*) infinitive ▷ *sm* infinity; (*Ling*) infinitive; **all'~** (*senza fine*) endlessly

infinocchi'are [infinok'kjare] /19/ *vt* (*fam*) to hoodwink

infischi'arsi [infis'kjarsi] /19/ *vpr*: **~ di** not to care about

in'fisso *sm* fixture; (*di porta, finestra*) frame

inflazi'one [inflat'tsjone] *sf* inflation

in'fliggere [in'fliddʒere] /104/ *vt* to inflict

in'flissi *ecc vb vedi* **infliggere**

influ'ente *ag* influential; **influ'enza** *sf* influence; (*Med*) influenza, flu; **influenza aviaria** bird flu; **influenza suina** swine flu

influen'zare [influen'tsare] /72/ *vt* to influence, have an influence on

influ'ire /55/ *vi*: **~ su** to influence

in'flusso *sm* influence

infon'dato, -a *ag* unfounded, groundless

in'fondere /25/ *vt*: **~ qc in qn** to instill sth in sb

infor'mare /72/ *vt* to inform, tell; **informarsi** *vpr*: **informarsi (di** o **su)** to inquire (about)

infor'matico, -a, -ci, -che *ag* computer *cpd* ▷ *sf* computer science

informa'tivo, -a *ag* informative

infor'mato, -a *ag* informed; **tenersi ~** to keep o.s. (well-) informed

informa'tore *sm* informer

informazi'one [informat'tsjone] *sf* piece of information; **informazioni** *sfpl* information *sg*: **chiedere un'~** to ask for (some) information

in'forme *ag* shapeless

informico'larsi /72/ *vpr*: **mi si è informicolata una gamba** I've got pins and needles in my leg

infortu'nato, -a *ag* injured, hurt ▷ *sm/f* injured person

infor'tunio *sm* accident; **~ sul lavoro** industrial accident, accident at work

infra'dito *sm inv* (*calzatura*) flip flop (BRIT), thong (US)

infrazi'one [infrat'tsjone] *sf*: **~ a** breaking of, violation of

infredda'tura *sf* slight cold

infreddo'lito, -a *ag* cold, chilled

infu'ori *av out*: **all'~** outwards; **all'~ di** (*eccetto*) except, with the exception of

infuri'are /19/ *vi* to rage; **infuriarsi** *vpr* to fly into a rage

infusi'one *sf* infusion

in'fuso, -a *pp di* **infondere** ▷ *sm* infusion

Ing. *abbr* = **ingegnere**

ingaggi'are [ingad'dʒare] /62/ *vt* (*assumere con compenso*) to take on, hire; (*Sport*) to sign on; (*Mil*) to engage

ingan'nare /72/ *vt* to deceive; (*fisco*) to cheat; (*eludere*) to dodge, elude; (*fig: tempo*) to while away ▷ *vi* (*apparenza*) to be deceptive;

ingannarsi *vpr* to be mistaken, be wrong

in'ganno *sm* deceit, deception; (*azione*) trick; (*menzogna, frode*) cheat, swindle; (*illusione*) illusion

inge'gnarsi [indʒeɲ'narsi] /15/ *vpr* to do one's best, try hard; **~ per vivere** to live by one's wits

inge'gnere [indʒeɲ'ɲere] *sm* engineer; **~ civile/navale** civil/ naval engineer; **ingegne'ria** *sf* engineering; **ingegnere genetica** genetic engineering

in'gegno [in'dʒeɲɲo] *sm* (*intelligenza*) intelligence, brains *pl*; (*capacità creativa*) ingenuity; (*disposizione*) talent; **inge'gnoso, -a** *ag* ingenious, clever

ingelo'sire /55/ *vt* to make jealous ▷ *vi* (*anche*: **ingelosirsi**) to become jealous

in'gente [in'dʒente] *ag* huge, enormous

ingenuità [indʒenui'ta] *sf* ingenuousness

in'genuo, -a [in'dʒɛnuo] *ag* naïve

> Attenzione! In inglese esiste la parola *ingenious*, che però significa *ingegnoso*.

inge'rire [indʒe'rire] /55/ *vt* to ingest

inges'sare [indʒes'sare] /72/ *vt* (*Med*) to put in plaster; **ingessa'tura** *sf* plaster

Inghil'terra [ingil'tɛrra] *sf*: **l'~** England

inghiot'tire [ingjot'tire] /17/ *vt* to swallow

ingial'lire [indʒal'lire] /55/ *vi* to go yellow

inginocchi'arsi [indʒinok'kjarsi] /19/ *vpr* to kneel (down)

ingiù [in'dʒu] *av* down, downwards

ingi'uria [in'dʒurja] *sf* insult; (*fig: danno*) damage

ingius'tizia [indʒus'tittsja] *sf* injustice

ingi'usto, -a [in'dʒusto] *ag* unjust, unfair

in'glese *ag* English ▷ *smf* Englishman/ woman ▷ *sm* (Ling) English; **gli Inglesi** the English; **andarsene** *o* **filare all'~** to take French leave

ingoi'are /19/ *vt* to gulp (down); (fig) to swallow (up)

ingol'fare /72/ *vt*, **ingol'farsi** *vpr* to flood

ingom'brante *ag* cumbersome

ingom'brare /72/ *vt* (strada) to block; (stanza) to clutter up

in'gordo, -a *ag*: ~ **di** greedy for; (fig) greedy *o* avid for

in'gorgo, -ghi *sm* blockage, obstruction; (anche: ~ **stradale**) traffic jam

ingoz'zare [ingot'tsare] /72/ *vt* (persona) to stuff; **ingozzarsi** *vpr*: **ingozzarsi (di)** to stuff o.s. (with)

ingra'naggio [ingra'naddʒo] *sm* (Tecn) gear; (di orologio) mechanism; **gli ingranaggi della burocrazia** the bureaucratic machinery

ingra'nare /72/ *vi* to mesh, engage ▷ *vt* to engage; ~ **la marcia** to get into gear

ingrandi'mento *sm* enlargement; extension

ingran'dire /55/ *vt* (anche Fot) to enlarge; (estendere) to extend; (Ottica, fig) to magnify ▷ *vi* (anche: **ingrandirsi**) to become larger *o* bigger; (aumentare) to grow, increase; (espandersi) to expand

ingras'sare /72/ *vt* to make fat; (animali) to fatten; (lubrificare) to oil, lubricate ▷ *vi* (anche: **ingrassarsi**) to get fat, put on weight

in'grato, -a *ag* ungrateful; (lavoro) thankless, unrewarding

ingredi'ente *sm* ingredient

in'gresso *sm* (porta) entrance; (atrio) hall; (l'entrare) entrance, entry; (facoltà di entrare) admission; **"~ libero"** "admission free"

ingros'sare /72/ *vt* to increase; (folla, livello) to swell ▷ *vi* (anche: **ingrossarsi**) to increase; to swell

in'grosso *av*: **all'~** (Comm) wholesale; (all'incirca) roughly, about

ingua'ribile *ag* incurable

'inguine *sm* (Anat) groin

ini'bire /55/ *vt* to forbid, prohibit; (Psic) to inhibit; **inibirsi** *vpr* to restrain o.s.

ini'bito, -a *ag* inhibited ▷ *sm/f* inhibited person

iniet'tare /72/ *vt* to inject; **iniezi'one** *sf* injection

ininterrotta'mente *av* non-stop, continuously

ininter'rotto, -a *ag* unbroken; (rumore) uninterrupted

inizi'ale [init'tsjale] *ag*, *sf* initial

inizi'are [init'tsjare] /19/ *vi*, *vt* to begin, start; ~ **qn a** to initiate sb into; (pittura ecc) to introduce sb to; ~ **a fare qc** to start doing sth

inizia'tiva [inittsja'tiva] *sf* initiative; ~ **privata** private enterprise

i'nizio [i'nittsjo] *sm* beginning; **all'~** at the beginning, at the start; **dare ~ a qc** to start sth, get sth going

innaffi'are *ecc* = **annaffiare** *ecc*

innamo'rare /72/ *vt* to enchant; **innamorarsi** *vpr*: **innamorarsi (di qn)** to fall in love (with sb)

innamo'rato, -a *ag*: **innamorato (di)** (che nutre amore) in love (with); **innamorato di** (appassionato) very fond of ▷ *sm/f* lover; (anche scherzoso) sweetheart

innanzi'tutto [innantsi'tutto] *av* first of all

in'nato, -a *ag* innate

innatu'rale *ag* unnatural

inne'gabile *ag* undeniable

innervo'sire /55/ *vt*: ~ **qn** to get on sb's nerves; **innervosirsi** *vpr* to get irritated *o* upset

innes'care /20/ *vt* to prime

'inno *sm* hymn; ~ **nazionale** national anthem

inno'cente [inno'tʃɛnte] *ag* innocent

in'nocuo, -a *ag* innocuous, harmless

innova'tivo, -a ag innovative
innume'revole ag innumerable
inol'trare /72/ vt (Amm) to pass on, forward
i'noltre av besides, moreover
inon'dare /72/ vt to flood
inoppor'tuno, -a ag untimely, ill-timed; (poco adatto) inappropriate; (momento) inopportune
inorri'dire /55/ vt to horrify ▷ vi to be horrified
inosser'vato, -a ag (non notato) unobserved; (non rispettato) not observed, not kept
inossi'dabile ag stainless
INPS sigla m (= Istituto Nazionale Previdenza Sociale) social security service
inqua'drare /72/ vt (foto, immagine) to frame; (fig) to situate, set
inqui'eto, -a ag restless; (preoccupato) worried, anxious
inqui'lino, -a sm/f tenant
inquina'mento sm pollution
inqui'nare /72/ vt to pollute
insabbi'are /19/ vt (fig: pratica) to shelve; **insabbiarsi** vpr (arenarsi: barca) to run aground; (fig: pratica) to be shelved
insac'cati smpl (Cuc) sausages
insa'lata sf salad; **~ mista** mixed salad; **~ russa** (Cuc) Russian salad (comprised of cold diced cooked vegetables in mayonnaise); **insalati'era** sf salad bowl
insa'nabile ag (piaga) which cannot be healed; (situazione) irremediable; (odio) implacable
insa'puta sf: **all'~ di qn** without sb knowing
insedi'are /19/ vt (Amm) to install; **insediarsi** vpr to take up office; (colonia, profughi ecc) to settle
in'segna [in'seɲɲa] sf sign; (emblema) sign, emblem; (bandiera) flag, banner
insegna'mento [inseɲɲa'mento] sm teaching

inse'gnante [inseɲ'ɲante] ag teaching ▷ smf teacher; **~ di sostegno** teaching assistant
inse'gnare [inseɲ'ɲare] /15/ vt, vi to teach; **~ a qn qc** to teach sb sth; **~ a qn a fare qc** to teach sb (how) to do sth
insegui'mento sm pursuit, chase
insegu'ire /45/ vt to pursue, chase
insena'tura sf inlet, creek
insen'sato, -a ag senseless, stupid
insen'sibile ag (anche fig) insensitive
inse'rire /55/ vt to insert; (Elettr) to connect; (allegare) to enclose; (annuncio) to put in, place; **inserirsi** vpr (fig): **inserirsi in** to become part of
inservi'ente smf attendant
inserzi'one [inser'tsjone] sf insertion; (avviso) advertisement; **fare un'~ sul giornale** to put an advertisement in the newspaper
insetti'cida, -i [insetti'tʃida] sm insecticide
in'setto sm insect
insi'curo, -a ag insecure
insi'eme av together ▷ prep: **~ a** o **con** together with ▷ sm whole; (Mat, servizio, assortimento) set; (Moda) ensemble, outfit; **tutti ~** all together; **tutto ~** all together; (in una volta) at one go; **nell'~** on the whole; **d'~** (veduta ecc) overall
in'signe [in'siɲɲe] ag (persona) famous, distinguished; (città, monumento) notable
insignifi'cante [insiɲɲifi'kante] ag insignificant
insinu'are /72/ vt (fig) to insinuate, imply; **~ qc in** (introdurre) to slip o slide sth into; **insinuarsi** vpr: **insinuarsi in** to seep into; (fig) to creep into; to worm one's way into
in'sipido, -a ag insipid
insis'tente ag insistent; (pioggia, dolore) persistent
in'sistere /11/ vi: **~ su qc** to insist on sth; **~ in qc/a fare** (perseverare) to persist in sth/in doing

insoddis'fatto, -a *ag* dissatisfied
insoffe'rente *ag* intolerant
insolazi'one [insolat'tsjone] *sf* (Med) sunstroke
inso'lente *ag* insolent
in'solito, -a *ag* unusual, out of the ordinary
inso'luto, -a *ag* (non risolto) unsolved
in'somma *av* (in breve, in conclusione) in short; (dunque) well ▷ *escl* for heaven's sake!
in'sonne *ag* sleepless; **in'sonnia** *sf* insomnia, sleeplessness
inson'nolito, -a *ag* sleepy, drowsy
insoppor'tabile *ag* unbearable
in'sorgere [in'sordʒere] /109/ *vi* (ribellarsi) to rise up, rebel; (apparire) to come up, arise
in'sorsi *ecc vb vedi* **insorgere**
insospet'tire /55/ *vt* to make suspicious ▷ *vi* (anche: **insospettirsi**) to become suspicious
inspi'rare /72/ *vt* to breathe in, inhale
in'stabile *ag* (carico, indole) unstable; (tempo) unsettled; (equilibrio) unsteady
instal'lare /72/ *vt* to install
instan'cabile *ag* untiring, indefatigable
instau'rare /72/ *vt* to establish, introduce
insuc'cesso [insut'tʃesso] *sm* failure, flop
insuffici'ente [insuffi'tʃente] *ag* insufficient; (compito, allievo) inadequate; **insuffici'enza** *sf* insufficiency; inadequacy; (Ins) fail; **insufficienza di prove** (Dir) lack of evidence; **insufficienza renale** renal insufficiency
insu'lina *sf* insulin
in'sulso, -a *ag* (sciocco) inane, silly; (persona) dull, insipid
insul'tare /72/ *vt* to insult, affront
in'sulto *sm* insult, affront
intac'care /20/ *vt* (fare tacche) to cut into; (corrodere) to corrode; (fig:

cominciare ad usare: risparmi) to break into; (: ledere) to damage
intagli'are [intaʎ'ʎare] /27/ *vt* to carve
in'tanto *av* (nel frattempo) meanwhile, in the meantime; (per cominciare) just to begin with; **~ che** while
inta'sare /72/ *vt* to choke (up), block (up); (Aut) to obstruct, block; **intasarsi** *vpr* to become choked o blocked
intas'care /20/ *vt* to pocket
in'tatto, -a *ag* intact; (puro) unsullied
intavo'lare /72/ *vt* to start, enter into
inte'grale *ag* complete; (pane, farina) wholemeal (BRIT), wholewheat (US); **calcolo ~** (Mat) integral calculus
inte'grante *ag*: **parte ~** integral part
inte'grare /72/ *vt* to complete; (Mat) to integrate; **integrarsi** *vpr* (persona) to become integrated
integra'tore *sm*: **integratori alimentari** nutritional supplements
integrità *sf* integrity
'integro, -a *ag* (intatto, intero) complete, whole; (retto) upright
intelaia'tura *sf* frame; (fig) structure, framework
intel'letto *sm* intellect; **intellettu'ale** *ag, smf* intellectual
intelli'gente [intelli'dʒente] *ag* intelligent
intem'perie *sfpl* bad weather *sg*
in'tendere /120/ *vt* (comprendere) to understand; (udire) to hear; (significare) to mean; (avere intenzione): **~ fare qc** to intend o mean to do sth; **intendersi** *vpr* (conoscere): **intendersi di** to know a lot about, be a connoisseur of; (accordarsi) to get on (well); **intendersela con qn** (avere una relazione amorosa) to have an affair with sb; **intendi'tore, -'trice** *sm/f* connoisseur, expert
inten'sivo, -a *ag* intensive
in'tenso, -a *ag* intense

in'tento, -a _ag_ (teso, assorto): **~ (a)** intent (on), absorbed (in) ▷ _sm_ aim, purpose

intenzio'nale [intentsjo'nale] _ag_ intentional

intenzi'one [inten'tsjone] _sf_ intention; (Dir) intent; **avere ~ di fare qc** to intend to do sth, have the intention of doing sth

interat'tivo, -a _ag_ interactive

intercet'tare [intertʃet'tare] /72/ _vt_ to intercept

intercity [inter'siti] _sm inv_ (Ferr) ≈ intercity (train)

inter'detto, -a _pp di_ **interdire** ▷ _ag_ forbidden, prohibited; (sconcertato) dumbfounded ▷ _sm_ (Rel) interdict

interes'sante _ag_ interesting; **essere in stato ~** to be expecting (a baby)

interes'sare /72/ _vt_ to interest; (concernere) to concern, be of interest to; (far intervenire): **~ qn a** to draw sb's attention to ▷ _vi_: **~ a** to interest, matter to; **interessarsi** _vpr_ (mostrare interesse): **interessarsi a** to take an interest in, be interested in; (occuparsi): **interessarsi di** to take care of

inte'resse _sm_ (anche Comm) interest

inter'faccia, -ce [inter'fattʃa] _sf_ (Inform) interface

interfe'renza [interfe'rɛntsa] _sf_ interference

interfe'rire /55/ _vi_ to interfere

interiezi'one [interjet'tsjone] _sf_ exclamation, interjection

interi'nale _ag_: **lavoro ~** temporary work (through an agency)

interi'ora _sfpl_ entrails

interi'ore _ag_ inner _cpd_; **parte ~** inside

inter'medio, -a _ag_ intermediate

inter'nare /72/ _vt_ (arrestare) to intern; (Med) to commit (to a mental institution)

inter'nauta _smf_ Internet user

internazio'nale [internattsjo'nale] _ag_ international

'Internet ['internet] _sf_ Internet; **in ~** on the Internet

in'terno, -a _ag_ (di dentro) internal, interior, inner; (: mare) inland; (nazionale) domestic; (allievo) boarding ▷ _sm_ inside, interior; (di paese) interior; (fodera) lining; (di appartamento) flat (BRIT) o apartment (US) (number); (Tel) extension ▷ _sm/f_ (Ins) boarder; **interni** _smpl_ (Cine) interior shots; **all'~** inside; **Ministero degli Interni** Ministry of the Interior, ≈ Home Office (BRIT), ≈ Department of the Interior (US)

in'tero, -a _ag_ (integro, intatto) whole, entire; (completo, totale) complete; (numero) whole; (non ridotto: biglietto) full; (latte) full-cream

interpel'lare /72/ _vt_ to consult

interpre'tare /72/ _vt_ to interpret; **in'terprete** _smf_ interpreter; (Teat) actor (actress), performer; (Mus) performer; **farsi interprete di** to act as a spokesman for

interregio'nale [interredʒo'nale] _sm_ train that travels between two or more regions of Italy

interro'gare /80/ _vt_ to question; (Ins) to test; **interrogazi'one** _sf_ questioning _no pl_; (Ins) oral test

inter'rompere /97/ _vt_ to interrupt; (studi, trattative) to break off, interrupt; **interrompersi** _vpr_ to break off, stop

interrut'tore _sm_ switch

interruzi'one [interrut'tsjone] _sf_ interruption; break

interur'bano, -a _ag_ inter-city ▷ _sf_ long-distance call

inter'vallo _sm_ interval; (spazio) space, gap

interve'nire /128/ _vi_ (partecipare): **~ a** to take part in; (intromettersi) (anche Pol) to intervene; (Med: operare) to operate; **inter'vento** _sm_ participation; (intromissione) intervention; (Med) operation;

fare un intervento nel corso di (*dibattito, programma*) to take part in
inter'vista *sf* interview;
intervis'tare /72/ *vt* to interview
intes'tare /72/ *vt* (*lettera*) to address; (*proprietà*): **~ a** to register in the name of; **~ un assegno a qn** to make out a cheque to sb
intestato, -a *ag* (*proprietà, casa, conto*) in the name of; (*assegno*) made out to;
carta intestata headed paper
intes'tino *sm* (*Anat*) intestine
intimidazi'one [intimidat'tsjone] *sf* intimidation
intimi'dire /55/ *vt* to intimidate ▷ *vi* (*anche*: **intimidirsi**) to grow shy
intimità *sf* intimacy; privacy; (*familiarità*) familiarity
'intimo, -a *ag* intimate; (*affetti, vita*) private; (*fig: profondo*) inmost ▷ *sm* (*persona*) intimate o close friend; (*dell'animo*) bottom, depths *pl*: **parti intime** (*Anat*) private parts
in'tingolo *sm* sauce; (*pietanza*) stew
intito'lare /72/ *vt* to give a title to; (*dedicare*) to dedicate; **intitolarsi** *vpr* (*libro, film*) to be called
intolle'rabile *ag* intolerable
intolle'rante *ag* intolerant
in'tonaco, -ci o **-chi** *sm* plaster
into'nare /72/ *vt* (*canto*) to start to sing; (*armonizzare*) to match; **intonarsi** *vpr* (*colori*) to go together; **intonarsi a** (*carnagione*) to suit; (*abito*) to go with, match
inton'tito, -a *ag* stunned, dazed; **~ dal sonno** stupid with sleep
in'toppo *sm* stumbling block, obstacle
in'torno *av* around; **~ a** (*attorno a*) around; (*riguardo, circa*) about
intossi'care /20/ *vt* to poison; **intossicazi'one** *sf* poisoning
intralci'are [intral'tʃare] /14/ *vt* to hamper, hold up
ntransi'tivo, -a *ag, sm* intransitive
ntrapren'dente *ag* enterprising, go-ahead

intra'prendere /81/ *vt* to undertake
intrat'tabile *ag* intractable
intratte'nere /121/ *vt* to entertain; (*chiacchierando*) to engage in conversation; **intrattenersi** *vpr* to linger; **intrattenersi su qc** to dwell on sth
intrave'dere /127/ *vt* to catch a glimpse of; (*fig*) to foresee
intrecci'are [intret'tʃare] /14/ *vt* (*capelli*) to plait, braid; (*intessere: anche fig*) to weave, interweave, intertwine
intri'gante *ag* scheming ▷ *smf* schemer, intriguer
in'trinseco, -a, -ci, -che *ag* intrinsic
in'triso, -a *ag*: **~ (di)** soaked (in)
intro'durre /90/ *vt* to introduce; (*chiave ecc*): **~ qc in** to insert sth into; (*persona: far entrare*) to show in; **introdursi** *vpr* (*moda, tecniche*) to be introduced; **introdursi in** (*persona: penetrare*) to enter; (*entrare furtivamente*) to steal o slip into; **introduzi'one** *sf* introduction
in'troito *sm* income, revenue
intro'mettersi /63/ *vpr* to interfere, meddle; (*interporsi*) to intervene
in'truglio [in'truʎʎo] *sm* concoction
intrusi'one *sf* intrusion; interference
in'truso, -a *sm/f* intruder
intu'ire /55/ *vt* to perceive by intuition; (*rendersi conto*) to realize; **in'tuito** *sm* intuition; (*perspicacia*) perspicacity
inu'mano, -a *ag* inhuman
inumi'dire /55/ *vt* to dampen, moisten; **inumidirsi** *vpr* to become damp o wet
i'nutile *ag* useless; (*superfluo*) pointless, unnecessary
inutil'mente *av* (*senza risultato*) in vain; (*senza utilità, scopo*) unnecessarily
inva'dente *ag* (*fig*) interfering, nosey
in'vadere /52/ *vt* to invade; (*affollare*) to swarm into, overrun; (*acque*) to flood

inva'ghirsi [inva'girsi] /55/ *vpr*: **~ di** to take a fancy to

invalidità *sf* infirmity; disability; (*Dir*) invalidity

in'valido, -a *ag* (*infermo*) infirm, invalid; (*al lavoro*) disabled; (*Dir: nullo*) invalid ▷ *sm/f* invalid; person with a disability

in'vano *av* in vain

invasi'one *sf* invasion

inva'sore, invadi'trice [invadi'tritʃe] *ag* invading ▷ *sm/f* invader

invecchi'are [invek'kjare] /19/ *vi* (*persona*) to grow old; (*vino, popolazione*) to age; (*moda*) to become dated ▷ *vt* to age; (*far apparire più vecchio*) to make look older

in'vece [in'vetʃe] *av* instead; (*al contrario*) on the contrary; **~ di** instead of

inve'ire /55/ *vi*: **~ contro** to rail against

inven'tare /72/ *vt* to invent; (*pericoli, pettegolezzi*) to make up, invent

inven'tario *sm* inventory; (*Comm*) stocktaking *no pl*

inven'tore, -'trice *sm/f* inventor

invenzi'one [inven'tsjone] *sf* invention; (*bugia*) lie, story

inver'nale *ag* winter *cpd*; (*simile all'inverno*) wintry

in'verno *sm* winter

invero'simile *ag* unlikely

inversi'one *sf* inversion; reversal; **"divieto d'~"** (*Aut*) "no U-turns"

in'verso, -a *ag* opposite; (*Mat*) inverse ▷ *sm* contrary, opposite; **in senso ~** in the opposite direction; **in ordine ~** in reverse order

inver'tire /45/ *vt* to invert, reverse; **~ la marcia** (*Aut*) to do a U-turn

investi'gare /80/ *vt, vi* to investigate; **investiga'tore, -'trice** *sm/f* investigator, detective; **investigatore privato** private investigator

investi'mento *sm* (*Econ*) investment

inves'tire /45/ *vt* (*denaro*) to invest; (*veicolo: pedone*) to knock down; (: *altro veicolo*) to crash into; (*apostrofare*) to assail; (*incaricare*): **~ qn di** to invest sb with

invi'are /60/ *vt* to send; **invi'ato, -a** *sm/f* envoy; (*Stampa*) correspondent; **inviato speciale** (*Pol*) special envoy; (*di giornale*) special correspondent

in'vidia *sf* envy; **invidi'are** /19/ *vt*: **invidiare qn (per qc)** to envy sb (for sth); **invidiare qc a qn** to envy sb sth; **invidi'oso, -a** *ag* envious

in'vio, -'vii *sm* sending; (*insieme di merci*) consignment; (*tasto*) Return (key), Enter (key)

invipe'rito, -a *ag* furious

invi'sibile *ag* invisible

invi'tare /72/ *vt* to invite; **~ qn a fare** to invite sb to do; **invi'tato, -a** *sm/f* guest; **in'vito** *sm* invitation

invo'care /20/ *vt* (*chiedere: aiuto, pace*) to cry out for; (*appellarsi: la legge, Dio*) to appeal to, invoke

invogli'are [invoʎ'ʎare] /27/ *vt*: **~ qn a fare** to tempt sb to do, induce sb to do

involon'tario, -a *ag* (*errore*) unintentional; (*gesto*) involuntary

invol'tino *sm* (*Cuc*) roulade

in'volto *sm* (*pacco*) parcel; (*fagotto*) bundle

in'volucro *sm* cover, wrapping

inzup'pare [intsup'pare] /72/ *vt* to soak; **inzupparsi** *vpr* to get soaked

'io *pron* I ▷ *sm inv*: **,io** the ego, the self; **io stesso(a)** I myself

i'odio *sm* iodine

l'onio *sm*: **lo ~, il mar ~** the Ionian (Sea)

ipermer'cato *sm* hypermarket

ipertensi'one *sf* high blood pressure hypertension

iper'testo *sm* hypertext; **ipertestu'ale** *ag* (*Inform*): **collegamento** *o* **link ipertestuale** hyperlink

ip'nosi *sf* hypnosis; **ipnotiz'zare** /72/ *vt* to hypnotize

ipocri'sia sf hypocrisy

i'pocrita, -i, -e ag hypocritical ▷ smf hypocrite

ipo'teca, -che sf mortgage

i'potesi sf inv hypothesis

'ippico, -a, -ci, -che ag horse cpd ▷ sf horseracing

ippocas'tano sm horse chestnut

ip'podromo sm racecourse

ippo'potamo sm hippopotamus

'ipsilon sf o m inv (lettera) Y, y; (: dell'alfabeto greco) epsilon

IR abbr (= Interregionale) long distance train which stops frequently

ira'cheno, -a [ira'kɛno] ag, sm/f Iraqi

I'ran sm: **l'~** Iran

irani'ano, -a ag, smf Iranian

I'raq sm: **l'~** Iraq

'iride sf (arcobaleno) rainbow; (Anat, Bot) iris

'iris sm inv iris

Ir'landa sf: **l'~** Ireland; **l'~ del Nord** Northern Ireland, Ulster; **la Repubblica d'~** Eire, the Republic of Ireland; **irlan'dese** ag Irish ▷ smf Irishman/woman; **gli Irlandesi** the Irish

iro'nia sf irony; **i'ronico, -a, -ci, -che** ag ironic(al)

irragio'nevole [irradʒo'nevole] ag irrational; (persona, pretese, prezzo) unreasonable

irrazio'nale [irrattsjo'nale] ag irrational

irre'ale ag unreal

irrego'lare ag irregular; (terreno) uneven

irremo'vibile ag (fig) unshakeable, unyielding

irrequi'eto, -a ag restless

irresis'tibile ag irresistible

irrespon'sabile ag irresponsible

irri'gare /80/ vt (annaffiare) to irrigate; (fiume ecc) to flow through

irrigi'dire [irridʒi'dire] /55/ vt to stiffen; **irrigidirsi** vpr to stiffen

irri'sorio, -a ag derisory

irri'tare /72/ vt (mettere di malumore) to irritate, annoy; (Med) to irritate; **irritarsi** vpr (stizzirsi) to become irritated o annoyed; (Med) to become irritated

ir'rompere /97/ vi: **~ in** to burst into

irru'ente ag (fig) impetuous, violent

ir'ruppi ecc vb vedi **irrompere**

irruzi'one [irrut'tsjone] sf: **fare ~ in** to burst into; (polizia) to raid

is'crissi ecc vb vedi **iscrivere**

is'critto, -a pp di **iscrivere** ▷ smf member; **per o in ~** in writing

is'crivere /105/ vt to register, enter; (persona): **~ (a)** to register (in), enrol (in); **iscriversi** vpr: **iscriversi (a)** (club, partito) to join; (università) to register o enrol (at); (esame, concorso) to register o enter (for); **iscrizi'one** sf (epigrafe ecc) inscription; (a scuola, società ecc) enrolment, registration; (registrazione) registration

Is'lam sm: **l'~** Islam

Is'landa sf: **l'~** Iceland; **islan'dese** ag Icelandic ▷ smf Icelander ▷ sm (Ling) Icelandic

'isola sf island; **~ pedonale** (Aut) pedestrian precinct

isola'mento sm isolation; (Tecn) insulation

iso'lante ag insulating ▷ sm insulator

iso'lare /72/ vt to isolate; (Tecn) to insulate; (: acusticamente) to soundproof; **isolarsi** vpr to isolate o.s.; **iso'lato, -a** ag isolated; insulated ▷ sm (edificio) block

ispet'tore, -'trice sm/f inspector

ispezio'nare [ispettsjo'nare] /72/ vt to inspect

'ispido, -a ag bristly, shaggy

ispi'rare /72/ vt to inspire

Isra'ele sm: **l'~** Israel; **israeli'ano, -a** ag, sm/f Israeli

is'sare /72/ vt to hoist

istan'taneo, -a ag instantaneous ▷ sf (Fot) snapshot

is'tante sm instant, moment; **all'~, sull'~** instantly, immediately

is'terico, -a, -ci, -che *ag* hysterical

isti'gare /80/ *vt* to incite

is'tinto *sm* instinct

istitu'ire /55/ *vt* (*fondare*) to institute, found; (*porre: confronto*) to establish; (*intraprendere: inchiesta*) to set up

isti'tuto *sm* institute; (*di università*) department; (*ente, Dir*) institution; **~ di bellezza** beauty salon; **~ di credito** bank, banking institution; **~ di ricerca** research institute

istituzi'one [istitut'tsjone] *sf* institution

'istmo *sm* (*Geo*) isthmus

'istrice ['istritʃe] *sm* porcupine

istru'ito, -a *ag* educated

istrut'tore, -'trice *sm/f* instructor ▷ *ag*: **giudice ~** examining (BRIT) o committing (US) magistrate

istruzi'one [istrut'tsjone] *sf* (*gen*) training; (*Ins, cultura*) education; (*direttiva*) instruction; **istruzioni** *sfpl* (*norme*) instructions; **istruzioni per l'uso** instructions (for use); **~ obbligatoria** (*Ins*) compulsory education

l'talia *sf*: **l'~** Italy

itali'ano, -a *ag* Italian ▷ *sm/f* Italian ▷ *sm* (*Ling*) Italian; **gli Italiani** the Italians

itine'rario *sm* itinerary

'ittico, -a, -ci, -che *ag* fish *cpd*; fishing *cpd*

Iugos'lavia *sf* = **Jugoslavia**

'I.V.A. *sigla f* (= *imposta sul valore aggiunto*) VAT

jazz [dʒaz] *sm* jazz

jeans [dʒinz] *smpl* jeans

Jeep® [dʒip] *sm inv* jeep

'jogging ['dʒɔgiŋ] *sm* jogging; **fare ~** to go jogging

'jolly ['dʒɔli] *sm inv* joker

joys'tick [dʒois'tik] *sm inv* joystick

ju'do [dʒu'dɔ] *sm* judo

Jugos'lavia [jugoz'lavja] *sf* (*Storia*): **la ~** Yugoslavia; **la ex-~** former Yugoslavia; **jugos'lavo, -a** *ag, sm/f* (*Storia*) Yugoslav(ian)

K, k ['kappa] *sf o m inv* (*lettera*) K, k
▷ *abbr* (= *kilo-, chilo-*) k; (*Inform*) K; **K come Kursaal** ≈ K for King
kami'kaze [kami'kaddze] *sm inv* kamikaze
kara'oke [kara'oke] *sm inv* karaoke
karatè *sm* karate
ka'yak [ka'jak] *sm inv* kayak
Kenia ['kenja] *sm:* **il ~** Kenya
kg *abbr* (= *chilogrammo*) kg
killer *sm inv* gunman, hired gun
kitsch [kitʃ] *sm* kitsch
kiwi ['kiwi] *sm inv* kiwi (fruit)
km *abbr* (= *chilometro*) km
K.'O. [kappa'o] *sm inv* knockout
ko'ala [ko'ala] *sm inv* koala (bear)
koso'varo, -a *ag, sm/f* Kosovan
Kosovo *sm* Kosovo
krapfen (*Cuc*) *sm inv* doughnut
Ku'wait [ku'vait] *sm:* **il ~** Kuwait

l *abbr* (= *litro*) l
l' *det vedi* **la; lo; il**
la *det f* (*dav V* **l'**) the ▷ *pron* (*dav V* **l'**: *oggetto: persona*) her; (: *cosa*) it; (: *forma di cortesia*) you; *vedi anche* **il**
là *av* there; **di là** (*da quel luogo*) from there; (*in quel luogo*) in there; (*dall'altra parte*) over there; **di là di** beyond; **per di là** that way; **più in là** further on; (*tempo*) later on; **fatti in là** move up; **là dentro/sopra/sotto** in/up o on/under there; *vedi anche* **quello**
labbro *sm* (*pl f* **labbra**) (*Anat*) lip
labi'rinto *sm* labyrinth, maze
labora'torio *sm* (*di ricerca*) laboratory; (*di arti, mestieri*) workshop; **~ linguistico** language laboratory
labori'oso, -a *ag* (*faticoso*) laborious; (*attivo*) hard-working
lacca, -che *sf* lacquer
laccio ['lattʃo] *sm* noose; (*legaccio, tirante*) lasso; (*di scarpa*) lace; **~ emostatico** tourniquet

lace'rare [latʃe'rare] /72/ vt to tear to shreds, lacerate; **lacerarsi** vpr to tear

'lacrima sf tear; **in lacrime** in tears; **lacri'mogeno, -a** ag: **gas lacrimogeno** tear gas

la'cuna sf (fig) gap

'ladro sm thief

laggiù [lad'dʒu] av down there; (di là) over there

la'gnarsi [laɲ'ɲarsi] /15/ vpr: **~ (di)** to complain (about)

'lago, -ghi sm lake

la'guna sf lagoon

'laico, -a, -ci, -che ag (apostolato) lay; (vita) secular; (scuola) non-denominational ▷ sm/f layman/woman

'lama sf blade ▷ sm inv (Zool) llama; (Rel) lama

lamen'tare /72/ vt to lament; **lamentarsi** vpr (emettere lamenti) to moan, groan; (rammaricarsi): **lamentarsi (di)** to complain (about)

lamen'tela sf complaining no pl

la'metta sf razor blade

'lamina sf (lastra sottile) thin sheet (o layer o plate); **~ d'oro** gold leaf; gold foil

'lampada sf lamp; **~ a petrolio/a gas** oil/gas lamp; **~ da tavolo** table lamp

lampa'dario sm chandelier

lampa'dina sf light bulb; **~ tascabile** pocket torch (BRIT), flashlight (US)

lam'pante ag (fig: evidente) crystal clear, evident

lampeggi'are [lamped'dʒare] /62/ vi (luce, fari) to flash ▷ vb impers: **lampeggia** there's lightning; **lampeggia'tore** sm (Aut) indicator

lampi'one sm street light o lamp (BRIT)

'lampo sm (Meteor) flash of lightning; (di luce, fig) flash

lam'pone sm raspberry

'lana sf wool; **~ d'acciaio** steel wool; **pura ~ vergine** pure new wool; **~ di vetro** glass wool

lan'cetta [lan'tʃetta] sf (indice) pointer, needle; (di orologio) hand

'lancia, -ce ['lantʃa] sf (arma) lance; (: picca) spear; (di pompa antincendio) nozzle; (imbarcazione) launch; **~ di salvataggio** lifeboat

lanciafi'amme [lantʃa'fjamme] sm inv flamethrower

lanci'are [lan'tʃare] /14/ vt to throw, hurl, fling; (Sport) to throw; (far partire: automobile) to get up to full speed; (bombe) to drop; (razzo, prodotto, moda) to launch; **lanciarsi** vpr: **lanciarsi contro/su** to throw o hurl o fling o.s. against/on; **lanciarsi in** (fig) to embark on

lanci'nante [lantʃi'nante] ag (dolore) shooting, throbbing; (grido) piercing

'lancio ['lantʃo] sm throwing no pl; throw; dropping no pl; drop; launching no pl; launch; **~ del disco** (Sport) throwing the discus; **~ del peso** (Sport) putting the shot

'languido, -a ag (fiacco) languid, weak; (tenero, malinconico) languishing

lan'terna sf lantern; (faro) lighthouse

'lapide sf (di sepolcro) tombstone; (commemorativa) plaque

'lapsus sm inv slip

'lardo sm bacon fat, lard

lar'ghezza [lar'gettsa] sf width; breadth; looseness; generosity; **~ di vedute** broad-mindedness

'largo, -a, -ghi, -ghe ag wide; broad; (maniche) wide; (abito: troppo ampio) loose; (fig) generous ▷ sm width; breadth; (mare aperto): **il ~** the open sea ▷ sf: **stare o tenersi alla larga (da qn/qc)** to keep one's distance (from sb/sth), keep away (from sb/sth); **~ due metri** two metres wide; **~ di spalle** broad-shouldered; **di larghe vedute** broad-minded; **su larga scala** on a large scale; **di manica larga** generous, open-handed; **al ~ di Genova** off (the coast of) Genoa;

farsi ~ tra la folla to push one's way through the crowd

'**larice** ['laritʃe] sm (Bot) larch

larin'gite [larin'dʒite] sf laryngitis

'**larva** sf larva; (fig) shadow

la'sagne [la'zaɲɲe] sfpl lasagna sg

lasci'are [laʃʃare] /14/ vt to leave; (abbandonare) to leave, abandon, give up; (cessare di tenere) to let go of ▷ vb aus: **~ qn fare qc** to let sb do sth; **lasciarsi** vpr (persone) to part; (coppia) to split up; **~ andare** o **correre** o **perdere** to let things go their own way; **~ stare qc/qn** to leave sth/sb alone; **lasciarsi andare/truffare** to let o.s. go/be cheated

'**laser** ['lazer] ag, sm inv: **(raggio) ~** laser (beam)

lassa'tivo, -a ag, sm laxative

'**lasso** sm: **~ di tempo** interval, lapse of time

las'sù av up there

'**lastra** sf (di pietra) slab; (di metallo, Fot) plate; (di ghiaccio, vetro) sheet; (radiografica) X-ray (plate)

lastri'cato sm paving

late'rale ag lateral, side cpd; (uscita, ingresso ecc) side cpd ▷ sm (Calcio) half-back

la'tino, -a ag, sm Latin

lati'tante smf fugitive (from justice)

lati'tudine sf latitude

'**lato, -a** ag (fig) wide, broad; **in senso ~** broadly speaking ▷ sm side; (fig) aspect, point of view

'**latta** sf tin (plate); (recipiente) tin, can

lat'tante ag unweaned

'**latte** sm milk; **~ detergente** cleansing milk o lotion; **~ intero** full-cream milk; **~ a lunga conservazione** UHT milk, long-life milk; **~ magro** o **scremato** skimmed milk; **~ secco** o **in polvere** dried o powdered milk; **~ solare** suntan lotion; **latti'cini** smpl dairy o milk products

at'tina sf (di birra ecc) can

at'tuga, -ghe sf lettuce

'**laurea** sf degree; **~ in ingegneria** engineering degree; **~ in lettere** ≈ arts degree

● **LAUREA**
●
● The laurea is awarded to students
● who successfully complete their
● degree courses. Traditionally,
● this takes between four and six
● years; a major element of the final
● examinations is the presentation
● and discussion of a dissertation.
● A shorter, more vocational course
● of study, taking from two to three
● years, is also available; at the end
● of this time students receive a
● diploma called the laurea breve.

laure'are /72/ vt to confer a degree on; **laurearsi** vpr to graduate

laure'ato, -a ag, sm/f graduate

'**lauro** sm laurel

'**lauto, -a** ag (pranzo, mancia) lavish

'**lava** sf lava

la'vabo sm washbasin

la'vaggio [la'vaddʒo] sm washing no pl; **~ del cervello** brainwashing no pl; **~ a secco** dry-cleaning

la'vagna [la'vaɲɲa] sf (Geo) slate; (di scuola) blackboard; **~ interattiva** interactive whiteboard

la'vanda sf (anche Med) wash; (Bot) lavender; **lavande'ria** sf laundry; **lavanderia automatica** launderette; **lavanderia a secco** dry-cleaner's; **lavan'dino** sm sink

lavapi'atti smf inv dishwasher

la'vare /72/ vt to wash; **lavarsi** vpr to wash, have a wash; **~ a secco** to dry-clean; **lavarsi le mani/i denti** to wash one's hands/clean one's teeth

lava'secco sf o m inv dry-cleaner's

lavasto'viglie [lavasto'viʎʎe] sf o m inv (macchina) dishwasher

lava'trice [lava'tritʃe] sf washing machine

la'vello sm (kitchen) sink

lavo'rare /72/ vi to work; (fig: bar, studio ecc) to do good business ▷ vt to work; **~ a** to work on; **~ a maglia** to knit; **lavorarsi qn** (fig: convincere) to work on sb; **lavora'tivo, -a** ag working; **lavora'tore, -'trice** sm/f worker ▷ ag working

la'voro sm work; (occupazione) job, work no pl; (opera) piece of work, job; (Econ) labour; **che ~ fa?** what do you do?; **lavori forzati** hard labour sg: **~ interinale** o **in affitto** temporary work

le det fpl the ▷ pron (oggetto) them; (: a lei, a essa) (to) her; (: forma di cortesia) (to) you; vedi anche **il**

le'ale ag loyal; (sincero) sincere; (onesto) fair

'lecca 'lecca sm inv lollipop

leccapi'edi smf inv (peg) toady, bootlicker

lec'care /20/ vt to lick; (gatto: latte ecc) to lick o lap up; (fig) to flatter; **leccarsi i baffi** to lick one's lips

leccherò ecc [lekke'rɔ] vb vedi **leccare**

'leccio ['lettʃo] sm holm oak, ilex

leccor'nia sf titbit, delicacy

'lecito, -a ['lɛtʃito] ag permitted, allowed

'lega, -ghe sf league; (di metalli) alloy

le'gaccio [le'gattʃo] sm string, lace

le'gale ag legal ▷ sm lawyer; **legaliz'zare** /72/ vt to legalize; (documento) to authenticate

le'game sm (corda, fig: affettivo) tie, bond; (nesso logico) link, connection

le'gare /80/ vt (prigioniero, capelli, cane) to tie (up); (libro) to bind; (Chim) to alloy; (fig: collegare) to bind, join ▷ vi (far lega) to unite; (fig) to get on well

le'genda [le'dʒɛnda] sf (di carta geografica ecc); = **leggenda**

'legge ['lɛddʒe] sf law

leg'genda [led'dʒɛnda] sf (narrazione) legend; (di carta geografica ecc) key, legend

'leggere ['lɛddʒere] /61/ vt, vi to read

legge'rezza [ledd3e'rettsa] sf lightness; thoughtlessness; fickleness

leg'gero, -a [led'dʒɛro] ag light; (agile, snello) nimble, agile, light; (tè, caffè) weak; (fig: non grave, piccolo) slight; (: spensierato) thoughtless; (: incostante) fickle; free and easy; **alla leggera** thoughtlessly

leg'gio, -'gii [led'dʒio] sm lectern; (Mus) music stand

legherò ecc [lege'rɔ] vb vedi **legare**

legisla'tivo, -a [ledʒizla'tivo] ag legislative

legisla'tura [ledʒizla'tura] sf legislature

le'gittimo, -a [le'dʒittimo] ag legitimate; (fig: giustificato, lecito) justified, legitimate; **legittima difesa** (Dir) self-defence (BRIT), self-defense (US)

'legna ['leɲɲa] sf firewood

'legno ['leɲɲo] sm wood; (pezzo di legno) piece of wood; **di ~** wooden; **~ compensato** plywood

le'gume sm (Bot) pulse; **legumi** smpl pulses

'lei pron (soggetto) she; (oggetto: per dare rilievo, con preposizione) her; (forma di cortesia: anche: **L~**) you ▷ sm: **dare del ~ a qn** to address sb as "lei"; **~ stessa** she herself; you yourself

● **LEI**
●
● lei is the third person singular
● pronoun. It is used in Italian to
● address an adult whom you do not
● know or with whom you are on
● formal terms.

lenta'mente av slowly

'lente sf (Ottica) lens sg: **~ d'ingrandimento** magnifying glass; **lenti** sfpl (occhiali) lenses; **lenti a contatto, lenti corneali** contact lenses; **lenti (a contatto) morbide/rigide** soft/hard contact lenses

len'tezza [len'tettsa] *sf* slowness
len'ticchia [len'tikkja] *sf* (Bot) lentil
len'tiggine [len'tiddʒine] *sf* freckle
'lento, -a *ag* slow; (molle: fune) slack; (non stretto: vite, abito) loose ▷ *sm* (ballo) slow dance
'lenza ['lɛntsa] *sf* fishing line
lenzu'olo [len'tswɔlo] *sm* sheet
le'one *sm* lion; **L~** Leo
lepo'rino, -a *ag*: **labbro ~** harelip
'lepre *sf* hare
'lercio, -a, -ci, -ce ['lɛrtʃo] *ag* filthy
lesi'one *sf* (Med) lesion; (Dir) injury, damage; (Edil) crack
les'sare /72/ *vt* (Cuc) to boil
'lessi *ecc vb vedi* **leggere**
'lessico, -ci *sm* vocabulary; (dizionario) lexicon
'lesso, -a *ag* boiled ▷ *sm* boiled meat
le'tale *ag* lethal; fatal
leta'maio *sm* dunghill
le'tame *sm* manure, dung
le'targo, -ghi *sm* lethargy; (Zool) hibernation
'lettera *sf* letter; **lettere** *sfpl* (letteratura) literature *sg*; (studi umanistici) arts (subjects); **alla ~** literally; **in lettere** in words, in full
lettera'mente *av* literally
lette'rario, -a *ag* literary
lette'rato, -a *ag* well-read, scholarly
lettera'tura *sf* literature
let'tiga, -ghe *sf* (barella) stretcher
let'tino *sm* cot (BRIT); crib (US); (per il sole) sun lounger; **~ solare** sunbed
'letto, -a *pp di* **leggere** ▷ *sm* bed; **andare a ~** to go to bed; **~ a castello** bunk beds *pl*; **~ a una piazza/a due piazze** *o* **matrimoniale** single/double bed
let'tore, -'trice *sm/f* reader; (Ins) (foreign language) assistant (BRIT), (foreign) teaching assistant (US) ▷ *sm* (Tecn): **~ di libri digitali** e-reader; **~ ottico (di caratteri)** optical character reader; **~ CD/DVD** CD/DVD player; **~ MP3/MP4** MP3/MP4 player

let'tura *sf* reading

> Attenzione! In inglese esiste la parola *lecture*, che però significa *lezione* oppure *conferenza*.

leuce'mia [leutʃe'mia] *sf* leukaemia
'leva *sf* lever; (Mil) conscription; **far ~ su qn** to work on sb; **~ del cambio** (Aut) gear lever
le'vante *sm* east; (vento) East wind; **il L~** the Levant
le'vare /72/ *vt* (occhi, braccio) to raise; (sollevare, togliere: tassa, divieto) to lift; (: indumenti) to take off, remove; (rimuovere) to take away; (: dal di sopra) to take off; (: dal di dentro) to take out
leva'toio, -a *ag*: **ponte ~** drawbridge
lezi'one [let'tsjone] *sf* lesson; (all'università, sgridata) lecture; **fare ~** to teach; to lecture; **dare una ~ a qn** to teach sb a lesson; **lezioni private** private lessons
li *pron pl* (oggetto) them
lì *av* there; **di** *o* **da lì** from there; **per di lì** that way; **di lì a pochi giorni** a few days later; **lì per lì** there and then; at first; **essere lì (lì) per fare** to be on the point of doing, be about to do; **lì dentro** in there; **lì sotto** under there; **lì sopra** on there; up there; *vedi anche* **quello**
liba'nese *ag, sm/f* Lebanese *inv*
Li'bano *sm*: **il ~** the Lebanon
'libbra *sf* (peso) pound
li'beccio [li'bettʃo] *sm* south-west wind
li'bellula *sf* dragonfly
libe'rale *ag, smf* liberal
liberaliz'zare [liberalid'dzare] /72/ *vt* to liberalize
libe'rare /72/ *vt* (rendere libero: prigioniero) to release; (: popolo) to free, liberate; (sgombrare: passaggio) to clear; (: stanza) to vacate; (produrre: energia) to release; **liberarsi** *vpr*: **liberarsi di qc/qn** to get rid of sth/sb; **liberazi'one** *sf* (di prigioniero)

release, freeing; (*di popolo*) liberation; rescuing

● **LIBERAZIONE**
●
● The *Liberazione* is a national
● holiday which falls on 25 April. It
● commemorates the liberation of
● Italy in 1945 from German forces
● and Mussolini's government
● and marks the end of the war on
● Italian soil.

'libero, -a *ag* free; (*strada*) clear; (*non occupato: posto ecc*) vacant; free; not taken; empty; not engaged; **~ di fare qc** free to do sth; **~ da** free from; **~ arbitrio** free will; **~ professionista** self-employed professional person; **~ scambio** free trade; **libertà** *sf inv* freedom; (*tempo disponibile*) free time ▷ *sfpl* (*licenza*) liberties; **essere in libertà provvisoria/vigilata** to be released without bail/be on probation

'Libia *sf*: **la ~** Libya; **'libico, -a, -ci, -che** *ag*, *sm/f* Libyan

li'bidine *sf* lust

li'braio *sm* bookseller

li'brarsi /72/ *vpr* to hover

libre'ria *sf* (*bottega*) bookshop; (*mobile*) bookcase

> Attenzione! In inglese esiste la parola *library*, che però significa *biblioteca*.

li'bretto *sm* booklet; (*taccuino*) notebook; (*Mus*) libretto; **~ degli assegni** chequebook; **~ di circolazione** (*Aut*) logbook; **~ di risparmio** (savings) bankbook, passbook; **~ universitario** student's report book

'libro *sm* book; **~ di cassa** cash book; **~ mastro** ledger; **~ paga** payroll; **~ di testo** textbook

li'cenza [li'tʃɛntsa] *sf* (*permesso*) permission, leave; (*di pesca, caccia, circolazione*) permit, licence; (*Mil*)

leave; (*Ins*) school-leaving certificate; (*libertà*) liberty; licence; (*sfrenatezza*) licentiousness; **andare in ~** (*Mil*) to go on leave

licenzia'mento [litʃentsja'mento] *sm* dismissal

licenzi'are [litʃen'tsjare] /19/ *vt* (*impiegato*) to dismiss; (*Comm: per eccesso di personale*) to make redundant; (*Ins*) to award a certificate to; **licenziarsi** *vpr* (*impiegato*) to resign, hand in one's notice; (*Ins*) to obtain one's school-leaving certificate

li'ceo [li'tʃɛo] *sm* (*Ins*) secondary (*BRIT*) o high (*US*) school (*for 14- to 19-year-olds*)

'lido *sm* beach, shore

'Liechtenstein ['liktənstain] *sm*: **il ~** Liechtenstein

li'eto, -a *ag* happy, glad; **"molto ~"** (*nelle presentazioni*) "pleased to meet you"

li'eve *ag* light; (*di poco conto*) slight; (*sommesso: voce*) faint, soft

lievi'tare /72/ *vi* (*anche fig*) to rise ▷ *vt* to leaven

li'evito *sm* yeast; **~ di birra** brewer's yeast

'ligio, -a, -gi, -gie ['lidʒo] *ag* faithful, loyal

'lilla, lillà *sm inv* lilac

'lima *sf* file; **~ da unghie** nail file

limacci'oso, -a [limat'tʃoso] *ag* slimy; muddy

li'mare /72/ *vt* to file (down); (*fig*) to polish

limi'tare /72/ *vt* to limit, restrict; (*circoscrivere*) to bound, surround; **limitarsi** *vpr*: **limitarsi nel mangiare** to limit one's eating; **limitarsi a qc/a fare qc** to limit o.s. to sth/to doing sth

'limite *sm* limit; (*confine*) border, boundary; **~ di velocità** speed limit

limo'nata *sf* lemonade (*BRIT*), (lemon) soda (*US*); (*spremuta*) lemon squash (*BRIT*), lemonade (*US*)

li'mone sm (pianta) lemon tree; (frutto) lemon

'limpido, -a ag (acqua) limpid, clear; (cielo) clear

lince ['lintʃe] sf lynx

linci'are [lin'tʃare] /14/ vt to lynch

'linea sf line; (di mezzi pubblici di trasporto: itinerario) route; (: servizio) service; **a grandi linee** in outline; **mantenere la ~** to look after one's figure; : **aereo di ~** airliner; **nave di ~** liner; **volo di ~** scheduled flight; **~ aerea** airline; **~ di partenza/ d'arrivo** (Sport) starting/finishing line; **~ di tiro** line of fire

linea'menti smpl features; (fig) outlines

line'are ag linear; (fig) coherent, logical

line'etta sf (trattino) dash; (d'unione) hyphen

lin'gotto sm ingot, bar

'lingua sf (Anat, Cuc) tongue; (idioma) language; **mostrare la ~** to stick out one's tongue; **di ~ italiana** Italian-speaking; **~ madre** mother tongue; **una ~ di terra** a spit of land

lingu'aggio [lin'gwaddʒo] sm language

lingu'etta sf (di strumento) reed; (di scarpa, Tecn) tongue; (di busta) flap

'lino sm (pianta) flax; (tessuto) linen

li'noleum sm inv linoleum, lino

liposuzi'one [liposut'tsjone] sf liposuction

liqui'dare /72/ vt (società, beni, persona: uccidere) to liquidate; (persona: sbarazzarsene) to get rid of; (conto, problema) to settle; (Comm: merce) to sell off, clear; **liquidazi'one** sf liquidation; (di conto) settlement; (di merce) clearance sale

liquidità sf liquidity

'liquido, -a ag, sm liquid; **~ per freni** brake fluid

liqui'rizia [likwi'rittsja] sf liquorice

li'quore sm liqueur

'lira sf (unità monetaria) lira; (Mus) lyre; **~ sterlina** pound sterling

'lirico, -a, -ci, -che ag lyric(al); (Mus) lyric; **cantante/teatro ~** opera singer/house

Lis'bona sf Lisbon

'lisca, -sche sf (di pesce) fishbone

lisci'are [liʃʃare] /14/ vt to smooth; (fig) to flatter

'liscio, -a, -sci, -sce ['liʃʃo] ag smooth; (capelli) straight; (mobile) plain; (bevanda alcolica) neat; (fig) straightforward, simple ▷ av: **andare ~** to go smoothly; **passarla liscia** to get away with it

'liso, -a ag worn out, threadbare

'lista sf (elenco) list; **~ elettorale** electoral roll; **~ delle spese** shopping list; **~ dei vini** wine list; **~ delle vivande** menu

lis'tino sm list; **~ dei cambi** (foreign) exchange rate; **~ dei prezzi** price list

'lite sf quarrel, argument; (Dir) lawsuit

liti'gare /80/ vi to quarrel; (Dir) to litigate

li'tigio [li'tidʒo] sm quarrel

lito'rale ag coastal, coast cpd ▷ sm coast

'litro sm litre

livel'lare /72/ vt to level, make level

li'vello sm level; (fig) level, standard; **ad alto ~** (fig) high-level; **~ del mare** sea level

'livido, -a ag livid; (per percosse) bruised, black and blue; (cielo) leaden ▷ sm bruise

Li'vorno sf Livorno, Leghorn

'lizza ['littsa] sf lists pl: **scendere in ~** to enter the lists

lo det m (dav s impura, gn, pn, ps, x, z; dav V l') the ▷ pron (dav V l', oggetto: persona) him; (: cosa) it; **lo sapevo** I knew it; **lo so** I know; **sii buono, anche se lui non lo è** be good, even if he isn't; vedi anche **il**

lo'cale ag local ▷ sm room; (luogo pubblico) premises pl: **~ notturno** nightclub; **località** sf inv locality

lo'canda sf inn

locomo'tiva sf locomotive

locuzi'one [lokut'tsjone] sf phrase, expression

lo'dare /72/ vt to praise

'lode sf praise; (Ins): **laurearsi con 110 e ~** ≈ to graduate with first-class honours (BRIT), ≈ to graduate summa cum laude (US)

'loden sm inv (stoffa) loden; (cappotto) loden overcoat

lo'devole ag praiseworthy

loga'ritmo sm logarithm

log'garsi /72/ vpr (Inform) to log in

'loggia, -ge ['lɔddʒa] sf (Archit) loggia; (circolo massonico) lodge; **loggi'one** sm (di teatro): **il loggione** the Gods sg

'logico, -a, -ci, -che ['lɔdʒiko] ag logical

logo'rare /72/ vt to wear out; (sciupare) to waste; **logorarsi** vpr to wear out; (fig) to wear o.s. out

'logoro, -a ag (stoffa) worn out, threadbare; (persona) worn out

Lombar'dia sf: **la ~** Lombardy

lom'bata sf (taglio di carne) loin

lom'brico, -chi sm earthworm

londi'nese ag London cpd ▷ smf Londoner

'Londra sf London

lon'gevo, -a [lon'dʒevo] ag long-lived

longi'tudine [londʒi'tudine] sf longitude

lonta'nanza [lonta'nantsa] sf distance; absence

lon'tano, -a ag (distante) distant, faraway; (assente) absent; (vago: sospetto) slight, remote; (tempo: remoto) far-off, distant; (parente) distant, remote ▷ av far; **è lontana la casa?** is it far to the house?, is the house far from here?; **è ~ un chilometro** it's a kilometre away o a kilometre from here; **più ~** farther; **da** o **di ~** from a distance; **~ da** a long way from; **è molto ~ da qui?** is it far from here?; **alla lontana** slightly, vaguely

lo'quace [lo'kwatʃe] ag talkative, loquacious; (fig: gesto ecc) eloquent

'lordo, -a ag dirty, filthy; (peso, stipendio) gross

'loro pron pl (oggetto, con preposizione) them; (complemento di termine) to them; (soggetto) they; (forma di cortesia: anche: **L~**) you; to you; **il (la) ~, i (le) ~** det their; (forma di cortesia: anche: **L~**) your ▷ pron theirs; (forma di cortesia: anche: **L~**) yours; **~ stessi(e)** they themselves; you yourselves

'losco, -a, -schi, -sche ag (fig) shady, suspicious

'lotta sf struggle, fight; (Sport) wrestling; **~ libera** all-in wrestling; **lot'tare** /72/ vi to fight, struggle; to wrestle

lotte'ria sf lottery; (di gara ippica) sweepstake

'lotto sm (gioco) (state) lottery; (parte) lot; (Edil) site

○ **LOTTO**
○
○ The Lotto is an official lottery run
○ by the Italian Finance Ministry.
○ It consists of a weekly draw of
○ numbers and is very popular.

lozi'one [lot'tsjone] sf lotion

lubrifi'cante sm lubricant

lubrifi'care /20/ vt to lubricate

luc'chetto [luk'ketto] sm padlock

lucci'care [luttʃi'kare] /20/ vi to sparkle; (oro) to glitter; (stella) to twinkle

'luccio ['luttʃo] sm (Zool) pike

'lucciola ['luttʃola] sf (Zool) firefly; glow-worm

'luce ['lutʃe] sf light; (finestra) window; **alla ~ di** by the light of; **fare ~ su qc** (fig) to shed o throw light on sth; **~ del sole/della luna** sun/moonlight

lucer'nario [lutʃer'narjo] sm skylight

lu'certola [lu'tʃertola] sf lizard

luci'dare [lutʃi'dare] /72/ vt to polish

lucida'trice [lutʃidaˈtritʃe] *sf* floor polisher

'lucido, -a [ˈlutʃido] *ag* shining, bright; (*lucidato*) polished; (*fig*) lucid ▷ *sm* shine, lustre; (*per scarpe ecc*) polish; (*disegno*) tracing

'lucro *sm* profit, gain

'luglio [ˈluʎʎo] *sm* July

'lugubre *ag* gloomy

'lui *pron* (*soggetto*) he; (*oggetto: per dare rilievo, con preposizione*) him; **~ stesso** he himself

lu'maca, -che *sf* slug; (*chiocciola*) snail

lumi'noso, -a *ag* (*che emette luce*) luminous; (*cielo, colore, stanza*) bright; (*sorgente*) of light, light *cpd*; (*fig: sorriso*) bright, radiant

'luna *sf* moon; **~ nuova/piena** new/full moon; **~ di miele** honeymoon

'luna park *sm inv* amusement park, funfair

lu'nare *ag* lunar, moon *cpd*

lu'nario *sm* almanac; **sbarcare il ~** to make ends meet

lu'natico, -a, -ci, -che *ag* whimsical, temperamental

lunedì *sm inv* Monday; **di** *o* **il ~** on Mondays

lun'ghezza [lunˈgettsa] *sf* length; **~ d'onda** (*Fisica*) wavelength

'lungo, -a, -ghi, -ghe *ag* long; (*lento: persona*) slow; (*diluito: caffè, brodo*) weak, watery, thin ▷ *sm* length ▷ *prep* along; **~ 3 metri** 3 metres long; **a ~** for a long time; **a ~ andare** in the long run; **di gran lunga** (*molto*) by far; **andare in ~** *o* **per le lunghe** to drag on; **saperla lunga** to know what's what; **in ~ e in largo** far and wide, all over; **~ il corso dei secoli** throughout the centuries

lungo'mare *sm* promenade

lu'notto *sm* (*Aut*) rear *o* back window; **~ termico** heated rear window

'luogo, -ghi *sm* place; (*posto: di incidente ecc*) scene, site; (*punto, passo di libro*) passage; **in ~ di** instead of; **in**

primo ~ in the first place; **aver ~** to take place; **dar ~ a** to give rise to; **~ comune** commonplace; **~ di nascita** birthplace; (*Amm*) place of birth; **~ di provenienza** place of origin

'lupo, -a *sm/f* wolf/she-wolf

'luppolo *sm* (*Bot*) hop

'lurido, -a *ag* filthy

lusin'gare /80/ *vt* to flatter

Lussem'burgo *sm* (*stato*): **il ~** Luxembourg ▷ *sf* (*città*) Luxembourg

'lusso *sm* luxury; **di ~** luxury *cpd*; **lussu'oso, -a** *ag* luxurious

lus'suria *sf* lust

lus'trino *sm* sequin

'lutto *sm* mourning; **essere in/portare il ~** to be in/wear mourning

m

m. *abbr* = **mese**; **metro**; **miglia**; **monte**

ma *cong* but; **ma insomma!** for goodness sake!; **ma no!** of course not!

'**macabro, -a** *ag* gruesome, macabre

macché [mak'ke] *escl* not at all!, certainly not!

macche'roni [makke'roni] *smpl* macaroni *sg*

'**macchia** ['makkja] *sf* stain, spot; (*chiazza di diverso colore*) spot, splash, patch; (*tipo di boscaglia*) scrub; **darsi/vivere alla ~** (*fig*) to go into/live in hiding; **macchi'are** /19/ *vt* (*sporcare*) to stain, mark; **macchiarsi** *vpr* (*persona*) to get o.s. dirty; (*stoffa*) to stain; to get stained *o* marked

macchi'ato, -a [mak'kjato] *ag* (*pelle, pelo*) spotted; **~ di** stained with; **caffè ~** coffee with a dash of milk

'**macchina** ['makkina] *sf* machine; (*motore, locomotiva*) engine; (*automobile*) car; (*fig: meccanismo*) machinery; **andare in ~** (*Aut*) to go by car; (*Stampa*) to go to press; **~ da cucire** sewing machine; **~ fotografica** camera; **~ da presa** cine *o* movie camera; **~ da scrivere** typewriter; **~ a vapore** steam engine

macchi'nario [makki'narjo] *sm* machinery

macchi'nista, -i [makki'nista] *sm* (*di treno*) engine-driver; (*di nave*) engineer

Mace'donia [matʃe'dɔnja] *sf* Macedonia

mace'donia [matʃe'dɔnja] *sf* fruit salad

macel'laio [matʃel'lajo] *sm* butcher

macelle'ria *sf* butcher's (shop)

ma'cerie [ma'tʃɛrje] *sfpl* rubble *sg*, debris *sg*

ma'cigno [ma'tʃinno] *sm* (*masso*) rock, boulder

maci'nare [matʃi'nare] /72/ *vt* to grind; (*carne*) to mince (BRIT), grind (US)

macrobi'otico, -a *ag* macrobiotic ▷ *sf* macrobiotics *sg*

Ma'donna *sf* (*Rel*) Our Lady

mador'nale *ag* enormous, huge

'**madre** *sf* mother; (*matrice di bolletta*) counterfoil ▷ *ag inv* mother *cpd*; **ragazza ~** unmarried mother; **scena ~** (*Teat*) principal scene; (*fig*) terrible scene

madre'lingua *sf* mother tongue, native language

madre'perla *sf* mother-of-pearl

ma'drina *sf* godmother

maestà *sf inv* majesty

ma'estra *sf vedi* **maestro**

maes'trale *sm* north-west wind, mistral

ma'estro, -a *sm/f* (*Ins: anche:* **~ di scuola** *o* **elementare**) primary (BRIT) *o* grade school (US) teacher; (*esperto*) expert ▷ *sm* (*artigiano, fig: guida*) master; (*Mus*) maestro ▷ *ag* (*principale*) main; (*di grande abilità*) masterly, skilful; **maestra d'asilo** nursery teacher; **~ di cerimonie** master of ceremonies

'mafia sf Mafia

'maga, -ghe sf sorceress

ma'gari escl (esprime desiderio): **~ fosse vero!** if only it were true!; **ti piacerebbe andare in Scozia? — ~!** would you like to go to Scotland? — I certainly would! ▷ av (anche) even; (forse) perhaps

magaz'zino [magad'dzino] sm warehouse; **grande ~** department store

> Attenzione! In inglese esiste la parola *magazine*, che però significa *rivista*.

'maggio ['maddʒo] sm May

maggio'rana [maddʒo'rana] sf (Bot) (sweet) marjoram

maggio'ranza [maddʒo'rantsa] sf majority

maggior'domo [maddʒor'dɔmo] sm butler

maggi'ore [mad'dʒore] ag (comparativo: più grande) bigger, larger; taller; greater; (: più vecchio: sorella, fratello) older, elder; (: di grado superiore) senior; (: più importante: Mil, Mus) major; (superlativo) biggest, largest; tallest; greatest; oldest, eldest ▷ smf (di grado) superior; (di età) elder; (Mil) major; (: Aer) squadron leader; **la maggior parte** the majority; **andare per la ~** (cantante, attore ecc) to be very popular; **maggio'renne** ag of age ▷ smf person who has come of age

ma'gia [ma'dʒia] sf magic; **'magico, -a, -ci, -che** ag magic; (fig) fascinating, charming, magical

nagis'trato [madʒis'trato] sm magistrate

maglia ['maʎʎa] sf stitch; (lavoro ai ferri) knitting no pl; (tessuto, Sport) jersey; (maglione) jersey, sweater; (di catena) link; (di rete) mesh; **~ diritta/rovescia** plain/purl; **magli'etta**

sf (canottiera) vest; (tipo camicia) T-shirt

magli'one [maʎ'ʎone] sm jumper, sweater

ma'gnetico, -a, -ci, -che ag magnetic

ma'gnifico, -a, -ci, -che [maɲ'nifiko] ag magnificent, splendid; (ospite) generous

ma'gnolia [maɲ'nɔlja] sf magnolia

'mago, -ghi sm (stregone) magician, wizard; (illusionista) magician

ma'grezza [ma'grettsa] sf thinness

'magro, -a ag (very) thin, skinny; (carne) lean; (formaggio) low-fat; (fig: scarso, misero) meagre, poor; (: meschino: scusa) poor, lame; **mangiare di ~** not to eat meat

'mai av (nessuna volta) never; (talvolta) ever; **non ... ~** never; **~ più** never again; **come ~?** why (o how) on earth?; **chi/dove/quando ~?** whoever/wherever/whenever?

mai'ale sm (Zool) pig; (carne) pork

mail ['meil] sf inv = **e-mail**

maio'nese sf mayonnaise

'mais sm maize

mai'uscolo, -a ag (lettera) capital; (fig) enormous, huge

mala'fede sf bad faith

malan'dato, -a ag (persona: di salute) in poor health; (: di condizioni finanziarie) badly off; (trascurato) shabby

ma'lanno sm (disgrazia) misfortune; (malattia) ailment

mala'pena sf: **a ~** hardly, scarcely

ma'laria sf (Med) malaria

ma'lato, -a ag ill, sick; (gamba) bad; (pianta) diseased ▷ sm/f sick person; (in ospedale) patient; **malat'tia** sf (infettiva ecc) illness, disease; (cattiva salute) illness, sickness; (di pianta) disease

mala'vita sf underworld

mala'voglia [mala'vɔʎʎa] sf: **di ~** av unwillingly, reluctantly

Mala'ysia sf Malaysia

mal'concio, -a, -ci, -ce
[mal'kontʃo] *ag* in a sorry state
malcon'tento *sm* discontent
malcos'tume *sm* immorality
mal'destro, -a *ag* (*inabile*) inexpert,
inexperienced; (*goffo*) awkward
'**male** *av* badly ▷ *sm* (*ciò che è ingiusto,
disonesto*) evil; (*danno, svantaggio*)
harm; (*sventura*) misfortune; (*dolore
fisico, morale*) pain, ache; **sentirsi ~**
to feel ill; **aver mal di cuore/fegato**
to have a heart/liver complaint;
**aver mal di denti/d'orecchi/di
testa** to have toothache/earache/a
headache; **aver mal di gola** to have
a sore throat; **aver ~ ai piedi** to have
sore feet; **far ~** (*dolere*) to hurt; **far ~
alla salute** to be bad for one's health;
far del ~ a qn to hurt *o* harm sb;
restare *o* **rimanere ~** to be sorry; to
be disappointed, to be hurt; **trattar
~ qn** to ill-treat sb; **andare a ~** to go
off *o* bad; **come va? — non c'è ~** how
are you? — not bad; **di ~ in peggio**
from bad to worse; **mal d'auto**
carsickness; **mal di mare** seasickness
male'detto, -a *pp di* **maledire** ▷ *ag*
cursed, damned; (*fig fam*) damned,
blasted
male'dire /38/ *vt* to curse;
maledizi'one *sf* curse; **maledizione!**
damn it!
maledu'cato, -a *ag* rude, ill-
mannered
maleducazi'one
[maledukat'tsjone] *sf* rudeness
ma'lefico, -a, -ci, -che *ag* (*influsso,
azione*) evil
ma'lessere *sm* indisposition, slight
illness; (*fig*) uneasiness
malfa'mato, -a *ag* notorious
malfat'tore, -'trice *sm/f*
wrongdoer
mal'fermo, -a *ag* unsteady, shaky;
(*salute*) poor, delicate
mal'grado *prep* in spite of, despite
▷ *cong* although; **mio** *o* **tuo** *ecc* **~**
against my (*o* your *ecc*) will

ma'ligno, -a [ma'liɲɲo] *ag*
(*malvagio*) malicious, malignant;
(*Med*) malignant
malinco'nia *sf* melancholy, gloom;
malin'conico, -a, -ci, -che *ag*
melancholy
malincu'ore: **a ~** *av* reluctantly,
unwillingly
malin'teso, -a *ag* misunderstood;
(*riguardo, senso del dovere*) mistaken,
wrong ▷ *sm* misunderstanding;
c'è stato un ~ there's been a
misunderstanding
ma'lizia [ma'littsja] *sf* (*malignità*)
malice; (*furbizia*) cunning;
(*espediente*) trick; **malizi'oso, -a** *ag*
malicious; cunning; (*vivace, birichino*)
mischievous
malme'nare /72/ *vt* to beat up
ma'locchio [ma'lɔkkjo] *sm* evil eye
ma'lora *sf*: **andare in ~** to go to
the dogs
ma'lore *sm* (sudden) illness
mal'sano, -a *ag* unhealthy
'**malta** *sf* (*Edil*) mortar
mal'tempo *sm* bad weather
'**malto** *sm* malt
maltrat'tare /72/ *vt* to ill-treat
malu'more *sm* bad mood; (*irritabilità*)
bad temper; (*discordia*) ill feeling; **di ~**
in a bad mood
'**malva** *sf* (*Bot*) mallow ▷ *ag, sm inv*
mauve
mal'vagio, -a, -gi, -gie [mal'vadʒo]
ag wicked, evil
malvi'vente *sm* criminal
malvolenti'eri *av* unwillingly,
reluctantly
'**mamma** *sf* mum(my); **~ mia!** my
goodness!
mam'mella *sf* (*Anat*) breast; (*di vacca,
capra ecc*) udder
mam'mifero *sm* mammal
ma'nata *sf* (*colpo*) slap; (*quantità*)
handful
man'canza [man'kantsa] *sf*
lack; (*carenza*) shortage, scarcity;
(*fallo*) fault; (*imperfezione*) failing,

shortcoming; **per ~ di tempo** through lack of time; **in ~ di meglio** for lack of anything better

man'care /20/ vi (essere insufficiente) to be lacking; (venir meno) to fail; (sbagliare) to be wrong, make a mistake; (non esserci) to be missing, not to be there; (essere lontano): **~ (da)** to be away (from) ▷ vt to miss; **~ di** to lack; **~ a** (promessa) to fail to keep; **tu mi manchi** I miss you; **mancò poco che morisse** he very nearly died; **mancano ancora 10 sterline** we're still £10 short; **manca un quarto alle 6** it's a quarter to 6

mancherò ecc [manke'rɔ] vb vedi **mancare**

'mancia, -ce ['mantʃa] sf tip; **~ competente** reward

manci'ata [man'tʃata] sf handful

man'cino, -a [man'tʃino] ag (braccio) left; (persona) left-handed; (fig) underhand

manda'rancio [manda'rantʃo] sm clementine

man'dare /72/ vt to send; (far funzionare: macchina) to drive; (emettere) to send out; (: grido) to give, utter, let out; **~ avanti** (fig: famiglia) to provide for; (: fabbrica) to run, look after; **~ giù** to send down; (anche fig) to swallow; **~ via** to send away; (licenziare) to fire

manda'rino sm mandarin (orange); (cinese) mandarin

man'data sf (quantità) lot, batch; (di chiave) turn; **chiudere a doppia ~** to double-lock

man'dato sm (incarico) commission; (Dir: provvedimento) warrant; (di deputato ecc) mandate; (ordine di pagamento) postal o money order; **~ d'arresto** warrant for arrest

man'dibola sf mandible, jaw

'mandorla sf almond; **'mandorlo** sm almond tree

'mandria sf herd

maneggi'are [maned'dʒare] /62/ vt (creta, cera) to mould, work, fashion; (arnesi, utensili) to handle; (: adoperare) to use; (fig: persone, denaro) to handle, deal with; **ma'neggio** sm moulding; handling; use; (intrigo) plot, scheme; (per cavalli) riding school

ma'nesco, -a, -schi, -sche ag free with one's fists

ma'nette sfpl handcuffs

manga'nello sm club

mangi'are [man'dʒare] /62/ vt to eat; (intaccare) to eat into o away; (Carte, Scacchi: ecc) to take ▷ vi to eat ▷ sm eating; (cibo) food; (cucina) cooking; **mangiarsi le parole** to mumble; **mangiarsi le unghie** to bite one's nails

man'gime [man'dʒime] sm fodder

'mango, -ghi sm mango

ma'nia sf (Psic) mania; (fig) obsession, craze; **ma'niaco, -a, -ci, -che** ag suffering from a mania; **maniaco (di)** obsessed (by), crazy (about)

'manica, -che sf sleeve; (fig: gruppo) gang, bunch; (Geo): **la M~, il Canale della M~** the (English) Channel; **essere di ~ larga/stretta** to be easy-going/strict; **~ a vento** (Aer) wind sock

mani'chino [mani'kino] sm (di sarto, vetrina) dummy

'manico, -ci sm handle; (Mus) neck

mani'comio sm psychiatric hospital; (fig) madhouse

mani'cure sf o m inv manicure ▷ sf inv manicurist

mani'era sf way, manner; (stile) style, manner; **maniere** sfpl (comportamento) manners; **in ~ che** so that; **in ~ da** so as to; **in tutte le maniere** at all costs

manifes'tare /72/ vt to show, display; (esprimere) to express; (rivelare) to reveal, disclose ▷ vi to demonstrate; **manifestazi'one** sf show, display, expression; (sintomo)

m

sign, symptom; (*dimostrazione pubblica*) demonstration; (*cerimonia*) event

mani'festo, -a *ag* obvious, evident ▷ *sm* poster, bill; (*scritto ideologico*) manifesto

ma'niglia [ma'niʎʎa] *sf* handle; (*sostegno: negli autobus ecc*) strap

manipo'lare /72/ *vt* to manipulate; (*alterare: vino*) to adulterate

man'naro, -a *ag*: **lupo ~** werewolf

'mano, -i *sf* hand; (*strato: di vernice ecc*) coat; **a ~** by hand; **di prima ~** (*notizia*) first-hand; **di seconda ~** second-hand; **man ~** little by little, gradually; **man ~ che** as; **darsi** *o* **stringersi la ~** to shake hands; **mettere le mani avanti** (*fig*) to safeguard o.s.; **restare a mani vuote** to be left empty-handed; **venire alle mani** to come to blows; **mani in alto!** hands up!

mano'dopera *sf* labour

ma'nometro *sm* gauge, manometer

mano'mettere /63/ *vt* (*alterare*) to tamper with; (*aprire indebitamente*) to break open illegally

ma'nopola *sf* (*dell'armatura*) gauntlet; (*guanto*) mitt; (*di impugnatura*) hand-grip; (*pomello*) knob

manos'critto, -a *ag* handwritten ▷ *sm* manuscript

mano'vale *sm* labourer

mano'vella *sf* handle; (*Tecn*) crank

ma'novra *sf* manoeuvre (BRIT), maneuver (US); (*Ferr*) shunting

man'sarda *sf* attic

mansi'one *sf* task, duty, job

mansu'eto, -a *ag* gentle, docile

man'tello *sm* cloak; (*fig: di neve ecc*) blanket, mantle; (*Zool*) coat

mante'nere /121/ *vt* to maintain; (*adempiere: promesse*) to keep, abide by; (*provvedere a*) to support, maintain; **mantenersi** *vpr*: **mantenersi calmo/giovane** to stay calm/young

'Mantova *sf* Mantua

manu'ale *ag* manual ▷ *sm* (*testo*) manual, handbook

ma'nubrio *sm* handle; (*di bicicletta ecc*) handlebars *pl*; (*Sport*) dumbbell

manutenzi'one [manuten'tsjone] *sf* maintenance, upkeep; (*d'impianti*) maintenance, servicing

'manzo ['mandzo] *sm* (*Zool*) steer; (*carne*) beef

'mappa *sf* (*Geo*) map; **mappa'mondo** *sm* map of the world; (*globo girevole*) globe

mara'tona *sf* marathon

'marca, -che *sf* (*Comm: di prodotti*) brand; (*contrassegno, scontrino*) ticket, check; **prodotti di (gran) ~** high-class products; **~ da bollo** official stamp

mar'care /20/ *vt* (*munire di contrassegno*) to mark; (*a fuoco*) to brand; (*Sport: gol*) to score; (*: avversario*) to mark; (*accentuare*) to stress; **~ visita** (*Mil*) to report sick

marcherò ecc [marke'rɔ] *vb vedi* **marcare**

mar'chese, -a [mar'keze] *sm/f* marquis *o* marquess/marchioness

marchi'are [mar'kjare] /19/ *vt* to brand

'marcia, -ce ['martʃa] *sf* (*anche Mus, Mil*) march; (*funzionamento*) running; (*il camminare*) walking; (*Aut*) gear; **mettere in ~** to start; **mettersi in ~** to get moving; **far ~ indietro** (*Aut*) to reverse; (*fig*) to back-pedal

marciapi'ede [martʃa'pjɛde] *sm* (*di strada*) pavement (BRIT), sidewalk (US); (*Ferr*) platform

marci'are [mar'tʃare] /14/ *vi* to march; (*andare, treno, macchina*) to go; (*funzionare*) to run, work

'marcio, -a, -ci, -ce ['martʃo] *ag* (*frutta, legno*) rotten, bad; (*Med*) festering; (*fig*) corrupt, rotten

mar'cire [mar'tʃire] /55/ *vi* (*andare a male*) to go bad, rot; (*suppurare*) to fester; (*fig*) to rot, waste away

'**marco, -chi** sm (unità monetaria) mark

'**mare** sm sea; **in ~** at sea; **andare al ~** (in vacanza ecc) to go to the seaside; **il ~ del Nord** the North Sea

ma'**rea** sf tide; **alta/bassa ~** high/low tide

mareggi'**ata** [mared'dʒata] sf heavy sea

mare'**moto** sm seaquake

maresci'**allo** [mareʃʃallo] sm (Mil) marshal; (sottufficiale) warrant officer

marga'**rina** sf margarine

marghe'**rita** [marge'rita] sf (ox-eye) daisy, marguerite

'**margine** ['mardʒine] sm margin; (di bosco, via) edge, border

mariju'**ana** [mæri'wa:nə] sf marijuana

ma'**rina** sf navy; (costa) coast; (quadro) seascape; **~ mercantile** merchant navy (BRIT) o marine (US); **~ militare** ≈ Royal Navy (BRIT), ≈ Navy (US)

mari'**naio** sm sailor

mari'**nare** /72/ vt (Cuc) to marinate; **~ la scuola** to play truant

ma'**rino, -a** ag sea cpd, marine

mario'**netta** sf puppet

ma'**rito** sm husband

ma'**rittimo, -a** ag maritime, sea cpd

marmel'**lata** sf jam; (di agrumi) marmalade

mar'**mitta** sf (recipiente) pot; (Aut) silencer; **~ catalitica** catalytic converter

'**marmo** sm marble

mar'**motta** sf (Zool) marmot

maroc'**chino, -a** [marok'kino] ag, sm/f Moroccan

Ma'**rocco** sm: **il ~** Morocco

mar'**rone** ag inv brown ▷ sm (Bot) chestnut

> Attenzione! In inglese esiste la parola maroon, che però indica un altro colore, il rosso bordeaux.

mar'**supio** sm (Zool) pouch, marsupium

marte'**dì** sm inv Tuesday; **di** o **il ~** on Tuesdays; **~ grasso** Shrove Tuesday

martel'**lare** /72/ vt to hammer ▷ vi (pulsare) to throb; (: cuore) to thump

mar'**tello** sm hammer; (di uscio) knocker; **~ pneumatico** pneumatic drill

'**martire** smf martyr

mar'**xista, -i, -e** ag, smf Marxist

marza'**pane** [martsa'pane] sm marzipan

'**marzo** ['martso] sm March

mascal'**zone** [maskal'tsone] sm rascal, scoundrel

mas'**cara** sm inv mascara

ma'**scella** [maʃʃella] sf (Anat) jaw

'**maschera** ['maskera] sf mask; (travestimento) disguise; (per un ballo ecc) fancy dress; (Teat, Cine) usher/usherette; (personaggio del teatro) stock character; **masche'rare** /72/ vt to mask; (travestire) to disguise; to dress up; (fig: celare) to hide, conceal; (Mil) to camouflage; **mascherarsi** vpr: **mascherarsi da** to disguise o.s. as; to dress up as; (fig) to masquerade as

mas'**chile** [mas'kile] ag masculine; (sesso, popolazione) male; (abiti) men's; (per ragazzi, scuola) boys'

maschi'**lista, -i, -e** ag, smf (uomo) (male) chauvinist, sexist; (donna) sexist

'**maschio, -a** ['maskjo] ag (Biol) male; (virile) manly ▷ sm (anche Zool, Tecn) male; (uomo) man; (ragazzo) boy; (figlio) son

masco'**lino, -a** ag masculine

'**massa** sf mass; (di gente) mass, multitude; (Elettr) earth; **una ~ di** (di errori ecc) heaps of, masses of; **in ~** (Comm) in bulk; (tutti insieme) en masse; **adunata in ~** mass meeting; **manifestazione/cultura di ~** mass demonstration/culture

mas'**sacro** sm massacre, slaughter; (fig) mess, disaster

massaggi'**are** [massad'dʒare] /62/ vt to massage

mas'saggio [mas'saddʒo] *sm* massage; **~ cardiaco** cardiac massage

mas'saia *sf* housewife

masse'rizie [masse'rittsje] *sfpl* (household) furnishings

mas'siccio, -a, -ci, -ce [mas'sittʃo] *ag (oro, legno)* solid; *(palazzo)* massive; *(corporatura)* stout ▷ *sm (Geo)* massif

'massima *sf vedi* **massimo**

massi'male *sm* maximum; *(Comm)* ceiling, limit

'massimo, -a *ag*, *sm* maximum ▷ *sf (sentenza, regola)* maxim; *(Meteor)* maximum temperature; **in linea di massima** generally speaking; **al ~** at (the) most

'masso *sm* rock, boulder

masteriz'zare [masterid'dzare] /72/ *vt (CD, DVD)* to burn

masterizza'tore [masteriddza'tore] *sm* CD burner *o* writer

masti'care /20/ *vt* to chew

'mastice ['mastitʃe] *sm* mastic; *(per vetri)* putty

mas'tino *sm* mastiff

ma'tassa *sf* skein

mate'matico, -a, -ci, -che *ag* mathematical ▷ *sm/f* mathematician ▷ *sf* mathematics *sg*

materas'sino *sm* mat; **~ gonfiabile** air bed

mate'rasso *sm* mattress; **~ a molle** spring *o* interior-sprung mattress

ma'teria *sf (Fisica)* matter; *(Tecn, Comm)* material, matter *no pl*; *(disciplina)* subject; *(argomento)* subject matter, material; **in ~ di** *(per quanto concerne)* on the subject of; **materie prime** raw materials

materi'ale *ag* material; *(fig: grossolano)* rough, rude ▷ *sm* material; *(insieme di strumenti ecc)* equipment *no pl*, materials *pl*

maternità *sf* motherhood, maternity; *(reparto)* maternity ward

ma'terno, -a *ag (amore, cura ecc)* maternal, motherly; *(nonno)* maternal; *(lingua, terra)* mother *cpd*

ma'tita *sf* pencil; **matite colorate** coloured pencils; **~ per gli occhi** eyeliner (pencil)

ma'tricola *sf (registro)* register; *(numero)* registration number; *(nell'università)* freshman, fresher

ma'trigna [ma'triɲɲa] *sf* stepmother

matrimoni'ale *ag* matrimonial, marriage *cpd*

matri'monio *sm* marriage, matrimony; *(durata)* marriage, married life; *(cerimonia)* wedding

mat'tina *sf* morning

'matto, -a *ag* mad, crazy; *(fig: falso)* false, imitation ▷ *sm/f* madman/ woman; **avere una voglia matta di qc** to be dying for sth

mat'tone *sm* brick; *(fig)*: **questo libro/film è un ~** this book/film is heavy going

matto'nella *sf* tile

matu'rare /72/ *vi (anche: maturarsi) (frutta, grano)* to ripen; *(ascesso)* to come to a head; *(fig: persona, idea, Econ)* to mature ▷ *vt* to ripen, to (make) mature

maturità *sf* maturity; *(di frutta)* ripeness, maturity; *(Ins)* school-leaving examination, ≈ GCE A-levels (BRIT)

ma'turo, -a *ag* mature; *(frutto)* ripe, mature

max. *abbr (= massimo)* max

maxis'chermo [maksis'kermo] *sm* giant screen

'mazza ['mattsa] *sf (bastone)* club; *(martello)* sledge-hammer; *(Sport: da golf)* club; *(: da baseball, cricket)* bat

maz'zata [mat'tsata] *sf (anche fig)* heavy blow

'mazzo ['mattso] *sm (di fiori, chiavi ecc)* bunch; *(di carte da gioco)* pack

me *pron* me; **me stesso, me stessa** myself; **sei bravo quanto me** you are as clever as I (am) *o* as me

mec'canico, -a, -ci, -che ag
mechanical ▷ sm mechanic
mecca'nismo sm mechanism
me'daglia [me'daʎʎa] sf medal
me'desimo, -a ag same; (in persona):
io ~ I myself
'media sf vedi **medio**
medi'ante prep by means of
media'tore, -'trice sm/f mediator;
(Comm) middle man, agent
medi'care /20/ vt to treat; (ferita)
to dress
medi'cina [medi'tʃina] sf medicine;
~ legale forensic medicine
'medico, -a, -ci, -che ag medical
▷ sm doctor; **~ generico** general
practitioner, GP
medie'vale ag medieval
'medio, -a ag average; (punto, ceto)
middle; (altezza, statura) medium
▷ sm (dito) middle finger ▷ sf average;
(Mat) mean; (Ins: voto) end-of-term
average; **medie** sfpl vedi **scuola
media**; **licenza media** leaving
certificate awarded at the end of 3 years
of secondary education; **in media** on
average
medi'ocre ag mediocre; poor
medi'tare /72/ vt to ponder over,
meditate on; (progettare) to plan,
think out ▷ vi to meditate
mediter'raneo, -a ag
Mediterranean; **il (mare) M~** the
Mediterranean (Sea)
me'dusa sf (Zool) jellyfish
mega sm inv (Inform) meg
mega'byte sm inv (Inform) megabyte
me'gafono sm megaphone
'meglio ['mɛʎʎo] av, ag inv better;
(con senso superlativo) best ▷ sm (la
cosa migliore): **il ~** the best (thing);
faresti ~ ad andartene you had
better leave; **alla ~** as best one can;
andar di bene in ~ to get better and
better; **fare del proprio ~** to do one's
best; **per il ~** for the best; **aver la ~
su qn** to get the better of sb
mela sf apple; **~ cotogna** quince

mela'grana sf pomegranate
melan'zana [melan'dzana] sf
aubergine (BRIT), eggplant (US)
melato'nina sf melatonin
'melma sf mud, mire
'melo sm apple tree
melo'dia sf melody
me'lone sm (musk) melon
'membro sm (pl m **membri**) member;
(pl f **membra**) (arto) limb
memo'randum sm inv
memorandum
me'moria sf memory; **memorie**
sfpl (opera autobiografica) memoirs;
a ~ (imparare, sapere) by heart; **a ~
d'uomo** within living memory
mendi'cante smf beggar

PAROLA CHIAVE

'meno av **1** (in minore misura) less;
dovresti mangiare meno you
should eat less, you shouldn't eat
so much
2 (comparativo): **meno ... di** not as ...
as, less ... than; **sono meno alto di
te** I'm not as tall as you (are), I'm less
tall than you (are); **meno ... che** not
as ... as, less ... than; **meno che mai**
less than ever; **è meno intelligente
che ricco** he's more rich than
intelligent; **meno fumo più mangio**
the less I smoke the more I eat
3 (superlativo) least; **il meno dotato
degli studenti** the least gifted of
the students; **è quello che compro
meno spesso** it's the one I buy
least often
4 (Mat) minus; **8 meno 5** 8 minus 5,
8 take away 5; **sono le 8 meno un
quarto** it's a quarter to 8; **meno 5
gradi** 5 degrees below zero, minus
5 degrees; **mille euro in meno** a
thousand euros less
5 (fraseologia): **quanto meno
poteva telefonare** he could at least
have phoned; **non so se accettare
o meno** I don't know whether to

m

accept or not; **fare a meno di qc/qn** to do without sth/sb; **non potevo fare a meno di ridere** I couldn't help laughing; **meno male!** thank goodness!; **meno male che sei arrivato** it's a good job that you've come

▶ *ag inv* (*tempo, denaro*) less; (*errori, persone*) fewer; **ha fatto meno errori di tutti** he made fewer mistakes than anyone, he made the fewest mistakes of all

▶ *sm inv* **1**: **il meno** (*il minimo*) the least; **parlare del più e del meno** to talk about this and that **2** (*Mat*) minus

▶ *prep* (*eccetto*) except (for), apart from; **a meno che, a meno di** unless; **a meno che non piova** unless it rains; **non posso, a meno di prendere ferie** I can't, unless I take some leave

meno'pausa *sf* menopause
'**mensa** *sf* (*locale*) canteen; (: *Mil*) mess; (: *nelle università*) refectory
men'sile *ag* monthly ▷ *sm* (*periodico*) monthly (magazine); (*stipendio*) monthly salary
'**mensola** *sf* bracket; (*ripiano*) shelf; (*Archit*) corbel
'**menta** *sf* mint; (*anche*: **~ piperita**) peppermint; (*bibita*) peppermint cordial; (*caramella*) mint, peppermint
men'tale *ag* mental; **mentalità** *sf inv* mentality
'**mente** *sf* mind; **imparare/sapere qc a ~** to learn/know sth by heart; **avere in ~ qc** to have sth in mind; **passare di ~ a qn** to slip sb's mind
men'tire /17/ *vi* to lie
'**mento** *sm* chin
'**mentre** *cong* (*temporale*) while; (*avversativo*) whereas
menù *sm inv* (set) menu; **~ turistico** set *o* tourists' menu
menzio'nare [mentsjo'nare] /72/ *vt* to mention

men'zogna [men'tsɔɲɲa] *sf* lie
mera'viglia [mera'viʎʎa] *sf* amazement, wonder; (*persona, cosa*) marvel, wonder; **a ~** perfectly, wonderfully; **meravigli'are** /27/ *vt* to amaze, astonish; **meravigliarsi** *vpr*: **meravigliarsi (di)** to marvel (at); (*stupirsi*) to be amazed (at), be astonished (at); **meravigli'oso, -a** *ag* wonderful, marvellous (BRIT), marvelous (US)
mer'cante *sm* merchant; **~ d'arte** art dealer
merca'tino *sm* (*rionale*) local street market; (*Econ*) unofficial stock market
mer'cato *sm* market; **~ dei cambi** exchange market; **~ nero** black market
'**merce** ['mɛrtʃe] *sf* goods *pl*, merchandise
mercé [mer'tʃe] *sf* mercy
merce'ria [mertʃe'ria] *sf* (*articoli*) haberdashery (BRIT), notions *pl* (US); (*bottega*) haberdasher's shop (BRIT), notions store (US)
mercoledì *sm inv* Wednesday; **di** *o* **il ~** on Wednesdays; **~ delle Ceneri** Ash Wednesday
mer'curio *sm* mercury
'**merda** *sf* (*fam!*) shit (!)
me'renda *sf* afternoon snack
meren'dina *sf* snack
meridi'ano, -a *ag* (*di mezzogiorno*) midday *cpd*, noonday ▷ *sm* meridian ▷ *sf* (*orologio*) sundial
meridio'nale *ag* southern ▷ *smf* southerner
meridi'one *sm* south
me'ringa, -ghe *sf* (*Cuc*) meringue
meri'tare /72/ *vt* to deserve, merit ▷ *vb impers*: **merita andare** it's worth going
meri'tevole *ag* worthy
'**merito** *sm* merit; (*valore*) worth; **dare ~ a qn di** to give sb credit for; **finire a pari ~** to finish joint first (*o* second *ecc*); to tie; **in ~ a** as regards, with regard to

mer'letto sm lace

'merlo sm (Zool) blackbird; (Archit) battlement

mer'luzzo [mer'luttso] sm (Zool) cod

mes'chino, -a [mes'kino] ag wretched; (scarso) scanty, poor; (persona: gretta) mean; (: limitata) narrow-minded, petty

mesco'lare /72/ vt to mix; (vini, colori) to blend; (mettere in disordine) to mix up, muddle up; (carte) to shuffle

'mese sm month

'messa sf (Rel) mass; ~ in moto starting; ~ in piega set; ~ a punto (Tecn) adjustment; (Aut) tuning; (fig) clarification; ~ in scena = messinscena

messag'gero [messad'dʒero] sm messenger

messaggi'arsi [messad'dʒarsi] /72/ vpr to text; messaggiamoci we'll text each other

messag'gino [messad'dʒino] sm (di telefonino) text (message)

mes'saggio [mes'saddʒo] sm message

messag'gistica [messad'dʒistica] sf: ~ immediata (Inform) instant messaging; programma di ~ immediata instant messenger

mes'sale sm (Rel) missal

messi'cano, -a ag, sm/f Mexican

'Messico sm: il ~ Mexico

messin'scena [messin'ʃɛna] sf (Teat) production

'messo, -a pp di mettere ▷ sm messenger

mesti'ere sm (professione) job; (: manuale) trade; (: artigianale) craft; (fig: abilità nel lavoro) skill, technique; essere del ~ to know the tricks of the trade

'mestolo sm (Cuc) ladle

mestruazi'one [mestruat'tsjone] sf menstruation

'meta sf destination; (fig) aim, goal

metà sf inv half; (punto di mezzo) middle; dividere qc a o per ~ to divide sth in half, halve sth; fare a ~ (di qc con qn) to go halves (with sb in sth); a ~ prezzo at half price; a ~ strada halfway

meta'done sm methadone

me'tafora sf metaphor

me'tallico, -a, -ci, -che ag (di metallo) metal cpd; (splendore, rumore ecc) metallic

me'tallo sm metal

metalmec'canico, -a, -ci, -che ag engineering cpd ▷ sm engineering worker

me'tano sm methane

meteoro'logico, -a, -ci, -che [meteoro'lɔdʒiko] ag meteorological, weather cpd

me'ticcio, -a, -ci, -ce [me'tittʃo] sm/f half-caste (!), half-breed (!)

me'todico, -a, -ci, -che ag methodical

'metodo sm method

'metro sm metre; (nastro) tape measure; (asta) (metre) rule

metropoli'tano, -a ag metropolitan ▷ sf underground (BRIT), subway (US)

metroses'suale ag metrosexual

'mettere /63/ vt to put; (abito) to put on; (: portare) to wear; (installare: telefono) to put in; (fig: provocare): ~ fame/allegria a qn to make sb hungry/happy; (supporre): mettiamo che ... let's suppose o say that ...; mettersi vpr (persona) to put o.s.; (oggetto) to go; (disporsi: faccenda) to turn out; mettersi a (cominciare) to begin to, start to; mettersi a sedere to sit down; mettersi al lavoro to set to work; mettersi a letto to get into bed; (per malattia) to take to one's bed; mettersi il cappello to put on one's hat; mettersi con qn (in società) to team up with sb; (in coppia) to start going out with sb; metterci: metterci molta cura/molto tempo to take a lot of care/a lot of time; mettercela tutta to do one's best;

m

~ **a tacere** qn/qc to keep sb/sth quiet; ~ **su casa** to set up house; ~ **su un negozio** to start a shop; ~ **via** to put away

mezza'notte [meddza'nɔtte] *sf* midnight

'mezzo, -a ['mɛddzo] *ag* half; **un ~ litro/panino** half a litre/ roll ▷ *av* half-; ~ **morto** half-dead ▷ *sm (metà)* half; *(parte centrale: di strada ecc)* middle; *(per raggiungere un fine)* means *sg*; *(veicolo)* vehicle; *(nell'indicare l'ora)*: **le nove e ~** half past nine; **mezzogiorno e ~** half past twelve; **mezzi** *smpl (possibilità economiche)* means; **di mezza età** middle-aged; **un soprabito di mezza stagione** a spring (o autumn) coat; **di ~** middle, in the middle; **andarci di ~** *(patir danno)* to suffer; **levarsi** o **togliersi di ~** to get out of the way; **in ~ a** in the middle of; **per** o **a ~ di** by means of; **mezzi di comunicazione di massa** mass media *pl*: **mezzi pubblici** public transport *sg*: **mezzi di trasporto** means of transport

mezzogi'orno [meddzo'dʒorno] *sm* midday, noon; **a ~** at 12 (o'clock) o midday o noon; **il ~ d'Italia** southern Italy

mi *pron (dav lo, la, li, le, ne diventa* **me**: *oggetto)* me; *(complemento di termine)* (to) me; *(riflessivo)* myself ▷ *sm (Mus)* E; *(: solfeggiando la scala)* mi

miago'lare /72/ *vi* to miaow, mew

'mica *av (fam)*: **non ... ~** not ... at all; **non sono ~ stanco** I'm not a bit tired; **non sarà ~ partito?** he wouldn't have left, would he?; ~ **male** not bad

'miccia, -ce ['mittʃa] *sf* fuse

micidi'ale [mitʃi'djale] *ag* fatal; *(dannosissimo)* deadly

micro'fibra *sf* microfibre

mi'crofono *sm* microphone

micros'copio *sm* microscope

mi'dollo *(pl f* **midolla**) *sm (Anat)* marrow; ~ **osseo** bone marrow

mi'ele *sm* honey

'miglia ['miʎʎa] *sfpl di* **miglio¹**

migli'aio [miʎ'ʎajo] *(pl f* **migliaia**) *sm* thousand; **un ~ (di)** about a thousand; **a migliaia** by the thousand, in thousands

'miglio¹ [miʎ'ʎo] *(pl f* **miglia**) *sm (unità di misura)* mile; ~ **marino** o **nautico** nautical mile

'miglio² ['miʎʎo] *sm (Bot)* millet

migliora'mento [miʎʎora'mento] *sm* improvement

miglio'rare [miʎʎo'rare] /72/ *vt, vi* to improve

migli'ore [miʎ'ʎore] *ag (comparativo)* better; *(superlativo)* best ▷ *sm*: **il ~** the best (thing) ▷ *smf*: **il (la) ~** the best (person); **il miglior vino di questa regione** the best wine in this area

'mignolo ['miɲɲolo] *sm (Anat)* little finger, pinkie; *(: dito del piede)* little toe

Mi'lano *sf* Milan

miliar'dario, -a *sm/f* millionaire

mili'ardo *sm* thousand million , billion *(us)*

mili'one *sm* million

mili'tante *ag, smf* militant

mili'tare /72/ *vi (Mil)* to be a soldier, serve; *(fig: in un partito)* to be a militant ▷ *ag* military ▷ *sm* serviceman; **fare il ~** to do one's military service

'mille *(pl* **mila**) *num* a o one thousand; **diecimila** ten thousand; ~ **euro** one thousand euros

mil'lennio *sm* millennium

millepi'edi *sm inv* centipede

mil'lesimo, -a *ag, sm* thousandth

milli'grammo *sm* milligram(me)

mil'limetro *sm* millimetre

'milza ['miltsa] *sf (Anat)* spleen

mimetiz'zare [mimetid'dzare] /72/ *vt* to camouflage; **mimetizzarsi** *vpr* to camouflage o.s.

'mimo *sm (attore, componimento)* mime

mi'mosa sf mimosa

min. abbr (= minuto, minimo) min

mina sf (esplosiva) mine; (di matita) lead

mi'naccia, -ce [mi'nattʃa] sf threat; **minacci'are** /14/ vt to threaten; **minacciare qn di morte** to threaten to kill sb; **minacciare di fare qc** to threaten to do sth

mi'nare /72/ vt (Mil) to mine; (fig) to undermine

mina'tore sm miner

mine'rale ag, sm mineral

mine'rario, -a ag (delle miniere) mining; (dei minerali) ore cpd

mi'nestra sf soup; **~ in brodo** noodle soup; **~ di verdura** vegetable soup

minia'tura sf miniature

mini'bar sm inv minibar

mini'era sf mine

mini'gonna sf miniskirt

minimo, -a ag minimum, least, slightest; (piccolissimo) very small, slight; (il più basso) lowest, minimum ▷ sm minimum; **al ~** at least; **girare al ~** (Aut) to idle

minis'tero sm (Pol, Rel) ministry; (governo) government; **M~ delle Finanze** Ministry of Finance, ≈ Treasury

mi'nistro sm (Pol, Rel) minister

mino'ranza [mino'rantsa] sf minority

mi'nore ag (comparativo) less; (più piccolo) smaller; (numero) lower; (inferiore) lower, inferior; (meno importante) minor; (più giovane) younger; (superlativo) least; smallest; lowest, least important, youngest ▷ smf = **minorenne**

mino'renne ag under age ▷ smf minor, person under age

mi'nuscolo, -a ag (scrittura, carattere) small; (piccolissimo) tiny ▷ sf small letter

mi'nuto, -a ag tiny, minute; (pioggia) fine; (corporatura) delicate, fine

'mio (f 'mia, pl mi'ei o 'mie) det: **il ~, la mia** ecc my ▷ pron: **il ~, la mia** ecc mine; **i miei** my family; **un ~ amico** a friend of mine

'miope ag short-sighted

'mira sf (anche fig) aim; **prendere la ~** to take aim; **prendere di ~ qn** (fig) to pick on sb

mi'racolo sm miracle

mi'raggio [mi'raddʒo] sm mirage

mi'rare /72/ vi: **~ a** to aim at; **mi'rato, -a** ag targetted

mi'rino sm (Tecn) sight; (Fot) viewer, viewfinder

mir'tillo sm bilberry (BRIT), blueberry (US), whortleberry

mi'scela [miʃ'ʃɛla] sf mixture; (di caffè) blend

'mischia ['miskja] sf scuffle; (Rugby) scrum, scrummage

mis'cuglio [mis'kuʎʎo] sm mixture, hotchpotch, jumble

'mise vb vedi **mettere**

mise'rabile ag (infelice) miserable, wretched; (povero) poverty-stricken; (di scarso valore) miserable

mi'seria sf extreme poverty; (infelicità) misery

miseri'cordia sf mercy, pity

'misero, -a ag miserable, wretched; (povero) poverty-stricken; (insufficiente) miserable

'misi vb vedi **mettere**

mi'sogino [mi'zɔdʒino] sm misogynist

'missile sm missile

missio'nario, -a ag, smf missionary

missi'one sf mission

misteri'oso, -a ag mysterious

mis'tero sm mystery

'misto, -a ag mixed; (scuola) mixed, coeducational ▷ sm mixture

mis'tura sf mixture

mi'sura sf measure; (misurazione, dimensione) measurement; (taglia) size; (provvedimento) measure, step;

(*moderazione*) moderation; (*Mus*) time; (: *divisione*) bar; (*fig: limite*) bounds *pl*, limit; **nella ~ in cui** inasmuch as, insofar as; **su ~** made to measure

misu'rare /72/ *vt* (*ambiente, stoffa*) to measure; (*terreno*) to survey; (*abito*) to try on; (*pesare*) to weigh; (*fig: parole ecc*) to weigh up; (: *spese, cibo*) to limit ▷ *vi* to measure; **misurarsi** *vpr*: **misurarsi con qn** to have a confrontation with sb; (*competere*) to compete with sb

'**mite** *ag* mild

'**mitico, -a, -ci, -che** *ag* mythical

'**mito** *sm* myth; **mitolo'gia, -'gie** *sf* mythology

'**mitra** *sf* (*Rel*) mitre ▷ *sm inv* (*arma*) sub-machine gun

mit'tente *smf* sender

mm *abbr* (= *millimetro*) mm

'**mobile** *ag* mobile; (*parte di macchina*) moving; (*Dir: bene*) movable, personal ▷ *sm* (*arredamento*) piece of furniture; **mobili** *smpl* (*mobilia*) furniture *sg*

mocas'sino *sm* moccasin

'**moda** *sf* fashion; **alla ~, di ~** fashionable, in fashion

modalità *sf inv* formality

mo'della *sf* model

mo'dello *sm* model; (*stampo*) mould ▷ *ag inv* model *cpd*

'**modem** *sm inv* modem

modera'tore, -'trice *sm/f* moderator

mo'derno, -a *ag* modern

mo'desto, -a *ag* modest

'**modico, -a, -ci, -che** *ag* reasonable, moderate

mo'difica, -che *sf* modification

modifi'care /20/ *vt* to modify, alter

'**modo** *sm* way, manner; (*mezzo*) means, way; (*occasione*) opportunity; (*Ling*) mood; (*Mus*) mode; **modi** *smpl* (*maniere*) manners; **a suo ~, a ~ suo** in his own way; **ad** *o* **in ogni ~** anyway; **di** *o* **in ~ che** so that; **in ~ da** so as to; **in tutti i modi** at all costs;

(*comunque sia*) anyway; (*in ogni caso*) in any case; **in qualche ~** somehow or other; **~ di dire** turn of phrase; **per ~ di dire** so to speak

'**modulo** *sm* (*modello*) form; (*Archit: lunare, di comando*) module

mo'gano *sm* mahogany

'**mogio, -a, -gi, -gie** ['mɔdʒo] *ag* down in the dumps, dejected

'**moglie** ['moʎʎe] *sf* wife

mo'ine *sfpl* cajolery *sg*; (*leziosità*) affectation *sg*

mo'lare /72/ *sm* (*dente*) molar

'**mole** *sf* mass; (*dimensioni*) size; (*edificio grandioso*) massive structure

moles'tare /72/ *vt* to bother, annoy; **mo'lestia** *sf* annoyance, bother; **recar molestia a qn** to bother sb; **molestie sessuali** sexual harassment *sg*

'**molla** *sf* spring; **molle** *sfpl* (*per camino*) tongs

mol'lare /72/ *vt* to release, let go; (*Naut*) to ease; (*fig: ceffone*) to give ▷ *vi* (*cedere*) to give in

'**molle** *ag* soft; (*muscoli*) flabby

mol'letta *sf* (*per capelli*) hairgrip; (*per panni stesi*) clothes peg (BRIT) *o* pin (US)

mol'lica, -che *sf* crumb, soft part

mol'lusco, -schi *sm* mollusc

'**molo** *sm* breakwater; jetty

moltipli'care /20/ *vt* to multiply; **moltiplicarsi** *vpr* to multiply; (*richieste*) to increase in number; **moltiplicazi'one** *sf* multiplication

PAROLA CHIAVE

'**molto, -a** *det* (*quantità*) a lot of, much; (*numero*) a lot of, many; **molto pane/carbone** a lot of bread/coal; **molta gente** a lot of people, many people; **molti libri** a lot of books, many books; **non ho molto tempo** I haven't got much time; **per molto (tempo)** for a long time

▷ *av* **1** a lot, (very) much; **viaggia**

molto he travels a lot; **non viaggia molto** he doesn't travel much o a lot **2** (*intensivo: con aggettivi, avverbi*) very; (*: con participio passato*) (very) much; **molto buono** very good; **molto migliore, molto meglio** much o a lot better
▶ *pron* much, a lot

momentanea'mente *av* at the moment, at present
momen'taneo, -a *ag* momentary, fleeting
mo'mento *sm* moment; **da un ~ all'altro** at any moment; (*all'improvviso*) suddenly; **al ~ di fare** just as I was (*o* were *o* he was *ecc*) doing; **a momenti** (*da un mo'mento all'altro*) any time o a moment now; (*quasi*) nearly; **per il ~** for the time being; **dal ~ che** ever since; (*dato che*) since
'monaca, -che *sf* nun
'Monaco *sf* Monaco; **~ (di Baviera)** Munich
'monaco, -ci *sm* monk
monar'chia *sf* monarchy
monas'tero *sm* (*di monaci*) monastery; (*di monache*) convent
mon'dano, -a *ag* (*anche fig*) worldly; (*dell'alta società*) society *cpd*; fashionable
mondi'ale *ag* (*campionato, popolazione*) world *cpd*; (*influenza*) world-wide
'mondo *sm* world; (*grande quantità*): **un ~ di** lots of, a host of; **il gran** o **bel ~** high society
mo'nello, -a *sm/f* street urchin; (*ragazzo vivace*) scamp, imp
mo'neta *sf* coin; (*Econ: valuta*) currency; (*denaro spicciolo*) (small) change; **~ estera** foreign currency; **~ legale** legal tender
mongol'fiera *sf* hot-air balloon
'monitor *sm inv* (*Tecn, TV*) monitor
monolo'cale *sm* ≈ studio flat
mono'polio *sm* monopoly

mo'notono, -a *ag* monotonous
monovo'lume *sf inv* (*anche*: **automobile ~**) people carrier, MPV
mon'sone *sm* monsoon
monta'carichi [monta'kariki] *sm inv* hoist, goods lift
mon'taggio [mon'taddʒo] *sm* (*Tecn*) assembly; (*Cine*) editing
mon'tagna [mon'taɲɲa] *sf* mountain; (*zona montuosa*): **la ~** the mountains *pl*: **andare in ~** to go to the mountains; **montagne russe** roller coaster *sg*, big dipper *sg* (BRIT)
monta'naro, -a *ag* mountain *cpd*
▷ *sm/f* mountain dweller
mon'tano, -a *ag* mountain *cpd*; alpine
mon'tare /72/ *vt* to go (*o* come) up; (*cavallo*) to ride; (*apparecchiatura*) to set up, assemble; (*Cuc*) to whip; (*Zool*) to cover; (*incastonare*) to mount, set; (*Cine*) to edit; (*Fot*) to mount ▷ *vi* to go (*o* come) up; (*aumentare di livello, volume*) to rise; (*a cavallo*): **~ bene/male** to ride well/badly
monta'tura *sf* assembling *no pl*; (*di occhiali*) frames *pl*; (*di gioiello*) mounting, setting; (*fig*): **~ pubblicitaria** publicity stunt
'monte *sm* mountain; **a ~** upstream; **mandare a ~ qc** to upset sth, cause sth to fail; **il M~ Bianco** Mont Blanc; **~ di pietà** pawnshop; **~ premi** prize
mon'tone *sm* (*Zool*) ram; **carne di ~** mutton
montu'oso, -a *ag* mountainous
monu'mento *sm* monument
mo'quette [mɔ'kɛt] *sf* fitted carpet
'mora *sf* (*del rovo*) blackberry; (*del gelso*) mulberry; (*Dir*) delay; (*: somma*) arrears *pl*
mo'rale *ag* moral ▷ *sf* (*scienza*) ethics *sg*, moral philosophy; (*complesso di norme*) moral standards *pl*, morality; (*condotta*) morals *pl*; (*insegnamento morale*) moral ▷ *sm* morale; **essere giù di ~** to be feeling down

m

morbido | 152

'morbido, -a *ag* soft; (*pelle*) soft, smooth

> Attenzione! In inglese esiste la parola *morbid*, che però significa *morboso*.

mor'billo *sm* (*Med*) measles *sg*
'morbo *sm* disease
mor'boso, -a *ag* (*fig*) morbid
mordere /64/ *vt* to bite; (*addentare*) to bite into
mor'fina *sf* morphine
mori'bondo, -a *ag* dying, moribund
mo'rire /65/ *vi* to die; (*abitudine, civiltà*) to die out; **~ di fame** to die of hunger; (*fig*) to be starving; **~ di noia/paura** to be bored/scared to death; **fa un caldo da ~** it's terribly hot
mormo'rare /72/ *vi* to murmur; (*brontolare*) to grumble
'moro, -a *ag* dark(-haired), dark(-complexioned)
'morsa *sf* (*Tecn*) vice; (*fig: stretta*) grip
morsi'care /20/ *vt* to nibble (at), gnaw (at); (*insetto*) to bite
'morso, -a *pp di* **mordere** ▷ *sm* bite; (*di insetto*) sting; (*parte della briglia*) bit; **i morsi della fame** pangs of hunger
morta'della *sf* (*Cuc*) mortadella (*type of salted pork meat*)
mor'taio *sm* mortar
mor'tale *ag, sm* mortal
'morte *sf* death
'morto, -a *pp di* **morire** ▷ *ag* dead ▷ *sm/f* dead man/woman; **i morti** the dead; **fare il ~** (*nell'acqua*) to float on one's back; **il Mar M~** the Dead Sea
mo'saico, -ci *sm* mosaic
'Mosca *sf* Moscow
'mosca, -sche *sf* fly; **~ cieca** blind-man's buff
mosce'rino [moʃʃe'rino] *sm* midge, gnat
mos'chea [mos'kɛa] *sf* mosque
'moscio, -a, -sci, -sce ['moʃʃo] *ag* (*fig*) lifeless

mos'cone *sm* (*Zool*) bluebottle; (*barca*) pedalo; (: *a remi*) kind of pedalo with oars
'mossa *sf* movement; (*nel gioco*) move
'mossi *ecc vb vedi* **muovere**
'mosso, -a *pp di* **muovere** ▷ *ag* (*mare*) rough; (*capelli*) wavy; (*Fot*) blurred
mos'tarda *sf* mustard; **~ di Cremona** pickled fruit with mustard
'mostra *sf* exhibition, show; (*ostentazione*) show; **in ~** on show; **far ~ di** (*fingere*) to pretend; **far ~ di sé** to show off
mos'trare /72/ *vt* to show
'mostro *sm* monster; **mostru'oso, -a** *ag* monstrous
mo'tel *sm inv* motel
moti'vare /72/ *vt* (*causare*) to cause; (*giustificare*) to justify, account for
mo'tivo *sm* (*causa*) reason, cause; (*movente*) motive; (*letterario*) (central) theme; (*disegno*) motif, design, pattern; (*Mus*) motif; **per quale ~?** why?, for what reason?
'moto *sm* (*anche Fisica*) motion; (*movimento, gesto*) movement; (*esercizio fisico*) exercise; (*sommossa*) rising, revolt; (*commozione*) feeling, impulse ▷ *sf inv* (*motocicletta*) motorbike; **mettere in ~** to set in motion; (*Aut*) to start up
motoci'cletta *sf* motorcycle
motoci'clista, -i, -e *smf* motorcyclist
mo'tore, -'trice *ag* motor; (*Tecn*) driving ▷ *sm* engine, motor; **a ~** motor *cpd*, power-driven; **~ a combustione interna/a reazione** internal combustion/jet engine; **~ di ricerca** (*Inform*) search engine; **moto'rino** *sm* moped; **motorino di avviamento** (*Aut*) starter
motos'cafo *sm* motorboat
'motto *sm* (*battuta scherzosa*) witty remark; (*frase emblematica*) motto, maxim
'mouse ['maus] *sm inv* (*Inform*) mouse

mo'vente *sm* motive

movi'mento *sm* movèment; (*fig*) activity, hustle and bustle; (*Mus*) tempo, movement

mozi'one [mot'tsjone] *sf* (*Pol*) motion

mozza'rella [mottsa'rɛlla] *sf* mozzarella

mozzi'cone [mottsi'kone] *sm* stub, butt, end; (*anche*: **~ di sigaretta**) cigarette end

'**mucca, -che** *sf* cow; **~ pazza**; mad cow disease

mucchio ['mukkjo] *sm* pile, heap; (*fig*): **un ~ di** lots of, heaps of

muco, -chi *sm* mucus

'**muffa** *sf* mould , mildew

mug'gire [mud'dʒire] /55/ *vi* (*vacca*) to low, moo; (*toro*) to bellow; (*fig*) to roar

mu'ghetto [mu'getto] *sm* lily of the valley

mu'lino *sm* mill; **~ a vento** windmill

'**mulo** *sm* mule

'**multa** *sf* fine

multi'etnico, -a, -ci, -che *ag* multiethnic

multiraz'ziale [multirat'tsjale] *ag* multiracial

multi'sala *ag inv* multiscreen

multivitami'nico, -a, -ci, -che *ag*: **complesso ~** multivitamin

'**mummia** *sf* mummy

'**mungere** ['mundʒere] /5/ *vt* (*anche fig*) to milk

munici'pale [munitʃi'pale] *ag* municipal; town *cpd*

muni'cipio [muni'tʃipjo] *sm* town council, corporation; (*edificio*) town hall

munizi'oni [munit'tsjoni] *sfpl* (*Mil*) ammunition *sg*

'**munsi** *ecc vb vedi* **mungere**

mu'oio *ecc vb vedi* **morire**

mu'overe /66/ *vt* to move; (*ruota, macchina*) to drive; (*sollevare*: *questione, obiezione*) to raise, bring up; (: *accusa*) to make, bring forward;

muoversi *vpr* to move; **muoviti!** hurry up!, get a move on!

'**mura** *sfpl vedi* **muro**

mu'rale *ag* wall *cpd*; mural

mura'tore *sm* mason; (*con mattoni*) bricklayer

'**muro** *sm* wall

'**muschio** ['muskjo] *sm* (*Zool*) musk; (*Bot*) moss

musco'lare *ag* muscular, muscle *cpd*

'**muscolo** *sm* (*Anat*) muscle

mu'seo *sm* museum

museru'ola *sf* muzzle

'**musica** *sf* music; **~ da ballo/camera** dance/chamber music; **musi'cale** *ag* musical; **musi'cista, -i, -e** *smf* musician

'**müsli** ['mysli] *sm* muesli

'**muso** *sm* muzzle; (*di auto, aereo*) nose; **tenere il ~** to sulk

mus(s)ul'mano, -a *ag, sm/f* Muslim, Moslem

'**muta** *sf* (*di animali*) moulting; (*di serpenti*) sloughing; (*per immersioni subacquee*) diving suit; (*gruppo di cani*) pack

mu'tande *sfpl* (*da uomo*) (under)pants

'**muto, -a** *ag* (*Med*) with a speech impairment; (*emozione, dolore: Cine*) silent; (*Ling*) silent, mute; (*carta geografica*) blank; **~ per lo stupore ecc** speechless with amazement *etc*

'**mutuo, -a** *ag* (*reciproco*) mutual ▷ *sm* (*Econ*) (long-term) loan

m

N *abbr* (= *nord*) N

n *abbr* (= *numero*) no.

'nafta *sf* naphtha; (*per motori diesel*) diesel oil

nafta'lina *sf* (*Chim*) naphthalene; (*tarmicida*) mothballs *pl*

'naia *sf* (*Mil*) *slang term for national service*

na'ïf [na'if] *ag inv* naïve

'nanna *sf* (*linguaggio infantile*): **andare a ~** to go to beddy-byes

'nano, -a *ag, sm/f* dwarf (!)

napole'tano, -a *ag, sm/f* Neapolitan

'Napoli *sf* Naples

nar'ciso [nar'tʃizo] *sm* narcissus

nar'cotico, -ci *sm* narcotic

na'rice [na'ritʃe] *sf* nostril

nar'rare /72/ *vt* to tell the story of, recount

narra'tivo, -a *ag* narrative ▷ *sf* (*branca*) fiction

na'sale *ag* nasal

'nascere ['naʃʃere] /67/ *vi* (*bambino*) to be born; (*pianta*) to come *o* spring up; (*fiume*) to rise, have its source; (*sole*) to rise; (*dente*) to come through; (*fig: derivare, conseguire*): **~ da** to arise from, be born out of; **è nata nel 1952** she was born in 1952; **'nascita** *sf* birth

nas'condere /68/ *vt* to hide, conceal; **nascondersi** *vpr* to hide; **nascon'diglio** *sm* hiding place; **nascon'dino** *sm* (*gioco*) hide-and-seek; **nas'cosi** *ecc vb vedi* **nascondere**; **nas'costo, -a** *pp di* **nascondere** ▷ *ag* hidden; **di nascosto** secretly

na'sello *sm* (*Zool*) hake

'naso *sm* nose

'nastro *sm* ribbon; (*magnetico, isolante: Sport*) tape; **~ adesivo** adhesive tape; **~ trasportatore** conveyor belt

nas'turzio [nas'turtsjo] *sm* nasturtium

na'tale *ag* of one's birth ▷ *sm* (*Rel*): **N~** Christmas; (*giorno della nascita*) birthday; **nata'lizio, -a** *ag* (*del Natale*) Christmas *cpd*

'natica, -che *sf* (*Anat*) buttock

'nato, -a *pp di* **nascere** ▷ *ag*: **un attore ~** a born actor; **nata Pieri** née Pieri

na'tura *sf* nature; **pagare in ~** to pay in kind; **~ morta** still life

natu'rale *ag* natural

natural'mente *av* naturally; (*certamente, sì*) of course

natu'rista, -i, -e *ag, sm/f* naturist, nudist

naufra'gare /80/ *vi* (*nave*) to be wrecked; (*persona*) to be shipwrecked; (*fig*) to fall through; **'naufrago, -ghi** *sm* castaway, shipwreck victim

'nausea *sf* nausea; **nause'ante** *ag* (*odore*) nauseating; (*sapore*) disgusting; (*fig*) sickening

'nautico, -a, -ci, -che *ag* nautical

na'vale *ag* naval

na'vata sf (anche: ~ **centrale**) nave; (anche: ~ **laterale**) aisle

'**nave** sf ship, vessel; ~ **cisterna** tanker; ~ **da guerra** warship; ~ **passeggeri** passenger ship

na'vetta sf shuttle; (servizio di collegamento) shuttle (service)

navi'cella [navi'tʃella] sf (di aerostato) gondola; ~ **spaziale** spaceship

navi'gare /80/ vi to sail; ~ **in Internet** to surf the Net; **naviga'tore** sm: **navigatore satellitare** satnav; **navigazi'one** sf navigation

nazio'nale [nattsjo'nale] ag national ▷ sf (Sport) national team; **nazionalità** sf inv nationality

nazi'one [nat'tsjone] sf nation

naziskin ['nɑ:tsiskin] sm inv Nazi skinhead

NB abbr (= nota bene) NB

PAROLA CHIAVE

ne pron 1 (di lui, lei, loro) of him/her/ them; about him/her/them; **ne riconosco la voce** I recognize his (o her) voice

2 (di questa, quella cosa) of it; about it; **ne voglio ancora** I want some more (of it o them); **non parliamone più!** let's not talk about it any more!

3 (con valore partitivo): **hai dei libri? — sì, ne ho** have you any books? — yes, I have (some); **hai del pane? — no, non ne ho** have you any bread? — no, I haven't any; **quanti anni hai? — ne ho 17** how old are you? — I'm 17

▷ av (moto da luogo, da lì) from there; **ne vengo ora** I've just come from there

né cong: **né ... né** neither ... nor; **né l'uno né l'altro lo vuole** neither of them wants it; **non parla né l'italiano né il tedesco** he speaks neither Italian nor German, he doesn't speak either Italian or

German; **non piove né nevica** it isn't raining or snowing

ne'anche [ne'anke] av, cong not even; **non ... ~** not even; ~ **se volesse potrebbe venire** he couldn't come even if he wanted to; **non l'ho visto — neanch'io** I didn't see him — neither did I o I didn't either; ~ **per idea** o **sogno!** not on your life!

'**nebbia** sf fog; (foschia) mist

necessaria'mente av necessarily

neces'sario, -a [netʃes'sarjo] ag necessary

necessità [netʃessi'ta] sf inv necessity; (povertà) need, poverty

necro'logio [nekro'lɔdʒo] sm obituary notice

ne'gare /80/ vt to deny; (rifiutare) to deny, refuse; ~ **di aver fatto/che** to deny having done/that; **nega'tivo, -a** ag, sf, sm negative

negherò ecc [nege'rɔ] vb vedi **negare**

negli'gente [negli'dʒɛnte] ag negligent, careless

negozi'ante [negot'tsjante] smf trader, dealer; (bottegaio) shopkeeper (BRIT), storekeeper (US)

negozi'are [negot'tsjare] /19/ vt to negotiate ▷ vi: ~ **in** to trade o deal in; **negozi'ato** sm negotiation

ne'gozio [ne'gɔttsjo] sm (locale) shop (BRIT), store (US)

'**negro, -a** ag, sm/f (peg) black person

ne'mico, -a, -ci, -che ag hostile; (Mil) enemy cpd ▷ sm/f enemy; **essere ~ di** to be strongly averse o opposed to

nem'meno av, cong = **neanche**

'**neo** sm mole; (fig) (slight) flaw

'**neon** sm (Chim) neon

neo'nato, -a ag newborn ▷ sm/f newborn baby

neozelan'dese [neoddzelan'dese] ag New Zealand cpd ▷ smf New Zealander

Ne'pal sm: **il ~** Nepal

nep'pure av, cong = **neanche**

n

'nero, -a ag black; (scuro) dark ▷ sm black; **il Mar N~** the Black Sea

'nervo sm (Anat) nerve; (Bot) vein; **avere i nervi** to be on edge; **dare sui nervi a qn** to get on sb's nerves; **ner'voso, -a** ag nervous; (irritabile) irritable ▷ sm (fam): **far venire il nervoso a qn** to get on sb's nerves

'nespola sf (Bot) medlar; (fig) blow, punch

'nesso sm connection, link

PAROLA CHIAVE

nes'suno, -a (det: dav sm **nessun** + C, V, **nessuno** + s impura, gn, pn, ps, x, z; dav sf **nessuna** + C, **nessun'** + V) det
1 (non uno) no; (: espressione negativa) + any; **non c'è nessun libro** there isn't any book, there is no book; **nessun altro** no one else, nobody else; **nessun'altra cosa** nothing else; **in nessun luogo** nowhere
2 (qualche) any; **hai nessuna obiezione?** do you have any objections?
▷ pron 1 (non uno) no one, nobody; (espressione negativa) + any(one); **nessuno è venuto, non è venuto nessuno** nobody came
2 (cosa: espressione negativa) none; (: espressione negativa) + any
3 (qualcuno) anyone, anybody; **ha telefonato nessuno?** did anyone phone?

net'tare vt to clean
net'tezza [net'tettsa] sf cleanness, cleanliness; **~ urbana** cleansing department
'netto, -a ag (pulito) clean; (chiaro) clear, clear-cut; (deciso) definite; (Econ) net
nettur'bino sm dustman (BRIT), garbage collector (US)
neu'trale ag neutral
'neutro, -a ag neutral; (Ling) neuter ▷ sm (Ling) neuter

'neve sf snow; **nevi'care** /20/ vb impers to snow; **nevi'cata** sf snowfall
ne'vischio [ne'viskjo] sm sleet
ne'voso, -a ag snowy; snow-covered
nevral'gia [nevral'dʒia] sf neuralgia
nevras'tenico, -a, -ci, -che ag (Med) neurasthenic; (fig) hot-tempered
ne'vrosi sf inv neurosis
ne'vrotico, -a, -ci, -che ag, sm/f (anche fig) neurotic
'nicchia ['nikkja] sf niche; (naturale) cavity, hollow; **~ di mercato** (Comm) niche market
nicchi'are [nik'kjare] /19/ vi to shilly-shally, hesitate
'nichel ['nikel] sm nickel
nico'tina sf nicotine
'nido sm nest; **a ~ d'ape** (tessuto ecc) honeycomb cpd

PAROLA CHIAVE

ni'ente pron 1 (nessuna cosa) nothing; **niente può fermarlo** nothing can stop him; **niente di niente** absolutely nothing; **grazie! — di niente!** thank you! — not at all!; **nient'altro** nothing else; **nient'altro che** nothing but, just, only; **niente affatto** not at all, not in the least; **come se niente fosse** as if nothing had happened; **cose da niente** trivial matters; **per niente** (gratis, invano) for nothing
2 (qualcosa): **hai bisogno di niente?** do you need anything?
3: **non ... niente** nothing; (espressione negativa) + anything; **non ho visto niente** I saw nothing, I didn't see anything; **non ho niente da dire** I have nothing o haven't anything to say
▷ sm nothing; **un bel niente** absolutely nothing; **basta un niente per farla piangere** the slightest thing is enough to make her cry
▷ av (in nessuna misura): **non ... niente** not ... at all; **non è (per) niente buono** it isn't good at all

Ni'geria [ni'dʒɛrja] *sf*: **la ~** Nigeria

'ninfa *sf* nymph

nin'fea *sf* water lily

ninna'nanna *sf* lullaby

'ninnolo *sm* (*gingillo*) knick-knack

ni'pote *smf* (*di zii*) nephew (niece); (*di nonni*) grandson(-daughter), grandchild

'nitido, -a *ag* clear; (*specchio*) bright

ni'trire /55/ *vi* to neigh

ni'trito (*di cavallo*) neighing *no pl*; neigh; (*Chim*) nitrite

nitroglice'rina [nitroglitʃe'rina] *sf* nitroglycerine

no *av* (*risposta*) no; **vieni o no?** are you coming or not?; **perché no?** why not?; **lo conosciamo? — tu no ma io sì** do we know him? — you don't but I do; **verrai, no?** you'll come, won't you?

'nobile *ag* noble ▷ *smf* noble, nobleman/woman

'nocca, -che *sf* (*Anat*) knuckle

'noccio *ecc* ['nɔttʃo] *vb vedi* **nuocere**

nocci'ola [not'tʃɔla] *sf* hazelnut ▷ *ag inv* (*anche: color ~*) hazel, light brown

noccio'lina [nottʃo'lina] *sf* (*anche: ~ americana*) peanut

'nocciolo ['nɔttʃolo] *sm* (*di frutto*) stone; (*fig*) heart, core

'noce ['nɔtʃe] *sm* (*albero*) walnut tree ▷ *sf* (*frutto*) walnut; **~ di cocco** coconut; **~ moscata** nutmeg

no'cevo *ecc* [no'tʃevo] *vb vedi* **nuocere**

no'civo, -a [no'tʃivo] *ag* harmful, noxious

'nocqui *ecc* [no'tʃivo] *vb vedi* **nuocere**

'nodo *sm* (*di cravatta, legname, Naut*) knot; (*Aut, Ferr*) junction; (*Med, Astr, Bot*) node; (*fig: legame*) bond, tie; (: *punto centrale*) heart, crux; **avere un ~ alla gola** to have a lump in one's throat

no-'global [no-'global] *smf inv* anti-globalization protester ▷ *ag inv* (*movimento, manifestante*) anti-globalization

'noi *pron* (*soggetto*) we; (*oggetto: per dare rilievo, con preposizione*) us; **~ stessi(e)** we ourselves; (*oggetto*) ourselves

'noia *sf* boredom; (*disturbo, impaccio*) bother *no pl*, trouble *no pl*; **avere qn/qc a ~** not to like sb/sth; **mi è venuto a ~** I'm tired of it; **dare ~ a** to annoy; **avere delle noie con qn** to have trouble with sb

noi'oso, -a *ag* boring; (*fastidioso*) annoying, troublesome

> Attenzione! In inglese esiste la parola *noisy*, che però significa *rumoroso*.

noleggi'are [noled'dʒare] /62/ *vt* (*prendere a noleggio*) to hire (BRIT), rent; (*dare a noleggio*) to hire out (BRIT), rent out; (*aereo, nave*) to charter; **no'leggio** *sm* hire (BRIT), rental; charter

'nomade *ag* nomadic ▷ *smf* nomad

'nome *sm* name; (*Ling*) noun; **in o a ~ di** in the name of; **di o per ~** (*chiamato*) called, named; **conoscere qn di ~** to know sb by name; **~ d'arte** stage name; **~ di battesimo** Christian name; **~ di famiglia** surname; **~ utente** login, username

no'mignolo [no'miɲɲolo] *sm* nickname

'nomina *sf* appointment

nomi'nale *ag* nominal; (*Ling*) noun *cpd*

nomi'nare /72/ *vt* to name; (*eleggere*) to appoint; (*citare*) to mention

nomina'tivo, -a *ag* (*intestato*) registered; (*Ling*) nominative ▷ *sm* (*Amm*) name; (*Ling*) nominative

non *av* not ▷ *prefisso* non-; **grazie — non c'è di che** thank you — don't mention it; *vedi anche* **affatto, appena** *ecc*

nonché [non'ke] *cong* (*tanto più, tanto meno*) let alone; (*e inoltre*) as well as

noncu'rante *ag*: **~ (di)** careless (of), indifferent (to)

n

nonno | 158

'**nonno, -a** sm/f grandfather/
mother; (in senso più familiare)
grandma/grandpa; **nonni** smpl
grandparents

non'nulla sm inv: **un ~** nothing,
a trifle

'**nono, -a** num ninth

nonos'tante prep in spite of,
notwithstanding ▷ cong although,
even though

nontiscordardimé sm inv (Bot)
forget-me-not

nord sm north ▷ ag inv north;
northern; **il Mare del N~** the
North Sea; **nor'dest** sm north-east;
nor'dovest sm north-west

'**norma** sf (principio) norm; (regola)
regulation, rule; (consuetudine)
custom, rule; **a ~ di legge** according
to law, as laid down by law; **norme
di sicurezza** safety regulations;
norme per l'uso instructions
for use

nor'male ag normal; standard cpd

normal'mente av normally

norve'gese [norve'dʒese] ag, sm/f,
sm Norwegian

Nor'vegia sf: **la ~** Norway

nostal'gia [nostal'dʒia] sf (di casa,
paese) homesickness; (del passato)
nostalgia

nos'trano, -a ag local; national;
(pianta, frutta) home-produced

'**nostro, -a** det: **il (la) ~(a)** ecc our
▷ pron: **il (la) ~(a)** ecc ours ▷ sm: **il ~**
our money; our belongings; **i nostri**
our family; our own people; **è dei
nostri** he's one of us

'**nota** sf (segno) mark; (comunicazione
scritta: Mus) note; (fattura) bill;
(elenco) list; **degno di ~** noteworthy,
worthy of note

no'taio sm notary

no'tare /72/ vt (segnare: errori) to
mark; (registrare) to note (down),
write down; (rilevare, osservare)
to note, notice; **farsi ~** to get o.s.
noticed

no'tevole ag (talento) notable,
remarkable; (peso) considerable

no'tifica, -che sf notification

no'tizia [no'tittsja] sf (piece of)
news sg; (informazione) piece of
information; **notizi'ario** sm (Radio,
TV, Stampa) news sg

'**noto, -a** ag (well-)known

notorietà sf fame; notoriety

no'torio, -a ag well-known; (peg)
notorious

not'tambulo, -a sm/f night-bird (fig)

not'tata sf night

'**notte** sf night; **di ~** at night; (durante
la notte) in the night, during the
night; **~ bianca** sleepless night

not'turno, -a ag nocturnal; (servizio,
guardiano) night cpd

no'vanta num ninety; **novan'tesimo,
-a** num ninetieth

'**nove** num nine

nove'cento [nove'tʃento] num nine
hundred ▷ sm: **il N~** the twentieth
century

no'vella sf (Letteratura) short story

no'vello, -a ag (piante, patate) new;
(insalata, verdura) early; (sposo)
newly-married

no'vembre sm November

novità sf inv novelty; (innovazione)
innovation; (cosa originale, insolita)
something new; (notizia) (piece of)
news sg: **le ~ della moda** the latest
fashions

nozi'one [not'tsjone] sf notion, idea

'**nozze** ['nɔttse] sfpl wedding sg,
marriage sg: **~ d'argento/d'oro**
silver/golden wedding sg

'**nubile** ag (donna) unmarried, single

'**nuca, -che** sf nape of the neck

nucle'are ag nuclear

'**nucleo** sm nucleus; (gruppo) team,
unit, group; (Mil, Polizia) squad; **il ~
familiare** the family unit

nu'dista, -i, -e sm/f nudist

'**nudo, -a** ag (persona) bare, naked,
nude; (membra) bare, naked;
(montagna) bare ▷ sm (Arte) nude

'nulla *pron, av* = **niente** ▷ *sm*: **il ~** nothing

nullità *sf inv* nullity; (*persona*) nonentity

'nullo, -a *ag* useless, worthless; (*Dir*) null (and void); (*Sport*): **incontro ~** draw

nume'rale *ag, sm* numeral

nume'rare /72/ *vt* to number

nu'merico, -a, -ci, -che *ag* numerical

'numero *sm* number; (*romano, arabo*) numeral; (*di spettacolo*) act, turn; **~ civico** house number; **~ di scarpe** shoe size; **~ di telefono** telephone number; **nume'roso, -a** *ag* numerous, many; (*folla, famiglia*) large

nu'occio *ecc* ['nwɔttʃo] *vb vedi* **nuocere**

nu'ocere ['nwɔtʃere] /69/ *vi*: **~ a** to harm, damage

nu'ora *sf* daughter-in-law

nuo'tare /72/ *vi* to swim; (*galleggiare: oggetti*) to float; **nuota'tore, -'trice** *sm/f* swimmer; **nu'oto** *sm* swimming

nu'ova *sf vedi* **nuovo**

nuova'mente *av* again

Nu'ova Ze'landa [-dze'landa] *sf*: **la ~** New Zealand

nu'ovo, -a *ag* new ▷ *sf* (*notizia*) (piece of) news *sg*: **di ~** again; **~ fiammante** *o* **di zecca** brand-new

nutri'ente *ag* nutritious, nourishing

nutri'mento *sm* food, nourishment

nu'trire /45/ *vt* to feed; (*fig: sentimenti*) to harbour (BRIT), harbor (US), nurse; **nutrirsi** *vpr*: **nutrirsi di** to feed on, to eat

'nuvolo, -a *ag* cloudy ▷ *sf* cloud; **nuvo'loso, -a** *ag* cloudy

nuzi'ale [nut'tsjale] *ag* nuptial; wedding *cpd*

'nylon ['nailən] *sm* nylon

o *cong* (*dav V spesso* **od**) or; **o ... o** either ... or; **o l'uno o l'altro** either (of them)

O. *abbr* (= *ovest*) W

'oasi *sf inv* oasis

obbedi'ente *ecc vedi* **ubbidiente** *ecc*

obbli'gare /80/ *vt* (*Dir*) to bind; (*costringere*): **~ qn a fare** to force *o* oblige sb to do; **obbliga'torio, -a** *ag* compulsory, obligatory; **'obbligo, -ghi** *sm* obligation; (*dovere*) duty; **avere l'obbligo di fare** to be obliged to do; **essere d'obbligo** (*discorso, applauso*) to be called for

o'beso, -a *ag* obese

obiet'tare /72/ *vt*: **~ che** to object that; **~ su qc** to object to sth, raise objections concerning sth

obiet'tivo, -a *ag* objective ▷ *sm* (*Ottica, Fot*) lens *sg*, objective; (*Mil, fig*) objective

obiet'tore *sm* objector; **~ di coscienza** conscientious objector

obiezi'one [objet'tsjone] *sf* objection

obi'torio *sm* morgue

o'bliquo, -a *ag* oblique; *(inclinato)* slanting; *(fig)* devious, underhand

oblite'rare /72/ *vt (francobollo)* to cancel; *(biglietto)* to stamp

oblò *sm inv* porthole

'oboe *sm (Mus)* oboe

'oca *(pl* **oche)** *sf* goose

occasi'one *sf (caso favorevole)* opportunity; *(causa, motivo, circostanza)* occasion; *(Comm)* bargain; **d'~** *(a buon prezzo)* bargain *cpd; (usato)* secondhand

occhi'aia [ok'kjaja] *sf* eye socket; **avere le occhiaie** to have shadows under one's eyes

occhi'ali [ok'kjali] *smpl* glasses, spectacles; **~ da sole/da vista** sunglasses/(prescription) glasses

occhi'ata [ok'kjata] *sf* look, glance; **dare un'~ a** to have a look at

occhi'ello [ok'kjɛllo] *sm* buttonhole; *(asola)* eyelet

'occhio ['ɔkkjo] *sm* eye; **~!** careful!, watch out!; **a ~ nudo** with the naked eye; **a quattr'occhi** privately, tête-à-tête; **dare all'~** *o* **nell'~ a qn** to catch sb's eye; **fare l'~ a qc** to get used to sth; **tenere d'~ qn** to keep an eye on sb; **vedere di buon/mal ~ qc** to look favourably/unfavourably on sth

occhio'lino [okkjo'lino] *sm:* **fare l'~ a qn** to wink at sb

occiden'tale [ottʃiden'tale] *ag* western ▷ *smf* Westerner

occi'dente [ottʃi'dɛnte] *sm* west; *(Pol)* **l'O~** the West; **a ~** in the west

occor'rente *ag* necessary ▷ *sm* all that is necessary

occor'renza [okkor'rɛntsa] *sf* necessity, need; **all'~** in case of need

oc'correre /28/ *vi* to be needed, be required ▷ *vb impers:* **occorre farlo** it must be done; **occorre che tu parta** you must leave, you'll have to leave; **mi occorrono i soldi** I need the money

Attenzione! In inglese esiste il verbo to occur, che però significa succedere.

oc'culto, -a *ag* hidden, concealed; *(scienze, forze)* occult

occu'pare /72/ *vt* to occupy; *(manodopera)* to employ; *(ingombrare)* to occupy, take up; **occuparsi** *vpr* to occupy o.s., keep o.s. busy; *(impiegarsi)* to get a job; **occuparsi di** *(interessarsi)* to take an interest in; *(prendersi cura di)* to look after, take care of; **occu'pato, -a** *ag (Mil, Pol)* occupied; *(persona: affaccendato)* busy; *(posto, sedia)* taken; *(toilette, Tel)* engaged; **la linea è occupata** the line's engaged; **occupazi'one** *sf* occupation; *(impiego, lavoro)* job; *(Econ)* employment

o'ceano *sm* ocean

'ocra *sf* ochre

'OCSE *sigla f (= Organizzazione per la Cooperazione e lo Sviluppo Economico)* OECD

ocu'lare *ag* ocular, eye *cpd;* **testimone ~** eye witness

ocu'lato, -a *ag (attento)* cautious, prudent; *(accorto)* shrewd

ocu'lista, -i, -e *smf* eye specialist, oculist

odi'are /19/ *vt* to hate, detest

odi'erno, -a *ag* today's, of today; *(attuale)* present

'odio *sm* hatred; **avere in ~ qc/qn** to hate *o* detest sth/sb; **odi'oso, -a** *ag* hateful, odious

'odo *ecc vb vedi* **udire**

odo'rare /72/ *vt (annusare)* to smell; *(profumare)* to perfume, scent ▷ *vi:* **~ (di)** to smell (of)

o'dore *sm* smell; **gli odori** *(Cuc)* (aromatic) herbs

of'fendere /36/ *vt* to offend; *(violare)* to break, violate; *(insultare)* to insult; *(ferire)* to hurt; **offendersi** *vpr (con senso reciproco)* to insult one another; *(risentirsi):* **offendersi (di)** to take offence (at), be offended (by)

offe'rente *sm* (*in aste*): **al migliore ~** to the highest bidder

of'ferto, -a *pp di* **offrire** ▷ *sf* offer; (*donazione: anche Rel*) offering; (*in gara d'appalto*) tender; (*in aste*) bid; (*Econ*) supply; **fare un'offerta** to make an offer; (*per appalto*) to tender; (*ad un'asta*) to bid; **"offerte d'impiego"** "situations vacant"; **offerta speciale** special offer

offeso, -a *pp di* **offendere** ▷ *ag* offended; (*fisicamente*) hurt, injured ▷ *sm/f* offended party ▷ *sf* insult, affront; (*Mil*) attack; (*Dir*) offence

offi'cina [offi'tʃina] *sf* workshop

offrire /70/ *vt* to offer; **offrirsi** *vpr* (*proporsi*) to offer (o.s.), volunteer; (*occasione*) to present itself; (*esporsi*): **offrirsi a** to expose o.s. to; **ti offro da bere** I'll buy you a drink

offus'care /20/ *vt* to obscure, darken; (*fig: intelletto*) to dim, cloud; (: *fama*) to obscure, overshadow; **offuscarsi** *vpr* to grow dark; to cloud, grow dim; to be obscured

ogget'tivo, -a [oddʒet'tivo] *ag* objective

og'getto [od'dʒetto] *sm* object; (*materia, argomento*) subject (matter); **oggetti smarriti** lost property *sg*

oggi ['oddʒi] *av, sm* today; **~ a otto** a week today; **oggigi'orno** *av* nowadays

OGM [odʒi'ɛmme] *sigla mpl* (= *organismi geneticamente modificati*) GMO

ogni ['oɲɲi] *det* every, each; (*tutti*) all; (*con valore distributivo*) every; **~ uomo è mortale** all men are mortal; **viene ~ due giorni** he comes every two days; **~ cosa** everything; **ad ~ costo** at all costs, at any price; **in ~ luogo** everywhere; **~ tanto** every so often; **~ volta che** every time that

Ognis'santi [oɲɲis'santi] *sm* All Saints' Day

o'gnuno [oɲ'ɲuno] *pron* everyone, everybody

O'landa *sf*: **l'~** Holland; **olan'dese** *ag* Dutch ▷ *sm* (*Ling*) Dutch ▷ *smf* Dutchman/woman; **gli Olandesi** the Dutch

ole'andro *sm* oleander

oleo'dotto *sm* oil pipeline

ole'oso, -a *ag* oily; (*che contiene olio*) oil-yielding

ol'fatto *sm* sense of smell

oli'are /19/ *vt* to oil

oli'era *sf* oil cruet

Olim'piadi *sfpl* Olympic Games; **o'limpico, -a, -ci, -che** *ag* Olympic

'olio *sm* oil; **sott'~** (*Cuc*) in oil; **~ di fegato di merluzzo** cod liver oil; **~ d'oliva** olive oil; **~ di semi** vegetable oil; **oli essenziali** essential oils

o'liva *sf* olive; **o'livo** *sm* olive tree

'olmo *sm* elm

OLP *sigla f* (= *Organizzazione per la Liberazione della Palestina*) PLO

ol'traggio [ol'traddʒo] *sm* outrage; offence, insult; (*Dir*): **~ a pubblico ufficiale** insulting a public official; (*Dir*): **~ al pudore** indecent behaviour (*BRIT*) o behavior (*US*)

ol'tranza [ol'trantsa] *sf*: **a ~** to the last, to the bitter end

'oltre *av* (*più in là*) further; (*di più: aspettare*) longer, more ▷ *prep* (*di là da*) beyond, over, on the other side of; (*più di*) more than, over; (*in aggiunta a*) besides; (*eccetto*): **~ a** except, apart from; **oltrepas'sare** /72/ *vt* to go beyond, exceed

o'maggio [o'maddʒo] *sm* (*dono*) gift; (*segno di rispetto*) homage, tribute; **omaggi** *smpl* (*complimenti*) respects; **in ~** (*copia, biglietto*) complimentary; **rendere ~ a** to pay homage o tribute to

ombe'lico, -chi *sm* navel

'ombra *sf* (*zona non assolata, fantasma*) shade; (*sagoma scura*) shadow; **sedere all'~** to sit in the shade; **restare nell'~** (*fig*) to remain in obscurity

O

om'brello *sm* umbrella; **ombrel'lone** *sm* beach umbrella

om'bretto *sm* eyeshadow

O.M.C. *sigla f* (= *Organizzazione Mondiale del Commercio*) WTO

ome'lette [ɔmə'lɛt] *sf inv* omelet(te)

ome'lia *sf* (*Rel*) homily, sermon

omeopa'tia *sf* hom(o)eopathy

omertà *sf* conspiracy of silence

o'mettere /63/ *vt* to omit, leave out; **~ di fare** to omit o fail to do

omi'cida, -i, -e [omi'tʃida] *ag* homicidal, murderous ▷ *smf* murderer/murderess

omi'cidio [omi'tʃidjo] *sm* murder; **~ colposo** culpable homicide

o'misi *ecc vb vedi* **omettere**

omissi'one *sf* omission; **~ di soccorso** (*Dir*) failure to stop and give assistance

omogeneiz'zato [omodʒeneid'dzato] *sm* baby food

omo'geneo, -a [omo'dʒɛneo] *ag* homogeneous

o'monimo, -a *sm/f* namesake ▷ *sm* (*Ling*) homonym

omosessu'ale *ag, smf* homosexual

O.M.S. *sigla f* = **Organizzazione Mondiale della Sanità**

On. *abbr* (*Pol*); = **onorevole**

'onda *sf* wave; **mettere** o **mandare in ~** (*Radio, TV*) to broadcast; **andare in ~** (*Radio, TV*) to go on the air; **onde corte/medie/lunghe** short/medium/long wave *sg*

'onere *sm* burden; **oneri fiscali** taxes

onestà *sf* honesty

o'nesto, -a *ag* (*probo, retto*) honest; (*giusto*) fair; (*casto*) chaste, virtuous

ONG *sigla f inv* (= *Organizzazione Non Governativa*) NGO

onnipo'tente *ag* omnipotent

ono'mastico, -ci *sm* name day

ono'rare /72/ *vt* to honour (*BRIT*), honor (*US*); (*far onore a*) to do credit to

ono'rario, -a *ag* honorary ▷ *sm* fee

o'nore *sm* honour (*BRIT*), honor (*US*); **in ~ di** in honour of; **fare gli onori**

di casa to play host (o hostess); **fare ~ a** to honour; (*pranzo*) to do justice to; (*famiglia*) to be a credit to; **farsi ~** to distinguish o.s.; **ono'revole** *ag* honourable (*BRIT*), honorable (*US*) ▷ *smf* (*Pol*) ≈ Member of Parliament (*BRIT*), ≈ Congressman/woman (*US*)

on'tano *sm* (*Bot*) alder

O.N.U. *sigla f* (= *Organizzazione delle Nazioni Unite*) UN, UNO

o'paco, -a, -chi, -che *ag* (*vetro*) opaque; (*metallo*) dull, matt

o'pale *sm* o *f* opal

'opera *sf* work; (*azione rilevante*) action, deed, work; (*Mus*) work, opus; (: *melodramma*) opera; (: *teatro*) opera house; (*ente*) institution, organization; **~ d'arte** work of art; **~ lirica** (grand) opera; **opere pubbliche (OO.PP.)** public works

ope'raio, -a *ag* working-class; workers' ▷ *sm/f* worker; **classe operaia** working class

ope'rare /72/ *vt* to carry out, make; (*Med*) to operate on ▷ *vi* to operate, work; (*rimedio*) to act, work; (*Med*) to operate; **operarsi** *vpr* (*Med*) to have an operation; **operarsi d'appendicite** to have one's appendix out; **operazi'one** *sf* operation

ope'retta *sf* (*Mus*) operetta, light opera

opini'one *sf* opinion; **l'~ pubblica** public opinion

'oppio *sm* opium

op'pongo *ecc vb vedi* **opporre**

op'porre /77/ *vt* to oppose; **opporsi** *vpr*: **opporsi (a qc)** to oppose (sth); to object (to sth); **~ resistenza/un rifiuto** to offer resistance/to refuse

opportu'nista, -i, -e *smf* opportunist

opportunità *sf inv* opportunity; (*convenienza*) opportuneness, timeliness

oppor'tuno, -a *ag* timely, opportune

op'posi ecc vb vedi **opporre**

opposizi'one [oppozit'tsjone] sf opposition; (Dir) objection

op'posto, -a pp di **opporre** ▷ ag opposite; (opinioni) conflicting ▷ sm opposite, contrary; **all'~** on the contrary

oppressi'one sf oppression

oppri'mente ag (caldo, noia) oppressive; (persona) tiresome; (deprimente) depressing

op'primere /50/ vt (premere, gravare) to weigh down; (estenuare: caldo) to suffocate, oppress; (tiranneggiare: popolo) to oppress

op'pure cong or (else)

op'tare /72/ vi: **~ per** to opt for

o'puscolo sm booklet, pamphlet

opzi'one [op'tsjone] sf option

'ora sf (60 minuti) hour; (momento) time; **che ~ è?, che ore sono?** what time is it?; **non veder l'~ di fare** to long to do, look forward to doing; **di buon'~** early; **alla buon'~!** at last!; **~ legale** o **estiva** summer time (BRIT), daylight saving time (US); **~ di cena** dinner time; **~ locale** local time; **~ di pranzo** lunchtime; **~ di punta** (Aut) rush hour

o'racolo sm oracle

o'rale ag, sm oral

o'rario, -a ag hourly; (fuso, segnale) time cpd; (velocità) per hour ▷ sm timetable, schedule; (di ufficio, visite ecc) hours pl; time(s); **in ~** on time

o'rata sf (Zool) sea bream

ora'tore, -'trice sm/f speaker; orator

'orbita sf (Astr, Fisica) orbit; (Anat) (eye-)socket

or'chestra [or'kɛstra] sf orchestra

orchi'dea [orki'dɛa] sf orchid

or'digno [or'diɲɲo] sm: **~ esplosivo** explosive device

ordi'nale ag, sm ordinal

ordi'nare /72/ vt (mettere in ordine) to arrange, organize; (Comm) to order; (prescrivere: medicina) to prescribe;

(comandare): **~ a qn di fare qc** to order o command sb to do sth; (Rel) to ordain

ordi'nario, -a ag (comune) ordinary; everyday; standard; (grossolano) coarse, common ▷ sm ordinary; (Ins: di università) full professor

ordi'nato, -a ag tidy, orderly

ordinazi'one [ordinat'tsjone] sf (Comm) order; (Rel) ordination; **eseguire qc su ~** to make sth to order

'ordine sm order; (carattere): **d'~ pratico** of a practical nature; **all'~** (Comm) (assegno) to order; **di prim'~** first-class; **fino a nuovo ~** until further notice; **essere in ~** (documenti) to be in order; (persona, stanza) to be tidy; **mettere in ~** to put in order, tidy (up); **~ del giorno** (di seduta) agenda; (Mil) order of the day; **~ di pagamento** (Comm) order for payment; **l'~ pubblico** law and order; **ordini (sacri)** (Rel) holy orders

orec'chino [orek'kino] sm earring

o'recchio [o'rekkjo] (pl f **orecchie**) sm (Anat) ear

orecchi'oni [orek'kjoni] smpl (Med) mumps sg

o'refice [o'refitʃe] sm goldsmith; jeweller; **orefice'ria** sf (arte) goldsmith's art; (negozio) jeweller's (shop)

'orfano, -a ag orphan(ed) ▷ sm/f orphan; **~ di padre/madre** fatherless/motherless

orga'netto sm barrel organ; (fam: armonica a bocca) mouth organ; (: fisarmonica) accordion

or'ganico, -a, -ci, -che ag organic ▷ sm personnel, staff

organi'gramma, -i sm organization chart

orga'nismo sm (Biol) organism; (Anat, Amm) body, organism

organiz'zare [organid'dzare] /72/ vt to organize; **organizzarsi** vpr to

o

get organized; **organizzazi'one** sf organization

'**organo** sm organ; (di congegno) part; (portavoce) spokesman/woman, mouthpiece

'**orgia, -ge** ['ɔrdʒa] sf orgy

or'**goglio** [or'ɡoʎʎo] sm pride; **orgogli'oso, -a** ag proud

orien'tale ag (paese, regione) eastern; (tappeti, lingua, civiltà) oriental; east

orienta'mento sm positioning; orientation; direction; **senso di ~** sense of direction; **perdere l'~** to lose one's bearings; **~ professionale** careers guidance

orien'tare /72/ vt (situare) to position; **orientarsi** vpr to find one's bearings; (fig: tendere) to tend, lean; (indirizzarsi): **orientarsi verso** to take up, go in for

ori'ente sm east; **l'O~** the East, the Orient; **a ~** in the east

o'rigano sm oregano

origi'nale [oridʒi'nale] ag original; (bizzarro) eccentric ▷ sm original

origi'nario, -a [oridʒi'narjo] ag original; **essere ~ di** to be a native of; (provenire da) to originate from; (animale, pianta) to be native to

o'rigine [o'ridʒine] sf origin; **all'~** originally; **d'~ inglese** of English origin; **dare ~ a** to give rise to

origli'are [oriʎ'ʎare] /27/ vi: **~ (a)** to eavesdrop (on)

o'rina sf urine

ori'nare /72/ vi to urinate ▷ vt to pass

orizzon'tale [oriddzon'tale] ag horizontal

oriz'zonte [orid'dzonte] sm horizon

'**orlo** sm edge, border; (di recipiente) rim, brim; (di vestito ecc) hem

'**orma** sf (di persona) footprint; (di animale) track; (impronta, traccia) mark, trace

or'mai av by now, by this time; (adesso) now; (quasi) almost, nearly

ormeggi'are [ormed'dʒare] /62/ vt (Naut) to moor

or'mone sm hormone

ornamen'tale ag ornamental, decorative

or'nare /72/ vt to adorn, decorate; **ornarsi** vpr: **ornarsi (di)** to deck o.s. (out) (with)

ornitolo'gia [ornitolo'dʒia] sf ornithology

'**oro** sm gold; **d'~, in ~** gold cpd; **d'~** (colore, occasione) golden; (persona) marvellous

oro'logio [oro'lɔdʒo] sm clock; (da tasca, da polso) watch; **~ da polso** wristwatch; **~ al quarzo** quartz watch

o'roscopo sm horoscope

or'rendo, -a ag (spaventoso) horrible, awful; (bruttissimo) hideous

or'ribile ag horrible

or'rore sm horror; **avere in ~ qn/qc** to loathe o detest sb/sth; **mi fanno ~** I loathe o detest them

orsacchi'otto [orsak'kjɔtto] sm teddy bear

'**orso** sm bear; **~ bruno/bianco** brown/polar bear

or'taggio [or'taddʒo] sm vegetable

or'tensia sf hydrangea

or'tica, -che sf (stinging) nettle

orti'caria sf nettle rash

'**orto** sm vegetable garden, kitchen garden; (Agr) market garden (BRIT), truck farm (US); **~ botanico** botanical garden(s)

orto'dosso, -a ag orthodox

ortogra'fia sf spelling

orto'pedico, -a, -ci, -che ag orthopaedic ▷ sm orthopaedic specialist

orzai'olo [ordza'jɔlo] sm (Med) stye

'**orzo** ['ɔrdzo] sm barley

o'sare /72/ vt, vi to dare; **~ fare** to dare (to) do

oscenità [oʃʃeni'ta] sf inv obscenity

o'sceno, -a [oʃʃɛno] ag obscene; (ripugnante) ghastly

oscil'lare [oʃʃil'lare] /72/ vi (pendolo) to swing; (dondolare: al vento ecc) to rock; (*variare*) to fluctuate; (*Tecn*) to oscillate; (*fig*): **~ fra** to waver *o* hesitate between

oscu'rare /72/ *vt* to darken, obscure; (*fig*) to obscure; **oscurarsi** *vpr* (*cielo*) to darken, cloud over; (*persona*): **si oscurò in volto** his face clouded over

oscurità *sf* (*vedi ag*) darkness; obscurity

os'curo, -a *ag* dark; (*fig*) obscure; (*vita, natali*) humble, lowly ▷ *sm*: **all'~** in the dark; **tenere qn all'~ di qc** to keep sb in the dark about sth

ospe'dale *sm* hospital

ospi'tale *ag* hospitable

ospi'tare /72/ *vt* to give hospitality to; (*albergo*) to accommodate

'ospite *smf* (*persona che ospita*) host/hostess; (*persona ospitata*) guest

os'pizio [os'pittsjo] *sm* (*per vecchi ecc*) home

osser'vare /72/ *vt* to observe, watch; (*esaminare*) to examine; (*notare, rilevare*) to notice, observe; (*Dir: la legge*) to observe, respect; (*mantenere: silenzio*) to keep, observe; **far ~ qc a qn** to point sth out to sb; **osservazi'one** *sf* observation; (*di legge ecc*) observance; (*considerazione critica*) observation, remark; (*rimprovero*) reproof; **in osservazione** under observation

ossessio'nare /72/ *vt* to obsess, haunt; (*tormentare*) to torment, harass

ossessi'one *sf* obsession

os'sia *cong* that is, to be precise

'ossido *sm* oxide; **~ di carbonio** carbon monoxide

ossige'nare [ossidʒe'nare] /72/ *vt* to oxygenate; (*decolorare*) to bleach; **acqua ossigenata** hydrogen peroxide

os'sigeno *sm* oxygen

'osso (*pl f* **ossa**) *sm* (*Anat*) bone; **d'~** (*bottone ecc*) of bone, bone *cpd*; **~ di seppia** cuttlebone

ostaco'lare /72/ *vt* to block, obstruct

os'tacolo *sm* obstacle; (*Equitazione*) hurdle, jump

os'taggio [os'taddʒo] *sm* hostage

os'tello *sm* hostel; **~ della gioventù** youth hostel

osten'tare /72/ *vt* to make a show of, flaunt

oste'ria *sf* inn

os'tetrico, -a, -ci, -che *ag* obstetric ▷ *sm* obstetrician

'ostia *sf* (*Rel*) host; (*per medicinali*) wafer

'ostico, -a, -ci, -che *ag* (*fig*) harsh; difficult, tough; unpleasant

os'tile *ag* hostile

osti'narsi /72/ *vpr* to insist, dig one's heels in; **~ a fare** to persist (obstinately) in doing; **osti'nato, -a** *ag* (*caparbio*) obstinate; (*tenace*) persistent, determined

'ostrica, -che *sf* oyster

> ▌ Attenzione! In inglese esiste la parola *ostrich*, che però significa *struzzo*.

ostru'ire /55/ *vt* to obstruct, block

o'tite *sf* ear infection

ot'tanta *num* eighty

ot'tavo, -a *num* eighth

otte'nere /121/ *vt* to obtain, get; (*risultato*) to achieve, obtain

'ottico, -a, -ci, -che *ag* (*della vista: nervo*) optic; (*dell'ottica*) optical ▷ *sm* optician ▷ *sf* (*scienza*) optics *sg*; (*Fot: lenti, prismi ecc*) optics *pl*

ottima'mente *av* excellently, very well

otti'mismo *sm* optimism; **otti'mista, -i, -e** *smf* optimist

'ottimo, -a *ag* excellent, very good

'otto *num* eight

ot'tobre *sm* October

otto'cento [otto'tʃɛnto] *num* eight hundred ▷ *sm*: **l'O~** the nineteenth century

ot'tone *sm* brass; **gli ottoni** (*Mus*) the brass

ottu'rare /72/ *vt* to close (up); (*dente*) to fill; **otturarsi** *vpr* to become *o* get

blocked up; **otturazi'one** *sf* closing
(up); (*dentaria*) filling
ot'tuso, -a *ag* (*Mat, fig*) obtuse;
(*suono*) dull
o'vaia *sf* (*Anat*) ovary
o'vale *ag, sm* oval
o'vatta *sf* cotton wool; (*per imbottire*)
padding, wadding
'ovest *sm* west
o'vile *sm* pen, enclosure
ovulazi'one [ovulat'tsjone] *sf*
ovulation
'ovulo *sm* (*Fisiol*) ovum
o'vunque *av* = **dovunque**
ovvi'are /19/ *vi*: ~ **a** to obviate
'ovvio, -a *ag* obvious
ozi'are [ot'tsjare] /19/ *vi* to laze
around, idle
'ozio ['ɔttsjo] *sm* idleness; (*tempo
libero*) leisure; **ore d'~** leisure time;
stare in ~ to be idle
o'zono [od'dzɔno] *sm* ozone

P *abbr* (= *parcheggio*) P; (*Aut*)
(= *principiante*) L
p. *abbr* (= *pagina*) p
pac'chetto [pak'ketto] *sm* packet;
~ **azionario** (*Finanza*) shareholding
'pacco, -chi *sm* parcel; (*involto*)
bundle; ~ **postale** parcel
'pace ['patʃe] *sf* peace; **darsi ~** to
resign o.s.; **fare (la) ~ con qn** to
make it up with sb
pa'cifico, -a, -ci, -che [pa'tʃifiko]
ag (*persona*) peaceable; (*vita*)
peaceful; (*fig: indiscusso*)
indisputable; (: *ovvio*) obvious, clear
▷ *sm*: **il P~, l'Oceano P~** the Pacific
(Ocean)
paci'fista, -i, -e [patʃi'fista] *smf*
pacifist
pa'della *sf* frying pan; (*per infermi*)
bedpan
padigli'one [padiʎ'ʎone] *sm*
pavilion
'Padova *sf* Padua

'**padre** sm father
pa'drino sm godfather
padro'nanza [padro'nantsa] sf
command, mastery
pa'drone, -a sm/f master/mistress;
(proprietario) owner; (datore di lavoro)
employer; **essere ~ di sé** to be in
control of o.s.; **~/padrona di casa**
master/mistress of the house; (per gli
inquilini) landlord/lady
pae'saggio [pae'zaddʒo] sm
landscape
pa'ese sm (nazione) country, nation;
(terra) country, land; (villaggio)
village; **~ di provenienza** country
of origin; **i Paesi Bassi** the
Netherlands
'**paga, -ghe** sf pay, wages pl
paga'mento sm payment
pa'gare /80/ vt to pay; (acquisto, fig,
colpa) to pay for; (contraccambiare) to
repay, pay back ▷ vi to pay; **quanto
l'ha pagato?** how much did you
pay for it?; **~ con carta di credito**
to pay by credit card; **~ in contanti**
to pay cash
pa'gella [pa'dʒɛlla] sf (Ins) report
card
pagherò [page'rɔ] sm inv
acknowledgement of a debt, IOU
'**pagina** ['padʒina] sf page; **Pagine
bianche** phone book, telephone
directory; **Pagine Gialle**® Yellow
Pages®
'**paglia** ['paʎʎa] sf straw
pagli'accio [paʎ'ʎattʃo] sm clown
pagli'etta [paʎ'ʎetta] sf (cappello per
uomo) (straw) boater; (per tegami ecc)
steel wool
pa'gnotta [paɲ'ɲɔtta] sf round loaf
'**Pakistan** sm: **il ~** Pakistan
'**pala** sf shovel; (di remo, ventilatore,
elica) blade; (di ruota) paddle
pa'lato sm palate
pa'lazzo [pa'lattso] sm (reggia)
palace; (edificio) building; **~ di
giustizia** courthouse; **~ dello sport**
sports stadium

'**palco, -chi** sm (Teat) box; (tavolato)
platform, stand; (ripiano) layer
palco'scenico, -ci [palkoʃ'ʃɛniko]
sm (Teat) stage
pa'lese ag clear, evident
Pales'tina sf: **la ~** Palestine
palesti'nese ag, smf Palestinian
pa'lestra sf gymnasium; (esercizio
atletico) exercise, training; (fig)
training ground, school
pa'letta sf spade; (per il focolare)
shovel; (del capostazione) signalling
disc
pa'letto sm stake, peg; (spranga) bolt
'**palio** sm (gara): **il P~** horse race run at
Siena; **mettere qc in ~** to offer sth
as a prize

● **PALIO**
●
●
● The Palio is a horse race which
● takes place in a number of Italian
● towns, the most famous being
● the 'Palio di Siena'. The Tuscan
● race dates back to the thirteenth
● century; nowadays it is usually
● held twice a year, on 2 July and 16
● August, in the Piazza del Campo. 10
● of the 17 city districts or 'contrade'
● take part; the winner is the first
● horse to complete the course,
● whether or not it still has its
● rider. The race is preceded by a
● procession of 'contrada' members
● in historical dress.

'**palla** sf ball; (pallottola) bullet; **~ di
neve** snowball; **~ ovale** rugby
ball; **pallaca'nestro** sf basketball;
palla'mano [palla'mano] sf
handball; **pallanu'oto** sf water polo;
palla'volo sf volleyball
palleggi'are [palled'dʒare] /62/ vi
(Calcio) to practise (BRIT) o practice
(US) with the ball; (Tennis) to knock up
pallia'tivo sm palliative; (fig) stopgap
measure
'**pallido, -a** ag pale

P

pal'lina sf (bilia) marble
pallon'cino [pallon'tʃino] sm balloon; (lampioncino) Chinese lantern
pal'lone sm (palla) ball; (Calcio) football; (aerostato) balloon; **gioco del ~** football
pal'lottola sf pellet; (proiettile) bullet
'palma sf (Anat); = **palmo**; (Bot, simbolo) palm; **~ da datteri** date palm
'palmo sm (Anat) palm; **restare con un ~ di naso** to be badly disappointed
'palo sm (legno appuntito) stake; (sostegno) pole; **fare da** o **il ~** (fig) to act as look-out
palom'baro sm diver
pal'pare /72/ vt to feel, finger
'palpebra sf eyelid
pa'lude sf marsh, swamp
pancar'rè sm sliced bread
pan'cetta [pan'tʃetta] sf (Cuc) bacon
pan'china [pan'kina] sf garden seat; (di giardino pubblico) (park) bench
'pancia, -ce ['pantʃa] sf belly, stomach; **mettere** o **fare ~** to be getting a paunch; **avere mal di ~** to have stomach ache o a sore stomach
panci'otto [pan'tʃɔtto] sm waistcoat
'pancreas sm inv pancreas
'panda sm inv panda
pande'mia sf pandemic
'pane sm bread; (pagnotta) loaf (of bread); (forma): **un ~ di burro/ cera** ecc a pat of butter/bar of wax etc; **guadagnarsi il ~** to earn one's living; **~ a cassetta** sliced bread; **~ integrale** wholemeal bread; **~ di Spagna** sponge cake; **~ tostato** toast
panette'ria sf (forno) bakery; (negozio) baker's (shop), bakery
panetti'ere, -a sm/f baker
panet'tone sm a kind of spiced brioche with sultanas (eaten at Christmas)
pangrat'tato sm breadcrumbs pl

'panico, -a, -ci, -che ag, sm panic
pani'ere sm basket
pani'ficio [pani'fitʃo] sm (forno) bakery; (negozio) baker's (shop), bakery
pa'nino sm roll; **~ caldo** toasted sandwich; **~ imbottito** filled roll; sandwich
panino'teca, -che sf sandwich bar
'panna sf (Cuc) cream; (Aut); = **panne**; **~ da cucina** cooking cream; **~ montata** whipped cream
'panne [pan] sf inv (Aut): **essere in ~** to have broken down
pan'nello sm panel; **~ solare** solar panel
'panno sm cloth; **panni** smpl (abiti) clothes; **mettiti nei miei panni** (fig) put yourself in my shoes
pan'nocchia [pan'nɔkkja] sf (di mais ecc) ear
pan'nolino sm (per bambini) nappy (BRIT), diaper (US)
panno'lone sm incontinence pad
pano'rama, -i sm panorama
panta'loni smpl trousers (BRIT), pants (US), pair sg of trousers o pants
pan'tano sm bog
pan'tera sf panther
pan'tofola sf slipper
'papa, -i sm pope
pa'pà sm inv dad(dy)
pa'pavero sm poppy
'pappa sf baby cereal; **~ reale** royal jelly
pappa'gallo sm parrot; (fig: uomo) Romeo, wolf
pa'rabola sf (Mat) parabola; (Rel) parable
para'bolico, -a, -ci, -che ag (Mat) parabolic; vedi anche **antenna**
para'brezza [para'breddza] sm inv (Aut) windscreen (BRIT), windshield (US)
paraca'dute sm inv parachute
para'diso sm paradise
parados'sale ag paradoxical

para'fulmine *sm* lightning conductor

pa'raggi [pa'raddʒi] *smpl*: **nei ~ in** the vicinity, in the neighbourhood (*BRIT*) o neighborhood (*US*)

parago'nare /72/ *vt*: **~ con/a** to compare with/to

para'gone *sm* comparison; (*esempio analogo*) analogy, parallel; **reggere al ~** to stand comparison

pa'ragrafo *sm* paragraph

pa'ralisi *sf inv* paralysis

paral'lelo, -a *ag* parallel ▷ *sm* (*Geo*) parallel; (*comparazione*): **fare un ~ tra** to draw a parallel between

para'lume *sm* lampshade

pa'rametro *sm* parameter

para'noia *sf* paranoia; **para'noico, -a, -ci, -che** *ag, sm/f* paranoid

para'occhi [para'ɔkki] *smpl* blinkers

paraolim'piadi *sfpl* paralympics

para'petto *sm* parapet

pa'rare /72/ *vt* (*addobbare*) to adorn, deck; (*proteggere*) to shield, protect; (*scansare: colpo*) to parry; (*Calcio*) to save ▷ *vi*: **dove vuole andare a ~?** what are you driving at?

pa'rata *sf* (*Sport*) save; (*Mil*) review, parade

para'urti *sm inv* (*Aut*) bumper

para'vento *sm* folding screen; **fare da ~ a qn** (*fig*) to shield sb

par'cella [par'tʃɛlla] *sf* account, fee (*of lawyer etc*)

parcheggi'are [parked'dʒare] /62/ *vt* to park; **parcheggia'tore, -'trice** [parkedd'ʒatore] *sm/f* parking attendant

par'cheggio *sm* parking *no pl*; (*luogo*) car park; (*singolo posto*) parking space

par'chimetro [par'kimetro] *sm* parking meter

'parco, -chi *sm* park; (*spazio per deposito*) depot; (*complesso di veicoli*) fleet

par'cometro *sm* (Pay and Display) ticket machine

pa'recchio, -a [pa'rekkjo] *det* quite a lot of; (*tempo*) quite a lot of, a long

pareggi'are [pared'dʒare] /62/ *vt* to make equal; (*terreno*) to level, make level; (*bilancio, conti*) to balance ▷ *vi* (*Sport*) to draw; **pa'reggio** *sm* (*Econ*) balance; (*Sport*) draw

pa'rente *smf* relative, relation

Attenzione! In inglese esiste la parola *parent*, che però significa *genitore*.

paren'tela *sf* (*vincolo di sangue, fig*) relationship

pa'rentesi *sf* (*segno grafico*) bracket, parenthesis; (*frase incisa*) parenthesis; (*digressione*) parenthesis, digression

pa'rere /71/ *sm* (*opinione*) opinion; (*consiglio*) advice, opinion; **a mio ~** in my opinion ▷ *vi* to seem, appear ▷ *vb impers*: **pare che** it seems o appears that; they say that; **mi pare che** it seems to me that; **mi pare di sì/no** I think so/don't think so; **fai come ti pare** do as you like; **che ti pare del mio libro?** what do you think of my book?

pa'rete *sf* wall

'pari *ag inv* (*uguale*) equal, same; (*in giochi*) equal, drawn, tied; (*Mat*) even ▷ *sm inv* (*Pol: di Gran Bretagna*) peer ▷ *smf inv* peer, equal; **copiato ~ ~** copied word for word; **alla ~** on the same level; **ragazza alla ~** au pair (girl); **mettersi alla ~ con** to place o.s. on the same level as; **mettersi in ~ con** to catch up with; **andare di ~ passo con qn** to keep pace with sb

Pa'rigi [pa'ridʒi] *sf* Paris

pari'gino, -a [pari'dʒino] *ag, sm/f* Parisian

pa'rità *sf* parity, equality; (*Sport*) draw, tie

parlamen'tare /72/ *ag* parliamentary ▷ *smf* ≈ Member of Parliament (*BRIT*), ≈ Congressman/ woman (*US*) ▷ *vi* to negotiate, parley

parla'mento *sm* parliament

P

parlan'tina sf (fam) talkativeness;
  avere ~ to have the gift of the gab

par'lare /72/ vi to speak, talk;
  (confidare cose segrete) to talk ▷ vt to
  speak; **~ (a qn) di** to speak o talk (to
  sb) about

parmigi'ano, -a [parmi'dʒano] sm
  (grana) Parmesan (cheese)

pa'rola sf word; (facoltà) speech;
  parole sfpl (chiacchiere) talk sg:
  chiedere la ~ to ask permission to
  speak; **prendere la ~** to take the
  floor; **~ d'onore** word of honour; **~
  d'ordine** (Mil) password; **parole
  incrociate** crossword (puzzle)
  sg; **paro'laccia, -ce** sf bad word,
  swearword

parrò ecc vb vedi **parere**

par'rocchia [par'rɔkkja] sf parish;
  (chiesa) parish church

par'rucca, -che sf wig

parrucchi'ere, -a [parruk'kjɛre]
  sm/f hairdresser ▷ sm barber

'**parte** sf part; (lato) side; (quota
  spettante a ciascuno) share; (direzione)
  direction; (Pol) party; faction;
  (Dir) party; **a ~** ag separate ▷ av
  separately; **scherzi a ~** joking aside;
  a ~ ciò apart from that; **da ~** (in
  disparte) to one side, aside; **mettere/
  prendere da ~** to put/take aside;
  d'altra ~ on the other hand; **da ~ di**
  (per conto di) on behalf of; **da ~ mia**
  as far as I'm concerned, as for me;
  da ~ a ~ right through; **da nessuna
  ~** nowhere; **da questa ~** (in questa
  direzione) this way; **da ogni ~** on all

sides, everywhere; (moto da luogo)
  from all sides; **prendere ~ a qc** to
  take part in sth; **mettere qn a ~ di
  qc** to inform sb of sth

parteci'pare [partetʃi'pare] /72/
  vi: **~ a** to take part in, participate
  in; (utili ecc) to share in; (spese ecc) to
  contribute to; (dolore, successo di qn)
  to share (in)

parteggi'are [parted'dʒare] /62/
  vi: **~ per** to side with, be on the side of

par'tenza [par'tɛntsa] sf departure;
  (Sport) start; **essere in ~** to be about
  to leave, be leaving

parti'cipio [parti'tʃipjo] sm
  participle

partico'lare ag (specifico) particular;
  (proprio) personal, private; (speciale)
  special, particular; (caratteristico)
  distinctive, characteristic; (fuori
  dal comune) peculiar ▷ sm detail,
  particular; **in ~** in particular,
  particularly

par'tire /45/ vi to go, leave;
  (allontanarsi) to go (o drive ecc) away o
  off; (petardo, colpo) to go off; (fig: avere
  inizio, Sport) to start; **sono partita
  da Roma alle 7** I left Rome at 7; **il
  volo parte da Ciampino** the flight
  leaves from Ciampino; **a ~ da** from

par'tita sf (Comm) lot, consignment;
  (Econ: registrazione) entry, item;
  (Carte, Sport: gioco) game;
  (: competizione) match, game; **~ di
  caccia** hunting party; **numero di ~
  IVA** VAT registration number

par'tito sm (Pol) party; (decisione)
  decision, resolution; (persona da
  maritare) match

'**parto** sm (Med) labour (BRIT), labor
  (US), delivery, (child)birth

'**parvi** ecc vb vedi **parere**

parzi'ale [par'tsjale] ag (limitato)
  partial; (non obiettivo) biased, partial

pasco'lare /72/ vt, vi to graze

'**pascolo** sm pasture

'**Pasqua** sf Easter

Pasqu'etta sf Easter Monday

pas'sabile *ag* fairly good, passable
pas'saggio [pas'saddʒo] *sm* passing *no pl*, passage; (*traversata*) crossing *no pl*, passage; (*luogo, prezzo della traversata, brano di libro ecc*) passage; (*su veicolo altrui*) lift (BRIT), ride; (*Sport*) pass; **di ~** (*persona*) passing through; **~ pedonale/a livello** pedestrian/level (BRIT) *o* grade (US) crossing
passamon'tagna [passamon'taɲɲa] *sm inv* balaclava
pas'sante *smf* passer-by ▷ *sm* loop
passa'porto *sm* passport
pas'sare /72/ *vi* (*andare*) to go; (*veicolo, pedone*) to pass (by), go by; (*fare una breve sosta: postino ecc*) to come, call; (: *amico: per fare una visita*) to call *o* drop in; (*sole, aria, luce*) to get through; (*trascorrere: giorni, tempo*) to pass, go by; (*fig: proposta di legge*) to be passed; (: *dolore*) to pass, go away; (*Carte*) to pass ▷ *vt* (*attraversare*) to cross; (*trasmettere: messaggio*): **~ qc a qn** to pass sth on to sb; (*dare*): **~ qc a qn** to pass sth to sb, give sb sth; (*trascorrere: tempo*) to spend; (*superare: esame*) to pass; (*triturare: verdura*) to strain; (*approvare*) to pass, approve; (*oltrepassare, sorpassare: anche fig*) to go beyond, pass; (*fig: subire*) to go through; **~ da ... a** to pass from ... to; **~ di padre in figlio** to be handed down *o* to pass from father to son; **~ per** (*anche fig*) to go through; **~ per stupido/un genio** to be taken for a fool/a genius; **~ sopra** (*anche fig*) to pass over; **~ attraverso** (*anche fig*) to go through; **~ alla storia** to pass into history; **~ a un esame** to go up (to the next class) after an exam; **~ inosservato** to go unnoticed; **~ di moda** to go out of fashion; **le passo il Signor X** (*al telefono*) here is Mr X; I'm putting you through to Mr X; **lasciar ~ qn/ qc** to let sb/sth through; : **come te la passi?** how are you getting on *o* along?

passa'tempo *sm* pastime, hobby
pas'sato, -a *ag* past; (*sfiorito*) faded ▷ *sm* past; (*Ling*) past (tense); **~ prossimo** (*Ling*) present perfect; **~ remoto** (*Ling*) past historic; **~ di verdura** (*Cuc*) vegetable purée
passeg'gero, -a [passed'dʒero] *ag* passing ▷ *sm/f* passenger
passeggi'are [passed'dʒare] /62/ *vi* to go for a walk; (*in veicolo*) to go for a drive; **passeggi'ata** *sf* walk; drive; (*luogo*) promenade; **fare una passeggiata** to go for a walk (*o* drive); **passeg'gino** [passed'dʒino] *sm* pushchair (BRIT), stroller (US)
passe'rella *sf* footbridge; (*di nave, aereo*) gangway; (*pedana*) catwalk
'passero *sm* sparrow
passi'one *sf* passion
pas'sivo, -a *ag* passive ▷ *sm* (*Ling*) passive; (*Econ*) debit; (*complesso dei debiti*) liabilities *pl*
'passo *sm* step; (*andatura*) pace; (*rumore*) (foot)step; (*orma*) footprint; (*passaggio, fig: brano*) passage; (*valico*) pass; **a ~ d'uomo** at walking pace; **~ (a)** step by step; **fare due** *o* **quattro passi** to go for a walk *o* stroll; **di questo ~** at this rate; **"~ carraio"** vehicle entrance — keep clear"
'pasta *sf* (*Cuc*) dough; (: *impasto per dolce*) pastry; (*anche*: **~ alimentare**) pasta; (*massa molle di materia*) paste; (*fig: indole*) nature; **paste** *sfpl* (*pasticcini*) pastries; **~ in brodo** noodle soup; **~ sfoglia** puff pastry *o* paste (US)
pastasci'utta [pastaʃ'ʃutta] *sf* pasta
pas'tella *sf* batter
pas'tello *sm* pastel
pas'ticca, -che *sf* = **pastiglia**
pasticce'ria [pastittʃe'ria] *sf* (*pasticcini*) pastries *pl*, cakes *pl*; (*negozio*) cake shop; (*arte*) confectionery
pasticci'ere, -a [pastit'tʃere] *sm/f* pastrycook; confectioner

pastic'cino [pastit'tʃino] sm petit four

pas'ticcio [pas'tittʃo] sm (Cuc) pie; (lavoro disordinato, imbroglio) mess; **trovarsi nei pasticci** to get into trouble

pas'tiglia [pas'tiʎʎa] sf pastille, lozenge

pas'tina sf small pasta shapes used in soup

'pasto sm meal

pas'tore sm shepherd; (Rel) pastor, minister; (anche: **cane ~**) sheepdog; **~ tedesco** (Zool) Alsatian (dog) (BRIT) German shepherd (dog)

pa'tata sf potato; **patate fritte** chips (BRIT), French fries; **pata'tine** sfpl (potato) crisps (BRIT) o chips (US); **patatine fritte** chips

pâté [pa'te] sm inv pâté

pa'tente sf licence; (anche: **~ di guida**) driving licence (BRIT), driver's license (US); **~ a punti** driving licence with penalty points

> Attenzione! In inglese esiste la parola patent, che però significa brevetto.

paternità sf paternity, fatherhood

pa'tetico, -a, -ci, -che ag pathetic; (commovente) moving, touching

pa'tibolo sm gallows sg, scaffold

'patina sf (su rame ecc) patina; (sulla lingua) fur, coating

pa'tire /55/ vt, vi to suffer

pa'tito, -a sm/f enthusiast, fan, lover

patolo'gia [patolo'dʒia] sf pathology

'patria sf homeland

pa'trigno [pa'triɲɲo] sm stepfather

patri'monio sm estate, property; (fig) heritage

pa'trono sm (Rel) patron saint; (socio di patronato) patron; (Dir) counsel

patteggi'are [patted'dʒare] /62/ vt, vi to negotiate; (Dir) to plea-bargain

patti'naggio [patti'naddʒo] sm skating; **~ a rotelle/sul ghiaccio** roller-/ice-skating

patti'nare /72/ vi to skate; **~ sul ghiaccio** to ice-skate; **pattina'tore, -'trice** sm/f skater

'pattino sm skate; (di slitta) runner; (Aer) skid; (Tecn) sliding block; **pattini (da ghiaccio)** (ice) skates; **pattini in linea** rollerblades®; **pattini a rotelle** roller skates

'patto sm (accordo) pact, agreement; (condizione) term, condition; **a ~ che** on condition that

pat'tuglia [pat'tuʎʎa] sf (Mil) patrol

pattu'ire /55/ vt to reach an agreement on

pattumi'era sf (dust)bin (BRIT), ashcan (US)

pa'ura sf fear; **aver ~ di/di fare/che** to be frightened o afraid of/of doing/ that; **far ~ a** to frighten; **per ~ di/ che** for fear of/that; **pau'roso, -a** ag (che fa paura) frightening; (che ha paura) fearful, timorous

'pausa sf (sosta) break; (nel parlare, Mus) pause

pavi'mento sm floor

> Attenzione! In inglese esiste la parola pavement, che però significa marciapiede.

pa'vone sm peacock

pazien'tare [pattsjen'tare] /72/ vi to be patient

pazi'ente [pat'tsjɛnte] ag, smf patient; **pazi'enza** sf patience

paz'zesco, -a, -schi, -sche [pat'tsesko] ag mad, crazy

paz'zia [pat'tsia] sf (Med) madness, insanity; (di azione, decisione) madness, folly

'pazzo, -a ['pattso] ag (Med) mad, insane; (strano) wild, mad ▷ sm/f madman/woman; **~ di** (gioia, amore ecc) mad o crazy with; **~ per qc/qn** mad o crazy about sth/sb

PC sigla m inv (= personal computer) PC; **PC portatile** laptop

pec'care /20/ vi to sin; (fig) to err

pec'cato sm sin; **è un ~ che** it's a pity that; **che ~!** what a shame o pity!

peccherò *ecc* [pekke'rɔ] *vb vedi* **peccare**

'pece ['petʃe] *sf* pitch

Pe'chino [pe'kino] *sf* Beijing

'pecora *sf* sheep; **peco'rino** *sm* sheep's milk cheese

pe'daggio [pe'daddʒo] *sm* toll

pedago'gia [pedago'dʒia] *sf* pedagogy, educational methods *pl*

peda'lare /72/ *vi* to pedal; (*andare in bicicletta*) to cycle

pe'dale *sm* pedal

pe'dana *sf* footboard; (*Sport: nel salto*) springboard; (: *nella scherma*) piste

pe'dante *ag* pedantic ▷ *smf* pedant

pe'data *sf* (*impronta*) footprint; (*colpo*) kick; **prendere a pedate qn/qc** to kick sb/sth

pedi'atra, -i, -e *smf* paediatrician

pedi'cure *sm inv, f inv* chiropodist

pe'dina *sf* (*della dama*) draughtsman (BRIT), draftsman (US); (*fig*) pawn

pedi'nare /72/ *vt* to shadow, tail

pe'dofilo, -a *ag, sm/f* paedophile

pedo'nale *ag* pedestrian

pe'done, -a *sm/f* pedestrian ▷ *sm* (*Scacchi*) pawn

'peggio ['peddʒo] *av, ag inv* worse ▷ *sm o f*: **il o la ~** the worst; **alla ~** at worst, if the worst comes to the worst; **peggio'rare** /72/ *vt* to make worse, worsen ▷ *vi* to grow worse, worsen; **peggi'ore** *ag* (*comparativo*) worse; (*superlativo*) worst ▷ *smf*: **il (la) peggiore** the worst (person)

'pegno ['peɲɲo] *sm* (*Dir*) security, pledge; (*nei giochi di società*) forfeit; (*fig*) pledge, token; **dare in ~ qc** to pawn sth

pe'lare /72/ *vt* (*spennare*) to pluck; (*spellare*) to skin; (*sbucciare*) to peel; (*fig*) to make pay through the nose

pe'lato, -a *ag* peeled; **(pomodori) pelati** peeled tomatoes

'pelle *sf* skin; (*di animale*) skin, hide; (*cuoio*) leather; **avere la ~ d'oca** to have goose pimples *o* goose flesh

pellegri'naggio [pellegri'naddʒo] *sm* pilgrimage

pelle'rossa (*pl* **pellirosse**) *smf* (*peg*) Red Indian (!)

pelli'cano *sm* pelican

pel'liccia, -ce [pel'littʃa] *sf* (*mantello di animale*) fur; (*indumento*) fur coat; **~ ecologica** fake fur

pel'licola *sf* (*membrana sottile*) film, layer; (*Fot, Cine*) film

'pelo *sm* hair; (*pelame*) coat, hair; (*pelliccia*) fur; (*di tappeto*) pile; (*di liquido*) surface; **per un ~: per un ~ non ho perduto il treno;** I very nearly missed the train; **c'è mancato un ~ che affogasse** he narrowly escaped drowning; **pe'loso, -a** *ag* hairy

'peltro *sm* pewter

pe'luche [pə'lyʃ] *sm* plush; **giocattoli di ~** soft toys

pe'luria *sf* down

'pena *sf* (*Dir*) sentence; (*punizione*) punishment; (*sofferenza*) sadness *no pl*, sorrow; (*fatica*) trouble *no pl*, effort; (*difficoltà*) difficulty; **far ~** to be pitiful; **mi fai ~** I feel sorry for you; **prendersi** *o* **darsi la ~ di fare** to go to the trouble of doing; **~ di morte** death sentence; **~ pecuniaria** fine; **pe'nale** *ag* penal

pen'dente *ag* hanging; leaning ▷ *sm* (*ciondolo*) pendant; (*orecchino*) drop earring

'pendere /8/ *vi* (*essere appeso*): **~ da** to hang from; (*essere inclinato*) to lean; (*fig: incombere*): **~ su** to hang over

pen'dio, -ii *sm* slope, slant; (*luogo in pendenza*) slope

'pendola *sf* pendulum clock

pendo'lare *smf* commuter

pendo'lino *sm* high-speed train

pene'trante *ag* piercing, penetrating

pene'trare /72/ *vi* to come *o* get in ▷ *vt* to penetrate; **~ in** to enter; (*proiettile*) to penetrate; (*acqua, aria*) to go *o* come into

penicil'lina [penitʃil'lina] *sf* penicillin

pe'nisola *sf* peninsula

penitenzi'ario [peniten'tsjarjo] *sm* prison

'penna *sf* (*di uccello*) feather; (*per scrivere*) pen; **penne** *sfpl* (*Cuc*) quills (*type of pasta*); **~ a feltro/ stilografica/a sfera** felt-tip/ fountain/ballpoint pen

penna'rello *sm* felt(-tip) pen

pen'nello *sm* brush; (*per dipingere*) (paint)brush; **a ~** (*perfettamente*) to perfection, perfectly; **~ per la barba** shaving brush

pen'netta *sf* (*Inform*) dongle; **~ USB** memory stick

pe'nombra *sf* half-light, dim light

pen'sare /72/ *vi* to think ▷ *vt* to think; (*inventare, escogitare*) to think out; **~ a** to think of; (*amico, vacanze*) to think of *o* about; (*problema*) to think about; **~ di fare qc** to think of doing sth; **ci penso io** I'll see to *o* take care of it

pensi'ero *sm* thought; (*modo di pensare, dottrina*) thinking *no pl*; (*preoccupazione*) worry, care, trouble; **stare in ~ per qn** to be worried about sb; **pensie'roso, -a** *ag* thoughtful

'pensile *ag* hanging ▷ *sm* (*in cucina*) wall cupboard

pensio'nato, -a *sm/f* pensioner

pensi'one *sf* (*al prestatore di lavoro*) pension; (*vitto e alloggio*) board and lodging; (*albergo*) boarding house; **andare in ~** to retire; **mezza ~** half board; **~ completa** full board

pen'tirsi /45/ *vpr*: **~ di** to repent of; (*rammaricarsi*) to regret, be sorry for

'pentola *sf* pot; **~ a pressione** pressure cooker

pe'nultimo, -a *ag* last but one (*BRIT*), next to last, penultimate

penzo'lare [pendzo'lare] /72/ *vi* to dangle, hang loosely

'pepe *sm* pepper; **~ macinato/in grani/nero** ground/whole/black pepper

peperon'cino [peperon'tʃino] *sm* chilli pepper

pepe'rone *sm*: **~ (rosso)** red pepper, capsicum; (*piccante*) chili

pe'pita *sf* nugget

PAROLA CHIAVE

per *prep* **1** (*moto attraverso luogo*) through; **i ladri sono passati per la finestra** the thieves got in (*o* out) through the window; **l'ho cercato per tutta la casa** I've searched the whole house *o* all over the house for it

2 (*moto a luogo*) for, to; **partire per la Germania/il mare** to leave for Germany/the sea; **il treno per Roma** the Rome train, the train for *o* to Rome

3 (*stato in luogo*): **seduto/sdraiato per terra** sitting/lying on the ground

4 (*tempo*) for; **per anni/lungo tempo** for years/a long time; **per tutta l'estate** throughout the summer, all summer long; **lo rividi per Natale** I saw him again at Christmas; **lo faccio per lunedì** I'll do it for Monday

5 (*mezzo, maniera*) by; **per lettera/ ferrovia/via aerea** by letter/ rail/airmail; **prendere qn per un braccio** to take sb by the arm

6 (*causa, scopo*) for; **assente per malattia** absent because of *o* through *o* owing to illness; **ottimo per il mal di gola** excellent for sore throats

7 (*limitazione*) for; **è troppo difficile per lui** it's too difficult for him; **per quel che mi riguarda** as far as I'm concerned; **per poco che sia** however little it may be; **per questa volta ti perdono** I'll forgive you this time

8 (*prezzo, misura*) for; (: *distributivo*) a, per; **venduto per 3 milioni** sold for 3 million; **15 euro per persona** 15 euros a *o* per person; **uno per volta**

one at a time; **uno per uno** one by one; **5 per cento** 5 per cent; **3 per 4 fa 12** 3 times 4 equals 12; **dividere/moltiplicare 12 per 4** to divide/multiply 12 by 4

9 (*in qualità di*) as; (*al posto di*) for; **avere qn per professore** to have sb as a teacher; **ti ho preso per Mario** I mistook you for Mario, I thought you were Mario; **dare per morto qn** to give sb up for dead

10 (*seguito da vb: finale*): **per fare qc** (so as) to do sth, in order to do sth; (: *causale*): **per aver fatto qc** for having done sth; (: *consecutivo*): **è abbastanza grande per andarci da solo** he's big enough to go on his own

'pera *sf* pear

per'bene *ag inv* respectable, decent ▷ *av* (*con cura*) properly, well

percentu'ale [pertʃentu'ale] *sf* percentage

perce'pire [pertʃe'pire] /55/ *vt* (*sentire*) to perceive; (*ricevere*) to receive

○ **PAROLA CHIAVE**

perché [per'ke] *av* why; **perché no?** why not?; **perché non vuoi andarci?** why don't you want to go?; **spiegami perché l'hai fatto** tell me why you did it

▷ *cong* **1** (*causale*) because; **non posso uscire perché ho da fare** I can't go out because *o* as I've a lot to do

2 (*finale*) in order that, so that; **te lo do perché tu lo legga** I'm giving it to you so (that) you can read it

3 (*consecutivo*): **è troppo forte perché si possa batterlo** he's too strong to be beaten

▷ *sm inv* reason; **il perché di** the reason for

perciò [per'tʃɔ] *cong* so, for this *o* that reason

per'correre /28/ *vt* (*luogo*) to go all over; (: *paese*) to travel up and down, go all over; (*distanza*) to cover

per'corso, -a *pp di* **percorrere** ▷ *sm* (*tragitto*) journey; (*tratto*) route

percu'otere /106/ *vt* to hit, strike

percussi'one *sf* percussion; **strumenti a ~** (*Mus*) percussion instruments

'perdere /73/ *vt* to lose; (*lasciarsi sfuggire*) to miss; (*sprecare: tempo, denaro*) to waste ▷ *vi* to lose; (*serbatoio ecc*) to leak; **perdersi** *vpr* (*smarrirsi*) to get lost; (*svanire*) to disappear, vanish; **saper ~** to be a good loser; **lascia ~!** forget it!, never mind!

perdigi'orno [perdi'dʒorno] *sm inv, f inv* idler, waster

'perdita *sf* loss; (*spreco*) waste; (*fuoriuscita*) leak; **siamo in ~** (*Comm*) we are running at a loss; **a ~ d'occhio** as far as the eye can see

perdo'nare /72/ *vt* to pardon, forgive; (*scusare*) to excuse, pardon

per'dono *sm* forgiveness; (*Dir*) pardon

perduta'mente *av* desperately, passionately

pe'renne *ag* eternal, perpetual, perennial; (*Bot*) perennial

perfetta'mente *av* perfectly; **sai ~ che ...** you know perfectly well that ...

per'fetto, -a *ag* perfect ▷ *sm* (*Ling*) perfect (tense)

perfeziona'mento [perfettsjona'mento] *sm*: **~ (di)** improvement (in), perfection (of); **corso di ~** proficiency course

perfezio'nare [perfettsjo'nare] /72/ *vt* to improve, perfect; **perfezionarsi** *vpr* to improve

perfezi'one [perfet'tsjone] *sf* perfection

per'fino *av* even

perfo'rare /72/ *vt* to perforate, to punch a hole (*o* holes) in; (*banda, schede*) to punch; (*trivellare*) to drill

perga'mena *sf* parchment

P

perico'lante *ag* precarious

pe'ricolo *sm* danger; **mettere in ~** to endanger, put in danger; **perico'loso, -a** *ag* dangerous

perife'ria *sf (di città)* outskirts *pl*

pe'rifrasi *sf inv* circumlocution

pe'rimetro *sm* perimeter

peri'odico, -a, -ci, -che *ag* periodic(al); *(Mat)* recurring ▷ *sm* periodical

pe'riodo *sm* period

peripe'zie [peripet'tsie] *sfpl* ups and downs, vicissitudes

pe'rito, -a *ag* expert, skilled ▷ *sm/f* expert; *(agronomo, navale)* surveyor; **un ~ chimico** a qualified chemist

peri'zoma, -i [peri'dzoma] *sm* G-string

'perla *sf* pearl; **per'lina** *sf* bead

perlus'trare /72/ *vt* to patrol

perma'loso, -a *ag* touchy

perma'nente *ag* permanent ▷ *sf* permanent wave, perm; **perma'nenza** *sf* permanence; *(soggiorno)* stay

perme'are /72/ *vt* to permeate

per'messo, -a *pp di* **permettere** ▷ *sm (autorizzazione)* permission, leave; *(dato a militare, impiegato)* leave; *(licenza)* licence, permit; *(Mil: foglio)* pass; **~?, è ~?** *(posso entrare?)* may I come in?; *(posso passare?)* excuse me; **~ di lavoro/pesca** work/fishing permit; **~ di soggiorno** residence permit

per'mettere /63/ *vt* to allow, permit; **~ a qn qc/di fare qc** to allow sb sth/to do sth; **permettersi qc/di fare qc** to allow o.s. sth/to do sth; *(avere la possibilità)* to afford sth/to do sth

per'misi *ecc vb vedi* **permettere**

per'nacchia [per'nakkja] *sf (fam)*: **fare una ~** to blow a raspberry

per'nice [per'nitʃe] *sf* partridge

'perno *sm* pivot

pernot'tare /72/ *vi* to spend the night, stay overnight

'pero *sm* pear tree

però *cong (ma)* but; *(tuttavia)* however, nevertheless

perpendico'lare *ag, sf* perpendicular

per'plesso, -a *ag* perplexed, puzzled; uncertain

perqui'sire /55/ *vt* to search; **perquisizi'one** *sf (police)* search

'perse *ecc vb vedi* **perdere**

persecuzi'one [persekut'tsjone] *sf* persecution

persegui'tare /72/ *vt* to persecute

perseve'rante *ag* persevering

'persi *ecc vb vedi* **perdere**

persi'ano, -a *ag* Persian ▷ *sf* shutter; **persiana avvolgibile** roller blind

per'sino *av* = **perfino**

persis'tente *ag* persistent

'perso, -a *pp di* **perdere**

per'sona *sf* person; *(qualcuno)*: **una ~** someone, somebody; *(espressione)* anyone o anybody

perso'naggio [perso'naddʒo] *sm (persona ragguardevole)* personality, figure; *(tipo)* character, individual; *(Letteratura)* character

perso'nale *ag* personal ▷ *sm* staff; personnel; *(figura fisica)* build

personalità *sf inv* personality

perspi'cace [perspi'katʃe] *ag* shrewd, discerning

persu'adere /88/ *vt*: **~ qn (di qc/a fare)** to persuade sb (of sth/to do)

per'tanto *cong (quindi)* so, therefore

'pertica, -che *sf* pole

perti'nente *ag*: **~ (a)** relevant (to), pertinent (to)

per'tosse *sf* whooping cough

perturbazi'one [perturbat'tsjone] *sf* disruption; disturbance; **~ atmosferica** atmospheric disturbance

per'vadere /52/ *vt* to pervade

per'verso, -a *ag* perverted; perverse

perver'tito, -a *sm/f* pervert

p.es. *abbr* (= *per esempio*) e.g.

pe'sante *ag* heavy

pe'sare /72/ *vt* to weigh ▷ *vi (avere un peso)* to weigh; *(essere pesante)* to be heavy; (fig) to carry weight; **~ su** (fig) to lie heavy on; to influence; to hang over; **tutta la responsabilità pesa su di lui** all the responsibility rests on his shoulders; **è una situazione che mi pesa** it's a difficult situation for me; **il suo parere pesa molto** his opinion counts for a lot

'**pesca** (pl **pesche**) sf (frutto) peach; (il pescare) fishing; **andare a ~** to go fishing; **~ di beneficenza** (lotteria) lucky dip; **~ con la lenza** angling

pes'care /20/ vt (pesce) to fish for; to catch; (qc nell'acqua) to fish out; (fig: trovare) to get hold of, find

pesca'tore sm fisherman; (con lenza) angler

'**pesce** ['peʃʃe] sm fish (gen inv); **Pesci** (dello zodiaco) Pisces; **~ d'aprile!** April Fool!; **~ rosso** goldfish; **~ spada** swordfish; **pesce'cane** sm shark

pesche'reccio [peske'rettʃo] sm fishing boat

pesche'ria [peske'ria] sf fishmonger's (shop) (BRIT), fish store (US)

pescherò ecc [peske'rɔ] vb vedi **pescare**

'**peso** sm weight; (Sport) shot; **essere di ~ a qn** (fig) to be a burden to sb; **rubare sul ~** to give short weight; **~ lordo/netto** gross/net weight; **~ piuma/mosca/gallo/medio/ massimo** (Pugilato) feather/fly/ bantam/middle/heavyweight

pessi'mismo sm pessimism; **pessi'mista, -i, -e** ag pessimistic ▷ smf pessimist

'**pessimo, -a** ag very bad, awful

pes'tare /72/ vt to tread on, trample on; (sale, pepe) to grind; (uva, aglio) to crush; (fig: picchiare): **~ qn** to beat sb up

'**peste** sf plague; (persona) nuisance, pest

pes'tello sm pestle

'**petalo** sm (Bot) petal

pe'tardo sm firecracker, banger (BRIT)

petizi'one [petit'tsjone] sf petition

petroli'era sf (nave) oil tanker

pe'trolio sm oil, petroleum; (per lampada, fornello) paraffin

> Attenzione! In inglese esiste la parola petrol, che però significa benzina.

pettego'lare /72/ vi to gossip

pettego'lezzo [pettego'leddzo] sm gossip no pl; **fare pettegolezzi** to gossip

pet'tegolo, -a ag gossipy ▷ sm/f gossip

petti'nare /72/ vt to comb (the hair of); **pettinarsi** vpr to comb one's hair; **pettina'tura** sf (acconciatura) hairstyle

'**pettine** sm comb; (Zool) scallop

petti'rosso sm robin

'**petto** sm chest; (seno) breast, bust; (Cuc: di carne bovina) brisket; (di pollo ecc) breast; **a doppio ~** (abito) double-breasted

petu'lante ag insolent

'**pezza** ['pɛttsa] sf piece of cloth; (toppa) patch; (cencio) rag, cloth

pez'zente [pet'tsɛnte] smf beggar

'**pezzo** ['pɛttso] sm (gen) piece; (brandello, frammento) piece, bit; (di macchina, arnese ecc) part; (Stampa) article; **aspettare un ~** to wait quite a while o some time; **in** o **a pezzi** in pieces; **andare a pezzi** to break into pieces; **un bel ~ d'uomo** a fine figure of a man; **abito a due pezzi** two-piece suit; **~ di cronaca** (Stampa) report; **~ grosso** (fig) bigwig; **~ di ricambio** spare part

pi'accio ecc ['pjattʃo] vb vedi **piacere**

pia'cente [pja'tʃɛnte] ag attractive

pia'cere [pja'tʃere] /74/ vi to please ▷ sm pleasure; (favore) favour (BRIT), favor (US); **una ragazza che piace** a likeable girl; (attraente) an attractive girl; **mi piace** I like it; **quei ragazzi non mi piacciono** I don't like those boys; **gli ~bbe andare al cinema** he would like to go to the cinema;

il suo discorso è piaciuto molto his speech was well received; **"~!"** (nelle presentazioni) "pleased to meet you!"; **~ (di conoscerla)** nice to meet you; **con ~** certainly, with pleasure; **per ~** please; **fare un ~ a qn** to do sb a favour; **pia'cevole** ag pleasant, agreeable

pi'acqui ecc vb vedi **piacere**

pi'aga, -ghe sf (lesione) sore; (ferita: anche fig) wound; (fig: flagello) scourge, curse; (: persona) pest, nuisance

piagnuco'lare [pjaɲɲuko'lare] /72/ vi to whimper

pianeggi'ante [pjaned'dʒante] ag flat, level

piane'rottolo sm landing

pia'neta sm (Astr) planet

pi'angere ['pjandʒere] /75/ vi to cry, weep; (occhi) to water ▷ vt to cry, weep; (lamentare) to bewail, lament; **~ la morte di qn** to mourn sb's death

pianifi'care /20/ vt to plan

pia'nista, -i, -e smf pianist

pi'ano, -a ag (piatto) flat, level; (Mat) plane; (chiaro) clear, plain ▷ av (adagio) slowly; (a bassa voce) softly; (con cautela) slowly, carefully ▷ sm (Mat) plane; (Geo) plain; (livello) level, plane; (di edificio) floor; (programma) plan; (Mus) piano; **pian ~** very slowly; (poco a poco) little by little; **al ~ terra** on the ground floor; **in primo/secondo ~** in the foreground/background; **di primo ~** (fig) prominent, high-ranking

piano'forte sm piano, pianoforte

piano'terra sm inv = **piano terra**

pi'ansi ecc vb vedi **piangere**

pi'anta sf (Bot) plant; (Anat: anche: ~ **del piede**) sole (of the foot); (grafico) plan; (cartina topografica) map; **in ~ stabile** on the permanent staff; **pian'tare** /72/ vt to plant; (conficcare) to drive o hammer in; (tenda) to put up, pitch; (fig: lasciare) to leave, desert; **piantarsi** vpr: **piantarsi**

davanti a qn to plant o.s. in front of sb; **piantala!** (fam) cut it out!

pianter'reno sm ground floor

pian'tina sf (di edificio, città) (small) map; (Bot) (small) plant

pia'nura sf plain

pi'astra sf plate; (di pietra) slab; (di fornello) hotplate; **panino alla ~** ≈ toasted sandwich; **~ di registrazione** tape deck

pias'trella sf tile

pias'trina sf (Mil) identity disc (BRIT) o tag (US)

piatta'forma sf (anche fig) platform

piat'tino sm saucer

pi'atto, -a ag flat; (fig: scialbo) dull ▷ sm (recipiente, vivanda) dish; (portata) course; (parte piana) flat (part); **piatti** smpl (Mus) cymbals; **~ fondo** soup dish; **~ forte** main course; **~ del giorno** dish of the day, plat du jour; **~ dei giradischi** turntable; **~ piano** dinner plate

pi'azza ['pjattsa] sf square; (Comm) market; **far ~ pulita** to make a clean sweep; **~ d'armi** (Mil) parade ground; **piaz'zale** sm (large) square

piaz'zola [pjat'tsɔla] sf (Aut) lay-by; (di tenda) pitch

pic'cante ag hot, pungent; (fig) racy; biting

pic'chetto [pik'ketto] sm (Mil, di scioperanti) picket; (di tenda) peg

picchi'are [pik'kjare] /19/ vt (persona: colpire) to hit, strike; (: prendere a botte) to beat (up); (battere) to beat; (sbattere) to bang ▷ vi (bussare) to knock; (: con forza) to bang; (colpire) to hit, strike; (sole) to beat down; **picchi'ata** sf (Aer) dive

'picchio ['pikkjo] sm woodpecker

pic'cino, -a [pit'tʃino] ag tiny, very small

picci'one [pit'tʃone] sm pigeon

'picco, -chi sm peak; **a ~** vertically

'piccolo, -a ag small; (oggetto, mano, di età: bambino) small, little; (dav sostantivo: di breve durata, viaggio)

pic'cone sm pick(-axe)

pic'cozza [pik'kɔttsa] sf ice-axe

pic'nic sm inv picnic

pi'docchio [pi'dɔkkjo] sm louse

pi'ede sm foot; (di mobile) leg; **in piedi** standing; **a piedi** on foot; **a piedi nudi** barefoot; **su due piedi** (fig) at once; **prendere ~** (fig) to gain ground, catch on; **sul ~ di guerra** (Mil) ready for action; **~ di porco** crowbar

pi'ega, -ghe sf (piegatura, Geo) fold; (di gonna) pleat; (di pantaloni) crease; (grinza) wrinkle, crease; **prendere una brutta o cattiva ~** (fig) to take a turn for the worse

pie'gare /80/ vt to fold; (braccia, gambe, testa) to bend ▷ vi to bend; **piegarsi** vpr to bend; (fig): **piegarsi (a)** to yield (to), submit (to)

piegherò ecc [pjege'rɔ] vb vedi **piegare**

pie'ghevole ag pliable, flexible; (porta) folding

Pie'monte sm: **il ~** Piedmont

pi'ena sf vedi **pieno**

pi'eno, -a ag full; (muro, mattone) solid ▷ sm (colmo) height, peak; (carico) full load ▷ sf (di fiume) flood, spate; **~ di** full of; **in ~ giorno** in broad daylight; **fare il ~** (di benzina) to fill up (with petrol)

piercing ['pirsing] sm: **farsi il ~ all'ombelico** to have one's navel pierced

pietà sf pity; (Rel) piety; **senza ~** pitiless, ruthless; **avere ~ di** (compassione) to pity, feel sorry for; (misericordia) to have pity o mercy on

pie'tanza [pje'tantsa] sf dish, course

pie'toso, -a ag (compassionevole) pitying, compassionate; (che desta pietà) pitiful

pi'etra sf stone; **~ preziosa** precious stone, gem

piffero sm (Mus) pipe

short; (fig) mean, petty ▷ sm/f child, little one

pigi'ama [pi'dʒama] sm pyjamas pl

pigli'are [piʎ'ʎare] /27/ vt to take, grab; (afferrare) to catch

pigna ['piɲɲa] sf pine cone

pi'gnolo, -a [piɲ'ɲɔlo] ag pernickety

pi'grizia [pi'grittsja] sf laziness

pigro, -a ag lazy

PIL sigla m (= prodotto interno lordo) GDP

pila sf (catasta, di ponte) pile; (Elettr) battery; (torcia) torch (BRIT), flashlight

pi'lastro sm pillar

pile ['pail] sm inv fleece

pillola sf pill; **prendere la ~** to be on the pill

pi'lone sm (di ponte) pier; (di linea elettrica) pylon

pi'lota, -i, -e smf pilot; (Aut) driver ▷ ag inv pilot cpd; **~ automatico** automatic pilot

pinaco'teca, -che sf art gallery

pi'neta sf pinewood

ping-pong [piŋ'pɔŋ] sm table tennis

pingu'ino sm (Zool) penguin

pinna sf fin; (di cetaceo, per nuotare) flipper

pino sm pine (tree); **pi'nolo** sm pine kernel

pinza ['pintsa] sf pliers pl; (Med) forceps pl; (Zool) pincer

pinzette [pin'tsette] sfpl tweezers

pi'oggia, -ge ['pjɔddʒa] sf rain; **~ acida** acid rain

pi'olo sm peg; (di scala) rung

piom'bare /72/ vi to fall heavily; (gettarsi con impeto): **~ su** to fall upon, assail ▷ vt (dente) to fill; **piomba'tura** sf (di dente) filling

piom'bino sm (sigillo) (lead) seal; (del filo a piombo) plummet; (Pesca) sinker

pi'ombo sm (Chim) lead; **a ~** (cadere) straight down; **senza ~** (benzina) unleaded

pioni'ere, -a sm/f pioneer

pi'oppo sm poplar

pi'overe /76/ vb impers to rain ▷ vi (fig: scendere dall'alto) to rain down;

(*affluire in gran numero*): **~ in** to pour into; **pioviggi'nare** /72/ vb impers to drizzle; **pio'voso, -a** ag rainy

pi'ovra sf octopus

pi'ovve ecc vb vedi **piovere**

'**pipa** sf pipe

pipì sf (fam): **fare ~** to have a wee (wee)

pipis'trello sm (Zool) bat

pi'ramide sf pyramid

pi'rata, -i sm pirate; **~ informatico** hacker; **~ della strada** hit-and-run driver

Pire'nei smpl: **i ~** the Pyrenees

pi'romane smf pyromaniac; arsonist

pi'roscafo sm steamer, steamship

pisci'are [piʃʃare] /14/ vi (fam!) to piss (!), pee (!)

pi'scina [piʃʃina] sf (swimming) pool

pi'sello sm pea

piso'lino sm nap

'**pista** sf (traccia) track, trail; (di stadio) track; (di pattinaggio) rink; (da sci) run; (Aer) runway; (di circo) ring; **~ da ballo** dance floor

pis'tacchio [pis'takkjo] sm pistachio (tree); pistachio (nut)

pis'tola sf pistol, gun

pis'tone sm piston

pi'tone sm python

pit'tore, -'trice sm/f painter; **pitto'resco, -a, -schi, -sche** ag picturesque

pit'tura sf painting; **pittu'rare** /72/ vt to paint

○ **PAROLA CHIAVE**

più av **1** (*in maggiore quantità*) more; **più del solito** more than usual; **in più, di più** more; **ne voglio di più** I want some more; **ci sono 3 persone in o di più** there are 3 more o extra people; **più o meno** more or less; **per di più** (*inoltre*) what's more, moreover

2 (*comparativo*) more; (: se monosillabo, spesso) + ...er; **più ... di/che** more ...

than; **lavoro più di te/di Paola** I work harder than you/than Paola; **è più intelligente che ricco** he's more intelligent than rich

3 (*superlativo*) most; (: se monosillabico, spesso) + ...est; **il più grande/intelligente** the biggest/most intelligent; **è quello che compro più spesso** that's the one I buy most often; **al più presto** as soon as possible; **al più tardi** at the latest

4 (*negazione*): **non ... più** no more, no longer; **non ho più soldi** I've got no more money, I don't have any more money; **non lavoro più** I'm no longer working, I don't work any more; **a più non posso** (*gridare*) at the top of one's voice; (*correre*) as fast as one can

5 (*Mat*) plus; **4 più 5 fa 9** 4 plus 5 equals 9; **più 5 gradi** 5 degrees above freezing, plus 5

▶ prep plus

▶ ag inv **1**: **più ... (di)** more ... (than); **più denaro/tempo** more money/time; **più persone di quante ci aspettassimo** more people than we expected

2 (*numerosi, diversi*) several; **l'aspettai per più giorni** I waited for it for several days

▶ sm **1** (*la maggior parte*): **il più è fatto** most of it is done

2 (*Mat*) plus (sign)

3: **i più** the majority

---

pi'uma sf feather; **piu'mino** sm (eider)down; (*per letto*) eiderdown; (: tipo danese) duvet, continental quilt; (*giacca*) quilted jacket (with goose-feather padding); (*per cipria*) powder puff; (*per spolverare*) feather duster

piut'tosto av rather; **~ che** (*anziché*) rather than

'**pizza** ['pittsa] sf pizza; **pizze'ria** sf place where pizzas are made, sold or eaten

pizzi'care [pittsi'kare] /20/ vt
(stringere) to nip, pinch; (pungere)
to sting; to bite; (Mus) to pluck ▷ vi
(prudere) to itch, be itchy; (cibo) to be
hot o spicy

'pizzico ['pittsiko] sm (pizzicotto)
pinch, nip; (piccola quantità) pinch,
dash; (d'insetto) sting; bite

pizzi'cotto [pittsi'kɔtto] sm
pinch, nip

'pizzo ['pittso] sm (merletto) lace;
(barbetta) goatee beard

plagi'are [pla'dʒare] /62/ vt (copiare)
to plagiarize

plaid [plɛd] sm inv (travelling) rug
(BRIT), lap robe (US)

pla'nare /72/ vi (Aer) to glide

'plasma sm plasma

plas'mare /72/ vt to mould , shape

'plastico, -a, -ci, -che ag plastic
▷ sf (arte) plastic arts pl; (Med) plastic
surgery; (sostanza) plastic; **plastica
facciale** face lift

'platano sm plane tree

pla'tea sf (Teat) stalls pl

'platino sm platinum

plau'sibile ag plausible

pleni'lunio sm full moon

'plettro sm plectrum

pleu'rite sf pleurisy

'plico, -chi sm (pacco) parcel; **in ~ a
parte** (Comm) under separate cover

plo'tone sm (Mil) platoon; **~
d'esecuzione** firing squad

plu'rale ag, sm plural

P.M. abbr (Pol) = **Pubblico Ministero**;
(= Polizia Militare) MP

PMI sigla fpl (= Piccole e Medie Imprese)
SME

pneu'matico, -a, -ci, -che ag
inflatable; (Tecn) pneumatic ▷ sm
(Aut) tyre (BRIT), tire (US)

po' av, sm vedi **poco**

⃝ **PAROLA CHIAVE**

'poco, -a, -chi, -che ag (quantità)
little, not much; (numero) few, not
many; **poco pane/denaro/spazio**
little o not much bread/money/space;
poche persone/idee few o not many
people/ideas; **ci vediamo tra poco**
(sottinteso: tempo) see you soon
▷ av **1** (in piccola quantità) little, not
much; (: numero limitato) few, not
many; **guadagna poco** he doesn't
earn much, he earns little
2 (con ag, av) (a) little, not very; **è
poco più vecchia di lui** she's a little
o slightly older than him; **sta poco
bene** he isn't very well
3 (tempo): **poco dopo/prima** shortly
afterwards/before; **il film dura
poco** the film doesn't last very long;
ci vediamo molto poco we don't see
each other very often, we hardly ever
see each other
4: **un po'** a little, a bit; **è un po'
corto** it's a little o a bit short;
arriverà fra un po' he'll arrive
shortly o in a little while
5: **a dir poco** to say the least; **a
poco a poco** little by little; **per poco
non cadevo** I nearly fell; **è una
cosa da poco** it's nothing, it's of no
importance; **una persona da poco**
a worthless person
▷ pron (a) little

podcast ['pɔdkast] sm podcast

po'dere sm (Agr) farm

'podio sm dais, platform; (Mus)
podium

po'dismo sm (Sport: marcia) walking;
(: corsa) running

poe'sia sf (arte) poetry;
(componimento) poem

po'eta, -essa sm/f poet/poetess

poggi'are [pod'dʒare] /62/ vt to
lean, rest; (posare) to lay, place;
poggia'testa sm inv (Aut) headrest

'poggio ['pɔddʒo] sm hillock, knoll

poi av then; (alla fine) finally, at last; **e
~** (inoltre) and besides; **questa ~ (è
bella)!** (ironico) that's a good one!

poiché [poi'ke] cong since, as

'poker sm poker

po'lacco, -a, -chi, -che ag Polish ▷ sm/f Pole

po'lare ag polar

po'lemico, -a, -ci, -che ag polemical, controversial ▷ sf controversy

po'lenta sf (Cuc) sort of thick porridge made with maize flour

'polipo sm polyp

polisti'rolo sm polystyrene

po'litica, -che sf vedi **politico**; **politica'mente** av politically; **politicamente corretto** politically correct

po'litico, -a, -ci, -che ag political ▷ sm/f politician ▷ sf politics sg; (linea di condotta) policy

poli'zia [polit'tsia] sf police; **~ giudiziaria** ≈ Criminal Investigation Department (CID) (BRIT), Federal Bureau of Investigation (FBI) (US); **~ stradale** traffic police; **polizi'esco, -a, -schi, -sche** ag police cpd; (film, romanzo) detective cpd; **polizi'otto** sm policeman; **cane poliziotto** police dog; **donna poliziotto** policewoman; **poliziotto di quartiere** local police officer

○ **POLIZIA DI STATO**
○
○ The remit of the polizia di stato
○ is to maintain public order, to
○ uphold the law, and to prevent and
○ investigate crime. This is a civilian
○ branch of the police force; male
○ and female officers perform similar
○ duties. The polizia di stato reports to
○ the Minister of the Interior.

po'lizza ['polittsa] sf (Comm) bill; **~ di assicurazione** insurance policy; **~ di carico** bill of lading

pol'laio sm henhouse

'pollice ['pollitʃe] sm thumb

'polline sm pollen

'pollo sm chicken

pol'mone sm lung; **~ d'acciaio** (Med) iron lung; **polmo'nite** sf pneumonia; **polmonite atipica** SARS

'polo sm (Geo, Fisica) pole; (gioco) polo; **il ~ sud/nord** the South/North Pole

Po'lonia sf: **la ~** Poland

'polpa sf flesh, pulp; (carne) lean meat

pol'paccio [pol'pattʃo] sm (Anat) calf

polpas'trello sm fingertip

pol'petta sf (Cuc) meatball

'polpo sm octopus

pol'sino sm cuff

'polso sm (Anat) wrist; (pulsazione) pulse; (fig: forza) drive, vigour

pol'trire /55/ vi to laze about

pol'trona sf armchair; (Teat: posto) seat in the front stalls (BRIT) o the orchestra (US)

'polvere sf dust; (sostanza ridotta minutissima) powder, dust; **caffè in ~** instant coffee; **latte in ~** dried o powdered milk; **sapone in ~** soap powder; **~ pirica** o **da sparo** gunpowder

po'mata sf ointment, cream

po'mello sm knob

pome'riggio [pome'riddʒo] sm afternoon

'pomice ['pomitʃe] sf pumice

'pomo sm (mela) apple; (ornamentale) knob; (di sella) pommel; **~ d'Adamo** (Anat) Adam's apple

pomo'doro sm tomato; **pomodori pelati** skinned tomatoes

'pompa sf pump; (sfarzo) pomp (and ceremony); **~ antincendio** fire hose; **~ di benzina** petrol (BRIT) o gas (US) pump; (distributore) filling o gas (US) station; **impresa di pompe funebri** funeral parlour sg (BRIT), undertaker's sg; **pom'pare** /72/ vt to pump; (trarre) to pump out; (gonfiare d'aria) to pump up

pom'pelmo sm grapefruit

pompi'ere sm fireman

po'nente sm west

'pongo vb vedi **porre**

'poni vb vedi **porre**

'ponte sm bridge; (di nave) deck; (anche: **~ di comando**) bridge; (impalcatura) scaffold; **fare il ~** (fig) to take the extra day off; (between 2 public holidays): **governo ~** interim government; **~ aereo** airlift; **~ levatoio** drawbridge; **~ sospeso** suspension bridge

pon'tefice sm (Rel) pontiff

'popcorn ['pɔpkɔːn] sm inv popcorn

popo'lare /72/ ag popular; (quartiere, clientela) working-class ▷ vt (rendere abitato) to populate; **popolarsi** vpr to fill with people, get crowded; **popolazi'one** sf population

'popolo sm people

'poppa sf (di nave) stern; (fam: mammella) breast

porcel'lana [portʃel'lana] sf porcelain, china; (oggetto) piece of porcelain

porcel'lino, -a [portʃel'lino] sm/f piglet; **~ d'India** guinea pig

porche'ria [porke'ria] sf filth, muck; (fig: oscenità) obscenity; (: azione disonesta) dirty trick; (: cosa mal fatta) rubbish

por'cile [por'tʃile] sm pigsty

por'cino, -a [por'tʃino] ag of pigs, pork cpd ▷ sm (fungo) type of edible mushroom

'porco, -ci sm pig; (carne) pork

porcos'pino sm porcupine

'porgere ['pɔrdʒere] /115/ vt to hand, give; (tendere) to hold out

pornogra'fia sf pornography; **porno'grafico, -a, -ci, -che** ag pornographic

'poro sm pore

'porpora sf purple

'porre /77/ vt (mettere) to put; (collocare) to place; (posare) to lay (down), put (down); (fig: supporre): **poniamo (il caso) che ...** let's suppose that ...

'porro sm (Bot) leek; (Med) wart

'porsi ecc vb vedi **porgere**

'porta sf door; (Sport) goal

porta...: portaba'gagli sm inv (facchino) porter; (Aut, Ferr) luggage rack; **porta-'CD** sm inv (mobile) CD rack; (astuccio) CD holder; **porta'cenere** sm inv ashtray; **portachi'avi** sm inv keyring; **porta'erei** sf inv (nave) aircraft carrier; **portafi'nestra** (pl **portefinestre**) sf French window; **porta'foglio** sm wallet; (Pol, Borsa) portfolio; **portafor'tuna** sm inv lucky charm; mascot

por'tale sm (di chiesa, Inform) portal

porta'mento sm carriage, bearing

portamo'nete sm inv purse

por'tante ag (muro ecc) supporting, load-bearing

portan'tina sf sedan chair; (per ammalati) stretcher

portaom'brelli sm inv umbrella stand

porta'pacchi [porta'pakki] sm inv (di moto, bicicletta) luggage rack

porta'penne [porta'penne] sm inv pen holder; (astuccio) pencil case

por'tare /72/ vt (sostenere, sorreggere: peso, bambino, pacco) to carry; (indossare: abito, occhiali) to wear; (: capelli lunghi) to have; (avere: nome, titolo) to have, bear; (recare): **~ qc a qn** to take (o bring) sth to sb; (fig: sentimenti) to bear

portasiga'rette sm inv cigarette case

por'tata sf (vivanda) course; (Aut) carrying (o loading) capacity; (di arma) range; (volume d'acqua) (rate of) flow; (fig: limite) scope, capability; (: importanza) impact, import; **alla ~ di tutti** (conoscenza) within everybody's capabilities; (prezzo) within everybody's means; **a/fuori ~ (di)** within/out of reach (of); **a ~ di mano** within (arm's) reach

por'tatile ag portable

por'tato, -a ag (incline): **~ a** inclined o apt to

p

portau'ovo *sm inv* eggcup

porta'voce [porta'votʃe] *smf inv*
spokesman/woman

por'tento *sm* wonder, marvel

porti'era *sf* (Aut) door

porti'ere *sm* (portinaio) concierge,
caretaker; (di hotel) porter; (nel calcio)
goalkeeper

porti'naio, -a *sm/f* concierge,
caretaker

portine'ria *sf* caretaker's lodge

'porto, -a *pp di* **porgere** ▷ *sm*
(Naut) harbour, port ▷ *sm inv* port
(wine); **~ d'armi** gun licence (BRIT) o
license (US)

Porto'gallo *sm*: **il ~** Portugal;
porto'ghese *ag, smf, sm*
Portuguese *inv*

por'tone *sm* main entrance, main
door

portu'ale *ag* harbour *cpd*, port *cpd*
▷ *sm* dock worker

porzi'one [por'tsjone] *sf* portion,
share; (di cibo) portion, helping

'posa *sf* (Fot) exposure; (atteggiamento,
di modello) pose

po'sare /72/ *vt* to put (down), lay
(down) ▷ *vi* (ponte, edificio, teoria):
~ su to rest on; (Fot: atteggiarsi) to
pose; **posarsi** *vpr* (ape, aereo) to land;
(uccello) to alight; (sguardo) to settle

po'sata *sf* piece of cutlery

pos'critto *sm* postscript

'posi *ecc vb vedi* **porre**

posi'tivo, -a *ag* positive

posizi'one [pozit'tsjone] *sf* position;
prendere ~ (fig) to take a stand; **luci
di ~** (Aut) sidelights

pos'porre /77/ *vt* to place after;
(differire) to postpone, defer

posse'dere /107/ *vt* to own, possess;
(qualità, virtù) to have, possess

posses'sivo, -a *ag* possessive

pos'sesso *sm* ownership *no pl*;
possession

posses'sore *sm* owner

pos'sibile *ag* possible ▷ *sm*: **fare
tutto il ~** to do everything possible;

nei limiti del ~ as far as possible;
al più tardi ~ as late as possible;
possibilità *sf inv* possibility ▷ *sfpl*
(mezzi) means; **aver la possibilità di
fare** to be in a position to do; to have
the opportunity to do

possi'dente *smf* landowner

possi'edo *ecc vb vedi* **possedere**

'posso *ecc vb vedi* **potere**

'posta *sf* (servizio) post, postal
service; (corrispondenza) post,
mail; (ufficio postale) post office;
(nei giochi d'azzardo) stake; **poste**
sfpl (amministrazione) post office; **~
aerea** airmail; **~ elettronica** E-mail,
e-mail, electronic mail; **~ ordinaria**
≈ second-class mail; **~ prioritaria**
first class (post); **ministro delle
Poste e Telecomunicazioni**
Postmaster General; **pos'tale** *ag*
postal, post office *cpd*

posteggi'are [posted'dʒare] /62/
vt, vi to park; **pos'teggio** *sm* car park
(BRIT), parking lot (US); (di taxi) rank
(BRIT), stand (US)

'poster *sm inv* poster

posteri'ore *ag* (dietro) back; (dopo)
later ▷ *sm* (fam: sedere) behind

postici'pare [postitʃi'pare] /72/ *vt* to
defer, postpone

pos'tino *sm* postman (BRIT),
mailman (US)

'posto, -a *pp di* **porre** ▷ *sm* (sito,
posizione) place; (impiego) job; (spazio
libero) room, space; (di parcheggio)
space; (sedile: al teatro, in treno ecc)
seat; (Mil) post; **a ~** (in ordine) in
place, tidy; (fig) settled; (persona)
reliable; **mettere a ~** to tidy (up), put
in order; (faccende) to straighten out;
al ~ di in place of; **sul ~** on the spot;
~ di blocco roadblock; **~ di lavoro**
job; **~ di polizia** police station; **posti
in piedi** (Teat, in autobus) standing
room

po'tabile *ag* drinkable; **acqua ~**
drinking water

po'tare /72/ *vt* to prune

po'tassio *sm* potassium

po'tente *ag* (*nazione*) strong, powerful; (*veleno, farmaco*) potent, strong; **po'tenza** *sf* power; (*forza*) strength

potenzi'ale [poten'tsjale] *ag, sm* potential

PAROLA CHIAVE

po'tere /78/ *sm* power; **al potere** (*partito ecc*) in power; **potere d'acquisto** purchasing power
▶ *vb aus* **1** (*essere in grado di*) can, be able to; **non ha potuto ripararlo** he couldn't *o* he wasn't able to repair it; **non è potuto venire** he couldn't *o* he wasn't able to come; **spiacente di non poter aiutare** sorry not to be able to help
2 (*avere il permesso*) can, may, be allowed to; **posso entrare?** can *o* may I come in?; **posso chiederti, dove sei stato?** where, may I ask, have you been?
3 (*eventualità*) may, might, could; **potrebbe essere vero** it might *o* could be true; **può aver avuto un incidente** he may *o* might *o* could have had an accident; **può darsi** perhaps; **può darsi** *o* **può essere che non venga** he may *o* might not come
4 (*augurio*): **potessi almeno parlargli!** if only I could speak to him!
5 (*suggerimento*): **potresti almeno scusarti!** you could at least apologize!
▶ *vt* can, be able to; **può molto per noi** he can do a lot for us; **non ne posso più** (*per stanchezza*) I'm exhausted; (*per rabbia*) I can't take any more

potrò *ecc vb vedi* **potere**

povero, -a *ag* poor; (*disadorno*) plain, bare ▶ *sm/f* poor man/woman; **i poveri** the poor; **~ di** lacking in,

having little; **povertà** *sf* poverty; **povertà energetica** fuel poverty

poz'zanghera [pot'tsangera] *sf* puddle

'pozzo ['pottso] *sm* well; (*cava: di carbone*) pit; (*di miniera*) shaft; **~ petrolifero** oil well

P.R.A. [pra] *sigla m* (= *Pubblico Registro Automobilistico*) ≈ DVLA

pran'zare [pran'dzare] /72/ *vi* to dine, have dinner, to lunch, have lunch

'pranzo ['prandzo] *sm* dinner; (*a mezzogiorno*) lunch

'prassi *sf* usual procedure

'pratica, -che *sf* practice; (*esperienza*) experience; (*conoscenza*) knowledge, familiarity; (*tirocinio*) training, practice; (*Amm: affare*) matter, case; (*: incartamento*) file, dossier; **in ~** (*praticamente*) in practice; **mettere in ~** to put into practice

prati'cabile *ag* (*progetto*) practicable, feasible; (*luogo*) passable, practicable

pratica'mente *av* (*in modo pratico*) in a practical way, practically; (*quasi*) practically, almost

prati'care /20/ *vt* to practise; (*Sport: tennis ecc*) to play; (*: nuoto, scherma ecc*) to go in for; (*eseguire: apertura, buco*) to make; **~ uno sconto** to give a discount

'pratico, -a, -ci, -che *ag* practical; **~ di** (*esperto*) experienced *o* skilled in; (*familiare*) familiar with

'prato *sm* meadow; (*di giardino*) lawn

preav'viso *sm* notice; **telefonata con ~** personal *o* person to person call

pre'cario, -a *ag* precarious; (*Ins*) temporary

precauzi'one [prekaut'tsjone] *sf* caution, care; (*misura*) precaution

prece'dente [pretʃe'dɛnte] *ag* previous ▶ *sm* precedent; **il discorso/film ~** the previous *o* preceding speech/film; **senza precedenti** unprecedented;

precedenti penali criminal record sg; **prece'denza** sf priority, precedence; (Aut) right of way

pre'cedere [pre'tʃedere] /29/ vt to precede, go o (come) before

precipi'tare [pretʃipi'tare] /72/ vi (cadere) to fall headlong; (fig: situazione) to get out of control ▷ vt (gettare dall'alto in basso) to hurl, fling; (fig: affrettare) to rush; **precipitarsi** vpr (gettarsi) to hurl o fling o.s.; (affrettarsi) to rush; **precipi'toso, -a** ag (caduta, fuga) headlong; (fig: avventato) rash, reckless; (: affrettato) hasty, rushed

preci'pizio [pretʃi'pittsjo] sm precipice; **a ~** (fig) (correre) headlong

precisa'mente [pretʃiza'mente] av (gen) precisely; (con esattezza) exactly

preci'sare [pretʃi'zare] /72/ vt to state, specify; (spiegare) to explain (in detail)

precisi'one [pretʃi'zjone] sf precision; accuracy

pre'ciso, -a [pre'tʃizo] ag (esatto) precise; (accurato) accurate, precise; (deciso: idea) precise, definite; (uguale): **2 vestiti precisi** 2 dresses exactly the same; **sono le 9 precise** it's exactly 9 o'clock

pre'cludere /3/ vt to block, obstruct

pre'coce [pre'kɔtʃe] ag early; (bambino) precocious; (vecchiaia) premature

precon'cetto, -a [prekon'tʃetto] sm preconceived idea, prejudice

precur'sore sm forerunner, precursor

'preda sf (bottino) booty; (animale, fig) prey; **essere ~ di** to fall prey to; **essere in ~ a** to be prey to

'predica, -che sf sermon; (fig) lecture, talking-to

predi'care /20/ vt, vi to preach

predi'cato sm (Ling) predicate

predi'letto, -a pp di **prediligere** ▷ ag, sm/f favourite

predi'ligere [predi'lidʒere] /117/ vt to prefer, have a preference for

pre'dire /38/ vt to foretell, predict

predis'porre /77/ vt to get ready, prepare; **~ qn a qc** to predispose sb to sth

predizi'one [predit'tsjone] sf prediction

prefazi'one [prefat'tsjone] sf preface, foreword

prefe'renza [prefe'rɛntsa] sf preference

prefe'rire /55/ vt to prefer, like better; **~ il caffè al tè** to prefer coffee to tea, like coffee better than tea

pre'figgersi [pre'fiddʒersi] /79/ vpr: **~ uno scopo** to set o.s. a goal

pre'fisso, -a pp di **prefiggersi** ▷ sm (Ling) prefix; (Tel) dialling (BRIT) o dial (US) code

pre'gare /80/ vi to pray ▷ vt (Rel) to pray to; (implorare) to beg; (chiedere): **~ qn di fare** to ask sb to do; **farsi ~** to need coaxing o persuading

pre'gevole [pre'dʒevole] ag valuable

pregherò ecc [prege'rɔ] vb vedi **pregare**

preghi'era [pre'gjɛra] sf (Rel) prayer; (domanda) request

pregi'ato, -a [pre'dʒato] ag (opera) valuable; **vino ~** vintage wine

'pregio ['predʒo] sm (stima) esteem, regard; (qualità) (good) quality, merit; (valore) value, worth

pregiudi'care [predʒudi'kare] /20/ vt to prejudice, harm, be detrimental to

pregiu'dizio [predʒu'dittsjo] sm (idea errata) prejudice; (danno) harm no pl

'prego escl (a chi ringrazia) don't mention it!; (invitando qn ad accomodarsi) please sit down!; (invitando qn ad andare prima) after you!

pregus'tare /72/ vt to look forward to

prele'vare /72/ vt (denaro) to withdraw; (campione) to take; (polizia) to take, capture

preli'evo sm (Banca) withdrawal; (Med) **fare un ~ (di)** to take a sample (of); **fare un ~ di sangue** to take a blood sample

prelimi'nare ag preliminary

'premere /29/ vt to press ▷ vi: **~ su** to press down on; (fig) to put pressure on; **~ a** (fig) (importare) to matter to

pre'mettere /63/ vt to put before; (dire prima) to start by saying, state first

premi'are /19/ vt to give a prize to; (fig: merito, onestà) to reward

premiazi'one [premjat'tsjone] sf prize giving

'premio sm prize; (ricompensa) reward; (Comm) premium; (Amm: indennità) bonus

pre'misi ecc vb vedi **premettere**

premu'nirsi /55/ vpr: **~ di** to provide o.s. with; **~ contro** to protect o.s. from, guard o.s. against

pre'mura sf (fretta) haste, hurry; (riguardo) attention, care; **premure** sfpl (attenzioni, cure) care sg: **aver ~** to be in a hurry; **far ~ a qn** to hurry sb; **usare ogni ~ nei riguardi di qn** to be very attentive to sb; **premu'roso, -a** ag thoughtful, considerate

'prendere /81/ vt to take; (andare a prendere) to get, fetch; (ottenere) to get; (guadagnare) to get, earn; (catturare: ladro, pesce) to catch; (collaboratore, dipendente) to take on; (passeggero) to pick up; (chiedere: somma, prezzo) to charge, ask; (trattare: persona) to handle ▷ vi (colla, cemento) to take; (pianta) to take; (fuoco: nel camino) to catch; (voltare): **~ a destra** to turn (to the) right; **prendersi** vpr (azzuffarsi): **prendersi a pugni** to come to blows; **prende qualcosa?** (da bere, da mangiare) would you like something to eat (o drink)?; **prendo un caffè** I'll have a coffee; **~ qn/qc per** (scambiare) to take sb/sth for; **~ fuoco** to catch fire; **~ parte a** to take part in;

prendersi cura di qn/qc to look after sb/sth; **prendersela** (adirarsi) to get annoyed; (preoccuparsi) to get upset, worry

preno'tare /72/ vt to book, reserve; **prenotazi'one** [prenotat'tsjone] sf booking, reservation

preoccu'pare /72/ vt to worry; to preoccupy; **preoccuparsi** vpr: **preoccuparsi di qn/qc** to worry about sb/sth; **preoccuparsi per qn** to be anxious for sb; **preoccupazi'one** sf worry, anxiety

prepa'rare /72/ vt to prepare; (esame, concorso) to prepare for; **prepararsi** vpr (vestirsi) to get ready; **prepararsi a qc/a fare** to get ready o prepare (o.s.) for sth/to do; **~ da mangiare** to prepare a meal; **prepa'tivi** smpl preparations

preposizi'one [prepozit'tsjone] sf (Ling) preposition

prepo'tente ag (persona) domineering, arrogant; (bisogno, desiderio) overwhelming, pressing ▷ smf bully

'presa sf taking no pl; catching no pl; (di città) capture; (indurimento: di cemento) setting; (appiglio, Sport) hold; (di acqua, gas) (supply) point; (piccola quantità: di sale ecc) pinch; (Carte) trick; **~ (di corrente)** socket; (al muro) point; **far ~** (colla) to set; **ha fatto ~ sul pubblico** (fig) it caught the public's imagination; **essere alle prese con qc** (fig) to be struggling with sth; **~ d'aria** air inlet

pre'sagio [pre'zadʒo] sm omen

'presbite ag long-sighted

pres'crivere /105/ vt to prescribe

'prese ecc vb vedi **prendere**

presen'tare /72/ vt to present; (Amm: inoltrare) to submit; (far conoscere): **~ qn (a)** to introduce sb (to); **presentarsi** vpr (recarsi, farsi vedere) to present o.s., appear; (farsi conoscere) to introduce o.s.; (occasione) to arise; **presentarsi**

come **candidato** (*Pol*) to stand (*BRIT*) *o* run (*US*) as a candidate; **presentarsi bene/male** to have a good/poor appearance

pre'sente *ag* present; (*questo*) this ▷ *sm* present; **i presenti** those present; **aver ~ qc/qn** to remember sth/sb; **tener ~ qn/qc** to keep sb/ sth in mind

presenti'mento *sm* premonition

pre'senza [pre'zɛntsa] *sf* presence; (*aspetto esteriore*) appearance; **~ di spirito** presence of mind

pre'sepe, pre'sepio *sm* crib

preser'vare /72/ *vt* to protect; to save; **preserva'tivo** *sm* sheath, condom

'presi *ecc vb vedi* **prendere**

'preside *smf* (*Ins*) head (teacher) (*BRIT*), principal (*US*); (*di facoltà universitaria*) dean; **~ di facoltà** (*Università*) dean of faculty

presi'dente *sm* (*Pol*) president; (*di assemblea, Comm*) chairman; **P~ del Consiglio (dei Ministri)** ≈ Prime Minister

presi'edere /29/ *vt* to preside over ▷ *vi*: **~ a** to direct, be in charge of

pressap'poco *av* about, roughly

pres'sare /72/ *vt* to press

pressi'one *sf* pressure; **far ~ su qn** to put pressure on sb; **~ sanguigna** blood pressure; **~ atmosferica** atmospheric pressure

'presso *av* (*vicino*) nearby, close at hand ▷ *prep* (*vicino a*) near; (*accanto a*) beside, next to; (*in casa di*): **~ qn** at sb's home; (*nelle lettere*) care of, c/o; (*alle dipendenza di*): **lavora ~ di noi** he works for *o* with us ▷ *smpl*: **nei pressi di** near, in the vicinity of

pres'tante *ag* good-looking

pres'tare /72/ *vt*: **~ (qc a qn)** to lend (sb sth *o* sth to sb); **prestarsi** *vpr* (*offrirsi*): **prestarsi a fare** to offer to do; (*essere adatto*): **prestarsi a** to lend itself to, be suitable for; **~ aiuto** to

lend a hand; **~ ascolto** *o* **orecchio** to listen; **~ attenzione** to pay attention; **~ fede a qc/qn** to give credence to sth/sb; **prestazi'one** *sf* (*Tecn, Sport*) performance

prestigia'tore, -'trice [prestidʒa'tore] *sm/f* conjurer

pres'tigio [pres'tidʒo] *sm* (*potere*) prestige; (*illusione*): **gioco di ~** conjuring trick

'prestito *sm* lending *no pl*; loan; **dar in ~** to lend; **prendere in ~** to borrow

'presto *av* (*tra poco*) soon; (*in fretta*) quickly; (*di buon'ora*) early; **a ~** see you soon; **fare ~ a fare qc** to hurry up and do sth; (*non costare fatica*) to have no trouble doing sth; **si fa ~ a criticare** it's easy to criticize

pre'sumere /12/ *vt* to presume, assume

pre'sunsi *ecc vb vedi* **presumere**

presuntu'oso, -a *ag* presumptuous

presunzi'one [prezun'tsjone] *sf* presumption

'prete *sm* priest

preten'dente *smf* pretender ▷ *sm* (*corteggiatore*) suitor

pre'tendere /120/ *vt* (*esigere*) to demand, require; (*sostenere*): **~ che** to claim that; **pretende di aver sempre ragione** he thinks he's always right

> Attenzione! In inglese esiste il verbo *to pretend*, che però significa *far finta*.

pre'teso, -a *pp di* **pretendere** ▷ *sf* (*esigenza*) claim, demand; (*presunzione, sfarzo*) pretentiousness; **senza pretese** unpretentious

pre'testo *sm* pretext, excuse

preva'lere /126/ *vi* to prevail

preve'dere /82/ *vt* (*indovinare*) to foresee; (*presagire*) to foretell; (*considerare*) to make provision for

preve'nire /128/ *vt* (*anticipare*) to forestall; (: *domanda*) to anticipate; (*evitare*) to avoid, prevent

preven'tivo, -a *ag* preventive ▷ *sm* (Comm) estimate

prevenzi'one [preven'tsjone] *sf* prevention; (*preconcetto*) prejudice

previ'dente *ag* showing foresight; prudent; **previ'denza** *sf* foresight; **istituto di previdenza** provident institution; **previdenza sociale** social security (BRIT), welfare (US)

pre'vidi *ecc vb vedi* **prevedere**

previsi'one *sf* forecast, prediction; **previsioni meteorologiche** *o* **del tempo** weather forecast *sg*

pre'visto, -a *pp di* **prevedere** ▷ *sm*: **piú/meno del ~** more/less than expected

prezi'oso, -a [pret'tsjoso] *ag* precious; (*aiuto, consiglio*) invaluable ▷ *sm* jewel; valuable

prez'zemolo [pret'tsemolo] *sm* parsley

'prezzo ['prɛttso] *sm* price; **~ d'acquisto/di vendita** purchase/ selling price

prigi'one [pri'dʒone] *sf* prison; **prigioni'ero, -a** *ag* captive ▷ *sm/f* prisoner

'prima *sf vedi* **primo** ▷ *av* before; (*in anticipo*) in advance, beforehand; (*per l'addietro*) at one time, formerly; (*più presto*) sooner, earlier; (*in primo luogo*) first ▷ *cong*: **~ di fare/che parta** before doing/he leaves; **~ di** before; **~ o poi** sooner or later

pri'mario, -a *ag* primary; (*principale*) chief, leading, primary ▷ *sm/f* (*medico*) chief physician

prima'tista, -i, -e *smf* (Sport) record holder

pri'mato *sm* supremacy; (Sport) record

prima'vera *sf* spring

primi'tivo, -a *ag* primitive; (*significato*) original

pri'mizie [pri'mittsje] *sfpl* early produce *sg*

'primo, -a *ag* first; (*fig*) initial; basic; prime ▷ *sm/f* first (one) ▷ *sm* (Cuc)

first course; (*in date*): **il ~ luglio** the first of July ▷ *sf* (Teat) first night; (Cine) première; (Aut) first (gear); **le prime ore del mattino** the early hours of the morning; **ai primi di maggio** at the beginning of May; **viaggiare in prima** to travel first-class; **in ~ luogo** first of all, in the first place; **di prim'ordine** *o* **prima qualità** first-class, first-rate; **in un ~ tempo** *o* **momento** at first; **prima donna** leading lady; (*di opera lirica*) prima donna

primordi'ale *ag* primordial

'primula *sf* primrose

princi'pale [printʃi'pale] *ag* main, principal ▷ *sm* manager, boss

principal'mente [printʃipal'mente] *av* mainly, principally

'principe ['printʃipe] *sm* prince; **~ ereditario** crown prince; **princi'pessa** *sf* princess

principi'ante [printʃi'pjante] *smf* beginner

prin'cipio [prin'tʃipjo] *sm* (*inizio*) beginning, start; (*origine*) origin, cause; (*concetto, norma*) principle; **principi** *smpl* (*concetti fondamentali*) principles; **al** *o* **in ~** at first; **per ~** on principle; **una questione di ~** a matter of principle

priorità *sf* priority

priori'tario, -a *ag* of utmost importance; (*interesse*) overriding

pri'vare /72/ *vt*: **~ qn di** to deprive sb of; **privarsi** *vpr*: **privarsi di** to go *o* do without

pri'vato, -a *ag* private ▷ *sm/f* private citizen; **in ~** in private

privilegi'are [privile'dʒare] /62/ *vt* to grant a privilege to

privilegi'ato, -a [privile'dʒato] *ag* (*individuo, classe*) privileged; (*trattamento, Comm: credito*) preferential; **azioni privilegiate** preference shares (BRIT), preferred stock (US)

P

privi'legio [privi'lɛdʒo] *sm* privilege
'privo, -a *ag*: **~ di** without, lacking
pro *prep* for, on behalf of ▷ *sm inv* (*utilità*) advantage, benefit; **a che ~?** what's the use?; **il ~ e il contro** the pros and cons
pro'babile *ag* probable, likely; **probabilità** *sf inv* probability
probabil'mente *av* probably
pro'blema, -i *sm* problem
pro'boscide [pro'bɔʃʃide] *sf* (*di elefante*) trunk
pro'cedere [pro'tʃɛdere] /29/ *vi* to proceed; (*comportarsi*) to behave; (*iniziare*): **~ a** to start; **~ contro** (*Dir*) to start legal proceedings against; **proce'dura** *sf* (*Dir*) procedure
proces'sare [protʃes'sare] /72/ *vt* (*Dir*) to try
processi'one [protʃes'sjone] *sf* procession
pro'cesso [pro'tʃɛsso] *sm* (*Dir*) trial; proceedings *pl*; (*metodo*) process
pro'cinto [pro'tʃinto] *sm*: **in ~ di fare** about to do, on the point of doing
procla'mare /72/ *vt* to proclaim
procre'are /72/ *vt* to procreate
procu'rare /72/ *vt*: **~ qc a qn** (*fornire*) to get *o* obtain sth for sb; (*causare*: *noie ecc*) to bring *o* give sb sth
pro'digio [pro'didʒo] *sm* marvel, wonder; (*persona*) prodigy
pro'dotto, -a *pp di* **produrre** ▷ *sm* product; **prodotti agricoli** farm produce *sg*
pro'duco *ecc vb vedi* **produrre**
pro'durre /90/ *vt* to produce
pro'dussi *ecc vb vedi* **produrre**
produzi'one *sf* production; (*rendimento*) output
Prof. *abbr* (= *professore*) Prof
profa'nare /72/ *vt* to desecrate
profes'sare /72/ *vt* to profess; (*medicina ecc*) to practise
professio'nale *ag* professional
professi'one *sf* profession; **professio'nista, -i, -e** *smf* professional

profes'sore, -'essa *sm/f* (*Ins*) teacher; (*: di università*) lecturer; (*: titolare di cattedra*) professor
pro'filo *sm* profile; (*breve descrizione*) sketch, outline; **di ~** in profile
pro'fitto *sm* advantage, profit, benefit; (*fig: progresso*) progress; (*Comm*) profit
profondità *sf inv* depth
pro'fondo, -a *ag* deep; (*rancore, meditazione*) profound ▷ *sm* depth(s), bottom; **~ 8 metri** 8 metres deep
'profugo, -a, -ghi, -ghe *sm/f* refugee
profu'mare /72/ *vt* to perfume ▷ *vi* to be fragrant; **profumarsi** *vpr* to put on perfume *o* scent
profu'mato, -a *ag* (*fiore, aria*) fragrant; (*fazzoletto, saponetta*) scented; (*pelle*) sweet-smelling; (*persona*) with perfume on
profume'ria *sf* perfumery; (*negozio*) perfume shop
pro'fumo *sm* (*prodotto*) perfume, scent; (*fragranza*) scent, fragrance
proget'tare [prodʒet'tare] /72/ *vt* to plan; (*edificio*) to plan, design; **pro'getto** *sm* plan; (*idea*) plan, project; **progetto di legge** bill
pro'gramma, -i *sm* programme; (*TV, Radio*) programmes *pl*; (*Ins*) syllabus, curriculum; (*Inform*) program; **program'mare** /72/ *vt* (*TV, Radio*) to put on; (*Inform*) to program; (*Econ*) to plan; **programma'tore, -'trice** *sm/f* (*Inform*) computer programmer (*BRIT*) *o* programer (*US*)
progre'dire /55/ *vi* to progress, make progress
pro'gresso *sm* progress *no pl*; **fare progressi** to make progress
proi'bire /55/ *vt* to forbid, prohibit
proiet'tare /72/ *vt* (*gen, Geom, Cine*) to project; (*: presentare*) to show, screen; (*luce, ombra*) to throw, cast, project; **proi'ettile** *sm* projectile, bullet, shell *etc*; **proiet'tore** *sm* (*Cine*) projector; (*Aut*) headlamp; (*Mil*)

searchlight; **proiezi'one** *sf* (*Cine*) projection; showing

prolife'rare /72/ *vi* (*fig*) to proliferate

pro'lunga, -ghe *sf* (*di cavo elettrico ecc*) extension

prolun'gare /80/ *vt* (*discorso, attesa*) to prolong; (*linea, termine*) to extend

prome'moria *sm inv* memorandum

pro'messa *sf* promise

pro'mettere /63/ *vt* to promise ▷ *vi* to be *o* look promising; **~ a qn di fare** to promise sb that one will do

promi'nente *ag* prominent

pro'misi *ecc vb vedi* **promettere**

promon'torio *sm* promontory, headland

promozi'one [promot'tsjone] *sf* promotion

promu'overe /66/ *vt* to promote

proni'pote *smf* (*di nonni*) great-grandchild, great-grandson/granddaughter; (*di zii*) great-nephew/niece

pro'nome *sm* (*Ling*) pronoun

pron'tezza [pron'tettsa] *sf* readiness; quickness; promptness

'pronto, -a *ag* ready; (*rapido*) fast, quick, prompt; **~!** (*Tel*) hello!; **~ all'ira** quick-tempered; **~ soccorso** (*trattamento*) first aid; (*reparto*) A&E (*BRIT*), ER (*US*)

prontu'ario *sm* manual, handbook

pro'nuncia [pro'nuntʃa] *sf* pronunciation

pronunci'are [pronun'tʃare] /14/ *vt* (*parola, sentenza*) to pronounce; (*dire*) to utter; (*discorso*) to deliver

propa'ganda *sf* propaganda

pro'pendere /8/ *vi*: **~ per** to favour, lean towards

propi'nare /72/ *vt* to administer

pro'porre /77/ *vt* (*suggerire*): **~ qc (a qn)** to suggest sth (to sb); (*candidato*) to put forward; (*legge, brindisi*) to propose; **~ di fare** to suggest *o* propose doing; **proporsi di fare** to propose *o* intend to do; **proporsi una meta** to set o.s. a goal

proporzio'nale [proportsjo'nale] *ag* proportional

proporzi'one [propor'tsjone] *sf* proportion; **in ~ a** in proportion to; **proporzioni** *sfpl* (*dimensioni*) proportions; **di vaste proporzioni** huge

pro'posito *sm* (*intenzione*) intention, aim; (*argomento*) subject, matter; **a ~ di** regarding, with regard to; **di ~** (*apposta*) deliberately, on purpose; **a ~** by the way; **capitare a ~** (*cosa, persona*) to turn up at the right time

proposizi'one [propozit'tsjone] *sf* (*Ling*) clause; (: *periodo*) sentence

pro'posto, -a *pp di* **proporre** ▷ *sf* proposal; (*suggerimento*) suggestion; **proposta di legge** bill

proprietà *sf inv* (*ciò che si possiede*) property, estate; (*caratteristica*) property; (*correttezza*) correctness; **~ privata** private property; **proprie'tario, -a** *sm/f* owner; (*di albergo ecc*) proprietor, owner; (*per l'inquilino*) landlord/lady

'proprio, -a *ag* (*possessivo*) own; (: *impersonale*) one's; (*esatto*) exact, correct, proper; (*senso, significato*) literal; (*Ling: nome*) proper; (*particolare*) **~ di** characteristic of, peculiar to ▷ *av* (*precisamente*) just, exactly; (*davvero*) really; (*affatto*): **non ... ~** not ... at all; **l'ha visto con i (suoi) propri occhi** he saw it with his own eyes

proro'gare /80/ *vt* to extend; (*differire*) to postpone, defer

'prosa *sf* prose

pro'sciogliere [proʃ'ʃɔʎʎere] /103/ *vt* to release; (*Dir*) to acquit

prosciu'gare [proʃʃu'gare] /80/ *vt* (*terreni*) to drain, reclaim; **prosciugarsi** *vpr* to dry up

prosci'utto [proʃ'ʃutto] *sm* ham; **~ cotto/crudo** cooked/cured ham

prosegui'mento *sm* continuation; **buon ~!** all the best!; (*a chi viaggia*) enjoy the rest of your journey!

prosegu'ire /45/ *vt* to carry on with, continue ▷ *vi* to carry on, go on
prospe'rare /72/ *vi* to thrive
prospet'tare /72/ *vt* (*esporre*) to point out, show; **prospettarsi** *vpr* to look, appear
prospet'tiva *sf* (*Arte*) perspective; (*veduta*) view; (*fig: previsione, possibilità*) prospect
pros'petto *sm* (*Disegno*) elevation; (*veduta*) view, prospect; (*facciata*) façade, front; (*tabella*) table; (*sommario*) summary
prossimità *sf* nearness, proximity; **in ~ di** near (to), close to
'prossimo, -a *ag* (*che viene subito dopo*) next; (*parente*) close; (*vicino*): **~ a** near (to), close to ▷ *sm* neighbour, fellow man
prostitu'irsi /55/ *vpr* to prostitute o.s.
prosti'tuta *sf* prostitute
protago'nista, -i, -e *smf* protagonist
pro'teggere [pro'tɛddʒere] /83/ *vt* to protect
prote'ina *sf* protein
pro'tendere /120/ *vt* to stretch out
pro'testa *sf* protest
protes'tante *ag, smf* Protestant
protes'tare /72/ *vt, vi* to protest
pro'tetto, -a *pp di* **proteggere**
protezi'one [protet'tsjone] *sf* protection; (*patrocinio*) patronage
pro'totipo *sm* prototype
pro'trarre /123/ *vt* (*prolungare*) to prolong; **protrarsi** *vpr* to go on, continue
protube'ranza [protube'rantsa] *sf* protuberance, bulge
'prova *sf* (*esperimento, cimento*) test, trial; (*tentativo*) attempt, try; (*Mat*) proof *no pl*; (*Dir*) evidence *no pl*, proof *no pl*; (*Ins*) exam, test; (*Teat*) rehearsal; (*di abito*) fitting; **a ~ di** (*in testimonianza di*) as proof of; **a ~ di fuoco** fireproof; **mettere alla ~** to put to the test; **giro di ~** test *o* trial

run; **fino a ~ contraria** until (it's) proved otherwise; **~ generale** (*Teat*) dress rehearsal
pro'vare /72/ *vt* (*sperimentare*) to test; (*tentare*) to try, attempt; (*assaggiare*) to try, taste; (*sperimentare in sé*) to experience; (*sentire*) to feel; (*cimentare*) to put to the test; (*dimostrare*) to prove; (*abito*) to try on; **~ a fare** to try *o* attempt to do
proveni'enza [prove'njɛntsa] *sf* origin, source
prove'nire /128/ *vi*: **~ da** to come from
pro'venti *smpl* revenue *sg*
pro'verbio *sm* proverb
pro'vetta *sf* test tube; **bambino in ~** test-tube baby
pro'vider [pro'vaider] *sm inv* (*Inform*) service provider
pro'vincia [pro'vintʃa], **-ce** *o* **-cie** *sf* province
pro'vino *sm* (*Cine*) screen test; (*campione*) specimen
provo'cante *ag* (*attraente*) provocative
provo'care /20/ *vt* (*causare*) to cause, bring about; (*eccitare: riso, pietà*) to arouse; (*irritare, sfidare*) to provoke; **provocazi'one** *sf* provocation
provve'dere /82/ *vi* (*prendere un provvedimento*) to take steps, act; (*disporre*): **~ (a)** to provide (for); **provvedi'mento** *sm* measure; (*di previdenza*) precaution
provvi'denza [provvi'dɛntsa] *sf*: **la ~** providence
provvigi'one [provvi'dʒone] *sf* (*Comm*) commission
provvi'sorio, -a *ag* temporary
prov'vista *sf* supply
'prua *sf* (*Naut*) bow(s), prow
pru'dente *ag* cautious, prudent; (*assennato*) sensible, wise; **pru'denza** *sf* prudence, caution; wisdom
'prudere /29/ *vi* to itch, be itchy
'prugna ['pruɲɲa] *sf* plum; **~ secca** prune

pru'rito sm itchiness no pl; itch

P.S. abbr (= postscriptum) PS ▷ sigla f (Polizia) = **Pubblica Sicurezza**

pseu'donimo sm pseudonym

psica'nalisi sf psychoanalysis

psicana'lista, -i, -e smf psychoanalyst

'psiche ['psike] sf (Psic) psyche

psichi'atra, -i, -e [psi'kjatra] smf psychiatrist; **psichi'atrico, -a, -ci, -che** ag psychiatric

psicolo'gia [psikolo'dʒia] sf psychology; **psico'logico, -a, -ci, -che** ag psychological; **psi'cologo, -a, -gi, -ghe** sm/f psychologist

psico'patico, -a, -ci, -che ag psychopathic ▷ sm/f psychopath

pubbli'care /20/ vt to publish

pubblicazi'one [pubblikat'tsjone] sf publication

pubblici'tà [pubblitʃi'ta] sf (diffusione) publicity; (attività) advertising; (annunci nei giornali) advertisements pl

'pubblico, -a, -ci, -che ag public; (statale, scuola ecc) state cpd ▷ sm public; (spettatori) audience; **in ~** in public; **~ funzionario** civil servant; **P~ Ministero** Public Prosecutor's Office; **la Pubblica Sicurezza** the police

pube sm (Anat) pubis

puber'tà sf puberty

pu'dico, -a, -ci, -che ag modest

pu'dore sm modesty

pue'rile ag childish

pugi'lato [pudʒi'lato] sm boxing

pugile ['pudʒile] sm boxer

pugna'lare [puɲɲa'lare] /72/ vt to stab

pu'gnale [puɲ'ɲale] sm dagger

pugno ['puɲɲo] sm fist; (colpo) punch; (quantità) fistful

pulce ['pultʃe] sf flea

pul'cino [pul'tʃino] sm chick

pu'lire /55/ vt to clean; (lucidare) to polish; **pu'lito, -a** ag (anche fig) clean; (ordinato) neat, tidy; **puli'tura**

sf cleaning; **pulitura a secco** dry-cleaning; **puli'zia** sf cleaning; (condizione) cleanness; **fare le pulizie** to do the cleaning, do the housework; **pulizia etnica** ethnic cleansing

'pullman sm inv coach

pul'lover sm inv pullover, jumper

pullu'lare /72/ vi to swarm, teem

pul'mino sm minibus

'pulpito sm pulpit

pul'sante sm (push-)button

pul'sare /72/ vi to pulsate, beat

pul'viscolo sm fine dust; **~ atmosferico** specks pl of dust

'puma sm inv puma

pun'gente [pun'dʒɛnte] ag prickly; stinging; (anche fig) biting

'pungere ['pundʒere] /84/ vt to prick; (insetto, ortica) to sting; (freddo) to bite

pungigli'one [pundʒiʎ'ʎone] sm sting

pu'nire /55/ vt to punish; **punizi'one** sf punishment; (Sport) penalty

'punsi ecc vb vedi **pungere**

'punta sf point; (parte terminale) tip, end; (di monte) peak; (di costa) promontory; (minima parte) touch, trace; **in ~ di piedi** on tiptoe; **ore di ~** peak hours; **uomo di ~** front-rank o leading man

pun'tare /72/ vt (piedi a terra, gomiti sul tavolo) to plant; (dirigere: pistola) to point; (scommettere): **~ su** to bet on ▷ vi (mirare): **~ a** to aim at; (avviarsi): **~ su** to head o make for; (fig: contare): **~ su** to count o rely on

pun'tata sf (gita) short trip; (scommessa) bet; (parte di opera) instalment; **romanzo a puntate** serial

puntegg'iatura [puntedd ʒa'tura] sf (Ling) punctuation

pun'teggio [pun'tedd ʒo] sm score

puntel'lare /72/ vt to support

pun'tello sm prop, support

pun'tina sf: ~ **da disegno** drawing pin

pun'tino sm dot; **fare qc a** ~ to do sth properly

'**punto, -a** pp di **pungere** ▷ sm point; (segno, macchiolina) dot; (Ling) full stop; (di indirizzo e-mail) dot; (posto) spot; (a scuola) mark; (nel cucire, nella maglia, Med) stitch ▷ av: **non ... ~** not ... at all; ~ **cardinale** point of the compass, cardinal point; ~ **debole** weak point; ~ **esclamativo/interrogativo** exclamation/question mark; ~ **nero** (comedone) blackhead; ~ **di partenza** (anche fig) starting point; ~ **di riferimento** landmark; (fig) point of reference; ~ **di vendita** retail outlet; ~ **e virgola** semicolon; ~ **di vista** (fig) point of view

puntu'ale ag punctual

pun'tura sf (di ago) prick; (di insetto) sting, bite; (Med) puncture; (: iniezione) injection; (dolore) sharp pain

> Attenzione! In inglese esiste la parola puncture, che si usa per indicare la foratura di una gomma.

punzecchi'are [puntsek'kjare] /19/ vt to prick; (fig) to tease

può vb vedi **potere**

pu'pazzo [pu'pattso] sm puppet

pu'pillo, -a sm/f (Dir) ward ▷ sf (Anat) pupil

purché [pur'ke] cong provided that, on condition that

'**pure** cong (tuttavia) and yet, nevertheless; (anche se) even if ▷ av (anche) too, also; **pur di** (al fine di) just to; **faccia ~!** go ahead!, please do!

purè sm, **pu'rea** sf (Cuc) purée; (di patate) mashed potatoes pl

pu'rezza [pu'rettsa] sf purity

pur'gante sm (Med) purgative, purge

purga'torio sm purgatory

purifi'care /20/ vt to purify; (metallo) to refine

'**puro, -a** ag pure; (acqua) clear, limpid; (vino) undiluted; **puro'sangue** sm inv, f inv thoroughbred

pur'troppo av unfortunately

pus sm pus

'**pustola** sf pimple

puti'ferio sm rumpus, row

put'tana sf (fam!) whore (!)

puz'zare [put'tsare] /72/ vi to stink

'**puzzo** ['puttso] sm stink, foul smell

'**puzzola** ['puttsola] sf polecat

puzzo'lente [puttso'lɛnte] ag stinking

P.V.C. [pivi'tʃi] sigla m (= polyvinyl chloride) PVC

q *abbr* (= *quintale*) q

qua *av* here; **in ~** (*verso questa parte*) this way; **da un anno in ~** for a year now; **da quando in ~?** since when?; **per di ~** (*passare*) this way; **al di ~ di** (*fiume, strada*) on this side of; **~ dentro/fuori** *ecc* in/out here *ecc*; *vedi anche* **questo**

qua'derno *sm* notebook; (*per scuola*) exercise book

qua'drante *sm* quadrant; (*di orologio*) face

qua'drare /72/ *vi* (*bilancio*) to balance, tally; **~ (con)** to correspond (with) ▷ *vt* (*Mat*) to square; **non mi quadra** I don't like it; **qua'drato, -a** *ag* square; (*fig: equilibrato*) level-headed, sensible; (: *peg*) square ▷ *sm* (*Mat*) square; (*Pugilato*) ring; **5 al quadrato** 5 squared

quadri'foglio [kwadri'fɔʎʎo] *sm* four-leaf clover

quadri'mestre *sm* (*periodo*) four-month period; (*Ins*) term

'quadro *sm* (*pittura*) painting, picture; (*quadrato*) square; (*tabella*) table, chart; (*Tecn*) board, panel; (*Teat*) scene; (*fig: scena, spettacolo*) sight; (: *descrizione*) outline, description; **quadri** *smpl* (*Pol*) party organizers; (*Comm*) managerial staff; (*Mil*) cadres; (*Carte*) diamonds

'quadruplo, -a *ag, sm* quadruple

quaggiù [kwad'dʒu] *av* down here

'quaglia ['kwaʎʎa] *sf* quail

PAROLA CHIAVE

'qualche ['kwalke] *det* **1** some, a few; (*in interrogative*) any; **ho comprato qualche libro** I've bought some *o* a few books; **qualche volta** sometimes; **hai qualche sigaretta?** have you any cigarettes?
2 (*uno*): **c'è qualche medico?** is there a doctor?; **in qualche modo** somehow
3 (*un certo, parecchio*) some; **un personaggio di qualche rilievo** a figure of some importance
4: **qualche cosa** = **qualcosa**

qual'cosa *pron* something; (*in espressioni interrogative*) anything; **qualcos'altro** something else; anything else; **~ di nuovo** something new; anything new; **~ da mangiare** something to eat; anything to eat; **c'è ~ che non va?** is there something *o* anything wrong?

qual'cuno *pron* (*persona*) someone, somebody; (: *in espressioni interrogative*) anyone, anybody; (*alcuni*) some; **~ è favorevole a noi** some are on our side; **qualcun altro** someone *o* somebody else; anyone *o* anybody else

PAROLA CHIAVE

'quale (*spesso troncato in* **qual**) *det* **1** (*interrogativo*) what; (: *scegliendo tra*

due o più cose o persone) which; **quale uomo/denaro?** what man/money?; which man/money?; **quali sono i tuoi programmi?** what are your plans?; **quale stanza preferisci?** which room do you prefer?
2 *(relativo, come)*: **il risultato fu quale ci si aspettava** the result was as expected
3 *(in elenchi)* such as, like; **piante quali l'edera** plants such as *o* like ivy
4 *(esclamativo)* what; **quale disgrazia!** what bad luck!
▶ *pron* **1** *(interrogativo)* which; **quale dei due scegli?** which of the two do you want?
2 *(relativo)*: **il (la) quale** *(persona) (soggetto)* who; *(oggetto, con preposizione)* whom; *(cosa)* which; *(possessivo)* whose; **suo padre, il quale è avvocato, ...** his father, who is a lawyer, ...; **il signore con il quale parlavo** the gentleman to whom I was speaking; **l'albergo al quale ci siamo fermati** the hotel where we stayed *o* which we stayed at; **la signora della quale ammiriamo la bellezza** the lady whose beauty we admire
▶ *av* as; **quale sindaco di questa città** as mayor of this town

qua'lifica, -che *sf* qualification; *(titolo)* title
qualifi'cato, -a *ag (dotato di qualifica)* qualified; *(esperto, abile)* skilled; **non mi ritengo ~ per questo lavoro** I don't think I'm qualified for this job; **è un medico molto ~** he is a very distinguished doctor
qualificazi'one *sf*: **gara di ~** *(Sport)* qualifying event
qualità *sf inv* quality; **in ~ di** in one's capacity as
qua'lora *cong* in case, if
qual'siasi, qua'lunque *det (inv)* any; *(quale che sia)* whatever; *(discriminativo)* whichever; *(posposto,*

mediocre) poor, indifferent; ordinary; **mettiti un vestito ~** put on any old dress; **~ cosa** anything; **~ cosa accada** whatever happens; **a ~ costo** at any cost, whatever the cost; **l'uomo ~** the man in the street; **~ persona** anyone, anybody

'**quando** *cong, av* when; **~ sarò ricco** when I'm rich; **da ~** *(dacché)* since; *(interrogativo)*: **da ~ sei qui?** how long have you been here?; **quand'anche** even if
quantità *sf inv* quantity; **una ~ di** *(gran numero)* a great deal of; a lot of; **in grande ~** in large quantities

PAROLA CHIAVE

'**quanto, -a** *det* **1** *(interrogativo: quantità)* how much; *(: numero)* how many; **quanto pane/denaro?** how much bread/money?; **quanti libri/ragazzi?** how many books/boys?; **quanto tempo?** how long?; **quanti anni hai?** how old are you?
2 *(esclamativo)*: **quante storie!** what a lot of nonsense!; **quanto tempo sprecato!** what a waste of time!
3 *(relativo: quantità)* as much ... as; *(: numero)* as many ... as; **ho quanto denaro mi occorre** I have as much money as I need; **prendi quanti libri vuoi** take as many books as you like
▶ *pron* **1** *(interrogativo: quantità)* how much; *(: numero)* how many; *(: tempo)* how long; **quanto mi dai?** how much will you give me?; **quanti me ne hai portati?** how many did you bring me?; **da quanto sei qui?** how long have you been here?; **quanti ne abbiamo oggi?** what's the date today?
2 *(relativo: quantità)* as much as; *(: numero)* as many as; **farò quanto posso** I'll do as much as I can; **possono venire quanti sono stati invitati** all those who have been invited can come

▶ *av* **1** (*interrogativo: con ag, av*) how; (: *con vb*) how much; **quanto stanco ti sembrava?** how tired did he seem to you?; **quanto corre la tua moto?** how fast can your motorbike go?; **quanto costa?** how much does it cost?; **quant'è?** how much is it?
2 (*esclamativo: con ag, av*) how; (: *con vb*) how much; **quanto sono felice!** how happy I am!; **sapessi quanto abbiamo camminato!** if you knew how far we've walked!; **studierò quanto posso** I'll study as much as o all I can; **quanto prima** as soon as possible
3: in quanto (*in qualità di*) as; (*perché, per il fatto che*) as, since; **(in) quanto a** (*per ciò che riguarda*) as for, as regards
4: per quanto (*nonostante, anche se*) however; **per quanto si sforzi, non ce la farà** try as he may, he won't manage it; **per quanto sia brava, fa degli errori** however good she may be, she makes mistakes

qua'ranta *num* forty
quaran'tena *sf* quarantine
quaran'tesimo, -a *num* fortieth
quaran'tina *sf*: **una ~ (di)** about forty
quarta *sf vedi* **quarto**
quar'tetto *sm* quartet(te)
quarti'ere *sm* district, area; (*Mil*) quarters *pl*: **~ generale** headquarters *pl*
quarto, -a *ag* fourth ▷ *sm* fourth; (*quarta parte*) quarter ▷ *sf* (*Aut*) fourth (gear); **le 6 e un ~** a quarter past (*BRIT*) o after (*US*) 6; **~ d'ora** quarter of an hour; **quarti di finale** quarter finals
quarzo ['kwartso] *sm* quartz
quasi *av* almost, nearly ▷ *cong* (*anche:* **~ che**) as if; **(non) ... ~ mai** hardly ever; **~ ~ me ne andrei** I've half a mind to leave
quassù *av* up here

quat'tordici [kwat'torditʃi] *num* fourteen
quat'trini *smpl* money *sg*, cash *sg*
'quattro *num* four; **in ~ e quattr'otto** in less than no time; **quattro'cento** *num* four hundred ▷ *sm*: **il Quattrocento** the fifteenth century

PAROLA CHIAVE

'quello, -a (*dav sm* **quel** + C, **quell'** + V, **quello** + *s impura, gn, pn, ps, x, z*; *pl* **quei** + C, **quegli** + V *o s impura, gn, pn, ps, x, z*; *dav sf* **quella** + C, **quell'** + V; *pl* **quelle**) *det* that; (*pl*) those; **quella casa** that house; **quegli uomini** those men; **voglio quella camicia** (**lì** *o* **là**) I want that shirt
▶ *pron* **1** (*dimostrativo*) that one; (: *pl*) those ones; (: *ciò*) that; **conosci quella?** do you know her?; **prendo quello bianco** I'll take the white one; **chi è quello?** who's that?; **prendiamo quello** (**lì** *o* **là**) let's take that one (there)
2 (*relativo*): **quello(a) che** (*persona*) the one (who); (*cosa*) the one (which), the one (that); **quelli(e) che** (*persone*) those who; (*cose*) those which; **è lui quello che non voleva venire** he's the one who didn't want to come; **ho fatto quello che potevo** I did what I could

'quercia, -ce ['kwertʃa] *sf* oak (tree); (*legno*) oak
que'rela *sf* (*Dir*) (legal) action
que'sito *sm* question, query; problem
questio'nario *sm* questionnaire
questi'one *sf* problem, question; (*controversia*) issue; (*litigio*) quarrel; **in ~** in question; **è ~ di tempo** it's a matter o question of time

PAROLA CHIAVE

'questo, -a *det* **1** (*dimostrativo*) this; (: *pl*) these; **questo libro** (**qui** *o*

q

qua) this book; **io prendo questo cappotto, tu quello** I'll take this coat, you take that one; **quest'oggi** today; **questa sera** this evening **2** (*enfatico*): **non fatemi più prendere di queste paure** don't frighten me like that again ▸ *pron* (*dimostrativo*) this (one); (: *pl*) these (ones); (: *ciò*) this; **prendo questo (qui** o **qua)** I'll take this one; **preferisci questi o quelli?** do you prefer these (ones) or those (ones)?; **questo intendevo io** this is what I meant; **vengono Paolo e Luca: questo da Roma, quello da Palermo** Paolo and Luca are coming: the former from Palermo, the latter from Rome

ques'tura *sf* police headquarters *pl*
qui *av* here; **da** o **di ~** from here; **di ~ in avanti** from now on; **di ~ a poco/una settimana** in a little while/a week's time; **~ dentro/sopra/vicino** in/up/near here; *vedi anche* **questo**
quie'tanza [kwje'tantsa] *sf* receipt
qui'ete *sf* quiet, quietness; calmness; stillness; peace
qui'eto, -a *ag* quiet; (*notte*) calm, still; (*mare*) calm
'quindi *av* then ▸ *cong* therefore, so
'quindici ['kwinditʃi] *num* fifteen; **~ giorni** a fortnight (BRIT), two weeks
quindi'cina [kwindi'tʃina] *sf* (*serie*): **una ~ (di)** about fifteen; **fra una ~ di giorni** in a fortnight (BRIT) o two weeks
quinta *sf vedi* **quinto**
quin'tale *sm* quintal (100 kg)
'quinto, -a *num* fifth ▸ *sf* (*Aut*) fifth (gear)
quiz [kwidz] *sm inv* (*domanda*) question; (*anche*: **gioco a ~**) quiz game
'quota *sf* (*parte*) quota, share; (*Aer*) height, altitude; (*Ippica*) odds *pl*:

prendere/perdere ~ (*Aer*) to gain/lose height o altitude; **~ d'iscrizione** enrolment fee; (*ad un club*) membership fee
quotidi'ano, -a *ag* daily; (*banale*) everyday ▸ *sm* (*giornale*) daily (paper)
quozi'ente [kwot'tsjɛnte] *sm* (*Mat*) quotient; **~ d'intelligenza** intelligence quotient, IQ

r

R, r ['ɛrre] *sm o f (lettera)* R, r; **R come Roma** ≈ R for Robert (*BRIT*), R for Roger (*US*)

'rabbia *sf (ira)* anger, rage; *(accanimento, furia)* fury; *(Med: idrofobia)* rabies *sg*

rab'bino *sm* rabbi

rabbi'oso, -a *ag* angry, furious; *(facile all'ira)* quick-tempered; *(forze, acqua ecc)* furious, raging; *(Med)* rabid, mad

rabbo'nire /55/ *vt* to calm down

rabbrivi'dire /55/ *vi* to shudder, shiver

raccapez'zarsi [rakkapet'tsarsi] /72/ *vpr*: **non ~** to be at a loss

raccapricci'ante [rakkaprit'tʃante] *ag* horrifying

accatta'palle *sm inv (Sport)* ballboy

accat'tare /72/ *vt* to pick up

ac'chetta [rak'ketta] *sf (per tennis)* racket; *(per ping-pong)* bat; **~ da neve** snowshoe; **~ da sci** ski stick

racchi'udere [rak'kjudere] /22/ *vt* to contain

rac'cogliere [rak'kɔʎʎere] /23/ *vt* to collect; *(raccattare)* to pick up; *(frutti, fiori)* to pick, pluck; *(Agr)* to harvest; *(approvazione, voti)* to win

raccogli'tore [rakkoʎʎi'tore] *sm (cartella)* folder, binder

rac'colta *sf vedi* **raccolto**

rac'colto, -a *pp di* **raccogliere** ▷ *ag (persona: pensoso)* thoughtful; *(luogo: appartato)* secluded, quiet ▷ *sm (Agr)* crop, harvest ▷ *sf* collecting *no pl*; collection; *(Agr)* harvesting *no pl*, gathering *no pl*; harvest, crop; *(adunata)* gathering; **raccolta differenziata** *(dei rifiuti)* separate collection of different kinds of household waste

raccoman'dabile *ag* (highly) commendable; **è un tipo poco ~** he is not to be trusted

raccoman'dare /72/ *vt* to recommend; *(affidare)* to entrust; **~ a qn di fare qc** to recommend that sb does sth

raccoman'dato, -a *ag (lettera, pacco)* recorded-delivery ▷ *sf (anche:* **lettera raccomandata**) recorded-delivery letter

raccon'tare /72/ *vt*: **~ (a qn)** *(dire)* to tell (sb); *(narrare)* to relate (to sb), tell (sb) about; **rac'conto** *sm* telling *no pl*, relating *no pl*; *(fatto raccontato)* story, tale; **racconti per bambini** children's stories

rac'cordo *sm (Tecn: giunzione)* connection, joint; **~ anulare** *(Aut)* ring road (*BRIT*), beltway (*US*); **~ autostradale** slip road (*BRIT*), entrance (*o exit*) ramp (*US*); **~ ferroviario** siding; **~ stradale** link road

racimo'lare [ratʃimo'lare] /72/ *vt (fig)* to scrape together, glean

'rada *sf (natural)* harbour (*BRIT*) *o* harbor (*US*)

'radar *sm inv* radar

raddoppi·are /19/ *vt, vi* to double
raddriz·zare [raddrit'tsare] /72/ *vt* to straighten; (*fig: correggere*) to put straight, correct
'**radere** /85/ *vt* (*barba*) to shave off; (*mento*) to shave; (*fig: rasentare*) to graze; to skim; **radersi** *vpr* to shave (o.s.); **~ al suolo** to raze to the ground
radi·are /19/ *vt* to strike off
radia·tore *sm* radiator
radiazi·one [radjat'tsjone] *sf* (*Fisica*) radiation; (*cancellazione*) striking off
radi·cale *ag* radical ▷ *sm* (*Ling*) root; **radicali liberi** free radicals
ra'dicchio [ra'dikkjo] *sm* variety of chicory
ra'dice [ra'ditʃe] *sf* root
'**radio** *sf inv* radio ▷ *sm* (*Chim*) radium; **radioat·tivo, -a** *ag* radioactive; **radio'cronaca, -che** *sf* radio commentary; **radiogra'fia** *sf* radiography; (*foto*) X-ray photograph
radi·oso, -a *ag* radiant
radios·veglia [radjoz'veʎʎa] *sf* radio alarm
'**rado, -a** *ag* (*capelli*) sparse, thin; (*visite*) infrequent; **di ~** rarely
radu·nare /72/ *vt*, **radu·narsi** *vpr* to gather, assemble
ra'dura *sf* clearing
raf'fermo, -a *ag* stale
'**raffica, -che** *sf* (*Meteor*) gust (of wind); **~ di colpi** (*di fucile*) burst of gunfire
raffigu·rare /72/ *vt* to represent
raffi'nato, -a *ag* refined
raffor'zare [raffor'tsare] /72/ *vt* to reinforce
raffredda'mento *sm* cooling
raffred'dare /72/ *vt* to cool; (*fig*) to dampen, have a cooling effect on; **raffreddarsi** *vpr* to grow cool *o* cold; (*prendere un raffreddore*) to catch a cold; (*fig*) to cool (off)
raffred'dato, -a *ag* (*Med*): **essere ~** to have a cold
raffred'dore *sm* (*Med*) cold

raf'fronto *sm* comparison
'**rafia** *sf* (*fibra*) raffia
'**rafting** ['rafting] *sm* white-water rafting
ra'gazzo, -a [ra'gattso] *sm/f* boy/ girl; (*fam: fidanzato*) boyfriend/ girlfriend; **ragazzi** *smpl* (*figli*) kids; **ragazza madre** unmarried mother; **ciao ragazzi!** (*gruppo*) hi guys!
raggi·ante [rad'dʒante] *ag* radiant, shining
'**raggio** ['raddʒo] *sm* (*di sole ecc*) ray; (*Mat, distanza*) radius; (*di ruota ecc*) spoke; **~ d'azione** range; **raggi X** X-rays
raggi·rare [raddʒi'rare] /72/ *vt* to take in, trick
raggi'ungere [rad'dʒundʒere] /5/ *vt* to reach; (*persona: riprendere*) to catch up (with); (*bersaglio*) to hit; (*fig: meta*) to achieve
raggomito'larsi /72/ *vpr* to curl up
raggranel'lare /72/ *vt* to scrape together
raggrup'pare /72/ *vt* to group (together)
ragiona'mento [radʒona'mento] *sm* reasoning *no pl*; arguing *no pl*; argument
ragio'nare [radʒo'nare] /72/ *vi* to reason; (*discorrere*): **~ (di)** to argue (about)
ragi'one [ra'dʒone] *sf* reason; (*dimostrazione, prova*) argument, reason; (*diritto*) right; **aver ~** to be right; **aver ~ di qn** to get the better of sb; **dare ~ a qn** (*persona*) to side with sb; (*fatto*) to prove sb right; **in ~ di** at the rate of; to the amount of; according to; **a** *o* **con ~** rightly, justly; **perdere la ~** to become insane; (*fig*) to take leave of one's senses; **a ragion veduta** after due consideration; **~ sociale** (*Comm*) corporate name
ragione'ria [radʒone'ria] *sf* accountancy; (*ufficio*) accounts department

ragio'nevole [radʒo'nevole] *ag* reasonable

ragioni'ere, -a [radʒo'njεre] *sm/f* accountant

ragli'are [raʎ'ʎare] /27/ *vi* to bray

ragna'tela [raɲɲa'tela] *sf* cobweb, spider's web

'ragno ['raɲɲo] *sm* spider

ragù *sm inv* (*Cuc*) meat sauce (*for pasta*); stew

RAI-TV [raiti'vu] *sigla f* (= *Radio televisione italiana*) Italian Broadcasting Company

ralle'grare /72/ *vt* to cheer up; **rallegrarsi** *vpr* to cheer up; (*provare allegrezza*) to rejoice; **rallegrarsi con qn** to congratulate sb

rallen'tare /72/ *vt* to slow down; (*fig*) to lessen, slacken ▷ *vi* to slow down

rallenta'tore *sm* (*Cine*) slow-motion camera; **al ~** (*anche fig*) in slow motion

raman'zina [raman'dzina] *sf* lecture, telling-off

'rame *sm* (*Chim*) copper

rammari'carsi /20/ *vpr*: **~ (di)** (*rincrescersi*) to be sorry (about), regret; (*lamentarsi*) to complain (about)

rammen'dare /72/ *vt* to mend; (*calza*) to darn

'ramo *sm* branch

ramo'scello [ramoʃ'ʃello] *sm* twig

'rampa *sf* flight (of stairs); **~ di lancio** launching pad

rampi'cante *ag* (*Bot*) climbing

'rana *sf* frog

'rancido, -a ['rantʃido] *ag* rancid

ran'core *sm* rancour, resentment

ran'dagio, -a, -gi, -gie *o* **-ge** [ran'dadʒo] *ag* (*gatto, cane*) stray

ran'dello *sm* club, cudgel

'rango, -ghi *sm* (*grado*) rank; (*condizione sociale*) station

rannicchi'arsi [rannik'kjarsi] /19/ *vpr* to crouch, huddle

rannuvo'larsi /72/ *vpr* to cloud over, become overcast

'rapa *sf* (*Bot*) turnip

ra'pace [ra'patʃe] *ag* (*animale*) predatory; (*fig*) rapacious, grasping ▷ *sm* bird of prey

ra'pare /72/ *vt* (*capelli*) to crop, cut very short

rapida'mente *av* quickly, rapidly

rapidità *sf* speed

'rapido, -a *ag* fast; (*esame, occhiata*) quick, rapid ▷ *sm* (*Ferr*) express (train)

rapi'mento *sm* kidnapping; (*fig*) rapture

ra'pina *sf* robbery; **~ in banca** bank robbery; **~ a mano armata** armed robbery; **rapi'nare** /72/ *vt* to rob; **rapina'tore, -'trice** *sm/f* robber

ra'pire /55/ *vt* (*cose*) to steal; (*persone*) to kidnap; (*fig*) to enrapture, delight; **rapi'tore, -'trice** *sm/f* kidnapper

rap'porto *sm* (*resoconto*) report; (*legame*) relationship; (*Mat, Tecn*) ratio; **rapporti sessuali** sexual intercourse *sg*

rappre'saglia [rappre'saʎʎa] *sf* reprisal, retaliation

rappresen'tante *smf* representative

rappresen'tare /72/ *vt* to represent; (*Teat*) to perform; **rappresentazi'one** *sf* representation; performing *no pl*; (*spettacolo*) performance

rara'mente *av* seldom, rarely

rare'fatto, -a *ag* rarefied

'raro, -a *ag* rare

ra'sare /72/ *vt* (*barba ecc*) to shave off; (*siepi, erba*) to trim, cut; **rasarsi** *vpr* to shave (o.s.)

raschi'are [ras'kjare] /19/ *vt* to scrape; (*macchia, fango*) to scrape off ▷ *vi* to clear one's throat

ra'sente *prep*: **~ (a)** close to, very near

'raso, -a *pp di* **radere** ▷ *ag* (*barba*) shaved; (*capelli*) cropped; (*con misure di capacità*) level; (*pieno: bicchiere*) full to the brim ▷ *sm* (*tessuto*) satin; **~ terra** close to the ground; **un cucchiaio ~** a level spoonful

ra'soio sm razor; **~ elettrico** electric shaver o razor

ras'segna [ras'seɲɲa] sf (Mil) inspection, review; (esame) inspection; (resoconto) review, survey; (pubblicazione letteraria ecc) review; (mostra) exhibition, show; **passare in ~** (Mil: fig) to review

rasse'gnare [rasseɲ'ɲare] /15/ vt: **~ le dimissioni** to resign; **rassegnarsi** vpr (accettare): **rassegnarsi (a qc/a fare)** to resign o.s. (to sth/to doing)

rassicu'rare /72/ vt to reassure

rasso'dare /72/ vt to harden, stiffen; **rassodarsi** vpr to harden, to strengthen

rassomigli'anza [rassomiʎ'ʎantsa] sf resemblance

rassomigli'are [rassomiʎ'ʎare] /27/ vi: **~ a** to resemble, look like

rastrel'lare /72/ vt to rake; (fig: perlustrare) to comb

ras'trello sm rake

'rata sf (quota) instalment; **pagare a rate** to pay by instal(l)ments o on hire purchase (BRIT)

ratifi'care /20/ vt (Dir) to ratify

'ratto sm (Dir) abduction; (Zool) rat

rattop'pare /72/ vt to patch

rattris'tare /72/ vt to sadden; **rattristarsi** vpr to become sad

'rauco, -a, -chi, -che ag hoarse

rava'nello sm radish

ravi'oli smpl ravioli sg

ravvi'vare /72/ vt to revive; (fig) to brighten up, enliven

razio'nale [rattsjo'nale] ag rational

razio'nare [rattsjo'nare] /72/ vt to ration

razi'one [rat'tsjone] sf ration; (porzione) portion, share

'razza ['rattsa] sf race; (Zool) breed; (discendenza, stirpe) stock, race; (sorta) sort, kind

razzi'ale [rat'tsjale] ag racial

raz'zismo [rat'tsizmo] sm racism, racialism

raz'zista, -i, -e [rat'tsista] ag, smf racist, racialist

'razzo ['raddzo] sm rocket

RC sigla = **Reggio Calabria**; (= partito della Rifondazione Comunista) left-wing Italian political party

re sm inv king; (Mus) D; (: solfeggiando la scala) re; **i Re Magi** the Three Wise Men, the Magi

rea'gire [rea'dʒire] /55/ vi to react

re'ale ag real; (di, da re) royal ▷ sm: **il ~** reality

reality [ri'aliti] sm inv reality show

realiz'zare [realid'dzare] /72/ vt (progetto ecc) to realize, carry out; (sogno, desiderio) to realize, fulfil; (scopo) to achieve; (Comm: titoli ecc) to realize; (Calcio: ecc) to score; **realizzarsi** vpr to be realized

real'mente av really, actually

realtà sf inv reality

re'ato sm offence

reat'tore sm (Fisica) reactor; (Aer: aereo) jet; (: motore) jet engine

reazio'nario, -a [reattsjo'narjo] ag (Pol) reactionary

reazi'one [reat'tsjone] sf reaction

'rebus sm inv rebus; (fig) puzzle; enigma

recapi'tare /72/ vt to deliver

re'capito sm (indirizzo) address; (consegna) delivery; **~ telefonico** phone number; **~ a domicilio** home delivery (service)

re'care /20/ vt (portare) to bring; **recarsi** vpr: **recarsi in città/a scuola** to go into town/to school

re'cedere [re'tʃɛdere] /29/ vi to withdraw

recensi'one [retʃen'sjone] sf review

re'cente [re'tʃɛnte] ag recent; **di ~** recently; **recente'mente** av recently

re'cidere [re'tʃidere] /34/ vt to cut off, chop off

recin'tare [retʃin'tare] /72/ vt to enclose, fence off

re'cinto [re'tʃinto] sm enclosure; (ciò che recinge) fence; surrounding wall

recipi'ente [retʃi'pjɛnte] *sm* container

re'ciproco, -a, -ci, -che [re'tʃiproko] *ag* reciprocal

'recita ['rɛtʃita] *sf* performance

reci'tare [retʃi'tare] /72/ *vt (poesia, lezione)* to recite; *(dramma)* to perform; *(ruolo)* to play o act (the part of)

recla'mare /72/ *vi* to complain ▷ *vt (richiedere)* to demand

re'clamo *sm* complaint

recli'nabile *ag (sedile)* reclining

reclusi'one *sf (Dir)* imprisonment

'recluta *sf* recruit

re'condito, -a *ag* secluded; *(fig)* secret, hidden

'record *ag inv* record *cpd* ▷ *sm inv* record; **in tempo ~, a tempo di ~** in record time; **detenere il ~ di** to hold the record for; **~ mondiale** world record

recriminazi'one [rekriminat'tsjone] *sf* recrimination

recupe'rare *ecc* = **ricuperare** *ecc*

redargu'ire /55/ *vt* to rebuke

re'dassi *ecc vb vedi* **redigere**

reddi'tizio, -a [reddi'tittsjo] *ag* profitable

'reddito *sm* income; *(dello Stato)* revenue; *(di un capitale)* yield

re'densi *ecc vb vedi* **redimere**

re'dento, -a *pp di* **redimere**

re'digere [re'didʒere] /47/ *vt* to write; *(contratto)* to draw up

re'dimere /86/ *vt* to deliver; *(Rel)* to redeem

'redini *sfpl* reins

'reduce ['rɛdutʃe] *ag:* **~ da** returning from, back from ▷ *smf* survivor

refe'rendum *sm inv* referendum

refe'renza [refe'rɛntsa] *sf* reference

re'ferto *sm* medical report

rega'lare /72/ *vt* to give (as a present), make a present of

re'galo *sm* gift, present

re'gata *sf* regatta

'reggere ['rɛddʒere] /87/ *vt (tenere)* to hold; *(sostenere)* to support, bear, hold up; *(portare)* to carry, bear; *(resistere)* to withstand; *(dirigere: impresa)* to manage, run; *(governare)* to rule, govern; *(Ling)* to take, be followed by ▷ *vi (resistere):* **~ a** to stand up to, hold out against; *(sopportare):* **~ a** to stand; *(durare)* to last; *(fig: teoria ecc)* to hold water; **reggersi** *vpr (stare ritto)* to stand

'reggia, -ge ['rɛddʒa] *sf* royal palace

reggi'calze [reddʒi'kaltse] *sm inv* suspender belt

reggi'mento [reddʒi'mento] *sm (Mil)* regiment

reggi'seno [reddʒi'seno] *sm* bra

re'gia, -'gie [re'dʒia] *sf (TV, Cine: ecc)* direction

re'gime [re'dʒime] *sm (Pol)* regime; *(Dir: aureo, patrimoniale ecc)* system; *(Med)* diet; *(Tecn) (engine)* speed

re'gina [re'dʒina] *sf* queen

regio'nale [redʒo'nale] *ag* regional ▷ *sm* local train *(stopping frequently)*

regi'one [re'dʒone] *sf (gen)* region; *(territorio)* region, district, area; *see note* **"regione"**

re'gista, -i, -e [re'dʒista] *smf (TV, Cine ecc)* director

regis'trare [redʒis'trare] /72/ *vt (Amm)* to register; *(Comm)* to enter; *(notare)* to report, note; *(canzone, conversazione: strumento di misura)* to record; *(mettere a punto)* to adjust, regulate; **~ i bagagli** to check in one's luggage; **registra'tore** *sm (strumento)* recorder, register; *(magnetofono)* tape recorder; **registratore di cassa** cash register; **registratore a cassette** cassette recorder

re'gistro [re'dʒistro] *sm* register; *(Dir)* registry; *(Comm):* **~ (di cassa)** ledger; **~ di bordo** logbook

re'gnare [reɲ'ɲare] /15/ *vi* to reign, rule

'regno ['renno] sm kingdom; (*periodo*) reign; (*fig*) realm; **il ~ animale/ vegetale** the animal/vegetable kingdom; **il R~ Unito** the United Kingdom

'regola sf rule; **a ~ d'arte** duly; perfectly; **avere le carte in ~** to have one's papers in order

rego'labile ag adjustable

regola'mento sm (*complesso di norme*) regulations pl; (*di debito*) settlement; **~ di conti** (*fig*) settling of scores

rego'lare /72/ ag regular; (*in regola: documento*) in order ▷ vt to regulate, control; (*apparecchio*) to adjust, regulate; (*questione, conto, debito*) to settle; **regolarsi** vpr (*comportarsi*) to behave, act; **regolarsi nel bere/ nello spendere** (*moderarsi*) to control one's drinking/spending

rela'tivo, -a ag relative

relazi'one [relat'tsjone] sf (*fra cose, persone*) relation(ship); (*resoconto*) report, account

rele'gare /80/ vt to banish; (*fig*) to relegate

religi'one [reli'dʒone] sf religion

religi'oso, -a [reli'dʒoso] ag religious

re'liquia sf relic

re'litto sm wreck; (*fig*) down-and-out

re'mare /72/ vi to row

remini'scenze [reminiʃ'ʃentse] sfpl reminiscences

remis'sivo, -a ag submissive, compliant

'remo sm oar

re'moto, -a ag remote

'rendere /88/ vt (*ridare*) to return, give back; (: *saluto ecc*) to return; (*produrre*) to yield, bring in; (*esprimere, tradurre*) to render; **~ qc possibile** to make sth possible; **~ grazie a qn** to thank sb; **~ omaggio a qn** to honour sb; **~ un servizio a qn** to do sb a service; **~ una testimonianza** to give evidence; **~ la visita** to pay a return visit; **non so se rendo l'idea** I don't know whether I'm making myself clear

rendi'mento sm (*reddito*) yield; (*di manodopera, Tecn*) efficiency; (*capacità*) output; (*di studenti*) performance

'rendita sf (*di individuo*) private o unearned income; (*Comm*) revenue; **~ annua** annuity

'rene sm kidney

'renna sf reindeer inv

re'parto sm department, section; (*Mil*) detachment

repel'lente ag repulsive

repen'taglio [repen'taʎʎo] sm: **mettere a ~** to jeopardize, risk

repen'tino, -a ag sudden, unexpected

reper'torio sm (*Teat*) repertory; (*elenco*) index, (alphabetical) list

'replica, -che sf repetition; reply, answer; (*obiezione*) objection; (*Teat, Cine*) repeat performance; (*copia*) replica

repli'care /20/ vt (*ripetere*) to repeat; (*rispondere*) to answer, reply

repressi'one sf repression

re'presso, -a pp di **reprimere**

re'primere /50/ vt to suppress, repress

re'pubblica, -che sf republic

reputazi'one [reput'tsjone] sf reputation

requi'sire /55/ vt to requisition

requi'sito sm requirement

'resa sf (*l'arrendersi*) surrender; (*restituzione, rendimento*) return; **~ dei conti** rendering of accounts; (*fig*) day of reckoning

'resi ecc vb vedi **rendere**

resi'dente ag resident; **residenzi'ale** ag residential

re'siduo, -a ag residual, remaining ▷ sm remainder; (*Chim*) residue

'resina sf resin

resis'tente ag (*che resiste*): **~ a** resistant to; (*forte*) strong; (*duraturo*) long-lasting, durable; **~ al caldo**

heat-resistant; **resis'tenza** sf
resistance; (di persona: fisica) stamina,
endurance; (: mentale) endurance,
resistance

● **RESISTENZA**
●
● The Italian Resistenza fought
● against both the Nazis and
● the Fascists during the Second
● World War. It was particularly
● active after the fall of the
● Fascist government on 25 July
● 1943, throughout the German
● occupation and during the period
● of Mussolini's Republic of Salò
● in northern Italy. Resistance
● members spanned the whole
● political spectrum and played a
● vital role in the Liberation and
● in the formation of the new
● democratic government.

re'sistere /11/ vi to resist; **~ a** (assalto,
tentazioni) to resist; (dolore) to
withstand; (non patir danno) to be
resistant to

reso'conto sm report, account

res'pingere [res'pindʒere] /114/ vt to
drive back, repel; (rifiutare) to reject;
(Ins: bocciare) to fail

respi'rare /72/ vi to breathe; (fig)
to get one's breath; to breathe
again ▷ vt to breathe (in), inhale;
respirazi'one sf breathing;
respirazione artificiale artificial
respiration; **res'piro** sm breathing
no pl; (singolo atto) breath; (fig)
respite, rest; **mandare un respiro di
sollievo** to give a sigh of relief

respon'sabile ag responsible ▷ smf
person responsible; (capo) person
in charge; **~ di** responsible for; (Dir)
liable for; **responsabilità** sf inv
responsibility; (legale) liability

res'ponso sm answer

'ressa sf crowd, throng

'ressi ecc vb vedi **reggere**

res'tare /72/ vi (rimanere) to remain,
stay; (avanzare) to be left, remain; **~
orfano/cieco** to become o be left an
orphan/become blind; **~ d'accordo**
to agree; **non resta più niente**
there's nothing left; **restano pochi
giorni** there are only a few days left

restau'rare /72/ vt to restore

res'tio, -a, -'tii, -'tie ag: **~ a**
reluctant to

restitu'ire /55/ vt to return, give
back; (energie, forze) to restore

'resto sm remainder, rest; (denaro)
change; (Mat) remainder; **resti** smpl
leftovers; (di città) remains; **del ~**
moreover, besides; **tenga pure il
~** keep the change; **resti mortali**
(mortal) remains

res'tringere [res'trindʒere] /117/ vt
to reduce; (vestito) to take in; (stoffa)
to shrink; (fig) to restrict, limit;
restringersi vpr (strada) to narrow;
(stoffa) to shrink

'rete sf net; (di recinzione) wire
netting; (Aut, Ferr, di spionaggio
ecc) network; (fig) trap, snare;
segnare una ~ (Calcio) to score
a goal; **~ ferroviaria/stradale/
di distribuzione** railway/road/
distribution network; **~ del letto**
(sprung) bed base; **~ sociale** social
network; **~ (televisiva)** (sistema)
network; (canale) channel; **la R~**
the web

reti'cente [reti'tʃɛnte] ag reticent

retico'lato sm grid; (rete metallica)
wire netting; (di filo spinato) barbed
wire fence

'retina sf (Anat) retina

re'torico, -a, -ci, -che ag rhetorical

retribu'ire /55/ vt to pay

'retro sm inv back ▷ av (dietro): **vedi ~**
see over(leaf)

retro'cedere [retro'tʃɛdere] /29/ vi
to withdraw ▷ vt (Calcio) to relegate;
(Mil) to degrade

re'trogrado, -a ag (fig) reactionary,
backward-looking

retro'marcia [retro'martʃa] *sf* (*Aut*) reverse; (: *dispositivo*) reverse gear

retro'scena [retroʃʃena] *sf inv* (*Teat*) backstage ▷ *sm inv*: **i ~** (*fig*) the behind-the-scenes activities

retrovi'sore *sm* (*Aut*) (rear-view) mirror

'retta *sf* (*Mat*) straight line; (*di convitto*) charge for bed and board; (*fig: ascolto*): **dar ~ a** to listen to, pay attention to

rettango'lare *ag* rectangular

ret'tangolo, -a *ag* right-angled ▷ *sm* rectangle

ret'tifica, -che *sf* rectification, correction

'rettile *sm* reptile

retti'lineo, -a *ag* rectilinear

'retto, -a *pp di* **reggere** ▷ *ag* straight; (*onesto*) honest, upright; (*giusto, esatto*) correct, proper, right; **angolo ~** (*Mat*) right angle

ret'tore *sm* (*Rel*) rector; (*di università*) ≈ chancellor

retwit'tare /72/ *vt* (*su Twitter*) to retweet

reuma'tismo *sm* rheumatism

revisi'one *sf* auditing *no pl*; audit; servicing *no pl*; overhaul; review; revision; **~ contabile interna** internal audit

revi'sore *sm*: **~ di conti/bozze** auditor/proofreader

re'vival [ri'vaivəl] *sm inv* revival

'revoca *sf* revocation

revo'care /20/ *vt* to revoke

re'volver *sm inv* revolver

ri'abbia *ecc vb vedi* **riavere**

riabili'tare /72/ *vt* to rehabilitate

riabilitazi'one [riabilitat'tsjone] *sf* rehabilitation

rianimazi'one [rianimat'tsjone] *sf* (*Med*) resuscitation; **centro di ~** intensive care unit

ria'prire /9/ *vt*, **ria'prirsi** *vpr* to reopen, open again

ri'armo *sm* (*Mil*) rearmament

rias'sumere /12/ *vt* (*riprendere*) to resume; (*impiegare di nuovo*) to re-employ; (*sintetizzare*) to summarize;

rias'sunto, -a *pp di* **riassumere** ▷ *sm* summary

riattac'care /20/ *vt* (*attaccare di nuovo*): **~ (a)** (*manifesto, francobollo*) to stick back (on); (*bottone*) to sew back (on); (*quadro, chiavi*) to hang back up (on); **~ (il telefono o il ricevitore)** to hang up (the receiver)

ri'avere /13/ *vt* to have again; (*avere indietro*) to get back; (*riacquistare*) to recover; **riaversi** *vpr* to recover

riba'dire /55/ *vt* (*fig*) to confirm

ri'balta *sf* flap; (*Teat: proscenio*) front of the stage; **luci della ~** footlights *pl*; (*fig*) limelight

ribal'tabile *ag* (*sedile*) tip-up

ribal'tare /72/ *vt*, *vi* (*anche*: **ribaltarsi**) to turn over, tip over

ribas'sare /72/ *vt* to lower, bring down ▷ *vi* to come down, fall

ri'battere /1/ *vt* to return, hit back; (*confutare*) to refute; **~ che** to retort that

ribel'larsi /72/ *vpr*: **~ (a)** to rebel (against); **ri'belle** *ag* (*soldati*) rebel; (*ragazzo*) rebellious ▷ *smf* rebel

'ribes *sm inv* currant; **~ nero** blackcurrant; **~ rosso** redcurrant

ri'brezzo [ri'breddzo] *sm* disgust, loathing; **far ~ a** to disgust

ribut'tante *ag* disgusting, revolting

rica'dere /18/ *vi* to fall again; (*scendere a terra: fig: nel peccato ecc*) to fall back; (*vestiti, capelli ecc*) to hang (down); (*riversarsi: fatiche, colpe*): **~ su** to fall on; **rica'duta** *sf* (*Med*) relapse

rica'mare /72/ *vt* to embroider

ricambi'are /19/ *vt* to change again; (*contraccambiare*) to return, repay; **ri'cambio** *sm* exchange, return; (*Fisiol*) metabolism

ri'camo *sm* embroidery

ricapito'lare /72/ *vt* to recapitulate, sum up

ricari'care /20/ *vt* (*arma, macchina fotografica*) to reload; (*penna, pipa*) to refill; (*orologio, giocattolo*) to rewind; (*Elettr*) to recharge

ricat'tare /72/ vt to blackmail; **ri'catto** sm blackmail

rica'vare /72/ vt (estrarre) to draw out, extract; (ottenere) to obtain, gain

ric'chezza [rik'kettsa] sf wealth; (fig) richness

'**riccio, -a, -ci, -ce** ['rittʃo] ag curly ▷ sm (Zool) hedgehog; (anche: ~ **di mare**) sea urchin; '**ricciolo** sm curl

'**ricco, -a, -chi, -che** ag rich; (persona, paese) rich, wealthy ▷ sm/f rich man/ woman; **i ricchi** the rich; ~ **di** full of; (risorse, fauna ecc) rich in

ri'cerca, -che [ri'tʃerka] sf search; (indagine) investigation, inquiry; (studio): **la ~** research; **una ~** a piece of research; ~ **di mercato** market research

ricer'care [ritʃer'kare] /20/ vt (motivi, cause) to look for, try to determine; (successo, piacere) to pursue; (onore, gloria) to seek; **ricer'cato, -a** ag (apprezzato) much sought-after; (affettato) studied, affected ▷ sm/f (Polizia) wanted man/woman

ricerca'tore, -'trice [ritʃerka'tore] sm/f (Ins) researcher

ri'cetta [ri'tʃetta] sf (Med) prescription; (Cuc) recipe

ricettazi'one [ritʃettat'tsjone] sf (Dir) receiving (stolen goods)

ri'cevere [ri'tʃevere] /29/ vt to receive; (stipendio, lettera) to get, receive; (accogliere: ospite) to welcome; (vedere: cliente, rappresentante ecc) to see; **ricevi'mento** sm receiving no pl; (trattenimento) reception; **ricevi'tore** sm (Tecn) receiver; **rice'vuta** sf receipt; **accusare ricevuta di qc** (Comm) to acknowledge receipt of sth; **ricevuta fiscale** official receipt (for tax purposes); **ricevuta di ritorno** (Posta) advice of receipt

richia'mare [rikja'mare] /72/ vt (chiamare indietro, ritelefonare) to call back; (ambasciatore, truppe) to recall; (rimproverare) to reprimand; (attirare) to attract, draw; **richiamarsi** vpr: **richiamarsi a** (riferirsi a) to refer to

richi'edere [ri'kjɛdere] /21/ vt to ask again for; (chiedere: per sapere) to ask; (: per avere) to ask for; (Amm: documenti) to apply for; (esigere) to need, require; (chiedere indietro): ~ **qc** to ask for sth back

richi'esto, -a [ri'kjɛsto] pp di **richiedere** ▷ sf (domanda) request; (Amm) application, request; (esigenza) demand, request; **a richiesta** on request

rici'claggio [ritʃi'kladdʒo] sm recycling

rici'clare [ritʃi'klare] /72/ vt to recycle

'**ricino** ['ritʃino] sm: **olio di ~** castor oil

ricognizi'one [rikoɲɲit'tsjone] sf (Mil) reconnaissance; (Dir) recognition, acknowledgement

ricominci'are [rikomin'tʃare] /14/ vt, vi to start again, begin again

ricom'pensa sf reward

ricompen'sare /72/ vt to reward

riconcili'are [rikontʃi'ljare] /19/ vt to reconcile; **riconciliarsi** vpr to be reconciled

ricono'scente [rikonoʃʃɛnte] ag grateful

rico'noscere [riko'noʃʃere] /26/ vt to recognize; (Dir: figlio, debito) to acknowledge; (ammettere: errore) to admit, acknowledge

rico'perto, -a pp di **ricoprire**

ricopi'are /19/ vt to copy

rico'prire /9/ vt (coprire) to cover; (occupare: carica) to hold

ricor'dare /72/ vt to remember, recall; (richiamare alla memoria): ~ **qc a qn** to remind sb of sth; **ricordarsi** vpr: **ricordarsi (di)** to remember; **ricordarsi di qc/di aver fatto** to remember sth/having done

ri'cordo sm memory; (regalo) keepsake, souvenir; (di viaggio) souvenir

ricor'rente *ag* recurrent, recurring;
  ricor'renza *sf* recurrence; (*festività*)
  anniversary

ri'correre /28/ *vi* (*ripetersi*) to recur; ~
  a (*rivolgersi*) to turn to; (*Dir*) to appeal
  to; (*servirsi di*) to have recourse to

ricostitu'ente *ag* (*Med*): **cura** ~ tonic

ricostru'ire /55/ *vt* (*casa*) to rebuild;
  (*fatti*) to reconstruct

ri'cotta *sf* soft white unsalted cheese
  made from sheep's milk

ricove'rare /72/ *vt* to give shelter
  to; ~ **qn in ospedale** to admit sb
  to hospital

ri'covero *sm* shelter, refuge; (*Mil*)
  shelter; (*Med*) admission (to hospital)

ricreazi'one [rikreat'tsjone] *sf*
  recreation, entertainment; (*Ins*)
  break

ri'credersi /29/ *vpr* to change one's
  mind

ricupe'rare /72/ *vt* (*rientrare in
  possesso di*) to recover, get back;
  (*tempo perduto*) to make up for; (*Naut*)
  to salvage; (: *naufraghi*) to rescue;
  (*delinquente*) to rehabilitate; ~ **lo
  svantaggio** (*Sport*) to close the gap

ridacchi'are [ridak'kjare] /19/ *vi*
  to snigger

ri'dare /33/ *vt* to return, give back

'ridere /89/ *vi* to laugh; (*deridere,
  beffare*): ~ **di** to laugh at, make fun of

ri'dicolo, -a *ag* ridiculous, absurd

ridimensio'nare /72/ *vt* to
  reorganize; (*fig*) to see in the right
  perspective

ri'dire /38/ *vt* to repeat; (*criticare*) to
  find fault with; to object to; **trova
  sempre qualcosa da** ~ he always
  manages to find fault

ridon'dante *ag* redundant

ri'dotto, -a *pp di* **ridurre** ▷ *ag*
  (*biglietto*) reduced; (*formato*) small

ri'duco *ecc vb vedi* **ridurre**

ri'durre /90/ *vt* (*anche Chim, Mat*) to
  reduce; (*prezzo, spese*) to cut, reduce;
  (*accorciare: opera letteraria*) to abridge;
  (: *Radio, TV*) to adapt; **ridursi** *vpr*

(*diminuirsi*) to be reduced, shrink;
  ridursi a to be reduced to; **ridursi
  a pelle e ossa** to be reduced to skin
  and bone; **ri'dussi** *ecc vb vedi* **ridurre**;

ridut'tore *sm* (*Tecn, Chim*) reducer;
  (*Elettr*) adaptor; **riduzi'one** *sf*
  reduction; abridgement; adaptation

ri'ebbi *ecc vb vedi* **riavere**

riem'pire /91/ *vt* to fill (up); (*modulo*)
  to fill in *o* out; **riempirsi** *vpr* to fill (up);
  ~ **qc di** to fill sth (up) with

rien'tranza [rien'trantsa] *sf* recess;
  indentation

rien'trare /72/ *vi* (*entrare di nuovo*)
  to go (*o* come) back in; (*tornare*) to
  return; (*fare una rientranza*) to go
  in, curve inwards; to be indented;
  (*riguardare*): ~ **in** to be included
  among, form part of

riepilo'gare /80/ *vt* to summarize
  ▷ *vi* to recapitulate

ri'esco *ecc vb vedi* **riuscire**

ri'fare /53/ *vt* to do again; (*ricostruire*)
  to make again; (*nodo*) to tie again, do
  up again; (*imitare*) to imitate, copy;
  rifarsi *vpr* (*risarcirsi*): **rifarsi di** to
  make up for; (*vendicarsi*): **rifarsi di
  qc su qn** to get one's own back on sb
  for sth; (*riferirsi*): **rifarsi a** to go back
  to; to follow; ~ **il letto** to make the
  bed; **rifarsi una vita** to make a new
  life for *o.s*

riferi'mento *sm* reference; **in** *o* **con** ~
  a with reference to

rife'rire /55/ *vt* (*riportare*) to report
  ▷ *vi* to do a report; **riferirsi** *vpr*:
  riferirsi a to refer to

rifi'nire /55/ *vt* to finish off, put the
  finishing touches to

rifiu'tare /72/ *vt* to refuse; ~ **di fare**
  to refuse to do; **rifi'uto** *sm* refusal;
  rifiuti *smpl* (*spazzatura*) rubbish *sg*,
  refuse *sg*

riflessi'one *sf* (*Fisica, meditazione*)
  reflection; (*il pensare*) thought,
  reflection; (*osservazione*) remark

rifles'sivo, -a *ag* (*persona*)
  thoughtful, reflective; (*Ling*) reflexive

ri'flesso, -a pp di **riflettere** ▷ sm (di luce, allo specchio) reflection; (Fisiol) reflex; **di** o **per ~** indirectly

riflessolo'gia [riflessolo'dʒia] sf: reflexology

ri'flettere /92/ vt to reflect ▷ vi to think; **riflettersi** vpr to be reflected; **~ su** to think over

riflet'tore sm reflector; (proiettore) floodlight; (Mil) searchlight

ri'flusso sm flowing back; (della marea) ebb; **un'epoca di ~** an era of nostalgia

ri'forma sf reform; **la R~** (Rel) the Reformation

riforma'torio sm (Dir) community home (BRIT), reformatory (US)

riforni'mento sm supplying, providing; restocking; (di carburante) refuelling; **rifornimenti** smpl (provviste) supplies, provisions

rifor'nire /55/ vt (fornire di nuovo: casa ecc) to restock; (provvedere): **~ di** to supply o provide with; **rifornirsi** vpr: **rifornirsi di qc** to stock up on sth

rifugi'arsi [rifu'dʒarsi] /62/ vpr to take refuge; **rifugi'ato, -a** sm/f refugee

ri'fugio [ri'fudʒo] sm refuge, shelter; (in montagna) shelter; **~ antiaereo** air-raid shelter

'riga, -ghe sf line; (striscia) stripe; (di persone, cose) line, row; (regolo) ruler; (scriminatura) parting; **mettersi in ~** to line up; **a righe** (foglio) lined; (vestito) striped

ri'gare /80/ vt (foglio) to rule ▷ vi: **~ diritto** (fig) to toe the line

rigatti'ere sm junk dealer

ri'ghello [ri'gɛllo] sm ruler

righerò ecc [rige'rɔ] vb vedi **rigare**

'rigido, -a ['ridʒido] ag rigid, stiff; (membra ecc, indurite) stiff; (Meteor) harsh, severe; (fig) strict

rigogli'oso, -a [rigoʎ'ʎoso] ag (pianta) luxuriant; (fig: commercio, sviluppo) thriving

ri'gore sm (Meteor) harshness, rigours pl; (fig) severity, strictness; (anche: **calcio di ~**) penalty; **di ~** compulsory; **a rigor di termini** strictly speaking

riguar'dare /72/ vt to look at again; (considerare) to regard, consider; (concernere) to regard, concern; **riguardarsi** vpr (aver cura di sé) to look after o.s.

rigu'ardo sm (attenzione) care; (considerazione) regard, respect; **~ a** concerning, with regard to; **non aver riguardi nell'agire/nel parlare** to act/speak freely

rilasci'are [rilaʃ'ʃare] /14/ vt (rimettere in libertà) to release; (Amm: documenti) to issue

rilas'sare /72/ vt to relax; **rilassarsi** vpr to relax; (fig: disciplina) to become slack

rile'gare /80/ vt (libro) to bind

ri'leggere [ri'lɛddʒere] /61/ vt to reread, read again; (rivedere) to read over

ri'lento: a ~ av slowly

rile'vante ag considerable; important

rile'vare /72/ vt (ricavare) to find; (notare) to notice; (mettere in evidenza) to point out; (venire a conoscere: notizia) to learn; (raccogliere: dati) to gather, collect; (Topografia) to survey; (Mil) to relieve; (Comm) to take over

rili'evo sm (Arte, Geo) relief; (fig: rilevanza) importance; (osservazione) point, remark; (Topografia) survey; **dar ~ a** o **mettere in ~ qc** (fig) to bring sth out, highlight sth

rilut'tante ag reluctant

'rima sf rhyme; (verso) verse; **far ~ con** to rhyme with; **rispondere a qn per le rime** to give sb tit for tat

riman'dare /72/ vt to send again; (restituire, rinviare) to send back, return; **~ qc (a)** (differire) to postpone sth o put sth off (till); **~ qn a** (fare *riferimento*) to refer sb to; **essere rimandato** (*Ins*) to have to resit one's exams

ri'mando *sm* (*rinvio*) return; (*dilazione*) postponement; (*riferimento*) cross-reference

rima'nente *ag* remaining ▷ *sm* rest, remainder; **i rimanenti** (*persone*) the rest of them, the others

rima'nere /93/ *vi* (*restare*) to remain, stay; (*avanzare*) to be left, remain; (*restare stupito*) to be amazed; **rimangono poche settimane a Pasqua** there are only a few weeks left till Easter; **~ vedovo** to be left a widower; **~ confuso/sorpreso** to be confused/surprised; **rimane da vedere se** it remains to be seen whether

rimangi'are [riman'dʒare] /62/ *vt* to eat again; **rimangiarsi la parola/una promessa** (*fig*) to go back on one's word/one's promise

ri'mango *ecc vb vedi* **rimanere**

rimargi'nare [rimardʒi'nare] /72/ *vt, vi*, **rimarginarsi** *vpr* to heal

rimbal'zare [rimbal'tsare] /72/ *vi* to bounce back, rebound; (*proiettile*) to ricochet

rimbam'bito, -a *ag* senile, in one's dotage

rimboc'care /20/ *vt* (*coperta*) to tuck in; (*maniche, pantaloni*) to turn *o* roll up

rimbom'bare /72/ *vi* to resound

rimbor'sare /72/ *vt* to pay back, repay

rimedi'are /19/ *vi*: **~ a** to remedy ▷ *vt* (*fam: procurarsi*) to get *o* scrape together

ri'medio *sm* (*medicina*) medicine; (*cura, fig*) remedy, cure

ri'mettere /63/ *vt* (*mettere di nuovo*) to put back; (*Comm: merci*) to deliver; (: *denaro*) to remit; (*vomitare*) to bring up; (*perdere: anche*: **rimetterci**) to lose; (*indossare di nuovo*): **~ qc** to put sth back on, put sth on again;

(*affidare*) to entrust; (*decisione*) to refer; (*condonare*) to remit; **rimettersi al bello** (*tempo*) to clear up; **rimettersi in salute** to get better, recover one's health

ri'misi *ecc vb vedi* **rimettere**

'rimmel® *sm inv* mascara

rimoder'nare /72/ *vt* to modernize

rimorchi'are [rimor'kjare] /19/ *vt* to tow; (*fig: ragazza*) to pick up

ri'morchio [ri'morkjo] *sm* tow; (*veicolo*) trailer

ri'morso *sm* remorse

rimozi'one [rimot'tsjone] *sf* removal; (*da un impiego*) dismissal; (*Psic*) repression

rimpatri'are /19/ *vi* to return home ▷ *vt* to repatriate

rimpi'angere [rim'pjandʒere] /75/ *vt* to regret; (*persona*) to miss; **rimpi'anto, -a** *pp di* **rimpiangere** ▷ *sm* regret

rimpiaz'zare [rimpjat'tsare] /72/ *vt* to replace

rimpiccio'lire [rimpittʃo'lire] /55/ *vt* to make smaller ▷ *vi* (*anche*: **rimpicciolirsi**) to become smaller

rimpin'zare [rimpin'tsare] /72/ *vt*: **~ di** to cram *o* stuff with; **rimpinzarsi** *vpr*: **rimpinzarsi (di qc)** to stuff o.s. (with sth)

rimprove'rare /72/ *vt* to rebuke, reprimand

rimu'overe /66/ *vt* to remove; (*destituire*) to dismiss

Rinasci'mento [rinaʃʃi'mento] *sm*: **il ~** the Renaissance

ri'nascita [ri'naʃʃita] *sf* rebirth, revival

rinca'rare /72/ *vt* to increase the price of ▷ *vi* to go up, become more expensive

rinca'sare /72/ *vi* to go home

rinchi'udere [rin'kjudere] /22/ *vt* to shut (up *o* lock) up; **rinchiudersi** *vpr*: **rinchiudersi in** to shut o.s. up in; **rinchiudersi in se stesso** to withdraw into o.s.

rin'correre /28/ vt to chase, run after

rin'corso, -a pp di **rincorrere** ▷ sf short run

rin'crescere [rin'kreʃʃere] /30/ vb impers: **mi rincresce che/di non poter fare** I'm sorry that/I can't do, I regret that/being unable to do

rinfacci'are [rinfat'tʃare] /14/ vt (fig): **~ qc a qn** to throw sth in sb's face

rinfor'zare [rinfor'tsare] /72/ vt to reinforce, strengthen ▷ vi (anche: **rinforzarsi**) to grow stronger

rinfres'care /20/ vt (atmosfera, temperatura) to cool (down); (abito, pareti) to freshen up ▷ vi (tempo) to grow cooler; **rinfrescarsi** vpr (ristorarsi) to refresh o.s.; (lavarsi) to freshen up; **rin'fresco, -schi** sm (festa) party; **rinfreschi** smpl refreshments

rin'fusa sf: **alla ~** in confusion, higgledy-piggledy

ringhi'are [rin'gjare] /19/ vi to growl, snarl

ringhi'era [rin'gjɛra] sf railing; (delle scale) banister(s)

ringiova'nire [rindʒova'nire] /55/ vt: **~ qn** (vestito, acconciatura ecc) to make sb look younger; (vacanze ecc) to rejuvenate sb ▷ vi (anche: **ringiovanirsi**) to become (o look) younger

ringrazia'mento [ringrattsja'mento] sm thanks pl

ringrazi'are [ringrat'tsjare] /19/ vt to thank; **~ qn di qc** to thank sb for sth

rinne'gare /80/ vt (fede) to renounce; (figlio) to disown, repudiate

rinno'vabile ag (contratto, energia) renewable

rinnova'mento sm renewal; (economico) revival

rinno'vare /72/ vt to renew; (ripetere) to repeat, renew

rinoce'ronte [rinotʃe'ronte] sm rhinoceros

rino'mato, -a ag renowned, celebrated

rintracci'are [rintrat'tʃare] /14/ vt to track down

rintro'nare /72/ vi to boom, roar ▷ vt (assordare) to deafen; (stordire) to stun

rinunci'are [rinun'tʃare] /14/ vi: **~ a** to give up, renounce; **~ a fare qc** to give up doing sth

rinvi'are /60/ vt (rimandare indietro) to send back, return; **~ qc (a)** (differire) to postpone sth o put sth off (till); (seduta) to adjourn sth (till); **~ qn a** (fare un rimando) to refer sb to

rin'vio, -'vii sm (rimando) return; (differimento) postponement; (: di seduta) adjournment; (in un testo) cross-reference; **~ a giudizio** (Dir) indictment

riò ecc vb vedi **riavere**

ri'one sm district, quarter

riordi'nare /72/ vt (rimettere in ordine) to tidy; (riorganizzare) to reorganize

riorganiz'zare [riorganid'dzare] /72/ vt to reorganize

ripa'gare /80/ vt to repay

ripa'rare /72/ vt (proteggere) to protect, defend; (correggere: male, torto) to make up for; (: errore) to put right; (aggiustare) to repair ▷ vi (mettere rimedio): **~ a** to make up for; **ripararsi** vpr (rifugiarsi) to take refuge o shelter; **riparazi'one** sf (di un torto) reparation; (di guasto, scarpe) repairing no pl; repair; (risarcimento) compensation

ri'paro sm (protezione) shelter, protection; (rimedio) remedy

ripar'tire /45/ vt (dividere) to divide up; (distribuire) to share out ▷ vi to set off again; to leave again

ripas'sare /72/ vi to come (o go) back ▷ vt (scritto, lezione) to go over (again)

ripen'sare /72/ vi to think; (cambiare idea) to change one's mind; (tornare col pensiero): **~ a** to recall

ripercu'otersi /106/ vpr: **~ su** (fig) to have repercussions on

ripercussi'one sf (fig): **avere una ~ o delle ripercussioni su** to have repercussions on

ripes'care /20/ vt (pesce) to catch again; (persona, cosa) to fish out; (fig: ritrovare) to dig out

ri'petere /1/ vt to repeat; (ripassare) to go over; **ripetizi'one** sf repetition; (di lezione) revision; **ripetizioni** sfpl (Ins) private tutoring o coaching sg

ripi'ano sm (di mobile) shelf

ri'picca sf: **per ~** out of spite

'ripido, -a ag steep

ripie'gare /80/ vt to refold; (piegare più volte) to fold (up) ▷ vi (Mil) to retreat, fall back; (fig: accontentarsi): **~ su** to make do with

ripi'eno, -a ag full; (Cuc) stuffed; (: panino) filled ▷ sm (Cuc) stuffing

ri'pone vb vedi **riporre**

ri'pongo ecc vb vedi **riporre**

ri'porre /77/ vt (porre al suo posto) to put back, replace; (mettere via) to put away; (fiducia, speranza): **~ qc in qn** to place o put sth in sb

ripor'tare /72/ vt (portare indietro) to bring (o take) back; (riferire) to report; (citare) to quote; (vittoria) to gain; (successo) to have; (Mat) to carry; **riportarsi** vpr: **riportarsi a** (anche fig) to go back to; (riferirsi a) to refer to; **~ danni** to suffer damage

ripo'sare /72/ vt to rest ▷ vi to rest; **riposarsi** vpr to rest

ri'posi ecc vb vedi **riporre**

ri'poso sm rest; (Mil): **~!** at ease!; **a ~** (in pensione) retired; **giorno di ~** day off

ripos'tiglio [ripos'tiλλo] sm lumber room

ri'prendere /81/ vt (prigioniero, fortezza) to recapture; (prendere indietro) to take back; (ricominciare: lavoro) to resume; (andare a prendere) to fetch, come back for; (assumere di nuovo: impiegati) to take on again, re-employ; (rimproverare) to tell off; (restringere: abito) to take in; (Cine) to shoot; **riprendersi** vpr to recover; (correggersi) to correct o.s.

ri'preso, -a pp di **riprendere** ▷ sf recapture; resumption; (economica, da malattia, emozione) recovery; (Aut) acceleration no pl; (Teat, Cine) rerun; (Cine: presa) shooting no pl; shot; (Sport) second half; (Pugilato) round; **a più riprese** on several occasions, several times; **ripresa cinematografica** shot

ripristi'nare /72/ vt to restore

ripro'durre /90/ vt to reproduce; **riprodursi** vpr (Biol) to reproduce; (riformarsi) to form again

ripro'vare /72/ vt (provare di nuovo: gen) to try again; (: vestito) to try on again; (: sensazione) to experience again ▷ vi (tentare): **~ (a fare qc)** to try (to do sth) again; **riproverò più tardi** I'll try again later

ripudi'are /19/ vt to repudiate, disown

ripu'gnante [ripuɲ'ɲante] ag disgusting, repulsive

ri'quadro sm square; (Archit) panel

ri'saia sf paddy field

risa'lire /98/ vi (ritornare in su) to go back up; **~ a** (ritornare con la mente) to go back to; (datare da) to date back to, go back to

risal'tare /72/ vi (fig: distinguersi) to stand out; (Archit) to project, jut out

risa'puto, -a ag: **è ~ che ...** everyone knows that ..., it's common knowledge that ...

risarci'mento [risartʃi'mento] sm: **~ (di)** compensation (for); **aver diritto al ~ dei danni** to be entitled to damages

risar'cire [risar'tʃire] /55/ vt (cose) to pay compensation for; (persona): **~ qn di qc** to compensate sb for sth

ri'sata sf laugh

riscalda'mento sm heating; **~ centrale** central heating

riscal'dare /72/ vt (scaldare) to heat; (: mani, persona) to warm; (minestra) to reheat; **riscaldarsi** vpr to warm up

ris'catto sm ransom; redemption
rischia'rare [riskja'rare] /72/ vt
(illuminare) to light up; (colore) to
make lighter; **rischiararsi** vpr (tempo)
to clear up; (cielo) to clear; (fig: volto)
to brighten up; **rischiararsi la voce**
to clear one's throat
rischi'are [ris'kjare] /19/ vt to risk
▷ vi: **~ di fare qc** to risk o run the risk
of doing sth
'rischio ['riskjo] sm risk; **rischi'oso,
-a** ag risky, dangerous
risciac'quare /72/ vt to rinse
riscon'trare /72/ vt (rilevare) to find
riscri'vibile ag (CD, DVD) rewritable
riscu'otere /106/ vt (ritirare una
somma dovuta) to collect; (: stipendio)
to draw, collect; (assegno) to cash;
(fig: successo ecc) to win, earn
'rise ecc vb vedi **ridere**
risenti'mento sm resentment
risen'tire /45/ vt to hear again;
(provare) to feel ▷ vi: **~ di** to feel (o
show) the effects of; **risentirsi** vpr:
risentirsi di o **per** to take offence
(BRIT) o offense (US) at, resent;
risen'tito, -a ag resentful
ri'serbo ecc vb vedi **ridere**
ri'serva sf reserve; (di caccia, pesca)
preserve; (restrizione, di indigeni)
reservation; **tenere di ~** to keep
in reserve
riser'vare /72/ vt (tenere in serbo) to
keep, put aside; (prenotare) to book,
reserve; **riser'vato, -a** ag (prenotato:
fig: persona) reserved; (confidenziale)
confidential
'risi ecc vb vedi **ridere**
risi'edere /29/ vi: **~ a** o **in** to reside in
'risma sf (di carta) ream; (fig) kind,
sort
'riso¹, -a pp di **ridere** ▷ sm (il ridere): **un
~** a laugh; **il ~** laughter
'riso² sm (pianta) rice
riso'lino sm snigger
ri'solsi ecc vb vedi **risolvere**
ri'solto, -a pp di **risolvere**
riso'luto, -a ag determined, resolute

risoluzi'one [risolut'tsjone] sf
solving no pl; (Mat) solution;
(decisione, di schermo, immagine)
resolution
ri'solvere /94/ vt (difficoltà,
controversia) to resolve; (problema) to
solve; (decidere): **~ di fare** to resolve
to do; **risolversi** vpr (decidersi):
risolversi a fare to make up
one's mind to do; (andare a finire):
risolversi in to end up, turn out;
risolversi in nulla to come to
nothing
riso'nanza [riso'nantsa] sf
resonance; **aver vasta ~** (fig) (fatto
ecc) to be known far and wide
ri'sorgere [ri'sordʒere] /109/ vi
to rise again; **risorgi'mento** sm
revival; **il Risorgimento** (Storia) the
Risorgimento

⬤ **RISORGIMENTO**
⬤
⬤
⬤ The Risorgimento, the period
⬤ stretching from the early
⬤ nineteenth century to 1861 and the
⬤ proclamation of the Kingdom of
⬤ Italy, saw considerable upheaval
⬤ and change. Political and
⬤ personal freedom took on new
⬤ importance as the events of the
⬤ French Revolution unfolded. The
⬤ Risorgimento paved the way for the
⬤ unification of Italy in 1871.

ri'sorsa sf expedient, resort; **risorse
umane** human resources
ri'sorsi ecc vb vedi **risorgere**
ri'sotto sm (Cuc) risotto
risparmi'are /19/ vt to save; (non
uccidere) to spare ▷ vi to save; **~ qc a
qn** to spare sb sth
ris'parmio sm saving no pl; (denaro)
savings pl; **risparmi** smpl (denaro)
savings
rispecchi'are [rispek'kjare] /19/ vt
to reflect
rispet'tabile ag respectable

rispet'tare /72/ vt to respect; **farsi ~** to command respect

rispet'tivo, -a ag respective

ris'petto sm respect; **rispetti** smpl (saluti) respects, regards; **~ a** (in paragone a) compared to; (in relazione a) as regards, as for

ris'pondere /95/ vi to answer, reply; (freni) to respond; **~ a** (domanda) to answer, reply to; (persona) to answer; (invito) to reply to; (provocazione, veicolo, apparecchio) to respond to; (corrispondere a) to correspond to; (speranze, bisogno) to answer; **~ a qn di qc** (essere responsabile) to be answerable to sb for sth

ris'posto, -a pp di **rispondere** ▷ sf answer, reply; **in risposta a** in reply to

'rissa sf brawl

ris'tampa sf reprinting no pl; reprint

risto'rante sm restaurant

ris'tretto, -a pp di **restringere** ▷ ag (racchiuso) enclosed, hemmed in; (angusto) narrow; (Cuc: brodo) thick; (: caffè) extra strong; **~ (a)** (limitato) restricted o limited (to)

ristruttu'rare /72/ vt (azienda) to reorganize; (edificio) to restore; (appartamento) to alter; (crema, balsamo) to repair

risucchi'are [risuk'kjare] /19/ vt to suck in

risul'tare /72/ vi (dimostrarsi) to prove (to be), turn out (to be); (riuscire): **~ vincitore** to emerge as the winner; **~ da** (provenire) to result from, be the result of; **mi risulta che ...** I understand that ...; **non mi risulta** not as far as I know; **risul'tato** sm result

risuo'nare /72/ vi (rimbombare) to resound

risurrezi'one [risurret'tsjone] sf (Rel) resurrection

risusci'tare [risuʃʃi'tare] /72/ vt to resuscitate, restore to life; (fig) to revive, bring back ▷ vi to rise (from the dead)

ris'veglio [riz'veʎʎo] sm waking up; (fig) revival

ris'volto sm (di giacca) lapel; (di pantaloni) turn-up; (di manica) cuff; (di tasca) flap; (di libro) inside flap; (fig) implication

ritagli'are [rita'ʎʎare] /27/ vt (tagliar via) to cut out

ritar'dare /72/ vi (persona, treno) to be late; (orologio) to be slow ▷ vt (rallentare) to slow down; (impedire) to delay, hold up; (differire) to postpone, delay

ri'tardo sm delay; (di persona aspettata) lateness no pl; (fig: mentale) learning difficulty; **in ~** late

ri'tegno [ri'teɲɲo] sm restraint

rite'nere /121/ vt (trattenere) to hold back; (: somma) to deduct; (giudicare) to consider, believe

ri'tengo vb vedi **ritenere**

ri'tenni ecc vb vedi **ritenere**

riterrò ecc vb vedi **ritenere**

ritiene ecc vb vedi **ritenere**

riti'rare /72/ vt to withdraw; (Pol: richiamare) to recall; (andare a prendere: pacco ecc) to collect, pick up; **ritirarsi** vpr to withdraw; (da un'attività) to retire; (stoffa) to shrink; (marea) to recede

'ritmo sm rhythm; (fig) rate; (: della vita) pace, tempo

'rito sm rite; **di ~** usual, customary

ritoc'care /20/ vt (disegno, fotografia) to touch up; (testo) to alter

ritor'nare /72/ vi to return, go (o come) back, get back; (ripresentarsi) to recur; (ridiventare): **~ ricco** to become rich again ▷ vt (restituire) to return, give back

ritor'nello sm refrain

ri'torno sm return; **essere di ~** to be back; **avere un ~ di fiamma** (Aut) to backfire; (fig: persona) to be back in love again

ri'trarre /123/ vt (trarre indietro, via) to withdraw; (distogliere: sguardo) to turn away; (*rappresentare*) to portray, depict; (*ricavare*) to get, obtain

ritrat'tare /72/ *vt* (*disdire*) to retract, take back; (*trattare nuovamente*) to deal with again

ri'tratto, -a *pp di* **ritrarre** ▷ *sm* portrait

ritro'vare /72/ *vt* to find; (*salute*) to regain; (*persona*) to find; to meet again; **ritrovarsi** *vpr* (*essere, capitare*) to find o.s.; (*raccapezzarsi*) to find one's way; (*con senso reciproco*) to meet (again)

'ritto, -a *ag* (*in piedi*) standing, on one's feet; (*levato in alto*) erect, raised; (: *capelli*) standing on end; (*posto verticalmente*) upright

ritu'ale *ag, sm* ritual

riuni'one *sf* (*adunanza*) meeting; (*riconciliazione*) reunion

riu'nire /55/ *vt* (*ricongiungere*) to join (together); (*riconciliare*) to reunite, bring together (again); **riunirsi** *vpr* (*adunarsi*) to meet; (*tornare a stare insieme*) to be reunited

riu'scire [riuʃʃire] /125/ *vi* (*uscire di nuovo*) to go out again, go back out; (*aver esito: fatti, azioni*) to go, turn out; (*aver successo*) to succeed, be successful; (*essere, apparire*) to be, prove; (*raggiungere il fine*) to manage, succeed; **~ a fare qc** to manage *o* be able to do sth

'riva *sf* (*di fiume*) bank; (*di lago, mare*) shore

ri'vale *smf* rival; **rivalità** *sf* rivalry

rivalu'tare /72/ *vt* (*Econ*) to revalue

rive'dere /127/ *vt* to see again; (*ripassare*) to revise; (*verificare*) to check

'ivedrò *ecc vb vedi* **rivedere**

ive'lare /72/ *vt* to reveal; (*divulgare*) to reveal, disclose; (*dare indizio*) to reveal, show; **rivelarsi** *vpr* (*manifestarsi*) to be revealed; **rivelarsi onesto** *ecc* to prove to be honest *etc*; **rivelazi'one** *sf* revelation

rivendi'care /20/ *vt* to claim, demand

rivendi'tore, -'trice *smf* retailer; **~ autorizzato** (*Comm*) authorized dealer

ri'verbero *sm* (*di luce, calore*) reflection; (*di suono*) reverberation

rivesti'mento *sm* covering; coating

rives'tire /45/ *vt* to dress again; (*ricoprire*) to cover; (*con vernice*) to coat; (*fig: carica*) to hold

ri'vidi *ecc vb vedi* **rivedere**

ri'vincita [ri'vintʃita] *sf* (*Sport*) return match; (*fig*) revenge

ri'vista *sf* review; (*periodico*) magazine, review; (*Teat*) revue; variety show

ri'volgere [ri'vɔldʒere] /96/ *vt* (*attenzione, sguardo*) to turn, direct; (*parole*) to address; **rivolgersi** *vpr* to turn round; **rivolgersi a** (*fig*) (*dirigersi per informazioni*) to go and see, go and speak to; (*ufficio*) to enquire at

ri'volsi *ecc vb vedi* **rivolgere**

ri'volta *sf* revolt, rebellion

rivol'tella *sf* revolver

rivoluzio'nare [rivoluttsjo'nare] /72/ *vt* to revolutionize

rivoluzio'nario, -a [rivoluttsjo'narjo] *ag, sm/f* revolutionary

rivoluzi'one [rivolut'tsjone] *sf* revolution

riz'zare [rit'tsare] /72/ *vt* to raise, erect; **rizzarsi** *vpr* to stand up; (*capelli*) to stand on end

'roba *sf* stuff, things *pl*; (*possessi, beni*) belongings *pl*, things *pl*, possessions *pl*; **~ da mangiare** things to eat, food; **~ da matti!** it's sheer madness *o* lunacy!

'robot *sm inv* robot

ro'busto, -a *ag* robust, sturdy; (*solido: catena*) strong

roc'chetto [rok'ketto] *sm* reel, spool

'roccia, -ce ['rɔttʃa] *sf* rock; **fare ~** (*Sport*) to go rock climbing

'roco, -a, -chi, -che *ag* hoarse

ro'daggio [ro'daddʒo] *sm* running (BRIT) *o* breaking (US) in; **in ~** running *o* breaking in

rodi'tore *sm* (*Zool*) rodent

rodo'dendro *sm* rhododendron

ro'gnone [roɲ'ɲone] *sm* (*Cuc*) kidney

'rogo, -ghi *sm* (*per cadaveri*) (funeral) pyre; (*supplizio*): **il ~** the stake

rol'lio *sm* roll(ing)

'Roma *sf* Rome

Roma'nia *sf*: **la ~** Romania

ro'manico, -a, -ci, -che *ag* Romanesque

ro'mano, -a *ag, sm/f* Roman

ro'mantico, -a, -ci, -che *ag* romantic

romanzi'ere [roman'dzjɛre] *sm* novelist

ro'manzo, -a [ro'mandzo] *ag* (*Ling*) romance *cpd* ▷ *sm* novel; **~ d'appendice** serial (story); **~ poliziesco, ~ giallo** detective story; **~ rosa** romantic novel

'rombo *sm* rumble, thunder, roar; (*Mat*) rhombus; (*Zool*) turbot; brill

'rompere /97/ *vt* to break; (*conversazione, fidanzamento*) to break off ▷ *vi* to break; **rompersi** *vpr* to break; **mi rompe le scatole** (*fam*) he (*o* she) is a pain in the neck; **rompersi un braccio** to break an arm; **rompis'catole** *smf inv* (*fam*) pest, pain in the neck

'rondine *sf* (*Zool*) swallow

ron'zare [ron'dzare] /72/ *vi* to buzz, hum

ron'zio, -ii [ron'dzio] *sm* buzzing

'rosa *sf* rose ▷ *ag inv*, *sm* pink; **ro'sato, -a** *ag* pink, rosy ▷ *sm* (*vino*) rosé (wine)

rosicchi'are [rosik'kjare] /19/ *vt* to gnaw (at); (*mangiucchiare*) to nibble (at)

rosma'rino *sm* rosemary

roso'lare /72/ *vt* (*Cuc*) to brown

roso'lia *sf* (*Med*) German measles *sg*, rubella

ro'sone *sm* rosette; (*vetrata*) rose window

'rospo *sm* (*Zool*) toad

ros'setto *sm* (*per labbra*) lipstick

'rosso, -a *ag, sm, sm/f* red; **il mar R~** the Red Sea; **~ d'uovo** egg yolk

rosticce'ria [rostittʃe'ria] *sf* shop selling roast meat and other cooked food

ro'taia *sf* rut, track; (*Ferr*) rail

ro'tella *sf* small wheel; (*di mobile*) castor

roto'lare /72/ *vt, vi* to roll; **rotolarsi** *vpr* to roll (about)

'rotolo *sm* roll; **andare a rotoli** (*fig*) to go to rack and ruin

ro'tondo, -a *ag* round

'rotta *sf* (*Aer, Naut*) course, route; (*Mil*) rout; **a ~ di collo** at breakneck speed; **essere in ~ con qn** to be on bad terms with sb

rotta'mare /72/ *vt* to scrap old vehicles in return for incentives

rottama'zione [rottamat'tsjone] *sf* (*come incentivo*) the scrapping of old vehicles in return for incentives

rot'tame *sm* fragment, scrap, broken bit; **rottami** *smpl* (*di nave aereo ecc*) wreckage *sg*

'rotto, -a *pp di* **rompere** ▷ *ag* broken; (*calzoni*) torn, split ▷ *sm*: **per il ~ della cuffia** by the skin of one's teeth

rot'tura *sf* breaking *no pl*; break; (*di rapporti*) breaking off; (*Med*) fracture, break

rou'lotte [ru'lɔt] *sf inv* caravan

ro'vente *ag* red-hot

'rovere *sm* oak

ro'vescia [ro'veʃʃa] *sf*: **alla ~** upside-down; inside-out; **oggi mi va tutto alla ~** everything is going wrong (for me) today

rovesci'are [roveʃʃare] /14/ *vt* (*versare in giù*) to pour; (*: accidentalmente*) to spill; (*capovolgere*) to turn upside down; (*gettare a terra*) to knock down; (*fig: governo*) to overthrow; (*piegare all'indietro: testa*) to throw back;

rovesciarsi vpr (sedia, macchina) to overturn; (barca) to capsize; (liquido) to spill; (fig: situazione) to be reversed
ro'vescio [ro'vɛʃʃo] sm other side, wrong side; (della mano) back; (di moneta) reverse; (pioggia) sudden downpour; (fig) setback; (Maglia: anche: **punto ~**) purl (stitch); (Tennis) backhand (stroke); **a ~** upside-down; (con l'esterno all'interno) inside-out; **capire qc a ~** to misunderstand sth
ro'vina; **rovine** sfpl (ruderi) ruins; **andare in ~** (andare a pezzi) to collapse; (fig) to go to rack and ruin; **mandare qc/qn in ~** to ruin sth/sb
rovi'nare /72/ vi to collapse, fall down ▷ vt (danneggiare: fig) to ruin; **rovinarsi** vpr (persona) to ruin o.s.; (oggetto, vestito) to be ruined
rovis'tare /72/ vt (casa) to ransack; (tasche) to rummage in (o through)
'rovo sm (Bot) blackberry o bramble bush
'rozzo, -a ['roddzo] ag rough, coarse
ru'bare /72/ vt to steal; **~ qc a qn** to steal sth from sb
rubi'netto sm tap, faucet (US)
ru'bino sm ruby
ru'brica, -che sf (di giornale) column; (quadernetto) index book; address book; **~ d'indirizzi** address book; **~ telefonica** list of telephone numbers
rudere sm (rovina) ruins pl
rudimen'tale ag rudimentary, basic
rudi'menti smpl rudiments; basic principles; basic knowledge sg
ruffi'ano sm pimp
ruga, -ghe sf wrinkle
ruggine ['ruddʒine] sf rust
rug'gire [rud'dʒire] /55/ vi to roar
rugi'ada [ru'dʒada] sf dew
ru'goso, -a ag wrinkled
rul'lino sm (Fot) (roll of) film, spool
rullo sm (di tamburi) roll; (arnese cilindrico, Tip) roller; **~ compressore** steam roller; **~ di pellicola** roll of film
rum sm rum
ru'meno, -a ag, sm/f, sm Romanian

rumi'nare /72/ vt (Zool) to ruminate
ru'more sm: **un ~** a noise, a sound; **il ~** noise; **rumo'roso, -a** ag noisy
Attenzione! In inglese esiste la parola rumour, che però significa voce nel senso di diceria.
ru'olo sm (Teat, fig) role, part; (elenco) roll, register, list; **di ~** permanent, on the permanent staff
ru'ota sf wheel; **~ anteriore/posteriore** front/back wheel; **~ di scorta** spare wheel
ruo'tare /72/ vt, vi to rotate
'rupe sf cliff
'ruppi ecc vb vedi **rompere**
ru'rale ag rural, country cpd
ru'scello [ruʃʃello] sm stream
'ruspa sf excavator
rus'sare /72/ vi to snore
'Russia sf: **la ~** Russia; **'russo, -a** ag, sm/f, sm Russian
'rustico, -a, -ci, -che ag rustic; (fig) rough, unrefined
rut'tare /72/ vi to belch; **'rutto** sm belch
'ruvido, -a ag rough, coarse

S

S. *abbr* (= sud) S; (= santo) St

sa *vb vedi* **sapere**

'sabato *sm* Saturday; **di** *o* **il ~ on** Saturdays

'sabbia *sf* sand; **sabbie mobili** quicksand(s pl); **sabbi'oso, -a** *ag* sandy

'sacca, -che *sf* bag; (*bisaccia*) haversack; **~ da viaggio** travelling bag

sacca'rina *sf* saccharin(e)

saccheggi'are [sakked'dʒare] /62/ *vt* to sack, plunder

sac'chetto [sak'ketto] *sm* (small) bag; (small) sack; **~ di carta/di plastica** paper/plastic bag

'sacco, -chi *sm* bag; (*per carbone ecc*) sack; (*Anat, Biol*) sac; (*tela*) sacking; (*saccheggio*) sack(ing); (*fig: grande quantità*): **un ~ di** lots of, heaps of; **~ a pelo** sleeping bag; **~ per i rifiuti** bin bag

sacer'dote [satʃer'dɔte] *sm* priest

sacrifi'care /20/ *vt* to sacrifice; **sacrificarsi** *vpr* to sacrifice o.s.; (*privarsi di qc*) to make sacrifices

sacri'ficio [sakri'fitʃo] *sm* sacrifice

'sacro, -a *ag* sacred

'sadico, -a, -ci, -che *ag* sadistic ▷ *sm/f* sadist

sa'etta *sf* arrow; (*fulmine*) thunderbolt; flash of lightning

sa'fari *sm inv* safari

sag'gezza [sad'dʒettsa] *sf* wisdom

'saggio, -a, -gi, -ge ['saddʒo] *ag* wise ▷ *sm* (*persona*) sage; (*operazione sperimentale*) test; (*fig: prova*) proof; (*campione indicativo*) sample; (*scritto*) essay

Sagit'tario [sadʒit'tarjo] *sm* Sagittarius

'sagoma *sf* (*profilo*) outline, profile; (*forma*) form, shape; (*Tecn*) template; (*bersaglio*) target; (*fig: persona*) character

'sagra *sf* festival

sagres'tano *sm* sacristan; sexton

sagres'tia *sf* sacristy

Sa'hara [sa'ara] *sm*: **il (Deserto del) ~** the Sahara (Desert)

sai *vb vedi* **sapere**

'sala *sf* hall; (*stanza*) room; (*Cine: di proiezione*) cinema; **~ d'aspetto** waiting room; **~ da ballo** ballroom; **~ per concerti** concert hall; **~ giochi** amusement arcade; **~ operatoria** operating theatre (BRIT) *o* room (US); **~ da pranzo** dining room

sa'lame *sm* salami *no pl*, salami sausage

sala'moia *sf* (*Cuc*) brine

sa'lato, -a *ag* (*sapore*) salty; (*Cuc*) salted, salt *cpd*; (*fig: prezzi*) steep, stiff

sal'dare /72/ *vt* (*congiungere*) to join, bind; (*parti metalliche*) to solder; (: *con saldatura autogena*) to weld; (*conto*) to settle, pay

'saldo, -a *ag* (*resistente, forte*) strong, firm; (*fermo*) firm, steady, stable; (*fig*) firm, steadfast ▷ *sm* (*svendita*) sale; (*di conto*) settlement; (*Econ*) balance;

saldi *smpl* (Comm) sales; **essere ~ nella propria fede** (fig) to stick to one's guns

'**sale** *sm* salt; **ha poco ~ in zucca** he doesn't have much sense; **~ grosso** cooking salt; **~ fino** table salt

'**salgo** *ecc vb vedi* **salire**

'**salice** ['salitʃe] *sm* willow; **~ piangente** weeping willow

sali'ente *ag* (fig) salient, main

sali'era *sf* salt cellar

sa'lire /98/ *vi* to go (o come) up; (aereo ecc) to climb, go up; (passeggero) to get on; (sentiero, prezzi, livello) to go up, rise ▷ *vt* (scale, gradini) to go (o come) up; **~ su** to climb (up); **~ sul treno/sull'autobus** to board the train/the bus; **~ in macchina** to get into the car; **sa'lita** *sf* climb, ascent; (erta) hill, slope; **in salita** *ag, av* uphill

sa'liva *sf* saliva

'**salma** *sf* corpse

'**salmo** *sm* psalm

sal'mone *sm* salmon

sa'lone *sm* (stanza) sitting room, lounge; (in albergo) lounge; (su nave) lounge, saloon; (mostra) show, exhibition; **~ di bellezza** beauty salon

sa'lotto *sm* lounge, sitting room; (mobilio) lounge suite

sal'pare /72/ *vi* (Naut) to set sail; (anche: **~ l'ancora**) to weigh anchor

'**salsa** *sf* (Cuc) sauce; **~ di pomodoro** tomato sauce

sal'siccia, -ce [sal'sittʃa] *sf* pork sausage

sal'tare /72/ *vi* to jump, leap; (esplodere) to blow up, explode; (: **valvola**) to blow; (venir via) to pop off; (non aver luogo: corso ecc) to be cancelled ▷ *vt* to jump (over), leap (over); (fig: pranzo, capitolo) to skip, miss (out); (Cuc) to sauté; **far ~** to blow up; to burst open; **~ fuori** to turn up

saltel'lare /72/ *vi* to skip; to hop

'**salto** *sm* jump; (Sport) jumping; **fare un ~** to jump, leap; **fare un ~ da qn** to pop over to sb's (place); **~ in alto/lungo** high/long jump; **~ con l'asta** pole vaulting; **~ mortale** somersault

saltu'ario, -a *ag* occasional, irregular

sa'lubre *ag* healthy, salubrious

sa'lume *sm* (Cuc) cured pork; **salumi** *smpl* cured pork meats

salume'ria *sf* delicatessen

salu'tare /72/ *ag* healthy; (fig) salutary, beneficial ▷ *vt* (per dire buon giorno, fig) to greet; (per dire addio) to say goodbye to; (Mil) to salute

sa'lute *sf* health; **~!** (a chi starnutisce) bless you!; (nei brindisi) cheers!; **bere alla ~ di qn** to drink (to) sb's health

sa'luto *sm* (gesto) wave; (parola) greeting; (Mil) salute

salvada'naio *sm* moneybox, piggy bank

salva'gente [salva'dʒɛnte] *sm* (Naut) lifebuoy; (stradale: pl inv) traffic island; **~ a ciambella** lifebelt; **~ a giubbotto** lifejacket (BRIT), life preserver (US)

salvaguar'dare /72/ *vt* to safeguard

sal'vare /72/ *vt* to save; (trarre da un pericolo) to rescue; (proteggere) to protect; **salvarsi** *vpr* to save o.s.; to escape; **salvas'chermo** *sm* (Inform) screen saver; **salva'slip** *sm inv* panty liner; **salva'taggio** *sm* rescue

'**salve** *escl* (fam) hi!

'**salvia** *sf* (Bot) sage

salvi'etta *sf* napkin; **~ umidificata** baby wipe

'**salvo, -a** *ag* safe, unhurt, unharmed; (fuori pericolo) safe, out of danger ▷ *sm*: **in ~** = safe ▷ *prep* (eccetto) except; **~ che** (a meno che) unless; (eccetto che) except (that); **mettere qc in ~** to put sth in a safe place; **~ imprevisti** barring accidents

sam'buco *sm* elder (tree)

'**sandalo** *sm* (Bot) sandalwood; (calzatura) sandal

'**sangue** *sm* blood; **farsi cattivo ~** to fret, get worked up; **~ freddo** (fig)

sang-froid, calm; **a ~ freddo** in cold
blood; **sangui'nare** /72/ *vi* to bleed
sanità *sf* health; (*salubrità*)
healthiness; **Ministero della S~**
Department of Health; **~ mentale**
sanity
sani'tario, -a *ag* health *cpd*;
(*condizioni*) sanitary ▷ *sm* (*Amm*)
doctor; **sanitari** (*impianti*) bathroom
o sanitary fittings
'sanno *vb vedi* **sapere**
'sano, -a *ag* healthy; (*denti,
costituzione*) healthy, sound; (*integro*)
whole, unbroken; (*fig: politica,
consigli*) sound; **~ di mente** sane; **di
sana pianta** completely, entirely; **~
e salvo** safe and sound
San Silvestro [san sil'vestro] *sm*
(*giorno*) New Year's Eve
'santo, -a *ag* holy; (*fig*) saintly;
(*seguito da nome proprio: dav sm* **san**
+ C, **sant'** +V, **santo** + *s impura, gn,
pn, ps, x, z; dav sf* **santa** + C, **sant'** +
V) saint ▷ *sm/f* saint; **la Santa Sede**
the Holy See
santu'ario *sm* sanctuary
sanzi'one [san'tsjone] *sf* sanction;
(*penale, civile*) sanction, penalty
sa'pere /99/ *vt* to know; (*essere capace
di*): **so nuotare** I know how to swim,
I can swim ▷ *vi*: **~ di** (*aver sapore*) to
taste of; (*aver odore*) to smell of ▷ *sm*
knowledge; **far ~ qc a qn** to inform
sb about sth, let sb know sth; **mi sa
che non sia vero** I don't think that's
true; **non lo so** I don't know; **non so
l'inglese** I don't speak English
sa'pone *sm* soap; **~ da bucato**
washing soap
sa'pore *sm* taste, flavour; **sapo'rito,
-a** *ag* tasty
sappi'amo *vb vedi* **sapere**
saprò *ecc vb vedi* **sapere**
sarà *ecc vb vedi* **essere**
saraci'nesca, -sche [saratʃi'neska]
sf (*serranda*) rolling shutter
sar'castico, -a, -ci, -che *ag*
sarcastic

Sar'degna [sar'deɲɲa] *sf*: **la ~**
Sardinia
sar'dina *sf* sardine
'sardo, -a *ag, sm/f* Sardinian
sa'rei *ecc vb vedi* **essere**
SARS *sf* (= *severe acute respiratory
syndrome*) SARS
'sarta *sf vedi* **sarto**
'sarto, -a *sm/f* tailor/dressmaker
'sasso *sm* stone; (*ciottolo*) pebble;
(*masso*) rock
sas'sofono *sm* saxophone
sas'soso, -a *ag* stony; pebbly
'Satana *sm* Satan
satelli'tare *ag* satellite *cpd*
sa'tellite *sm, ag* satellite
'satira *sf* satire
'sauna *sf* sauna
sazi'are [sat'tsjare] /19/ *vt* to satisfy,
satiate; **saziarsi** *vpr*: **saziarsi (di)** to
eat one's fill (of); (*fig*): **saziarsi di** to
grow tired o weary of
'sazio, -a ['sattsjo] *ag*: **~ (di)** sated
(with), full (of); (*fig: stufo*) fed up
(with), sick (of); **sono ~** I'm full (up)
sba'dato, -a *ag* careless, inattentive
sbadigli'are [zbadiʎ'ʎare] /27/ *vi* to
yawn; **sba'diglio** *sm* yawn
sbagli'are [zbaʎ'ʎare] /27/ *vt* to make
a mistake in, get wrong ▷ *vi* to make
a mistake (o mistakes), be mistaken;
(*ingannarsi*) to be wrong; (*operare in
modo non giusto*) to err; **sbagliarsi**
vpr to make a mistake, be mistaken,
be wrong; **~ la mira/strada** to miss
one's target/take the wrong road
sbagli'ato, -a [zbaʎ'ʎato] *ag* (*gen*)
wrong; (*compito*) full of mistakes;
(*conclusione*) erroneous
'sbaglio *sm* mistake, error; (*morale*)
error; **fare uno ~** to make a mistake
sbalor'dire /55/ *vt* to stun, amaze
▷ *vi* to be stunned, be amazed
sbal'zare [zbal'tsare] /72/ *vt* to
throw, hurl ▷ *vi* (*balzare*) to bounce;
(*saltare*) to leap, bound
sban'dare /72/ *vi* (*Naut*) to list; (*Aut*)
to skid; (*Aer*) to bank

sba'raglio [zbaˈraʎʎo] *sm* rout; defeat; **gettarsi allo ~** to risk everything

sbaraz'zarsi [zbaratˈtsarsi] /72/ *vpr*: **~ di** to get rid of, rid o.s. of

sbar'care /20/ *vt* (*passeggeri*) to disembark; (*merci*) to unload ▷ *vi* to disembark

'sbarra *sf* bar; (*di passaggio a livello*) barrier; (*Dir*): **mettere/presentarsi alla ~** to bring/appear before the court

sbar'rare /72/ *vt* (*strada ecc*) to block, bar; (*assegno*) to cross; **~ il passo** to bar the way; **~ gli occhi** to open one's eyes wide

'sbattere /1/ *vt* (*porta*) to bang, slam; (*tappeti, ali, Cuc*) to beat; (*urtare*) to knock, hit ▷ *vi* (*porta, finestra*) to bang; (*agitarsi: ali, vele ecc*) to flap; **me ne sbatto!** (*fam*) I don't give a damn!

sba'vare /72/ *vi* to dribble; (*colore*) to smear, smudge

'sberla *sf* slap

sbia'dire /55/ *vi* to fade ▷ *vt* to fade; **sbia'dito, -a** *ag* faded; (*fig*) colourless, dull

sbian'care /20/ *vt* to whiten; (*tessuto*) to bleach ▷ *vi* (*impallidire*) to grow pale *o* white

sbirci'ata [zbirˈtʃata] *sf*: **dare una ~ a qc** to glance at sth, have a look at sth

sbloc'care /20/ *vt* to unblock, free; (*freno*) to release; (*prezzi, affitti*) to free from controls; **sbloccarsi** *vpr* (*gen*) to become unblocked; (*passaggio, strada*) to clear, become unblocked

sboc'care /20/ *vi*: **~ in** (*fiume*) to flow into; (*strada*) to lead into; (*persona*) to come (out) into; (*fig: concludersi*) to end (up) in

sboc'cato, -a *ag* (*persona*) foul-mouthed; (*linguaggio*) foul

sbocci'are [zbotˈtʃare] /14/ *vi* (*fiore*) to bloom, open (out)

sbol'lire /55/ *vi* (*fig*) to cool down, calm down

'sbornia *sf* (*fam*): **prendersi una ~** to get plastered

sbor'sare /72/ *vt* (*denaro*) to pay out

sbot'tare /72/ *vi*: **~ in una risata/ per la collera** to burst out laughing/ explode with anger

sbotto'nare /72/ *vt* to unbutton, undo

sbrai'tare /72/ *vi* to yell, bawl

sbra'nare /72/ *vt* to tear to pieces

sbricio'lare [zbritʃoˈlare] /72/ *vt*, **sbricio'larsi** *vpr* to crumble

sbri'gare /80/ *vt* to deal with; **sbrigarsi** *vpr* to hurry (up)

'sbronza [ˈzbrontsa] (*fam*) *sf* (*ubriaco*): **prendersi una ~** to get plastered

sbron'zarsi [zbronˈtsarsi] /72/ *vpr* (*fam*) to get plastered

'sbronzo, -a [ˈzbrontso] *ag* (*fam*) plastered

sbruf'fone, -a *sm/f* boaster

sbu'care /20/ *vi* to come out, emerge; (*improvvisamente*) to pop out (*o* up)

sbucci'are [zbutˈtʃare] /14/ *vt* (*arancia, patata*) to peel; (*piselli*) to shell; **sbucciarsi un ginocchio** to graze one's knee

sbucherò *ecc* [zbukeˈrɔ] *vb vedi* **sbucare**

sbuf'fare /72/ *vi* (*persona, cavallo*) to snort; (*: ansimare*) to puff, pant; (*treno*) to puff

sca'broso, -a *ag* (*fig: difficile*) difficult, thorny; (*: imbarazzante*) embarrassing; (*: sconcio*) indecent

scacchi'era [skakˈkjɛra] *sf* chessboard

scacci'are [skatˈtʃare] /14/ *vt* to chase away *o* out, drive away *o* out

'scaddi *ecc vb vedi* **scadere**

sca'dente *ag* shoddy, of poor quality

sca'denza [skaˈdɛntsa] *sf* (*di cambiale, contratto*) maturity; (*di passaporto*) expiry date; **a breve/ lunga ~** short-/long-term; **data di ~** expiry date

sca'dere /18/ *vi (contratto ecc)* to expire; *(debito)* to fall due; *(valore, forze, peso)* to decline, go down

sca'fandro *sm (di palombaro)* diving suit; *(di astronauta)* spacesuit

scaf'fale *sm* shelf; *(mobile)* set of shelves

'scafo *sm (Naut, Aer)* hull

scagio'nare [skadʒo'nare] /72/ *vt* to exonerate, free from blame

'scaglia ['skaʎʎa] *sf (Zool)* scale; *(scheggia)* chip, flake

scagli'are [skaʎ'ʎare] /27/ *vt (lanciare: anche fig)* to hurl, fling; **scagliarsi** *vpr*: **scagliarsi su** *o* **contro** to hurl *o* fling o.s. at; *(fig)* to rail at

'scala *sf (a gradini ecc)* staircase, stairs *pl*; *(a pioli, di corda)* ladder; *(Mus, Geo, di colori, valori, fig)* scale; **scale** *sfpl (scalinata)* stairs; **su larga** *o* **vasta ~** on a large scale; **su ~ ridotta** on a small scale; **~ a libretto** stepladder; **~ mobile** escalator; *(Econ)* sliding scale; **~ mobile (dei salari)** index-linked pay scale

sca'lare /72/ *vt (Alpinismo, muro)* to climb, scale; *(debito)* to scale down, reduce

scalda'bagno [skalda'baɲɲo] *sm* water heater

scal'dare /72/ *vt* to heat; **scaldarsi** *vpr* to warm up, heat up; *(al fuoco, al sole)* to warm o.s.; *(fig)* to get excited

scal'fire /55/ *vt* to scratch

scali'nata *sf* staircase

sca'lino *sm (anche fig)* step; *(di scala a pioli)* rung

'scalo *sm (Naut)* slipway; *(: porto d'approdo)* port of call; *(Aer)* stopover; **fare ~ (a)** *(Naut)* to call (at), put in (at); *(Aer)* to land (at), make a stop (at); **~ merci** *(Ferr)* goods *(BRIT)* o freight yard

scalop'pina *sf (Cuc)* escalope

scal'pello *sm* chisel

scal'pore *sm* noise, row; **far ~** *(notizia)* to cause a sensation *o* a stir

'scaltro, -a *ag* cunning, shrewd

'scalzo, -a ['skaltso] *ag* barefoot

scambi'are /19/ *vt* to exchange; *(confondere)*: **~ qn/qc per** to take *o* mistake sb/sth for; **mi hanno scambiato il cappello** they've given me the wrong hat; **scambiarsi** *vpr (auguri, confidenze, visite)* to exchange

'scambio *sm* exchange; *(Ferr)* points *pl*: **fare (uno) ~** to make a swap

scampa'gnata [skampaɲ'ɲata] *sf* trip to the country

scam'pare /72/ *vt (salvare)* to rescue, save; *(evitare: morte, prigione)* to escape ▷ *vi*: **~ (a qc)** to survive (sth), escape (sth); **scamparla bella** to have a narrow escape

'scampo *sm (salvezza)* escape; *(Zool)* prawn; **cercare ~ nella fuga** to seek safety in flight

'scampolo *sm* remnant

scanala'tura *sf (incavo)* channel, groove

scandagli'are [skandaʎ'ʎare] /27/ *vt (Naut)* to sound; *(fig)* to sound out; to probe

scandaliz'zare [skandalid'dzare] /72/ *vt* to shock, scandalize; **scandalizzarsi** *vpr* to be shocked

'scandalo *sm* scandal

Scandi'navia *sf*: **la ~** Scandinavia; **scandi'navo, -a** *ag, sm/f* Scandinavian

'scanner ['skanner] *sm inv* scanner

scansafa'tiche [skansafa'tike] *smf inv* idler, loafer

scan'sare /72/ *vt (rimuovere)* to move (aside), shift; *(schivare: schiaffo)* to dodge; *(sfuggire)* to avoid; **scansarsi** *vpr* to move aside

scan'sia *sf* shelves *pl*; *(per libri)* bookcase

'scanso *sm*: **a ~ di** in order to avoid, as a precaution against

scanti'nato *sm* basement

scapacci'one [skapat'tʃone] *sm* clout

scapes'trato, -a *ag* dissolute

'scapola sf shoulder blade

'scapolo sm bachelor

scappa'mento sm (Aut) exhaust

scap'pare /72/ vi (fuggire) to escape; (andare via in fretta) to rush off; **~ di prigione** to escape from prison; **~ di mano** (oggetto) to slip out of one's hands; **~ di mente a qn** to slip sb's mind; **lasciarsi ~** (occasione, affare) to let go by; **mi scappò detto** I let it slip; **scappa'toia** sf way out

scara'beo sm beetle

scarabocchi'are [skarabok'kjare] /19/ vt to scribble, scrawl; **scara'bocchio** sm scribble, scrawl

scara'faggio [skara'faddʒo] sm cockroach

scaraman'zia [skaraman'tsia] sf: **per ~** for luck

scaraven'tare /72/ vt to fling, hurl; **scaraventarsi** vpr to fling o.s.

scarce'rare [skartʃe'rare] /72/ vt to release (from prison)

scardi'nare /72/ vt: **~ una porta** to take a door off its hinges

scari'care /20/ vt (merci, camion ecc) to unload; (passeggeri) to set down, put off; (da Internet) to download; (arma) to unload; (: sparare, anche Elettr) to discharge; (corso d'acqua) to empty, pour; (fig: liberare da un peso) to unburden, relieve; **scaricarsi** vpr (orologio) to run o wind down; (batteria, accumulatore) to go flat o dead; (fig: rilassarsi) to unwind; (: sfogarsi) to let off steam

scarico, -a, -chi, -che ag unloaded; (orologio) run down; (batteria, accumulatore) dead, flat ▷ sm (di merci, materiali) unloading; (di immondizie) dumping, tipping (BRIT); (Tecn: deflusso) draining; (: dispositivo) drain; (Aut) exhaust

scarlat'tina sf scarlet fever

scar'latto, -a ag scarlet

scarpa sf shoe; **scarpe da ginnastica** gym shoes; **scarpe da tennis** tennis shoes

scar'pata sf escarpment

scarpi'era sf shoe rack

scar'pone sm boot; **scarponi da montagna** climbing boots; **scarponi da sci** ski-boots

scarseggi'are [skarsed'dʒare] /62/ vi to be scarce; **~ di** to be short of, lack

'scarso, -a ag (insufficiente) insufficient, meagre; (povero: annata) poor, lean; (Ins: voto) poor; **~ di** lacking in; **3 chili scarsi** just under 3 kilos, barely 3 kilos

scar'tare /72/ vt (pacco) to unwrap; (idea) to reject; (Mil) to declare unfit for military service; (carte da gioco) to discard; (Calcio) to dodge (past) ▷ vi to swerve

'scarto sm (cosa scartata, anche Comm) reject; (di veicolo) swerve; (differenza) gap, difference

scassi'nare /72/ vt to break, force

scate'nare /72/ vt (fig) to incite, stir up; **scatenarsi** vpr (temporale) to break; (rivolta) to break out; (persona: infuriarsi) to rage

'scatola sf box; (di latta) tin (BRIT), can; **cibi in ~** tinned (BRIT) o canned foods; **~ cranica** cranium; **scato'lone** sm (big) box

scat'tare /72/ vt (fotografia) to take ▷ vi (congegno, molla ecc) to be released; (balzare) to spring up; (Sport) to put on a spurt; (fig: per l'ira) to fly into a rage; **~ in piedi** to spring to one's feet

'scatto sm (dispositivo) release; (: di arma da fuoco) trigger mechanism; (rumore) click; (balzo) jump, start; (Sport) spurt; (fig: di ira ecc) fit; (: di stipendio) increment; **di ~** suddenly

scaval'care /20/ vt (ostacolo) to pass (o climb) over; (fig) to get ahead of, overtake

sca'vare /72/ vt (terreno) to dig; (legno) to hollow out; (pozzo, galleria) to bore; (città sepolta ecc) to excavate

'scavo sm excavating no pl; excavation

'scegliere ['ʃeʎʎere] /100/ vt to choose, select

sce'icco, -chi [ʃe'ikko] sm sheik

'scelgo ecc ['ʃelgo] vb vedi **scegliere**

scel'lino [ʃel'lino] sm shilling

'scelto, -a ['ʃelto] pp di **scegliere** ▷ ag (gruppo) carefully selected; (frutta, verdura) choice, top quality; (Mil: specializzato) crack cpd, highly skilled ▷ sf choice; (selezione) selection, choice; **frutta o formaggi a scelta** choice of fruit or cheese; **di prima scelta** top grade o quality

'scemo, -a ['ʃemo] ag stupid, silly

'scena ['ʃena] sf (gen) scene; (palcoscenico) stage; **le scene** (fig) (teatro) the stage; **andare in ~** to be staged o put on o performed; **mettere in ~** to stage; **fare una ~** to make a scene

sce'nario [ʃe'narjo] sm scenery; (di film) scenario

sce'nata [ʃe'nata] sf row, scene

'scendere ['ʃendere] /101/ vi to go (o come) down; (strada, sole) to go down; (notte) to fall; (passeggero: fermarsi) to get out, alight; (fig: temperatura, prezzi) to fall, drop ▷ vt (scale, pendio) to go (o come) down; **~ dalle scale** to go (o come) down the stairs; **~ dal treno** to get off o out of the train; **~ dalla macchina** to get out of the car; **~ da cavallo** to dismount, get off one's horse

sceneggi'ato [ʃenedʒ'dʒato] sm television drama

'scettico, -a, -ci, -che ['ʃettiko] ag sceptical

'scettro ['ʃettro] sm sceptre

'scheda ['skɛda] sf (index) card; **~ elettorale** ballot paper; **~ di memoria** (Inform) memory card; **~ ricaricabile** (Tel) top-up card; **~ telefonica** phone card; **sche'dario** sm file; (mobile) filing cabinet

sche'dina [ske'dina] sf ≈ pools coupon (BRIT)

'scheggia, -ge ['skeddʒa] sf splinter, sliver

'scheletro ['skɛletro] sm skeleton

'schema, -i ['skɛma] sm (diagramma) diagram, sketch; (progetto, abbozzo) outline, plan

'scherma ['skerma] sf fencing

scher'maglia [sker'maʎʎa] sf (fig) skirmish

'schermo ['skermo] sm shield, screen; (Cine, TV) screen; **a ~ panoramico** (TV) widescreen

scher'nire [sker'nire] /55/ vt to mock, sneer at

scher'zare [sker'tsare] /72/ vi to joke

'scherzo ['skertso] sm joke; (tiro) trick; (Mus) scherzo; **è uno ~!** (una cosa facile) it's child's play!, it's easy!; **per ~** in jest; for a joke o a laugh; **fare un brutto ~ a qn** to play a nasty trick on sb

schiaccia'noci [skjattʃa'notʃi] sm inv nutcracker

schiacci'are [skjat'tʃare] /14/ vt (dito) to crush; (noci) to crack; **~ un pisolino** to have a nap; **schiacciarsi** vpr (appiattirsi) to get squashed; (frantumarsi) to get crushed

schiaffeggi'are [skjaffed'dʒare] /62/ vt to slap

schi'affo ['skjaffo] sm slap

schian'tare [skjan'tare] /72/ vt to break; **schiantarsi** vpr to break (up), shatter

schia'rire [skja'rire] /55/ vt to lighten, make lighter ▷ vi (anche: **schiarirsi**) to grow lighter; (tornar sereno) to clear, brighten up; **schiarirsi la voce** to clear one's throat

schiavitù [skjavi'tu] sf slavery

schi'avo, -a ['skjavo] sm/f slave

schi'ena ['skjɛna] sf (Anat) back; **schie'nale** sm (di sedia) back

schi'era ['skjɛra] sf (Mil) rank; (gruppo) group, band

schiera'mento [skjera'mento] sm (Mil, Sport) formation; (fig) alliance

schie'rare [skje'rare] /72/ vt
(esercito) to line up, draw up, marshal;
schierarsi vpr to line up; (fig):
schierarsi con o **dalla parte di/
contro qn** to side with/oppose sb

'schifo ['skifo] sm disgust; **fare ~**
(essere fatto male, dare pessimi risultati)
to be awful; **mi fa ~** it makes me sick,
it's disgusting; **quel libro è uno ~**
that book's rotten; **schi'foso, -a** ag
disgusting, revolting; (molto scadente)
rotten, lousy

schioc'care /20/ vt (frusta) to crack;
(dita) to snap; (lingua) to click; **~ le
labbra** to smack one's lips

schi'udere ['skjudere] /22/ vt,
schi'udersi vpr to open

schi'uma ['skjuma] sf foam; (di
sapone) lather; (di latte) froth; (fig:
feccia) scum

schi'vare [ski'vare] /72/ vt to dodge,
avoid

'schivo, -a ['skivo] ag (ritroso) stand-
offish, reserved; (timido) shy

schiz'zare [skit'tsare] /72/ vt
(spruzzare) to spurt, squirt; (sporcare)
to splash, spatter; (fig: abbozzare) to
sketch ▷ vi to spurt, squirt; (saltar
fuori) to dart up (o off ecc)

schizzi'noso, -a [skittsi'noso] ag
fussy, finicky

'schizzo ['skittso] sm (di liquido) spurt;
splash, spatter; (abbozzo) sketch

sci [ʃi] sm inv (attrezzo) ski; (attività)
skiing; **~ di fondo** cross-country
skiing, ski touring (us); **~ d'acqua** o
nautico water-skiing

'scia ['ʃia] (pl **scie**) sf (di imbarcazione)
wake; (di profumo) trail

scià [ʃa] sm inv shah

sci'abola ['ʃabola] sf sabre

scia'callo [ʃa'kallo] sm jackal

sciac'quare [ʃak'kware] /72/ vt
to rinse

scia'gura [ʃa'gura] sf disaster,
calamity; misfortune

scialac'quare [ʃalak'kware] /72/ vt
to squander

sci'albo, -a ['ʃalbo] ag pale, dull; (fig)
dull, colourless

sci'alle ['ʃalle] sm shawl

scia'luppa [ʃa'luppa] sf (anche: **~ di
salvataggio**) lifeboat

sci'ame ['ʃame] sm swarm

sci'are [ʃi'are] /60/ vi to ski

sci'arpa ['ʃarpa] sf scarf; (fascia) sash

scia'tore, -'trice [ʃia'tore] sm/f
skier

sci'atto, -a ['ʃatto] ag (persona)
slovenly, unkempt

scien'tifico, -a, -ci, -che
[ʃen'tifiko] ag scientific

sci'enza ['ʃentsa] sf science;
(sapere) knowledge; **scienze** sfpl
(Ins) science sg: **scienze naturali**
natural sciences; **scienzi'ato, -a** sm/f
scientist

'scimmia ['ʃimmja] sf monkey

scimpanzé [ʃimpan'tse] sm inv
chimpanzee

'scindere ['ʃindere] /102/,
'scindersi vpr to split (up)

scin'tilla [ʃin'tilla] sf spark;
scintil'lare /72/ vi to spark; (acqua,
occhi) to sparkle

scioc'chezza [ʃok'kettsa] sf
stupidity no pl; stupid o foolish thing;
dire sciocchezze to talk nonsense

sci'occo, -a, -chi, -che ['ʃokko] ag
stupid, foolish

sci'ogliere ['ʃɔʎʎere] /103/ vt (nodo)
to untie; (capelli) to loosen; (persona,
animale) to untie, release; (neve,
zucchero ecc) to dissolve; (fig: mistero)
to solve; (porre fine a: contratto) to
cancel; (: società, matrimonio) to
dissolve; (: riunione) to bring to an
end; (fig: persona) **~ da** to release
from; (neve) to melt; **sciogliersi** vpr
to loosen, come untied; to melt; to
dissolve; (assemblea, corteo, duo) to
break up; **~ i muscoli** to limber up;
scioglilingua [ʃoʎʎi'lingwa] sm inv
tongue-twister

sci'olgo ecc ['ʃɔlgo] vb vedi
sciogliere

sci'olto, -a ['ʃɔlto] *pp di* **sciogliere**
▷ *ag* loose; *(agile)* agile, nimble;
supple; *(disinvolto)* free and easy;
versi sciolti *(Poesia)* blank verse

sciope'rare [ʃope'rare] /72/ *vi* to
strike, go on strike

sci'opero ['ʃɔpero] *sm* strike; **fare
~** to strike; **~ bianco** work-to-rule
(BRIT), slowdown (US); **~ selvaggio**
wildcat strike; **~ a singhiozzo**
on-off strike

scio'via [ʃio'via] *sf* ski lift

scip'pare [ʃip'pare] /72/ *vt*: **~ qn** to
snatch sb's bag

sci'rocco [ʃi'rɔkko] *sm* sirocco

sci'roppo [ʃi'rɔppo] *sm* syrup

'scisma, -i ['ʃizma] *sm* (Rel) schism

scissi'one [ʃis'sjone] *sf* (anche fig)
split, division; (Fisica) fission

'scisso, -a ['ʃisso] *pp di* **scindere**

sciu'pare [ʃu'pare] /72/ *vt* (abito,
libro, appetito) to spoil, ruin; (tempo,
denaro) to waste

scivo'lare [ʃivo'lare] /72/ *vi* to slide
o glide along; (involontariamente) to
slip, slide; **'scivolo** *sm* slide; (Tecn)
chute; **scivo'loso, -a** *ag* slippery

scle'rosi *sf* sclerosis

scoc'care /20/ *vt* (freccia) to shoot
▷ *vi* (guizzare) to shoot up; (battere:
ora) to strike

scoccherò *ecc* [skokke'rɔ] *vb vedi*
scoccare

scocci'are [skot'tʃare] /14/ *vt* to
bother, annoy; **scocciarsi** *vpr* to be
bothered *o* annoyed

sco'della *sf* bowl

scodinzo'lare [skodintso'lare] /72/
vi to wag its tail

scogli'era [skoʎ'ʎɛra] *sf* reef;
(rupe) cliff

'scoglio ['skɔʎʎo] *sm* (al mare) rock

scoi'attolo *sm* squirrel

scola'pasta *sm inv* colander

scolapi'atti *sm inv* drainer (for
plates)

sco'lare /72/ *ag*: **età ~** school age ▷ *vt*
to drain ▷ *vi* to drip

scola'resca *sf* schoolchildren *pl*,
pupils *pl*

sco'laro, -a *sm/f* pupil, schoolboy/
girl

> Attenzione! In inglese esiste la
> parola *scholar*, che però significa
> *studioso*.

sco'lastico, -a, -ci, -che *ag* (gen)
scholastic; (libro, anno, divisa)
school *cpd*

scol'lato, -a *ag* (vestito) low-cut, low-
necked; (donna) wearing a low-cut
dress (o blouse ecc)

scolla'tura *sf* neckline

scolle'gare /80/ *vt* (fili, apparecchi)
to disconnect; **scollegarsi** *vpr* (da
Internet) to disconnect; (da chat-line)
to log off

'scolo *sm* drainage

scolo'rire /55/ *vt* to fade; to discolour
(BRIT), discolor (US) ▷ *vi* (anche:
scolorirsi) to fade; to become
discoloured; (impallidire) to turn pale

scol'pire /55/ *vt* to carve, sculpt

scombusso'lare /72/ *vt* to upset

scom'messo, -a *pp di* **scommettere**
▷ *sf* bet, wager

scom'mettere /63/ *vt, vi* to bet

scomo'dare /72/ *vt* to trouble,
bother, disturb; **scomodarsi** *vpr* to
put o.s. out; **scomodarsi a fare** to
go to the bother *o* trouble of doing

'scomodo, -a *ag* uncomfortable;
(sistemazione, posto) awkward,
inconvenient

scompa'rire /7/ *vi* (sparire) to
disappear, vanish; (fig) to be
insignificant

scomparti'mento *sm*
compartment

scompigli'are [skompiʎ'ʎare]
/27/ *vt* (cassetto, capelli) to mess up,
disarrange; (fig: piani) to upset

scomuni'care /20/ *vt* to
excommunicate

'sconcio, -a, -ci, -ce ['skontʃo] *ag*
(osceno) indecent, obscene ▷ *sm*
disgrace

scon'figgere [skon'fiddʒere] /104/ vt to defeat, overcome

sconfi'nare /72/ vi to cross the border; (in proprietà privata) to trespass; (fig): **~ da** to stray o digress from

scon'fitto, -a pp di **sconfiggere** ▷ sf defeat

scon'forto sm despondency

sconge'lare [skondʒe'lare] /72/ vt to defrost

scongiu'rare [skondʒu'rare] /72/ vt (implorare) to beseech, entreat, implore; (eludere: pericolo) to ward off, avert; **scongi'uro** sm (esorcismo) exorcism; **fare gli scongiuri** to touch wood (BRIT), knock on wood (US)

scon'nesso, -a ag incoherent

sconosci'uto, -a [skonoʃʃuto] ag unknown; new, strange ▷ sm/f stranger; unknown person

sconsigli'are [skonsiʎ'ʎare] /27/ vt: **~ qc a qn** to advise sb against sth; **~ qn dal fare qc** to advise sb not to do o against doing sth

sconso'lato, -a ag inconsolable; desolate

scon'tare /72/ vt (Comm: detrarre) to deduct; (: debito) to pay off; (: cambiale) to discount; (pena) to serve; (colpa, errori) to pay for, suffer for

scon'tato, -a ag (previsto) foreseen, taken for granted; **dare per ~ che** to take it for granted that

scon'tento, -a ag: **~ (di)** discontented o dissatisfied (with) ▷ sm dissatisfaction

'sconto sm discount; **fare o concedere uno ~** to give a discount; **uno ~ del 10%** a 10% discount

scon'trarsi /72/ vpr (treni ecc) to crash, collide; (venire ad uno scontro: fig) to clash; **~ con** to crash into, collide with

scon'trino sm ticket; (di cassa) receipt

'scontro sm clash, encounter; (di veicoli) crash, collision

scon'troso, -a ag sullen, surly; (permaloso) touchy

sconveni'ente ag unseemly, improper

scon'volgere [skon'vɔldʒere] /96/ vt to throw into confusion, upset; (turbare) to shake, disturb, upset; **scon'volto, -a** pp di **sconvolgere**

'scooter ['skuter] sm inv scooter

'scopa sf broom; (Carte) Italian card game; **sco'pare** /72/ vt to sweep

sco'perto, -a pp di **scoprire** ▷ ag uncovered; (capo) uncovered, bare; (macchina) open; (Mil) exposed, without cover; (conto) overdrawn ▷ sf discovery

'scopo sm aim, purpose; **a che ~?** what for?

scoppi'are /19/ vi (spaccarsi) to burst; (esplodere) to explode; (fig) to break out; **~ in pianto** o **a piangere** to burst out crying; **~ dalle risa** o **dal ridere** to split one's sides laughing

scoppiet'tare /72/ vi to crackle

'scoppio sm explosion; (di tuono, arma ecc) crash, bang; (fig: di risa, ira) fit; (di pneumatico) bang; (fig: di guerra) outbreak; **a ~ ritardato** delayed-action

sco'prire /9/ vt to discover; (liberare da ciò che copre) to uncover; (: monumento) to unveil; **scoprirsi** vpr to put on lighter clothes; (fig) to give o.s. away

scoraggi'are [skorad'dʒare] /62/ vt to discourage; **scoraggiarsi** vpr to become discouraged, lose heart

scorcia'toia [skortʃa'toja] sf short cut

'scorcio ['skortʃo] sm (Arte) foreshortening; (di secolo, periodo) end, close; **~ panoramico** vista

scor'dare /72/ vt to forget; **scordarsi** vpr: **scordarsi di qc/di fare** to forget sth/to do

'scorgere ['skɔrdʒere] /59/ *vt* to make out, distinguish, see

scorpacci'ata [skorpat'tʃata] *sf*: **fare una ~ (di)** to stuff o.s. (with), eat one's fill (of)

scorpi'one *sm* scorpion; **S~** Scorpio

'scorrere /28/ *vt* (*giornale, lettera*) to run o skim through ▷ *vi* (*liquido, fiume*) to run, flow; (*fune*) to run; (*cassetto, porta*) to slide easily; (*tempo*) to pass (by)

scor'retto, -a *ag* incorrect; (*sgarbato*) impolite; (*sconveniente*) improper

scor'revole *ag* (*porta*) sliding; (*fig: stile*) fluent, flowing

'scorsi *ecc vb vedi* **scorgere**

'scorso, -a *pp di* **scorrere** ▷ *ag* last

scor'soio, -a *ag*: **nodo ~** noose

'scorta *sf* (*di personalità, convoglio*) escort; (*provvista*) supply, stock

scor'tese *ag* discourteous, rude

'scorza ['skɔrdza] *sf* (*di albero*) bark; (*di agrumi*) peel, skin

sco'sceso, -a [skoʃʃeso] *ag* steep

'scosso, -a *pp di* **scuotere** ▷ *ag* (*turbato*) shaken, upset ▷ *sf* jerk, jolt, shake; (*Elettr, fig*) shock; **scossa di terremoto** earth tremor

scos'tante *ag* (*fig*) off-putting (BRIT), unpleasant

scotch [skɔtʃ] *sm inv* (*whisky*) Scotch®; (*nastro adesivo*) Scotch tape®, Sellotape®

scot'tare /72/ *vt* (*ustionare*) to burn; (: *con liquido bollente*) to scald ▷ *vi* to burn; (*caffè*) to be too hot; **scottarsi** *vpr* to burn/scald o.s.; (*fig*) to have one's fingers burnt; **scotta'tura** *sf* burn; scald

'scotto, -a *ag* overcooked ▷ *sm* (*fig*): **pagare lo ~ (di)** to pay the penalty (for)

sco'vare /72/ *vt* to drive out, flush out; (*fig*) to discover

'Scozia ['skɔttsja] *sf*: **la ~** Scotland; **scoz'zese** *ag* Scottish ▷ *smf* Scot

scredi'tare /72/ *vt* to discredit

'screen saver ['skriin'sɛivər] *sm inv* (*Inform*) screen saver

scre'mato, -a *ag* skimmed; **parzialmente ~** semi-skimmed

screpo'lato, -a *ag* (*labbra*) chapped; (*muro*) cracked

'screzio ['skrɛttsjo] *sm* disagreement

scricchio'lare [skrikkjo'lare] /72/ *vi* to creak, squeak

'scrigno ['skriɲɲo] *sm* casket

scrimina'tura *sf* parting

'scrissi *ecc vb vedi* **scrivere**

'scritto, -a *pp di* **scrivere** ▷ *ag* written ▷ *sm* writing; (*lettera*) letter, note ▷ *sf* inscription

scrit'toio *sm* writing desk

scrit'tore, -'trice *sm/f* writer

scrit'tura *sf* writing; (*Comm*) entry; (*contratto*) contract; (*Rel*): **la Sacra S~** the Scriptures *pl*

scrittu'rare /72/ *vt* (*Teat, Cine*) to sign up, engage; (*Comm*) to enter

scriva'nia *sf* desk

'scrivere /105/ *vt* to write; **come si scrive?** how is it spelt?, how do you write it?

scroc'cone, -a *sm/f* scrounger

'scrofa *sf* (*Zool*) sow

scrol'lare /72/ *vt* to shake; **scrollarsi** *vpr* (*anche fig*) to give o.s. a shake; **~ le spalle/il capo** to shrug one's shoulders/shake one's head

'scrupolo *sm* scruple; (*meticolosità*) care, conscientiousness

scrupo'loso, -a *ag* scrupulous; conscientious

scru'tare /72/ *vt* to scrutinize; (*intenzioni, causa*) to examine, scrutinize

scu'cire [sku'tʃire] /31/ *vt* (*orlo ecc*) to unpick, undo; **scucirsi** *vpr* to come unstitched

scude'ria *sf* stable

scu'detto *sm* (*Sport*) (championship) shield; (*distintivo*) badge

'scudo *sm* shield

sculacci'are [skulat'tʃare] /14/ *vt* to spank

scul'tore, -'trice *sm/f* sculptor

scul'tura *sf* sculpture

scu'ola *sf* school; **~ elementare** o **primaria** primary (BRIT) o grade (US) school (for children from 6 to 11 years of age); **~ guida** driving school; **~ media** secondary (BRIT) o high (US) school; **~ dell'obbligo** compulsory education; **scuole serali** evening classes, night school *sg*: **~ tecnica** technical college

scu'otere /106/ *vt* to shake

'scure *sf* axe

'scuro, -a *ag* dark; (fig: espressione) grim ▷ *sm* darkness; dark colour (BRIT) o color (US); (imposta) (window) shutter; **verde/rosso** ecc **~** dark green/red etc

'scusa *sf* excuse; **scuse** *sfpl* apology *sg*, apologies; **chiedere ~ a qn (per)** to apologize to sb (for); **chiedo ~** I'm sorry; (disturbando ecc) excuse me

scu'sare /72/ *vt* to excuse; **scusarsi** *vpr*: **scusarsi (di)** to apologize (for); **(mi) scusi** I'm sorry; (per richiamare l'attenzione) excuse me

sde'gnato, -a [zdeɲ'ɲato] *ag* indignant, angry

'sdegno ['zdeɲɲo] *sm* scorn, disdain

sdolci'nato, -a [zdoltʃi'nato] *ag* mawkish, oversentimental

sdrai'arsi /19/ *vpr* to stretch out, lie down

'sdraio *sm*: **sedia a ~** deck chair

sdruccio'levole [zdruttʃo'levole] *ag* slippery

PAROLA CHIAVE

se *pron vedi* **si**

▶ *cong* **1** (condizionale, ipotetica) if; **se nevica non vengo** I won't come if it snows; **sarei rimasto se me l'avessero chiesto** I would have stayed if they'd asked me; **non puoi fare altro se non telefonare** all you can do is phone; **se mai** if, if ever; **siamo noi se mai che le siamo**

grati it is we who should be grateful to you; **se no** (altrimenti) or (else), otherwise

2 (in frasi dubitative, interrogative indirette) if, whether; **non so se scrivere o telefonare** I don't know whether o if I should write or phone

sé *pron* (gen) oneself; (esso, essa, lui, lei, loro) itself; himself; herself; themselves; **sé stesso(a)** *pron* oneself; itself; himself; herself

seb'bene *cong* although, though

sec. *abbr* (= secolo) c.

'secca *sf vedi* **secco**

sec'care /20/ *vt* to dry; (prosciugare) to dry up; (fig: importunare) to annoy, bother ▷ *vi* to dry; to dry up; **seccarsi** *vpr* to dry; to dry up; (fig) to grow annoyed

sec'cato, -a *ag* (fig: infastidito) bothered, annoyed; (: stufo) fed up

secca'tura *sf* (fig) bother *no pl*, trouble *no pl*

seccherò ecc [sekke'rɔ] *vb vedi* **seccare**

secchi'ello *sm* bucket; **~ del ghiaccio** ice bucket

'secchio ['sekkjo] *sm* bucket, pail

'secco, -a, -chi, -che *ag* dry; (fichi, pesce) dried; (foglie, ramo) withered; (magro: persona) thin, skinny; (fig: risposta, modo di fare) curt, abrupt; (: colpo) clean, sharp ▷ *sm* (siccità) drought ▷ *sf* (del mare) shallows *pl*: **restarci ~** (morire sul colpo) to drop dead; **tirare a ~** (barca) to beach; **rimanere a ~** (fig) to be left in the lurch

seco'lare *ag* age-old, centuries-old; (laico, mondano) secular

'secolo *sm* century; (epoca) age

se'conda *sf vedi* **secondo**

secon'dario, -a *ag* secondary

se'condo, -a *ag* second ▷ *sm* second; (di pranzo) main course ▷ *sf* (Aut) second (gear) ▷ *prep* according to; (nel modo prescritto) in accordance with; **seconda classe** second-class; **di seconda mano** second-hand; **viaggiare in seconda** to travel second-class; **a seconda di** according to; in accordance with; **~ me** in my opinion, to my mind

'**sedano** *sm* celery

seda'tivo, -a *ag, sm* sedative

'**sede** *sf (di ditta: principale)* head office; *(di organizzazione)* headquarters *pl*: **~ centrale** head office; **~ sociale** registered office

seden'tario, -a *ag* sedentary

se'dere /107/ *vi* to sit, be seated

'**sedia** *sf* chair; **~ elettrica** electric chair; **~ a rotelle** wheelchair

'**sedici** ['sedit∫i] *num* sixteen

se'dile *sm* seat; *(panchina)* bench

sedu'cente [sedu't∫ɛnte] *ag* seductive; *(proposta)* very attractive

se'durre /90/ *vt* to seduce

se'duta *sf* session, sitting; *(riunione)* meeting; **~ stante** *(fig)* immediately; **~ spiritica** seance

seduzi'one [sedut'tsjone] *sf* seduction; *(fascino)* charm, appeal

SEeO *abbr (= salvo errori e omissioni)* E & OE

'**sega, -ghe** *sf* saw

'**segale** *sf* rye

se'gare /80/ *vt* to saw; *(recidere)* to saw off

'**seggio** ['sɛddʒo] *sm* seat; **~ elettorale** polling station

'**seggiola** ['sɛddʒola] *sf* chair; **seggio'lone** *sm (per bambini)* highchair

seggio'via [sɛddʒo'via] *sf* chairlift

segherò *ecc* [sege'rɔ] *vb vedi* **segare**

segna'lare [seɲɲa'lare] /72/ *vt (avvertire)* to signal; *(menzionare)* to indicate; *(: fatto, risultato, aumento)* to report; *(: errore, dettaglio)* to point out; *(persona)* to single out

se'gnale [seɲ'ɲale] *sm* signal; *(cartello):* **~ stradale** road sign; **~ acustico** acoustic o sound signal; **~ d'allarme** alarm; *(Ferr)* communication cord; **~ orario** *(Radio)* time signal

segna'libro [seɲɲa'libro] *sm (anche Inform)* bookmark

se'gnare [seɲ'ɲare] /15/ *vt* to mark; *(prendere nota)* to note; *(indicare)* to indicate, mark; *(Sport: goal)* to score

'**segno** ['seɲɲo] *sm* sign; *(impronta, contrassegno)* mark; *(limite)* limit, bounds *pl*; *(bersaglio)* target; **fare ~ di sì/no** to nod (one's head)/shake one's head; **fare ~ a qn di fermarsi** to motion (to) sb to stop; **cogliere** o **colpire nel ~** *(fig)* to hit the mark; **~ zodiacale** star sign

segre'tario, -a *sm/f* secretary; **~ comunale** town clerk; **S~ di Stato** Secretary of State

segrete'ria *sf (di ditta, scuola)* (secretary's) office; *(d'organizzazione internazionale)* secretariat; *(Pol: ecc: carica)* office of Secretary; **~ telefonica** answering machine

se'greto, -a *ag* secret ▷ *sm* secret; secrecy *no pl* ▷ *sf* dungeon; **in ~** in secret, secretly

segu'ace [se'gwat∫e] *smf* follower, disciple

segu'ente *ag* following, next

segu'ire /45/ *vt (anche su Twitter)* to follow; *(frequentare: corso)* to attend ▷ *vi* to follow; *(continuare: testo)* to continue

segui'tare /72/ *vt* to continue, carry on with ▷ *vi* to continue, carry on

'**seguito** *sm (scorta)* suite, retinue; *(discepoli)* followers *pl*; *(favore)* following; *(continuazione)* continuation; *(conseguenza)* result; **di ~** at a stretch, on end; **in ~** later on; **in ~ a, a ~ di** following; *(a causa di)* as a result of, owing to

'**sei** *vb vedi* **essere** ▷ *num* six

sei'cento [sei't∫ɛnto] *num* six hundred ▷ *sm*: **il S~** the seventeenth century

selci'ato [sel't∫ato] *sm* cobbled surface

selezio'nare [selettsjo'nare] /72/ *vt* to select

selezi'one [selet'tsjone] *sf* selection

'sella *sf* saddle

sel'lino *sm* saddle

selvag'gina [selvad'dʒina] *sf* (*animali*) game

sel'vaggio, -a, -gi, -ge [sel'vaddʒo] *ag* wild; (*tribù*) savage, uncivilized; (*fig*) savage, brutal ▷ *sm/f* savage

sel'vatico, -a, -ci, -che *ag* wild

se'maforo *sm* (*Aut*) traffic lights *pl*

sem'brare /72/ *vi* to seem ▷ *vb impers:* **sembra che** it seems that; **mi sembra che** it seems to me that; I think (that); **~ di essere** to seem to be

'seme *sm* seed; (*sperma*) semen; (*Carte*) suit

se'mestre *sm* half-year, six-month period

semifi'nale *sf* semifinal

semi'freddo *sm* ice-cream dessert

semi'nare /72/ *vt* to sow

semi'nario *sm* seminar; (*Rel*) seminary

seminter'rato *sm* basement; (*appartamento*) basement flat (*BRIT*) o apartment (*US*)

'semola *sf:* **~ di grano duro** durum wheat

semo'lino *sm* semolina

'semplice ['semplitʃe] *ag* simple; (*di un solo elemento*) single

'sempre *av* always; (*ancora*) still; **posso ~ tentare** I can always o still try; **da ~** always; **per ~** forever; **una volta per ~** once and for all; **~ che** provided (that); **~ più** more and more; **~ meno** less and less

sempre'verde *ag, sm* o *f* (*Bot*) evergreen

'senape *sf* (*Cuc*) mustard

se'nato *sm* senate; **sena'tore, -'trice** *sm/f* senator

'senno *sm* judgment, (common) sense; **col ~ di poi** with hindsight

'seno *sm* (*Anat: petto, mammella*) breast; (: *grembo, anche fig*) womb; (: *cavità*) sinus

sen'sato, -a *ag* sensible

sensazio'nale [sensattsjo'nale] *ag* sensational

sensazi'one [sensat'tsjone] *sf* feeling, sensation; **fare ~** to cause a sensation, create a stir; **avere la ~ che** to have a feeling that

sen'sibile *ag* sensitive; (*ai sensi*) perceptible; (*rilevante, notevole*) appreciable, noticeable; **~ a** sensitive to

> Attenzione! In inglese esiste la parola *sensible*, che però significa *ragionevole*.

sensibiliz'zare [sensibilid'dzare] /72/ *vt* (*fig*) to make aware, awaken

'senso *sm* (*Fisiol, istinto*) sense; (*impressione, sensazione*) feeling, sensation; (*significato*) meaning, sense; (*direzione*) direction; **sensi** *smpl* (*coscienza*) consciousness *sg*; (*sensualità*) senses; **fare ~ a** (*ripugnare*) to disgust, repel; **ciò non ha ~** that doesn't make sense; **~ comune** common sense; **in ~ orario/antiorario** clockwise/anticlockwise; **~ di colpa** sense of guilt; **a ~ unico** one-way; **"~ vietato"** (*Aut*) "no entry"

sensu'ale *ag* sensual; sensuous

sen'tenza [sen'tentsa] *sf* (*Dir*) sentence; (*massima*) maxim

senti'ero *sm* path

sentimen'tale *ag* sentimental; (*vita, avventura*) love *cpd*

senti'mento *sm* feeling

senti'nella *sf* sentry

sen'tire /45/ *vt* (*percepire al tatto, fig*) to feel; (*udire*) to hear; (*ascoltare*) to listen to; (*odore*) to smell; (*avvertire con il gusto, assaggiare*) to taste ▷ *vi:* **~ di** (*avere sapore*) to taste of; (*avere odore*) to smell of; **sentirsi** *vpr* (*uso reciproco*) to be in touch; **sentirsi bene/male** to feel well/unwell o ill; **sentirsi di fare qc** (*essere disposto*) to feel like doing sth

sen'tito, -a *ag* (*sincero*) sincere, warm; **per ~ dire** by hearsay

S

'senza ['sɛntsa] *prep, cong* without; **~ dir nulla** without saying a word; **fare ~ qc** to do without sth; **~ di me** without me; **~ che io lo sapessi** without me o my knowing; **~ amici** friendless; **senz'altro** of course, certainly; **~ dubbio** no doubt; **~ scrupoli** unscrupulous

sepa'rare /72/ *vt* to separate; (*dividere*) to divide; (*tenere distinto*) to distinguish; **separarsi** *vpr* (*coniugi*) to separate, part; (*amici*) to part, leave each other; **separarsi da** (*coniuge*) to separate o part from; (*amico, socio*) to part company with; (*oggetto*) to part with; **sepa'rato, -a** *ag* (*letti, conto ecc*) separate; (*coniugi*) separated

seppel'lire /55/ *vt* to bury

'seppi *ecc vb vedi* **sapere**

'seppia *sf* cuttlefish ▷ *ag inv* sepia

se'quenza [se'kwɛntsa] *sf* sequence

seques'trare /72/ *vt* (*Dir*) to impound; (*rapire*) to kidnap; **se'questro** *sm* (*Dir*) impoundment; **sequestro di persona** kidnapping

'sera *sf* evening; **di ~** in the evening; **domani ~** tomorrow evening, tomorrow night; **se'rale** *ag* evening *cpd*; **se'rata** *sf* evening; (*ricevimento*) party

ser'bare /72/ *vt* to keep; (*mettere da parte*) to put aside; **~ rancore/odio verso qn** to bear sb a grudge/hate sb

serba'toio *sm* tank; (*cisterna*) cistern

'Serbia *sf*: **la ~** Serbia

'serbo, -a *ag* Serbian ▷ *sm/f* Serbian, Serb ▷ *sm* (*Ling*) Serbian; (*il serbare*): **mettere/tenere** o **avere in ~ qc** to put/keep sth aside

se'reno, -a *ag* (*tempo, cielo*) clear; (*fig*) serene, calm

ser'gente [ser'dʒɛnte] *sm* (*Mil*) sergeant

'serie *sf inv* (*successione*) series *inv*; (*gruppo, collezione di chiavi ecc*) set; (*Sport*) division; league; (*Comm*): **modello di ~/fuori ~** standard/ custom-built model; **in ~** in quick succession; (*Comm*) mass *cpd*

serietà *sf* seriousness; reliability

'serio, -a *ag* serious; (*impiegato*) responsible, reliable; (*ditta, cliente*) reliable, dependable; **sul ~** (*davvero*) really, truly; (*seriamente*) seriously, in earnest

ser'pente *sm* snake; **~ a sonagli** rattlesnake

'serra *sf* greenhouse; hothouse

ser'randa *sf* roller shutter

serra'tura *sf* lock

'server ['server] *sm inv* (*Inform*) server

ser'vire /45/ *vt* to serve; (*clienti: al ristorante*) to wait on; (*: al negozio*) to serve, attend to; (*fig: giovare*) to aid, help; (*Carte*) to deal ▷ *vi* (*Tennis*) to serve; (*essere utile*): **~ a qn** to be of use to sb; **servirsi** *vpr* (*usare*): **servirsi di** to use; (*prendere: cibo*): **servirsi (di)** to help o.s. (to); (*essere cliente abituale*): **servirsi da** to be a regular customer at, go to; **~ qc/a fare** (*utensile ecc*) to be used for sth/for doing; **~ (a qn) da** to serve as (for sb); **serviti pure!** help yourself!

servizi'evole [servit'tsjevole] *ag* obliging, willing to help

ser'vizio [ser'vittsjo] *sm* service; (*al ristorante, sul conto*) service (charge); (*Stampa, TV, Radio*) report; (*da tè, caffè ecc*) set, service; **servizi** *smpl* (*di casa*) kitchen and bathroom; (*Econ*) services; **essere di ~** to be on duty; **fuori ~** (*telefono ecc*) out of order; **~ compreso/escluso** service included/not included; **~ assistenza clienti** customer service; **~ di posate** set of cutlery; **~ militare** military service; **servizi segreti** secret service *sg*

ses'santa *num* sixty; **sessan'tesimo, -a** *num* sixtieth

sessi'one *sf* session

'sesso *sm* sex; **sessu'ale** *ag* sexual, sex *cpd*

ses'tante *sm* sextant

'sesto, -a num sixth

'seta sf silk

'sete sf thirst; **avere ~** to be thirsty

'setola sf bristle

'setta sf sect

set'tanta num seventy; **settan'tesimo, -a** num seventieth

set'tare /72/ vt (Inform) to set up

'sette num seven

sette'cento [sette'tʃɛnto] num seven hundred ▷ sm: **il S~** the eighteenth century

set'tembre sm September

settentrio'nale ag northern

settentri'one sm north

setti'mana sf week; **settima'nale** ag, sm weekly

○ **SETTIMANA BIANCA**
○
○ *Settimana bianca* is the name given
○ to a week-long winter-sports
○ holiday taken by many Italians
○ some time in the skiing season.

settimo, -a num seventh

set'tore sm sector

severità sf severity

se'vero, -a ag severe

sevizi'are [sevit'tsjare] /19/ vt to torture

sezio'nare [settsjo'nare] /72/ vt to divide into sections; (Med) to dissect

sezi'one [set'tsjone] sf section

sfacchi'nata [sfakki'nata] sf (fam) chore, drudgery no pl

sfacci'ato, -a [sfat'tʃato] ag (maleducato) cheeky, impudent; (vistoso) gaudy

sfa'mare /72/ vt to feed; (cibo) to fill; **sfamarsi** vpr to satisfy one's hunger, fill o.s. up

sfasci'are [sfaʃ'ʃare] /14/ vt (ferita) to unbandage; (distruggere) to smash, shatter; **sfasciarsi** vpr (rompersi) to smash, shatter

sfavo'revole ag unfavourable

sfera sf sphere

sfer'rare /72/ vt (fig: colpo) to land, deal; (: attacco) to launch

'sfida sf challenge

sfi'dare /72/ vt to challenge; (fig) to defy, brave

sfi'ducia [sfi'dutʃa] sf distrust, mistrust

sfi'gato, -a (fam) ag: **essere ~** (sfortunato) to be unlucky

sfigu'rare /72/ vt (persona) to disfigure; (quadro, statua) to deface ▷ vi (far cattiva figura) to make a bad impression

sfi'lare /72/ vt (ago) to unthread; (abito, scarpe) to slip off ▷ vi (truppe) to march past, parade; (atleti) to parade; **sfilarsi** vpr (perle ecc) to come unstrung; (orlo, tessuto) to fray; (calza) to run, ladder; **sfi'lata** sf (Mil) parade; (di manifestanti) march; **sfilata di moda** fashion show

'sfinge ['sfindʒe] sf sphinx

sfi'nito, -a ag exhausted

sfio'rare /72/ vt to brush (against); (argomento) to touch upon

sfio'rire /55/ vi to wither, fade

sfo'cato, -a ag (Fot) out of focus

sfoci'are [sfo'tʃare] /14/ vi: **~ in** to flow into; (fig: malcontento) to develop into

sfode'rato, -a ag (vestito) unlined

sfo'gare /80/ vt to vent; **sfogarsi** vpr (sfogare la propria rabbia) to give vent to one's anger; (confidarsi): **sfogarsi (con)** to pour out one's feelings (to); **non sfogarti su di me!** don't take your bad temper out on me!

sfoggi'are [sfod'dʒare] /62/ vt, vi to show off

'sfoglia sf sheet of pasta dough; **pasta ~** (Cuc) puff pastry

sfogli'are /27/ vt (libro) to leaf through

'sfogo, -ghi sm (eruzione cutanea) rash; (fig) outburst; **dare ~ a** (fig) to give vent to

sfon'dare /72/ vt (porta) to break down; (scarpe) to wear a hole in;

(*cesto, scatola*) to burst, knock the bottom out of; (*Mil*) to break through ▷ *vi* (*riuscire*) to make a name for o.s.

'sfondo *sm* background

sfor'mato *sm* (*Cuc*) type of soufflé

sfor'tuna *sf* misfortune, ill luck *no pl*; **avere ~** to be unlucky; **sfortu'nato, -a** *ag* unlucky; (*impresa, film*) unsuccessful

sfor'zare [sfor'tsare] /72/ *vt* to force; **sforzarsi** *vpr*: **sforzarsi di** *o* **a** *o* **per fare** to try hard to do

'sforzo ['sfɔrtso] *sm* effort; (*tensione eccessiva, Tecn*) strain; **fare uno ~** to make an effort

sfrat'tare /72/ *vt* to evict; **'sfratto** *sm* eviction

sfrecci'are [sfret'tʃare] /14/ *vi* to shoot *o* flash past

sfre'gare /80/ *vt* (*strofinare*) to rub; (*graffiare*) to scratch; **sfregarsi le mani** to rub one's hands; **~ un fiammifero** to strike a match

sfregi'are [sfre'dʒare] /62/ *vt* to slash, gash; (*persona*) to disfigure; (*quadro*) to deface

sfre'nato, -a *ag* (*fig*) unrestrained, unbridled

sfron'tato, -a *ag* shameless

sfrutta'mento *sm* exploitation

sfrut'tare /72/ *vt* (*terreno*) to overwork, exhaust; (*miniera*) to exploit, work; (*fig: operai, occasione, potere*) to exploit

sfug'gire [sfud'dʒire] /31/ *vi* to escape; **~ a** (*custode*) to escape (from); (*morte*) to escape; **~ a qn** (*dettaglio, nome*) to escape sb; **~ di mano a qn** to slip out of sb's hand (*o* hands)

sfu'mare /72/ *vt* (*colori, contorni*) to soften, shade off ▷ *vi* to shade (off), fade; (*fig: svanire*) to vanish, disappear; (: *speranze*) to come to nothing

sfuma'tura *sf* shading off *no pl*; (*tonalità*) shade, tone; (*fig*) touch, hint

sfuri'ata *sf* (*scatto di collera*) fit of anger; (*rimprovero*) sharp rebuke

sga'bello *sm* stool

sgabuz'zino [zgabud'dzino] *sm* lumber room

sgambet'tare /72/ *vi* to kick one's legs about

sgam'betto *sm*: **far lo ~ a qn** to trip sb up; (*fig*) to oust sb

sganci'are [zgan'tʃare] /14/ *vt* to unhook; (*Ferr*) to uncouple; (*bombe: da aereo*) to release, drop; (*fig: fam: soldi*) to fork out; **sganciarsi** *vpr* (*fig*): **sganciarsi (da)** to get away (from)

sganghe'rato, -a [zgange'rato] *ag* (*porta*) off its hinges; (*auto*) ramshackle; (*riso*) wild, boisterous

sgar'bato, -a *ag* rude, impolite

'sgarbo *sm*: **fare uno ~ a qn** to be rude to sb

sgargi'ante [zgar'dʒante] *ag* gaudy, showy

sgattaio'lare /72/ *vi* to sneak away *o* off

sge'lare [zdʒe'lare] /72/ *vi, vt* to thaw

sghignaz'zare [zgiɲɲat'tsare] /72/ *vi* to laugh scornfully

sgob'bare /72/ *vi* (*scolaro*) to swot; (*operaio*) to slog

sgombe'rare /72/, **sgomb'rare** *vt* (*tavolo, stanza*) to clear; (*evacuare: piazza, città*) to evacuate ▷ *vi* to move

'sgombro, -a *ag*: **~ (di)** clear (of), free (from) ▷ *sm* (*Zool*) mackerel; (*anche*: **sgombero**) clearing; vacating; evacuation; (*trasloco*) removal

sgonfi'are /19/ *vt* to let down, deflate; **sgonfiarsi** *vpr* to go down

'sgonfio, -a *ag* (*pneumatico, pallone*) flat

'sgorbio *sm* blot; scribble

sgra'devole *ag* unpleasant, disagreeable

sgra'dito, -a *ag* unpleasant, unwelcome

sgra'nare /72/ *vt* (*piselli*) to shell; **~ gli occhi** to open one's eyes wide

sgran'chire [zgran'kire] /55/ vt, **sgranchirsi** [zgran'kirsi] vpr to stretch; **sgranchirsi le gambe** to stretch one's legs

sgranocchi'are [zgranok'kjare] /19/ vt to munch

'sgravio sm: ~ **fiscale** o **contributivo** tax relief

sgrazi'ato, -a [zgrat'tsjato] ag clumsy, ungainly

sgri'dare /72/ vt to scold

sgual'cire [zgwal'tʃire] /55/ vt to crumple (up), crease

sgual'drina sf (peg) slut (!)

sgu'ardo sm (occhiata) look, glance; (espressione) look (in one's eye)

sguaz'zare [zgwat'tsare] /72/ vi (nell'acqua) to splash about; (nella melma) to wallow; ~ **nell'oro** to be rolling in money

sguinzagli'are [zgwintsaʎ'ʎare] /27/ vt to let off the leash; (fig: persona): ~ **qn dietro a qn** to set sb on sb

sgusci'are [zguʃ'ʃare] /14/ vt to shell ▷ vi (sfuggire di mano) to slip; ~ **via** to slip o slink away

'shampoo ['ʃampo] sm inv shampoo

'shiatzu ['tʃiatsu] sm inv shiatsu

shock [ʃɔk] sm inv shock

PAROLA CHIAVE

si (dav lo, la, li, le, ne diventa **se**) pron
1 (riflessivo: maschile) himself; (: femminile) herself; (: neutro) itself; (: impersonale) oneself; (: pl) themselves; **lavarsi** to wash (oneself); **si è tagliato** he has cut himself; **si credono importanti** they think a lot of themselves

2 (riflessivo, con complemento oggetto): **lavarsi le mani** to wash one's hands; **si sta lavando i capelli** he (o she) is washing his (o her) hair

3 (reciproco) one another, each other; **si amano** they love one another o each other

4 (passivo): **si ripara facilmente** it is easily repaired

5 (impersonale): **si dice che ...** they o people say that ...; **si vede che è vecchio** one o you can see that it's old

6 (noi) we; **tra poco si parte** we're leaving soon

sì av yes; **un giorno sì e uno no** every other day

'sia ecc vb vedi **essere**

si'amo vb vedi **essere**

si'cario sm hired killer

sicché [sik'ke] cong (perciò) so (that), therefore; (e quindi) (and) so

siccità [sittʃi'ta] sf drought

sic'come cong since, as

Si'cilia [si'tʃilja] sf: **la ~** Sicily; **sicili'ano, -a** [sitʃi'ljano] ag, sm/f Sicilian

si'cura sf safety catch; (Aut) safety lock

sicu'rezza [siku'rettsa] sf safety; security; confidence; certainty; **di ~** safety cpd; **la ~ stradale** road safety

si'curo, -a ag safe; (ben difeso) secure; (fiducioso) confident; (certo) sure, certain; (notizia, amico) reliable; (esperto) skilled ▷ av (anche: **di ~**) certainly; **essere/mettere al ~** to be safe/put in a safe place; **~ di sé** self-confident, sure of o.s.; **sentirsi ~** to feel safe o secure

si'edo ecc vb vedi **sedere**

si'epe sf hedge

si'ero sm (Med) serum; **sieronega'tivo, -a** ag HIV-negative; **sieroposi'tivo, -a** ag HIV-positive

si'ete vb vedi **essere**

si'filide sf syphilis

Sig. abbr (= signore) Mr

siga'retta sf cigarette; ~ **elettronica** e-cigarette

'sigaro sm cigar

Sigg. abbr (= signori) Messrs

sigil'lare [sidʒil'lare] /72/ vt to seal

si'gillo [si'dʒillo] sm seal

'sigla sf initials pl; (abbreviazione) acronym, abbreviation;

S

~ automobilistica *abbreviation of province on vehicle number plate*; **~ musicale** signature tune

Sig.na *abbr* (= *signorina*) Miss

signifi'care [siɲɲifi'kare] /20/ *vt* to mean; **signifi'cato** *sm* meaning

si'gnora [siɲ'ɲora] *sf* lady; **la ~ X** Mrs X; **buon giorno S~/Signore/ Signorina** good morning; (*deferente*) good morning Madam/Sir/Madam; (*quando si conosce il nome*) good morning Mrs/Mr/Miss X; **Gentile S~/Signore/Signorina** (*in una lettera*) Dear Madam/Sir/Madam; **il signor Rossi e ~** Mr Rossi and his wife; **signore e signori** ladies and gentlemen

si'gnore [siɲ'ɲore] *sm* gentleman; (*padrone*) lord, master; (*Rel*) **il S~** the Lord; **il signor X** Mr X; **i signori Bianchi** (*coniugi*) Mr and Mrs Bianchi; *vedi anche* **signora**

signo'rile [siɲɲo'rile] *ag* refined

signo'rina [siɲɲo'rina] *sf* young lady; **la ~ X** Miss X; *vedi anche* **signora**

Sig.ra *abbr* (= *signora*) Mrs

silenzia'tore [silentsja'tore] *sm* silencer

si'lenzio [si'lɛntsjo] *sm* silence; **fare ~** to be quiet, stop talking; **silenzi'oso, -a** *ag* silent, quiet

si'licio [si'litʃo] *sm* silicon

sili'cone *sm* silicone

'sillaba *sf* syllable

si'luro *sm* torpedo

SIM [sim] *sigla f inv* (*Tel*): **~ card** SIM card

simboleggi'are [simboled'dʒare] /62/ *vt* to symbolize

'simbolo *sm* symbol

'simile *ag* (*analogo*) similar; (*di questo tipo*): **un uomo ~** such a man, a man like this; **libri simili** such books; **~ a** similar to; **i suoi simili** one's fellow men; one's peers

simme'tria *sf* symmetry

simpa'tia *sf* (*qualità*) pleasantness; (*inclinazione*) liking; **avere ~ per**

qn to like sb, have a liking for sb; **sim'patico, -a, -ci, -che** *ag* (*persona*) nice, pleasant, likeable; (*casa, albergo ecc*) nice, pleasant

> Attenzione! In inglese esiste la parola *sympathetic*, che però significa *comprensivo*.

simpatiz'zare [simpatid'dzare] /72/ *vi*: **~ con** to take a liking to

simu'lare /72/ *vt* to sham, simulate; (*Tecn*) to simulate

simul'taneo, -a *ag* simultaneous

sina'goga, -ghe *sf* synagogue

sincerità [sintʃeri'ta] *sf* sincerity

sin'cero, -a [sin'tʃero] *ag* sincere; (*onesto*) genuine; heartfelt

sinda'cale *ag* (trade-)union *cpd*

sinda'cato *sm* (*di lavoratori*) (trade) union; (*Amm, Econ, Dir*) syndicate, trust, pool

'sindaco, -ci *sm* mayor

sinfo'nia *sf* (*Mus*) symphony

singhioz'zare [singjot'tsare] /72/ *vi* to sob; to hiccup

singhi'ozzo [sin'gjottso] *sm* sob; (*Med*) hiccup; **avere il ~** to have the hiccups; **a ~** (*fig*) by fits and starts

'single ['singol] *ag inv*, *smf inv* single

singo'lare *ag* (*insolito*) remarkable, singular; (*Ling*) singular ▷ *sm* (*Ling*) singular; (*Tennis*): **~ maschile/ femminile** men's/women's singles

'singolo, -a *ag* single, individual ▷ *sm* (*persona*) individual; (*Tennis*); = **singolare**

si'nistro, -a *ag* left, left-hand; (*fig*) sinister ▷ *sm* (*incidente*) accident ▷ *sf* (*Pol*) left (wing); **a sinistra** on the left; (*direzione*) to the left

si'nonimo *sm* synonym; **~ di** synonymous with

sin'tassi *sf* syntax

'sintesi *sf* synthesis; (*riassunto*) summary, résumé

sin'tetico, -a, -ci, -che *ag* synthetic

sintetiz'zare [sintetid'dzare] /72/ *vt* to synthesize; (*riassumere*) to summarize

sinto'matico, -a, -ci, -che *ag* symptomatic

'sintomo *sm* symptom

sintoniz'zare [sintonid'dzare] /72/ *vt* to tune (in); **sintonizzarsi** *vpr*: **sintonizzarsi su** to tune in to

si'pario *sm* (*Teat*) curtain

si'rena *sf* (*apparecchio*) siren; (*nella mitologia, fig*) siren, mermaid

'Siria *sf*: **la ~** Syria

si'ringa, -ghe *sf* syringe

'sismico, -a, -ci, -che *ag* seismic

sis'tema, -i *sm* system; (*metodo*) method, way; **~ nervoso** nervous system; **~ operativo** (*Inform*) operating system; **~ solare** solar system

siste'mare /72/ *vt* (*mettere a posto*) to tidy, put in order; (*risolvere: questione*) to sort out, settle; (*procurare un lavoro a*) to find a job for; (*dare un alloggio a*) to settle, find accommodation (*BRIT*) *o* accommodations (*US*) for; **sistemarsi** *vpr* (*problema*) to be settled; (*persona: trovare alloggio*) to find accommodation(s); (: *trovarsi un lavoro*) to get fixed up with a job; **ti sistemo io!** I'll soon sort you out!

siste'matico, -a, -ci, -che *ag* systematic

sistemazi'one [sistemat'tsjone] *sf* arrangement, order; settlement; employment; accommodation (*BRIT*), accommodations (*US*)

'sito *sm*: **~ Internet** website

situ'ato, -a *ag*: **~ a/su** situated at/on

situazi'one [situat'tsjone] *sf* situation

ski-lift [ski'lift] *sm inv* ski tow

slacci'are [zlat'tʃare] /14/ *vt* to undo, unfasten

slanci'ato, -a [zlan'tʃato] *ag* slender

'slancio *sm* dash, leap; (*fig*) surge; **di ~** impetuously

'slavo, -a *ag* Slav(onic), Slavic

sle'ale *ag* disloyal; (*concorrenza ecc*) unfair

sle'gare /80/ *vt* to untie

slip [zlip] *sm inv* briefs *pl*

'slitta *sf* sledge; (*trainata*) sleigh

slit'tare /72/ *vi* to slip, slide; (*Aut*) to skid

s.l.m. *abbr* (= *sul livello del mare*) a.s.l.

slo'gare /80/ *vt* (*Med*) to dislocate

sloggi'are [zlod'dʒare] /62/ *vt* (*inquilino*) to turn out ▷ *vi* to move out

Slo'vacchia [zlo'vakkja] *sf* Slovakia

slo'vacco, -a, -ci, -che *ag, sm/f* Slovak

Slo'venia *sf* Slovenia

slo'veno, -a *ag, sm/f* Slovene, Slovenian ▷ *sm* (*Ling*) Slovene

smacchi'are [zmak'kjare] /19/ *vt* to remove stains from; **smacchia'tore** *sm* stain remover

'smacco, -chi *sm* humiliating defeat

smagli'ante [zmaʎ'ʎante] *ag* brilliant, dazzling

smaglia'tura [zmaʎʎa'tura] *sf* (*su maglia, calza*) ladder; (*sulla pelle*) stretch mark

smalizi'ato, -a [smalit'tsjato] *ag* shrewd, cunning

smalti'mento *sm* (*di rifiuti*) disposal

smal'tire /55/ *vt* (*merce*) to sell off; (*rifiuti*) to dispose of; (*cibo*) to digest; (*peso*) to lose; (*rabbia*) to get over; **~ la sbornia** to sober up

'smalto *sm* (*anche di denti*) enamel; (*per ceramica*) glaze; **~ per unghie** nail varnish

smantel'lare /72/ *vt* to dismantle

smarri'mento *sm* loss; (*fig*) bewilderment; dismay

smar'rire /55/ *vt* to lose; (*non riuscire a trovare*) to mislay; **smarrirsi** *vpr* (*perdersi*) to lose one's way, get lost; (: *oggetto*) to go astray

'smartphone ['zmartfɔn] *sm inv* smartphone

smasche'rare [zmaske'rare] /72/ *vt* to unmask

SME *abbr* = **Stato Maggiore Esercito** ▷ *sigla m* (= *Sistema Monetario Europeo*) EMS

smen'tire /55/ vt (negare) to deny; (testimonianza) to refute; **smentirsi** vpr to be inconsistent

sme'raldo sm emerald

'smesso, -a pp di **smettere**

'smettere /63/ vt to stop; (vestiti) to stop wearing ▷ vi to stop, cease; **~ di fare** to stop doing

'smilzo, -a ['zmiltso] ag thin, lean

sminu'ire /72/ vt to diminish, lessen; (fig) to belittle

sminuz'zare [zminut'tsare] /72/ vt to break into small pieces; to crumble

'smisi ecc vb vedi **smettere**

smis'tare /72/ vt (pacchi ecc) to sort; (Ferr) to shunt

smisu'rato, -a ag boundless, immeasurable; (grandissimo) immense, enormous

'smoking ['smoukiŋ] sm inv dinner jacket

smon'tare /72/ vt (mobile, macchina ecc) to take to pieces, dismantle; (fig: scoraggiare) to dishearten ▷ vi (scendere: da cavallo) to dismount; (: da treno) to get off; (terminare il lavoro) to stop (work); **smontarsi** vpr to lose heart; to lose one's enthusiasm

'smorfia sf grimace; (atteggiamento lezioso) simpering; **fare smorfie** to make faces; to simper

'smorto, -a ag (viso) pale, wan; (colore) dull

smor'zare [zmor'tsare] /72/ vt (suoni) to deaden; (colori) to tone down; (luce) to dim; (sete) to quench; (entusiasmo) to dampen; **smorzarsi** vpr (suono, luce) to fade; (entusiasmo) to dampen

sms ['ɛsse'ɛmme'ɛsse] sm inv text (message)

smu'overe /66/ vt to move, shift; (fig: commuovere) to move; (: dall'inerzia) to rouse, stir

snatu'rato, -a ag inhuman, heartless

'snello, -a ag (agile) agile; (svelto) slender, slim

sner'vante ag (attesa, lavoro) exasperating

sniffare [znif'fare] /72/ vt (fam: cocaina) to snort

snob'bare /72/ vt to snub

sno'dare /72/ vt (rendere agile, mobile) to loosen; **snodarsi** vpr (articolarsi) to come loose; (strada, fiume) to bend; (strada, fiume) to wind

sno'dato, -a ag (articolazione, persona) flexible; (fune ecc) undone

so vb vedi **sapere**

sobbar'carsi /20/ vpr: **~ a** to take on, undertake

'sobrio, -a ag sober

socchi'udere [sok'kjudere] /22/ vt (porta) to leave ajar; (occhi) to half-close; **socchi'uso, -a** pp di **socchiudere**

soc'correre /28/ vt to help, assist

soccorri'tore, -'trice sm/f rescuer

soc'corso, -a pp di **soccorrere** ▷ sm help, aid, assistance; **~ stradale** breakdown service

soci'ale [so'tʃale] ag social; (di associazione) club cpd, association cpd

socia'lismo [sotʃa'lizmo] sm socialism; **socia'lista, -i, -e** ag, smf socialist; **socializ'zare** [sotʃalid'dzare] /72/ vi to socialize

società [sotʃe'ta] sf inv society; (sportiva) club; (Comm) company; **~ per azioni** joint-stock company; **~ a responsabilità limitata** type of limited liability company

soci'evole [so'tʃevole] ag sociable

'socio ['sɔtʃo] sm (Dir, Comm) partner; (membro di associazione) member

'soda sf (Chim) soda; (acqua gassata) soda (water)

soddisfa'cente [soddisfa'tʃɛnte] ag satisfactory

soddis'fare /41/ vt, vi: **~ (a)** to satisfy; (impegno) to fulfil; (debito) to pay off; (richiesta) to meet, comply with; **soddis'fatto, -a** pp di **soddisfare** ▷ ag satisfied; **essere soddisfatto di** to be satisfied o pleased with; **soddisfazi'one** sf satisfaction

'**sodo, -a** ag firm, hard; (uovo) hard-boiled ▷ av (picchiare, lavorare) hard; **dormire ~** to sleep soundly

sofà sm inv sofa

soffe'renza [soffe'rɛntsa] sf suffering

sof'ferto, -a pp di **soffrire**

soffi'are /19/ vt to blow; (notizia, segreto) to whisper ▷ vi to blow; (sbuffare) to puff (and blow); **soffiarsi il naso** to blow one's nose; **~ qc/qn a qn** (fig) to pinch o steal sth/sb from sb; **~ via qc** to blow sth away

soffi'ata sf (fam) tip-off; **fare una ~ alla polizia** to tip off the police

'**soffice** ['sɔffitʃe] ag soft

'**soffio** sm (di vento) breath; (Med) murmur

sof'fitta sf attic

sof'fitto sm ceiling

soffo'cante ag suffocating, stifling

soffo'care /20/ vi (anche: **soffocarsi**) to suffocate, choke ▷ vt to suffocate, choke; (fig) to stifle, suppress

sof'frire /70/ vt to suffer, endure; (sopportare) to bear, stand ▷ vi to suffer; to be in pain; **~ (di) qc** (Med) to suffer from sth

sof'fritto, -a pp di **soffriggere** ▷ sm (Cuc) fried mixture of herbs, bacon and onions

sofisti'cato, -a ag sophisticated; (vino) adulterated

'**software** ['sɔftwɛə] sm: **~ applicativo** applications package

sogget'tivo, -a [soddʒet'tivo] ag subjective

sog'getto, -a [sod'dʒɛtto] ag: **~ a** (sottomesso) subject to; (esposto) (a variazioni, danni ecc) subject o liable to ▷ sm subject

soggezi'one [soddʒet'tsjone] sf subjection; (timidezza) awe; **avere ~ di qn** to stand in awe of sb; to be ill at ease in sb's presence

soggi'orno [sod'dʒorno] sm (permanenza) stay; (stanza) living room

'**soglia** ['sɔʎʎa] sf doorstep; (anche fig) threshold

sogli'ola ['sɔʎʎola] sf (Zool) sole

so'gnare [soɲ'ɲare] /15/ vt, vi to dream; **~ a occhi aperti** to daydream

'**sogno** ['soɲɲo] sm dream

'**soia** sf (Bot) soya

sol sm (Mus) G; (: solfeggiando la scala) so(h)

so'laio sm (soffitta) attic

sola'mente av only, just

so'lare ag solar, sun cpd

'**solco, -chi** sm (scavo, fig: ruga) furrow; (incavo) rut, track; (di disco) groove

sol'dato sm soldier; **~ semplice** private

'**soldo** sm (fig): **non vale un ~** it's not worth a penny; **soldi** smpl (denaro) money sg: **non ho soldi** I haven't got any money

'**sole** sm sun; (luce) sun(light); (tempo assolato) sun(shine); **prendere il ~** to sunbathe

soleggi'ato, -a [soled'dʒato] ag sunny

so'lenne ag solemn

so'lere /108/ vb impers: **come suole accadere** as is usually the case, as usually happens

soli'dale ag: **essere ~ con qn** to be in agreement with sb

solidarietà sf solidarity

'**solido, -a** ag solid; (forte, robusto) sturdy, solid; (fig: ditta) sound, solid ▷ sm (Mat) solid

so'lista, -i, -e ag solo ▷ smf soloist

solita'mente av usually, as a rule

soli'tario, -a ag (senza compagnia) solitary, lonely; (solo, isolato) solitary, lone; (deserto) lonely ▷ sm (gioiello, gioco) solitaire

'**solito, -a** ag usual; **essere ~ fare** to be in the habit of doing; **di ~** usually;

più tardi del ~ later than usual;
come al ~ as usual
soli'tudine sf solitude
sol'letico sm tickling; **soffrire il ~** to
be ticklish
solleva'mento sm raising; lifting;
(ribellione) revolt; **~ pesi** (Sport)
weight-lifting
solle'vare /72/ vt to lift, raise; (fig:
persona: alleggerire): **~ (da)** to relieve
(of); (: dar conforto) to comfort,
relieve; (: questione) to raise; (: far
insorgere) to stir (to revolt); **sollevarsi**
vpr to rise; (fig: riprendersi) to recover;
(: ribellarsi) to rise up
solli'evo sm relief; (conforto) comfort
'solo, -a ag alone; (in senso spirituale:
isolato) lonely; (unico): **un ~ libro**
only one book, a single book; (con ag
numerale): **veniamo noi tre soli** just
o only the three of us are coming ▷ av
(soltanto) only, just; **non ~ ... ma
anche** not only ... but also; **fare qc
da ~** to do sth (all) by oneself
sol'tanto av only
sol'lubile ag (sostanza) soluble
soluzi'one [solut'tsjone] sf solution
sol'vente ag, sm solvent
so'maro sm ass, donkey
somigli'anza [somiʎ'ʎantsa] sf
resemblance
somigli'are [somiʎ'ʎare] /27/ vi:
~ a to be like, resemble; (nell'aspetto
fisico) to look like; **somigliarsi** vpr to
be (o look) alike
'somma sf (Mat) sum; (di denaro) sum
(of money)
som'mare /72/ vt to add up;
(aggiungere) to add; **tutto sommato**
all things considered
som'mario, -a ag (racconto, indagine)
brief; (giustizia) summary ▷ sm
summary
sommer'gibile [sommer'dʒibile]
sm submarine
som'merso, -a pp di **sommergere**
sommità sf inv summit, top; (fig)
height

som'mossa sf uprising
'sonda sf (Med, Meteor, Aer) probe;
(Mineralogia) drill ▷ ag inv: **pallone** m
~ weather balloon
son'daggio [son'daddʒo] sm
sounding; probe; boring, drilling;
(indagine) survey; **~ d'opinioni**
opinion poll
son'dare /72/ vt (Naut) to sound;
(atmosfera, piaga) to probe;
(Mineralogia) to bore, drill; (fig:
opinione ecc) to survey, poll
so'netto sm sonnet
son'nambulo, -a sm/f sleepwalker
sonnel'lino sm nap
son'nifero sm sleeping drug (o pill)
'sonno sm sleep; **aver ~** to be sleepy;
prendere ~ to fall asleep
'sono vb vedi **essere**
so'noro, -a ag (ambiente) resonant;
(voce) sonorous, ringing; (onde: Cine)
sound cpd
sontu'oso, -a ag sumptuous; lavish
sop'palco, -chi sm mezzanine
soppor'tare /72/ vt (subire: perdita,
spese) to bear, sustain; (soffrire: dolore)
to bear, endure; (cosa: freddo) to
withstand; (persona: freddo, vino) to
take; (tollerare) to put up with, tolerate

> Attenzione! In inglese esiste il
> verbo to support, che però non
> significa sopportare.

sop'primere /50/ vt (carica, privilegi
ecc) to do away with; (pubblicazione)
to suppress; (parola, frase) to delete
'sopra prep (gen) on; (al di sopra di, più
in alto di) above; over; (riguardo a) on,
about ▷ av on top; (attaccato, scritto)
on it; (al di sopra) above; (al piano
superiore) upstairs; **donne ~ i 30 anni**
women over 30 (years of age); **abito
di ~** I live upstairs; **dormirci ~** (fig)
to sleep on it
so'prabito sm overcoat
soprac'ciglio [soprat'tʃiʎʎo] (pl f
sopracciglia) sm eyebrow
sopraf'fare /41/ vt to overcome,
overwhelm

soprallu'ogo, -ghi *sm (di esperti)* inspection; *(di polizia)* on-the-spot investigation

sopram'mobile *sm* ornament

soprannatu'rale *ag* supernatural

sopran'nome *sm* nickname

so'prano, -a *sm/f (persona)* soprano ▷ *sm (voce)* soprano

soprappensi'ero *av* lost in thought

sopras'salto *sm*: **di ~** with a start; suddenly

soprasse'dere /107/ *vi*: **~ a** to delay, put off

soprat'tutto *av (anzitutto)* above all; *(specialmente)* especially

sopravvalu'tare /72/ *vt* to overestimate

soprav'vento *sm*: **avere/prendere il ~ su qn** to have/get the upper hand over sb

sopravvis'suto, -a *pp di* **sopravvivere**

soprav'vivere /130/ *vi* to survive; *(continuare a vivere)*: **~ (in)** to live on (in); **~ a** *(incidente ecc)* to survive; *(persona)* to outlive

so'pruso *sm* abuse of power; **subire un ~** to be abused

soq'quadro *sm*: **mettere a ~** to turn upside-down

sor'betto *sm* sorbet, water ice

sor'dina *sf*: **in ~** softly; *(fig)* on the sly

'sordo, -a *ag* deaf; *(rumore)* muffled; *(dolore)* dull; *(odio, rancore)* silent ▷ *sm/f* deaf person; **sordo'muto, -a** *ag* hearing- and speech-impaired ▷ *sm/f* person with a hearing- and speech-impairment

so'rella *sf* sister; **sorel'lastra** *sf* stepsister; *(con genitore in comune)* half sister

sor'gente [sor'dʒɛnte] *sf (acqua che sgorga)* spring; *(di fiume, Fisica, fig)* source

'sorgere ['sordʒere] /109/ *vi* to rise; *(scaturire)* to spring, rise; *(fig: difficoltà)* to arise

sorni'one, -a *ag* sly

sorpas'sare /72/ *vt (Aut)* to overtake; *(fig)* to surpass; *(: eccedere)* to exceed, go beyond; **~ in altezza** to be higher than; *(persona)* to be taller than

sorpren'dente *ag* surprising

sor'prendere /81/ *vt (cogliere: in flagrante ecc)* to catch; *(stupire)* to surprise; **sorprendersi** *vpr*: **sorprendersi (di)** to be surprised (at); **sor'preso, -a** *pp di* **sorprendere** ▷ *sf* surprise; **fare una sorpresa a qn** to give sb a surprise

sor'reggere [sor'reddʒere] /87/ *vt* to support, hold up; *(fig)* to sustain; **sorreggersi** *vpr (tenersi ritto)* to stay upright

sor'ridere /89/ *vi* to smile; **sor'riso, -a** *pp di* **sorridere** ▷ *sm* smile

'sorsi *ecc vb vedi* **sorgere**

'sorso *sm* sip

'sorta *sf* sort, kind; **di ~** whatever, of any kind at all

'sorte *sf (fato)* fate, destiny; *(evento fortuito)* chance; **tirare a ~** to draw lots

sor'teggio [sor'teddʒo] *sm* draw

sorvegli'ante [sorveʎ'ʎante] *smf (di carcere)* guard, warder (BRIT); *(di fabbrica ecc)* supervisor

sorvegli'anza [sorveʎ'ʎantsa] *sf* watch; supervision; *(Polizia, Mil)* surveillance

sorvegli'are [sorveʎ'ʎare] /27/ *vt (bambino, bagagli, prigioniero)* to watch, keep an eye on; *(malato)* to watch over; *(territorio, casa)* to watch o keep watch over; *(lavori)* to supervise

sorvo'lare /72/ *vt (territorio)* to fly over ▷ *vi*: **~ su** *(fig)* to skim over

S.O.S. *sigla m* mayday, SOS

'sosia *sm inv* double

sos'pendere /8/ *vt (appendere)* to hang (up); *(interrompere, privare di una carica)* to suspend; *(rimandare)* to defer; *(appendere)* to hang

sospet'tare /72/ *vt* to suspect ▷ *vi*: **~ di** to suspect; *(diffidare)* to be suspicious of

S

sos'petto, -a *ag* suspicious ▷ *sm* suspicion; **sospet'toso, -a** *ag* suspicious

sospi'rare /72/ *vi* to sigh ▷ *vt* to long for, yearn for; **sos'piro** *sm* sigh

'sosta *sf* (*fermata*) stop, halt; (*pausa*) pause, break; **senza ~** non-stop, without a break

sostan'tivo *sm* noun, substantive

sos'tanza [sos'tantsa] *sf* substance; **sostanze** *sfpl* (*ricchezze*) wealth *sg*, possessions; **in ~** in short, to sum up

sos'tare /72/ *vi* (*fermarsi*) to stop (for a while), stay; (*fare una pausa*) to take a break

sos'tegno [sos'teɲɲo] *sm* support

soste'nere /121/ *vt* to support; (*prendere su di sé*) to take on, bear; (*resistere*) to withstand, stand up to; (*affermare*): **~ che** to maintain that; **sostenersi** *vpr* to hold o.s. up, support o.s.; (*fig*) to keep up one's strength; **~ gli esami** to sit exams

sostenta'mento *sm* maintenance, support

sostitu'ire /55/ *vt* (*mettere al posto di*): **~ qn/qc a** to substitute sb/sth for; (*prendere il posto di*) to replace, take the place of

sosti'tuto, -a *sm/f* substitute

sostituzi'one [sostitut'tsjone] *sf* substitution; **in ~ di** as a substitute for, in place of

sotta'ceti [sotta't∫eti] *smpl* pickles

sot'tana *sf* (*sottoveste*) underskirt; (*gonna*) skirt; (*Rel*) soutane, cassock

sotter'fugio [sotter'fudʒo] *sm* subterfuge

sotter'raneo, -a *ag* underground ▷ *sm* cellar

sotter'rare /72/ *vt* to bury

sot'tile *ag* thin; (*figura, caviglia*) thin, slim, slender; (*fine: polvere, capelli*) fine; (*fig: leggero*) light; (*: vista*) sharp, keen; (*: olfatto*) fine, discriminating; (*: mente*) subtle; shrewd ▷ *sm*: **non andare per il ~** not to mince matters

sottin'teso, -a *pp di* **sottintendere** ▷ *sm* allusion; **parlare senza sottintesi** to speak plainly

'sotto *prep* (*gen*) under; (*più in basso di*) below ▷ *av* underneath, beneath; below; **(al piano) di ~** downstairs; **~ il monte** at the foot of the mountain; **~ la pioggia/il sole** in the rain/sun(shine); **siamo ~ Natale/ Pasqua** it's nearly Christmas/Easter; **~ forma di** in the form of; **~ terra** underground; **chiuso ~ vuoto** vacuum packed

sotto'fondo *sm* background; **~ musicale** background music

sottoline'are /72/ *vt* to underline; (*fig*) to emphasize, stress

sottoma'rino, -a *ag* (*flora*) submarine; (*cavo, navigazione*) underwater ▷ *sm* (*Naut*) submarine

sottopas'saggio [sottopas'saddʒo] *sm* (*Aut*) underpass; (*pedonale*) subway, underpass

sotto'porre /77/ *vt* (*costringere*) to subject; (*fig: presentare*) to submit; **sottoporsi** *vpr* to submit; **sottoporsi a** (*subire*) to undergo

sotto'sopra *av* upside-down

sotto'terra *av* underground

sotto'titolo *sm* subtitle

sottovalu'tare /72/ *vt* to underestimate

sotto'veste *sf* underskirt

sotto'voce [sotto'vot∫e] *av* in a low voice

sottovu'oto *av*: **confezionare ~** to vacuum-pack ▷ *ag*: **confezione** *f* **~** vacuum pack

sot'trarre /123/ *vt* (*Mat*) to subtract, take away; **sottrarsi** *vpr*: **sottrarsi a** (*sfuggire*) to escape; (*evitare*) to avoid; **~ qn/qc a** (*togliere*) to remove sb/sth from; (*salvare*) to save *o* rescue sb/sth from; **~ qc a qn** (*rubare*) to steal sth from sb; **sottrazi'one** *sf* subtraction; (*furto*) removal

souve'nir [suv(ə)'nir] *sm inv* souvenir

sovi'etico, -a, -ci, -che *ag* Soviet ▷ *sm/f* Soviet citizen

sovrac'carico, -a, -chi, -che *ag*: **~ (di)** overloaded (with) ▷ *sm* excess load; **~ di lavoro** extra work

sovraffol'lato, -a *ag* overcrowded

sovrannatu'rale *ag* **= soprannaturale**

so'vrano, -a *ag* sovereign; (*fig: sommo*) supreme ▷ *sm/f* sovereign, monarch

sovrap'porre /77/ *vt* to place on top of, put on top of

sovvenzi'one [sovven'tsjone] *sf* subsidy, grant

'sozzo, -a ['sottso] *ag* filthy, dirty

S.p.A. *abbr vedi* **società per azioni**

spac'care /20/ *vt* to split, break; (*legna*) to chop; **spaccarsi** *vpr* to split, break; **spacca'tura** *sf* split

spaccherò *ecc* [spakke'rɔ] *vb vedi* **spaccare**

spacci'are /14/ *vt* (*vendere*) to sell (off); (*mettere in circolazione*) to circulate; (*droga*) to peddle, push; **spacciarsi** *vpr*: **spacciarsi per** (*farsi credere*) to pass o.s. off as, pretend to be; **spaccia'tore, -'trice** [spattʃa'tore] *sm/f* (*di droga*) pusher; (*di denaro falso*) dealer; **'spaccio** *sm*: **spaccio (di)** (*di merce rubata, droga*) trafficking (in); (*di denaro falso*) passing (of); (*vendita*) sale; (*bottega*) shop

'spacco, -chi *sm* (*fenditura*) split, crack; (*strappo*) tear; (*di gonna*) slit

spac'cone *smf* boaster, braggart

'spada *sf* sword

spae'sato, -a *ag* disorientated, lost

spa'ghetti [spa'getti] *smpl* (*Cuc*) spaghetti *sg*

'Spagna ['spaɲɲa] *sf*: **la ~** Spain; **spa'gnolo, -a** *ag* Spanish ▷ *sm/f* Spaniard ▷ *sm* (*Ling*) Spanish; **gli Spagnoli** the Spanish

'spago, -ghi *sm* string, twine

spai'ato, -a *ag* (*calza, guanto*) odd

spalan'care /20/ *vt*, **spalan'carsi** *vpr* to open wide

spa'lare /72/ *vt* to shovel

'spalla *sf* shoulder; (*fig: Teat*) stooge; **spalle** *sfpl* (*dorso*) back

spalli'era *sf* (*di sedia ecc*) back; (*di letto: da capo*) head(board); (: *da piedi*) foot(board); (*Ginnastica*) wall bars *pl*

spal'lina *sf* (*di sottoveste, maglietta*) strap; (*imbottitura*) shoulder pad

spal'mare /72/ *vt* to spread

'spalti *smpl* (*di stadio*) terraces

spamming ['spammin] *sm* (*Internet*) spamming

'spandere /110/ *vt* to spread; (*versare*) to pour (out)

spa'rare /72/ *vt* to fire ▷ *vi* (*far fuoco*) to fire; (*tirare*) to shoot; **spara'toria** *sf* exchange of shots

sparecchi'are [sparek'kjare] /19/ *vt*: **~ (la tavola)** to clear the table

spa'reggio [spa'reddʒo] *sm* (*Sport*) play-off

'spargere ['spardʒere] /111/ *vt* (*sparpagliare*) to scatter; (*versare: vino*) to spill; (: *lacrime, sangue*) to shed; (*diffondere*) to spread; (*emanare*) to give off (*o* out); **spargersi** *vpr* to spread

spa'rire /112/ *vi* to disappear, vanish

spar'lare /72/ *vi*: **~ di** to run down, speak ill of

'sparo *sm* shot

spar'tire /55/ *vt* (*eredità, bottino*) to share out; (*avversari*) to separate

spar'tito *sm* (*Mus*) score

sparti'traffico *sm inv* (*Aut*) central reservation (BRIT), median (strip) (US)

sparvi'ero *sm* (*Zool*) sparrowhawk

spasi'mante *sm* suitor

spassio'nato, -a *ag* dispassionate, impartial

'spasso *sm* (*divertimento*) amusement, enjoyment; **andare a ~** to go out for a walk; **essere a ~** (*fig*) to be out of work; **mandare qn a ~** (*fig*) to give sb the sack

'spatola *sf* spatula; (*di muratore*) trowel

spa'valdo, -a *ag* arrogant, bold

spaventa'passeri *sm inv* scarecrow

spaven'tare /72/ *vt* to frighten, scare; **spaventarsi** *vpr* to become frightened, become scared; to get a fright; spa'vento *sm* fear, fright; **far spavento a qn** to give sb a fright; spaven'toso, -a *ag* frightening, terrible; (*fig: fam*) tremendous, fantastic

spazien'tirsi [spattsjen'tirsi] /55/ *vpr* to lose one's patience

'spazio ['spattsjo] *sm* space; ~ **aereo** airspace; **spazi'oso, -a** *ag* spacious

spazzaca'mino [spattsaka'mino] *sm* chimney sweep

spazza'neve [spattsa'neve] *sm inv* snowplough

spaz'zare [spat'tsare] /72/ *vt* to sweep; (*foglie ecc*) to sweep up; (*cacciare*) to sweep away; **spazza'tura** *sf* sweepings *pl*; (*immondizia*) rubbish; **spaz'zino** *sm* street sweeper

'spazzola ['spattsola] *sf* brush; ~ **per abiti** clothesbrush; ~ **da capelli** hairbrush; **spazzo'lare** /72/ *vt* to brush; **spazzo'lino** *sm* (small) brush; **spazzolino da denti** toothbrush

specchi'arsi [spek'kjarsi] /19/ *vpr* to look at o.s. in a mirror; (*riflettersi*) to be mirrored, be reflected

specchi'etto [spek'kjetto] *sm* (*tabella*) table, chart; ~ **da borsetta** pocket mirror; ~ **retrovisore** (*Aut*) rear-view mirror

'specchio ['spekkjo] *sm* mirror

speci'ale [spe'tʃale] *ag* special; **specia'lista, -i, -e** *smf* specialist; **specialità** *sf inv* speciality; (*branca di studio*) special field, speciality; **specializzazi'one** *sf* specialization; **special'mente** *av* especially, particularly

'specie ['spetʃe] *sf inv* (*Biol, Bot, Zool*) species *inv*; (*tipo*) kind, sort ⊳ *av* especially, particularly; **una ~ di** a kind of; **fare ~ a qn** to surprise sb; **la ~ umana** mankind

specifi'care [spetʃifi'kare] /20/ *vt* to specify, state

spe'cifico, -a, -ci, -che [spe'tʃifiko] *ag* specific

specu'lare /72/ *vi*: ~ **su** (*Comm*) to speculate in; (*sfruttare*) to exploit; (*meditare*) to speculate on; **speculazi'one** *sf* speculation

spe'dire /55/ *vt* to send

'spegnere ['speɲɲere] /113/ *vt* (*fuoco, sigaretta*) to put out, extinguish; (*apparecchio elettrico*) to turn o switch off; (*gas*) to turn off; (*fig: suoni, passioni*) to stifle; (*debito*) to cancel; **spegnersi** *vpr* to go out; to go off; (*morire*) to pass away; **puoi ~ la luce?** could you switch off the light?

spel'lare /72/ *vt* (*scuoiare*) to skin; **spellarsi** *vpr* to peel

'spendere /8/ *vt* to spend

'spengo *ecc vb vedi* **spegnere**

'spensi *ecc vb vedi* **spegnere**

spensie'rato, -a *ag* carefree

'spento, -a *pp di* **spegnere** ⊳ *ag* (*suono*) muffled; (*colore*) dull; (*sigaretta*) out; (*civiltà, vulcano*) extinct

spe'ranza [spe'rantsa] *sf* hope

spe'rare /72/ *vt* to hope for ⊳ *vi*: ~ **in** to trust in; ~ **che/di fare** to hope that/to do; **lo spero, spero di sì** I hope so

sper'duto, -a *ag* (*isolato*) out-of-the-way; (*persona: smarrita, a disagio*) lost

sperimen'tale *ag* experimental

sperimen'tare /72/ *vt* to experiment with, test; (*fig*) to test, put to the test

'sperma, -i *sm* sperm

spe'rone *sm* spur

sperpe'rare /72/ *vt* to squander

'spesa *sf* (*soldi spesi*) expense; (*costo*) cost; (*acquisto*) purchase; (*fam: acquisto del cibo quotidiano*) shopping; **spese postali** postage *sg*: **spese di viaggio** travelling (*BRIT*) o traveling (*US*) expenses 'spesso, -a *ag* (*fitto*) thick; (*frequente*) frequent ▷ *av* often; **spesse volte** frequently, often

spes'sore *sm* thickness

Spett. *abbr vedi* **spettabile**

spet'tabile *ag* (*in lettere, abbr* Spett.): **~ ditta X** Messrs X and Co

spet'tacolo *sm* (*rappresentazione*) performance, show; (*vista, scena*) sight; **dare o ~ di sé** to make an exhibition o a spectacle of o.s.

spet'tare /72/ *vi*: **~ a** (*decisione*) to be up to; (*stipendio*) to be due to; **spetta a lei decidere** it's up to you to decide

spetta'tore, -'trice *sm/f* (*Cine, Teat*) member of the audience; (*di avvenimento*) onlooker, witness

spettego'lare /72/ *vi* to gossip

spetti'nato, -a *ag* dishevelled

'spettro *sm* (*fantasma*) spectre; (*Fisica*) spectrum

'spezie ['spɛttsje] *sfpl* (*Cuc*) spices

spez'zare [spet'tsare] /72/ *vt* (*rompere*) to break; (*fig: interrompere*) to break up; **spezzarsi** *vpr* to break

spezza'tino [spettsa'tino] *sm* (*Cuc*) stew

spezzet'tare [spettset'tare] /72/ *vt* to break up (o chop) into small pieces

'spia *sf* spy; (*confidente della polizia*) informer; (*Elettr*) indicating light; warning light; (*fessura*) peephole; (*fig: sintomo*) sign, indication

spia'cente [spja'tʃɛnte] *ag* sorry; **essere ~ di qc/di fare qc** to be sorry about sth/for doing sth

spia'cevole [spja'tʃevole] *ag* unpleasant, disagreeable

spi'aggia, -ge ['spjaddʒa] *sf* beach; **~ libera** public beach

spia'nare /72/ *vt* (*terreno*) to level, make level; (*edificio*) to raze to the ground; (*pasta*) to roll out; (*rendere liscio*) to smooth (out)

spi'are /60/ *vt* to spy on

spi'azzo ['spjattso] *sm* open space; (*radura*) clearing

'spicchio ['spikkjo] *sm* (*di agrumi*) segment; (*di aglio*) clove; (*parte*) piece, slice

spicci'are [spit'tʃare] /14/ *vt* to finish off; **spicciarsi** *vpr* to hurry up

'spicciolo, -a ['spittʃolo] *ag*: **moneta spicciola** (small) change; **spiccioli** *smpl* (small) change

'spicco, -chi *sm*: **fare ~** to stand out; **di ~** outstanding; (*tema*) main, principal

spie'dino *sm* (*utensile*) skewer; (*cibo*) kebab

spi'edo *sm* (*Cuc*) spit

spie'gare /80/ *vt* (*far capire*) to explain; (*tovaglia*) to unfold; (*vele*) to unfurl; **spiegarsi** *vpr* to explain o.s., make o.s. clear; **~ qc a qn** to explain sth to sb; **spiegazi'one** *sf* explanation

spieghe'rò *ecc* [spjege'rɔ] *vb vedi* **spiegare**

spie'tato, -a *ag* ruthless, pitiless

spiffe'rare /72/ *vt* (*fam*) to blurt out, blab

'spiffero *sm* draught (BRIT), draft (US)

'spiga, -ghe *sf* (*Bot*) ear

spigli'ato, -a [spiʎ'ʎato] *ag* self-possessed, self-confident

'spigolo *sm* corner; (*Geom*) edge

'spilla *sf* brooch; (*da cravatta, cappello*) pin; **~ di sicurezza o da balia** safety pin

'spillo *sm* pin; **~ di sicurezza o da balia** safety pin; **~ di sicurezza** (*Mil*) (safety) pin

spi'lorcio, -a, -ci, -ce [spi'lortʃo] *ag* mean, stingy

'spina *sf* (*Bot*) thorn; (*Zool*) spine, prickle; (*di pesce*) bone; (*Elettr*) plug; (*di botte*) bunghole; **birra alla ~** draught beer; **~ dorsale** (*Anat*) backbone

spi'nacio [spi'natʃo] *sm* spinach *no pl*; (*Cuc*): **spinaci** spinach *sg*

spi'nello *sm* (*Droga: gergo*) joint

'spingere ['spindʒere] /114/ *vt* to push; (*condurre: anche fig*) to drive;

S

(*stimolare*): **~ qn a fare** to urge *o* press sb to do

spi'noso, -a *ag* thorny, prickly

'**spinsi** *ecc vb vedi* **spingere**

'**spinto, -a** *pp di* **spingere** ▷ *sf* (*urto*) push; (*Fisica*) thrust; (*fig: stimolo*) incentive, spur; (: *appoggio*) string-pulling *no pl*; **dare una spinta a qn** (*fig*) to pull strings for sb

spio'naggio [spio'naddʒo] *sm* espionage, spying

spion'cino [spion'tʃino] *sm* peephole

spi'raglio [spi'raʎʎo] *sm* (*fessura*) chink, narrow opening; (*raggio di luce, fig*) gleam

spi'rale *sf* spiral; (*contraccettivo*) coil; **a ~** spiral(-shaped)

spiri'tato, -a *ag* possessed; (*fig: persona, espressione*) wild

spiri'tismo *sm* spiritualism

'**spirito** *sm* (*Rel, Chim, disposizione d'animo, di legge ecc, fantasma*) spirit; (*pensieri, intelletto*) mind; (*arguzia*) wit; (*umorismo*) humour, wit; **lo S~ Santo** the Holy Spirit *o* Ghost

spirito'saggine [spirito'saddʒine] *sf* witticism; (*peg*) wisecrack

spiri'toso, -a *ag* witty

spiritu'ale *ag* spiritual

'**splendere** /29/ *vi* to shine

'**splendido, -a** *ag* splendid; (*splendente*) shining; (*sfarzoso*) magnificent, splendid

splen'dore *sm* splendour; (*luce intensa*) brilliance, brightness

spogli'are [spoʎ'ʎare] /27/ *vt* (*svestire*) to undress; (*privare, fig: depredare*): **~ qn di qc** to deprive sb of sth; (*togliere ornamenti: anche fig*): **~ qn/qc di** to strip sb/sth of; **spogliarsi** *vpr* to undress, strip; **spogliarsi di** (*ricchezze ecc*) to deprive o.s. of, give up; (*pregiudizi*) to rid o.s. of; **spoglia'rello** *sm* striptease; **spoglia'toio** *sm* dressing room; (*di scuola ecc*) cloakroom; (*Sport*) changing room

'**spola** *sf* (*bobina*) spool; **fare la ~ (fra)** to go to and fro *o* shuttle (between)

spolve'rare /72/ *vt* (*anche Cuc*) to dust; (*con spazzola*) to brush; (*con battipanni*) to beat; (*fig*) to polish off ▷ *vi* to dust

spon'taneo, -a *ag* spontaneous; (*persona*) unaffected, natural

spor'care /20/ *vt* to dirty, make dirty; (*fig*) to sully, soil; **sporcarsi** *vpr* to get dirty

spor'cizia [spor'tʃittsja] *sf* (*stato*) dirtiness; (*sudiciume*) dirt, filth; (*cosa sporca*) dirt *no pl*, something dirty

'**sporco, -a, -chi, -che** *ag* dirty, filthy

spor'genza [spor'dʒɛntsa] *sf* projection

'**sporgere** ['spɔrdʒere] /115/ *vt* to put out, stretch out ▷ *vi* (*venire in fuori*) to stick out; **sporgersi** *vpr* to lean out; **~ querela contro qn** (*Dir*) to take legal action against sb

'**sporsi** *ecc vb vedi* **sporgere**

sport *sm inv* sport

spor'tello *sm* (*di treno, auto ecc*) door; (*di banca, ufficio*) window, counter; **~ automatico** (*Banca*) cash dispenser, automated telling machine

spor'tivo, -a *ag* (*gara, giornale*) sports *cpd*; (*persona*) sporty; (*abito*) casual; (*spirito, atteggiamento*) sporting

'**sposa** *sf* bride; (*moglie*) wife

sposa'lizio [spoza'littsjo] *sm* wedding

spo'sare /72/ *vt* to marry; (*fig: idea, fede*) to espouse; **sposarsi** *vpr* to get married, marry; **sposarsi con qn** to marry sb, get married to sb; **spo'sato, -a** *ag* married

'**sposo** *sm* (*bride*)groom; (*marito*) husband

spos'sato, -a *ag* exhausted, weary

spos'tare /72/ *vt* to move, shift; (*cambiare: orario*) to change; **spostarsi** *vpr* to move

'**spranga, -ghe** *sf* (*sbarra*) bar

spre'care /20/ *vt* to waste

spre'gevole [spre'dʒevole] *ag* contemptible, despicable

'spremere /62/ *vt* to squeeze

spremia'grumi *sm inv* lemon squeezer

spre'muta *sf* fresh fruit juice; ~ **d'arancia** fresh orange juice

sprez'zante [spret'tsante] *ag* scornful, contemptuous

sprofon'dare /72/ *vi* to sink; (*casa*) to collapse; (*suolo*) to give way, subside

spro'nare /72/ *vt* to spur (on)

sproporzio'nato, -a [sproportsjo'nato] *ag* disproportionate, out of all proportion

sproporzi'one [spropor'tsjone] *sf* disproportion

spro'posito *sm* blunder; **a ~** at the wrong time; (*rispondere, parlare*) irrelevantly

sprovve'duto, -a *ag* inexperienced, naïve

sprov'visto, -a *ag* (*mancante*): **~ di** lacking in, without; **alla sprovvista** unawares

spruz'zare [sprut'tsare] /72/ *vt* (*a nebulizzazione*) to spray; (*aspergere*) to sprinkle; (*inzaccherare*) to splash

spugna ['spuɲɲa] *sf* (*Zool*) sponge; (*tessuto*) towelling

spuma *sf* (*schiuma*) foam; (*bibita*) fizzy drink

spu'mante *sm* sparkling wine

pun'tare /72/ *vt* (*coltello*) to break the point of; (*capelli*) to trim ▷ *vi* (*uscire: germogli*) to sprout; (*: capelli*) to begin to grow; (*: denti*) to come through; (*apparire*) to appear (suddenly)

pun'tino *sm* snack

punto *sm* (*Teat, Mus*) cue; (*fig*) starting point; **dare lo ~ a** (*fig*) to give rise to

pu'tare /72/ *vt* to spit out; (*fig*) to belch (out) ▷ *vi* to spit

quadra *sf* (*strumento*) (set) square; (*gruppo*) team, squad; (*di operai*)

gang, squad; (*Mil*) squad; (*: Aer, Naut*) squadron; (*Sport*) team; **lavoro a squadre** teamwork

squagli'arsi [skwaʎ'ʎarsi] /27/ *vpr* to melt; (*fig*) to sneak off

squa'lifica, -che *sf* disqualification

squalifi'care /20/ *vt* to disqualify

'squallido, -a *ag* wretched, bleak

'squalo *sm* shark

'squama *sf* scale

squarcia'gola [skwartʃa'gola]: **a ~** *av* at the top of one's voice

squattri'nato, -a *ag* penniless

squili'brato, -a *ag* (*Psic*) unbalanced

squil'lante *ag* shrill, sharp

squil'lare /72/ *vi* (*campanello, telefono*) to ring (out); (*tromba*) to blare; **'squillo** *sm* ring, ringing *no pl*; blare ▷ *sf inv* (*anche:* **ragazza squillo**) call girl

squi'sito, -a *ag* exquisite; (*cibo*) delicious; (*persona*) delightful

squit'tire /55/ *vi* (*uccello*) to squawk; (*topo*) to squeak

sradi'care /20/ *vt* to uproot; (*fig*) to eradicate

srego'lato, -a *ag* (*senza ordine: vita*) disorderly; (*smodato*) immoderate; (*dissoluto*) dissolute

S.r.l. *abbr vedi* **società a responsabilità limitata**

sroto'lare /72/ *vt,* **sroto'larsi** *vpr* to unroll

SS *sigla* = **Sassari**

S.S.N. *abbr* (= *Servizio Sanitario Nazionale*) ≈ NHS

sta *ecc vb vedi* **stare**

'stabile *ag* stable, steady; (*tempo: non variabile*) settled; (*Teat: compagnia*) resident ▷ *sm* (*edificio*) building

stabili'mento *sm* (*edificio*) establishment; (*fabbrica*) plant, factory

stabi'lire /55/ *vt* to establish; (*fissare: prezzi, data*) to fix; (*decidere*) to decide; **stabilirsi** *vpr* (*prendere dimora*) to settle

stac'care /20/ *vt* (*levare*) to detach, remove; (*separare: anche fig*) to

S

separate, divide; (*strappare*) to tear off (*o* out); (*scandire: parole*) to pronounce clearly; (*Sport*) to leave behind; **staccarsi** *vpr* (*bottone ecc*) to come off; (*scostarsi*): **staccarsi (da)** to move away (from); (*fig: separarsi*): **staccarsi da** to leave; **non ~ gli occhi da qn** not to take one's eyes off sb

'**stadio** *sm* (*Sport*) stadium; (*periodo, fase*) phase, stage

'**staffa** *sf* (*di sella, Tecn*) stirrup; **perdere le staffe** (*fig*) to fly off the handle

staffetta *sf* (*messo*) dispatch rider; (*Sport*) relay race

stagio'nale [stadʒo'nale] *ag* seasonal

stagio'nato, -a [stadʒo'nato] *ag* seasoned matured; (*scherzoso: attempato*) getting on in years

stagi'one [sta'dʒone] *sf* season; **alta/bassa ~** high/low season

sta'gista, -i, -e [sta'dʒista] *smf* trainee, intern (*US*)

'**stagno, -a** ['staɲɲo] *ag* watertight; (*a tenuta d'aria*) airtight ▷ *sm* (*acquitrino*) pond; (*Chim*) tin

sta'gnola [staɲ'ɲɔla] *sf* tinfoil

'**stalla** *sf* (*per bovini*) cowshed; (*per cavalli*) stable

stal'lone *sm* stallion

stamat'tina *av* this morning

stam'becco, -chi *sm* ibex

stami'nale *ag*: **cellula ~** stem cell

'**stampa** *sf* (*Tip, Fot: tecnica*) printing; (*impressione, copia fotografica*) print; (*insieme di quotidiani, giornalisti ecc*): **la ~** the press

stam'pante *sf* (*Inform*) printer

stam'pare /72/ *vt* to print; (*pubblicare*) to publish; (*coniare*) to strike, coin; (*imprimere: anche fig*) to impress

stampa'tello *sm* block letters *pl*

stam'pella *sf* crutch

'**stampo** *sm* mould; (*fig: indole*) type, kind, sort

sta'nare /72/ *vt* to drive out

stan'care /20/ *vt* to tire, make tired; (*annoiare*) to bore; (*infastidire*) to annoy; **stancarsi** *vpr* to get tired, tire o.s. out; **stancarsi (di)** to grow weary (of), grow tired (of)

stan'chezza [stan'kettsa] *sf* tiredness, fatigue

'**stanco, -a, -chi, -che** *ag* tired; **~ di** tired of, fed up with

stan'ghetta [stan'getta] *sf* (*di occhiali*) leg; (*Mus, di scrittura*) bar

'**stanno** *vb vedi* **stare**

sta'notte *av* tonight; (*notte passata*) last night

'**stante** *prep*: **a sé ~** (*appartamento, casa*) independent, separate

stan'tio, -a, -tii, -tie *ag* stale; (*burro*) rancid; (*fig*) old

stan'tuffo *sm* piston

'**stanza** ['stantsa] *sf* room; (*Poesia*) stanza; **~ da bagno** bathroom; **~ da letto** bedroom

stap'pare /72/ *vt* to uncork; (*tappo a corona*) to uncap

'**stare** /116/ *vi* (*restare in un luogo*) to stay, remain; (*abitare*) to stay, live; (*essere situato*) to be, be situated; (*anche: ~ in piedi*) to stand; (*essere, trovarsi*) to be; (*seguito da gerundio*): **sta studiando** he's studying; **se stesse in me** if it were up to me, if it depended on me; **~ per fare qc** to be about to do sth; **starci** (*esserci spazio*): **nel baule non ci sta più niente** there's no more room in the boot; (*accettare*) to accept; **ci stai?** is that okay with you?; **~ a** (*attenersi a*) to follow, stick to; (*seguito dall'infinito*): **stiamo a discutere** we're talking; (*toccare a*): **sta a te giocare** it's your turn to play; **~ a qn** (*abiti ecc*) to fit sb; **queste scarpe mi stanno strette** these shoes are tight for me; **il rosso ti sta bene** red suits you; **come sta?** how are you?; **io sto bene/male** I'm very well/not very well

starnu'tire /55/ *vi* to sneeze;
  star'nuto *sm* sneeze
sta'sera *av* this evening, tonight
sta'tale *ag* state *cpd*, government *cpd*
  ▷ *smf* state employee, local authority
  employee; (*nell'amministrazione*) ≈
  civil servant; **strada ~** ≈ trunk (BRIT)
  o main road
sta'tista, -i *sm* statesman
sta'tistico, -a, -ci, -che *ag*
  statistical ▷ *sf* statistics *sg*
'stato, -a *pp di* **essere**; **stare** ▷ *sm*
  (*condizione*) state, condition; (*Pol*)
  state; (*Dir*) status; **essere in ~**
  d'accusa (*Dir*) to be committed for
  trial; **~ d'assedio/d'emergenza**
  state of siege/emergency; **~ civile**
  (*Amm*) marital status; **~ d'animo**
  mood; **~ maggiore** (*Mil*) general
  staff; **gli Stati Uniti (d'America)** the
  United States (of America)
'statua *sf* statue
statuni'tense *ag* United States *cpd*,
  of the United States
sta'tura *sf* (*Anat*) height, stature;
  (*fig*) stature
sta'tuto *sm* (*Dir*) statute;
  constitution
sta'volta *av* this time
stazio'nario, -a [stattsjo'narjo] *ag*
  stationary; (*fig*) unchanged
stazi'one [stat'tsjone] *sf* station;
  (*balneare, invernale ecc*) resort;
  ~ degli autobus bus station; **~**
  balneare seaside resort; **~**
  ferroviaria railway (BRIT) *o* railroad
  (US) station; **~ invernale** winter
  sports resort; **~ di polizia** police
  station (*in small town*); **~ di servizio**
  service *o* petrol (BRIT) *o* filling
  station
stecca, -che *sf* stick; (*di ombrello*)
  rib; (*di sigarette*) carton; (*Med*) splint;
  (*stonatura*): **fare una ~** to sing (*o* play)
  a wrong note
stec'cato *sm* fence
stella *sf* star; **~ alpina** (*Bot*)
  edelweiss; **~ cadente** *o* **filante**

shooting star; **~ di mare** (*Zool*)
  starfish
'stelo *sm* stem; (*asta*) rod; **lampada a**
  ~ standard lamp
'stemma, -i *sm* coat of arms
'stemmo *vb vedi* **stare**
stempi'ato, -a *ag* with a receding
  hairline
'stendere /120/ *vt* (*braccia, gambe*)
  to stretch (out); (*tovaglia*) to spread
  (out); (*bucato*) to hang out; (*mettere*
  a giacere) to lay (down); (*spalmare:*
  colore) to spread; (*mettere per iscritto*)
  to draw up; **stendersi** *vpr* (*coricarsi*)
  to stretch out, lie down; (*estendersi*)
  to extend, stretch
stenogra'fia *sf* shorthand
sten'tare /72/ *vi*: **~ a fare** to find it
  hard to do, have difficulty doing
'stento *sm* (*fatica*) difficulty; **stenti**
  smpl (*privazioni*) hardship *sg*, privation
  sg: **a ~** with difficulty, barely
'sterco *sm* dung
'stereo *ag inv* stereo ▷ *sm inv*
  (*impianto*) stereo
sterile *ag* sterile; (*terra*) barren; (*fig*)
  futile, fruitless
steriliz'zare [sterilid'dzare] /72/ *vt*
  to sterilize
ster'lina *sf* pound (sterling)
stermi'nare /72/ *vt* to exterminate,
  wipe out
stermi'nato, -a *ag* immense;
  endless
ster'minio *sm* extermination,
  destruction
'sterno *sm* (*Anat*) breastbone
ste'roide *sm* steroid
ster'zare [ster'tsare] /72/ *vt, vi* (*Aut*)
  to steer; **'sterzo** *sm* steering; (*volante*)
  steering wheel
'stessi *ecc vb vedi* **stare**
'stesso, -a *ag* same; (*rafforzativo:*
  in persona, proprio): **il re ~** the king
  himself *o* in person ▷ *pron*: **lo(la)**
  ~(a) the same (one); **i suoi stessi**
  avversari lo ammirano even his
  enemies admire him; **fa lo ~** it

doesn't matter; **per me è lo ~** it's all the same to me, it doesn't matter to me; vedi **io; tu** ecc

ste'sura sf drafting no pl, drawing up no pl; (documento) draft

'stetti ecc vb vedi **stare**

'stia ecc vb vedi **stare**

sti'lare /72/ vt to draw up, draft

'stile sm style; **~ libero** freestyle; **sti'lista, -i, -e** smf designer

stilo'grafica, -che sf (anche: **penna ~**) fountain pen

'stima sf esteem; valuation; assessment, estimate

sti'mare /72/ vt (persona) to esteem, hold in high regard; (terreno, casa ecc) to value; (stabilire in misura approssimativa) to estimate, assess; (ritenere): **~ che** to consider that; **stimarsi fortunato** to consider o.s. (to be) lucky

stimo'lare /72/ vt to stimulate; (incitare): **~ qn (a fare)** to spur sb on (to do)

'stimolo sm (anche fig) stimulus

'stingere ['stindʒere] /37/ vt, vi (anche: **stingersi**) to fade; **'stinto, -a** pp di **stingere**

sti'pare /72/ vt to cram, pack; **stiparsi** vpr (accalcarsi) to crowd, throng

sti'pendio sm salary

'stipite sm (di porta, finestra) jamb

stipu'lare /72/ vt (redigere) to draw up

sti'rare /72/ vt (abito) to iron; (distendere) to stretch; (strappare: muscolo) to strain; **stirarsi** vpr to stretch (o.s.)

stiti'chezza [stiti'kettsa] sf constipation

'stitico, -a, -ci, -che ag constipated

'stiva sf (di nave) hold

sti'vale sm boot

'stizza ['stittsa] sf anger, vexation

'stoffa sf material, fabric; (fig): **aver la ~ di** to have the makings of

'stomaco, -chi sm stomach; **dare di ~** to vomit, be sick

sto'nato, -a ag (persona) off-key; (strumento) off-key, out of tune

stop sm inv (Telegrafia) stop; (Aut: cartello) stop sign; (: fanalino d'arresto) brake-light

'storcere ['stɔrtʃere] /106/ vt to twist; **storcersi** vpr to writhe, twist; **~ il naso** (fig) to turn up one's nose; **storcersi la caviglia** to twist one's ankle

stor'dire /55/ vt (intontire) to stun, daze; **stor'dito, -a** ag stunned

'storia sf (scienza, avvenimenti) history; (racconto, bugia) story; (faccenda, questione) business no pl; (pretesto) excuse, pretext; **storie** sfpl (smancerie) fuss sg; **'storico, -a, -ci, -che** ag historic(al) ▷ sm/f historian

stori'one sm (Zool) sturgeon

'stormo sm (di uccelli) flock

'storpio, -a ag crippled, maimed

'storsi ecc vb vedi **storcere**

'storto, -a pp di **storcere** ▷ ag (chiodo) twisted, bent; (gamba, quadro) crooked ▷ sf (distorsione) sprain, twist

sto'viglie [sto'viʎʎe] sfpl dishes pl, crockery sg

'strabico, -a, -ci, -che ag squint-eyed; (occhi) squint

strac'chino [strak'kino] sm type of soft cheese

stracci'are [strat'tʃare] /14/ vt to tear; **stracciarsi** vpr to tear

'straccio, -a, -ci, -ce ['strattʃo] ag: **carta straccia** waste paper ▷ sm rag; (per pulire) cloth, duster; **stracci** smpl (indumenti) rags; **si è ridotto a uno ~** he's worn himself out; **non ha uno ~ di lavoro** he's not got a job of any sort

'strada sf road; (di città) street; (cammino, via, fig) way; **~ facendo** on the way; **essere fuori ~** (fig) to be on the wrong track; **fare** o **farsi ~** (fig) to get on in life; **~ senza uscita** dead end; **stra'dale** ag road cpd

strafalci'one [strafal'tʃone] sm blunder, howler

stra'fare /53/ vi to overdo it

strafot'tente ag: **è ~** he doesn't give a damn, he couldn't care less

'strage ['stradʒe] sf massacre, slaughter

stralu'nato, -a ag (occhi) rolling; (persona) beside o.s., very upset

'strambo, -a ag strange, queer

strampa'lato, -a ag odd, eccentric

stra'nezza [stra'nettsa] sf strangeness

strango'lare /72/ vt to strangle

strani'ero, -a ag foreign ▷ sm/f foreigner

Attenzione! In inglese esiste la parola stranger, che però significa sconosciuto oppure estraneo.

'strano, -a ag strange, odd

straordi'nario, -a ag extraordinary; (treno ecc) special ▷ sm (lavoro) overtime

strapi'ombo sm overhanging rock; **a ~** overhanging

strap'pare /72/ vt (gen) to tear, rip; (pagina ecc) to tear off, tear out; (sradicare) to pull up; (fig) to wrest sth from sb; (togliere): **~ qc a qn** to snatch sth from sb; **strapparsi** vpr (lacerarsi) to rip, tear; (rompersi) to break; **strapparsi un muscolo** to tear a muscle; **'strappo** sm pull, tug; (lacerazione) tear, rip; **fare uno strappo alla regola** to make an exception to the rule; **strappo muscolare** torn muscle

strari'pare /72/ vi to overflow

'strascico, -chi ['straʃʃiko] sm (di abito) train; (conseguenza) after-effect

strata'gemma, -i [strata'dʒɛmma] sm stratagem

strate'gia, -'gie [strate'dʒia] sf strategy; **stra'tegico, -a, -ci, -che** ag strategic

'strato sm layer; (rivestimento) coat, coating; (Geo, fig) stratum; (Meteor) stratus; **~ d'ozono** ozone layer

strat'tone sm tug, jerk; **dare uno ~ a qc** to tug o jerk sth, give sth a tug o jerk

strava'gante ag odd, eccentric

'strazio ['strattsjo] sm torture; (fig: cosa fatta male): **essere uno ~** to be appalling

'strega, -ghe sf witch

stre'gare /80/ vt to bewitch

stre'gone sm (mago) wizard; (di tribù) witch doctor

strepi'toso, -a ag clamorous, deafening; (fig: successo) resounding

stres'sante ag stressful

stres'sato, -a ag under stress

stretch [stretʃ] ag inv stretch

'stretta sf vedi **stretto**

stretta'mente av tightly; (rigorosamente) strictly

'stretto, -a pp di **stringere** ▷ ag (corridoio, limiti) narrow; (gonna, scarpe, nodo, curva) tight; (intimo: parente, amico) close; (rigoroso: osservanza) strict; (preciso: significato) precise, exact ▷ sm (braccio di mare) strait ▷ sf (di mano) grasp; (finanziaria) squeeze; (fig: dolore, turbamento) pang; **a denti stretti** with clenched teeth; **lo ~ necessario** the bare minimum; **una stretta di mano** a handshake; **essere alle strette** to have one's back to the wall; **stret'toia** sf bottleneck; (fig) tricky situation

stri'ato, -a ag streaked

'stridulo, -a ag shrill

stril'lare /72/ vt, vi to scream, shriek; **'strillo** sm scream, shriek

strimin'zito, -a [strimin'tsito] ag (misero) shabby; (molto magro) skinny

strimpel'lare /72/ vt (Mus) to strum

'stringa, -ghe sf lace

strin'gato, -a ag (fig) concise

'stringere ['strindʒere] /117/ vt (avvicinare due cose) to press (together), squeeze (together); (tenere stretto) to hold tight, clasp, clutch; (pugno, mascella, denti) to clench; (*labbra*) to compress; (*avvitare*) to tighten; (*abito*) to take in; (*scarpe*) to pinch, be tight for; (*fig: concludere: patto*) to make; (*: accelerare: passo*) to quicken ▷ vi (*essere stretto*) to be tight; (*tempo: incalzare*) to be pressing

'**strinsi** *ecc vb vedi* **stringere**

'**striscia, -sce** ['striʃʃa] *sf* (*di carta, tessuto ecc*) strip; (*riga*) stripe; **strisce (pedonali)** zebra crossing *sg*

strisci'are [striʃʃare] /14/ *vt* (*piedi*) to drag; (*muro, macchina*) to graze ▷ vi to crawl, creep

'**striscio** ['striʃʃo] *sm* graze; (*Med*) smear; **colpire di ~** to graze

strisci'one [striʃʃone] *sm* banner

strito'lare /72/ *vt* to grind

striz'zare [strit'tsare] /72/ *vt* (*panni*) to wring (out); **~ l'occhio** to wink

'**strofa** *sf* strophe

strofi'naccio [strofi'nattʃo] *sm* duster, cloth; (*per piatti*) dishcloth; (*per pavimenti*) floorcloth

strofi'nare /72/ *vt* to rub

stron'care /20/ *vt* to break off; (*fig: ribellione*) to suppress, put down; (*: film, libro*) to tear to pieces

'**stronzo** ['strontso] *sm* (*sterco*) turd; (*fam!: persona*) shit (!)

stroz'zare [strot'tsare] /72/ *vt* (*soffocare*) to choke, strangle

struc'care /20/ *vt* to remove make-up from; **struccarsi** *vpr* to remove one's make-up

strumen'tale *ag* (*Mus*) instrumental

strumentaliz'zare [strumentalid'dzare] /72/ *vt* to exploit, use to one's own ends

stru'mento *sm* (*arnese, fig*) instrument, tool; (*Mus*) instrument; **~ a corda** *o* **ad arco/a fiato** string(ed)/wind instrument

'**strutto** *sm* lard

strut'tura *sf* structure

'**struzzo** ['struttso] *sm* ostrich

stuc'care /20/ *vt* (*muro*) to plaster; (*vetro*) to putty; (*decorare con stucchi*) to stucco

'**stucco, -chi** *sm* plaster; (*da vetri*) putty; (*ornamentale*) stucco; **rimanere di ~** (*fig*) to be dumbfounded

stu'dente, -'essa *sm/f* student; (*scolaro*) pupil, schoolboy/girl

studi'are /19/ *vt* to study

'**studio** *sm* studying; (*ricerca, saggio, stanza*) study; (*di professionista*) office; (*di artista, Cine, TV, Radio*) studio; (*di medico*) surgery (BRIT), office (US); **studi** *smpl* (*Ins*) studies

studi'oso, -a *ag* studious, hardworking ▷ *sm/f* scholar

'**stufa** *sf* stove; **~ elettrica** electric fire *o* heater

stu'fare /72/ *vt* (*Cuc*) to stew; (*fig: fam*) to bore; **stufarsi** *vpr* (*fam*): **stufarsi (di)** (*fig*) to get fed up (with); '**stufo, -a** *ag* (*fam*): **essere stufo di** to be fed up with, be sick and tired of

stu'oia *sf* mat

stupefa'cente [stupefa'tʃente] *ag* stunning, astounding ▷ *sm* drug, narcotic

stu'pendo, -a *ag* marvellous, wonderful

stupi'daggine [stupi'daddʒine] *sf* stupid thing (to do *o* say)

stupidità *sf* stupidity

'**stupido, -a** *ag* stupid

stu'pire /55/ *vt* to amaze, stun ▷ vi (*anche*: **stupirsi**); **~ (di)** to be amazed (at), be stunned (by)

stu'pore *sm* amazement, astonishment

stu'prare /72/ *vt* to rape

'**stupro** *sm* rape

stu'rare /72/ *vt* (*lavandino*) to clear

stuzzica'denti [stuttsika'dɛnti] *sm* toothpick

stuzzi'care [stuttsi'kare] /20/ *vt* (*ferita ecc*) to poke (at), prod (at); (*fig*) to tease; (*: appetito*) to whet;

(: *curiosità*) to stimulate; **~ i denti** to pick one's teeth

⬭ **PAROLA CHIAVE**

su (*su + il* = **sul**, *su + lo* = **sullo**, *su + l'* = **sull'**, *su + la* = **sulla**, *su + i* = **sui**, *su + gli* = **sugli**, *su + le* = **sulle**) *prep* 1 (*gen*) on; (*moto*) on(to); (*in cima a*) on (top of); **mettilo sul tavolo** put it on the table; **un paesino sul mare** a village by the sea

2 (*argomento*) about, on; **un libro su Cesare** a book on o about Caesar

3 (*circa*) about; **costerà sui 3 milioni** it will cost about 3 million; **una ragazza sui 17 anni** a girl of about 17 (years of age)

4: **su misura** made to measure; **su richiesta** on request; **3 casi su dieci** 3 cases out of 10

▷ *av* 1 (*in alto, verso l'alto*) up; **vieni su** come on up; **guarda su** look up; **su le mani!** hands up!; **in su** (*verso l'alto*) up(wards); (*in poi*) onwards; **dai 20 anni in su** from the age of 20 onwards

2 (*addosso*) on; **cos'hai su?** what have you got on?

▷ *escl* come on!; **su coraggio!** come on, cheer up!

su'bacqueo, -a *ag* underwater ▷ *sm* skin-diver

sub'buglio [sub'buʎʎo] *sm* confusion, turmoil

'subdolo, -a *ag* underhand, sneaky

suben'trare /72/ *vi*: **~ a qn in qc** to take over sth from sb

su'bire /55/ *vt* to suffer, endure

'subito *av* immediately, at once, straight away

subodo'rare /72/ *vt* (*insidia ecc*) to smell, suspect

subordi'nato, -a *ag* subordinate; (*dipendente*): **~ a** dependent on, subject to

suc'cedere [sut'tʃɛdere] /118/ *vi* (*accadere*) to happen; **~ a** (*prendere il posto di*) to succeed; (*venire dopo*) to follow; **cos'è successo?** what happened?; **succes'sivo, -a** *ag* successive; **suc'cesso, -a** *pp di* **succedere** ▷ *sm* (*esito*) outcome; (*buona riuscita*) success; **di successo** (*libro, personaggio*) successful

succhi'are [suk'kjare] /19/ *vt* to suck (up)

succhi'otto [suk'kjɔtto] *sm* dummy (BRIT), pacifier (US), comforter (US)

suc'cinto, -a [sut'tʃinto] *ag* (*discorso*) succinct; (*abito*) brief

'succo, -chi *sm* juice; (*fig*) essence, gist; **~ di frutta/pomodoro** fruit/ tomato juice

succur'sale *sf* branch (office)

sud *sm* south ▷ *ag inv* south; (*regione*) southern

Su'dafrica *sm*: **il ~** South Africa; **sudafri'cano, -a** *ag, sm/f* South African

Suda'merica *sm*: **il ~** South America

su'dare /72/ *vi* to perspire, sweat; **~ freddo** to come out in a cold sweat

su'dato, -a *ag* (*persona, mani*) sweaty; (*fig: denaro*) hard-earned ▷ *sf* (*anche fig*) sweat; **una vittoria sudata** a hard-won victory; **ho fatto una bella sudata per finirlo in tempo** it was a real sweat to get it finished in time

suddi'videre /43/ *vt* to subdivide

su'dest *sm* south-east

'sudicio, -a, -ci, -ce ['suditʃo] *ag* dirty, filthy

su'doku *sm inv* sudoku

su'dore *sm* perspiration, sweat

su'dovest *sm* south-west

suffici'ente [suffi'tʃɛnte] *ag* enough, sufficient; (*borioso*) self-important; (*Ins*) satisfactory; **suffici'enza** *sf* self-importance; (*Ins*) pass mark; **a sufficienza** enough; **ne ho avuto a sufficienza!** I've had enough of this!

suf'fisso *sm* (*Ling*) suffix

S

suggeri'mento [suddʒeri'mento] *sm* suggestion; (*consiglio*) piece of advice, advice *no pl*

sugge'rire [suddʒe'rire] /55/ *vt* (*risposta*) to tell; (*consigliare*) to advise; (*proporre*) to suggest; (*Teat*) to prompt

suggestio'nare [suddʒestjo'nare] /72/ *vt* to influence

sugges'tivo, -a [suddʒes'tivo] *ag* (*paesaggio*) evocative; (*teoria*) interesting, attractive

'sughero ['sugero] *sm* cork

'sugo, -ghi *sm* (*succo*) juice; (*di carne*) gravy; (*condimento*) sauce; (*fig*) gist, essence

sui'cida, -i, -e [sui'tʃida] *ag* suicidal ▷ *smf* suicide

suici'darsi [suitʃi'darsi] /72/ *vpr* to commit suicide

sui'cidio [sui'tʃidjo] *sm* suicide

su'ino, -a *ag*: **carne suina** pork ▷ *sm* pig

sul'tano, -a *sm/f* sultan (sultana)

'suo (*f* **'sua**, *pl* **'sue, su'oi**) *det*: **il ~, la sua** *ecc* (*di lui*) his; (*di lei*) her; (*di esso*) its; (*con valore indefinito*) one's, his/her; (*forma di cortesia: anche*: **S~**) your ▷ *pron*: **il ~, la sua** *ecc* his; hers; yours; **i ~i** his (*o* her *ecc*) family

su'ocero, -a ['swɔtʃero] *sm/f* father/mother-in-law

su'ola *sf* (*di scarpa*) sole

su'olo *sm* (*terreno*) ground; (*terra*) soil

suo'nare /72/ *vt* (*Mus*) to play; (*campana*) to ring; (*ore*) to strike; (*clacson, allarme*) to sound ▷ *vi* to play; (*telefono, campana*) to ring; (*ore*) to strike; (*clacson, fig: parole*) to sound

suone'ria *sf* alarm

su'ono *sm* sound

su'ora *sf* (*Rel*) nun; **Suor Maria** Sister Maria

'super *ag inv*: (**benzina**) **~** ≈ four-star (petrol) (BRIT), ≈ premium (US)

supe'rare /72/ *vt* (*oltrepassare: limite*) to exceed, surpass; (*percorrere*) to cover; (*attraversare: fiume*) to cross; (*sorpassare: veicolo*) to overtake; (*fig*: *essere più bravo di*) to surpass, outdo; (: *difficoltà*) to overcome; (: *esame*) to get through; **~ qn in altezza/peso** to be taller/heavier than sb; **ha superato la cinquantina** he's over fifty (years of age)

su'perbia *sf* pride; **su'perbo, -a** *ag* proud; (*fig*) magnificent, superb

superfici'ale [superfi'tʃale] *ag* superficial

super'ficie, -ci [super'fitʃe] *sf* surface

su'perfluo, -a *ag* superfluous

superi'ore *ag* (*piano, arto, classi*) upper; (*più elevato: temperatura, livello*): **~ (a)** higher (than); (*migliore*): **~ (a)** superior (to)

superla'tivo, -a *ag, sm* superlative

supermer'cato *sm* supermarket

su'perstite *ag* surviving ▷ *smf* survivor

superstizi'one [superstit'tsjone] *sf* superstition; **superstizi'oso, -a** *ag* superstitious

super'strada *sf* ≈ expressway

su'pino, -a *ag* supine

supplemen'tare *ag* extra; (*treno*) relief *cpd*; (*entrate*) additional

supple'mento *sm* supplement

sup'plente *smf* temporary member of staff; supply (*o* substitute) teacher

'supplica, -che *sf* (*preghiera*) plea; (*domanda scritta*) petition, request

suppli'care /20/ *vt* to implore, beseech

sup'plizio [sup'plittsjo] *sm* torture

sup'pongo, sup'poni *ecc vb vedi* **supporre**

sup'porre /77/ *vt* to suppose; **supponiamo che ...** let's *o* just suppose that ...

sup'porto *sm* (*sostegno*) support

sup'posta *sf* (*Med*) suppository

su'premo, -a *ag* supreme

surge'lare [surdʒe'lare] /72/ *vt* to (deep-)freeze

surge'lato, -a [surdʒe'lato] *ag* (deep-)frozen ▷ *smpl*: **i surgelati** frozen food *sg*

sur'plus *sm inv* (Econ) surplus

surriscal'dare /72/ *vt* to overheat

suscet'tibile [suʃʃet'tibile] *ag* (sensibile) touchy, sensitive

susci'tare [suʃʃi'tare] /72/ *vt* to provoke, arouse

su'sina *sf* plum

sussegu'ire /45/ *vt* to follow; **susseguirsi** *vpr* to follow one another

sus'sidio *sm* subsidy; **sussidi didattici/audiovisivi** teaching/audiovisual aids

sussul'tare /72/ *vi* to shudder

sussur'rare /72/ *vt, vi* to whisper, murmur; **sus'surro** *sm* whisper, murmur

sva'gare /80/ *vt* (divertire) to amuse; **svagarsi** *vpr* to amuse o.s.

'svago, -ghi *sm* (riposo) relaxation; (ricreazione) amusement; (passatempo) pastime

svaligi'are [zvali'dʒare] /62/ *vt* to rob, burgle (BRIT), burglarize (US)

svalu'tare /72/ *vt* (Econ) to devalue; **svalutarsi** *vpr* (Econ) to be devalued

svalutazi'one *sf* devaluation

sva'nire /55/ *vi* to disappear, vanish

svantaggi'ato, -a [zvantad'dʒato] *ag* at a disadvantage

svan'taggio [zvan'taddʒo] *sm* disadvantage; (inconveniente) drawback, disadvantage

svari'ato, -a *ag* varied; (numeroso) various

'svastica, -che *sf* swastika

sve'dese *ag* Swedish ▷ *smf* Swede ▷ *sm* (Ling) Swedish

'sveglia ['zveʎʎa] *sf* waking up; (orologio) alarm (clock); **~ telefonica** alarm call

svegli'are [zveʎ'ʎare] /27/ *vt* to wake up; (fig) to awaken, arouse; **svegliarsi** *vpr* to wake up; (fig) to be revived, reawaken

'sveglio, -a ['zveʎʎo] *ag* awake; (fig) quick-witted

sve'lare /72/ *vt* to reveal

'svelto, -a *ag* (passo) quick; (mente) quick, alert; **alla svelta** quickly

'svendere /29/ *vt* to sell off, clear

'svendita *sf* (Comm) (clearance) sale

'svengo *ecc vb vedi* **svenire**

sveni'mento *sm* fainting fit, faint

sve'nire /128/ *vi* to faint

sven'tare /72/ *vt* to foil, thwart

sven'tato, -a *ag* (distratto) scatterbrained; (imprudente) rash

svento'lare /72/ *vt, vi* to wave, flutter

sven'tura *sf* misfortune

sverrò *ecc vb vedi* **svenire**

sves'tire /45/ *vt* to undress; **svestirsi** *vpr* to get undressed

'Svezia ['zvɛttsja] *sf*: **la ~** Sweden

svi'are /60/ *vt* to divert; (fig) to lead astray

svi'gnarsela [zviɲ'ɲarsela] /72/ *vpr* to slip away, sneak off

svilup'pare /72/ *vt*, **svilup'parsi** *vpr* to develop

sviluppa'tore, -trice *sm/f* (Inform) developer

svi'luppo *sm* development

'svincolo *sm* (stradale) motorway (BRIT) o expressway (US) intersection

'svista *sf* oversight

svi'tare /72/ *vt* to unscrew

'Svizzera ['zvittsera] *sf*: **la ~** Switzerland; **'svizzero, -a** ['zvittsero] *ag, sm/f* Swiss

svogli'ato, -a [zvoʎ'ʎato] *ag* listless; (pigro) lazy

'svolgere ['zvɔldʒere] /96/ *vt* to unwind; (srotolare) to unroll; (fig: argomento) to develop; (: piano, programma) to carry out; **svolgersi** *vpr* to unwind; to unroll; (fig: aver luogo) to take place; (: procedere) to go on

'svolsi *ecc vb vedi* **svolgere**

'svolta *sf* (atto) turning no pl; (curva) turn, bend; (fig) turning-point

svol'tare /72/ *vi* to turn

svuo'tare /72/ *vt* to empty (out)

S

T, t [ti] *sf o m inv (lettera)* T, t; **T come Taranto** ≈ T for Tommy

t *abbr* = **tonnellata**

tabacche'ria [tabakke'ria] *sf* tobacconist's (shop)

ta'bacco, -chi *sm* tobacco

ta'bella *sf (tavola)* table; *(elenco)* list

tabel'lone *sm (per pubblicità)* billboard; *(in stazione)* timetable board

'tablet ['tablet] *sm inv (Inform)* tablet

TAC *sigla f (Med)* (= *Tomografia Assiale Computerizzata*) CAT

tac'chino [tak'kino] *sm* turkey

'tacco, -chi *sm* heel; **tacchi a spillo** stiletto heels

taccu'ino *sm* notebook

ta'cere [ta'tʃere] /119/ *vi* to be silent *o* quiet; *(smettere di parlare)* to fall silent ▷ *vt* to keep to oneself, say nothing about; **far ~ qn** to make sb be quiet; *(fig)* to silence sb

ta'chimetro [ta'kimetro] *sm* speedometer

'tacqui *ecc vb vedi* **tacere**

ta'fano *sm* horsefly

'taglia ['taʎʎa] *sf (statura)* height; *(misura)* size; *(riscatto)* ransom; *(ricompensa)* reward; **taglie forti** *(Abbigliamento)* outsize

taglia'carte [taʎʎa'karte] *sm inv* paperknife

tagli'ando [taʎ'ʎando] *sm* coupon

tagli'are [taʎ'ʎare] /27/ *vt* to cut; *(recidere, interrompere)* to cut off; *(intersecare)* to cut across, intersect; *(carne)* to carve; *(vini)* to blend ▷ *vi* to cut; *(prendere una scorciatoia)* to take a short-cut; **tagliarsi** *vpr* to cut o.s.; **~ la strada a qn** to cut across in front of sb; **~ corto** *(fig)* to cut short; **~ la corda** *(fig)* to sneak off; **~ i ponti (con)** *(fig)* to break off relations (with); **mi sono tagliato** I've cut myself

taglia'telle [taʎʎa'tɛlle] *sfpl* tagliatelle *pl*

taglia'unghie [taʎʎa'ungje] *sm inv* nail clippers *pl*

tagli'ente [taʎ'ʎɛnte] *ag* sharp

'taglio ['taʎʎo] *sm (anche fig)* cut; cutting *no pl*; *(parte tagliente)* cutting edge; *(di abito)* cut, style; *(di stoffa)* length; *(di vini)* blending; **di ~** on edge, edgeways; **banconote di piccolo/grosso ~** notes of small/large denomination; **~ cesareo** Caesarean section

tailan'dese *ag, smf, sm* Thai

Tai'landia *sf*: **la ~** Thailand

'talco *sm* talcum powder

PAROLA CHIAVE

'tale *det* **1** *(simile, così grande)* such; **un(a) tale ...** such a ...; **non accetto tali discorsi** I won't allow such talk; **è di una tale arroganza** he is so arrogant; **fa una tale confusione!** he makes such a mess!
2 *(persona o cosa indeterminata)* such-and-such; **il giorno tale**

all'ora tale on such-and-such a day at such-and-such a time; **la tal persona** that person; **ha telefonato una tale Giovanna** somebody called Giovanna phoned
3 (*nelle similitudini*): **tale ... tale** like ... like; **tale padre tale figlio** like father, like son; **hai il vestito tale quale il mio** your dress is just *o* exactly like mine
▶ *pron* (*indefinito, persona*): **un(a) tale** someone; **quel** (*o* **quella**) **tale** that person, that man (*o* woman); **il tal dei tali** what's-his-name

tale'bano *sm* Taliban
ta'lento *sm* talent
talis'mano *sm* talisman
tallon'cino [tallon'tʃino] *sm* counterfoil
tal'lone *sm* heel
tal'mente *av* so
'talpa *sf* (*Zool: anche fig*) mole
tal'volta *av* sometimes, at times
tambu'rello *sm* tambourine
tam'buro *sm* drum
Ta'migi [ta'midʒi] *sm*: **il ~** the Thames
tampo'nare /72/ *vt* (*otturare*) to plug; (*urtare: macchina*) to crash *o* ram into
tam'pone *sm* (*Med*) wad, pad; (*per timbri*) ink-pad; (*respingente*) buffer; **~ assorbente** tampon
'tana *sf* lair, den
'tanga *sm inv* G-string
tan'gente [tan'dʒɛnte] *ag* (*Mat*): **~ a** tangential to ▶ *sf* tangent; (*quota*) share
tangenzi'ale [tandʒen'tsjale] *sf* (*strada*) bypass
'tanica *sf* (*contenitore*) jerry can

PAROLA CHIAVE

'tanto, -a *det* **1** (*molto: quantità*) a lot of, much; (*: numero*) a lot of, many; **tanto tempo** a lot of time, a long time; **tanti auguri!** all the best!;

tante grazie many thanks; **tante volte** many times, often; **ogni tanti chilometri** every so many kilometres
2 (*così tanto: quantità*) so much, such a lot of; (*: numero*) so many, such a lot of; **ho aspettato per tanto tempo** I waited so long *o* for such a long time
3: **tanto ... quanto** (*quantità*) as much ... as; (*numero*) as many ... as; **ho tanta pazienza quanta ne hai tu** I have as much patience as you have *o* as you; **ha tanti amici quanti nemici** he has as many friends as he has enemies
▶ *pron* **1** (*molto*) much, a lot; (*così tanto*) so much, such a lot; **tanti, -e** many, a lot; so many; such a lot; **credevo ce ne fosse tanto** I thought there was (such) a lot, I thought there was plenty
2: **tanto quanto** (*denaro*) as much as; (*cioccolatini*) as many as; **ne ho tanto quanto basta** I have as much as I need; **due volte tanto** twice as much
3 (*indeterminato*) so much; **tanto per l'affitto, tanto per il gas** so much for the rent, so much for the gas; **costa un tanto al metro** it costs so much per metre; **di tanto in tanto, ogni tanto** every so often; **tanto vale che ...** I (*o* we *ecc*) may as well ...; **tanto meglio!** so much the better!; **tanto peggio per lui!** so much the worse for him!
▶ *av* **1** (*molto*) very; **vengo tanto volentieri** I'd be very glad to come; **non ci vuole tanto a capirlo** it doesn't take much to understand it
2 (*così tanto: con ag, av*) so; (*: con vb*) so much, such a lot; **è tanto bella!** she's so beautiful!; **non urlare tanto (forte)** don't shout so much; **sto tanto meglio adesso** I'm so much better now; **tanto ... che** so ... (that); **tanto ... da** so ... as
3: **tanto ... quanto** as ... as; **conosco tanto Carlo quanto suo**

padre I know both Carlo and his father; **non è poi tanto complicato quanto sembra** it's not as difficult as it seems; **tanto più insisti, tanto più non mollerà** the more you insist, the more stubborn he'll be; **quanto più … tanto meno** the more … the less

4 (*solamente*) just; **tanto per cambiare/scherzare** just for a change/a joke; **una volta tanto** for once

5 (*a lungo*) (for) long
▶ *cong* after all

'**tappa** *sf* (*luogo di sosta, fermata*) stop, halt; (*parte di un percorso*) stage, leg; (*Sport*) lap; **a tappe** in stages

tap'pare /72/ *vt* to plug, stop up; (*bottiglia*) to cork; **tapparsi** *vpr*: **tapparsi in casa** to shut o.s. up at home; **tapparsi la bocca** to shut up; **tapparsi le orecchie** to turn a deaf ear

tappa'rella *sf* rolling shutter

tappe'tino *sm* (*per auto*) car mat; **~ antiscivolo** (*da bagno*) non-slip mat; **~ del mouse** mouse mat

tap'peto *sm* carpet; (*anche:* **tappetino**) rug; (*Sport*): **andare al ~** to go down for the count; **mettere sul ~** (*fig*) to bring up for discussion

tappez'zare [tappet'tsare] /72/ *vt* (*con carta*) to paper; (*rivestire*): **~ qc (di)** to cover sth (with); **tappezze'ria** *sf* (*tessuto*) tapestry; (*carta da parati*) wallpaper; (*arte*) upholstery; **far da tappezzeria** (*fig*) to be a wallflower

'**tappo** *sm* stopper; (*in sughero*) cork

tar'dare /72/ *vi* to be late ▷ *vt* to delay; **~ a fare** to delay doing

'**tardi** *av* late; **più ~** later (on); **al più ~** at the latest; **sul ~** (*verso sera*) late in the day; **far ~** to be late; (*restare alzato*) to stay up late; **è troppo ~** it's too late

'**targa, -ghe** *sf* plate; (*Aut*) number (*BRIT*) *o* license (*US*) plate; **targ'hetta**

sf (*con nome: su porta*) nameplate; (*: su bagaglio*) name tag

ta'riffa *sf* (*gen*) rate, tariff; (*di trasporti*) fare; (*elenco*) price list; tariff

'**tarlo** *sm* woodworm

'**tarma** *sf* moth

ta'rocco, -chi *sm* tarot card; **tarocchi** *smpl* (*gioco*) tarot *sg*

tarta'ruga, -ghe *sf* tortoise; (*di mare*) turtle; (*materiale*) tortoiseshell

tar'tina *sf* canapé

tar'tufo *sm* (*Bot*) truffle

'**tasca, -sche** *sf* pocket; **tas'cabile** *ag* (*libro*) pocket *cpd*

'**tassa** *sf* (*imposta*) tax; (*doganale*) duty; (*per iscrizione, a scuola ecc*) fee; **~ di circolazione/di soggiorno** road/tourist tax

tas'sare /72/ *vt* to tax; to levy a duty on

tas'sello *sm* plug; (*assaggio*) wedge

tassì *sm inv* = **taxi**; **tas'sista, -i, -e** *smf* taxi driver

'**tasso** *sm* (*di natalità, d'interesse ecc*) rate; (*Bot*) yew; (*Zool*) badger; **~ di cambio/d'interesse** rate of exchange/interest

tas'tare /72/ *vt* to feel; **~ il terreno** (*fig*) to see how the land lies

tasti'era *sf* keyboard

tastie'rino *sm* keypad

'**tasto** *sm* key; (*tatto*) touch, feel

tas'toni *av*: **procedere (a) ~** to grope one's way forward

'**tatto** *sm* (*senso*) touch; (*fig*) tact; **duro al ~** hard to the touch; **aver ~** to be tactful, have tact

tatu'aggio [tatu'addʒo] *sm* tattooing; (*disegno*) tattoo

tatu'are /72/ *vt* to tattoo

TAV [tav] *sigla m* (*inv*), *sigla f* (*inv*) (= *treno alta velocità*) high-speed train; (*sistema*) high-speed rail system

'**tavola** *sf* table; (*asse*) plank, board; (*lastra*) tablet; (*quadro*) panel (painting); (*illustrazione*) plate; **~ calda** snack bar; **~ rotonda** (*fig*) round table; **~ a vela** windsurfer

tavo'letta *sf* tablet, bar; **a ~** (*Aut*) flat out

tavo'lino *sm* small table; (*scrivania*) desk

'tavolo *sm* table

'taxi *sm inv* taxi

'tazza ['tattsa] *sf* cup; **~ da caffè/tè** coffee/tea cup; **una ~ di caffè/tè** a cup of coffee/tea

TBC *abbr f* (= *tubercolosi*) TB

te *pron* (*soggetto: in forme comparative, oggetto*) you

tè *sm inv* tea; (*trattenimento*) tea party

tea'trale *ag* theatrical

te'atro *sm* theatre

techno ['tɛkno] *ag inv* (*musica*) techno

'tecnico, -a, -ci, -che *ag* technical ▷ *sm/f* technician ▷ *sf* technique; (*tecnologia*) technology

tecnolo'gia [teknolo'dʒia] *sf* technology

te'desco, -a, -schi, -sche *ag, sm/f, sm* German

te'game *sm* (*Cuc*) pan

'tegola *sf* tile

tei'era *sf* teapot

tel. *abbr* (= *telefono*) tel.

'tela *sf* (*tessuto*) cloth; (*per vele, quadri*) canvas; (*dipinto*) canvas, painting; **di ~** (*calzoni*) (heavy) cotton *cpd*; (*scarpe, borsa*) canvas *cpd*; **~ cerata** oilcloth

te'laio *sm* (*apparecchio*) loom; (*struttura*) frame

tele'camera *sf* television camera

teleco'mando *sm* remote control

tele'cronaca, -che *sf* television report

telefo'nare /72/ *vi* to telephone, ring; (*fare una chiamata*) to make a phone call ▷ *vt* to telephone; **~ a qn** to phone o ring o call sb (up)

telefo'nata *sf* (*telephone*) call; **~ a carico del destinatario** reverse charge (*BRIT*) o collect (*US*) call

tele'fonico, -a, -ci, -che *ag* (tele) phone *cpd*

telefo'nino *sm* mobile phone

te'lefono *sm* telephone; **~ a gettoni** ≈ pay phone; **~ fisso** landline

telegior'nale [teledʒor'nale] *sm* television news (programme)

tele'gramma, -i *sm* telegram

telela'voro *sm* teleworking

teleno'vela *sf* soap opera

Tele'pass® *sm inv* automatic payment card for use on Italian motorways

telepa'tia *sf* telepathy

teles'copio *sm* telescope

teleselezi'one [teleselet'tsjone] *sf* direct dialling

telespetta'tore, -'trice *sm/f* (television) viewer

tele'vendita *sf* teleshopping

televisi'one *sf* television

televi'sore *sm* television set

'tema, -i *sm* theme; (*Ins*) essay, composition

te'mere /29/ *vt* to fear, be afraid of; (*essere sensibile a: freddo, calore*) to be sensitive to ▷ *vi* to be afraid; (*essere preoccupato*): **~ per** to worry about, fear for; **~ di/che** to be afraid of/that

temperama'tite *sm inv* pencil sharpener

tempera'mento *sm* temperament

tempera'tura *sf* temperature

tempe'rino *sm* penknife

tem'pesta *sf* storm; **~ di sabbia/ neve** sand/snowstorm

'tempia *sf* (*Anat*) temple

'tempio *sm* (*edificio*) temple

'tempo *sm* (*Meteor*) weather; (*cronologico*) time; (*epoca*) time, times *pl*; (*di film, gioco: parte*) part; (*Mus*) time; (*: battuta*) beat; (*Ling*) tense; **che ~ fa?** what's the weather like?; **un ~** once; **~ fa** some time ago; **al ~ stesso** o **a un ~** at the same time; **per ~** early; **aver fatto il proprio ~** to have had its (o his *ecc*) day; **primo/ secondo ~** (*Teat*) first/second part; (*Sport*) first/second half; **in ~ utile** in due time o course; **a ~ pieno** full-time; **~ libero** free time

t

tempo'rale *ag* temporal ▷ *sm*
(*Meteor*) (thunder)storm

tempo'raneo, -a *ag* temporary

te'nace [te'natʃe] *ag* strong, tough;
(*fig*) tenacious

te'naglie [te'naʎʎe] *sfpl* pincers *pl*

'tenda *sf* (*riparo*) awning; (*di finestra*)
curtain; (*per campeggio ecc*) tent

ten'denza [ten'dɛntsa] *sf* tendency;
(*orientamento*) trend; **avere ~ a o per
qc** to have a bent for sth

'tendere /120/ *vt* (*allungare al
massimo*) to stretch, draw tight;
(*porgere: mano*) to hold out; (*fig:
trappola*) to lay, set ▷ *vi*: **~ a qc/a
fare** to tend towards sth/to do; **~
l'orecchio** to prick up one's ears; **il
tempo tende al caldo** the weather
is getting hot; **un blu che tende al
verde** a greenish blue

'tendine *sm* tendon, sinew

ten'done *sm* (*da circo*) big top

'tenebre *sfpl* darkness *sg*

te'nente *sm* lieutenant

te'nere /121/ *vt* to hold; (*conservare,
mantenere*) to keep; (*ritenere,
considerare*) to consider; (*occupare:
spazio*) to take up, occupy; (*seguire:
strada*) to keep to ▷ *vi* to hold;
(*colori*) to be fast; (*dare importanza*):
~ a to care about; **~ a fare** to want
to do, be keen to do; **tenersi** *vpr*
(*stare in una determinata posizione*)
to stand; (*stimarsi*) to consider o.s.;
(*aggrapparsi*): **tenersi a** to hold on
to; (*attenersi*): **tenersi a** to stick to;
~ una conferenza to give a lecture;
~ conto di qc to take sth into
consideration; **~ presente qc** to bear
sth in mind

'tenero, -a *ag* tender; (*pietra, cera,
colore*) soft; (*fig*) tender, loving

'tengo *ecc vb vedi* **tenere**

'tenni *ecc vb vedi* **tenere**

'tennis *sm* tennis

ten'nista, -i, -e *smf* tennis player

te'nore *sm* (*tono*) tone; (*Mus*) tenor;
~ di vita (*livello*) standard of living

tensi'one *sf* tension

ten'tare /72/ *vt* (*indurre*) to tempt;
(*provare*): **~ qc/di fare** to attempt
o try sth/to do; **tenta'tivo** *sm*
attempt; **tentazi'one** *sf* temptation

tenten'nare /72/ *vi* to shake, be
unsteady; (*fig*) to hesitate, waver

ten'toni *av*: **andare a ~** (*anche fig*) to
grope one's way

'tenue *ag* (*sottile*) fine; (*colore*) soft;
(*fig*) slender, slight

te'nuta *sf* (*capacità*) capacity; (*divisa*)
uniform; (*abito*) dress; (*Agr*) estate;
a ~ d'aria airtight; **~ di strada**
roadholding power

teolo'gia [teolo'dʒia] *sf* theology

teo'ria *sf* theory

te'pore *sm* warmth

tep'pista, -i *sm* hooligan

tera'pia *sf* therapy; **~ intensiva**
intensive care

tergicris'tallo [terdʒikris'tallo]
sm windscreen (BRIT) o windshield
(US) wiper

tergiver'sare [terdʒiver'sare] /72/ *vi*
to shilly-shally

ter'male *ag* thermal; **stazione**
sf **~** spa

'terme *sfpl* thermal baths

termi'nale *ag*, *sm* terminal

termi'nare /72/ *vt* to end; (*lavoro*) to
finish ▷ *vi* to end

'termine *sm* term; (*fine, estremità*)
end; (*di territorio*) boundary, limit;
contratto a ~ (*Comm*) forward
contract; **a breve/lungo ~** short-/
long-term; **parlare senza mezzi
termini** to talk frankly, not to mince
one's words

ter'mometro *sm* thermometer

'termos *sm inv* = **thermos**

termosi'fone *sm* radiator

ter'mostato *sm* thermostat

'terra *sf* (*gen, Elettr*) earth; (*sostanza*)
soil, earth; (*opposto al mare*) land *no
pl*; (*regione, paese*) land; (*argilla*) clay;
terre *sfpl* (*possedimenti*) lands, land
sg: **a o per ~** (*stato*) on the ground (o

floor); (*moto*) to the ground, down; **mettere a ~** to earth

terra'cotta *sf* terracotta; **vasellame** *sm* **di ~** earthenware

terra'ferma *sf* dry land, terra firma; (*continente*) mainland

ter'razza [ter'rattsa] *sf*, **ter'razzo** [ter'rattso] *sm* terrace

terre'moto *sm* earthquake

ter'reno, -a *ag* (*vita, beni*) earthly ▷ *sm* (*suolo, fig*) ground; (*Comm*) land *no pl*, plot (of land); site; (*Sport, Mil*) field

ter'restre *ag* (*superficie*) of the earth, earth's; (*di terra: battaglia, animale*) land *cpd*; (*Rel*) earthly, worldly

ter'ribile *ag* terrible, dreadful

terrifi'cante *ag* terrifying

ter'rina *sf* tureen

territori'ale *ag* territorial

terri'torio *sm* territory

ter'rore *sm* terror; **terro'rismo** *sm* terrorism; **terro'rista, -i, -e** *smf* terrorist

terroriz'zare [terrorid'dzare] /72/ *vt* to terrorize

terza ['tɛrtsa] *sf vedi* **terzo**

ter'zino [ter'tsino] *sm* (*Calcio*) fullback, back

terzo, -a ['tɛrtso] *ag* third ▷ *sm* (*frazione*) third; (*Dir*) third party ▷ *sf* (*Aut*) third (gear); (*Ins: elementare*) third year at primary school; (*: media*) third year at secondary school; (*: superiore*) sixth year at secondary school; **terzi** *smpl* (*altri*) others, other people; **la terza pagina** (*Stampa*) the Arts page

teschio ['tɛskjo] *sm* skull

tesi *ecc vb vedi* **tendere**

teso, -a *pp di* **tendere** ▷ *ag* (*tirato*) taut, tight; (*fig*) tense

te'soro *sm* treasure; **il Ministero del T~** the Treasury

tessera *sf* (*documento*) card

tes'suto *sm* fabric, material; (*Biol*) tissue

test ['tɛst] *sm inv* test

testa *sf* head; (*di cose: estremità, parte anteriore*) head, front; **di ~** (*vettura ecc*) front; **fare di ~ propria** to go one's own way; **in ~** (*Sport*) in the lead; **tenere ~ a qn** (*nemico ecc*) to stand up to sb; **una ~ d'aglio** a bulb of garlic; **~ o croce?** heads or tails?; **avere la ~ dura** to be stubborn; **~ di serie** (*Tennis*) seed, seeded player

testa'mento *sm* (*atto*) will; **l'Antico/ il Nuovo T~** (*Rel*) the Old/New Testament

tes'tardo, -a *ag* stubborn, pig-headed

tes'tata *sf* (*parte anteriore*) head; (*intestazione*) heading

tes'ticolo *sm* testicle

testi'mone *smf* (*Dir*) witness; **~ oculare** eye witness

testimoni'are /19/ *vt* to testify; (*fig*) to bear witness to, to testify to ▷ *vi* to give evidence, testify

testo *sm* text; **fare ~** (*opera, autore*) to be authoritative; **questo libro non fa ~** this book is not essential reading

tes'tuggine [tes'tuddʒine] *sf* tortoise; (*di mare*) turtle

tetano *sm* (*Med*) tetanus

tetto *sm* roof; **tet'toia** *sf* roofing; canopy

tet'tuccio [tet'tuttʃo] *sm*: **~ apribile** (*Aut*) sunroof

Tevere *sm*: **il ~** the Tiber

TG [tid'dʒi], **tg** *abbr m* (= *telegiornale*) TV news *sg*

thermos® ['tɛrmos] *sm inv* vacuum *o* Thermos® flask

ti *pron* (*dav lo, la, li, le, ne diventa* **te**, *oggetto*) you; (*complemento di termine*) (to) you; (*riflessivo*) yourself

Tibet *sm*: **il ~** Tibet

tibia *sf* tibia, shinbone

tic *sm inv* tic, (nervous) twitch; (*fig*) mannerism

ticchet'tio [tikket'tio] *sm* (*di macchina da scrivere*) clatter; (*di orologio*) ticking; (*della pioggia*) patter '**ticket** *sm inv* (Med) prescription charge (BRIT)

ti'ene *ecc vb vedi* **tenere**

ti'epido, -a *ag* lukewarm, tepid

'**tifo** *sm* (Med) typhus; (fig): **fare il ~ per** to be a fan of

ti'fone *sm* typhoon

ti'foso, -a *sm/f* (Sport: ecc) fan

tigì [ti'dʒi] *sm inv* TV news

'**tiglio** ['tiʎʎo] *sm* lime (tree), linden (tree)

'**tigre** *sf* tiger

tim'brare /72/ *vt* to stamp; (annullare: francobolli) to postmark; **~ il cartellino** to clock in

'**timbro** *sm* stamp; (Mus) timbre, tone

'**timido, -a** *ag* shy; timid

'**timo** *sm* thyme

ti'mone *sm* (Naut) rudder

ti'more *sm* (paura) fear; (rispetto) awe

'**timpano** *sm* (Anat) eardrum

'**tingere** ['tindʒere] /37/ *vt* to dye

'**tinsi** *ecc vb vedi* **tingere**

'**tinta** *sf* (materia colorante) dye; (colore) shade

tintin'nare /72/ *vi* to tinkle

tinto'ria *sf* (lavasecco) dry cleaner's (shop)

tin'tura *sf* (operazione) dyeing; (colorante) dye; **~ di iodio** tincture of iodine

'**tipico, -a, -ci, -che** *ag* typical

'**tipo** *sm* type; (genere) kind, type; (fam) chap, fellow; **che ~ di…?** what kind of …?

tipogra'fia *sf* typography; (procedimento) letterpress (printing); (officina) printing house

T.I.R. *sigla m* (= Transports Internationaux Routiers) International Heavy Goods Vehicle

ti'rare /72/ *vt* (gen) to pull; (chiudere: tenda ecc) to draw, pull; (tracciare, disegnare) to draw, trace; (lanciare: sasso, palla) to throw; (stampare) to print; (pistola, freccia) to fire; (estrarre): **~ qc da** to take o pull sth out of; to get sth out of; to extract sth from

▷ *vi* (pipa, camino) to draw; (vento) to blow; (abito) to be tight; (fare fuoco) to fire; (fare del tiro, Calcio) to shoot; **~ a indovinare** to take a guess; **~ sul prezzo** to bargain; **~ avanti** *vi* to struggle on; *vt* to keep going; **~ fuori** (estrarre) to take out, pull out; **~ giù** (abbassare) to bring down, to lower; (da scaffale ecc) to take down; **~ su** to pull up; (capelli) to put up; (fig: bambino) to bring up; **tirar dritto** to keep right on going; **~ via** (togliere) to take off; **tirarsi indietro** to move back; (fig) to back out; **tirati su!** cheer up!

tira'tura *sf* (azione) printing; (di libro) (print) run; (di giornale) circulation

'**tirchio, -a** ['tirkjo] *ag* mean, stingy

'**tiro** *sm* shooting *no pl*, firing *no pl*; (colpo, sparo) shot; (di palla: lancio) throwing *no pl*; throw; (fig) trick; **cavallo da ~** draught (BRIT) o draft (US) horse; **~ a segno** target shooting; (luogo) shooting range; **~ con l'arco** archery

tiro'cinio [tiro'tʃinjo] *sm* apprenticeship; (professionale) training

ti'roide *sf* thyroid (gland)

Tir'reno *sm*: **il (mar) ~** the Tyrrhenian Sea

ti'sana *sf* herb tea

tito'lare *smf* incumbent; (proprietario) owner; (Calcio) regular player

'**titolo** *sm* title; (di giornale) headline; (diploma) qualification; (Comm) security; (: azione) share; **a che ~?** for what reason?; **a ~ di amicizia** out of friendship; **a ~ di premio** as a prize; **~ di credito** share; **titoli di stato** government securities; **titoli di testa** (Cine) credits

titu'bante *ag* hesitant, irresolute

toast [toust] *sm inv* toasted sandwich (generally with ham and cheese)

toc'cante *ag* touching

toc'care /20/ vt to touch; (*tastare*) to feel; (*fig: riguardare*) to concern; (: *commuovere*) to touch, move; (: *pungere*) to hurt, wound; (: *far cenno a: argomento*) to touch on, mention ▷ vi: **~ a** (*accadere*) to happen to; (*spettare*) to be up to; **tocca a te difenderci** it's up to you to defend us; **a chi tocca?** whose turn is it?; **mi toccò pagare** I had to pay; **~ il fondo** (*in acqua*) to touch the bottom

toccherò ecc [tokke'rɔ] vb vedi **toccare**

togliere ['tɔʎʎere] /122/ vt (*rimuovere*) to take away (o off), remove; (*riprendere, non concedere più*) to take away, remove; (*Mat*) to take away, subtract; **~ qc a qn** to take sth (away) from sb; **ciò non toglie che ...** nevertheless ..., be that as it may ...; **togliersi il cappello** to take off one's hat

toilette [twa'lɛt] sf inv toilet; (*mobile*) dressing table

Tokyo sf Tokyo

tolgo ecc vb vedi **togliere**

tolle'rare /72/ vt to tolerate

tolsi ecc vb vedi **togliere**

'tomba sf tomb

tom'bino sm manhole cover

'tombola sf (*gioco*) tombola; (*ruzzolone*) tumble

'tondo, -a ag round

'tonfo sm splash; (*rumore sordo*) thud; (*caduta*) **fare un ~** to take a tumble

tonifi'care /20/ vt (*muscoli, pelle*) to tone up; (*irrobustire*) to invigorate, brace

tonnel'lata sf ton

'tonno sm tuna (fish)

'tono sm (*gen, Mus*) tone; (*di pezzo*) key; (*di colore*) shade, tone

ton'silla sf tonsil

'tonto, -a ag dull, stupid

to'pazio [to'pattsjo] sm topaz

'topo sm mouse

'toppa sf (*serratura*) keyhole; (*pezza*) patch

to'race [to'ratʃe] sm chest

'torba sf peat

torcere ['tɔrtʃere] /106/ vt to twist; **torcersi** vpr to twist, writhe

'torcia, -ce ['tɔrtʃa] sf torch; **~ elettrica** torch (BRIT), flashlight (US)

torci'collo [tortʃi'kɔllo] sm stiff neck

'tordo sm thrush

To'rino sf Turin

tor'menta sf snowstorm

tormen'tare /72/ vt to torment; **tormentarsi** vpr to fret, worry o.s.

tor'nado sm tornado

tor'nante sm hairpin bend (BRIT) o curve (US)

tor'nare /72/ vi to return, go (o come) back; (*ridiventare: anche fig*) to become (again); (*riuscire giusto, esatto: conto*) to work out; (*risultare*) to turn out (o be), prove (to be); **~ a casa** to go (o come) home; **~ utile** to prove o turn out (to be) useful; **torno a casa martedì** I'm going home on Tuesday

tor'neo sm tournament

'tornio sm lathe

'toro sm bull; **T~** Taurus

'torre sf tower; (*Scacchi*) rook, castle; **~ di controllo** (*Aer*) control tower

tor'rente sm torrent

torri'one sm keep

tor'rone sm nougat

'torsi ecc vb vedi **torcere**

torsi'one sf twisting; (*Tecn*) torsion

'torso sm torso, trunk; (*Arte*) torso

'torsolo sm (*di cavolo ecc*) stump; (*di frutta*) core

'torta sf cake

tortel'lini smpl (*Cuc*) tortellini

'torto, -a pp di **torcere** ▷ ag (*ritorto*) twisted; (*storto*) twisted, crooked ▷ sm (*ingiustizia*) wrong; (*colpa*) fault; **a ~** wrongly; **aver ~** to be wrong

tor'tora sf turtle dove

tor'tura sf torture; **tortu'rare** /72/ vt to torture

to'sare /72/ vt (*pecora*) to shear; (*siepe*) to clip

t

Tos'cana *sf*: la ~ Tuscany

'tosse *sf* cough; **ho la ~** I've got a cough

'tossico, -a, -ci, -che *ag* toxic; (*Econ*): **titolo ~** toxic asset

tossicodipen'dente *smf* drug addict

tos'sire /55/ *vi* to cough

tosta'pane *sm inv* toaster

to'tale *ag, sm* total

toto'calcio [toto'kaltʃo] *sm* gambling pool betting on football results ≈ (football) pools *pl* (BRIT)

to'vaglia [to'vaʎʎa] *sf* tablecloth; **tovagli'olo** *sm* napkin

tra *prep* (*di due persone, cose*) between; (*di più persone, cose*) among(st); (*tempo: entro*) within, in; **litigano ~ (di) loro** they're fighting amongst themselves; **~ 5 giorni** in 5 days' time; **~ breve** *o* **poco** soon; **~ sé e sé** (*parlare ecc*) to oneself; **sia detto ~ noi ...** between you and me ...

trabocca're /20/ *vi* to overflow

trabocchetto [trabok'ketto] *sm* (*fig*) trap

'traccia, -ce ['trattʃa] *sf* (*segno, striscia*) trail, track; (*orma*) tracks *pl*; (*residuo, testimonianza*) trace, sign; (*abbozzo*) outline

tracci'are [trat'tʃare] /14/ *vt* to trace, mark (out); (*disegnare*) to draw; (*fig: abbozzare*) to outline

tra'chea [tra'kɛa] *sf* windpipe, trachea

tra'colla *sf* shoulder strap; **borsa a ~** shoulder bag

tradi'mento *sm* betrayal; (*Dir, Mil*) treason

tra'dire /55/ *vt* to betray; (*coniuge*) to be unfaithful to; (*doveri: mancare*) to fail in; (*rivelare*) to give away, reveal

tradizio'nale [tradittsjo'nale] *ag* traditional

tradizi'one [tradit'tsjone] *sf* tradition

tra'durre /90/ *vt* to translate; (*spiegare*) to render, convey;

tradut'tore, -'trice *sm/f* translator; **traduzi'one** *sf* translation

'trae *vb vedi* **trarre**

traffi'cante *smf* dealer; (*peg*) trafficker

traffi'care /20/ *vi* (*affaccendarsi*) to busy o.s.; (*commerciare*): **~ (in)** to trade (in), deal (in) ▷ *vt* (*peg*) to traffic in

'traffico, -ci *sm* traffic; (*commercio*) trade, traffic; **~ di armi/droga** arms/drug trafficking

tra'gedia [tra'dʒɛdja] *sf* tragedy

'traggo *ecc vb vedi* **trarre**

tra'ghetto [tra'getto] *sm* ferry(boat)

'tragico, -a, -ci, -che ['tradʒiko] *ag* tragic

tra'gitto [tra'dʒitto] *sm* (*passaggio*) crossing; (*viaggio*) journey

tragu'ardo *sm* (*Sport*) finishing line; (*fig*) goal, aim

'trai *ecc vb vedi* **trarre**

traiet'toria *sf* trajectory

trai'nare /72/ *vt* to drag, haul; (*rimorchiare*) to tow

tralasci'are [tralaʃ'ʃare] /14/ *vt* (*studi*) to neglect; (*dettagli*) to leave out, omit

tra'liccio [tra'littʃo] *sm* (*Elettr*) pylon

tram *sm inv* tram

'trama *sf* (*filo*) weft, woof; (*fig: argomento, maneggio*) plot

traman'dare /72/ *vt* to pass on, hand down

tram'busto *sm* turmoil

tramez'zino [tramed'dzino] *sm* sandwich

'tramite *prep* through

tramon'tare /72/ *vi* to set, go down; **tra'monto** *sm* setting; (*del sole*) sunset

trampo'lino *sm* (*per tuffi*) springboard, diving board; (*per lo sci*) ski-jump

tra'nello *sm* trap

'tranne *prep* except (for), but (for); **~ che** unless

tranquil'lante *sm* (*Med*) tranquillizer

tranquillità *sf* calm, stillness; quietness; peace of mind

tranquilliz'zare [trankwillid'dzare] /72/ *vt* to reassure

> Attenzione! In inglese esiste il verbo *to tranquillize*, che però significa "calmare con un tranquillante".

tran'quillo, -a *ag* calm, quiet; (*bambino, scolaro*) quiet; (*sereno*) with one's mind at rest; **sta' ~** don't worry

transazi'one [transat'tsjone] *sf* compromise; (*Dir*) settlement; (*Comm*) transaction, deal

tran'senna *sf* barrier

trans'genico, -a, -ci, -che [trans'dʒɛniko] *ag* genetically modified

tran'sigere [tran'sidʒere] /47/ *vi* (*venire a patti*) to compromise, come to an agreement

transi'tabile *ag* passable

transi'tare /72/ *vi* to pass

transi'tivo, -a *ag* transitive

'transito *sm* transit; **di ~** (*merci*) in transit; (*stazione*) transit *cpd*; **"divieto di ~"** "no entry"

'trapano *sm* (*utensile*) drill; (*Med*) trepan

trape'lare /72/ *vi* to leak, drip; (*fig*) to leak out

tra'pezio [tra'pɛttsjo] *sm* (*Mat*) trapezium; (*attrezzo ginnico*) trapeze

trapian'tare /72/ *vt* to transplant; **trapi'anto** *sm* transplanting; (*Med*) transplant; **trapianto cardiaco** heart transplant

'trappola *sf* trap

tra'punta *sf* quilt

'trarre /123/ *vt* to draw, pull; (*portare*) to take; (*prendere, tirare fuori*) to take (out), draw; (*derivare*) to obtain; **~ origine da qc** to have its origins *o* originate in sth

trasa'lire /55/ *vi* to start, jump

trasan'dato, -a *ag* shabby

trasci'nare [traʃʃi'nare] /72/ *vt* to drag; **trascinarsi** *vpr* to drag o.s. along; (*fig*) to drag on

tras'correre /28/ *vt* (*tempo*) to spend, pass ▷ *vi* to pass

tras'crivere /105/ *vt* to transcribe

trascu'rare /72/ *vt* to neglect; (*non considerare*) to disregard

trasferi'mento *sm* transfer; (*trasloco*) removal, move; **~ di chiamata** (*Tel*) call forwarding

trasfe'rire /55/ *vt* to transfer; **trasferirsi** *vpr* to move; **tras'ferta** *sf* transfer; (*indennità*) travelling expenses *pl*; (*Sport*) away game

trasfor'mare /72/ *vt* to transform, change; **trasformarsi** *vpr* to be transformed; **trasformarsi in qc** to turn into sth; **trasforma'tore** *sm* (*Elettr*) transformer

trasfusi'one *sf* (*Med*) transfusion

trasgre'dire /55/ *vt* to disobey, contravene

traslo'care /20/ *vt* to move, transfer; **tras'loco, -chi** *sm* removal

tras'mettere /63/ *vt* (*passare*): **~ qc a qn** to pass sth on to sb; (*mandare*) to send; (*Tecn, Tel, Med*) to transmit; (*TV, Radio*) to broadcast; **trasmissi'one** *sf* (*gen, Fisica, Tecn*) transmission; (*passaggio*) transmission, passing on; (*TV, Radio*) broadcast

traspa'rente *ag* transparent

traspor'tare /72/ *vt* to carry, move; (*merce*) to transport, convey; **lasciarsi ~ (da qc)** (*fig*) to let o.s. be carried away (by sth); **tras'porto** *sm* transport

'trassi *ecc vb vedi* **trarre**

trasver'sale *ag* cross(-); (*retta*) transverse; running at right angles

'tratta *sf* (*Econ*) draft; **la ~ delle bianche** the white slave trade

tratta'mento *sm* treatment; (*servizio*) service

trat'tare /72/ *vt* (*gen*) to treat; (*commerciare*) to deal in; (*svolgere: argomento*) to discuss, deal with;

(*negoziare*) to negotiate ▷ *vi*: **~ di** to deal with; **~ con** (*persona*) to deal with; **si tratta di ...** it's about ...

tratte'nere /121/ *vt* (*far rimanere: persona*) to detain; (*intrattenere: ospiti*) to entertain; (*tenere, frenare, reprimere*) to hold back, keep back; (*astenersi dal consegnare*) to hold, keep; (*detrarre: somma*) to deduct; **trattenersi** *vpr* (*astenersi*) to restrain o.s., stop o.s.; (*soffermarsi*) to stay, remain

trat'tino *sm* dash; (*in parole composte*) hyphen

'**tratto, -a** *pp di* **trarre** ▷ *sm* (*di penna, matita*) stroke; (*parte*) part, piece; (*di strada*) stretch; (*di mare, cielo*) expanse; (*di tempo*) period (of time)

trat'tore *sm* tractor

tratto'ria *sf* (small) restaurant

'**trauma, -i** *sm* trauma

tra'vaglio [tra'vaʎʎo] *sm* (*angoscia*) pain, suffering; (*Med*) pains *pl*

trava'sare /72/ *vt* to decant

tra'versa *sf* (*trave*) crosspiece; (*via*) sidestreet; (*Ferr*) sleeper (BRIT), (railroad) tie (US); (*Calcio*) crossbar

traver'sata *sf* crossing; (*Aer*) flight, trip

traver'sie *sfpl* mishaps, misfortunes

tra'verso, -a *ag* oblique; **di ~** *ag* askew ▷ *av* sideways; **andare di ~** (*cibo*) to go down the wrong way; **guardare di ~** to look askance at

travesti'mento *sm* disguise

traves'tire /45/ *vt* to disguise; **travestirsi** *vpr* to disguise o.s.

tra'volgere [tra'vɔldʒere] /96/ *vt* to sweep away, carry away; (*fig*) to overwhelm

tre *num* three

'**treccia, -ce** ['trettʃa] *sf* plait, braid

tre'cento [tre'tʃɛnto] *num* three hundred ▷ *sm*: **il T~** the fourteenth century

'**tredici** ['treditʃi] *num* thirteen

'**tregua** *sf* truce; (*fig*) respite

tre'mare /72/ *vi*: **~ di** (*freddo ecc*) to shiver o tremble with; (*paura, rabbia*) to shake o tremble with

tre'mendo, -a *ag* terrible, awful

⬛ Attenzione! In inglese esiste la parola *tremendous*, che però significa *enorme* oppure *fantastico, strepitoso*.

'**tremito** *sm* trembling *no pl*; shaking *no pl*; shivering *no pl*

'**treno** *sm* train; **~ di gomme** set of tyres o (BRIT) o tires (US); **~ merci** goods (BRIT) o freight train; **~ viaggiatori** passenger train

○ **TRENI**
○
○
○ There are several different types
○ of train in Italy. "Regionali" and
○ "interregionali" are local trains
○ which stop at every small town
○ and village; the former operate
○ within regional boundaries,
○ while the latter may cross them.
○ "Diretti" are ordinary trains for
○ which passengers do not pay a
○ supplement; the main difference
○ from "espressi" is that the latter
○ are long-distance and mainly run
○ at night. "Intercity" and "eurocity"
○ are faster and entail a supplement.
○ "Rapidi" only contain first-class
○ seats, and the high-speed
○ "pendolino", which offers both
○ first- and second-class travel, runs
○ between the major cities.

'**trenta** *num* thirty; **tren'tesimo, -a** *num* thirtieth; **tren'tina** *sf*: **una trentina (di)** thirty or so, about thirty

trepi'dante *ag* anxious

triango'lare *ag* triangular

tri'angolo *sm* triangle

tri'bù *sf inv* tribe

tri'buna *sf* (*podio*) platform; (*in aule ecc*) gallery; (*di stadio*) stand

tribu'nale *sm* court

tri'ciclo [tri'tʃiklo] sm tricycle
tri'foglio [tri'fɔʎʎo] sm clover
'triglia ['triʎʎa] sf red mullet
tri'mestre sm period of three months; (Ins) term, quarter (us); (Comm) quarter
trin'cea [trin'tʃea] sf trench
trion'fare /72/ vi to triumph, win; **~ su** to triumph over, overcome; **tri'onfo** sm triumph
tripli'care /20/ vt to triple
'triplo, -a ag triple; treble ▷ sm: **il ~ (di)** three times as much (as); **la spesa è tripla** it costs three times as much
'trippa sf (Cuc) tripe
'triste ag sad; (luogo) dreary, gloomy
tri'tare /72/ vt to mince, grind (us)
trivi'ale ag vulgar, low
tro'feo sm trophy
'tromba sf (Mus) trumpet; (Aut) horn; **~ d'aria** whirlwind; **~ delle scale** stairwell
trom'bone sm trombone
trom'bosi sf thrombosis
tron'care /20/ vt to cut off; (spezzare) to break off
'tronco, -a, -chi, -che ag cut off; broken off; (Ling) truncated; (fig) cut short ▷ sm (Bot, Anat) trunk; (fig: tratto) section; **licenziare qn in ~** to fire sb on the spot
'trono sm throne
tropi'cale ag tropical

PAROLA CHIAVE

'troppo, -a det (in eccesso: quantità) too much; (: numero) too many; **c'era troppa gente** there were too many people; **fa troppo caldo** it's too hot
▷ pron (in eccesso: quantità) too much; (: numero) too many; **ne hai messo troppo** you've put in too much; **meglio troppi che pochi** better too many than too few
▷ av (eccessivamente: con ag, av) too; (: con vb) too much; **troppo amaro/tardi** too bitter/late; **lavora troppo** he works too much; **costa troppo** it costs too much; **di troppo** too much; too many; **qualche tazza di troppo** a few cups too many; **5 euro di troppo** 5 euros too much; **essere di troppo** to be in the way

'trota sf trout
'trottola sf spinning top
tro'vare /72/ vt to find; (giudicare): **trovo che** I find o think that; **trovarsi** vpr (reciproco: incontrarsi) to meet; (essere, stare) to be; (arrivare, capitare) to find o.s.; **andare a ~ qn** to go and see sb; **~ qn colpevole** to find sb guilty; **trovarsi bene/male** (in un luogo, con qn) to get on well/badly
truc'care /20/ vt (falsare) to fake; (attore ecc) to make up; (travestire) to disguise; (Sport) to fix; (Aut) to soup up; **truccarsi** vpr to make up (one's face)
'trucco, -chi sm trick; (cosmesi) make-up
'truffa sf fraud, swindle; **truffare** /72/ vt to swindle, cheat
truffa'tore, -'trice sm/f swindler, cheat
'truppa sf troop
tu pron you; **tu stesso(a)** you yourself; **dare del tu a qn** to address sb as "tu"
'tubo sm tube; (per conduttore) pipe; **~ digerente** (Anat) alimentary canal, digestive tract; **~ di scappamento** (Aut) exhaust pipe
tuf'fare /72/ vt to plunge; **tuffarsi** vpr to plunge, dive
'tuffo sm dive; (breve bagno) dip
tuli'pano sm tulip
tu'more sm (Med) tumour
Tuni'sia sf: **la ~** Tunisia
'tuo (f'**tua**, pl'**tuoi**, '**tue**) det: **il ~, la tua** ecc your ▷ pron: **il ~, la tua** ecc yours
tuo'nare /72/ vi to thunder; **tuona** it is thundering, there's some thunder
tu'ono sm thunder

tu'orlo *sm* yolk
tur'bante *sm* turban
tur'bare /72/ *vt* to disturb, trouble
tur'bato, -a *ag* upset; (*preoccupato, ansioso*) anxious
turbo'lenza [turbo'lɛntsa] *sf* turbulence
tur'chese [tur'kese] *sf* turquoise
Tur'chia [tur'kia] *sf*: **la ~** Turkey
'turco, -a, -chi, -che *ag* Turkish ▷ *sm/f* Turk (Turkish woman) ▷ *sm* (*Ling*) Turkish; **parlare ~** (*fig*) to talk double Dutch
tu'rismo *sm* tourism; tourist industry; **~ sessuale** sex tourism; **tu'rista, -i, -e** *smf* tourist; **tu'ristico, -a, -ci, -che** *ag* tourist *cpd*
'turno *sm* turn; (*di lavoro*) shift; **di ~** (*soldato, medico, custode*) on duty; **a ~** (*rispondere*) in turn; (*lavorare*) in shifts; **fare a ~ a fare qc** to take turns to do sth; **è il suo ~** it's your (*o* his *ecc*) turn
'turpe *ag* filthy, vile
'tuta *sf* overalls *pl*; (*Sport*) tracksuit
tu'tela *sf* (*Dir: di minore*) guardianship; (: *protezione*) protection; (*difesa*) defence
tutor ['tiutor] *sm inv* (*Aut*) speed monitoring system
tutta'via *cong* nevertheless, yet

PAROLA CHIAVE

'tutto, -a *det* **1** (*intero*) all; **tutto il latte** all the milk; **tutta la notte** all night, the whole night; **tutto il libro** the whole book; **tutta una bottiglia** a whole bottle
2 (*pl, collettivo*) all; every; **tutti i libri** all the books; **tutte le notti** every night; **tutti i venerdì** every Friday; **tutti gli uomini** all the men; (*collettivo*) all men; **tutto l'anno** all year long; **tutti e due** both *o* each of us (*o* them *o* you); **tutti e cinque** all five of us (*o* them *o* you)
3 (*completamente*): **era tutta sporca** she was all dirty; **tremava tutto** he was trembling all over; **è tutta sua madre** she's just *o* exactly like her mother
4: **a tutt'oggi** so far, up till now; **a tutta velocità** at full *o* top speed
▶ *pron* **1** (*ogni cosa*) everything, all; (*qualsiasi cosa*) anything; **ha mangiato tutto** he's eaten everything; **tutto considerato** all things considered; **100 euro in tutto** 100 euros in all; **in tutto eravamo 50** there were 50 of us in all
2: **tutti, e** (*ognuno*) all, everybody; **vengono tutti** they are all coming, everybody's coming; **tutti quanti** all and sundry
▶ *av* (*completamente*) entirely, quite; **è tutto il contrario** it's quite *o* exactly the opposite; **tutt'al più: saranno stati tutt'al più una cinquantina** there were about fifty of them at (the very) most; **tutt'al più possiamo prendere un treno** if the worst comes to the worst we can take a train; **tutt'altro** on the contrary; **è tutt'altro che felice** he's anything but happy; **tutt'a un tratto** suddenly
▶ *sm*: **il tutto** the whole lot, all of it

tut'tora *av* still
TV [ti'vu] *sf inv* (= *televisione*) TV ▷ *sigla* = **Treviso**
twit'tare /72/ *vt* (*su Twitter*) to tweet

u

ubbidi'ente ag obedient
ubbi'dire /55/ vi to obey; **~ a** to obey;
(veicolo, macchina) to respond to
ubria'care /20/ vt: **~ qn** to get sb
drunk; (alcool) to make sb drunk; (fig) to
make sb's head spin o reel; **ubriacarsi**
vpr to get drunk; **ubriacarsi di** (fig) to
become intoxicated with
ubri'aco, -a, -chi, -che ag, sm/f
drunk
uc'cello [ut't∫ello] sm bird
uc'cidere [ut't∫idere] /34/ vt to kill;
uccidersi vpr (suicidarsi) to kill o.s.;
(perdere la vita) to be killed
u'dire /124/ vt to hear
u'dito sm (sense of) hearing
UE sigla f (= Unione Europea) EU
UEM sigla f (= Unione economica e
monetaria) EMU
'uffa escl tut!
uffici'ale [uffi't∫ale] ag official ▷ sm
(Amm) official, officer; (Mil) officer;
~ di stato civile registrar

uf'ficio [uf'fit∫o] sm (gen) office;
(dovere) duty; (mansione) task,
function, job; (agenzia) agency,
bureau; (Rel) service; **d'~** ag office
cpd; official ▷ av officially; **~ di
collocamento** employment office;
~ informazioni information bureau;
~ oggetti smarriti lost property
office (BRIT), lost and found (US);
~ postale post office; **~ vendite/
del personale** sales/personnel
department
uffici'oso, -a [uffi't∫oso] ag unofficial
uguagli'anza [ugwaʎ'ʎantsa] sf
equality
uguagli'are [ugwaʎ'ʎare] /27/ vt
to make equal; (essere uguale) to
equal, be equal to; (livellare) to level;
uguagliarsi vpr: **uguagliarsi a** o **con
qn** (paragonarsi) to compare o.s. to sb
ugu'ale ag equal; (identico) identical,
the same; (uniforme) level, even ▷ av:
costano ~ they cost the same; **sono
bravi ~** they're equally good
UIL sigla f (= Unione Italiana del Lavoro)
trade union federation
'ulcera ['ult∫era] sf ulcer
U'livo sm (Pol) centre-left coalition
ulteri'ore ag further
ultima'mente av lately, of late
ulti'mare /72/ vt to finish, complete
'ultimo, -a ag (finale) last; (estremo)
farthest, utmost; (recente:
notizia, moda) latest; (fig: sommo,
fondamentale) ultimate ▷ sm/f last
(one); **fino all'~** to the last, until
the end; **da ~, in ~** in the end; **per ~**
(entrare, arrivare) last; **abitare all'~
piano** to live on the top floor
ultravio'letto, -a ag ultraviolet
ulu'lare /72/ vi to howl
umanità sf humanity
u'mano, -a ag human; (comprensivo)
humane
umidità sf dampness; humidity
'umido, -a ag damp; (mano, occhi)
moist; (clima) humid ▷ sm dampness,
damp; **carne in ~** stew

'**umile** *ag* humble

umili'are /19/ *vt* to humiliate; **umiliarsi** *vpr* to humble o.s.

u'more *sm* (*disposizione d'animo*) mood; (*carattere*) temper; **di buon/cattivo ~** in a good/bad mood

umo'rismo *sm* humour (BRIT), humor (US); **avere il senso dell'~** to have a sense of humour; **umo'ristico, -a, -ci, -che** *ag* humorous, funny

u'nanime *ag* unanimous

unci'netto [untʃi'netto] *sm* crochet hook

un'cino [un'tʃino] *sm* hook

undi'cenne [undi'tʃɛnne] *ag, smf* eleven-year-old

undi'cesimo, -a [undi'tʃɛzimo] *ag* eleventh

'**undici** ['unditʃi] *num* eleven

ungere ['undʒere] /5/ *vt* to grease, oil; (*Rel*) to anoint; (*fig*) to flatter, butter up

unghe'rese [unge'rese] *ag, smf, sm* Hungarian

Unghe'ria [unge'ria] *sf*: **l'~** Hungary

'**unghia** ['ungja] *sf* (*Anat*) nail; (*di animale*) claw; (*di rapace*) talon; (*di cavallo*) hoof

ungu'ento *sm* ointment

'**unico, -a, -ci, -che** *ag* (*solo*) only; (*ineguagliabile*) unique; (*singolo: binario*) single; **è figlio ~** he's an only child

unifi'care /20/ *vt* to unite, unify; (*sistemi*) to standardize; **unificazi'one** *sf* uniting; unification; standardization

uni'forme *ag* uniform; (*superficie*) even ▷ *sf* (*divisa*) uniform

uni'one *sf* union; (*fig: concordia*) unity, harmony; **U~ Europea** European Union; **ex U~ Sovietica** former Soviet Union

u'nire /55/ *vt* to unite; (*congiungere*) to join, connect; (*: ingredienti, colori*) to combine; (*in matrimonio*) to unite, join together; **unirsi** *vpr* to unite; (*in matrimonio*) to be joined together;

~ qc a to unite sth with; to join o connect sth with; to combine sth with; **unirsi a** (*gruppo, società*) to join

unità *sf inv* (*unione, concordia*) unity; (*Mat, Mil, Comm, di misura*) unit; **~ di misura** unit of measurement

u'nito, -a *ag* (*paese*) united; (*amici, famiglia*) close; **in tinta unita** plain, self-coloured

univer'sale *ag* universal; general

università *sf inv* university

uni'verso *sm* universe

PAROLA CHIAVE

'**uno, -a** (*dav sm* **un** + C, V, **uno** + *s impura, gn, pn, ps, x, z*; *dav sf* **un'** + V, **una** + C) *det* **1** a; (*dav vocale*) an; **un bambino** a child; **una strada** a street; **uno zingaro** a gypsy **2** (*intensivo*): **ho avuto una paura!** I got such a fright!

▶ *pron* **1** one; **prendine uno** take one (of them); **l'uno o l'altro** either (of them); **l'uno e l'altro** both (of them); **aiutarsi l'un l'altro** to help one another o each other; **sono entrati l'uno dopo l'altro** they came in one after the other

2 (*un tale*) someone, somebody

3 (*con valore impersonale*) one, you; **se uno vuole** if one wants, if you want

▶ *num* one; **una mela e due pere** one apple and two pears; **uno più uno fa due** one plus one equals two, one and one are two

▶ *sf*: **è l'una** it's one (o'clock)

'**unsi** *ecc vb vedi* **ungere**

'**unto, -a** *pp di* **ungere** ▷ *ag* greasy, oily ▷ *sm* grease

u'omo (*pl* **uomini**) *sm* man; **da ~** (*abito, scarpe*) men's, for men; **~ d'affari** businessman; **~ di paglia** stooge; **~ politico** politician; **~ rana** frogman

u'ovo (*pl f* **uova**) *sm* egg; **~ affogato** o **in camicia** poached egg; **~ bazzotto/sodo** soft-/hard-boiled egg; **~ alla coque** boiled egg; **~ di Pasqua** Easter egg; **~ al tegame** o **all'occhio di bue** fried egg; **uova strapazzate** scrambled eggs

ura'gano sm hurricane

urba'nistica sf town planning

ur'bano, -a ag urban, city cpd, town cpd; (Tel: chiamata) local; (fig) urbane

ur'gente [ur'dʒɛnte] ag urgent; **ur'genza** sf urgency; **in caso d'urgenza** in (case of) an emergency; **d'urgenza** ag emergency; av urgently, as a matter of urgency

ur'lare /72/ vi (persona) to scream, yell; (animale, vento) to howl ▷ vt to scream, yell

'urlo (pl m **urli** o pl f **urla**) sm scream, yell; howl

URP sigla m (= Ufficio Relazioni con il Pubblico) PR Office

urrà escl hurrah!

U.R.S.S. sigla f = **Unione delle Repubbliche Socialiste Sovietiche**; **l'~** the USSR

ur'tare /72/ vt to bump into, knock against, crash into; (fig: irritare) to annoy ▷ vi: **~ contro** o **in** to bump into, knock against; (fig: imbattersi) to come up against; **urtarsi** vpr (reciproco: scontrarsi) to collide; (: fig) to clash; (irritarsi) to get annoyed

'USA smpl: **gli ~** the USA

u'sanza [u'zantsa] sf custom; (moda) fashion

u'sare /72/ vt to use, employ ▷ vi (essere di moda) to be fashionable; (servirsi): **~ di** to use; (diritto) to exercise; (essere solito): **~ fare** to be in the habit of doing, be accustomed to doing ▷ vb impers: **qui usa così** it's the custom round here; **u'sato, -a** ag used; (consumato) worn; (di seconda mano) used, second-hand ▷ sm second-hand goods pl

u'scire [uʃʃire] /125/ vi (gen) to come out; (partire, andare a passeggio, a uno spettacolo ecc) to go out; (essere sorteggiato: numero) to come up;

~ da (gen) to leave; (posto) to go (o come) out of, leave; (solco, vasca ecc) to come out of; (muro) to stick out of; (competenza ecc) to be outside; (infanzia, adolescenza) to leave behind; (famiglia nobile ecc) to come from; **~ da** o **di casa** to go out; (fig) to leave home; **~ in automobile** to go out in the car, go for a drive; **~ di strada** (Aut) to go off o leave the road

u'scita [uʃʃita] sf (passaggio, varco) exit, way out; (per divertimento) outing; (Econ: somma) expenditure; (Teat) entrance; (fig: battuta) witty remark; **~ di sicurezza** emergency exit

usi'gnolo [uziɲ'nɔlo] sm nightingale

'uso sm (utilizzazione) use; (esercizio) practice; (abitudine) custom; **a ~ di** for (the use of); **d'~** (corrente) in use; **fuori ~** out of use; **per ~ esterno** for external use only

usti'one sf burn

usu'ale ag common, everyday

u'sura sf usury; (logoramento) wear (and tear)

uten'sile sm tool, implement; **utensili da cucina** kitchen utensils

u'tente smf user

'utero sm uterus

'utile ag useful ▷ sm (vantaggio) advantage, benefit; (Econ: profitto) profit

utiliz'zare [utilid'dzare] /72/ vt to use, make use of, utilize

UVA abbr (= ultravioletto prossimo) UVA

'uva sf grapes pl: **~ passa** raisins pl: **~ spina** gooseberry

UVB abbr (= ultravioletto lontano) UVB

u

v. *abbr* (= *vedi*) v.

va, va' *vb vedi* **andare**

va'cante *ag* vacant

va'canza [va'kantsa] *sf* (*riposo, ferie*) holiday(s *pl*) (BRIT), vacation (US); (*giorno di permesso*) day off, holiday; **vacanze** *sfpl* (*periodo di ferie*) holidays, vacation *sg*: **essere/andare in ~** to be/go on holiday *o* vacation; **vacanze estive** summer holiday(s) *o* vacation; **vacanze natalizie** Christmas holidays *o* vacation

> Attenzione! In inglese esiste la parola *vacancy* che però indica un posto vacante o una camera disponibile.

'vacca, -che *sf* cow

vacci'nare [vattʃi'nare] /72/ *vt* to vaccinate

vac'cino [vat'tʃino] *sm* (*Med*) vaccine

vacil'lare [vatʃil'lare] /72/ *vi* to sway, wobble; (*fiamma, luce*) to flicker; (*fig: memoria, coraggio*) to be failing, falter

'vacuo, -a *ag* (*fig*) empty, vacuous

'vado *ecc vb vedi* **andare**

vaga'bondo, -a *sm/f* tramp, vagrant

va'gare /80/ *vi* to wander

vagherò *ecc* [vage'rɔ] *vb vedi* **vagare**

va'gina [va'dʒina] *sf* vagina

'vaglia ['vaʎʎa] *sm inv* money order; **~ postale** postal order

vagli'are [vaʎ'ʎare] /27/ *vt* to sift; (*fig*) to weigh up

'vago, -a, -ghi, -ghe *ag* vague

va'gone *sm* (*Ferr: per passeggeri*) coach; (: *per merci*) truck, wagon; **~ letto** sleeper, sleeping car; **~ ristorante** dining *o* restaurant car

'vai *vb vedi* **andare**

vai'olo *sm* smallpox

va'langa, -ghe *sf* avalanche

va'lere /126/ *vi* (*avere forza, potenza*) to have influence; (*essere valido*) to be valid; (*avere vigore, autorità*) to hold, apply; (*essere capace: poeta, studente*) to be good, be able ▷ *vt* (*prezzo, sforzo*) to be worth; (*corrispondere*) to correspond to; (*procurare*): **~ qc a qn** to earn sb sth; **valersi** *vpr*: **valersi di** to make use of, take advantage of; **far ~** (*autorità ecc*) to assert; **vale a dire** that is to say; **~ la pena** to be worth the effort *o* worth it

'valgo *ecc vb vedi* **valere**

vali'care /20/ *vt* to cross

'valico, -chi *sm* (*passo*) pass

'valido, -a *ag* valid; (*rimedio*) effective; (*aiuto*) real; (*persona*) worthwhile

vali'getta *sf* briefcase; **~ ventiquattrore** overnight bag *o* case

va'ligia, -gie *o* **-ge** [va'lidʒa] *sf* (*suit*) case; **fare le valigie** to pack (up)

'valle *sf* valley; **a ~** (*di fiume*) downstream; **scendere a ~** to go downhill

va'lore *sm* (*gen*) value; (*merito*) merit, worth; (*coraggio*) valour , courage; (*Finanza: titolo*) security; **valori** *smpl* (*oggetti preziosi*) valuables

valoriz'zare [valorid'dzare] /72/ vt (*terreno*) to develop; (*fig*) to make the most of

va'luta sf currency, money; (*Banca*): **~ 15 gennaio** interest to run from January 15th

valu'tare /72/ vt (*casa, gioiello, fig*) to value; (*stabilire: peso, entrate, fig*) to estimate

'valvola sf (*Tecn, Anat*) valve; (*Elettr*) fuse

'valzer ['valtser] sm inv waltz

vam'pata sf (*di fiamma*) blaze; (*di calore*) blast; (: *al viso*) flush

vam'piro sm vampire

vanda'lismo sm vandalism

'vandalo sm vandal

vaneggi'are [vaned'dʒare] /62/ vi to rave

'vanga, -ghe sf spade

van'gelo [van'dʒɛlo] sm gospel

va'niglia [va'niʎʎa] sf vanilla

vanità sf vanity; (*di promessa*) emptiness; (*di sforzo*) futility; **vani'toso, -a** ag vain, conceited

'vanno vb vedi **andare**

'vano, -a ag vain ⊳ sm (*spazio*) space; (*apertura*) opening; (*stanza*) room

van'taggio [van'taddʒo] sm advantage; **essere/portarsi in ~** (*Sport*) to be in/take the lead; **vantaggi'oso, -a** ag advantageous, favourable

van'tare /72/ vt to praise, speak highly of; **vantarsi** vpr: **vantarsi (di/di aver fatto)** to boast o brag (about/about having done)

'vanvera sf: **a ~** haphazardly; **parlare a ~** to talk nonsense

va'pore sm vapour; (*anche*: **~ acqueo**) steam; (*nave*) steamer; **a ~** (*turbina ecc*) steam cpd; **al ~** (*Cuc*) steamed

va'rare /72/ vt (*Naut, fig*) to launch; (*Dir*) to pass

var'care /20/ vt to cross

'varco, -chi sm passage; **aprirsi un ~ tra la folla** to push one's way through the crowd

vare'china [vare'kina] sf bleach

vari'abile ag variable; (*tempo, umore*) changeable, variable ⊳ sf (*Mat*) variable

vari'cella [vari'tʃɛlla] sf chickenpox

vari'coso, -a ag varicose

varietà sf inv variety ⊳ sm inv variety show

'vario, -a ag varied; (*parecchi: col sostantivo al pl*) various; (*mutevole: umore*) changeable

'varo sm (*Naut, fig*) launch; (*di leggi*) passing

varrò ecc vb vedi **valere**

Var'savia sf Warsaw

va'saio sm potter

'vasca, -sche sf basin; (*anche*: **~ da bagno**) bathtub, bath

vas'chetta [vas'ketta] sf (*per gelato*) tub; (*per sviluppare fotografie*) dish

vase'lina sf vaseline

'vaso sm (*recipiente*) pot; (: *barattolo*) jar; (: *decorativo*) vase; (*Anat*) vessel; **~ da fiori** vase; (*per piante*) flowerpot

vas'soio sm tray

'vasto, -a ag vast, immense

Vati'cano sm: **il ~** the Vatican

ve pron, av vedi **vi**

vecchi'aia [vek'kjaja] sf old age

'vecchio, -a ['vɛkkjo] ag old ⊳ sm/f old man/woman; **i vecchi** the old

ve'dere /127/ vt, vi to see; **vedersi** vpr to meet, see one another; **avere a che ~ con** to have to do with; **far ~ qc a qn** to show sb sth; **farsi ~** to show o.s.; (*farsi vivo*) to show one's face; **vedi di non farlo** make sure o see you don't do it; **non (ci) si vede** (è *buio ecc*) you can't see a thing; **non lo posso ~** (*fig*) I can't stand him

ve'detta sf (*sentinella, posto*) look-out; (*Naut*) patrol boat

'vedovo, -a sm/f widower (widow)

vedrò ecc vb vedi **vedere**

ve'duta sf view; **vedute** sfpl (*fig: opinioni*) views; **di larghe o ampie vedute** broad-minded; **di vedute limitate** narrow-minded

vege'tale [vedʒe'tale] *ag, sm* vegetable

vegetari'ano, -a [vedʒeta'rjano] *ag, sm/f* vegetarian

vegetazi'one [vedʒetat'tsjone] *sf* vegetation

'vegeto, -a ['vɛdʒeto] *ag (pianta)* thriving; *(persona)* strong, vigorous

'veglia ['veʎʎa] *sf* wakefulness; *(sorveglianza)* watch; *(trattenimento)* evening gathering; **fare la ~ a un malato** to watch over a sick person

vegli'one [veʎ'ʎone] *sm* ball, dance; **~ di Capodanno** New Year's Eve party

ve'icolo *sm* vehicle

'vela *sf (Naut: tela)* sail; *(: sport)* sailing

ve'leno *sm* poison; **vele'noso, -a** *ag* poisonous

veli'ero *sm* sailing ship

vel'luto *sm* velvet; **~ a coste** cord

'velo *sm* veil; *(tessuto)* voile

ve'loce [ve'lotʃe] *ag* fast, quick ▷ *av* fast, quickly; **velocità** *sf* speed; **a forte velocità** at high speed; **velocità di crociera** cruising speed

'vena *sf (gen)* vein; *(filone)* vein, seam; *(fig: ispirazione)* inspiration; *(: umore)* mood; **essere in ~ di qc** to be in the mood for sth

ve'nale *ag (prezzo, valore)* market *cpd*; *(fig)* venal; mercenary

ven'demmia *sf (raccolta)* grape harvest; *(quantità d'uva)* grape crop, grapes *pl*; *(vino ottenuto)* vintage

'vendere /29/ *vt* to sell; **"vendesi"** "for sale"

ven'detta *sf* revenge

vendi'care /20/ *vt* to avenge; **vendicarsi** *vpr*: **vendicarsi (di)** to avenge o.s. (for); *(per rancore)* to take one's revenge (for); **vendicarsi su qn** to revenge o.s. on sb

'vendita *sf* sale; **la ~** *(attività)* selling; *(smercio)* sales *pl*; **in ~** on sale; **~ all'asta** sale by auction; **~ per telefono** telesales *sg*

vene'rare /72/ *vt* to venerate

venerdì *sm inv* Friday; **di** *o* **il ~** on Fridays; **V~ Santo** Good Friday

ve'nereo, -a *ag* venereal

Ve'nezia [ve'nɛttsja] *sf* Venice

'vengo *ecc vb vedi* **venire**

veni'ale *ag* venial

ve'nire /128/ *vi* to come; *(riuscire: dolce, fotografia)* to turn out; *(come ausiliare: essere)*: **viene ammirato da tutti** he is admired by everyone; **~ da** to come from; **quanto viene?** how much does it cost?; **far ~** *(mandare a chiamare)* to send for; **~ giù** to come down; **~ meno** *(svenire)* to faint; **~ meno a qc** not to fulfil sth; **~ su** to come up; **~ via** to come away; **~ a trovare qn** to come and see sb

'venni *ecc vb vedi* **venire**

ven'taglio [ven'taʎʎo] *sm* fan

ven'tata *sf* gust (of wind)

ven'tenne *ag*: **una ragazza ~** a twenty-year-old girl, a girl of twenty

ven'tesimo, -a *num* twentieth

'venti *num* twenty

venti'lare /72/ *vt (stanza)* to air, ventilate; *(fig: idea, proposta)* to air; **ventila'tore** *sm* ventilator, fan

ven'tina *sf*: **una ~ (di)** around twenty, twenty or so

'vento *sm* wind

'ventola *sf (Aut, Tecn)* fan

ven'tosa *sf (Zool)* sucker; *(di gomma)* suction pad

ven'toso, -a *ag* windy

'ventre *sm* stomach

'vera *sf* wedding ring

vera'mente *av* really

ve'randa *sf* veranda(h)

ver'bale *ag* verbal ▷ *sm (di riunione)* minutes *pl*

'verbo *sm (Ling)* verb; *(parola)* word; *(Rel)*: **il V~** the Word

'verde *ag, sm* green; **~ bottiglia/ oliva** bottle/olive green; **essere al ~** to be broke

ver'detto *sm* verdict

ver'dura *sf* vegetables *pl*

'vergine ['vɛrdʒine] *sf* virgin; **V~** Virgo ▷ *ag* virgin; (*ragazza*): **essere ~** to be a virgin

ver'gogna [ver'goɲɲa] *sf* shame; (*timidezza*) shyness, embarrassment; **vergo'gnarsi** /15/ *vpr*: **vergognarsi (di)** to be o feel ashamed (of); to be shy (about), be embarrassed (about); **vergo'gnoso, -a** *ag* ashamed; (*timido*) shy, embarrassed; (*causa di vergogna: azione*) shameful

ve'rifica, -che *sf* checking *no pl*; check

verifi'care /20/ *vt* (*controllare*) to check; (*confermare*) to confirm, bear out

verità *sf inv* truth

'verme *sm* worm

ver'miglio [ver'miʎʎo] *sm* vermilion, scarlet

ver'nice [ver'nitʃe] *sf* (*colorazione*) paint; (*trasparente*) varnish; (*pelle*) patent leather; **"~ fresca"** "wet paint"; **vernici'are** /14/ *vt* to paint; to varnish

'vero, -a *ag* (*veridico: fatti, testimonianza*) true; (*autentico*) real ▷ *sm* (*verità*) truth; (*realtà*) (real) life; **un ~ e proprio delinquente** a real criminal, an out and out criminal

vero'simile *ag* likely, probable

verrò *ecc vb vedi* **venire**

ver'ruca, -che *sf* wart

versa'mento *sm* (*pagamento*) payment; (*deposito di denaro*) deposit

ver'sante *sm* slopes *pl*, side

ver'sare /72/ *vt* (*fare uscire: vino, farina*) to pour (out); (*spargere: lacrime, sangue*) to shed; (*rovesciare*) to spill; (*Econ*) to pay; (: *depositare*) to deposit, pay in

versa'tile *ag* versatile

versi'one *sf* version; (*traduzione*) translation

'verso *sm* (*di poesia*) verse, line; (*di animale, uccello, venditore ambulante*) cry; (*direzione*) direction; (*modo*) way; (*di foglio di carta*) verso; (*di moneta*) reverse; **versi** *smpl* (*poesia*) verse *sg* ▷ *prep* (*in direzione di*) toward(s); (*nei pressi di*) near, around (about); (*in senso*

temporale) about, around; (*nei confronti di*) for; **non c'è ~ di persuaderlo** there's no way of persuading him, he can't be persuaded; **~ di me** towards me; **~ sera** towards evening

'vertebra *sf* vertebra

verte'brale *ag* vertebral; **colonna ~** spinal column, spine

verti'cale *ag, sf* vertical

'vertice ['vɛrtitʃe] *sm* summit, top; (*Mat*) vertex; **conferenza al ~** (*Pol*) summit conference

ver'tigine [ver'tidʒine] *sf* dizziness *no pl*; dizzy spell; (*Med*) vertigo; **avere le vertigini** to feel dizzy

ve'scica, -che [veʃʃika] *sf* (*Anat*) bladder; (*Med*) blister

'vescovo *sm* bishop

'vespa *sf* wasp

ves'taglia [ves'taʎʎa] *sf* dressing gown

ves'tire /45/ *vt* (*bambino, malato*) to dress; (*avere indosso*) to have on, wear; **vestirsi** *vpr* to dress, get dressed; **ves'tito, -a** *ag* dressed ▷ *sm* garment; (*da donna*) dress; (*da uomo*) suit; **vestiti** *smpl* (*indumenti*) clothes; **vestito di bianco** dressed in white

veteri'nario, -a *ag* veterinary ▷ *sm* veterinary surgeon (*BRIT*), veterinarian (*US*), vet

'veto *sm inv* veto

ve'traio *sm* glassmaker; (*per finestre*) glazier

ve'trato, -a *ag* (*porta, finestra*) glazed; (*che contiene vetro*) glass *cpd* ▷ *sf* glass door (o window); (*di chiesa*) stained glass window; **carta vetrata** sandpaper

ve'trina *sf* (*di negozio*) (shop) window; (*armadio*) display cabinet; **vetri'nista, -i, -e** *smf* window dresser

'vetro *sm* glass; (*per finestra, porta*) pane (of glass)

'vetta *sf* peak, summit, top

vet'tura *sf* (*carrozza*) carriage; (*Ferr*) carriage (*BRIT*), car (*US*); (*auto*) car (*BRIT*), automobile (*US*)

vezzeggia'tivo [vettseddʒa'tivo]
sm (*Ling*) term of endearment
vi (*dav lo, la, li, le, ne diventa* **ve**) *pron*
(*oggetto*) you; (*complemento di termine*)
(to) you; (*riflessivo*) yourselves;
(*reciproco*) each other ▷ *av* (*lì*) there;
(*qui*) here; (*per questo/quel luogo*)
through here/there; **vi è/sono**
there is/are
'via *sf* (*gen*) way; (*strada*) street;
(*sentiero, pista*) path, track; (*Amm:
procedimento*) channels *pl* ▷ *prep*
(*passando per*) via, by way of ▷ *av*
away ▷ *escl* go away!; (*suvvia*) come
on!; (*Sport*) go! ▷ *sm* (*Sport*) starting
signal; **per ~ di** (*a causa di*) because
of, on account of; **in** *o* **per ~** on the
way; **in ~ di guarigione** on the
road to recovery; **per ~ aerea** by
air; (*lettere*) by airmail; **andare/
essere ~** to go/be away; **~ ~ che** (*a
mano a mano*) as; **dare il ~** (*Sport*)
to give the starting signal; **dare il
~ a** (*fig*) to start; **in ~ provvisoria**
provisionally; **V~ lattea** (*Astr*) Milky
Way; **~ di mezzo** middle course; **non
c'è ~ di scampo** *o* **d'uscita** there's
no way out
via'dotto *sm* viaduct
viaggi'are [viad'dʒare] /62/ *vi*
to travel; **viaggia'tore, -'trice** *ag*
travelling ▷ *sm* traveller , passenger
vi'aggio *sm* travel(ling); (*tragitto*)
journey, trip; **buon ~!** have a good
trip!; **~ di nozze** honeymoon
vi'ale *sm* avenue
via'vai *sm* coming and going, bustle
vi'brare /72/ *vi* to vibrate
'vice ['vitʃe] *sm/f* deputy
vi'cenda [vi'tʃenda] *sf* event; **a ~**
in turn
vice'versa [vitʃe'vɛrsa] *av* vice versa;
da Roma a Pisa e ~ from Rome to
Pisa and back
vici'nanza [vitʃi'nantsa] *sf*
nearness, closeness
vi'cino, -a [vi'tʃino] *ag* (*gen*) near;
(*nello spazio*) near, nearby; (*accanto*)

next; (*nel tempo*) near, close at hand
▷ *sm/f* neighbour (BRIT), neighbor
(US) ▷ *av* near, close; **da ~** (*guardare*)
close up; (*esaminare, seguire*) closely;
(*conoscere*) well, intimately; **~ a** near
(to), close to; (*accanto a*) beside; **~ di
casa** neighbour
'vicolo *sm* alley; **~ cieco** blind alley
'video *sm inv* (*TV: schermo*) screen;
video'camera *sf* camcorder;
videocas'setta *sf* videocassette
videochia'mare [videokja'mare]
/72/ *vt* to video call
video: **video'clip** [video'klip] *sm
inv* videoclip; **videogi'oco, -chi**
[video'dʒɔko] *sm* video game;
videoregistra'tore *sm* video
(recorder); **videote'lefono** *sm*
videophone
'vidi *ecc vb vedi* **vedere**
vie'tare /72/ *vt* to forbid; (*Amm*) to
prohibit; **~ a qn di fare** to forbid sb to
do; to prohibit sb from doing
vie'tato, -a *ag* (*vedi vb*) forbidden;
prohibited; banned; **"~
fumare/l'ingresso"** "no smoking/
admittance"; **~ ai minori di 14/18
anni** prohibited to children under
14/18; **"senso ~"** (*Aut*) "no entry";
"sosta vietata" (*Aut*) "no parking"
Viet'nam *sm*: **il ~** Vietnam;
vietna'mita, -i, -e *ag, smf, sm*
Vietnamese *inv*
vi'gente [vi'dʒɛnte] *ag* in force
vi'gile ['vidʒile] *ag* watchful ▷ *sm*
(*anche:* **~ urbano**) policeman (*in
towns*); **~ del fuoco** fireman
vi'gilia [vi'dʒilja] *sf* (*giorno
antecedente*) eve; **la ~ di Natale**
Christmas Eve
vigli'acco, -a, -chi, -che
[viʎ'ʎakko] *ag* cowardly ▷ *sm/f*
coward
'vigna ['viɲɲa] *sf*, **vi'gneto**
[viɲ'ɲeto] *sm* vineyard
vi'gnetta [viɲ'ɲetta] *sf* cartoon; (*Aut:
anche:* **~ autostradale**) (: *tassa*) car
tax (*for motorways*); (: *adesivo*) sticker

showing that this tax has been paid

vi'gore *sm* vigour; *(Dir):* **essere/ entrare in ~** to be in/come into force

'vile *ag (spregevole)* low, mean, base; *(codardo)* cowardly

'villa *sf* villa

vil'laggio [vil'laddʒo] *sm* village; **~ turistico** holiday village

vil'lano, -a *ag* rude, ill-mannered

villeggia'tura [villeddʒa'tura] *sf* holiday(s *pl*) *(BRIT)*, vacation *(US)*

vil'letta *sf*, **vil'lino** *sm* small house (with a garden), cottage

'vimini *smpl* wicker; **mobili di ~** wicker furniture *sg*

'vincere ['vintʃere] /129/ *vt (in guerra, al gioco, a una gara)* to defeat, beat; *(premio, guerra, partita)* to win; *(fig)* to overcome, conquer ▷ *vi* to win; **~ qn in** *(abilità, bellezza)* to surpass sb in; **vinci'tore, -'trice** *sm/f* winner; *(Mil)* victor

vi'nicolo, -a *ag* wine *cpd*

'vino *sm* wine; **~ bianco/rosato/ rosso** white/rosé/red wine; **~ da pasto** table wine

'vinsi *ecc vb vedi* **vincere**

vi'ola *sf (Bot)* violet; *(Mus)* viola ▷ *ag*, *sm inv (colore)* purple

vio'lare /72/ *vt (chiesa)* to desecrate, violate; *(giuramento, legge)* to violate

violen'tare /72/ *vt* to use violence on; *(donna)* to rape

vio'lento, -a *ag* violent; **vio'lenza** *sf* violence; **violenza carnale** rape

vio'letto, -a *ag*, *sm (colore)* violet ▷ *sf (Bot)* violet

violi'nista, -i, -e *smf* violinist

vio'lino *sm* violin

violon'cello [violon'tʃello] *sm* cello

vi'ottolo *sm* path, track

VIP [vip] *sm inv*, *f inv (= Very Important Person)* VIP

'vipera *sf* viper, adder

vi'rale *ag (Inform)* viral

vi'rare /72/ *vi (Naut, Aer)* to turn; *(Fot)* to tone; **~ di bordo** to change course; *(Naut)* to tack

'virgola *sf (Ling)* comma; *(Mat)* point; **virgo'lette** *sfpl* inverted commas, quotation marks

vi'rile *ag (proprio dell'uomo)* masculine; *(non puerile, da uomo)* manly, virile

virtù *sf inv* virtue; **in** *o* **per ~ di** by virtue of, by

virtu'ale *ag* virtual

'virus *sm inv (anche Inform)* virus

'viscere ['viʃʃere] *sfpl (di animale)* entrails *pl*; *(fig)* bowels *pl*

'vischio ['viskjo] *sm (Bot)* mistletoe; *(pania)* birdlime

'viscido, -a ['viʃʃido] *ag* slimy

vi'sibile *ag* visible

visibilità *sf* visibility

visi'era *sf (di elmo)* visor; *(di berretto)* peak

visi'one *sf* vision; **prendere ~ di qc** to examine sth, look sth over; **prima/seconda ~** *(Cine)* first/second showing

visita *sf* visit; *(Med)* visit, call; *(: esame)* examination; **~ medica** medical examination; **~ guidata** guided tour; **visi'tare** /72/ *vt* to visit; *(Med)* to visit, call on; *(: esaminare)* to examine; **visita'tore, -'trice** *sm/f* visitor

vi'sivo, -a *ag* visual

'viso *sm* face

vi'sone *sm* mink

'vispo, -a *ag* quick, lively

'vissi *ecc vb vedi* **vivere**

'vista *sf (facoltà)* (eye)sight; *(veduta)* view; *(fatto di vedere):* **la ~ di** the sight of; **sparare a ~** to shoot on sight; **in ~** in sight; **perdere qn di ~** to lose sight of sb; *(fig)* to lose touch with sb; **far ~ di fare** to pretend to do; **a ~ d'occhio** as far as the eye can see; *(fig)* before one's very eyes

'visto, -a *pp di* **vedere** ▷ *sm* visa; **~ che** seeing (that)

vis'toso, -a *ag* gaudy, garish; *(ingente)* considerable

visu'ale *ag* visual

'vita *sf* life; *(Anat)* waist; **a ~** for life

vi'tale *ag* vital

vita'mina *sf* vitamin
'vite *sf* (*Bot*) vine; (*Tecn*) screw
vi'tello *sm* (*Zool*) calf; (*carne*) veal; (*pelle*) calfskin
'vittima *sf* victim
'vitto *sm* food; (*in un albergo ecc*) board; **~ e alloggio** board and lodging
vit'toria *sf* victory
'viva *escl*: **~ il re!** long live the king!
vi'vace [vi'vatʃe] *ag* (*vivo, animato*) lively; (: *mente*) lively, sharp; (*colore*) bright
vi'vaio *sm* (*di pesci*) hatchery; (*Agr*) nursery
viva'voce [viva'votʃe] *sm inv* (*dispositivo*) loudspeaker; **mettere in ~** to switch on the loudspeaker
vi'vente *ag* living, alive; **i viventi** the living
'vivere /130/ *vi* to live ▷ *vt* to live; (*passare: brutto momento*) to live through, go through; (*sentire: gioie, pene di qn*) to share ▷ *sm* life; (*anche:* **modo di ~**) way of life; **viveri** *smpl* (*cibo*) food *sg*, provisions; **~ di** to live on
'vivido, -a *ag* (*colore*) vivid, bright
vivisezi'one [viviset'tsjone] *sf* vivisection
'vivo, -a *ag* (*vivente*) alive, living; (: *animale*) live; (*fig*) lively; (: *colore*) bright, brilliant; **i vivi** the living; **~ e vegeto** hale and hearty; **farsi ~** to show one's face; to keep in touch; **ritrarre dal ~** to paint from life; **pungere qn nel ~** (*fig*) to cut sb to the quick
vivrò *ecc vb vedi* **vivere**
vizi'are [vit'tsjare] /19/ *vt* (*bambino*) to spoil; (*corrompere moralmente*) to corrupt; **vizi'ato, -a** *ag* spoilt; (*aria, acqua*) polluted
'vizio ['vittsjo] *sm* (*morale*) vice; (*cattiva abitudine*) bad habit; (*imperfezione*) flaw, defect; (*errore*) fault, mistake
V.le *abbr* = **viale**

vocabo'lario *sm* (*dizionario*) dictionary; (*lessico*) vocabulary
vo'cabolo *sm* word
vo'cale *ag* vocal ▷ *sf* vowel
vocazi'one [vokat'tsjone] *sf* vocation; (*fig*) natural bent
'voce ['votʃe] *sf* voice; (*diceria*) rumour; (*di un elenco: in bilancio*) item; **aver ~ in capitolo** (*fig*) to have a say in the matter
'voga *sf* (*Naut*) rowing; (*usanza*): **essere in ~** to be in fashion *o* in vogue
vo'gare /80/ *vi* to row
vogherò *ecc* [voge'rɔ] *vb vedi* **vogare**
'voglia ['vɔʎʎa] *sf* desire, wish; (*macchia*) birthmark; **aver ~ di qc/ di fare** to feel like sth/like doing; (*più forte*) to want sth/to do
'voglio *ecc* ['vɔʎʎo] *vb vedi* **volere**
'voi *pron* you; **voi'altri** *pron* you
vo'lante *ag* flying ▷ *sm* (steering) wheel
volan'tino *sm* leaflet
vo'lare /72/ *vi* (*uccello, aereo, fig*) to fly; (*cappello*) to blow away *o* off, fly away *o* off; **~ via** to fly away *o* off
vo'latile *ag* (*Chim*) volatile ▷ *sm* (*Zool*) bird
volente'roso, -a *ag* willing
volenti'eri *av* willingly; **"~"** "with pleasure", "I'd be glad to"

 PAROLA CHIAVE

vo'lere /131/ *sm* will, wish(es); **contro il volere di** against the wishes of; **per volere di qn** in obedience to sb's will *o* wishes
  ▷ *vt* **1** (*esigere, desiderare*) to want; **volere fare qc** to want to do sth; **volere che qn faccia qc** to want sb to do sth; **vorrei questo/fare** I would *o* I'd like this/to do; **come vuoi** as you like; **vuoi un caffè?** would you like a coffee?; **senza volere** (*inavvertitamente*) without meaning to, unintentionally

2 (*consentire*): **vogliate attendere, per piacere** please wait; **vogliamo andare?** shall we go?; **vuole essere così gentile da …?** would you be so kind as to …?; **non ha voluto ricevermi** he wouldn't see me
3: volerci (*essere necessario*) (*materiale, attenzione*) to be needed; (*tempo*) to take; **quanta farina ci vuole per questa torta?** how much flour do you need for this cake?; **ci vuole un'ora per arrivare a Venezia** it takes an hour to get to Venice
4: voler bene a qn (*amore*) to love sb; (*affetto*) to be fond of sb, like sb very much; **voler male a qn** to dislike sb; **volerne a qn** to bear sb a grudge; **voler dire** to mean

vol'gare *ag* vulgar
voli'era *sf* aviary
voli'tivo, -a *ag* strong-willed
volli *ecc vb vedi* **volere**
'volo *sm* flight; **colpire qc al ~** to hit sth as it flies past; **capire al ~** to understand straight away; **~ charter** charter flight; **~ di linea** scheduled flight
volontà *sf inv* will; **a ~** (*mangiare, bere*) as much as one likes; **buona/cattiva ~** goodwill/lack of goodwill
volontari'ato *sm* (*lavoro*) voluntary work
volon'tario, -a *ag* voluntary ▷ *sm* (*Mil*) volunteer
'volpe *sf* fox
'volta *sf* (*momento, circostanza*) time; (*turno, giro*) turn; (*curva*) turn, bend; (*Archit*) vault; (*direzione*): **partire alla ~ di** to set off for; **a mia** (*o tua ecc*) **~** in turn; **una ~** once; **una ~ sola** only once; **due volte** twice; **una cosa per ~** one thing at a time; **una ~ per tutte** once and for all; **a volte** at times, sometimes; **una ~ che** (*temporale*) once; (*causale*) since; **3 volte 4** 3 times 4

volta'faccia [volta'fattʃa] *sm inv* (*fig*) volte-face
vol'taggio [vol'taddʒo] *sm* (*Elettr*) voltage
vol'tare /72/ *vt* to turn; (*girare: moneta*) to turn over; (*rigirare*) to turn round ▷ *vi* to turn; **voltarsi** *vpr* to turn; to turn over; to turn round
volta'stomaco *sm* nausea; (*fig*) disgust
'volto, -a *pp di* **volgere** ▷ *sm* face
vo'lubile *ag* changeable, fickle
vo'lume *sm* volume
vomi'tare /72/ *vt, vi* to vomit;
'vomito *sm* vomiting *no pl*; vomit
'vongola *sf* clam
vo'race [vo'ratʃe] *ag* voracious, greedy
vo'ragine [vo'radʒine] *sf* abyss, chasm
vorrò *ecc vb vedi* **volere**
'vortice ['vɔrtitʃe] *sm* whirlwind; whirlpool; (*fig*) whirl
'vostro, -a *det*: **il (la) ~(a)** *ecc* your ▷ *pron*: **il (la) ~(a)** *ecc* yours
vo'tante *smf* voter
vo'tare /72/ *vi* to vote ▷ *vt* (*sottoporre a votazione*) to take a vote on; (*approvare*) to vote for; (*Rel*): **~ qc a** to dedicate sth to
'voto *sm* (*Pol*) vote; (*Ins*) mark (BRIT), grade (US); (*Rel*) vow; (: *offerta*) votive offering; **aver voti belli/brutti** (*Ins*) to get good/bad marks o grades
vs. *abbr* (= *vostro*) yr
vul'cano *sm* volcano
vulne'rabile *ag* vulnerable
vu'oi, vu'ole *vb vedi* **volere**
vuo'tare /72/ *vt*, **vuo'tarsi** *vpr* to empty
vu'oto, -a *ag* empty; (*fig: privo*): **~ di** (*senso ecc*) devoid of ▷ *sm* empty space, gap; (*spazio in bianco*) blank; (*Fisica*) vacuum; (*fig: mancanza*) gap, void; **a mani vuote** empty-handed; **~ d'aria** air pocket; **"~ a rendere"** "returnable bottle"

V

W X

'wafer ['vafer] *sm inv (Cuc, Elettr)*
   wafer
'water ['wɔ:təʳ] *sm inv* toilet
watt [vat] *sm inv* watt
WC *sm inv* WC
web [ueb] *sm:* **il ~** the web ▷ *ag inv:*
   pagina ~ webpage; **cercare nel ~** to
   search the web; **webcam** [web'kam]
   sf inv (Inform) webcam
'weekend ['wi:kend] *sm inv* weekend
'western ['wɛstern] *ag (Cine)* cowboy
   cpd ▷ *sm inv* western, cowboy film;
   ~ all'italiana spaghetti western
'whisky ['wiski] *sm inv* whisky
Wi-Fi [uai'fai] *(Inform) sm* Wi-Fi ▷ *ag
   inv* Wi-Fi
'windsurf ['windsə:f] *sm inv (tavola)*
   windsurfer; *(sport)* windsurfing
'würstel ['vyrstəl] *sm inv* frankfurter

xe'nofobo, -a [kse'nɔfobo] *ag*
   xenophobic ▷ *sm/f* xenophobe
xi'lofono [ksi'lɔfono] *sm* xylophone

Y Z

yacht [jɔt] *sm inv* yacht
'yoga ['jɔga] *ag inv, sm* yoga (*cpd*)
yogurt ['jɔgurt] *sm inv* yog(h)urt

zabai'one [dzaba'jone] *sm dessert made of egg yolks, sugar and marsala*
zaf'fata [tsaf'fata] *sf (tanfo)* stench
zaffe'rano [dzaffe'rano] *sm* saffron
zaf'firo [dzaf'firo] *sm* sapphire
zai'netto [dzai'netto] *sm* (small) rucksack
'zaino ['dzaino] *sm* rucksack
'zampa ['tsampa] *sf (di animale: gamba)* leg; (: *piede*) paw; **a quattro zampe** on all fours
zampil'lare [tsampil'lare] /72/ *vi* to gush, spurt
zan'zara [dzan'dzara] *sf* mosquito; **zanzari'era** *sf* mosquito net
'zappa ['tsappa] *sf* hoe
'zapping ['tsapɪŋ] *sm (TV)* channel-hopping
zar, za'rina [tsar, tsa'rina] *sm/f* tsar (tsarina)
'zattera ['dzattera] *sf* raft

z

'**zebra** ['dzɛbra] *sf* zebra; **zebre** *sfpl* (Aut) zebra crossing *sg* (BRIT), crosswalk *sg* (US)

'**zecca, -che** ['tsekka] *sf* (Zool) tick; (officina di monete) mint

'**zelo** ['dzɛlo] *sm* zeal

'**zenzero** ['dzendzero] *sm* ginger

'**zeppa** ['tseppa] *sf* wedge

'**zeppo, -a** ['tseppo] *ag*: ~ **di** crammed o packed with

zer'bino [dzer'bino] *sm* doormat

'**zero** ['dzɛro] *sm* zero, nought; **vincere per tre a ~** (Sport) to win three-nil

'**zia** ['tsia] *sf* aunt

zibel'lino [dzibel'lino] *sm* sable

'**zigomo** ['dzigomo] *sm* cheekbone

zig'zag [dzig'dzag] *sm inv* zigzag; **andare a ~** to zigzag

Zim'babwe [tsim'babwe] *sm*: **lo ~** Zimbabwe

'**zinco** ['dzinko] *sm* zinc

'**zingaro, -a** ['dzingaro] *sm/f* gipsy

'**zio** ['tsio] (*pl* **zii**) *sm* uncle

zip'pare /72/ *vt* (Inform: file) to zip

zi'tella [dzi'tɛlla] *sf* spinster; (peg) old maid

'**zitto, -a** ['tsitto] *ag* quiet, silent; **sta' ~!** be quiet!

'**zoccolo** ['tsɔkkolo] *sm* (calzatura) clog; (di cavallo ecc) hoof; (Archit) plinth; (di armadio) base

zodia'cale [dzodia'kale] *ag* zodiac *cpd*; **segno ~** sign of the zodiac

zo'diaco [dzo'diako] *sm* zodiac

'**zolfo** ['tsolfo] *sm* sulphur

'**zolla** ['dzolla] *sf* clod (of earth)

zol'letta [dzol'letta] *sf* sugar lump

'**zona** ['dzɔna] *sf* zone, area; **~ di depressione** (Meteor) trough of low pressure; **~ disco** (Aut) ≈ meter zone; **~ industriale** industrial estate; **~ pedonale** pedestrian precinct; **~ verde** (di abitato) green area

'**zonzo** ['dzondzo]: **a ~** *av* **andare a ~** to wander about, stroll about

'**zoo** ['dzɔo] *sm inv* zoo

zoolo'gia [dzoolo'dʒia] *sf* zoology

zoppi'care [tsoppi'kare] /20/ *vi* to limp; (fig: mobile) rickety

'**zoppo, -a** ['tsɔppo] *ag* lame; (fig: mobile) shaky, rickety

ZTL *sigla f* (= Zona a Traffico Limitato) controlled traffic zone

'**zucca, -che** ['tsukka] *sf* (Bot) marrow; pumpkin

zucche'rare [tsukke'rare] /72/ *vt* to put sugar in; **zucche'rato, -a** *ag* sweet, sweetened

zuccheri'era [tsukke'rjɛra] *sf* sugar bowl

'**zucchero** ['tsukkero] *sm* sugar; **~ di canna** cane sugar; **~ filato** candy floss, cotton candy (US)

zuc'china [tsuk'kina] *sf* courgette (BRIT), zucchini (US)

'**zuffa** ['tsuffa] *sf* brawl

'**zuppa** ['tsuppa] *sf* soup; (fig) mixture, muddle; **~ inglese** (Cuc) dessert made with sponge cake, custard and chocolate ≈ trifle (BRIT)

'**zuppo, -a** ['tsuppo] *ag*: **~ (di)** drenched (with), soaked (with)

Italian in focus

Introduction

Italian in focus gives you an introduction to various aspects of Italy and the Italian language. The following pages help you get to know the country where the language is spoken and the people who speak it.

Practical language tips and helpful notes on common translation difficulties will enable you to become a more confident Italian speaker. A useful correspondence section gives you all the information you need to be able to communicate effectively.

We've also included a number of links to useful websites, which will give you the opportunity to read more about Italy and the Italian language.

We hope you will enjoy using your *Italian in focus* supplement. We are sure it will help you find out more about Italy and Italians and become more confident in writing and speaking Italian.

Cominciamo!

Italy and its regions

©Collins Bartholomew Ltd 2016

Italy's neighbours

Italian is an official language in two Swiss cantons, Ticino and Grigioni, in the republic of San Marino and in Vatican City. Italian is also spoken in Malta, part of Croatia, and part of Slovenia.

Italy and its regions

The six biggest Italian cities

City	Name of inhabitants	Population
Roma	i romani	3,718,000
Milano	i milanesi	3,099,000
Napoli	i napoletani	2,202,000
Torino	i torinesi	1,765,000
Palermo	i palermitani	853,000
Bergamo	i bergamaschi	840,000

Italy consists of the mainland and two large islands, Sardegna and Sicilia, together with smaller islands such as Elba and Capri.

There are 20 administrative regions, five of which are *regioni autonome*, which have more decision-making powers than the others. Three of the 'autonomous regions' are in the north – Valle d'Aosta, Friuli-Venezia Giulia and Trentino-Alto Adige. The other two are the islands of Sardegna and Sicilia. Central government retains jurisdiction for matters such as defence, foreign affairs and the legal system, which affect the country as a whole.

Italy has only been a unified country since 1870. Before then parts of the peninsula were under the control of various countries, such as Spain, Austria and France. There was, and still is, a strong regional identity, with many people speaking one of the diverse local dialects. Nowadays everyone learns standard Italian at school; however, many people speak *dialetto* with neighbours, friends and family.

As is often the case in areas bordering other countries, there are some bilingual communities. For example, in the Trentino-Alto Adige area in the far north of Italy, the majority language is German and it is now co-official with Italian.

A snapshot of Italy

- In area, Italy (301, 000 km²) is somewhat bigger than the UK (244,000 km²).

- The Po (652 km) is Italy's longest river. It rises in the Alps and flows into the Adriatic near Venice.

- The population of Italy is about 59.8 million, which is slightly less than that of the UK. The birth rate is very low (1.2 children per woman). Deaths outnumber births.

- The Italian economy is the fourth biggest in the EU and eighth biggest in the world.

- Italy is the world's biggest wine-producing country.

- Gran Paradiso (4061m) is Italy's highest peak. Monte Bianco (Mont Blanc) (4810m) is higher but there is some debate as to whether it lies in France or Italy.

- 50.7 million tourists visit Italy every year, making it the 5th most popular tourist destination in the world.

- Italy has four active volcanoes: Etna, Vesuvius, Stromboli and Vulcano. Etna erupts frequently and is Europe's most active volcano.

Some useful links are:
www. governo.it
Website of the Italian government.
www.istat.it
The Italian statistics office.
www.enit.it
Italian state tourist board.

5

The Italian-speaking world

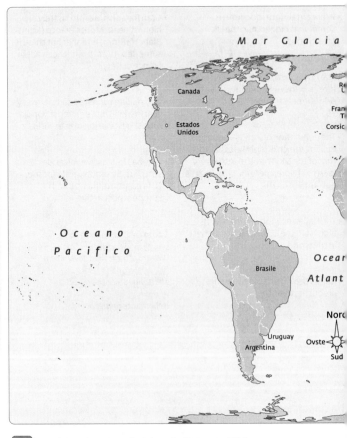

Countries or regions where Italian is the mother tongue or an official language

Countries with large numbers of Italian speakers

Ártico

Germania
Slovenia
igioni Croazia
San Marino
Albania
Italia
Malta

Somalia

Oceano
Pacifico

Oceano
Indiano

Australia

©Collins Bartholomew Ltd 2016

Many Italians went to the Americas – particularly to the US and Argentina – and to Australia. There are 1½ million Italian speakers in Argentina and ¾ of a million in the US. Italian has had a major influence on the way Spanish is spoken in Argentina.

The Italian State

- Italy has dozens of political parties. The two main political groupings are the centre-right and the centre-left. The government tends to be formed by a coalition consisting of several parties.

- Italy has two houses of parliament: the Senate (*il Senato*) and the Chamber of Deputies (*la Camera dei Deputati*). The President of the Republic (*il Presidente della Repubblica*), who is the head of state, has a tenure of seven years.

- The Prime Minister (*il Presidente del Consiglio*) is the head of government.

- Inside Italy there are two tiny independent states: San Marino and Vatican City.

- San Marino is the smallest republic in Europe.

- Vatican City is the spiritual and administrative centre of the Roman Catholic Church. It has two official languages, Italian and Latin.

Italian words that have travelled the world

An important part of the language Italians took to foreign countries was to do with food – many immigrants opened cafés and restaurants. These days people all over the world drink cappuccinos and espressos, and eat ciabatta, spaghetti, minestrone and pizza.

While everyone is familiar with these food items, they may not realize that the Italian words themselves have interesting, highly descriptive meanings. Here are just a few:

• cappuccino
This comes from the word capuchin. Capuchins are friars whose habits are brown – the colour of cappuccino coffee.

• ciabatta
This means 'slipper'. The bread has this name because of its shape.

• macchiato
macchiato means 'stained' and describes the look of a dark coffee with a little spot of milk on it .

• spaghetti
spago means 'string' – so *spaghetti* are 'little strings'. There's another pasta called *orecchiette*. If you bear in mind that *un orecchio* is an ear, you can probably guess what this pasta looks like.

• tiramisù
This word doesn't describe the appearance of the dessert, but the effect it has, as it means 'pick-me-up' (a reference to the stimulating effect of the coffee it contains).

• vermicelli
This kind of pasta is very, very thin, and its name means 'little worms'.

Italian words used in English

Apart from lots of words to do with food, there are other Italian words that are very often used in English. Here are a few interesting examples:

• solo
This means 'alone' in Italian and was originally borrowed as a musical term – but it's now used in all kinds of contexts.

• fiasco
English has borrowed only one of this word's two senses: the other one is 'wine bottle'!

• piano
This is the Italian for 'soft'. When the pianoforte was invented it was so called because it could be played either soft (*piano*), or loud (*forte*), unlike its predecessor, the harpsichord.

• prima donna
This word for leading lady means 'first woman'. This is another musical term which has come to be used more generally.

• bimbo
Unlike in English, in Italian this is not a derogatory word for a woman – it just means 'little boy'. *Una bimba* is a little girl.

• al fresco
In Italian this doesn't mean 'outside' but 'in the cool', and in a figurative sense, 'in jail'.

English words used in Italian

Italians have as great an appetite for English words as other people have for Italian food. Words from every conceivable field are borrowed; daily life, popular culture, science, computing, sport, business and so on.

- Countless words are borrowed in their original form:

lo stress	la privacy
lo shopping	il gay
il fast food	il blues
il jazz	lo show
il talk show	il computer
il mouse	il golf
lo sport	il supporter
il record	il training
il manager	il target

In the plural, these words get a plural article (*i*, *gli* or *le*) but no final 's':

Singular	Plural
il talk show	i talk show
lo sport	gli sport
la star	le star

- Other words are Italianized, but still recognizably English:

chattare	to chat
craccare	to crack
dribblare	to dribble
sprintare	to sprint
scrollare	to scroll
standardizzare	to standardize
interfaccia	interface
reality	reality show

- Some words look English, but have taken on a different meaning:

un box	a garage
un golf	a cardigan (it also means the sport)
un ticket	a prescription charge
uno smoking	a dinner jacket
uno spot	a tv or radio advert

Improving your pronunciation

Italian sounds

Vowels

Each English vowel can be pronounced in several quite different ways – think of the sound the letter **i** has, for example, in the words m**i**lk, k**i**nd and c**i**rcus. Italian vowels vary much less in their pronunciation:

a – is like the *a* in father
e – is like the *e* in set
i – is like the *ee* in sheep OR is pronounced like *y* in yard
o – is like the *o* in orange
u – is like the *oo* in soon

Avoid saying Italian words like their English lookalikes: the *i* in *Milano* and in *aprile*, for example, is the long *ee* sound, not the short i used in Milan and April.

Unlike English, Italian is pronounced exactly as it is written, so *interessante*, for example, has five syllables, with a clearly pronounced vowel in each one: *in-te-res-san-te*.

• Italian vowels never disappear as they do in English words like interesting (int-res-ting) and camera (cam-ra). Always pronounce them fully.

• Italian vowels never have the indistinct 'uh' sound to be heard at the end of many English words, for example, host<u>el</u>, hospit<u>al</u> and cir<u>cus</u>. Always pronounce Italian vowels clearly.

• When **i** is pronounced **y**, make sure that it's **y** as in yard, not **y** as in very:

andiamo	an-dya-mo
	(not an-dy-a-mo)
ravioli	rav-yo-lee
	(not ra-vee-o-lee)
stazione	sta-zyo-ne
	(not sta-zee-o-ne)

Improving your pronunciation

Consonants

- The presence of a double consonant in Italian makes the consonant sound longer: *cat-ti-vo*, *inte-res-san-te*, *An-na*.

- *c* followed by *e* or *i* is pronounced **tch**, as in *centro* and *facile*.

- *ch* is pronounced **k**, as in *fuochi* and *chiuso*.

- *g* followed by *e* and *i* is pronounced *j*, as in *leggero* and *giardino*.

- *gh* is pronounced like *g* in get, as in *lunghi* and *spaghetti*.

- *gl* followed by *e* and *i* is normally pronounced like the **lli** in million, for example *luglio*, *bagagli*.

- *gn* is pronounced **ny**, for example *gnocchi*, *giugno*.

- *sc* followed by *e* and *i* is pronounced **sh**, as in *lasciare* and *sciare*.

Stress

- Italian words are usually stressed on the next to the last syllable, for example *cucina*, *studente*, *straniero*, *diciassette*, *parlare*, *avere*.

- If a word is spelled with an accent on the last vowel, for example, *fedeltà*, *università*, *però*, *così*, *caffè*, *perché*, put the stress on this vowel.

- Some words are stressed on other syllables; the 'they' form of verbs, for example, usually stresses the third to last syllable: *capiscono* (= they understand); *parlano* (= they speak).

- Other words, such as *semplice*, *macchina*, *vendere* and *camera* stress the first syllable. Be aware that words aren't always stressed as you'd expect and when in doubt look in the dictionary: you'll see that in each headword there's a mark that looks like an apostrophe. The syllable immediately following this apostrophe is the one you stress.

A useful link is:
www.accademiadellacrusca.it
National language academy of Italy.

Improving your fluency

Conversational words and phrases

In English we insert lots of words and phrases, such as *so, then, by the way*, into our conversation, to give our thoughts a structure and often to show our attitude. The Italian words below do the same thing. If you use them you'll sound more fluent and natural.

- *allora*
  Allora, che facciamo stasera? (= so)

- *va bene*
  Va bene, ho capito. (= okay)

- *ecco*
  Ecco perché non sono venuti.
  (= that's)
  Ecco Mario! (= here's)
  Eccolo! (= there … is)

- *forse*
  Sì, ma **forse** hanno ragione.
  (= maybe)

- *certo*
  Certo che puoi. (= of course)

- *dunque*
  Dunque, come dicevo … (= well)
  Dunque ha ragione lui. (= so)

- *può darsi*
  Sì, lo so, ma **può darsi** che …
  (= perhaps)

- *purtroppo*
  Sì, **purtroppo**. (= unfortunately)

- *sinceramente*
  Sinceramente, non m'importa niente.
  (= really)

- *comunque*
  Comunque, non è sempre così.
  (= however)

- *senz'altro*
  Mi scriverai? – **Senz'altro**!
  (= of course)
  È **senz'altro** meglio lui. (= definitely)

- *davvero*
  Ha pagato lui. – **Davvero**? (= really)

Improving your fluency

Varying the words you use to get your message across will also make you sound more fluent in Italian. For example, instead of *Mi piace molto* *il calcio*, you could say *Il calcio è la mia passione*. Here are some other suggestions.

Saying what you like or dislike

Adoro le ciliege.	I love …
Mi è piaciuto molto il tuo regalo.	I (really) liked …
Non mi piace il tennis.	I don't like …
Il suo ultimo film *non mi piace per niente*.	I don't like … (at all).
Detesto mentire.	I hate …

Expressing your opinion

Credo che sia giusto.	I think …
Penso che costino di più.	I think …
Sono sicuro/sicura che ti piacerà.	I'm sure …
Secondo me è stato un errore.	In my opinion …
A mio parere vincerà lui.	In my opinion …
A me sembra che qualche volta …	It seems to me …

Agreeing or disagreeing

Ha ragione.	You're right.
Giusto!	Quite right!
(Non) sono d'accordo.	I (don't) agree.
Non direi.	I wouldn't say so.
Certo!	Of course!

Correspondence

The following section on correspondence has been designed to help you communicate confidently in written as well as spoken Italian. Sample letters, emails and sections on text messaging and making telephone calls will ensure that you have all the vocabulary you need to correspond successfully.

Text messaging

un sms *(esse emme esse)* = text message
mandare un sms a qualcuno = to text somebody

Abbreviation	Italian	English
+ tardi	*più tardi*	later
+o-	*più o meno*	more or less
ba	*bacio*	kiss
bn	*bene*	well
C6?	*ci sei?*	are you there?
cs	*cosa*	what
c ved	*ci vediamo*	see you soon
dv	*dove*	where
k6?	*chi sei?*	who are you?
ke cs?	*che cosa?*	what?
tu6	*tu sei*	you are
k	*che*	that, what
qd	*quando*	when
nn	*non*	not
k fai?	*che fai?*	what are you doing?
qnd	*quando*	when
TVB	*ti voglio bene*	I love you
TVTB	*ti voglio tanto bene*	I love you so much
x	*per*	for
xke	*perché*	because
xke?	*perché?*	why?
TAT	*ti amo tanto*	love you loads

Writing an email

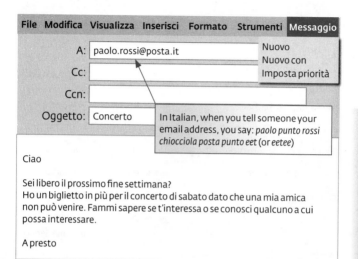

| File | Modifica | Visualizza | Inserisci | Formato | Strumenti | Messaggio |

A: paolo.rossi@posta.it

Nuovo
Nuovo con
Imposta priorità

Cc:

Ccn:

Oggetto: Concerto

In Italian, when you tell someone your email address, you say: *paolo punto rossi chiocciola posta punto eet* (or *eetee*)

Ciao

Sei libero il prossimo fine settimana?
Ho un biglietto in più per il concerto di sabato dato che una mia amica non può venire. Fammi sapere se t'interessa o se conosci qualcuno a cui possa interessare.

A presto

file	file	*rispondi*	reply
modifica	edit	*rispondi a tutti*	reply to all
visualizza	view	*inoltrare*	to forward
formato	format	*allega*	attachment
inserisci	insert	*A*	to
?	help	*Cc (copia carbone)*	cc (carbon copy)
strumenti	tools	*Ccn (copia carbone nascosta)*	bcc (blind carbon copy)
scrivere	to compose	*oggetto*	subject
help	help	*Da*	from
invia	send	*dat*	date
crea messaggio	new message		

Here is some additional useful Internet vocabulary:

ADSL	broadband	Internet	the Internet
avanti	forward	la Rete	the (World-Wide) Web
cartella	folder	motore di ricerca	search engine
cercare	to search	navigare in Internet	to surf the Net
cliccare	to click	pagina iniziale	home page
collegamenti	links	pagina web	web page
collegarsi	to log on	preferiti	favourites
copiare	to copy	programma	program
cronologia	history	provider	Internet Service Provider
domande frequenti	FAQs	salvare	to save
fare doppio click	to double-click	scaricare	to download
finestra	window	scollegarsi	to log off
foglio di calcolo	spreadsheet	sito Internet	website
icona	icon	stampare	print
impostazioni	settings	tagliare	to cut
incollare	to paste	tastiera	keyboard
indietro	back	visualizzare	to view

Writing a personal letter

Siena, 5 giugno 2017

Cara Maria,

ti ringrazio moltissimo del biglietto che mi hai mandato per il mio compleanno, che è arrivato proprio il giorno della mia festa!

Mi dispiace che tu non sia potuta venire a Milano per il mio compleanno e spero che ti sia ripresa dopo l'influenza. Mi piacerebbe poterti incontrare presto perché ho molte novità da raccontarti. Forse tra due settimane verrò a Torino con degli amici. Pensi di essere libera il giorno 12? Ti telefono la prossima settimana, così ci mettiamo d'accordo.

Baci,

Anna

Writing a personal letter

Other ways of starting a personal letter	Other ways of ending a personal letter
Carissima Maria *Mia cara Maria* *Cari Luigi e Silvia*	*Un abbraccio* *Bacioni* *Con affetto* *A presto*

Some useful phrases

Ti ringrazio per la tua lettera.	Thank you for your letter.
Mi ha fatto piacere ricevere tue notizie.	It was lovely to hear from you.
Scusami se non ti ho scritto prima.	I'm sorry I didn't reply sooner.
Salutami tanto Lucia.	Give my love to Lucia.
Tanti saluti anche da Paolo.	Paolo sends his best wishes.
Scrivi presto!	Write soon!

Writing a formal letter

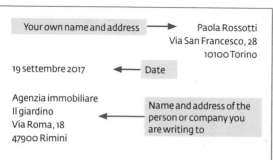

Your own name and address ⟶   Paola Rossotti
                              Via San Francesco, 28
                                    10100 Torino

19 settembre 2017 ⟵ Date

Agenzia immobiliare
Il giardino   Name and address of the
Via Roma, 18   ⟵   person or company you
47900 Rimini   are writing to

OGGETTO: Richiesta di rimborso

Egr. signori,
vi scrivo per presentare reclamo in merito all'appartamento
che ho affittato nel condominio Le Torri per il periodo 5-12
agosto. Avevo espressamente richiesto un appartamento
con due camere e invece mi è stato assegnato un
appartamento con una camera sola; mancava inoltre
il condizionatore d'aria di cui il contratto di locazione fa
specifica menzione.
Chiedo quindi un rimborso di 1000 euro comprensivo
della differenza tra la tariffa che ho pagato per un
appartamento con due camere e aria condizionata e quella
per un appartamento con una camera sola senza aria
condizionata, e di un risarcimento per i disagi subiti.

Allego fotocopia del contratto di locazione.

Distinti saluti

Paola Rossotti

Writing a formal letter

Other ways of starting a formal letter	Other ways of ending a formal letter
Egregio signore, *Gentile signora,* *Egregio Signor Paolozzo,* *Gentile Signora Paolozzo,* *Spett. Ditta,* (when writing to a firm)	*Distinti saluti* *Le porgo i miei più distinti saluti* *Cordiali saluti*

Some useful phrases

La ringrazio della sua lettera del ...	Thank you for your letter of ...
In riferimento a ...	With reference to ...
Vi prego di inviarmi ...	Please send me ...
In attesa di una sua risposta la ringrazio per l'attenzione.	I look forward to hearing from you.
La ringrazio in anticipo per ...	Thank you in advance for ...

Agenzia immobiliare
Il giardino
Via Roma, 18 ← The house number comes after the street name, and the postcode comes before the name of the town.
47900 Rimini

Making a call

Asking for information

Qual è il prefisso di Livorno?	What's the code for Livorno?
Cosa devo fare per ottenere la linea esterna?	How do I get an outside line?
Può darmi il numero dell'interno della Signora Busi?	Could you give me Ms Busi's extension number?

When your number answers

Buongiorno, c'è Andrea?	Hello! Is Andrea there?
Potrei parlare con Lucia, per favore?	Could I speak to Lucia, please?
Parla la Signora de Maggio?	Is that Mrs de Maggio?
Può chiedergli/chiederle di richiamarmi?	Could you ask him/her to call me back?
Richiamo fra mezz'ora.	I'll call back in half an hour.
Posso lasciare un messaggio, per favore?	Could I leave a message, please?

When you answer the telephone

Pronto!	Hello!
Chi parla?	Who's speaking?
Sono Marco.	It's Marco speaking.
Sì, sono io.	Speaking.
Vuole lasciare un messaggio?	Would you like to leave a message?

What you may hear

Chi devo dire?	Who shall I say is calling?
Le passo la comunicazione.	I'm putting you through now.
Attenda in linea.	Please hold.
Non risponde nessuno.	There's no reply.
La linea è occupata.	The line is engaged (*Brit*)/busy (*US*).
Vuole lasciare un messaggio?	Would you like to leave a message?

If you have a problem

Scusi, ho sbagliato numero.	Sorry, I dialled the wrong number.
La linea è molto disturbata.	This is a very bad line.
Qui non c'è campo.	There's no signal here.
Ho la batteria quasi scarica.	My battery's low.
Non ti sento.	I can't hear you.

Italian phrases and sayings

In Italian, as in many languages, people use vivid expressions based on images from their experience of real life. We've grouped the common expressions below according to the type of image they use. For fun, we have given you the word-for-word translation as well as the English equivalent.

Food and drink

dire pane al pane e vino al vino
word for word:
→ to call a spade a spade
to call bread bread and wine wine

Se non è zuppa è pan bagnato.
word for word:
→ It's much of a muchness.
if it's not soup it's wet bread

rendere pan per focaccia
word for word:
→ to give as good as you get
to give bread for focaccia

avere le mani in pasta
word for word:
→ to have a finger in the pie
to have your hands in the dough

lavorare per la pagnotta
word for word:
→ to earn your living
to work for your loaf

Ormai la frittata è fatta.
word for word:
→ The damage is done.
the omelette is made now

Weather

fare il bello e il cattivo tempo
word for word:
→ to do as one pleases
to make the good and bad weather

una tempesta in un bicchier d'acqua
word for word:
→ a storm in a teacup
a storm in a glass of water

sposa bagnata sposa fortunata
word for word:
→ rain on your wedding day is lucky
wet bride, lucky bride

Italian phrases and sayings

Animals

prendere due piccioni con una fava
word for word:

→ to kill two birds with one stone
to get two pigeons with one broad bean

Quando il gatto non c'è i topi ballano.
word for word:

→ When the cat's away the mice will play.
when the cat's not there the mice dance

Chi dorme non piglia pesci.
word for word:

→ The early bird catches the worm.
if you're asleep you don't catch any fish

In bocca al lupo!
word for word:

→ Break a leg!
into the wolf's mouth!

Meglio un uovo oggi che una gallina domani.
word for word:

→ A bird in the hand is worth two in the bush.
better an egg today than a hen tomorrow

L'ospite è come il pesce, dopo tre giorni puzza.
word for word:

→ It's nice when they come and it's nice when they go.
guests are like fish – after three days they start to smell

Parts of the body

essere un pugno in un occhio
word for word:

→ to be an eyesore
to be a punch in the eye

Chi non ha testa ha gambe.
word for word:

→ Use your head to save your legs.
people who have no head have legs

rimanere a bocca aperta
word for word:

→ to be amazed
to be left open-mouthed

avere le mani bucate
word for word:

→ to spend money like water
to have holes in your hands

Italian phrases and sayings

nascere con la camicia   → to be born with a silver spoon in your
                                   mouth
    word for word: *to be born with with a shirt on*

sudare sette camicie   → to work like a dog
    word for word: *to sweat seven shirts*

tirare qualcuno per la giacca   → to twist someone's arm
    word for word: *to pull someone by the coat*

Se sono rose fioriranno.   → The proof of the pudding is in the
                                   eating.
    word for word: *if they're roses they'll bloom*

fare di ogni erba un fascio   → to lump everything together
    word for word: *to put all the grasses into one bundle*

Non sono tutte rose e fiori.   → It's not all a bed of roses.
    word for word: *it's not all roses and flowers*

Rosso di sera, bel tempo si spera.   → Red sky at night, shepherd's delight.
    word for word: *(if the sky's) red at night you can hope*
                                    for good weather

vedere tutto nero   → to look on the black side
    word for word: *to see everything as black*

Al buio tutti i gatti sono neri.   → At night all cats are grey.
    word for word: *in the dark all cats are black*

Some common translation difficulties

On the following pages we have shown some of the translation difficulties you are most likely to come across. We hope that the tips we have given will help you to avoid these common pitfalls when writing or speaking Italian.

How to say 'you' in Italian

There are three ways of saying *you* in Italian: **tu** and **lei** are used to speak to one person, and **voi** is used to speak to more than one person.

• Use **tu** when you are speaking to a person you know well, or to a child. If you are a student you can call another student **tu**.

| And how old are you, Roberto? | → | E **tu**, Roberto, quanti anni hai? |

• Use **lei** when speaking to strangers, or anyone you're not on familiar terms with. As you get to know someone better they may suggest that you call each other **tu** instead of **lei**. In shops, hotels and restaurants customers are always addressed as **lei**.

| Would you like a coffee too, madam? | → | Vuole un caffè anche **lei**, signora? |

It may seem potentially confusing that **lei** also means 'she', but in practice it's quite obvious that if someone speaks directly to you using **lei**, the meaning is *you*.

• Use **voi** when you are speaking to more than one person.

| Where are you boys from? | → | **Voi**, ragazzi, di dove siete? |

'You' has to go with the verb in English, but in Italian you often use the verb alone:

How old are you?	→	Quanti anni hai?
You speak good Italian, madam.	→	Parla bene l'italiano, signora.
You're young.	→	Siete giovani.

Some common translation difficulties

You use the words **tu**, **lei** and **voi** to attract someone's attention, or for the sake of emphasis.

Tu cosa pensi?	→ What do <u>you</u> think?
Lei quale preferisce?	→ Which one do <u>you</u> prefer?

Showing possession

In English -'s is a common way of showing who or what something belongs to. In Italian you have to use **di**:

my brother**'s** car	→ *la macchina **di** mio fratello*
Maria**'s** house	→ *la casa **di** Maria*

Translating 'to like'

There are two ways of saying you like something, depending on whether it is singular or plural:

I like Italy. → **Mi piace** *l'Italia.*
word-for-word meaning of Italian: *to me is pleasing Italy*

I like dogs. → **Mi piacciono** *i cani.*
word-for-word meaning of Italian: *to me are pleasing dogs*

If you bear in mind the word-for-word meaning of the Italian you'll have no trouble deciding whether to use **piace** or **piacciono**.

To say 'we like', change **mi** to **ci**.

We like the sea.	→ **Ci piace** *il mare.*
We like his films.	→ **Ci piacciono** *i suoi film.*

Some common translation difficulties

If you want to ask someone if they like something:

• Use **ti** when asking someone you know well.

    Do you like my shoes?   ➔ **Ti piacciono** le mie scarpe?

• Use **le** when speaking politely

    Do you like Italian food, madam? ➔ **Le piace** la cucina italiana, signora?

• Use **vi** when talking to more than one person.

    Do you like football, boys?   ➔ **Vi piace** il calcio, ragazzi?

Translating -ing

The English -*ing* form is used to talk about something you are doing or were doing. This can be translated into Italian by using the Italian present continuous tense (the verb form that ends **-ando** or **-endo**).

    They were gett**ing** bored.   ➔ Si stavano annoi**ando**.
    He's read**ing** the paper.   ➔ Sta legg**endo** il giornale.
    She's talk**ing** to Mum.   ➔ Sta parl**ando** con la mamma.

It is, however, just as common to translate the –*ing* form in English with the present simple tense in Italian.

    He's read**ing** the paper.   ➔ **Legge** il giornale.
    She's talk**ing** to Mum.   ➔ **Parla** con la mamma.

In other cases the Italian infinitive (the verb form that ends in **-are**, **-ere**, or **-ire**) is often used where the -*ing* form is used in English.

• Use the infinitive when talking about activities:

    I love **reading**.   ➔ Mi piace moltissimo **leggere**.
    We don't like **walking**.   ➔ Non ci piace **camminare**.
    Smoking is bad for you. ➔ **Fumare** fa male.

Some common translation difficulties

Use the infinitive to translate prepositions such as *without* + *-ing*
(**senza** + infinitive), *before* + *-ing* (**prima di** + infinitive), *after* + *-ing*
(**dopo aver** + past participle).

He went away **without saying** anything.	→ *È andato via **senza dire** niente.*
Before opening the packet, read the instructions.	→ ***Prima di aprire** il pacchetto, leggi le istruzioni.*
After making a phone call she went out.	→ ***Dopo aver** telefonato è uscita.*

More on prepositions

Sentences that have no preposition in English may contain a preposition
in Italian. The dictionary can help you with these. For example:

They started **laughing**.	→ *Hanno cominciato **a ridere**.*
Have you finished **eating**?	→ *Hai finito **di mangiare**?*
When did you stop **smoking**?	→ *Quando hai smesso **di fumare**?*

Saying Sorry

• To apologize about something, use **scusi** to someone you're on formal
terms with, and **scusa** to a friend. Use **scusate** to more than one person.

Sorry.	→ *Scusi.*
Sorry I'm late.	→ *Scusi il ritardo.*
Sorry, Paola, I've got to go.	→ *Scusa, Paola, devo andare.*
Sorry to disturb you.	→ *Scusate il disturbo.*

• **Scusi** is also used to mean *'excuse me'* when you stop somebody to ask
something.

Excuse me, where is the station?	→ *Scusi, dov'è la stazione?*

Some common translation difficulties

When you haven't heard what someone said, say **come, scusi**?

• To express regret use **mi dispiace**:

My grandfather has died. –
   Oh, **I'm sorry**.
	→ *È morto mio nonno. –*
	   *Oh, **mi dispiace**.*

I haven't got time, **sorry**.	→ *Non ho tempo, **mi dispiace**.*
I'm sorry but I can't come.	→ ***Mi dispiace** ma non posso venire.*
I'm sorry for them.	→ ***Mi dispiace** per loro.*

Translating 'to be'

'To be' usually corresponds to **essere**, but remember:

• In phrases describing how you feel, use **avere**:

I **am** hot/cold	→ **ho** *caldo/freddo*
they **are** hungry/thirsty	→ **hanno** *fame/sete*
he **is** scared	→ **ha** *paura*

• To describe the weather, use **fare**:

It**'s** nice weather today.	→ ***Fa** bel tempo oggi.*

• To say your age, use **avere**:

I**'m** fifteen.	→ **Ho** *quindici anni.*

• To talk about your health, use **stare**:

I**'m** fine, thanks.	→ ***Sto** bene, grazie*

Some common translation difficulties

'Have' or 'have got' usually correspond to *avere*:

I've **got** two brothers.	→ **Ho** due fratelli.
Have you **got** a bike?	→ **Hai** una bici?
I**'ve** spent a lot of money.	→ **Ho** speso molti soldi.
What **have** you done?	→ Cos'**hai** fatto?

Remember, though that 'have' and 'has' are translated by *essere*:

• In the perfect tense of some common verbs such as to go (*andare*), to come (*venire*) and to arrive (*arrivare*):

Where **have** they gone?	→ Dove **sono** andati?
She **has** come too.	→ **È** venuta anche lei.
We**'ve** arrived.	→ **Siamo** arrivati.

• In the perfect tense of all reflexive verbs:

I**'ve** hurt myself.	→ Mi **sono** fatto male.
Has she had a good time?	→ Si **è** divertita?

A [eɪ] n (Mus) la m; **A road** n (BRIT Aut) ≈ strada statale; **A to Z®** n stradario

---

KEYWORD

a [ə] (before vowel or silent h: an) indef art
1 un, uno (+ s impure, gn, pn, ps, x, z),
una f, un' + vowel; **a book** un libro; **a mirror** uno specchio; **an apple** una mela; **she's a doctor** è medico
2 (instead of the number "one") un(o),
una f; **a year ago** un anno fa; **a hundred/thousand pounds** cento/mille sterline
3 (in expressing ratios, prices etc) a,
per; **3 a day/week** 3 al giorno/alla settimana; **10 km an hour** 10 km all'ora; **£5 a person** 5 sterline a persona or per persona

A2 n abbr (BRIT Scol) seconda parte del diploma di studi superiori chiamato "A level"

AA n abbr (BRIT: = Automobile Association) ≈ A.C.I. m; (= Alcoholics Anonymous) A.A. f

AAA n abbr (= American Automobile Association) ≈ A.C.I. m

aback [ə'bæk] adv: **to be taken ~** essere sbalordito/a

abandon [ə'bændən] vt abbandonare ▷ n abbandono; **with ~** sfrenatamente, spensieratamente

abattoir ['æbətwɑːʳ] n (BRIT) mattatoio

abbey ['æbɪ] n abbazia, badia

abbreviation [əbriːvɪ'eɪʃən] n abbreviazione f

abdomen ['æbdəmən] n addome m

abduct [æb'dʌkt] vt rapire

abide [ə'baɪd] vt sopportare; **I can't ~ it/him** non lo posso soffrire or sopportare; **abide by** vt fus conformarsi a

ability [ə'bɪlɪtɪ] n abilità f inv

able ['eɪbl] adj capace; **to be ~ to do sth** essere capace di fare qc, poter fare qc

abnormal [æb'nɔːməl] adj anormale

aboard [ə'bɔːd] adv a bordo ▷ prep a bordo di

abolish [ə'bɒlɪʃ] vt abolire

abolition [æbəu'lɪʃən] n abolizione f

abort [ə'bɔːt] vt abortire; **abortion** [ə'bɔːʃən] n aborto; **to have an abortion** abortire

---

KEYWORD

about [ə'baut] adv **1** (approximately) circa, quasi; **about a hundred/thousand** un centinaio/migliaio, circa cento/mille; **it takes about 10 hours** ci vogliono circa 10 ore; **at about 2 o'clock** verso le 2; **I've just about finished** ho quasi finito
2 (referring to place) qua e là, in giro; **to leave things lying about** lasciare delle cose in giro; **to run about** correre qua e là; **to walk about** camminare

3: **to be about to do sth** stare per fare qc

▶ *prep* **1** (*relating to*) su, di; **a book about London** un libro su Londra; **what is it about?** di che si tratta?; (*book, film etc*) di cosa tratta?; **we talked about it** ne abbiamo parlato; **what** *or* **how about doing this?** che ne dici di fare questo?

2 (*referring to place*): **to walk about the town** camminare per la città; **her clothes were scattered about the room** i suoi vestiti erano sparsi *or* in giro per tutta la stanza

above [ə'bʌv] *adv, prep* sopra; **mentioned ~** suddetto; **~ all** soprattutto

abroad [ə'brɔːd] *adv* all'estero

abrupt [ə'brʌpt] *adj* (*sudden*) improvviso/a; (*gruff, blunt*) brusco/a

abscess ['æbsɪs] *n* ascesso

absence ['æbsəns] *n* assenza

absent ['æbsənt] *adj* assente; **absent-minded** *adj* distratto/a

absolute ['æbsəluːt] *adj* assoluto/a; **absolutely** [-'luːtlɪ] *adv* assolutamente

absorb [əb'sɔːb] *vt* assorbire; **to be ~ed in a book** essere immerso in un libro; **absorbent cotton** [əb'zɔːbənt-] *n* (*US*) cotone *m* idrofilo; **absorbing** *adj* avvincente, molto interessante

abstain [əb'steɪn] *vi*: **to ~ (from)** astenersi (da)

abstract ['æbstrækt] *adj* astratto/a

absurd [əb'səːd] *adj* assurdo/a

abundance [ə'bʌndəns] *n* abbondanza

abundant [ə'bʌndənt] *adj* abbondante

abuse *n* [ə'bjuːs] abuso; (*insults*) ingiurie *fpl* ▶ *vt* [ə'bjuːz] abusare di; **abusive** *adj* ingiurioso/a

abysmal [ə'bɪzməl] *adj* spaventoso/a

academic [ækə'dɛmɪk] *adj* accademico/a; (*pej: issue*) puramente formale ▶ *n* universitario/a;

academic year *n* anno accademico

academy [ə'kædəmɪ] *n* (*learned body*) accademia; (*school*) scuola privata; **~ of music** conservatorio

accelerate [æk'sɛləreɪt] *vt, vi* accelerare; **acceleration** *n* accelerazione *f*; **accelerator** *n* acceleratore *m*

accent ['æksɛnt] *n* accento

accept [ək'sɛpt] *vt* accettare; **acceptable** *adj* accettabile; **acceptance** *n* accettazione *f*

access ['æksɛs] *n* accesso; **accessible** [æk'sɛsəbl] *adj* accessibile

accessory [æk'sɛsərɪ] *n* accessorio; (*Law*): **~ to** complice *m/f* di

accident ['æksɪdənt] *n* incidente *m*; (*chance*) caso; **I've had an ~** ho avuto un incidente; **by ~** per caso; **accidental** [-'dɛntl] *adj* accidentale; **accidentally** [-'dɛntlɪ] *adv* per caso; **Accident and Emergency Department** *n* (BRIT) pronto soccorso; **accident insurance** *n* assicurazione *f* contro gli infortuni

acclaim [ə'kleɪm] *n* acclamazione *f*

accommodate [ə'kɔmədeɪt] *vt* alloggiare; (*oblige, help*) favorire

accommodation [əkɔmə'deɪʃən] *n*, (*US*) **accommodations** *n pl* alloggio

accompaniment [ə'kʌmpənɪmənt] *n* accompagnamento

accompany [ə'kʌmpənɪ] *vt* accompagnare

accomplice [ə'kʌmplɪs] *n* complice *m/f*

accomplish [ə'kʌmplɪʃ] *vt* compiere; (*goal*) raggiungere; **accomplishment** *n* compimento; realizzazione *f*

accord [ə'kɔːd] *n* accordo ▶ *vt* accordare; **of his own ~** di propria iniziativa; **accordance** *n*: **in accordance with** in conformità con; **according**: **according to**

prep secondo; **accordingly** *adv* in conformità

account [ə'kaunt] *n* (*Comm*) conto; (*report*) descrizione *f*; **accounts** *npl* (*Comm*) conti *mpl*; **of little ~** di poca importanza; **on ~** in acconto; **on no ~** per nessun motivo; **on ~ of** a causa di; **to take into ~, take ~ of** tener conto di; **account for** *vt fus* (*explain*) spiegare; giustificare; **accountable** *adj*: **accountable (to)** responsabile (verso); **accountant** [ə'kauntənt] *n* ragioniere/a; **account number** *n* numero di conto

accumulate [ə'kju:mjuleit] *vt* accumulare ▷ *vi* accumularsi

accuracy ['ækjurəsi] *n* precisione *f*

accurate ['ækjurit] *adj* preciso/a; **accurately** *adv* precisamente

accusation [ækju'zeiʃən] *n* accusa

accuse [ə'kju:z] *vt* accusare; **accused** *n* accusato/a

accustomed [ə'kʌstəmd] *adj*: **~ to** abituato/a a

ace [eis] *n* asso

ache [eik] *n* male *m*, dolore *m* ▷ *vi* (*be sore*) far male, dolere; **my head ~s** mi fa male la testa

achieve [ə'tʃi:v] *vt* (*aim*) raggiungere; (*victory, success*) ottenere; **achievement** *n* compimento; successo

acid ['æsid] *adj* acido/a ▷ *n* acido

acknowledge [ək'nɒlidʒ] *vt* (*fact*) riconoscere; (*letter: also*: **~ receipt of**) accusare ricevuta di; **acknowledgement** *n* riconoscimento; (*of letter*) conferma

acne ['ækni] *n* acne *f*

acorn ['eikɔ:n] *n* ghianda

acoustic [ə'ku:stik] *adj* acustico/a

acquaintance [ə'kweintəns] *n* conoscenza; (*person*) conoscente *m/f*

acquire [ə'kwaiəʳ] *vt* acquistare; **acquisition** [ækwi'ziʃən] *n* acquisto

acquit [ə'kwit] *vt* assolvere; **to ~ o.s. well** comportarsi bene

acre ['eikəʳ] *n* acro (= 4047 m²)

acronym ['ækrənim] *n* acronimo

across [ə'krɒs] *prep* (*on the other side*) dall'altra parte di; (*crosswise*) attraverso ▷ *adv* dall'altra parte; in larghezza; **to run/swim ~** attraversare di corsa/a nuoto; **~ from** di fronte a

acrylic [ə'krilik] *adj* acrilico/a

act [ækt] *n* atto; (*in music-hall etc*) numero; (*Law*) decreto ▷ *vi* agire; (*Theat*) recitare; (*pretend*) fingere ▷ *vt* (*part*) recitare; **to ~ as** agire da; **act up** (*col*) *vi* (*person*) comportarsi male; (*knee, back, injury*) fare male; (*machine*) non funzionare; **acting** *adj* che fa le funzioni di ▷ *n* (*of actor*) recitazione *f*; **to do some acting** fare del teatro (*or* del cinema)

action ['ækʃən] *n* azione *f*; (*Mil*) combattimento; (*Law*) processo ▷ *vt* (*Comm: request*) evadere; (*tasks*) portare a termine; **to take ~** agire; **out of ~** fuori combattimento; (*machine etc*) fuori servizio; **action replay** *n* (*TV*) replay *m inv*

activate ['æktiveit] *vt* (*mechanism*) fare funzionare, attivare

active ['æktiv] *adj* attivo/a; **actively** *adv* (*participate*) attivamente; (*discourage, dislike*) vivamente

activist ['æktivist] *n* attivista *m/f*

activity [æk'tiviti] *n* attività *f inv*; **activity holiday** *n* vacanza attiva (*in bici, a cavallo, in barca, a vela ecc.*)

actor ['æktəʳ] *n* attore *m*

actress ['æktris] *n* attrice *f*

actual ['æktjuəl] *adj* reale, vero/a

▌ Be careful not to translate *actual* by the Italian word *attuale*.

actually ['æktjuəli] *adv* veramente; (*even*) addirittura

▌ Be careful not to translate *actually* by the Italian word *attualmente*.

acupuncture ['ækjupʌŋktʃəʳ] *n* agopuntura

acute [ə'kju:t] *adj* acuto/a; (*mind, person*) perspicace

AD adv abbr (= Anno Domini) d. C.

ad [æd] n abbr = **advertisement**

adamant ['ædəmənt] adj irremovibile

adapt [ə'dæpt] vt adattare ▷ vi: **to ~ (to)** adattarsi (a); **adapter, adaptor** n (Elec) adattatore m

add [æd] vt aggiungere ▷ vi: **to ~ to** (increase) aumentare ▷ n (Internet): **thanks for the ~** grazie per avermi aggiunto (come amico); **add up** vt (figures) addizionare ▷ vi (fig): **it doesn't ~ up** non ha senso; **it doesn't ~ up to much** non è un granché

addict ['ædɪkt] n tossicomane m/f; (fig) fanatico/a; **addicted** [ə'dɪktɪd] adj: **to be addicted to** (drink etc) essere dedito/a a; (fig: football etc) essere tifoso/a di; **addiction** [ə'dɪkʃən] n (Med) tossicodipendenza; **addictive** [ə'dɪktɪv] adj che dà assuefazione

addition [ə'dɪʃən] n addizione f; (thing added) aggiunta; **in ~** inoltre; **in ~ to** oltre; **additional** adj supplementare

additive ['ædɪtɪv] n additivo

address [ə'drɛs] n indirizzo; (talk) discorso ▷ vt indirizzare; (speak to) fare un discorso a; (issue) affrontare; **my ~ is …** il mio indirizzo è…; **address book** n rubrica

adequate ['ædɪkwɪt] adj adeguato/a; sufficiente

adhere [əd'hɪər] vi: **to ~ to** aderire a; (fig: rule, decision) seguire

adhesive [əd'hiːzɪv] n adesivo; **~ tape** (BRIT: for parcels etc) nastro adesivo; (us Med) cerotto adesivo

adjacent [ə'dʒeɪsənt] adj adiacente; **~ to** accanto a

adjective ['ædʒɛktɪv] n aggettivo

adjoining [ə'dʒɔɪnɪŋ] adj accanto inv, adiacente

adjourn [ə'dʒəːn] vt rimandare ▷ vi essere aggiornato/a

adjust [ə'dʒʌst] vt aggiustare; (Comm: change) rettificare ▷ vi: **to**

~ (to) adattarsi (a); **adjustable** adj regolabile; **adjustment** n (Psych) adattamento; (of machine) regolazione f; (of prices, wages) aggiustamento

administer [əd'mɪnɪstər] vt amministrare; (justice) somministrare; **administration** [ədmɪnɪs'treɪʃən] n amministrazione f; **administrative** [əd'mɪnɪstrətɪv] adj amministrativo/a

administrator [əd'mɪnɪstreɪtər] n amministratore/trice

admiral ['ædmərəl] n ammiraglio

admiration [ædmə'reɪʃən] n ammirazione f

admire [əd'maɪər] vt ammirare; **admirer** n ammiratore/trice

admission [əd'mɪʃən] n ammissione f; (to exhibition, nightclub etc) ingresso; (confession) confessione f

admit [əd'mɪt] vt ammettere; far entrare; (agree) riconoscere; **admit to** vt fus riconoscere; **admittance** n ingresso; **admittedly** adv bisogna pur riconoscere (che)

adolescent [ædəu'lɛsnt] adj, n adolescente m/f

adopt [ə'dɔpt] vt adottare; **adopted** adj adottivo/a; **adoption** [ə'dɔpʃən] n adozione f

adore [ə'dɔːr] vt adorare

adorn [ə'dɔːn] vt ornare

Adriatic [eɪdrɪ'ætɪk] n: **the ~ (Sea)** il mare Adriatico, l'Adriatico

adrift [ə'drɪft] adv alla deriva

ADSL n abbr (= asymmetric digital subscriber line) ADSL m

adult ['ædʌlt] n adulto/a ▷ adj adulto/a; (work, education) per adulti; **adult education** n scuola per adulti

adultery [ə'dʌltərɪ] n adulterio

advance [əd'vɑːns] n avanzamento; (money) anticipo ▷ adj (booking etc) in anticipo ▷ vt (date, money) anticipare ▷ vi avanzare; **in ~** in anticipo; **do I need to book in ~?** occorre che

prenoti in anticipo?; **advanced** adj
avanzato/a; (Scol: studies) superiore

advantage [əd'vɑːntɪdʒ] n (also
Tennis) vantaggio; **to take ~ of**
approfittarsi di

advent ['ædvənt] n avvento; **A~**
(Rel) Avvento

adventure [əd'vɛntʃər] n avventura;
adventurous [əd'vɛntʃərəs] adj
avventuroso/a

adverb ['ædvəːb] n avverbio

adversary ['ædvəsərɪ] n
avversario/a

adverse ['ædvəːs] adj avverso/a

advert ['ædvəːt] n abbr (BRIT)
= **advertisement**

advertise ['ædvətaɪz] vi, vt fare
pubblicità or réclame (a), fare
un'inserzione (per vendere); **to ~
for** (staff) cercare tramite annuncio;
advertisement [əd'vəːtɪsmənt]
n (Comm) réclame f inv, pubblicità
f inv; (in classified ads) inserzione f;
advertiser n azienda che reclamizza
un prodotto; (in newspaper)
inserzionista m/f; **advertising**
['ædvətaɪzɪŋ] n pubblicità

advice [əd'vaɪs] n consigli mpl;
piece of ~ consiglio; **to take legal ~**
consultare un avvocato

advisable [əd'vaɪzəbl] adj
consigliabile

advise [əd'vaɪz] vt consigliare; **to
~ sb of sth** informare qn di qc; **to ~
sb against sth/against doing sth**
sconsigliare qc a qn/a qn di fare qc;
adviser n consigliere/a; (in business)
consulente m/f, consigliere/a;
advisory [-ərɪ] adj consultivo/a

advocate n ['ædvəkɪt] (upholder)
sostenitore/trice; (Law) avvocato
(difensore) ▷ vt ['ædvəkeɪt]
propugnare

Aegean (Sea) [iː'dʒiːən-] n (mare
m) Egeo

aerial ['ɛərɪəl] n antenna ▷ adj
aereo/a

aerobics [ɛə'rəubɪks] n aerobica

aeroplane ['ɛərəpleɪn] (BRIT) n
aeroplano

aerosol ['ɛərəsɔl] (BRIT) n aerosol
m inv

affair [ə'fɛər] n affare m; (also: **love
~**) relazione f amorosa; **affairs**
(business) affari

affect [ə'fɛkt] vt toccare; (influence)
influire su, incidere su; (feign) fingere;
affected adj affettato/a; **affection**
[ə'fɛkʃən] n affetto; **affectionate** adj
affettuoso/a

afflict [ə'flɪkt] vt affliggere

affluent ['æfluənt] adj ricco/a; **the ~
society** la società del benessere

afford [ə'fɔːd] vt permettersi;
(provide) fornire; **affordable** adj (che
ha un prezzo) abbordabile

Afghanistan [æf'gænɪstɑːn] n
Afganistan m

afraid [ə'freɪd] adj impaurito/a; **to
be ~ of** aver paura di; **to be ~ of
doing** or **to do** aver paura di fare;
to be ~ that aver paura che; **I'm ~
so!** ho paura di sì!; **I'm ~ not** no, mi
dispiace

Africa ['æfrɪkə] n Africa; **African** adj,
n africano/a; **African-American** adj,
n afroamericano/a

after ['ɑːftər] prep, adv dopo ▷ conj
dopo che; **what/who are you ~?**
che/chi cerca?; **~ he left/having
done** dopo che se ne fu andato/dopo
aver fatto; **to name sb ~ sb** dare a
qn il nome di qn; **it's twenty ~ eight**
(US) sono le otto e venti; **to ask ~ sb**
chiedere di qn; **~ you!** dopo di lei!;
~ all dopo tutto; **after-effects** npl
conseguenze fpl; (of illness) postumi
mpl; **aftermath** n conseguenze fpl;
in the aftermath of nel periodo
dopo; **afternoon** n pomeriggio;
after-shave (lotion) ['ɑːftəʃeɪv-]
n dopobarba m inv; **aftersun**
['ɑːftəsʌn] adj: **aftersun (lotion/
cream)** (lozione f/crema) doposole
m inv; **afterwards**, (US) **afterward**
adv dopo

again [ə'gɛn] adv di nuovo; **to begin/ see ~** ricominciare/rivedere; **not ... ~** non ... più; **~ and ~** ripetutamente

against [ə'gɛnst] prep contro

age [eɪdʒ] n età f inv ▷ vt, vi invecchiare; **he is 20 years of ~** ha 20 anni; **~d 10** di 10 anni; **to come of ~** diventare maggiorenne; **it's been ~s since ...** sono secoli che ...; **the ~d** gli anziani; **age group** n generazione f; **age limit** n limite m d'età

agency ['eɪdʒənsɪ] n agenzia

agenda [ə'dʒɛndə] n ordine m del giorno

agent ['eɪdʒənt] n agente m

aggravate ['ægrəveɪt] vt aggravare; (annoy) esasperare

aggression [ə'grɛʃən] n aggressione f

aggressive [ə'grɛsɪv] adj aggressivo/a

agile ['ædʒaɪl] adj agile

agitated ['ædʒɪteɪtɪd] adj agitato/a, turbato/a

AGM n abbr = **annual general meeting**

ago [ə'gəʊ] adv: **2 days ~** 2 giorni fa; **not long ~** poco tempo fa; **how long ~?** quanto tempo fa?

agony ['ægənɪ] n dolore m atroce; **I was in ~** avevo dei dolori atroci

agree [ə'griː] vt (price) pattuire ▷ vi: **to ~ (with)** essere d'accordo (con); (Ling) concordare (con); **to ~ to sth/ to do sth** accettare qc/di fare qc; **to ~ that** (admit) ammettere che; **to ~ on sth** accordarsi su qc; **garlic doesn't ~ with me** l'aglio non mi va; **agreeable** adj gradevole; (willing) disposto/a; **agreed** adj (time, place) stabilito/a; **agreement** n accordo; **in agreement** d'accordo

agricultural [ægrɪ'kʌltʃərəl] adj agricolo/a

agriculture ['ægrɪkʌltʃəʳ] n agricoltura

ahead [ə'hɛd] adv avanti; davanti; **~ of** davanti a; (fig: schedule etc) in anticipo su; **~ of time** in anticipo; **go right or straight ~** tiri diritto

aid [eɪd] n aiuto ▷ vt aiutare; **in ~ of** a favore di

aide [eɪd] n (person) aiutante m/f

AIDS [eɪdz] n abbr (= acquired immune deficiency or immunodeficiency syndrome) AIDS f

ailing ['eɪlɪŋ] adj sofferente; (fig: economy, industry etc) in difficoltà

ailment ['eɪlmənt] n indisposizione f

aim [eɪm] vt: **to ~ sth at** (gun) mirare qc a, puntare qc a; (camera, remark) rivolgere qc a; (missile) lanciare qc contro ▷ vi (also: **take ~**) prendere la mira ▷ n mira; **to ~ at** mirare a; **to ~ to do** aver l'intenzione di fare

ain't [eɪnt] (col) = **am not; aren't; isn't**

air [ɛəʳ] n aria ▷ vt (room, bed) arieggiare; (clothes) far prendere aria a; (idea, grievance) esprimere pubblicamente ▷ cpd (currents) d'aria; (attack) aereo/a; **to throw sth into the ~** lanciare qc in aria; **by ~** (travel) in aereo; **to be on the ~** (Radio, TV) (programme) essere in onda; **airbag** n airbag m inv; **airbed** n (BRIT) materassino; **airborne** ['ɛəbɔːn] adj (plane) in volo; (troops) aerotrasportato/a; **as soon as the plane was airborne** appena l'aereo ebbe decollato; **air-conditioned** adj con or ad aria condizionata; **air conditioning** n condizionamento d'aria; **aircraft** n (pl inv) apparecchio; **airfield** n campo d'aviazione; **Air Force** n aviazione f militare; **air hostess** n (BRIT) hostess f inv; **airing cupboard** ['ɛərɪŋ-] n armadio riscaldato per asciugare panni; **airlift** n ponte m aereo; **airline** n linea aerea; **airliner** n aereo di linea; **airmail** n posta aerea; **by airmail** per via or posta aerea; **airplane** n (US) aeroplano; **airport** n aeroporto; **air raid** n incursione f aerea; **airsick** adj: **to be airsick** soffrire di mal d'aereo;

airspace n spazio aereo; **airstrip** n pista d'atterraggio; **air terminal** n air-terminal m inv; **airtight** adj ermetico/a; **air traffic controller** n controllore m del traffico aereo; **airy** adj arioso/a; (manners) noncurante

aisle [aɪl] n (of church) navata laterale; navata centrale; (of plane) corridoio; **aisle seat** n (on plane) posto sul corridoio

ajar [ə'dʒɑ:ʳ] adj socchiuso/a

à la carte [ɑ:lɑ:'kɑ:t] adv alla carta

alarm [ə'lɑ:m] n allarme m ⊳ vt allarmare; (person) mettere in ansia; **alarm call** n (in hotel etc) sveglia; **could I have an alarm call at 7 am, please?** vorrei essere svegliato alle 7, per favore; **alarm clock** n sveglia; **alarmed** adj (person) allarmato/a; (house, car etc) dotato/a di allarme; **alarming** adj allarmante, preoccupante

Albania [æl'beɪnɪə] n Albania

albeit [ɔ:l'bi:ɪt] conj sebbene + sub, benché + sub

album ['ælbəm] n album m inv

alcohol ['ælkəhɔl] n alcool m; **alcohol-free** adj analcolico/a; **alcoholic** [-'hɔlɪk] adj alcolico/a ⊳ n alcolizzato/a

alcove ['ælkəuv] n alcova

ale [eɪl] n birra

alert [ə'lə:t] adj vigile ⊳ n allarme m ⊳ vt: **to ~ sb (to sth)** avvertire qn (di qc); **to ~ sb to the dangers of sth** mettere qn in guardia contro qc

algebra ['ældʒɪbrə] n algebra

Algeria [æl'dʒɪərɪə] n Algeria

alias ['eɪlɪəs] adv alias ⊳ n pseudonimo, falso nome m

alibi ['ælɪbaɪ] n alibi m inv

alien ['eɪlɪən] n straniero/a; (extraterrestrial) alieno/a ⊳ adj: **~ (to)** estraneo/a (a); **alienate** vt alienare

alight [ə'laɪt] adj acceso/a ⊳ vi scendere; (bird) posarsi

align [ə'laɪn] vt allineare

alike [ə'laɪk] adj simile ⊳ adv allo stesso modo; **to look ~** assomigliarsi

alive [ə'laɪv] adj vivo/a; (active) attivo/a

KEYWORD

all [ɔ:l] adj tutto/a; **all day** tutto il giorno; **all night** tutta la notte; **all men** tutti gli uomini; **all five came** sono venuti tutti e cinque; **all the books** tutti i libri; **all the food** tutto il cibo; **all the time** tutto il tempo; (always) sempre; **all his life** tutta la vita

⊳ pron **1** tutto/a; **I ate it all, I ate all of it** l'ho mangiato tutto; **all of us went** tutti noi siamo andati; **all of the boys went** tutti i ragazzi sono andati

2 (in phrases): **above all** soprattutto; **after all** dopotutto; **at all: not at all** (in answer to question) niente affatto; (in answer to thanks) prego!, di niente!, s'immagini!; **I'm not at all tired** non sono affatto stanco; **anything at all will do** andrà bene qualsiasi cosa; **all in all** tutto sommato

⊳ adv: **all alone** tutto/a solo/a; **it's not as hard as all that** non è poi così difficile; **all the more/the better** tanto più/meglio; **all but** quasi; **the score is two all** il punteggio è di due a due or è due pari

Allah ['ælə] n Allah m

allegation [ælɪ'geɪʃən] n asserzione f

alleged [ə'lɛdʒd] adj presunto/a; **allegedly** [ə'lɛdʒɪdlɪ] adv secondo quanto si asserisce

allegiance [ə'li:dʒəns] n fedeltà

allergic [ə'lə:dʒɪk] adj: **~ to** allergico/a a

allergy ['ælədʒɪ] n allergia

alleviate [ə'li:vɪeɪt] vt sollevare

alley ['ælɪ] n vicolo

alliance [ə'laɪəns] n alleanza

allied ['ælaɪd] adj alleato/a

alligator ['ælɪgeɪtəʳ] n alligatore m

all-in ['ɔːlɪn] *adj*, *adv* (BRIT: *charge*) tutto compreso

allocate ['æləkeɪt] *vt*: **to ~ sth to** assegnare qc a

allot [ə'lɔt] *vt*: **to ~ sth to** (*duties*) assegnare qc a

all-out ['ɔːlaut] *adj* (*effort etc*) totale ▷ *adv*: **to go all out for** mettercela tutta per

allow [ə'lau] *vt* (*practice, behaviour*) permettere; (*sum to spend etc*) accordare; (*sum, time estimated*) dare; (*concede*): **to ~ that** ammettere che; **to ~ sb to do** permettere a qn di fare; **he is ~ed to (do it)** lo può fare; **allow for** *vt fus* tener conto di; **allowance** *n* (*money received*) assegno; (*for travelling, accommodation*) indennità *f inv*; (*Tax*) detrazione *f* di imposta; **to make allowance(s) for** tener conto di

all right *adv* (*feel, work*) bene; (*as answer*) va bene

ally *n* ['ælaɪ] alleato

almighty [ɔːl'maɪtɪ] *adj* onnipotente; (*row etc*) colossale

almond ['ɑːmənd] *n* mandorla

almost ['ɔːlməust] *adv* quasi

alone [ə'ləun] *adj*, *adv* solo/a; **to leave sb ~** lasciare qn in pace; **to leave sth ~** lasciare stare qc; **let ~ ...** figuriamoci poi ..., tanto meno ...

along [ə'lɔŋ] *prep* lungo ▷ *adv*: **is he coming ~?** viene con noi?; **he was hopping/limping ~** veniva saltellando/zoppicando; **~ with** insieme con; **all ~** (*all the time*) sempre, fin dall'inizio; **alongside** *prep* accanto a; lungo ▷ *adv* accanto

aloof [ə'luːf] *adj* distaccato/a ▷ *adv* a distanza, in disparte; **to stand ~** tenersi a distanza or in disparte

aloud [ə'laud] *adv* ad alta voce

alphabet ['ælfəbɛt] *n* alfabeto

Alps [ælps] *npl*: **the ~** le Alpi

already [ɔːl'rɛdɪ] *adv* già

alright ['ɔːl'raɪt] *adv* (BRIT) = **all right**

also ['ɔːlsəu] *adv* anche

altar ['ɔltə*] *n* altare *m*

alter ['ɔltə*] *vt*, *vi* alterare; **alteration** [ɔltə'reɪʃən] *n* modificazione *f*, alterazione *f*; **alterations** (*Sewing, Archit*) modifiche *fpl*; **timetable subject to alteration** orario soggetto a variazioni

alternate *adj* [ɔl'təːnɪt] alterno/a; (US: *plan etc*) alternativo/a ▷ *vi* ['ɔltəneɪt]: **to ~ (with)** alternarsi (a); **on ~ days** ogni due giorni

alternative [ɔl'təːnətɪv] *adj* alternativo/a ▷ *n* (*choice*) alternativa; **alternatively** *adv* come alternativa

although [ɔːl'ðəu] *conj* benché + *sub*, sebbene + *sub*

altitude ['æltɪtjuːd] *n* altitudine *f*

altogether [ɔːltə'gɛðə*] *adv* del tutto, completamente; (*on the whole*) tutto considerato; (*in all*) in tutto

aluminium [ælju'mɪnɪəm], (US) **aluminum** [ə'luːmɪnəm] *n* alluminio

always ['ɔːlweɪz] *adv* sempre

Alzheimer's ['æltshaɪməz] *n* (*also*: **~ disease**) morbo di Alzheimer

am [æm] *vb see* **be**

amalgamate [ə'mælgəmeɪt] *vt* amalgamare ▷ *vi* amalgamarsi

amass [ə'mæs] *vt* ammassare

amateur ['æmətə*] *n* dilettante *m/f* ▷ *adj* (*Sport*) dilettante

amaze [ə'meɪz] *vt* stupire; **amazed** *adj* sbalordito/a; **to be amazed (at)** essere sbalordito/a (da); **amazement** *n* stupore *m*; **amazing** *adj* sorprendente, sbalorditivo/a

Amazon ['æməzən] *n* (*Mythology*) Amazzone *f*; **the ~** il Rio delle Amazzoni ▷ *cpd* (*basin, jungle*) amazzonico/a

ambassador [æm'bæsədə*] *n* ambasciatore/trice

amber ['æmbə*] *n* ambra; **at ~** (BRIT Aut) giallo

ambiguous [æm'bɪgjuəs] *adj* ambiguo/a

ambition [æm'bɪʃən] *n* ambizione *f*; **ambitious** [æm'bɪʃəs] *adj* ambizioso/a

ambulance ['æmbjuləns] *n* ambulanza

ambush ['æmbuʃ] *n* imboscata

amen ['ɑ:'mɛn] *excl* così sia, amen

amend [ə'mɛnd] *vt* (*law*) emendare; (*text*) correggere; **to make ~s** fare ammenda; **amendment** *n* emendamento; correzione *f*

amenities [ə'mi:nɪtɪz] *npl* attrezzature *fpl* ricreative e culturali

America [ə'mɛrɪkə] *n* America; **American** *adj*, *n* americano/a; **American football** *n* (BRIT) football *m* americano

amicable ['æmɪkəbl] *adj* amichevole

amid(st) [ə'mɪd(st)] *prep* in mezzo a

ammunition [æmju'nɪʃən] *n* munizioni *fpl*

amnesty ['æmnɪstɪ] *n* amnistia; **to grant an ~ to** concedere l'amnistia a, amnistiare

among(st) [ə'mʌŋ(st)] *prep* fra, tra, in mezzo a

amount [ə'maunt] *n* somma; ammontare *m*; (*quantity*) quantità *f inv* ▷ *vi*: **to ~ to** (*total*) ammontare a; (*be same as*) essere come

amp(ère) ['æmp(ɛə')] *n* ampere *m inv*

ample ['æmpl] *adj* ampio/a; spazioso/a; (*enough*): **this is ~** questo è più che sufficiente

amplifier ['æmplɪfaɪə'] *n* amplificatore *m*

amputate ['æmpjuteɪt] *vt* amputare

Amtrak ['æmtræk] (US) *n* società ferroviaria americana

amuse [ə'mju:z] *vt* divertire; **amusement** *n* divertimento; **amusement arcade** *n* sala giochi; **amusement park** *n* luna park *m inv*

amusing [ə'mju:zɪŋ] *adj* divertente

an [æn, ən, n] *indef art see* **a**

anaemia [ə'ni:mɪə] *n* anemia

anaemic [ə'ni:mɪk] *adj* anemico/a

anaesthetic [ænɪs'θɛtɪk] *adj* anestetico/a ▷ *n* anestetico

analog(ue) ['ænəlɒg] *adj* (*watch*, *computer*) analogico/a

analogy [ə'nælədʒɪ] *n* analogia; **to draw an ~ between** fare un'analogia tra

analyse, (US) **analyze** ['ænəlaɪz] *vt* analizzare; **analysis** (*pl* **analyses**) [ə'næləsɪs, -si:z] *n* analisi *f inv*; **analyst** ['ænəlɪst] *n* (*political analyst etc*) analista *m/f*; (US) (psic) analista *m/f*

analyze ['ænəlaɪz] *vt* (US) = **analyse**

anarchy ['ænəkɪ] *n* anarchia

anatomy [ə'nætəmɪ] *n* anatomia

ancestor ['ænsɪstə'] *n* antenato/a

anchor ['æŋkə'] *n* ancora ▷ *vi* (*also*: **to drop ~**) gettare l'ancora ▷ *vt* ancorare; **to weigh ~** salpare *or* levare l'ancora

anchovy ['æntʃəvɪ] *n* acciuga

ancient ['eɪnʃənt] *adj* antico/a; (*person*, *car*) vecchissimo/a

and [ænd] *conj* e (*often 'ed' before vowel*); **~ so on** e così via; **try ~ come** cerca di venire; **he talked ~ talked** non la finiva di parlare; **better ~ better** sempre meglio

Andes ['ændi:z] *npl*: **the ~** le Ande

anemia *etc* [ə'ni:mɪə] (US) = **anaemia** *etc*

anesthetic [ænɪs'θɛtɪk] (US) = **anaesthetic**

angel ['eɪndʒəl] *n* angelo

anger ['æŋgə'] *n* rabbia

angina [æn'dʒaɪnə] *n* angina pectoris

angle ['æŋgl] *n* angolo; **from their ~** dal loro punto di vista

angler ['æŋglə'] *n* pescatore *m* con la lenza

Anglican ['æŋglɪkən] *adj*, *n* anglicano/a

angling ['æŋglɪŋ] *n* pesca con la lenza

angrily ['æŋgrɪlɪ] *adv* con rabbia

angry ['æŋgrɪ] adj arrabbiato/a, furioso/a; (wound) infiammato/a; **to be ~ with sb/at sth** essere in collera con qn/per qc; **to get ~** arrabbiarsi; **to make sb ~** fare arrabbiare qn

anguish ['æŋgwɪʃ] n angoscia

animal ['ænɪməl] adj animale ▷ n animale m

animated ['ænɪmeɪtɪd] adj animato/a

animation [ænɪ'meɪʃən] n animazione f

aniseed ['ænɪsiːd] n semi mpl di anice

ankle ['æŋkl] n caviglia

annex n ['ænɛks] (BRIT: also: **~e**) edificio annesso ▷ vt [ə'nɛks] annettere

anniversary [ænɪ'vəːsərɪ] n anniversario

announce [ə'naʊns] vt annunciare; **announcement** n annuncio; (letter, card) partecipazione f; **announcer** n (Radio, TV: between programmes) annunciatore/trice; (: in a programme) presentatore/trice

annoy [ə'nɔɪ] vt dare fastidio a; **don't get ~ed!** non irritarti!; **annoying** adj irritante

annual ['ænjʊəl] adj annuale ▷ n (Bot) pianta annua; (book) annuario; **annually** adv annualmente

anonymous [ə'nɔnɪməs] adj anonimo/a

anorak ['ænəræk] n giacca a vento

anorexia [ænə'rɛksɪə] n (Med: also: **~ nervosa**) anoressia

anorexic [ænə'rɛksɪk] adj, n anoressico/a

another [ə'nʌðər] adj: **~ book** (one more) un altro libro, ancora un libro; (a different one) un altro libro ▷ pron un altro (un'altra), ancora uno/a; see also **one**

answer ['ɑːnsər] n risposta; soluzione f ▷ vi rispondere ▷ vt (reply to) rispondere a; (problem) risolvere; (prayer) esaudire; **in ~**

to your letter in risposta alla sua lettera; **to ~ the phone** rispondere (al telefono); **to ~ the bell** rispondere al campanello; **to ~ the door** aprire la porta; **answer back** vi ribattere; **answerphone** n (esp BRIT) segreteria telefonica

ant [ænt] n formica

Antarctic [ænt'ɑːktɪk] n: **the ~** l'Antartide f

antelope ['æntɪləʊp] n antilope f

antenatal ['æntɪ'neɪtl] adj prenatale

antenna (pl **antennae**) [æn'tɛnə, -niː] n antenna

anthem ['ænθəm] n: **national ~** inno nazionale

anthology [æn'θɔlədʒɪ] n antologia

anthrax ['ænθræks] n antrace m

anthropology [ænθrə'pɔlədʒɪ] n antropologia

anti- ['æntɪ] prefix anti...; **antibiotic** ['æntɪbaɪ'ɔtɪk] n antibiotico; **antibody** ['æntɪbɔdɪ] n anticorpo

anticipate [æn'tɪsɪpeɪt] vt prevedere; pregustare; (wishes, request) prevenire; **anticipation** [æntɪsɪ'peɪʃən] n anticipazione f; (expectation) aspettativa fpl

anticlimax ['æntɪ'klaɪmæks] n: **it was an ~** fu una completa delusione

anticlockwise ['æntɪ'klɔkwaɪz] adj, adv in senso antiorario

antics ['æntɪks] npl buffonerie fpl

anti: antidote ['æntɪdəʊt] n antidoto; **antifreeze** ['æntɪfriːz] n anticongelante m; **anti-globalization** [æntɪgləʊbəlaɪ'zeɪʃən] n antiglobalizzazione f; **antihistamine** [æntɪ'hɪstəmɪn] n antistaminico; **antiperspirant** ['æntɪ'pəːspərənt] adj antitraspirante

antique [æn'tiːk] n antichità f inv ▷ adj antico/a; **antique shop** n negozio d'antichità

antiseptic [æntɪ'sɛptɪk] n antisettico

antisocial ['æntɪ'səʊʃəl] adj asociale

antiviral [æntɪ'vaɪərəl] *adj (Med)* antivirale

antivirus [æntɪ'vaɪərəs] *adj (Comput)* antivirus *inv*; **antivirus software** *n* antivirus *m inv*

antlers ['æntləz] *npl* palchi *mpl*

anxiety [æŋ'zaɪətɪ] *n* ansia, (*keenness*): **~ to do** smania di fare

anxious ['æŋkʃəs] *adj* ansioso/a, inquieto/a; (*worrying*) angosciante; (*keen*): **~ to do/that** impaziente di fare/che + *sub*

KEYWORD

any ['ɛnɪ] *adj* 1 (*in questions etc*): **have you any butter?** hai del burro?, hai un po' di burro?; **have you any children?** hai bambini?; **if there are any tickets left** se ci sono ancora (dei) biglietti, se c'è ancora qualche biglietto
2 (*with negative*): **I haven't any money/books** non ho soldi/libri
3 (*no matter which*) qualsiasi, qualunque; **choose any book you like** scegli un libro qualsiasi
4 (*in phrases*): **in any case** in ogni caso; **any day now** da un giorno all'altro; **at any moment** in qualsiasi momento, da un momento all'altro; **at any rate** ad ogni modo
▶ *pron* 1 (*in questions, with negative*): **have you got any?** ne hai?; **can any of you sing?** qualcuno di voi sa cantare?; **I haven't any (of them)** non ne ho
2 (*no matter which one(s)*): **take any of those books (you like)** prendi uno qualsiasi di quei libri
▶ *adv* 1 (*in questions etc*): **do you want any more soup/sandwiches?** vuoi ancora un po' di minestra/degli altri panini?; **are you feeling any better?** ti senti meglio?
2 (*with negative*): **I can't hear him any more** non lo sento più; **don't wait any longer** non aspettare più

anybody ['ɛnɪbɔdɪ] *pron (in interrogative sentences*) qualcuno; (*in negative sentences*) nessuno; (*no matter who*) chiunque; **can you see ~?** vedi qualcuno *or* nessuno?; **if ~ should phone ...** se telefona qualcuno ...; **I don't see ~** non vedo nessuno; **~ could do it** chiunque potrebbe farlo

anyhow ['ɛnɪhau] *adv (at any rate*) ad ogni modo, comunque; (*haphazard*): **do it ~ you like** fallo come ti pare; **I shall go ~** ci andrò lo stesso *or* comunque; **she leaves things just ~** lascia tutto come capita

anyone ['ɛnɪwʌn] *pron* = **anybody**

anything ['ɛnɪθɪŋ] *pron (in interrogative sentences*) qualcosa, niente; (*with negative*) niente; **you can say ~ you like** (*no matter what*) puoi dire quello che ti pare; **can you see ~?** vedi niente *or* qualcosa?; **if ~ happens to me ...** se mi dovesse succedere qualcosa ...; **I can't see ~** non vedo niente; **~ will do** va bene qualsiasi cosa *or* tutto; **~ else?** (*in shop*) basta (così)?; **it can cost ~ between £15 and £20** può costare qualcosa come 15 o 20 sterline

anytime ['ɛnɪtaɪm] *adv* in qualunque momento; quando vuole

anyway ['ɛnɪweɪ] *adv (at any rate*) ad ogni modo, comunque; (*besides*) ad ogni modo

anywhere ['ɛnɪwɛəʳ] *adv (in interrogative sentences*) da qualche parte; (*with negative*) da nessuna parte; (*no matter where*) da qualsiasi *or* qualunque parte, dovunque; **can you see him ~?** lo vedi da qualche parte?; **I don't see him ~** non lo vedo da nessuna parte; **~ in the world** dovunque nel mondo

apart [ə'pɑːt] *adv (to one side*) a parte; (*separately*) separatamente; **with one's legs ~** con le gambe divaricate; **10 miles/a long way ~** a 10 miglia di distanza/molto lontani

l'uno dall'altro; **to take ~** smontare;
~ from a parte, eccetto

apartment [ə'pɑ:tmənt] n (US)
appartamento; (room) locale m;
apartment building n (US) stabile
m, caseggiato

apathy ['æpəθɪ] n apatia

ape [eɪp] n scimmia ▷ vt
scimmiottare

aperitif [ə'perɪti:f] n aperitivo

aperture ['æpətʃuəʳ] n apertura

APEX n abbr (= advance purchase
excursion) APEX m inv

apologize [ə'pɒlədʒaɪz] vi: **to ~
(for sth to sb)** scusarsi (di qc a qn),
chiedere scusa (a qn per qc)

apology [ə'pɒlədʒɪ] n scuse fpl

apostrophe [ə'pɒstrəfɪ] n (sign)
apostrofo

app n abbr (col: Comput) = **application**
applicazione f

appal, (US) **appall** [ə'pɔ:l] vt
atterrire; sconvolgere; **appalling** adj
spaventoso/a

apparatus [æpə'reɪtəs] n apparato;
(in gymnasium) attrezzatura

apparent [ə'pærənt] adj evidente;
apparently adv evidentemente

appeal [ə'pi:l] vi (Law) appellarsi
alla legge ▷ n (Law) appello; (request)
richiesta; (charm) attrattiva; **to ~ for**
chiedere (con insistenza); **to ~ to**
(person) appellarsi a; (thing) piacere
a; **it doesn't ~ to me** mi dice poco;
appealing adj (attractive) attraente

appear [ə'pɪəʳ] vi apparire; (Law)
comparire; (publication) essere
pubblicato/a; (seem) sembrare;
it would ~ that sembra che;
appearance n apparizione f;
apparenza; (look, aspect) aspetto

appendicitis [əpendɪ'saɪtɪs] n
appendicite f

appendix (pl **appendices**)
[ə'pendɪks, -si:z] n appendice f

appetite ['æpɪtaɪt] n appetito

appetizer ['æpɪtaɪzəʳ] n stuzzichino

applaud [ə'plɔ:d] vt, vi applaudire

applause [ə'plɔ:z] n applauso

apple ['æpl] n mela; **apple pie** n
torta di mele

appliance [ə'plaɪəns] n apparecchio

applicable [ə'plɪkəbl] adj
applicabile; **to be ~ to** essere valido
per; **the law is ~ from January** la
legge entrerà in vigore in gennaio

applicant ['æplɪkənt] n candidato/a

application [æplɪ'keɪʃən] n
applicazione f; (for a job, a grant etc)
domanda; (Comput) applicazione f;
application form n modulo per la
domanda

apply [ə'plaɪ] vt: **to ~ (to)** (paint,
ointment) dare (a); (theory, technique)
applicare (a) ▷ vi: **to ~ to** (ask)
rivolgersi a; (be suitable for, relevant
to) riguardare, riferirsi a; **to ~ (for)**
(permit, grant, job) fare domanda
(per); **to ~ o.s. to** dedicarsi a

appoint [ə'pɔɪnt] vt nominare;
appointment n nomina;
(arrangement to meet) appuntamento;
to make an appointment with sb
prendere un appuntamento con qn; **I
have an appointment (with) ...** ho
un appuntamento (con) ...

appraisal [ə'preɪzl] n valutazione f

appreciate [ə'pri:ʃieɪt] vt (like)
apprezzare; (be grateful for) essere
riconoscente di; (be aware of) rendersi
conto di ▷ vi (Comm) aumentare;
I'd ~ your help ti sono grato per
l'aiuto; **appreciation** [əpri:ʃɪ'eɪʃən]
n apprezzamento; (Finance) aumento
del valore

apprehension [æprɪ'hɛnʃən] n
(fear) inquietudine f

apprehensive [æprɪ'hɛnsɪv] adj
apprensivo/a

apprentice [ə'prɛntɪs] n
apprendista m/f

approach [ə'prəutʃ] vi avvicinarsi
▷ vt (come near) avvicinarsi a; (ask,
apply to) rivolgersi a; (subject, passer-
by) avvicinare ▷ n approccio; accesso;
(to problem) modo di affrontare

appropriate vt [ə'prəuprieit] (take) appropriarsi di ▷ adj [ə'prəupriːt] appropriato/a, adatto/a

approval [ə'pruːvəl] n approvazione f; **on ~** (Comm) in prova, in esame

approve [ə'pruːv] vt, vi approvare; **approve of** vt fus approvare

approximate adj [ə'prɒksɪmɪt] approssimativo/a; **approximately** adv circa

Apr. abbr (= April) apr.

apricot ['eɪprɪkɒt] n albicocca

April ['eɪprəl] n aprile m; **~ fool!** pesce d'aprile!; **April Fools' Day** n vedi nota "April Fools' Day"

- **APRIL FOOLS' DAY**

- April Fools' Day è il primo aprile, il
- giorno degli scherzi e delle burle.
- Il nome deriva dal fatto che, se
- una persona cade nella trappola
- che gli è stata tesa, fa la figura del
- fool, cioè dello sciocco. Di recente
- gli scherzi stanno diventando
- sempre più elaborati, e persino
- i giornalisti a volte inventano
- vicende incredibili per burlarsi
- dei lettori.

apron ['eɪprən] n grembiule m

apt [æpt] adj (suitable) adatto/a; (able) capace; (likely): **to be ~ to do** avere tendenza a fare

aquarium [ə'kwɛərɪəm] n acquario

Aquarius [ə'kwɛərɪəs] n Acquario

Arab ['ærəb] adj, n arabo/a

Arabia [ə'reɪbɪə] n Arabia; **Arabian** [ə'reɪbɪən] adj arabo/a; **Arabic** ['ærəbɪk] adj arabico/a, arabo/a ▷ n arabo; **Arabic numerals** npl numeri mpl arabi, numerazione f araba

arbitrary ['ɑːbɪtrərɪ] adj arbitrario/a

arbitration [ɑːbɪ'treɪʃən] n (Law) arbitrato; (Industry) arbitraggio

arc [ɑːk] n arco

arcade [ɑː'keɪd] n portico; (passage with shops) galleria

arch [ɑːtʃ] n arco; (of foot) arco plantare ▷ vt inarcare

archaeology [ɑːkɪ'ɒlədʒɪ] n archeologia

archbishop [ɑːtʃ'bɪʃəp] n arcivescovo

archeology [ɑːkɪ'ɒlədʒɪ] = **archaeology**

architect ['ɑːkɪtɛkt] n architetto; **architectural** [ɑːkɪ'tɛktʃərəl] adj architettonico/a; **architecture** ['ɑːkɪtɛktʃə] n architettura

archive ['ɑːkaɪv] n (also Comput) archivio; **archives** npl archivi mpl

Arctic ['ɑːktɪk] adj artico/a ▷ n: **the ~** l'Artico

are [ɑːʳ] vb see **be**

area ['ɛərɪə] n (Geom) area; (zone) zona; (: smaller) settore m; **area code** n (us Tel) prefisso

arena [ə'riːnə] n arena

aren't [ɑːnt] = **are not**

Argentina [ɑːdʒən'tiːnə] n Argentina; **Argentinian** [-'tɪnɪən] adj, n argentino/a

arguably ['ɑːgjuəblɪ] adv: **it is ~ ...** si può sostenere che sia ...

argue ['ɑːgjuː] vi (quarrel) litigare; (reason) ragionare; **to ~ that** sostenere che

argument ['ɑːgjumənt] n (reasons) argomento; (quarrel) lite f

Aries ['ɛəriːz] n Ariete m

arise (pt **arose**, pp **arisen**) [ə'raɪz, ə'rəuz, ə'rɪzn] vi (opportunity, problem) presentarsi

arithmetic [ə'rɪθmətɪk] n aritmetica

arm [ɑːm] n braccio ▷ vt armare; **~ in ~** a braccetto; see also **arms**; **armchair** n poltrona

armed [ɑːmd] adj armato/a; **armed robbery** n rapina a mano armata

armour, (us) **armor** ['ɑːməʳ] n armatura; (Mil: tanks) mezzi mpl blindati

armpit ['ɑːmpɪt] n ascella

armrest ['ɑːmrɛst] n bracciolo

arms [ɑ:mz] *npl* (*weapons*) armi *fpl*

army ['ɑ:mɪ] *n* esercito

aroma [ə'rəumə] *n* aroma; **aromatherapy** *n* aromaterapia

arose [ə'rəuz] *pt of* **arise**

around [ə'raund] *adv* attorno, intorno ▷ *prep* intorno a; (*fig: about*): **~ £5/3 o'clock** circa 5 sterline/le 3; **is he ~?** è in giro?

arouse [ə'rauz] *vt* (*sleeper*) svegliare; (*curiosity, passions*) suscitare

arrange [ə'reɪndʒ] *vt* sistemare; (*programme*) preparare; **to ~ to do sth** mettersi d'accordo per fare qc; **arrangement** *n* sistemazione *f*; (*agreement*) accordo; **arrangements** *npl* (*plans etc*) progetti *mpl*, piani *mpl*

array [ə'reɪ] *n*: **~ of** fila di

arrears [ə'rɪəz] *npl* arretrati *mpl*; **to be in ~ with one's rent** essere in arretrato con l'affitto

arrest [ə'rɛst] *vt* arrestare; (*sb's attention*) attirare ▷ *n* arresto; **under ~** in arresto

arrival [ə'raɪvəl] *n* arrivo; (*person*) arrivato/a; **a new ~** un nuovo venuto; (*baby*) un neonato

arrive [ə'raɪv] *vi* arrivare; **arrive at** *vt fus* arrivare a

arrogance ['ærəgəns] *n* arroganza

arrogant ['ærəgənt] *adj* arrogante

arrow ['ærəu] *n* freccia

arse [ɑ:s] *n* (*col!*) culo (!)

arson ['ɑ:sn] *n* incendio doloso

art [ɑ:t] *n* arte *f*; (*craft*) mestiere *m*; *see also* **arts**; **art college** *n* scuola di belle arti

artery ['ɑ:tərɪ] *n* arteria

art gallery *n* galleria d'arte

arthritis [ɑ:'θraɪtɪs] *n* artrite *f*

artichoke ['ɑ:tɪtʃəuk] *n* carciofo; **Jerusalem ~** topinambur *m inv*

article ['ɑ:tɪkl] *n* articolo; **articles** *npl* (BRIT Law: *training*) contratto di tirocinio; **~s of clothing** indumenti *mpl*

articulate *adj* [ɑ:'tɪkjulɪt] (*person*) che si esprime forbitamente; (*speech*)

articolato/a ▷ *vi* [ɑ:'tɪkjuleɪt] articolare

artificial [ɑ:tɪ'fɪʃəl] *adj* artificiale

artist ['ɑ:tɪst] *n* artista *m/f*; **artistic** [ɑ:'tɪstɪk] *adj* artistico/a

arts [ɑ:ts] *npl* (Scol) lettere *fpl*

art school *n* scuola d'arte

KEYWORD

as [æz] *conj* **1** (*referring to time*) mentre; **as the years went by** col passare degli anni; **he came in as I was leaving** arrivò mentre stavo uscendo; **as from tomorrow** da domani

2 (*in comparisons*): **as big as** grande come; **twice as big as** due volte più grande di; **as much/many as** tanto quanto/tanti quanti; **as soon as possible** prima possibile

3 (*since, because*) dal momento che, siccome

4 (*referring to manner, way*) come; **do as you wish** fa' come vuoi; **as she said** come ha detto lei

5 (*concerning*): **as for** *or* **to that** per quanto riguarda *or* quanto a quello

6: **as if** *or* **though** come se; **he looked as if he was ill** sembrava stare male; *see also* **long**; **such**; **well**

▷ *prep*: **he works as a driver** fa l'autista; **as chairman of the company, he ...** come presidente della compagnia, lui ...; **he gave me it as a present** me lo ha regalato

a.s.a.p. *abbr* (= *as soon as possible*) prima possibile

asbestos [æz'bɛstəs] *n* asbesto, amianto

ASBO *n abbr* (BRIT: = *antisocial behaviour order*) provvedimento restrittivo per comportamento antisociale

ascent [ə'sɛnt] *n* salita

ash [æʃ] *n* (*dust*) cenere *f*; **~ (tree)** frassino

ashamed [ə'ʃeɪmd] *adj* vergognoso/a; **to be ~ of** vergognarsi di

ashore [ə'ʃɔːʳ] *adv* a terra

ashtray ['æʃtreɪ] *n* portacenere *m*

Ash Wednesday *n* Mercoledì *m inv* delle Ceneri

Asia ['eɪʃə] *n* Asia; **Asian** *adj, n* asiatico/a

aside [ə'saɪd] *adv* da parte ▷ *n* a parte *m*

ask [ɑːsk] *vt* (*question*) domandare; (*invite*) invitare; **to ~ sb sth/sb to do sth** chiedere qc a qn/a qn di fare qc; **to ~ sb about sth** chiedere a qn di qc; **to ~ (sb) a question** fare una domanda (a qn); **to ~ sb out to dinner** invitare qn a mangiare fuori; **ask for** *vt fus* chiedere; **it's just ~ing for trouble** *or* **for it** è proprio (come) andarsela a cercare

asleep [ə'sliːp] *adj* addormentato/a; **to be ~** dormire; **to fall ~** addormentarsi

AS level *n abbr* (= *Advanced Subsidiary level*) prima parte del diploma di studi superiori chiamato "A level"

asparagus [əs'pærəgəs] *n* asparagi *mpl*

aspect ['æspɛkt] *n* aspetto

aspiration [æspə'reɪʃən] *n* aspirazione *f*; **aspirations** *npl* aspirazioni *fpl*

aspire [əs'paɪəʳ] *vi*: **to ~ to** aspirare a

aspirin ['æsprɪn] *n* aspirina

ass [æs] *n* asino; (*col*) scemo/a; (*US col!*) culo (!)

assassin [ə'sæsɪn] *n* assassino; **assassinate** [ə'sæsɪneɪt] *vt* assassinare

assault [ə'sɔːlt] *n* (*Mil*) assalto; (*gen: attack*) aggressione *f* ▷ *vt* assaltare; aggredire; (*sexually*) violentare

assemble [ə'sɛmbl] *vt* riunire; (*Tech*) montare ▷ *vi* riunirsi

assembly [ə'sɛmblɪ] *n* (*meeting*) assemblea; (*construction*) montaggio

assert [ə'səːt] *vt* asserire; (*insist on*) far valere; **assertion** [ə'səːʃən] *n* asserzione *f*

assess [ə'sɛs] *vt* valutare; **assessment** *n* valutazione *f*

asset ['æsɛt] *n* vantaggio; **assets** *npl* (*Comm: of individual*) beni *mpl*; (: *of company*) attivo

assign [ə'saɪn] *vt*: **to ~ (to)** (*task*) assegnare (a); (*resources*) riservare (a); (*cause, meaning*) attribuire (a); **to ~ a date to sth** fissare la data di qc; **assignment** *n* compito

assist [ə'sɪst] *vt* assistere, aiutare; **assistance** *n* assistenza, aiuto; **assistant** *n* assistente *m/f*; (*BRIT: also*: **shop assistant**) commesso/a

associate *adj* [ə'səuʃɪɪt] associato/a; (*member*) aggiunto/a ▷ *n* [ə'səuʃɪɪt] collega *m/f* ▷ *vt* [ə'səuʃɪeɪt] associare ▷ *vi* [ə'səuʃɪeɪt]: **to ~ with sb** frequentare qn

association [əsəusɪ'eɪʃən] *n* associazione *f*

assorted [ə'sɔːtɪd] *adj* assortito/a

assortment [ə'sɔːtmənt] *n* assortimento

assume [ə'sjuːm] *vt* supporre; (*responsibilities etc*) assumere; (*attitude, name*) prendere

assumption [ə'sʌmpʃən] *n* supposizione *f*, ipotesi *f inv*; (*of power*) assunzione *f*

assurance [ə'ʃuərəns] *n* assicurazione *f*; (*self-confidence*) fiducia in se stesso

assure [ə'ʃuəʳ] *vt* assicurare

asterisk ['æstərɪsk] *n* asterisco

asthma ['æsmə] *n* asma

astonish [ə'stɔnɪʃ] *vt* stupire; **astonished** *adj* stupito/a, sorpreso/a; **to be astonished (at)** essere stupito/a (da); **astonishing** *adj* sorprendente, stupefacente; **I find it astonishing that ...** mi stupisce che ...; **astonishment** *n* stupore *m*

astound [ə'staund] *vt* sbalordire

astray [ə'streɪ] adv: **to go ~** smarrirsi; **to lead ~** portare sulla cattiva strada

astrology [əs'trɒlədʒɪ] n astrologia

astronaut ['æstrənɔːt] n astronauta m/f

astronomer [əs'trɒnəmə*] n astronomo/a

astronomical [æstrə'nɒmɪkl] adj astronomico/a

astronomy [əs'trɒnəmɪ] n astronomia

astute [əs'tjuːt] adj astuto/a

asylum [ə'saɪləm] n asilo; (lunatic asylum) manicomio

○ **KEYWORD**

at [æt] prep **1** (referring to position, direction) a; **at the top** in cima; **at the desk** al banco, alla scrivania; **at home/school** a casa/scuola; **at the baker's** dal panettiere; **to look at sth** guardare qc; **to throw sth at sb** lanciare qc a qn
2 (referring to time) a; **at 4 o'clock** alle 4; **at night** di notte; **at Christmas** a Natale; **at times** a volte
3 (referring to rates, speed etc) a; **at £1 a kilo** a 1 sterlina al chilo; **two at a time** due alla volta, due per volta; **at 50 km/h** a 50 km/h
4 (referring to manner): **at a stroke** d'un solo colpo; **at peace** in pace
5 (referring to activity): **to be at work** essere al lavoro; **to play at cowboys** giocare ai cowboy; **to be good at sth/doing sth** essere bravo in qc/a fare qc
6 (referring to cause): **shocked/surprised/annoyed at sth** colpito da/sorpreso da/arrabbiato per qc; **I went at his suggestion** ci sono andato dietro suo consiglio n
▶ n (@ symbol) chiocciola

ate [eɪt] pt of **eat**

atheist ['eɪθɪɪst] n ateo/a

Athens ['æθɪnz] n Atene f

athlete ['æθliːt] n atleta m/f

athletic [æθ'lɛtɪk] adj atletico/a; **athletics** n atletica

Atlantic [ət'læntɪk] adj atlantico/a ▷ n: **the ~ (Ocean)** l'Atlantico, l'Oceano Atlantico

atlas ['ætləs] n atlante m

ATM abbr (= automated telling machine) (sportello) Bancomat® m inv

atmosphere ['ætməsfɪə*] n atmosfera

atom ['ætəm] n atomo; **atomic** [ə'tɒmɪk] adj atomico/a; **atom(ic) bomb** n bomba atomica

atrocity [ə'trɒsɪtɪ] n atrocità f inv

attach [ə'tætʃ] vt attaccare; (document, letter) allegare; (importance etc) attribuire; **to be ~ed to sb/sth** (to like) essere affezionato/a a qn/qc; **attachment** [ə'tætʃmənt] n (tool) accessorio; (love): **attachment (to)** affetto (per)

attack [ə'tæk] vt attaccare; (person) aggredire; (task etc) iniziare; (problem) affrontare ▷ n attacco; (also: **heart ~**) infarto; **attacker** n aggressore m

attain [ə'teɪn] vt (also: **~ to**) arrivare a, raggiungere

attempt [ə'tɛmpt] n tentativo ▷ vt tentare; **to make an ~ on sb's life** attentare alla vita di qn

attend [ə'tɛnd] vt frequentare; (meeting, talk) andare a; (patient) assistere; **attend to** vt fus (needs, affairs etc) prendersi cura di; (customer) occuparsi di; **attendance** n (being present) presenza; (people present) gente f presente; **attendant** n custode m/f; persona di servizio ▷ adj concomitante

■ Be careful not to translate attend by the Italian word attendere.

attention [ə'tɛnʃən] n attenzione f; (Mil) attenti!; **for the ~ of** (Admin) per l'attenzione di

attic ['ætɪk] n soffitta

attitude ['ætɪtjuːd] n
atteggiamento; (posture) posa
attorney [ə'təːnɪ] n (lawyer)
avvocato; (having proxy) mandatario;
Attorney General n (BRIT)
Procuratore m Generale; (US)
Ministro della Giustizia
attract [ə'trækt] vt attirare;
attraction [ə'trækʃən] n (gen pl:
pleasant things) attrattiva; (Physics,
fig: towards sth) attrazione f;
attractive adj attraente
attribute n ['ætrɪbjuːt] attributo ⊳ vt
[ə'trɪbjuːt]: **to ~ sth to** attribuire qc a
aubergine ['əubəʒiːn] n melanzana
auburn ['ɔːbən] adj tizianesco/a
auction ['ɔːkʃən] n (also: **sale by ~**)
asta ⊳ vt (also: **sell by ~**) vendere
all'asta; (also: **put up for ~**) mettere
all'asta
audible ['ɔːdɪbl] adj udibile
audience ['ɔːdɪəns] n (people)
pubblico; spettatori mpl; ascoltatori
mpl; (interview) udienza
audit ['ɔːdɪt] vt rivedere, verificare
audition [ɔː'dɪʃən] n audizione f
auditor ['ɔːdɪtər] n revisore m
auditorium [ɔːdɪ'tɔːrɪəm] n sala,
auditorio
Aug. abbr (= August) ago., ag.
August ['ɔːgəst] n agosto
aunt [ɑːnt] n zia; **auntie, aunty**
['ɑːntɪ] n zietta
au pair ['əu'peər] n (also: **~ girl**)
(ragazza f) alla pari inv
aura ['ɔːrə] n aura
austerity [ɔs'tɛrɪtɪ] n austerità f inv
Australia [ɔs'treɪlɪə] n Australia;
Australian adj, n australiano/a
Austria ['ɔstrɪə] n Austria; **Austrian**
adj, n austriaco/a
authentic [ɔː'θɛntɪk] adj
autentico/a
author ['ɔːθər] n autore/trice
authority [ɔː'θɔrɪtɪ] n autorità f inv;
(permission) autorizzazione f; **the
authorities** npl (government etc) le
autorità

authorize ['ɔːθəraɪz] vt autorizzare
auto ['ɔːtəu] n (US) auto f inv;
autobiography [ɔːtəbaɪ'ɔgrəfɪ]
n autobiografia; **autograph**
['ɔːtəgrɑːf] n autografo ⊳ vt
firmare; **automatic** [ɔːtə'mætɪk]
adj automatico/a ⊳ n (gun) arma
automatica; (car) automobile
f con cambio automatico;
(washing machine) lavatrice f
automatica; **automatically** adv
automaticamente; **automobile**
['ɔːtəməbiːl] n (US) automobile
f; **autonomous** [ɔː'tɔnəməs]
adj autonomo/a; **autonomy**
[ɔː'tɔnəmɪ] n autonomia
autumn ['ɔːtəm] n autunno
auxiliary [ɔːg'zɪlɪərɪ] adj ausiliario/a
⊳ n ausiliare m/f
avail [ə'veɪl] vt: **to ~ o.s. of** servirsi
di; approfittarsi di ⊳ n: **to no ~**
inutilmente
availability [əveɪlə'bɪlɪtɪ] n
disponibilità
available [ə'veɪləbl] adj disponibile
avalanche ['ævəlɑːnʃ] n valanga
Ave. abbr = **avenue**
avenue ['ævənjuː] n viale m; (fig)
strada, via
average ['ævərɪdʒ] n media ⊳ adj
medio/a ⊳ vt (also: **~ out at**) essere in
media di; **on ~** in media
avert [ə'vəːt] vt evitare, prevenire;
(one's eyes) distogliere
avid ['ævɪd] adj (supporter etc)
accanito/a
avocado [ævə'kɑːdəu] n (BRIT: also:
~ pear) avocado m inv
avoid [ə'vɔɪd] vt evitare
await [ə'weɪt] vt aspettare
awake [ə'weɪk] (pt awoke, pp
awoken or **awaked**) vt svegliare ⊳ vi
svegliarsi ⊳ adj sveglio/a
award [ə'wɔːd] n premio; (Law)
decreto; (sum) risarcimento ⊳ vt
assegnare; (Law: damages) decretare
aware [ə'wɛər] adj: **~ of** (conscious)
conscio/a di; (informed) informato/a

di; **to become ~ of** accorgersi di;
awareness n consapevolezza
away [ə'weɪ] adj, adv via; lontano/a;
  two kilometres ~ a due chilometri
  di distanza; **two hours ~ by car**
  a due ore di distanza in macchina;
  the holiday was two weeks ~
  mancavano due settimane alle
  vacanze; **he's ~ for a week** è andato
  via per una settimana; **to take
  ~** portare via; **he was working/
  pedalling ~** lavorava/pedalava più
  che poteva; **to fade ~** scomparire
awe [ɔː] n timore m
awe-inspiring ['ɔːɪnspaɪərɪŋ],
  awesome ['ɔːsəm] adj imponente
awful ['ɔːfəl] adj terribile; **an ~ lot
  of** (people, cars, dogs) un numero
  incredibile di; (jam, flowers) una
  quantità incredibile di; **awfully** adv
  (very) terribilmente
awkward ['ɔːkwəd] adj (clumsy)
  goffo/a; (inconvenient) scomodo/a;
  (embarrassing) imbarazzante
awoke [ə'wəuk] pt of **awake**
awoken [ə'wəukən] pp of **awake**
axe, (US) **ax** [æks] n scure f ▷ vt
  (project etc) abolire; (jobs) sopprimere
axle ['æksl] n (also: **~-tree**) asse m
ay(e) [aɪ] excl (yes) sì
azalea [ə'zeɪlɪə] n azalea

B [biː] n (Mus) si m; **B road** n (BRIT Aut)
  ≈ strada secondaria
BA n abbr = **Bachelor of Arts**
baby ['beɪbɪ] n bambino/a; **baby
  carriage** n (US) carrozzina; **baby-sit**
  vi fare il (or la) babysitter; **baby-sitter**
  n baby-sitter mf inv; **baby wipe** n
  salvietta umidificata
bachelor ['bætʃələʳ] n scapolo;
  B~ of Arts/Science (BA/BSc) ≈
  laureato/a in lettere/scienze
back [bæk] n (of person, horse) dorso,
  schiena; (as opposed to front) dietro;
  (of hand) dorso; (of train) coda; (of
  chair) schienale m; (of page) rovescio;
  (of book) retro; (Football) difensore m
  ▷ vt (candidate) appoggiare; (horse:
  at races) puntare su; (car) guidare a
  marcia indietro ▷ vi indietreggiare;
  (car etc) fare marcia indietro ▷ adj
  (in compounds) posteriore, di dietro
  ▷ adv (not forward) indietro; (returned):
  he's ~ è tornato; **he ran ~** tornò

indietro di corsa; **throw the ball ~** (*restitution*) ritira la palla; **can I have it ~?** posso riaverlo?; **he called ~** (*again*) ha richiamato; **~ seats/ wheels** (*Aut*) sedili *mpl*/ruote *fpl* posteriori; **back down** *vi* (*fig*) fare marcia indietro; **back out** *vi* (*of promise*) tirarsi indietro; **back up** *vt* (*support*) appoggiare, sostenere; (*Comput*) fare una copia di riserva di; **backache** ['bækeɪk] *n* mal *m* di schiena; **backbencher** ['bækbentʃə*] *parlamentare che non ha incarichi né al governo né all'opposizione*; **backbone** *n* spina dorsale; **back door** *n* porta sul retro; **backfire** *vi* (*Aut*) dar ritorni di fiamma; (*plans*) fallire; **backgammon** *n* tavola reale; **background** *n* sfondo; (*of events*) background *m inv*; (*basic knowledge*) base *f*; (*experience*) esperienza; **family background** ambiente *m* familiare; **backing** *n* (*fig*) appoggio; **backlog** *n*: **backlog of work** lavoro arretrato; **backpack** *n* zaino; **backpacker** *n chi viaggia con zaino e sacco a pelo*; **backslash** *n* backslash *m inv*, barra obliqua inversa; **backstage** *adv* nel retroscena; **backstroke** *n* nuoto sul dorso; **backup** *adj* (*train, plane*) supplementare; (*Comput*) di riserva ▷ *n* (*support*) appoggio, sostegno; (*also:* **backup file**) file *m inv* di riserva; **backward** *adj* (*movement*) indietro *inv*; (*person*) tardivo/a; (*country*) arretrato/a; **backwards** *adv* indietro; (*fall, walk*) all'indietro; **back yard** *n* cortile *m* sul retro
bacon ['beɪkən] *n* pancetta
bacteria [bæk'tɪərɪə] *npl* batteri *mpl*
bad [bæd] *adj* cattivo/a; (*child*) cattivello/a; (*meat, food*) andato/a a male; **his ~ leg** la sua gamba malata; **to go ~** andare a male
badge [bædʒ] *n* insegna; (*of policeman*) stemma *m*
badger ['bædʒə*] *n* tasso

badly ['bædlɪ] *adv* (*work, dress etc*) male; **~ wounded** gravemente ferito; **he needs it ~** ne ha gran bisogno
bad-mannered [bæd'mænəd] *adj* maleducato/a, sgarbato/a
badminton ['bædmɪntən] *n* badminton *m*
bad-tempered [bæd'tɛmpəd] *adj* irritabile; (*in bad mood*) di malumore
bag [bæg] *n* sacco; (*handbag etc*) borsa; **~s of** (*col*) (*lots of*) un sacco di
baggage *n* bagagli *mpl*; **baggage allowance** *n* peso bagaglio consentito; **baggage claim, baggage reclaim** *n* ritiro *m* bagaglio *inv*
baggy *adj* largo/a, sformato/a
bagpipes *npl* cornamusa
bail [beɪl] *n* cauzione *f* ▷ *vt* (*prisoner: also:* **grant ~ to**) concedere la libertà provvisoria su cauzione a; (*Naut: also:* **~ out**) aggottare; **on ~** in libertà provvisoria su cauzione
bait [beɪt] *n* esca ▷ *vt* (*hook*) innescare; (*trap*) munire di esca; (*fig*) tormentare
bake [beɪk] *vt* cuocere al forno ▷ *vi* cuocersi al forno; **baked beans** [-biːnz] *npl* fagioli *mpl* in salsa di pomodoro; **baked potato** *n* patata (con la buccia) cotta al forno; **baker** *n* fornaio/a, panettiere/a; **bakery** *n* panetteria; **baking** *n* cottura (al forno); **baking powder** *n* lievito in polvere
balance ['bæləns] *n* equilibrio; (*Comm: sum*) bilancio; (*remainder*) resto; (*scales*) bilancia ▷ *vt* tenere in equilibrio; (*budget*) far quadrare; (*account*) pareggiare; (*compensate*) contrappesare; **~ of trade/ payments** bilancia commerciale/ dei pagamenti; **balanced** *adj* (*personality, diet*) equilibrato/a; **balance sheet** *n* bilancio
balcony ['bælkənɪ] *n* balcone *m*; (*in theatre*) balconata

bald [bɔːld] *adj* calvo/a; *(tyre)* liscio/a
Balearics [bælɪˈærɪks], **Balearic**
Islands *npl:* **the ~** le Baleari *fpl*
ball [bɔːl] *n* palla; *(football)* pallone
m; (for golf) pallina; *(of wool, string)*
gomitolo; *(dance)* ballo; **to play ~**
(with sb) *(fig)* stare al gioco (di qn)
ballerina [bæləˈriːnə] *n* ballerina
ballet [ˈbæleɪ] *n* balletto; **ballet**
dancer *n* ballerino/a classico/a
balloon [bəˈluːn] *n* pallone *m*
ballot [ˈbælət] *n* scrutinio
ball-point pen [ˈbɔːlpɔɪnt-] *n* penna
a sfera
ballroom [ˈbɔːlrum] *n* sala da ballo
Baltic [ˈbɔːltɪk] *adj, n:* **the ~ Sea** il
(mar) Baltico
bamboo [bæmˈbuː] *n* bambù *m*
ban [bæn] *n* interdizione *f* ▷ *vt*
interdire
banana [bəˈnɑːnə] *n* banana
band [bænd] *n* banda; *(at a dance)*
orchestra; *(Mil)* fanfara
bandage [ˈbændɪdʒ] *n* benda, fascia
Band-Aid® [ˈbændeɪd] *n (US)*
cerotto
B & B *n abbr =* **bed and breakfast**
bandit [ˈbændɪt] *n* bandito
bang [bæŋ] *n (of door)* lo sbattere;
(blow) colpo ▷ *vt* battere
(violentemente); *(door)* sbattere ▷ *vi*
scoppiare; sbattere
Bangladesh [bɑːŋɡləˈdɛʃ] *n*
Bangladesh *m*
bangle [ˈbæŋɡl] *n* braccialetto
bangs [bæŋz] *npl (US: fringe)* frangia,
frangetta
banish [ˈbænɪʃ] *vt* bandire
banister(s) [ˈbænɪstə(z)] *n(pl)*
ringhiera
banjo [ˈbændʒəu] *(pl* **banjoes** *or*
banjos) *n* banjo *m inv*
bank [bæŋk] *n* banca, banco; *(of river,
lake)* riva, sponda; *(of earth)* banco
▷ *vi (Aviat)* inclinarsi in virata; **bank**
on *vt fus* contare su; **bank account**
n conto in banca; **bank balance** *n*
saldo; **a healthy bank balance** un

solido conto in banca; **bank card** *n*
carta *f* assegni *inv*; **bank charges**
npl (BRIT) spese *fpl* bancarie; **banker**
n banchiere *m*; **bank holiday** *n*
(BRIT) giorno di festa; *vedi nota* **"bank**
holiday"; **banking** *n* attività
bancaria; professione *f* di banchiere;
bank manager *n* direttore *m* di
banca; **banknote** *n* banconota

● **BANK HOLIDAY**
●
● Una *bank holiday*, in Gran
● Bretagna, è una giornata in cui
● le banche e molti negozi sono
● chiusi. Generalmente *il bank*
● *holiday* cadono di lunedì e molti
● ne approfittano per fare una
● breve vacanza fuori città. Di
● conseguenza, durante questi fine
● settimana lunghi ("*bank holiday*
● *weekend*") si verifica un notevole
● aumento del traffico sulle strade,
● negli aeroporti e nelle stazioni e
● molte località turistiche registrano
● il tutto esaurito.

bankrupt [ˈbæŋkrʌpt] *adj* fallito/a;
to go ~ fallire; **bankruptcy** *n*
fallimento
bank statement *n* estratto conto
banner [ˈbænəʳ] *n* striscione *m*
bannister(s) [ˈbænɪstə(z)] *n(pl) see*
banister(s)
banquet [ˈbæŋkwɪt] *n* banchetto
baptism [ˈbæptɪzəm] *n* battesimo
baptize [bæpˈtaɪz] *vt* battezzare
bar [bɑːʳ] *n (rod)* barra; *(of window etc)*
sbarra; *(of chocolate)* tavoletta; *(fig)*
ostacolo; restrizione *f*; *(pub)* bar *m*
inv; (counter) banco; *(Mus)* battuta
▷ *vt (road, window)* sbarrare; *(person)*
escludere; *(activity)* interdire; **~ of**
soap saponetta; **the B~** *(Law)*
l'Ordine *m* degli avvocati; **behind**
~s *(prisoner)* dietro le sbarre; **~ none**
senza eccezione
barbaric [bɑːˈbærɪk] *adj* barbarico/a

barbecue ['bɑːbɪkjuː] n barbecue m inv

barbed wire ['bɑːbd-] n filo spinato

barber ['bɑːbəʳ] n barbiere m; **barber's (shop)**, (US) **barber shop** n barbiere m

bar code n codice m a barre

bare [bɛəʳ] adj nudo/a ▷ vt scoprire, denudare; (teeth) mostrare; **the ~ essentials, the ~ necessities** lo stretto necessario; **barefoot** adj, adv scalzo/a; **barely** adv appena

bargain ['bɑːgɪn] n (transaction) contratto; (good buy) affare m ▷ vi contrattare; **into the ~** per giunta; **bargain for** vt fus (col): **to ~ for sth** aspettarsi qc; **he got more than he ~ed for** gli è andata peggio di quel che si aspettasse

barge [bɑːdʒ] n chiatta; **barge in** vi (walk in) piombare dentro; (interrupt talk) intromettersi a sproposito

bark [bɑːk] n (of tree) corteccia; (of dog) abbaio ▷ vi abbaiare

barley ['bɑːlɪ] n orzo

barmaid ['bɑːmeɪd] n cameriera al banco

barman ['bɑːmən] n (irreg) barista m

barn [bɑːn] n granaio

barometer [bəˈrɔmɪtəʳ] n barometro

baron ['bærən] n barone m; **baroness** n baronessa

barracks ['bærəks] npl caserma

barrage ['bærɑːʒ] n (Mil, dam) sbarramento; (fig) fiume m

barrel ['bærəl] n barile m; (of gun) canna

barren ['bærən] adj sterile; (soil) arido/a

barrette [bəˈrɛt] n (US) fermaglio per capelli

barricade [bærɪˈkeɪd] n barricata

barrier ['bærɪəʳ] n barriera

barring ['bɑːrɪŋ] prep salvo

barrister ['bærɪstəʳ] n (BRIT) avvocato/essa

barrow ['bærəu] n (cart) carriola

bartender ['bɑːtɛndəʳ] n (US) barista m

base [beɪs] n base f ▷ adj vile ▷ vt: **to ~ sth on** basare qc su

baseball ['beɪsbɔːl] n baseball m; **baseball cap** n berretto da baseball

basement ['beɪsmənt] n seminterrato; (of shop) piano interrato

bases ['beɪsiːz] npl of **basis**

bash [bæʃ] vt (col) picchiare

basic ['beɪsɪk] adj (principles, precautions, rules) elementare; **basically** ['beɪsɪklɪ] adv fondamentalmente, sostanzialmente; **basics** npl: **the basics** l'essenziale m

basil ['bæzl] n basilico

basin ['beɪsn] n (vessel, also Geo) bacino; (also: **wash~**) lavabo

basis (pl **bases**) ['beɪsɪs, -siːz] n base f; **on a part-time ~** part-time; **on a trial ~** in prova

basket ['bɑːskɪt] n cesta; (smaller) cestino; (with handle) paniere m; **basketball** n pallacanestro f

bass [beɪs] n (Mus) basso

bastard ['bɑːstəd] n bastardo/a; (col!) stronzo (!)

bat [bæt] n pipistrello; (for baseball etc) mazza; (BRIT: for table tennis) racchetta ▷ vt: **he didn't ~ an eyelid** non battè ciglio

batch [bætʃ] n (of bread) infornata; (of papers) cumulo

bath (pl **baths**) [bɑːθ, bɑːðz] n bagno; (bathtub) vasca da bagno ▷ vt far fare il bagno a; **to have a ~** fare un bagno; see also **baths**

bathe [beɪð] vi fare il bagno ▷ vt (wound etc) lavare

bathing ['beɪðɪŋ] n bagni mpl; **bathing costume**, (US) **bathing suit** n costume m da bagno

bath: bathrobe ['bɑːθrəub] n accappatoio; **bathroom** ['bɑːθrum] n stanza da bagno; **baths** [bɑːðz] npl bagni mpl pubblici; **bath towel** n

asciugamano da bagno; **bathtub** n
(vasca da) bagno

baton ['bætən] n (Mus) bacchetta;
(Athletics) testimone m; (club)
manganello

batter ['bætə'] vt battere ▷ n
pastetta; **battered** adj (hat)
sformato/a; (pan) ammaccato/a

battery ['bætərɪ] n batteria; (of torch)
pila; **battery farming** n allevamento
in batteria

battle ['bætl] n battaglia ▷ vi
battagliare, lottare; **battlefield** n
campo di battaglia

bay [beɪ] n (of sea) baia; **to hold sb at
~** tenere qn a bada

bazaar [bə'zɑ:'] n bazar m inv; vendita
di beneficenza

BBC n abbr = **British Broadcasting
Corporation**

BC adv abbr (= before Christ) a.C.

 KEYWORD

be [biː] (pt **was, were**, pp **been**) aux
vb **1** (with present participle, forming
continuous tenses): **what are you
doing?** che fai?, che stai facendo?;
they're coming tomorrow vengono
domani; **I've been waiting for her
for hours** sono ore che l'aspetto
2 (with pp, forming passives) essere; **to
be killed** essere or venire ucciso/a;
the box had been opened la scatola
era stata aperta; **the thief was
nowhere to be seen** il ladro non si
trovava da nessuna parte
3 (in tag questions): **it was fun,
wasn't it?** è stato divertente, no?;
he's good-looking, isn't he? è un
bell'uomo, vero?; **she's back, is she?**
così è tornata, eh?
4 (+ to + infinitive): **the house is
to be sold** abbiamo (or hanno etc)
intenzione di vendere casa; **you're
to be congratulated for all your
work** dovremo farvi i complimenti
per tutto il vostro lavoro; **he's not to
open it** non deve aprirlo
▶ vb + complement **1** (gen) essere; **I'm
English** sono inglese; **I'm tired** sono
stanco/a; **I'm hot/cold** ho caldo/
freddo; **he's a doctor** è medico; **2
and 2 are 4** 2 più 2 fa 4; **be careful!**
sta attento/a!; **be good** sii buono/a
2 (of health) stare; **how are you?**
come sta?; **he's very ill** sta molto
male
3 (of age): **how old are you?** quanti
anni hai?; **I'm sixteen (years old)**
ho sedici anni
4 (cost) costare; **how much was the
meal?** quant'era or quanto costava il
pranzo?; **that'll be £5, please** (sono)
5 sterline, per favore
▶ vi **1** (exist, occur etc) essere, esistere;
the best singer that ever was il
migliore cantante mai esistito or
di tutti tempi; **be that as it may**
comunque sia, sia come sia; **so be it**
sia pure, e sia
2 (referring to place) essere, trovarsi; **I
won't be here tomorrow** non ci sarò
domani; **Edinburgh is in Scotland**
Edimburgo si trova in Scozia

3 (*referring to movement*): **where have you been?** dove sei stato?; **I've been to China** sono stato in Cina
▶*impers vb* **1** (*referring to time, distance*) essere; **it's 5 o'clock** sono le 5; **it's the 28th of April** è il 28 aprile; **it's 10 km to the village** di qui al paese sono 10 km
2 (*referring to the weather*) fare; **it's too hot/cold** fa troppo caldo/freddo; **it's windy** c'è vento
3 (*emphatic*): **it's me** sono io; **it was Maria who paid the bill** è stata Maria che ha pagato il conto

beach [biːtʃ] *n* spiaggia ▷ *vt* tirare in secco
beacon ['biːkən] *n* (*lighthouse*) faro; (*marker*) segnale *m*
bead [biːd] *n* perlina; **beads** *npl* (*necklace*) collana
beak [biːk] *n* becco
beam [biːm] *n* trave *f*; (*of light*) raggio ▷ *vi* brillare
bean [biːn] *n* fagiolo; (*coffee bean*) chicco; **runner ~** fagiolino; **beansprouts** *npl* germogli *mpl* di soia
bear [bɛəʳ] (*pt* **bore**, *pp* **borne**) *n* orso ▷ *vt* portare; (*produce*) generare; (*endure*) sopportare ▷ *vi*: **to ~ right/left** piegare a destra/sinistra
beard [bɪəd] *n* barba
bearer ['bɛərəʳ] *n* portatore *m*
bearing ['bɛərɪŋ] *n* portamento; (*connection*) rapporto; **bearings** *npl* (*also*: **ball ~s**) cuscinetti *mpl* a sfere; **to take a ~** fare un rilevamento; **to find one's ~s** orientarsi
beast [biːst] *n* bestia
beat [biːt] *n* colpo; (*of heart*) battito; (*Mus*) tempo, battuta; (*of policeman*) giro ▷ *vt* (*pt* **beat**, *pp* **beaten**) battere; (*eggs, cream*) sbattere; **off the ~en track** fuori mano; **~ it!** (*col*) fila!, fuori dai piedi!; **beat up** *vt* (*col: person*) picchiare; (*eggs*) sbattere; **beating** *n* botte *fpl*

beautiful ['bjuːtɪful] *adj* bello/a; **beautifully** *adv* splendidamente
beauty ['bjuːtɪ] *n* bellezza; **beauty parlour** [-'pɑːləʳ], (*US*) **beauty parlor** *n* salone *m* di bellezza; **beauty salon** *n* istituto di bellezza; **beauty spot** *n* (*BRIT Tourism*) luogo pittoresco
beaver ['biːvəʳ] *n* castoro
became [bɪ'keɪm] *pt of* **become**
because [bɪ'kɔz] *conj* perché; **~ of** a causa di
beckon ['bɛkən] *vt* (*also*: **~ to**) chiamare con un cenno
become [bɪ'kʌm] *vt* (*irreg: like* **come**) diventare; **to ~ fat/thin** ingrassarsi/dimagrire
bed [bɛd] *n* letto; (*of flowers*) aiuola; (*of coal, clay*) strato; **bed and breakfast** *n* (*terms*) camera con colazione; (*place*) ≈ pensione *f* familiare; *vedi nota* **"bed and breakfast (B & B)"**; **bedclothes** ['bɛdkləʊðz] *npl* coperte *fpl* e lenzuola *fpl*; **bedding** *n* coperte e lenzuola *fpl*; **bed linen** *n* biancheria da letto; **bedroom** *n* camera da letto; **bedside** *n*: **at sb's bedside** al capezzale di qn; **bedside lamp** *n* lampada da comodino; **bedside table** *n* comodino; **bedsit(ter)** ['bɛdsɪt(əʳ)] *n* (*BRIT*) monolocale *m*; **bedspread** *n* copriletto; **bedtime** *n*: **it's bedtime** è ora di andare a letto

● **BED AND BREAKFAST (B & B)**
●
● I *bed and breakfasts*, anche *B & Bs*,
● sono piccole pensioni a conduzione
● familiare, in case private o fattorie,
● dove si affittano camere e viene
● servita al mattino la tradizionale
● colazione all'inglese. Queste
● pensioni offrono un servizio di
● camera con prima colazione,
● appunto *bed and breakfast*, a
● prezzi più contenuti rispetto agli
● alberghi.

bee [biː] n ape f

beech [biːtʃ] n faggio

beef [biːf] n manzo; **roast ~** arrosto di manzo; **beefburger** n hamburger m inv; **Beefeater** n guardia della Torre di Londra

been [biːn] pp of **be**

beer [bɪəʳ] n birra; **beer garden** n (BRIT) giardino (di pub)

beet [biːt] (US) n (also: **red ~**) barbabietola rossa

beetle ['biːtl] n scarafaggio; coleottero

beetroot ['biːtruːt] n (BRIT) barbabietola

before [bɪˈfɔːʳ] prep (in time) prima di; (in space) davanti a ▷ conj prima che + sub; prima di ▷ adv prima; **~ going** prima di andare; **~ she goes** prima che vada; **the week ~** la settimana prima; **I've seen it ~** l'ho già visto; **I've never seen it ~** è la prima volta che lo vedo; **beforehand** adv in anticipo

beg [bɛg] vi chiedere l'elemosina ▷ vt (also: **~ for**) chiedere in elemosina; (favour) chiedere; **to ~ sb to do** pregare qn di fare

began [bɪˈgæn] pt of **begin**

beggar ['bɛgəʳ] n mendicante m/f

begin (pt **began**, pp **begun**) [bɪˈgɪn, bɪˈgæn, bɪˈgʌn] vt, vi cominciare; **to ~ doing** or **to do sth** incominciare or iniziare a fare qc; **beginner** n principiante m/f; **beginning** n inizio, principio

begun [bɪˈgʌn] pp of **begin**

behalf [bɪˈhɑːf] n: **on ~ of** per conto di; a nome di

behave [bɪˈheɪv] vi comportarsi; (well: also: **~ o.s.**) comportarsi bene; **behaviour**, (US) **behavior** [bɪˈheɪvjəʳ] n comportamento, condotta

behind [bɪˈhaɪnd] prep dietro; (followed by pronoun) dietro di; (time) in ritardo con ▷ adv dietro; (leave, stay) indietro ▷ n didietro; **~ the scenes**

dietro le quinte; **to be ~ (schedule) with sth** essere indietro con qc

beige [beɪʒ] adj beige inv

Beijing [beɪˈdʒɪŋ] n Pechino f

being ['biːɪŋ] n essere m

belated [bɪˈleɪtɪd] adj tardo/a

belch [bɛltʃ] vi ruttare ▷ vt (gen: also: **~ out**: smoke etc) eruttare

Belgian ['bɛldʒən] adj, n belga m/f

Belgium ['bɛldʒəm] n Belgio

belief [bɪˈliːf] n (opinion) opinione f, convinzione f; (trust, faith) fede f

believe [bɪˈliːv] vt, vi credere; **to ~ in** (God) credere in; (ghosts) credere a; (method) avere fiducia in; **believer** n (Rel) credente m/f; (in idea, activity): **to be a believer in** credere in

bell [bɛl] n campana; (small, on door, electric) campanello

bellboy ['bɛlbɔɪ], (US) **bellhop** ['bɛlhɔp] n ragazzo d'albergo, fattorino d'albergo

bellow ['bɛləu] vi muggire

bell pepper (esp US) n peperone m

belly ['bɛlɪ] n pancia; **bellybutton** n ombelico

belong [bɪˈlɔŋ] vi: **to ~ to** appartenere a; (club etc) essere socio di; **this book ~s here** questo libro va qui; **belongings** npl cose fpl, roba

beloved [bɪˈlʌvɪd] adj adorato/a

below [bɪˈləu] prep sotto, al di sotto di ▷ adv sotto, di sotto; giù; **see ~** vedi sotto or oltre

belt [bɛlt] n cintura; (Tech) cinghia ▷ vt (thrash) picchiare ▷ vi (col) filarsela; **beltway** n (US: Aut: ring road) circonvallazione f; (: motorway) autostrada

bemused [bɪˈmjuːzd] adj perplesso/a, stupito/a

bench [bɛntʃ] n panca; (in workshop, Pol) banco; **the B~** (Law) la Corte

bend [bɛnd] (pt, pp **bent**) vt curvare; (leg, arm) piegare ▷ vi curvarsi; piegarsi ▷ n (in road) curva; (in pipe, river) gomito; **bend down** vi chinarsi; **bend over** vi piegarsi

beneath [bɪ'niːθ] *prep* sotto, al di sotto di; (*unworthy of*) indegno/a di ▷ *adv* sotto, di sotto

beneficial [bɛnɪ'fɪʃəl] *adj* che fa bene; vantaggioso/a

benefit ['bɛnɪfɪt] *n* beneficio, vantaggio; (*allowance of money*) indennità *f inv* ▷ *vt* far bene a ▷ *vi*: **he'll ~ from it** ne trarrà beneficio or profitto

benign [bɪ'naɪn] *adj* (*person, smile*) benevolo/a; (*Med*) benigno/a

bent [bɛnt] *pt, pp of* **bend** ▷ *n* inclinazione *f* ▷ *adj* (col: *dishonest*) losco/a; **to be ~ on** essere deciso/a a

bereaved [bɪ'riːvd] *npl*: **the ~** i familiari in lutto

beret ['bɛreɪ] *n* berretto

Berlin [bəː'lɪn] *n* Berlino *f*

Bermuda [bəː'mjuːdə] *n* le Bermude

berry ['bɛrɪ] *n* bacca

berth [bəːθ] *n* (*bed*) cuccetta; (*for ship*) ormeggio ▷ *vi* (*in harbour*) entrare in porto; (*at anchor*) gettare l'ancora

beside [bɪ'saɪd] *prep* accanto a; **to be ~ o.s. (with anger)** essere fuori di sé; **that's ~ the point** non c'entra; **besides** [bɪ'saɪdz] *adv* inoltre, per di più ▷ *prep* oltre a; (*except*) a parte

best [bɛst] *adj* migliore ▷ *adv* meglio; **the ~ part of** (*quantity*) la maggior parte di; **at ~** tutt'al più; **to make the ~ of sth** cavare il meglio possibile da qc; **to do one's ~** fare del proprio meglio; **to the ~ of my knowledge** per quel che ne so; **to the ~ of my ability** al massimo delle mie capacità; **best-before date** *n* (*Comm*): **"best-before date: ..."** da consumarsi preferibilmente entro il...; **best man** *n* (*irreg*) testimone *m* dello sposo; **bestseller** *n* bestseller *m inv*

bet [bɛt] *n* scommessa ▷ *vt, vi* (*pt, pp* **bet** or **betted**) scommettere; **to ~ sb sth** scommettere qc con qn

betray [bɪ'treɪ] *vt* tradire

better ['bɛtəʳ] *adj* migliore ▷ *adv* meglio ▷ *vt* migliorare ▷ *n*: **to get**

the ~ of avere la meglio su; **you had ~ do it** è meglio che lo faccia; **he thought ~ of it** cambiò idea; **to get ~** migliorare

betting ['bɛtɪŋ] *n* scommesse *fpl*; **betting shop** *n* (*BRIT*) ufficio dell'allibratore

between [bɪ'twiːn] *prep* tra ▷ *adv* in mezzo, nel mezzo

beverage ['bɛvərɪdʒ] *n* bevanda

beware [bɪ'wɛəʳ] *vt, vi*: **to ~ (of)** stare attento/a (a); **"~ of the dog"** "attenti al cane"

bewildered [bɪ'wɪldəd] *adj* sconcertato/a, confuso/a

beyond [bɪ'jɔnd] *prep* (*in space*) oltre; (*exceeding*) al di sopra di ▷ *adv* di là; **~ doubt** senza dubbio; **~ repair** irreparabile

bias ['baɪəs] *n* (*prejudice*) pregiudizio; (*preference*) preferenza; **bias(s)ed** *adj* parziale

bib [bɪb] *n* bavaglino

Bible ['baɪbl] *n* Bibbia

bicarbonate of soda [baɪ'kɑːbənɪt-] *n* bicarbonato (di sodio)

biceps ['baɪsɛps] *n* bicipite *m*

bicycle ['baɪsɪkl] *n* bicicletta; **bicycle pump** *n* pompa della bicicletta

bid [bɪd] (*pt* **bade** or **bid**, *pp* **bidden** or **bid**) *n* offerta; (*attempt*) tentativo ▷ *vi* fare un'offerta ▷ *vt* fare un'offerta di; **to ~ sb good day** dire buon giorno a qn; **bidder** *n*: **the highest bidder** il maggior offerente

bidet ['biːdeɪ] *n* bidè *m inv*

big [bɪg] *adj* grande; grosso/a; **Big Apple** *n vedi nota* **"Big Apple"**; **bigheaded** ['bɪg'hɛdɪd] *adj* presuntuoso/a; **big toe** *n* alluce *m*

● **BIG APPLE**
●
● Tutti sanno che *The Big Apple*, la
● Grande Mela, è New York (*"apple"*
● in gergo significa grande città),
● ma sicuramente i soprannomi

di altre città americane non sono così conosciuti. Chicago è soprannominata "theWindy City" perché è ventosa, New Orleans si chiama "the Big Easy" per il modo di vivere tranquillo e rilassato dei suoi abitanti, e l'industria automobilistica ha fatto sì che Detroit fosse soprannominata "Motown".

bike [baɪk] n bici f inv; **bike lane** n pista ciclabile

bikini [bɪˈkiːnɪ] n bikini m inv

bilateral [baɪˈlætərl] adj bilaterale

bilingual [baɪˈlɪŋgwəl] adj bilingue

bill [bɪl] n conto; (Pol) atto; (Us: banknote) banconota; (of bird) becco; (of show) locandina; **may I have the ~ please?** posso avere il conto per piacere?; **"stick or post no ~s"** "divieto di affissione"; **to fit or fill the ~** (fig) fare al caso; **billboard** n tabellone m; **billfold** [ˈbɪlfəʊld] n (Us) portafoglio

billiards [ˈbɪljədz] n biliardo

billion [ˈbɪljən] n (BRIT) bilione m; (Us) miliardo

bin [bɪn] n (for coal, rubbish) bidone m; (for bread) cassetta; (BRIT: also: **dust~**) pattumiera; (: also: **litter ~**) cestino

bind (pt, pp **bound**) [baɪnd, baʊnd] vt legare; (oblige) obbligare ▷ n (col) scocciatura

binge [bɪndʒ] n (col): **to go on a ~** fare baldoria; **binge drinker** n persona che di norma beve troppo

bingo [ˈbɪŋgəʊ] n gioco simile alla tombola

binoculars [bɪˈnɔkjuləz] npl binocolo

bio... [baɪə...] prefix bio; **biochemistry** [baɪəʊˈkɛmɪstrɪ] n biochimica; **biodegradable** [ˈbaɪəʊdɪˈgreɪdəbl] adj biodegradabile; **biofuel** [ˈbaɪəʊfjuəl] n biocarburante; **biography** [baɪˈɔgrəfɪ] n biografia; **biological** adj biologico/a; **biology**

[baɪˈɔlədʒɪ] n biologia; **biometric** [baɪəʊˈmɛtrɪk] adj biometrico/a

bipolar [baɪˈpəʊləʳ] adj bipolare

birch [bəːtʃ] n betulla

bird [bəːd] n uccello; (BRIT col: girl) bambola; **bird flu** n influenza aviaria; **bird of prey** n (uccello) rapace m; **birdwatching** n birdwatching m

Biro® [ˈbaɪrəʊ] n biro® f inv

birth [bəːθ] n nascita; **to give ~ to** dare alla luce, partorire; **birth certificate** n certificato di nascita; **birth control** n controllo delle nascite; contraccezione f; **birthday** n compleanno ▷ cpd di compleanno; **birthmark** n voglia; **birthplace** n luogo di nascita

biscuit [ˈbɪskɪt] n (BRIT) biscotto

bishop [ˈbɪʃəp] n vescovo

bistro [ˈbiːstrəʊ] n bistrò m inv

bit [bɪt] pt of **bite** ▷ n pezzo; (of horse) morso; (Comput) bit m inv; **a ~ of** un po' di; **a ~ mad/dangerous** un po' matto/pericoloso; **~ by ~** a poco a poco

bitch [bɪtʃ] n (dog) cagna; (col!) puttana (!)

bite [baɪt] vt, vi (pt **bit**, pp **bitten**) mordere; (insect) pungere ▷ n morso; (insect bite) puntura; (mouthful) boccone m; **let's have a ~ to eat** mangiamo un boccone; **to ~ one's nails** mangiarsi le unghie

bitten [ˈbɪtn] pp of **bite**

bitter [ˈbɪtəʳ] adj amaro/a; (wind, criticism) pungente ▷ n (BRIT: beer) birra amara

bizarre [bɪˈzɑːʳ] adj bizzarro/a

black [blæk] adj nero/a ▷ n nero ▷ vt (BRIT Industry) boicottare; **~ coffee** caffè m inv nero; **to give sb a ~ eye** fare un occhio nero a qn; **in the ~** (in credit) in attivo; **black out** vi (faint) svenire; **blackberry** n mora; **blackbird** n merlo; **blackboard** n lavagna; **blackcurrant** n ribes m inv; **black ice** n strato trasparente di ghiaccio; **blackmail** n ricatto ▷ vt ricattare;

black market n mercato nero; **blackout** n oscuramento; (fainting) svenimento; (TV) interruzione f delle trasmissioni; **black pepper** n pepe m nero; **black pudding** n sanguinaccio; **Black Sea** n: **the Black Sea** il mar Nero
bladder ['blædə^r] n vescica
blade [bleɪd] n lama; (of oar) pala; **~ of grass** filo d'erba
blame [bleɪm] n colpa ▷ vt: **to ~ sb/ sth for sth** dare la colpa di qc a qn/ qc; **who's to ~?** chi è colpevole?
bland [blænd] adj mite; (taste) blando/a
blank [blæŋk] adj bianco/a; (look) distratto/a ▷ n spazio vuoto; (cartridge) cartuccia a salve
blanket ['blæŋkɪt] n coperta
blast [blɑːst] n (of wind) raffica; (bomb blast) esplosione f ▷ vt far saltare
blatant ['bleɪtənt] adj flagrante
blaze [bleɪz] n (fire) incendio; (fig) vampata; splendore m ▷ vi (fire) ardere, fiammeggiare; (guns) sparare senza sosta; (fig: eyes) ardere ▷ vt: **to ~ a trail** (fig) tracciare una via nuova; **in a ~ of publicity** circondato da grande pubblicità
blazer ['bleɪzə^r] n blazer m inv
bleach [bliːtʃ] n (also: **household ~**) varechina ▷ vt (material) candeggiare; **bleachers** npl (US Sport) posti mpl di gradinata
bleak [bliːk] adj tetro/a
bled [blɛd] pt, pp of **bleed**
bleed (pt, pp **bled**) [bliːd, blɛd] vi sanguinare; **my nose is ~ing** mi viene fuori sangue dal naso
blemish ['blɛmɪʃ] n macchia
blend [blɛnd] n miscela ▷ vt mescolare ▷ vi (colours etc: also: **~ in**) armonizzare; **blender** n (Culin) frullatore m
bless (pt, pp **blessed** or **blest**) [blɛs, blɛst] vt benedire; **~ you!** (sneezing) salute!; **blessing** n benedizione f; fortuna
blew [bluː] pt of **blow**
blight [blaɪt] vt (hopes etc) deludere; (life) rovinare
blind [blaɪnd] adj cieco/a ▷ n (for window) avvolgibile m; (Venetian blind) veneziana ▷ vt accecare; **~ people** i ciechi; **blind alley** n vicolo cieco; **blindfold** n benda ▷ adj, adv bendato/a ▷ vt bendare gli occhi a
blink [blɪŋk] vi battere gli occhi; (light) lampeggiare
bliss [blɪs] n estasi f
blister ['blɪstə^r] n (on skin) vescica; (on paintwork) bolla ▷ vi (paint) coprirsi di bolle
blizzard ['blɪzəd] n bufera di neve
bloated ['bləʊtɪd] adj gonfio/a
blob [blɔb] n (drop) goccia; (stain, spot) macchia
block [blɔk] n blocco; (in pipes) ingombro; (toy) cubo; (of buildings) isolato ▷ vt bloccare; **the sink is ~ed** il lavandino è otturato; **block up** vt bloccare; (pipe) ingorgare, intasare; **blockade** [blɔ'keɪd] n blocco; **blockage** n ostacolo; **blockbuster** n grande successo; **block capitals** npl stampatello; **block letters** npl stampatello
blog [blɔg] n blog m inv ▷ vi scrivere blog, bloggare
blogger ['blɔgə^r] n (Comput) blogger mf inv
blogging ['blɔgɪŋ] n blogging m ▷ adj: **~ website** sito di blogging
blogosphere ['blɔgəsfɪə^r] n blogosfera
bloke [bləʊk] n (BRIT col) tizio
blond(e) [blɔnd] n ▷ adj biondo/a
blood [blʌd] n sangue m; **blood donor** n donatore/trice di sangue; **blood group** n gruppo sanguigno; **blood poisoning** n setticemia; **blood pressure** n pressione f sanguigna; **bloodshed** n spargimento di sangue; **bloodshot** adj: **bloodshot eyes** occhi iniettati di sangue; **bloodstream** n flusso del sangue; **blood test** n analisi f inv del sangue; **blood transfusion** n trasfusione f di sangue; **blood type** n

gruppo sanguigno; **blood vessel** n vaso sanguigno; **bloody** adj (fight) sanguinoso/a; (nose) sanguinante; (BRIT col!): **this bloody …** questo maledetto …; **bloody awful/good** (col!) veramente terribile/buono; **a bloody awful day** (col!) una giornata di merda (!)

bloom [bluːm] n fiore m ▷ vi essere in fiore

blossom [ˈblɒsəm] n fiore m; (with pl sense) fiori mpl ▷ vi essere in fiore

blot [blɒt] n macchia ▷ vt macchiare

blouse [blauz] n camicetta

blow [bləʊ] (pt **blew**, pp **blown**) n colpo ▷ vi soffiare ▷ vt (fuse) far saltare; (wind) spingere; (instrument) suonare; **to ~ one's nose** soffiarsi il naso; **to ~ a whistle** fischiare; **blow away** vi volare via ▷ vt portare via; **blow out** vi scoppiare; **blow up** vi saltare in aria ▷ vt far saltare in aria; (tyre) gonfiare; (Phot) ingrandire; **blow-dry** n messa in piega a föhn

blown [bləʊn] pp of **blow**

blue [bluː] adj azzurro/a; (depressed) giù inv; **~ film/joke** film/barzelletta pornografico(a); **out of the ~** (fig) all'improvviso; **bluebell** n giacinto di bosco; **blueberry** n mirtillo; **blue cheese** n formaggio tipo gorgonzola; **blues** npl: **the blues** (Mus) il blues; **to have the blues** (col) (feeling) essere a terra; **bluetit** n cinciarella

bluff [blʌf] vi bluffare ▷ n bluff m inv ▷ adj (person) brusco/a; **to call sb's ~** mettere alla prova il bluff di qn

blunder [ˈblʌndəʳ] n abbaglio ▷ vi prendere un abbaglio

blunt [blʌnt] adj smussato/a; (point) spuntato/a; (person) brusco/a

blur [bləːʳ] n forma indistinta ▷ vt offuscare; **blurred** adj (photo) mosso/a; (TV) sfuocato/a

blush [blʌʃ] vi arrossire ▷ n rossore m; **blusher** n fard m inv

board [bɔːd] n tavola; (on wall) tabellone m; (committee) consiglio,

comitato; (in firm) consiglio d'amministrazione; (Naut, Aviat): **on ~** a bordo ▷ vi salire a bordo di; (train) salire su; **full ~** (BRIT) pensione f completa; **half ~** (BRIT) mezza pensione; **~ and lodging** vitto e alloggio; **to go by the ~** venir messo/a da parte; **board game** n gioco da tavolo; **boarding card** n (Aviat, Naut) carta d'imbarco; **boarding pass** n (BRIT) = **boarding card**; **boarding school** n collegio; **board room** n sala del consiglio

boast [bəʊst] vi: **to ~ (about or of)** vantarsi (di)

boat [bəʊt] n nave f; (small) barca

bob [bɒb] vi (boat, cork on water: also: **~ up and down**) andare su e giù

bobby pin [ˈbɒbɪ-] (US) n fermaglio per capelli

body [ˈbɒdɪ] n corpo; (of car) carrozzeria; (of plane) fusoliera; (fig: group) gruppo; (: organization) associazione f, organizzazione f; (quantity) quantità f inv; **body-building** n culturismo; **bodyguard** n guardia del corpo; **bodywork** n carrozzeria

bog [bɒg] n palude f ▷ vt: **to get ~ged down** (fig) impantanarsi

bogus [ˈbəʊgəs] adj falso/a; finto/a

boil [bɔɪl] vt, vi bollire ▷ n (Med) foruncolo; **to come to the** or (US) **a ~** raggiungere l'ebollizione; **~ed egg** uovo alla coque; **~ed potatoes** patate fpl bollite or lesse; **boil over** vi traboccare (bollendo); **boiler** n caldaia; **boiling** adj bollente; **I'm boiling (hot)** (col) sto morendo di caldo; **boiling point** n punto di ebollizione

bold [bəʊld] adj audace; (child) impudente; (colour) deciso/a

Bolivia [bəˈlɪvɪə] n Bolivia

Bolivian [bəˈlɪvɪən] adj, n boliviano/a

bollard [ˈbɒləd] n (Aut) colonnina luminosa

Bollywood [ˈbɒlɪwʊd] n Bollywood f

bolt [bəult] n chiavistello; (with nut) bullone m ⊳ adv: **~ upright** diritto/a come un fuso ⊳ vt serrare; (also: **~ together**) imbullonare; (food) mangiare in fretta ⊳ vi scappare via

bomb [bɔm] n bomba ⊳ vt bombardare; **bombard** [bɔm'bɑːd] vt bombardare; **bomber** n (Aviat) bombardiere m; (terrorist) dinamitardo/a; **bomb scare** n stato di allarme (per sospetta presenza di una bomba)

bond [bɔnd] n legame m; (binding promise, Finance) obbligazione f; (Comm): **in ~** in attesa di sdoganamento

bone [bəun] n osso; (of fish) spina, lisca ⊳ vt disossare; togliere le spine a

bonfire ['bɔnfaɪə'] n falò m inv

bonnet ['bɔnɪt] n cuffia; (BRIT: of car) cofano

bonus ['bəunəs] n premio; (fig) sovrappiù m inv

boo [buː] excl ba! ⊳ vt fischiare

book [buk] n libro; (of stamps etc) blocchetto ⊳ vt (ticket, seat, room) prenotare; (driver) multare; (football player) ammonire; **books** npl (Comm) conti mpl; **book in** vi (BRIT: at hotel) prendere una camera; **book up** vt riservare, prenotare; **the hotel is ~ed up** l'albergo è al completo; **all seats are ~ed up** è tutto esaurito; **bookcase** n libreria; **booking** n (BRIT) prenotazione f; **booking office** n (BRIT: Rail) biglietteria; (Theat) botteghino; **book-keeping** n contabilità; **booklet** n opuscolo, libriccino; **bookmaker** n allibratore m; **bookmark** n segnalibro ⊳ vt (Comput) mettere un segnalibro a; (Internet) aggiungere a "Preferiti"; **bookseller** n libraio; **bookshelf** n mensola (per libri); **bookshop** n libreria

boom [buːm] n (noise) rimbombo; (busy period) boom m inv ⊳ vi rimbombare; andare a gonfie vele

boost [buːst] n spinta ⊳ vt spingere

boot [buːt] n stivale m; (for hiking) scarpone m da montagna; (for football etc) scarpa; (BRIT: of car) portabagagli m inv ⊳ vt (Comput) inizializzare; **to ~** (in addition) per giunta, in più

booth [buːð] n (at fair) baraccone m; (of cinema, telephone etc) cabina

booze [buːz] (col) n alcool m

border ['bɔːdə'] n orlo; margine m; (of a country) frontiera; (for flowers) aiuola (laterale) ⊳ vt (road) costeggiare; **the B~s** la zona di confine tra l'Inghilterra e la Scozia; **border on** vt fus confinare con; **borderline** n: **on the borderline** incerto/a

bore [bɔː'] pt of **bear** ⊳ vt (hole) scavare; (person) annoiare ⊳ n (person) seccatore/trice; (of gun) calibro; **bored** adj annoiato/a; **to be bored** annoiarsi; **he's bored to tears** or **bored to death** or **bored stiff** è annoiato a morte; **boredom** n noia

boring ['bɔːrɪŋ] adj noioso/a

born [bɔːn] adj: **to be ~** nascere; **I was ~ in 1960** sono nato nel 1960

borne [bɔːn] pp of **bear**

borough ['bʌrə] n comune m

borrow ['bɔrəu] vt: **to ~ sth (from sb)** prendere in prestito qc (da qn)

Bosnia-Herzegovina ['bɔznɪəhɜːtzə'gəuviːnə] n Bosnia-Erzegovina; **Bosnian** ['bɔznɪən] adj, n bosniaco/a

bosom ['buzəm] n petto; (fig) seno

boss [bɔs] n capo ⊳ vt (also: **~ about** or **around**) comandare a bacchetta; **bossy** adj prepotente

both [bəuθ] adj entrambi/e, tutt'e due ⊳ pron: **~ of them** entrambi/e ⊳ adv: **they sell ~ meat and poultry** vendono insieme la carne ed il pollame; **~ of us went, we ~ went** ci siamo andati tutt'e due

bother ['bɔðə'] vt (worry) preoccupare; (annoy) infastidire ⊳ vi (also: **~ o.s.**) preoccuparsi ⊳ n: **it is a ~ to have to do** è una seccatura dover fare; **it was no ~** non c'era problema; **to ~ doing sth** darsi la pena di fare qc

bottle ['bɔtl] n bottiglia; (baby's) biberon m inv ⊳ vt imbottigliare; **bottle bank** n contenitore m per la raccolta del vetro; **bottle-opener** n apribottiglie m inv

bottom ['bɔtəm] n fondo; (buttocks) sedere m ⊳ adj più basso/a, ultimo/a; **at the ~ of** in fondo a

bought [bɔːt] pt, pp of **buy**

boulder ['bəuldər] n masso (tondeggiante)

bounce [bauns] vi (ball) rimbalzare; (cheque) essere restituito/a ⊳ vt far rimbalzare ⊳ n (rebound) rimbalzo; **bouncer** (col) n buttafuori m inv

bound [baund] pt, pp of **bind** ⊳ n (gen pl) limite m; (leap) salto ⊳ vi saltare ⊳ vt (limit) delimitare ⊳ adj: **~ by law** obbligato/a per legge; **to be ~ to do sth** (obliged) essere costretto/a a fare qc; **he's ~ to fail** (likely) fallirà di certo; **~ for** diretto/a a; **out of ~s** il cui accesso è vietato

boundary ['baundrɪ] n confine m

bouquet [buːkeɪ] n bouquet m inv

bourbon ['buəbən] n (us: also: **~ whiskey**) bourbon m inv

bout [baut] n periodo; (of malaria etc) attacco; (Boxing etc) incontro

boutique [buːtiːk] n boutique f inv

bow¹ [bəu] n nodo; (weapon) arco; (Mus) archetto

bow² [bau] n (with body) inchino; (Naut: also: **~s**) prua ⊳ vi inchinarsi; (yield): **to ~ to** or **before** sottomettersi a

bowels [bauəlz] npl intestini mpl; (fig) viscere fpl

bowl [bəul] n (for eating) scodella; (for washing) bacino; (ball) boccia ⊳ vi (Cricket) servire (la palla); **bowler** ['bəulər] n (Cricket) lanciatore m; (BRIT: also: **bowler hat**) bombetta; **bowling** ['bəulɪŋ] n (game) gioco delle bocce; **bowling alley** n pista da

bowling; **bowling green** n campo di bocce; **bowls** [bəulz] n gioco delle bocce

bow tie n cravatta a farfalla

box [bɔks] n scatola; (also: **cardboard ~**) (scatola di) cartone m; (Theat) palco ⊳ vi fare pugilato ⊳ vt mettere in (una) scatola, inscatolare; **boxer** n (person) pugile m; **boxer shorts** ['bɔksəfɔːts] npl boxer; **a pair of boxer shorts** un paio di boxer; **boxing** n (Sport) pugilato; **Boxing Day** n (BRIT) ≈ Santo Stefano; vedi nota **"Boxing Day"**; **boxing gloves** npl guantoni mpl da pugile; **boxing ring** n ring m inv; **box office** n biglietteria

- **BOXING DAY**

- Il Boxing Day è un giorno di festa
- e cade in genere il 26 dicembre.
- Prende il nome dall'usanza di
- donare pacchi regalo natalizi, un
- tempo chiamati "Christmas boxes", a
- fornitori e dipendenti.

boy [bɔɪ] n ragazzo

boycott ['bɔɪkɔt] n boicottaggio ⊳ vt boicottare

boyfriend ['bɔɪfrɛnd] n ragazzo

bra [brɑː] n reggipetto, reggiseno

brace [breɪs] n (on teeth) apparecchio correttore; (tool) trapano ⊳ vt rinforzare, sostenere; **to ~ o.s.** (fig) farsi coraggio; see also **braces**

bracelet ['breɪslɪt] n braccialetto

braces ['breɪsɪz] npl (BRIT) bretelle fpl

bracket ['brækɪt] n (Tech) mensola; (group) gruppo; (Typ) parentesi f inv ⊳ vt mettere fra parentesi

brag [bræg] vi vantarsi

braid [breɪd] n (trimming) passamano; (of hair) treccia

brain [breɪn] n cervello; **brains** npl (intelligence) cervella fpl; **he's got ~s** è intelligente

braise [breɪz] vt brasare

brake [breɪk] n (on vehicle) freno ▷ vi frenare; **brake light** n (fanalino dello) stop m inv

bran [bræn] n crusca

branch [brɑːntʃ] n ramo; (Comm) succursale f; **branch off** vi diramarsi; **branch out** vi: **to ~ out into** intraprendere una nuova attività nel ramo di

brand [brænd] n marca; (fig) tipo ▷ vt (cattle) marcare (a ferro rovente); **brand name** n marca; **brand-new** adj nuovo/a di zecca

brandy ['brændɪ] n brandy m inv

brash [bræʃ] adj sfacciato/a

brass [brɑːs] n ottone m; **the ~** (Mus) gli ottoni; **brass band** n fanfara

brat [bræt] n (pej) marmocchio, monello/a

brave [breɪv] adj coraggioso/a ▷ vt affrontare; **bravery** n coraggio

brawl [brɔːl] n rissa

Brazil [brə'zɪl] n Brasile m; **Brazilian** adj, n brasiliano/a

breach [briːtʃ] vt aprire una breccia in ▷ n (gap) breccia, varco; (breaking): **~ of contract** rottura di contratto; **~ of the peace** violazione f dell'ordine pubblico

bread [brɛd] n pane m; **breadbin** n cassetta f portapane inv; **breadbox** n (us) cassetta f portapane inv; **breadcrumbs** npl briciole fpl; (Culin) pangrattato

breadth [brɛtθ] n larghezza; (fig: of knowledge etc) ampiezza

break [breɪk] (pt **broke**, pp **broken**) vt rompere; (law) violare ▷ vi rompersi; (storm) scoppiare; (weather) cambiare; (dawn) spuntare; (news) saltare fuori ▷ n (gap) breccia; (fracture) rottura; (rest, also Scol) intervallo; (: short) pausa; (chance) possibilità f inv; **to ~ one's leg** etc rompersi la gamba etc; **to ~ a record** battere un primato; **to ~ the news to sb** comunicare per primo la notizia a qn; **to ~ even** coprire le

spese; **~ free** or **loose** liberarsi; **break down** vt (figures, data) analizzare; (door etc) buttare giù, abbattere; (resistance) stroncare ▷ vi crollare; (Med) avere un esaurimento (nervoso); (Aut) guastarsi; **break in** vt (horse etc) domare ▷ vi (burglar) fare irruzione; **break into** vt fus (house) fare irruzione in; **break off** vi (speaker) interrompersi; (branch) troncarsi ▷ vt (talks, engagement) rompere; **break out** vi evadere; **to ~ out in spots** coprirsi di macchie; **break up** vi (partnership) sciogliersi; (friends) separarsi; **the line's** or **you're ~ing up** la linea è disturbata ▷ vt fare in pezzi, spaccare; (fight etc) interrompere, far cessare; (marriage) finire; **breakdown** n (Aut) guasto; (in communications) interruzione f; (of marriage) rottura; (Med: also: **nervous breakdown**) esaurimento nervoso; (of payments, statistics etc) resoconto; **breakdown truck, breakdown van** n carro m attrezzi inv

breakfast ['brɛkfəst] n colazione f

break-in n irruzione f;

breakthrough n (fig) passo avanti

breast [brɛst] n (of woman) seno; (chest, Culin) petto; **breast-feed** vt, vi (irreg: like **feed**) allattare (al seno); **breast-stroke** n nuoto a rana

breath [brɛθ] n respiro; **out of ~** senza fiato

Breathalyser® ['brɛθəlaɪzəʳ] (BRIT) n alcoltest m inv

breathe [briːð] vt, vi respirare; **breathe in** vi inspirare ▷ vt respirare; **breathe out** vi, vt espirare; **breathing** n respiro, respirazione f

breath: breathless ['brɛθlɪs] adj senza fiato; **breathtaking** ['brɛθteɪkɪŋ] adj mozzafiato inv; **breath test** n ≈ prova del palloncino

bred [brɛd] pt, pp of **breed**

breed [briːd] (pt, pp **bred**) vt allevare ▷ vi riprodursi ▷ n razza; (type, class) varietà f inv

breeze [briːz] n brezza
breezy ['briːzɪ] adj allegro/a
brew [bruː] vt (tea) fare un infuso
di; (beer) fare ▷ vi (storm, fig: trouble
etc) prepararsi; **brewery** n fabbrica
di birra
bribe [braɪb] n bustarella ▷ vt
comprare; **bribery** n corruzione f
bric-a-brac ['brɪkəbræk] n bric-
a-brac m
brick [brɪk] n mattone m; **bricklayer**
n muratore m
bride [braɪd] n sposa; **bridegroom**
n sposo; **bridesmaid** n damigella
d'onore
bridge [brɪdʒ] n ponte m; (Naut)
ponte di comando; (of nose) dorso;
(Cards, Dentistry) bridge m inv ▷ vt (fig:
gap) colmare
bridle ['braɪdl] n briglia
brief [briːf] adj breve ▷ n (Law)
comparsa; (gen) istruzioni fpl ▷ vt:
to ~ sb (about sth) mettere qn
al corrente (di qc); see also **briefs**;
briefcase n cartella; **briefing**
n istruzioni fpl, briefing m inv;
briefly adv (speak, visit, explain, say)
brevemente; (glimpse, glance) di
sfuggita
brigadier [brɪgə'dɪər] n generale m
di brigata
bright [braɪt] adj luminoso/a;
(person) sveglio/a; (colour) vivace
brilliant ['brɪljənt] adj brillante;
(light, smile) radioso/a; (col)
splendido/a
brim [brɪm] n orlo
brine [braɪn] n (Culin) salamoia
bring (pt, pp **brought**) [brɪŋ, brɔːt]
vt portare; **bring about** vt causare;
bring back vt riportare; **bring down**
vt (lower) far scendere; (shoot down)
abbattere; (government) far cadere;
bring in vt (person) fare entrare;
(object) portare; (Pol: bill) presentare;
(: legislation) introdurre; (Law: verdict)
emettere; (produce: income) rendere;
bring on vt (illness, attack) causare,

provocare; (player, substitute) far
scendere in campo; **bring out** vt
(meaning) mettere in evidenza; (new
product) lanciare; (book) pubblicare,
fare uscire; **bring up** vt allevare;
(question) introdurre
brink [brɪŋk] n orlo
brisk [brɪsk] adj (person, tone)
spiccio/a; (trade etc) vivace; (pace)
svelto/a
bristle ['brɪsl] n setola ▷ vi rizzarsi;
bristling with irto/a di
Brit [brɪt] n abbr (col) (= British person)
britannico/a
Britain ['brɪtən] n (also: **Great ~**)
Gran Bretagna
British ['brɪtɪʃ] adj britannico/a; **the
~ Isles** n pl le Isole Britanniche
Briton ['brɪtən] n britannico/a
brittle ['brɪtl] adj fragile
broad [brɔːd] adj largo/a; (distinction)
generale; (accent) spiccato/a;
in ~ daylight in pieno giorno;
broadband adj (Comput) a banda
larga, ADSL ▷ n banda larga,
ADSL m inv; **broad bean** n fava;
broadcast (pt, pp **broadcast**) n
trasmissione f ▷ vt trasmettere per
radio (or per televisione) ▷ vi fare una
trasmissione; **broaden** vt allargare
▷ vi allargarsi; **broadly** adv (fig) in
generale; **broad-minded** adj di
mente aperta
broccoli ['brɔkəlɪ] n broccoli mpl
brochure ['brəuʃjuər] n dépliant
m inv
broil [brɔɪl] vt cuocere a fuoco vivo
broiler ['brɔɪlər] (us) n (grill) griglia
broke [brəuk] pt of **break** ▷ adj (col)
squattrinato/a
broken ['brəukən] pp of **break** ▷ adj
rotto/a; **a ~ leg** una gamba rotta; **in
~ French/English** in un francese/
inglese stentato
broker ['brəukər] n agente m
bronchitis [brɔŋ'kaɪtɪs] n
bronchite f
bronze [brɔnz] n bronzo

brooch [brəʊtʃ] n spilla
brood [bru:d] n covata ▷ vi (person) rimuginare
broom [brum] n scopa; (Bot) ginestra
Bros. abbr (= brothers) F.lli
broth [brɒθ] n brodo
brothel ['brɒθəl] n bordello
brother ['brʌðər] n fratello; **brother-in-law** n cognato
brought [brɔ:t] pt, pp of **bring**
brow [braʊ] n fronte f; (rare, gen: also: **eye~**) sopracciglio; (of hill) cima
brown [braʊn] adj bruno/a, marrone; (tanned) abbronzato/a ▷ n (colour) color m bruno or marrone ▷ vt (Culin) rosolare; **brown bread** n pane m integrale, pane nero
Brownie ['braʊnɪ] n giovane esploratrice f
brown rice n riso greggio
brown sugar n zucchero greggio
browse [braʊz] vi (in bookshop etc) curiosare; **to ~ through a book** sfogliare un libro; **browser** n (Comput) browser m inv
bruise [bru:z] n (on person) livido ▷ vt farsi un livido a
brunette [bru:'nɛt] n bruna
brush [brʌʃ] n spazzola; (for painting, shaving) pennello; (quarrel) schermaglia ▷ vt spazzolare; (also: ~ past, ~ against) sfiorare
Brussels ['brʌslz] n Bruxelles f; **Brussels sprout** [spraʊt] n cavolo di Bruxelles
brutal ['bru:tl] adj brutale
BSc n abbr (Univ) = **Bachelor of Science**
BSE n abbr (= bovine spongiform encephalopathy) encefalite f bovina spongiforme
bubble ['bʌbl] n bolla ▷ vi ribollire; (sparkle, fig) essere effervescente; **bubble bath** n bagno m schiuma inv; **bubble gum** n gomma americana
buck [bʌk] n maschio (di camoscio, caprone, coniglio ecc); (US col) dollaro ▷ vi sgroppare; **to pass the ~ (to**

sb) scaricare (su di qn) la propria responsabilità
bucket ['bʌkɪt] n secchio; **bucket list** n elenco di cose da fare prima di morire
buckle ['bʌkl] n fibbia ▷ vt allacciare ▷ vi (wheel etc) piegarsi
bud [bʌd] n gemma; (of flower) bocciolo ▷ vi germogliare; (flower) sbocciare
Buddhism ['bʊdɪzəm] n buddismo
Buddhist ['bʊdɪst] adj, n buddista (m/f)
buddy ['bʌdɪ] n (US) compagno
budge [bʌdʒ] vt scostare; (fig) smuovere ▷ vi spostarsi; smuoversi
budgerigar ['bʌdʒərɪgɑ:r] n pappagallino
budget ['bʌdʒɪt] n bilancio preventivo ▷ vi: **to ~ for sth** fare il bilancio per qc
budgie ['bʌdʒɪ] n = **budgerigar**
buff [bʌf] adj color camoscio inv ▷ n (col: enthusiast) appassionato/a
buffalo ['bʌfələʊ] (pl **buffalo** or **buffaloes**) n bufalo; (US) bisonte m
buffer ['bʌfər] n respingente m; (Comput) memoria tampone, buffer m inv ▷ vi (Comput) fare il buffering, trasferire nella memoria tampone; **buffering** n buffering m inv, trasferimento nella memoria tampone
buffet n ['bʊfeɪ] (food, BRIT: bar) buffet m inv ▷ vt ['bʌfɪt] sferzare; **buffet car** n (BRIT Rail) ≈ servizio ristoro
bug [bʌg] n (insect) insetto; (fig: germ) virus m inv; (spy device) microfono spia; (Comput) bug m inv ▷ vt mettere sotto controllo; (annoy) scocciare
buggy ['bʌgɪ] n (baby buggy) passeggino
build [bɪld] n (of person) corporatura ▷ vt (pt, pp **built**) costruire; **build up** vt (reputation) consolidare; (increase) incrementare; **builder** n costruttore m; **building** n costruzione f; edificio; (also: **building trade**) edilizia; **building site** n cantiere m

di costruzione; **building society** n società immobiliare e finanziaria
built [bɪlt] pt, pp of **build; built-in** adj (cupboard) a muro; (device) incorporato/a; **built-up area** ['bɪltʌp-] n abitato
bulb [bʌlb] n (Bot) bulbo; (Elec) lampadina
Bulgaria [bʌl'gɛərɪə] n Bulgaria; **Bulgarian** adj bulgaro/a ▷ n bulgaro/a; (Ling) bulgaro
bulge [bʌldʒ] n rigonfiamento ▷ vi essere protuberante or rigonfio/a; **to be bulging with** essere pieno/aor zeppo/a di
bulimia [bə'lɪmɪə] n bulimia
bulimic [bjuː'lɪmɪk] adj, n bulimico/a
bulk [bʌlk] n massa, volume m; **the ~ of** il grosso di; **(to buy) in ~** (comprare) in grande quantità; (Comm) (comprare) all'ingrosso; **bulky** adj grosso/a, voluminoso/a
bull [bul] n toro m; (male elephant, whale) maschio
bulldozer ['buldəuzəʳ] n bulldozer m inv
bullet ['bulɪt] n pallottola
bulletin ['bulɪtɪn] n bollettino; **bulletin board** n (Comput) bulletin board m inv
bullfight ['bulfaɪt] n corrida; **bullfighter** n torero; **bullfighting** n tauromachia
bully ['bulɪ] n prepotente m ▷ vt angariare; (frighten) intimidire
bum [bʌm] n (col: backside) culo; (tramp) vagabondo/a
bumblebee ['bʌmblbiː] n bombo
bump [bʌmp] n (in car) piccolo tamponamento; (jolt) scossa; (on road etc) protuberanza; (on head) bernoccolo ▷ vt battere; **bump into** vt fus scontrarsi con; (meet) imbattersi in; **bumper** n paraurti m inv ▷ adj: **bumper harvest** raccolto eccezionale; **bumpy** ['bʌmpɪ] adj (road) dissestato/a
bun [bʌn] n focaccia; (of hair) crocchia

bunch [bʌntʃ] n (of flowers, keys) mazzo; (of bananas) casco; (of people) gruppo; **~ of grapes** grappolo d'uva; **bunches** npl (in hair) codine fpl
bundle ['bʌndl] n fascio ▷ vt (also: **~ up**) legare in un fascio; (put): **to ~ sth/sb into** spingere qc/qn in
bungalow ['bʌngələu] n bungalow m inv
bungee jumping ['bʌndʒiː'dʒʌmpɪŋ] n salto nel vuoto da ponti, grattacieli ecc con un cavo fissato alla caviglia
bunion ['bʌnjən] n callo (al piede)
bunk [bʌŋk] n cuccetta; **bunk beds** npl letti mpl a castello
bunker ['bʌŋkəʳ] n (coal store) ripostiglio per il carbone; (Mil, Golf) bunker m inv
bunny ['bʌnɪ] n (also: **~ rabbit**) coniglietto
buoy [bɔɪ] n boa; **buoyant** adj galleggiante; (fig) vivace
burden ['bəːdn] n carico, fardello ▷ vt caricare; **to ~ sb with** caricare qn di
bureau (pl **bureaux**) ['bjuərəu, -z] n (BRIT: writing desk) scrivania; (US: chest of drawers) cassettone m; (office) ufficio, agenzia
bureaucracy [bjuə'rɔkrəsɪ] n burocrazia
bureaucrat ['bjuərəkræt] n burocrate m/f
bureau de change [-də'ʃɑ̃ʒ] (pl **bureaux de change**) n cambiavalute m inv
bureaux [bjuə'rəuz] npl of **bureau**
burger ['bəːgəʳ] n hamburger m inv
burglar ['bəːgləʳ] n scassinatore m; **burglar alarm** n (allarme m) antifurto m inv; **burglary** n furto con scasso
burial ['bɛrɪəl] n sepoltura
burn [bəːn] vt, vi (pt, pp **burned** or **burnt**) bruciare ▷ n bruciatura, scottatura; **burn down** vt distruggere col fuoco; **burn out** vt (writer etc): **to ~ o.s. out** esaurirsi;

burning adj in fiamme; (sand) che scotta; (ambition) bruciante

Burns Night n vedi nota "Burns Night"

burnt [bəːnt] pt, pp of **burn**

burp [bəːp] (col) n rutto ▷ vi ruttare

burrow ['bʌrəu] n tana ▷ vt scavare

burst [bəːst] (pt, pp **burst**) vt far scoppiare or esplodere ▷ vi esplodere; (tyre) scoppiare ▷ n scoppio; (also: ~ pipe) rottura nel tubo, perdita; **a ~ of speed** uno scatto (di velocità); **to ~ into flames/tears** scoppiare in fiamme/lacrime; **to be ~ing with** essere pronto a scoppiare di; **to ~ out laughing** scoppiare a ridere; **burst into** vt fus (room etc) irrompere in

bury ['bɛrɪ] vt seppellire

bus [bʌs] (pl **buses**) n autobus m inv; **bus conductor** n autista m/f (dell'autobus)

bush [buʃ] n cespuglio; (scrub land) macchia; **to beat about the ~** menare il cane per l'aia

business ['bɪznɪs] n (matter) affare m; (trading) affari mpl; (firm) azienda; (job, duty) lavoro; **to be away on ~** essere andato via per affari; **it's none of my ~** questo non mi riguarda; **he means ~** non scherza; **business class** n (Aviat) business class f; **businesslike** adj serio/a; efficiente; **businessman** n (irreg) uomo d'affari; **business trip** n

viaggio d'affari; **businesswoman** n (irreg) donna d'affari

busker ['bʌskə'] n (BRIT) suonatore/trice ambulante

bus: **bus pass** n tessera dell'autobus; **bus shelter** n pensilina (alla fermata dell'autobus); **bus station** n stazione f delle corriere, autostazione f; **bus stop** n fermata d'autobus

bust [bʌst] n busto; (Anat) seno ▷ adj (col: broken) rotto/a; **to go ~** fallire

bustling ['bʌslɪŋ] adj animato/a

busy ['bɪzɪ] adj occupato/a; (shop, street) molto frequentato/a ▷ vt: **to ~ o.s.** darsi da fare; **busy signal** n (US Tel) segnale m di occupato

KEYWORD

but [bʌt] conj ma; **I'd love to come, but I'm busy** vorrei tanto venire, ma ho da fare

▶ prep (apart from, except) eccetto, tranne, meno; **he was nothing but trouble** non dava altro che guai; **no-one but him can do it** nessuno può farlo tranne lui; **but for you/your help** se non fosse per te/per il tuo aiuto; **anything but that** tutto ma non questo

▶ adv (just, only) solo, soltanto; **she's but a child** è solo una bambina; **had I but known** se solo avessi saputo; **I can but try** tentar non nuoce; **all but finished** quasi finito

butcher ['butʃə'] n macellaio ▷ vt macellare; **~'s (shop)** macelleria

butler ['bʌtlə'] n maggiordomo

butt [bʌt] n (cask) grossa botte f; (of gun) calcio; (of cigarette) mozzicone m; (BRIT fig: target) oggetto ▷ vt cozzare

butter ['bʌtə'] n burro ▷ vt imburrare; **buttercup** n ranuncolo

butterfly ['bʌtəflaɪ] n farfalla; (Swimming: also: ~ **stroke**) (nuoto a) farfalla

buttocks ['bʌtəks] *npl* natiche *fpl*
button ['bʌtn] *n* bottone *m*; (*US: badge*) distintivo ▷ *vt* (*also:* **~ up**) abbottonare ▷ *vi* abbottonarsi
buy [baɪ] *vt* (*pt, pp* **bought**) comprare ▷ *n* acquisto; **to ~ sb sth/sth from sb** comprare qc per qn/qc da qn; **to ~ sb a drink** offrire da bere a qn; **buy out** *vt* (*business*) rilevare; **buy up** *vt* accaparrare; **buyer** *n* compratore/trice
buzz [bʌz] *n* ronzio; (*col: phone call*) colpo di telefono ▷ *vi* ronzare; **buzzer** ['bʌzər] *n* cicalino

KEYWORD

by [baɪ] *prep* **1** (*referring to cause, agent*) da; **killed by lightning** ucciso da un fulmine; **surrounded by a fence** circondato da uno steccato; **a painting by Picasso** un quadro di Picasso
2 (*referring to method, manner, means*): **by bus/car/train** in autobus/macchina/treno, con l'autobus/la macchina/il treno; **to pay by cheque** pagare con (un) assegno; **by moonlight** al chiaro di luna; **by saving hard, he ...** risparmiando molto, lui ...
3 (*via, through*) per; **we came by Dover** siamo venuti via Dover
4 (*close to, past*) accanto a; **the house by the river** la casa sul fiume; **a holiday by the sea** una vacanza al mare; **she sat by his bed** si sedette accanto al suo letto; **she rushed by me** mi è passata accanto correndo; **I go by the post office every day** passo davanti all'ufficio postale ogni giorno
5 (*not later than*) per, entro; **by 4 o'clock** per *or* entro le 4; **by this time tomorrow** domani a quest'ora; **by the time I got here it was too late** quando sono arrivato era ormai troppo tardi

6 (*during*): **by day/night** di giorno/notte
7 (*amount*) a; **by the kilo** a chili; **paid by the hour** pagato all'ora; **one by one** uno per uno; **little by little** a poco a poco
8 (*Math: measure*): **to divide/multiply by 3** dividere/moltiplicare per 3; **it's broader by a metre** è un metro più largo, è più largo di un metro
9 (*according to*) per; **to play by the rules** attenersi alle regole; **it's all right by me** per me va bene
10: **(all) by oneself** (tutto/a) solo/a; **he did it (all) by himself** lo ha fatto (tutto) da solo
11: **by the way** a proposito; **this wasn't my idea by the way** tra l'altro l'idea non è stata mia
▷ *adv* **1** *see* **go**; **pass** *etc*
2: **by and by** (*in past*) poco dopo; (*in future*) fra breve; **by and large** nel complesso

bye(-bye) ['baɪ('baɪ)] *excl* ciao!, arrivederci!
by-election ['baɪɪlɛkʃən] *n* (*BRIT*) elezione *f* straordinaria
bypass ['baɪpɑːs] *n* circonvallazione *f*; (*Med*) by-pass *m inv* ▷ *vt* fare una deviazione intorno a
byte [baɪt] *n* (*Comput*) byte *m inv*, bicarattere *m*

C

C [si:] n (Mus) do
cab [kæb] n taxi m inv; (of train, truck) cabina
cabaret ['kæbəreɪ] n cabaret m inv
cabbage ['kæbɪdʒ] n cavolo
cabin ['kæbɪn] n capanna; (on ship) cabina; **cabin crew** n equipaggio
cabinet ['kæbɪnɪt] n (Pol) consiglio dei ministri; (furniture) armadietto; (also: **display ~**) vetrinetta; **cabinet minister** n ministro (membro del Consiglio)
cable ['keɪbl] n cavo; fune f; (Tel) cablogramma m ▷ vt telegrafare; **cable-car** n funivia; **cable television** n televisione f via cavo
cactus (pl **cacti**) ['kæktəs, -taɪ] n cactus m inv
café ['kæfeɪ] n caffè m inv
cafeteria [kæfɪ'tɪərɪə] n self-service m inv
caffein(e) ['kæfi:n] n caffeina
cage [keɪdʒ] n gabbia

cagoule [kə'gu:l] n K-way® m inv
cake [keɪk] n (large) torta; (small) pasticcino; **~ of soap** saponetta
calcium ['kælsɪəm] n calcio
calculate ['kælkjuleɪt] vt calcolare; **calculation** [kælkju'leɪʃən] n calcolo; **calculator** n calcolatrice f
calendar ['kæləndər] n calendario
calf (pl **calves**) [kɑ:f, kɑ:vz] n (of cow) vitello; (of other animals) piccolo; (also: **~skin**) (pelle f di) vitello; (Anat) polpaccio
calibre, (us) **caliber** ['kælɪbər] n calibro
call [kɔ:l] vt (gen, also Tel) chiamare; (meeting, strike) indire ▷ vi chiamare; (visit: also: **~ in**, **~ round**) passare ▷ n (shout) grido, urlo; (also: **telephone ~**) telefonata; **to be ~ed** (person, object) chiamarsi; **to be on ~** essere a disposizione; **call back** vi (return) ritornare; (Tel) ritelefonare, richiamare; **can you ~ back later?** può richiamare più tardi?; **call for** vt fus richiedere; (collect) passare a prendere; **call in** vt (doctor, expert, police) chiamare, far venire; **call off** vt disdire; **call on** vt fus (visit) passare da; (request): **to ~ on sb to do** chiedere a qn di fare; **call out** vi (in pain) urlare; (to person) chiamare; **call up** vt (Mil) richiamare; (Tel) telefonare a; **callbox** n (BRIT) cabina telefonica; **call centre**, (us) **call center** n centro informazioni telefoniche; **caller** n persona che chiama; visitatore/trice
callous ['kæləs] adj indurito/a, insensibile
calm [kɑ:m] adj calmo/a ▷ n calma ▷ vt calmare; **calm down** vi calmarsi ▷ vt calmare; **calmly** adv con calma
Calor gas® ['kælər-] n butano
calorie ['kælərɪ] n caloria
calves [kɑ:vz] npl of **calf**
camcorder ['kæmkɔ:dər] n videocamera
came [keɪm] pt of **come**

camel ['kæməl] n cammello
camera ['kæmərə] n macchina
fotografica; (Cine, TV) cinepresa; **in ~**
a porte chiuse; **cameraman** n (irreg)
cameraman m inv; **camera phone**
n telefono cellulare con fotocamera
integrata
camouflage ['kæməflɑːʒ] n
(Mil, Zool) mimetizzazione f ▷ vt
mimetizzare
camp [kæmp] n campeggio; (Mil)
campo ▷ vi accamparsi ▷ adj
effeminato/a
campaign [kæm'peɪn] n (Mil, Pol etc)
campagna ▷ vi: **to ~ (for/against)**
(also fig) fare una campagna (per/
contro); **campaigner** n: **campaigner
for** fautore/trice di; **campaigner
against** oppositore/trice di
camp: campbed n (BRIT)
brandina; **camper** ['kæmpəʳ] n
campeggiatore/trice; (vehicle)
camper m inv; **campground** n (US)
campeggio; **camping** ['kæmpɪŋ]
n campeggio; **to go camping**
andare in campeggio; **camp site**
['kæmpsaɪt] n campeggio
campus ['kæmpəs] n campus m inv
can¹ [kæn] n (of milk) scatola; (of
oil) bidone m; (of water) tanica; (tin)
scatola ▷ vt mettere in scatola

KEYWORD

can² [kæn] (negative **cannot, can't**,
conditional, pt **could**) aux vb **1** (be able
to) potere; **I can't go any further**
non posso andare oltre; **you can
do it if you try** sei in grado di farlo –
basta provarci; **I'll help you all I can**
ti aiuterò come potrò; **I can't see
you** non ti vedo
2 (know how to) sapere, essere capace
di; **I can swim** so nuotare; **can you
speak French?** parla francese?
3 (may) potere; **could I have a
word with you?** posso parlarle un
momento?

4 (expressing disbelief, puzzlement etc):
it can't be true! non può essere
vero!; **what CAN he want?** cosa può
mai volere?
5 (expressing possibility, suggestion etc):
he could be in the library può darsi
che sia in biblioteca; **she could have
been delayed** può aver avuto un
contrattempo

Canada ['kænədə] n Canada m;
Canadian [kə'neɪdɪən] adj, n
canadese (m/f)
canal [kə'næl] n canale m
canary [kə'nɛərɪ] n canarino
Canary Islands, Canaries
[kə'nɛərɪz] npl: **the ~** le (isole)
Canarie
cancel ['kænsəl] vt annullare; (train)
sopprimere; (cross out) cancellare;
cancellation [kænsə'leɪʃən] n
annullamento; soppressione
f; cancellazione f; (Tourism)
prenotazione f annullata
cancer ['kænsəʳ] n cancro, **C~** (sign)
Cancro
candidate ['kændɪdeɪt] n
candidato/a
candle ['kændl] n candela; (in church)
cero; **candlestick** n bugia; (bigger,
ornate) candeliere m
candy ['kændɪ] n zucchero candito;
(US) caramella; caramelle fpl;
candy bar (US) n lungo biscotto, in
genere ricoperto di cioccolata; **candy-
floss** ['kændɪflɔs] n (BRIT) zucchero
filato
cane [keɪn] n canna; (for baskets,
chairs etc) bambù m; (Scol) verga ▷ vt
(BRIT Scol) punire a colpi di verga
canister ['kænɪstəʳ] n scatola
metallica
cannabis ['kænəbɪs] n canapa
indiana
canned ['kænd] adj (food) in scatola
cannon ['kænən] (pl **cannon** or
cannons) n (gun) cannone m
cannot ['kænɔt] = **can not**

canoe [kə'nu:] n canoa; **canoeing** n canottaggio

canon ['kænən] n (clergyman) canonico; (standard) canone m

can opener [-əunpər] n apriscatole m inv

can't [kænt] = **can not**

canteen [kæn'ti:n] n mensa; (BRIT: of cutlery) portaposate m inv
> Be careful not to translate canteen by the Italian word cantina.

canter ['kæntər] vi andare al piccolo galoppo

canvas ['kænvəs] n tela

canvass ['kænvəs] vi (Pol): **to ~ for** raccogliere voti per ▷ vt fare un sondaggio di

canyon ['kænjən] n canyon m inv

cap [kæp] n (also BRIT Football: hat) berretto; (of pen) coperchio; (of bottle) tappo; (contraceptive) diaframma m ▷ vt (outdo) superare; (limit) fissare un tetto (a)

capability [keɪpə'bɪlɪtɪ] n capacità f inv, abilità f inv

capable ['keɪpəbl] adj capace

capacity [kə'pæsɪtɪ] n capacità f inv; (of lift etc) capienza

cape [keɪp] n (garment) cappa; (Geo) capo

caper ['keɪpər] n (Culin) cappero; (prank) scherzetto

capital ['kæpɪtl] n (also: ~ city) capitale f; (money) capitale m; (also: ~ letter) (lettera) maiuscola; **capitalism** n capitalismo; **capitalist** adj, n capitalista (m/f); **capital punishment** n pena capitale

Capitol ['kæpɪtl] n: **the ~** il Campidoglio

Capricorn ['kæprɪkɔ:n] n Capricorno

capsize [kæp'saɪz] vt capovolgere ▷ vi capovolgersi

capsule ['kæpsju:l] n capsula

captain ['kæptɪn] n capitano

caption ['kæpʃən] n leggenda

captivity [kæp'tɪvɪtɪ] n prigionia

capture ['kæptʃər] vt catturare; (Comput) registrare ▷ n cattura; (data capture) registrazione f or rilevazione f di dati

car [kɑ:r] n macchina, automobile f; (Rail) vagone m

carafe [kə'ræf] n caraffa

caramel ['kærəməl] n caramello

carat ['kærət] n carato; **18 ~ gold** oro a 18 carati

caravan ['kærəvæn] n (BRIT) roulotte f inv; (of camels) carovana; **caravan site** n (BRIT) campeggio per roulotte

carbohydrate [kɑ:bəu'haɪdreɪt] n carboidrato

carbon ['kɑ:bən] n carbonio; **carbon copy** n copia f carbone inv; **carbon dioxide** [-daɪ'ɔksaɪd] n diossido di carbonio; **carbon footprint** n impronta di carbonio; **carbon monoxide** [-mɔ'nɔksaɪd] n monossido di carbonio; **carbon-neutral** adj carbon neutral, ad emissioni zero CO_2

car boot sale n vedi nota **"car boot sale"**

- **CAR BOOT SALE**
-
- Il car boot sale è un mercatino
- dell'usato molto popolare in Gran
- Bretagna. Normalmente ha luogo
- in un parcheggio o in un grande
- spiazzo, e la merce viene in genere
- esposta nei bagagliai, in inglese
- appunto "boots", aperti delle
- macchine.

carburettor, (US) **carburetor** [kɑ:bju'retər] n carburatore m

card [kɑ:d] n carta; (visiting card etc) biglietto; (Christmas card etc) cartolina; **cardboard** n cartone m; **card game** n gioco di carte

cardigan ['kɑ:dɪgən] n cardigan m inv

cardinal ['kɑ:dɪnl] adj, n cardinale (m)

cardphone ['kɑːdfəun] n telefono a scheda (magnetica)

care [kɛəʳ] n cura, attenzione f; (worry) preoccupazione f ▷ vi: **to ~ about** curarsi di; (thing, idea) interessarsi di; **in sb's ~** alle cure di qn; **to take ~** fare attenzione; **to take ~ of** curarsi di; (details, arrangements, bill, problem) occuparsi di; **I don't ~** non me ne importa; **I couldn't ~ less** non me ne importa un bel niente; **~ of (c/o)** presso; **care for** vt fus aver cura di; (like) voler bene a

career [kə'rɪəʳ] n carriera ▷ vi (also: **~ along**) andare di (gran) carriera

care: carefree ['kɛəfriː] adj sgombro/a di preoccupazioni; **careful** ['kɛəful] adj attento/a; (cautious) cauto/a; **(be) careful!** attenzione!; **carefully** adv con cura; cautamente; **caregiver** (US) n (professional) badante m/f; (unpaid) persona che si prende cura di un parente malato o anziano; **careless** ['kɛəlɪs] adj negligente; (heedless) spensierato/a; **carelessness** n negligenza, mancanza di tatto; **carer** ['kɛərəʳ] n chi si occupa di un familiare anziano o invalido; **caretaker** ['kɛəteɪkəʳ] n custode m

car-ferry ['kɑːfɛrɪ] n traghetto

cargo ['kɑːgəu] (pl **cargoes**) n carico

car hire n autonoleggio

Caribbean [kærɪ'biːən] adj: **the ~ (Sea)** il Mar dei Caraibi

caring ['kɛərɪŋ] adj (person) premuroso/a; (society, organization) umanitario/a

carnation [kɑː'neɪʃən] n garofano

carnival ['kɑːnɪvəl] n (public celebration) carnevale m; (US: funfair) luna park m inv

carol ['kærəl] n: **(Christmas) ~** canto di Natale

carousel [kærə'sɛl] n (US) giostra

car park n (BRIT) parcheggio

carpenter ['kɑːpɪntəʳ] n carpentiere m

carpet ['kɑːpɪt] n tappeto ▷ vt coprire con tappeto

car rental n (US) autonoleggio

carriage ['kærɪdʒ] n vettura; (of goods) trasporto; **carriageway** n (BRIT: part of road) carreggiata

carrier ['kærɪəʳ] n (of disease) portatore/trice; (Comm) impresa di trasporti; **carrier bag** n (BRIT) sacchetto

carrot ['kærət] n carota

carry ['kærɪ] vt (person) portare; (vehicle) trasportare; (involve: responsibilities etc) comportare; (Med) essere portatore/trice di ▷ vi (sound) farsi sentire; **to be** or **get carried away** (fig) farsi trascinare; **carry on** vi: **to ~ on with sth/doing** continuare qc/a fare ▷ vt mandare avanti; **carry out** vt (orders) eseguire; (investigation) svolgere

cart [kɑːt] n carro ▷ vt (col) trascinare

carton ['kɑːtən] n (box) scatola di cartone; (of yogurt) cartone m; (of cigarettes) stecca

cartoon [kɑː'tuːn] n (in newspaper etc) vignetta; (comic strip) fumetto; (Cine, TV) cartone m animato

cartridge ['kɑːtrɪdʒ] n (for gun, pen) cartuccia; (music tape) cassetta

carve [kɑːv] vt (meat) trinciare; (wood, stone) intagliare; **carving** n (in wood etc) scultura

car wash n lavaggio auto

case [keɪs] n caso; (Law) causa, processo; (box) scatola; (BRIT: also: **suit~**) valigia; **in ~ of** in caso di; **in ~ he** caso mai lui; **in any ~** in ogni caso; **just in ~** in caso di bisogno

cash [kæʃ] n (coins, notes) soldi mpl, denaro ▷ vt incassare; **I haven't got any ~** non ho contanti; **to pay (in) ~** pagare in contanti; **~ with order/on delivery (COD)** pagamento all'ordinazione/alla consegna; **cashback** n (discount) sconto; (*at supermarket etc*) anticipo di contanti ottenuto presso la cassa di un negozio tramite una carta di debito; **cash card** *n* (*BRIT*) carta per prelievi automatici; **cash desk** *n* (*BRIT*) cassa; **cash dispenser** *n* (*BRIT*) sportello automatico

cashew [kæ'ʃuː] *n* (*also:* **~ nut**) anacardio

cashier [kæ'ʃɪəʳ] *n* cassiere/a

cashmere ['kæʃmɪəʳ] *n* cachemire *m*

cash point *n* sportello bancario automatico, Bancomat® *m inv*

cash register *n* registratore *m* di cassa

casino [kə'siː'nəu] *n* casinò *m inv*

casket ['kɑːskɪt] *n* cofanetto; (*US*: *coffin*) bara

casserole ['kæsərəul] *n* casseruola; **chicken ~** pollo in casseruola

cassette [kæ'sɛt] *n* cassetta; **cassette player** *n* riproduttore *m* a cassette

cast [kɑːst] *vt* (*pt, pp* **cast**) (*throw*) gettare; (*metal*) gettare, fondere; (*Theat*): **to ~ sb as Hamlet** scegliere qn per la parte di Amleto ▷ *n* (*Theat*) cast *m inv*; (*also:* **plaster ~**) ingessatura; **to ~ one's vote** votare, dare il voto; **cast off** *vi* (*Naut*) salpare

castanets [kæstə'nɛts] *npl* castagnette *fpl*

caster sugar ['kɑːstə-] *n* (*BRIT*) zucchero semolato

cast iron *n* ghisa ▷ *adj*: **cast-iron** (*lit*) di ghisa; (*fig*: *will, alibi*) di ferro

castle ['kɑːsl] *n* castello

casual ['kæʒjul] *adj* (*chance*) casuale, fortuito/a; (*irregular*: *work etc*) avventizio/a; (*unconcerned*) noncurante, indifferente; **~ wear** casual *m*

casualty ['kæʒjultɪ] *n* ferito/a; (*dead*) morto/a, vittima; (*Med*: *department*) pronto soccorso

cat [kæt] *n* gatto

catalogue, (*US*) **catalog** ['kætələg] *n* catalogo ▷ *vt* catalogare

catalytic converter [kætə'lɪtɪk kən'vəːtəʳ] *n* marmitta catalitica, catalizzatore *m*

cataract ['kætərækt] *n* (*also Med*) cateratta

catarrh [kə'tɑːʳ] *n* catarro

catastrophe [kə'tæstrəfɪ] *n* catastrofe *f*

catch [kætʃ] (*pt, pp* **caught**) *vt* prendere; (*ball*) afferrare; (*person: by surprise*) sorprendere; (*attention*) attirare; (*comment, whisper*) cogliere; (*person*) raggiungere ▷ *vi* (*fire*) prendere ▷ *n* (*fish etc caught*) retata; (*of ball*) presa; (*trick*) inganno; (*Tech*) gancio; (*game*) catch *m inv*; **to ~ fire** prendere fuoco; **to ~ sight of** scorgere; **catch up** *vi* mettersi in pari ▷ *vt* (*also:* **~ up with**) raggiungere; **catching** ['kætʃɪŋ] *adj* (*Med*) contagioso/a

category ['kætɪgərɪ] *n* categoria

cater ['keɪtəʳ]; **cater for** *vt fus* (*BRIT*: *needs*) provvedere a; (: *readers, consumers*) incontrare i gusti di; (*Comm*: *provide food*) provvedere alla ristorazione di

caterpillar ['kætəpɪləʳ] *n* bruco

cathedral [kə'θiːdrəl] *n* cattedrale *f*, duomo

Catholic ['kæθəlɪk] *adj, n* (*Rel*) cattolico/a

Catseye® ['kæts'aɪ] *n* (*BRIT Aut*) catarifrangente *m*

cattle ['kætl] *npl* bestiame *m*, bestie *fpl*

catwalk ['kætwɔːk] *n* passerella

caught [kɔːt] *pt, pp of* **catch**

cauliflower ['kɔlɪflauəʳ] *n* cavolfiore *m*

cause [kɔːz] *n* causa ▷ *vt* causare

caution ['kɔːʃən] *n* prudenza; (*warning*) avvertimento ▷ *vt* avvertire; ammonire; **cautious** ['kɔːʃəs] *adj* cauto/a, prudente

cave [keɪv] *n* caverna, grotta; **cave in** *vi* (*roof etc*) crollare

caviar(e) ['kævɪɑːʳ] *n* caviale *m*

cavity ['kævɪtɪ] n cavità f inv
cc abbr (= cubic centimetre) cc; (on letter etc) = **carbon copy**
CCTV n abbr (= closed-circuit television) televisione f a circuito chiuso
CD n abbr (= compact disk) CD m inv; (player) lettore m CD inv; **CD burner** n masterizzatore m (di) CD; **CD player** n lettore m CD; **CD-ROM** ['si:'di:'rɔm] n abbr (= compact disc read-only memory) CD-ROM m inv
cease [si:s] vt, vi cessare; **ceasefire** n cessate il fuoco m inv
cedar ['si:də'] n cedro
ceilidh ['keɪlɪ] n festa con musiche e danze popolari scozzesi o irlandesi
ceiling ['si:lɪŋ] n soffitto; (fig: upper limit) tetto
celebrate ['sɛlɪbreɪt] vt, vi celebrare; **celebration** [sɛlɪ'breɪʃən] n celebrazione f
celebrity [sɪ'lɛbrɪtɪ] n celebrità f inv
celery ['sɛlərɪ] n sedano
cell [sɛl] n cella; (of revolutionaries, Biol) cellula; (Elec) elemento (di batteria)
cellar ['sɛlə'] n sottosuolo; cantina
cello ['tʃɛləʊ] n violoncello
cellophane® ['sɛləfeɪn] n cellophane® m
cellphone ['sɛlfəʊn] n cellulare m
Celsius ['sɛlsɪəs] adj Celsius inv
Celtic ['kɛltɪk, 'sɛltɪk] adj celtico/a
cement [sə'mɛnt] n cemento
cemetery ['sɛmɪtrɪ] n cimitero
censor ['sɛnsə'] n censore m ▷ vt censurare; **censorship** n censura
census ['sɛnsəs] n censimento
cent [sɛnt] n (of dollar, euro) centesimo; see also **per cent**
centenary [sɛn'ti:nərɪ], (US) **centennial** [sɛn'tɛnɪəl] n centenario
center ['sɛntə'] n, vt (US) = **centre**
centi...: centigrade ['sɛntɪgreɪd] adj centigrado/a; **centimetre**, (US) **centimeter** ['sɛntɪmi:tə'] n centimetro; **centipede** ['sɛntɪpi:d] n centopiedi m inv
central ['sɛntrəl] adj centrale; **Central America** n America centrale; **central heating** n riscaldamento centrale; **central reservation** n (BRIT Aut) banchina f spartitraffico inv
centre, (US) **center** ['sɛntə'] n centro ▷ vt centrare; (concentrate): **to ~ (on)** concentrare (su); **centre-forward** n (Sport) centroavanti m inv; **centre-half** n (Sport) centromediano
century ['sɛntjurɪ] n secolo; **in the twentieth ~** nel ventesimo secolo
CEO n abbr = **chief executive officer**
ceramic [sɪ'ræmɪk] adj ceramico/a
cereal ['si:rɪəl] n cereale m
ceremony ['sɛrɪmənɪ] n cerimonia; **to stand on ~** fare complimenti
certain ['sə:tən] adj certo/a; **to make ~ of** assicurarsi di; **for ~** per certo, di sicuro; **certainly** adv certamente, certo; **certainty** n certezza
certificate [sə'tɪfɪkɪt] n certificato, diploma m
certify ['sə:tɪfaɪ] vt certificare; (award diploma to) conferire un diploma a; (declare insane) dichiarare pazzo/a
cf. abbr (= compare) cfr
CFC n abbr (= chlorofluorocarbon) CFC m inv
chain [tʃeɪn] n catena ▷ vt (also: **~ up**) incatenare; **chain-smoke** vi fumare una sigaretta dopo l'altra
chair [tʃɛə'] n sedia; (armchair) poltrona; (of university) cattedra; (of meeting) presidenza ▷ vt (meeting) presiedere; **chairlift** n seggiovia; **chairman** n (irreg) presidente m; **chairperson** n presidente/essa; **chairwoman** n (irreg) presidentessa
chalet ['ʃæleɪ] n chalet m inv
chalk [tʃɔ:k] n gesso; **chalkboard** (US) n lavagna
challenge ['tʃælɪndʒ] n sfida ▷ vt sfidare; (statement, right)

mettere in dubbio; **to ~ sb to do** sfidare qn a fare; **challenging** adj (task) impegnativo/a; (remark) provocatorio/a; (look) di sfida

chamber ['tʃeɪmbə^r] n camera; **chambermaid** n cameriera

champagne [ʃæm'peɪn] n champagne m inv

champion ['tʃæmpɪən] n campione/essa; **championship** n campionato

chance [tʃɑːns] n caso; (opportunity) occasione f; (likelihood) possibilità f inv ▷ vt: **to ~ it** rischiare, provarci ▷ adj fortuito/a; **to take a ~** rischiare; **by ~** per caso

chancellor ['tʃɑːnsələ^r] n cancelliere m; **C~ of the Exchequer** (BRIT) Cancelliere m dello Scacchiere

chandelier [ʃændə'lɪə^r] n lampadario

change [tʃeɪndʒ] vt cambiare; (transform): **to ~ sb into** trasformare qn in ▷ vi cambiare; (change one's clothes) cambiarsi; (be transformed): **to ~ into** trasformarsi in ▷ n cambiamento; (money) resto; **to ~ one's mind** cambiare idea; **a ~ of clothes** un cambio (di vestiti); **for a ~** tanto per cambiare; **small ~** spiccioli mpl; **keep the ~** tenga il resto; **sorry, I don't have any ~** mi dispiace, non ho spiccioli; **change over** vi (from sth to sth) passare; (players etc) scambiarsi (di posto o di campo) ▷ vt cambiare; **changeable** adj (weather) variabile; **change machine** n distributore m automatico di monete; **changing room** n (BRIT: in shop) camerino; (Sport) spogliatoio

channel ['tʃænl] n canale m; (of river, sea) alveo ▷ vt canalizzare; **Channel Tunnel** n: **the Channel Tunnel** il tunnel sotto la Manica

chant [tʃɑːnt] n canto; salmodia ▷ vt cantare; salmodiare

chaos ['keɪɒs] n caos m

chaotic [keɪ'ɔtɪk] adj caotico/a

chap [tʃæp] n (BRIT col: man) tipo

chapel ['tʃæpl] n cappella

chapped [tʃæpt] adj (skin, lips) screpolato/a

chapter ['tʃæptə^r] n capitolo

character ['kærɪktə^r] n carattere m; (in novel, film) personaggio; **characteristic** ['kærɪktə'rɪstɪk] adj caratteristico/a ▷ n caratteristica; **characterize** ['kærɪktəraɪz] vt caratterizzare; (describe): **to characterize (as)** descrivere (come)

charcoal ['tʃɑːkəul] n carbone m di legna

charge [tʃɑːdʒ] n accusa; (cost) prezzo; (responsibility) responsabilità ▷ vt (gun, battery, Mil: enemy) caricare; (customer) fare pagare a; (sum) fare pagare; (Law): **to ~ sb (with)** accusare qn (di) ▷ vi (gen with, up, along etc) lanciarsi; **charges** npl: **bank ~s** commissioni fpl bancarie; **to reverse the ~s** (Tel) fare una telefonata a carico del destinatario; **to take ~ of** incaricarsi di; **to be in ~ of** essere responsabile per; **how much do you ~ for this repair?** quanto chiede per la riparazione?; **to ~ an expense (up) to sb** addebitare una spesa a qn; **charge card** n (of shop) carta f clienti inv; **charger** n (also: **battery charger**) caricabatterie m inv; (old: warhorse) destriero

charismatic [kærɪz'mætɪk] adj carismatico/a

charity ['tʃærɪtɪ] n carità; (organization) opera pia; **charity shop** n (BRIT) negozi che vendono articoli di seconda mano e devolvono il ricavato in beneficenza

charm [tʃɑːm] n fascino; (on bracelet) ciondolo ▷ vt affascinare, incantare; **charming** adj affascinante

chart [tʃɑːt] n tabella; grafico; (map) carta nautica ▷ vt fare una carta nautica di; **charts** npl (Mus) hit parade f

charter ['tʃɑːtə^r] vt (plane) noleggiare ▷ n (document) carta; **chartered accountant** ['tʃɑːtəd-] n (BRIT) ragioniere/a professionista; **charter flight** n volo m charter inv

chase [tʃeɪs] vt inseguire; (also: ~ **away**) cacciare ▷ n caccia

chat [tʃæt] vi (also: **have a ~**) chiacchierare; (on the internet) chattare ▷ n chiacchierata; (on the internet) chat f inv; **chat up** vt (BRIT col: girl, boy) abbordare; **chat room** n (Internet) chat f inv; **chat show** n (BRIT) talk show m inv

chatter ['tʃætə^r] vi (person) ciarlare; (bird) cinguettare; (teeth) battere ▷ n ciarle fpl; cinguettio

chauffeur ['ʃəʊfə^r] n autista m

chauvinist ['ʃəʊvɪnɪst] n (also: **male ~**) maschilista m; (nationalist) sciovinista m/f

cheap [tʃiːp] adj a buon mercato, economico/a; (joke) grossolano/a; (poor quality) di cattiva qualità ▷ adv a buon mercato; **cheap day return** n biglietto ridotto di andata e ritorno valido in giornata; **cheaply** adv a buon prezzo, a buon mercato

cheat [tʃiːt] vi imbrogliare; (at school) copiare ▷ vt ingannare ▷ n imbroglione m; **to ~ sb out of sth** defraudare qn di qc; **cheat on** vt fus (husband, wife) tradire

Chechnya [tʃɪtʃˈnjɑː] n Cecenia

check [tʃɛk] vt verificare; (passport, ticket) controllare; (halt) fermare; (restrain) contenere ▷ n verifica; controllo; (curb) freno; (us: bill) conto; (pattern: gen pl) quadretti mpl; (us) = **cheque** ▷ adj (pattern, cloth) a quadretti; **check in** vi (in hotel) registrare; (at airport) presentarsi all'accettazione ▷ vt (luggage) depositare; **check off** vt segnare; **check out** vi (from hotel) saldare il conto; **check up** vi: **to ~ up (on sth)** investigare (qc); **to ~ up on sb** informarsi sul conto di qn;

checkbook n (us) = **chequebook**; **checkers** n (us) dama; **check-in** n (also: **check-in desk**) (at airport) check-in m inv, accettazione f (bagagli inv); **checking account** n (us) conto corrente; **checklist** n lista di controllo; **checkmate** n scaccomatto; **checkout** n (in supermarket) cassa; **checkpoint** n posto di blocco; **checkroom** n (us) deposito m bagagli inv; **checkup** n (Med) controllo medico

cheddar ['tʃedə^r] n formaggio duro di latte di mucca di colore bianco o arancione

cheek [tʃiːk] n guancia; (impudence) faccia tosta; **cheekbone** n zigomo; **cheeky** adj sfacciato/a

cheer [tʃɪə^r] vt applaudire; (gladden) rallegrare ▷ vi applaudire ▷ n grido (di incoraggiamento); **cheers** npl (of approval, encouragement) applausi mpl; evviva mpl; **~s!** salute!; **cheer up** vi rallegrarsi, farsi animo ▷ vt rallegrare; **cheerful** adj allegro/a

cheerio ['tʃɪərɪ'əʊ] excl (BRIT) ciao!

cheerleader ['tʃɪəliːdə^r] n cheerleader f inv

cheese [tʃiːz] n formaggio; **cheeseburger** n cheeseburger m inv; **cheesecake** n specie di torta di ricotta, a volte con frutta

chef [ʃef] n capocuoco

chemical ['kemɪkl] adj chimico/a ▷ n prodotto chimico

chemist ['kemɪst] n (BRIT: pharmacist) farmacista m/f; (scientist) chimico/a; **~'s shop** n (BRIT) farmacia; **chemistry** n chimica

cheque, (us) **check** [tʃɛk] n assegno; **chequebook** n libretto degli assegni; **cheque card** n carta f assegni inv

cherry ['tʃerɪ] n ciliegia; (also: **~ tree**) ciliegio

chess [tʃes] n scacchi mpl

chest [tʃest] n petto; (box) cassa

chestnut ['tʃesnʌt] n castagna; (also: **~ tree**) castagno

chest of drawers n cassettone m
chew [tʃuː] vt masticare; **chewing gum** n chewing gum m
chic [ʃiːk] adj elegante
chick [tʃɪk] n pulcino; (col) pollastrella
chicken [ˈtʃɪkɪn] n pollo; (col: coward) coniglio; **chicken out** vi (col) avere fifa; **chickenpox** n varicella
chickpea [ˈtʃɪkpiː] n cece m
chief [tʃiːf] n capo ▷ adj principale; **chief executive**, (US) **chief executive officer** n direttore m generale; **chiefly** adv per lo più, soprattutto
child (pl **children**) [tʃaɪld, ˈtʃɪldrən] n bambino/a; **child abuse** n molestie fpl a minori; **child benefit** n (BRIT) ≈ assegni mpl familiari; **childbirth** n parto; **child-care** n il badare ai bambini; **childhood** n infanzia; **childish** adj puerile; **child minder** [-ˈmaɪndəʳ] n (BRIT) bambinaia; **children** [ˈtʃɪldrən] npl of **child**
Chile [ˈtʃɪlɪ] n Cile m
Chilean [ˈtʃɪlɪən] adj, n cileno/a
chill [tʃɪl] n freddo; (Med) infreddatura ▷ vt raffreddare; **chill out** vi (esp US col) darsi una calmata
chilli, (US) **chili** [ˈtʃɪlɪ] n peperoncino
chilly [ˈtʃɪlɪ] adj freddo/a, fresco/a; **to feel ~** sentirsi infreddolito/a
chimney [ˈtʃɪmnɪ] n camino
chimpanzee [tʃɪmpænˈziː] n scimpanzé m inv
chin [tʃɪn] n mento
China [ˈtʃaɪnə] n Cina
china [ˈtʃaɪnə] n porcellana
Chinese [tʃaɪˈniːz] adj cinese ▷ n (pl inv) cinese m/f; (Ling) cinese m
chip [tʃɪp] n (gen pl: Culin) patatina fritta; (: US: also: **potato ~**) patatina; (of wood, glass, stone) scheggia; (microchip) chip m inv ▷ vt (cup, plate) scheggiare; **chip and PIN** n sistema m chip e PIN; **chip and PIN machine** lettore m di carte chip e PIN; **chip and PIN card** carta chip e PIN; **chip shop** n (BRIT) vedi nota **"chip shop"**

● **CHIP SHOP**
●
● I chip shops, anche chiamati fish-
● and-chip shops, sono friggitorie che
● vendono principalmente filetti di
● pesce impanati e patatine fritte
● che un tempo venivano serviti
● ai clienti avvolti in carta di giornale.

chiropodist [kɪˈrɔpədɪst] n (BRIT) pedicure mf inv
chisel [ˈtʃɪzl] n cesello
chives [tʃaɪvz] npl erba cipollina
chlorine [ˈklɔːriːn] n cloro
choc-ice [ˈtʃɔkaɪs] n (BRIT) gelato ricoperto di cioccolato
chocolate [ˈtʃɔklɪt] n (substance) cioccolato, cioccolata; (drink) cioccolata; (a sweet) cioccolatino
choice [tʃɔɪs] n scelta ▷ adj scelto/a
choir [ˈkwaɪəʳ] n coro
choke [tʃəuk] vi soffocare ▷ vt soffocare; (block) ingombrare ▷ n (Aut) valvola dell'aria; **to be ~d with** essere intasato/a
cholesterol [kəˈlɛstərɔl] n colesterolo
chook [tʃuk] n (AUST, NZ col) gallina
choose (pt **chose**, pp **chosen**) [tʃuːz, tʃəuz, ˈtʃəuzn] vt scegliere; **to ~ to do** decidere di fare; preferire fare
chop [tʃɔp] vt (wood) spaccare; (Culin: also: **~ up**) tritare ▷ n (Culin) costoletta; **chop down** vt (tree) abbattere; **chop off** vt tagliare; **chopsticks** [ˈtʃɔpstɪks] npl bastoncini mpl cinesi
chord [kɔːd] n (Mus) accordo
chore [tʃɔːʳ] n faccenda; **household ~s** faccende fpl domestiche
chorus [ˈkɔːrəs] n coro; (repeated part of song, also fig) ritornello
chose [tʃəuz] pt of **choose**
chosen [ˈtʃəuzn] pp of **choose**
Christ [kraɪst] n Cristo
christen [ˈkrɪsn] vt battezzare; **christening** n battesimo

Christian ['krɪstɪən] *adj, n* cristiano/a; **Christianity** [krɪstɪ'ænɪtɪ] *n* cristianesimo; **Christian name** *n* nome *m* di battesimo

Christmas ['krɪsməs] *n* Natale *m*; **happy** *or* **merry ~!** Buon Natale!; **Christmas card** *n* cartolina di Natale; **Christmas carol** *n* canto natalizio; **Christmas Day** *n* il giorno di Natale; **Christmas Eve** *n* la vigilia di Natale; **Christmas pudding** *n* (*esp* BRIT) specie di budino con frutta secca, spezie e brandy; **Christmas tree** *n* albero di Natale

chrome [krəum] *n* cromo

chronic ['krɔnɪk] *adj* cronico/a

chrysanthemum [krɪ'sænθəməm] *n* crisantemo

chubby ['tʃʌbɪ] *adj* paffuto/a

chuck [tʃʌk] *vt* buttare, gettare; **to ~ (up** *or* **in)** (BRIT) piantare; **chuck out** *vt* buttar fuori

chuckle ['tʃʌkl] *vi* ridere sommessamente

chum [tʃʌm] *n* compagno/a

chunk [tʃʌŋk] *n* pezzo

church [tʃə:tʃ] *n* chiesa; **churchyard** *n* sagrato

churn [tʃə:n] *n* (*for butter*) zangola; (*also:* **milk ~**) bidone *m*

chute [ʃu:t] *n* (*also:* **rubbish ~**) canale *m* di scarico; (BRIT: *children's slide*) scivolo

chutney ['tʃʌtnɪ] *n* salsa piccante (di frutta, zucchero e spezie)

CIA *n abbr* (US: = *Central Intelligence Agency*) C.I.A. *f*

CID *n abbr* (BRIT: = *Criminal Investigation Department*) ≈ polizia giudiziaria

cider ['saɪdə^r] *n* sidro

cigar [sɪ'gɑ:^r] *n* sigaro

cigarette [sɪgə'rɛt] *n* sigaretta; **cigarette lighter** *n* accendino

cinema ['sɪnəmə] *n* cinema *m inv*

cinnamon ['sɪnəmən] *n* cannella

circle ['sə:kl] *n* cerchio; (*of friends etc*) circolo; (*in cinema*) galleria ▷ *vi* girare in circolo ▷ *vt* (*surround*) circondare; (*move round*) girare intorno a

circuit ['sə:kɪt] *n* circuito

circular ['sə:kjulə^r] *adj* circolare ▷ *n* circolare *f*

circulate ['sə:kjuleɪt] *vi* circolare ▷ *vt* far circolare; **circulation** [sə:kju'leɪʃən] *n* circolazione *f*; (*of newspaper*) tiratura

circumstances ['sə:kəmstənsɪz] *npl* circostanze *fpl*; (*financial condition*) condizioni *fpl* finanziarie

circus ['sə:kəs] *n* circo

cite [saɪt] *vt* citare

citizen ['sɪtɪzn] *n* (*of country*) cittadino/a; (*of town*) abitante *m/f*; **citizenship** *n* cittadinanza

citrus fruit ['sɪtrəs-] *n* agrume *m*

city ['sɪtɪ] *n* città *f inv*; **the C~** la Città di Londra (*centro commerciale*); **city centre** *n* centro della città; **City Technology College** *n* (BRIT) istituto tecnico superiore (*finanziato dall'industria*)

civic ['sɪvɪk] *adj* civico/a

civil ['sɪvɪl] *adj* civile; **civilian** [sɪ'vɪlɪən] *adj, n* borghese (*m/f*)

civilization [sɪvɪlaɪ'zeɪʃən] *n* civiltà *f inv*

civilized ['sɪvɪlaɪzd] *adj* civilizzato/a; (*fig*) cortese

civil: civil law *n* codice *m* civile; (*study*) diritto civile; **civil rights** *npl* diritti *mpl* civili; **civil servant** *n* impiegato/a statale; **Civil Service** *n* amministrazione *f* statale; **civil war** *n* guerra civile

CJD *n abbr* (= *Creutzfeld-Jakob disease*) malattia di Creutzfeldt-Jakob

claim [kleɪm] *vt* (*rights etc*) rivendicare; (*damages*) richiedere; (*assert*) sostenere ▷ *vi* (*for insurance*) fare una domanda d'indennizzo ▷ *n* rivendicazione *f*; pretesa; richiesta; **claim form** *n* (*gen*) modulo di richiesta; (*for expenses*) modulo di rimborso spese

clam [klæm] *n* vongola

clamp [klæmp] n pinza; morsa ▷ vt stringere con una morsa; (Aut: wheel) applicare le ganasce a

clan [klæn] n clan m inv

clap [klæp] vi applaudire

claret ['klærət] n vino di Bordeaux

clarify ['klærɪfaɪ] vt chiarificare, chiarire

clarinet [klærɪ'nɛt] n clarinetto

clarity ['klærɪtɪ] n chiarezza

clash [klæʃ] n frastuono; (fig) scontro ▷ vi scontrarsi; cozzare

clasp [klɑːsp] n (hold) stretta; (of necklace, bag) fermaglio, fibbia ▷ vt stringere

class [klɑːs] n classe f ▷ vt classificare

classic ['klæsɪk] adj classico/a ▷ n classico/a; **classical** adj classico/a

classification [klæsɪfɪ'keɪʃən] n classificazione f

classify ['klæsɪfaɪ] vt classificare

classmate ['klɑːsmeɪt] n compagno/a di classe

classroom ['klɑːsrum] n aula

classy ['klɑːsɪ] adj (col) chic inv, elegante

clatter ['klætər] n tintinnio; scalpitio ▷ vi tintinnare; scalpitare

clause [klɔːz] n clausola; (Ling) proposizione f

claustrophobic [klɔːstrə'fəubɪk] adj claustrofobico/a

claw [klɔː] n (of bird of prey) artiglio; (of lobster) pinza

clay [kleɪ] n argilla

clean [kliːn] adj pulito/a; (outline, break, movement) netto/a ▷ vt pulire; **clean up** vt (also fig) ripulire; **cleaner** n (person) uomo (donna) delle pulizie; **cleaner's** n (also: **dry cleaner's**) tintoria; **cleaning** n pulizia

cleanser ['klɛnzər] n detergente m

clear [klɪər] adj chiaro/a; (glass etc) trasparente; (road, way) libero/a; (conscience) pulito/a ▷ vt sgombrare; liberare; (table) sparecchiare; (Law: suspect) discolpare; (obstacle) superare; (cheque) fare la compensazione di ▷ vi

(weather) rasserenarsi; (fog) andarsene ▷ adv: ~ **of** distante da; **clear away** vt (things, clothes, etc) mettere a posto; **to ~ away the dishes** sparecchiare la tavola; **clear up** vt mettere in ordine; (mystery) risolvere; **clearance** n (removal) sgombro; (permission) autorizzazione f, permesso; **clear-cut** adj ben delineato/a, distinto/a; **clearing** n radura; **clearly** adv chiaramente; **clearway** n (BRIT) strada con divieto di sosta

clench [klɛntʃ] vt stringere

clergy ['kləːdʒɪ] n clero

clerk [klɑːk, US kləːrk] n (BRIT) impiegato/a; (US) commesso/a

clever ['klɛvər] adj (mentally) intelligente; (deft, skilful) abile; (device, arrangement) ingegnoso/a

cliché ['kliːʃeɪ] n cliché m inv

click [klɪk] vi scattare; (Comput) cliccare ▷ vt: **to ~ one's tongue** schioccare la lingua; **to ~ one's heels** battere i tacchi

client ['klaɪənt] n cliente m/f

cliff [klɪf] n scogliera scoscesa, rupe f

climate ['klaɪmɪt] n clima m; **climate change** n cambiamenti mpl climatici

climax ['klaɪmæks] n culmine m; (sexual) orgasmo

climb [klaɪm] vi salire; (clamber) arrampicarsi ▷ vt salire; (Climbing) scalare ▷ n salita; arrampicata; scalata; **climb down** vi scendere; (BRIT fig) far marcia indietro; **climber** n rocciatore/trice; alpinista m/f; **climbing** n alpinismo

clinch [klɪntʃ] vt (deal) concludere

cling (pt, pp **clung**) [klɪŋ, klʌŋ] vi: **to ~ (to)** tenersi stretto/a (a), aggrapparsi (a); (clothes) aderire strettamente (a)

clingfilm® ['klɪŋfɪlm] n pellicola trasparente (per alimenti)

clinic ['klɪnɪk] n clinica

clip [klɪp] n (for hair) forcina; (also: **paper ~**) graffetta; (TV, Cine)

sequenza ▷ vt attaccare insieme;
(hair, nails) tagliare; (hedge) tosare;
clipping n (from newspaper) ritaglio

cloak [kləuk] n mantello ▷ vt
avvolgere; **cloakroom** n (for coats
etc) guardaroba m inv; (BRIT: W.C.)
gabinetti mpl

clock [klɔk] n orologio; **clock in,
clock on** vi timbrare il cartellino
(all'entrata); **clock off, clock out**
vi timbrare il cartellino (all'uscita);
clockwise adv in senso orario;
clockwork n movimento or
meccanismo a orologeria ▷ adj
a molla

clog [klɔg] n zoccolo ▷ vt intasare ▷ vi
(also: ~ **up**) intasarsi, bloccarsi

clone [kləun] n clone m

close¹ [kləus] adj vicino/a; (watch)
stretto/a; (examination) attento/a;
(contest) combattuto/a; (weather)
afoso/a ▷ adv vicino, dappresso; ~
to vicino a; ~ **by, ~ at hand** qui (or lì)
vicino; **a ~ friend** un amico intimo;
to have a ~ shave (fig) scamparla
bella

close² [kləuz] vt chiudere ▷ vi
(shop etc) chiudere; (lid, door etc)
chiudersi; (end) finire ▷ n (end)
fine f; **close down** vi cessare
(definitivamente); **closed** adj
chiuso/a

closely ['kləuslɪ] adv (examine, watch)
da vicino; **we are ~ related** siamo
parenti stretti

closet ['klɔzɪt] n (cupboard) armadio

close-up ['kləusʌp] n primo piano

closing time n orario di chiusura

closure ['kləuʒər] n chiusura

clot [klɔt] n (also: **blood ~**) coagulo;
(col: idiot) scemo/a ▷ vi coagularsi

cloth [klɔθ] n (material) tessuto,
stoffa; (BRIT: also: **tea~**) strofinaccio

clothes [kləuðz] npl abiti mpl,
vestiti mpl; **clothes line** n corda (per
stendere il bucato); **clothes peg**, (US)
clothes pin n molletta

clothing ['kləuðɪŋ] n = **clothes**

cloud [klaud] n nuvola; **cloud over**
vi rannuvolarsi; (fig) offuscarsi;
cloudy adj nuvoloso/a; (liquid)
torbido/a

clove [kləuv] n chiodo di garofano;
clove of garlic n spicchio d'aglio

clown [klaun] n pagliaccio ▷ vi (also:
~ **about, ~ around**) fare il pagliaccio

club [klʌb] n (society) club m inv,
circolo; (weapon, Golf) mazza ▷ vt
bastonare ▷ vi: **to ~ together**
associarsi; **clubs** npl (Cards) fiori mpl;
club class n (Aviat) classe f club inv

clue [klu:] n indizio; (in crosswords)
definizione f; **I haven't a ~** non ho la
minima idea

clump [klʌmp] n (of flowers, trees)
gruppo; (of grass) ciuffo

clumsy ['klʌmzɪ] adj goffo/a

clung [klʌŋ] pt, pp of **cling**

cluster ['klʌstər] n gruppo ▷ vi
raggrupparsi

clutch [klʌtʃ] n (grip, grasp) presa,
stretta; (Aut) frizione f ▷ vt afferrare,
stringere forte

cm abbr (= centimetre) cm

Co. abbr = **county**; (= company) C., C.ia

c/o abbr (= care of) presso

coach [kəutʃ] n (bus) pullman m
inv; (horse-drawn, of train) carrozza;
(Sport) allenatore/trice; (tutor) chi
dà ripetizioni ▷ vt allenare; dare
ripetizioni a; **coach station** (BRIT) n
stazione f delle corriere; **coach trip** n
viaggio in pullman

coal [kəul] n carbone m

coalition [kəuə'lɪʃən] n coalizione f

coarse [kɔ:s] adj (salt, sand etc)
grosso/a; (cloth, person) rozzo/a

coast [kəust] n costa ▷ vi (with cycle
etc) scendere a ruota libera; **coastal**
adj costiero/a; **coastguard** n guardia
costiera; **coastline** n linea costiera

coat [kəut] n cappotto; (of animal)
pelo; (of paint) mano f ▷ vt coprire;
coat hanger n attaccapanni m inv;
coating n rivestimento

coax [kəuks] vt indurre (con moine)

cob [kɔb] n see **corn**
cobbled ['kɔbld] adj: **~ street** strada pavimentata a ciottoli
cobweb ['kɔbwɛb] n ragnatela
cocaine [kə'keɪn] n cocaina
cock [kɔk] n (rooster) gallo; (male bird) maschio ▷ vt (gun) armare; **cockerel** n galletto
cockney ['kɔknɪ] n cockney mf inv (abitante dei quartieri popolari dell'East End di Londra)
cockpit ['kɔkpɪt] n abitacolo
cockroach ['kɔkrəʊtʃ] n blatta
cocktail ['kɔkteɪl] n cocktail m inv
cocoa ['kəʊkəʊ] n cacao
coconut ['kəʊkənʌt] n noce f di cocco
cod [kɔd] n merluzzo
C.O.D. abbr = **cash on delivery**
code [kəʊd] n codice m
coeducational ['kəʊɛdju'keɪʃənl] adj misto/a
coffee ['kɔfɪ] n caffè m inv; **coffee bar** n (BRIT) caffè m inv; **coffee bean** n grano or chicco di caffè; **coffee break** n pausa per il caffè; **coffee maker** n bollitore m per il caffè; **coffeepot** n caffettiera; **coffee shop** n ≈ caffè m inv; **coffee table** n tavolino
coffin ['kɔfɪn] n bara
cog [kɔg] n dente m
cognac ['kɔnjæk] n cognac m inv
coherent [kəʊ'hɪərənt] adj coerente
coil [kɔɪl] n rotolo; (Aut, Elec) bobina; (contraceptive) spirale f ▷ vt avvolgere
coin [kɔɪn] n moneta ▷ vt (word) coniare
coincide [kəʊɪn'saɪd] vi coincidere; **coincidence** [kəʊ'ɪnsɪdəns] n combinazione f
Coke® [kəʊk] n coca f inv
coke [kəʊk] n coke m
colander ['kɔləndəʳ] n colino
cold [kəʊld] adj freddo/a ▷ n freddo; (Med) raffreddore m; **it's ~** fa freddo; **to be ~** (person) aver freddo; (object) essere freddo/a; **to catch ~** prendere freddo; **to catch a ~** prendere un

raffreddore; **in ~ blood** a sangue freddo; **cold sore** n erpete m
coleslaw ['kəʊlslɔː] n insalata di cavolo bianco
colic ['kɔlɪk] n colica
collaborate [kə'læbəreɪt] vi collaborare
collapse [kə'læps] vi crollare ▷ n crollo; (Med) collasso
collar ['kɔləʳ] n (of coat, shirt) colletto; (for dog) collare m; **collarbone** n clavicola
colleague ['kɔliːg] n collega m/f
collect [kə'lɛkt] vt (gen) raccogliere; (as a hobby) fare collezione di; (BRIT: call for) prendere; (money owed, pension) riscuotere; (donations, subscriptions) fare una colletta di ▷ vi adunarsi, riunirsi; (rubbish etc) ammucchiarsi ▷ (us Tel): **to call ~** fare una chiamata a carico del destinatario; **collection** [kə'lɛkʃən] n collezione f; raccolta; (for money) colletta; **collective** adj collettivo/a ▷ n collettivo; **collector** [kə'lɛktəʳ] n collezionista m/f
college ['kɔlɪdʒ] n college m inv; (of technology, agriculture etc) istituto superiore
collide [kə'laɪd] vi: **to ~ (with)** scontrarsi (con)
collision [kə'lɪʒən] n collisione f, scontro
cologne [kə'ləʊn] n (also: **eau de ~**) acqua di colonia
Colombia [kə'lɔmbɪə] n Colombia; **Colombian** adj, n colombiano/a
colon ['kəʊlən] n (sign) due punti mpl; (Med) colon m inv
colonel ['kəːnl] n colonnello
colonial [kə'ləʊnɪəl] adj coloniale
colony ['kɔlənɪ] n colonia
colour, (us) **color** ['kʌləʳ] n colore m ▷ vt colorare; (tint, dye) tingere; (fig: affect) influenzare ▷ vi (blush) arrossire; **colour in** vt colorare; **colour-blind** adj daltonico/a; **coloured** adj (photo) a colori; (col!:

person) di colore; **colour film** n (*for camera*) pellicola a colori; **colourful** *adj* pieno/a di colore, a vivaci colori; (*personality*) colorato/a; **colouring** n (*substance*) colorante m; (*complexion*) colorito; **colour television** n televisione f a colori

column ['kɔləm] n colonna

coma ['kəumə] n coma m inv

comb [kəum] n pettine m ▷ vt (*hair*) pettinare; (*area*) battere a tappeto

combat ['kɔmbæt] n combattimento ▷ vt combattere, lottare contro

combination [kɔmbɪ'neɪʃən] n combinazione f

combine [kəm'baɪn] vt: **to ~ (with)** combinare (con); (*one quality with another*): **to ~ sth with sth** unire qc a qc ▷ vi unirsi; (*Chem*) combinarsi ▷ n ['kɔmbaɪn] (*Econ*) associazione f

come (*pt* **came**, *pp* **come**) [kʌm, keɪm] vi venire; arrivare; **to ~ to** (*decision etc*) raggiungere; **I've ~ to like him** ha cominciato a piacermi; **to ~ undone/loose** slacciarsi/ allentarsi; **come across** vt fus trovare per caso; **come along** vi (*pupil, work*) fare progressi; **~ along!** avanti!, andiamo!, forza!; **come back** vi ritornare; **come down** vi scendere; (*prices*) calare; (*buildings*) essere demolito/a; **come from** vt fus venire da; provenire da; **come in** vi entrare; **come off** vi (*button*) staccarsi; (*stain*) andar via; (*attempt*) riuscire; **come on** vi (*lights*) accendersi; (*electricity*) entrare in funzione; (*pupil, undertaking*) fare progressi; **~ on!** avanti!, andiamo!, forza!; **come out** vi uscire; (*stain*) andare via; **come round** vi (*after faint, operation*) riprendere conoscenza, rinvenire; **come to** vi rinvenire; **come up** vi (*sun*) salire; (*problem*) sorgere; (*event*) essere in arrivo; (*in conversation*) saltar fuori; **come up with** vt fus: **he**

came up with an idea venne fuori con un'idea

comeback ['kʌmbæk] n (*Theat etc*) ritorno

comedian [kə'mi:dɪən] n comico

comedy ['kɔmɪdɪ] n commedia

comet ['kɔmɪt] n cometa

comfort ['kʌmfət] n comodità f inv, benessere m; (*relief*) consolazione f, conforto ▷ vt consolare, confortare; **comfortable** adj comodo/a; (*financially*) agiato/a; **comfort station** n (us) gabinetti mpl

comic ['kɔmɪk] adj (also: **~al**) comico/a ▷ n comico; (*BRIT: magazine*) giornaletto; **comic book** n (us) giornalino (a fumetti); **comic strip** n fumetto

comma ['kɔmə] n virgola

command [kə'mɑ:nd] n ordine m, comando; (*Mil: authority*) comando; (*mastery*) padronanza ▷ vt comandare; **to ~ sb to do** ordinare a qn di fare; **commander** n capo; (*Mil*) comandante m

commemorate [kə'mɛməreɪt] vt commemorare

commence [kə'mɛns] vt, vi cominciare; **commencement** n (us Univ) cerimonia di consegna dei diplomi

commend [kə'mɛnd] vt lodare; raccomandare

comment ['kɔmɛnt] n commento ▷ vi: **to ~ (on)** fare commenti (su); **commentary** ['kɔməntərɪ] n commentario; (*Sport*) radiocronaca; telecronaca; **commentator** ['kɔməntəɪtə'] n commentatore/ trice; (*Sport*) radiocronista m/f; telecronista m/f

commerce ['kɔmə:s] n commercio

commercial [kə'mə:ʃəl] adj commerciale ▷ n (TV, Radio) pubblicità f inv; **commercial break** n intervallo pubblicitario

commission [kə'mɪʃən] n commissione f ▷ vt (*work of art*) commissionare; **out of ~** (Naut) in disarmo; **commissioner** n (Police) questore m

commit [kə'mɪt] vt (act) commettere; (to sb's care) affidare; **to ~ o.s. (to do)** impegnarsi (a fare); **to ~ suicide** suicidarsi; **commitment** n impegno; promessa

committee [kə'mɪtɪ] n comitato, commissione f

commodity [kə'mɔdɪtɪ] n prodotto, articolo

common ['kɔmən] adj comune; (pej) volgare; (usual) normale ▷ n terreno comune; **in ~** in comune; see also **Commons**; **commonly** adv comunemente, usualmente; **commonplace** adj banale, ordinario/a; **Commons** npl (BRIT Pol): **the (House of) Commons** la Camera dei Comuni; **common sense** n buon senso; **Commonwealth** n: **the Commonwealth** il Commonwealth

COMMONWEALTH

Il Commonwealth è un'associazione di stati sovrani indipendenti e di alcuni territori annessi che facevano parte dell'antico Impero Britannico. Ancora oggi molti stati del Commonwealth riconoscono simbolicamente il sovrano brittanico come capo di stato, e i loro rappresentanti si riuniscono per discutere questioni di comune interesse.

communal ['kɔmjuːnl] adj (for common use) pubblico/a

commune n ['kɔmjuːn] (group) comune f ▷ vi [kə'mjuːn]: **to ~ with** mettersi in comunione con

communicate [kə'mjuːnɪkeɪt] vt comunicare, trasmettere ▷ vi: **to ~ (with)** comunicare (con)

communication [kəmjuːnɪ'keɪʃən] n comunicazione f

communion [kə'mjuːnɪən] n (also: **Holy C~**) comunione f

communism ['kɔmjunɪzəm] n comunismo; **communist** adj, n comunista (m/f)

community [kə'mjuːnɪtɪ] n comunità f inv; **community centre**, (US) **community center** n circolo ricreativo; **community service** n (BRIT) ≈ lavoro sostitutivo

commute [kə'mjuːt] vi fare il pendolare ▷ vt (Law) commutare; **commuter** n pendolare m/f

compact adj [kəm'pækt] compatto/a ▷ n ['kɔmpækt] (also: **powder ~**) portacipria m inv; **compact disc** n compact disc m inv; **compact disc player** n lettore m CD inv

companion [kəm'pænjən] n compagno/a

company ['kʌmpənɪ] n (also Comm, Mil, Theat) compagnia; **to keep sb ~** tenere compagnia a qn; **company car** n macchina (di proprietà) della ditta; **company director** n amministratore m, consigliere m di amministrazione

comparable ['kɔmpərəbl] adj simile; **~ to** or **with** paragonabile a

comparative [kəm'pærətɪv] adj relativo/a; (adjective, adverb etc) comparativo/a; **comparatively** adv relativamente

compare [kəm'pɛəʳ] vt: **to ~ sth/ sb with/to** confrontare qc/qn con/a ▷ vi: **to ~ (with)** reggere il confronto (con); **comparison** [kəm'pærɪsn] n confronto; **in comparison with** confronto a

compartment [kəm'pɑːtmənt] n compartimento; (Rail) scompartimento

compass ['kʌmpəs] n bussola; **(a pair of) ~es** (Math) compasso; **within the ~ of** entro i limiti di

compassion [kəm'pæʃən] n compassione f

compatible [kəm'pætɪbl] *adj*
compatibile

compel [kəm'pɛl] *vt* costringere,
obbligare; **compelling** *adj* (*fig:
argument*) irresistibile

compensate ['kɔmpənseɪt] *vt*
risarcire ▷ *vi*: **to ~ for** compensare;
compensation [kɔmpən'seɪʃən]
n compensazione *f*; (*money*)
risarcimento

compete [kəm'piːt] *vi* (*take part*)
concorrere; (*vie*): **to ~ (with)** fare
concorrenza (a)

competent ['kɔmpɪtənt] *adj*
competente

competition [kɔmpɪ'tɪʃən] *n* gara;
concorso; (*Econ*) concorrenza

competitive [kəm'pɛtɪtɪv] *adj*
(*sports*) agonistico/a; (*person*)
che ha spirito di competizione;
che ha spirito agonistico; (*Econ*)
concorrenziale

competitor [kəm'pɛtɪtər] *n*
concorrente *m/f*

complacent [kəm'pleɪsnt] *adj*
compiaciuto/a di sé

complain [kəm'pleɪn] *vi* lagnarsi,
lamentarsi; **complaint** *n* lamento;
(*in shop etc*) reclamo; (*Med*) malattia

complement *n* ['kɔmplɪmənt]
complemento; (*especially of ship's crew
etc*) effettivo ▷ *vt* ['kɔmplɪmənt]
(*enhance*) accompagnarsi bene a;
complementary [kɔmplɪ'mɛntərɪ]
adj complementare

complete [kəm'pliːt] *adj*
completo/a ▷ *vt* completare;
(*form*) riempire; **completely** *adv*
completamente; **completion** *n*
completamento

complex ['kɔmplɛks] *adj*
complesso/a ▷ *n* (*Psych, buildings etc*)
complesso

complexion [kəm'plɛkʃən] *n* (*of
face*) carnagione *f*

compliance [kəm'plaɪəns] *n*
acquiescenza; **in ~ with** (*orders,
wishes etc*) in conformità con

complicate ['kɔmplɪkeɪt] *vt*
complicare; **complicated** *adj*
complicato/a; **complication**
[kɔmplɪ'keɪʃən] *n* complicazione *f*

compliment *n* ['kɔmplɪmənt]
complimento ▷ *vt* ['kɔmplɪmənt]
fare un complimento a;
complimentary [kɔmplɪ'mɛntərɪ]
adj complimentoso/a, elogiativo/a;
(*free*) in omaggio

comply [kəm'plaɪ] *vi*: **to ~ with**
assentire a; conformarsi a

component [kəm'pəunənt] *adj*,
componente (*m*)

compose [kəm'pəuz] *vt* (*music,
poem etc*) comporre; **to ~ o.s.**
ricomporsi; **~d of** composto/a di;
composer *n* (*Mus*) compositore/
trice; **composition** [kɔmpə'zɪʃən] *n*
composizione *f*

composure [kəm'pəuʒər] *n* calma

compound ['kɔmpaund] *n* (*Chem,
Ling*) composto; (*enclosure*) recinto
▷ *adj* composto/a

comprehension [kɔmprɪ'hɛnʃən]
n comprensione *f*

comprehensive [kɔmprɪ'hɛnsɪv]
adj completo/a; **comprehensive
(school)** *n* (BRIT) scuola secondaria
aperta a tutti

> Be careful not to translate
> *comprehensive* by the Italian word
> *comprensivo*.

compress *vt* [kəm'prɛs] comprimere
▷ *n* ['kɔmprɛs] (*Med*) compressa

comprise [kəm'praɪz] *vt* (*also*: **be ~d
of**) comprendere

compromise ['kɔmprəmaɪz] *n*
compromesso ▷ *vt* compromettere
▷ *vi* venire a un compromesso

compulsive [kəm'pʌlsɪv] *adj* (*liar,
gambler*) che non riesce a controllarsi;
(*viewing, reading*) cui non si può fare
a meno

compulsory [kəm'pʌlsərɪ] *adj*
obbligatorio/a

computer [kəm'pjuːtər] *n* computer
m inv, elaboratore *m* elettronico;

computer game n gioco per computer; **computer-generated** adj realizzato/a al computer; **computerize** vt computerizzare; **computer programmer** n programmatore/trice; **computer programming** n programmazione f di computer; **computer science** n informatica; **computer studies** npl informatica; **computing** n informatica

con [kɔn] vt (col) truffare ▷ n truffa
conceal [kən'siːl] vt nascondere
concede [kən'siːd] vt concedere; (admit) ammettere
conceited [kən'siːtɪd] adj presuntuoso/a, vanitoso/a
conceive [kən'siːv] vt concepire ▷ vi concepire un bambino
concentrate ['kɔnsəntreɪt] vi concentrarsi ▷ vt concentrare
concentration [kɔnsən'treɪʃən] n concentrazione f
concept ['kɔnsɛpt] n concetto
concern [kən'səːn] n affare m; (Comm) azienda, ditta; (anxiety) preoccupazione f ▷ vt riguardare; **to be ~ed (about)** preoccuparsi (di); **concerning** prep riguardo a, circa
concert ['kɔnsət] n concerto; **concert hall** n sala da concerti
concerto [kən'tʃəːtəu] n concerto
concession [kən'sɛʃən] n concessione f
concise [kən'saɪs] adj conciso/a
conclude [kən'kluːd] vt concludere; **conclusion** [kən'kluːʒən] n conclusione f
concrete ['kɔŋkriːt] n calcestruzzo ▷ adj concreto/a; di calcestruzzo
concussion [kən'kʌʃən] n commozione f cerebrale
condemn [kən'dɛm] vt condannare; (building) dichiarare pericoloso/a
condensation [kɔndɛn'seɪʃən] n condensazione f
condense [kən'dɛns] vi condensarsi ▷ vt condensare

condition [kən'dɪʃən] n condizione f; (disease) malattia ▷ vt condizionare; **on ~ that** a condizione che + sub, a condizione di; **conditional** adj condizionale; **to be conditional upon** dipendere da; **conditioner** n (for hair) balsamo; (for fabrics) ammorbidente m
condo ['kɔndəu] n abbr (US col) = **condominium**
condom ['kɔndəm] n preservativo
condominium [kɔndə'mɪnɪəm] n (US) condominio
condone [kən'dəun] vt condonare
conduct n ['kɔndʌkt] condotta ▷ vt [kən'dʌkt] condurre; (manage) dirigere; amministrare; (Mus) dirigere; **to ~ o.s.** comportarsi; **conducted tour** [kən'dʌktɪd-] n gita accompagnata; **conductor** n (of orchestra) direttore m d'orchestra; (on bus) bigliettaio; (US Rail) controllore m; (Elec) conduttore m
cone [kəun] n cono; (Bot) pigna; (traffic cone) birillo
confectionery [kən'fɛkʃənərɪ] n dolciumi mpl
confer [kən'fəːr] vt: **to ~ sth on** conferire qc a ▷ vi conferire
conference ['kɔnfərns] n congresso
confess [kən'fɛs] vt confessare, ammettere ▷ vi confessarsi; **confession** [kən'fɛʃən] n confessione f
confide [kən'faɪd] vi: **to ~ in** confidarsi con
confidence ['kɔnfɪdns] n confidenza; (trust) fiducia; (also: **self-~**) sicurezza di sé; **in ~** (speak, write) in confidenza, confidenzialmente; **confident** adj sicuro/a; sicuro/a di sé; **confidential** [kɔnfɪ'dɛnʃəl] adj riservato/a, confidenziale
confine [kən'faɪn] vt limitare; (shut up) rinchiudere; **confined** adj (space) ristretto/a

confirm [kən'fəːm] vt confermare;
confirmation [kɔnfə'meɪʃən] n
conferma; (Rel) cresima
confiscate ['kɔnfɪskeɪt] vt
confiscare
conflict n ['kɔnflɪkt] conflitto ▷ vi
[kən'flɪkt] essere in conflitto
conform [kən'fɔːm] vi: **to ~ (to)**
conformarsi (a)
confront [kən'frʌnt] vt (enemy,
danger) affrontare; **confrontation**
[kɔnfrən'teɪʃən] n scontro
confuse [kən'fjuːz] vt (one thing
with another) confondere; **confused**
adj confuso/a; **confusing** adj
che fa confondere; **confusion**
[kən'fjuːʒən] n confusione f
congestion [kən'dʒɛstʃən] n
congestione f
congratulate [kən'grætjuleɪt]
vt: **to ~ sb (on)** congratularsi con
qn (per or di); **congratulations**
[kəngrætju'leɪʃənz] npl auguri
mpl; (on success) complimenti
mpl; **congratulations (on)**
congratulazioni fpl (per)
congregation [kɔngrɪ'geɪʃən] n
congregazione f
congress ['kɔngrɛs] n congresso;
congressman ['kɔngrɛsmən] n
(irreg: US) membro del Congresso;
congresswoman ['kɔngrɛswumən]
n (irreg: US) (donna) membro del
Congresso
conifer ['kɔnɪfər] n conifero
conjugate ['kɔndʒugeɪt] vt
coniugare
conjugation [kɔndʒə'geɪʃən] n
coniugazione f
conjunction [kən'dʒʌŋkʃən] n
congiunzione f
conjure ['kʌndʒər] vi fare giochi di
prestigio
connect [kə'nɛkt] vt connettere,
collegare; (Elec) collegare; (fig)
associare ▷ vi (train): **to ~ with**
essere in coincidenza con; **to
be ~ed with** (associated) aver

rapporti con; **connecting flight** n
volo in coincidenza; **connection**
[kə'nɛkʃən] n relazione f,
rapporto; (Elec) connessione f; (Tel)
collegamento; (train, plane etc)
coincidenza
conquer ['kɔŋkər] vt conquistare;
(feelings) vincere
conquest ['kɔŋkwɛst] n conquista
cons [kɔnz] npl see **pro**;
convenience
conscience ['kɔnʃəns] n coscienza
conscientious [kɔnʃɪ'ɛnʃəs] adj
coscienzioso/a
conscious ['kɔnʃəs] adj consapevole;
(Med) cosciente; **consciousness** n
consapevolezza; (Med) coscienza
consecutive [kən'sɛkjutɪv] adj
consecutivo/a; **on 3 ~ occasions** 3
volte di fila
consensus [kən'sɛnsəs] n consenso;
the ~ of opinion l'opinione f
unanime or comune
consent [kən'sɛnt] n consenso ▷ vi:
to ~ (to) acconsentire (a)
consequence ['kɔnsɪkwəns] n
conseguenza, risultato; importanza
consequently ['kɔnsɪkwəntlɪ] adv
di conseguenza, dunque
conservation [kɔnsə'veɪʃən] n
conservazione f
conservative [kən'səːvətɪv] adj,
n conservatore/trice; (cautious)
cauto/a; **C~** adj, n (BRIT Pol)
conservatore/trice
conservatory [kən'səːvətrɪ]
n (greenhouse) serra; (Mus)
conservatorio
consider [kən'sɪdər] vt considerare;
(take into account) tener conto
di; **to ~ doing sth** considerare la
possibilità di fare qc; **considerable**
[kən'sɪdərəbl] adj considerevole,
notevole; **considerably** adv
notevolmente, decisamente;
considerate [kən'sɪdərɪt] adj
premuroso/a; **consideration**
[kənsɪdə'reɪʃən] n considerazione

f; **considering** [kən'sɪdərɪŋ] *prep* in considerazione di

consignment [kən'saɪnmənt] *n (of goods)* consegna; spedizione *f*

consist [kən'sɪst] *vi*: **to ~ of** constare di, essere composto/a di

consistency [kən'sɪstənsɪ] *n* consistenza; *(fig)* coerenza *f*

consistent [kən'sɪstənt] *adj* coerente

consolation [kɔnsə'leɪʃən] *n* consolazione *f*

console *vt* [kən'səul] consolare ▷ *n* ['kɔnsəul] quadro di comando

consonant ['kɔnsənənt] *n* consonante *f*

conspicuous [kən'spɪkjuəs] *adj* cospicuo/a

conspiracy [kən'spɪrəsɪ] *n* congiura, cospirazione *f*

constable ['kʌnstəbl] *n (BRIT)* ≈ poliziotto, agente *m* di polizia; **chief ~** ≈ questore *m*

constant ['kɔnstənt] *adj* costante; continuo/a; **constantly** *adv* costantemente; continuamente

constipated ['kɔnstɪpeɪtɪd] *adj* stitico/a; **constipation** [kɔnstɪ'peɪʃən] *n* stitichezza

constituency [kən'stɪtjuənsɪ] *n* collegio elettorale

constitute ['kɔnstɪtjuːt] *vt* costituire

constitution [kɔnstɪ'tjuːʃən] *n* costituzione *f*

constraint [kən'streɪnt] *n* costrizione *f*

construct [kən'strʌkt] *vt* costruire; **construction** [kən'strʌkʃən] *n* costruzione *f*; **constructive** *adj* costruttivo/a

consul ['kɔnsl] *n* console *m*; **consulate** ['kɔnsjulɪt] *n* consolato

consult [kən'sʌlt] *vt*: **to ~ sb (about sth)** consultare qn (su *or* riguardo a qc); **consultant** *n (Med)* consulente *m* medico; *(other specialist)* consulente; **consultation**

[kɔnsəl'teɪʃən] *n (discussion)* consultazione *f*; *(Med, Law)* consulto; **consulting room** [kən'sʌltɪŋ-] *n (BRIT)* ambulatorio

consume [kən'sjuːm] *vt* consumare; **consumer** *n* consumatore/trice

consumption [kən'sʌmpʃən] *n* consumo

cont. *abbr (= continued)* segue

contact ['kɔntækt] *n* contatto; *(person)* conoscenza ▷ *vt* mettersi in contatto con; **contact lenses** *npl* lenti *fpl* a contatto

contagious [kən'teɪdʒəs] *adj (also fig)* contagioso/a

contain [kən'teɪn] *vt* contenere; **to ~ o.s.** contenersi; **container** *n* recipiente *m*; *(for shipping etc)* container *m inv*

contaminate [kən'tæmɪneɪt] *vt* contaminare

cont'd *abbr (= continued)* segue

contemplate ['kɔntəmpleɪt] *vt* contemplare; *(consider)* pensare a *(or* di)

contemporary [kən'tɛmpərərɪ] *adj, n* contemporaneo/a

contempt [kən'tɛmpt] *n* disprezzo; **~ of court** *(Law)* oltraggio alla Corte

contend [kən'tɛnd] *vt*: **to ~ that** sostenere che ▷ *vi*: **to ~ with** lottare contro

content¹ ['kɔntɛnt] *n* contenuto; **contents** *npl (of box, case etc)* contenuto; **(table of) ~s** indice *m*

content² [kən'tɛnt] *adj* contento/a, soddisfatto/a ▷ *vt* contentare, soddisfare; **contented** [kən'tɛntɪd] *adj* contento/a, soddisfatto/a

contest *n* ['kɔntɛst] lotta; *(competition)* gara, concorso ▷ *vt* [kən'tɛst] contestare; *(Law)* impugnare; *(compete for)* contendersi; **contestant** [kən'tɛstənt] *n* concorrente *m/f*; *(in fight)* avversario/a

context ['kɔntɛkst] *n* contesto

continent ['kɒntɪnənt] n
continente m; **the C~** (BRIT)
l'Europa continentale; **continental**
[kɒntɪ'nɛntl] adj continentale;
continental breakfast n colazione
f all'europea (senza piatti caldi);
continental quilt n (BRIT) piumino

continual [kən'tɪnjuəl] adj
continuo/a; **continually** adv di
continuo

continue [kən'tɪnjuː] vi continuare
▷ vt continuare; (start again)
riprendere

continuity [kɒntɪ'njuːɪtɪ] n
continuità; (Cine) (ordine m della)
sceneggiatura

continuous [kən'tɪnjuəs] adj
continuo/a, ininterrotto/a;
continuous assessment n
(BRIT) valutazione f continua;
continuously adv (repeatedly)
continuamente; (uninterruptedly)
ininterrottamente

contour ['kɒntuəʳ] n contorno,
profilo; (also: **~ line**) curva di livello

contraception [kɒntrə'sɛpʃən] n
contraccezione f

contraceptive [kɒntrə'sɛptɪv]
adj contraccettivo/a ▷ n
contraccettivo

contract n ['kɒntrækt] contratto
▷ vi [kən'trækt] (become smaller)
contrarsi; (Comm): **to ~ to do sth**
fare un contratto per fare qc ▷ vt
[kən'trækt] (illness) contrarre;
contractor n imprenditore m

contradict [kɒntrə'dɪkt] vt
contraddire; **contradiction**
[kɒntrə'dɪkʃən] n contraddizione
f; **to be in contradiction with**
discordare con

contrary¹ ['kɒntrərɪ] adj
contrario/a; (unfavourable) avverso/a,
contrario/a ▷ n contrario; **on the ~**
al contrario; **unless you hear to the
~** salvo contrordine

contrary² [kən'trɛərɪ] adj (perverse)
bisbetico/a

contrast n ['kɒntrɑːst] contrasto
▷ vt [kən'trɑːst] mettere in
contrasto; **in ~ to** or **with**
contrariamente a

contribute [kən'trɪbjuːt] vi
contribuire ▷ vt: **to ~ £10/an article
to** dare 10 sterline/un articolo a; **to ~
to** contribuire a; (newspaper) scrivere
per; **contribution** [kɒntrɪ'bjuːʃən]
n contributo; **contributor**
[kən'trɪbjutəʳ] n (to newspaper)
collaboratore/trice

control [kən'trəul] vt (firm,
operation etc) dirigere; (check)
controllare ▷ n controllo; **controls**
npl (of vehicle etc) comandi mpl; **to
be in ~ of** avere il controllo di; **to
go out of ~** (car) non rispondere
ai comandi; (situation) sfuggire di
mano; **control tower** n (Aviat) torre
f di controllo

controversial [kɒntrə'vəːʃl] adj
controverso/a, polemico/a

controversy ['kɒntrəvəːsɪ] n
controversia, polemica

convenience [kən'viːnɪəns] n
comodità f inv; **at your ~** a suo
comodo; **all modern ~s**, (BRIT)
all mod cons tutte le comodità
moderne

convenient [kən'viːnɪənt] adj
comodo/a

> Be careful not to translate
> convenient by the Italian word
> conveniente.

convent ['kɒnvənt] n convento

convention [kən'vɛnʃən] n
convenzione f; (meeting) convegno;
conventional adj convenzionale

conversation [kɒnvə'seɪʃən] n
conversazione f

conversely [kɒn'vəːslɪ] adv al
contrario, per contro

conversion [kən'vəːʃən] n
conversione f; (BRIT: of house)
trasformazione f, rimodernamento

convert vt [kən'vəːt] (Rel, Comm)
convertire; (alter) trasformare ▷ n

['kɔnvə:t] convertito/a; **convertible**
n macchina decappottabile
convey [kən'veɪ] vt trasportare;
(thanks) comunicare; (idea) dare;
conveyor belt [kən'veɪə'-] n nastro
trasportatore
convict vt [kən'vɪkt] dichiarare
colpevole ▷ n ['kɔnvɪkt] carcerato/a;
conviction [kən'vɪkʃən] n
condanna; (belief) convinzione f
convince [kən'vɪns] vt: **to ~ sb (of
sth/that)** convincere qn (di qc/
che), persuadere qn (di qc/che);
convinced adj: **convinced of/that**
convinto/a di/che; **convincing** adj
convincente
convoy ['kɔnvɔɪ] n convoglio
cook [kuk] vt cucinare, cuocere
▷ vi cuocere; (person) cucinare ▷ n
cuoco/a; **cookbook** ['kukbuk] n
= **cookery book**; **cooker** n fornello,
cucina; **cookery** n cucina; **cookery
book** n (BRIT) libro di cucina; **cookie**
n (US) biscotto; (Comput) cookie m inv;
cooking n cucina
cool [ku:l] adj fresco/a; (not afraid)
calmo/a; (unfriendly) freddo/a ▷ vt
raffreddare; (room) rinfrescare ▷ vi
(water) raffreddarsi; (air) rinfrescarsi;
cool down vi raffreddarsi; (fig:
person, situation) calmarsi; **cool
off** vi (become calmer) calmarsi; (lose
enthusiasm) perdere interesse
cop [kɔp] n (col) sbirro
cope [kəup] vi: **to ~ with** (problems)
far fronte a
copper ['kɔpə'] n rame m; (col:
policeman) sbirro
copy ['kɔpɪ] n copia ▷ vt copiare;
copyright n diritto d'autore
coral ['kɔrəl] n corallo
cord [kɔ:d] n corda; (Elec) filo; **cords**
npl (trousers) calzoni mpl (di velluto) a
coste; **cordless** adj senza cavo
corduroy ['kɔ:dərɔɪ] n fustagno
core [kɔ:'] n (of fruit) torsolo; (of
organization etc) cuore m ▷ vt estrarre
il torsolo da

coriander [kɔrɪ'ændə'] n coriandolo
cork [kɔ:k] n sughero; (of bottle)
tappo; **corkscrew** n cavatappi m inv
corn [kɔ:n] n (BRIT: wheat) grano; (US:
maize) granturco; (on foot) callo; **~ on
the cob** (Culin) pannocchia cotta
corned beef ['kɔ:nd-] n carne f di
manzo in scatola
corner ['kɔ:nə'] n angolo; (Aut)
curva ▷ vt intrappolare; mettere
con le spalle al muro; (Comm: market)
accaparrare ▷ vi prendere una curva
corner shop n (BRIT) piccolo negozio
di generi alimentari
cornflakes ['kɔ:nfleɪks] npl fiocchi
mpl di granturco
cornflour ['kɔ:nflauə'] n (BRIT)
farina finissima di granturco
cornstarch ['kɔ:nsta:tʃ] n (US)
= **cornflour**
Cornwall ['kɔ:nwəl] n Cornovaglia
coronary ['kɔrənərɪ] n: **~
(thrombosis)** trombosi f coronaria
coronation [kɔrə'neɪʃən] n
incoronazione f
coroner ['kɔrənə'] n magistrato
incaricato di indagare la causa di morte
in circostanze sospette
corporal ['kɔ:prəl] n
caporalmaggiore m ▷ adj: **~
punishment** pena corporale
corporate ['kɔ:pərɪt] adj
comune; (Comm) costituito/a (in
corporazione)
corporation [kɔ:pə'reɪʃən] n (of
town) consiglio comunale; (Comm)
ente m
corps (pl **corps**) [kɔ:, kɔ:z] n corpo
corpse [kɔ:ps] n cadavere m
correct [kə'rekt] adj (accurate)
corretto/a, esatto/a; (proper)
corretto/a ▷ vt correggere;
correction [kə'rekʃən] n correzione f
correspond [kɔrɪs'pɔnd] vi
corrispondere; **correspondence** n
corrispondenza; **correspondent** n
corrispondente m/f; **corresponding**
adj corrispondente

corridor ['kɔrɪdɔːʳ] n corridoio

corrode [kə'rəud] vt corrodere ▷ vi corrodersi

corrupt [kə'rʌpt] adj corrotto/a; (Comput) alterato/a ▷ vt corrompere; **corruption** n corruzione f

Corsica ['kɔːsɪkə] n Corsica

cosmetic [kɔz'mɛtɪk] n cosmetico; **cosmetic surgery** n chirurgia plastica

cosmopolitan [kɔzmə'pɔlɪtn] adj cosmopolita

cost [kɔst] (pt, pp **cost**) n costo ▷ vi costare ▷ vt stabilire il prezzo di; **costs** npl (Law) spese fpl; **how much does it ~?** quanto costa?

co-star ['kəustɑːʳ] n attore/trice della stessa importanza del protagonista

Costa Rica ['kɔstə'riːkə] n Costa Rica

costly ['kɔstlɪ] adj costoso/a, caro/a

cost-of-living ['kɔstəv'lɪvɪŋ] adj: **~ allowance** indennità f inv di contingenza

costume ['kɔstjuːm] n costume m; (lady's suit) tailleur m inv; (BRIT: also: **swimming ~**) costume da bagno

cosy, (US) **cozy** ['kəuzɪ] adj intimo/a; **I'm very ~ here** sto proprio bene qui

cot [kɔt] n (BRIT: child's) lettino; (US: folding bed) brandina

cottage ['kɔtɪdʒ] n cottage m inv; **cottage cheese** n fiocchi mpl di latte magro

cotton ['kɔtn] n cotone m; **~ dress** etc vestito etc di cotone; **cotton on** vi (col): **to ~ on (to sth)** afferrare (qc); **cotton bud** n (BRIT) cotton fioc® m inv; **cotton candy** (US) n zucchero filato; **cotton wool** n (BRIT) cotone m idrofilo

couch [kautʃ] n sofà m inv

cough [kɔf] vi tossire ▷ n tosse f; **I've got a ~** ho la tosse; **cough mixture, cough syrup** n sciroppo per la tosse

could [kud] pt of **can²**

couldn't ['kudnt] = **could not**

council ['kaunsl] n consiglio; **city or town ~** consiglio comunale; **council estate** n (BRIT) quartiere m di case popolari; **council house** n (BRIT) casa popolare; **councillor** n consigliere/a; **council tax** n (BRIT) tassa comunale sulla proprietà

counsel ['kaunsl] n avvocato; consultazione f ▷ vt: **to ~ sth/sb to do sth** consigliare qc/a qn di fare qc; **counselling**, (US) **counseling** n (Psych) assistenza psicologica; **counsellor**, (US) **counselor** n consigliere/a; (US) avvocato

count [kaunt] vi contare ▷ n conto; (nobleman) conte m; **count in** vt (col) includere; **~ me in** ci sto anch'io; **count on** vt fus contare su; **countdown** n conto alla rovescia

counter ['kauntəʳ] n banco ▷ vt opporsi a ▷ adv: **~ to** contro; in opposizione a; **counter-clockwise** ['kauntə'klɔkwaɪz] (US) adv in senso antiorario

counterfeit ['kauntəfɪt] n contraffazione f, falso ▷ vt contraffare, falsificare ▷ adj falso/a

counterpart ['kauntəpɑːt] n (of document etc) copia; (of person) corrispondente m/f

counterterrorism ['kauntə'terərɪzəm] n antiterrorismo

countess ['kauntɪs] n contessa

countless ['kauntlɪs] adj innumerevole

country ['kʌntrɪ] n paese m; (native land) patria; (as opposed to town) campagna; (region) regione f; **country and western (music)** n musica country e western, country m; **country house** n villa in campagna; **countryside** n campagna

county ['kauntɪ] n contea

coup (pl **coups**) [kuː, kuːz] n colpo; (also: **~ d'état**) colpo di Stato

couple ['kʌpl] *n* coppia; **a ~ of** un paio di

coupon ['ku:pɔn] *n* buono; (*Comm*) coupon *m inv*

courage ['kʌrɪdʒ] *n* coraggio; **courageous** *adj* coraggioso/a

courgette [kuə'ʒɛt] *n* (*BRIT*) zucchina

courier ['kurɪəʳ] *n* corriere *m*; (*for tourists*) guida

course [kɔ:s] *n* corso; (*of ship*) rotta; (*for golf*) campo; (*part of meal*) piatto; **of ~** senz'altro, naturalmente; **~ (of action)** modo d'agire; **a ~ of treatment** (*Med*) una cura

court [kɔ:t] *n* corte *f*; (*Tennis*) campo ▷ *vt* fare la corte a; **to take to ~** citare in tribunale

courtesy ['kə:təsɪ] *n* cortesia; **by ~ of** per gentile concessione di; **courtesy bus, courtesy coach** *n* navetta gratuita (*di hotel, aeroporto*)

court: court-house *n* (*US*) palazzo di giustizia; **courtroom** ['kɔ:trum] *n* tribunale *m*; **courtyard** ['kɔ:tjɑ:d] *n* cortile *m*

cousin ['kʌzn] *n* cugino/a; **first ~** cugino di primo grado

cover ['kʌvəʳ] *vt* coprire; (*book, table*) rivestire; (*include*) comprendere; (*Press*) fare un servizio su ▷ *n* (*of pan*) coperchio; (*over furniture*) fodera; (*of bed*) copriletto; (*of book*) copertina; (*shelter*) riparo; (*Comm, Insurance, of spy*) copertura; **covers** *npl* (*on bed*) lenzuola *fpl* e coperte *fpl*; **to take to ~** mettersi al riparo; **under ~** al riparo; **under ~ of darkness** protetto dall'oscurità; **under separate ~** (*Comm*) a parte, in plico separato; **cover up** *vi*: **to ~ up for sb** (*fig*) coprire qn; **coverage** *n* (*Press, TV, Radio*): **to give full coverage to** fare un ampio servizio su; **cover charge** *n* coperto; **cover-up** *n* occultamento (*di informazioni*)

cow [kau] *n* vacca ▷ *vt* (*person*) intimidire

coward ['kauəd] *n* vigliacco/a; **cowardly** *adj* vigliacco/a

cowboy ['kaubɔɪ] *n* cow-boy *m inv*

cozy ['kəuzɪ] *adj* (*US*) = **cosy**

crab [kræb] *n* granchio

crack [kræk] *n* fessura, crepa; incrinatura; (*noise*) schiocco; (*: of gun*) scoppio; (*Drugs*) crack *m inv* ▷ *vt* spaccare; incrinare; (*whip*) schioccare; (*nut*) schiacciare; (*solve: problem, case*) risolvere; (*: code*) decifrare ▷ *cpd* (*troops*) fuori classe; **to ~ jokes** dire battute, scherzare; **to get ~ing** (*col*) darsi una mossa; **crack down on** *vt fus* prendere serie misure contro, porre freno a; **cracked** *adj* (*col*) matto/a; **cracker** ['krækəʳ] *n* cracker *m inv*; (*firework*) petardo

crackle ['krækl] *vi* crepitare

cradle ['kreɪdl] *n* culla

craft [krɑ:ft] *n* mestiere *m*; (*cunning*) astuzia; (*boat*) naviglio; **craftsman** *n* artigiano; **craftsmanship** *n* abilità

cram [kræm] *vi* (*for exams*) prepararsi (in gran fretta) ▷ *vt* (*fill*): **to ~ sth with** riempire qc di; (*put*): **to ~ sth into** stipare qc in

cramp [kræmp] *n* crampo; **I've got ~ in my leg** ho un crampo alla gamba; **cramped** *adj* ristretto/a

cranberry ['krænbərɪ] *n* mirtillo

crane [kreɪn] *n* gru *f inv*

crap [kræp] *n* (*col!*) fesserie *fpl*; **to have a ~** cacare (!)

crash [kræʃ] *n* fragore *m*; (*of car*) incidente *m*; (*of plane*) caduta; (*Stock Exchange*) crollo ▷ *vt* fracassare ▷ *vi* (*plane*) fracassarsi; (*car*) avere un incidente; (*two cars*) scontrarsi; (*business etc*) fallire, andare in rovina; **crash course** *n* corso intensivo; **crash helmet** *n* casco

crate [kreɪt] *n* cassa

crave [kreɪv] *vt*, *vi*: **to ~ (for)** desiderare ardentemente

crawl [krɔ:l] *vi* strisciare carponi; (*vehicle*) avanzare lentamente ▷ *n* (*Swimming*) crawl *m*

crayfish ['kreɪfɪʃ] n inv (freshwater) gambero (d'acqua dolce); (saltwater) gambero

crayon ['kreɪən] n matita colorata

craze [kreɪz] n mania

crazy ['kreɪzɪ] adj matto/a; (col: keen): **to be ~ about sb** essere pazzo di qn; **to be ~ about sth** andare matto per qc

creak [kriːk] vi cigolare, scricchiolare

cream [kriːm] n crema; (fresh) panna ▷ adj (colour) color crema inv; **cream cheese** n formaggio fresco; **creamy** adj cremoso/a

crease [kriːs] n grinza; (deliberate) piega ▷ vt sgualcire ▷ vi sgualcirsi

create [kriː'eɪt] vt creare; **creation** [kriː'eɪʃən] n creazione f; **creative** adj creativo/a; **creator** n creatore/ trice

creature ['kriːtʃər] n creatura

crèche [krɛʃ] n asilo infantile

credentials [krɪ'dɛnʃlz] npl credenziali fpl

credibility [krɛdɪ'bɪlɪtɪ] n credibilità

credible ['krɛdɪbl] adj credibile; (witness, source) attendibile

credit ['krɛdɪt] n credito; onore m ▷ vt (Comm) accreditare; (believe: also: **give ~ to**) credere, prestar fede a; **to ~ sb with sth** (fig) attribuire qc a qn; **to be in ~** (person) essere creditore/ trice; (bank account) essere coperto/a; see also **credits**; **credit card** n carta di credito; **credit crunch** n improvvisa stretta di credito

credits ['krɛdɪts] npl (Cine) titoli mpl

creek [kriːk] n insenatura; (us) piccolo fiume m

creep (pt, pp **crept**) [kriːp, krɛpt] vi avanzare furtivamente (or pian piano)

cremate [krɪ'meɪt] vt cremare

crematorium (pl **crematoria**) [krɛmə'tɔːrɪəm, -'tɔːrɪə] n forno crematorio

crept [krɛpt] pt, pp of **creep**

crescent ['krɛsnt] n (shape) mezzaluna; (street) strada semicircolare

cress [krɛs] n crescione m

crest [krɛst] n cresta; (of coat of arms) cimiero

crew [kruː] n equipaggio; **crew-neck** n girocollo

crib [krɪb] n culla ▷ vt (col) copiare

cricket ['krɪkɪt] n (insect) grillo; (game) cricket m; **cricketer** n giocatore m di cricket

crime [kraɪm] n crimine m; **criminal** ['krɪmɪnl] adj, n criminale (m/f)

crimson ['krɪmzn] adj color cremisi inv

cringe [krɪndʒ] vi acquattarsi; (in embarrassment) sentirsi sprofondare

cripple ['krɪpl] n (col!) zoppo/a ▷ vt azzoppare

crisis (pl **crises**) ['kraɪsɪs, -siːz] n crisi f inv

crisp [krɪsp] adj croccante; (fig) frizzante; vivace; deciso/a; **crispy** adj croccante

criterion (pl **criteria**) [kraɪ'tɪərɪən, -'tɪərɪə] n criterio

critic ['krɪtɪk] n critico/a; **critical** adj critico/a; **criticism** ['krɪtɪsɪzəm] n critica; **criticize** ['krɪtɪsaɪz] vt criticare

Croat ['krəuæt] adj, n = **Croatian**

Croatia [krəu'eɪʃə] n Croazia; **Croatian** adj croato/a ▷ n croato/a; (Ling) croato

crockery ['krɔkərɪ] n vasellame m

crocodile ['krɔkədaɪl] n coccodrillo

crocus ['krəukəs] n croco

croissant ['krwasã] n brioche f inv, croissant m inv

crook [kruk] n (col) truffatore m; (of shepherd) bastone m; **crooked** ['krukɪd] adj curvo/a, storto/a; (person, action) disonesto/a

crop [krɔp] n (produce) coltivazione f; (amount produced) raccolto; (riding crop) frustino ▷ vt (hair) rapare; **crop up** vi presentarsi

cross [krɔs] n croce f; (Biol) incrocio ▷ vt (street etc) attraversare; (arms, legs, Biol) incrociare; (cheque) sbarrare ▷ adj di cattivo umore; **cross off** vt cancellare (tirando una riga con la penna); **cross out** vt cancellare; **cross over** vi attraversare; **cross-Channel ferry** ['krɔs'tʃænl-] n traghetto che attraversa la Manica; **crosscountry (race)** n cross-country m inv; **crossing** n incrocio; (sea-passage) traversata; (also: **pedestrian crossing**) passaggio pedonale; **crossing guard** (US) n dipendente comunale che aiuta i bambini ad attraversare la strada; **crossroads** n incrocio; **crosswalk** n (US) strisce fpl pedonali, passaggio pedonale; **crossword** n cruciverba m inv

crotch [krɔtʃ] n (Anat) inforcatura; (of garment) pattina

crouch [krautʃ] vi acquattarsi; rannicchiarsi

crouton ['kru:tɔn] n crostino

crow [krəu] n (bird) cornacchia; (of cock) canto del gallo ▷ vi (cock) cantare

crowd [kraud] n folla ▷ vt affollare, stipare ▷ vi: **to ~ round/in** affollarsi intorno a/in; **crowded** adj affollato/a; **crowded with** stipato/a di

crown [kraun] n corona; (of head) calotta cranica; (of hat) cocuzzolo; (of hill) cima ▷ vt incoronare; (fig: career) coronare; **crown jewels** npl gioielli mpl della Corona

crucial ['kru:ʃl] adj cruciale, decisivo/a

crucifix ['kru:sɪfɪks] n crocifisso

crude [kru:d] adj (materials) greggio/a; non raffinato/a; (fig: basic) crudo/a, primitivo/a; (: vulgar) rozzo/a, grossolano/a ▷ n (also: **~ oil**) (petrolio) greggio

cruel ['kruəl] adj crudele; **cruelty** n crudeltà f inv

cruise [kru:z] n crociera ▷ vi andare a velocità di crociera; (taxi) circolare

crumb [krʌm] n briciola

crumble ['krʌmbl] vt sbriciolare ▷ vi sbriciolarsi; (plaster etc) sgretolarsi; (land, earth) franare; (building, fig) crollare

crumpet ['krʌmpɪt] n specie di frittella

crumple ['krʌmpl] vt raggrinzare, spiegazzare

crunch [krʌntʃ] vt sgranocchiare; (underfoot) scricchiolare ▷ n (fig) punto or momento cruciale; **crunchy** adj croccante

crush [krʌʃ] n folla; (love): **to have a ~ on sb** avere una cotta per qn; (drink): **lemon ~** spremuta di limone ▷ vt schiacciare; (crumple) sgualcire

crust [krʌst] n crosta; **crusty** adj (bread) croccante; (person) brontolone/a; (remark) brusco/a

crutch [krʌtʃ] n gruccia

cry [kraɪ] vi piangere; (shout) urlare ▷ n urlo, grido; **cry out** vi, vt gridare

crystal ['krɪstl] n cristallo

cub [kʌb] n cucciolo; (also: **~ scout**) lupetto

Cuba ['kju:bə] n Cuba

Cuban ['kju:bən] adj, n cubano/a

cube [kju:b] n cubo ▷ vt (Math) elevare al cubo; **cubic** adj cubico/a; **cubic metre** etc metro etc cubo

cubicle ['kju:bɪkl] n scompartimento separato; cabina

cuckoo ['kuku:] n cucù m inv

cucumber ['kju:kʌmbə^r] n cetriolo

cuddle ['kʌdl] vt abbracciare, coccolare ▷ vi abbracciarsi

cue [kju:] n stecca; (Theat etc) segnale m

cuff [kʌf] n (BRIT: of shirt, coat etc) polsino; (US: on trousers) risvolto; **off the ~** improvvisando; **cufflink** ['kʌflɪŋk] n gemello

cuisine [kwɪ'zi:n] n cucina

cul-de-sac ['kʌldəsæk] n vicolo cieco

cull [kʌl] vt (ideas etc) scegliere ▷ n (of animals) abbattimento selettivo

culminate ['kʌlmɪneɪt] vi: **to ~ in** culminare con

culprit ['kʌlprɪt] n colpevole m/f
cult [kʌlt] n culto
cultivate ['kʌltɪveɪt] vt (also fig) coltivare
cultural ['kʌltʃərəl] adj culturale
culture ['kʌltʃəʳ] n (also fig) cultura
cumin ['kʌmɪn] n (spice) cumino
cunning ['kʌnɪŋ] n astuzia, furberia ▷ adj astuto/a, furbo/a
cup [kʌp] n tazza; (prize, of bra) coppa
cupboard ['kʌbəd] n armadio
cup final n (BRIT Football) finale f di coppa
curator [kjuə'reɪtəʳ] n direttore m (di museo ecc)
curb [kə:b] vt tenere a freno ▷ n freno; (US) bordo del marciapiede
curdle ['kə:dl] vi cagliare
cure [kjuəʳ] vt guarire; (Culin) trattare; affumicare; essiccare ▷ n rimedio
curfew ['kə:fju:] n coprifuoco
curiosity [kjuərɪ'ɔsɪtɪ] n curiosità
curious ['kjuərɪəs] adj curioso/a
curl [kə:l] n riccio ▷ vt ondulare; (tightly) arricciare ▷ vi arricciarsi; **curl up** vi rannicchiarsi; **curler** n bigodino; **curly** ['kə:lɪ] adj ricciuto/a
currant ['kʌrnt] n (dried) uvetta; (bush, fruit) ribes m inv
currency ['kʌrnsɪ] n moneta; **to gain ~** (fig) acquistare larga diffusione
current ['kʌrnt] adj corrente ▷ n corrente f; **current account** n (BRIT) conto corrente; **current affairs** npl attualità fpl; **currently** adv attualmente
curriculum (pl **curriculums** or **curricula**) [kə'rɪkjuləm, -lə] n curriculum m inv; **curriculum vitae** [-'vi:taɪ] n curriculum vitae m inv
curry ['kʌrɪ] n curry m inv ▷ vt: **to ~ favour with** cercare di attirarsi i favori di; **curry powder** n curry m
curse [kə:s] vt maledire ▷ vi bestemmiare ▷ n maledizione f; bestemmia

cursor ['kə:səʳ] n (Comput) cursore m
curt [kə:t] adj secco/a
curtain ['kə:tn] n tenda; (Theat) sipario
curve [kə:v] n curva ▷ vi curvarsi; **curved** adj curvo/a
cushion ['kuʃən] n cuscino ▷ vt (shock) fare da cuscinetto a
custard ['kʌstəd] n (for pouring) crema
custody ['kʌstədɪ] n (of child) custodia; **to take sb into ~** mettere qn in detenzione preventiva
custom ['kʌstəm] n costume m; consuetudine f; (Comm) clientela
customer ['kʌstəməʳ] n cliente m/f
customized ['kʌstəmaɪzd] adj (car) fuoriserie inv
customs ['kʌstəmz] npl dogana; **customs officer** n doganiere m
cut [kʌt] (pt, pp **cut**) vt tagliare; (shape, make) intagliare; (reduce) ridurre ▷ vi tagliare ▷ n taglio; (in salary etc) riduzione f; **I've ~ myself** mi sono tagliato; **to ~ a tooth** mettere un dente; **cut back** vt (plants) tagliare; (production, expenditure) ridurre; **cut down** vt (tree) abbattere; **cut down on** vt fus ridurre; **cut off** vt tagliare; (fig) isolare; **cut out** vt tagliare; eliminare; (picture) ritagliare; **cut up** vt tagliare a pezzi; **cutback** n riduzione f
cute [kju:t] adj carino/a
cutlery ['kʌtlərɪ] n posate fpl
cutlet ['kʌtlɪt] n costoletta; (nut cutlet) cotoletta vegetariana
cut-price, (US) **cut-rate** adj a prezzo ridotto; **cutting** ['kʌtɪŋ] adj tagliente ▷ n (Press) ritaglio (di giornale); (from plant) talea
CV n abbr = **curriculum vitae**
cwt. abbr = **hundredweight**
cyberbullying ['saɪbəbuliɪŋ] n bullismo informatico
cybercafé ['saɪbəkæfeɪ] n cybercaffè m inv

cybercrime ['saɪbəkraɪm] *n*
delinquenza informatica
cyberspace ['saɪbəspeɪs] *n*
ciberspazio
cycle ['saɪkl] *n* ciclo; (*bicycle*)
bicicletta ▷ *vi* andare in bicicletta;
cycle hire *n* noleggio *m* biciclette
inv; **cycle lane** *n* pista ciclabile;
cycle path *n* pista ciclabile;
cycling ['saɪklɪŋ] *n* ciclismo; **to
go on a cycling holiday** (*BRIT*) fare
una vacanza in bicicletta; **cyclist**
['saɪklɪst] *n* ciclista *m/f*
cyclone ['saɪkləʊn] *n* ciclone *m*
cylinder ['sɪlɪndəʳ] *n* cilindro
cymbals ['sɪmblz] *npl* piatti *mpl*
cynical ['sɪnɪkl] *adj* cinico/a
Cypriot ['sɪprɪət] *adj, n* cipriota (*m/f*)
Cyprus ['saɪprəs] *n* Cipro
cyst [sɪst] *n* cisti *f inv*; **cystitis**
[sɪ'staɪtɪs] *n* cistite *f*
czar [zɑːʳ] *n* zar *m inv*
Czech [tʃɛk] *adj* ceco/a ▷ *n* ceco/a;
(*Ling*) ceco; **Czech Republic** *n*: **the
Czech Republic** la Repubblica Ceca

d

D [diː] *n* (*Mus*) re *m*
dab [dæb] *vt* (*eyes, wound*) tamponare;
(*paint, cream*) applicare (con leggeri
colpetti)
dad [dæd], **daddy** ['dædɪ] *n* babbo,
papà *m inv*
daffodil ['dæfədɪl] *n* trombone *m*,
giunchiglia
daft [dɑːft] *adj* sciocco/a
dagger ['dægəʳ] *n* pugnale *m*
daily ['deɪlɪ] *adj* quotidiano/a,
giornaliero/a ▷ *n* quotidiano ▷ *adv*
tutti i giorni
dairy ['dɛərɪ] *n* (*shop*) latteria; (*on
farm*) caseificio ▷ *cpd* caseario/a;
dairy produce *n* latticini *mpl*
daisy ['deɪzɪ] *n* margherita
dam [dæm] *n* diga ▷ *vt* sbarrare;
costruire dighe su
damage ['dæmɪdʒ] *n* danno,
danni *mpl*; (*fig*) danno ▷ *vt*
danneggiare; **damages** *npl* (*Law*)
danni *mpl*

damn | 346

damn [dæm] vt condannare; (curse)
maledire ▷ n (col): **I don't give a ~**
non me ne frega niente ▷ adj (col: also:
~ed): **this ~ ...** questo maledetto ...;
~ (it)! accidenti!

damp [dæmp] adj umido/a ▷ n
umidità, umido ▷ vt (also: **~en**: cloth,
rag) inumidire, bagnare; (: enthusiasm
etc) spegnere

dance [dɑːns] n danza, ballo; (ball)
ballo ▷ vi ballare; **dance floor** n pista
da ballo; **dancer** n danzatore/trice;
(professional) ballerino/a; **dancing**
['dɑːnsɪŋ] n danza, ballo

dandelion ['dændɪlaɪən] n dente
m di leone

dandruff ['dændrəf] n forfora

Dane [deɪn] n danese m/f

danger ['deɪndʒəʳ] n pericolo;
there is a ~ of fire c'è pericolo di
incendio; **in ~** in pericolo; **he was
in ~ of falling** rischiava di cadere;
dangerous adj pericoloso/a

dangle ['dæŋgl] vt dondolare; (fig) far
balenare ▷ vi pendolare

Danish ['deɪnɪʃ] adj danese ▷ n (Ling)
danese m

dare [dɛəʳ] vt: **to ~ sb to do** sfidare
qn a fare ▷ vi: **to ~ (to) do sth** osare
fare qc; **I ~ say** (I suppose) immagino
(che); **daring** adj audace, ardito/a
▷ n audacia

dark [dɑːk] adj (night, room) buio/a,
scuro/a; (colour, complexion) scuro/a;
(fig) cupo/a, tetro/a, nero/a ▷ n: **in
the ~** al buio; **in the ~ about** (fig)
all'oscuro di; **after ~** a notte fatta;
darken vt (colour) scurire ▷ vi (sky,
room) oscurarsi; **darkness** n oscurità,
buio; **darkroom** n camera oscura

darling ['dɑːlɪŋ] adj caro/a ▷ n tesoro

dart [dɑːt] n freccetta; (Sewing) pince
f inv ▷ vi: **to ~ towards** precipitarsi
verso; **to ~ along** passare come un
razzo; **to ~ away/along** sfrecciare
via/lungo; **dartboard** n bersaglio
(per freccette); **darts** n tiro al
bersaglio (con freccette)

dash [dæʃ] n (sign) lineetta; (small
quantity: of liquid) goccio, goccino ▷ vt
(missile) gettare; (hopes) infrangere
▷ vi: **to ~ towards** precipitarsi verso

dashboard ['dæʃbɔːd] n (Aut)
cruscotto

data ['deɪtə] npl dati mpl; **database**
n database m inv, base f di dati;
data processing n elaborazione f
(elettronica) dei dati

date [deɪt] n data; (appointment)
appuntamento; (fruit) dattero ▷ vt
datare; (person) uscire con; **what's
the ~ today?** quanti ne abbiamo
oggi?; **~ of birth** data di nascita; **to
~** (until now) fino a oggi; **dated** adj
passato/a di moda

daughter ['dɔːtəʳ] n figlia;
daughter-in-law n nuora

daunting ['dɔːntɪŋ] adj non
invidiabile

dawn [dɔːn] n alba ▷ vi (day)
spuntare; **it ~ed on him that ...** gli è
venuto in mente che ...

day [deɪ] n giorno; (as duration)
giornata; (period of time, age) tempo,
epoca; **the ~ before** il giorno avanti
or prima; **the ~ after, the following
~** il giorno dopo, il giorno seguente;
the ~ before yesterday l'altroieri;
the ~ after tomorrow dopodomani;
by ~ di giorno; **day care centre**
n scuola materna; **daydream** vi
sognare a occhi aperti; **daylight** n
luce f del giorno; **day return** n (BRIT)
biglietto giornaliero di andata e
ritorno; **daytime** n giorno; **day-to-
day** adj (routine, life, organization)
quotidiano/a; **day trip** n gita (di
un giorno)

dazed [deɪzd] adj stordito/a

dazzle ['dæzl] vt abbagliare;
dazzling adj (light) abbagliante;
(colour) violento/a; (smile) smagliante

DC abbr (= direct current) c.c.

dead [dɛd] adj morto/a; (numb)
intirizzito/a; (telephone) muto/a;
(battery) scarico/a ▷ adv

assolutamente, perfettamente; **the dead** npl i morti; **he was shot ~** fu colpito a morte; **~ tired** stanco/a morto/a; **to stop ~** fermarsi di colpo; **dead end** n vicolo cieco; **deadline** n scadenza; **deadly** adj mortale; (weapon, poison) micidiale; **Dead Sea** n: **the Dead Sea** il mar Morto

deaf [dɛf] adj sordo/a; **deafen** vt assordare; **deafening** adj fragoroso/a, assordante

deal [diːl] n accordo; (business deal) affare m ▷ vt (pt, pp **dealt** [dɛlt]) (blow, cards) dare; **a great ~ of** molto/a; **deal with** vt fus (Comm) fare affari con, trattare con; (handle) occuparsi di; (be about: book etc) trattare di; **dealer** n commerciante m/f; **dealings** npl (Comm) relazioni fpl; (relations) rapporti mpl

dealt [dɛlt] pt, pp of **deal**

dean [diːn] n (Rel) decano; (Scol) preside m di facoltà (or di collegio)

dear [dɪəʳ] adj caro/a ▷ n: **my ~** caro mio/cara mia ▷ excl: **~ me!** Dio mio!; **D~ Sir/Madam** (in letter) Egregio Signore/Egregia Signora; **D~ Mr/ Mrs X** Gentile Signor/Signora X; **dearly** adv (love) moltissimo; (pay) a caro prezzo

death [dɛθ] n morte f; (Admin) decesso; **death penalty** n pena di morte; **death sentence** n condanna a morte

debate [dɪˈbeɪt] n dibattito ▷ vt dibattere; discutere

debit [ˈdɛbɪt] n debito ▷ vt: **to ~ a sum to sb** or **to sb's account** addebitare una somma a qn; **debit card** n carta di debito

debris [ˈdɛbriː] n detriti mpl

debt [dɛt] n debito; **to be in ~** essere indebitato/a

debug [diːˈbʌg] vt (Comput) localizzare e rimuovere errori in

debut [ˈdeɪbjuː] n debutto

Dec. abbr (= December) dic.

decade [ˈdɛkeɪd] n decennio

347 | dedicate

decaffeinated [dɪˈkæfɪneɪtɪd] adj decaffeinato/a

decay [dɪˈkeɪ] n decadimento; (also: **tooth ~**) carie f ▷ vi (rot) imputridire

deceased [dɪˈsiːst] n: **the ~** il (la) defunto(a)

deceit [dɪˈsiːt] n inganno; **deceive** [dɪˈsiːv] vt ingannare

December [dɪˈsɛmbəʳ] n dicembre m

decency [ˈdiːsənsɪ] n decenza

decent [ˈdiːsənt] adj decente; (respectable) per bene; (kind) gentile

deception [dɪˈsɛpʃən] n inganno

deceptive [dɪˈsɛptɪv] adj ingannevole

decide [dɪˈsaɪd] vt (person) far prendere una decisione a; (question, argument) risolvere, decidere ▷ vi decidere, decidersi; **to ~ to do/ that** decidere di fare/che; **to ~ on** decidere per

decimal [ˈdɛsɪməl] adj, n decimale (m)

decision [dɪˈsɪʒən] n decisione f

decisive [dɪˈsaɪsɪv] adj decisivo/a; (manner, person) deciso/a

deck [dɛk] n (Naut) ponte m; **top ~** imperiale m; **record ~** piatto (giradischi); (of cards) mazzo; **deckchair** n sedia a sdraio

declaration [dɛkləˈreɪʃən] n dichiarazione f

declare [dɪˈklɛəʳ] vt dichiarare

decline [dɪˈklaɪn] n (decay) declino; (lessening) ribasso ▷ vt declinare; rifiutare ▷ vi declinare; diminuire

decorate [ˈdɛkəreɪt] vt (adorn, give a medal to) decorare; (paint and paper) tinteggiare e tappezzare; **decoration** [dɛkəˈreɪʃən] n (medal etc, adornment) decorazione f; **decorator** n decoratore/trice

decrease n [ˈdiːkriːs] diminuzione f ▷ vt, vi [diːˈkriːs] diminuire

decree [dɪˈkriː] n decreto

dedicate [ˈdɛdɪkeɪt] vt consacrare; (book etc) dedicare; **dedicated** adj coscienzioso/a; (Comput)

specializzato/a, dedicato/a;
dedication [dɛdɪˈkeɪʃən] n (*devotion*)
dedizione f; (*in book*) dedica
deduce [dɪˈdjuːs] vt dedurre
deduct [dɪˈdʌkt] vt: **to ~ sth
(from)** dedurre qc (da); **deduction**
[dɪˈdʌkʃən] n deduzione f
deed [diːd] n azione f, atto; (*Law*) atto
deem [diːm] vt (*formal*) giudicare,
ritenere; **to ~ it wise to do** ritenere
prudente fare
deep [diːp] adj profondo/a ▷ adv:
spectators stood 20 ~ c'erano
20 file di spettatori; **4 metres ~**
profondo(a) 4 metri; **how ~ is
the water?** quanto è profonda
l'acqua?; **deep-fry** vt friggere
in olio abbondante; **deeply** adv
profondamente
deer [dɪəʳ] n (*pl inv*): **the ~** i cervidi
(*Zool*); **(red) ~** cervo; **(fallow) ~**
daino; **(roe) ~** capriolo
default [dɪˈfɔːlt] n (*Comput: also: ~
value*) default m inv; **by ~** (*Sport*) per
abbandono
defeat [dɪˈfiːt] n sconfitta ▷ vt (*team,
opponents*) sconfiggere
defect n [ˈdiːfɛkt] difetto ▷ vi
[dɪˈfɛkt]: **to ~ to the enemy/the
West** passare al nemico/all'Ovest;
defective [dɪˈfɛktɪv] adj difettoso/a
defence, (*us*) **defense** [dɪˈfɛns]
n difesa
defend [dɪˈfɛnd] vt difendere;
defendant n imputato/a; **defender**
n difensore/a
defense [dɪˈfɛns] n (*us*) = **defence**
defensive [dɪˈfɛnsɪv] adj difensivo/a
▷ n: **on the ~** sulla difensiva
defer [dɪˈfəːʳ] vt (*postpone*) differire,
rinviare
defiance [dɪˈfaɪəns] n sfida; **in ~ of**
a dispetto di; **defiant** [dɪˈfaɪənt] adj
(*attitude*) di sfida; (*person*) ribelle
deficiency [dɪˈfɪʃənsɪ] n deficienza,
carenza; **deficient** adj deficiente;
insufficiente; **to be deficient in**
mancare di

deficit [ˈdɛfɪsɪt] n disavanzo, deficit
m inv
define [dɪˈfaɪn] vt definire
definite [ˈdɛfɪnɪt] adj (*fixed*)
definito/a, preciso/a; (*clear, obvious*)
ben definito/a, esatto/a; (*Ling*)
determinativo/a; **he was ~ about
it** ne era sicuro; **definitely** adv
indubbiamente
definition [dɛfɪˈnɪʃən] n definizione f
deflate [diːˈfleɪt] vt sgonfiare
deflect [dɪˈflɛkt] vt deflettere,
deviare
defraud [dɪˈfrɔːd] vt: **to ~ (of)**
defraudare (di)
defriend [diːˈfrɛnd] vt (*Internet*)
cancellare dagli amici
defrost [diːˈfrɒst] vt (*fridge*)
disgelare
defuse [diːˈfjuːz] vt disinnescare; (*fig*)
distendere
defy [dɪˈfaɪ] vt sfidare; (*efforts etc*)
resistere a; **it defies description**
supera ogni descrizione
degree [dɪˈgriː] n grado; (*Scol*) laurea
(universitaria); **a (first) ~ in maths**
una laurea in matematica; **by ~s**
(*gradually*) gradualmente, a poco
a poco; **to some ~** fino a un certo
punto, in certa misura
dehydrated [diːhaɪˈdreɪtɪd] adj
disidratato/a; (*milk, eggs*) in polvere
de-icer [ˈdiːaɪsəʳ] n sbrinatore m
delay [dɪˈleɪ] vt ritardare ▷ vi: **to ~ (in
doing sth)** ritardare (a fare qc) ▷ n
ritardo; **to be ~ed** subire un ritardo;
(*person*) essere trattenuto/a
delegate n [ˈdɛlɪgɪt] delegato/a ▷ vt
[ˈdɛlɪgeɪt] delegare
delete [dɪˈliːt] vt cancellare
deli [ˈdɛlɪ] n = **delicatessen**
deliberate adj [dɪˈlɪbərɪt]
(*intentional*) intenzionale; (*slow*)
misurato/a ▷ vi [dɪˈlɪbəreɪt]
deliberare, riflettere; **deliberately**
adv (*on purpose*) deliberatamente
delicacy [ˈdɛlɪkəsɪ] n delicatezza
delicate [ˈdɛlɪkɪt] adj delicato/a

delicatessen [dɛlikəˈtɛsn] n ≈ salumeria

delicious [dɪˈlɪʃəs] adj delizioso/a, squisito/a

delight [dɪˈlaɪt] n delizia, gran piacere m ▷ vt dilettare; **to take ~ in** divertirsi a; **delighted** adj: **delighted (at** or **with sth)** contentissimo/a (di qc), felice (di qc); **to be delighted to do sth/ that** essere felice di fare qc/che + sub; **delightful** adj delizioso/a; incantevole

delinquent [dɪˈlɪŋkwənt] adj, n delinquente (m/f)

deliver [dɪˈlɪvəʳ] vt (mail) distribuire; (goods) consegnare; (speech) pronunciare; (Med) far partorire; **delivery** n distribuzione f; consegna; (of speaker) dizione f; (Med) parto

delusion [dɪˈluːʒən] n illusione f

de luxe [dəˈlʌks] adj di lusso

delve [dɛlv] vi: **to ~ into** frugare in; (subject) far ricerche in

demand [dɪˈmɑːnd] vt richiedere; (rights) rivendicare ▷ n richiesta; (Econ) domanda; (claim) rivendicazione f; **in ~** ricercato/a, richiesto/a; **on ~** a richiesta; **demanding** adj (boss) esigente; (work) impegnativo/a

demise [dɪˈmaɪz] n decesso

demo [ˈdɛməu] n abbr (col) (= demonstration) manifestazione f

democracy [dɪˈmɔkrəsɪ] n democrazia; **democrat** [ˈdɛməkræt] n democratico/a; **democratic** [dɛməˈkrætɪk] adj democratico/a

demolish [dɪˈmɔlɪʃ] vt demolire

demolition [dɛməˈlɪʃən] n demolizione f

demon [ˈdiːmən] n (also fig) demonio ▷ cpd: **a ~ squash player** un mago dello squash; **a ~ driver** un guidatore folle

demonstrate [ˈdɛmənstreɪt] vt dimostrare, provare ▷ vi: **to ~ (for/against)** dimostrare (per/contro), manifestare (per/contro); **demonstration** [dɛmənˈstreɪʃən] n dimostrazione f; (Pol) manifestazione f, dimostrazione; **demonstrator** n (Pol) dimostrante m/f; (Comm) dimostratore/trice

demote [dɪˈməut] vt far retrocedere

den [dɛn] n tana, covo; (room) buco

denial [dɪˈnaɪəl] n diniego; rifiuto

denim [ˈdɛnɪm] n tessuto di cotone ritorto; see also **denims**

denims [ˈdɛnɪmz] npl blue jeans mpl

Denmark [ˈdɛnmɑːk] n Danimarca

denomination [dɪnɔmɪˈneɪʃən] n (of money) valore m; (Rel) confessione f

denounce [dɪˈnauns] vt denunciare

dense [dɛns] adj fitto/a; (smoke) denso/a; (col: stupid) ottuso/a, duro/a

density [ˈdɛnsɪtɪ] n densità f inv

dent [dɛnt] n ammaccatura ▷ vt (also: **make a ~ in**) ammaccare

dental [ˈdɛntl] adj dentale; **dental floss** [-flɔs] n filo interdentale; **dental surgery** n studio dentistico

dentist [ˈdɛntɪst] n dentista m/f

denture(s) [ˈdɛntʃə(z)] n(pl) dentiera

deny [dɪˈnaɪ] vt negare; (refuse) rifiutare

deodorant [diːˈəudərənt] n deodorante m

depart [dɪˈpɑːt] vi partire; **to ~ from** (fig) deviare da

department [dɪˈpɑːtmənt] n (Comm) reparto; (Scol) sezione f, dipartimento; (Pol) ministero; **department store** n grande magazzino

departure [dɪˈpɑːtʃəʳ] n partenza; (fig): **~ from** deviazione f da; **a new ~** una svolta (decisiva); **departure lounge** n sala d'attesa

depend [dɪˈpɛnd] vi: **to ~ (up)on** dipendere da; (rely on) contare su; **it ~s** dipende; **~ing on the result …** a seconda del risultato …; **dependant** n persona a carico; **dependent** adj: **to be dependent (on)** dipendere

(da); (*child, relative*) essere a carico (di)
▷ *n* = **dependant**

depict [dɪˈpɪkt] *vt* (*in picture*)
dipingere; (*in words*) descrivere

deport [dɪˈpɔːt] *vt* deportare;
espellere

deposit [dɪˈpɒzɪt] *n* (*Comm, Geo*)
deposito; (*of ore, oil*) giacimento;
(*Chem*) sedimento; (*part payment*)
acconto; (*for hired goods etc*) cauzione
f ▷ *vt* depositare; dare in acconto;
(*luggage etc*) mettere *or* lasciare in
deposito; **deposit account** *n* conto
vincolato

depot [ˈdɛpəu] *n* deposito; (*US*)
stazione *f* ferroviaria

depreciate [dɪˈpriːʃɪeɪt] *vi* svalutarsi

depress [dɪˈprɛs] *vt* deprimere;
(*price, wages*) abbassare; (*press
down*) premere; **depressed** *adj*
(*person*) depresso/a, abbattuto/a;
(*market, trade*) in ribasso; (*industry*)
in crisi; **depressing** *adj* deprimente;
depression [dɪˈprɛʃən] *n*
depressione *f*

deprive [dɪˈpraɪv] *vt*: **to ~ sb
of** privare qn di; **deprived** *adj*
disgraziato/a

dept. *abbr* = **department**

depth [dɛpθ] *n* profondità *f inv*; **in
the ~s of** nel profondo di; nel cuore
di; **to be out of one's ~** (*BRIT*)
(*swimmer*) essere dove non si tocca;
(*fig*) non sentirsi all'altezza della
situazione

deputy [ˈdɛpjutɪ] *n* (*second in
command*) vice *m/f*; (*US: also: ~
sheriff*) vice-sceriffo ▷ *cpd*: **~ head**
(*BRIT*) (*Scol*) vicepreside *m/f*

derail [dɪˈreɪl] *vt*: **to be ~ed**
deragliare

derelict [ˈdɛrɪlɪkt] *adj* abbandonato/a

derive [dɪˈraɪv] *vt*: **to ~ sth from**
derivare qc da; trarre qc da ▷ *vi*: **to ~
from** derivare da

descend [dɪˈsɛnd] *vt, vi* discendere,
scendere; **to ~ from** discendere da;
to ~ to (*lying, begging*) abbassarsi a;

descendant *n* discendente *m/f*;
descent [dɪˈsɛnt] *n* discesa; (*origin*)
discendenza, famiglia

describe [dɪsˈkraɪb] *vt* descrivere;
description [dɪsˈkrɪpʃən] *n*
descrizione *f*; (*sort*) genere *m*, specie *f*

desert *n* [ˈdɛzət] deserto ▷ *vt* [dɪˈzəːt]
lasciare, abbandonare ▷ *vi* [dɪˈzəːt]
(*Mil*) disertare; **deserted** [dɪˈzəːtɪd]
adj deserto/a

deserve [dɪˈzəːv] *vt* meritare

design [dɪˈzaɪn] *n* (*sketch*) disegno;
(*layout, shape*) linea; (*pattern*)
fantasia; (*intention*) intenzione *f*
▷ *vt* disegnare; progettare; **design
and technology** (*BRIT Scol*)
progettazione *f* e tecnologie *fpl*

designate *vt* [ˈdɛzɪgneɪt] designare
▷ *adj* [ˈdɛzɪgnɪt] designato/a

designer [dɪˈzaɪnə*r*] *n* (*Tech*)
disegnatore/trice; (*fashion designer*)
disegnatore/trice di moda

desirable [dɪˈzaɪərəbl] *adj*
desiderabile; **it is ~ that** è opportuno
che + *sub*

desire [dɪˈzaɪə*r*] *n* desiderio, voglia
▷ *vt* desiderare, volere

desk [dɛsk] *n* (*in office*) scrivania; (*for
pupil*) banco; (*BRIT: in shop, restaurant*)
cassa; (*in hotel*) ricevimento; (*at
airport*) accettazione *f*; **desktop** *n*
desktop *m inv*; **desktop publishing** *n*
desktop publishing *m*

despair [dɪsˈpɛə*r*] *n* disperazione *f*
▷ *vi*: **to ~ of** disperare di

despatch [dɪsˈpætʃ] *n, vt* = **dispatch**

desperate [ˈdɛspərɪt] *adj*
disperato/a; (*fugitive*) capace
di tutto; **to be ~ for sth/to do**
volere disperatamente qc/fare;
desperately *adv* disperatamente;
(*very*) terribilmente, estremamente;
desperation [dɛspəˈreɪʃən] *n*
disperazione *f*

despise [dɪsˈpaɪz] *vt* disprezzare,
sdegnare

despite [dɪsˈpaɪt] *prep* malgrado, a
dispetto di, nonostante

dessert [dɪ'zəːt] n dolce m; frutta;
dessertspoon n cucchiaio da dolci
destination [dɛstɪ'neɪʃən] n
destinazione f
destined ['dɛstɪnd] adj: **to be ~ to
do sth** essere destinato(a) a fare qc;
~ for London diretto a Londra
destiny ['dɛstɪnɪ] n destino
destroy [dɪs'trɔɪ] vt distruggere
destruction [dɪs'trʌkʃən] n
distruzione f
destructive [dɪs'trʌktɪv] adj
distruttivo/a
detach [dɪ'tætʃ] vt staccare,
distaccare; **detached** adj (attitude)
distante; **detached house** n villa
detail ['diːteɪl] n particolare
m, dettaglio ▷ vt dettagliare,
particolareggiare; **in ~** nei
particolari; **detailed** adj
particolareggiato/a
detain [dɪ'teɪn] vt trattenere; (in
captivity) detenere
detect [dɪ'tɛkt] vt scoprire, scorgere;
(Med, Police, Radar etc) individuare;
detection [dɪ'tɛkʃən] n scoperta;
individuazione f; **detective** n
investigatore/trice; **detective story**
n giallo
detention [dɪ'tɛnʃən] n detenzione
f; (Scol) permanenza forzata per
punizione
deter [dɪ'təː'] vt dissuadere
detergent [dɪ'təːdʒənt] n detersivo
deteriorate [dɪ'tɪərɪəreɪt] vi
deteriorarsi
determination [dɪtəːmɪ'neɪʃən] n
determinazione f
determine [dɪ'təːmɪn] vt
determinare; **determined** adj
(person) risoluto/a, deciso/a; **to
be determined to do sth** essere
determinato or deciso a fare qc
deterrent [dɪ'tɛrənt] n deterrente
m; **to act as a ~** fungere da
deterrente
detest [dɪ'tɛst] vt detestare
detour ['diːtuə'] n deviazione f

detox ['diːtɔks] n disintossicazione f
detract [dɪ'trækt] vi: **to ~ from**
detrarre da
detrimental [dɛtrɪ'mɛntl] adj: **~ to**
dannoso/a a, nocivo/a a
devastating ['dɛvəsteɪtɪŋ] adj
devastatore/trice, sconvolgente
develop [dɪ'vɛləp] vt sviluppare;
(habit) prendere (gradualmente) ▷ vi
svilupparsi; (facts, symptoms: appear)
manifestarsi, rivelarsi; **developing
country** n paese m in via di sviluppo;
development n sviluppo
device [dɪ'vaɪs] n (apparatus)
congegno
devil ['dɛvl] n diavolo; demonio
devious ['diːvɪəs] adj (person)
subdolo/a
devise [dɪ'vaɪz] vt escogitare,
concepire
devote [dɪ'vəut] vt: **to ~ sth
to** dedicare qc a; **devoted** adj
devoto/a; **to be devoted to**
essere molto affezionato/a a a;
devotion [dɪ'vəuʃən] n devozione
f, attaccamento; (Rel) atto di
devozione, preghiera
devour [dɪ'vauə'] vt divorare
devout [dɪ'vaut] adj pio/a, devoto/a
dew [djuː] n rugiada
diabetes [daɪə'biːtiːz] n diabete m
diabetic [daɪə'bɛtɪk] adj, n diabetico/a
diagnose [daɪəg'nəuz] vt
diagnosticare
diagnosis (pl **diagnoses**)
[daɪəg'nəusɪs, -siːz] n diagnosi f inv
diagonal [daɪ'ægənl] adj, n
diagonale (f)
diagram ['daɪəgræm] n
diagramma m
dial ['daɪəl] n quadrante m; (on
radio) lancetta; (on telephone) disco
combinatore ▷ vt (number) fare
dialect ['daɪəlɛkt] n dialetto
dialling code ['daɪəlɪŋ-], (US) **area
code** n prefisso
dialling tone ['daɪəlɪŋ-], (US) **dial
tone** n segnale m di linea libera

d

dialogue ['daɪəlɒg], (US) **dialog** n dialogo

diameter [daɪ'æmɪtər] n diametro

diamond ['daɪəmənd] n diamante m; (shape) rombo; **diamonds** npl (Cards) quadri mpl

diaper ['daɪəpər] n (US) pannolino

diarrhoea, (US) **diarrhea** [daɪə'riːə] n diarrea

diary ['daɪərɪ] n (daily account) diario; (book) agenda

dice [daɪs] n (pl inv) dado ▷ vt (Culin) tagliare a dadini

dictate vt [dɪk'teɪt] dettare; **dictation** [dɪk'teɪʃən] n (to secretary etc) dettatura; (Scol) dettato

dictator [dɪk'teɪtər] n dittatore m

dictionary ['dɪkʃənrɪ] n dizionario

did [dɪd] pt of **do**

didn't ['dɪdnt] = **did not**

die [daɪ] vi morire; **to be dying for sth/to do sth** morire dalla voglia di qc/di fare qc; **die down** vi abbassarsi; **die out** vi estinguersi

diesel ['diːzl] n (vehicle) diesel m inv

diet ['daɪət] n alimentazione f; (restricted food) dieta ▷ vi (also: **be on a ~**) stare a dieta

differ ['dɪfər] vi: **to ~ from sth** differire da qc; essere diverso/a da qc; **to ~ from sb over sth** essere in disaccordo con qn su qc; **difference** n differenza; (quarrel) screzio; **different** adj diverso/a; **differentiate** [dɪfə'rɛnʃɪeɪt] vi differenziarsi; **to differentiate between** discriminare fra, fare differenza fra; **differently** adv diversamente

difficult ['dɪfɪkəlt] adj difficile; **difficulty** n difficoltà f inv

dig [dɪg] (pt, pp **dug**) vt (hole) scavare; (garden) vangare ▷ n (prod) gomitata; (fig) frecciata; (Archaeology) scavo; **dig up** vt (tree etc) sradicare; (information) scavare fuori

digest vt [daɪ'dʒɛst] digerire ▷ n ['daɪdʒɛst] compendio; **digestion** [dɪ'dʒɛstʃən] n digestione f

digit ['dɪdʒɪt] n cifra; (finger) dito; **digital** adj digitale; **digital camera** n fotocamera digitale; **digital TV** n televisione f digitale

dignified ['dɪgnɪfaɪd] adj dignitoso/a

dignity ['dɪgnɪtɪ] n dignità

digs [dɪgz] npl (BRIT col) camera ammobiliata

dilemma [daɪ'lɛmə] n dilemma m

dill [dɪl] n aneto

dilute [daɪ'luːt] vt diluire; (with water) annacquare

dim [dɪm] adj (light, eyesight) debole; (memory, outline) vago/a; (room) in penombra; (col: stupid) ottuso/a, tonto/a ▷ vt (light) abbassare

dime [daɪm] n (US) = **10 cents**

dimension [dɪ'mɛnʃən] n dimensione f

diminish [dɪ'mɪnɪʃ] vt, vi diminuire

din [dɪn] n chiasso, fracasso

dine [daɪn] vi pranzare; **diner** n (person) cliente m/f; (US: eating place) tavola calda

dinghy ['dɪŋgɪ] n gommone m; (also: **sailing ~**) dinghy m inv

dingy ['dɪndʒɪ] adj grigio/a

dining car ['daɪnɪŋ-] (BRIT) n vagone m ristorante

dining room n sala da pranzo

dining table n tavolo da pranzo

dinkum ['dɪŋkʌm] adj (AUST, NZ col) genuino/a

dinner ['dɪnər] n (lunch) pranzo; (evening meal) cena; (public) banchetto; **dinner jacket** n smoking m inv; **dinner party** n cena; **dinner time** n ora di pranzo (or cena)

dinosaur ['daɪnəsɔːr] n dinosauro

dip [dɪp] n discesa; (in sea) bagno; (Culin) salsetta ▷ vt immergere; bagnare; (BRIT Aut: lights) abbassare ▷ vi abbassarsi

diploma [dɪ'pləʊmə] n diploma m

diplomacy [dɪ'pləʊməsɪ] n diplomazia

diplomat ['dɪpləmæt] n
diplomatico; **diplomatic**
[dɪplə'mætɪk] adj diplomatico/a
dipstick ['dɪpstɪk] n (Aut) indicatore
m di livello dell'olio
dire [daɪəʳ] adj terribile; estremo/a
direct [daɪ'rɛkt] adj diretto/a ▷ vt
dirigere; (order): **to ~ sb to do sth**
dare direttive a qn di fare qc ▷ adv
direttamente; **can you ~ me to ...?** mi
può indicare la strada per ...?; **direct
debit** n (Banking) addebito effettuato
per ordine di un cliente di banca
direction [dɪ'rɛkʃən] n direzione f;
directions npl (advice) chiarimenti
mpl; **~s for use** istruzioni fpl; **sense
of ~** senso dell'orientamento
directly [dɪ'rɛktlɪ] adv (in straight line)
direttamente; (at once) subito
director [dɪ'rɛktəʳ] n direttore/trice,
amministratore/trice; (Theat, Cine,
TV) regista m/f
directory [dɪ'rɛktərɪ] n elenco;
directory enquiries, (US) **directory
assistance** n (Tel) informazioni fpl
elenco abbonati
dirt [dɜːt] n sporcizia; immondizia;
(earth) terra; **dirty** adj sporco/a ▷ vt
sporcare
disability [dɪsə'bɪlɪtɪ] n invalidità f
inv; (Law) incapacità f inv
disabled [dɪs'eɪbld] adj (mentally)
ritardato/a; **~ people** gli invalidi
disadvantage [dɪsəd'vɑːntɪdʒ] n
svantaggio
disagree [dɪsə'griː] vi (differ)
discordare; (be against, think
otherwise): **to ~ (with)** essere in
disaccordo (con), dissentire (da);
disagreeable adj sgradevole;
(person) antipatico/a; **disagreement**
n disaccordo; (quarrel) dissapore m
disappear [dɪsə'pɪəʳ] vi scomparire;
disappearance n scomparsa
disappoint [dɪsə'pɔɪnt] vt deludere;
disappointed adj deluso/a;
disappointing adj deludente;
disappointment n delusione f

disapproval [dɪsə'pruːvəl] n
disapprovazione f
disapprove [dɪsə'pruːv] vi: **to ~ of**
disapprovare
disarm [dɪs'ɑːm] vt disarmare;
disarmament n disarmo
disaster [dɪ'zɑːstəʳ] n disastro;
disastrous [dɪ'zɑːstrəs] adj
disastroso/a
disbelief ['dɪsbə'liːf] n incredulità
disc [dɪsk] n disco; (Comput) = **disk**
discard [dɪs'kɑːd] vt (old things)
scartare; (fig) abbandonare
discharge vt [dɪs'tʃɑːdʒ] (duties)
compiere; (Elec, waste etc) scaricare;
(Med) emettere; (patient) dimettere;
(employee) licenziare; (soldier)
congedare; (defendant) liberare ▷ n
['dɪstʃɑːdʒ] (Elec) scarica; (Med)
emissione f; licenziamento; congedo;
liberazione f
discipline ['dɪsɪplɪn] n disciplina ▷ vt
disciplinare; (punish) punire
disc jockey n disc jockey m inv
disclose [dɪs'kləuz] vt rivelare,
svelare
disco ['dɪskəu] n abbr discoteca
discoloured, (US) **discolored**
[dɪs'kʌləd] adj scolorito/a, ingiallito/a
discomfort [dɪs'kʌmfət] n disagio;
(lack of comfort) scomodità f inv
disconnect [dɪskə'nɛkt] vt
sconnettere, staccare; (Elec, Radio)
staccare; (gas, water) chiudere
discontent [dɪskən'tɛnt] n
scontentezza
discontinue [dɪskən'tɪnjuː] vt
smettere, cessare; **"~d"** (Comm)
"fuori produzione"
discount n ['dɪskaunt] sconto ▷ vt
[dɪs'kaunt] scontare; (report, idea etc)
non badare a
discourage [dɪs'kʌrɪdʒ] vt
scoraggiare
discover [dɪs'kʌvəʳ] vt scoprire;
discovery n scoperta
discredit [dɪs'krɛdɪt] vt screditare;
mettere in dubbio

discreet [dɪ'skriːt] *adj* discreto/a
discrepancy [dɪ'skrɛpənsɪ] *n* discrepanza
discretion [dɪ'skrɛʃən] *n* discrezione *f*; **use your own ~** giudichi lei
discriminate [dɪ'skrɪmɪneɪt] *vi*: **to ~ between** distinguere tra; **to ~ against** discriminare contro; **discrimination** [dɪskrɪmɪ'neɪʃən] *n* discriminazione *f*; (*judgement*) discernimento
discuss [dɪ'skʌs] *vt* discutere; (*debate*) dibattere; **discussion** [dɪ'skʌʃən] *n* discussione *f*; **discussion forum** *n* (*Comput*) forum *m inv* di discussione
disease [dɪ'ziːz] *n* malattia
disembark [dɪsɪm'bɑːk] *vt, vi* sbarcare
disgrace [dɪs'greɪs] *n* vergogna; (*disfavour*) disgrazia ▷ *vt* disonorare, far cadere in disgrazia; **disgraceful** *adj* scandaloso/a, vergognoso/a
disgruntled [dɪs'grʌntld] *adj* scontento/a, di cattivo umore
disguise [dɪs'gaɪz] *n* travestimento ▷ *vt*: **to ~ o.s. as** travestirsi da; **in ~** travestito/a
disgust [dɪs'gʌst] *n* disgusto, nausea ▷ *vt* disgustare, far schifo a; **disgusted** [dɪs'gʌstɪd] *adj* indignato/a; **disgusting** [dɪs'gʌstɪŋ] *adj* disgustoso/a, ripugnante
dish [dɪʃ] *n* piatto; **to do** *or* **wash the ~es** fare i piatti; **dishcloth** *n* strofinaccio dei piatti
dishonest [dɪs'ɔnɪst] *adj* disonesto/a
dishtowel ['dɪʃtauəl] *n* strofinaccio dei piatti
dishwasher ['dɪʃwɔʃəʳ] *n* lavastoviglie *f inv*
disillusion [dɪsɪ'luːʒən] *vt* disilludere, disingannare
disinfectant [dɪsɪn'fɛktənt] *n* disinfettante *m*
disintegrate [dɪs'ɪntɪgreɪt] *vi* disintegrarsi

disk [dɪsk] *n* (*Comput*) disco; **double-sided ~** disco a doppia faccia; **disk drive** *n* disk drive *m inv*; **diskette** *n* (*Comput*) dischetto
dislike [dɪs'laɪk] *n* antipatia, avversione *f*; (*gen pl*) cosa che non piace ▷ *vt*: **he ~s it** non gli piace
dislocate ['dɪsləkeɪt] *vt* slogare
disloyal [dɪs'lɔɪəl] *adj* sleale
dismal ['dɪzml] *adj* triste, cupo/a
dismantle [dɪs'mæntl] *vt* (*machine*) smontare
dismay [dɪs'meɪ] *n* costernazione *f* ▷ *vt* sgomentare
dismiss [dɪs'mɪs] *vt* congedare; (*employee*) licenziare; (*idea*) scacciare; (*Law*) respingere; **dismissal** *n* congedo; licenziamento
disobedient [dɪsə'biːdɪənt] *adj* disubbidiente
disobey [dɪsə'beɪ] *vt* disubbidire a
disorder [dɪs'ɔːdəʳ] *n* disordine *m*; (*rioting*) tumulto; (*Med*) disturbo
disorganized [dɪs'ɔːgənaɪzd] *adj* (*person, life*) disorganizzato/a; (*system, meeting*) male organizzato/a
disown [dɪs'əun] *vt* rinnegare, disconoscere
dispatch [dɪs'pætʃ] *vt* spedire, inviare ▷ *n* spedizione *f*, invio; (*Mil, Press*) dispaccio
dispel [dɪs'pɛl] *vt* dissipare, scacciare
dispense [dɪs'pɛns] *vt* distribuire, amministrare; **dispenser** *n* (*container*) distributore *m*
disperse [dɪs'pəːs] *vt* disperdere; (*knowledge*) disseminare ▷ *vi* disperdersi
display [dɪs'pleɪ] *n* esposizione *f*; (*of feeling etc*) manifestazione *f*; (*screen*) schermo ▷ *vt* mostrare; (*goods*) esporre; (*pej*) ostentare
displease [dɪs'pliːz] *vt* dispiacere a, scontentare; **~d with** scontento/a di
disposable [dɪs'pəuzəbl] *adj* (*pack etc*) a perdere; (*income*) disponibile
disposal [dɪs'pəuzl] *n* (*of rubbish*) smaltimento; (*of property etc*)

cessione f; **at one's ~** alla sua disposizione

dispose [dɪsˈpəʊz] vt disporre; **dispose of** vt fus sbarazzarsi di; **disposition** [dɪspəˈzɪʃən] n disposizione f; (temperament) carattere m

disproportionate [dɪsprəˈpɔːʃənət] adj sproporzionato/a

dispute [dɪsˈpjuːt] n disputa; (also: **industrial ~**) controversia (sindacale) ⊳ vt contestare; (matter) discutere; (victory) disputare

disqualify [dɪsˈkwɒlɪfaɪ] vt (Sport) squalificare; **to ~ sb from sth/ from doing** rendere qn incapace a qc/a fare; squalificare qn da qc/da fare; **to ~ sb from driving** ritirare la patente a qn

disregard [dɪsrɪˈgɑːd] vt non far caso a, non badare a

disrupt [dɪsˈrʌpt] vt disturbare; (public transport) creare scompiglio in; **disruption** [dɪsˈrʌpʃən] n disordine m; interruzione f

dissatisfaction [dɪssætɪsˈfækʃən] n scontentezza, insoddisfazione f

dissatisfied [dɪsˈsætɪsfaɪd] adj: **~ (with)** scontento/a or insoddisfatto/a (di)

dissect [dɪˈsɛkt] vt sezionare

dissent [dɪˈsɛnt] n dissenso

dissertation [dɪsəˈteɪʃən] n tesi f inv, dissertazione f

dissolve [dɪˈzɒlv] vt dissolvere, sciogliere; (Comm, Pol, marriage) sciogliere ⊳ vi dissolversi, sciogliersi

distance [ˈdɪstns] n distanza; **in the ~** in lontananza

distant [ˈdɪstnt] adj lontano/a, distante; (manner) riservato/a, freddo/a

distil, (us) **distill** [dɪsˈtɪl] vt distillare; **distillery** n distilleria

distinct [dɪsˈtɪŋkt] adj distinto/a; **as ~ from** a differenza di; **distinction** [dɪsˈtɪŋkʃən] n distinzione f; (in exam) lode f; **distinctive** adj distintivo/a

distinguish [dɪsˈtɪŋgwɪʃ] vt distinguere; discernere; **distinguished** adj (eminent) eminente

distort [dɪsˈtɔːt] vt distorcere; (Tech) deformare

distract [dɪsˈtrækt] vt distrarre; **distracted** adj distratto/a; **distraction** [dɪsˈtrækʃən] n distrazione f

distraught [dɪsˈtrɔːt] adj stravolto/a

distress [dɪsˈtrɛs] n angoscia ⊳ vt affliggere; **distressing** adj doloroso/a

distribute [dɪsˈtrɪbjuːt] vt distribuire; **distribution** [dɪstrɪˈbjuːʃən] n distribuzione f; **distributor** n distributore m

district [ˈdɪstrɪkt] n (of country) regione f; (of town) quartiere m; (Admin) distretto; **district attorney** n (US) ≈ sostituto procuratore m della Repubblica

distrust [dɪsˈtrʌst] n diffidenza, sfiducia ⊳ vt non aver fiducia in

disturb [dɪsˈtəːb] vt disturbare; **disturbance** n disturbo; (by drunks etc) disordini mpl; **disturbed** adj (worried, upset) turbato/a; **to be emotionally disturbed** avere turbe emotive; **disturbing** adj sconvolgente

ditch [dɪtʃ] n fossa ⊳ vt (col) piantare in asso

ditto [ˈdɪtəʊ] adv idem

dive [daɪv] n tuffo; (of submarine) immersione f ⊳ vi tuffarsi; immergersi; **diver** n tuffatore/trice; palombaro

diverse [daɪˈvəːs] adj vario/a

diversion [daɪˈvəːʃən] n (BRIT Aut) deviazione f; (distraction) divertimento

diversity [daɪˈvəːsɪtɪ] n diversità f inv, varietà f inv

divert [daɪˈvəːt] vt deviare

divide [dɪˈvaɪd] vt dividere; (separate) separare ⊳ vi dividersi; **divided**

d

highway *n* (*US*) strada a doppia carreggiata

divine [dɪ'vaɪn] *adj* divino/a

diving ['daɪvɪŋ] *n* tuffo; **diving board** *n* trampolino

division [dɪ'vɪʒən] *n* divisione *f*; separazione *f*; (*Football*) serie *f inv*

divorce [dɪ'vɔ:s] *n* divorzio ▷ *vt* divorziare da; (*dissociate*) separare; **divorced** *adj* divorziato/a; **divorcee** [dɪvɔ:'si:] *n* divorziato/a

D.I.Y. *n abbr* (*BRIT*) = **do-it-yourself**

dizzy ['dɪzɪ] *adj*: **to feel ~** avere il capogiro

DJ *n abbr* = **disc jockey**

DNA *n abbr* (= *deoxyribonucleic acid*) DNA *m*; **DNA test** *n* test *m inv* del DNA

 KEYWORD

do [du:] (*pt* **did**, *pp* **done**) *aux vb* **1** (*in negative constructions*) non tradotto; **I don't understand** non capisco **2** (*to form questions*) non tradotto; **didn't you know?** non lo sapevi?; **why didn't you come?** perché non sei venuto? **3** (*for emphasis, in polite expressions*): **she does seem rather late** sembra essere piuttosto in ritardo; **do sit down** si accomodi la prego, prego si sieda; **do take care!** mi raccomando, stai attento! **4** (*used to avoid repeating vb*): **she swims better than I do** lei nuota meglio di me; **do you agree? — yes, I do/no, I don't** sei d'accordo? — sì/no; **she lives in Glasgow — so do I** lei vive a Glasgow — anch'io; **he asked me to help him and I did** mi ha chiesto di aiutarlo ed io l'ho fatto **5** (*in question tags*): **you like him, don't you?** ti piace, vero?; **I don't know him, do I?** non lo conosco, vero?

▷ *vt* (*gen: carry out, perform etc*) fare; **what are you doing tonight?** che fai stasera?; **to do the cooking** cucinare; **to do the washing-up** fare i piatti; **to do one's teeth** lavarsi i denti; **to do one's hair/nails** farsi i capelli/le unghie; **the car was doing 100** la macchina faceva i 100 all'ora

▷ *vi* **1** (*act, behave*) fare; **do as I do** faccia come me, faccia come faccio io **2** (*get on, fare*) andare; **he's doing well/badly at school** va bene/male a scuola; **how do you do?** piacere! **3** (*suit*) andare bene; **this room will do** questa stanza va bene **4** (*be sufficient*) bastare; **will £10 do?** basteranno 10 sterline?; **that'll do** basta così; **that'll do!** (*in annoyance*) ora basta!; **to make do (with)** arrangiarsi (con)

▷ *n* (*col: party etc*) festa; **it was rather a grand do** è stato un ricevimento piuttosto importante

do away with *vt fus* (*col: kill*) far fuori; (*abolish*) abolire

do up *vt* (*laces*) allacciare; (*dress, buttons*) abbottonare; (*renovate: room, house*) rimettere a nuovo, rifare

do with *vt fus* (*need*) aver bisogno di; (*be connected*): **what has it got to do with you?** e tu che c'entri?; **I won't have anything to do with it** non voglio avere niente a che farci; **it has to do with money** si tratta di soldi

do without *vi* fare senza ▷ *vt fus* fare a meno di

dock [dɔk] *n* (*Naut*) bacino; (*Law*) banco degli imputati ▷ *vi* entrare in bacino; (*Space*) agganciarsi; **docks** *npl* (*Naut*) dock *m inv*

doctor ['dɔktə'] *n* medico/a; (*PhD etc*) dottore/essa ▷ *vt* (*food, drink*) adulterare; **Doctor of Philosophy, PhD** *n* dottorato di ricerca; (*person*) titolare *m/f* di un dottorato di ricerca

document *n* ['dɔkjumənt] documento; **documentary** [dɔkju'mɛntərɪ] *adj* (*evidence*) documentato/a ▷ *n* documentario;

documentation [dɔkjumən'teɪʃən] n documentazione f

dodge [dɔdʒ] n trucco; schivata ▷ vt schivare, eludere

dodgy ['dɔdʒɪ] adj (BRIT col: uncertain) rischioso/a; (untrustworthy) sospetto/a

does [dʌz] see **do**

doesn't ['dʌznt] = **does not**

dog [dɔg] n cane m ▷ vt (follow closely) pedinare; (fig: memory etc) perseguitare; **doggy bag** n sacchetto per gli avanzi (da portare a casa)

do-it-yourself ['du:ɪtjɔ:'sɛlf] n il far da sé

dole [dəul] n (BRIT) sussidio di disoccupazione; **to be on the ~** vivere del sussidio

doll [dɔl] n bambola

dollar ['dɔləʳ] n dollaro

dolphin ['dɔlfɪn] n delfino

dome [dəum] n cupola

domestic [də'mɛstɪk] adj (duty, happiness, animal) domestico/a; (policy, affairs, flights) nazionale; **domestic appliance** n elettrodomestico

dominant ['dɔmɪnənt] adj dominante

dominate ['dɔmɪneɪt] vt dominare

domino ['dɔmɪnəu] (pl **dominoes**) n domino; **dominoes** npl (game) gioco del domino

donate [də'neɪt] vt donare; **donation** [də'neɪʃən] n donazione f

done [dʌn] pp of **do**

dongle ['dɔŋgl] n (Comput) chiavetta, pennetta

donkey ['dɔŋkɪ] n asino

donor ['dəunəʳ] n donatore/trice; **donor card** n tessera di donatore di organi

don't [dəunt] = **do not**

donut ['dəunʌt] n (us) = **doughnut**

doodle ['du:dl] vi scarabocchiare

doom [du:m] n destino; rovina ▷ vt: **to be ~ed (to failure)** essere predestinato/a (a fallire)

door [dɔ:ʳ] n porta; **doorbell** n campanello; **door handle** n maniglia;

doorknob ['dɔ:nɔb] n pomello, maniglia; **doorstep** n gradino della porta; **doorway** n porta

dope [dəup] n (col: drugs) roba ▷ vt (horse etc) drogare

dormitory ['dɔ:mɪtrɪ] n dormitorio; (us) casa dello studente

DOS [dɔs] n abbr (= disk operating system) DOS m

dosage ['dəusɪdʒ] n posologia

dose [dəus] n dose f; (bout) attacco

dot [dɔt] n punto; macchiolina ▷ vt: **~ted with** punteggiato(a) di; **on the ~** in punto; **dotcom** [dɔt'kɔm] n azienda che opera in Internet; **dotted line** ['dɔtɪd-] n linea punteggiata

double ['dʌbl] adj doppio/a ▷ adv (twice): **to cost ~ sth** costare il doppio (di qc) ▷ n sosia m inv ▷ vt raddoppiare; (fold) piegare doppio or in due ▷ vi raddoppiarsi; **on the ~, (BRIT) at the ~** a passo di corsa; **double back** vi (person) tornare sui propri passi; **double bass** n contrabbasso; **double bed** n letto matrimoniale; **double-check** vt, vi ricontrollare; **double-click** vi (Comput) fare doppio click; **double-cross** ['dʌbl'krɔs] vt fare il doppio gioco con; **doubledecker** n autobus m inv a due piani; **double glazing** n (BRIT) doppi vetri mpl; **double room** n camera matrimoniale; **doubles** n (Tennis) doppio; **double yellow lines** npl (BRIT Aut) linea gialla doppia continua che segnala il divieto di sosta

doubt [daut] n dubbio ▷ vt dubitare di; **to ~ that** dubitare che + sub; **doubtful** adj dubbioso/a, incerto/a; (person) equivoco/a; **doubtless** adv indubbiamente

dough [dəu] n pasta, impasto; **doughnut, (us) donut** n bombolone m

dove [dʌv] n colombo/a

down [daun] n piumino ▷ adv giù, di sotto ▷ prep giù per ▷ vt (col: drink)

scolarsi; **~ with X!** abbasso X!;
down-and-out n barbone m;
downfall n caduta; rovina; **downhill**
adv: **to go downhill** andare in
discesa; (business) lasciarsi andare;
andare a rotoli
Downing Street ['daʊnɪŋ-] n:
10 ~ residenza del primo ministro
inglese

○ **DOWNING STREET**
○
○ Downing Street è la via di
○ Westminster che porta da
○ Whitehall al parco di St James dove,
○ al numero 10, si trova la residenza
○ del primo ministro inglese. Nella
○ stessa via, al numero 11, si trova
○ la residenza del Cancelliere dello
○ Scacchiere. Spesso si usa Downing
○ Street per indicare il governo
○ britannico.

down: download vt (Comput)
scaricare; **downloadable** adj
(Comput) scaricabile; **downright** adj
franco/a; (refusal) assoluto/a
Down's syndrome n sindrome f
di Down
down: downstairs adv di sotto; al
piano inferiore; **down-to-earth** adj
pratico/a; **downtown** adv in città;
down under adv (Australia etc) agli
antipodi; **downward** adj ▷ adv in giù,
in discesa; **downwards** ['daʊnwədz]
adv in giù, in discesa
doz. abbr = **dozen**
doze [dəʊz] vi sonnecchiare
dozen ['dʌzn] n dozzina; **a ~ books**
una dozzina di libri; **80p a ~** 80 pence
la dozzina; **~s of times** centinaia or
migliaia di volte
Dr, Dr. abbr (= doctor) Dr, Dott./
Dott.ssa; (in street names) = **dozen**
drab [dræb] adj tetro/a, grigio/a
draft [drɑːft] n abbozzo; (Pol) bozza;
(Comm) tratta; (US Mil: call-up) leva
▷ vt abbozzare; see also **draught**

drag [dræg] vt trascinare; (river)
dragare ▷ vi trascinarsi ▷ n (col)
noioso/a; (: task) noia; (women's
clothing): **in ~** travestito (da donna)
dragon ['drægən] n drago
dragonfly ['drægənflaɪ] n libellula
drain [dreɪn] n (for sewage) fogna;
(on resources) salasso ▷ vt (land,
marshes) prosciugare; (vegetables)
scolare ▷ vi (water) defluire; **drainage**
n prosciugamento; fognatura;
drainpipe n tubo di scarico
drama ['drɑːmə] n (art) dramma
m, teatro; (play) commedia; (event)
dramma; **dramatic** [drə'mætɪk] adj
drammatico/a
drank [dræŋk] pt of **drink**
drape [dreɪp] vt drappeggiare; see
also **drapes**; **drapes** [dreɪps] npl (US:
curtains) tende fpl
drastic ['dræstɪk] adj drastico/a
draught, (US) **draft** [drɑːft] n
corrente f d'aria; (Naut) pescaggio;
on ~ (beer) alla spina; **draught beer**
n birra alla spina; **draughts** n (BRIT)
(gioco della) dama
draw [drɔː] (pt **drew**, pp **drawn**) vt
tirare; (take out) estrarre; (attract)
attirare; (picture) disegnare; (money) ritirare ▷ vi
(Sport) pareggiare ▷ n pareggio;
(in lottery) estrazione f; **to ~ near**
avvicinarsi; **draw out** vi (lengthen)
allungarsi ▷ vt (money) ritirare; **draw
up** vi (stop) arrestarsi, fermarsi
▷ vt (chair) avvicinare; (document)
compilare; **drawback** n svantaggio,
inconveniente m
drawer [drɔːʳ] n cassetto
drawing ['drɔːɪŋ] n disegno;
drawing pin n (BRIT) puntina da
disegno; **drawing room** n salotto
drawn [drɔːn] pp of **draw**
dread [drɛd] n terrore m ▷ vt tremare
all'idea di; **dreadful** adj terribile
dream [driːm] n sogno ▷ vt, vi (pt,
pp **dreamed** or **dreamt** [drɛmt])
sognare; **dreamer** n sognatore/trice

dreamt [drɛmt] *pt, pp of* **dream**
dreary ['drɪərɪ] *adj* tetro/a;
monotono/a
drench [drɛntʃ] *vt* inzuppare
dress [drɛs] *n* vestito; (*no pl: clothing*)
abbigliamento ▷ *vt* vestire; (*wound*)
fasciare ▷ *vi* vestirsi; **to get ~ed**
vestirsi; **dress up** *vi* vestirsi a festa;
(*in fancy dress*) vestirsi in costume;
dress circle (BRIT) *n* prima galleria;
dresser *n* (*furniture*) credenza; (US)
cassettone *m*; **dressing** *n* (*Med*)
benda; (*Culin*) condimento; **dressing
gown** *n* (BRIT) vestaglia; **dressing
room** *n* (*Theat*) camerino; (*Sport*)
spogliatoio; **dressing table** *n*
toilette *f inv*; **dressmaker** *n* sarta
drew [druː] *pt of* **draw**
dribble ['drɪbl] *vi* (*baby*) sbavare ▷ *vt*
(*ball*) dribblare
dried [draɪd] *adj* (*fruit, beans*) secco/a;
(*eggs, milk*) in polvere
drier ['draɪə'] *n* = **dryer**
drift [drɪft] *n* (*of current etc*) direzione
f; forza; (*of sand, snow*) cumulo;
turbine *m*; (*general meaning*) senso
▷ *vi* (*boat*) essere trasportato/a dalla
corrente; (*sand, snow*) ammucchiarsi
drill [drɪl] *n* trapano; (*Mil*)
esercitazione *f* ▷ *vt* trapanare;
(*soldiers*) addestrare ▷ *vi* (*for oil*) fare
trivellazioni
drink [drɪŋk] *n* bevanda, bibita;
(*alcoholic drink*) bicchierino; (*sip*) sorso
▷ *vt, vi* (*pt* **drank**, *pp* **drunk**) bere;
to have a ~ bere qualcosa; **a ~ of
water** un po' d'acqua; **drink-driving**
n guida in stato di ebbrezza; **drinker**
n bevitore/trice; **drinking water** *n*
acqua potabile
drip [drɪp] *n* goccia; (*dripping*)
sgocciolio; (*Med*) fleboclisi *f inv* ▷ *vi*
gocciolare; (*washing, tap*) sgocciolare
drive [draɪv] (*pt* **drove**, *pp* **driven**)
n [draɪv,
drəuv, 'drɪvn] *n* passeggiata *or*
giro in macchina; (*also*: **~way**)
viale *m* d'accesso; (*energy*) energia;
(*campaign*) campagna; (*also*: **disk ~**)

disk drive *m inv* ▷ *vt* guidare; (*nail*)
piantare; (*push*) cacciare, spingere;
(*Tech: motor*) azionare; far funzionare
▷ *vi* (*Aut: at controls*) guidare; (: *travel*)
andare in macchina; **left-/right-
hand ~** guida a sinistra/destra; **to ~
sb mad** far impazzire qn; **drive out**
vt (*force out*) cacciare, mandare via;
drive-in *adj, n* (*esp US*) drive-in (*m inv*)
driven ['drɪvn] *pp of* **drive**
driver ['draɪvə'] *n* conducente *m/f*;
(*of taxi*) tassista *m*; (*chauffeur: of bus*)
autista *m/f*; **driver's license** *n* (US)
patente *f* di guida
driveway ['draɪvweɪ] *n* viale *m*
d'accesso
driving ['draɪvɪŋ] *n* guida; **driving
instructor** *n* istruttore/trice di
scuola guida; **driving lesson** *n*
lezione *f* di guida; **driving licence** *n*
(BRIT) patente *f* di guida; **driving test**
n esame *m* di guida
drizzle ['drɪzl] *n* pioggerella
droop [druːp] *vi* (*flower*) appassire;
(*head, shoulders*) chinarsi
drop [drɔp] *n* (*of water*) goccia;
(*lessening*) diminuzione *f*; (*fall*) caduta
▷ *vt* lasciar cadere; (*name from list*)
lasciare fuori ▷ *vi* cascare; (*wind,
temperature, price*) calare, abbassarsi;
(*voice*) abbassarsi; **drops** *npl* (*Med*)
gocce *fpl*; **drop in** *vi* (*col: visit*): **to ~ in
(on)** fare un salto (da), passare (da);
drop off *vi* (*sleep*) addormentarsi
▷ *vt*: **to ~ sb off** far scendere qn;
drop out *vi* (*withdraw*) ritirarsi;
(*student etc*) smettere di studiare
drought [draut] *n* siccità *f inv*
drove [drəuv] *pt of* **drive**
drown [draun] *vt* affogare; (*fig: noise*)
soffocare
drowsy ['drauzɪ] *adj* sonnolento/a,
assonnato/a
drug [drʌg] *n* farmaco; (*narcotic*)
droga ▷ *vt* drogare; **to be on ~s**
drogarsi; (*Med*) prendere medicinali;
hard/soft ~s droghe pesanti/
leggere; **drug addict** *n* tossicomane

d

m/f; **drug dealer** *n* trafficante *m/f* di droga; **druggist** *n* (*US*) farmacista *m/f;* **drugstore** ['drʌgstɔ:'] *n* (*US*) *negozio di generi vari e di articoli di farmacia con un bar*

drum [drʌm] *n* tamburo; (*for oil, petrol*) fusto ▷ *vi* tamburellare; **drums** *npl* (*set of drums*) batteria; **drummer** *n* batterista *m/f*

drunk [drʌŋk] *pp of* **drink** ▷ *adj* ubriaco/a, ebbro/a ▷ *n* ubriacone/a; **drunken** *adj* ubriaco/a, da ubriaco

dry [draɪ] *adj* secco/a; (*day, clothes*) asciutto/a ▷ *vt* seccare; (*clothes, hair, hands*) asciugare ▷ *vi* asciugarsi; **dry off** *vi* asciugarsi ▷ *vt* asciugare; **dry up** *vi* seccarsi; **dry-cleaner's** *n* lavasecco *m inv;* **dry-cleaning** *n* pulitura a secco; **dryer** *n* (*for hair*) föhn *m inv,* asciugacapelli *m inv;* (*for clothes*) asciugabiancheria *m inv;* (*US: spin-dryer*) centrifuga

DSS *n abbr* (*BRIT:* = Department of Social Security*) ministero della Previdenza sociale*

DTP *n abbr* (= desk-top publishing) desktop publishing *m inv*

dual ['djuəl] *adj* doppio/a; **dual carriageway** *n* (*BRIT*) strada a doppia carreggiata

dubious ['dju:bɪəs] *adj* dubbio/a

Dublin ['dʌblɪn] *n* Dublino *f*

duck [dʌk] *n* anatra ▷ *vi* abbassare la testa

due [dju:] *adj* dovuto/a; (*expected*) atteso/a; (*fitting*) giusto/a ▷ *n* dovuto ▷ *adv:* **~ north** diritto verso nord

duel ['djuəl] *n* duello

duet [dju:'ɛt] *n* duetto

dug [dʌg] *pt, pp of* **dig**

duke [dju:k] *n* duca *m*

dull [dʌl] *adj* (*light*) debole; (*boring*) noioso/a; (*slow-witted*) ottuso/a; (*sound, pain*) sordo/a; (*weather, day*) fosco/a, scuro/a ▷ *vt* (*pain, grief*) attutire; (*mind, senses*) intorpidire

dumb [dʌm] *adj* (*pej*) muto/a; (*stupid*) stupido/a

dummy ['dʌmɪ] *n* (*tailor's model*) manichino; (*Tech, Comm*) riproduzione *f;* (*BRIT: for baby*) tettarella ▷ *adj* falso/a, finto/a

dump [dʌmp] *n* (*also:* **rubbish ~**) mucchio di rifiuti (*place*) discarica ▷ *vt* (*put down*) scaricare; mettere giù; (*get rid of*) buttar via

dumpling ['dʌmplɪŋ] *n specie di gnocco*

dune [dju:n] *n* duna

dungarees [dʌŋgə'ri:z] *npl* tuta

dungeon ['dʌndʒən] *n* prigione *f* sotterranea

duplex ['dju:plɛks] *n* (*US: house*) *casa con muro divisorio in comune con un'altra;* (: *also:* **~ apartment**) appartamento su due piani

duplicate *n* ['dju:plɪkət] doppio ▷ *vt* ['dju:plɪkeɪt] duplicare; **in ~** in duplice copia

durable ['djuərəbl] *adj* durevole; (*clothes, metal*) resistente

duration [djuə'reɪʃən] *n* durata

during ['djuərɪŋ] *prep* durante, nel corso di

dusk [dʌsk] *n* crepuscolo

dust [dʌst] *n* polvere *f* ▷ *vt* (*furniture*) spolverare; (*cake etc*): **to ~ with** cospargere con; **dustbin** *n* (*BRIT*) pattumiera; **duster** *n* straccio per la polvere; **dustman** *n* (*irreg: BRIT*) netturbino; **dustpan** *n* pattumiera; **dusty** *adj* polveroso/a

Dutch [dʌtʃ] *adj* olandese ▷ *n* (*Ling*) olandese *m* ▷ *adv:* **to go ~** or **d~** (*col*) fare alla romana; **the ~** gli Olandesi; **Dutchman** (**Dutchwoman**) *n* (*irreg*) olandese *m/f*

duty ['dju:tɪ] *n* dovere *m;* (*tax*) dazio, tassa; **on ~** di servizio; **off ~** libero(a), fuori servizio; **duty-free** *adj* esente da dazio

duvet ['du:veɪ] (*BRIT*) *n* piumino, piumone *m*

DVD *n abbr* (= digital versatile or video disc) DVD *m inv;* **DVD burner** *n*

masterizzatore m (di) DVD; **DVD player** n lettore m DVD
DVD writer n masterizzatore m (di) DVD
dwarf [dwɔːf] n (col!) nano/a ▷ vt far apparire piccolo
dwell (pt, pp **dwelt**) [dwɛl, dwɛlt] vi dimorare; **dwell on** vt fus indugiare su
dwelt [dwɛlt] pt, pp of **dwell**
dwindle ['dwɪndl] vi diminuire
dye [daɪ] n tintura ▷ vt tingere
dying ['daɪɪŋ] adj morente, moribondo/a
dynamic [daɪ'næmɪk] adj dinamico/a
dynamite ['daɪnəmaɪt] n dinamite f
dyslexia [dɪs'lɛksɪə] n dislessia
dyslexic [dɪs'lɛksɪk] adj, n dislessico/a

E [iː] n (Mus) mi m
E111 n abbr (formerly) (also: **form ~**) E111 (modulo UE per rimborso spese mediche)
each [iːtʃ] adj ogni, ciascuno/a ▷ pron ciascuno/a, ognuno/a; **~ one** ognuno(a); **~ other** si (or ci etc); **they hate ~ other** si odiano (l'un l'altro); **you are jealous of ~ other** siete gelosi l'uno dell'altro; **they have 2 books ~** hanno 2 libri ciascuno
eager ['iːgər] adj impaziente; desideroso/a; ardente; **to be ~ for** essere desideroso di, aver gran voglia di
eagle ['iːgl] n aquila
ear [ɪər] n orecchio; (of corn) pannocchia; **earache** n mal m d'orecchi; **eardrum** n timpano
earl [əːl] (BRIT) n conte m
earlier ['əːlɪər] adj precedente ▷ adv prima
early ['əːlɪ] adv presto, di buon'ora; (ahead of time) in anticipo ▷ adj

primo/a; (*quick: reply*) veloce; **at an ~ hour** di buon'ora; **have an ~ night/ start** vada a letto/parta presto; **in the ~ spring/19th century** all'inizio della primavera/dell'Ottocento; **early retirement** n prepensionamento

earmark ['ɪəmɑːk] vt: **to ~ sth for** destinare qc a

earn [əːn] vt guadagnare; (*rest, reward*) meritare

earnest ['əːnɪst] adj serio/a; **in ~** sul serio

earnings ['əːnɪŋz] npl guadagni mpl; (*salary*) stipendio

ear: **earphones** ['ɪəfəʊnz] npl cuffia; **earplugs** npl tappi mpl per le orecchie; **earring** n orecchino

earth [əːθ] n terra ▷ vt (BRIT Elec) mettere a terra; **earthquake** n terremoto

ease [iːz] n agio, comodo ▷ vt (*soothe*) calmare; (*loosen*) allentare; **at ~** a proprio agio; (*Mil*) a riposo; **to ~ sth out/in** tirare fuori/infilare qc con delicatezza; facilitare l'uscita/l'entrata di qc

easily ['iːzɪlɪ] adv facilmente

east [iːst] n est m ▷ adj dell'est ▷ adv a oriente; **the E~** l'Oriente m; (*Pol*) i Paesi dell'Est; **eastbound** ['iːstbaʊnd] adj (*traffic*) diretto/a a est; (*carriageway*) che porta a est

Easter ['iːstə*] n Pasqua; **Easter egg** n uovo di Pasqua

eastern ['iːstən] adj orientale, d'oriente; (*Pol*) dell'est

Easter Sunday n domenica di Pasqua

easy ['iːzɪ] adj facile; (*manner*) disinvolto/a ▷ adv: **to take it** or **things ~** prendersela con calma; **easy-going** adj accomodante

eat (pt **ate**, pp **eaten**) [iːt, eɪt, 'iːtn] vt mangiare; **eat out** vi mangiare fuori

eavesdrop ['iːvzdrɔp] vi: **to ~ (on a conversation)** origliare (una conversazione)

e-book ['iːbuk] n libro elettronico

e-business ['iːbɪznɪs] n (*company*) azienda che opera in Internet; (*commerce*) commercio elettronico

EC n abbr (= European Community) CE f

eccentric [ɪk'sɛntrɪk] adj, n eccentrico/a

echo ['ɛkəʊ] (pl **echoes**) n eco m or f ▷ vt ripetere; fare eco a ▷ vi echeggiare; dare un eco

e-cigarette ['iːsɪgærɛt] n sigaretta elettronica

eclipse [ɪ'klɪps] n eclissi f inv

eco-friendly [iːkəʊ'frɛndlɪ] adj ecologico/a

ecological [iːkə'lɔdʒɪkəl] adj ecologico/a

ecology [ɪ'kɔlədʒɪ] n ecologia

e-commerce [iː'kɔməːs] n commercio elettronico

economic [iːkə'nɔmɪk] adj economico/a; **economical** adj economico/a; (*person*) economo/a; **economics** n economia ▷ npl (*financial aspect*) lato finanziario

economist [ɪ'kɔnəmɪst] n economista m/f

economize [ɪ'kɔnəmaɪz] vi risparmiare, fare economia

economy [ɪ'kɔnəmɪ] n economia; **economy class** n (Aviat etc) classe f turistica; **economy class syndrome** n sindrome f della classe economica

ecstasy ['ɛkstəsɪ] n estasi f inv; **ecstatic** [ɛks'tætɪk] adj estatico/a, in estasi

eczema ['ɛksɪmə] n eczema m

edge [ɛdʒ] n margine m; (*of table, plate, cup*) orlo; (*of knife etc*) taglio ▷ vt bordare; **on ~** (*fig*) = **edgy**; **to ~ away from** sgattaiolare da

edgy ['ɛdʒɪ] adj nervoso/a

edible ['ɛdɪbl] adj commestibile; (*meal*) mangiabile

Edinburgh ['ɛdɪnbərə] n Edimburgo

edit ['ɛdɪt] vt curare; **edition** [ɪ'dɪʃən] n edizione f; **editor** n (*in newspaper*) redattore/trice;

redattore/trice capo; (*of sb's work*) curatore/trice; **editorial** [ɛdɪ'tɔːrɪəl] *adj* redazionale, editoriale ▷ *n* editoriale *m*

Be careful not to translate *editor* by the Italian word *editore*.

educate ['ɛdjukeɪt] *vt* istruire; educare; **educated** *adj* istruito/a

education [ɛdju'keɪʃən] *n* (*teaching*) insegnamento; (*schooling*) istruzione *f*; **educational** *adj* pedagogico/a; scolastico/a; istruttivo/a

eel [iːl] *n* anguilla

eerie ['ɪərɪ] *adj* che fa accapponare la pelle

effect [ɪ'fɛkt] *n* effetto ▷ *vt* effettuare; **to take ~** (*law*) entrare in vigore; (*drug*) fare effetto; **in ~** effettivamente; **effective** *adj* efficace; (*actual*) effettivo/a; **effectively** *adv* efficacemente; effettivamente; **effects** *npl* (*Theat*) effetti *mpl* scenici; (*property*) effetti *mpl*

efficiency [ɪ'fɪʃənsɪ] *n* efficienza; rendimento effettivo

efficient [ɪ'fɪʃənt] *adj* efficiente; **efficiently** *adv* efficientemente; efficacemente

effort ['ɛfət] *n* sforzo; **effortless** *adj* senza sforzo, facile

e.g. *adv abbr* (= *exempli gratia*) per esempio, p.es.

egg [ɛg] *n* uovo; **hard-boiled/soft-boiled ~** uovo sodo/alla coque; **eggcup** *n* portauovo *m inv*; **eggplant** *n* (*esp us*) melanzana; **eggshell** *n* guscio d'uovo; **egg white** *n* albume *m*, bianco d'uovo; **egg yolk** *n* tuorlo, rosso (d'uovo)

ego ['iːgəu] *n* ego *m inv*

Egypt ['iːdʒɪpt] *n* Egitto; **Egyptian** [ɪ'dʒɪpʃən] *adj*, *n* egiziano/a

eight [eɪt] *num* otto; **eighteen** *num* diciotto; **eighteenth** *num* diciottesimo/a; **eighth** [eɪtθ] *num* ottavo/a; **eightieth** ['eɪtɪɪθ] *num* ottantesimo/a; **eighty** *num* ottanta

Eire ['ɛərə] *n* Repubblica d'Irlanda

either ['aɪðəʳ] *adj* l'uno/a o l'altro/a; (*both, each*) ciascuno/a; **on ~ side** su ciascun lato ▷ *pron*: **~ (of them)** (o) l'uno/a o l'altro/a; **I don't like ~** non mi piace né l'uno né l'altro ▷ *adv* neanche; **no, I don't ~** no, neanch'io ▷ *conj*: **~ good or bad** o buono o cattivo

eject [ɪ'dʒɛkt] *vt* espellere; lanciare

elaborate *adj* [ɪ'læbərɪt] elaborato/a, minuzioso/a ▷ *vt* [ɪ'læbəreɪt] elaborare ▷ *vi* [ɪ'læbəreɪt] fornire i dettagli

elastic [ɪ'læstɪk] *adj* elastico/a ▷ *n* elastico; **elastic band** *n* (*BRIT*) elastico

elbow ['ɛlbəu] *n* gomito

elder ['ɛldəʳ] *adj* maggiore, più vecchio/a ▷ *n* (*tree*) sambuco; **one's ~s** i più anziani; **elderly** *adj* anziano/a ▷ *npl*: **the elderly** gli anziani

eldest ['ɛldɪst] *adj*, *n*: **the ~ (child)** il (la) maggiore (dei bambini)

elect [ɪ'lɛkt] *vt* eleggere; **to ~ to do** decidere di fare ▷ *adj*: **the president ~** il presidente designato; **election** [ɪ'lɛkʃən] *n* elezione *f*; **electoral** [ɪ'lɛktərəl] *adj* elettorale; **electorate** *n* elettorato

electric [ɪ'lɛktrɪk] *adj* elettrico/a; **electrical** *adj* elettrico/a; **electric blanket** *n* coperta elettrica; **electric fire** *n* stufa elettrica; **electrician** [ɪlɛk'trɪʃən] *n* elettricista *m*; **electricity** [ɪlɛk'trɪsɪtɪ] *n* elettricità; **electric shock** *n* scossa (elettrica); **electrify** [ɪ'lɛktrɪfaɪ] *vt* (*Rail*) elettrificare; (*audience*) elettrizzare

electronic [ɪlɛk'trɔnɪk] *adj* elettronico/a; **electronic mail** *n* posta elettronica; **electronics** *n* elettronica

elegance ['ɛlɪgəns] *n* eleganza

elegant ['ɛlɪgənt] *adj* elegante

element ['ɛlɪmənt] *n* elemento; (*of heater, kettle etc*) resistenza

elementary [ɛlɪ'mɛntərɪ] *adj*
elementare; **elementary school** *n*
(*us*) scuola elementare
elephant ['ɛlɪfənt] *n* elefante/essa
elevate ['ɛlɪveɪt] *vt* elevare
elevator ['ɛlɪveɪtəʳ] *n* elevatore *m*;
(*us:* lift) ascensore *m*
eleven [ɪ'lɛvn] *num* undici; **eleventh**
adj undicesimo/a
eligible ['ɛlɪdʒəbl] *adj* eleggibile; (*for
membership*) che ha i requisiti
eliminate [ɪ'lɪmɪneɪt] *vt* eliminare
elm [ɛlm] *n* olmo
eloquent ['ɛləkwənt] *adj* eloquente
else [ɛls] *adv* altro; **something
~** qualcos'altro; **somewhere ~**
altrove; **everywhere ~** in qualsiasi
altro luogo; **nobody ~** nessun altro;
where ~? in quale altro luogo?; **little
~** poco altro; **elsewhere** *adv* altrove
elusive [ɪ'lu:sɪv] *adj* elusivo/a
email ['i:meɪl] *n abbr* (= *electronic
mail*) posta elettronica, e-mail *m*
or f inv ▷ *vt* mandare un messaggio
di posta elettronica *or* un e-mail a;
email address *n* indirizzo di posta
elettronica
embankment [ɪm'bæŋkmənt] *n* (*of
road, railway*) massicciata
embargo [ɪm'bɑːgəu] *n* (*pl
embargoes*) (*Comm, Naut*) embargo
▷ *vt* mettere l'embargo su; **to put an
~ on sth** mettere l'embargo su qc
embark [ɪm'bɑːk] *vi*: **to ~ (on)**
imbarcarsi (su) ▷ *vt* imbarcare; **to ~
on** (*fig*) imbarcarsi in
embarrass [ɪm'bærəs] *vt*
imbarazzare; **embarrassed** *adj*
imbarazzato/a; **embarrassing** *adj*
imbarazzante; **embarrassment** *n*
imbarazzo
embassy ['ɛmbəsɪ] *n* ambasciata
embrace [ɪm'breɪs] *vt* abbracciare
▷ *vi* abbracciarsi ▷ *n* abbraccio
embroider [ɪm'brɔɪdəʳ] *vt* ricamare;
embroidery *n* ricamo
embryo ['ɛmbrɪəu] *n* embrione *m*
emerald ['ɛmərəld] *n* smeraldo

emerge [ɪ'məːdʒ] *vi* emergere
emergency [ɪ'məːdʒənsɪ] *n*
emergenza; **in an ~** in caso di
emergenza; **emergency brake** (*us*)
n freno a mano; **emergency exit**
n uscita di sicurezza; **emergency
landing** *n* atterraggio forzato;
emergency room (*us Med*) *n* pronto
soccorso
emergency service *n* servizio di
pronto intervento
emigrate ['ɛmɪgreɪt] *vi* emigrare;
emigration [ɛmɪ'greɪʃən] *n*
emigrazione *f*
eminent ['ɛmɪnənt] *adj* eminente
emission [ɪ'mɪʃən] *n* (*of gas,
radiation*) emissione *f*
emit [ɪ'mɪt] *vt* emettere
emoticon [ɪ'məutɪkən] *n* (*Comput*)
faccina
emotion [ɪ'məuʃən] *n* emozione *f*;
emotional *adj* (*person*) emotivo/a;
(*scene*) commovente; (*tone, speech*)
carico/a d'emozione
emperor ['ɛmpərəʳ] *n* imperatore *m*
emphasis ['ɛmfəsɪs,
-siːz] *n* (*pl emphases*) enfasi *f inv*; importanza
emphasize ['ɛmfəsaɪz] *vt* (*word,
point*) sottolineare; (*feature*) mettere
in evidenza
empire ['ɛmpaɪəʳ] *n* impero
employ [ɪm'plɔɪ] *vt* impiegare;
employee [ɪmplɔɪ'iː] *n*
impiegato/a; **employer** *n* principale
m/f, datore *m* di lavoro; **employment**
n impiego; **employment agency** *n*
agenzia di collocamento
empower [ɪm'pauəʳ] *vt*: **to ~ sb to
do** concedere autorità a qn di fare
empress ['ɛmprɪs] *n* imperatrice *f*
emptiness ['ɛmptɪnɪs] *n* vuoto
empty ['ɛmptɪ] *adj* vuoto/a; (*threat,
promise*) vano/a ▷ *vt* vuotare ▷ *vi*
vuotarsi; (*liquid*) scaricarsi; **empty-
handed** *adj* a mani vuote
EMU *n abbr* (= *economic and monetary
union*) UEM *f*
emulsion [ɪ'mʌlʃən] *n* emulsione *f*

enable [ɪˈneɪbl] vt: **to ~ sb to do** permettere a qn di fare

enamel [ɪˈnæməl] n smalto; **enamel paint** n vernice f a smalto

enchanting [ɪnˈtʃɑːntɪŋ] adj incantevole, affascinante

encl. abbr (on letters etc) = enclosed, enclosure) all., alleg.

enclose [ɪnˈkləʊz] vt (land) circondare, recingere; (letter etc): **to ~ (with)** allegare (con); **please find ~d** trovi qui accluso

enclosure [ɪnˈkləʊʒəʳ] n recinto

encore [ɔŋˈkɔːʳ] excl, n bis (m inv)

encounter [ɪnˈkaʊntəʳ] n incontro ▷ vt incontrare

encourage [ɪnˈkʌrɪdʒ] vt incoraggiare; **encouragement** n incoraggiamento

encouraging [ɪnˈkʌrɪdʒɪŋ] adj incoraggiante

encyclop(a)edia [ɛnsaɪkləʊˈpiːdɪə] n enciclopedia

end [ɛnd] n fine f; (aim) fine m; (of table) bordo estremo; (of pointed object) punta ▷ vt finire; (also: **bring to an ~, put an ~ to**) mettere fine a ▷ vi finire; **in the ~** alla fine; **on ~** (object) ritto(a); **to stand on ~** (hair) rizzarsi; **for hours on ~** per ore e ore; **end up** vi: **to ~ up in** finire in

endanger [ɪnˈdeɪndʒəʳ] vt mettere in pericolo

endearing [ɪnˈdɪərɪŋ] adj accattivante

endeavour, (us) **endeavor** [ɪnˈdɛvəʳ] n sforzo, tentativo ▷ vi: **to ~ to do** cercare or sforzarsi di fare

ending [ˈɛndɪŋ] n fine f, conclusione f; (Ling) desinenza

endless [ˈɛndlɪs] adj senza fine

endorse [ɪnˈdɔːs] vt (cheque) girare; (approve) approvare, appoggiare; **endorsement** n approvazione f; (on driving licence) contravvenzione registrata sulla patente

endurance [ɪnˈdjuərəns] n resistenza; pazienza

endure [ɪnˈdjuəʳ] vt sopportare, resistere a ▷ vi durare

enemy [ˈɛnəmɪ] adj, n nemico/a

energetic [ɛnəˈdʒɛtɪk] adj energico/a, attivo/a

energy [ˈɛnədʒɪ] n energia

enforce [ɪnˈfɔːs] vt (Law) applicare, far osservare

engaged [ɪnˈgeɪdʒd] adj (BRIT: busy, in use) occupato/a; (betrothed) fidanzato/a; **the line's ~** (BRIT) la linea è occupata; **to get ~** fidanzarsi; **engaged tone** n (BRIT Tel) segnale m di occupato

engagement [ɪnˈgeɪdʒmənt] n impegno, obbligo; appuntamento; (to marry) fidanzamento; **engagement ring** n anello di fidanzamento

engaging [ɪnˈgeɪdʒɪŋ] adj attraente

engine [ˈɛndʒɪn] n (Aut) motore m; (Rail) locomotiva

engineer [ɛndʒɪˈnɪəʳ] n ingegnere m; (BRIT: for domestic appliances) tecnico; (us Rail) macchinista m; **engineering** n ingegneria

England [ˈɪŋglənd] n Inghilterra

English [ˈɪŋglɪʃ] adj inglese ▷ n (Ling) inglese m; **the English** npl gli Inglesi; **English Channel** n: **the English Channel** il Canale della Manica; **Englishman** n (irreg) inglese m; **Englishwoman** n (irreg) inglese f

engrave [ɪnˈgreɪv] vt incidere

engraving [ɪnˈgreɪvɪŋ] n incisione f

enhance [ɪnˈhɑːns] vt accrescere

enjoy [ɪnˈdʒɔɪ] vt godere; (have: success, fortune) avere; **to ~ o.s.** godersela, divertirsi; **enjoyable** adj piacevole; **enjoyment** n piacere m, godimento

enlarge [ɪnˈlɑːdʒ] vt ingrandire ▷ vi: **to ~ on** (subject) dilungarsi su; **enlargement** n (Phot) ingrandimento

enlist [ɪnˈlɪst] vt arruolare; (support) procurare ▷ vi arruolarsi

enormous [ɪˈnɔːməs] adj enorme

enough [ɪ'nʌf] *adj, n*: **~ time/books** assai tempo/libri; **have you got ~?** ne ha abbastanza *or* a sufficienza? ▷ *adv*: **big ~** abbastanza grande; **he has not worked ~** non ha lavorato abbastanza; **~!** basta!; **that's ~, thanks** basta così, grazie; **I've had ~ of him** ne ho abbastanza di lui; **... which, funnily ~** ... che, strano a dirsi

enquire [ɪn'kwaɪəʳ] *vt, vi* (*esp BRIT*) = **inquire**

enquiry [ɪn'kwaɪərɪ] *n* (*esp BRIT*) = **inquiry**

enrage [ɪn'reɪdʒ] *vt* fare arrabbiare

enrich [ɪn'rɪtʃ] *vt* arricchire

enrol, (*us*) **enroll** [ɪn'rəul] *vt* iscrivere ▷ *vi* iscriversi; **enrolment**, (*us*) **enrollment** *n* iscrizione *f*

en route [ɔn'ruːt] *adv*: **~ for/from/to** in viaggio per/da/a

en suite [ɔn'swiːt] *adj*: **room with ~ bathroom** camera con bagno

ensure [ɪn'ʃuəʳ] *vt* assicurare; garantire

entail [ɪn'teɪl] *vt* comportare

enter ['ɛntəʳ] *vt* entrare in; (*army*) arruolarsi in; (*competition*) partecipare a; (*sb for a competition*) iscrivere; (*write down*) registrare; (*Comput*) inserire ▷ *vi* entrare

enterprise ['ɛntəpraɪz] *n* (*undertaking, company*) impresa; (*spirit*) iniziativa; **free ~** liberalismo economico; **private ~** iniziativa privata; **enterprising** ['ɛntəpraɪzɪŋ] *adj* intraprendente

entertain [ɛntə'teɪn] *vt* divertire; (*invite*) ricevere; (*idea, plan*) nutrire; **entertainer** *n* comico/a; **entertaining** *adj* divertente; **entertainment** *n* (*amusement*) divertimento; (*show*) spettacolo

enthusiasm [ɪn'θuːzɪæzəm] *n* entusiasmo

enthusiast [ɪn'θuːzɪæst] *n* entusiasta *m/f*; **enthusiastic** [ɪnθuːzɪ'æstɪk] *adj* entusiasta, entusiastico/a; **to be enthusiastic**

about sth/sb essere appassionato di qc/entusiasta di qn

entire [ɪn'taɪəʳ] *adj* intero/a; **entirely** *adv* completamente, interamente

entitle [ɪn'taɪtl] *vt* (*give right*): **to ~ sb to sth/to do** dare diritto a qn a qc/a fare; **entitled** *adj* (*book*) che si intitola; **to be entitled to sth** avere diritto a qc; **to be entitled to do sth** avere il diritto di fare qc

entrance *n* ['ɛntrns] entrata, ingresso; (*of person*) entrata ▷ *vt* [ɪn'trɑːns] incantare, rapire; **to gain ~ to** (*university etc*) essere ammesso a; **entrance examination** *n* esame *m* di ammissione; **entrance fee** *n* tassa d'iscrizione; (*to museum etc*) prezzo d'ingresso; **entrance ramp** *n* (*us Aut*) rampa di accesso; **entrant** ['ɛntrnt] *n* partecipante *m/f*; concorrente *m/f*

entrepreneur ['ɔntrəprə'nəː'] *n* imprenditore *m*

entrust [ɪn'trʌst] *vt*: **to ~ sth to** affidare qc a

entry ['ɛntrɪ] *n* entrata; (*way in*) entrata, ingresso; (*item: on list*) iscrizione *f*; (*in dictionary*) voce *f*; **"no ~"** "vietato l'ingresso"; (*Aut*) "divieto di accesso"; **entry phone** *n* citofono

envelope ['ɛnvələup] *n* busta

envious ['ɛnvɪəs] *adj* invidioso/a

environment [ɪn'vaɪərənmənt] *n* ambiente *m*; **environmental** [ɪnvaɪərən'mɛntl] *adj* ecologico/a; ambientale; **environmentally** [ɪnvaɪərən'mɛntəlɪ] *adv*: **environmentally sound/friendly** che rispetta l'ambiente

envisage [ɪn'vɪzɪdʒ] *vt* immaginare; prevedere

envoy ['ɛnvɔɪ] *n* inviato/a

envy ['ɛnvɪ] *n* invidia ▷ *vt* invidiare; **to ~ sb sth** invidiare qn per qc

epic ['ɛpɪk] *n* poema *m* epico ▷ *adj* epico/a

epidemic [ɛpɪ'dɛmɪk] *n* epidemia

epilepsy ['ɛpɪlɛpsɪ] *n* epilessia

epileptic [ɛpɪ'lɛptɪk] *adj, n* epilettico/a; **epileptic fit** *n* attacco epilettico
episode ['ɛpɪsəud] *n* episodio
equal ['iːkwl] *adj, n* pari (m/f) ▷ *vt* uguagliare; **~ to** (*task*) all'altezza di; **equality** [iː'kwɔlɪtɪ] *n* uguaglianza; **equalize** *vi* pareggiare; **equally** *adv* ugualmente
equation [ɪ'kweɪʃən] *n* (*Math*) equazione *f*
equator [ɪ'kweɪtər] *n* equatore *m*
equip [ɪ'kwɪp] *vt* equipaggiare, attrezzare; **to ~ sb/sth with** fornire qn/qc di; **to be well ~ped** (*office etc*) essere ben attrezzato/a; **he is well ~ped for the job** ha i requisiti necessari per quel lavoro; **equipment** *n* attrezzatura; (*electrical etc*) apparecchiatura
equivalent [ɪ'kwɪvələnt] *adj, n* equivalente (m); **to be ~ to** equivalere a
ER *abbr* (*BRIT*) = **Elizabeth Regina**; (*US Med*) = **emergency room**
era ['ɪərə] *n* era, età *f inv*
erase [ɪ'reɪz] *vt* cancellare; **eraser** *n* gomma
e-reader ['iːriːdər] *n* e-reader *m inv*, lettore *m* di libri digitali
erect [ɪ'rɛkt] *adj* eretto/a ▷ *vt* costruire; (*assemble*) montare; **erection** [ɪ'rɛkʃən] *n* (*also Physiol*) erezione *f*; (*of building*) costruzione *f*; (*of machinery*) montaggio
ERM *n abbr* (= *Exchange Rate Mechanism*) ERM *m*, meccanismo dei tassi di cambio
erode [ɪ'rəud] *vt* erodere; (*metal*) corrodere
erosion [ɪ'rəuʒən] *n* erosione *f*
erotic [ɪ'rɔtɪk] *adj* erotico/a
errand ['ɛrənd] *n* commissione *f*
erratic [ɪ'rætɪk] *adj* imprevedibile; (*person, mood*) incostante
error ['ɛrər] *n* errore *m*
erupt [ɪ'rʌpt] *vi* (*volcano*) mettersi (*or* essere) in eruzione; (*war, crisis*) scoppiare; **eruption** [ɪ'rʌpʃən] *n* eruzione *f*; scoppio

escalate ['ɛskəleɪt] *vi* intensificarsi
escalator ['ɛskəleɪtər] *n* scala mobile
escape [ɪ'skeɪp] *n* evasione *f*; fuga; (*of gas etc*) fuga, fuoriuscita ▷ *vi* fuggire; (*from jail*) evadere, scappare; (*leak*) uscire ▷ *vt* sfuggire a; **to ~ from** (*place*) fuggire da; (*person*) sfuggire a
escort *n* ['ɛskɔːt] scorta; (*to dance etc*): **her ~** il suo cavaliere ▷ *vt* [ɪ'skɔːt] scortare; accompagnare
especially [ɪ'spɛʃlɪ] *adv* specialmente; (*above all*) soprattutto; (*specifically*) espressamente
espionage ['ɛspɪənɑːʒ] *n* spionaggio
essay ['ɛseɪ] *n* (*Scol*) composizione *f*; (*Literature*) saggio
essence ['ɛsns] *n* essenza
essential [ɪ'sɛnʃl] *adj* essenziale ▷ *n* elemento essenziale; **essentially** *adv* essenzialmente; **essentials** *npl*: **the essentials** l'essenziale *msg*
establish [ɪ'stæblɪʃ] *vt* stabilire; (*business*) mettere su; (*one's power etc*) affermare; **establishment** *n* stabilimento; **the Establishment** la classe dirigente; l'establishment *m*
estate [ɪ'steɪt] *n* proprietà *f inv*; (*Law*) beni *mpl*, patrimonio; (*BRIT: also: housing ~*) complesso edilizio; **estate agent** *n* (*BRIT*) agente *m* immobiliare; **estate car** *n* (*BRIT*) giardiniera
estimate *n* ['ɛstɪmət] stima; (*Comm*) preventivo ▷ *vt* ['ɛstɪmeɪt] stimare, valutare
etc. *abbr* (= *et cetera*) ecc., etc.
eternal [ɪ'təːnl] *adj* eterno/a
eternity [ɪ'təːnɪtɪ] *n* eternità
ethical ['ɛθɪkl] *adj* etico/a, morale; **ethics** ['ɛθɪks] *n* etica ▷ *npl* morale *f*
Ethiopia [iːθɪ'əupɪə] *n* Etiopia
ethnic ['ɛθnɪk] *adj* etnico/a; **ethnic minority** *n* minoranza etnica
e-ticket ['iːtɪkɪt] *n* biglietto elettronico
EU *n abbr* (= *European Union*) UE *f*
euro ['juərəu] *n* (*currency*) euro *m inv*

Europe ['juərəp] n Europa;
European [juərə'pi:ən] adj, n
europeo/a; **European Community**
n Comunità Europea; **European
Union** n Unione f europea

Eurostar® ['juərəustɑːᵣ] n
Eurostar® m inv

evacuate [ɪ'vækjueɪt] vt evacuare

evade [ɪ'veɪd] vt (tax) evadere; (duties
etc) sottrarsi a; (person) schivare

evaluate [ɪ'væljueɪt] vt valutare

evaporate [ɪ'væpəreɪt] vi evaporare

eve [iːv] n: **on the ~ of** alla vigilia di

even ['iːvn] adj regolare; (number)
pari inv ▷ adv anche, perfino; **~ if, ~
though** anche se; **~ more** ancora di
più; **~ so** ciò nonostante; **not ~ ...**
nemmeno ...; **to get ~ with sb** dare
la pari a qn

evening ['iːvnɪŋ] n sera; (as
duration, event) serata; **in the ~** la
sera; **evening class** n corso serale;
evening dress n (woman's) abito da
sera; **in evening dress** (man) in abito
scuro; (woman) in abito lungo

event [ɪ'vɛnt] n avvenimento; (Sport)
gara; **in the ~ of** in caso di; **eventful**
adj denso/a di eventi

eventual [ɪ'vɛntʃuəl] adj finale

> Be careful not to translate
> eventual by the Italian word
> eventuale.

eventually [ɪ'vɛntʃuəlɪ] adv alla fine

> Be careful not to translate
> eventually by the Italian word
> eventualmente.

ever ['ɛvəᵣ] adv mai; (at all times)
sempre; **the best ~** il migliore che
ci sia mai stato; **have you ~ seen
it?** l'hai mai visto?; **~ so pretty**
così bello(a); **~ since** adv da allora;
conj sin da quando; **evergreen** n
sempreverde m

every ['ɛvrɪ] adj ogni; **~ day** tutti i
giorni, ogni giorno; **~ other/third
day** ogni due/tre giorni; **~ other
car** una macchina su due; **~ now
and then** ogni tanto, di quando in

quando; **everybody** pron ognuno,
tutti pl; **everyday** adj quotidiano/a;
di ogni giorno; **everyone** ['ɛvrɪwʌn]
= **everybody**; **everything** pron
tutto, ogni cosa; **everywhere** adv
dappertutto; (wherever) ovunque

evict [ɪ'vɪkt] vt sfrattare

evidence ['ɛvɪdəns] n (proof) prova;
(of witness) testimonianza; **to show
~ of** (sign) dare segni di; **to give ~**
deporre

evident ['ɛvɪdənt] adj evidente;
evidently adv evidentemente

evil ['iːvl] adj cattivo/a, maligno/a
▷ n male m

evoke [ɪ'vəuk] vt evocare

evolution [iːvə'luːʃən] n evoluzione f

evolve [ɪ'vɔlv] vt elaborare ▷ vi
svilupparsi, evolversi

ewe [juː] n pecora

ex (col) [ɛks] n: **my ex** il (la) mio/a ex

ex- [ɛks] prefix ex

exact [ɪg'zækt] adj esatto/a ▷ vt:
to ~ sth (from) estorcere qc
(da); esigere qc (da); **exactly** adv
esattamente

exaggerate [ɪg'zædʒəreɪt] vt,
vi esagerare; **exaggeration**
[ɪgzædʒə'reɪʃən] n esagerazione f

exam [ɪg'zæm] n abbr (Scol)
= **examination**

examination [ɪgzæmɪ'neɪʃən] n
(Scol) esame m; (Med) controllo

examine [ɪg'zæmɪn] vt esaminare;
examiner n esaminatore/trice

example [ɪg'zɑːmpl] n esempio; **for
~** ad or per esempio

exasperated [ɪg'zɑːspəreɪtɪd] adj
esasperato/a

excavate ['ɛkskəveɪt] vt scavare

exceed [ɪk'siːd] vt superare; (one's
powers, time limit) oltrepassare;
exceedingly adv eccessivamente

excel [ɪk'sɛl] vi eccellere ▷ vt
sorpassare; **to ~ o.s.** (BRIT) superare
se stesso

excellence ['ɛksələns] n eccellenza

excellent ['ɛksələnt] adj eccellente

369 | **expand**

except [ɪkˈsɛpt] prep (also: **~ for,
~ing**) salvo, all'infuori di, eccetto
▷ vt escludere; **~ if/when** salvo
se/quando; **~ that** salvo che;
exception [ɪkˈsɛpʃən] n eccezione
f; **to take exception to** trovare a
ridire su; **exceptional** [ɪkˈsɛpʃənl]
adj eccezionale; **exceptionally**
[ɪkˈsɛpʃənəlɪ] adv eccezionalmente
excerpt [ˈɛksəːpt] n estratto
excess [ɪkˈsɛs] n eccesso; **excess
baggage** n bagaglio in eccedenza;
excessive adj eccessivo/a
exchange [ɪksˈtʃeɪndʒ] n scambio;
(also: **telephone ~**) centralino
▷ vt: **to ~ (for)** scambiare (con);
exchange rate n tasso di cambio
excite [ɪkˈsaɪt] vt eccitare; **to get
~d** eccitarsi; **excited** adj: **to get
excited** essere elettrizzato/a;
excitement n eccitazione
f; agitazione f; **exciting** adj
avventuroso/a; (film, book)
appassionante
exclaim [ɪkˈskleɪm] vi esclamare;
exclamation [ɛkskləˈmeɪʃən] n
esclamazione f; **exclamation mark**,
(US) **exclamation point** n punto
esclamativo
exclude [ɪkˈskluːd] vt escludere
excluding [ɪkˈskluːdɪŋ] prep: **~ VAT**
IVA esclusa
exclusion [ɪkˈskluːʒən] n esclusione
f; **to the ~ of** escludendo
exclusive [ɪkˈskluːsɪv] adj
esclusivo/a; **~ of VAT** IVA esclusa;
exclusively adv esclusivamente
excruciating [ɪkˈskruːʃɪeɪtɪŋ] adj
straziante, atroce
excursion [ɪkˈskəːʃən] n escursione
f, gita
excuse n [ɪkˈskjuːs] scusa ▷ vt
[ɪkˈskjuːz] scusare; **to ~ sb from**
(activity) dispensare qn da; **~ me!** mi
scusi!; **now if you will ~ me, ...** ora,
mi scusi ma …
ex-directory [ˈɛksdɪˈrɛktərɪ] adj
(BRIT): **to be ~** non essere sull'elenco

execute [ˈɛksɪkjuːt] vt (prisoner)
giustiziare; (plan etc) eseguire;
execution [ɛksɪˈkjuːʃən] n
esecuzione f
executive [ɪgˈzɛkjutɪv] n (Comm)
dirigente m; (Pol) esecutivo ▷ adj
esecutivo/a
exempt [ɪgˈzɛmpt] adj: **~ (from)**
esentato/a (da) ▷ vt: **to ~ sb from**
esentare qn da
exercise [ˈɛksəsaɪz] n (keep fit)
moto; (Scol, Mil etc) esercizio ▷ vt
esercitare; (patience) usare; (dog)
portar fuori ▷ vi (also: **take ~**) fare
del movimento or moto; **exercise
book** n quaderno
exert [ɪgˈzəːt] vt esercitare; **to ~
o.s.** sforzarsi; **exertion** [ɪgˈzəːʃən]
n sforzo
exhale [ɛksˈheɪl] vt, vi espirare
exhaust [ɪgˈzɔːst] n (also: **~ fumes**)
scappamento; (also: **~ pipe**) tubo
di scappamento ▷ vt esaurire;
exhausted adj esaurito/a;
exhaustion [ɪgˈzɔːstʃən] n
esaurimento; **nervous exhaustion**
sovraffaticamento mentale
exhibit [ɪgˈzɪbɪt] n (Art) oggetto
esposto; (Law) documento or
oggetto esibito ▷ vt esporre;
(courage, skill) dimostrare;
exhibition [ɛksɪˈbɪʃən] n mostra,
esposizione f
exhilarating [ɪgˈzɪləreɪtɪŋ] adj
esilarante; stimolante
exile [ˈɛksaɪl] n esilio; (person)
esiliato/a ▷ vt esiliare
exist [ɪgˈzɪst] vi esistere; **existence**
n esistenza; **existing** adj esistente;
attuale
exit [ˈɛksɪt] n uscita ▷ vi (Comput,
Theat) uscire; **exit ramp** n (US Aut)
rampa di uscita
exotic [ɪgˈzɔtɪk] adj esotico/a
expand [ɪkˈspænd] vt espandere;
(influence) estendere; (horizons)
allargare ▷ vi (gas) espandersi; (metal)
dilatarsi

e

expansion [ɪk'spænʃən] n (gen) espansione f; (of town, economy) sviluppo; (of metal) dilatazione f

expect [ɪk'spɛkt] vt (anticipate) prevedere, aspettarsi, prevedere or aspettarsi che + sub; (require) richiedere, esigere; (suppose) supporre; (await, also baby) aspettare ▷ vi: **to be ~ing** essere in stato interessante; **to ~ sb to do** aspettarsi che qn faccia; **expectation** [ɛkspɛk'teɪʃən] n aspettativa; speranza

expedition [ɛkspə'dɪʃən] n spedizione f

expel [ɪk'spɛl] vt espellere

expenditure [ɪk'spɛndɪtʃəʳ] n spesa

expense [ɪk'spɛns] n spesa; (high cost) costo; **expenses** npl (Comm) spese fpl, indennità fpl; **at the ~ of** a spese di; **expense account** n conto m spese inv

expensive [ɪk'spɛnsɪv] adj caro/a, costoso/a

experience [ɪk'spɪərɪəns] n esperienza ▷ vt (pleasure) provare; (hardship) soffrire; **experienced** adj esperto/a

experiment n [ɪk'spɛrɪmənt] esperimento, esperienza ▷ vi [ɪk'spɛrɪmɛnt] fare esperimenti; **experimental** [ɪkspɛrɪ'mɛntl] adj sperimentale; **at the experimental stage** in via di sperimentazione

expert ['ɛkspəːt] adj, n esperto/a; **expertise** [ɛkspəː'tiːz] n competenza

expire [ɪk'spaɪəʳ] vi (period of time, licence) scadere; **expiry** n scadenza; **expiry date** n (of medicine, food item) data di scadenza

explain [ɪk'spleɪn] vt spiegare; **explanation** [ɛksplə'neɪʃən] n spiegazione f

explicit [ɪk'splɪsɪt] adj esplicito/a

explode [ɪk'spləud] vi esplodere

exploit n ['ɛksplɔɪt] impresa ▷ vt [ɪk'splɔɪt] sfruttare; **exploitation** [ɛksplɔɪ'teɪʃən] n sfruttamento

explore [ɪk'splɔːʳ] vt esplorare; (possibilities) esaminare; **explorer** n esploratore/trice

explosion [ɪk'spləuʒən] n esplosione f; **explosive** [ɪk'spləusɪv] adj esplosivo/a ▷ n esplosivo

export vt [ɛk'spɔːt] esportare ▷ n ['ɛkspɔːt] esportazione f; articolo di esportazione ▷ cpd d'esportazione; **exporter** n esportatore m

expose [ɪk'spəuz] vt esporre; (unmask) smascherare; **exposed** adj (land, house) esposto/a; **exposure** [ɪk'spəuʒəʳ] n esposizione f; (Phot) posa; (Med) assideramento

express [ɪk'sprɛs] adj (definite) chiaro/a, espresso/a; (BRIT: letter etc) espresso inv ▷ n (train) espresso ▷ vt esprimere; **expression** [ɪk'sprɛʃən] n espressione f; **expressway** n (US: urban motorway) autostrada che attraversa la città

exquisite [ɛk'skwɪzɪt] adj squisito/a

extend [ɪk'stɛnd] vt (visit) protrarre; (road, deadline) prolungare; (building) ampliare; (offer) offrire, porgere ▷ vi (land) estendersi; **extension** [ɪk'stɛnʃən] n (of road, term) prolungamento; (of contract, deadline) proroga; (building) annesso; (to wire, table) prolunga; (telephone) interno; (: in private house) apparecchio supplementare; **extension cable** or **lead** n (Elec) prolunga

extensive [ɪk'stɛnsɪv] adj esteso/a, ampio/a; (damage) su larga scala; (inquiries, coverage, discussion) esauriente; (use) grande

extent [ɪk'stɛnt] n estensione f; **to some ~** fino a un certo punto; **to what ~?** fino a che punto?; **to such an ~ that ...** a tal punto che ...; **to the ~ of ...** fino al punto di ...

exterior [ɛk'stɪərɪəʳ] adj esteriore, esterno/a ▷ n esteriore m, esterno; aspetto (esteriore)

external [ɛk'stəːnl] adj esterno/a, esteriore

extinct [ɪk'stɪŋkt] *adj* estinto/a; **extinction** [ɪk'stɪŋkʃən] *n* estinzione *f*

extinguish [ɪk'stɪŋgwɪʃ] *vt* estinguere

extra ['ɛkstrə] *adj* extra *inv*, supplementare ▷ *adv* (*in addition*) di più ▷ *n* extra *m inv*; (*surcharge*) supplemento; (*Theat*) comparso

extract *vt* [ɪk'strækt] estrarre; (*money, promise*) strappare ▷ *n* ['ɛkstrækt] estratto; (*passage*) brano

extradite ['ɛkstrədaɪt] *vt* estradare

extraordinary [ɪk'strɔːdnrɪ] *adj* straordinario/a

extravagance [ɪk'strævəgəns] *n* sperpero; (*thing bought*) stravaganza

extravagant [ɪk'strævəgənt] *adj* (*in spending*) prodigo/a; (: *tastes*) dispendioso/a; esagerato/a

> Be careful not to translate *extravagant* by the Italian word *stravagante*.

extreme [ɪk'striːm] *adj* estremo/a ▷ *n* estremo; **extremely** *adv* estremamente

extremist [ɪk'striːmɪst] *adj, n* estremista (*m/f*)

extrovert ['ɛkstrəvəːt] *n* estroverso/a

eye [aɪ] *n* occhio; (*of needle*) cruna ▷ *vt* osservare; **to keep an ~ on** tenere d'occhio; **eyeball** *n* globo dell'occhio; **eyebrow** *n* sopracciglio; **eyedrops** *npl* gocce *fpl* oculari, collirio; **eyelash** *n* ciglio; **eyelid** *n* palpebra; **eyeliner** *n* eye-liner *m inv*; **eyeshadow** *n* ombretto; **eyesight** *n* vista; **eye witness** *n* testimone *m/f* oculare

F [ɛf] *n* (*Mus*) fa *m*

fabric ['fæbrɪk] *n* stoffa, tessuto

fabulous ['fæbjuləs] *adj* favoloso/a; (*super*) favoloso/a, fantastico/a

face [feɪs] *n* faccia, viso, volto; (*expression*) faccia; (*of clock*) quadrante *m*; (*of building*) facciata ▷ *vt* fronteggiare; (*fig*) affrontare; **~ down** (*person*) bocconi; (*object*) a faccia in giù; **to pull a ~** fare una smorfia; **in the ~ of** (*difficulties etc*) di fronte a; **on the ~ of it** a prima vista; **~ to ~** faccia a faccia; **face up to** *vt fus* affrontare, far fronte a; **face cloth** *n* (*BRIT*) guanto di spugna; **face pack** *n* (*BRIT*) maschera di bellezza

facial ['feɪʃəl] *adj* facciale, del viso ▷ *n* trattamento del viso

facilitate [fə'sɪlɪteɪt] *vt* facilitare

facility [fə'sɪlɪtɪ] *n* facilità; **facilities** *npl* attrezzature *fpl*; **credit facilities** facilitazioni *fpl* di credito

fact [fækt] *n* fatto; **in ~** in effetti

faction ['fækʃən] n fazione f
factor ['fæktə'] n fattore m
factory ['fæktərɪ] n fabbrica,
stabilimento

▌ Be careful not to translate *factory*
by the Italian word *fattoria*.

factual ['fæktjuəl] adj che si attiene
ai fatti
faculty ['fækəltɪ] n facoltà f inv; (US)
corpo insegnante
fad [fæd] n mania; capriccio
fade [feɪd] vi sbiadire, sbiadirsi; (light,
sound, hope) attenuarsi, affievolirsi;
(flower) appassire; **fade away** vi
(sound) affievolirsi
fag [fæg] n (BRIT: col: cigarette) cicca
Fahrenheit ['fɑːrənhaɪt] n
Fahrenheit m inv
fail [feɪl] vt (exam) non superare;
(candidate) bocciare; (courage,
memory) mancare a ▷ vi fallire;
(student) essere respinto/a; (eyesight,
health, light) venire a mancare; **to ~
to do sth** (neglect) mancare di fare
qc; (be unable) non riuscire a fare
qc; **without ~** senza fallo; certamente;
failing n difetto ▷ prep in mancanza
di; **failure** ['feɪljə'] n fallimento;
(person) fallito/a; (mechanical etc)
guasto
faint [feɪnt] adj debole; (recollection)
vago/a; (mark) indistinto/a ▷ n
(Med) svenimento ▷ vi svenire; **to
feel ~** sentirsi svenire; **faintest** adj:
I haven't the faintest idea non
ho la più pallida idea; **faintly** adv
debolmente; vagamente
fair [fɛə'] adj (person, decision)
giusto/a, equo/a; (quite large,
quite good) discreto/a; (hair etc)
biondo/a; (skin, complexion) chiaro/a;
(weather) bello/a, clemente ▷ adv:
to play ~ giocare correttamente
▷ n fiera; (BRIT: funfair) luna park m
inv; **fairground** n luna park m inv;
fair-haired [fɛə'hɛəd] adj (person)
biondo/a; **fairly** adv equamente;
(quite) abbastanza; **fair trade** n

commercio equo e solidale; **fairway**
n (Golf) fairway m inv
fairy ['fɛərɪ] n fata; **fairy tale** n fiaba
faith [feɪθ] n fede f; (trust) fiducia;
(sect) religione f, fede f; **faithful** adj
fedele; **faithfully** adv fedelmente;
yours faithfully (BRIT) (in letters)
distinti saluti
fake [feɪk] n imitazione f; (picture)
falso; (person) impostore/a ▷ adj
falso/a ▷ vt (accounts) falsificare;
(illness) fingere; (painting)
contraffare
falcon ['fɔːlkən] n falco, falcone m
fall [fɔːl] n caduta; (in temperature)
abbassamento; (in price) ribasso;
(US: autumn) autunno ▷ vi (pt **fell**, pp
fallen) cadere; (temperature, price)
scendere; **to ~ flat** (on one's face)
cadere bocconi; (joke) fare cilecca;
(plan) fallire; **fall apart** vi cadere a
pezzi; **fall down** vi (person) cadere;
(building, hopes) crollare; **fall for**
vt fus (person) prendere una cotta
per; **to ~ for a trick** (or **a story**
etc) cascarci; **fall off** vi cadere;
(diminish) diminuire, abbassarsi; **fall
out** vi (hair, teeth) cadere; (friends
etc) litigare; **fall through** vi (plan,
project) fallire
fallen ['fɔːlən] pp of **fall**
fallout ['fɔːlaut] n fall-out m
falls npl (waterfall) cascate fpl
false [fɔːls] adj falso/a; **under ~
pretences** con l'inganno; **false
alarm** n falso allarme m; **false teeth**
npl (BRIT) denti mpl finti
fame [feɪm] n fama, celebrità
familiar [fə'mɪlɪə'] adj familiare;
(close) intimo/a; **to be ~
with** conoscere; **familiarize**
[fə'mɪlɪəraɪz] vt: **to familiarize o.s.
with** familiarizzare con
family ['fæmɪlɪ] n famiglia; **family
doctor** n medico di famiglia; **family
planning** n pianificazione f familiare
famine ['fæmɪn] n carestia
famous ['feɪməs] adj famoso/a

fan [fæn] n (folding) ventaglio; (machine) ventilatore m; (person) ammiratore/trice; tifoso/a ▷ vt far vento a; (fire, quarrel) alimentare

fanatic [fə'nætɪk] n fanatico/a

fan belt n cinghia del ventilatore

fan club n fan club m inv

fancy ['fænsɪ] n immaginazione f, fantasia; (whim) capriccio ▷ adj (hat) stravagante; (hotel, food) speciale ▷ vt (feel like, want) aver voglia di; (imagine) immaginare; **to take a ~ to** incapricciarsi di; **he fancies her** gli piace; **fancy dress** n costume m (per maschera)

fan heater n (BRIT) stufa ad aria calda

fantasize ['fæntəsaɪz] vi fantasticare, sognare

fantastic [fæn'tæstɪk] adj fantastico/a

fantasy ['fæntəsɪ] n fantasia, immaginazione f; fantasticheria; chimera

fanzine ['fænziːn] n rivista specialistica (per appassionati)

FAQ abbr (= frequently asked question(s)) FAQ

far [fɑːʳ] adj lontano/a ▷ adv lontano; (much, greatly) molto; **is it ~ from here?** è molto lontano da qui?; **how ~?** quanto lontano?; (referring to activity etc) fino a dove?; **how ~ is the town centre?** quanto dista il centro da qui?; **~ away, ~ off** lontano, distante; **~ better** assai migliore; **~ from** lontano da; **by ~** di gran lunga; **go as ~ as the farm** vada fino alla fattoria; **as ~ as I know** per quel che so

farce [fɑːs] n farsa

fare [fɛəʳ] n (on trains, buses) tariffa; (in taxi) prezzo della corsa; (food) vitto, cibo; **half ~** metà tariffa; **full ~** tariffa intera

Far East n: **the ~** l'Estremo Oriente m

farewell [fɛə'wɛl] excl, n addio

farm [fɑːm] n fattoria, podere m ▷ vt coltivare; **farmer** n coltivatore/ trice, agricoltore/trice; **farmhouse** n fattoria; **farming** n (gen) agricoltura; (of crops) coltivazione f; (of animals) allevamento; **farmyard** n aia

far-reaching [fɑː'riːtʃɪŋ] adj di vasta portata

fart [fɑːt] (col!) n scoreggia (!) ▷ vi scoreggiare (!)

farther ['fɑːðəʳ] adv più lontano ▷ adj più lontano/a

farthest ['fɑːðɪst] adv superlative of **far**

fascinate ['fæsɪneɪt] vt affascinare; **fascinated** adj affascinato/a; **fascinating** adj affascinante; **fascination** [fæsɪ'neɪʃən] n fascino

fascist ['fæʃɪst] adj, n fascista (m/f)

fashion ['fæʃən] n moda; (manner) maniera, modo ▷ vt foggiare, formare; **in ~** alla moda; **out of ~** passato/a di moda; **fashionable** adj alla moda, di moda; **fashionista** [fæʃə'nɪstə] n fashionista m/f, maniaco/a della moda; **fashion show** n sfilata di moda

fast [fɑːst] adj rapido/a, svelto/a, veloce; (clock): **to be ~** andare avanti; (dye, colour) solido/a ▷ adv rapidamente; (stuck, held) saldamente ▷ n digiuno ▷ vi digiunare; **~ asleep** profondamente addormentato

fasten ['fɑːsn] vt chiudere, fissare; (coat) abbottonare, allacciare ▷ vi chiudersi, fissarsi; abbottonarsi, allacciarsi

fast food n fast food m inv

fat [fæt] adj grasso/a; (book, profit etc) grosso/a ▷ n grasso

fatal ['feɪtl] adj fatale; mortale; disastroso/a; **fatality** [fə'tælɪtɪ] n (road death etc) morto/a, vittima; **fatally** adv a morte

fate [feɪt] n destino; (of person) sorte f

father ['fɑːðəʳ] n padre m; **Father Christmas** n Babbo Natale; **father-in-law** n suocero

fatigue [fə'ti:g] n stanchezza
fattening ['fætnɪŋ] adj (food) che fa
ingrassare
fatty ['fætɪ] adj (food) grasso/a ▷ n
(col) ciccione/a
faucet ['fɔːsɪt] n (US) rubinetto
fault [fɔːlt] n colpa; (Tennis) fallo;
(defect) difetto; (Geo) faglia ▷ vt
criticare; **it's my ~** è colpa mia; **to
find ~ with** trovare da ridire su; **at ~**
in fallo; **faulty** adj difettoso/a
fauna ['fɔːnə] n fauna
favour, (US) **favor** ['feɪvə'] n favore
m ▷ vt (proposition) favorire, essere
favorevole a; (pupil etc) favorire;
(team, horse) dare per vincente;
to do sb a ~ fare un favore or una
cortesia a qn; **in ~ of** in favore di; **to
find ~ with sb** (person) entrare nelle
buone grazie di qn; (suggestion) avere
l'approvazione di qn; **favourable** adj
favorevole; **favourite** ['feɪvrɪt] adj,
n favorito/a
fawn [fɔːn] n daino ▷ adj (also:
~-coloured) marrone chiaro inv ▷ vi:
to ~ (up)on adulare servilmente
fax [fæks] n (document, machine)
facsimile m inv, telecopia; (machine)
telecopiatrice f ▷ vt teletrasmettere,
spedire via fax
FBI n abbr (US: = Federal Bureau of
Investigation) FBI f
fear [fɪə'] n paura, timore m ▷ vt
aver paura di, temere; **for ~ of** per
paura di; **fearful** adj pauroso/a;
(sight, noise) terribile, spaventoso/a;
fearless adj intrepido/a, senza paura
feasible ['fi:zəbl] adj fattibile,
realizzabile
feast [fi:st] n festa, banchetto; (Rel:
also: **~ day**) festa ▷ vi banchettare
feat [fi:t] n impresa, fatto insigne
feather ['feðə'] n penna
feature ['fi:tʃə'] n caratteristica;
(article) articolo ▷ vt (film) avere come
protagonista ▷ vi figurare; **features**
npl (of face) fisionomia; **feature film**
n film m inv principale

Feb. [fɛb] abbr (= February) feb.
February ['fɛbruərɪ] n febbraio
fed [fɛd] pt, pp of **feed**
federal ['fɛdərəl] adj federale
federation [fɛdə'reɪʃən] n
federazione f
fed up adj: **to be ~** essere stufo/a
fee [fi:] n pagamento; (of doctor,
lawyer) onorario; (for examination)
tassa d'esame; **school ~s** tasse fpl
scolastiche
feeble ['fi:bl] adj debole
feed [fi:d] n (of baby) pappa; (of
animal) mangime m; (on printer)
meccanismo di alimentazione ▷ vt
(pt, pp **fed**) nutrire; (baby) allattare;
(horse etc) dare da mangiare a; (fire,
machine) alimentare ▷ vi (baby,
animal) mangiare; **to ~ data/
information into sth** inserire dati/
informazioni in qc; **feedback** n
feed-back m
feel [fi:l] n (sense of touch) tatto; (of
substance) consistenza ▷ vt (pt, pp
felt) toccare; palpare; tastare; (cold,
pain, anger) sentire; (think, believe): **to
~ that** pensare che; **to ~ hungry/
cold** aver fame/freddo; **to ~ lonely/
better** sentirsi solo/meglio; **I don't
~ well** non mi sento bene; **it ~s soft**
è morbido al tatto; **to ~ like** (want)
aver voglia di; **to ~ about or around
for** cercare a tastoni; **feeling** n
sensazione f; (emotion) sentimento
feet [fi:t] npl of **foot**
fell [fɛl] pt of **fall** ▷ vt (tree) abbattere
fellow ['fɛləu] n individuo, tipo;
(comrade) compagno; (of learned
society) membro cpd; **fellow citizen** n
concittadino/a; **fellow countryman**
n (irreg) compatriota m; **fellow
men** npl simili mpl; **fellowship** n
associazione f; compagnia; (Scol)
specie di borsa di studio universitaria
felony ['fɛlənɪ] n reato, crimine m
felt [fɛlt] pt, pp of **feel** ▷ n feltro
female ['fi:meɪl] n (Zool) femmina;
(pej: woman) donna, femmina ▷ adj

(sex, character) femminile; (Biol, Elec) femmina inv; (vote etc) di donne

feminine ['feminin] adj, n femminile (m)

feminist ['feminist] n femminista m/f

fence [fens] n recinto ▷ vt (also: ~ in) recingere ▷ vi; (Sport) tirare di scherma; **fencing** n (Sport) scherma

fend [fend] vi: **to ~ for o.s.** arrangiarsi; **fend off** vt (attack, attacker) respingere, difendersi da

fender ['fendər] n parafuoco; (on boat) parabordo; (US) parafango; paraurti m inv

fennel ['fenl] n finocchio

ferment vi [fə'ment] fermentare ▷ n ['fə:ment] (fig) agitazione f, eccitazione f

fern [fə:n] n felce f

ferocious [fə'rəuʃəs] adj feroce

ferret ['ferit] n furetto

ferry ['feri] n (small) traghetto; (large: also: ~**boat**) nave f traghetto inv ▷ vt traghettare

fertile ['fə:tail] adj fertile; (Biol) fecondo/a; **fertilize** ['fə:tilaiz] vt fertilizzare; fecondare; **fertilizer** ['fə:tilaizər] n fertilizzante m

festival ['festivəl] n (Rel) festa; (Art, Mus) festival m inv

festive ['festiv] adj di festa; **the ~ season** (BRIT: Christmas) il periodo delle feste

fetch [fetʃ] vt andare a prendere; (sell for) essere venduto/a per

fête [feit] n festa

fetus ['fi:təs] n (US) = **foetus**

feud [fju:d] n contesa, lotta

fever ['fi:vər] n febbre f; **feverish** adj febbrile

few [fju:] adj pochi/e ▷ pron alcuni/e; **a ~ ...** qualche ...; **fewer** adj meno inv; meno numerosi/e; **fewest** adj il minor numero di

fiancé [fi'ɑ̃:ŋsei] n fidanzato; **fiancée** n fidanzata

fiasco [fi'æskəu] n fiasco

fib [fib] n piccola bugia

fibre, (US) **fiber** ['faibər] n fibra; **fibreglass**, (US) **fiberglass** n fibra di vetro

fickle ['fikl] adj incostante, capriccioso/a

fiction ['fikʃən] n narrativa, romanzi mpl; (sth made up) finzione f; **fictional** adj immaginario/a

fiddle ['fidl] n (Mus) violino; (cheating) imbroglio; truffa ▷ vt (BRIT: accounts) falsificare, falsare; **fiddle with** vt fus gingillarsi con

fidelity [fi'deliti] n fedeltà; (accuracy) esattezza

field [fi:ld] n campo; **field marshal** n feldmaresciallo

fierce [fiəs] adj (look) fiero/a; (fighting) accanito/a; (wind) furioso/a; (heat) intenso/a; (animal, person, attack) feroce

fifteen [fif'ti:n] num quindici; **fifteenth** num quindicesimo/a

fifth [fifθ] num quinto/a

fiftieth ['fiftiiθ] num cinquantesimo/a

fifty ['fifti] num cinquanta; **fifty-fifty** adj: **a fifty-fifty chance** una possibilità su due ▷ adv: **to go fifty-fifty with sb** fare a metà con qn

fig [fig] n fico

fight (pt, pp **fought**) [fait, fɔ:t] n zuffa, rissa; (Mil) battaglia, combattimento; (against cancer etc) lotta ▷ vt (person) azzuffarsi con; (enemy: also Mil) combattere; (cancer, alcoholism, emotion) lottare contro, combattere; (election) partecipare a ▷ vi combattere; **fight off** vt (attack, attacker) respingere; (disease, sleep, urge) lottare contro; **fighting** n combattimento

figure ['figər] n figura; (number, cipher) cifra ▷ vt (think: esp US) pensare ▷ vi (appear) figurare; **figure out** vt riuscire a capire; calcolare

file [fail] n (tool) lima; (dossier) incartamento; (folder) cartellina;

(row) fila; *(Comput)* archivio ▷ *vt (nails, wood)* limare; *(papers)* archiviare; *(Law: claim)* presentare; passare agli atti; **filing cabinet** ['faɪlɪŋ-] *n* casellario

Filipino [fɪlɪ'piːnəu] *n* filippino/a; *(Ling)* tagal *m*

fill [fɪl] *vt* riempire; *(job)* coprire ▷ *n*: **to eat one's ~** mangiare a sazietà; **fill in** *vt (hole)* riempire; *(form)* compilare; **fill out** *vt (form, receipt)* riempire; **fill up** *vt* riempire; **~ it up, please** *(Aut)* il pieno, per favore

fillet ['fɪlɪt] *n* filetto; **fillet steak** *n* bistecca di filetto

filling ['fɪlɪŋ] *n (Culin)* impasto, ripieno; *(for tooth)* otturazione *f*; **filling station** *n* stazione *f* di rifornimento

film [fɪlm] *n (Cine)* film *m inv*; *(Phot)* pellicola, rullino; *(of powder, liquid)* sottile strato ▷ *vt (scene)* filmare ▷ *vi* girare; **film star** *n* divo/a dello schermo

filter ['fɪltər] *n* filtro ▷ *vt* filtrare; **filter lane** *n* (BRIT Aut) corsia di svincolo

filth [fɪlθ] *n* sporcizia; **filthy** *adj* lordo/a, sozzo/a; *(language)* osceno/a

fin [fɪn] *n (of fish)* pinna

final ['faɪnl] *adj* finale, ultimo/a; definitivo/a ▷ *n (Sport)* finale *f*; **finals** *npl (Scol)* esami *mpl* finali; **finale** [fɪ'nɑːlɪ] *n* finale *m*; **finalist** ['faɪnəlɪst] *n (Sport)* finalista *m/f*; **finalize** ['faɪnəlaɪz] *vt* mettere a punto; **finally** ['faɪnəlɪ] *adv (lastly)* alla fine; *(eventually)* finalmente

finance [faɪ'næns] *n* finanza; *(capital)* capitale *m* ▷ *vt* finanziare; **finances** *npl (funds)* finanze *fpl*; **financial** [faɪ'nænʃəl] *adj* finanziario/a; **financial year** *n* anno finanziario, esercizio finanziario

find [faɪnd] *vt (pt, pp* **found)** trovare; *(lost object)* ritrovare ▷ *n* trovata, scoperta; **to ~ sb guilty** *(Law)* giudicare qn colpevole; **find out** *vt (truth, secret)* scoprire; *(person)* cogliere in fallo ▷ *vi*: **to ~ out about** informarsi su; *(by chance)* venire a sapere; **findings** *npl (Law)* sentenza, conclusioni *fpl*; *(of report)* conclusioni

fine [faɪn] *adj* bello/a; ottimo/a; *(thin, subtle)* fine ▷ *adv (well)* molto bene ▷ *n (Law)* multa ▷ *vt (Law)* multare; **to be ~** *(person)* stare bene; *(weather)* far bello; **fine arts** *npl* belle arti *fpl*

finger ['fɪŋɡər] *n* dito ▷ *vt* toccare, tastare; **little/index ~** mignolo/ (dito) indice *m*; **fingernail** *n* unghia; **fingerprint** *n* impronta digitale; **fingertip** *n* punta del dito

finish ['fɪnɪʃ] *n* fine *f*; *(polish etc)* finitura ▷ *vt, vi* finire; **to ~ doing sth** finire di fare qc; **to ~ first/second** arrivare primo/secondo; **finish off** *vt* compiere; *(kill)* uccidere; **finish up** *vi, vt* finire

Finland ['fɪnlənd] *n* Finlandia; **Finn** [fɪn] *n* finlandese *m/f*; **Finnish** *adj* finlandese ▷ *n (Ling)* finlandese *m*

fir [fəːr] *n* abete *m*

fire [faɪər] *n* fuoco; *(destructive)* incendio; *(gas fire, electric fire)* stufa ▷ *vt (discharge)*: **to ~ a gun** fare fuoco; *(arrow)* sparare; *(fig)* infiammare; *(dismiss)* licenziare ▷ *vi* sparare, far fuoco; **~!** al fuoco!; **on ~** in fiamme; **fire alarm** *n* allarme *m* d'incendio; **firearm** *n* arma da fuoco; **fire brigade** [-brɪ'ɡeɪd], *(us)* **fire department** *n* (corpo dei) pompieri *mpl*; **fire engine** *n* autopompa; **fire escape** *n* scala di sicurezza; **fire exit** *n* uscita di sicurezza; **fire extinguisher** [-ɪk'stɪŋɡwɪʃər] *n* estintore *m*; **fireman** *n (irreg)* pompiere *m*; **fireplace** *n* focolare *m*; **fire station** *n* caserma dei pompieri; **firetruck** *(us) n* = **fire engine**; **firewall** *n (Internet)* firewall *m inv*; **firewood** ['faɪəwud] *n* legna; **fireworks** *npl* fuochi *mpl* d'artificio

firm [fəːm] *adj* fermo/a ▷ *n* ditta, azienda; **firmly** *adv* fermamente

first [fəːst] *adj* primo/a ▷ *adv* (*before others*) il primo, la prima; (*before other things*) per primo; (*when listing reasons etc*) per prima cosa ▷ *n* (*person: in race*) primo/a; (*BRIT Scol*) laurea con lode; (*Aut*) prima; **at ~** dapprima, all'inizio; **~ of all** prima di tutto; **first aid** *n* pronto soccorso; **first-aid kit** *n* cassetta pronto soccorso; **first-class** *adj* di prima classe; **first-hand** *adj* di prima mano; **first lady** *n* (*US*) moglie *f* del presidente; **firstly** *adv* in primo luogo; **first name** *n* prenome *m*; **first-rate** *adj* di prima qualità, ottimo/a

fiscal ['fɪskəl] *adj* fiscale; **~ year** anno fiscale

fish [fɪʃ] *n* pesce *m* ▷ *vt* (*river, area*) pescare in ▷ *vi* pescare; **to go ~ing** andare a pesca; **fish-and-chip shop** [fɪʃən'tʃɪp-] *n* ≈ friggitoria; *see* **chip shop**; **fisherman** *n* (*irreg*) pescatore *m*; **fish fingers** *npl* (*BRIT*) bastoncini *mpl* di pesce (surgelati); **fishing** *n* pesca; **fishing boat** *n* barca da pesca; **fishing line** *n* lenza; **fishmonger** *n* pescivendolo; **fishmonger's (shop)** pescheria; **fish sticks** *npl* (*US*) = **fish fingers**; **fishy** ['fɪʃɪ] *adj* (*tale, story*) sospetto/a

fist [fɪst] *n* pugno

fit [fɪt] *adj* (*Med, Sport*) in forma; (*proper*) adatto/a, appropriato/a; conveniente ▷ *vt* (*clothes*) stare bene a; (*put in, attach*) mettere; installare; (*equip*) fornire, equipaggiare ▷ *vi* (*clothes*) stare bene; (*parts*) andare bene, adattarsi; (*in space, gap*) entrare ▷ *n* (*Med*) accesso, attacco; **~ to** in grado di; **~ for** adatto(a) a; degno(a) di; **this dress is a tight/good ~** questo vestito è stretto/sta bene; **~ of anger/enthusiasm** accesso d'ira/d'entusiasmo; **fit in** *vi* accordarsi; adattarsi; **fitness** *n* (*Med*) forma fisica; **fitted** *adj*: **fitted carpet** moquette *f* inv; **fitted cupboards** armadi *mpl* a muro; **fitted kitchen** (*BRIT*) cucina componibile; **fitting** *adj* appropriato/a ▷ *n* (*of dress*) prova; (*of piece of equipment*) montaggio, aggiustaggio; **fitting room** *n* (*in shop*) camerino; **fittings** ['fɪtɪŋz] *npl* (*in building*) impianti *mpl*

five [faɪv] *num* cinque; **fiver** *n* (*col: BRIT*) biglietto da cinque sterline; (*: US*) biglietto da cinque dollari

fix [fɪks] *vt* fissare; (*mend*) riparare; (*meal, drink*) preparare ▷ *n*: **to be in a ~** essere nei guai; **fix up** *vt* (*date, meeting*) fissare; **to ~ sb up with sth** procurare qc a qn; **fixed** [fɪkst] *adj* (*prices etc*) fisso/a; **fixture** ['fɪkstʃər] *n* impianto (fisso); (*Sport*) incontro (del calendario sportivo)

fizzy ['fɪzɪ] *adj* frizzante; gassato/a

flag [flæg] *n* bandiera; (*also: ~stone*) pietra da lastricare ▷ *vi* stancarsi; affievolirsi; **flagpole** ['flægpəul] *n* albero

flair [flɛər] *n* (*for business etc*) fiuto; (*for languages etc*) facilità; (*style*) stile *m*

flak [flæk] *n* (*Mil*) fuoco d'artiglieria; (*col: criticism*) critiche *fpl*

flake [fleɪk] *n* (*of rust, paint*) scaglia; (*of snow, soap powder*) fiocco ▷ *vi* (*also: ~ off*) sfaldarsi

flamboyant [flæm'bɔɪənt] *adj* sgargiante

flame [fleɪm] *n* fiamma

flamingo [flə'mɪŋgəu] *n* fenicottero, fiammingo

flammable ['flæməbl] *adj* infiammabile

flan [flæn] *n* (*BRIT*) flan *m inv*

flank [flæŋk] *n* fianco ▷ *vt* fiancheggiare

flannel ['flænl] *n* (*BRIT: also: face ~*) guanto di spugna; (*fabric*) flanella

flap [flæp] *n* (*of pocket, envelope*) lembo ▷ *vt* (*wings*) battere ▷ *vi* (*sail, flag*) sbattere; (*col: also: be in a ~*) essere in agitazione

flare [flɛər] *n* razzo; (*in skirt etc*) svasatura; **flares** (*trousers*)

f

pantaloni *mpl* a zampa d'elefante;
flare up *vi* andare in fiamme; (*fig: person*) infiammarsi di rabbia; (: *revolt*) scoppiare
flash [flæʃ] *n* vampata; (*also:* **news ~**) notizia *f* lampo *inv*; (*Phot*) flash *m inv* ▷ *vt* accendere e spegnere; (*send: message*) trasmettere; (: *look, smile*) lanciare ▷ *vi* brillare; (*light on ambulance, eyes etc*) lampeggiare; **in a ~** in un lampo; **to ~ one's headlights** accendere i fari; **he ~ed by** *or* **past** ci passò davanti come un lampo; **flashback** *n* flashback *m inv*; **flashbulb** *n* cubo *m* flash *inv*; **flashlight** *n* lampadina tascabile
flask [flɑːsk] *n* fiasco; (*also:* **vacuum ~**) thermos® *m inv*
flat [flæt] *adj* piatto/a; (*tyre*) sgonfio/a, a terra; (*battery*) scarico/a; (*beer*) svampito/a; (*denial*) netto/a; (*Mus*) bemolle *inv*; (: *voice*) stonato/a ▷ *n* (BRIT: *rooms*) appartamento; (*Mus*) bemolle *m*; (*Aut*) pneumatico sgonfio ▷ *adv*: **(to work) ~ out** (lavorare) a più non posso; **~ rate of pay** tariffa unica di pagamento; **flatten** *vt* (*also:* **flatten out**) appiattire; (*house, city*) abbattere
flatter ['flætə'] *vt* lusingare; **flattering** *adj* lusinghiero/a; (*clothes etc*) che dona
flaunt [flɔːnt] *vt* fare mostra di
flavour, (US) **flavor** ['fleɪvə'] *n* gusto ▷ *vt* insaporire, aggiungere sapore a; **what ~s do you have?** che gusti avete?; **vanilla-~ed** al gusto di vaniglia; **flavouring** *n* essenza (artificiale)
flaw [flɔː] *n* difetto; **flawless** *adj* senza difetti
flea [fliː] *n* pulce *f*; **flea market** *n* mercato delle pulci
flee (*pt, pp* **fled**) [fliː, flɛd] *vt* fuggire da ▷ *vi* fuggire, scappare
fleece [fliːs] *n* vello ▷ *vt* (*col*) pelare
fleet [fliːt] *n* flotta; (*of lorries etc*) convoglio; (*of cars*) parco

fleeting ['fliːtɪŋ] *adj* fugace, fuggitivo/a; (*visit*) volante
Flemish ['flɛmɪʃ] *adj* fiammingo/a
flesh [flɛʃ] *n* carne *f*; (*of fruit*) polpa
flew [fluː] *pt of* **fly**
flex [flɛks] *n* filo (flessibile) ▷ *vt* flettere; (*muscles*) contrarre; **flexibility** *n* flessibilità; **flexible** *adj* flessibile; **flexitime** ['flɛksɪtaɪm] *n* orario flessibile
flick [flɪk] *n* colpetto; scarto ▷ *vt* dare un colpetto a; **flick through** *vt fus* sfogliare
flicker ['flɪkə'] *vi* tremolare
flies [flaɪz] *npl of* **fly**
flight [flaɪt] *n* volo; (*escape*) fuga; (*also:* **~ of steps**) scalinata; **flight attendant** *n* (US) steward *m*, hostess *f inv*
flimsy ['flɪmzɪ] *adj* (*fabric*) leggero/a; (*building*) poco solido/a; (*excuse*) debole
flinch [flɪntʃ] *vi* ritirarsi; **to ~ from** tirarsi indietro di fronte a
fling (*pt, pp* **flung**) [flɪŋ, flʌŋ] *vt* lanciare, gettare
flint [flɪnt] *n* selce *f*; (*in lighter*) pietrina
flip [flɪp] *vt* (*switch*) far scattare; (*coin*) lanciare in aria
flip-flops ['flɪpflɒps] *npl* (*esp* BRIT: *sandals*) infradito *mpl*
flipper ['flɪpə'] *n* pinna
flirt [flɜːt] *vi* flirtare ▷ *n* civetta
float [fləʊt] *n* galleggiante *m*; (*in procession*) carro; (*sum of money*) somma ▷ *vi* galleggiare
flock [flɒk] *n* (*of sheep, Rel*) gregge *m*; (*of birds*) stormo ▷ *vi*: **to ~ to** accorrere in massa a
flood [flʌd] *n* alluvione *f*; (*of letters etc*) marea ▷ *vt* allagare; (*people*) invadere ▷ *vi* (*place*) allagarsi; (*people*): **to ~ into** riversarsi in; **flooding** *n* inondazione *f*; **floodlight** *n* riflettore *m* ▷ *vt* illuminare a giorno
floor [flɔː'] *n* pavimento; (*storey*) piano; (*of sea, valley*) fondo ▷ *vt*

(*knock down*) atterrare; (*silence*) far tacere; **on the ~** sul pavimento, per terra; **ground ~**, (*US*) **first ~** pianterreno; **first ~**, (*US*) **second ~** primo piano; **floorboard** n tavellone m di legno; **flooring** n (*floor*) pavimento; (*material*) materiale m per pavimentazioni; **floor show** n spettacolo di varietà

lop [flɒp] n fiasco ▷ vi far fiasco; (*fall*) lasciarsi cadere; **floppy** ['flɒpɪ] *adj* floscio/a, molle

lora ['flɔːrə] n flora

loral ['flɔːrl] *adj* floreale

lorence ['flɒrəns] n Firenze f

lorentine ['flɒrəntaɪn] *adj* fiorentino/a

lorist ['flɒrɪst] n fioraio/a; **florist's (shop)** n fioraio/a

lotation [fləʊ'teɪʃən] n (*Comm*) lancio

lour ['flaʊər] n farina

lourish ['flʌrɪʃ] vi fiorire ▷ n (*bold gesture*): **with a ~** con ostentazione

low [fləʊ] n flusso; circolazione f ▷ vi fluire; (*traffic, blood in veins*) circolare; (*hair*) scendere

lower ['flaʊər] n fiore m ▷ vi fiorire; **flower bed** n aiuola; **flowerpot** n vaso da fiori

lown [fləʊn] pp of **fly**

l. oz. *abbr* = **fluid ounce**

luctuate ['flʌktjʊeɪt] vi fluttuare, oscillare

luent ['fluːənt] *adj* (*speech*) facile, sciolto/a; corrente; **he speaks ~ Italian, he's ~ in Italian** parla l'italiano correntemente

luff [flʌf] n lanugine f; **fluffy** *adj* lanuginoso/a; (*toy*) di peluche

luid ['fluːɪd] *adj* fluido/a ▷ n fluido; **fluid ounce** n (*BRIT*) = 0.028 l; 0.05 pints

luke [fluːk] n (*col*) colpo di fortuna

lung [flʌŋ] pt, pp of **fling**

luorescent [fluə'rɛsnt] *adj* fluorescente

fluoride ['fluəraɪd] n fluoruro

flurry ['flʌrɪ] n (*of snow*) tempesta; **a ~ of activity/excitement** un'intensa attività/un'improvvisae agitazione

flush [flʌʃ] n rossore m; (*fig: of youth, beauty etc*) rigoglio, pieno vigore ▷ vt ripulire con un getto d'acqua ▷ vi arrossire ▷ *adj*: **~ with** a livello di, pari a; **to ~ the toilet** tirare l'acqua

flute [fluːt] n flauto

flutter ['flʌtər] n agitazione f; (*of wings*) battito ▷ vi (*bird*) battere le ali

fly (pt **flew**, pp **flown**) [flaɪ, fluː, fləʊn] n (*insect*) mosca; (*on trousers: also:* **flies**) patta ▷ vt pilotare; (*passengers, cargo*) trasportare (in aereo); (*distances*) percorrere ▷ vi volare; (*passengers*) andare in aereo; (*escape*) fuggire; (*flag*) sventolare; **fly away** vi volar via; **fly-drive** n: **fly-drive holiday** fly and drive m inv; **flying** n (*activity*) aviazione f; (*action*) volo ▷ *adj*: **flying visit** visita volante; **with flying colours** con risultati brillanti; **flying saucer** n disco volante; **flyover** n (*BRIT: bridge*) cavalcavia m inv

FM *abbr* = **frequency modulation**

foal [fəʊl] n puledro

foam [fəʊm] n schiuma; (*also:* **~ rubber**) gommapiuma® ▷ vi schiumare; (*soapy water*) fare la schiuma

focus ['fəʊkəs] n (pl **focuses**) fuoco; (*of interest*) centro ▷ vt (*field glasses etc*) mettere a fuoco ▷ vi: **to ~ on** (*with camera*) mettere a fuoco; (*person*) fissare lo sguardo su; **in ~** a fuoco; **out of ~** sfocato/a

foetus, (*US*) **fetus** ['fiːtəs] n feto

fog [fɒg] n nebbia; **foggy** *adj*: **it's foggy** c'è nebbia; **fog lamp**, (*US*) **fog light** n (*Aut*) faro m antinebbia inv

foil [fɔɪl] vt confondere, frustrare ▷ n lamina di metallo; (*also:* **kitchen ~**) foglio di alluminio; (*Fencing*) fioretto; **to act as a ~ to** (*fig*) far risaltare

fold [fəʊld] n (*bend, crease*) piega;
(*Agr*) ovile m; (*fig*) gregge m ▷ vt
piegare; **to ~ one's arms** incrociare
le braccia; **fold up** vi (*map etc*)
piegarsi; (*business*) crollare ▷ vt (*map
etc*) piegare, ripiegare; **folder** n (*for
papers*) cartella; cartellina; **folding**
adj (*chair, bed*) pieghevole
foliage ['fəʊlɪɪdʒ] n fogliame m
folk [fəʊk] npl gente f ▷ cpd popolare;
folks npl: **my ~s** i miei; **folklore**
['fəʊklɔːʳ] n folclore m; **folk music**
n musica folk inv; **folksong** n canto
popolare
follow ['fɒləʊ] vt (*also on Twitter*)
seguire ▷ vi seguire; (*result*)
conseguire, risultare; **he ~ed suit**
lui ha fatto lo stesso; **follow up** vt
(*letter, offer*) fare seguito a; (*case*)
seguire; **follower** n seguace m/f;
following adj seguente ▷ n seguito,
discepoli mpl; **follow-up** n seguito
fond [fɒnd] adj (*memory, look*)
tenero/a, affettuoso/a; **to be ~ of**
volere bene a; **she's ~ of swimming**
le piace nuotare
food [fuːd] n cibo; **food mixer** n
frullatore m; **food poisoning** n
intossicazione f alimentare; **food
processor** [-'prəʊsɛsə] n tritatutto
m inv elettrico; **food stamp** n (*US*)
buono alimentare dato agli indigenti
fool [fuːl] n sciocco/a; (*Culin*) frullato
▷ vt ingannare ▷ vi (*gen*): **~ around**
fare lo sciocco; **fool about, fool
around** vi (*waste time*) perdere
tempo; **foolish** adj scemo/a,
stupido/a; imprudente; **foolproof**
adj (*plan etc*) sicurissimo/a
foot [fut] n (*pl* **feet** [fiːt]) piede m;
(*measure*) piede (= 304 mm; = 12 inches);
(*of animal*) zampa ▷ vt (*bill*) pagare;
on ~ a piedi; **footage** n (*Cine: length*)
≈ metraggio; (: *material*) sequenza;
foot and mouth (disease) n afta
epizootica; **football** n pallone m;
(*sport: BRIT*) calcio; (: *US*) football
m americano; **footballer** n (*BRIT*)

= **football player**; **football match**
n (*BRIT*) partita di calcio; **football
player** n (*BRIT: also:* **footballer**)
calciatore m; (*US*) giocatore m di
football americano; **footbridge** n
passerella; **foothills** npl contrafforti
fpl; **foothold** n punto d'appoggio;
footing n (*fig*) posizione f; **to lose
one's footing** mettere un piede
in fallo; **footnote** n nota (a piè di
pagina); **footpath** n sentiero; (*in
street*) marciapiede m; **footprint** n
orma, impronta; **footstep** n passo;
footwear n calzatura

 KEYWORD

for [fɔːʳ] prep **1** (*indicating destination,
intention, purpose*) per; **the train for
London** il treno per Londra; **he went
for the paper** è andato a prendere il
giornale; **it's time for lunch** è ora di
pranzo; **what's it for?** a che serve?;
what for? (*why*) perché?
2 (*on behalf of, representing*) per; **to
work for sb/sth** lavorare per qn/qc;
I'll ask him for you glielo chiederò a
nome tuo; **G for George** ≈ G come
George
3 (*because of*) per, a causa di; **for this
reason** per questo motivo
4 (*with regard to*) per; **it's cold for
July** è freddo per luglio; **for everyone
who voted yes, 50 voted no** per
ogni voto a favore ce n'erano 50 contro
5 (*in exchange for*) per; **I sold it for £5**
l'ho venduto per 5 sterline
6 (*in favour of*) per, a favore di; **are
you for or against us?** sei con noi o
contro di noi?; **I'm all for it** sono
completamente a favore
7 (*referring to distance, time*) per;
there are roadworks for 5 km
ci sono lavori in corso per 5 km; **he
was away for 2 years** è stato via
per 2 anni; **she will be away for a
month** starà via un mese; **it hasn't
rained for 3 weeks** non piove da

3 settimane; **can you do it for tomorrow?** può farlo per domani? 8 (*with infinitive clauses*): **it is not for me to decide** non sta a me decidere; **it would be best for you to leave** sarebbe meglio che lei se ne andasse; **there is still time for you to do it** ha ancora tempo per farlo; **for this to be possible ...** perché ciò sia possibile ...

9 (*in spite of*) nonostante; **for all his complaints, he's very fond of her** nonostante le sue lamentele, le vuole molto bene

▶ *conj* (*since, as: formal*) dal momento che, poiché

forbid (*pt* **forbad(e)**, *pp* **forbidden**) [fə'bɪd, -'bæd, -'bɪdn] *vt* vietare, interdire; **to ~ sb to do sth** proibire a qn di fare qc; **forbidden** *pt of* **forbid** ▶ *adj* (*food*) proibito/a; (*area, territory*) vietato/a; (*word, subject*) tabù *inv*

force [fɔːs] *n* forza ▶ *vt* forzare; **forced** *adj* forzato/a; **forceful** *adj* forte, vigoroso/a

ford [fɔːd] *n* guado

fore [fɔːʳ] *n*: **to come to the ~** mettersi in evidenza; **forearm** ['fɔːrɑːm] *n* avambraccio; **forecast** ['fɔːkɑːst] *n* (*irreg: like* **cast**) previsione *f* ▶ *vt* prevedere; **forecourt** ['fɔːkɔːt] *n* (*of garage*) corte *f* esterna; **forefinger** ['fɔːfɪŋgəʳ] *n* (*dito*) indice *m*; **forefront** ['fɔːfrʌnt] *n*: **in the forefront of** all'avanguardia di; **foreground** ['fɔːgraʊnd] *n* primo piano; **forehead** ['fɒrɪd] *n* fronte *f*

foreign ['fɒrən] *adj* straniero/a; (*trade*) estero/a; (*object, matter*) estraneo/a; **foreign currency** *n* valuta estera; **foreigner** *n* straniero/a; **foreign exchange** *n* cambio di valuta; (*currency*) valuta estera; **Foreign Office** *n* (*BRIT*) Ministero degli Esteri; **foreign secretary** *n* (*BRIT*) ministro degli Affari esteri

fore: foreman ['fɔːmən] *n* (*irreg*) caposquadra *m*; **foremost** ['fɔːməʊst] *adj* principale; più in vista ▶ *adv*: **first and foremost** innanzitutto; **forename** *n* nome *m* di battesimo

forensic [fə'rɛnsɪk] *adj*: **~ medicine** medicina legale

foresee [fɔː'siː] *vt* (*irreg: like* **see**) prevedere; **foreseeable** *adj* prevedibile

forest ['fɒrɪst] *n* foresta; **forestry** ['fɒrɪstrɪ] *n* silvicoltura

forever [fə'rɛvəʳ] *adv* per sempre; (*endlessly*) sempre, di continuo

foreword ['fɔːwəːd] *n* prefazione *f*

forfeit ['fɔːfɪt] *vt* perdere; (*one's happiness, health*) giocarsi

forgave [fə'geɪv] *pt of* **forgive**

forge [fɔːdʒ] *n* fucina ▶ *vt* (*signature*) contraffare, falsificare; (*wrought iron*) fucinare, foggiare; **forger** *n* contraffattore *m*; **forgery** *n* falso; (*activity*) contraffazione *f*

forget (*pt* **forgot**, *pp* **forgotten**) [fə'gɛt, -'gɒt, -'gɒtn] *vt, vi* dimenticare; **forgetful** *adj* di corta memoria; **forgetful of** dimentico(a) di

forgive (*pt* **forgave**, *pp* **forgiven**) [fə'gɪv, -'geɪv, -'gɪvn] *vt* perdonare; **to ~ sb for sth/for doing sth** perdonare qc a qn/a qn di aver fatto qc

forgot [fə'gɒt] *pt of* **forget**

forgotten [fə'gɒtn] *pp of* **forget**

fork [fɔːk] *n* (*for eating*) forchetta; (*for gardening*) forca; (*of roads, railways*) bivio, biforcazione *f* ▶ *vi* (*road*) biforcarsi

forlorn [fə'lɔːn] *adj* (*person*) sconsolato/a; (*cottage*) abbandonato/a; (*attempt*) disperato/a; (*hope*) vano/a

form [fɔːm] *n* forma; (*Scol*) classe *f*; (*questionnaire*) modulo ▶ *vt* formare; **in top ~** in gran forma

formal ['fɔːməl] adj formale; (gardens) simmetrico/a, regolare; **formality** [fɔː'mælɪtɪ] n formalità f inv

format ['fɔːmæt] n formato ▷ vt (Comput) formattare

formation [fɔː'meɪʃən] n formazione f

former ['fɔːmər] adj vecchio/a (before n), ex inv (before n); **the ~ ... the latter** quello ... questo; **formerly** adv in passato

formidable ['fɔːmɪdəbl] adj formidabile

formula ['fɔːmjulə] n formula

fort [fɔːt] n forte m

forthcoming [fɔːθ'kʌmɪŋ] adj (event) prossimo/a; (help) disponibile; (character) aperto/a, comunicativo/a

fortieth ['fɔːtɪɪθ] num quarantesimo/a

fortify ['fɔːtɪfaɪ] vt (city) fortificare; (person) armare

fortnight ['fɔːtnaɪt] n (BRIT) quindici giorni mpl, due settimane fpl; **fortnightly** adj bimensile ▷ adv ogni quindici giorni

fortress ['fɔːtrɪs] n fortezza, rocca

fortunate ['fɔːtʃənɪt] adj fortunato/a; **it is ~ that** è una fortuna che + sub; **fortunately** adv fortunatamente

fortune ['fɔːtʃən] n fortuna; **fortune-teller** ['fɔːtʃəntɛlər] n indovino/a

forty ['fɔːtɪ] num quaranta

forum ['fɔːrəm] n foro

forward ['fɔːwəd] adj (ahead of schedule) in anticipo; (movement, position) in avanti; (not shy) sfacciato/a ▷ n (Sport) avanti m inv ▷ vt (letter) inoltrare; (parcel, goods) spedire; (career, plans) promuovere, appoggiare; **to move ~** avanzare; **forwarding address** n nuovo recapito cui spedire la posta; **forwards** adv avanti; **forward slash** n barra obliqua

fossick ['fɔsɪk] vi (AUST, NZ col)

cercare; **to ~ in a drawer** rovistare in un cassetto

fossil ['fɔsl] adj, n fossile (m)

foster ['fɔstər] vt incoraggiare, nutrire; (child) avere in affidamento; **foster child** n bambino/a preso/a in affidamento; **foster mother** n madre f affidataria

fought [fɔːt] pt, pp of **fight**

foul [faul] adj (smell, food) cattivo/a; (weather) brutto/a; (language) osceno/a ▷ n (Football) fallo ▷ vt sporcare; **foul play** n: **foul play is not suspected** si è scartata l'ipotesi dell'atto criminale

found [faund] pt, pp of **find** ▷ vt (establish) fondare; **foundation** [faun'deɪʃən] n (act) fondazione f; (base) base f; (also: **foundation cream**) fondo tinta; **foundations** npl (of building) fondamenta fpl

founder ['faundər] n fondatore/trice ▷ vi affondare

fountain ['fauntɪn] n fontana; **fountain pen** n penna stilografica

four [fɔːr] num quattro; **on all ~s** a carponi; **four-letter word** n parolaccia; **four-poster** n (also: **four-poster bed**) letto a quattro colonne; **fourteen** num quattordici; **fourteenth** num quattordicesimo/a; **fourth** num quarto/a; **four-wheel drive** ['fɔːwiːl-] n (Aut): **with four-wheel drive** con quattro ruote motrici

fowl [faul] n pollame m; volatile m

fox [fɔks] n volpe f ▷ vt confondere

foyer ['fɔɪeɪ] n atrio; (Theat) ridotto

fracking ['frækɪŋ] n fracking m inv

fraction ['frækʃən] n frazione f

fracture ['fræktʃər] n frattura

fragile ['frædʒaɪl] adj fragile

fragment ['frægmənt] n frammento

fragrance ['freɪɡrəns] n fragranza, profumo

frail [freɪl] adj debole, delicato/a

frame [freɪm] n (of building) armatura; (of human, animal) ossatura, corpo; (*of picture*) cornice *f*; (*of door, window*) telaio; (*of spectacles: also:* **~s**) montatura ▷ *vt* (*picture*) incorniciare; **framework** *n* struttura

France [frɑːns] *n* Francia

franchise ['fræntʃaɪz] *n* (*Pol*) diritto di voto; (*Comm*) concessione *f*

frank [fræŋk] *adj* franco/a, aperto/a ▷ *vt* (*letter*) affrancare; **frankly** *adv* francamente, sinceramente

frantic ['fræntɪk] *adj* frenetico/a

fraud [frɔːd] *n* truffa; (*Law*) frode *f*; (*person*) impostore/a

fraught [frɔːt] *adj*: **~ with** pieno(a) di, intriso(a) da

fray [freɪ] *vt* logorare ▷ *vi* logorarsi

freak [friːk] *n* fenomeno, mostro

freckle ['frɛkl] *n* lentiggine *f*

free [friː] *adj* libero/a; (*gratis*) gratuito/a ▷ *vt* (*prisoner, jammed person*) liberare; (*jammed object*) districare; **~ (of charge)** gratuitamente; **freedom** ['friːdəm] *n* libertà; **Freefone®** *n* ≈ numero verde; **free gift** *n* regalo, omaggio; **free kick** *n* calcio libero; **freelance** *adj* indipendente; **freely** *adv* liberamente; (*liberally*) liberalmente; **Freepost®** *n* affrancatura a carica del destinatario; **free-range** *adj* (*hen*) ruspante; (*eggs*) di gallina ruspante; **freeway** *n* (*us*) superstrada; **free will** *n* libero arbitrio; **of one's own free will** di spontanea volontà

freeze (*pt* **froze**, *pp* **frozen**) [friːz, frəʊz, 'frəʊzn] *vi* gelare ▷ *vt* gelare; (*food*) congelare; (*prices, salaries*) bloccare ▷ *n* gelo; blocco; **freezer** *n* congelatore *m*; **freezing** ['friːzɪŋ] *adj* (*wind, weather*) gelido/a ▷ *n* (*also:* **freezing point**) punto di congelamento; **3 degrees below freezing** 3 gradi sotto zero

freight [freɪt] *n* (*goods*) merce *f*, merci *fpl*; (*money charged*) spese *fpl* di trasporto; **freight train** *n* (*us*) treno *m* merci *inv*

French [frɛntʃ] *adj* francese ▷ *n* (*Ling*) francese *m*; **the French** *npl* i Francesi; **French bean** *n* fagiolino; **French bread** *n* baguette *f inv*; **French dressing** *n* (*Culin*) condimento per insalata; **French fried potatoes**, (*us*) **French fries** *npl* patate *fpl* fritte; **Frenchman** *n* (*irreg*) francese *m*; **French stick** *n* baguette *f inv*; **French window** *n* portafinestra; **Frenchwoman** *n* (*irreg*) francese *f*

frenzy ['frɛnzɪ] *n* frenesia

frequency ['friːkwənsɪ] *n* frequenza

frequent *adj* ['friːkwənt] frequente ▷ *vt* [frɪ'kwɛnt] frequentare; **frequently** *adv* frequentemente, spesso

fresh [frɛʃ] *adj* fresco/a; (*new*) nuovo/a; (*cheeky*) sfacciato/a; **freshen** *vi* (*wind, air*) rinfrescare; **freshen up** *vi* rinfrescarsi; **fresher** *n* (*BRIT Scol: col*) = **freshman**; **freshly** *adv* di recente, di fresco; **freshman** *n* (*irreg*) (*Scol*) matricola; **freshwater** *adj* (*fish*) d'acqua dolce

fret [frɛt] *vi* agitarsi, affliggersi

Fri. *abbr* (= *Friday*) ven.

friction ['frɪkʃən] *n* frizione *f*, attrito

Friday ['fraɪdɪ] *n* venerdì *m inv*

fridge [frɪdʒ] *n* (*BRIT*) frigo, frigorifero

fried [fraɪd] *pt, pp of* **fry** ▷ *adj* fritto/a

friend [frɛnd] *n* amico/a ▷ *vt* (*Internet*) aggiungere tra gli amici; **friendly** *adj* amichevole; **friendship** *n* amicizia

fries [fraɪz] *npl* (*esp us*) patate *fpl* fritte

frigate ['frɪgɪt] *n* (*Naut: modern*) fregata

fright [fraɪt] *n* paura, spavento; **to take ~** spaventarsi; **frighten** *vt* spaventare, far paura a; **frightened** *adj* spaventato/a; **frightening** *adj* spaventoso/a, pauroso/a; **frightful** *adj* orribile

frill [frɪl] *n* balza

fringe [frɪndʒ] *n* (*BRIT: of hair*) frangia; (*edge: of forest etc*) margine *m*

Frisbee® ['frɪzbɪ] n frisbee® m inv
fritter ['frɪtə^r] n frittella
frivolous ['frɪvələs] adj frivolo/a
fro [frəu] adv: **to and ~** avanti e
indietro
frock [frɔk] n vestito
frog [frɔg] n rana; **frogman**
['frɔgmən] n (irreg) uomo m rana inv

⊙ **KEYWORD**

from [frɔm] prep 1 (indicating starting
place, origin etc) da; **where do you
come from?, where are you from?**
da dove viene?, di dov'è?; **from
London to Glasgow** da Londra a
Glasgow; **a letter from my sister**
una lettera da mia sorella; **tell him
from me that ...** gli dica da parte
mia che ...
2 (indicating time) da; **from one
o'clock to** or **until** or **till two** dall'una
alle due; **from January (on)** da
gennaio, a partire da gennaio
3 (indicating distance) da; **the hotel is
1 km from the beach** l'albergo è a 1
km dalla spiaggia
4 (indicating price, number etc) da;
prices range from £10 to £50 i
prezzi vanno dalle 10 alle 50 sterline
5 (indicating difference) da; **he
can't tell red from green** non sa
distinguere il rosso dal verde
6 (because of, on the basis of): **from
what he says** da quanto dice lui;
weak from hunger debole per
la fame

front [frʌnt] n (of house, dress)
davanti m inv; (of train) testa; (of book)
copertina; (promenade: also: **sea ~**)
lungomare m; (Mil, Pol, Meteor) fronte
m; (fig: appearances) fronte f ▷ adj
primo/a; anteriore, davanti inv; **in ~
(of)** davanti (a); **front door** n porta
d'entrata; (of car) sportello anteriore;
frontier ['frʌntɪə^r] n frontiera; **front
page** n prima pagina; **front-wheel**

drive ['frʌntwiːl-] n trasmissione
f anteriore
frost [frɔst] n gelo; (also: **hoar~**)
brina; **frostbite** n congelamento;
frosting n (US: on cake) glassa; **frosty**
adj (weather, look, welcome) gelido/a
froth ['frɔθ] n spuma; schiuma
frown [fraun] vi accigliarsi
froze [frəuz] pt of **freeze**
frozen ['frəuzn] pp of **freeze**
fruit [fruːt] n (pl inv) frutto;
(collectively) frutta; **fruit juice** n
succo di frutta; **fruit machine** n
(BRIT) macchina f mangiasoldi inv;
fruit salad n macedonia
frustrate [frʌs'treɪt] vt frustrare;
frustrated adj frustrato/a
fry (pt, pp **fried**) [fraɪ, -d] vt friggere
▷ npl: **the small ~** i pesci piccoli;
frying pan n padella
ft. abbr = **foot**; **feet**
fudge [fʌdʒ] n (Culin) specie di
caramella a base di latte, burro e
zucchero
fuel [fjuəl] n (for heating) combustibile
m; (for propelling) carburante m; **fuel
poverty** n povertà energetica; **fuel
tank** n deposito m nafta inv; (on
vehicle) serbatoio (della benzina)
fulfil [ful'fɪl] vt (function) compiere;
(order) eseguire; (wish, desire)
soddisfare, appagare
full [ful] adj pieno/a; (details, skirt)
ampio/a ▷ adv: **to know ~ well that**
sapere benissimo che; **I'm ~ (up)**
sono sazio; **a ~ two hours** due ore
intere; **at ~ speed** a tutta velocità; **in
~** per intero; **full-length** adj (portrait)
in piedi; (film) a lungometraggio;
(coat, novel) lungo/a; **full moon** n
luna piena; **full-scale** adj (plan, model)
in grandezza naturale; (attack, search,
retreat) su vasta scala; **full stop** n
punto; **full-time** adj, adv (work) a
tempo pieno; **fully** adv interamente,
pienamente, completamente
fumble ['fʌmbl] vi brancolare;
fumble with vt fus trafficare con

fume [fju:m] vi essere furioso/a; **fumes** npl esalazioni fpl, vapori mpl

fun [fʌn] n divertimento, spasso; **to have ~** divertirsi; **for ~** per scherzo; **to make ~ of** prendersi gioco di

function ['fʌŋkʃən] n funzione f; cerimonia, ricevimento ▷ vi funzionare

fund [fʌnd] n fondo, cassa; (source) fondo; (store) riserva; **funds** npl (money) fondi mpl

fundamental [fʌndə'mɛntl] adj fondamentale

funeral ['fju:nərəl] n funerale m; **funeral director** n impresario di pompe funebri; **funeral parlour** [-'pɑːlər] n impresa di pompe funebri

fun fair ['fʌnfɛər] n luna park m inv

fungus (pl **fungi**) ['fʌŋgəs, -gaɪ] n fungo; (mould) muffa

funnel ['fʌnl] n imbuto; (of ship) ciminiera

funny ['fʌnɪ] adj divertente, buffo/a; (strange) strano/a, bizzarro/a

fur [fəːr] n pelo; pelliccia; (BRIT: in kettle etc) deposito calcare; **fur coat** n pelliccia

furious ['fjuərɪəs] adj furioso/a; (effort) accanito/a

furnish ['fəːnɪʃ] vt ammobiliare; (supply) fornire; **furnishings** npl mobili mpl, mobilia

furniture ['fəːnɪtʃər] n mobili mpl; **piece of ~** mobile m

furry ['fəːrɪ] adj (animal) peloso/a

further ['fəːðər] adj supplementare, altro/a; nuovo/a; più lontano/a ▷ adv più lontano; (more) di più; (moreover) inoltre ▷ vt favorire, promuovere; **further education** n ≈ corsi mpl di formazione; **college of further education** istituto statale con corsi specializzati (di formazione professionale, aggiornamento professionale ecc); **furthermore** [fəːðə'mɔːr] adv inoltre, per di più

furthest ['fəːðɪst] adv superlative of **far**

fury ['fjuərɪ] n furore m

fuse, (US) **fuze** [fjuːz] n fusibile m; (for bomb etc) miccia, spoletta ▷ vt fondere; (Elec): **to ~ the lights** far saltare i fusibili ▷ vi fondersi; **fuse box** n cassetta dei fusibili

fusion ['fjuːʒən] n fusione f

fuss [fʌs] n agitazione f; (complaining) storie fpl; **to make a ~** fare delle storie; **fussy** adj (person) puntiglioso/a, esigente; che fa le storie; (dress) carico/a di fronzoli; (style) elaborato/a

future ['fjuːtʃər] adj futuro/a ▷ n futuro, avvenire m; (Ling) futuro; **futures** npl (Comm) operazioni fpl a termine; **in ~** in futuro

fuze [fjuːz] n, vt, vi (US) = **fuse**

fuzzy ['fʌzɪ] adj (Phot) indistinto/a, sfocato/a; (hair) crespo/a

g

G [dʒiː] n (Mus) sol m

g abbr (= gram, gravity) g

G8 n abbr (Pol: = Group of Eight) G8 m

G20 n abbr (Pol: = Group of Twenty) G20 m

gadget ['gædʒɪt] n aggeggio

Gaelic ['geɪlɪk] adj gaelico/a ▷ n (language) gaelico

gag [gæg] n bavaglio; (joke) facezia, scherzo ▷ vt imbavagliare

gain [geɪn] n guadagno, profitto ▷ vt guadagnare ▷ vi (watch) andare avanti; (benefit): **to ~ (from)** trarre beneficio (da); **to ~ 3lbs (in weight)** aumentare di 3 libbre; **gain (up)on** vt fus guadagnare terreno su

gal. abbr = **gallon**

gala ['gɑːlə] n gala; **swimming ~** manifestazione f di nuoto

galaxy ['gæləksɪ] n galassia

gale [geɪl] n vento forte; burrasca

gall bladder ['gɔːl-] n cistifellea

gallery ['gælərɪ] n galleria

gallon ['gælən] n gallone m (Brit = 4.543 l; 8 pints; US = 3.785 l)

gallop ['gæləp] n galoppo ▷ vi galoppare

gallstone ['gɔːlstəun] n calcolo biliare

gamble ['gæmbl] n azzardo, rischio calcolato ▷ vt, vi giocare; **to ~ on** (fig) giocare su; **gambler** n giocatore/trice d'azzardo; **gambling** ['gæmblɪŋ] n gioco d'azzardo

game [geɪm] n gioco; (event) partita; (Tennis) game m inv; (Hunting, Culin) selvaggina ▷ adj (ready): **to be ~ (for sth/to do)** essere pronto/a (a qc/a fare); **games** npl (Scol) attività fpl sportive; **big ~** selvaggina grossa; **gamer** ['geɪmər] n chi gioca con i videogame; **games console** n console f inv dei videogame; **gameshow** ['geɪmʃəu] n gioco a premi; **gaming** ['geɪmɪŋ] n (Comput) il giocare con i videogame

gammon ['gæmən] n (bacon) quarto di maiale; (ham) prosciutto affumicato

gang [gæŋ] n banda, squadra ▷ vi: **to ~ up on sb** far combutta contro qn

gangster ['gæŋstər] n gangster m inv

gap [gæp] n (space) buco; (in time) intervallo; (difference): **~ (between)** divario (tra)

gape [geɪp] vi (person) restare a bocca aperta; (shirt, hole) essere spalancato/a

gap year n (Scol) anno di pausa preso prima di iniziare l'università, per lavorare o viaggiare

garage ['gærɑːʒ] n garage m inv; **garage sale** n vendita di oggetti usati nel garage di un privato

garbage ['gɑːbɪdʒ] (US) n immondizie fpl, rifiuti mpl; (col) sciocchezze fpl; **garbage can** n (US) bidone m della spazzatura; **garbage collector** n (US) spazzino/a

garden ['gɑːdn] n giardino; **gardens** npl (public) giardini pubblici;

garden centre n vivaio; **gardener** n giardiniere/a; **gardening** n giardinaggio

garlic ['gɑːlɪk] n aglio

garment ['gɑːmənt] n indumento

garnish ['gɑːnɪʃ] vt (food) guarnire

garrison ['gærɪsn] n guarnigione f ▷ vt guarnire

gas [gæs] n gas m inv; (us: gasoline) benzina ▷ vt asfissiare col gas; **gas cooker** n (BRIT) cucina a gas; **gas cylinder** n bombola del gas; **gas fire** n (BRIT) radiatore m a gas

gasket ['gæskɪt] n (Aut) guarnizione f

gasoline ['gæsəliːn] n (us) benzina

gasp [gɑːsp] n respiro affannoso, ansito ▷ vi ansimare, boccheggiare; (in surprise) restare senza fiato

gas: gas pedal (esp us) n pedale m dell'acceleratore; **gas station** (us) distributore m di benzina; **gas tank** n (us Aut) serbatoio (di benzina)

gate [geɪt] n cancello; (at airport) uscita

gâteau (pl **gâteaux**) ['gætəu, -z] n torta

gatecrash ['geɪtkræʃ] (BRIT) vt partecipare senza invito a

gateway ['geɪtweɪ] n porta

gather ['gæðəʳ] vt (flowers, fruit) cogliere; (pick up) raccogliere; (assemble) radunare; raccogliere; (understand) capire; (Sewing) increspare ▷ vi (assemble) radunarsi; **to ~ speed** acquistare velocità; **gathering** n adunanza

gauge [geɪdʒ] n (instrument) indicatore m ▷ vt misurare; (fig) valutare

gave [geɪv] pt of **give**

gay [geɪ] adj (homosexual) omosessuale; (cheerful) gaio/a, allegro/a; (colour) vivace, vivo/a

gaze [geɪz] n sguardo fisso ▷ vi: **to ~ at** guardare fisso

GB abbr (= Great Britain) GB

GCSE n abbr (BRIT: = General Certificate of Secondary Education) diploma di

istruzione secondaria conseguito a 16 anni in Inghilterra e Galles

gear [gɪəʳ] n attrezzi mpl, equipaggiamento; (Tech) ingranaggio; (Aut) marcia ▷ vt (fig: adapt): **to ~ sth to** adattare qc a; **top** or **high/low/bottom ~** (us) quinta (or sesta)/seconda/prima; **in ~** in marcia; **gear up** vi: **to ~ up (to do)** prepararsi (a fare); **gear box** n scatola del cambio; **gear lever**, (us) **gear shift** n leva del cambio

geese [giːs] npl of **goose**

gel [dʒɛl] n gel m inv

gem [dʒɛm] n gemma

Gemini ['dʒɛmɪnaɪ] n Gemelli mpl

gender ['dʒɛndəʳ] n genere m

gene [dʒiːn] n (Biol) gene m

general ['dʒɛnərl] n generale m ▷ adj generale; **in ~** in genere; **general anaesthetic**, (us) **general anesthetic** n anestesia totale; **general election** n elezioni fpl generali; **generalize** vi generalizzare; **generally** adv generalmente; **general practitioner** n medico generico; **general store** n emporio

generate ['dʒɛnəreɪt] vt generare

generation [dʒɛnə'reɪʃən] n generazione f

generator ['dʒɛnəreɪtəʳ] n generatore m

generosity [dʒɛnə'rɔsɪtɪ] n generosità

generous ['dʒɛnərəs] adj generoso/a; (copious) abbondante

genetic [dʒɪ'nɛtɪk] adj genetico/a; **~ engineering** ingegneria genetica; **genetically modified** adj geneticamente modificato/a, transgenico/a; **genetics** [dʒɪ'nɛtɪks] n genetica

Geneva [dʒɪ'niːvə] n Ginevra

genitals ['dʒɛnɪtlz] npl genitali mpl

genius ['dʒiːnɪəs] n genio

Genoa ['dʒɛnəuə] n Genova

genome ['giːnəum] n genoma m inv

gent [dʒɛnt] n abbr = **gentleman**

g

gentle ['dʒɛntl] *adj* delicato/a;
(*person*) dolce

Be careful not to translate *gentle*
by the Italian word *gentile*.

gentleman ['dʒɛntlmən] *n*
(*irreg*) signore *m*; (*well-bred man*)
gentiluomo

gently ['dʒɛntlɪ] *adv* delicatamente

gents [dʒɛnts] *n* W.C. *m* (per signori)

genuine ['dʒɛnjuɪn] *adj* autentico/a;
sincero/a; **genuinely** *adv*
genuinamente

geographic(al) [dʒɪə'græfɪk(l)] *adj*
geografico/a

geography [dʒɪ'ɔgrəfɪ] *n* geografia

geology [dʒɪ'ɔlədʒɪ] *n* geologia

geometry [dʒɪ'ɔmətrɪ] *n* geometria

geranium [dʒɪ'reɪnɪəm] *n* geranio

geriatric [dʒɛrɪ'ætrɪk] *adj*
geriatrico/a

germ [dʒəːm] *n* (*Med*) microbo; (*Biol*,
fig) germe *m*

German ['dʒəːmən] *adj* tedesco/a
▷ *n* tedesco/a; (*Ling*) tedesco;
German measles (*BRIT*) *n* rosolia

Germany ['dʒəːmənɪ] *n* Germania

gesture ['dʒɛstjəʳ] *n* gesto

 KEYWORD

get [gɛt] (*pt, pp* **got**, (*US*) *pp* **gotten**) *vi*
1 (*become, be*) diventare, farsi; **to get
drunk** ubriacarsi; **to get killed** venire
or rimanere ucciso/a; **it's getting
late** si sta facendo tardi; **to get old**
invecchiare; **when do I get paid?**
quando mi pagate?; **to get tired**
stancarsi

2 (*go*): **to get to/from** andare a/da;
to get home arrivare *or* tornare a
casa; **how did you get here?** come
sei venuto?

3 (*begin*) mettersi a, cominciare a;
to get to know sb incominciare a
conoscere qn; **let's get going** *or*
started muoviamoci

4 (*modal aux vb*): **you've got to do
it** devi farlo

▷ *vt* **1**: **to get sth done** (*do*) fare qc;
(*have done*) far fare qc; **to get one's
hair cut** tagliarsi *or* farsi tagliare i
capelli; **to get sb to do sth** far fare
qc a qn

2 (*obtain: money, permission, results*)
ottenere; (*find: job, flat*) trovare; (*fetch:
person, doctor*) chiamare; (*object*)
prendere; **get me Mr Jones, please**
(*Tel*) mi passi il signor Jones, per
favore; **to get sth for sb** prendere
or procurare qc a qn; **can I get you a
drink?** le posso offrire da bere?

3 (*receive: present, letter, prize*) ricevere;
(*acquire: reputation*) farsi; **how much
did you get for the painting?**
quanto le hanno dato per il quadro?

4 (*catch*) prendere; **to get sb by
the arm/throat** afferrare qn per
un braccio/alla gola; **get him!**
prendetelo!

5 (*hit: target etc*) colpire

6 (*take, move*) portare; **to get sth to
sb** far avere qc a qn; **do you think
we'll get it through the door?** pensi
che riusciremo a farlo passare per
la porta?

7 (*catch, take: plane, bus etc*) prendere;
where do we get the ferry to …?
dove si prende il traghetto per …?

8 (*understand*) afferrare; **I've got it!** ci
sono arrivato!, ci sono!

9 (*hear*) sentire; **I'm sorry, I didn't
get your name** scusi, non ho capito
(*or* sentito) come si chiama

10 (*have, possess*): **to have got** avere;
how many have you got? quanti
ne ha?

get along *vi* (*agree*) andare d'accordo;
(*depart*) andarsene; (*manage*) = **get by**

get at *vt fus* (*attack*) prendersela con;
(*reach*) raggiungere, arrivare a

get away *vi* partire, andarsene;
(*escape*) scappare

get away with *vt fus* cavarsela;
farla franca

get back *vi* (*return*) ritornare, tornare
▷ *vt* riottenere, riavere; **when do we**

get back? quando ritorniamo?
get by vi (pass) passare; (manage) farcela
get down vi, vt fus scendere ▷ vt scendere; (depress) buttare giù
get down to vt fus (work) mettersi a (fare)
get in vi entrare; (train) arrivare; (arrive home) ritornare, tornare
get into vt fus entrare in; **to get into a rage** incavolarsi
get off vi (from train etc) scendere; (depart: person, car) andare via; (escape) cavarsela ▷ vt (remove: clothes, stain) levare ▷ vt fus (train, bus) scendere da
get on vi: **how did you get on?** com'è andata?; **to get on (with sb)** andare d'accordo (con qn) ▷ vt fus montare in; (horse) montare su
get out vi uscire; (of vehicle) scendere ▷ vt tirar fuori, far uscire
get out of vt fus uscire da; (duty etc) evitare
get over vt fus (illness) riaversi da
get round vt fus aggirare; (fig: person) rigirare
get through vi (Tel) avere la linea
get through to vt fus (Tel) parlare a
get together vi riunirsi ▷ vt raccogliere; (people) adunare
get up vi (rise) alzarsi ▷ vt fus salire su per
get up to vt fus (reach) raggiungere; (prank etc) fare

getaway ['gɛtəweɪ] n fuga
Ghana ['gɑːnə] n Ghana m
ghastly ['gɑːstlɪ] adj orribile, orrendo/a; (pale) spettrale
ghetto ['gɛtəu] n ghetto
ghost [gəust] n fantasma m, spettro
giant ['dʒaɪənt] n gigante/essa ▷ adj gigantesco/a, enorme
gift [gɪft] n regalo; (donation, ability) dono; **gifted** adj dotato/a; **gift shop**, (us) **gift store** n negozio di souvenir; **gift token**, **gift voucher** n buono (acquisto)

gig [gɪg] n (col: of musician) serata
gigabyte [giːgəbaɪt] n gigabyte m inv
gigantic [dʒaɪ'gæntɪk] adj gigantesco/a
giggle ['gɪgl] vi ridere sciocamente
gills [gɪlz] npl (of fish) branchie fpl
gilt [gɪlt] n doratura ▷ adj dorato/a
gimmick ['gɪmɪk] n trucco
gin [dʒɪn] n (liquor) gin m inv
ginger ['dʒɪndʒə^r] n zenzero
gipsy ['dʒɪpsɪ] n zingaro/a
giraffe [dʒɪ'rɑːf] n giraffa
girl [gəːl] n ragazza; (young unmarried woman) signorina; (daughter) figlia, figliola; **girlfriend** n (of girl) amica; (of boy) ragazza; **Girl Scout** n (us) Giovane Esploratrice f
gist [dʒɪst] n succo
give [gɪv] (pt **gave**, pp **given**) vt dare ▷ vi cedere; **~ to sb sth**, **~ sth to sb** dare qc a qn; **I'll ~ you £5 for it** te lo pago 5 sterline; **to ~ a cry/sigh** emettere un grido/sospiro; **to ~ a speech** fare un discorso; **give away** vt dare via; (disclose) rivelare; (bride) condurre all'altare; **give back** vt rendere; **give in** vi cedere ▷ vt consegnare; **give out** vt distribuire; annunciare; **give up** vi rinunciare ▷ vt rinunciare a; **to ~ up smoking** smettere di fumare; **to ~ o.s. up** arrendersi
given ['gɪvn] pp of **give** ▷ adj (fixed: time, amount) dato/a, determinato/a ▷ conj: **~ (that) ...** dato che ...; **~ the circumstances ...** date le circostanze ...
glacier ['glæsɪə^r] n ghiacciaio
glad [glæd] adj lieto/a, contento/a; **gladly** ['glædlɪ] adv volentieri
glamorous ['glæmərəs] adj affascinante, seducente
glamour, (us) **glamor** ['glæmə^r] n fascino
glance [glɑːns] n occhiata, sguardo ▷ vi: **to ~ at** dare un'occhiata a; **glance off** vt fus (bullet) rimbalzare su
gland [glænd] n ghiandola

glare [glɛəʳ] n (of anger) sguardo
furioso; (of light) riverbero, luce f
abbagliante; (of publicity) chiasso ▷ vi
abbagliare; **to ~ at** guardare male;
glaring adj (mistake) madornale

glass [glɑːs] n (substance) vetro;
(tumbler) bicchiere m; **glasses**
['glɑːsɪz] npl (spectacles) occhiali mpl

glaze [gleɪz] vt (door) fornire di vetri;
(pottery) smaltare ▷ n smalto

gleam [gliːm] vi luccicare

glen [glɛn] n valletta

glide [glaɪd] vi scivolare; (Aviat, birds)
planare; **glider** n (Aviat) aliante m

glimmer ['glɪməʳ] n barlume m

glimpse [glɪmps] n impressione f
fugace ▷ vt vedere di sfuggita

glint [glɪnt] vi luccicare

glisten ['glɪsn] vi luccicare

glitter ['glɪtəʳ] vi scintillare

global ['gləʊbl] adj globale;
globalization [gləʊbəlaɪ'zeɪʃən] n
globalizzazione f; **global warming** n
riscaldamento globale

globe [gləʊb] n globo, sfera

gloom [gluːm] n oscurità, buio;
(sadness) tristezza, malinconia;
gloomy adj scuro/a, fosco/a, triste

glorious ['glɔːrɪəs] adj glorioso/a,
magnifico/a

glory ['glɔːrɪ] n gloria; splendore m

gloss [glɔs] n (shine) lucentezza; (also:
~ paint) vernice f a olio

glossary ['glɔsərɪ] n glossario

glossy ['glɔsɪ] adj lucente

glove [glʌv] n guanto; **glove
compartment** n (Aut) vano
portaoggetti

glow [gləʊ] vi ardere; (face) essere
luminoso/a

glucose ['gluːkəʊs] n glucosio

glue [gluː] n colla ▷ vt incollare

GM adj abbr (= genetically modified)
geneticamente modificato/a; **GM
crop** n cultura GM

gm abbr = **gram**

GM-free [dʒiːɛm'friː] adj privo/a
di OGM

GMO n abbr (= genetically modified
organism) OGM m inv

GMT abbr (= Greenwich Mean Time) T.M.G.

gnaw [nɔː] vt rodere

go [gəʊ] vi (pt **went**, pp **gone**) andare;
(depart) partire, andarsene; (work)
funzionare; (time) passare; (break etc)
cedere; (be sold): **to go for £10** essere
venduto per 10 sterline; (fit, suit): **to
go with** andare bene con; (become):
to go pale diventare pallido/a; **to go
mouldy** ammuffire ▷ n (pl **goes**) (try)
to have a go (at) provare; **to be on the
go** essere in moto; **whose go is it?** a
chi tocca?; **he's going to do** sta per
fare; **to go for a walk** andare a fare
una passeggiata; **to go dancing/
shopping** andare a ballare/fare
la spesa; **just then the bell went**
proprio allora suonò il campanello;
how did it go? com'è andato?; **to
go round the back/by the shop**
passare da dietro/davanti al negozio;
go ahead vi andare avanti; **go away**
vi partire, andarsene; **go back** vi
tornare, ritornare; **go by** vi (years,
time) scorrere ▷ vt fus attenersi a,
seguire (alla lettera); prestar fede
a; **go down** vi scendere; (ship)
affondare; (sun) tramontare ▷ vt fus
scendere; **go for** vt fus (fetch) andare
a prendere; (like) andar matto/a per;
(attack) attaccare; saltare addosso
a; **go in** vi entrare; **go into** vt fus
entrare in; (investigate) indagare,
esaminare; (embark on) lanciarsi in;
go off vi partire, andar via; (food)
guastarsi; (explode) esplodere,
scoppiare; (event) passare ▷ vt
fus: **I've gone off chocolate** la
cioccolata non mi piace più; **the gun
went off** il fucile si scaricò; **go on** vi
continuare; (happen) succedere; **to
go on doing** continuare a fare; **go
out** vi uscire; (fire, light) spegnersi;
they went out for 3 years (couple)
sono stati insieme per 3 anni; **go
over** vi (ship) ribaltarsi ▷ vt fus

(*check*) esaminare; **go past** *vi* passare ▷ *vt fus* passare davanti a; **go round** *vi* (*circulate: news, rumour*) circolare; (*revolve*) girare; (*suffice*) bastare (per tutti); **to go round (to sb's)** (*visit*) passare (da qn); **to go round (by)** (*make a detour*) passare (per); **go through** *vt fus* (*town etc*) attraversare; (*files, papers*) vagliare attentamente; (*examine: list, book*) leggere da cima a fondo; **go up** *vi* salire; **go with** *vt fus* (*accompany*) accompagnare; **go without** *vt fus* fare a meno di

go-ahead ['gəʊəhɛd] *adj* intraprendente ▷ *n*: **to give sb/sth the ~** dare il via libera a qn/qc

goal [gəʊl] *n* (*Sport*) gol *m*, rete *f*; (: *place*) porta; (*fig: aim*) fine *m*, scopo; **goalkeeper** *n* portiere *m*; **goalpost** ['gəʊlpəʊst] *n* palo (della porta)

goat [gəʊt] *n* capra

gobble ['gɔbl] *vt* (*also:* **~ down**, **~ up**) ingoiare

god [gɔd] *n* dio; **G~** Dio; **godchild** *n* figlioccio/a; **goddaughter** *n* figlioccia; **goddess** *n* dea; **godfather** *n* padrino; **godmother** *n* madrina; **godson** *n* figlioccio

goggles ['gɔglz] *npl* occhiali *mpl* (di protezione)

going ['gəʊɪŋ] *n* (*conditions*) andare *m*, stato del terreno ▷ *adj*: **the ~ rate** la tariffa in vigore

gold [gəʊld] *n* oro ▷ *adj* d'oro; **golden** *adj* (*made of gold*) d'oro; (*gold in colour*) dorato/a; **goldfish** *n* pesce *m* dorato *or* rosso; **goldmine** *n* (*also fig*) miniera d'oro; **gold-plated** *adj* placcato/a oro *inv*

golf [gɔlf] *n* golf *m*; **golf ball** *n* (*for game*) pallina da golf; (*on typewriter*) pallina; **golf club** *n* circolo di golf; (*stick*) bastone *m or* mazza da golf; **golf course** *n* campo di golf; **golfer** *n* giocatore/trice di golf

gone [gɔn] *pp of* **go** ▷ *adj* partito/a

gong [gɔŋ] *n* gong *m inv*

good [gʊd] *adj* buono/a; (*kind*) buono/a, gentile; (*child*) bravo/a ▷ *n* bene *m*; **~!** bene!, ottimo!; **to be ~ at** essere bravo/a in; **to be ~ for** andare bene per; **it's ~ for you** fa bene; **to make ~** (*loss, damage*) compensare; **it's no ~ complaining** brontolare non serve a niente; **for ~** per sempre, definitivamente; **would you be ~ enough to …?** avrebbe la gentilezza di …?; **a ~ deal (of)** molto/a, una buona quantità (di); **a ~ many** molti/e; **~ morning!** buon giorno!; **~ afternoon/evening!** buona sera!; **~ night!** buona notte!; **goodbye** *excl* arrivederci!; **Good Friday** *n* Venerdì Santo; **good-looking** *adj* bello/a; **good-natured** *adj* affabile; **goodness** *n* (*of person*) bontà; **for goodness sake!** per amor di Dio!; **goodness gracious!** santo cielo!, mamma mia!; **goods** *npl* (*Comm etc*) merci *fpl*, articoli *mpl*; **goods train** *n* (BRIT) treno *m* merci *inv*; **goodwill** *n* amicizia, benevolenza

google ['gu:gl] *vt*, *vi* cercare con Google®

goose (*pl* **geese**) [gu:s, gi:s] *n* oca

gooseberry ['guzbərɪ] *n* uva spina; **to play ~** (BRIT) tenere la candela

goose bumps ['gu:sbʌmpz] *n*, **gooseflesh** ['gu:sflɛʃ] *n*, **goosepimples** ['gu:spɪmplz] *npl* pelle *f* d'oca

gorge [gɔ:dʒ] *n* gola ▷ *vt*: **to ~ o.s. (on)** ingozzarsi (di)

gorgeous ['gɔ:dʒəs] *adj* magnifico/a

gorilla [gə'rɪlə] *n* gorilla *m inv*

gosh [gɔʃ] *excl* (*col*) perdinci!

gospel ['gɔspl] *n* vangelo

gossip ['gɔsɪp] *n* chiacchiere *fpl*; pettegolezzi *mpl*; (*person*) pettegolo/a ▷ *vi* chiacchierare; **gossip column** *n* cronaca mondana

got [gɔt] *pt*, *pp of* **get**

gotten ['gɔtn] (US) *pp of* **get**

gourmet ['guəmeɪ] *n* buongustaio/a

govern ['gʌvən] vt governare;
government n governo; **governor**
['gʌvənəʳ] n (of state, bank) governatore
m; (of school, hospital) amministratore
m; (BRIT: of prison) direttore/trice
gown [gaun] n vestito lungo; (of
teacher, judge: BRIT) toga
GP n abbr = **general practitioner**
GPS n abbr (= global positioning system)
GPS m
grab [græb] vt afferrare, arraffare;
(property, power) impadronirsi di ▷ vi:
to ~ at cercare di afferrare
grace [greɪs] n grazia ▷ vt onorare;
5 days' ~ dilazione f di 5 giorni;
graceful adj elegante, aggraziato/a;
gracious ['greɪʃəs] adj grazioso/a,
misericordioso/a
grade [greɪd] n (Comm) qualità f
inv; classe f; categoria; (in hierarchy)
grado; (us Scol: mark) voto; (: school
class) classe ▷ vt classificare;
ordinare; graduare; **grade crossing**
n (us) passaggio a livello; **grade
school** n (us) scuola elementare or
primaria
gradient ['greɪdɪənt] n pendenza,
inclinazione m
gradual ['grædjuəl] adj graduale;
gradually adv man mano, a poco
a poco
graduate n ['grædjuɪt] laureato/a;
(us Scol) diplomato/a ▷ vi ['grædjueɪt]
laurearsi; diplomarsi; **graduation**
[grædju'eɪʃən] n cerimonia del
conferimento della laurea
graffiti [grə'fiːtɪ] npl graffiti mpl
graft [grɑːft] n (Agr, Med) innesto;
(col: bribery) corruzione f ▷ vt
innestare; **it's hard ~** (BRIT col) è un
lavoraccio
grain [greɪn] n grano; (of sand)
granello; (of wood) venatura
gram [græm] n grammo
grammar ['græməʳ] n grammatica;
grammar school n (BRIT) ≈ liceo
gramme [græm] n = **gram**
gran (col) [græn] n (BRIT) nonna

grand [grænd] adj grande,
magnifico/a; grandioso/a; **grandad**
(col) n = **granddad**; **grandchild** (pl
-children) n nipote m; **granddad**
n (col) nonno; **granddaughter**
n nipote f; **grandfather** n
nonno; **grandma** n (col) nonna;
grandmother n nonna; **grandpa** n
(col); = **granddad**; **grandparent** n
nonno/a; **grand piano** n pianoforte
m a coda; **Grand Prix** ['grɑ̃:'priː] n
(Aut) Gran Premio, Grand Prix m inv;
grandson n nipote m
granite ['grænɪt] n granito
granny ['grænɪ] n (col) nonna
grant [grɑːnt] vt accordare;
(a request) accogliere; (admit)
ammettere, concedere ▷ n (Scol)
borsa; (Admin) sussidio, sovvenzione
f; **to take sth for ~ed** dare qc per
scontato; **to take sb for ~ed** dare
per scontata la presenza di qn
grape [greɪp] n chicco d'uva, acino
grapefruit ['greɪpfruːt] n pompelmo
graph [grɑːf] n grafico; **graphic**
adj grafico/a; (vivid) vivido/a;
graphics n (art, process) grafica ▷ npl
illustrazioni fpl
grasp [grɑːsp] vt afferrare ▷ n (grip)
presa; (fig) potere m; comprensione f
grass [grɑːs] n erba; **grasshopper** n
cavalletta
grate [greɪt] n graticola (del focolare)
▷ vi cigolare, stridere ▷ vt (Culin)
grattugiare
grateful ['greɪtful] adj grato/a,
riconoscente
grater ['greɪtəʳ] n grattugia
gratitude ['grætɪtjuːd] n gratitudine f
grave [greɪv] n tomba ▷ adj grave,
serio/a
gravel ['grævl] n ghiaia
gravestone ['greɪvstəun] n pietra
tombale
graveyard ['greɪvjɑːd] n cimitero
gravity ['grævɪtɪ] n (Physics) gravità;
pesantezza; (seriousness) gravità,
serietà

gravy ['greɪvɪ] n intingolo della carne; salsa

gray [greɪ] adj (US) = **grey**

graze [greɪz] vi pascolare, pascere ▷ vt (touch lightly) sfiorare; (scrape) escoriare ▷ n (Med) escoriazione f

grease [gri:s] n (fat) grasso; (lubricant) lubrificante m ▷ vt ingrassare; lubrificare; **greasy** adj grasso/a, untuoso/a

great [greɪt] adj grande; (col) magnifico/a, meraviglioso/a; **Great Britain** n Gran Bretagna; **great-grandfather** n bisnonno; **great-grandmother** n bisnonna; **greatly** adv molto

Greece [gri:s] n Grecia

greed [gri:d] n (also: **~iness**) avarizia; (for food) golosità, ghiottoneria; **greedy** adj avido/a; goloso/a, ghiotto/a

Greek [gri:k] adj greco/a ▷ n greco/a; (Ling) greco

green [gri:n] adj verde; (inexperienced) inesperto/a, ingenuo/a ▷ n verde m; (stretch of grass) prato; (of golf course) green m inv; **greens** npl (vegetables) verdura; **green card** n (BRIT AUT) carta verde; (US Admin) permesso di soggiorno e di lavoro; **greengage** ['gri:ngeɪdʒ] n susina Regina Claudia; **greengrocer** n (BRIT) fruttivendolo/a, erbivendolo/a; **greenhouse** n serra; **greenhouse effect** n: **the greenhouse effect** l'effetto serra; **green tax** n tassa verde

Greenland ['gri:nlənd] n Groenlandia

green salad n insalata verde

greet [gri:t] vt salutare; **greeting** n saluto; **greeting(s) card** n cartolina d'auguri

grew [gru:] pt of **grow**

grey, (US) **gray** [greɪ] adj grigio/a; **grey-haired** adj dai capelli grigi; **greyhound** n levriere m

grid [grɪd] n grata; (Elec) rete f; **gridlock** ['grɪdlɔk] n (traffic jam)

paralisi f inv del traffico; **gridlocked** adj paralizzato/a dal traffico; (talks etc) in fase di stallo

grief [gri:f] n dolore m

grievance ['gri:vəns] n lagnanza

grieve [gri:v] vi affliggersi ▷ vt addolorare; **to ~ for sb** (dead person) piangere qn

grill [grɪl] n (on cooker) griglia; (also: **mixed ~**) grigliata mista ▷ vt (BRIT) cuocere ai ferri; (col: question) interrogare senza sosta

grille [grɪl] n grata; (Aut) griglia

grim [grɪm] adj sinistro/a, brutto/a

grime [graɪm] n sudiciume m

grin [grɪn] n sorriso smagliante ▷ vi: **to ~ (at)** fare un gran sorriso (a)

grind [graɪnd] (pt, pp **ground**) vt macinare; (make sharp) arrotare ▷ n (work) sgobbata

grip [grɪp] n impugnatura; presa; (holdall) borsa da viaggio ▷ vt (object) afferrare; (attention) catturare; **to come to ~s with** affrontare; cercare di risolvere; **gripping** ['grɪpɪŋ] adj avvincente

grit [grɪt] n ghiaia; (courage) fegato ▷ vt (road) coprire di sabbia; **to ~ one's teeth** stringere i denti

grits [grɪts] npl (US) macinato grosso (di avena etc)

groan [grəun] n gemito ▷ vi gemere

grocer ['grəusə'] n negoziante m di generi alimentari; **~'s (shop)** negozio di alimentari; **grocery** ['grəusərɪ] n (shop) (negozio di) alimentari; **groceries** npl provviste fpl

groin [grɔɪn] n inguine m

groom [gru:m] n palafreniere m; (also: **bride~**) sposo ▷ vt (horse) strigliare; (fig): **to ~ sb for** avviare qn a; **well-~ed** (person) curato/a

groove [gru:v] n scanalatura, solco

grope [grəup] vi: **to ~ for sth** cercare qc a tastoni

gross [grəus] adj grossolano/a; (Comm) lordo/a; **grossly** adv (greatly) molto

grotesque [grəʊ'tɛsk] adj grottesco/a

ground [graʊnd] pt, pp of **grind** ▷ n suolo, terra; (land) terreno; (Sport) campo; (reason: gen pl) ragione f; (us: also: **~ wire**) (presa a) terra ▷ vt (plane) tenere a terra; (us Elec) mettere la presa a terra a; **grounds** npl (of coffee etc) fondi mpl; (gardens etc) terreno, giardini mpl; **on/to the ~** per/a terra; **to gain/lose ~** guadagnare/perdere terreno; **ground floor** n pianterreno; **groundsheet** n (BRIT) telone m impermeabile; **groundwork** n preparazione f

group [gruːp] n gruppo ▷ vt (also: **~ together**) raggruppare ▷ vi (also: **~ together**) raggrupparsi

grouse [graʊs] n (pl inv: bird) tetraone m ▷ vi (complain) brontolare

grovel ['grɔvl] vi (fig): **to ~ (before)** strisciare (di fronte a)

grow (pt **grew**, pp **grown**) [grəʊ, gruː, grəʊn] vi crescere; (increase) aumentare; (develop) svilupparsi; (become): **to ~ rich/weak** arricchirsi/indebolirsi ▷ vt coltivare, far crescere; **grow on** vt fus: **that painting is ~ing on me** quel quadro più lo guardo più mi piace; **grow up** vi farsi grande, crescere

growl [graʊl] vi ringhiare

grown [grəʊn] pp of **grow**; **grown-up** n adulto/a, grande m/f

growth [grəʊθ] n crescita, sviluppo; (what has grown) crescita; (Med) escrescenza, tumore m

grub [grʌb] n larva; (col: food) roba (da mangiare)

grubby ['grʌbɪ] adj sporco/a

grudge [grʌdʒ] n rancore m ▷ vt: **to ~ sb sth** dare qc a qn di malavoglia; invidiare qc a qn; **to bear sb a ~ (for)** serbar rancore a qn (per)

gruelling, (us) **grueling** ['gruəlɪŋ] adj estenuante

gruesome ['gruːsəm] adj orribile

grumble ['grʌmbl] vi brontolare, lagnarsi

grumpy ['grʌmpɪ] adj scorbutico/a

grunt [grʌnt] vi grugnire

guarantee [gærən'tiː] n garanzia ▷ vt garantire

guard [gɑːd] n guardia; (one man) guardia, sentinella; (BRIT Rail) capotreno; (on machine) schermo protettivo; (also: **fire ~**) parafuoco ▷ vt fare la guardia a; **to ~ (against or from)** proteggere (da); **to be on one's ~** stare in guardia; **guardian** n custode m; (of minor) tutore/trice

guerrilla [gə'rɪlə] n guerrigliero

guess [gɛs] vi indovinare ▷ vt indovinare; (us) credere, pensare ▷ n congettura; **to take or have a ~** provare a indovinare

guest [gɛst] n ospite m/f; (in hotel) cliente m/f; **guest-house** n pensione f; **guest room** n camera degli ospiti

guidance ['gaɪdəns] n guida, direzione f

guide [gaɪd] n guida; (BRIT: also: **girl ~**) giovane esploratrice f ▷ vt guidare; **guidebook** n guida; **guide dog** n cane m guida inv; **guided tour** n visita guidata; **what time does the guided tour start?** a che ora comincia la visita guidata?; **guidelines** npl (fig) indicazioni fpl, linee fpl direttive

guild [gɪld] n arte f, corporazione f; associazione f

guilt [gɪlt] n colpevolezza; **guilty** adj colpevole

guinea pig ['gɪnɪ-] n cavia

guitar [gɪ'tɑːr] n chitarra; **guitarist** n chitarrista m/f

gulf [gʌlf] n golfo; (abyss) abisso

gull [gʌl] n gabbiano

gulp [gʌlp] vi deglutire; (from emotion) avere il nodo in gola ▷ vt (also: **~ down**) tracannare, inghiottire

gum [gʌm] n (Anat) gengiva; (glue) colla; (sweet) caramella gommosa; (also: **chewing-~**) chewing-gum m ▷ vt incollare

gun [gʌn] n fucile m; (small) pistola, rivoltella; (rifle) carabina; (shotgun) fucile da caccia; (cannon) cannone m; **gunfire** n spari mpl; **gunman** n (irreg) bandito armato; **gunpoint** n: **at gunpoint** sotto minaccia di fucile; **gunpowder** n polvere f da sparo; **gunshot** n sparo

gush [gʌʃ] vi sgorgare; (fig) abbandonarsi ad effusioni

gust [gʌst] n (of wind) raffica; (of smoke) buffata

gut [gʌt] n intestino, budello; **guts** npl (of animals) interiora fpl; (courage) fegato

gutter ['gʌtər] n (of roof) grondaia; (in street) cunetta

guy [gaɪ] n (also: ~rope) cavo or corda di fissaggio; (col: man) tipo, elemento; (figure) effigie di Guy Fawkes

Guy Fawkes Night [-'fɔːks-] n (BRIT) vedi nota **"Guy Fawkes Night"**

● **GUY FAWKES NIGHT**
●
● La sera del 5 novembre, in
● occasione della Guy Fawkes Night,
● altrimenti chiamata Bonfire Night,
● viene commemorato con falò
● e fuochi d'artificio il fallimento
● della Congiura delle Polveri contro
● Giacomo I nel 1605. La festa prende
● il nome dal principale congiurato
● della cospirazione, Guy Fawkes, la
● cui effigie viene bruciata durante i
● festeggiamenti.

gym [dʒɪm] n (also: ~nasium) palestra; (also: ~nastics) ginnastica; **gymnasium** [dʒɪm'neɪzɪəm] n palestra; **gymnast** ['dʒɪmnæst] n ginnasta m/f; **gymnastics** [dʒɪm'næstɪks] n, npl ginnastica; **gym shoes** npl scarpe fpl da ginnastica

gynaecologist, (US) **gynecologist** [gaɪnɪ'kɔlədʒɪst] n ginecologo/a

gypsy ['dʒɪpsɪ] n = **gipsy**

h

haberdashery ['hæbədæʃərɪ] (BRIT) n merceria

habit ['hæbɪt] n abitudine f; (costume) abito; (Rel) tonaca

habitat ['hæbɪtæt] n habitat m inv

hack [hæk] vt tagliare, fare a pezzi ▷ n (pej: writer) scribacchino/a; **hacker** ['hækər] n (Comput) pirata m informatico

had [hæd] pt, pp of **have**

haddock ['hædək] (pl **haddock** or **haddocks**) n eglefino

hadn't ['hædnt] = **had not**

haemorrhage, (US) **hemorrhage** ['hɛmərɪdʒ] n emorragia

haemorrhoids, (US) **hemorrhoids** ['hɛmərɔɪdz] npl emorroidi fpl

haggle ['hægl] vi mercanteggiare

Hague [heɪg] n: **The ~** L'Aia

hail [heɪl] n grandine f; (of criticism etc) pioggia ▷ vt (call) chiamare; (flag down: taxi) fermare; (greet) salutare

▷ vi grandinare; **hailstone** n chicco di grandine

hair [hɛəʳ] n capelli mpl; (single hair: on head) capello; (: on body) pelo; **to do one's ~** pettinarsi; **hairband** ['hɛəbænd] n (elastic) fascia per i capelli; (rigid) cerchietto; **hairbrush** n spazzola per capelli; **haircut** n taglio di capelli; **hairdo** ['hɛədu:] n acconciatura, pettinatura; **hairdresser** n parrucchiere/a; **hairdresser's** n parrucchiere/a; **hair-dryer** ['hɛədraɪəʳ] n asciugacapelli m inv; **hair gel** n gel m inv per capelli; **hair spray** n lacca per capelli; **hairstyle** n pettinatura, acconciatura; **hairy** adj irsuto/a; peloso/a; (col: frightening) spaventoso/a

haka ['hɑːkə] n (NZ) danza eseguita dai giocatori prima di una partita

hake [heɪk] (pl **hake** or **hakes**) n nasello

half [hɑːf] n (pl **halves**) mezzo, metà f inv ▷ adj mezzo/a ▷ adv a mezzo, a metà; **~ an hour** mezz'ora; **~ a dozen** mezza dozzina; **~ a pound** mezza libbra; **two and a ~** due e mezzo; **a week and a ~** una settimana e mezza; **~ (of it)** la metà; **~ (of)** la metà di; **to cut sth in ~** tagliare qc in due; **~ asleep** mezzo/a addormentato/a; **half board** (BRIT) n mezza pensione; **half-brother** n fratellastro; **half day** n mezza giornata; **half fare** n tariffa a metà prezzo; **half-hearted** adj tiepido/a; **half-hour** n mezz'ora; **half-price** adj ▷ adv a metà prezzo; **half term** n (BRIT Scol) vacanza a or di metà trimestre; **half-time** n (Sport) intervallo; **halfway** adv a metà strada

hall [hɔːl] n sala, salone m; (entrance way) entrata; **~ of residence** n (BRIT) casa dello studente

hallmark ['hɔːlmɑːk] n marchio di garanzia; (fig) caratteristica

hallo [hə'ləʊ] excl = **hello**

hall of residence (BRIT) n casa dello studente

Halloween ['hæləʊ'i:n] n vigilia d'Ognissanti

● **HALLOWEEN**
●
● Secondo la tradizione
● anglosassone, durante la notte
● di Halloween, il 31 di ottobre, è
● possibile vedere le streghe e i
● fantasmi. I bambini, travestiti
● da fantasmi, streghe, mostri o
● simili, vanno di porta in porta e
● raccolgono dolci e piccoli doni.

hallucination [həlu:sɪ'neɪʃən] n allucinazione f

hallway ['hɔ:lweɪ] n ingresso; corridoio

halo ['heɪləʊ] n (of saint etc) aureola

halt [hɔ:lt] n fermata ▷ vt fermare ▷ vi fermarsi

halve [hɑːv] vt (apple etc) dividere a metà; (expense) ridurre di metà

halves [hɑːvz] npl of **half**

ham [hæm] n prosciutto

hamburger ['hæmbə:gəʳ] n hamburger m inv

hamlet ['hæmlɪt] n paesetto

hammer ['hæməʳ] n martello ▷ vt martellare ▷ vi: **to ~ on** or **at the door** picchiare alla porta

hammock ['hæmək] n amaca

hamper ['hæmpəʳ] vt impedire ▷ n cesta

hamster ['hæmstəʳ] n criceto

hamstring ['hæmstrɪŋ] n (Anat) tendine m del ginocchio

hand [hænd] n mano f; (of clock) lancetta; (handwriting) scrittura; (at cards) mano; (: game) partita; (worker) operaio/a ▷ vt dare, passare; **to give sb a ~** dare una mano a qn; **at ~** a portata di mano; **in ~** a disposizione; (work) in corso; **to be on ~** (person) essere disponibile;

(*emergency services*) essere pronto/a a intervenire; **to ~** (*information etc*) a portata di mano; **on the one ~ ..., on the other ~** da un lato ..., dall'altro; **hand down** *vt* passare giù; (*tradition, heirloom*) tramandare; (*us: sentence, verdict*) emettere; **hand in** *vt* consegnare; **hand out** *vt* distribuire; **hand over** *vt* passare; cedere; **handbag** *n* borsetta; **hand baggage** *n* bagaglio a mano; **handbook** *n* manuale *m*; **handbrake** *n* freno a mano; **handcuffs** *npl* manette *fpl*; **handful** *n* manciata, pugno

handicap ['hændɪkæp] *n* handicap *m inv* ▷ *vt* handicappare

handkerchief ['hæŋkətʃɪf] *n* fazzoletto

handle ['hændl] *n* (*of door etc*) maniglia; (*of cup etc*) ansa; (*of knife etc*) impugnatura; (*of saucepan*) manico; (*for winding*) manovella ▷ *vt* toccare, maneggiare; (*deal with*) occuparsi di; (*treat: people*) trattare; **"~ with care"** "fragile"; **to fly off the ~** (*fig*) perdere le staffe, uscire dai gangheri

handlebar(s) ['hændlbɑː(z)] *n(pl)* manubrio

hand: hand luggage ['hændlʌgɪdʒ] *n* bagagli *mpl* a mano; **handmade** *adj* fatto/a a mano; **handout** *n* (*money, food*) elemosina; (*leaflet*) volantino; (*at lecture*) prospetto; **hands-free** *n, adj* (*telephone*) con auricolare; (*microphone*) vivavoce *inv*

handsome ['hænsəm] *adj* bello/a; (*profit, fortune*) considerevole

handwriting ['hændraɪtɪŋ] *n* scrittura

handy ['hændɪ] *adj* (*person*) bravo/a; (*close at hand*) a portata di mano; (*convenient*) comodo/a

hang (*pt, pp* **hung**) [hæŋ, hʌŋ] *vt* appendere; (*criminal*) impiccare ▷ *vi* (*painting*) essere appeso/a; (*hair*) scendere; (*drapery*) cadere; **to get**

the ~ of (doing) sth (*col*) cominiciare a capire (come si fa) qc; **hang about** *vi* bighellonare, ciondolare; **hang down** *vi* ricadere; **hang on** *vi* (*wait*) aspettare; **hang out** *vt* (*washing*) stendere (fuori); (*col: live*) stare ▷ *vi* penzolare, pendere; **hang round** *vi* = **hang around**; **hang up** *vi* (*Tel*) riattaccare ▷ *vt* appendere

hanger ['hæŋər] *n* gruccia

hang-gliding ['hæŋglaɪdɪŋ] *n* volo col deltaplano

hangover ['hæŋəʊvər] *n* (*after drinking*) postumi *mpl* di sbornia

hankie ['hæŋkɪ] *n abbr* = **handkerchief**

happen ['hæpən] *vi* accadere, succedere; **to ~ to do sth** fare qc per caso; **as it ~s** guarda caso; **what's ~ing?** cosa succede?

happily ['hæpɪlɪ] *adv* felicemente; fortunatamente

happiness ['hæpɪnɪs] *n* felicità, contentezza

happy ['hæpɪ] *adj* felice, contento/a; **~ with** (*arrangements etc*) soddisfatto/a di; **to be ~ to do** (*willing*) fare volentieri; **~ birthday!** buon compleanno!

harass ['hærəs] *vt* molestare; **harassment** *n* molestia

harbour, (*us*) **harbor** ['hɑːbər] *n* porto ▷ *vt* (*hope*) nutrire; (*fear*) avere; (*grudge*) covare; (*criminal*) dare rifugio a

hard [hɑːd] *adj* duro/a ▷ *adv* (*work*) sodo; (*think, try*) bene; **to look ~ at** guardare fissamente; esaminare attentamente; **no ~ feelings!** senza rancore!; **to be ~ of hearing** essere duro/a d'orecchio; **to be ~ done by** essere trattato/a ingiustamente; **hardback** *n* libro rilegato; **hardboard** *n* legno precompresso; **hard disk** *n* (*Comput*) disco rigido; **harden** *vt* indurire

hardly ['hɑ:dlɪ] adv (scarcely) appena;
it's ~ the case non è proprio il caso; **~
anyone/anywhere** quasi nessuno/
da nessuna parte; **~ ever** quasi mai
hard: hardship ['hɑ:dʃɪp] n avversità
f inv; privazioni fpl; **hard shoulder**
n (BRIT Aut) corsia d'emergenza;
hard-up (col) al verde; **hardware**
['hɑ:dwɛəʳ] n ferramenta fpl;
(Comput) hardware m; (Mil)
armamenti mpl; **hardware shop**,
(US) **hardware store** n (negozio
di) ferramenta fpl; **hard-working**
[hɑ:d'wə:kɪŋ] adj lavoratore/trice
hardy ['hɑ:dɪ] adj robusto/a; (plant)
resistente al gelo
hare [hɛəʳ] n lepre f
harm [hɑ:m] n male m; (wrong)
danno ▷ vt (person) fare male a;
(thing) danneggiare; **out of ~'s way**
al sicuro; **harmful** adj dannoso/a;
harmless adj innocuo/a;
inoffensivo/a
harmony ['hɑ:mənɪ] n armonia
harness ['hɑ:nɪs] n (for horse)
bardatura, finimenti mpl; (for
child) briglie fpl; (safety harness)
imbracatura ▷ vt (horse) bardare;
(resources) sfruttare
harp [hɑ:p] n arpa ▷ vi: **to ~ on
about** insistere tediosamente su
harsh [hɑ:ʃ] adj (life, winter) duro/a;
(judge, criticism) severo/a; (sound)
rauco/a; (colour) chiassoso/a; (light)
violento/a
harvest ['hɑ:vɪst] n raccolto;
(of grapes) vendemmia ▷ vt
fare il raccolto di, raccogliere;
vendemmiare
has [hæz] see **have**
hashtag ['hæʃtæg] n (on Twitter)
hashtag m inv
hasn't ['hæznt] = **has not**
hassle ['hæsl] n (col) sacco di
problemi
haste [heɪst] n fretta; precipitazione
f; **hasten** ['heɪsn] vt affrettare ▷ vi:
to hasten (to) affrettarsi (a); **hastily**

adv in fretta, precipitosamente;
hasty adj affrettato/a, precipitoso/a
hat [hæt] n cappello
hatch [hætʃ] n (Naut: also: **~way**)
boccaporto; (also: **service ~**) portello
di servizio ▷ vi (bird) uscire dal guscio;
(egg) schiudersi
hatchback ['hætʃbæk] n (Aut) tre (or
cinque) porte f inv
hate [heɪt] vt odiare, detestare
▷ n odio; **hater** ['heɪtəʳ] n: **cop-~**
persona che odia i poliziotti; **woman-~**
misogino/a; **hatred** ['heɪtrɪd] n odio
haul [hɔ:l] vt trascinare, tirare ▷ n
(of fish) pescata; (of stolen goods etc)
bottino
haunt [hɔ:nt] vt (fear) pervadere;
(person) frequentare ▷ n rifugio; **this
house is ~ed** questa casa è abitata
da un fantasma; **haunted** adj
(castle etc) abitato/a dai fantasmi or
dagli spiriti; (look) ossessionato/a,
tormentato/a

KEYWORD

have [hæv] (pt, pp **had**) aux vb **1** (gen)
avere; essere; **to have arrived/
gone** essere arrivato/a/andato/a;
to have eaten/slept avere
mangiato/dormito; **he has been
kind/promoted** è stato gentile/
promosso; **having finished** or **when
he had finished, he left** dopo aver
finito, se n'è andato
2 (in tag questions): **you've done
it, haven't you?** l'hai fatto, (non è)
vero?; **he hasn't done it, has he?**
non l'ha fatto, vero?
3 (in short answers and questions):
**you've made a mistake — no
I haven't/so I have** ha fatto un
errore — ma no, niente affatto/sì,
è vero; **we haven't paid — yes we
have!** non abbiamo pagato — ma
sì che abbiamo pagato!; **I've been
there before, have you?** ci sono già
stato, e lei?

▶ *modal aux vb* (*be obliged*): **to have (got) to do sth** dover fare qc; **I haven't got** *or* **I don't have to wear glasses** non ho bisogno di portare gli occhiali

▶ *vt* **1** (*possess, obtain*) avere; **he has (got) blue eyes/dark hair** ha gli occhi azzurri/i capelli scuri; **have you got** *or* **do you have a car/phone?** ha la macchina/il telefono?; **may I have your address?** potrebbe darmi il suo indirizzo?; **you can have it for £5** te lo do per 5 sterline

2 (+ *noun: take, hold etc*): **to have breakfast/a swim/a bath** fare colazione/una nuotata/un bagno; **to have a cigarette** fumare una sigaretta; **to have dinner** cenare; **to have a drink** bere qualcosa; **to have lunch** pranzare

3: **to have sth done** far fare qc; **to have one's hair cut** tagliarsi *or* farsi tagliare i capelli; **to have sb do sth** far fare qc a qn

4 (*experience, suffer*) avere; **to have a cold/flu** avere il raffreddore/l'influenza; **she had her bag stolen** le hanno rubato la borsa

5 (*phrases: col*): **you've been had!** ci sei cascato!

have out *vt*: **to have it out with sb** (*settle a problem etc*) mettere le cose in chiaro con qn

haven ['heɪvn] *n* porto; (*fig*) rifugio
haven't ['hævnt] = **have not**
havoc ['hævək] *n* gran subbuglio; **to play ~ with sth** scombussolare qc
Hawaii [hə'waɪɪ] *n* le Hawaii
hawk [hɔːk] *n* falco
hawthorn ['hɔːθɔːn] *n* biancospino
hay [heɪ] *n* fieno; **hay fever** *n* febbre *f* da fieno; **haystack** *n* pagliaio
hazard ['hæzəd] *n* azzardo, ventura; (*risk*) pericolo, rischio ▷ *vt* (*guess, remark*) azzardare; **hazardous** *adj* pericoloso/a; **hazard warning lights** *npl* (*Aut*) luci *fpl* di emergenza

haze [heɪz] *n* foschia
hazel ['heɪzl] *n* (*tree*) nocciolo ▷ *adj* (*eyes*) (*color*) nocciola *inv*; **hazelnut** ['heɪzlnʌt] *n* nocciola
hazy ['heɪzɪ] *adj* fosco/a; (*idea*) vago/a
HD *abbr* (= *high definition*) HD, alta definizione
HDTV *n abbr* (= *high definition television*) televisore *m* HD, TV *f inv* ad alta definizione
he [hiː] *pron* lui, egli; **it is he who ...** è lui che ...
head [hɛd] *n* testa; (*leader*) capo; (*of school*) preside *m/f* ▷ *vt* (*list*) essere in testa a; (*group*) essere a capo di; **~s (or tails)** testa (o croce), pari (o dispari); **~ first** a capofitto, di testa; **~ over heels in love** pazzamente innamorato/a; **to ~ the ball** dare di testa alla palla; **head for** *vt fus* dirigersi verso; **head off** *vt* (*threat, danger*) sventare; **headache** *n* mal *m* di testa; **heading** *n* titolo; intestazione *f*; **headlamp** ['hɛdlæmp] *n* (BRIT) = **headlight**; **headlight** *n* fanale *m*; **headline** *n* titolo; **head office** *n* sede *f* (centrale); **headphones** *npl* cuffia; **headquarters** *npl* ufficio centrale; (*Mil*) quartiere *m* generale; **headroom** *n* (*in car*) altezza dell'abitacolo; (*under bridge*) altezza limite; **headscarf** *n* foulard *m inv*; **headset** *n* = **headphones**; **headteacher** *n* (*of primary school*) direttore/trice; (*of secondary school*) preside *m/f*; **head waiter** *n* capocameriere *m*
heal [hiːl] *vt, vi* guarire
health [hɛlθ] *n* salute *f*; **health care** *n* assistenza sanitaria; **health centre** *n* (BRIT) poliambulatorio; **health food** *n* alimenti *mpl* macrobiotici; **Health Service** *n*: **the Health Service** (BRIT) ≈ il Servizio Sanitario Statale; **healthy** *adj* (*person*) sano/a, in buona salute; (*climate*) salubre;

(appetite, attitude etc) sano/a; (economy) florido/a; (bank balance) solido/a

heap [hi:p] n mucchio ▷ vt (stones, sand): **to ~ (up)** ammucchiare; **~s (of)** (col) (lots) un mucchio (di)

hear (pt, pp **heard**) [hɪərˈ, həːd] vt sentire; (news) ascoltare ▷ vi sentire; **to ~ about** avere notizie di; sentire parlare di

hearing [ˈhɪərɪŋ] n (sense) udito; (of witnesses) audizione f; (of a case) udienza; **hearing aid** n apparecchio acustico

hearse [həːs] n carro funebre

heart [hɑːt] n cuore m; **hearts** npl (Cards) cuori mpl; **at ~** in fondo; **by ~** (learn, know) a memoria; **to take ~** farsi coraggio or animo; **to lose ~** perdere coraggio, scoraggiarsi; **heart attack** n attacco di cuore; **heartbeat** n battito del cuore; **heartbroken** adj: **to be heartbroken** avere il cuore spezzato; **heartburn** n bruciore m di stomaco; **heart disease** n malattia di cuore

hearth [hɑːθ] n focolare m

heartless [ˈhɑːtlɪs] adj senza cuore

hearty [ˈhɑːtɪ] adj caloroso/a; robusto/a, sano/a; vigoroso/a

heat [hi:t] n calore m; (fig) ardore m; fuoco; (Sport: also: **qualifying ~**) prova eliminatoria ▷ vt scaldare; **heat up** vi (liquids) scaldarsi; (room) riscaldarsi ▷ vt riscaldare; **heated** adj riscaldato/a; (argument) acceso/a; **heater** n radiatore m; (stove) stufa

heather [ˈhɛðər] n erica

heating [ˈhi:tɪŋ] n riscaldamento

heatwave [ˈhi:tweɪv] n ondata di caldo

heaven [ˈhɛvn] n paradiso, cielo; **heavenly** adj divino/a, celeste

heavily [ˈhɛvɪlɪ] adv pesantemente; (drink, smoke) molto

heavy [ˈhɛvɪ] adj pesante; (sea) grosso/a; (rain) forte; (weather) afoso/a; (drinker, smoker) gran (before noun)

Hebrew [ˈhi:bru:] adj ebreo/a ▷ n (Ling) ebraico

hectare [ˈhɛktɑːr] n (BRIT) ettaro

hectic [ˈhɛktɪk] adj movimentato/a

he'd [hi:d] = **he would; he had**

hedge [hɛdʒ] n siepe f ▷ vi essere elusivo/a; **to ~ one's bets** (fig) coprirsi dai rischi

hedgehog [ˈhɛdʒhɔg] n riccio

heed [hi:d] vt (also: **take ~ of**) badare a, far conto di

heel [hi:l] n (Anat) calcagno; (of shoe) tacco ▷ vt (shoe) rifare i tacchi a

hefty [ˈhɛftɪ] adj (person) solido/a; (parcel) pesante; (piece, price, profit) grosso/a

height [haɪt] n altezza; (high ground) altura; (fig: of glory) apice m; (: of stupidity) colmo; **heighten** vt (fig) accrescere

heir [ɛər] n erede m; **heiress** n erede f

held [hɛld] pt, pp of **hold**

helicopter [ˈhɛlɪkɔptər] n elicottero

hell [hɛl] n inferno; **oh ~!** (col) porca miseria!, accidenti!

he'll [hi:l] = **he will; he shall**

hello [həˈləu] excl buon giorno!; ciao! (to sb one addresses as "tu"); (surprise) ma guarda!

helmet [ˈhɛlmɪt] n casco

help [hɛlp] n aiuto; (charwoman) donna di servizio ▷ vt aiutare; **~!** aiuto!; **can you ~ me?** può aiutarmi? **~ yourself (to bread)** si serva (del pane); **he can't ~ it** non ci può far niente; **help out** vi aiutare ▷ vt: **to ~ sb out** aiutare qn; **helper** n aiutante m/f, assistente m/f; **helpful** adj di grande aiuto; (useful) utile; **helping** n porzione f; **helpless** adj impotente; debole; **helpline** n ≈ telefono amico; (Comm) servizio m informazioni inv (a pagamento)

hem [hɛm] n orlo ▷ vt fare l'orlo a

hemisphere [ˈhɛmɪsfɪər] n emisfero

hemorrhage ['hɛmərɪdʒ] *n* (US)
= **haemorrhage**

hemorrhoids ['hɛmərɔɪdz] *npl* (US)
= **haemorrhoids**

hen [hɛn] *n* gallina; (*female bird*)
femmina

hence [hɛns] *adv* (*therefore*) dunque;
2 years ~ di qui a 2 anni

hen night *n* (*col*) addio al nubilato

hepatitis [hɛpə'taɪtɪs] *n* epatite *f*

her [hə:ʳ] *pron* (*direct*) la, l' + *vowel*;
(*indirect*) le; (*stressed, after prep*) lei
▷ *adj* il (la) suo/a, i (le) suoi (sue); *see
also* **me; my**

herb [hə:b] *n* erba; **herbal** *adj* di erbe;
herbal tea tisana

herd [hə:d] *n* mandria

here [hɪəʳ] *adv* qui, qua ▷ *excl* ehi!; **~!**
(*at roll call*) presente!; **~ is, ~ are** ecco;
~ he/she is eccolo/eccola

hereditary [hɪ'rɛdɪtrɪ] *adj*
ereditario/a

heritage ['hɛrɪtɪdʒ] *n* eredità; (*of
country, nation*) retaggio

hernia ['hə:nɪə] *n* ernia

hero ['hɪərəu] (*pl* **heroes**) *n* eroe *m*;
heroic [hɪ'rəuɪk] *adj* eroico/a

heroin ['hɛrəuɪn] *n* eroina (*droga*)

heroine ['hɛrəuɪn] *n* eroina (*donna*)

heron ['hɛrən] *n* airone *m*

herring ['hɛrɪŋ] *n* aringa

hers [hə:z] *pron* il (la) suo/a, i (le) suoi
(sue); *see also* **mine¹**

herself [hə:'sɛlf] *pron* (*reflexive*) si;
(*emphatic*) lei stessa; (*after prep*) se
stessa, sé; *see also* **oneself**

he's [hi:z] = **he is; he has**

hesitant ['hɛzɪtənt] *adj* esitante,
indeciso/a

hesitate ['hɛzɪteɪt] *vi*: **to ~ (about/
to do)** esitare (su/a fare); **hesitation**
[hɛzɪ'teɪʃən] *n* esitazione *f*

heterosexual [hɛtərəu'sɛksjuəl]
adj, n eterosessuale (*m/f*)

hexagon ['hɛksəgən] *n* esagono

hey [heɪ] *excl* ehi!

heyday ['heɪdeɪ] *n*: **the ~ of** i bei
giorni di, l'età d'oro di

HGV *n abbr* = **heavy goods vehicle**

hi [haɪ] *excl* ciao!

hibernate ['haɪbəneɪt] *vi* ibernare

hiccough, hiccup ['hɪkʌp] *vi*
singhiozzare

hid [hɪd] *pt of* **hide**

hidden ['hɪdn] *pp of* **hide**

hide [haɪd] (*pt* **hid**, *pp* **hidden**) *n*
(*skin*) pelle *f* ▷ *vt*: **to ~ sth (from sb)**
nascondere qc (a qn) ▷ *vi*: **to ~ (from
sb)** nascondersi (da qn)

hideous ['hɪdɪəs] *adj* laido/a;
orribile

hiding ['haɪdɪŋ] *n* (*beating*)
bastonata; **to be in ~** (*concealed*)
tenersi nascosto/a

hi-fi ['haɪfaɪ] *adj, n abbr* (= *high fidelity*)
hi-fi (*m*) *inv*

high [haɪ] *adj* alto/a; (*speed, respect,
number*) grande; (*wind*) forte;
(*voice*) acuto/a ▷ *adv* alto, in alto;
20m ~ alto/a 20m; **highchair** *n*
seggiolone *m*; **high-class** *adj*
(*neighbourhood*) elegante; (*hotel*)
di prim'ordine; (*person*) di gran
classe; (*food*) raffinato/a; **higher
education** *n* istruzione *f* superiore
or universitaria; **high heels** *npl*
(*heels*) tacchi *mpl* alti; (*shoes*) scarpe
fpl con i tacchi alti; **high jump** *n*
(*Sport*) salto in alto; **highlands** *npl*
zona montuosa; **the Highlands**
le Highlands scozzesi; **highlight** *n*
(*fig: of event*) momento culminante;
(*in hair*) colpo di sole ▷ *vt* mettere
in evidenza; **highlights** *npl* (*in hair*)
colpi *mpl* di sole; **highlighter** *n* (*pen*)
evidenziatore *m*; **highly** *adv* molto;
to speak highly of parlare molto
bene di; **highness** *n*: **Her Highness**
Sua Altezza; **high-rise** *n* (*also*:
high-rise block, high-rise building)
palazzone *m*; **high school** *n* scuola
secondaria; (*US*) istituto d'istruzione
secondaria; **high season** *n* (BRIT)
alta stagione; **high street** *n* (BRIT)
strada principale; **high-tech** (*col*) *adj*
high-tech *inv*; **highway** ['haɪweɪ] *n*

strada maestra; **Highway Code** n (BRIT) codice m della strada

hijack ['haɪdʒæk] vt dirottare; **hijacker** n dirottatore/trice

hike [haɪk] vi fare un'escursione a piedi ▷ n escursione f a piedi; **hiker** n escursionista m/f; **hiking** n escursioni fpl a piedi

hilarious [hɪ'lɛərɪəs] adj (behaviour, event) spassosissimo/a

hill [hɪl] n collina, colle m; (fairly high) montagna; (on road) salita; **hillside** n fianco della collina; **hill walking** n escursioni fpl in collina; **hilly** ['hɪlɪ] adj collinoso/a

him [hɪm] pron (direct) lo, l' + vowel; (indirect) gli; (stressed, after prep) lui; **himself** pron (reflexive) si; (emphatic) lui stesso; (after prep) se stesso, sé; see also **oneself**

hind [haɪnd] adj posteriore ▷ n cerva

hinder ['hɪndər] vt ostacolare

hindsight ['haɪndsaɪt] n: **with (the benefit of) ~** con il senno di poi

Hindu ['hɪnduː] n indù mf inv; **Hinduism** n (Rel) induismo

hinge [hɪndʒ] n cardine m ▷ vi (fig): **to ~ on** dipendere da

hint [hɪnt] n (suggestion) allusione f; (advice) consiglio; (sign) accenno ▷ vt: **to ~ that** lasciar capire che ▷ vi: **to ~ at** accennare a, alludere a

hip [hɪp] n anca, fianco

hippie ['hɪpɪ] n hippy mf inv

hippo ['hɪpəʊ] (pl **hippos**) n ippopotamo

hippopotamus (pl **hippopotamuses** or **hippopotami**) [hɪpə'pɔtəməs, -'pɔtəmaɪ] n ippopotamo

hippy ['hɪpɪ] n = **hippie**

hire ['haɪər] vt (BRIT: car, equipment) noleggiare; (worker) assumere, dare lavoro a ▷ n nolo, noleggio; **for ~** da nolo; (taxi) libero/a; **hire(d) car** n (BRIT) macchina a nolo; **hire purchase** n (BRIT) acquisto (or vendita) rateale

his [hɪz] adj, pron il (la) suo (sua), i (le) suoi (sue); see also **my**; **mine**[1]

Hispanic [hɪs'pænɪk] adj ispanico/a

hiss [hɪs] vi fischiare; (cat, snake) sibilare

historian [hɪ'stɔːrɪən] n storico/a

historic(al) [hɪ'stɔrɪk(l)] adj storico/a

history ['hɪstərɪ] n storia

hit [hɪt] vt (pt, pp **hit**) colpire; picchiare; (knock against) battere; (reach: target) raggiungere; (collide with: car) urtare contro; (fig: affect) colpire; (find: problem) incontrare ▷ n colpo; (success, song) successo; **to ~ it off with sb** andare molto d'accordo con qn; **hit back** vi: **to ~ back at sb** restituire il colpo a qn

hitch [hɪtʃ] vt (fasten) attaccare; (also: **~ up**) tirare su ▷ n (difficulty) intoppo, difficoltà f inv; **to ~ a lift** fare l'autostop; **hitch-hike** vi fare l'autostop; **hitch-hiker** n autostoppista m/f; **hitch-hiking** n autostop m

hi-tech ['haɪ'tɛk] adj high-tech inv

hitman ['hɪtmæn] n (col) sicario

HIV n abbr: **~-negative/-positive** adj sieronegativo/a/sieropositivo/a

hive [haɪv] n alveare m

hoard [hɔːd] n (of food) provviste fpl; (of money) gruzzolo ▷ vt ammassare

hoarse [hɔːs] adj rauco/a

hoax [həʊks] n scherzo; falso allarme

hob [hɔb] n piastra (con fornelli)

hobble ['hɔbl] vi zoppicare

hobby ['hɔbɪ] n hobby m inv, passatempo

hobo ['həʊbəʊ] n (US) vagabondo

hockey ['hɔkɪ] n hockey m; **hockey stick** n bastone m da hockey

hog [hɔg] n maiale m ▷ vt (fig) arraffare; **to go the whole ~** farlo fino in fondo

Hogmanay [hɔgmə'neɪ] n (SCOTTISH) ≈ San Silvestro

hoist [hɔɪst] n paranco ▷ vt issare

hold [həʊld] (*pt, pp* **held**) *vt* tenere; (*contain*) contenere; (*keep back*) trattenere; (*believe*) mantenere; considerare; (*possess*) avere, possedere; detenere ▷ *vi* (*withstand pressure*) tenere; (*be valid*) essere valido/a ▷ *n* presa; (*control*): **to have a ~ over** avere controllo su; (*Naut*) stiva; **~ the line!** (*Tel*) resti in linea!; **to catch** *or* **get (a) ~ of** afferrare; **hold back** *vt* trattenere; (*secret*) tenere celato/a; **hold on** *vi* tener fermo; (*wait*) aspettare; **~ on!** (*Tel*) resti in linea!; **hold out** *vt* offrire ▷ *vi* (*resist*): **to ~ out (against)** resistere (a); **hold up** *vt* (*raise*) alzare; (*support*) sostenere; (*delay*) ritardare; (*rob*) assaltare; **holdall** *n* (BRIT) borsone *m*; **holder** *n* (*container*) contenitore *m*; (*of ticket, title*) possessore (posseditrice); (*of office etc*) incaricato/a; (*of record*) detentore/trice

hole [həʊl] *n* buco, buca

holiday ['hɔlədɪ] *n* vacanza; (*day off*) giorno di vacanza; (*public*) giorno festivo; **to be on ~** essere in vacanza; **holiday camp** *n* (BRIT) (*also:* **holiday centre**) ≈ villaggio (di vacanze); **holiday home** *n* seconda casa (*per le vacanze*); **holiday job** *n* (BRIT) ≈ lavoro estivo; **holiday-maker** *n* (BRIT) villeggiante *m/f*; **holiday resort** *n* luogo di villeggiatura

Holland ['hɔlənd] *n* Olanda

hollow ['hɔləʊ] *adj* cavo/a; (*container, claim*) vuoto/a; (*laugh*) forzato/a; (*sound*) cavernoso/a ▷ *n* cavità *f inv*; (*in land*) valletta, depressione *f*; **hollow out** *vt* scavare

holly ['hɔlɪ] *n* agrifoglio

Hollywood ['hɔlɪwʊd] *n* Hollywood *f*

holocaust ['hɔləkɔːst] *n* olocausto

holy ['həʊlɪ] *adj* santo/a; (*bread*) benedetto/a, consacrato/a

home [həʊm] *n* casa; (*country*) patria; (*institution*) casa, ricovero ▷ *cpd* familiare; (*cooking etc*) casalingo/a; (*Econ, Pol*) nazionale, interno/a; (*Sport*) di casa ▷ *adv* a casa; in patria; (*right in: nail etc*) fino in fondo; **at ~** a casa; (*in situation*) a proprio agio; **to go** (*or* **come**) **~** tornare a casa (*or* in patria); **make yourself at ~** si metta a suo agio; **home address** *n* indirizzo di casa; **homeland** *n* patria; **homeless** *adj* senza tetto; spatriato/a; **homely** ['həʊmlɪ] *adj* semplice, alla buona; accogliente; **home-made** *adj* casalingo/a; **home match** *n* partita in casa; **Home Office** *n* (BRIT) ministero degli Interni; **home owner** *n* proprietario/a di casa; **home page** *n* (*Comput*) home page *f inv*; **Home Secretary** *n* (BRIT) ministro degli Interni; **homesick** *adj*: **to be homesick** avere la nostalgia; **home town** *n* città *f inv* natale; **homework** *n* compiti *mpl* (*per casa*)

homicide ['hɔmɪsaɪd] *n* (US) omicidio

homoeopathic, (US) **homeopathic** ['həʊmɪəʊ'pæθɪk] *adj* omeopatico/a

homoeopathy, (US) **homeopathy** [həʊmɪ'ɔpəθɪ] *n* omeopatia

homosexual [hɔməʊ'sɛksjʊəl] *adj, n* omosessuale (*m/f*)

honest ['ɔnɪst] *adj* onesto/a; sincero/a; **honestly** *adv* onestamente; sinceramente; **honesty** *n* onestà

honey ['hʌnɪ] *n* miele *m*; **honeymoon** *n* luna di miele, viaggio di nozze; **honeysuckle** ['hʌnɪsʌkl] *n* (*Bot*) caprifoglio

Hong Kong ['hɔŋ'kɔŋ] *n* Hong Kong *f*

honorary ['ɔnərərɪ] *adj* onorario/a; (*duty, title*) onorifico/a

honour, (US) **honor** ['ɔnəʳ] *vt* onorare ▷ *n* onore *m*; **honourable**, (US) **honorable** *adj* onorevole; **honours degree** *n* (*Scol*) laurea (con corso di studi di 4 o 5 anni)

h

hood [hud] n cappuccio; (on cooker) cappa; (BRIT Aut) capote f; (US Aut) cofano

hoof (pl **hoofs** or **hooves**) [hu:f, hu:vz] n zoccolo

hook [huk] n gancio; (for fishing) amo ▷ vt uncinare; (dress) agganciare

hooligan ['hu:lɪɡən] n giovinastro, teppista m

hoop [hu:p] n cerchio

hooray [hu:'reɪ] excl = **hurrah**

hoot [hu:t] vi (Aut) suonare il clacson; (siren) ululare; (owl) gufare

Hoover® ['hu:vər] n (BRIT) aspirapolvere m inv ▷ vt pulire con l'aspirapolvere

hooves [hu:vz] npl of **hoof**

hop [hɔp] vi saltellare, saltare; (on one foot) saltare su una gamba

hope [həup] vt: **to ~ that/to do** sperare che/di fare ▷ vi sperare ▷ n speranza; **I ~ so/not** spero di sì/no; **hopeful** adj (person) pieno/a di speranza; (situation) promettente; **hopefully** adv con speranza; **hopefully he will recover** speriamo che si riprenda; **hopeless** adj senza speranza, disperato/a; (useless) inutile

hops [hɔps] npl luppoli mpl

horizon [hə'raɪzn] n orizzonte m; **horizontal** [hɔrɪ'zɔntl] adj orizzontale

hormone ['hɔ:məun] n ormone m

horn [hɔ:n] n (Zool, Mus) corno; (Aut) clacson m inv

horoscope ['hɔrəskəup] n oroscopo

horrendous [hɔ'rɛndəs] adj orrendo/a

horrible ['hɔrɪbl] adj orribile, tremendo/a

horrid ['hɔrɪd] adj orrido/a; (person) odioso/a

horrific [hɔ'rɪfɪk] adj (accident) spaventoso/a; (film) orripilante

horrifying ['hɔrɪfaɪɪŋ] adj terrificante

horror ['hɔrər] n orrore m; **horror film** n film m inv dell'orrore

hors d'œuvre [ɔ:'də:vrə] n antipasto

horse [hɔ:s] n cavallo; **horseback** adj, adv a cavallo: **on horseback** adj, adv a cavallo; **horse chestnut** n ippocastano; **horsepower** n cavallo (vapore); **horse-racing** n ippica; **horseradish** n rafano; **horse riding** n (BRIT) equitazione f

hose [həuz] n (also: **~pipe**) tubo; (also: **garden ~**) tubo per annaffiare

hospital ['hɔspɪtl] n ospedale m

hospitality [hɔspɪ'tælɪtɪ] n ospitalità

host [həust] n ospite m; (Rel) ostia; (large number): **a ~ of** una schiera di

hostage ['hɔstɪdʒ] n ostaggio/a

hostel ['hɔstl] n ostello; (also: **youth ~**) ostello della gioventù

hostess ['həustɪs] n ospite f; (BRIT Aviat) hostess f inv

hostile ['hɔstaɪl] adj ostile

hostility [hɔ'stɪlɪtɪ] n ostilità f inv

hot [hɔt] adj caldo/a; (as opposed to only warm) molto caldo/a; (spicy) piccante; (fig) accanito/a; ardente; violento/a, focoso/a; **to be ~** (person) aver caldo; (thing) essere caldo/a; (Meteor) far caldo; **hot dog** n hot dog m inv

hotel [həu'tɛl] n albergo

hotspot ['hɔtspɔt] n (Comput: also: **wireless ~**) hotspot m inv Wi-Fi

hot-water bottle [hɔt'wɔ:tə-] n borsa dell'acqua calda

hound [haund] vt perseguitare ▷ n segugio

hour ['auər] n ora; **hourly** adj (ad) ogni ora

house n [haus, 'hauzɪz] casa; (Pol) camera; (Theat) sala; pubblico; spettacolo ▷ vt [hauz] (person) ospitare, alloggiare; **on the ~** (fig) offerto/a dalla casa; **household** n famiglia; casa; **householder** n padrone/a di casa; (head of house) capofamiglia m/f; **housekeeper** n governante f; **housekeeping** n (work) governo della casa; (also: **housekeeping money**) soldi mpl per le spese di casa; **housewife** n (irreg) massaia, casalinga; **house wine** n vino della casa; **housework** n faccende fpl domestiche

housing ['hauzɪŋ] n alloggio; **housing development**, (BRIT) **housing estate** n zona residenziale con case popolari e/o private

hover ['hɔvə'] vi (bird) librarsi; **hovercraft** n hovercraft m inv

how [hau] adv come; **~ are you?** come sta?; **~ do you do?** piacere!; **~ far is it to …?** quanto è lontano …?; **~ long have you been here?** da quanto tempo è qui?; **~ lovely!** che bello!; **~ many?** quanti/e?; **~ much?** quanto/a?; **~ many people/much milk?** quante persone/quanto latte?; **~ old are you?** quanti anni ha?

however [hau'ɛvə'] adv in qualsiasi modo o maniera che; (+ adjective) per quanto + sub; (in questions) come ▷ conj comunque, però

howl [haul] vi ululare; (baby, person) urlare

HP n abbr (BRIT) = **hire purchase**

hp abbr (Aut) = **horsepower**

HQ n abbr (= headquarters) Q.G.

hr abbr (= hour) h

hrs abbr (= hours) h

HTML n abbr (= hypertext markup language) HTML m inv

hubcap ['hʌbkæp] n coprimozzo

huddle ['hʌdl] vi: **to ~ together** rannicchiarsi l'uno contro l'altro

huff [hʌf] n: **in a ~** stizzito/a

hug [hʌg] vt abbracciare; (shore, kerb) stringere

huge [hju:dʒ] adj enorme, immenso/a

hull [hʌl] n (of ship) scafo

hum [hʌm] vt (tune) canticchiare ▷ vi canticchiare; (insect, plane, tool) ronzare

human ['hju:mən] adj (irreg) umano/a ▷ n essere m umano

humane [hju:'meɪn] adj umanitario/a

humanitarian [hju:mænɪ'tɛərɪən] adj umanitario/a

humanity [hju:'mænɪtɪ] n umanità

human rights npl diritti mpl dell'uomo

humble ['hʌmbl] adj umile, modesto/a ▷ vt umiliare

humid ['hju:mɪd] adj umido/a; **humidity** [hju:'mɪdɪtɪ] n umidità

humiliate [hju:'mɪlɪeɪt] vt umiliare; **humiliating** adj umiliante; **humiliation** [hju:mɪlɪ'eɪʃən] n umiliazione f

hummus ['huməs] n purè di ceci

humorous ['hju:mərəs] adj umoristico/a; (person) buffo/a

humour, (US) **humor** ['hju:mə'] n umore m ▷ vt assecondare

hump [hʌmp] n gobba

hunch [hʌntʃ] n (premonition) intuizione f

hundred ['hʌndrəd] num cento; **~s of people** centinaia fpl di persone; **hundredth** [-ɪdθ] num centesimo/a

hung [hʌŋ] pt, pp of **hang**

Hungarian [hʌŋ'gɛərɪən] adj ungherese ▷ n ungherese m/f; (Ling) ungherese m

Hungary ['hʌŋgərɪ] n Ungheria

hunger ['hʌŋgə'] n fame f ▷ vi: **to ~ for** desiderare ardentemente

hungry ['hʌŋgrɪ] adj affamato/a; **to be ~** aver fame

hunt [hʌnt] vt (seek) cercare; (Sport) cacciare ▷ vi: **to ~ (for)** andare a caccia (di) ▷ n caccia; **hunter** n cacciatore m; **hunting** n caccia

hurdle ['hə:dl] n (Sport, fig) ostacolo

hurl [hə:l] vt lanciare con violenza

hurrah [hu'ra:], **hurray** [hu'reɪ] excl urra!, evviva!

hurricane ['hʌrɪkən] n uragano

hurry ['hʌrɪ] n fretta ▷ vi (also: **~ up**) affrettarsi ▷ vt (also: **~ up**: person) affrettare; (: work) far in fretta; **to**

be in a ~ aver fretta; **hurry up** vi
sbrigarsi

hurt [hə:t] (pt, pp **hurt**) vt (cause pain
to) far male a; (injure, fig) ferire ▷ vi
far male

husband ['hʌzbənd] n marito

hush [hʌʃ] n silenzio, calma ▷ vt
zittire

husky ['hʌskɪ] adj roco/a ▷ n cane m
eschimese

hut [hʌt] n rifugio; (shed) ripostiglio

hyacinth ['haɪəsɪnθ] n giacinto

hydrangea [haɪ'dreɪnʒə] n ortensia

hydrofoil ['haɪdrəfɔɪl] n aliscafo

hydrogen ['haɪdrədʒən] n idrogeno

hygiene ['haɪdʒi:n] n igiene f;
hygienic [haɪ'dʒi:nɪk] adj igienico/a

hymn [hɪm] n inno; cantica

hype [haɪp] n (col) battage m inv
pubblicitario

hyperlink ['haɪpəlɪŋk] n link m inv
ipertestuale

hyphen ['haɪfn] n trattino

hypnotize ['hɪpnətaɪz] vt
ipnotizzare

hypocrite ['hɪpəkrɪt] n ipocrita m/f

hypocritical [hɪpə'krɪtɪkl] adj
ipocrita

hypothesis (pl **hypotheses**)
[haɪ'pɔθɪsɪs, -si:z] n ipotesi f inv

hysterical [hɪ'sterɪkl] adj isterico/a

hysterics [hɪ'sterɪks] npl accesso di
isteria; (laughter) attacco di riso

I [aɪ] pron io

ice [aɪs] n ghiaccio; (on road) gelo ▷ vt
(cake) glassare ▷ vi (also: ~ **over**)
ghiacciare; (also: ~ **up**) gelare;
iceberg n iceberg m inv; **ice cream**
n gelato; **ice cube** n cubetto di
ghiaccio; **ice hockey** n hockey m
su ghiaccio

Iceland ['aɪslənd] n Islanda;
Icelander n islandese m/f; **Icelandic**
[aɪs'lændɪk] adj islandese ▷ n (Ling)
islandese m

ice: ice lolly n (BRIT) ghiacciolo;
ice rink n pista di pattinaggio; **ice
skating** n pattinaggio sul ghiaccio

icing ['aɪsɪŋ] n (Culin) glassa; **icing
sugar** (BRIT) n zucchero a velo

icon ['aɪkɔn] n icona

icy ['aɪsɪ] adj ghiacciato/a; (weather,
temperature) gelido/a

I'd [aɪd] = **I would; I had**

ID card n = **identity card**

idea [aɪ'dɪə] n idea

ideal [aɪˈdɪəl] *adj, n* ideale *(m)*;
ideally [aɪˈdɪəlɪ] *adv* perfettamente,
assolutamente; **ideally the book
should have ...** l'ideale sarebbe che il
libro avesse ...
identical [aɪˈdɛntɪkl] *adj* identico/a
identification [aɪdɛntɪfɪˈkeɪʃən] *n*
identificazione *f*; **means of ~** carta
d'identità
identify [aɪˈdɛntɪfaɪ] *vt* identificare
identity [aɪˈdɛntɪtɪ] *n* identità *f inv*;
identity card *n* carta d'identità;
identity theft *n* furto d'identità
ideology [aɪdɪˈɔlədʒɪ] *n* ideologia
idiom [ˈɪdɪəm] *n* idioma *m*; *(phrase)*
espressione *f* idiomatica
idiot [ˈɪdɪət] *n* idiota *m/f*
idle [ˈaɪdl] *adj* inattivo/a; *(lazy)*
pigro/a, ozioso/a; *(unemployed)*
disoccupato/a; *(question, pleasures)*
ozioso/a ▷ *vi (engine)* girare al minimo
idol [ˈaɪdl] *n* idolo
idyllic [ɪˈdɪlɪk] *adj* idillico/a
i.e. *abbr (that is)* cioè
if [ɪf] *conj* se; **if I were you ...** se fossi
in te ..., io al tuo posto ...; **if so** se è
così; **if not** se no; **if only** se solo *or*
soltanto
ignite [ɪgˈnaɪt] *vt* accendere ▷ *vi*
accendersi
ignition [ɪgˈnɪʃən] *n (Aut)* accensione
f; **to switch on/off the ~** accendere/
spegnere il motore
ignorance [ˈɪgnərəns] *n* ignoranza;
to keep sb in ~ of sth tenere qn
all'oscuro di qc
ignorant [ˈɪgnərənt] *adj* ignorante;
to be ~ of *(subject)* essere ignorante
in; *(events)* essere ignaro/a di
ignore [ɪgˈnɔːʳ] *vt* non tener conto di;
(person, fact) ignorare
ill [ɪl] *adj (sick)* malato/a; *(bad)*
cattivo/a ▷ *n* male *m*; **to take** *or* **be
taken ~** ammalarsi; **to speak/think
~ of sb** parlar/pensar male di qn
I'll [aɪl] = **I will; I shall**
illegal [ɪˈliːgl] *adj* illegale
illegible [ɪˈlɛdʒɪbl] *adj* illeggibile

illegitimate [ɪlɪˈdʒɪtɪmət] *adj*
illegittimo/a
ill health *n* problemi *mpl* di salute
illiterate [ɪˈlɪtərət] *adj* analfabeta,
illetterato/a; *(letter)* scorretto/a
illness [ˈɪlnɪs] *n* malattia
illuminate [ɪˈluːmɪneɪt] *vt*
illuminare
illusion [ɪˈluːʒən] *n* illusione *f*
illustrate [ˈɪləstreɪt] *vt* illustrare
illustration [ɪləˈstreɪʃən] *n*
illustrazione *f*
IM *n (= instant messaging)* messaggeria
istantanea
I'm [aɪm] = **I am**
image [ˈɪmɪdʒ] *n* immagine *f*; *(public
face)* immagine (pubblica)
imaginary [ɪˈmædʒɪnərɪ] *adj*
immaginario/a
imagination [ɪmædʒɪˈneɪʃən] *n*
immaginazione *f*, fantasia
imaginative [ɪˈmædʒɪnətɪv] *adj*
immaginoso/a
imagine [ɪˈmædʒɪn] *vt* immaginare
imam [ɪˈmɑːm] *n* imam *m inv*
imbalance [ɪmˈbæləns] *n* squilibrio
imitate [ˈɪmɪteɪt] *vt* imitare;
imitation [ɪmɪˈteɪʃən] *n* imitazione *f*
immaculate [ɪˈmækjulət] *adj*
immacolato/a; *(dress, appearance)*
impeccabile
immature [ɪməˈtjuəʳ] *adj*
immaturo/a
immediate [ɪˈmiːdɪət] *adj*
immediato/a; **immediately** *adv*
(at once) subito, immediatamente;
immediately next to proprio
accanto a
immense [ɪˈmɛns] *adj* immenso/a;
enorme; **immensely** *adv*
immensamente
immerse [ɪˈməːs] *vt* immergere
immigrant [ˈɪmɪgrənt] *n*
immigrante *m/f*; *(already established)*
immigrato/a; **immigration**
[ɪmɪˈgreɪʃən] *n* immigrazione *f*
imminent [ˈɪmɪnənt] *adj* imminente
immoral [ɪˈmɔrl] *adj* immorale

immortal [ɪˈmɔːtl] *adj, n* immortale (*m/f*)

immune [ɪˈmjuːn] *adj*: **~ (to)** immune (da); **immune system** *n* sistema *m* immunitario

immunize [ˈɪmjunaɪz] *vt* immunizzare

impact [ˈɪmpækt] *n* impatto

impair [ɪmˈpɛəʳ] *vt* danneggiare

impartial [ɪmˈpɑːʃl] *adj* imparziale

impatience [ɪmˈpeɪʃəns] *n* impazienza

impatient [ɪmˈpeɪʃənt] *adj* impaziente; **to get** or **grow ~** perdere la pazienza

impeccable [ɪmˈpɛkəbl] *adj* impeccabile

impending [ɪmˈpɛndɪŋ] *adj* imminente

imperative [ɪmˈpɛrətɪv] *adj* imperativo/a; necessario/a, urgente; (*voice*) imperioso/a

imperfect [ɪmˈpəːfɪkt] *adj* imperfetto/a; (*goods etc*) difettoso/a ▷ *n* (*Ling: also:* **~ tense**) imperfetto

imperial [ɪmˈpɪərɪəl] *adj* imperiale; (*measure*) legale

impersonal [ɪmˈpəːsənl] *adj* impersonale

impersonate [ɪmˈpəːsəneɪt] *vt* spacciarsi per, fingersi; (*Theat*) imitare

impetus [ˈɪmpətəs] *n* impeto

implant [ɪmˈplɑːnt] *vt* (*Med*) innestare; (*fig: idea, principle*) inculcare

implement *n* [ˈɪmplɪmənt] attrezzo; (*for cooking*) utensile *m* ▷ *vt* [ˈɪmplɪmɛnt] effettuare

implicate [ˈɪmplɪkeɪt] *vt* implicare

implication [ɪmplɪˈkeɪʃən] *n* implicazione *f*; **by ~** implicitamente

implicit [ɪmˈplɪsɪt] *adj* implicito/a; (*complete*) completo/a

imply [ɪmˈplaɪ] *vt* insinuare; suggerire

impolite [ɪmpəˈlaɪt] *adj* scortese

import *vt* [ɪmˈpɔːt] importare ▷ *n* [ˈɪmpɔːt] (*Comm*) importazione *f*

importance [ɪmˈpɔːtns] *n* importanza

important [ɪmˈpɔːtnt] *adj* importante; **it's not ~** non ha importanza

importer [ɪmˈpɔːtəʳ] *n* importatore/trice

impose [ɪmˈpəuz] *vt* imporre ▷ *vi*: **to ~ on sb** sfruttare la bontà di qn; **imposing** [ɪmˈpəuzɪŋ] *adj* imponente

impossible [ɪmˈpɔsɪbl] *adj* impossibile

impotent [ˈɪmpətnt] *adj* impotente

impoverished [ɪmˈpɔvərɪʃt] *adj* impoverito/a

impractical [ɪmˈpræktɪkl] *adj* non pratico/a

impress [ɪmˈprɛs] *vt* impressionare; (*mark*) imprimere, stampare; **to ~ sth on sb** far capire qc a qn

impression [ɪmˈprɛʃən] *n* impressione *f*; **to be under the ~ that** avere l'impressione che

impressive [ɪmˈprɛsɪv] *adj* notevole

imprison [ɪmˈprɪzn] *vt* imprigionare; **imprisonment** *n* imprigionamento

improbable [ɪmˈprɔbəbl] *adj* improbabile; (*excuse*) inverosimile

improper [ɪmˈprɔpəʳ] *adj* scorretto/a; (*unsuitable*) inadatto/a, improprio/a; sconveniente, indecente

improve [ɪmˈpruːv] *vt* migliorare ▷ *vi* migliorare; (*pupil etc*) fare progressi; **improvement** *n* miglioramento; progresso

improvise [ˈɪmprəvaɪz] *vt, vi* improvvisare

impulse [ˈɪmpʌls] *n* impulso; **to act on ~** agire d'impulso or impulsivamente; **impulsive** [ɪmˈpʌlsɪv] *adj* impulsivo/a

KEYWORD

in [ɪn] *prep* 1 (*indicating place, position*) in; **in the house/garden** in casa/

giardino; **in the box** nella scatola; **in the fridge** nel frigorifero; **I have it in my hand** ce l'ho in mano; **in town/ the country** in città/campagna; **in school** a scuola; **in here/there** qui/lì dentro

2 (*with place names, of town, region, country*): **in London** a Londra; **in England** in Inghilterra; **in the United States** negli Stati Uniti; **in Yorkshire** nello Yorkshire

3 (*indicating time: during, in the space of*) in; **in spring/summer** in primavera/estate; **in 1988** nel 1988; **in May** in *or* a maggio; **I'll see you in July** ci vediamo a luglio; **in the afternoon** nel pomeriggio; **at 4 o'clock in the afternoon** alle 4 del pomeriggio; **I did it in 3 hours/days** l'ho fatto in 3 ore/giorni; **I'll see you in 2 weeks** *or* **in 2 weeks' time** ci vediamo tra 2 settimane

4 (*indicating manner etc*) a; **in a loud/ soft voice** a voce alta/bassa; **in pencil** a matita; **in English/French** in inglese/francese; **the boy in the blue shirt** il ragazzo con la camicia blu

5 (*indicating circumstances*): **in the sun** al sole; **in the shade** all'ombra; **in the rain** sotto la pioggia; **a rise in prices** un aumento dei prezzi

6 (*indicating mood, state*): **in tears** in lacrime; **in anger** per la rabbia; **in despair** disperato/a; **in good condition** in buono stato, in buone condizioni; **to live in luxury** vivere nel lusso

7 (*with ratios, numbers*): **1 in 10** 1 su 10; **20 pence in the pound** 20 pence per sterlina; **they lined up in twos** si misero in fila per due

8 (*referring to people, works*) in; **the disease is common in children** la malattia è comune nei bambini; **in (the works of) Dickens** in Dickens

9 (*indicating profession etc*) in; **to be in teaching** fare l'insegnante, insegnare; **to be in publishing** lavorare nell'editoria

10 (*after superlative*) di; **the best in the class** il migliore della classe

11 (*with present participle*): **in saying this** dicendo questo, nel dire questo

▸ *adv*: **to be in** (*person: at home, work*) esserci; (*train, ship, plane*) essere arrivato/a; (*in fashion*) essere di moda; **to ask sb in** invitare qn ad entrare; **to run/limp** *etc* **in** entrare di corsa/zoppicando *etc*

▸ *n*: **the ins and outs of the problem** tutti gli aspetti del problema

inability [ɪnə'bɪlɪtɪ] *n* incapacità

inaccurate [ɪn'ækjurət] *adj* inesatto/a; impreciso/a

inadequate [ɪn'ædɪkwət] *adj* insufficiente

inadvertently [ɪnəd'və:tntlɪ] *adv* senza volerlo

inappropriate [ɪnə'prəuprɪət] *adj* non adatto/a; (*word, expression*) improprio/a

inaugurate [ɪ'nɔ:gjureɪt] *vt* inaugurare; (*president, official*) insediare

Inc. *abbr* (*us*: = *incorporated*) S.A.

incapable [ɪn'keɪpəbl] *adj*: **~ (of doing sth)** incapace (di fare qc)

incense *n* ['ɪnsɛns] incenso ▸ *vt* [ɪn'sɛns] (*anger*) infuriare

incentive [ɪn'sentɪv] *n* incentivo

inch [ɪntʃ] *n* pollice *m* (= 25 *mm*; 12 *in a foot*); **within an ~ of** a un pelo da; **he wouldn't give an ~** (*fig*) non ha ceduto di un millimetro

incidence ['ɪnsɪdns] *n* (*of crime, disease*) incidenza

incident ['ɪnsɪdnt] *n* incidente *m*; (*in book*) episodio

incidentally [ɪnsɪ'dɛntəlɪ] *adv* (*by the way*) a proposito

inclination [ɪnklɪ'neɪʃən] *n* inclinazione *f*

incline n ['ɪnklaɪn] pendenza, pendio ▷ vt [ɪn'klaɪn] inclinare ▷ vi (surface) essere inclinato/a; **to be ~d to do** tendere a fare; essere propenso/a a fare

include [ɪn'kluːd] vt includere, comprendere; **including** prep compreso/a, incluso/a; **inclusion** [ɪn'kluːʒən] n inclusione f; **inclusive** [ɪn'kluːsɪv] adj incluso/a, compreso/a; **inclusive of tax** etc tasse etc comprese

income ['ɪnkʌm] n reddito; **income support** n (BRIT) sussidio di indigenza or povertà; **income tax** n imposta sul reddito

incoming ['ɪnkʌmɪŋ] adj (passengers, flight, mail) in arrivo; (government, tenant) subentrante; **~ tide** marea montante

incompatible [ɪnkəm'pætɪbl] adj incompatibile

incompetence [ɪn'kɔmpɪtns] n incompetenza, incapacità

incompetent [ɪn'kɔmpɪtnt] adj incompetente, incapace

incomplete [ɪnkəm'pliːt] adj incompleto/a

inconsistent [ɪnkən'sɪstnt] adj incoerente; **~ with** in contraddizione con

inconvenience [ɪnkən'viːnjəns] n inconveniente m; (trouble) disturbo ▷ vt disturbare

inconvenient [ɪnkən'viːnjənt] adj scomodo/a

incorporate [ɪn'kɔːpəreɪt] vt incorporare; (contain) contenere

incorrect [ɪnkə'rɛkt] adj scorretto/a; (statement) inesatto/a

increase n ['ɪnkriːs] aumento ▷ vi [ɪn'kriːs] aumentare; **increasingly** adv sempre più

incredible [ɪn'krɛdɪbl] adj incredibile; **incredibly** adv incredibilmente

incur [ɪn'kəːʳ] vt (expenses) incorrere; (debt) contrarre; (loss) subire; (anger, risk) esporsi a

indecent [ɪn'diːsnt] adj indecente

indeed [ɪn'diːd] adv infatti; veramente; **yes ~!** certamente!

indefinitely [ɪn'dɛfɪnɪtlɪ] adv (wait) indefinitamente

independence [ɪndɪ'pɛndns] n indipendenza; **Independence Day** n (US) vedi nota **"Independence Day"**

INDEPENDENCE DAY

Negli Stati Uniti il 4 luglio si festeggia l'*Independence Day*, il giorno in cui è stata firmata, nel 1776, la Dichiarazione di Indipendenza con la quale tredici colonie britanniche dichiaravano la propria indipendenza dalla Gran Bretagna e la propria appartenenza agli Stati Uniti d'America.

independent [ɪndɪ'pɛndnt] adj indipendente; **independent school** n (BRIT) istituto scolastico indipendente che si autofinanzia

index ['ɪndɛks] n (pl **indexes**: in book) indice m; (: in library etc) catalogo; (pl **indices**: ratio, sign) indice m

India ['ɪndɪə] n India; **Indian** adj, n indiano/a

indicate ['ɪndɪkeɪt] vt indicare; **indication** [ɪndɪ'keɪʃən] n indicazione f, segno; **indicative** [ɪn'dɪkətɪv] adj: **indicative of** indicativo/a di ▷ n (Ling) indicativo; **to be indicative of sth** essere indicativo/a or un indice di qc; **indicator** ['ɪndɪkeɪtəʳ] n (Aut) indicatore m di direzione, freccia

indices ['ɪndɪsiːz] npl of **index**

indict [ɪn'daɪt] vt accusare; **indictment** [ɪn'daɪtmənt] n accusa

indifference [ɪn'dɪfrəns] n indifferenza

indifferent [ɪn'dɪfrənt] adj indifferente; (poor) mediocre

indigenous [ɪn'dɪdʒɪnəs] *adj*
indigeno/a

indigestion [ɪndɪ'dʒɛstʃən] *n*
indigestione *f*

indignant [ɪn'dɪgnənt] *adj*: **~ (at
sth/with sb)** indignato/a (per qc/
contro qn)

indirect [ɪndɪ'rɛkt] *adj* indiretto/a

indispensable [ɪndɪ'spɛnsəbl] *adj*
indispensabile

individual [ɪndɪ'vɪdjuəl] *n* individuo
▷ *adj* individuale; *(characteristic)*
particolare, originale; **individually**
adv singolarmente, uno/a per uno/a

Indonesia [ɪndəu'niːzɪə] *n*
Indonesia

indoor ['ɪndɔːʳ] *adj* da interno; *(plant)*
d'appartamento; *(swimming pool)*
coperto/a; *(sport, games)* fatto/a
al coperto; **indoors** [ɪn'dɔːz] *adv*
all'interno

induce [ɪn'djuːs] *vt* persuadere;
(bring about, Med) provocare

indulge [ɪn'dʌldʒ] *vt (whim)*
compiacere, soddisfare; *(child)*
viziare ▷ *vi*: **to ~ in sth** concedersi
qc; abbandonarsi a qc; **indulgent** *adj*
indulgente

industrial [ɪn'dʌstrɪəl] *adj*
industriale; *(injury)* sul lavoro;
industrial estate (BRIT) *n*
zona industriale; **industrialist**
[ɪn'dʌstrɪəlɪst] *n* industriale
m; **industrial park** *n* (US) zona
industriale

industry ['ɪndəstrɪ] *n* industria;
(diligence) operosità

inefficient [ɪnɪ'fɪʃənt] *adj*
inefficiente

inequality [ɪnɪ'kwɔlɪtɪ] *n*
ineguaglianza

inevitable [ɪn'ɛvɪtəbl] *adj*
inevitabile; **inevitably** *adv*
inevitabilmente

inexpensive [ɪnɪk'spɛnsɪv] *adj* poco
costoso/a

inexperienced [ɪnɪk'spɪərɪənst] *adj*
inesperto/a, senza esperienza

inexplicable [ɪnɪk'splɪkəbl] *adj*
inesplicabile

infamous ['ɪnfəməs] *adj* infame

infant ['ɪnfənt] *n* bambino/a

infantry ['ɪnfəntrɪ] *n* fanteria

infant school *n* (BRIT) scuola
elementare *(per bambini dall'età di
5 a 7 anni)*

infect [ɪn'fɛkt] *vt* infettare;
infection [ɪn'fɛkʃən] *n* infezione
f; **infectious** [ɪn'fɛkʃəs] *adj*
(disease) infettivo/a, contagioso/a;
(person, laughter, enthusiasm)
contagioso/a

infer [ɪn'fəːʳ] *vt*: **to ~ (from)** dedurre
(da), concludere (da)

inferior [ɪn'fɪərɪəʳ] *adj* inferiore;
(goods) di qualità scadente ▷ *n*
inferiore *m/f*; *(in rank)* subalterno/a

infertile [ɪn'fəːtaɪl] *adj* sterile

infertility [ɪnfəː'tɪlɪtɪ] *n* sterilità

infested [ɪn'fɛstɪd] *adj*: **~ (with)**
infestato/a (di)

infinite ['ɪnfɪnɪt] *adj* infinito/a;
infinitely *adv* infinitamente

infirmary [ɪn'fəːmərɪ] *n* ospedale *m*;
(in school, factory) infermeria

inflamed [ɪn'fleɪmd] *adj*
infiammato/a

inflammation [ɪnflə'meɪʃən] *n*
infiammazione *f*

inflatable [ɪn'fleɪtəbl] *adj*
gonfiabile

inflate [ɪn'fleɪt] *vt (tyre, balloon)*
gonfiare; *(fig)* esagerare; gonfiare;
inflation [ɪn'fleɪʃən] *n* (Econ)
inflazione *f*

inflexible [ɪn'flɛksɪbl] *adj*
inflessibile, rigido/a

inflict [ɪn'flɪkt] *vt*: **to ~ on**
infliggere a

influence ['ɪnfluəns] *n* influenza
▷ *vt* influenzare; **under the ~ of
alcohol** sotto l'influenza *or* l'effetto
dell'alcool; **influential** [ɪnflu'ɛnʃl]
adj influente

influx ['ɪnflʌks] *n* afflusso

info ['ɪnfəu] *n* (col) = **information**

inform [ɪn'fɔːm] vt: **to ~ sb (of)** informare qn (di) ▷ vi: **to ~ on sb** denunciare qn

informal [ɪn'fɔːml] adj informale; (announcement, invitation) non ufficiale

information [ɪnfə'meɪʃən] n informazioni fpl; particolari mpl; **a piece of ~** un'informazione; **information office** n ufficio m informazioni inv; **information technology** n informatica

informative [ɪn'fɔːmətɪv] adj istruttivo/a

infra-red [ɪnfrə'rɛd] adj infrarosso/a

infrastructure ['ɪnfrəstrʌktʃəʳ] n infrastruttura

infrequent [ɪn'friːkwənt] adj infrequente, raro/a

infuriate [ɪn'fjuərɪeɪt] vt rendere furioso/a

infuriating [ɪn'fjuərɪeɪtɪŋ] adj molto irritante

ingenious [ɪn'dʒiːnjəs] adj ingegnoso/a

ingredient [ɪn'griːdɪənt] n ingrediente m; elemento

inhabit [ɪn'hæbɪt] vt abitare; **inhabitant** [ɪn'hæbɪtnt] n abitante m/f

inhale [ɪn'heɪl] vt inalare ▷ vi (in smoking) aspirare; **inhaler** n inalatore m

inherent [ɪn'hɪərənt] adj: **~ (in or to)** inerente (a)

inherit [ɪn'hɛrɪt] vt ereditare; **inheritance** n eredità

inhibit [ɪn'hɪbɪt] vt (Psych) inibire; **inhibition** [ɪnhɪ'bɪʃən] n inibizione f

initial [ɪ'nɪʃl] adj iniziale ▷ n iniziale f ▷ vt siglare; **initials** npl (of name) iniziali fpl; (as signature) sigla; **initially** adv inizialmente, all'inizio

initiate [ɪ'nɪʃɪeɪt] vt (start) avviare; intraprendere; iniziare; (person) iniziare; **to ~ sb into a secret** mettere qn a parte di un segreto; **to**

~ proceedings against sb (Law) intentare causa a or contro qn

initiative [ɪ'nɪʃətɪv] n iniziativa

inject [ɪn'dʒɛkt] vt (liquid) iniettare; (person) fare un'iniezione a; (money): **to ~ sb with sth** fare a qn un'iniezione di qc; **to ~ into** immettere in; **injection** [ɪn'dʒɛkʃən] n iniezione f, puntura

injure ['ɪndʒəʳ] vt ferire; (damage: reputation etc) nuocere a; **injured** adj ferito/a; **injury** ['ɪndʒərɪ] n ferita

injustice [ɪn'dʒʌstɪs] n ingiustizia

ink [ɪŋk] n inchiostro; **ink-jet printer** ['ɪŋkdʒɛt-] n stampante f a getto d'inchiostro

inland adj ['ɪnlənd] interno/a ▷ adv [ɪn'lænd] all'interno; **Inland Revenue** n (BRIT) Fisco

in-laws ['ɪnlɔːz] npl suoceri mpl; famiglia del marito (or della moglie)

inmate ['ɪnmeɪt] n (in prison) carcerato/a; (in asylum) ricoverato/a

inn [ɪn] n locanda

inner ['ɪnəʳ] adj interno/a, interiore; **inner city** n centro di una zona urbana

inning ['ɪnɪŋ] n (US Baseball) ripresa; **~s** (Cricket) turno di battuta

innocence ['ɪnəsns] n innocenza

innocent ['ɪnəsnt] adj innocente

innovation [ɪnəu'veɪʃən] n innovazione f

innovative ['ɪnəu'veɪtɪv] adj innovativo/a

in-patient ['ɪnpeɪʃənt] n ricoverato/a

input ['ɪnput] n input m

inquest ['ɪnkwɛst] n inchiesta

inquire [ɪn'kwaɪəʳ] vi informarsi ▷ vt domandare, informarsi di or su; **inquiry** n domanda; (Law) indagine f, investigazione f; **"inquiries"** "informazioni"

ins. abbr = **inches**

insane [ɪn'seɪn] adj matto/a, pazzo/a; (Med) alienato/a

insanity [ɪnˈsænɪtɪ] n follia; (Med) alienazione f mentale

insect [ˈɪnsɛkt] n insetto; **insect repellent** n insettifugo

insecure [ɪnsɪˈkjuəʳ] adj malsicuro/a; (person) insicuro/a

insecurity [ɪnsɪˈkjuərɪtɪ] n mancanza di sicurezza

insensitive [ɪnˈsɛnsɪtɪv] adj insensibile

insert [ɪnˈsəːt] vt inserire, introdurre

inside [ɪnˈsaɪd] n interno, parte f interiore ▷ adj interno/a, interiore ▷ adv dentro, all'interno ▷ prep dentro, all'interno di; (of time): **~ 10 minutes** entro 10 minuti; **insides** npl (col) ventre m; **~ out** adv alla rovescia; **to turn sth ~ out** rivoltare qc; **to know sth ~ out** conoscere qc a fondo; **inside lane** n (Aut) corsia di marcia

insight [ˈɪnsaɪt] n acume m, perspicacia; (glimpse, idea) percezione f

insignificant [ɪnsɪɡˈnɪfɪknt] adj insignificante

insincere [ɪnsɪnˈsɪəʳ] adj insincero/a

insist [ɪnˈsɪst] vi insistere; **to ~ on doing** insistere per fare; **to ~ that** insistere perché + sub; (claim) sostenere che; **insistent** adj insistente

insomnia [ɪnˈsɒmnɪə] n insonnia

inspect [ɪnˈspɛkt] vt ispezionare; (BRIT: ticket) controllare; **inspection** [ɪnˈspɛkʃən] n ispezione f; controllo; **inspector** n ispettore/trice; (BRIT: on buses, trains) controllore m

inspiration [ɪnspəˈreɪʃən] n ispirazione f; **inspire** [ɪnˈspaɪəʳ] vt ispirare; **inspiring** adj stimolante

instability [ɪnstəˈbɪlɪtɪ] n instabilità

install [ɪnˈstɔːl], (US) **instal** vt installare; **installation** [ɪnstəˈleɪʃən] n installazione f

instalment, (US) **installment** [ɪnˈstɔːlmənt] n rata; (of TV serial etc)

puntata; **in ~s** (pay) a rate; (receive) una parte per volta; (publication) a fascicoli

instance [ˈɪnstəns] n esempio, caso; **for ~** per or ad esempio; **in the first ~** in primo luogo

instant [ˈɪnstənt] n istante m, attimo ▷ adj immediato/a; urgente; (coffee, food) in polvere; **instantly** adv immediatamente, subito; **instant messaging** n messaggeria istantanea

instead [ɪnˈstɛd] adv invece; **~ of** invece di

instinct [ˈɪnstɪŋkt] n istinto; **instinctive** adj istintivo/a

institute [ˈɪnstɪtjuːt] n istituto ▷ vt istituire, stabilire; (inquiry) avviare; (proceedings) iniziare

institution [ɪnstɪˈtjuːʃən] n istituzione f; istituto (d'istruzione); istituto (psichiatrico)

instruct [ɪnˈstrʌkt] vt: **to ~ sb in sth** insegnare qc a qn; **to ~ sb to do** dare ordini a qn di fare; **instruction** [ɪnˈstrʌkʃən] n istruzione f; **instructions (for use)** istruzioni per l'uso; **instructor** n istruttore/trice; (for skiing) maestro/a

instrument [ˈɪnstrumənt] n strumento; **instrumental** [ɪnstruˈmɛntl] adj (Mus) strumentale; **to be instrumental in sth/in doing sth** contribuire fattivamente a qc/a fare qc

insufficient [ɪnsəˈfɪʃənt] adj insufficiente

insulate [ˈɪnsjuleɪt] vt isolare; **insulation** [ɪnsjuˈleɪʃən] n isolamento

insulin [ˈɪnsjulɪn] n insulina

insult n [ˈɪnsʌlt] insulto, affronto ▷ vt [ɪnˈsʌlt] insultare; **insulting** adj offensivo/a, ingiurioso/a

insurance [ɪnˈʃuərəns] n assicurazione f; **fire/life ~** assicurazione contro gli incendi/sulla vita; **insurance company** n società

i

di assicurazioni; **insurance policy** n polizza d'assicurazione

insure [ɪnˈʃuəʳ] vt assicurare

intact [ɪnˈtækt] adj intatto/a

intake [ˈɪnteɪk] n (Tech) immissione f; (of food) consumo; (BRIT: of pupils etc) afflusso

integral [ˈɪntɪɡrəl] adj integrale; (part) integrante

integrate [ˈɪntɪɡreɪt] vt integrare ▷ vi integrarsi

integrity [ɪnˈtɛɡrɪtɪ] n integrità

intellect [ˈɪntəlɛkt] n intelletto; **intellectual** [ɪntəˈlɛktjuəl] adj, n intellettuale (m/f)

intelligence [ɪnˈtɛlɪdʒəns] n intelligenza; (Mil etc) informazioni fpl

intelligent [ɪnˈtɛlɪdʒənt] adj intelligente

intend [ɪnˈtɛnd] vt (gift etc): **to ~ sth for** destinare qc a; **to ~ to do** aver l'intenzione di fare

intense [ɪnˈtɛns] adj intenso/a; (person) di forti sentimenti

intensify [ɪnˈtɛnsɪfaɪ] vt intensificare

intensity [ɪnˈtɛnsɪtɪ] n intensità

intensive [ɪnˈtɛnsɪv] adj intensivo/a; **intensive care** n terapia intensiva; **intensive care unit** n reparto terapia intensiva

intent [ɪnˈtɛnt] n intenzione f ▷ adj: **~ (on)** intento/a (a), immerso/a (in); **to all ~s and purposes** a tutti gli effetti; **to be ~ on doing sth** essere deciso a fare qc

intention [ɪnˈtɛnʃən] n intenzione f; **intentional** adj intenzionale, deliberato/a

interact [ɪntərˈækt] vi interagire; **interaction** [ɪntərˈækʃən] n azione f reciproca, interazione f; **interactive** adj (Comput) interattivo/a

intercept [ɪntəˈsɛpt] vt intercettare; (person) fermare

interchange n [ˈɪntətʃeɪndʒ] (exchange) scambio; (on motorway) incrocio pluridirezionale

intercourse [ˈɪntəkɔːs] n rapporti mpl

interest [ˈɪntrɪst] n interesse m; (Comm: stake, share) interessi mpl ▷ vt interessare; **interested** adj interessato/a; **to be interested in** interessarsi di; **interesting** adj interessante; **interest rate** n tasso di interesse

interface [ˈɪntəfeɪs] n (Comput) interfaccia

interfere [ɪntəˈfɪəʳ] vi: **to ~ (in)** (quarrel, other people's business) immischiarsi (in); **to ~ with** (object) toccare; (plans, duty) interferire con; **interference** [ɪntəˈfɪərəns] n interferenza

interim [ˈɪntərɪm] adj provvisorio/a ▷ n: **in the ~** nel frattempo

interior [ɪnˈtɪərɪəʳ] n interno; (of country) entroterra ▷ adj interno/a; (minister) degli Interni; **interior design** n architettura d'interni

intermediate [ɪntəˈmiːdɪət] adj intermedio/a

intermission [ɪntəˈmɪʃən] n pausa; (Theat, Cine) intermissione f, intervallo

intern vt [ɪnˈtəːn] internare ▷ n [ˈɪntəːn] (US) medico interno

internal [ɪnˈtəːnl] adj interno/a; **Internal Revenue, Internal Revenue Service** n (US) Fisco

international [ɪntəˈnæʃənl] adj internazionale ▷ n (BRIT Sport) incontro internazionale

Internet [ˈɪntənɛt] n: **the ~** Internet f; **Internet café** n cybercaffè m inv; **Internet Service Provider** n Provider m inv; **Internet user** n utente m/f Internet

interpret [ɪnˈtəːprɪt] vt interpretare ▷ vi fare da interprete; **interpretation** [ɪntəːprɪˈteɪʃən] n interpretazione f; **interpreter** n interprete m/f

interrogate [ɪnˈtɛrəugeɪt] vt interrogare; **interrogation**

[ɪntɛrəu'geɪʃən] n interrogazione f; (of suspect etc) interrogatorio

interrogative [ɪntə'rɔgətɪv] adj interrogativo/a ▷ n (Ling) interrogativo

interrupt [ɪntə'rʌpt] vt, vi interrompere; **interruption** [ɪntə'rʌpʃən] n interruzione f

intersection [ɪntə'sɛkʃən] n intersezione f; (of roads) incrocio

interstate ['ɪntərsteɪt] (US) n fra stati

interval ['ɪntəvl] n intervallo; **at ~s** a intervalli

intervene [ɪntə'viːn] vi (time) intercorrere; (event, person) intervenire

interview ['ɪntəvjuː] n (Radio, TV etc) intervista; (for job) colloquio ▷ vt intervistare; avere un colloquio con; **interviewer** n intervistatore/trice

intimate adj ['ɪntɪmət] intimo/a; (knowledge) profondo/a ▷ vt ['ɪntɪmeɪt] lasciar capire

intimidate [ɪn'tɪmɪdeɪt] vt intimidire, intimorire

intimidating [ɪn'tɪmɪdeɪtɪŋ] adj (sight) spaventoso/a; (appearance, figure) minaccioso/a

into ['ɪntu] prep dentro, in; **come ~ the house** entra in casa; **he worked late ~ the night** lavorò fino a tarda notte; **~ Italian** in italiano

intolerant [ɪn'tɔlərnt] adj: **~ (of)** intollerante (di)

intranet ['ɪntrənɛt] n Intranet f

intransitive [ɪn'trænsɪtɪv] adj intransitivo/a

intricate ['ɪntrɪkət] adj intricato/a, complicato/a

intrigue [ɪn'triːg] n intrigo ▷ vt affascinare; **intriguing** adj affascinante

introduce [ɪntrə'djuːs] vt introdurre; **to ~ sb (to sb)** presentare qn (a qn); **to ~ sb to** (pastime, technique) iniziare qn a; **introduction** [ɪntrə'dʌkʃən] n introduzione f; (of person)

presentazione f; (to new experience) iniziazione f; **introductory** adj introduttivo/a

intrude [ɪn'truːd] vi (person) intromettersi; **to ~ on**; intromettersi in; **intruder** n intruso/a

intuition [ɪntjuː'ɪʃən] n intuizione f

inundate ['ɪnʌndeɪt] vt: **to ~ with** inondare di

invade [ɪn'veɪd] vt invadere

invalid n ['ɪnvəlɪd] malato/a; (with disability) invalido/a ▷ adj [ɪn'vælɪd] (not valid) invalido/a, non valido/a

invaluable [ɪn'væljuəbl] adj prezioso/a; inestimabile

invariably [ɪn'vɛərɪəblɪ] adv invariabilmente; sempre

invasion [ɪn'veɪʒən] n invasione f

invent [ɪn'vɛnt] vt inventare; **invention** [ɪn'vɛnʃən] n invenzione f; **inventor** n inventore m

inventory ['ɪnvəntrɪ] n inventario

inverted commas [ɪn'vəːtɪd-] npl (BRIT) virgolette fpl

invest [ɪn'vɛst] vt investire ▷ vi: **to ~ in** investire in

investigate [ɪn'vɛstɪgeɪt] vt investigare, indagare; (crime) fare indagini su; **investigation** [ɪnvɛstɪ'geɪʃən] n investigazione f; (of crime) indagine f

investigator [ɪn'vɛstɪgeɪtər] n investigatore/trice; **a private ~** un investigatore privato, un detective

investment [ɪn'vɛstmənt] n investimento

investor [ɪn'vɛstər] n investitore/trice; (shareholder) azionista m/f

invisible [ɪn'vɪzɪbl] adj invisibile

invitation [ɪnvɪ'teɪʃən] n invito

invite [ɪn'vaɪt] vt invitare; (opinions etc) sollecitare; **inviting** adj invitante, attraente

invoice ['ɪnvɔɪs] n fattura ▷ vt fatturare

involve [ɪn'vɔlv] vt (entail) richiedere, comportare; (associate): **to ~ sb (in)** implicare qn (in); coinvolgere qn (in); **involved** adj involuto/a, complesso/a; **to be involved in** essere coinvolto/a in; **involvement** n implicazione f; coinvolgimento

inward ['ɪnwəd] adj (movement) verso l'interno; (thought, feeling) interiore, intimo/a ▷ adv verso l'interno

iPod® ['aɪpɒd] n iPod® m inv

IQ n abbr (= intelligence quotient) quoziente m d'intelligenza

IRA n abbr (= Irish Republican Army) I.R.A. f

Iran [ɪ'rɑːn] n Iran m; **Iranian** [ɪ'reɪnɪən] adj, n iraniano/a

Iraq [ɪ'rɑːk] n Iraq m; **Iraqi** adj, n iracheno/a

Ireland ['aɪələnd] n Irlanda

iris ['aɪrɪs, -ɪz] n (pl **irises**) iride f; (Bot) giaggiolo, iride

Irish ['aɪrɪʃ] adj irlandese ▷ npl: **the ~** gli Irlandesi; **Irishman** n (irreg) irlandese m; **Irish Sea** n: **the Irish Sea** il mar d'Irlanda; **Irishwoman** n (irreg) irlandese f

iron ['aɪən] n ferro m; (for clothes) ferro da stiro ▷ adj di or in ferro ▷ vt (clothes) stirare

ironic(al) [aɪ'rɒnɪk(l)] adj ironico/a; **ironically** adv ironicamente

ironing ['aɪənɪŋ] n (act) stirare m; (clothes) roba da stirare; **ironing board** n asse f da stiro

irony ['aɪrənɪ] n ironia

irrational [ɪ'ræʃənl] adj irrazionale

irregular [ɪ'rɛɡjuləʳ] adj irregolare

irrelevant [ɪ'rɛləvənt] adj non pertinente

irresistible [ɪrɪ'zɪstɪbl] adj irresistibile

irresponsible [ɪrɪ'spɒnsɪbl] adj irresponsabile

irrigation [ɪrɪ'ɡeɪʃən] n irrigazione f

irritable ['ɪrɪtəbl] adj irritabile

irritate ['ɪrɪteɪt] vt irritare; **irritating** adj (person, sound etc) irritante; **irritation** [ɪrɪ'teɪʃən] n irritazione f

IRS n abbr (US) = **Internal Revenue Service**

is [ɪz] vb see **be**

ISDN n abbr (= Integrated Services Digital Network) ISDN f

Islam ['ɪzlɑːm] n Islam m; **Islamic** [ɪz'læmɪk] adj islamico/a

island ['aɪlənd] n isola; **islander** n isolano/a

isle [aɪl] n isola

isn't ['ɪznt] = **is not**

isolated ['aɪsəleɪtɪd] adj isolato/a

isolation [aɪsə'leɪʃən] n isolamento

ISP n abbr (Comput: = internet service provider) provider m inv

Israel ['ɪzreɪl] n Israele m; **Israeli** [ɪz'reɪlɪ] adj, n israeliano/a

issue ['ɪʃuː] n questione f, problema m; (of banknotes etc) emissione f; (of newspaper etc) numero ▷ vt (statement) rilasciare; (rations, equipment) distribuire; (book) pubblicare; (banknotes, cheques, stamps) emettere; **at ~** in gioco, in discussione; **to take ~ with sb (over sth)** prendere posizione contro qn (riguardo a qc); **to make an ~ of sth** fare un problema di qc

IT n abbr = **information technology**

KEYWORD

it [ɪt] pron **1** (specific: subject) esso/a; (: direct object) lo (la), l'; (: indirect object) gli (le); **where's my book? — it's on the table** dov'è il mio libro? — è sulla tavola; **I can't find it** non lo (or la) trovo; **give it to me** dammelo (or dammela); **about/ from/of it** ne; **I spoke to him about it** gliene ho parlato; **what did you learn from it?** quale insegnamento ne hai tratto?; **I'm proud of it** ne sono fiero; **put the book in it** mettici il libro; **did you go to it?** ci sei andato?

2 (impers): **it's raining** piove; **it's Friday tomorrow** domani è venerdì; **it's 6 o'clock** sono le 6; **who is it? — it's me** chi è? — sono io

Italian [ɪ'tæljən] adj italiano/a ▷ n italiano/a; (Ling) italiano; **the ~s** gli Italiani

italic [ɪ'tælɪk] adj corsivo/a; **italics** npl corsivo

Italy ['ɪtəlɪ] n Italia

ITC n abbr (BRIT: = Independent Television Commission) organo di controllo sulle reti televisive

itch [ɪtʃ] n prurito ▷ vi (person) avere il prurito; (part of body) prudere; **to be ~ing to do** avere una gran voglia di fare; **itchy** adj che prude; **my back is itchy** ho prurito alla schiena

it'd ['ɪtd] = **it would; it had**

item ['aɪtəm] n articolo; (on agenda) punto; (also: **news ~**) notizia

itinerary [aɪ'tɪnərərɪ] n itinerario

it'll ['ɪtl] = **it will; it shall**

its [ɪts] adj il (la) suo/a, i (le) suoi (sue)

it's [ɪts] = **it is; it has**

itself [ɪt'sɛlf] pron (emphatic) esso/a stesso/a; (reflexive) si

ITV n abbr (BRIT: = Independent Television) rete televisiva indipendente

I've [aɪv] = **I have**

ivory ['aɪvərɪ] n avorio

ivy ['aɪvɪ] n edera

jab [dʒæb] vt dare colpetti a; **to ~ sth into** affondare or piantare qc dentro ▷ n (Med: col) puntura

jack [dʒæk] n (Aut) cricco; (Cards) fante m

jacket ['dʒækɪt] n giacca; (of book) copertura; **jacket potato** n patata cotta al forno con la buccia

jackpot ['dʒækpɔt] n primo premio (in denaro)

Jacuzzi® [dʒə'kuːzɪ] n vasca per idromassaggio Jacuzzi®

jagged ['dʒægɪd] adj seghettato/a; (cliffs etc) frastagliato/a

jail [dʒeɪl] n prigione f ▷ vt mandare in prigione; **jail sentence** n condanna al carcere

jam [dʒæm] n marmellata; (also: **traffic ~**) ingorgo; (col) pasticcio ▷ vt (passage etc) ingombrare, ostacolare; (mechanism, drawer etc) bloccare; (Radio) disturbare con interferenze ▷ vi incepparsi; **to ~**

sth into forzare qc dentro; infilare qc a forza dentro

Jamaica [dʒə'meɪkə] n Giamaica

jammed [dʒæmd] adj (door) bloccato/a; (rifle, printer) inceppato/a

Jan. abbr (= January) gen., genn.

janitor ['dʒænɪtə'] n (caretaker) portiere m; (: Scol) bidello

January ['dʒænjuəri] n gennaio

Japan [dʒə'pæn] n Giappone m; **Japanese** [dʒæpə'ni:z] adj giapponese ▷ n (pl inv) giapponese m/f; (Ling) giapponese m

jar [dʒɑː'] n (container) barattolo, vasetto ▷ vi (sound) stridere; (colours etc) stonare

jargon ['dʒɑːgən] n gergo

javelin ['dʒævlɪn] n giavellotto

jaw [dʒɔː] n mascella

jazz [dʒæz] n jazz m

jealous ['dʒeləs] adj geloso/a; **jealousy** n gelosia

jeans [dʒiːnz] npl (blue-)jeans mpl

Jello® ['dʒeləu] n (US) gelatina di frutta

jelly ['dʒelɪ] n gelatina; **jellyfish** n medusa

jeopardize ['dʒepədaɪz] vt mettere in pericolo

jerk [dʒəːk] n sobbalzo, scossa, sussulto; (col) povero/a scemo/a ▷ vt dare una scossa a ▷ vi (vehicles) sobbalzare

Jersey ['dʒəːzɪ] n Jersey m

jersey ['dʒəːzɪ] n maglia; (fabric) jersey m

Jesus ['dʒiːzəs] n Gesù m

jet [dʒet] n (of gas, liquid) getto; (Aviat) aviogetto; **jet lag** n (problemi mpl dovuti allo) sbalzo dei fusi orari; **jet-ski** vi acquascooter m inv

jetty ['dʒetɪ] n molo

Jew [dʒuː] n ebreo

jewel ['dʒuːəl] n gioiello; **jeweller** (US) **jeweler** n orefice m, gioielliere/a; **jeweller's shop** oreficeria, gioielleria; **jewellery**, (US) **jewelry** n gioielli mpl; **jewelry store** (US) oreficeria, gioielleria

Jewish ['dʒuːɪʃ] adj ebreo/a, ebraico/a

jigsaw ['dʒɪgsɔː] n (also: ~ puzzle) puzzle m inv

job [dʒɔb] n lavoro; (employment) impiego, posto; **that's not my ~** non è compito mio; **it's a good ~ that …** meno male che …; **just the ~!** proprio quello che ci vuole!; **job centre** (BRIT) n ufficio di collocamento; **jobless** adj senza lavoro, disoccupato/a

jockey ['dʒɔkɪ] n fantino, jockey m inv ▷ vi: **to ~ for position** manovrare per una posizione di vantaggio

jog [dʒɔg] vt urtare ▷ vi (Sport) fare footing, fare jogging; **to ~ along** trottare; (fig) andare avanti pian piano; **to ~ sb's memory** rinfrescare la memoria di qn; **jogging** n footing m, jogging m

join [dʒɔɪn] vt unire, congiungere; (become member of) iscriversi a; (meet) raggiungere; riunirsi a ▷ vi (roads, rivers) confluire ▷ n giuntura; **join in** vt fus unirsi a ▷ vi partecipare; **join up** vi incontrarsi; (Mil) arruolarsi

joiner ['dʒɔɪnə'] n (BRIT) falegname m

joint [dʒɔɪnt] n (Tech) giuntura; giunto; (Anat) articolazione f, giuntura; (BRIT Culin) arrosto; (col: place) locale m; (: of cannabis) spinello ▷ adj comune; **joint account** n (at bank etc) conto comune; **jointly** adv in comune, insieme

joke [dʒəuk] n scherzo; (funny story) barzelletta; (also: **practical ~**) beffa ▷ vi scherzare; **to play a ~ on** fare uno scherzo a; **joker** n (Cards) matta, jolly m inv

jolly ['dʒɔlɪ] adj allegro/a, gioioso/a ▷ adv (BRIT col) veramente, proprio

jolt [dʒəult] n scossa, sobbalzo ▷ vt urtare

Jordan ['dʒɔːdən] n (country) Giordania; (river) Giordano

journal ['dʒəːnl] n giornale m; (periodical) rivista; (diary) diario;

journalism n giornalismo;
journalist n giornalista m/f

journey ['dʒə:nɪ] n viaggio; (distance covered) tragitto; **how was your ~?** com'è andato il viaggio?; **the ~ takes two hours** il viaggio dura due ore

joy [dʒɔɪ] n gioia; **joyrider** ['dʒɔɪraɪdə'] n chi ruba una macchina per andare a farsi un giro; **joy stick** ['dʒɔɪstɪk] n (Aviat) barra di comando; (Comput) joystick m inv

Jr. abbr = **junior**

judge [dʒʌdʒ] n giudice m/f ▷ vt giudicare

judo ['dʒu:dəu] n judo

jug [dʒʌg] n brocca, bricco

juggle ['dʒʌgl] vi fare giochi di destrezza; **juggler** n giocoliere/a

juice [dʒu:s] n succo; **juicy** ['dʒu:sɪ] adj succoso/a

Jul. abbr (= July) lug., lu.

July [dʒu:'laɪ] n luglio

jumble ['dʒʌmbl] n miscuglio ▷ vt (also: **~ up, ~ together**) mischiare; **jumble sale** (BRIT) n ≈ vendita di beneficenza

> **JUMBLE SALE**
>
> La jumble sale è un mercatino dove
> vengono venduti vari oggetti,
> per lo più di seconda mano; viene
> organizzata in chiese, scuole o
> circoli ricreativi. I proventi delle
> vendite vengono devoluti in
> beneficenza o usati per una giusta
> causa.

jumbo ['dʒʌmbəu] adj: **~ jet** jumbo-jet m inv; **~ size** formato gigante

jump [dʒʌmp] vi saltare, balzare; (start) sobbalzare; (increase) rincarare ▷ vt saltare ▷ n salto, balzo; sobbalzo

jumper ['dʒʌmpə'] n (BRIT: pullover) maglione m; (US: pinafore dress) scamiciato

jump leads, (US) **jumper cables** npl cavi mpl per batteria

Jun. abbr = **junior**

junction ['dʒʌŋkʃən] n (BRIT: of roads) incrocio; (of rails) nodo ferroviario

June [dʒu:n] n giugno

jungle ['dʒʌŋgl] n giungla

junior ['dʒu:nɪə'] adj, n: **he's ~ to me (by 2 years), he's my ~ (by 2 years)** è più giovane di me (di 2 anni); **he's ~ to me** (seniority) è al di sotto di me, ho più anzianità di lui; **junior high school** n (US) scuola media (da 12 a 15 anni); **junior school** n (BRIT) scuola elementare (da 8 a 11 anni)

junk [dʒʌŋk] n cianfrusaglie fpl; (cheap goods) robaccia; **junk food** n porcherie fpl

junkie ['dʒʌŋkɪ] n (col) drogato/a

junk mail n pubblicità f inv in cassetta

Jupiter ['dʒu:pɪtə'] n (planet) Giove m

jurisdiction [dʒuərɪs'dɪkʃən] n giurisdizione f; **it falls** or **comes within/outside our ~** è/non è di nostra competenza

jury ['dʒuərɪ] n giuria

just [dʒʌst] adj giusto/a ▷ adv: **he's ~ done it/left** lo ha appena fatto/è appena partito; **~ right** proprio giusto; **~ 2 o'clock** le 2 precise; **she's ~ as clever as you** è in gamba proprio quanto te; **~ as I arrived** proprio mentre arrivavo; **it was ~ before/enough/here** era poco prima/appena assai/proprio qui; **it's ~ me** sono solo io; **~ missed/caught** appena perso/preso; **~ listen to this!** senta un po' questo!; **it's ~ as well you didn't go** meno male che non ci sei andato

justice ['dʒʌstɪs] n giustizia

justification [dʒʌstɪfɪ'keɪʃən] n giustificazione f; (Typ) giustezza

justify ['dʒʌstɪfaɪ] vt giustificare

jut [dʒʌt] vi (also: **~ out**) sporgersi

juvenile ['dʒu:vənaɪl] adj giovane, giovanile; (court) dei minorenni; (books) per ragazzi ▷ n giovane m/f, minorenne m/f

K *n abbr* (= *one thousand*) mille ▷ *abbr*
(= *kilobyte*) K
kangaroo [kæŋgə'ru:] *n* canguro
karaoke [kɑ:rə'əuki] *n* karaoke *m inv*
karate [kə'rɑ:ti] *n* karate *m*
kebab [kə'bæb] *n* spiedino
keel [ki:l] *n* chiglia; **on an even ~** (*fig*)
in uno stato normale
keen [ki:n] *adj* (*interest, desire*)
vivo/a; (*eye, intelligence*) acuto/a;
(*competition*) serrato/a; (*edge*)
affilato/a; (*eager*) entusiasta; **to be
~ to do** *or* **on doing sth** avere una
gran voglia di fare qc; **to be ~ on sth**
essere appassionato/a di qc; **to be ~
on sb** avere un debole per qn
keep (*pt, pp* **kept**) [ki:p, kɛpt] *vt*
tenere; (*hold back*) trattenere;
(*feed: one's family etc*) mantenere,
sostentare; (*a promise*) mantenere;
(*chickens, bees, pigs etc*) allevare ▷ *vi*
(*food*) mantenersi; (*remain: in a certain
state or place*) restare ▷ *n* (*of castle*)
maschio; (*food etc*): **enough for his
~** abbastanza per vitto e alloggio;
to ~ doing sth continuare a fare
qc; fare qc di continuo; **to ~ sb
from doing/sth from happening**
impedire a qn di fare/che qc succeda;
to ~ sb busy/a place tidy tenere qn
occupato/a/un luogo in ordine; **to ~
sth to o.s.** tenere qc per sé; **to ~ sth
(back) from sb** celare qc a qn; **to ~
time** (*clock*) andar bene; **keep away**
vt: **to ~ sth/sb away from sb** tenere
qc/qn lontano da qn ▷ *vi*: **to ~ away
(from)** stare lontano (da); **keep back**
vt (*crowds, tears, money*) trattenere
▷ *vi* tenersi indietro; **keep off** *vt*
(*dog, person*) tenere lontano da ▷ *vi*
stare alla larga; **~ your hands off!**
non toccare!, giù le mani!; **"~ off the
grass"** "non calpestare l'erba"; **keep
on** *vi*: **to ~ on doing** continuare a
fare; **to ~ on (about sth)** continuare
a insistere (su qc); **keep out** *vt* tener
fuori; **"~ out"** "vietato l'accesso";
keep up *vt* continuare, mantenere
▷ *vi*: **to ~ up with** tener dietro a,
andare di pari passo con; (*work etc*)
farcela a seguire; **keeper** *n* custode
m/f, guardiano/a; **keeping** *n* (*care*)
custodia; **in keeping with** in
armonia con; in accordo con; **keeps**
n: **for keeps** (*col*) per sempre
kennel ['kɛnl] *n* canile *m*; **kennels** *npl*
canile *m*; **to put a dog in ~s** mettere
un cane al canile
Kenya ['kɛnjə] *n* Kenia *m*
kept [kɛpt] *pt, pp of* **keep**
kerb [kə:b] *n* (*BRIT*) orlo del
marciapiede
kerosene ['kɛrəsi:n] *n* cherosene *m*
ketchup ['kɛtʃəp] *n* ketchup *m inv*
kettle ['kɛtl] *n* bollitore *m*
key [ki:] *n* (*gen, Mus*) chiave *f*; (*of piano,
typewriter*) tasto ▷ *cpd* chiave *inv*;
key in *vt* (*text*) digitare; **keyboard**
n tastiera; **keyhole** *n* buco della
serratura; **keypad** *n* tastierino;
key ring *n* portachiavi *m inv*

kg *abbr* (= *kilogram*) Kg
khaki ['kɑːkɪ] *adj, n* cachi (*m*)
kick [kɪk] *vt* calciare, dare calci a; (*col: habit etc*) liberarsi di ▷ *vi* (*horse*) tirar calci ▷ *n* calcio; (*col: thrill*): **he does it for ~s** lo fa giusto per il piacere di farlo; **kick off** *vi* (*Sport*) dare il primo calcio; **kick-off** *n* (*Sport*) dinizio
kid [kɪd] *n* (*col: child*) ragazzino/a; (*animal, leather*) capretto ▷ *vi* (*col*) scherzare
kidnap ['kɪdnæp] *vt* rapire, sequestrare; **kidnapping** *n* sequestro (di persona)
kidney ['kɪdnɪ] *n* (*Anat*) rene *m*; (*Culin*) rognone *m*; **kidney bean** *n* fagiolo borlotto
kill [kɪl] *vt* uccidere, ammazzare ▷ *n* uccisione *f*; **killer** *n* uccisore *m*, killer *m inv*; assassino/a; **killing** *n* assassinio; (*col*): **to make a killing** fare un bel colpo
kiln [kɪln] *n* forno
kilo ['kiːləu] *n abbr* chilo; **kilobyte** *n* (*Comput*) kilobyte *m inv*; **kilogram(me)** ['kɪləugræm] *n* chilogrammo; **kilometre**, (*US*) **kilometer** ['kɪləmiːtə'] *n* chilometro; **kilowatt** ['kɪləuwɔt] *n* chilowatt *m inv*
kilt [kɪlt] *n* gonnellino scozzese
kin [kɪn] *n see* **next of kin**
kind [kaɪnd] *adj* gentile, buono/a ▷ *n* sorta, specie *f*; (*species*) genere *m*; **what ~ of ...?** che tipo di ...?; **to be two of a ~** essere molto simili; **in ~** (*Comm*) in natura
kindergarten ['kɪndəgɑːtn] *n* giardino d'infanzia
kindly ['kaɪndlɪ] *adj* pieno/a di bontà, benevolo/a ▷ *adv* con bontà, gentilmente; **will you ~ ...** vuole ... per favore
kindness ['kaɪndnɪs] *n* bontà, gentilezza
king [kɪŋ] *n* re *m inv*; **kingdom** *n* regno, reame *m*; **kingfisher** *n* martin *m inv* pescatore

king-size(d) ['kɪŋsaɪz(d)] *adj* super *inv*; **king-size(d) bed** *n* letto king-size
kiosk ['kiːɔsk] *n* edicola, chiosco; (BRIT: *also*: **telephone ~**) cabina (telefonica)
kipper ['kɪpə'] *n* aringa affumicata
kiss [kɪs] *n* bacio ▷ *vt* baciare; **to ~ (each other)** baciarsi; **~ of life** respirazione *f* bocca a bocca
kit [kɪt] *n* equipaggiamento, corredo; (*set of tools etc*) attrezzi *mpl*; (*for assembly*) scatola di montaggio
kitchen ['kɪtʃɪn] *n* cucina
kite [kaɪt] *n* (*toy*) aquilone *m*
kitten ['kɪtn] *n* gattino/a, micino/a
kiwi ['kiːwiː], **kiwi fruit** *n* kiwi *m inv*
km *abbr* (= *kilometre*) km
km/h *abbr* (= *kilometres per hour*) km/h
knack [næk] *n*: **to have the ~ of** avere l'abilità di
knee [niː] *n* ginocchio; **kneecap** *n* rotula
kneel [niːl] *vi* (*pt, pp* **knelt** [nɛlt]) (*also*: **~ down**) inginocchiarsi
knelt [nɛlt] *pt, pp of* **kneel**
knew [njuː] *pt of* **know**
knickers ['nɪkəz] *npl* (BRIT) mutandine *fpl*
knife [naɪf] *n* (*pl* **knives**) coltello ▷ *vt* accoltellare, dare una coltellata a
knight [naɪt] *n* cavaliere *m*; (*Chess*) cavallo
knit [nɪt] *vt* fare a maglia ▷ *vi* lavorare a maglia; (*broken bones*) saldarsi; **to ~ one's brows** aggrottare le sopracciglia; **knitting** *n* lavoro a maglia; **knitting needle** *n* ferro (da calza); **knitwear** *n* maglieria
knives [naɪvz] *npl of* **knife**
knob [nɔb] *n* bottone *m*; manopola
knock [nɔk] *vt* colpire; urtare; (*fig: col*) criticare ▷ *vi* (*at door etc*): **to ~ at/on** bussare a ▷ *n* bussata; colpo, botta; **knock down** *vt* abbattere; **knock off** *vi* (*col: finish*) smettere (di lavorare) ▷ *vt* (*from price*) far abbassare; (*col: steal*) sgraffignare;

k

knock out vt stendere; (Boxing) mettere K.O.; (defeat) battere; **knock over** vt (object) far cadere; (pedestrian) investire; **knockout** n (Boxing) knock out m inv ▷ cpd a eliminazione

knot [nɔt] n nodo ▷ vt annodare

know [nəu] vt (pt **knew** [njuː], pp **known** [nəun]) sapere; (person, author, place) conoscere; **to ~ how to do** sapere fare; **I don't ~** non lo so; **to ~ about** or **of sth/sb** conoscere qc/qn; **know-all** n sapientone/a; **know-how** n tecnica; pratica; **knowing** adj (look etc) d'intesa; **knowingly** adv (purposely) consapevolmente; (smile, look) con aria d'intesa; **know-it-all** n (US) = **know-all**

knowledge ['nɔlɪdʒ] n consapevolezza; (learning) conoscenza, sapere m; **knowledgeable** adj ben informato/a

known [nəun] pp of **know**

knuckle ['nʌkl] n nocca

koala [kəu'ɑːlə] n (also: ~ **bear**) koala m inv

Koran [kɔ'rɑːn] n Corano

Korea [kə'riːə] n Corea; **Korean** adj, n coreano/a

kosher ['kəuʃər] adj kasher inv

Kosovar, Kosovan ['kɔsəvɑr, 'kɔsəvən] adj kosovaro/a

Kosovo ['kusəvəu] n Kosovo

Kremlin ['krɛmlɪn] n: **the ~** il Cremlino

Kuwait [ku'weɪt] n Kuwait m

L abbr (BRIT) = **learner**

l abbr (= litre) l

lab [læb] n abbr (= laboratory) laboratorio

label ['leɪbl] n etichetta, cartellino; (brand: of record) casa ▷ vt etichettare

labor etc ['leɪbər] (US) = **labour** etc

laboratory [lə'bɔrətərɪ] n laboratorio

Labor Day n (US) festa del lavoro

labor union n (US) sindacato

Labour ['leɪbəʳ] n (BRIT Pol: also: **the ~ Party**) il partito laburista, i laburisti

labour, (US) **labor** ['leɪbəʳ] n (task) lavoro; (workmen) manodopera ▷ vi: **to ~ (at)** lavorare duro(a); **to be in ~** (Med) avere le doglie; **hard ~** lavori mpl forzati; **labourer,** (US) **laborer** ['leɪbərəʳ] n manovale m; **farm labourer** lavoratore m agricolo

lace [leɪs] n merletto, pizzo; (of shoe etc) laccio ▷ vt (shoe: also: **~ up**) allacciare

lack [læk] n mancanza ▷ vt mancare di; **through** or **for ~ of** per mancanza di; **to be ~ing** mancare; **to be ~ing in** mancare di

lacquer ['lækəʳ] n lacca

lacy ['leɪsɪ] adj (like lace) che sembra un pizzo

lad [læd] n ragazzo, giovanotto

ladder ['lædəʳ] n scala; (BRIT: in tights) smagliatura

ladle ['leɪdl] n mestolo

lady ['leɪdɪ] n signora; dama; **L~ Smith** lady Smith; **the ladies' (toilets)** i gabinetti per signore; **ladybird** ['leɪdɪbəːd], (US) **ladybug** ['leɪdɪbʌɡ] n coccinella

lag [læɡ] n (of time) lasso, intervallo ▷ vi (also: **~ behind**) trascinarsi ▷ vt (pipes) rivestire di materiale isolante

lager ['lɑːɡəʳ] n lager m inv

lagoon [ləˈɡuːn] n laguna

laid [leɪd] pt, pp of **lay**

laid-back [leɪdˈbæk] adj (col) rilassato/a, tranquillo/a

lain [leɪn] pp of **lie**

lake [leɪk] n lago

lamb [læm] n agnello

lame [leɪm] adj zoppo/a; (excuse etc) zoppicante

lament [ləˈmɛnt] n lamento ▷ vt lamentare, piangere

lamp [læmp] n lampada; **lamppost** ['læmppəust] (BRIT) n lampione m; **lampshade** ['læmpʃeɪd] n paralume m

land [lænd] n (as opposed to sea) terra (ferma); (country) paese m; (soil) terreno; suolo; (estate) terreni mpl, terre fpl ▷ vi (from ship) sbarcare; (Aviat) atterrare; (fig: fall) cadere ▷ vt (passengers) sbarcare; (goods) scaricare; **to ~ sb with sth** affibbiare qc a qn; **landing** n atterraggio; (of staircase) pianerottolo; **landing card** n carta di sbarco; **landlady** n padrona or proprietaria di casa; **landline** n telefono fisso; **landlord** n padrone m or proprietario di casa; (of pub etc) padrone m; **landmark** n punto di riferimento; (fig) pietra miliare; **landowner** ['lændəunəʳ] n proprietario/a terriero/a; **landscape** n paesaggio; **landslide** n (Geo) frana; (fig: Pol) valanga

lane [leɪn] n (in town) stradina; (Aut, in race) corsia; **"get in ~"** "immettersi in corsia"

language ['læŋɡwɪdʒ] n lingua; (way one speaks) linguaggio; **bad ~** linguaggio volgare; **language laboratory** n laboratorio linguistico

lantern ['læntn] n lanterna

lap [læp] n (of track) giro; **in** or **on one's ~** in grembo ▷ vt (also: **~ up**) papparsi, leccare ▷ vi (waves) sciabordare

lapel [ləˈpɛl] n risvolto

lapse [læps] n lapsus m inv; (longer) caduta ▷ vi (law, act) cadere; (ticket, passport, membership, contract) scadere; **to ~ into bad habits** pigliare cattive abitudini; **~ of time** spazio di tempo

laptop ['læptɔp] n (also: **~ computer**) laptop m inv

lard [lɑːd] n lardo

larder ['lɑːdəʳ] n dispensa

large [lɑːdʒ] adj grande; (person, animal) grosso/a; **at ~** (free) in libertà; (generally) in generale; nell'insieme; **largely** adv in gran parte; **large-scale** adj (map, drawing etc) in grande

scala; (*reforms, business activities*) su
vasta scala
lark [lɑːk] *n* (*bird*) allodola; (*joke*)
scherzo, gioco
larrikin [ˈlærɪkɪn] *n* (AUST, NZ *col*)
furfante *m/f*
laryngitis [lærɪnˈdʒaɪtɪs] *n*
laringite *f*
lasagne [ləˈzænjə] *n* lasagne *fpl*
laser [ˈleɪzəʳ] *n* laser *m*; **laser printer**
n stampante *f* laser *inv*
lash [læʃ] *n* frustata; (*also:* **eye~**)
ciglio ▷ *vt* frustare; (*tie*) legare; **to
~ to/together** legare a insieme;
lash out *vi*: **to ~ out (at** *or* **against
sb/sth)** attaccare violentemente
(qn/qc)
lass [læs] *n* ragazza
last [lɑːst] *adj* ultimo/a; (*week, month,
year*) scorso/a, passato/a ▷ *adv*
per ultimo ▷ *vi* durare; **~ week** la
settimana scorsa; **~ night** ieri sera,
la notte scorsa; **at ~** finalmente, alla
fine; **~ but one** penultimo/a; **lastly**
adv infine, per finire; **last-minute**
adj fatto/a (*or* preso/a *etc*) all'ultimo
momento
latch [lætʃ] *n* chiavistello; (*automatic
lock*) serratura a scatto; **latch on to**
vt fus (*cling to: person*) attaccarsi a,
appiccicarsi a; (: *idea*) afferrare, capire
late [leɪt] *adj* (*not on time*) in ritardo;
(*far on in day etc*) tardi *inv*; tardo/a;
(*former*) ex; (*dead*) defunto/a ▷ *adv*
tardi; (*behind time, schedule*) in
ritardo; **sorry I'm ~** scusi il ritardo;
the flight is two hours ~ il volo
ha due ore di ritardo; **it's too ~** è
troppo tardi; **of ~** di recente; **in the
~ afternoon** nel tardo pomeriggio;
in ~ May verso la fine di maggio;
latecomer *n* ritardatario/a; **lately**
adv recentemente; **later** [ˈleɪtəʳ]
adj (*date etc*) posteriore; (*version etc*)
successivo/a ▷ *adv* più tardi; **later on
today** oggi più tardi; **latest** [ˈleɪtɪst]
adj ultimo/a, più recente; **at the
latest** al più tardi

lather [ˈlɑːðəʳ] *n* schiuma di sapone
▷ *vt* insaponare
Latin [ˈlætɪn] *n* latino ▷ *adj* latino/a;
Latin America *n* America Latina;
Latin American *adj* sudamericano/a
latitude [ˈlætɪtjuːd] *n* latitudine *f*;
(*fig*) libertà d'azione
latter [ˈlætəʳ] *adj* secondo/a; più
recente ▷ *n*: **the ~** quest'ultimo, il
secondo
laugh [lɑːf] *n* risata ▷ *vi* ridere; **laugh
at** *vt fus* (*misfortune etc*) ridere di;
laughter *n* riso; risate *fpl*
launch [lɔːntʃ] *n* (*of rocket, product
etc*) lancio; (*of new ship*) varo; (*also:*
motor ~) lancia ▷ *vt* (*rocket, product*)
lanciare; (*ship, plan*) varare; **launch
into** *vt fus* lanciarsi in
launder [ˈlɔːndəʳ] *vt* lavare e stirare
Launderette® [lɔːnˈdrɛt], (US)
Laundromat® [ˈlɔːndrəmæt] *n*
lavanderia (automatica)
laundry [ˈlɔːndrɪ] *n* lavanderia;
(*clothes*) biancheria; (: *dirty*) panni
mpl da lavare
lava [ˈlɑːvə] *n* lava
lavatory [ˈlævətərɪ] *n* gabinetto
lavender [ˈlævəndəʳ] *n* lavanda
lavish [ˈlævɪʃ] *adj* copioso/a,
abbondante; (*giving freely*): **~ with**
prodigo/a di, largo/a in ▷ *vt*: **to ~ sth
on sb/sth** colmare qn/qc di qc
law [lɔː] *n* legge *f*; **civil/criminal
~** diritto civile/penale; **lawful** *adj*
legale, lecito/a; **lawless** *adj* senza
legge
lawn [lɔːn] *n* tappeto erboso;
lawnmower *n* tosaerba *m inv or f inv*
lawsuit [ˈlɔːsuːt] *n* processo, causa
lawyer [ˈlɔːjəʳ] *n* (*for sales, wills etc*) ≈
notaio; (*partner, in court*) ≈ avvocato/
essa
lax [læks] *adj* rilassato/a; negligente
laxative [ˈlæksətɪv] *n* lassativo
lay [leɪ] *pt of* **lie** ▷ *adj* laico/a; (*not
expert*) profano/a ▷ *vt* (*pt, pp* **laid**
[leɪd]) posare, mettere; (*eggs*) fare;
(*trap*) tendere; (*plans*) fare, elaborare;

to ~ the table apparecchiare la tavola; **lay down** vt mettere giù; (*rules etc*) formulare, fissare; **to ~ down the law** dettar legge; **to ~ down one's life** dare la propria vita; **lay off** vt (*workers*) licenziare; **lay on** vt (*provide*) fornire; **lay out** vt (*display*) presentare; **lay-by** n (BRIT) piazzola (di sosta)

layer ['leɪə^r] n strato

layman ['leɪmən] n (*irreg*) laico; profano

layout ['leɪaut] n lay-out m inv, disposizione f; (*Press*) impaginazione f

lazy ['leɪzɪ] adj pigro/a

lb. abbr (= pound (weight)) lb.

lead¹ (pt, pp **led**) [li:d, lɛd] n (*front position*) posizione f di testa; (*distance, time ahead*) vantaggio; (*clue*) indizio; (*Elec*) filo (elettrico); (*for dog*) guinzaglio; (*Theat*) parte f principale ▷ vt guidare, condurre; (*induce*) indurre; (*be leader of*) essere a capo di ▷ vi condurre; (*Sport*) essere in testa; **in the ~** in testa; **to ~ the way** fare strada; **lead up to** vt fus portare a

lead² [lɛd] n (*metal*) piombo; (*in pencil*) mina

leader ['li:də^r] n capo; leader m inv; (*in newspaper*) articolo di fondo; (*Sport*) chi è in testa; **leadership** n direzione f; capacità f di comando

lead-free ['lɛdfri:] adj senza piombo

leading ['li:dɪŋ] adj primo/a, principale

lead singer n cantante alla testa di un gruppo

leaf [li:f] n (pl **leaves**) foglia; **to turn over a new ~** cambiar vita; **leaf through** vt sfogliare

leaflet ['li:flɪt] n dépliant m inv; (*Pol, Rel*) volantino

league [li:g] n lega; (*Football*) campionato; **to be in ~ with** essere in lega con

leak [li:k] n (*out*) fuga; (*in*) infiltrazione f; (*security leak*) fuga d'informazioni ▷ vi (*roof, bucket*) perdere; (*liquid*) uscire; (*shoes*) lasciar passare l'acqua ▷ vt (*information*) divulgare

lean (pt, pp **leaned** or **leant**) [li:n, lɛnt] adj magro/a ▷ vt: **to ~ sth on** appoggiare qc su ▷ vi (*slope*) pendere; (*rest*): **to ~ against** appoggiarsi contro; essere appoggiato/a a; **to ~ on** appoggiarsi a; **lean forward** vi sporgersi in avanti; **lean over** vi inclinarsi; **leaning** n: **leaning (towards)** propensione f (per)

leant [lɛnt] pt, pp of **lean**

leap [li:p] n salto, balzo ▷ vi (pt, pp **leaped** or **leapt** [lɛpt]) saltare, balzare

leapt [lɛpt] pt, pp of **leap**

leap year n anno bisestile

learn (pt, pp **learned** or **learnt**) [lə:n, -t] vt, vi imparare; **to ~ (how) to do sth** imparare a fare qc; **to ~ about sth** (*hear*) apprendere qc; **learner** n principiante m/f; apprendista m/f; **he's a learner (driver)** (BRIT) sta imparando a guidare; **learning** n erudizione f, sapienza

learnt [lə:nt] pt, pp of **learn**

lease [li:s] n contratto d'affitto ▷ vt affittare

leash [li:ʃ] n guinzaglio

least [li:st] adj: **the ~** (+ noun) il (la) più piccolo/a, il (la) minimo/a; (*smallest amount of*) il (la) meno ▷ adv (+ verb) meno; **the ~** (+ adjective): **the ~ beautiful girl** la ragazza meno bella; **the ~ possible effort** il minimo sforzo possibile; **I have the ~ money** ho meno denaro di tutti; **at ~** almeno; **not in the ~** affatto, per nulla

leather ['lɛðə^r] n cuoio

leave (pt, pp **left**) [li:v, lɛft] vt lasciare; (*go away from*) partire da ▷ vi partire, andarsene; (*bus, train*) partire ▷ n (*time off*) congedo; (*Mil, consent*) licenza; **to be left** rimanere; **there's some milk left over** c'è rimasto del latte; **on ~** in congedo; **leave**

behind vt (also fig) lasciare; (forget) dimenticare; **leave out** vt omettere, tralasciare

leaves [li:vz] npl of **leaf**

Lebanon ['lɛbənən] n Libano

lecture ['lɛktʃə'] n conferenza; (Scol) lezione f ▷ vi fare conferenze; fare lezioni ▷ vt (scold) sgridare; **to ~ sb on** or **about sth** rimproverare qn or fare una ramanzina a qn per qc; **to give a ~ (on)** fare una conferenza (su); **lecture hall** n aula magna; **lecturer** ['lɛktʃərə'] n (BRIT: at university) professore/essa, docente m/f; **lecture theatre** n = **lecture hall**

led [lɛd] pt, pp of **lead¹**

ledge [lɛdʒ] n (of window) davanzale m; (on wall etc) sporgenza; (of mountain) cornice f, cengia

leek [li:k] n porro

left [lɛft] pt, pp of **leave** ▷ adj sinistro/a ▷ adv a sinistra ▷ n sinistra; **on the ~, to the ~** a sinistra; **the L~** (Pol) la sinistra; **left-hand** adj: **the left-hand side** il lato sinistro; **left-hand drive** adj guida a sinistra; **left-handed** adj mancino/a; **left-luggage locker** n armadietto per deposito bagagli; **left-luggage (office)** n deposito m bagagli inv; **left-overs** npl avanzi mpl, resti mpl; **left wing** n (Pol) sinistra ▷ adj: **left-wing** (Pol) di sinistra

leg [lɛg] n gamba; (of animal) zampa; (of furniture) piede m; (Culin: of chicken) coscia; (of journey) tappa; **1st/2nd ~** (Sport) partita di andata/ritorno

legacy ['lɛgəsɪ] n eredità f inv

legal ['li:gl] adj legale; **legal holiday** n (US) giorno festivo, festa nazionale; **legalize** vt legalizzare; **legally** adv legalmente; **legally binding** legalmente vincolante

legend ['lɛdʒənd] n leggenda; **legendary** ['lɛdʒəndərɪ] adj leggendario/a

leggings ['lɛgɪŋz] npl ghette fpl

legible ['lɛdʒəbl] adj leggibile

legislation [lɛdʒɪs'leɪʃən] n legislazione f

legislative ['lɛdʒɪslətɪv] adj legislativo/a

legitimate [lɪ'dʒɪtɪmət] adj legittimo/a

leisure ['lɛʒə'] n agio, tempo libero; ricreazioni fpl; **at ~** con comodo; **leisure centre** n centro di ricreazione; **leisurely** adj tranquillo/a, fatto/a con comodo or senza fretta

lemon ['lɛmən] n limone m; **lemonade** [lɛmə'neɪd] n limonata; **lemon tea** n tè m inv al limone

lend (pt, pp **lent**) [lɛnd, lɛnt] vt: **to ~ sth (to sb)** prestare qc (a qn)

length [lɛŋθ] n lunghezza; (distance) distanza; (section: of road, pipe etc) pezzo, tratto; **~ of time** periodo (di tempo); **at ~** (at last) finalmente, alla fine; (lengthily) a lungo; **lengthen** vt allungare, prolungare ▷ vi allungarsi; **lengthways** adv per il lungo; **lengthy** adj molto lungo/a

lens [lɛnz] n lente f; (of camera) obiettivo

Lent [lɛnt] n Quaresima

lent [lɛnt] pt, pp of **lend**

lentil ['lɛntl] n lenticchia

Leo ['li:əu] n Leone m

leopard ['lɛpəd] n leopardo

leotard ['li:ətɑ:d] n calzamaglia

leprosy ['lɛprəsɪ] n lebbra

lesbian ['lɛzbɪən] n lesbica

less [lɛs] adj, pron, adv, prep meno; **~ tax/10% discount** meno tasse/il 10% di sconto; **~ than you/ever** meno di lei/che mai; **~ than half** meno della metà; **~ and ~** sempre meno; **the ~ he works ...** meno lavora ...; **lessen** ['lɛsn] vi diminuire, attenuarsi ▷ vt diminuire, ridurre; **lesser** ['lɛsə'] adj minore, più piccolo/a; **to a lesser extent** or **degree** in grado or misura minore

lesson ['lɛsn] n lezione f; **to teach sb a ~** dare una lezione a qn

let (*pt, pp* **let**) [lɛt] *vt* lasciare; (BRIT: *lease*) dare in affitto; **to ~ sb do sth** lasciar fare qc a qn, lasciare che qn faccia qc; **to ~ sb know sth** far sapere qc a qn; **~'s go** andiamo; **~ him come** lo lasci venire; **"to ~"** "affittasi"; **let down** *vt* (*lower*) abbassare; (*dress*) allungare; (*hair*) sciogliere; (*disappoint*) deludere; (BRIT: *tyre*) sgonfiare; **let in** *vt* lasciare entrare; (*visitor etc*) far entrare; **let off** *vt* (*allow to go*) lasciare andare; (*firework etc*) far partire; **let out** *vt* lasciare uscire; (*scream*) emettere

lethal ['li:θl] *adj* letale, mortale

letter ['lɛtər] *n* lettera; **letterbox** (BRIT) *n* buca delle lettere

lettuce ['lɛtɪs] *n* lattuga, insalata

leukaemia, (US) **leukemia** [lu:'ki:mɪə] *n* leucemia

level ['lɛvl] *adj* piatto/a, piano/a; orizzontale ▷ *n* livello ▷ *vt* livellare, spianare; **to be ~ with** essere alla pari di; **to draw ~ with** mettersi alla pari di; **level crossing** *n* (BRIT) passaggio a livello

lever ['li:vər] *n* leva; **leverage** *n*: **leverage (on** *or* **with)** forza (su); (*fig*) ascendente *m* (su)

levy ['lɛvɪ] *n* tassa, imposta ▷ *vt* imporre

liability [laɪə'bɪlɪtɪ] *n* responsabilità *f inv*; (*handicap*) peso

liable ['laɪəbl] *adj* (*subject*): **~ to** soggetto/a a; passibile di; (*responsible*): **~ (for)** responsabile (di); (*likely*): **~ to do** propenso/a a fare

liaise [li:'eɪz] *vi*: **to ~ (with)** mantenere i contatti (con)

liar ['laɪər] *n* bugiardo/a

liberal ['lɪbərl] *adj* liberale; (*generous*): **to be ~ with** distribuire liberalmente; **Liberal Democrat** *n* liberaldemocratico/a

liberate ['lɪbəreɪt] *vt* liberare

liberation [lɪbə'reɪʃən] *n* liberazione *f*

liberty ['lɪbətɪ] *n* libertà *f inv*; **at ~** (*criminal*) in libertà; **at ~ to do** libero/a di fare

Libra ['li:brə] *n* Bilancia

librarian [laɪ'brɛərɪən] *n* bibliotecario/a

library ['laɪbrərɪ] *n* biblioteca

Libya ['lɪbɪə] *n* Libia

lice [laɪs] *npl of* **louse**

licence, (US) **license** ['laɪsns] *n* autorizzazione *f*, permesso; (Comm) licenza; (Radio, TV) canone *m*, abbonamento; (*also*: **driving ~**, (US) **driver's license**) patente *f* di guida; (*excessive freedom*) licenza

license ['laɪsns] *n* (US) = **licence** ▷ *vt* dare una licenza a; **licensed** *adj* (*for alcohol*) che ha la licenza di vendere bibite alcoliche; **license plate** *n* (*esp* US Aut) targa (automobilistica); **licensing hours** (BRIT) *npl* orario d'apertura (*di un pub*)

lick [lɪk] *vt* leccare; (*col: defeat*) stracciare; **to ~ one's lips** (*fig*) leccarsi i baffi

lid [lɪd] *n* coperchio; (*eyelid*) palpebra

lie [laɪ] *n* bugia, menzogna ▷ *vi* mentire, dire bugie; (*rest*) giacere, star disteso/a; (*object: be situated*) trovarsi, essere; **to tell ~s** raccontare *or* dire bugie; **to ~ low** (*fig*) latitare; **lie about, lie around** *vi* (*things*) essere in giro; (*person*) bighellonare; **lie down** *vi* stendersi, sdraiarsi

Liechtenstein ['lɪktənstaɪn] *n* Liechtenstein *m*

lie-in ['laɪɪn] *n* (BRIT): **to have a ~** rimanere a letto

lieutenant [lɛf'tɛnənt, US lu:'tɛnənt] *n* tenente *m*

life [laɪf] *n* (*pl* **lives**) vita ▷ *cpd* di vita; della vita; a vita; **to come to ~** rianimarsi; **life assurance** *n* (BRIT) = **life insurance**; **lifeboat** *n* scialuppa di salvataggio; **lifeguard** *n* bagnino; **life insurance** *n* assicurazione *f* sulla vita; **life jacket** *n* giubbotto di salvataggio;

lifelike adj che sembra vero/a; rassomigliante; **life preserver** [-prɪˈzɜːvəʳ] n (US) salvagente m; giubbotto di salvataggio; **life sentence** n (condanna all')ergastolo; **life style** n stile m di vita; **lifetime** [ˈlaɪftaɪm] n: **in his lifetime** durante la sua vita; **in a lifetime** nell'arco della vita; **in tutta la vita**; **the chance of a lifetime** un'occasione unica

lift [lɪft] vt sollevare; (ban, rule) levare ▷ vi (fog) alzarsi ▷ n (BRIT: elevator) ascensore m; **to give sb a ~** (BRIT) dare un passaggio a qn; **lift up** vt sollevare, alzare; **lift-off** n decollo

light (pt, pp **lighted**, pt, pp **lit**) [laɪt, lɪt] n luce f, lume m; (daylight) luce, giorno; (lamp) lampada; (Aut: rear light) luce f di posizione; (: headlamp) fanale m; (for cigarette etc): **have you got a ~?** ha da accendere? ▷ vt (candle, cigarette, fire) accendere; (room) illuminare ▷ adj (room, colour) chiaro/a; (not heavy, also fig) leggero/a; **lights** npl (Aut: traffic lights) semaforo; **to come to ~** venire alla luce, emergere; **to be lit by** essere illuminato/a da; **light up** vi illuminarsi ▷ vt illuminare; **light bulb** n lampadina; **lighten** vt (make less heavy) alleggerire; **lighter** n (also: **cigarette lighter**) accendino; **light-hearted** adj gioioso/a, gaio/a; **lighthouse** n faro; **lighting** n illuminazione f; **lightly** [ˈlaɪtlɪ] adv leggermente; **to get off lightly** cavarsela a buon mercato

lightning [ˈlaɪtnɪŋ] n lampo, fulmine m

lightweight [ˈlaɪtweɪt] adj (suit) leggero/a ▷ n (Boxing) peso leggero

like [laɪk] vt (person) volere bene a; (activity, object, food): **I ~ swimming/ that book/chocolate** mi piace nuotare/quel libro/il cioccolato ▷ prep come ▷ adj simile, uguale ▷ n: **the ~** uno/a uguale; **I would ~, I'd ~** mi piacerebbe, vorrei; **would you ~ a coffee?** gradirebbe un caffè?; **to be/look ~ sb/sth** somigliare a qn/ qc; **what does it look/taste ~?** che aspetto/gusto ha?; **what does it sound ~?** come fa?; **that's just ~ him** è proprio da lui; **do it ~ this** fallo così; **it is nothing ~ ...** non è affatto come ...; **his ~s and dislikes** i suoi gusti; **likeable** adj simpatico/a

likelihood [ˈlaɪklɪhud] n probabilità

likely [ˈlaɪklɪ] adj probabile; plausibile; **he's ~ to leave** probabilmente partirà, è probabile che parta; **not ~!** neanche per sogno!

likewise [ˈlaɪkwaɪz] adv similmente, nello stesso modo

liking [ˈlaɪkɪŋ] n: **~ (for)** debole m (per); **to be to sb's ~** piacere a qn

lilac [ˈlaɪlək] n lilla m inv

Lilo® [ˈlaɪləu] n materassino gonfiabile

lily [ˈlɪlɪ] n giglio

limb [lɪm] n arto

limbo [ˈlɪmbəu] n: **to be in ~** (fig) essere lasciato/a nel dimenticatoio

lime [laɪm] n (tree) tiglio; (fruit) limetta; (Geo) calce f

limelight [ˈlaɪmlaɪt] n: **in the ~** (fig) alla ribalta, in vista

limestone [ˈlaɪmstəun] n pietra calcarea; (Geo) calcare m

limit [ˈlɪmɪt] n limite m ▷ vt limitare; **limited** adj limitato/a, ristretto/a; **to be limited to** limitarsi a

limousine [ˈlɪməziːn] n limousine f inv

limp [lɪmp] n: **to have a ~** zoppicare ▷ vi zoppicare ▷ adj floscio/a, flaccido/a

line [laɪn] n linea; (rope) corda; (for fishing) lenza; (wire) filo; (of poem) verso; (row, series) fila, riga; coda; (on face) ruga ▷ vt (trees, crowd) fiancheggiare; (clothes) foderare (di); (box) rivestire or foderare (di); **in his ~ of business** nel suo ramo; **in ~ with** in linea con; **line up** vi allinearsi, mettersi in fila

▷ *vt* mettere in fila; (*event, celebration*) preparare

linear ['lɪnɪə'] *adj* lineare

linen ['lɪnɪn] *n* biancheria, panni *mpl*; (*cloth*) tela di lino

liner ['laɪnə'] *n* nave *f* di linea; **dustbin ~** sacchetto per la pattumiera

line-up ['laɪnʌp] *n* allineamento, fila; (*Sport*) formazione *f* di gioco

linger ['lɪŋgə'] *vi* attardarsi; indugiare; (*smell, tradition*) persistere

lingerie ['lænʒərɪ:] *n* biancheria intima (femminile)

linguist ['lɪŋgwɪst] *n* linguista *m/f*; poliglotta *m/f*; **linguistic** *adj* linguistico/a

lining ['laɪnɪŋ] *n* fodera

link [lɪŋk] *n* (*of a chain*) anello; (*relationship*) legame *m*; (*connection*) collegamento ▷ *vt* collegare, unire, congiungere; (*associate*): **to ~ with** *or* **to** collegare a; **link up** *vt* collegare, unire ▷ *vi* riunirsi; associarsi; **links** [lɪŋks] *npl* pista *or* terreno da golf

lion ['laɪən] *n* leone *m*; **lioness** *n* leonessa

lip [lɪp] *n* labbro; (*of cup etc*) orlo; **lipread** ['lɪprɪ:d] *vi* leggere sulle labbra; **lip salve** [-sælv] *n* burro di cacao; **lipstick** *n* rossetto

liqueur [lɪ'kjuə'] *n* liquore *m*

liquid ['lɪkwɪd] *n* liquido ▷ *adj* liquido/a; **liquidizer** *n* frullatore *m* (a brocca)

liquor ['lɪkə'] *n* alcool *m*; **liquor store** *n* (*us*) negozio di liquori

Lisbon ['lɪzbən] *n* Lisbona

lisp [lɪsp] *n* pronuncia blesa della "s"

list [lɪst] *n* lista, elenco ▷ *vt* (*write down*) mettere in lista; fare una lista di; (*enumerate*) elencare

listen ['lɪsn] *vi* ascoltare; **to ~ to** ascoltare; **listener** *n* ascoltatore/trice

lit [lɪt] *pt, pp of* **light**

liter ['lɪ:tə'] *n* (*us*) = **litre**

literacy ['lɪtərəsɪ] *n* il sapere leggere e scrivere

literal ['lɪtərl] *adj* letterale; **literally** *adv* alla lettera, letteralmente

literary ['lɪtərərɪ] *adj* letterario/a

literate ['lɪtərɪt] *adj* che sa leggere e scrivere

literature ['lɪtərɪtʃə'] *n* letteratura; (*brochures etc*) materiale *m*

litre, (*us*) **liter** ['lɪ:tə'] *n* litro

litter ['lɪtə'] *n* (*rubbish*) rifiuti *mpl*; (*young animals*) figliata; **litter bin** *n* (*BRIT*) cestino per rifiuti; **littered** *adj*: **littered with** coperto/a di

little ['lɪtl] *adj* (*small*) piccolo/a; (*not much*) poco/a ▷ *adv* poco; **a ~ bit** un pochino; **~ by ~** a poco a poco; **little finger** *n* mignolo

live¹ [lɪv] *vi* vivere; (*reside*) vivere, abitare; **where do you ~?** dove abita?; **live together** *vi* vivere insieme, convivere; **live up to** *vt fus* tener fede a, non venir meno a

live² [laɪv] *adj* (*animal*) vivo/a; (*wire*) sotto tensione; (*broadcast*) diretto/a; (*ammunition*) inesploso/a; (*performance*) dal vivo

livelihood ['laɪvlɪhud] *n* mezzi *mpl* di sostentamento

lively ['laɪvlɪ] *adj* vivace, vivo/a

liven up ['laɪvn-] *vt* (*discussion, evening*) animare ▷ *vi* ravvivarsi

liver ['lɪvə'] *n* fegato

lives [laɪvz] *npl of* **life**

livestock ['laɪvstɔk] *n* bestiame *m*

living ['lɪvɪŋ] *adj* vivo/a, vivente ▷ *n*: **to earn** *or* **make a ~** guadagnarsi la vita; **living room** *n* soggiorno

lizard ['lɪzəd] *n* lucertola

load [ləud] *n* (*weight*) peso; (*thing carried*) carico ▷ *vt* (*also*: **~ up**): **to ~ (with)** (*lorry, ship*) caricare (di); (*gun, camera*) caricare (con); **a ~ of**, **~s of** (*fig*) un sacco di; **to ~ a program** (*Comput*) caricare un programma; **loaded** *adj* (*question, word*) capzioso/a; (*col: rich*) pieno/a di soldi; **loaded (with)** (*vehicle*) carico/a (di)

loaf [ləuf] n (pl **loaves**) pane m, pagnotta

loan [ləun] n prestito ▷ vt dare in prestito; **on ~** in prestito

loathe [ləuð] vt detestare, aborrire

loaves [ləuvz] npl of **loaf**

lobby ['lɔbɪ] n atrio, vestibolo; (Pol: pressure group) gruppo di pressione ▷ vt fare pressione su

lobster ['lɔbstəʳ] n aragosta

local ['ləukl] adj locale ▷ n (BRIT: pub) ≈ bar m inv all'angolo; **the locals** npl la gente della zona; **local anaesthetic** n anestesia locale; **local authority** n ente m locale; **local government** n amministrazione f locale; **locally** ['ləukəlɪ] adv da queste parti; nel vicinato

locate [ləu'keɪt] vt (find) trovare; (situate) collocare; situare

location [ləu'keɪʃən] n posizione f; **on ~** (Cine) all'esterno

loch [lɔx] n lago

lock [lɔk] n (of door, box) serratura; (of canal) chiusa; (of hair) ciocca, riccio ▷ vt (with key) chiudere a chiave ▷ vi (door etc) chiudersi; (wheels) bloccarsi, incepparsi; **lock in** vt chiudere dentro (a chiave); **lock out** vt chiudere fuori; **lock up** vt (criminal, psychiatric patient) rinchiudere; (house) chiudere (a chiave) ▷ vi chiudere tutto (a chiave)

locker ['lɔkəʳ] n armadietto; **locker-room** n (us Sport) spogliatoio

locksmith ['lɔksmɪθ] n magnano

locomotive [ləukə'məutɪv] n locomotiva

lodge [lɔdʒ] n casetta, portineria; (hunting lodge) casino di caccia ▷ vi (person): **to ~ (with)** essere a pensione (presso or da); (bullet etc) conficcarsi ▷ vt (appeal etc) presentare, fare; **to ~ a complaint** presentare un reclamo; **lodger** n affittuario/a; (with room and meals) pensionante m/f

lodging ['lɔdʒɪŋ] n alloggio; see also **board**

loft [lɔft] n solaio, soffitta

log [lɔg] n (of wood) ceppo; (also: ~book) (Naut, Aviat) diario di bordo; (Aut) libretto di circolazione ▷ vt registrare; **log in, log on** vi (Comput) aprire una sessione (con codice di riconoscimento); **log off, log out** vi (Comput) terminare una sessione

logic ['lɔdʒɪk] n logica; **logical** adj logico/a

login ['lɔgɪn] n (Comput) nome m utente inv

logo ['ləugəu] n logo m inv

lol abbr (Internet, Tel: = laugh out loud) lol (morto dal ridere)

lollipop ['lɔlɪpɔp] n lecca lecca m inv

lolly ['lɔlɪ] n (col) lecca lecca m inv; (also: **ice ~**) ghiacciolo; (money) grana

London ['lʌndən] n Londra; **Londoner** n londinese m/f

lone [ləun] adj solitario/a

loneliness ['ləunlɪnɪs] n solitudine f, isolamento

lonely ['ləunlɪ] adj solo/a; solitario/a; isolato/a

long [lɔŋ] adj lungo/a ▷ adv a lungo, per molto tempo ▷ vi: **to ~ for sth/to do** desiderare qc/di fare; non veder l'ora di aver qc/di fare; **how ~ is this river/course?** quanto è lungo questo fiume/corso?; **6 metres ~** lungo 6 metri; **6 months ~** che dura 6 mesi, di 6 mesi; **all night ~** tutta la notte; **he no ~er comes** non viene più; **~ before** molto tempo prima; **before ~** (+ future) presto, fra poco; (+ past) poco tempo dopo; **don't be ~!** faccia presto!; **at ~ last** finalmente; **so** or **as ~ as** (while) finché; (provided that) sempre che + sub; **long-distance** adj (race) di fondo; (call) interurbano/a; **long-haul** ['lɔŋˌhɔːl] adj (flight) a lunga percorrenza inv; **longing** n desiderio, voglia, brama

longitude ['lɔŋgɪtjuːd] n longitudine f

long: long jump n salto in lungo;
long-life adj (milk) a lunga
conservazione; (batteries) di lunga
durata; **long-sighted** adj presbite;
long-standing adj di vecchia data;
long-term adj a lungo termine
loo [luː] n (BRIT col) W.C. m inv, cesso
look [luk] vi guardare; (seem)
sembrare, parere; (building etc): **to
~ south/on to the sea** dare a sud/
sul mare ▷ n sguardo; (appearance)
aspetto, aria; **looks** npl (good looks)
bellezza; **look after** vt fus occuparsi
di, prendersi cura di; (keep an eye on)
guardare, badare a; **look around**
vi guardarsi intorno; **look at** vt
fus guardare; **look back** vi: **to ~
back on** (event, period) ripensare a;
look down on vt fus (fig) guardare
dall'alto, disprezzare; **look for** vt
fus cercare; **look forward to** vt fus
non veder l'ora di; **~ing forward
to hearing from you** (in letter) in
attesa di una vostra gentile risposta;
look into vt fus esaminare; **look
out** vi (beware): **to ~ out (for)** stare
in guardia (per); **look out for** vt fus
cercare; **look round** vi (turn) girarsi,
voltarsi; (in shops) dare un'occhiata;
look through vt fus (papers, book)
scorrere; (telescope) guardare
attraverso; **look up** vi alzare gli
occhi; (improve) migliorare ▷ vt (word)
cercare; (friend) andare a trovare;
look up to vt fus avere rispetto per;
lookout n posto d'osservazione;
guardia; **to be on the lookout (for)**
stare in guardia (per)
loom [luːm] n telaio ▷ vi sorgere; (fig)
incombere
loony ['luːnɪ] n (col!) pazzo/a
loop [luːp] n cappio ▷ vt: **to ~ sth
round sth** passare qc intorno a qc;
loophole n via d'uscita; scappatoia
loose [luːs] adj (knot) sciolto/a;
(screw) allentato/a; (stone) cadente;
(clothes) ampio/a, largo/a; (animal)
in libertà, scappato/a; (life, morals)
dissoluto/a ▷ n: **to be on the ~** essere
in libertà; **loosely** adv senza stringere;
approssimativamente; **loosen**
['luːsn] vt sciogliere; (belt etc) allentare
loot [luːt] n bottino ▷ vt saccheggiare
lop-sided ['lɒp'saɪdɪd] adj non
equilibrato/a, asimmetrico/a
lord [lɔːd] n signore m; **L~ Smith** lord
Smith; **the L~** il Signore; **good L~!**
buon Dio!; **the (House of) L~s** (BRIT)
la Camera dei Lord
lorry ['lɒrɪ] n (BRIT) camion m inv;
lorry driver n (BRIT) camionista m
lose (pt, pp **lost**) [luːz, lɒst] vt perdere
▷ vi perdere; **to ~ (time)** (clock)
ritardare; **lose out** vi rimetterci;
loser n perdente m/f
loss [lɒs] n perdita; **to be at a ~**
essere perplesso/a
lost [lɒst] pt, pp of **lose** ▷ adj
perduto/a; **lost property**, (US) **lost
and found** n oggetti mpl smarriti
lot [lɒt] n (at auctions) lotto; (destiny)
destino, sorte f; **the ~** tutto/a
quanto/a; tutti/e quanti/e; **a ~**
molto; **a ~ of** una gran quantità di,
un sacco di; **~s of** molto/a; **to draw
~s (for sth)** tirare a sorte (per qc)
lotion ['ləʊʃən] n lozione f
lottery ['lɒtərɪ] n lotteria
loud [laʊd] adj forte, alto/a; (gaudy)
vistoso/a, sgargiante ▷ adv (speak etc)
forte; **out ~** (read etc) ad alta voce;
loudly adv fortemente, ad alta voce;
loudspeaker n altoparlante m
lounge [laʊndʒ] n salotto,
soggiorno; (of airport) sala d'attesa;
(BRIT: also: **~ bar**) bar m inv con
servizio a tavolino ▷ vi oziare
louse [laʊs] n (pl **lice**) pidocchio
lousy ['laʊzɪ] adj (col: fig) orrendo/a,
schifoso/a; **to feel ~** stare da cani
love [lʌv] n amore m ▷ vt amare; voler
bene a; **I ~ you** ti amo; **to ~ to do: I ~
to do** mi piace fare; **to be in ~ with**
essere innamorato/a di; **to fall in ~
with** innamorarsi di; **to make ~** fare
l'amore; **"15 ~"** (Tennis) "15 a zero";

love affair n relazione f; **love life** n vita sentimentale

lovely ['lʌvlɪ] adj bello/a; (delicious: smell, meal) buono/a

lover ['lʌvə^r] n amante m/f; (person in love) innamorato/a; (amateur): **a ~ of** un (un') amante di; un (un') appassionato/a di

loving ['lʌvɪŋ] adj affettuoso/a

low [ləʊ] adj basso/a ▷ adv in basso ▷ n (Meteor) depressione f; **to be ~ on** (supplies etc) avere scarsità di; **to feel ~** sentirsi giù; **low-alcohol** adj a basso contenuto alcolico; **low-calorie** adj a basso contenuto calorico

lower ['ləʊə^r] adj, adv comparative (bottom: of 2 things) più basso; (less important) meno importante ▷ vt calare; (price, eyes, voice) abbassare

low-fat ['ləʊ'fæt] adj magro/a

loyal ['lɔɪəl] adj fedele, leale; **loyalty** n fedeltà, lealtà; **loyalty card** n carta che offre sconti a clienti abituali

LP n abbr (= long-playing record) LP m

L-plate ['ɛlpleɪt] (BRIT) n ≈ contrassegno P principiante

Lt. abbr (= lieutenant) Ten.

Ltd abbr (= limited) ≈ S.r.l.

luck [lʌk] n fortuna, sorte f; **bad ~** sfortuna, mala sorte; **good ~** (buona) fortuna; **luckily** adv fortunatamente, per fortuna; **lucky** adj fortunato/a; (number etc) che porta fortuna

lucrative ['lu:krətɪv] adj lucrativo/a, lucroso/a, profittevole

ludicrous ['lu:dɪkrəs] adj ridicolo/a

luggage ['lʌgɪdʒ] n bagagli mpl; **luggage rack** n portabagagli m inv

lukewarm ['lu:kwɔ:m] adj tiepido/a

lull [lʌl] n intervallo di calma ▷ vt: **to ~ sb to sleep** cullare qn finché si addormenta

lullaby ['lʌləbaɪ] n ninnananna

lumber ['lʌmbə^r] n (wood) legname m; (junk) roba vecchia

luminous ['lu:mɪnəs] adj luminoso/a

lump [lʌmp] n pezzo; (in sauce) grumo; (swelling) gonfiore m; (also: **sugar ~**) zolletta ▷ vt (also: **~ together**) riunire, mettere insieme; **lump sum** n somma globale; **lumpy** adj (sauce) pieno/a di grumi; (bed) bitorzoluto/a

lunatic ['lu:nətɪk] adj pazzo/a, matto/a

lunch [lʌntʃ] n pranzo, colazione f; **lunch break** n intervallo del pranzo; **lunchtime** n ora di pranzo

lung [lʌŋ] n polmone m

lure [luə^r] n richiamo; lusinga ▷ vt attirare (con l'inganno)

lurk [lə:k] vi stare in agguato

lush [lʌʃ] adj lussureggiante

lust [lʌst] n lussuria; cupidigia; desiderio; (fig): **~ for** sete f di

Luxembourg ['lʌksəmbə:g] n (state) Lussemburgo m; (city) Lussemburgo f

luxurious [lʌgˈzjuərɪəs] adj sontuoso/a, di lusso

luxury ['lʌkʃərɪ] n lusso ▷ cpd di lusso

 Be careful not to translate luxury by the Italian word lussuria.

Lycra® ['laɪkrə] n lycra® f inv

lying ['laɪɪŋ] n bugie fpl, menzogne fpl ▷ adj bugiardo/a

lyric ['lɪrɪk] adj lirico/a; **lyrics** npl (of song) parole fpl

m

m *abbr* (= *metre*) m; = **mile; million**

MA *n abbr* = **Master of Arts**

ma [mɑ:] *n* (*col*) mamma

mac [mæk] *n* (*BRIT*) impermeabile *m*

macaroni [mækə'rəunɪ] *n* maccheroni *mpl*

Macedonia [mæsɪ'dəunɪə] *n* Macedonia; **Macedonian** [mæsɪ'dəunɪən] *adj* macedone ▷ *n* macedone *m/f*; (*Ling*) macedone *m*

machine [mə'ʃi:n] *n* macchina ▷ *vt* (*dress etc*) cucire a macchina; (*Tech*) lavorare (a macchina); **machine gun** *n* mitragliatrice *f*; **machinery** *n* macchinario, macchine *fpl*; (*fig*) macchina; **machine washable** *adj* lavabile in lavatrice

macho ['mætʃəu] *adj* macho *inv*

mackerel ['mækrəl] *n* (*pl inv*) sgombro

mackintosh ['mækɪntɔʃ] *n* (*BRIT*) impermeabile *m*

mad [mæd] *adj* matto/a, pazzo/a; (*foolish*) sciocco/a; (*angry*) furioso/a; **to be ~ (keen) about** *or* **on sth** (*col*) andar matto/a per qc

Madagascar [mædə'gæskəʳ] *n* Madagascar *m*

madam ['mædəm] *n* signora

mad cow disease *n* encefalite *f* bovina spongiforme

made [meɪd] *pt, pp of* **make**; **made-to-measure** *adj* (*BRIT*) fatto/a su misura; **made-up** ['meɪdʌp] *adj* (*story*) inventato/a

madly ['mædlɪ] *adv* follemente

madman ['mædmən] *n* (*irreg*) pazzo, alienato

madness ['mædnɪs] *n* pazzia

Madrid [mə'drɪd] *n* Madrid *f*

Mafia ['mæfɪə] *n* mafia *f*

mag. [mæg] *n abbr* (*BRIT col: Press*); = **magazine**

magazine [mægə'zi:n] *n* (*Press*) rivista; (*Radio, TV*) rubrica

> Be careful not to translate *magazine* by the Italian word *magazzino*.

maggot ['mægət] *n* baco, verme *m*

magic ['mædʒɪk] *n* magia ▷ *adj* magico/a; **magical** *adj* magico/a; **magician** [mə'dʒɪʃən] *n* mago/a

magistrate ['mædʒɪstreɪt] *n* magistrato; giudice *m/f*

magnet ['mægnɪt] *n* magnete *m*, calamita; **magnetic** [mæg'nɛtɪk] *adj* magnetico/a

magnificent [mæg'nɪfɪsnt] *adj* magnifico/a

magnify ['mægnɪfaɪ] *vt* ingrandire; **magnifying glass** *n* lente *f* d'ingrandimento

magpie ['mægpaɪ] *n* gazza

mahogany [mə'hɔgənɪ] *n* mogano

maid [meɪd] *n* domestica; (*in hotel*) cameriera

maiden name ['meɪdn-] *n* nome da *m* nubile *or* da ragazza

mail [meɪl] *n* posta ▷ *vt* spedire (per posta); **mailbox** *n* (*US*) cassetta delle lettere; **mailing list** *n* elenco d'indirizzi; **mailman** *n* (*irreg: US*) portalettere *m inv*, postino; **mail-order** *n* vendita (*or* acquisto) per corrispondenza

main [meɪn] *adj* principale ▷ *n* (*pipe*) conduttura principale; **the ~s** (*Elec*) la linea principale; **in the ~** nel complesso, nell'insieme; **main course** *n* (*Culin*) piatto principale, piatto forte; **mainland** *n* continente *m*; **mainly** *adv* principalmente, soprattutto; **main road** *n* strada principale; **mainstream** *n* (*fig*) corrente *f* principale; **main street** *n* strada principale

maintain [meɪn'teɪn] *vt* mantenere; (*affirm*) sostenere; **maintenance** ['meɪntənəns] *n* manutenzione *f*; (*alimony*) alimenti *mpl*

maisonette [meɪzə'nɛt] *n* (BRIT) appartamento a due piani

maize [meɪz] *n* granturco, mais *m*

majesty ['mædʒɪstɪ] *n* maestà *f inv*

major ['meɪdʒəʳ] *n* (*Mil*) maggiore *m* ▷ *adj* (*greater, Mus*) maggiore; (*in importance*) principale, importante

Majorca [mə'jɔːkə] *n* Maiorca

majority [mə'dʒɔrɪtɪ] *n* maggioranza

make [meɪk] *vt* (*pt, pp* **made**) fare; (*manufacture*) fare, fabbricare; (*cause to be*): **to ~ sb sad** *etc* rendere qn triste *etc*; (*force*): **to ~ sb do sth** costringere qn a fare qc, far fare qc a qn; (*equal*): **2 and 2 ~ 4** 2 più 2 fa 4 ▷ *n* fabbricazione *f*; (*brand*) marca; **to ~ a fool of sb** far fare a qn la figura dello scemo; **to ~ a profit** realizzare un profitto; **to ~ a loss** subire una perdita; **to ~ it** (*in time etc*) arrivare; (*succeed*) farcela; **what time do you ~ it?** che ora fai?; **to ~ do with** arrangiarsi con; **make off** *vi* svignarsela; **make out** *vt* (*write out*) scrivere; (: *cheque*) emettere; (*understand*) capire; (*see*) distinguere; (: *numbers*) decifrare; **make up** *vt* (*constitute*) formare; (*invent*) inventare; (*parcel*) fare ▷ *vi* conciliarsi; (*with cosmetics*) truccarsi; **make up**

for *vt fus* compensare; ricuperare; **makeover** ['meɪkəʊvəʳ] *n* cambio di immagine; **to give sb a makeover** far cambiare immagine a qn; **maker** *n* (*of programme etc*) creatore/ trice; (*manufacturer*) fabbricante *m*; **makeshift** *adj* improvvisato/a; **make-up** *n* trucco

making ['meɪkɪŋ] *n* (*fig*): **in the ~** in formazione; **he has the ~s of an actor** ha la stoffa dell'attore

malaria [mə'lɛərɪə] *n* malaria

Malaysia [mə'leɪzɪə] *n* Malaysia

male [meɪl] *n* (*Biol, Elec*) maschio ▷ *adj* maschile; (*animal, child*) maschio/a

malicious [mə'lɪʃəs] *adj* malevolo/a; (*Law*) doloso/a

malignant [mə'lɪɡnənt] *adj* (*Med*) maligno/a

mall [mɔːl] *n* (*also*: **shopping ~**) centro commerciale

mallet ['mælɪt] *n* maglio

malnutrition [mælnjuː'trɪʃən] *n* denutrizione *f*

malpractice [mæl'præktɪs] *n* prevaricazione *f*; negligenza

malt [mɔːlt] *n* malto

Malta ['mɔːltə] *n* Malta; **Maltese** [mɔːl'tiːz] *adj, n* (*pl inv*) maltese (*m/f*); (*Ling*) maltese *m*

mammal ['mæml] *n* mammifero

mammoth ['mæməθ] *adj* enorme, gigantesco/a

man [mæn] *n* (*pl* **men**) uomo ▷ *vt* fornire d'uomini; stare a; **an old ~** un vecchio; **~ and wife** marito e moglie

manage ['mænɪdʒ] *vi* farcela ▷ *vt* (*be in charge of*) occuparsi di; (*shop, restaurant*) gestire; **to ~ to do sth** riuscire a far qc; **manageable** *adj* maneggevole; (*task etc*) fattibile; **management** *n* amministrazione *f*, direzione *f*; **manager** *n* direttore *m*; (*of shop, restaurant*) gerente *m*; (*of artist, Sport*) manager *m inv*; **manageress** [mænɪdʒə'rɛs] *n* direttrice *f*; gerente *f*;

managerial [mænə'dʒɪərɪəl] *adj* dirigenziale; **managing director** ['mænɪdʒɪŋ-] *n* amministratore *m* delegato

mandarin ['mændərɪn] *n* (*person, fruit*) mandarino

mandate ['mændeɪt] *n* mandato

mandatory ['mændətərɪ] *adj* obbligatorio/a; ingiuntivo/a

mane [meɪn] *n* criniera

mangetout ['mɔnʒ'tu:] *n* pisello dolce, taccola

mango ['mæŋgəʊ] (*pl* **mangoes**) *n* mango

man: manhole ['mænhəʊl] *n* botola stradale; **manhood** ['mænhʊd] *n* età virile; virilità

mania ['meɪnɪə] *n* mania; **maniac** ['meɪnɪæk] *n* maniaco/a

manic ['mænɪk] *adj* (*behaviour, activity*) maniacale

manicure ['mænɪkjʊə'] *n* manicure *f inv*

manifest ['mænɪfɛst] *vt* manifestare ▷ *adj* manifesto/a, palese

manifesto [mænɪ'fɛstəʊ] *n* manifesto

manipulate [mə'nɪpjʊleɪt] *vt* manipolare

man: mankind [mæn'kaɪnd] *n* umanità, genere *m* umano; **manly** ['mænlɪ] *adj* virile; coraggioso/a; **man-made** *adj* sintetico/a; artificiale

manner ['mænə'] *n* maniera, modo, (*behaviour*) modo di fare; (*type, sort*): **all ~ of things** ogni genere di cosa; **manners** *npl* (*conduct*) maniere *fpl*; **bad ~s** maleducazione *f*; **all ~ of** ogni sorta di

manoeuvre, (*us*) **maneuver** [mə'nu:və'] *vt* manovrare ▷ *vi* far manovre ▷ *n* manovra

manpower ['mænpauə'] *n* manodopera

mansion ['mænʃən] *n* casa signorile

manslaughter ['mænslɔ:tə'] *n* omicidio preterintenzionale

mantelpiece ['mæntlpi:s] *n* mensola del caminetto

manual ['mænjuəl] *adj, n* manuale (*m*)

manufacture [mænju'fæktʃə'] *vt* fabbricare ▷ *n* fabbricazione *f*, manifattura; **manufacturer** *n* fabbricante *m*

manure [mə'njuə'] *n* concime *m*

manuscript ['mænjuskrɪpt] *n* manoscritto

many ['mɛnɪ] *adj* molti/e ▷ *pron* molti/e; **a great ~** moltissimi/e, un gran numero (di); **~ a ...** molti/e ...

map [mæp] *n* carta (geografica); (*of city*) cartina

maple ['meɪpl] *n* acero

mar [mɑ:'] *vt* sciupare

Mar. *abbr* (= *March*) mar.

marathon ['mærəθən] *n* maratona

marble ['mɑ:bl] *n* marmo; (*toy*) pallina, bilia

March [mɑ:tʃ] *n* marzo

march [mɑ:tʃ] *vi* marciare; sfilare ▷ *n* marcia

mare [mɛə'] *n* giumenta

margarine [mɑ:dʒə'ri:n] *n* margarina

margin ['mɑ:dʒɪn] *n* margine *m*; **marginal** *adj* marginale; **marginal seat** (*Pol*) seggio elettorale ottenuto con una stretta maggioranza; **marginally** *adv* (*bigger, better*) lievemente, di poco; (*different*) un po'

marigold ['mærɪgəʊld] *n* calendola

marijuana [mærɪ'wɑ:nə] *n* marijuana

marina [mə'ri:nə] *n* marina

marinade *n* [mærɪ'neɪd] marinata ▷ *vt* ['mærɪneɪd] = **marinate**

marinate ['mærɪneɪt] *vt* marinare

marine [mə'ri:n] *adj* (*animal, plant*) marino/a; (*forces, engineering*) marittimo/a ▷ *n* (*BRIT*) fante *m* di marina; (*US*) marine *m inv*

marital ['mærɪtl] *adj* maritale, coniugale; **~ status** stato coniugale

m

maritime ['mærɪtaɪm] *adj*
marittimo/a

marjoram ['mɑːdʒərəm] *n*
maggiorana

mark [mɑːk] *n* segno; (*stain*)
macchia; (*of skid etc*) traccia;
(BRIT Scol) voto; (Sport) bersaglio;
(*currency*) marco ▷ *vt* segnare; (*stain*)
macchiare; (*indicate*) indicare; (BRIT
Scol) dare un voto a; correggere; **to
~ time** segnare il passo; **marked** *adj*
spiccato/a, netto/a; **marker** *n* (*sign*)
segno; (*bookmark*) segnalibro

market ['mɑːkɪt] *n* mercato
▷ *vt* (Comm) mettere in vendita;
marketing *n* marketing *m*;
marketplace *n* (piazza del) mercato;
(*world of trade*) piazza, mercato;
market research *n* indagine *f* or
ricerca *f* di mercato

marmalade ['mɑːməleɪd] *n*
marmellata d'arance

maroon [mə'ruːn] *vt* (*fig*): **to be ~ed
(in** *or* **at)** essere abbandonato/a (in)
▷ *adj* bordeaux *inv*

marquee [mɑː'kiː] *n* padiglione *m*

marriage ['mærɪdʒ] *n* matrimonio;
marriage certificate *n* certificato di
matrimonio

married ['mærɪd] *adj* sposato/a; (*life,
love*) coniugale, matrimoniale

marrow ['mærəu] *n* midollo;
(*vegetable*) zucca

marry ['mærɪ] *vt* sposare, sposarsi
con; (*father, priest etc*) dare in
matrimonio ▷ *vi* (*also*: **get married**)
sposarsi

Mars [mɑːz] *n* (*planet*) Marte *m*

marsh [mɑːʃ] *n* palude *f*

marshal ['mɑːʃl] *n* maresciallo; (US:
fire marshal) capo; (: *police marshal*)
capitano ▷ *vt* (*thoughts, support*)
ordinare; (*soldiers*) adunare

martyr ['mɑːtəʳ] *n* martire *m/f*

marvel ['mɑːvl] *n* meraviglia ▷ *vi*: **to
~ (at)** meravigliarsi (di); **marvellous**,
(US) **marvelous** *adj* meraviglioso/a

Marxism ['mɑːksɪzəm] *n* marxismo

Marxist ['mɑːksɪst] *adj*, *n* marxista
(*m/f*)

marzipan ['mɑːzɪpæn] *n* marzapane
m

mascara [mæs'kɑːrə] *n* mascara
m inv

mascot ['mæskət] *n* mascotte *f inv*

masculine ['mæskjulɪn] *adj*
maschile; (*woman*) mascolino/a

mash [mæʃ] *vt* passare, schiacciare

mashed [mæʃt] *adj*: **~ potatoes**
purè *m* di patate

mask [mɑːsk] *n* maschera ▷ *vt*
mascherare

mason ['meɪsn] *n* (*also*: **stone~**)
scalpellino; (*also*: **free~**) massone *m*;
masonry *n* muratura

mass [mæs] *n* moltitudine *f*, massa;
(*Physics*) massa; (*Rel*) messa ▷ *cpd*
di massa ▷ *vi* ammassarsi; **the ~es**
(*ordinary people*) le masse; **~es of** (*col*)
una montagna di

massacre ['mæsəkəʳ] *n* massacro

massage ['mæsɑːʒ] *n* massaggio

massive ['mæsɪv] *adj* enorme,
massiccio/a

mass media *npl* mass media *mpl*

mass-produce ['mæsprə'djuːs] *vt*
produrre in serie

mast [mɑːst] *n* albero

master ['mɑːstəʳ] *n* padrone *m*;
(*teacher: in primary school, Art etc*)
maestro; (: *in secondary school*)
professore *m*; (*title for boys*): **M~ X**
Signorino X ▷ *vt* domare; (*learn*)
imparare a fondo; (*understand*)
conoscere a fondo; **mastermind**
n mente *f* superiore ▷ *vt* essere il
cervello di; **Master of Arts/Science**
n Master *m inv* in lettere/scienze;
masterpiece *n* capolavoro

masturbate ['mæstəbeɪt] *vi*
masturbarsi

mat [mæt] *n* stuoia; (*also*: **door~**)
stoino, zerbino; (*also*: **table ~**)
sottopiatto ▷ *adj* = **matt**

match [mætʃ] *n* fiammifero; (*game*)
partita, incontro; (*fig*) uguale *m/f*;

matrimonio; partito ▷ vt intonare; (*go well with*) andare benissimo con; (*equal*) uguagliare; (*correspond to*) corrispondere a; (*pair: also:* **~ up**) accoppiare ▷ vi intonarsi; **to be a good ~** andare bene; **matchbox** n scatola per fiammiferi; **matching** adj ben assortito/a

mate [meɪt] n compagno/a di lavoro; (*col: friend*) amico/a; (*animal*) compagno/a; (*in merchant navy*) secondo ▷ vi accoppiarsi

material [mə'tɪərɪəl] n (*substance*) materiale m, materia; (*cloth*) stoffa ▷ adj materiale; **materials** npl (*equipment etc*) materiali mpl

materialize [mə'tɪərɪəlaɪz] vi materializzarsi, realizzarsi

maternal [mə'tə:nl] adj materno/a

maternity [mə'tə:nɪtɪ] n maternità; **maternity hospital** n ≈ clinica ostetrica; **maternity leave** n congedo di maternità

math [mæθ] n abbr (US) = **mathematics**

mathematical [mæθə'mætɪkl] adj matematico/a

mathematician [mæθəmə'tɪʃən] n matematico/a

mathematics [mæθə'mætɪks] n matematica

maths [mæθs] n abbr (BRIT) = **mathematics**

matinée ['mætɪneɪ] n matinée f inv

matron ['meɪtrən] n (*in hospital*) capoinfermiera; (*in school*) infermiera

matt [mæt] adj opaco/a

matter ['mætə^r] n questione f; (*Physics*) materia, sostanza; (*content*) contenuto; (*Med: pus*) pus m ▷ vi importare; **matters** npl (*affairs*) questioni; **it doesn't ~** non importa; (*I don't mind*) non fa niente; **what's the ~?** che cosa c'è?; **no ~ what** qualsiasi cosa accada; **as a ~ of course** come cosa naturale; **as a ~ of fact** in verità

mattress ['mætrɪs] n materasso

mature [mə'tjuə^r] adj maturo/a; (*cheese*) stagionato/a ▷ vi maturare; stagionare; **mature student** n studente universitario che ha più di 25 anni; **maturity** n maturità

maul [mɔ:l] vt lacerare

mauve [məuv] adj malva inv

max. abbr = **maximum**

maximize ['mæksɪmaɪz] vt (*profits etc*) massimizzare; (*chances*) aumentare al massimo

maximum ['mæksɪməm] adj massimo/a ▷ n (pl **maxima**) massimo

May [meɪ] n maggio

may [meɪ] vi (*conditional* **might**) (*indicating possibility*): **he ~ come** può darsi che venga; (*be allowed to*): **~ I smoke?** posso fumare?; (*wishes*): **~ God bless you!** Dio la benedica!; **I might as well go** potrei anche andarmene

maybe ['meɪbi:] adv forse, può darsi; **~ he'll ...** può darsi che lui ... + sub, forse lui ...

May Day n il primo maggio

mayhem ['meɪhɛm] n cagnara

mayonnaise [meɪə'neɪz] n maionese f

mayor [mɛə^r] n sindaco; **mayoress** n sindaco (*donna*); moglie f del sindaco

maze [meɪz] n labirinto, dedalo

MD n abbr (= *Doctor of Medicine*) titolo di studio; (*Comm*) = **managing director**

me [mi:] pron mi, m' + *vowel or silent "h"*; (*stressed, after prep*) me; **he heard me** mi ha or m'ha sentito; **give me a book** dammi (*or* mi dia) un libro; **it's me** sono io; **with me** con me; **without me** senza di me

meadow ['mɛdəu] n prato

meagre, (US) **meager** ['mi:gə^r] adj magro/a

meal [mi:l] n pasto; (*flour*) farina; **mealtime** n l'ora di mangiare

mean [mi:n] adj (*with money*) avaro/a, gretto/a; (*unkind*) meschino/a, maligno/a; (*shabby*)

m

misero/a; (*average*) medio/a ▷ *vt* (*pt, pp* **meant**) (*signify*) significare, voler dire; (*intend*): **to ~ to do** aver l'intenzione di fare ▷ *n* mezzo; (*Math*) media; **to be ~t for** essere destinato/a a; **do you ~ it?** dice sul serio?; **what do you ~?** che cosa vuol dire?; *see also* **means**

meaning ['mi:nɪŋ] *n* significato, senso; **meaningful** *adj* significativo/a; **meaningless** *adj* senza senso

means [mi:nz] *npl* (*way, money*) mezzi *mpl*; **by means of** per mezzo di; **by all means** ma certo, prego

meant [mɛnt] *pt, pp of* **mean**

meantime ['mi:ntaɪm], **meanwhile** ['mi:nwaɪl] *adv* (*also:* **in the ~**) nel frattempo

measles ['mi:zlz] *n* morbillo

measure ['mɛʒəʳ] *vt, vi* misurare ▷ *n* misura; (*ruler*) metro

measurement ['mɛʒəmənt] *n* (*act*) misurazione *f*; (*measure*) misura; **chest/hip ~** giro petto/ fianchi; **to take sb's ~s** prendere le misure di qn

meat [mi:t] *n* carne *f*; **cold ~s** affettati *mpl*; **meatball** *n* polpetta di carne

Mecca ['mɛkə] *n* La Mecca; (*fig*): **a ~ (for)** la Mecca (di)

mechanic [mɪ'kænɪk] *n* meccanico; **mechanical** *adj* meccanico/a

mechanism ['mɛkənɪzəm] *n* meccanismo

medal ['mɛdl] *n* medaglia; **medallist**, (*us*) **medalist** *n* (*Sport*): **to be a gold medallist** essere medaglia d'oro

meddle ['mɛdl] *vi*: **to ~ in** immischiarsi in, mettere le mani in; **to ~ with** toccare

media ['mi:dɪə] *npl* media *mpl*

mediaeval [mɛdɪ'i:vl] *adj* = **medieval**

mediate ['mi:dɪeɪt] *vi* fare da mediatore/trice

medical ['mɛdɪkl] *adj* medico/a; **~ (examination)** *n* visita medica; **medical certificate** *n* certificato medico

medicated ['mɛdɪkeɪtɪd] *adj* medicato/a

medication [mɛdɪ'keɪʃən] *n* medicinali *mpl*, farmaci *mpl*

medicine ['mɛdsɪn] *n* medicina

medieval [mɛdɪ'i:vl] *adj* medievale

mediocre [mi:dɪ'əukəʳ] *adj* mediocre

meditate ['mɛdɪteɪt] *vi*: **to ~ (on)** meditare (su)

meditation [mɛdɪ'teɪʃən] *n* meditazione *f*

Mediterranean [mɛdɪtə'reɪnɪən] *adj* mediterraneo/a; **the ~ (Sea)** il (mare) Mediterraneo

medium ['mi:dɪəm] *adj* medio/a ▷ *n* (*pl* **media**: *means*) mezzo; (*pl* **mediums**: *person*) medium *m inv*; **medium-sized** *adj* (*tin etc*) di grandezza media; (*clothes*) di taglia media; **medium wave** *n* onde *fpl* medie

meek [mi:k] *adj* dolce, umile

meet (*pt, pp* **met**) [mi:t, mɛt] *vt* incontrare; (*for the first time*) fare la conoscenza di; (*go and fetch*) andare a prendere; (*fig*) affrontare; soddisfare; raggiungere ▷ *vi* incontrarsi; (*in session*) riunirsi; (*join: objects*) unirsi ▷ *n* (*BRIT Hunting*) raduno (dei partecipanti alla caccia alla volpe); (*US Sport*) raduno (sportivo); **I'll ~ you at the station** verrò a prenderla alla stazione; **pleased to ~ you!** piacere (di conoscerla)!; **meet up** *vi*: **to ~ up with sb** incontrare qn; **meet with** *vt fus* incontrare; **meeting** *n* incontro; (*session: of club etc*) riunione *f*; (*interview*) intervista; **she's at a meeting** (*Comm*) è in riunione; **meeting place** *n* luogo d'incontro

megabyte ['mɛgəbaɪt] *n* (*Comput*) megabyte *m inv*

megaphone ['mɛgəfəun] *n* megafono

megapixel ['mɛgəpɪksl] n
megapixel m inv
melancholy ['mɛlənkəlɪ] n
malinconia ▷ adj malinconico/a
melody ['mɛlədɪ] n melodia
melon ['mɛlən] n melone m
melt [mɛlt] vi (gen) sciogliersi,
struggersi; (metals) fondersi ▷ vt
sciogliere, struggere; fondere
member ['mɛmbər] n membro;
Member of Congress (US) n
membro del Congresso; **Member
of Parliament** (BRIT) n deputato/a;
**Member of the European
Parliament** (BRIT) n eurodeputato/a;
**Member of the House of
Representatives** (US) n membro
della Camera dei Rappresentanti;
**Member of the Scottish
Parliament** (BRIT) n deputato/a del
Parlamento scozzese; **membership**
n iscrizione f; (numero d')iscritti mpl,
membri mpl; **membership card** n
tessera (di iscrizione)
memento [mə'mɛntəu] n ricordo,
souvenir m inv
memo ['mɛməu] n appunto; (Comm
etc) comunicazione f di servizio
memorable ['mɛmərəbl] adj
memorabile
memorandum (pl **memoranda**)
[mɛmə'rændəm, -də] n appunto;
(Comm etc) comunicazione f di servizio
memorial [mɪ'mɔːrɪəl] n
monumento commemorativo ▷ adj
commemorativo/a
memorize ['mɛməraɪz] vt
memorizzare
memory ['mɛmərɪ] n (gen, Comput)
memoria; (recollection) ricordo;
memory stick n (Comput) stick m inv
di memoria
men [mɛn] npl of **man**
menace ['mɛnɪs] n minaccia ▷ vt
minacciare
mend [mɛnd] vt aggiustare, riparare;
(darn) rammendare ▷ n: **on the ~** in
via di guarigione

meningitis [mɛnɪn'dʒaɪtɪs] n
meningite f
menopause ['mɛnəupɔːz] n
menopausa
men's room n: **the ~** (esp US) la
toilette degli uomini
menstruation [mɛnstru'eɪʃən] n
mestruazione f
menswear ['mɛnzwɛər] n
abbigliamento maschile
mental ['mɛntl] adj mentale;
mental hospital n (pej) ospedale
m psichiatrico; **mentality**
[mɛn'tælɪtɪ] n mentalità f inv;
mentally adv: **to be mentally ill**
essere malato/a di mente
menthol ['mɛnθɒl] n mentolo
mention ['mɛnʃən] n menzione f
▷ vt menzionare, far menzione di;
don't ~ it! non c'è di che!, prego!
menu ['mɛnjuː] n (set menu, Comput)
menù m inv; (printed) carta
MEP n abbr = **Member of the
European Parliament**
mercenary ['məːsɪnərɪ] adj venale
▷ n mercenario
merchandise ['məːtʃəndaɪz] n
merci fpl
merchant ['məːtʃənt] n mercante m,
commerciante m; **merchant navy**,
(US) **merchant marine** n marina
mercantile
merciless ['məːsɪlɪs] adj
spietato/a
mercury ['məːkjurɪ] n mercurio
mercy ['məːsɪ] n pietà f; (Rel)
misericordia; **at the ~ of** alla
mercè di
mere [mɪər] adj semplice; **by a ~
chance** per mero caso; **merely** adv
semplicemente, non ... che
merge [məːdʒ] vt unire ▷ vi fondersi,
unirsi; (Comm) fondersi; **merger** n
(Comm) fusione f
meringue [mə'ræŋ] n meringa
merit ['mɛrɪt] n merito, valore m ▷ vt
meritare
mermaid ['məːmeɪd] n sirena

merry ['mɛrɪ] adj gaio/a, allegro/a;
M~ Christmas! Buon Natale!;
merry-go-round n carosello
mesh [mɛʃ] n maglia; rete f
mess [mɛs] n confusione f, disordine
m; (fig) pasticcio; (dirt) sporcizia; (Mil)
mensa; **mess about, mess around**
vi (col) trastullarsi; **mess with** vt fus
(col: challenge, confront) litigare con;
(: drugs, drinks) abusare di; **mess up**
vt (col) sporcare; fare un pasticcio
di; rovinare
message ['mɛsɪdʒ] n messaggio;
message board n (Comput) bacheca
elettronica
messenger ['mɛsɪndʒər] n
messaggero/a
Messrs, Messrs. ['mɛsəz] abbr (on
letters: = messieurs) Spett.
messy ['mɛsɪ] adj sporco/a;
disordinato/a
met [mɛt] pt, pp of **meet**
metabolism [mɛ'tæbəlɪzəm] n
metabolismo
metal ['mɛtl] n metallo; **metallic**
[mɛ'tælɪk] adj metallico/a
metaphor ['mɛtəfər] n metafora
meteor ['mi:tɪər] n meteora;
meteorite ['mi:tɪəraɪt] n meteorite
m
meteorology [mi:tɪə'rɔlədʒɪ] n
meteorologia
meter ['mi:tər] n (instrument)
contatore m; (parking meter)
parchimetro; (us: unit) = **metre**
method ['mɛθəd] n metodo;
methodical [mɪ'θɔdɪkl] adj
metodico/a
meths [mɛθs] (BRIT) n = **methylated
spirits**
methylated spirits ['mɛθɪleɪtɪd-]
n (BRIT: also: **meths**) alcool m
denaturato
meticulous [mɛ'tɪkjuləs] adj
meticoloso/a
metre, (us) meter ['mi:tər] n metro
metric ['mɛtrɪk] adj metrico/a
metro ['mɛtrəu] n metro m inv

metropolitan [mɛtrə'pɔlɪtən] adj
metropolitano/a
Mexican ['mɛksɪkən] adj, n
messicano/a
Mexico ['mɛksɪkəu] n Messico
mg abbr (= milligram) mg
mice [maɪs] npl of **mouse**
micro... ['maɪkrəu] prefix micro...;
microchip n microcircuito
integrato; **microphone** n microfono;
microscope n microscopio;
microwave n (also: **microwave
oven**) forno a microonde
mid [mɪd] adj: **~ May** metà maggio;
~ afternoon metà pomeriggio;
in ~ air a mezz'aria; **midday** n
mezzogiorno
middle ['mɪdl] n mezzo; centro;
(waist) vita ▷ adj di mezzo; **in the ~
of the night** nel cuore della notte;
middle-aged adj di mezza età;
Middle Ages npl: **the Middle Ages**
il Medioevo; **middle class** adj (also:
middle-class) ≈ borghese; **Middle
East** n: **the Middle East** il Medio
Oriente; **middle name** n secondo
nome m; **middle school** n (us) scuola
media per ragazzi dagli 11 ai 14 anni;
(BRIT) scuola media per ragazzi dagli 8 o
9 ai 12 o 13 anni
midge [mɪdʒ] n moscerino
midget ['mɪdʒɪt] n (col!) nano/a
midnight ['mɪdnaɪt] n mezzanotte f
midst [mɪdst] n: **in the ~ of** in
mezzo a
midsummer [mɪd'sʌmər] n mezza
or piena estate f
midway [mɪd'weɪ] adj, adv: **~
(between)** a mezza strada (fra); **~
(through)** a metà (di)
midweek [mɪd'wi:k] adv a metà
settimana
midwife (pl **midwives**) ['mɪdwaɪf,
-vz] n levatrice f
midwinter [mɪd'wɪntər] n pieno
inverno
might [maɪt] vb see **may** ▷ n potere
m, forza; **mighty** adj forte, potente

migraine ['mi:greɪn] n emicrania
migrant ['maɪgrənt] adj (bird) migratore/trice; (worker) emigrato/a
migrate [maɪ'greɪt] vi (bird) migrare; (person) emigrare
migration [maɪ'greɪʃən] n migrazione f
mike [maɪk] n abbr (= microphone) microfono
Milan [mɪ'læn] n Milano f
mild [maɪld] adj mite; (person, voice) dolce; (flavour) delicato/a; (illness) leggero/a; (interest) blando/a ⊳ n (beer) birra leggera; **mildly** ['maɪldlɪ] adv mitemente; dolcemente; delicatamente; leggermente; blandamente; **to put it mildly** a dire poco
mile [maɪl] n miglio; **mileage** n distanza in miglia, ≈ chilometraggio; **mileometer** [maɪ'lɒmɪtər] n (BRIT) = **milometer**; **milestone** ['maɪlstəun] n pietra miliare
military ['mɪlɪtərɪ] adj militare
militia [mɪ'lɪʃə] n milizia
milk [mɪlk] n latte m ⊳ vt (cow) mungere; (fig) sfruttare; **milk chocolate** n cioccolato al latte; **milkman** (irreg) lattaio; **milky** adj lattiginoso/a; (colour) latteo/a
mill [mɪl] n mulino; (small, for coffee, pepper etc) macinino; (factory) fabbrica; (spinning mill) filatura ⊳ vt macinare ⊳ vi (also: ~ **about**) brulicare
millennium (pl **millenniums** or **millennia**) [mɪ'lɛnɪəm, -'lɛnɪə] n millennio
milli... ['mɪlɪ] prefix milli...; **milligram(me)** n milligrammo; **millilitre**, (US) **milliliter** ['mɪlɪli:tər] n millilitro; **millimetre**, (US) **millimeter** n millimetro
million ['mɪljən] num milione m; **millionaire** n milionario, ≈ miliardario; **millionth** num milionesimo/a

milometer [maɪ'lɒmɪtər] n ≈ contachilometri m inv
mime [maɪm] n mimo ⊳ vt, vi mimare
mimic ['mɪmɪk] n imitatore/trice ⊳ vt imitare
min. abbr = **minute**; (= minimum) min.
mince [mɪns] vt tritare, macinare ⊳ n (BRIT Culin) carne f tritata or macinata; **mincemeat** n frutta secca tritata per uso in pasticceria; (US) carne f tritata or macinata; **mince pie** n specie di torta con frutta secca
mind [maɪnd] n mente f ⊳ vt (attend to, look after) badare a, occuparsi di; (be careful) fare attenzione a, stare attento/a a; (object to): **I don't ~ the noise** il rumore non mi dà alcun fastidio; **do you ~ if ...?** le dispiace se ...?; **I don't ~** non m'importa; **~ you, ...** sì, però va detto che ...; **never ~** non importa, non fa niente; (don't worry) non preoccuparti; **it is on my ~** mi preoccupa; **to my ~** secondo me, a mio parere; **to be out of one's ~** essere uscito/a di mente; **to keep sth in ~** non dimenticare qc; **to bear sth in ~** tener presente qc; **to make up one's ~** decidersi; **"~ the step"** "attenzione allo scalino"; **mindless** adj idiota
mine¹ [maɪn] pron il (la) mio/a; (pl) i (le) miei (mie); **this book is ~** questo libro è mio; **yours is red, ~ is green** il tuo è rosso, il mio è verde; **a friend of ~** un mio amico
mine² [maɪn] n miniera; (explosive) mina ⊳ vt (coal) estrarre; (ship, beach) minare; **minefield** ['maɪnfi:ld] n campo minato; **miner** ['maɪnər] n minatore m
mineral ['mɪnərəl] adj minerale ⊳ n minerale m; **mineral water** n acqua minerale
mingle ['mɪŋgl] vi: **to ~ with** mescolarsi a, mischiarsi con
miniature ['mɪnətʃər] adj in miniatura ⊳ n miniatura

m

minibar ['mɪnɪbɑːʳ] n minibar m inv
minibus ['mɪnɪbʌs] n minibus m inv
minicab ['mɪnɪkæb] n (BRIT) ≈ taxi m inv
minimal ['mɪnɪml] adj minimo/a
minimize ['mɪnɪmaɪz] vt minimizzare
minimum ['mɪnɪməm] n (pl **minima**) minimo ▷ adj minimo/a
mining ['maɪnɪŋ] n industria mineraria
miniskirt ['mɪnɪskəːt] n minigonna
minister ['mɪnɪstəʳ] n (BRIT Pol) ministro; (Rel) pastore m
ministry ['mɪnɪstrɪ] n ministero
minor ['maɪnəʳ] adj minore, di poca importanza; (Mus) minore ▷ n (Law) minorenne m/f
Minorca [mɪ'nɔːkə] n Minorca
minority [maɪ'nɔrɪtɪ] n minoranza
mint [mɪnt] n (plant) menta; (sweet) pasticca di menta ▷ vt (coins) battere; **the (Royal) M~** (BRIT), **the (US) M~** (US) la Zecca; **in ~ condition** come nuovo/a di zecca
minus ['maɪnəs] n (also: **~ sign**) segno meno ▷ prep meno
minute¹ ['mɪnɪt] n minuto; **minutes** npl (of meeting) verbale m
minute² [maɪ'njuːt] adj minuscolo/a; (detail) minuzioso/a
miracle ['mɪrəkl] n miracolo
miraculous [mɪ'rækjuləs] adj miracoloso/a
mirage ['mɪrɑːʒ] n miraggio
mirror ['mɪrəʳ] n specchio; (in car) specchietto
misbehave [mɪsbɪ'heɪv] vi comportarsi male
misc. abbr = **miscellaneous**
miscarriage ['mɪskærɪdʒ] n (Med) aborto spontaneo; **~ of justice** errore m giudiziario
miscellaneous [mɪsɪ'leɪnɪəs] adj (items) vario/a; (selection) misto/a
mischief ['mɪstʃɪf] n (naughtiness) birichineria; (maliciousness) malizia; **mischievous** adj birichino/a

misconception [mɪskən'sɛpʃən] n idea sbagliata
misconduct [mɪs'kɔndʌkt] n cattiva condotta; **professional ~** reato professionale
miser ['maɪzəʳ] n avaro
miserable ['mɪzərəbl] adj infelice; (wretched) miserabile; (weather) deprimente; (offer, failure) misero/a
misery ['mɪzərɪ] n (unhappiness) tristezza; (wretchedness) miseria
misfortune [mɪs'fɔːtʃən] n sfortuna
misgiving [mɪs'gɪvɪŋ] n dubbi mpl; **to have ~s about sth** essere diffidente or avere dei dubbi per quanto riguarda qc
misguided [mɪs'gaɪdɪd] adj sbagliato/a; poco giudizioso/a
mishap ['mɪshæp] n disgrazia
misinterpret [mɪsɪn'təːprɪt] vt interpretare male
misjudge [mɪs'dʒʌdʒ] vt giudicare male
mislay [mɪs'leɪ] vt (irreg) smarrire
mislead [mɪs'liːd] vt (irreg) sviare; **misleading** adj ingannevole
misplace [mɪs'pleɪs] vt smarrire
misprint ['mɪsprɪnt] n errore m di stampa
misrepresent [mɪsrɛprɪ'zɛnt] vt travisare
Miss [mɪs] n Signorina
miss [mɪs] vt (fail to get) perdere; (fail to hit) mancare; (fail to see): **you can't ~ it** non puoi non vederlo; (regret the absence of): **I ~ him/it** sento la sua mancanza ▷ vi mancare ▷ n (shot) colpo mancato; **we ~ed our train** abbiamo perso il treno; **miss out** (BRIT) omettere; **miss out on** vt fus (fun, party) perdersi; (chance, bargain) lasciarsi sfuggire
missile ['mɪsaɪl] n (Aviat) missile m; (object thrown) proiettile m
missing ['mɪsɪŋ] adj perso/a, smarrito/a; (removed) mancante; **~ person** scomparso/a; (after

disaster) disperso/a; **~ in action** (*Mil*) disperso/a; **to be ~** mancare

mission ['mɪʃən] *n* missione *f*; **missionary** *n* missionario/a

misspell [mɪs'spɛl] *vt* (*irreg: like* **spell**) sbagliare l'ortografia di

mist [mɪst] *n* nebbia, foschia ▷ *vi* (*also*: **~ over, ~ up**) annebbiarsi; (*BRIT*: *windows*) appannarsi

mistake [mɪs'teɪk] *n* sbaglio, errore *m* ▷ *vt* (*irreg: like* **take**) sbagliarsi di; fraintendere; **to ~ for** prendere per; **by ~** per sbaglio; **to make a ~** fare uno sbaglio *or* un errore, sbagliare; **there must be some ~** ci dev'essere un errore; **mistaken** *pp of* **mistake** ▷ *adj* (*idea etc*) sbagliato/a; **to be mistaken** sbagliarsi

mister ['mɪstər] *n* (*col*) signore *m*; *see* **Mr**

mistletoe ['mɪsltəu] *n* vischio

mistook [mɪs'tuk] *pt of* **mistake**

mistress ['mɪstrɪs] *n* padrona; (*lover*) amante *f*; (*BRIT Scol*) insegnante *f*

mistrust [mɪs'trʌst] *vt* diffidare di

misty ['mɪstɪ] *adj* nebbioso/a, brumoso/a

misunderstand [mɪsʌndə'stænd] *vt, vi* (*irreg*) capire male, fraintendere; **misunderstanding** *n* malinteso, equivoco; **there's been a misunderstanding** c'è stato un malinteso

misunderstood [mɪsʌndə'stud] *pt, pp of* **misunderstand**

misuse *n* [mɪs'juːs] cattivo uso; (*of power*) abuso ▷ *vt* [mɪs'juːz] far cattivo uso di; abusare di

mitt(en) ['mɪt(n)] *n* mezzo guanto; manopola

mix [mɪks] *vt* mescolare ▷ *vi* (*people*): **to ~ with** avere a che fare con ▷ *n* mescolanza; preparato; **mix up** *vt* mescolare; (*confuse*) confondere; **mixed** *adj* misto/a; **mixed grill** *n* (*BRIT*) misto alla griglia; **mixed salad** *n* insalata mista; **mixed-up** *adj* (*confused*) confuso/a; **mixer** *n*

(*for food: electric*) frullatore *m*; (*: hand*) frullino; **he is a good mixer** è molto socievole; **mixture** *n* mescolanza; (*blend: of tobacco etc*) miscela; (*Med*) sciroppo; **mix-up** *n* confusione *f*

ml *abbr* (= *millilitre(s)*) ml

mm *abbr* (= *millimetre*) mm

moan [məun] *n* gemito ▷ *vi* (*col: complain*): **to ~ (about)** lamentarsi (di)

moat [məut] *n* fossato

mob [mɔb] *n* calca ▷ *vt* accalcarsi intorno a

mobile ['məubaɪl] *adj* mobile ▷ *n* (*phone*) telefonino, cellulare *m*; (*Art*) mobile *m inv*; **mobile home** *n* grande roulotte *f inv* (*utilizzata come domicilio*); **mobile phone** *n* telefono portatile, telefonino

mobility [məu'bɪlɪtɪ] *n* mobilità; (*of applicant*) disponibilità a viaggiare

mobilize ['məubɪlaɪz] *vt* mobilitare ▷ *vi* mobilitarsi

mock [mɔk] *vt* deridere, burlarsi di ▷ *adj* falso/a; **mocks** *npl* (*BRIT col: Scol*) simulazione *f* degli esami; **mockery** *n* derisione *f*; **to make a mockery of** burlarsi di; (*exam*) rendere una farsa

mod cons ['mɔd'kɔnz] *npl abbr* (*BRIT*) = **modern conveniences**

mode [məud] *n* modo

model ['mɔdl] *n* modello; (*person: for fashion*) indossatore/trice; (*: for artist*) modello/a ▷ *vt* modellare ▷ *vi* fare l'indossatore (*or* l'indossatrice) ▷ *adj* (*small-scale: railway etc*) in miniatura; (*child, factory*) modello *inv*; **to ~ clothes** presentare degli abiti; **to ~ sb/sth on** modellare qn/qc su

modem ['məudɛm] *n* modem *m inv*

moderate *adj* ['mɔdərɪt] moderato/a ▷ *vi* ['mɔdəreɪt] moderarsi, placarsi ▷ *vt* moderare

moderation [mɔdə'reɪʃən] *n* moderazione *f*, misura; **in ~** in quantità moderata, con moderazione

m

modern ['mɔdən] *adj* moderno/a;
~ **conveniences** comodità *fpl*
moderne; ~ **languages** lingue
fpl moderne; **modernize** *vt*
modernizzare

modest ['mɔdɪst] *adj* modesto/a;
modesty *n* modestia

modification [mɔdɪfɪ'keɪʃən] *n*
modificazione *f*; **to make ~s** fare *or*
apportare delle modifiche

modify ['mɔdɪfaɪ] *vt* modificare

module ['mɔdjuːl] *n* modulo

mohair ['məuhεəʳ] *n* mohair *m*

Mohammed [məu'hæmɪd] *n*
Maometto

moist [mɔɪst] *adj* umido/a;
moisture ['mɔɪstʃəʳ] *n* umidità;
(*on glass*) goccioline *fpl* di vapore;
moisturizer ['mɔɪstʃəraɪzəʳ] *n*
idratante *f*

mold *etc* [məuld] (*US*) = **mould** *etc*

mole [məul] *n* (*animal, fig*) talpa;
(*spot*) neo

molecule ['mɔlɪkjuːl] *n* molecola

molest [məu'lεst] *vt* molestare

molten ['məultən] *adj* fuso/a

mom [mɔm] *n* (*US*) = **mum**

moment ['məumənt] *n* momento,
istante *m*; **at that ~** in quel
momento; **at the ~** al momento,
in questo momento; **momentarily**
['məuməntεrɪlɪ] *adv* per un
momento; (*US: very soon*) da un
momento all'altro; **momentary**
adj momentaneo/a, passeggero/a;
momentous [məu'mεntəs] *adj* di
grande importanza

momentum [məu'mεntəm] *n*
(*Physics*) momento; (*fig*) impeto; **to
gather ~** aumentare di velocità

mommy ['mɔmɪ] *n* (*US*) mamma

Mon. *abbr* (= *Monday*) lun.

Monaco ['mɔnəkəu] *n* Monaco *f*

monarch ['mɔnək] *n* monarca *m*;
monarchy *n* monarchia

monastery ['mɔnəstərɪ] *n*
monastero

Monday ['mʌndɪ] *n* lunedì *m inv*

monetary ['mʌnɪtərɪ] *adj*
monetario/a

money ['mʌnɪ] *n* denaro, soldi *mpl*;
money belt *n* marsupio (*per soldi*);
money order *n* vaglia *m inv*

mongrel ['mʌŋgrəl] *n* (*dog*) cane *m*
bastardo

monitor ['mɔnɪtəʳ] *n* (*TV, Comput*)
monitor *m inv* ▷ *vt* controllare

monk [mʌŋk] *n* monaco

monkey ['mʌŋkɪ] *n* scimmia

monologue ['mɔnələg] *n* monologo

monopoly [mə'nɔpəlɪ] *n* monopolio

monosodium glutamate
[mɔnə'səudɪəm'gluːtəmeɪt] *n*
glutammato di sodio

monotonous [mə'nɔtənəs] *adj*
monotono/a

monsoon [mɔn'suːn] *n* monsone *m*

monster ['mɔnstəʳ] *n* mostro

month [mʌnθ] *n* mese *m*; **monthly**
adj mensile ▷ *adv* al mese; ogni mese

monument ['mɔnjumənt] *n*
monumento

mood [muːd] *n* umore *m*; **to be
in a good/bad ~** essere di buon/
cattivo umore; **moody** *adj* (*variable*)
capriccioso/a, lunatico/a; (*sullen*)
imbronciato/a

moon [muːn] *n* luna; **moonlight** *n*
chiaro di luna

moor [muəʳ] *n* brughiera ▷ *vt* (*ship*)
ormeggiare ▷ *vi* ormeggiarsi

moose [muːs] *n* (*pl inv*) alce *m*

mop [mɔp] *n* lavapavimenti *m inv*;
(*also*: ~ **of hair**) zazzera ▷ *vt* lavare
con lo straccio; (*face*) asciugare;
mop up *vt* asciugare con uno
straccio

mope [məup] *vi* fare il broncio

moped ['məupεd] *n* (*BRIT*)
ciclomotore *m*

moral ['mɔrəl] *adj* morale ▷ *n*
morale *f*; **morals** *npl* (*principles*)
moralità

morale [mɔ'rɑːl] *n* morale *m*

morality [mə'rælɪtɪ] *n* moralità

morbid ['mɔːbɪd] *adj* morboso/a

KEYWORD

more [mɔːʳ] *adj* **1** (*greater in number etc*) più; **more people/letters than we expected** più persone/lettere di quante ne aspettavamo; **I have more wine/money than you** ho più vino/soldi di te; **I have more wine than beer** ho più vino che birra **2** (*additional*) altro/a, ancora; **do you want (some) more tea?** vuole dell'altro tè?, vuole ancora del tè?; **I have no** *or* **I don't have any more money** non ho più soldi
▸ *pron* **1** (*greater amount*) più; **more than 10** più di 10; **it cost more than we expected** è costato più di quanto ci aspettassimo
2 (*further or additional amount*) ancora; **is there any more?** ce n'è ancora?; **there's no more** non ce n'è più; **a little more** ancora un po'; **many/much more** molti/e/ molto/a di più
▸ *adv*: **more dangerous/easily (than)** più pericoloso/facilmente (di); **more and more** sempre di più; **more and more difficult** sempre più difficile; **more or less** più o meno; **more than ever** più che mai

moreover [mɔːˈrəuvəʳ] *adv* inoltre, di più
morgue [mɔːg] *n* obitorio
morning [ˈmɔːnɪŋ] *n* mattina, mattino; (*duration*) mattinata ▸ *cpd* del mattino; **in the ~** la mattina; **7 o'clock in the ~** le 7 di *or* della mattina; **morning sickness** *n* nausee *fpl* mattutine
Moroccan [məˈrɔkən] *adj, n* marocchino/a
Morocco [məˈrɔkəu] *n* Marocco
moron [ˈmɔːrɔn] *n* (*col!*) deficiente *m/f*
morphine [ˈmɔːfiːn] *n* morfina
morris dancing [ˈmɔrɪs-] *n vedi nota* "morris dancing"

MORRIS DANCING

Il *morris dancing* è una danza folcloristica inglese tradizionalmente riservata agli uomini. Vestiti di bianco e con dei campanelli attaccati alle caviglie, i ballerini eseguono una danza tenendo in mano dei fazzoletti bianchi e lunghi bastoni. Questa danza è molto popolare nelle feste paesane.

Morse [mɔːs] *n* (*also:* **~ code**) alfabeto Morse
mortal [ˈmɔːtl] *adj, n* mortale (*m*)
mortar [ˈmɔːtəʳ] *n* (*Constr*) malta; (*dish*) mortaio
mortgage [ˈmɔːɡɪdʒ] *n* ipoteca; (*loan*) prestito ipotecario ▸ *vt* ipotecare
mortician [mɔːˈtɪʃən] *n* (*US*) impresario di pompe funebri
mortified [ˈmɔːtɪfaɪd] *adj* umiliato/a
mortuary [ˈmɔːtjuərɪ] *n* camera mortuaria; obitorio
mosaic [məuˈzeɪɪk] *n* mosaico
Moscow [ˈmɔskəu] *n* Mosca
Moslem [ˈmɔzləm] *adj, n* = **Muslim**
mosque [mɔsk] *n* moschea
mosquito [mɔsˈkiːtəu] (*pl* **mosquitoes**) *n* zanzara
moss [mɔs] *n* muschio
most [məust] *adj* (*almost all*) la maggior parte di; (*largest, greatest*): **who has (the) ~ money?** chi ha più soldi di tutti? ▸ *pron* la maggior parte ▸ *adv* più; (*work, sleep etc*) di più; (*very*) molto, estremamente; **the ~** (*also + adjective*) il (la) più; **~ of** la maggior parte di; **~ of them** quasi tutti; **I saw ~** ho visto più io; **at the (very) ~** al massimo; **to make the ~ of** trarre il massimo vantaggio da; **a ~ interesting book** un libro estremamente interessante; **mostly** *adv* per lo più

m

MOT *n abbr* (BRIT) = **Ministry of Transport**; **the ~ (test)** *revisione obbligatoria degli autoveicoli*

motel [məu'tɛl] *n* motel *m inv*

moth [mɔθ] *n* farfalla notturna; tarma

mother ['mʌðə'] *n* madre *f* ▷ *vt* (*care for*) fare da madre a; **motherhood** *n* maternità; **mother-in-law** *n* suocera; **mother-of-pearl** [mʌðərəv'pə:l] *n* madreperla; **Mother's Day** *n* la festa della mamma; **mother-to-be** [mʌðətə'bi:] *n* futura mamma; **mother tongue** *n* madrelingua

motif [məu'ti:f] *n* motivo

motion ['məuʃən] *n* movimento, moto; (*gesture*) gesto; (*at meeting*) mozione *f* ▷ *vt, vi*: **to ~ (to) sb to do** fare cenno a qn di fare; **motionless** *adj* immobile; **motion picture** *n* film *m inv*

motivate ['məutɪveɪt] *vt* (*act, decision*) dare origine a, motivare; (*person*) spingere

motivation [məutɪ'veɪʃən] *n* motivazione *f*

motive ['məutɪv] *n* motivo

motor ['məutə'] *n* motore *m*; (BRIT col: *vehicle*) macchina ▷ *adj* (*industry, accident*) automobilistico/a; autoveicolo; **motorbike** *n* moto *f inv*; **motorboat** *n* motoscafo; **motorcar** *n* (BRIT) automobile *f*; **motorcycle** *n* motocicletta; **motorcyclist** *n* motociclista *m/f*; **motoring** *n* (BRIT) turismo automobilistico; **motorist** *n* automobilista *m/f*; **motor racing** *n* (BRIT) corse *fpl* automobilistiche; **motorway** *n* (BRIT) autostrada

motto ['mɔtəu] (*pl* **mottoes**) *n* motto

mould, (US) **mold** [məuld] *n* forma, stampo; (*mildew*) muffa ▷ *vt* formare; (*fig*) foggiare; **mouldy**, (US) **moldy** *adj* ammuffito/a; (*smell*) di muffa

mound [maund] *n* rialzo, collinetta; (*heap*) mucchio

mount [maunt] *n* (*Geo*) monte *m* ▷ *vt* montare; (*horse*) montare a ▷ *vi* salire; **mount up** *vi* (*build up*) accumularsi

mountain ['mauntɪn] *n* montagna ▷ *cpd* di montagna; **mountain bike** *n* mountain bike *f inv*; **mountaineer** [mauntɪ'nɪə'] *n* alpinista *m/f*; **mountaineering** [mauntɪ'nɪərɪŋ] *n* alpinismo; **mountainous** *adj* montagnoso/a; **mountain range** *n* catena montuosa

mourn [mɔ:n] *vt* piangere, lamentare ▷ *vi*: **to ~ (for sb)** piangere (la morte di qn); **mourner** *n* parente *m/f* (*or* amico/a) del defunto; **mourning** *n* lutto; **in mourning** in lutto

mouse (*pl* **mice**) [maus, maɪs] *n* topo; (*Comput*) mouse *m inv*; **mouse mat, mouse pad** *n* (*Comput*) tappetino del mouse

moussaka [mu'sɑ:kə] *n* moussaka

mousse [mu:s] *n* mousse *f inv*

moustache [məs'tɑ:ʃ], (US) **mustache** *n* baffi *mpl*

mouth [mauθ] *n* bocca; (*of river*) bocca, foce *f*; (*opening*) orifizio; **mouthful** *n* boccata; **mouth organ** *n* armonica; **mouthpiece** *n* (*Mus*) imboccatura, bocchino; (*person*) portavoce *mf inv*; **mouthwash** *n* collutorio

move [mu:v] *n* (*movement*) movimento; (*in game*) mossa; (: *turn to play*) turno; (*change: of house*) trasloco; (: *of job*) cambiamento ▷ *vt* muovere; (*change position of*) spostare; (*emotionally*) commuovere; (*Pol: resolution etc*) proporre ▷ *vi* (*gen*) muoversi, spostarsi; (*also:* **~ house**) cambiar casa, traslocare; **to ~ towards** andare verso; **to ~ sb to do sth** indurre *or* spingere qn a fare qc; **to get a ~ on** affrettarsi, sbrigarsi; **move back** *vi* (*return*) ritornare; **move in** *vi* (*to a house*) entrare (in nuova casa); (*police etc*) intervenire; **move off** *vi* partire; **move on** *vi*

riprendere la strada; **move out** vi
(of house) sgombrare; **move over**
vi spostarsi; **move up** vi avanzare;
movement ['mu:vmənt] n (gen)
movimento; (gesture) gesto; (of stars,
water, physical) moto

movie ['mu:vɪ] n film m inv; **the ~s**
il cinema; **movie theater** (us) n
cinema m inv

moving ['mu:vɪŋ] adj mobile;
(causing emotion) commovente

mow (pt **mowed**, pp **mowed** or
mown) [məu, -n] vt (grass) tagliare;
(corn) mietere; **mower** n (also: **lawn
mower**) tagliaerba m inv

Mozambique [məuzəm'bi:k] n
Mozambico

MP n abbr = **Member of Parliament**

MP3 n MP3 m inv; **MP3 player** n
lettore m MP3

mpg n abbr = **miles per gallon**

mph n abbr = **miles per hour**

Mr, (us) **Mr.** ['mɪstər] n: **Mr X** Signor
X, Sig. X

Mrs, (us) **Mrs.** ['mɪsɪz] n: **~ X** Signora
X, Sig.ra X

Ms, (us) **Ms.** [mɪz] n = **Miss**; **Mrs**; **Ms
X** ≈ Signora X, ≈ Sig.ra X

MS

In inglese si usa Ms al posto di "Mrs"
(Signora) o "Miss" (Signorina) per
evitare la distinzione tradizionale
tra le donne sposate e quelle nubili.

MSP n abbr = **Member of the
Scottish Parliament**

Mt abbr (Geo: = **mount**) M

KEYWORD

much [mʌtʃ] adj, pron molto/a; **he's
done so much work** ha lavorato così
tanto; **I have as much money as
you** ho tanti soldi quanti ne hai tu;
how much is it? quant'è?; **it costs
too much** costa troppo; **as much as**
you want quanto vuoi
▶ adv **1** (greatly) molto, tanto; **thank
you very much** molte grazie; **he's
very much the gentleman** è il vero
gentiluomo; **I read as much as I can**
leggo quanto posso; **as much as
you** tanto quanto te
2 (by far) molto; **it's much the
biggest company in Europe** è di
gran lunga la più grossa società in
Europa
3 (almost) grossomodo,
praticamente; **they're much the
same** sono praticamente uguali

muck [mʌk] n (dirt) sporcizia; **muck
up** vt (col: spoil) rovinare; **mucky** adj
(dirty) sporco/a, lordo/a

mucus ['mju:kəs] n muco

mud [mʌd] n fango

muddle ['mʌdl] n confusione f,
disordine m; pasticcio ▷ vt (also: **~ up**)
confondere

muddy ['mʌdɪ] adj fangoso/a

mudguard ['mʌdgɑ:d] n parafango

muesli ['mju:zlɪ] n muesli m inv

muffin ['mʌfɪn] n specie di pasticcino
soffice da tè

muffled ['mʌfld] adj smorzato/a,
attutito/a

muffler ['mʌflər] n (us: Aut)
marmitta; (: on motorbike)
silenziatore m

mug [mʌg] n (cup) tazzone m; (for
beer) boccale m; (col: face) muso;
(: fool) scemo/a ▷ vt (assault) assalire;
mugger ['mʌgər] n aggressore m;
mugging n aggressione f (a scopo
di rapina)

muggy ['mʌgɪ] adj afoso/a

mule [mju:l] n mulo

multicoloured, (us) **multicolored**
['mʌltɪkʌləd] adj multicolore,
variopinto/a

multimedia ['mʌltɪ'mi:dɪə] adj
multimedia inv

multinational [mʌltɪ'næʃənl] adj, n
multinazionale (f)

multiple ['mʌltɪpl] *adj* multiplo/a; molteplice ▷ *n* multiplo; **multiple choice (test)** *n* esercizi *mpl* a scelta multipla; **multiple sclerosis** [-sklɪ'rəusɪs] *n* sclerosi *f* a placche

multiplex ['mʌltɪplɛks] *n* (*also*: ~ **cinema**) cinema *m inv* multisale *inv*

multiplication [mʌltɪplɪ'keɪʃən] *n* moltiplicazione *f*

multiply ['mʌltɪplaɪ] *vt* moltiplicare ▷ *vi* moltiplicarsi

multistorey ['mʌltɪ'stɔ:rɪ] *adj* (*BRIT: building, car park*) a più piani

mum [mʌm] *n* (*BRIT col*) mamma ▷ *adj*: **to keep ~** non aprire bocca

mumble ['mʌmbl] *vt*, *vi* borbottare

mummy ['mʌmɪ] *n* (*BRIT: mother*) mamma; (*embalmed*) mummia

mumps [mʌmps] *n* orecchioni *mpl*

munch [mʌntʃ] *vt*, *vi* sgranocchiare

municipal [mju:'nɪsɪpl] *adj* municipale

mural ['mjuərəl] *n* dipinto murale

murder ['mə:dər] *n* assassinio, omicidio ▷ *vt* assassinare; **to commit ~** commettere un omicidio; **murderer** *n* omicida *m*, assassino

murky ['mə:kɪ] *adj* tenebroso/a

murmur ['mə:mər] *n* mormorio ▷ *vt*, *vi* mormorare

muscle ['mʌsl] *n* muscolo; (*fig*) forza; **muscular** ['mʌskjulər] *adj* muscolare; (*person, arm*) muscoloso/a

museum [mju:'zɪəm] *n* museo

mushroom ['mʌʃrum] *n* fungo ▷ *vi* svilupparsi rapidamente

music ['mju:zɪk] *n* musica; **musical** *adj* musicale; (*person*) portato/a per la musica ▷ *n* (*show*) commedia musicale; **musical instrument** *n* strumento musicale; **musician** [mju:'zɪʃən] *n* musicista *m/f*

Muslim ['mʌzlɪm] *adj*, *n* musulmano/a

muslin ['mʌzlɪn] *n* mussola

mussel ['mʌsl] *n* cozza

must [mʌst] *aux vb* (*obligation*): **I ~ do it** devo farlo; (*probability*): **he ~ be there by now** dovrebbe essere arrivato ormai; **I ~ have made a mistake** devo essermi sbagliato ▷ *n*: **this programme/trip is a ~** è un programma/viaggio da non perdersi

mustache ['mʌstæʃ] *n* (*US*) = **moustache**

mustard ['mʌstəd] *n* senape *f*, mostarda

mustn't ['mʌsnt] = **must not**

mute [mju:t] *adj*, *n* muto/a

mutilate ['mju:tɪleɪt] *vt* mutilare

mutiny ['mju:tɪnɪ] *n* ammutinamento

mutter ['mʌtər] *vt*, *vi* borbottare, brontolare

mutton ['mʌtn] *n* carne *f* di montone

mutual ['mju:tʃuəl] *adj* mutuo/a, reciproco/a

muzzle ['mʌzl] *n* muso; (*protective device*) museruola; (*of gun*) bocca ▷ *vt* mettere la museruola a

my [maɪ] *adj* il (la) mio/a; (*pl*) i (le) miei (mie); **my house** la mia casa; **my books** i miei libri; **my brother** mio fratello; **I've washed my hair/ cut my finger** mi sono lavato i capelli/tagliato

myself [maɪ'sɛlf] *pron* (*reflexive*) mi; (*emphatic*) io stesso/a; (*after prep*) me; *see also* **oneself**

mysterious [mɪs'tɪərɪəs] *adj* misterioso/a

mystery ['mɪstərɪ] *n* mistero

mystical ['mɪstɪkəl] *adj* mistico/a

mystify ['mɪstɪfaɪ] *vt* mistificare; (*puzzle*) confondere

myth [mɪθ] *n* mito; **mythology** [mɪ'θɔlədʒɪ] *n* mitologia

n

n/a abbr (= not applicable) non pertinente

nag [næg] vt tormentare ▷ vi brontolare in continuazione

nail [neɪl] n (human) unghia; (metal) chiodo ▷ vt inchiodare; **to ~ sb down to a date/price** costringere qn a un appuntamento/ad accettare un prezzo; **nailbrush** n spazzolino da or per unghie; **nailfile** n lima da or per unghie; **nail polish** n smalto da or per unghie; **nail polish remover** n acetone m, solvente m; **nail scissors** npl forbici fpl da or per unghie; **nail varnish** n (BRIT) = **nail polish**

naïve [naɪˈiːv] adj ingenuo/a

naked [ˈneɪkɪd] adj nudo/a

name [neɪm] n nome m; (reputation) nome, reputazione f ▷ vt (baby etc) chiamare; (plant, illness) nominare; (person, object) identificare; (price, date) fissare; **by ~** di nome; **she knows them all by ~** li conosce tutti per nome; **what's your ~?** come si chiama?; **namely** adv cioè

nanny [ˈnænɪ] n bambinaia

nap [næp] n (sleep) pisolino; (of cloth) peluria ▷ vi: **to be caught ~ping** essere preso alla sprovvista

napkin [ˈnæpkɪn] n tovagliolo

nappy [ˈnæpɪ] n (BRIT) pannolino

narcotic [nɑːˈkɒtɪk] n (Med) narcotico; **narcotics** npl (drugs) narcotici, stupefacenti mpl

narrative [ˈnærətɪv] n narrativa

narrator [nəˈreɪtər] n narratore/trice

narrow [ˈnærəu] adj stretto/a; (resources, means) limitato/a, modesto/a ▷ vi restringersi; **to have a ~ escape** farcela per un pelo; **narrow down** vt (search, investigation, possibilities) restringere; (list) ridurre; **narrowly** adv per un pelo; (time) per poco; **narrow-minded** adj meschino/a

nasal [ˈneɪzl] adj nasale

nasty [ˈnɑːstɪ] adj (unpleasant: person, remark) cattivo/a; (rude) villano/a; (smell, wound, situation) brutto/a

nation [ˈneɪʃən] n nazione f

national [ˈnæʃənl] adj nazionale ▷ n cittadino/a; **national anthem** n inno nazionale; **national dress** n costume m nazionale; **National Health Service** n (BRIT) ≈ Servizio sanitario nazionale; **National Insurance** n (BRIT) ≈ Previdenza Sociale; **nationalist** adj, n nazionalista (m/f); **nationality** [næʃəˈnælɪtɪ] n nazionalità f inv; **nationalize** vt nazionalizzare; **national park** n parco nazionale; **National Trust** n sovrintendenza ai beni culturali e ambientali

- **NATIONAL TRUST**
-
-
- Fondato nel 1895, il *National Trust*
- è un'organizzazione che si occupa
- della tutela e salvaguardia di edifici
- e monumenti di interesse storico e

nationwide | 450

● di territori di interesse ambientale
● nel Regno Unito.

nationwide ['neɪʃənwaɪd] *adj* diffuso/a in tutto il paese ▷ *adv* in tutto il paese

native ['neɪtɪv] *n* abitante *m/f* del paese ▷ *adj* indigeno/a; (*country*) natio/a; (*ability*) innato/a; **a ~ of Russia** un nativo della Russia; **a ~ speaker of French** una persona di madrelingua francese; **Native American** *n* discendente di tribù dell'America settentrionale

NATO ['neɪtəu] *n abbr* (= *North Atlantic Treaty Organization*) N.A.T.O. *f*

natural ['nætʃrəl] *adj* naturale; (*ability*) innato/a; (*manner*) semplice; **natural gas** *n* gas *m* metano; **natural history** *n* storia naturale; **naturally** *adv* naturalmente; (*by nature: gifted*) di natura; **natural resources** *npl* risorse *fpl* naturali

nature ['neɪtʃər] *n* natura; (*character*) natura, indole *f*; **by ~** di natura; **nature reserve** (BRIT) *n* parco naturale

naughty ['nɔːtɪ] *adj* (*child*) birichino/a, cattivello/a; (*story, film*) spinto/a

nausea ['nɔːsɪə] *n* (*Med*) nausea; (*fig: disgust*) schifo

naval ['neɪvl] *adj* navale

navel ['neɪvl] *n* ombelico

navigate ['nævɪgeɪt] *vt* percorrere navigando ▷ *vi* navigare; (*Aut*) fare da navigatore; **navigation** [nævɪ'geɪʃən] *n* navigazione *f*

navy ['neɪvɪ] *n* marina

Nazi ['nɑːtsɪ] *n* nazista (*m/f*)

NB *abbr* (= *nota bene*) N.B.

near [nɪər] *adj* vicino/a; (*relation*) prossimo/a ▷ *adv* vicino ▷ *prep* (*also*: **~ to**) vicino a, presso; (*in time*) verso ▷ *vt* avvicinarsi a; **nearby** [nɪə'baɪ] *adj* vicino/a ▷ *adv* vicino; **nearly** *adv* quasi; **I nearly lost it** per poco non lo perdevo; **near-sighted** [nɪə'saɪtɪd] *adj* miope

neat [niːt] *adj* (*person, room*) ordinato/a; (*work*) pulito/a; (*solution, plan*) ben indovinato/a, azzeccato/a; (*spirits*) liscio/a; **neatly** *adv* con ordine; (*skilfully*) abilmente

necessarily ['nɛsɪsrɪlɪ] *adv* necessariamente

necessary ['nɛsɪsrɪ] *adj* necessario/a

necessity [nɪ'sɛsɪtɪ] *n* necessità *f inv*

neck [nɛk] *n* collo; (*of garment*) colletto ▷ *vi* (*col*) pomiciare, sbaciucchiarsi; **~ and ~** testa a testa; **necklace** ['nɛklɪs] *n* collana; **necktie** ['nɛktaɪ] *n* cravatta

nectarine ['nɛktərɪn] *n* nocepesca

need [niːd] *n* bisogno ▷ *vt* aver bisogno di; **do you ~ anything?** ha bisogno di qualcosa?; **I ~ to do it** lo devo fare, bisogna che io lo faccia; **you don't ~ to go** non deve andare, non c'è bisogno che lei vada

needle ['niːdl] *n* ago; (*on record player*) puntina ▷ *vt* punzecchiare

needless ['niːdlɪs] *adj* inutile

needlework ['niːdlwəːk] *n* cucito

needn't ['niːdnt] = **need not**

needy ['niːdɪ] *adj* bisognoso/a

negative ['nɛgətɪv] *n* (*Phot*) negativo; (*Ling*) negazione *f* ▷ *adj* negativo/a

neglect [nɪ'glɛkt] *vt* trascurare ▷ *n* (*of person, duty*) negligenza; (*of child, house etc*) scarsa cura; **state of ~** stato di abbandono

negotiate [nɪ'gəuʃɪeɪt] *vi* negoziare ▷ *vt* (*Comm*) negoziare; (*obstacle*) superare; **negotiation** [nɪgəuʃɪ'eɪʃən] *n* trattativa; (*Pol*) negoziato

negotiator [nɪ'gəuʃɪeɪtər] *n* negoziatore/trice

neighbour, (*us*) **neighbor** ['neɪbər] *n* vicino/a; **neighbourhood** *n* vicinato; **neighbouring** *adj* vicino/a

neither ['naɪðər] *adj, pron* né l'uno/a né l'altro/a, nessuno/a dei (delle) due ▷ *conj* neanche, nemmeno, neppure

▷ adv: **~ good nor bad** né buono né cattivo; **I didn't move and ~ did Claude** io non mi mossi e nemmeno Claude; **... ~ did I refuse** ..., ma non ho nemmeno rifiutato

neon ['niːɔn] n neon m

Nepal [nɪ'pɔːl] n Nepal m

nephew ['nɛvjuː] n nipote m

nerve [nəːv] n nervo; (fig) coraggio; (impudence) faccia tosta; **he gets on my ~s** mi dà ai nervi; **a fit of ~s** una crisi di nervi

nervous ['nəːvəs] adj nervoso/a; (anxious) agitato/a, in apprensione; **nervous breakdown** n esaurimento nervoso

nest [nɛst] n nido ▷ vi fare il nido, nidificare

net [nɛt] n rete f ▷ adj netto/a ▷ vt (person, profit) ricavare un utile netto di; (fish etc) prendere con la rete; **the N~** (Internet) Internet f; **netball** n specie di pallacanestro

Netherlands ['nɛðələndz] npl: **the ~** i Paesi Bassi

netiquette ['nɛtɪkɛt] n netiquette f inv

nett [nɛt] adj = **net**

nettle ['nɛtl] n ortica

network ['nɛtwəːk] n rete f

neurotic [njuə'rɔtɪk] adj, n nevrotico/a

neuter ['njuːtər] adj neutro/a ▷ vt (cat etc) castrare

neutral ['njuːtrəl] adj neutro/a; (person, nation) neutrale ▷ n (Aut): **in ~** in folle

never ['nɛvər] adv (non...) mai; **~ again** mai più; **I'll ~ go there again** non ci vado più; **~ in my life** mai in vita mia; see also **mind**; **never-ending** adj interminabile; **nevertheless** [nɛvəðə'lɛs] adv tuttavia, ciò nonostante, ciò nondimeno

new [njuː] adj nuovo/a; (brand new) nuovo/a di zecca; **New Age** n New Age f inv; **newbie** ['njuːbɪ] n (Comput, Tech) utilizzatore/trice inesperto/a; (to a job or group) nuovo/a arrivato/a; (to a hobby or experience) neofita m/f; **newborn** adj neonato/a; **newcomer** ['njuːkʌmər] n nuovo/a venuto/a; **newly** adv di recente

news [njuːz] n notizie fpl; (Radio) giornale m radio; (TV) telegiornale m: **a piece of ~** una notizia; **news agency** n agenzia di stampa; **newsagent** n (BRIT) giornalaio; **newscaster** n (Radio, TV) annunciatore/trice; **newsdealer** ['njuːzdiːlər] n (US) = **newsagent**; **newsletter** n bollettino; **newspaper** n giornale m; **newsreader** n = **newscaster**

newt [njuːt] n tritone m

New Year n Anno Nuovo; **New Year's Day** n il Capodanno; **New Year's Eve** n la vigilia di Capodanno

New York [-'jɔːk] n New York f

New Zealand [-'ziːlənd] n Nuova Zelanda; **New Zealander** n neozelandese m/f

next [nɛkst] adj prossimo/a ▷ adv accanto; (in time) dopo; **~ to** accanto a; **~ to nothing** quasi niente; **~ please!** (avanti) il prossimo!; **~ time** la prossima volta; **the ~ day** il giorno dopo, l'indomani; **~ year** l'anno prossimo or venturo; **when do we meet ~?** quando ci rincontriamo?; **next door** adv, adj accanto inv; **next of kin** n parente m/f prossimo/a

NHS n abbr = **National Health Service**

nibble ['nɪbl] vt mordicchiare

nice [naɪs] adj (holiday, trip) piacevole; (flat, picture) bello/a; (person) simpatico/a, gentile; **nicely** adv bene

niche [niːʃ] n (Archit) nicchia

nick [nɪk] n taglietto; tacca ▷ vt (col) rubare; **in the ~ of time** appena in tempo

nickel ['nɪkl] n nichel m; (US) moneta da cinque centesimi di dollaro

nickname ['nɪkneɪm] n soprannome m

n

nicotine ['nɪkətiːn] n nicotina
niece [niːs] n nipote f
Nigeria [naɪ'dʒɪərɪə] n Nigeria
night [naɪt] n notte f; (evening) sera;
at ~ la sera; **by ~** di notte; **the ~
before last** l'altro ieri notte; l'altro
ieri sera; **night club** n locale m
notturno; **nightdress** n camicia da
notte; **nightie** ['naɪtɪ] n camicia da
notte; **night life** ['naɪtlaɪf] n vita
notturna; **nightly** ['naɪtlɪ] adj di ogni
notte or sera; (by night) notturno/a
▷ adv ogni notte or sera; **nightmare**
['naɪtmɛəʳ] n incubo; **night school** n
scuola serale; **nightshift** ['naɪtʃɪft] n
turno di notte; **night-time** n notte f
nil [nɪl] n nulla m; (BRIT Sport) zero
nine [naɪn] num nove; **nineteen** num
diciannove; **nineteenth** [naɪn'tiːnθ]
num diciannovesimo/a; **ninetieth**
['naɪntɪɪθ] num novantesimo/a;
ninety num novanta; **ninth** [naɪnθ]
num nono/a
nip [nɪp] vt pizzicare; (bite) mordere
nipple ['nɪpl] n (Anat) capezzolo
nitrogen ['naɪtrədʒən] n azoto

KEYWORD

no [nəu] adv (opposite of "yes") no; **are
you coming? — no (I'm not)** viene?
— no (non vengo); **would you like
some more? — no thank you** ne
vuole ancora un po'? — no, grazie
▶ adj (not any) nessuno/a; **I have no
money/time/books** non ho soldi/
tempo/libri; **no student would
have done it** nessuno studente lo
avrebbe fatto; **"no parking"** "divieto
di sosta"; **"no smoking"** "vietato
fumare"
▶ n (pl **noes**) no m inv

nobility [nəu'bɪlɪtɪ] n nobiltà
noble ['nəubl] adj nobile
nobody ['nəubədɪ] pron nessuno
nod [nɔd] vi accennare col capo, fare
un cenno; (in agreement) annuire

con un cenno del capo; (sleep)
sonnecchiare ▷ vt: **to ~ one's head**
fare di sì col capo ▷ n cenno; **nod off**
vi assopirsi
noise [nɔɪz] n rumore m; (din, racket)
chiasso; **noisy** adj (street, car)
rumoroso/a; (person) chiassoso/a
nominal ['nɔmɪnl] adj nominale;
(rent) simbolico/a
nominate ['nɔmɪneɪt] vt (propose)
proporre come candidato;
(elect) nominare; **nomination**
[nɔmɪ'neɪʃən] n nomina;
candidatura; **nominee** [nɔmɪ'niː] n
persona nominata; candidato/a
none [nʌn] pron (not one thing) niente;
(not one person) nessuno/a; **~ of you**
nessuno/a di voi; **I have ~ left** non ne
ho più; **he's ~ the worse for it** non
ne ha risentito
nonetheless ['nʌnðə'lɛs] adv
nondimeno
non-fiction [nɔn'fɪkʃən] n
saggistica
nonsense ['nɔnsəns] n sciocchezze fpl
non: non-smoker n non fumatore/
trice; **non-smoking** adj (person)
che non fuma; (area, section) per
non fumatori; **non-stick** adj
antiaderente, antiadesivo/a
noodles ['nuːdlz] npl taglierini mpl
noon [nuːn] n mezzogiorno
no one ['nəuwʌn] pron = **nobody**
nor [nɔːʳ] conj = **neither** ▷ adv see
neither
norm [nɔːm] n norma
normal ['nɔːml] adj normale;
normally adv normalmente
north [nɔːθ] n nord m, settentrione m
▷ adj nord inv, del nord, settentrionale
▷ adv verso nord; **North America**
n America del Nord; **North
American** adj, n nordamericano/a;
northbound ['nɔːθbaund] adj
(traffic) diretto/a a nord; (carriageway)
nord inv; **north-east** n nord-est m;
northeastern adj nordorientale;
northern ['nɔːðən] adj del nord,

settentrionale; **Northern Ireland** n Irlanda del Nord; **North Korea** n Corea del Nord; **North Pole** n: **the North Pole** il Polo Nord; **North Sea** n: **the North Sea** il mare del Nord; **north-west** n nord-ovest m; **northwestern** adj nordoccidentale

Norway ['nɔːweɪ] n Norvegia; **Norwegian** [nɔː'wiːdʒən] adj norvegese ▷ n norvegese m/f; (Ling) norvegese m

nose [nəuz] n naso; (of animal) muso; **nose about** vi aggirarsi; **nosebleed** n emorragia nasale; **nosey** ['nəuzɪ] adj curioso/a

nostalgia [nɔs'tældʒɪə] n nostalgia

nostalgic [nɔs'tældʒɪk] adj nostalgico/a

nostril ['nɔstrɪl] n narice f; (of horse) frogia

nosy ['nəuzɪ] adj = **nosey**

not [nɔt] adv non; **you must ~** or **mustn't do this** non deve fare questo; **it's too late, isn't it** or **is it ~?** è troppo tardi, vero?; **he is ~** or **isn't here** non è qui, non c'è; **~ that I don't like him** non che lo (lui) non mi piaccia; **~ yet/now** non ancora/ora

notable ['nəutəbl] adj notevole; **notably** ['nəutəblɪ] adv notevolmente; (in particular) in particolare

notch [nɔtʃ] n tacca; (in saw) dente m

note [nəut] n nota; (letter, banknote) biglietto ▷ vt: **to take ~ of** prendere nota di; **to take ~s** prendere appunti; **notebook** n taccuino; **noted** ['nəutɪd] adj celebre; **notepad** n bloc-notes m inv; **notepaper** n carta da lettere

nothing ['nʌθɪŋ] n nulla m, niente m; (zero) zero; **he does ~** non fa niente; **~ new** niente di nuovo; **for ~** per niente

notice ['nəutɪs] n avviso; (of leaving) preavviso ▷ vt notare, accorgersi di; **to take ~ of** fare attenzione a; **to bring sth to sb's ~** far notare qc a qn; **to hand in one's ~** licenziarsi;

at short ~ con un breve preavviso; **until further ~** fino a nuovo avviso; **noticeable** adj evidente

notify ['nəutɪfaɪ] vt: **to ~ sth to sb** notificare qc a qn; **to ~ sb of sth** avvisare qn di qc

notion ['nəuʃən] n idea; (concept) nozione f; **notions** ['nəuʃənz] npl (US: haberdashery) merceria

notorious [nəu'tɔːrɪəs] adj famigerato/a

notwithstanding [nɔtwɪθ'stændɪŋ] adv nondimeno ▷ prep nonostante, malgrado

nought [nɔːt] n zero

noun [naun] n nome m, sostantivo

nourish ['nʌrɪʃ] vt nutrire; **nourishment** n nutrimento

Nov. abbr (= November) nov.

novel ['nɔvl] n romanzo ▷ adj nuovo/a; **novelist** n romanziere/a; **novelty** n novità f inv

November [nəu'vɛmbəʳ] n novembre m

novice ['nɔvɪs] n principiante m/f; (Rel) novizio/a

now [nau] adv ora, adesso ▷ conj: **~ (that)** adesso che, ora che; **right ~** subito; **by ~** ormai; **just ~** proprio ora; **that's the fashion just ~** è la moda del momento; **I saw her just ~** l'ho vista proprio adesso; **~ and then, ~ and again** ogni tanto; **from ~ on** da ora in poi; **nowadays** ['nauədeɪz] adv oggidì

nowhere ['nəuwɛəʳ] adv in nessun luogo, da nessuna parte

nozzle ['nɔzl] n (of hose etc) boccaglio; (of fire extinguisher) lancia

nr abbr (BRIT) = **near**

nuclear ['njuːklɪəʳ] adj nucleare

nucleus (pl **nuclei**) ['njuːklɪəs, 'njuːklɪaɪ] n nucleo

nude [njuːd] adj nudo/a ▷ n (Art) nudo; **in the ~** tutto/a nudo/a

nudge [nʌdʒ] vt dare una gomitata a

nudist ['njuːdɪst] n nudista m/f

nudity ['njuːdɪtɪ] n nudità

n

nuisance ['nju:sns] *n*: **it's a ~** è una seccatura; **he's a ~** dà fastidio

numb [nʌm] *adj* intorpidito/a; **~ with** (*fear, grief*) paralizzato/a da; **~ with cold** intirizzito/a (dal freddo)

number ['nʌmbə^r] *n* numero ▷ *vt* numerare; (*include*) contare; **a ~ of** un certo numero di; **to be ~ed among** venire annoverato/a tra; **they were 10 in ~** erano in tutto 10; **number plate** *n* (BRIT Aut) targa; **Number Ten** *n* (BRIT: = 10 Downing Street) residenza del Primo Ministro del Regno Unito

numerical [nju:'mɛrɪkl] *adj* numerico/a

numerous ['nju:mərəs] *adj* numeroso/a

nun [nʌn] *n* suora, monaca

nurse [nə:s] *n* infermiere/a; (*also*: **~maid**) bambinaia ▷ *vt* (*patient, cold*) curare; (*baby*: BRIT) cullare; (: US) allattare, dare il latte a

nursery ['nə:sərɪ] *n* (*room*) camera dei bambini; (*institution*) asilo; (*for plants*) vivaio; **nursery rhyme** *n* filastrocca; **nursery school** *n* scuola materna; **nursery slope** *n* (BRIT Ski) pista per principianti

nursing ['nə:sɪŋ] *n* (*profession*) professione *f* di infermiere (*or* di infermiera); (*care*) cura; **nursing home** *n* casa di cura

nurture ['nə:tʃə^r] *vt* allevare; nutrire

nut [nʌt] *n* (*of metal*) dado; (*fruit*) noce *f* (*or* nocciola *or* mandorla *etc*); **he's ~s** (*col*) è matto

nutmeg ['nʌtmɛg] *n* noce *f* moscata

nutrient ['nju:trɪənt] *adj* nutriente ▷ *n* sostanza nutritiva

nutrition [nju:'trɪʃən] *n* nutrizione *f*

nutritious [nju:'trɪʃəs] *adj* nutriente

NVQ *n abbr* (BRIT) = **National Vocational Qualification**

nylon ['naɪlɔn] *n* nailon *m* ▷ *adj* di nailon

oak [əuk] *n* quercia ▷ *cpd* di quercia

OAP *n abbr* (BRIT) = **old-age pensioner**

oar [ɔ:^r] *n* remo

oasis (*pl* **oases**) [əu'eɪsɪs, əu'eɪsi:z] *n* oasi *f inv*

oath [əuθ] *n* giuramento; (*swear word*) bestemmia

oatmeal ['əutmi:l] *n* farina d'avena

oats [əuts] *npl* avena

obedience [ə'bi:dɪəns] *n* ubbidienza

obedient [ə'bi:dɪənt] *adj* ubbidiente

obese [əu'bi:s] *adj* obeso/a

obesity [əu'bi:sɪtɪ] *n* obesità

obey [ə'beɪ] *vt* ubbidire a; (*instructions, regulations*) osservare

obituary [ə'bɪtjuərɪ] *n* necrologia

object *n* ['ɔbdʒɪkt] oggetto; (*purpose*) scopo, intento; (*Ling*) complemento oggetto ▷ *vi* [əb'dʒɛkt]: **to ~ to** (*attitude*) disapprovare; (*proposal*) protestare contro, sollevare delle obiezioni contro; **I ~!** mi oppongo!;

he ~ed that ... obiettò che ...;
expense is no ~ non si bada a spese;
objection [əb'dʒɛkʃən] n obiezione
f; **objective** n obiettivo
obligation [ɔblɪ'geɪʃən] n obbligo,
dovere m; **"without ~"** "senza
impegno"
obligatory [ə'blɪgətərɪ] adj
obbligatorio/a
oblige [ə'blaɪdʒ] vt (do a favour) fare
una cortesia a; (force): **to ~ sb to do**
costringere qn a fare; **to be ~d to sb
for sth** essere grato a qn per qc
oblique [ə'bliːk] adj obliquo/a;
(allusion) indiretto/a
obliterate [ə'blɪtəreɪt] vt cancellare
oblivious [ə'blɪvɪəs] adj: **~ of**
incurante di; inconscio/a di
oblong ['ɔblɔŋ] adj oblungo/a ▷ n
rettangolo
obnoxious [əb'nɔkʃəs] adj odioso/a;
(smell) disgustoso/a, ripugnante
oboe ['əʊbəʊ] n oboe m
obscene [əb'siːn] adj osceno/a
obscure [əb'skjuəʳ] adj oscuro/a ▷ vt
oscurare; (hide: sense) nascondere
observant [əb'zəːvnt] adj attento/a

Be careful not to translate
observant by the Italian word
osservante.

observation [ɔbzə'veɪʃən] n
osservazione f; (by police etc)
sorveglianza
observatory [əb'zəːvətrɪ] n
osservatorio
observe [əb'zəːv] vt osservare;
(remark) fare osservare; **observer** n
osservatore/trice
obsess [əb'sɛs] vt ossessionare;
obsession [əb'sɛʃən] n ossessione f;
obsessive adj ossessivo/a
obsolete ['ɔbsəliːt] adj obsoleto/a
obstacle ['ɔbstəkl] n ostacolo
obstinate ['ɔbstɪnɪt] adj ostinato/a
obstruct [əb'strʌkt] vt (block)
ostruire, ostacolare; (halt) fermare;
(hinder) impedire; **obstruction**
[əb'strʌkʃən] n ostruzione f; ostacolo

obtain [əb'teɪn] vt ottenere
obvious ['ɔbvɪəs] adj ovvio/a,
evidente; **obviously** adv
ovviamente; **obviously!** certo!
occasion [ə'keɪʒən] n occasione f;
(event) avvenimento; **occasional**
adj occasionale; **occasionally** adv
ogni tanto
occult [ɔ'kʌlt] adj occulto/a ▷ n: **the
~** l'occulto
occupant ['ɔkjupənt] n occupante
m/f; (of boat, car etc) persona a bordo
occupation [ɔkju'peɪʃən] n
occupazione f; (job) mestiere m,
professione f
occupy ['ɔkjupaɪ] vt occupare; **to ~
o.s. by doing** occuparsi a fare
occur [ə'kəːʳ] vi accadere; (difficulty,
opportunity) capitare; **to ~ to sb**
venire in mente a qn; **occurrence** n
caso, fatto; presenza

Be careful not to translate *occur*
by the Italian word *occorrere*.

ocean ['əʊʃən] n oceano
o'clock [ə'klɔk] adv: **it is 5 ~** sono le 5
Oct. abbr (= October) ott.
October [ɔk'təʊbəʳ] n ottobre m
octopus ['ɔktəpəs] n polpo, piovra
odd [ɔd] adj (strange) strano/a,
bizzarro/a; (number) dispari inv; (not
of a set) spaiato/a; **60-~** 60 e oltre;
at ~ times di tanto in tanto; **the
~ one out** l'eccezione f; **oddly** adv
stranamente; **odds** npl (in betting)
quota
odometer [ɔ'dɔmɪtəʳ] n odometro
odour, (US) **odor** ['əʊdəʳ] n odore m;
(unpleasant) cattivo odore

 KEYWORD

of [ɔv, əv] prep **1** (gen) di; **a boy of 10**
un ragazzo di 10 anni; **a friend of
ours** un nostro amico; **that was
kind of you** è stato molto gentile
da parte sua
2 (expressing quantity, amount, dates
etc) di; **a kilo of flour** un chilo di

farina; **how much of this do you need?** quanto gliene serve?; **there were four of them** (people) erano in quattro; (objects) ce n'erano quattro; **three of us went** tre di noi sono andati; **the 5th of July** il 5 luglio
3 (from, out of) di, in; **made of wood** (fatto) di or in legno

  KEYWORD

off [ɔf] adv 1 (distance, time): **it's a long way off** è lontano; **the game is 3 days off** la partita è tra 3 giorni
2 (departure, removal) via; **to go off to Paris** andarsene a Parigi; **I must be off** devo andare via; **to take off one's coat** togliersi il cappotto; **the button came off** il bottone è venuto via or si è staccato; **10% off** con lo sconto del 10%
3 (not at work): **to have a day off** avere un giorno libero; **to be off sick** essere assente per malattia
▶ adj (engine) spento/a; (tap) chiuso/a; (cancelled) sospeso/a; (BRIT: food) andato/a a male; **on the off chance** nel caso; **to have an off day** non essere in forma
▶ prep 1 (motion, removal etc) da; (distant from) a poca distanza da; **a street off the square** una strada che parte dalla piazza
2: **to be off meat** non mangiare più la carne

offence, (US) **offense** [əˈfɛns] n (Law) contravvenzione f; (: more serious) reato; **to take ~ at** offendersi per
offend [əˈfɛnd] vt (person) offendere; **offender** n delinquente m/f; (against regulations) contravventore/trice
offense [əˈfɛns] n (US) = **offence**
offensive [əˈfɛnsɪv] adj offensivo/a; (smell etc) sgradevole, ripugnante ▶ n (Mil) offensiva

offer [ˈɔfəʳ] n offerta, proposta ▶ vt offrire; **"on ~"** (Comm) "in offerta speciale"
offhand [ɔfˈhænd] adj disinvolto/a, noncurante ▶ adv: **I can't tell you ~** non posso dirglielo su due piedi
office [ˈɔfɪs] n (place) ufficio; (position) carica; **doctor's ~** (US) ambulatorio; **to take ~** entrare in carica; **office block**, (US) **office building** n complesso di uffici; **office hours** npl orario d'ufficio; (US Med) orario di visite
officer [ˈɔfɪsəʳ] n (Mil etc) ufficiale m; (of organization) funzionario; (also: **police ~**) agente m di polizia
office worker n impiegato/a d'ufficio
official [əˈfɪʃl] adj (authorized) ufficiale ▶ n ufficiale m; (civil servant) impiegato/a statale; funzionario
off: off-licence n (BRIT) spaccio di bevande alcoliche; **off-line** adj, adv (Comput) off-line inv, non in linea; (: switched off) spento/a; **off-peak** adj (ticket etc) a tariffa ridotta; (time) non di punta; **off-putting** adj (BRIT) sgradevole; **off-season** adj, adv fuori stagione; **offset** [ˈɔfsɛt] vt (irreg: counteract) controbilanciare, compensare; **offshore** [ɔfˈʃɔːʳ] adj (breeze) di terra; (island) vicino alla costa; (fishing) costiero/a; **offside** [ˈɔfsaɪd] adj (Sport) fuori gioco; (Aut: with right-hand drive) destro/a; (: with left-hand drive) sinistro/a; **offspring** [ˈɔfsprɪŋ] n prole f, discendenza
often [ˈɔfn] adv spesso; **how ~ do you go?** quanto spesso ci va?
oh [əu] excl oh!
oil [ɔɪl] n olio; (petroleum) petrolio; (for central heating) nafta ▶ vt (machine) lubrificare; **oil filter** n (Aut) filtro dell'olio; **oil painting** n quadro a olio; **oil refinery** n raffineria di petrolio; **oil rig** n derrick m inv; (at

sea) piattaforma per trivellazioni subacquee; **oil slick** n chiazza d'olio; **oil tanker** n (ship) petroliera; (truck) autocisterna per petrolio; **oil well** n pozzo petrolifero; **oily** adj unto/a, oleoso/a; (food) grasso/a

ointment ['ɔɪntmənt] n unguento

O.K. [əu'keɪ] excl d'accordo! ▷ vt approvare ▷ adj non male inv; **is it ~?, are you ~?** tutto bene?

old [əuld] adj vecchio/a; (ancient) antico/a, vecchio/a; (person) vecchio/a, anziano/a; **how ~ are you?** quanti anni ha?; **he's 10 years ~** ha 10 anni; **~er brother/sister** fratello/sorella maggiore; **old age** n vecchiaia; **old-age pension** ['əuldeɪdʒ-] n (BRIT) pensione f di vecchiaia; **old-age pensioner** n (BRIT) pensionato/a; **old-fashioned** adj antiquato/a, fuori moda; (person) all'antica; **old people's home** n ricovero per anziani

olive ['ɒlɪv] n (fruit) oliva; (tree) olivo ▷ adj (also: **~-green**) verde oliva inv; **olive oil** n olio d'oliva

Olympic [əu'lɪmpɪk] adj olimpico/a; **the ~ Games, the ~s** i giochi olimpici, le Olimpiadi

omelet(te) ['ɒmlɪt] n omelette f inv

omen ['əumən] n presagio, augurio

ominous ['ɒmɪnəs] adj minaccioso/a; (event) di malaugurio

omit [əu'mɪt] vt omettere

KEYWORD

on [ɒn] prep 1 (indicating position) su; **on the wall** sulla parete; **on the left** a or sulla sinistra

2 (indicating means, method, condition etc): **on foot** a piedi; **on the train/plane** in treno/aereo; **on the telephone** al telefono; **on the radio/television** alla radio/ televisione; **to be on drugs** drogarsi; **on holiday** in vacanza

3 (referring to time): **on Friday** venerdì; **on Fridays** il or di venerdì; **on June 20th** il 20 giugno; **on Friday, June 20th** venerdì, 20 giugno; **a week on Friday** venerdì a otto; **on his arrival** al suo arrivo; **on seeing this** vedendo ciò

4 (about, concerning) su, di; **information on train services** informazioni sui collegamenti ferroviari; **a book on Goldoni/ physics** un libro su Goldoni/di or sulla fisica

▷ adv 1 (referring to dress, covering): **to have one's coat on** avere indosso il cappotto; **to put one's coat on** mettersi il cappotto; **what's she got on?** cosa indossa?; **she put her boots/gloves/hat on** si mise gli stivali/i guanti/il cappello; **screw the lid on tightly** avvita bene il coperchio

2 (further, continuously): **to walk on, go on** etc continuare, proseguire; **to read on** continuare a leggere; **on and off** ogni tanto

▷ adj 1 (in operation: machine, TV, light) acceso/a; (tap) aperto/a; (brake) inserito/a; **is the meeting still on?** (in progress) la riunione è ancora in corso?; (not cancelled) è confermato l'incontro?; **there's a good film on at the cinema** danno un buon film al cinema

2 (col): **that's not on!** (not acceptable) non si fa così!; (not possible) non se ne parla neanche!

once [wʌns] adv una volta ▷ conj non appena, quando; **~ he had left/it was done** dopo che se n'era andato/ fu fatto; **at ~** subito; (simultaneously) a un tempo; **~ a week** una volta alla settimana; **~ more** ancora una volta; **~ and for all** una volta per sempre; **~ upon a time there was …** c'era una volta …

oncoming ['ɒnkʌmɪŋ] adj (traffic) che viene in senso opposto

O

○ KEYWORD

one [wʌn] *num* uno/a; **one hundred and fifty** centocinquanta; **one day** un giorno
▶ *adj* **1** (*sole*) unico/a; **the one book which** l'unico libro che; **the one man who** l'unico che
2 (*same*) stesso/a; **they came in the one car** sono venuti nella stessa macchina
▶ *pron* **1**: **this one** questo/a; **that one** quello/a; **I've already got one/a red one** ne ho già uno/uno rosso; **one by one** uno per uno
2: **one another** l'un l'altro; **to look at one another** guardarsi; **to help one another** aiutarsi l'un l'altro *or* a vicenda
3 (*impersonal*) si; **one never knows** non si sa mai; **to cut one's finger** tagliarsi un dito; **one needs to eat** bisogna mangiare; **one-off** (*BRIT col*) *n* fatto eccezionale

oneself [wʌn'sɛlf] *pron* (*reflexive*) si; (*after prep*) sé, se stesso/a; **to do sth (by) ~** fare qc da sé; **to hurt ~** farsi male; **to keep sth for ~** tenere qc per sé; **to talk to ~** parlare da solo
one: one-shot [wʌn'ʃɔt] *n* (*US*) = **one-off**; **one-sided** *adj* (*decision, view, argument*) unilaterale; **one-to-one** *adj* (*relationship*) univoco/a; **one-way** *adj* (*street, traffic*) a senso unico
ongoing ['ɔngəuɪŋ] *adj* in corso; in attuazione
onion ['ʌnjən] *n* cipolla
on-line ['ɔnlaɪn] *adj, adv* (*Comput*) on-line *inv*
onlooker ['ɔnlukə^r] *n* spettatore/trice
only ['əunlɪ] *adv* solo, soltanto ▶ *adj* solo/a, unico/a ▶ *conj* solo che, ma; **an ~ child** un figlio unico; **not ~** non solo
on-screen [ɔn'skri:n] *adj* sullo schermo *inv*
onset ['ɔnsɛt] *n* inizio

onto ['ɔntu] *prep* su, sopra
onward(s) ['ɔnwəd(z)] *adv* (*move*) in avanti; **from this time onward(s)** d'ora in poi
oops [ups] *excl* ops! (*esprime rincrescimento per un piccolo contrattempo*); **~-a-daisy!** oplà!
ooze [u:z] *vi* stillare
opaque [əu'peɪk] *adj* opaco/a
open ['əupn] *adj* aperto/a; (*road*) libero/a; (*meeting*) pubblico/a ▶ *vt* aprire ▶ *vi* (*eyes, door, debate*) aprirsi; (*flower*) sbocciare; (*shop, bank, museum*) aprire; (*book etc: commence*) cominciare; **in the ~ (air)** all'aperto; **is it ~ to the public?** è aperto al pubblico?; **what time do you ~?** a che ora aprite?; **open-air** *adj* all'aperto; **opening** *n* apertura; (*opportunity*) occasione *f*, opportunità *f inv*; sbocco ▶ *adj* (*speech*) di apertura; **opening hours** *npl* orario d'apertura; **open learning** *n* sistema educativo secondo il quale lo studente ha maggior controllo e gestione delle modalità di apprendimento; **openly** *adv* apertamente; **open-minded** *adj* che ha la mente aperta; **open-necked** *adj* col collo slacciato; **open-plan** *adj* senza pareti divisorie; **Open University** *n* (*BRIT*) vedi nota **"Open University"**

● OPEN UNIVERSITY
●
● La *Open University* (OU), fondata
● in Gran Bretagna nel 1969,
● organizza corsi universitari per
● corrispondenza o via Internet,
● basati anche su lezioni che
● vengono trasmesse dalla *BBC*
● per radio e per televisione e su
● corsi estivi.

opera ['ɔpərə] *n* opera; **opera house** *n* opera; **opera singer** *n* cantante *m/f* d'opera *or* lirico/a

operate ['ɒpəreɪt] vt (machine) azionare, far funzionare; (system) usare ▷ vi funzionare; (drug, person) agire; **to ~ on sb (for)** (Med) operare qn (di)

operating room n (US) = **operating theatre**

operating theatre n (Med) sala operatoria

operation [ɒpə'reɪʃən] n operazione f; **to be in ~** (machine) essere in azione or funzionamento; (system) essere in vigore; **to have an ~ (for)** (Med) essere operato/a (di); **operational** adj d'esercizio; (ready for use or action) in funzione

operative ['ɒpərətɪv] adj (measure) operativo/a

operator ['ɒpəreɪtər] n (of machine) operatore/trice; (Tel) centralinista m/f

opinion [ə'pɪnjən] n opinione f, parere m; **in my ~** secondo me, a mio avviso; **opinion poll** n sondaggio di opinioni

opponent [ə'pəunənt] n avversario/a

opportunity [ɒpə'tju:nɪtɪ] n opportunità f inv, occasione f; **to take the ~ to do** or **of doing** cogliere l'occasione per fare

oppose [ə'pəuz] vt opporsi a; **~d to** contrario/a a; **as ~d to** in contrasto con

opposite ['ɒpəzɪt] adj opposto/a; (house etc) di fronte ▷ adv di fronte, dirimpetto ▷ prep di fronte a ▷ n opposto, contrario; **the ~ sex** l'altro sesso

opposition [ɒpə'zɪʃən] n opposizione f

oppress [ə'prɛs] vt opprimere

opt [ɒpt] vi: **to ~ for** optare per; **to ~ to do** scegliere di fare; **opt out** vi: **to ~ out of** ritirarsi da

optician [ɒp'tɪʃən] n ottico

optimism ['ɒptɪmɪzəm] n ottimismo

optimist ['ɒptɪmɪst] n ottimista m/f; **optimistic** [ɒptɪ'mɪstɪk] adj ottimistico/a

optimum ['ɒptɪməm] adj ottimale

option ['ɒpʃən] n scelta; (Scol) materia facoltativa; (Comm) opzione f; **optional** adj facoltativo/a; (Comm) a scelta

or [ɔːr] conj o, oppure; (with negative): **he hasn't seen or heard anything** non ha visto né sentito niente; **or else** se no, altrimenti; oppure

oral ['ɔːrəl] adj orale ▷ n esame m orale

orange ['ɒrɪndʒ] n (fruit) arancia ▷ adj arancione; **orange juice** n succo d'arancia; **orange squash** n succo d'arancia (da diluire con l'acqua)

orbit ['ɔːbɪt] n orbita ▷ vt orbitare intorno a

orchard ['ɔːtʃəd] n frutteto

orchestra ['ɔːkɪstrə] n orchestra; (US: seating) platea

orchid ['ɔːkɪd] n orchidea

ordeal [ɔː'diːl] n prova, travaglio

order ['ɔːdər] n ordine m; (Comm) ordinazione f ▷ vt ordinare; **to ~ sb to do** ordinare a qn di fare; **in ~** in ordine; (document) in regola; **in ~ to do** per fare; **in ~ that** affinché + sub; **a machine in working ~** una macchina che funziona bene; **out of ~** non in ordine; (machine, toilets) essere guasto/a; **to be on ~** essere stato ordinato; **order form** n modulo d'ordinazione; **orderly** n (Mil) attendente m; (Med) inserviente m ▷ adj (room) in ordine; (mind) metodico/a; (person) ordinato/a, metodico/a

ordinary ['ɔːdnrɪ] adj normale, comune; (pej) mediocre ▷ n: **out of the ~** diverso dal solito, fuori dell'ordinario

ore [ɔːr] n minerale m grezzo

oregano [ɒrɪ'gɑːnəu] n origano

organ ['ɔːgən] n organo; **organic** [ɔː'gænɪk] adj organico/a; (food,

o

produce) biologico/a; **organism** *n* organismo

organization [ɔːgənaɪˈzeɪʃən] *n* organizzazione *f*

organize [ˈɔːgənaɪz] *vt* organizzare; **to get ~d** organizzarsi; **organized** [ˈɔːgənaɪzd] *adj* organizzato/a; **organizer** *n* organizzatore/trice

orgasm [ˈɔːgæzəm] *n* orgasmo

orgy [ˈɔːdʒɪ] *n* orgia

oriental [ɔːrɪˈentl] *adj, n* orientale (*m/f*)

orientation [ɔːrɪenˈteɪʃən] *n* orientamento

origin [ˈɔrɪdʒɪn] *n* origine *f*

original [əˈrɪdʒɪnl] *adj* originale; (*earliest*) originario/a ▷ *n* originale *m*; **originally** *adv* (*at first*) all'inizio

originate [əˈrɪdʒɪneɪt] *vi*: **to ~ from** essere originario/a di; (*suggestion*) provenire da; **to ~ in** avere origine in

Orkneys [ˈɔːknɪz] *npl*: **the ~** (*also*: **the Orkney Islands**) le (isole) Orcadi

ornament [ˈɔːnəmənt] *n* ornamento; (*trinket*) ninnolo; **ornamental** [ɔːnəˈmɛntl] *adj* ornamentale

ornate [ɔːˈneɪt] *adj* molto ornato/a

orphan [ˈɔːfn] *n* orfano/a

orthodox [ˈɔːθədɔks] *adj* ortodosso/a

orthopaedic, (US) **orthopedic** [ɔːθəˈpiːdɪk] *adj* ortopedico/a

osteopath [ˈɔstɪəpæθ] *n* specialista *m/f* di osteopatia

ostrich [ˈɔstrɪtʃ] *n* struzzo

other [ˈʌðəʳ] *adj* altro/a ▷ *pron*: **the ~** l'altro/a; **the ~s** gli altri; **~ than** altro che; a parte; **otherwise** *adv*, *conj* altrimenti

otter [ˈɔtəʳ] *n* lontra

ouch [autʃ] *excl* ohi!, ahi!

ought [ɔːt] *aux vb*: **I ~ to do it** dovrei farlo; **this ~ to have been corrected** questo avrebbe dovuto essere corretto; **he ~ to win** dovrebbe vincere

ounce [auns] *n* oncia (= *28.35 g; 16 in a pound*)

our [auəʳ] *adj* il (la) nostro/a; (*pl*) i (le) nostri/e; **ours** *pron* il (la) nostro/a; (*pl*) i (le) nostri/e; *see also* **mine¹**; **ourselves** *pl pron* (*reflexive*) ci; (*after preposition*) noi; (*emphatic*) noi stessi/e; *see also* **oneself**

oust [aust] *vt* cacciare, espellere

KEYWORD

out [aut] *adv* (*gen*) fuori; **out here/there** qui/là fuori; **to speak out loud** parlare forte; **to have a night out** uscire una sera; **the boat was 10 km out** la barca era a 10 km dalla costa; **3 days out from Plymouth** a 3 giorni da Plymouth

▶ *prep*: **out of** (*outside, beyond*) fuori di; (*because of*) per; **out of 10** su 10; **out of petrol** senza benzina

out: outback [ˈautbæk] *n* (*in Australia*) interno, entroterra; **outbound** *adj*: **outbound (for** *or* **from)** in partenza (per *or* da); **outbreak** *n* scoppio; epidemia; **outburst** *n* scoppio; **outcast** [ˈautkɑːst] *n* esule *m/f*; (*socially*) paria *m inv*; **outcome** [ˈautkʌm] *n* esito, risultato; **outcry** [ˈautkraɪ] *n* protesta, clamore *m*; **outdated** [autˈdeɪtɪd] *adj* (*custom, clothes*) fuori moda; (*idea*) sorpassato/a; **outdoor** [autˈdɔːʳ] *adj* all'aperto; **outdoors** *adv* fuori; all'aria aperta

outer [ˈautəʳ] *adj* esteriore; **outer space** *n* spazio cosmico

outfit [ˈautfɪt] *n* (*clothes*) completo; (: *for sport*) tenuta

out: outgoing [ˈautgəuɪŋ] *adj* (*character*) socievole; **outgoings** *npl* (BRIT: *expenses*) spese *fpl*, uscite *fpl*; **outhouse** [ˈauthaus] *n* costruzione *f* annessa

outing [ˈautɪŋ] *n* gita; escursione *f*

out: outlaw [ˈautlɔː] *n* fuorilegge *m/f* ▷ *vt* bandire; **outlay** [ˈautleɪ] *n* spese *fpl*; (*investment*) sborsa; spese;

outlet ['autlɛt] n (for liquid etc) sbocco, scarico; (also: **retail outlet**) punto di vendita; (us Elec) presa di corrente;
outline ['autlaın] n contorno, profilo; (summary) abbozzo, grandi linee fpl ▷ vt (fig) descrivere a grandi linee;
outlook ['autluk] n prospettiva, vista; **outnumber** [aut'nʌmbə'] vt superare in numero; **out-of-date** adj (passport, ticket) scaduto/a; (clothes) fuori moda inv; **out-of-doors** [autəv'dɔ:z] adv all'aperto;
out-of-the-way adj (remote) fuori mano; **out-of-town** [,autəv'taun] adj (shopping centre etc) inv uori città;
outpatient ['autpeɪʃənt] n paziente m/f esterno/a; **outpost** ['autpəust] n avamposto; **output** ['autput] n produzione f; (Comput) output m inv
outrage ['autreɪdʒ] n oltraggio; scandalo ▷ vt oltraggiare;
outrageous [aut'reɪdʒəs] adj oltraggioso/a; scandaloso/a
outright adv [aut'raɪt] completamente; schiettamente; apertamente; sul colpo ▷ adj ['autraɪt] completo/a; schietto/a e netto/a
outset ['autsɛt] n inizio
outside [aut'saɪd] n esterno, esteriore m ▷ adj esterno/a, esteriore ▷ adv fuori, all'esterno ▷ prep fuori di, all'esterno di; **at the ~** (fig) al massimo; **outside lane** n (Aut) corsia di sorpasso; **outside line** n (Tel) linea esterna; **outsider** n (in race etc) outsider m inv; (stranger) straniero/a
out: outsize ['autsaɪz] adj (clothes) per taglie forti; **outskirts** ['autskə:ts] npl sobborghi mpl;
outspoken [aut'spəukən] adj molto franco/a; **outstanding** [aut'stændɪŋ] adj eccezionale, di rilievo; (unfinished) non completo/a; non evaso/a; non regolato/a
outward ['autwəd] adj (sign, appearances) esteriore; (journey) d'andata; **outwards** ['autwədz] adv (esp BRIT) = **outward**

outweigh [aut'weɪ] vt avere maggior peso di
oval ['əuvl] adj, n ovale (m)
ovary ['əuvəri] n ovaia
oven ['ʌvn] n forno; **oven glove** n guanto da forno; **ovenproof** adj da forno; **oven-ready** adj pronto/a da infornare
over ['əuvə'] adv al di sopra ▷ adj, adv (finished) finito/a, terminato/a; (too much) troppo; (remaining) che avanza ▷ prep su; sopra; (above) al di sopra di; (on the other side of) di là di; (more than) più di; (during) durante; **~ here** qui; **~ there** là; **all ~** (everywhere) dappertutto; (finished) tutto/a finito/a; **~ and ~ (again)** più e più volte; **~ and above** oltre (a); **to ask ~** invitare qn (a passare)
overall adj ['əuvərɔ:l] totale ▷ n ['əuvərɔ:l] (BRIT) grembiule m ▷ adv [əuvər'ɔ:l] nell'insieme, complessivamente; **overalls** npl tuta (da lavoro)
overboard ['əuvəbɔ:d] adv (Naut) fuori bordo, in acqua
overcame [əuvə'keɪm] pt of **overcome**
overcast ['əuvəka:st] adj (sky) coperto/a
overcharge [əuvə'tʃa:dʒ] vt: **to ~ sb for sth** far pagare troppo caro a qn per qc
overcoat ['əuvəkəut] n soprabito, cappotto
overcome [əuvə'kʌm] vt (irreg) superare; sopraffare
over: overcrowded [əuvə'kraudɪd] adj sovraffollato/a; **overdo** [əuvə'du:] vt (irreg) esagerare; (overcook) cuocere troppo; **overdone** [əuvə'dʌn] adj troppo cotto/a; **overdose** ['əuvədəus] n dose f eccessiva; **overdraft** ['əuvədra:ft] n scoperto (di conto); **overdrawn** [əuvə'drɔ:n] adj (account) scoperto/a; **overdue** [əuvə'dju:]

o

adj in ritardo; **overestimate** [əʊvərˈɛstɪmeɪt] *vt* sopravvalutare

overflow *vi* [əʊvəˈfləʊ] traboccare ▷ *n* [ˈəʊvəfləʊ] (*also*: ~ **pipe**) troppopieno

overgrown [əʊvəˈɡrəʊn] *adj* (*garden*) ricoperto/a di vegetazione

overhaul *vt* [əʊvəˈhɔːl] revisionare ▷ *n* [ˈəʊvəhɔːl] revisione *f*

overhead *adv* [əʊvəˈhɛd] di sopra ▷ *adj* [ˈəʊvəhɛd] aereo/a; (*lighting*) verticale ▷ *n* [ˈəʊvəhɛd] (*US*) = **overheads**; **overhead projector** *n* lavagna luminosa; **overheads** *npl* spese *fpl* generali

over: overhear [əʊvəˈhɪəʳ] *vt* (*irreg*) sentire (per caso); **overheat** [əʊvəˈhiːt] *vi* surriscaldarsi; **overland** *adj*, *adv* per via di terra; **overlap** *vi* [əʊvəˈlæp] sovrapporsi; **overleaf** [əʊvəˈliːf] *adv* a tergo; **overload** [əʊvəˈləʊd] *vt* sovraccaricare; **overlook** [əʊvəˈlʊk] *vt* (*have view of*) dare su; (*miss*) trascurare; (*forgive*) passare sopra a

overnight *adv* [əʊvəˈnaɪt] (*happen*) durante la notte; (*fig*) tutto d'un tratto ▷ *adj* [ˈəʊvənaɪt] di notte; **he stayed there ~** ci ha passato la notte; **overnight bag** *n* borsa da viaggio

overpass [ˈəʊvəpɑːs] *n* cavalcavia *m inv*

overpower [əʊvəˈpaʊəʳ] *vt* sopraffare; **overpowering** *adj* irresistibile; (*heat, stench*) soffocante

over: overreact [əʊvəriːˈækt] *vi* reagire in modo esagerato; **overrule** [əʊvəˈruːl] *vt* (*decision*) annullare; (*claim*) respingere; **overrun** [əʊvəˈrʌn] *vt* (*irreg: like* **run**) (*country etc*) invadere; (*time limit etc*) superare

overseas [əʊvəˈsiːz] *adv* oltremare; (*abroad*) all'estero ▷ *adj* (*trade*) estero/a; (*visitor*) straniero/a

oversee [əʊvəˈsiː] *vt* (*irreg*) sorvegliare

overshadow [əʊvəˈʃædəʊ] *vt* far ombra su; (*fig*) eclissare

oversight [ˈəʊvəsaɪt] *n* omissione *f*, svista

oversleep [əʊvəˈsliːp] *vi* (*irreg*) dormire troppo a lungo

overspend [əʊvəˈspɛnd] *vi* (*irreg*) spendere troppo; **we have overspent by 5000 dollars** abbiamo speso 5000 dollari di troppo

overt [əʊˈvəːt] *adj* palese

overtake [əʊvəˈteɪk] *vt* (*irreg*) sorpassare

over: overthrow [əʊvəˈθrəʊ] *vt* (*irreg: government*) rovesciare; **overtime** [ˈəʊvətaɪm] *n* (*lavoro*) straordinario

overtook [əʊvəˈtʊk] *pt of* **overtake**

over: overturn [əʊvəˈtəːn] *vt* rovesciare ▷ *vi* rovesciarsi; **overweight** [əʊvəˈweɪt] *adj* (*person*) troppo grasso/a; **overwhelm** [əʊvəˈwɛlm] *vt* sopraffare; sommergere; schiacciare; **overwhelming** *adj* (*victory, defeat*) schiacciante; (*heat, desire*) intenso/a

ow [aʊ] *excl* ahi!

owe [əʊ] *vt*: **to ~ sb sth, to ~ sth to sb** dovere qc a qn; **owing to** *prep* a causa di

owl [aʊl] *n* gufo

own [əʊn] *adj* proprio/a ▷ *vt* possedere; **a room of my ~** la mia propria camera; **to get one's ~ back** vendicarsi; **on one's ~** tutto/a solo/a; **own up** *vi* confessare; **owner** *n* proprietario/a; **ownership** *n* possesso

ox (*pl* **oxen**) [ɔks, ˈɔksn] *n* bue *m*

Oxbridge [ˈɔksbrɪdʒ] *n* le università di Oxford e/o Cambridge

oxen [ˈɔksn] *npl of* **ox**

oxygen [ˈɔksɪdʒən] *n* ossigeno

oyster [ˈɔɪstəʳ] *n* ostrica

oz. *abbr* = **ounce**

ozone [ˈəʊzəʊn] *n* ozono; **ozone-friendly** *adj* che non danneggia lo strato d'ozono; **ozone layer** *n* fascia d'ozono

p

PA n abbr = **personal assistant;
public address system**
p.a. abbr = **per annum**
pace [peɪs] n passo; (speed) passo;
velocità ▷ vi: **to ~ up and down**
camminare su e giù; **to keep ~ with**
camminare di pari passo a; (events)
tenersi al corrente di; **pacemaker** n
(Med) pacemaker m inv, stimolatore
m cardiaco; (Sport) chi fa l'andatura
Pacific [pə'sɪfɪk] n: **the ~ (Ocean)** il
Pacifico, l'Oceano Pacifico
pacifier ['pæsɪfaɪər] n (us: dummy)
succhiotto, ciuccio (col)
pack [pæk] n pacco; (us: of cigarettes)
pacchetto; (of hounds) muta; (of
thieves etc) banda; (of cards) mazzo
▷ vt (in suitcase etc) mettere; (box)
riempire; (cram) stipare, pigiare ▷ vi:
to ~ one's bags fare la valigia; **to
send sb ~ing** spedire via qn; **pack in**
(BRIT col) vi (watch, car) guastarsi ▷ vt

mollare, piantare; **~ it in!** piantala!,
dacci un taglio!; **pack off** vt (person)
spedire; **to ~ sb off** spedire via
qn; **pack up** vi (BRIT col: machine)
guastarsi; (person) far fagotto ▷ vt
(belongings, clothes) mettere in una
valigia; (goods, presents) imballare
package ['pækɪdʒ] n pacco; balla;
(also: **~ deal**) pacchetto; forfait m
inv; **package holiday** n vacanza
organizzata; **package tour** n viaggio
organizzato
packaging ['pækɪdʒɪŋ] n confezione
f, imballo
packed [pækt] adj (crowded)
affollato/a; **~ lunch** (BRIT) pranzo
al sacco
packet ['pækɪt] n pacchetto
packing ['pækɪŋ] n imballaggio
pact [pækt] n patto, accordo;
trattato
pad [pæd] n blocco; (to prevent friction)
cuscinetto; (col: flat) appartamentino
▷ vt imbottire; **padded** adj
imbottito/a
paddle ['pædl] n (oar) pagaia; (us: for
table tennis) racchetta da ping-pong
▷ vi sguazzare ▷ vt (boat) fare andare
a colpi di pagaia; **paddling pool** n
(BRIT) piscina per bambini
paddock ['pædək] n prato recintato;
(at racecourse) paddock m inv
padlock ['pædlɔk] n lucchetto
paedophile, (us) **pedophile**
['pi:dəufaɪl] adj, n pedofilo/a
page [peɪdʒ] n pagina; (also: **~
boy**) paggio ▷ vt (in hotel etc) (far)
chiamare
pager ['peɪdʒər] n (Tel) cercapersone
m inv
paid [peɪd] pt, pp of **pay** ▷ adj (work,
official) rimunerato/a; **to put ~ to**
(BRIT) mettere fine a
pain [peɪn] n dolore m; **to be in ~**
soffrire, aver male; **to take ~s to do**
mettercela tutta per fare; **painful**
adj doloroso/a, che fa male; (difficult)
difficile, penoso/a; **painkiller**

n antalgico, antidolorifico;
painstaking ['peɪnzteɪkɪŋ]
adj (*person*) sollecito/a; (*work*)
accurato/a
paint [peɪnt] *n* vernice *f*; colore *m*
▷ *vt* dipingere; (*door etc*) verniciare;
to ~ the door blue verniciare la
porta di azzurro; **paintbrush** *n*
pennello; **painter** *n* (*artist*) pittore
m; (*decorator*) imbianchino; **painting**
n pittura; verniciatura; (*picture*)
dipinto, quadro
pair [pɛəʳ] *n* (*of shoes, gloves etc*) paio;
(*of people*) coppia; duo *m inv*; **a ~ of
scissors/trousers** un paio di forbici/
pantaloni
pajamas [pə'dʒɑːməz] *npl* (*us*)
pigiama *m*
Pakistan [pɑːkɪ'stɑːn] *n* Pakistan *m*;
Pakistani *adj*, *n* pakistano/a
pal [pæl] *n* (*col*) amico/a,
compagno/a
palace ['pæləs] *n* palazzo
pale [peɪl] *adj* pallido/a ▷ *n*: **to be
beyond the ~** aver oltrepassato
ogni limite
Palestine ['pælɪstaɪn] *n* Palestina;
Palestinian [pælɪs'tɪnɪən] *adj*, *n*
palestinese (*m/f*)
palm [pɑːm] *n* (*Anat*) palma, palmo;
(*also*: **~ tree**) palma ▷ *vt*: **to ~ sth off
on sb** (*col*) rifilare qc a qn
pamper ['pæmpəʳ] *vt* viziare,
coccolare
pamphlet ['pæmflət] *n* dépliant
m inv
pan [pæn] *n* (*also*: **sauce~**)
casseruola; (*also*: **frying ~**) padella
pancake ['pænkeɪk] *n* frittella
panda ['pændə] *n* panda *m inv*
pandemic [pæn'dɛmɪk] *n* pandemia
pane [peɪn] *n* vetro
panel ['pænl] *n* (*of wood, cloth etc*)
pannello; (*Radio, TV*) giuria
panhandler ['pænhændləʳ] *n* (*us
col*) accattone/a
panic ['pænɪk] *n* panico ▷ *vi* perdere il
sangue freddo

panorama [pænə'rɑːmə] *n*
panorama *m*
pansy ['pænzɪ] *n* (*Bot*) viola
del pensiero, pensée *f inv*; (*col!*)
femminuccia
pant [pænt] *vi* ansare
panther ['pænθəʳ] *n* pantera
panties ['pæntɪz] *npl* slip *m*,
mutandine *fpl*
pantomime ['pæntəmaɪm] *n* (*BRIT*:
at Christmas) spettacolo natalizio;
(*tecnica*) pantomima

- **PANTOMIME**
-
-
- In Gran Bretagna la *pantomime*
- (abbreviata in *panto*) è una
- sorta di libera interpretazione
- delle favole più conosciute che
- vengono messe in scena nei teatri
- durante il periodo natalizio. Gli
- attori principali sono la dama,
- "*dame*", che è un uomo vestito da
- donna, il protagonista, "*principal
- boy*", che è una donna travestita da
- uomo, e il cattivo, "*villain*". È uno
- spettacolo per tutta la famiglia,
- che prevede la partecipazione del
- pubblico.

pants [pænts] *npl* mutande *fpl*, slip
m; (*us: trousers*) pantaloni *mpl*
paper ['peɪpəʳ] *n* carta; (*also*: **wall~**)
carta da parati, tappezzeria; (*also*:
news~) giornale *m*; (*study, article*)
saggio; (*exam*) prova scritta ▷ *adj*
di carta ▷ *vt* tappezzare; *see also*
papers; **paperback** *n* tascabile *m*;
edizione *f* economica; **paper bag**
n sacchetto di carta; **paper clip**
n graffetta, clip *f inv*; **papers** *npl*
(*also*: **identity papers**) carte *fpl*,
documenti *mpl*; **paper shop** *n* (*BRIT*)
giornalaio (*negozio*); **paperwork** *n*
lavoro amministrativo
paprika ['pæprɪkə] *n* paprica
par [pɑːʳ] *n* parità, pari *f*; (*Golf*) norma;
on a ~ with alla pari con

paracetamol [pærə'si:təmɔl] n
(BRIT) paracetamolo

parachute ['pærəʃu:t] n paracadute
m inv

parade [pə'reɪd] n parata ▷ vt (fig)
fare sfoggio di ▷ vi sfilare in parata

paradise ['pærədaɪs] n paradiso

paradox ['pærədɔks] n paradosso

paraffin ['pærəfɪn] n (BRIT): **~ (oil)**
paraffina

paragraph ['pærəgrɑ:f] n
paragrafo

parallel ['pærəlɛl] adj parallelo/a;
(fig) analogo/a ▷ n (line) parallela;
(fig, Geo) parallelo

paralysed ['pærəlaɪzd] adj
paralizzato/a

paralysis (pl **paralyses**) [pə'rælɪsɪs,
-si:z] n paralisi f inv

paramedic [pærə'mɛdɪk] n
paramedico

paranoid ['pærənɔɪd] adj
paranoico/a

parasite ['pærəsaɪt] n parassita m

parcel ['pɑ:sl] n pacco, pacchetto
▷ vt (also: **~ up**) impaccare

pardon ['pɑ:dn] n perdono; grazia
▷ vt perdonare; (Law) graziare; **~ me!**
mi scusi!; **I beg your ~!** scusi!; **(I beg
your) ~?, (US) ~ me?** prego?

parent ['pɛərənt] n padre m (or
madre f); **parents** npl genitori mpl;
parental [pə'rɛntl] adj dei genitori

Be careful not to translate parent
by the Italian word parente.

Paris ['pærɪs] n Parigi f

parish ['pærɪʃ] n parrocchia; (BRIT:
civil) ≈ municipio

Parisian [pə'rɪzɪən] adj, n
parigino/a

park [pɑ:k] n parco ▷ vt, vi
parcheggiare

parking ['pɑ:kɪŋ] n parcheggio; **"no
~"** "sosta vietata"; **parking lot** n (US)
posteggio, parcheggio; **parking
meter** n parchimetro; **parking
ticket** n multa per sosta vietata

parkway ['pɑ:kweɪ] n (US) viale m

parliament ['pɑ:ləmənt] n
parlamento; **parliamentary**
[pɑ:lə'mɛntərɪ] adj parlamentare

Parmesan [pɑ:mɪ'zæn] n (also: **~
cheese**) parmigiano

parole [pə'rəʊl] n: **on ~** in libertà per
buona condotta

parrot ['pærət] n pappagallo

parsley ['pɑ:slɪ] n prezzemolo

parsnip ['pɑ:snɪp] n pastinaca

parson ['pɑ:sn] n prete m; (Church of
England) parroco

part [pɑ:t] n parte f; (of machine)
pezzo; (US: in hair) scriminatura
▷ adj in parte ▷ adv = **partly** ▷ vt
separare ▷ vi (people) separarsi; **to
take ~ in** prendere parte a; **to take
sb's ~** parteggiare per qn, prendere
le parti di qn; **for my ~** per parte
mia; **for the most ~** in generale;
nella maggior parte dei casi; **to
take sth in good/bad ~** prendere
bene/male qc; **~ of speech** parte del
discorso; **part with** vt fus separarsi
da; rinunciare a

partial ['pɑ:ʃl] adj parziale; **to be ~ to**
avere un debole per

participant [pɑ:'tɪsɪpənt] n: **~ (in)**
partecipante m/f (a)

participate [pɑ:'tɪsɪpeɪt] vi: **to ~
(in)** prendere parte (a), partecipare
(a)

particle ['pɑ:tɪkl] n particella

particular [pə'tɪkjʊləʳ] adj
particolare; speciale; (fussy)
difficile; meticoloso/a; **particulars**
npl particolari mpl, dettagli mpl;
(information) informazioni fpl; **in
~** in particolare, particolarmente;
particularly adv particolarmente;
in particolare

parting ['pɑ:tɪŋ] n separazione f;
(BRIT: in hair) scriminatura ▷ adj
d'addio

partition [pɑ:'tɪʃən] n (Pol)
partizione f; (wall) tramezzo

partly ['pɑ:tlɪ] adv parzialmente;
in parte

P

partner ['pɑːtnə^r] n (Comm)
socio/a; (wife, husband etc, Sport)
compagno/a; (at dance) cavaliere
(dama); **partnership** n associazione
f; (Comm) società f inv

partridge ['pɑːtrɪdʒ] n pernice f

part-time ['pɑːt'taɪm] adj, adv a
orario ridotto

party ['pɑːtɪ] n (Pol) partito; (team)
squadra; (Law) parte f; (celebration)
ricevimento; serata; festa ▷ adj (Pol)
del partito, di partito

pass [pɑːs] vt (gen) passare; (place)
passare davanti a; (exam) passare,
superare; (candidate) promuovere;
(overtake, surpass) sorpassare,
superare; (approve) approvare ▷ vi
passare ▷ n (permit) lasciapassare m
inv; permesso; (in mountains) passo,
gola; (Sport) passaggio; (Scol): **to get
a ~** prendere la sufficienza; **could
you ~ the vegetables round?**
potrebbe far passare i contorni?; **to ~
sth through a hole** etc far passare qc
attraverso un buco etc; **to make a ~
at sb** (col) fare delle proposte or delle
avances a qn; **pass away** vi morire;
pass by vi passare ▷ vt trascurare;
pass on vt: **to ~ on (to)** passare (a);
pass out vi svenire; **pass over** vi
(die) spirare ▷ vt lasciare da parte;
pass up vt (opportunity) lasciarsi
sfuggire, perdere; **passable** adj (road)
praticabile; (work) accettabile

passage ['pæsɪdʒ] n (gen) passaggio;
(also: **~way**) corridoio; (in book)
brano, passo; (by boat) traversata

passenger ['pæsɪndʒə^r] n
passeggero/a

passer-by [pɑːsə'baɪ] n passante
m/f

passing place n (Aut) piazzola (di
sosta)

passion ['pæʃən] n passione f; amore
m; **passionate** adj appassionato/a;
passion fruit n frutto della passione

passive ['pæsɪv] adj (also Ling)
passivo/a

passport ['pɑːspɔːt] n passaporto;
passport control n controllo m
passaporti inv; **passport office** n
ufficio m passaporti inv

password ['pɑːswəːd] n parola
d'ordine

past [pɑːst] prep (further than) oltre,
di là di; dopo; (later than) dopo
▷ adv: **to run ~** passare di corsa
▷ adj passato/a; (president etc) ex inv
▷ n passato; **he's ~ forty** ha più di
quarant'anni; **ten ~ eight** le otto e
dieci; **for the ~ few days** da qualche
giorno; in questi ultimi giorni

pasta ['pæstə] n pasta

paste [peɪst] n (glue) colla; (Culin)
pâté m inv; pasta ▷ vt collare

pastel ['pæstl] adj pastello inv

pasteurized ['pæstəraɪzd] adj
pastorizzato/a

pastime ['pɑːstaɪm] n passatempo

pastor ['pɑːstə^r] n pastore m

past participle [-'pɑːtɪsɪpl] n (Ling)
participio passato

pastry ['peɪstrɪ] n pasta

pasture ['pɑːstʃə^r] n pascolo

pasty¹ ['pæstɪ] n pasticcio di carne

pasty² ['peɪstɪ] adj (complexion)
pallido/a, smorto/a

pat [pæt] vt accarezzare, dare un
colpetto (affettuoso) a

patch [pætʃ] n (of material) toppa;
(eye patch) benda; (spot) macchia
▷ vt (clothes) rattoppare; **a bad ~** un
brutto periodo; **patchy** adj irregolare

pâté ['pæteɪ] n pâté m inv

patent ['peɪtnt] n brevetto
▷ vt brevettare ▷ adj patente,
manifesto/a

paternal [pə'təːnl] adj paterno/a

paternity leave [pə'təːnɪtɪ-] n
congedo di paternità

path [pɑːθ] n sentiero, viottolo; viale
m; (fig) via, strada; (of planet, missile)
traiettoria

pathetic [pə'θɛtɪk] adj (pitiful)
patetico/a; (very bad) penoso/a

pathway ['pɑːθweɪ] n sentiero

patience ['peɪʃns] n pazienza; (BRIT Cards) solitario
patient ['peɪʃnt] n paziente m/f; malato/a ▷ adj paziente
patio ['pætɪəu] n terrazza
patriotic [pætrɪ'ɔtɪk] adj patriottico/a
patrol [pə'trəul] n pattuglia ▷ vt pattugliare; **patrol car** n autoradio f inv (della polizia)
patron ['peɪtrən] n (in shop) cliente m/f; (of charity) benefattore/trice; **~ of the arts** mecenate m/f
patronizing ['pætrənaɪzɪŋ] adj condiscendente
pattern ['pætən] n modello; (design) disegno, motivo; **patterned** adj a disegni, a motivi; (material) fantasia inv
pause [pɔːz] n pausa ▷ vi fare una pausa, arrestarsi
pave [peɪv] vt pavimentare; **to ~ the way for** aprire la via a
pavement ['peɪvmənt] n (BRIT) marciapiede m

> Be careful not to translate pavement by the Italian word pavimento.

pavilion [pə'vɪlɪən] n (Sport) edificio annesso ad un campo sportivo
paving ['peɪvɪŋ] n pavimentazione f
paw [pɔː] n zampa
pawn [pɔːn] n (Chess) pedone m; (fig) pedina ▷ vt dare in pegno; **pawnbroker** n prestatore m su pegno
pay [peɪ] (pt, pp paid) n stipendio; paga ▷ vt pagare ▷ vi (be profitable) rendere; **to ~ attention (to)** fare attenzione (a); **to ~ sb a visit** far visita a qn; **to ~ one's respects to sb** porgere i propri rispetti a qn; **pay back** vt rimborsare; **pay for** vt fus pagare; **pay in** vt versare; **pay off** vt (debts) saldare; (creditor) pagare; (workers) licenziare ▷ vi (scheme) funzionare; (patience) dare dei frutti; **pay out** vt (money) sborsare, tirar

fuori; (rope) far allentare; **pay up** vt saldare; **payable** adj pagabile; **pay-as-you-go** ['peɪəzjə'gəu] adj (mobile phone) con scheda prepagata; **pay day** n giorno di paga; **pay envelope** n (US) busta f paga inv; **payment** n pagamento; versamento; saldo; **payout** n pagamento; (in competition) premio; **pay packet** n (BRIT) busta f paga inv; **payphone** n cabina telefonica; **payroll** n ruolo (organico); **pay slip** n foglio m paga inv; **pay television** n televisione f a pagamento, pay-tv f inv
PC n abbr = **personal computer** ▷ adj abbr = **politically correct**
pc abbr = **per cent**
PDA n abbr (= personal digital assistant) PDA m inv
PE n abbr (= physical education) ed. fisica
pea [piː] n pisello
peace [piːs] n pace f; **peaceful** adj pacifico/a, calmo/a
peach [piːtʃ] n pesca
peacock ['piːkɔk] n pavone m
peak [piːk] n (of mountain) cima, vetta; (mountain itself) picco; (of cap) visiera; (fig) apice m; **peak hours** npl ore fpl di punta
peanut ['piːnʌt] n arachide f, nocciolina americana; **peanut butter** n burro di arachidi
pear [pɛər] n pera
pearl [pəːl] n perla
peasant ['pɛznt] n contadino/a
peat [piːt] n torba
pebble ['pɛbl] n ciottolo
peck [pɛk] vt (also: **~ at**) beccare ▷ n colpo di becco; (kiss) bacetto; **peckish** adj (BRIT col): **I feel peckish** ho un languorino
peculiar [pɪ'kjuːlɪər] adj strano/a, bizzarro/a; (particular) particolare; **~ to** tipico/a di
pedal ['pɛdl] n pedale m ▷ vi pedalare
pedalo ['pɛdələu] n pedalò m inv
pedestal ['pɛdəstl] n piedestallo

pedestrian [pɪ'dɛstrɪən] n
pedone/a ▷ adj pedonale; (fig)
prosaico/a, pedestre; **pedestrian
crossing** n (BRIT) passaggio
pedonale; **pedestrianized** adj:
a pedestrianized street una
zona pedonalizzata; **pedestrian
precinct,** (US) **pedestrian zone** n
zona pedonale

pedigree ['pɛdɪɡriː] n (of animal)
pedigree m inv; (fig) background m inv
▷ cpd (animal) di razza

pedophile ['piːdəʊfaɪl] (US) n
= **paedophile**

pee [piː] vi (col) pisciare

peek [piːk] vi guardare
furtivamente

peel [piːl] n buccia; (of orange, lemon)
scorza ▷ vt sbucciare ▷ vi (paint etc)
staccarsi

peep [piːp] n (look) sguardo furtivo,
sbirciata; (sound) pigolio ▷ vi
guardare furtivamente

peer [pɪə'] vi: **to ~ at** scrutare ▷ n
(noble) pari m inv; (equal) pari mf
inv, uguale m/f; (contemporary)
contemporaneo/a

peg [pɛɡ] n caviglia; (for coat etc)
attaccapanni m inv; (BRIT: also:
clothes ~) molletta

pelican ['pɛlɪkən] n pellicano;
pelican crossing n (BRIT Aut)
attraversamento pedonale con semaforo
a controllo manuale

pelt [pɛlt] vt: **to ~ sb (with)**
bombardare qn (con) ▷ vi (rain)
piovere a dirotto; (col: run) filare
▷ n pelle f

pelvis ['pɛlvɪs] n pelvi f inv, bacino

pen [pɛn] n penna; (for sheep) recinto

penalty ['pɛnltɪ] n penalità f inv;
sanzione f penale; (fine) ammenda;
(Sport) penalizzazione f

pence [pɛns] npl (BRIT) of **penny**

pencil ['pɛnsl] n matita ▷ vt (also:
~ in) scrivere a matita; **pencil
case** n astuccio per matite; **pencil
sharpener** n temperamatite m inv

pendant ['pɛndnt] n pendaglio

pending ['pɛndɪŋ] prep in attesa di
▷ adj in sospeso

penetrate ['pɛnɪtreɪt] vt penetrare

penfriend ['pɛnfrɛnd] n (BRIT)
corrispondente m/f

penguin ['pɛŋɡwɪn] n pinguino

penicillin [pɛnɪ'sɪlɪn] n penicillina

peninsula [pə'nɪnsjulə] n penisola

penis ['piːnɪs] n pene m

penitentiary [pɛnɪ'tɛnʃərɪ] n (US)
carcere m

penknife ['pɛnnaɪf] n temperino

penniless ['pɛnɪlɪs] adj senza un
soldo

penny (pl **pennies** or **pence**) ['pɛnɪ,
'pɛnɪz, pɛns] n (BRIT) penny m; (US)
centesimo

penpal ['pɛnpæl] n corrispondente
m/f

pension ['pɛnʃən] n pensione f;
pensioner n (BRIT) pensionato/a

pentagon ['pɛntəɡən] n
pentagono; **the P~** (US Pol) il
Pentagono

penthouse ['pɛnthaus] n
appartamento (di lusso) nell'attico

penultimate [pɪ'nʌltɪmət] adj
penultimo/a

people ['piːpl] npl gente f; persone
fpl; (citizens) popolo ▷ n (nation,
race) popolo; **4/several ~ came** 4/
parecchie persone sono venute; **~
say ...** si dice or la gente dice
che ...

pepper ['pɛpə'] n pepe m; (vegetable)
peperone m ▷ vt (fig): **to ~ with**
spruzzare di; **peppermint** n (sweet)
pasticca di menta

per [pə:'] prep per; a; **~ hour** all'ora;
~ kilo etc il chilo etc; **~ day** al giorno

perceive [pə'siːv] vt percepire;
(notice) accorgersi di

per cent adv per cento

percentage [pə'sɛntɪdʒ] n
percentuale f

perception [pə'sɛpʃən] n percezione
f; sensibilità; perspicacia

perch [pəːtʃ] n (fish) pesce m persico; (for bird) sostegno, ramo ▷ vi appollaiarsi

percussion [pəˈkʌʃən] n percussione f; (Mus) strumenti mpl a percussione

perfect [pəːfɪkt] adj perfetto/a ▷ n (also: ~ **tense**) perfetto, passato prossimo ▷ vt [pəˈfɛkt] perfezionare; mettere a punto; **perfection** [pəˈfɛkʃən] n perfezione f; **perfectly** adv perfettamente, alla perfezione

perform [pəˈfɔːm] vt (carry out) eseguire, fare; (symphony etc) suonare; (play, ballet) dare; (opera) fare ▷ vi suonare; recitare; **performance** n esecuzione f; (at theatre etc) rappresentazione f, spettacolo; (of an artist) interpretazione f; (of player etc) performance f; (of car, engine) prestazione f; **performer** n artista m/f

perfume [pəːfjuːm] n profumo

perhaps [pəˈhæps] adv forse

perimeter [pəˈrɪmɪtər] n perimetro

period [pɪərɪəd] n periodo; (Hist) epoca; (Scol) lezione f; (full stop) punto; (Med) mestruazioni fpl ▷ adj (costume, furniture) d'epoca; **periodical** [pɪərɪˈɔdɪkl] n periodico; **periodically** adv periodicamente

perish [pɛrɪʃ] vi perire, morire; (decay) deteriorarsi

perjury [pəːdʒərɪ] n spergiuro

perk [pəːk] n (col) vantaggio

perm [pəːm] n (for hair) permanente f

permanent [pəːmənənt] adj permanente; **permanently** adv definitivamente

permission [pəˈmɪʃən] n permesso

permit n [pəːmɪt] permesso ▷ vt [pəˈmɪt] permettere; **to ~ sb to do** permettere a qn di fare

perplex [pəˈplɛks] vt lasciare perplesso/a

persecute [pəːsɪkjuːt] vt perseguitare

persecution [pəːsɪˈkjuːʃən] n persecuzione f

persevere [pəːsɪˈvɪər] vi perseverare

Persian [pəːʃən] adj persiano/a ▷ n (Ling) persiano; **the ~ Gulf** n il Golfo Persico

persist [pəˈsɪst] vi: **to ~ (in doing)** persistere (nel fare); ostinarsi (a fare); **persistent** adj persistente; ostinato/a

person [pəːsn] n persona; **in ~** di or in persona, personalmente; **personal** adj personale; individuale; **personal assistant** n segretaria personale; **personal computer** n personal computer m inv; **personality** [pəːsəˈnælɪtɪ] n personalità f inv; **personally** adv personalmente; **to take sth personally** prendere qc come una critica personale; **personal organizer** n agenda; (electronic) agenda elettronica; **personal stereo** n walkman® m inv

personnel [pəːsəˈnɛl] n personale m

perspective [pəˈspɛktɪv] n prospettiva

perspiration [pəːspɪˈreɪʃən] n traspirazione f, sudore m

persuade [pəˈsweɪd] vt: **to ~ sb to do sth** persuadere qn a fare qc

persuasion [pəˈsweɪʒən] n persuasione f; (creed) convinzione f, credo

persuasive [pəˈsweɪsɪv] adj persuasivo/a

perverse [pəˈvəːs] adj perverso/a

pervert n [pəːvəːt] pervertito/a ▷ vt [pəˈvəːt] pervertire

pessimism [pɛsɪmɪzəm] n pessimismo

pessimist [pɛsɪmɪst] n pessimista m/f; **pessimistic** [pɛsɪˈmɪstɪk] adj pessimistico/a

pest [pɛst] n animale m (or insetto) pestifero; (fig) peste f

pester [pɛstər] vt tormentare, molestare

pesticide [pɛstɪsaɪd] n pesticida m

pet [pɛt] n animale m domestico; (favourite) favorito/a ▷ vt

P

accarezzare; **teacher's ~** favorito/a del maestro

petal ['pɛtl] n petalo

petite [pə'ti:t] adj piccolo/a e aggraziato/a

petition [pə'tɪʃən] n petizione f

petrified ['pɛtrɪfaɪd] adj (fig) morto/a di paura

petrol ['pɛtrəl] n (BRIT) benzina; **two/four-star ~** ≈ benzina normale/super

▎Be careful not to translate petrol by the Italian word petrolio.

petroleum [pə'trəʊlɪəm] n petrolio

petrol: petrol pump n (BRIT: in car, at garage) pompa di benzina; **petrol station** n (BRIT) stazione f di rifornimento; **petrol tank** n (BRIT) serbatoio della benzina

petticoat ['pɛtɪkəʊt] n sottana

petty ['pɛtɪ] adj (mean) meschino/a; (unimportant) insignificante

pew [pju:] n panca (di chiesa)

pewter ['pju:tər] n peltro

phantom ['fæntəm] n fantasma m

pharmacist ['fɑ:məsɪst] n farmacista m/f

pharmacy ['fɑ:məsɪ] n farmacia

phase [feɪz] n fase f, periodo; **phase in** vt introdurre gradualmente; **phase out** vt (machinery) eliminare gradualmente; (product) ritirare gradualmente; (job, subsidy) abolire gradualmente

PhD n abbr = **Doctor of Philosophy**

pheasant ['fɛznt] n fagiano

phenomena [fə'nɔmɪnə] npl of **phenomenon**

phenomenal [fɪ'nɔmɪnl] adj fenomenale

phenomenon (pl **phenomena**) [fə'nɔmɪnən, -nə] n fenomeno

Philippines ['fɪlɪpi:nz] npl: **the ~** le Filippine

philosopher [fɪ'lɔsəfər] n filosofo/a

philosophical [fɪlə'sɔfɪkl] adj filosofico/a

philosophy [fɪ'lɔsəfɪ] n filosofia

phlegm [flɛm] n flemma

phobia ['fəʊbjə] n fobia

phone [fəʊn] n telefono ▷ vt telefonare a ▷ vi telefonare; **to be on the ~** avere il telefono; (be calling) essere al telefono; **phone back** vt, vi richiamare; **phone up** vt telefonare a ▷ vi telefonare; **phone book** n guida del telefono, elenco telefonico; **phone box**, (US) **phone booth** n cabina telefonica; **phone call** n telefonata; **phonecard** n scheda telefonica; **phone number** n numero di telefono

phonetics [fə'nɛtɪks] n fonetica

phoney ['fəʊnɪ] adj falso/a, fasullo/a

photo ['fəʊtəʊ] n foto f inv; **photo album** n (new) album m inv per fotografie; (containing photos) album m inv delle fotografie; **photocopier** n fotocopiatrice f; **photocopy** n fotocopia ▷ vt fotocopiare

photograph ['fəʊtəgræf] n fotografia ▷ vt fotografare; **photographer** [fə'tɔgrəfər] n fotografo; **photography** [fə'tɔgrəfɪ] n fotografia

phrase [freɪz] n espressione f; (Ling) locuzione f; (Mus) frase f ▷ vt esprimere

phrasebook ['freɪzbʊk] n vocabolarietto

physical ['fɪzɪkl] adj fisico/a; **~ education** educazione f fisica; **physically** adv fisicamente

physician [fɪ'zɪʃən] n medico

physicist ['fɪzɪsɪst] n fisico

physics ['fɪzɪks] n fisica

physiotherapist [fɪzɪəʊ'θɛrəpɪst] n fisioterapista m/f

physiotherapy [fɪzɪəʊ'θɛrəpɪ] n fisioterapia

physique [fɪ'zi:k] n fisico, costituzione f

pianist ['pi:ənɪst] n pianista m/f

piano [pɪ'ænəʊ] n pianoforte m

pick [pɪk] n (tool: also: **~-axe**) piccone m ▷ vt scegliere; (gather) cogliere;

(remove) togliere; (lock) far scattare; **take your ~** scelga; **the ~ of** il fior fiore di; **to ~ one's nose** mettersi le dita nel naso; **to ~ one's teeth** pulirsi i denti con lo stuzzicadenti; **to ~ a fight/quarrel with sb** attaccar rissa/briga con qn; **pick on** vt fus (person) avercela con; **pick out** vt scegliere; (distinguish) distinguere; **pick up** vi (improve) migliorarsi ▷ vt raccogliere; (Police) prendere; (collect) passare a prendere; (Aut: give lift to) far salire; (person: for sexual encounter) rimorchiare; (learn) imparare; (Radio, TV, Tel) ricevere; **to ~ o.s. up** rialzarsi; **to ~ up speed** acquistare velocità

pickle ['pɪkl] n (also: **~s**) (as condiment) sottaceti mpl; (fig): **in a ~** nei pasticci ▷ vt mettere sottaceto; mettere in salamoia

pickpocket ['pɪkpɔkɪt] n borsaiolo

pickup ['pɪkʌp] n (BRIT: on record player) pick-up m inv; (small truck: also: **~ truck, ~ van**) camioncino

picnic ['pɪknɪk] n picnic m inv; **picnic area** n area per il picnic

picture ['pɪktʃəʳ] n quadro; (painting) pittura; (photograph) foto(grafia); (drawing) disegno; (film) film m inv ▷ vt raffigurarsi; **the ~s** (BRIT) il cinema; **to take a ~ of sb/sth** fare una foto a qn/di qc; **picture frame** n cornice m inv; **picture messaging** n picture messaging m, invio di messaggini con immagini

picturesque [pɪktʃə'rɛsk] adj pittoresco/a

pie [paɪ] n torta; (of meat) pasticcio

piece [piːs] n pezzo; (of land) appezzamento; (item): **a ~ of furniture/advice** un mobile/consiglio ▷ vt: **to ~ together** mettere insieme; **to take to ~s** smontare

pie chart n grafico a torta

pier [pɪəʳ] n molo; (of bridge etc) pila

pierce [pɪəs] vt forare; (with arrow etc) trafiggere; **pierced** adj: **I've**

got pierced ears ho i buchi per gli orecchini

pig [pɪg] n maiale m, porco

pigeon ['pɪdʒən] n piccione m

piggy bank ['pɪgɪ-] n salvadanaio

pigsty ['pɪgstaɪ] n porcile m

pigtail ['pɪgteɪl] n treccina

pike [paɪk] n (fish) luccio

pilchard ['pɪltʃəd] n specie di sardina

pile [paɪl] n (pillar, of books) pila; (heap) mucchio; (of carpet) pelo; **to ~ into** (car) stiparsi or ammucchiarsi in; **pile up** vt ammucchiare; **piles** [paɪlz] npl emorroidi fpl; **pileup** ['paɪlʌp] n (Aut) tamponamento a catena

pilgrimage ['pɪlgrɪmɪdʒ] n pellegrinaggio

pill [pɪl] n pillola; **to be on the ~** prendere la pillola

pillar ['pɪləʳ] n colonna

pillow ['pɪləʊ] n guanciale m; **pillowcase** n federa

pilot ['paɪlət] n pilota m/f ▷ cpd (scheme etc) pilota inv ▷ vt pilotare; **pilot light** n fiamma pilota

pimple ['pɪmpl] n foruncolo

PIN n abbr (= personal identification number) codice m segreto, PIN m inv

pin [pɪn] n spillo; (Tech) perno ▷ vt attaccare con uno spillo; **~s and needles** formicolio; **to ~ sth on sb** (fig) addossare la colpa di qc a qn; **pin down** vt (fig): **to ~ sb down** obbligare qn a pronunziarsi

pinafore ['pɪnəfɔːʳ] n (also: **~ dress**) scamiciato

pinch [pɪntʃ] n pizzicotto, pizzico ▷ vt pizzicare; (col: steal) grattare; **at a ~** in caso di bisogno

pine [paɪn] n (also: **~ tree**) pino ▷ vi: **to ~ for** struggersi dal desiderio di

pineapple ['paɪnæpl] n ananas m inv

ping [pɪŋ] n (noise) tintinnio; **Ping-Pong®** ['pɪŋpɔŋ] n ping-pong® m

pink [pɪŋk] adj rosa inv ▷ n (colour) rosa m inv; (Bot) garofano

pinpoint ['pɪnpɔɪnt] vt indicare con precisione

P

pint [paɪnt] *n* pinta (*Brit* = 0.57 l; *US* = 0.47 l); (*BRIT col: of beer*) ≈ birra grande

pioneer [paɪə'nɪər] *n* pioniere/a

pious ['paɪəs] *adj* pio/a

pip [pɪp] *n (seed)* seme *m*; (*BRIT: time signal on radio*) segnale *m* orario

pipe [paɪp] *n* tubo; (*for smoking*) pipa ▷ *vt* portare per mezzo di tubazione; **pipeline** *n* conduttura; (*for oil*) oleodotto; **piper** *n* piffero; suonatore/trice di cornamusa

pirate ['paɪərət] *n* pirata *m* ▷ *vt* riprodurre abusivamente

Pisces ['paɪsiːz] *n* Pesci *mpl*

piss [pɪs] *vi (col!)* pisciare; **pissed** *adj* (*BRIT col: drunk*) ubriaco/a fradicio/a

pistol ['pɪstl] *n* pistola

piston ['pɪstən] *n* pistone *m*

pit [pɪt] *n* buca, fossa; (*also: coal ~*) miniera; (*quarry*) cava ▷ *vt*: **to ~ sb against sb** opporre qn a qn

pitch [pɪtʃ] *n (Mus)* tono; (*fig*) grado, punto; (*BRIT Sport*) campo; (*tar*) pece *f* ▷ *vt (throw)* lanciare ▷ *vi (fall)* cascare; **to ~ a tent** piantare una tenda; **pitch-black** *adj* nero/a come la pece

pitfall ['pɪtfɔːl] *n* trappola

pith [pɪθ] *n (of plant)* midollo; (*of orange*) parte *f* interna della scorza; (*fig*) essenza, succo; vigore *m*

pitiful ['pɪtɪful] *adj (touching)* pietoso/a

pity ['pɪtɪ] *n* pietà ▷ *vt* aver pietà di; **what a ~!** che peccato!

pizza ['piːtsə] *n* pizza

placard ['plækɑːd] *n* affisso

place [pleɪs] *n* posto, luogo; (*proper position, rank, seat*) posto; (*house*) casa, alloggio; (*home*): **at/to his ~** a casa sua ▷ *vt (object)* posare, mettere; (*identify*) riconoscere; individuare; **to take ~** aver luogo; succedere; **out of ~** (*not suitable*) inopportuno/a; **in the first ~** in primo luogo; **to change ~s with sb** scambiare il posto con qn; **to ~ an order with sb (for)** fare un'ordinazione a qn (di); **to be ~d** (*in race, exam*) classificarsi; **place mat** *n*

sottopiatto; (*in linen etc*) tovaglietta; **placement** *n* collocamento; (*job*) lavoro

placid ['plæsɪd] *adj* placido/a, calmo/a

plague [pleɪg] *n* peste *f* ▷ *vt* tormentare

plaice [pleɪs] *n (pl inv)* pianuzza

plain [pleɪn] *adj (clear)* chiaro/a, palese; (*simple*) semplice; (*frank*) franco/a, aperto/a; (*not handsome*) bruttino/a; (*without seasoning etc*) scondito/a; naturale; (*in one colour*) tinta unita *inv* ▷ *adv* francamente, chiaramente ▷ *n* pianura; **plain chocolate** *n* cioccolato fondente; **plainly** *adv* chiaramente; (*frankly*) francamente

plaintiff ['pleɪntɪf] *n* attore/trice

plait [plæt] *n* treccia

plan [plæn] *n* pianta; (*scheme*) progetto, piano ▷ *vt (think in advance*) progettare; (*prepare*) organizzare ▷ *vi*: **to ~ (for)** far piani *or* progetti (per); **to ~ to do** progettare di fare

plane [pleɪn] *n (Aviat)* aereo; (*tree*) platano; (*tool*) pialla; (*Art, Math etc*) piano ▷ *adj* piano/a, piatto/a ▷ *vt* (*with tool*) piallare

planet ['plænɪt] *n* pianeta *m*

plank [plæŋk] *n* tavola, asse *f*

planning ['plænɪŋ] *n* progettazione *f*; **family ~** pianificazione delle nascite

plant [plɑːnt] *n* pianta; (*machinery*) impianto; (*factory*) fabbrica ▷ *vt* piantare; (*bomb*) mettere

plantation [plæn'teɪʃən] *n* piantagione *f*

plaque [plæk] *n* placca

plaster ['plɑːstər] *n* intonaco; (*also: ~ of Paris*) gesso; (*BRIT: also: sticking ~*) cerotto ▷ *vt* intonacare; ingessare; (*cover*): **to ~ with** coprire di; **plaster cast** *n (Med)* ingessatura, gesso; (*model, statue*) modello in gesso

plastic ['plæstɪk] *n* plastica ▷ *adj* (*made of plastic*) di *or* in plastica;

plastic bag n sacchetto di plastica;
plastic surgery n chirurgia plastica
plate [pleɪt] n (dish) piatto; (in book)
tavola; (dental plate) dentiera; **gold/
silver ~** vasellame m d'oro/d'argento
plateau (pl **plateaus** or **plateaux**)
['plætəu, -z] n altipiano
platform ['plætfɔːm] n (stage,
at meeting) palco; (BRIT: on bus)
piattaforma; (Rail) marciapiede m;
the train leaves from ~ 7 il treno
parte dal binario 7
platinum ['plætɪnəm] n platino
platoon [plə'tuːn] n plotone m
platter ['plætəʳ] n piatto
plausible ['plɔːzɪbl] adj plausibile,
credibile; (person) convincente
play [pleɪ] n gioco; (Theat)
commedia ▷ vt (game) giocare a;
(team, opponent) giocare contro;
(instrument, piece of music) suonare;
(record, tape) ascoltare; (play, part)
interpretare ▷ vi giocare; suonare;
recitare; **to ~ safe** giocare sul
sicuro; **play back** vt riascoltare,
risentire; **play up** vi (cause trouble)
fare i capricci; **player** n giocatore/
trice; (Theat) attore/trice; (Mus)
musicista m/f; **playful** adj
giocoso/a; **playground** n (in school)
cortile m per la ricreazione; (in park)
parco m giochi inv; **playgroup** n
giardino d'infanzia; **playing card**
n carta da gioco; **playing field** n
campo sportivo; **playschool** n
= **playgroup**; **playtime** n (Scol)
ricreazione f; **playwright** n
drammaturgo/a
plc abbr (BRIT: = public limited company)
società per azioni a responsabilità
limitata quotata in borsa
plea [pliː] n (request) preghiera,
domanda; (Law) (argomento di)
difesa
plead [pliːd] vt patrocinare; (give as
excuse) addurre a pretesto ▷ vi (Law)
perorare la causa; (beg): **to ~ with sb**
implorare qn

pleasant ['plɛznt] adj piacevole,
gradevole
please [pliːz] vt piacere a ▷ vi (think
fit): **do as you ~** faccia come le pare; **~!**
per piacere!, per favore!; (acceptance):
yes, ~ sì, grazie; **~ yourself!** come
ti (or le) pare!; **pleased** adj: **pleased
(with)** contento/a (di); **pleased to
meet you!** piacere!
pleasure ['plɛʒəʳ] n piacere m; **"it's
a ~"** "prego"
pleat [pliːt] n piega
pledge [plɛdʒ] n pegno; (promise)
promessa ▷ vt impegnare;
promettere
plentiful ['plɛntɪful] adj
abbondante, copioso/a
plenty ['plɛntɪ] n: **~ of** tanto/a,
molto/a; un'abbondanza di
pliers ['plaɪəz] npl pinza
plight [plaɪt] n situazione f critica
plod [plɔd] vi camminare a stento;
(fig) sgobbare
plonk [plɔŋk] (col) n (BRIT: wine) vino
da poco ▷ vt: **to ~ sth down** buttare
giù qc bruscamente
plot [plɔt] n congiura, cospirazione
f; (of story, play) trama; (of land)
lotto ▷ vt (mark out) fare la pianta
di; rilevare; (: diagram etc) tracciare;
(conspire) congiurare, cospirare ▷ vi
congiurare
plough, (US) **plow** [plau] n aratro
▷ vt (earth) arare; **to ~ money
into** (company etc) investire
danaro in; **ploughman**, (US)
plowman ['plaumən] n aratore m;
ploughman's lunch (BRIT) semplice
pasto a base di pane e formaggio
plow etc [plau] (US) = **plough** etc
ploy [plɔɪ] n stratagemma m
pluck [plʌk] vt (fruit) cogliere;
(musical instrument) pizzicare;
(bird) spennare; (hairs) togliere ▷ n
coraggio, fegato; **to ~ up courage**
farsi coraggio
plug [plʌg] n tappo; (Elec) spina; (Aut:
also: **spark(ing) ~**) candela ▷ vt (hole)

p

tappare; (col: advertise) spingere; **plug in** (Elec) vt attaccare a una presa; **plughole** n (BRIT) scarico

plum [plʌm] n (fruit) susina

plumber ['plʌmə*] n idraulico

plumbing ['plʌmɪŋ] n (trade) lavoro di idraulico; (piping) tubature fpl

plummet ['plʌmɪt] vi: **to ~ (down)** cadere a piombo

plump [plʌmp] adj grassoccio/a; **plump for** vt fus (col: choose) decidersi per

plunge [plʌndʒ] n tuffo; (fig) caduta ▷ vt immergere ▷ vi (dive) tuffarsi; (fall) cadere, precipitare; **to take the ~** saltare il fosso

plural ['pluərl] adj, n plurale (m)

plus [plʌs] n (also: **~ sign**) segno più ▷ prep più; **ten/twenty ~** più di dieci/venti

ply [plaɪ] n (of wool) capo ▷ vt (a trade) esercitare ▷ vi (ship) fare il servizio; **three ~ (wool)** lana a tre capi; **to ~ sb with drink** dare da bere continuamente a qn; **plywood** n legno compensato

PM n abbr = **prime minister**

p.m. adv abbr (= post meridiem) del pomeriggio

PMS n abbr (= premenstrual syndrome) sindrome f premestruale

PMT n abbr (= premenstrual tension) sindrome f premestruale

pneumatic [njuː'mætɪk] adj pneumatico/a; **~ drill** martello pneumatico

pneumonia [njuː'məunɪə] n polmonite f

poach [pəutʃ] vt (cook: egg) affogare; (: fish) cuocere in bianco; (steal) cacciare (or pescare) di frodo ▷ vi fare il bracconiere; **poached** adj (egg) affogato/a

PO box n abbr = **post office box**

pocket ['pɔkɪt] n tasca ▷ vt intascare; **to be out of ~** (BRIT) rimetterci; **pocketbook** n (US:

wallet) portafoglio; **pocket money** n paghetta, settimana

pod [pɔd] n guscio

podcast ['pɔdkɑːst] n podcast m inv

podiatrist [pɔ'diːətrɪst] n (US) callista m/f, pedicure m/f

podium ['pəudɪəm] n podio

poem ['pəuɪm] n poesia

poet ['pəuɪt] n poeta/essa; **poetic** [pəu'ɛtɪk] adj poetico/a; **poetry** n poesia

poignant ['pɔɪnjənt] adj struggente

point [pɔɪnt] n (gen) punto; (tip: of needle etc) punta; (Elec) presa (di corrente); (in time) punto, momento; (Scol) voto; (main idea, important part) nocciolo; (also: **decimal ~**): **2 ~ 3 (2.3)** 2 virgola 3 (2,3) ▷ vt (show) indicare; (gun etc): **to ~ sth at** puntare qc contro ▷ vi: **to ~ at** mostrare a dito; **points** npl (Aut) puntine fpl; (Rail) scambio; **to make a ~** fare un'osservazione; **to get/miss the ~** capire/non capire; **to come to the ~** venire al fatto; **to be on the ~ of doing sth** essere sul punto di or stare (proprio) per fare qc; **there's no ~ (in doing)** è inutile (fare); **~ of view** punto di vista; **point out** vt far notare; **point-blank** adv (also: **at point-blank range**) a bruciapelo; (fig) categoricamente; **pointed** adj (shape) aguzzo/a, appuntito/a; (remark) specifico/a; **pointer** n (needle) lancetta; (clue) indicazione f; (advice) consiglio; **pointless** adj inutile, vano/a

poison ['pɔɪzn] n veleno ▷ vt avvelenare; **poisonous** adj velenoso/a

poke [pəuk] vt (fire) attizzare; (jab with finger, stick etc) punzecchiare; (put): **to ~ sth in(to)** spingere qc dentro; **poke about, poke around** vi frugare; **poke out** vi (stick out) sporger fuori

poker ['pəukə*] n attizzatoio; (Cards) poker m

Poland ['pəʊlənd] *n* Polonia

polar ['pəʊləʳ] *adj* polare; **polar bear** *n* orso bianco

Pole [pəʊl] *n* polacco/a

pole [pəʊl] *n* (*of wood*) palo; (*Elec, Geo*) polo; **pole bean** *n* (*us: runner bean*) fagiolino; **pole vault** *n* salto con l'asta

police [pə'liːs] *n* polizia ▷ *vt* mantenere l'ordine in; **police car** *n* macchina della polizia; **police constable** *n* (*BRIT*) agente *m* di polizia; **police force** *n* corpo di polizia, polizia; **policeman** *n* (*irreg*) poliziotto, agente *m* di polizia; **police officer** *n* = **police constable**; **police station** *n* posto di polizia; **policewoman** *n* (*irreg*) donna *f* poliziotto *inv*

policy ['pɒlɪsɪ] *n* politica; (*also*: **insurance ~**) polizza (d'assicurazione)

polio ['pəʊlɪəʊ] *n* polio *f*

Polish ['pəʊlɪʃ] *adj* polacco/a ▷ *n* (*Ling*) polacco

polish ['pɒlɪʃ] *n* (*for shoes*) lucido; (*for floor*) cera; (*for nails*) smalto; (*shine*) lucentezza, lustro; (*fig: refinement*) raffinatezza ▷ *vt* lucidare; (*fig: improve*) raffinare; **polish off** *vt* (*food*) mangiarsi; **polished** *adj* (*fig*) raffinato/a

polite [pə'laɪt] *adj* cortese; **politeness** *n* cortesia

political [pə'lɪtɪkl] *adj* politico/a; **politically** *adv* politicamente; **politically correct** *adj* politicamente corretto/a

politician [pɒlɪ'tɪʃən] *n* politico

politics ['pɒlɪtɪks] *n* politica ▷ *npl* (*views, policies*) idee *fpl* politiche

poll [pəʊl] *n* scrutinio; (*votes cast*) voti *mpl*; (*also*: **opinion ~**) sondaggio (d'opinioni) ▷ *vt* ottenere

pollen ['pɒlən] *n* polline *m*

polling station ['pəʊlɪŋ-] *n* (*BRIT*) sezione *f* elettorale

pollute [pə'luːt] *vt* inquinare

pollution [pə'luːʃən] *n* inquinamento

polo ['pəʊləʊ] *n* polo; **polo neck** *n* collo alto; (*also*: **polo neck sweater**) dolcevita ▷ *adj* a collo alto; **polo shirt** *n* polo *f inv*

polyester [pɒlɪ'ɛstəʳ] *n* poliestere *m*

polystyrene [pɒlɪ'staɪriːn] *n* polistirolo

polythene ['pɒlɪθiːn] *n* politene *m*; **polythene bag** *n* sacchetto di plastica

pomegranate ['pɒmɪgrænɪt] *n* melagrana

pompous ['pɒmpəs] *adj* pomposo/a

pond [pɒnd] *n* pozza; stagno

ponder ['pɒndəʳ] *vt* ponderare, riflettere su

pony ['pəʊnɪ] *n* pony *m inv*; **ponytail** *n* coda di cavallo; **pony trekking** [-trɛkɪŋ] *n* (*BRIT*) escursione *f* a cavallo

poodle ['puːdl] *n* barboncino, barbone *m*

pool [puːl] *n* (*of rain*) pozza; (*pond*) stagno; (*also*: **swimming ~**) piscina; (*fig: of light*) cerchio; (*billiards*) specie di biliardo a buca ▷ *vt* mettere in comune; **typing ~** servizio comune di dattilografia; **to do the (football) ~s** ≈ giocare al totocalcio

poor [pʊəʳ] *adj* povero/a; (*mediocre*) mediocre, cattivo/a ▷ *npl*: **the ~** i poveri; **~ in** povero/a di; **poorly** *adv* poveramente; (*badly*) male ▷ *adj* indisposto/a, malato/a

pop [pɒp] *n* (*noise*) schiocco; (*Mus*) musica pop; (*us col: father*) babbo; (*col: drink*) bevanda gasata ▷ *vt* (*put*) mettere (in fretta) ▷ *vi* scoppiare; (*cork*) schioccare; **pop in** *vi* passare; **pop out** *vi* fare un salto fuori; **popcorn** *n* pop-corn *m*

poplar ['pɒpləʳ] *n* pioppo

popper ['pɒpəʳ] *n* bottone *m* a pressione

poppy ['pɒpɪ] *n* papavero

P

Popsicle® ['pɒpsɪkl] n (us: ice lolly) ghiacciolo

pop star n pop star f inv

popular ['pɒpjuləᵣ] adj popolare; (fashionable) in voga; **popularity** [pɒpju'lærɪtɪ] n popolarità

population [pɒpju'leɪʃən] n popolazione f

pop-up adj (Comput: menu, window) a comparsa

porcelain ['pɔːslɪn] n porcellana

porch [pɔːtʃ] n veranda

pore [pɔːᵣ] n poro ▷ vi: **to ~ over** essere immerso/a in

pork [pɔːk] n carne f di maiale; **pork chop** n braciola or costoletta di maiale; **pork pie** n (BRIT Culin) pasticcio di maiale in crosta

porn [pɔːn] (col) n pornografia ▷ adj porno inv; **pornographic** [pɔːnə'græfɪk] adj pornografico/a; **pornography** [pɔː'nɒgrəfɪ] n pornografia

porridge ['pɒrɪdʒ] n porridge m

port¹ [pɔːt] n porto; (Naut: left side) babordo; **~ of call** (porto di) scalo

port² [pɔːt] n (wine) porto

portable ['pɔːtəbl] adj portatile

porter ['pɔːtəᵣ] n (for luggage) facchino, portabagagli m inv; (doorkeeper) portiere m, portinaio

portfolio [pɔːt'fəʊlɪəʊ] n (case) cartella; (Pol, Econ) portafoglio; (of artist) raccolta dei propri lavori

portion ['pɔːʃən] n porzione f

portrait ['pɔːtreɪt] n ritratto

portray [pɔː'treɪ] vt fare il ritratto di; (character on stage) rappresentare; (in writing) ritrarre

Portugal ['pɔːtjʊgl] n Portogallo

Portuguese [pɔːtjʊ'giːz] adj portoghese ▷ n (pl inv) portoghese m/f; (Ling) portoghese m

pose [pəʊz] n posa ▷ vi posare; (pretend): **to ~ as** atteggiarsi a, posare a ▷ vt porre

posh [pɒʃ] adj (col) elegante; (family) per bene

position [pə'zɪʃən] n posizione f; (job) posto ▷ vt sistemare

positive ['pɒzɪtɪv] adj positivo/a; (certain) sicuro/a, certo/a; (definite) preciso/a; definitivo/a; **positively** adv (affirmatively, enthusiastically) positivamente; (decisively) decisamente; (really) assolutamente

possess [pə'zɛs] vt possedere; **possession** [pə'zɛʃən] n possesso; **possessions** npl (belongings) beni mpl; **possessive** adj possessivo/a

possibility [pɒsɪ'bɪlɪtɪ] n possibilità f inv

possible ['pɒsɪbl] adj possibile; **as big as ~** il più grande possibile; **possibly** adv (perhaps) forse; **if you possibly can** se le è possibile; **I cannot possibly come** proprio non posso venire

post [pəʊst] n (BRIT) posta; (: collection) levata; (job, situation) posto; (Mil) postazione f; (pole) palo; (on blog, social network) post m inv, commento ▷ vt (BRIT: send by post) impostare; (Mil) appostare; (notice) affiggere; (to internet: video) caricare; (: comment) mandare; (BRIT: appoint): **to ~ to** assegnare a; **postage** n affrancatura; **postal** adj postale; **postal order** n vaglia m inv postale; **postbox** (BRIT) n cassetta delle lettere; **postcard** n cartolina; **postcode** n (BRIT) codice m (di avviamento) postale

poster ['pəʊstəᵣ] n manifesto, affisso

postgraduate ['pəʊst'grædjuət] n laureato/a che continua gli studi

postman ['pəʊstmən] n (irreg) postino

postmark ['pəʊstmɑːk] n bollo or timbro postale

post-mortem [pəʊst'mɔːtəm] n autopsia

post office n (building) ufficio postale; **the Post Office** ≈ le Poste e Telecomunicazioni

postpone [pəʊst'pəʊn] vt rinviare

posture ['pɔstʃəʳ] n portamento; (pose) posa, atteggiamento

postwoman ['pəustwumən] (BRIT: irreg) n postina

pot [pɔt] n (for cooking) pentola; casseruola; (teapot) teiera; (coffeepot) caffettiera; (for plants, jam) vaso; (col: marijuana) erba ▷ vt (plant) piantare in vaso; **a ~ of tea for two** tè per due; **to go to ~** (col: work, performance) andare in malora

potato [pə'teɪtəu] (pl potatoes) n patata; **potato peeler** n sbucciapatate m inv

potent ['pəutnt] adj potente, forte

potential [pə'tenʃl] adj potenziale ▷ n possibilità fpl

pothole ['pɔthəul] n (in road) buca; (BRIT: underground) caverna

pot plant n pianta in vaso

potter ['pɔtəʳ] n vasaio ▷ vi (BRIT): **to ~ around, ~ about** lavoracchiare; **pottery** n ceramiche fpl; (factory) fabbrica di ceramiche

potty ['pɔtɪ] adj (col: mad) tocco/a ▷ n (child's) vasino

pouch [pautʃ] n borsa; (Zool) marsupio

poultry ['pəultrɪ] n pollame m

pounce [pauns] vi: **to ~ (on)** piombare (su)

pound [paund] n (weight) libbra; (money) (lira) sterlina ▷ vt (beat) battere; (crush) pestare, polverizzare ▷ vi (beat) battere, martellare; **pound sterling** n sterlina

pour [pɔːʳ] vt versare ▷ vi riversarsi; (rain) piovere a dirotto; **pour in** vi affluire in gran quantità; **pour out** vi (people) riversarsi fuori ▷ vt vuotare; versare; (fig) sfogare; **pouring** adj: **pouring rain** pioggia torrenziale

pout [paut] vi sporgere le labbra; fare il broncio

poverty ['pɔvətɪ] n povertà, miseria

powder ['paudəʳ] n polvere f ▷ vt: **~ed milk** latte m in polvere; **to ~ one's nose** incipriarsi il naso

power ['pauəʳ] n (strength) potenza, forza; (ability, Pol: of party, leader) potere m; (Elec) corrente f; **to be in ~** essere al potere; **power cut** n (BRIT) interruzione f or mancanza di corrente; **power failure** n interruzione f della corrente elettrica; **powerful** adj potente, forte; **powerless** adj impotente; **powerless to do** impossibilitato/a a fare; **power point** n (BRIT) presa di corrente; **power station** n centrale f elettrica

PP abbr (= pages) pp.; (= per procurationem): **pp J. Smith** per il Signor J. Smith

PR n abbr = **public relations**

practical ['præktɪkl] adj pratico/a; **practical joke** n beffa; **practically** adv praticamente

practice ['præktɪs] n pratica; (of profession) esercizio; (at football etc) allenamento; (business) gabinetto; clientela ▷ vt, vi (US) = **practise**; **in ~** (in reality) in pratica; **out of ~** fuori esercizio

practise, (US) **practice** ['præktɪs] vt (work at: piano, one's backhand etc) esercitarsi a; (train for: skiing, running etc) allenarsi a; (a sport, religion) praticare; (method) usare; (profession) esercitare ▷ vi esercitarsi; (train) allenarsi; (lawyer, doctor) esercitare; **practising** adj (Christian etc) praticante; (lawyer) che esercita la professione

practitioner [præk'tɪʃənəʳ] n professionista m/f

pragmatic [præg'mætɪk] adj pragmatico/a

prairie ['prɛərɪ] n prateria

praise [preɪz] n elogio, lode f ▷ vt elogiare, lodare

pram [præm] n (BRIT) carrozzina

prank [præŋk] n burla

prawn [prɔːn] n gamberetto; **prawn cocktail** n cocktail m inv di gamberetti

P

pray [preɪ] vi pregare; **prayer** [prɛə^r] n preghiera

preach [pri:tʃ] vt, vi predicare; **preacher** n predicatore/trice; (US: minister) pastore m

precarious [prɪ'kɛərɪəs] adj precario/a

precaution [prɪ'kɔ:ʃən] n precauzione f

precede [prɪ'si:d] vt precedere; **precedent** ['prɛsɪdənt] n precedente m; **preceding** [prɪ'si:dɪŋ] adj precedente

precinct ['pri:sɪŋkt] n (US) circoscrizione f

precious ['prɛʃəs] adj prezioso/a

precise [prɪ'saɪs] adj preciso/a; **precisely** adv precisamente

precision [prɪ'sɪʒən] n precisione f

predator ['prɛdətə^r] n predatore m

predecessor ['pri:dɪsɛsə^r] n predecessore/a

predicament [prɪ'dɪkəmənt] n situazione f difficile

predict [prɪ'dɪkt] vt predire; **predictable** adj prevedibile; **prediction** [prɪ'dɪkʃən] n predizione f

predominantly [prɪ'dɔmɪnəntlɪ] adv in maggior parte; soprattutto

preface ['prɛfəs] n prefazione f

prefect ['pri:fɛkt] n (BRIT: in school) studente/essa con funzioni disciplinari; (Admin: in Italy) prefetto

prefer [prɪ'fə:^r] vt preferire; **to ~ doing** or **to do** preferire fare; **preferable** ['prɛfrəbl] adj preferibile; **preferably** ['prɛfrəblɪ] adv preferibilmente; **preference** ['prɛfrəns] n preferenza

prefix ['pri:fɪks] n prefisso

pregnancy ['prɛgnənsɪ] n gravidanza

pregnant ['prɛgnənt] adj incinta adj f

prehistoric ['pri:hɪs'tɔrɪk] adj preistorico/a

prejudice ['prɛdʒudɪs] n pregiudizio; (harm) torto, danno; **prejudiced**

adj (view) prevenuto/a; **to be prejudiced against sb/sth** essere prevenuto contro qn/qc; **prejudiced (in favour of)** ben disposto/a (verso)

preliminary [prɪ'lɪmɪnərɪ] adj preliminare

prelude ['prɛlju:d] n preludio

premature ['prɛmətʃuə^r] adj prematuro/a

premier ['prɛmɪə^r] adj primo/a ▷ n (Pol) primo ministro

première ['prɛmɪɛə^r] n prima

Premier League n ≈ serie A

premises ['prɛmɪsɪz] npl locale m; **on the ~** sul posto; **business ~** locali commerciali

premium ['pri:mɪəm] n premio; **to be at a ~** essere ricercatissimo

premonition [prɛmə'nɪʃən] n premonizione f

preoccupied [pri:'ɔkjupaɪd] adj preoccupato/a

prepaid [pri:'peɪd] adj pagato/a in anticipo

preparation [prɛpə'reɪʃən] n preparazione f; **preparations** npl (for trip, war) preparativi mpl

preparatory school [prɪ'pærətərɪ-] n scuola elementare privata

prepare [prɪ'pɛə^r] vt preparare ▷ vi: **to ~ for** prepararsi a; **prepared** adj: **prepared to** pronto/a a

preposition [prɛpə'zɪʃən] n preposizione f

prep school ['prɛp-] n = **preparatory school**

prerequisite [pri:'rɛkwɪzɪt] n requisito indispensabile

preschool ['pri:'sku:l] adj (age) prescolastico/a; (child) in età prescolastica

prescribe [prɪ'skraɪb] vt (Med) prescrivere

prescription [prɪ'skrɪpʃən] n prescrizione f; (Med) ricetta

presence ['prɛzns] n presenza; **~ of mind** presenza di spirito

present ['prɛznt] *adj* presente; (*wife, residence, job*) presente ▷ *n* (*gift*) regalo; **the ~** il presente ▷ *vt* [prɪ'zɛnt] presentare; (*give*): **to ~ sb with sth** offrire qc a qn; **at ~** al momento; **to give sb a ~** fare un regalo a qn; **presentable** [prɪ'zɛntəbl] *adj* presentabile; **presentation** [prɛzn'teɪʃən] *n* presentazione *f*; (*ceremony*) consegna ufficiale; **present-day** *adj* attuale, d'oggigiorno; **presenter** *n* (*Radio, TV*) presentatore/trice; **presently** *adv* (*soon*) fra poco, presto; (*at present*) al momento; **present participle** *n* participio presente

preservation [prɛzə'veɪʃən] *n* preservazione *f*, conservazione *f*

preservative [prɪ'zə:vətɪv] *n* conservante *m*

preserve [prɪ'zə:v] *vt* (*keep safe*) preservare, proteggere; (*maintain*) conservare; (*food*) mettere in conserva ▷ *n* (*often pl: jam*) marmellata; (*fruit*) frutta sciroppata

preside [prɪ'zaɪd] *vi*: **to ~ (over)** presiedere (a)

president ['prɛzɪdənt] *n* presidente *m*; **presidential** [prɛzɪ'dɛnʃl] *adj* presidenziale

press [prɛs] *n* (*tool, machine*) pressa; (*for wine*) torchio; (*newspapers*) stampa ▷ *vt* (*push*) premere, pigiare; (*squeeze*) spremere; (: *hand*) stringere; (*clothes: iron*) stirare; (*pursue*) incalzare; (*insist*): **to ~ sth on sb** far accettare qc da qn ▷ *vi* premere; accalcare; **we are ~ed for time** ci manca il tempo; **to ~ for sth** insistere per avere qc; **press conference** *n* conferenza stampa; **pressing** *adj* urgente; **press stud** *n* (*BRIT*) bottone *m* a pressione; **press-up** *n* (*BRIT*) flessione *f* sulle braccia

pressure ['prɛʃəʳ] *n* pressione *f* ▷ *vt*: **to put ~ on sb (to do)** mettere qn sotto pressione (affinché faccia); **pressure cooker** *n* pentola a pressione; **pressure group** *n* gruppo di pressione

prestige [prɛs'ti:ʒ] *n* prestigio

prestigious [prɛs'tɪdʒəs] *adj* prestigioso/a

presumably [prɪ'zju:məblɪ] *adv* presumibilmente

presume [prɪ'zju:m] *vt* supporre

pretence, (*US*) **pretense** [prɪ'tɛns] *n* (*claim*) pretesa; **to make a ~ of doing** far finta di fare; **under false ~s** con l'inganno

pretend [prɪ'tɛnd] *vt* (*feign*) fingere ▷ *vi* far finta; **to ~ to do** far finta di fare

pretense [prɪ'tɛns] *n* (*US*) = **pretence**

pretentious [prɪ'tɛnʃəs] *adj* pretenzioso/a

pretext ['pri:tɛkst] *n* pretesto

pretty ['prɪtɪ] *adj* grazioso/a, carino/a ▷ *adv* abbastanza, assai

prevail [prɪ'veɪl] *vi* (*win, be usual*) prevalere; (*persuade*): **to ~ (up) on sb to do** persuadere qn a fare; **prevailing** *adj* dominante

prevalent ['prɛvələnt] *adj* (*belief*) predominante; (*customs*) diffuso/a; (*fashion*) corrente; (*disease*) comune

prevent [prɪ'vɛnt] *vt*: **to ~ sb from doing** impedire a qn di fare; **to ~ sth from happening** impedire che qc succeda; **prevention** [prɪ'vɛnʃən] *n* prevenzione *f*; **preventive** *adj* preventivo/a

preview ['pri:vju:] *n* (*of film*) anteprima

previous ['pri:vɪəs] *adj* precedente; anteriore; **previously** *adv* prima

prey [preɪ] *n* preda ▷ *vi*: **to ~ on** far preda di; **it was ~ing on his mind** lo stava ossessionando

price [praɪs] *n* prezzo ▷ *vt* (*goods*) fissare il prezzo di; valutare; **priceless** *adj* di valore inestimabile; **price list** *n* listino (dei) prezzi

prick [prɪk] *n* puntura ▷ *vt* pungere; **to ~ up one's ears** drizzare gli orecchi

p

prickly ['prɪklɪ] adj spinoso/a
pride [praɪd] n orgoglio; superbia
▷ vt: **to ~ o.s. on** essere orgoglioso/a di; vantarsi di
priest [priːst] n prete m, sacerdote m
primarily ['praɪmərɪlɪ] adv principalmente, essenzialmente
primary ['praɪmərɪ] adj primario/a; (first in importance) primo/a ▷ n (US: election) primarie fpl; **primary school** n (BRIT) scuola elementare
prime [praɪm] adj primario/a, fondamentale; (excellent) di prima qualità ▷ n: **in the ~ of life** nel fiore della vita ▷ vt (wood) preparare; (fig) mettere al corrente; **prime minister** n primo ministro
primitive ['prɪmɪtɪv] adj primitivo/a
primrose ['prɪmrəuz] n primavera
prince [prɪns] n principe m
princess [prɪn'sɛs] n principessa
principal ['prɪnsɪpl] adj principale ▷ n (of school, college etc) preside m/f; **principally** adv principalmente
principle ['prɪnsɪpl] n principio; **in ~** in linea di principio; **on ~** per principio
print [prɪnt] n (mark) impronta; (letters) caratteri mpl; (fabric) tessuto stampato; (Art, Phot) stampa ▷ vt imprimere; (publish) stampare, pubblicare; (write in capitals) scrivere in stampatello; **out of ~** esaurito/a; **print out** vt (Comput) stampare; **printer** n tipografo; (machine) stampante f; **print-out** n tabulato
prior ['praɪə'] adj precedente; (claim etc) più importante; **~ to doing** prima di fare
priority [praɪ'ɔrɪtɪ] n priorità f inv; precedenza
prison ['prɪzn] n prigione f ▷ cpd (system) carcerario/a; (conditions, food) nelle or delle prigioni; **prisoner** n prigioniero/a; **prisoner of war** prigioniero/a di guerra
pristine ['prɪstiːn] adj originario/a

privacy ['prɪvəsɪ] n solitudine f, intimità
private ['praɪvɪt] adj privato/a; personale ▷ n soldato semplice; **"~"** (on envelope) "riservata"; (on door) "privato"; **in ~** in privato; **privately** adv in privato; (within o.s.) dentro di sé; **private property** n proprietà privata; **private school** n scuola privata
privatize ['praɪvɪtaɪz] vt privatizzare
privilege ['prɪvɪlɪdʒ] n privilegio
prize [praɪz] n premio ▷ adj (example, idiot) perfetto/a; (bull, novel) premiato/a ▷ vt apprezzare, pregiare; **prize giving** n premiazione f; **prizewinner** n premiato/a
pro [prəu] n (Sport) professionista m/f ▷ prep pro; **the ~s and cons** il pro e il contro
probability [prɔbə'bɪlɪtɪ] n probabilità f inv; **in all ~** con ogni probabilità
probable ['prɔbəbl] adj probabile
probably ['prɔbəblɪ] adv probabilmente
probation [prə'beɪʃən] n: **on ~** (employee) in prova; (Law) in libertà vigilata
probe [prəub] n (Med, Space) sonda; (enquiry) indagine f, investigazione f ▷ vt sondare, esplorare; indagare
problem ['prɔbləm] n problema m
procedure [prə'siːdʒə'] n (Admin, Law) procedura; (method) metodo, procedimento
proceed [prə'siːd] vi (go forward) avanzare, andare avanti; (go about it) procedere; (continue): **to ~ (with)** continuare; **to ~ to** andare a; passare a; **to ~ to do** mettersi a fare; **proceedings** npl misure fpl; (Law) procedimento; (meeting) riunione f; (records) rendiconti mpl; atti mpl; **proceeds** ['prəusiːdz] npl profitto, incasso

process ['prəusɛs] n processo;
(*method*) metodo, sistema m ▷ vt
trattare; (*information*) elaborare
procession [prə'sɛʃən] n
processione f, corteo; **funeral ~**
corteo funebre
proclaim [prə'kleɪm] vt proclamare,
dichiarare
prod [prɔd] vt dare un colpetto a;
pungolare ▷ n colpetto
produce n ['prɔdju:s] (*Agr*) prodotto,
prodotti mpl ▷ vt [prə'dju:s]
produrre; (*show*) esibire, mostrare;
(*cause*) cagionare, causare; **producer**
n (*Theat, Cine, Agr*) produttore m
product ['prɔdʌkt] n prodotto;
production [prə'dʌkʃən] n
produzione f; **productive**
[prə'dʌktɪv] adj produttivo/a;
productivity [prɔdʌk'tɪvɪtɪ] n
produttività
Prof. abbr (= *professor*) Prof.
profession [prə'fɛʃən] n professione
f; **professional** n professionista
m/f ▷ adj professionale; (*work*) da
professionista
professor [prə'fɛsə^r] n professore
m (*titolare di una cattedra*); (*us*)
professore/essa
profile ['prəufaɪl] n profilo
profit ['prɔfɪt] n profitto; beneficio
▷ vi: **to ~ (by** or **from)** approfittare
(di); **profitable** adj redditizio/a
profound [prə'faund] adj
profondo/a
programme, (*us*) **program**
['prəugræm] n programma m ▷ vt
programmare; **programmer**, (*us*)
programer n programmatore/trice;
programming, (*us*) **programing** n
programmazione f
progress n ['prəugrɛs] progresso
▷ vi [prə'grɛs] avanzare, procedere;
(*also*: **make ~**) far progressi; **in ~** in
corso; **progressive** [prə'grɛsɪv] adj
progressivo/a; (*person*) progressista
prohibit [prə'hɪbɪt] vt proibire,
vietare

project n ['prɔdʒɛkt] (*plan*) piano;
(*venture*) progetto; (*Scol*) studio ▷ vt
[prə'dʒɛkt] proiettare ▷ vi (*stick out*)
sporgere; **projection** [prə'dʒɛkʃən]
n proiezione f; sporgenza; **projector**
[prə'dʒɛktə^r] n proiettore m
prolific [prə'lɪfɪk] adj (*artist etc*)
fecondo/a
prolong [prə'lɔŋ] vt prolungare
prom [prɔm] n abbr = **promenade;
promenade concert**; (*us: ball*) ballo
studentesco

- **PROM**
-
-
- In Gran Bretagna i *Proms* (=
- *promenade concerts*) sono concerti
- di musica classica, i più noti dei
- quali sono quelli eseguiti nella
- Royal Albert Hall a Londra.
- Prendono il nome dal fatto che
- in origine il pubblico li ascoltava
- stando in piedi o passeggiando.
- Negli Stati Uniti, invece, con *prom*
- si intende il ballo studentesco di
- un'università o di un college.

promenade [prɔmə'nɑ:d] n (*by sea*)
lungomare m
prominent ['prɔmɪnənt] adj
(*standing out*) prominente;
(*important*) importante
promiscuous [prə'mɪskjuəs] adj
(*sexually*) di facili costumi
promise ['prɔmɪs] n promessa ▷ vt,
vi promettere; **to ~ sb sth, to ~
sth to sb** promettere qc a qn; **to ~
(sb) that/to do sth** promettere (a
qn) che/di fare qc; **promising** adj
promettente
promote [prə'məut] vt promuovere;
(*venture, event*) organizzare;
promotion [prə'məuʃən] n
promozione f
prompt [prɔmpt] adj rapido/a,
svelto/a; puntuale; (*reply*) sollecito/a
▷ adv (*punctually*) in punto ▷ n
(*Comput*) prompt m inv ▷ vt incitare;

P

provocare; (Theat) suggerire a; **to ~ sb to do** spingere qn a fare; **promptly** adv prontamente; puntualmente

prone [prəun] adj (lying) prono/a; **~ to** propenso/a a, incline a

prong [prɔŋ] n rebbio, punta

pronoun ['prəunaun] n pronome m

pronounce [prə'nauns] vt pronunciare; **how do you ~ it?** come si pronuncia?

pronunciation [prənʌnsɪ'eɪʃən] n pronuncia

proof [pru:f] n prova; (of book) bozza; (Phot) provino ▷ adj: **~ against** a prova di

prop [prɔp] n sostegno, appoggio ▷ vt (also: **~ up**) sostenere, appoggiare; (lean): **to ~ sth against** appoggiare qc contro or a; **props** oggetti m inv di scena

propaganda [prɔpə'gændə] n propaganda

propeller [prə'pɛləʳ] n elica

proper ['prɔpəʳ] adj (suited, right) adatto/a, appropriato/a; (seemly) decente; (authentic) vero/a; (col: real) vero/a e proprio/a; **properly** ['prɔpəlɪ] adv (eat, study) bene; (behave) come si deve; **proper noun** n nome m proprio

property ['prɔpətɪ] n (things owned) beni mpl; (land, building, Chem etc, quality) proprietà f inv

prophecy ['prɔfɪsɪ] n profezia

prophet ['prɔfɪt] n profeta m

proportion [prə'pɔ:ʃən] n proporzione f; (share) parte f; **proportions** npl (size) proporzioni fpl; **proportional** adj proporzionale

proposal [prə'pəuzl] n proposta; (plan) progetto; (of marriage) proposta di matrimonio

propose [prə'pəuz] vt proporre, suggerire ▷ vi fare una proposta di matrimonio; **to ~ to do** proporsi di fare, aver l'intenzione di fare

proposition [prɔpə'zɪʃən] n proposizione f; (proposal) proposta

proprietor [prə'praɪətəʳ] n proprietario/a

prose [prəuz] n prosa

prosecute ['prɔsɪkju:t] vt (Law) perseguire; **prosecution** [prɔsɪ'kju:ʃən] n (accusing side) accusa; **prosecutor** n (also: **public prosecutor**) ≈ procuratore m della Repubblica

prospect n ['prɔspɛkt] prospettiva; (hope) speranza ▷ vt [prə'spɛkt] esplorare ▷ vi: **to ~ for gold** cercare l'oro; **prospective** [prə'spɛktɪv] adj (legislation, son-in-law) futuro/a; **prospects** (prɔspɛkts] npl (for work etc) prospettive fpl

prospectus [prə'spɛktəs] n prospetto, programma m

prosper ['prɔspəʳ] vi prosperare; **prosperity** [prɔ'spɛrɪtɪ] n prosperità; **prosperous** adj prospero/a

prostitute ['prɔstɪtju:t] n prostituta; **male ~** uomo che si prostituisce

protect [prə'tɛkt] vt proteggere, salvaguardare; **protection** n protezione f; **protective** adj protettivo/a

protein ['prəuti:n] n proteina

protest n ['prəutɛst] protesta ▷ vt, vi [prə'tɛst] protestare

Protestant ['prɔtɪstənt] adj, n protestante (m/f)

protester [prə'tɛstəʳ] n dimostrante m/f

protractor [prə'træktəʳ] n (Geom) goniometro

proud [praud] adj fiero/a, orgoglioso/a; (pej) superbo/a

prove [pru:v] vt dimostrare, provare ▷ vi: **to ~ (to be) correct** etc risultare vero/a etc; **to ~ o.s.** mostrare le proprie capacità

proverb ['prɔvə:b] n proverbio

provide [prə'vaɪd] vt fornire, provvedere; **to ~ sb with sth** fornire or provvedere qn di qc; **provide for**

vt fus provvedere a; *(future event)* prevedere; **provided** *conj*: **provided (that)** purché + *sub*, a condizione che + *sub*; **providing** [prə'vaɪdɪŋ] *conj* purché + *sub*, a condizione che + *sub*

province ['prɒvɪns] *n* provincia; **provincial** [prə'vɪnʃəl] *adj* provinciale

provision [prə'vɪʒən] *n (supply)* riserva; *(supplying)* provvista; rifornimento; *(stipulation)* condizione *f*; **provisions** *npl (food)* provviste *fpl*; **provisional** *adj* provvisorio/a

provocative [prə'vɒkətɪv] *adj (aggressive)* provocatorio/a; *(thought-provoking)* stimolante; *(seductive)* provocante

provoke [prə'vəʊk] *vt* provocare; incitare

prowl [praʊl] *vi (also:* **~ about, ~ around)** aggirarsi furtivamente ▷ *n*: **on the ~** in caccia

proximity [prɒk'sɪmɪtɪ] *n* prossimità

proxy ['prɒksɪ] *n*: **by ~** per procura

prudent ['pru:dnt] *adj* prudente

prune [pru:n] *n* prugna secca ▷ *vt* potare

pry [praɪ] *vi*: **to ~ into** ficcare il naso in

PS *n abbr (= postscript)* P.S.

pseudonym ['sju:dənɪm] *n* pseudonimo

psychiatric [saɪkɪ'ætrɪk] *adj* psichiatrico/a

psychiatrist [saɪ'kaɪətrɪst] *n* psichiatra *m/f*

psychic ['saɪkɪk] *adj (also:* **~al)** psichico/a; *(person)* dotato/a di qualità telepatiche

psychoanalysis *(pl* **-ses)** [saɪkəʊə'nælɪsɪs, -sɪːz] *n* psicanalisi *f inv*

psychological [saɪkə'lɒdʒɪkl] *adj* psicologico/a

psychologist [saɪ'kɒlədʒɪst] *n* psicologo/a

psychology [saɪ'kɒlədʒɪ] *n* psicologia

psychotherapy [saɪkəʊ'θɛrəpɪ] *n* psicoterapia

pt *abbr* = **pint**; *(= point)* pt

PTO *abbr (= please turn over)* v.r.

pub [pʌb] *n abbr (= public house)* pub *m inv*

puberty ['pju:bətɪ] *n* pubertà

public ['pʌblɪk] *adj* pubblico/a ▷ *n* pubblico; **in ~** in pubblico

publication [pʌblɪ'keɪʃən] *n* pubblicazione *f*

public: public company *n* ≈ società *f inv* per azioni *(costituita tramite pubblica sottoscrizione)*; **public convenience** *n (BRIT)* gabinetti *mpl*; **public holiday** *n (BRIT)* giorno festivo, festa nazionale; **public house** *n (BRIT)* pub *m inv*

publicity [pʌb'lɪsɪtɪ] *n* pubblicità

publicize ['pʌblɪsaɪz] *vt* rendere pubblico/a

public: public limited company *n* ≈ società per azioni a responsabilità limitata *(quotata in Borsa)*; **publicly** ['pʌblɪklɪ] *adv* pubblicamente; **public opinion** *n* opinione *f* pubblica; **public relations** *n* pubbliche relazioni *fpl*; **public school** *n (BRIT)* scuola privata; *(US)* scuola statale; **public transport** *n* mezzi *mpl* pubblici

publish ['pʌblɪʃ] *vt* pubblicare; **publisher** *n* editore *m*; **publishing** *n (industry)* editoria; *(of a book)* pubblicazione *f*

pub lunch *n*: **to go for a ~** andare a mangiare al pub

pudding ['pʊdɪŋ] *n* budino; *(BRIT: dessert)* dolce *m*; **black ~**, *(US)* **blood ~** sanguinaccio

puddle ['pʌdl] *n* pozza, pozzanghera

Puerto Rico ['pwɛ:təʊ'ri:kəʊ] *n* Portorico

puff [pʌf] *n* sbuffo ▷ *vi (pant)* ansare; **to ~ one's pipe** tirare sboccate di fumo; **puff pastry** *n* pasta sfoglia

pull [pʊl] *n (tug)* strattone *m* ▷ *vt* tirare; *(muscle)* strappare; *(trigger)*

P

premere ▷ vi tirare; **to give sth a ~** tirare su qc; **to ~ to pieces** fare a pezzi; **to ~ one's punches** (Boxing) risparmiare l'avversario; **to ~ one's weight** dare il proprio contributo; **to ~ o.s. together** ricomporsi, riprendersi; **to ~ sb's leg** prendere in giro qn; **pull apart** vt (break) fare a pezzi; **pull away** vi (move off: vehicle) muoversi, partire; (: boat) staccarsi dal molo, salpare; (draw back: person) indietreggiare; **pull back** vt (lever etc) tirare indietro; (curtains) aprire ▷ vi (from confrontation etc) tirarsi indietro; (Mil: withdraw) ritirarsi; **pull down** vt (house) demolire; (tree) abbattere; **pull in** vi (Aut: at the kerb) accostarsi; (Rail) entrare in stazione; **pull off** vt (clothes) togliere; (deal etc) portare a compimento; **pull out** vi partire; (Aut: come out of line) spostarsi sulla mezzeria ▷ vt staccare; far uscire; (withdraw) ritirare; **pull over** vi (Aut) accostare; **pull up** vi (stop) fermarsi ▷ vt (uproot) sradicare; (raise) sollevare

pulley ['pulɪ] n puleggia, carrucola

pullover ['puləʊvəʳ] n pullover m inv

pulp [pʌlp] n (of fruit) polpa

pulpit ['pulpɪt] n pulpito

pulse [pʌls] n polso; (Bot) legume m; **pulses** npl (Culin) legumi mpl

puma ['pjuːmə] n puma m inv

pump [pʌmp] n pompa; (shoe) scarpetta ▷ vt pompare; **pump up** vt gonfiare

pumpkin ['pʌmpkɪn] n zucca

pun [pʌn] n gioco di parole

punch [pʌntʃ] n (blow) pugno; (tool) punzone m; (drink) ponce m ▷ vt (hit): **to ~ sb/sth** dare un pugno a qn/qc; **punch-up** n (BRIT col) rissa

punctual ['pʌŋktjuəl] adj puntuale

punctuation [pʌŋktju'eɪʃən] n interpunzione f, punteggiatura

puncture ['pʌŋktʃəʳ] n foratura ▷ vt forare

> ⚠ Be careful not to translate *puncture* by the Italian word *puntura*.

punish ['pʌnɪʃ] vt punire; **punishment** n punizione f

punk [pʌŋk] n (also: **~ rocker**) punk mf inv; (also: **~ rock**) musica punk, punk rock m; (us col: hoodlum) teppista m

pup [pʌp] n cucciolo/a

pupil ['pjuːpl] n allievo/a; (Anat) pupilla

puppet ['pʌpɪt] n burattino

puppy ['pʌpɪ] n cucciolo/a, cagnolino/a

purchase ['pəːtʃɪs] n acquisto, compera ▷ vt comprare

pure [pjuəʳ] adj puro/a; **purely** ['pjuəlɪ] adv puramente

purify ['pjuərɪfaɪ] vt purificare

purity ['pjuərɪtɪ] n purezza

purple ['pəːpl] adj di porpora; viola inv

purpose ['pəːpəs] n intenzione f, scopo; **on ~** apposta

purr [pəːʳ] vi fare le fusa

purse [pəːs] n (BRIT) borsellino; (US) borsetta ▷ vt contrarre

pursue [pə'sjuː] vt inseguire; (fig: activity etc) continuare con; (: aim etc) perseguire

pursuit [pə'sjuːt] n inseguimento; (fig) ricerca; (pastime) passatempo

pus [pʌs] n pus m

push [puʃ] n spinta; (effort) grande sforzo; (drive) energia ▷ vt spingere; (button) premere; (fig) fare pubblicità a; (thrust): **to ~ sth (into)** ficcare qc (in) ▷ vi spingere; premere; **to ~ for** insistere per ottenere; **push in** vi introdursi a forza; **push off** vi (col) filare; **push on** vi (continue) continuare; **push over** vt far cadere; **push through** vi farsi largo spingendo ▷ vt (measure) far approvare; **pushchair** n (BRIT) passeggino; **pusher** n (also: **drug pusher**) spacciatore/trice (di droga);

push-up n (US: press-up) flessione f sulle braccia

puss [pus], **pussy(-cat)** ['pusɪ-] n micio

put (pt, pp **put**) [put] vt mettere, porre; (say) dire, esprimere; (a question) fare; (estimate) stimare; **put aside** vt (lay down: book etc) mettere da una parte, posare; (save) mettere da parte; (in shop) tenere da parte; **put away** vt (return) mettere a posto; **put back** vt (replace) rimettere (a posto); (postpone) rinviare; (delay) ritardare; **put by** vt (money) mettere da parte; **put down** vt (parcel etc) posare, mettere giù; (pay) versare; (in writing) mettere per iscritto; (revolt etc) sopprimere; (attribute) attribuire; **put forward** vt (ideas) avanzare, proporre; **put in** vt (application, complaint) presentare; (time, effort) mettere; **put off** vt (postpone) rimandare, rinviare; (discourage) dissuadere; **put on** vt (clothes, lipstick etc) mettere; (light etc) accendere; (play etc) mettere in scena; (food, meal) mettere su; (brake) mettere; **to ~ on weight** ingrassare; **to ~ on airs** darsi delle arie; **put out** vt mettere fuori; (one's hand) porgere; (light etc) spegnere; (inconvenience: person) scomodare; **put through** vt (Tel: caller) mettere in comunicazione; (: call) passare; (plan) far approvare; **put together** vt mettere insieme, riunire; (assemble: furniture) montare; (: meal) improvvisare; **put up** vt (raise) sollevare, alzare; (: umbrella) aprire; (: tent) montare; (pin up) affiggere; (hang) appendere; (build) costruire, erigere; (increase) aumentare; (accommodate) alloggiare; **put up with** vt fus sopportare

putt [pʌt] n colpo leggero; **putting green** n green m inv; campo da putting

puzzle ['pʌzl] n enigma m, mistero; (jigsaw) puzzle m; (also: **crossword ~**) parole fpl incrociate, cruciverba m inv ▷ vt confondere, rendere perplesso/a ▷ vi scervellarsi; **puzzled** adj perplesso/a; **puzzling** adj (question) poco chiaro/a; (attitude, set of instructions) incomprensibile

pyjamas (BRIT) [pə'dʒɑːməz] npl pigiama m

pylon ['paɪlən] n pilone m

pyramid ['pɪrəmɪd] n piramide f

Pyrenees [pɪrə'niːz] npl: **the ~** i Pirenei

P

q

quack [kwæk] *n* (*of duck*) qua qua *m inv*; (*pej: doctor*) ciarlatano/a

quadruple [kwɔ'drupl] *vt* quadruplicare ▷ *vi* quadruplicarsi

quail [kweɪl] *n* (*Zool*) quaglia ▷ *vi* (*person*): **to ~ at** *or* **before** perdersi d'animo davanti a

quaint [kweɪnt] *adj* bizzarro/a; (*old-fashioned*) antiquato/a e pittoresco/a

quake [kweɪk] *vi* tremare ▷ *n abbr* = **earthquake**

qualification [kwɔlɪfɪ'keɪʃən] *n* (*degree etc*) qualifica, titolo; (*ability*) competenza, qualificazione *f*; (*limitation*) riserva, restrizione *f*

qualified ['kwɔlɪfaɪd] *adj* qualificato/a; (*able*) competente, qualificato/a; (*limited*) condizionato/a; **~ for/to do** qualificato/a per/per fare

qualify ['kwɔlɪfaɪ] *vt* abilitare; (*limit: statement*) modificare, precisare ▷ *vi*: **to ~ (as)** qualificarsi (come); **to ~ (for)** acquistare i requisiti necessari (per); (*Sport*) qualificarsi (per *or* a)

quality ['kwɔlɪtɪ] *n* qualità *f inv*

qualm [kwɑːm] *n* dubbio; scrupolo

quantify ['kwɔntɪfaɪ] *vt* quantificare

quantity ['kwɔntɪtɪ] *n* quantità *f inv*

quarantine ['kwɔrntiːn] *n* quarantena

quarrel ['kwɔrl] *n* lite *f*, disputa ▷ *vi* litigare

quarry ['kwɔrɪ] *n* (*for stone*) cava; (*animal*) preda

quart [kwɔːt] *n* ≈ litro

quarter ['kwɔːtəʳ] *n* quarto; (*of year*) trimestre *m*; (*district*) quartiere *m*; (*us: 25 cents*) quarto di dollaro ▷ *vt* dividere in quattro; (*Mil*) alloggiare; **quarters** *npl* (*living quarters*) alloggio; (*Mil*) alloggi *mpl*, quadrato; **a ~ of an hour** un quarto d'ora; **quarter final** *n* quarto di finale; **quarterly** *adj* trimestrale ▷ *adv* trimestralmente ▷ *n* periodico trimestrale

quartet(te) [kwɔː'tɛt] *n* quartetto

quartz [kwɔːts] *n* quarzo

quay [kiː] *n* (*also*: **~side**) banchina

queasy ['kwiːzɪ] *adj* (*stomach*) delicato/a; **to feel ~** aver la nausea

queen [kwiːn] *n* (*gen*) regina; (*Cards etc*) regina, donna

queer [kwɪəʳ] *adj* strano/a, curioso/a ▷ *n* (*col!*) finocchio

quench [kwɛntʃ] *vt*: **to ~ one's thirst** dissetarsi

query ['kwɪərɪ] *n* domanda, questione *f* ▷ *vt* mettere in questione

quest [kwɛst] *n* cerca, ricerca

question ['kwɛstʃən] *n* domanda, questione *f* ▷ *vt* (*person*) interrogare; (*plan, idea*) mettere in questione *or* in dubbio; **it's a ~ of doing** si tratta di fare; **beyond ~** fuori di dubbio; **out of the ~** fuori discussione, impossibile; **questionable** *adj* discutibile; **question mark** *n* punto interrogativo; **questionnaire** [kwɛstʃə'nɛəʳ] *n* questionario

queue [kjuː] (BRIT) n coda, fila ▷ vi fare la coda

quiche [kiːʃ] n torta salata a base di uova, formaggio, prosciutto o altro

quick [kwɪk] adj rapido/a, veloce; (reply) pronto/a; (mind) pronto/a, acuto/a ▷ n: **cut to the ~** (fig) toccato/a sul vivo; **be ~!** fa presto!; **quickly** adv rapidamente, velocemente

quid [kwɪd] n (pl inv: BRIT col) sterlina

quiet ['kwaɪət] adj tranquillo/a, quieto/a; (ceremony) semplice ▷ n tranquillità, calma ▷ vt, vi (US) = **quieten**; **keep ~!** sta zitto!; **quieten** vi (also: **quieten down**) calmarsi, chetarsi ▷ vt calmare, chetare; **quietly** adv tranquillamente, calmamente; silenziosamente

quilt [kwɪlt] n trapunta; **continental ~** piumino

quirky ['kwəːkɪ] adj stravagante

quit [kwɪt] (pt, pp **quit** or **quitted**) vt mollare; (premises) lasciare, partire da ▷ vi (give up) mollare; (resign) dimettersi

quite [kwaɪt] adv (rather) assai; (entirely) completamente, del tutto; **I ~ understand** capisco perfettamente; **~ a few of them** non pochi di loro; **~ (so)!** esatto!; **that's not ~ right** non è proprio esatto

quits [kwɪts] adj: **~ (with)** pari (con); **let's call it ~** adesso siamo pari

quiver ['kwɪvəʳ] vi tremare, fremere

quiz [kwɪz] n (game) quiz m inv; indovinello ▷ vt interrogare

quota ['kwəʊtə] n quota

quotation [kwəʊ'teɪʃən] n citazione f; (of shares etc) quotazione f; (estimate) preventivo; **quotation marks** npl virgolette fpl

quote [kwəʊt] n citazione f ▷ vt (sentence) citare; (price) dare, fissare; (shares) quotare ▷ vi: **to ~ from** citare; **quotes** npl = **quotation marks**

r

rabbi ['ræbaɪ] n rabbino

rabbit ['ræbɪt] n coniglio

rabies ['reɪbiːz] n rabbia

RAC n abbr (BRIT: = Royal Automobile Club) ≈ A.C.I. m

raccoon [rə'kuːn], **racoon** n procione m

race [reɪs] n razza; (competition, rush) corsa ▷ vt (horse) far correre ▷ vi correre; (engine) imballarsi; **race car** n (US) = **racing car**; **racecourse** n campo di corse, ippodromo; **racehorse** n cavallo da corsa; **racetrack** n pista

racial ['reɪʃl] adj razziale

racing ['reɪsɪŋ] n corsa; **racing car** n (BRIT) macchina da corsa; **racing driver** n (BRIT) corridore m automobilista

racism ['reɪsɪzəm] n razzismo; **racist** adj, n razzista m/f

rack [ræk] n rastrelliera; (also: **luggage ~**) rete f, portabagagli

m inv; (*also:* **roof ~**) portabagagli;
(*dish rack*) scolapiatti *m inv* ▷ *vt:* **to
~ one's brains** scervellarsi; **~ed by**
torturato/a da

racket ['rækɪt] *n* (*for tennis*)
racchetta; (*noise*) fracasso; baccano;
(*swindle*) imbroglio, truffa; (*organized
crime*) racket *m inv*

racquet ['rækɪt] *n* racchetta

radar ['reɪdɑːʳ] *n* radar *m*

radiation [reɪdɪ'eɪʃən] *n*
irradiamento; (*radioactive*)
radiazione *f*

radiator ['reɪdɪeɪtəʳ] *n* radiatore *m*

radical ['rædɪkl] *adj* radicale

radio ['reɪdɪəu] *n* radio *f inv;* **on
the ~** alla radio; **radioactive**
['reɪdɪəu'æktɪv] *adj* radioattivo/a;
radio station *n* stazione *f* radio *inv*

radish ['rædɪʃ] *n* ravanello

RAF *n abbr* = **Royal Air Force**

raffle ['ræfl] *n* lotteria

raft [rɑːft] *n* zattera; (*also:* **life ~**)
zattera di salvataggio

rag [ræg] *n* straccio, cencio; (*pej:
newspaper*) giornalaccio, bandiera;
(*for charity*) iniziativa studentesca a
scopo benefico; **rags** *npl* (*torn clothes*)
stracci *mpl*, brandelli *mpl*

rage [reɪdʒ] *n* (*fury*) collera, furia
▷ *vi* (*person*) andare su tutte le furie;
(*storm*) infuriare; **it's all the ~** fa
furore

ragged ['rægɪd] *adj* (*edge*) irregolare;
(*cuff*) logoro/a; (*appearance*) pezzente

raid [reɪd] *n* (*Mil*) incursione *f;*
(*criminal*) rapina; (*by police*) irruzione
f ▷ *vt* fare un'incursione in; rapinare;
fare irruzione in

rail [reɪl] *n* (*on stair*) ringhiera; (*on
bridge, balcony*) parapetto; (*of ship*)
battagliola; **railcard** *n* (*BRIT*) tessera
di riduzione ferroviaria; **railing(s)**
n(pl) ringhiere *fpl;* **railroad** (*US*)
= **railway; railway** (*BRIT*) *n* ferrovia;
railway line *n* (*BRIT*) linea ferroviaria;
railway station *n* (*BRIT*) stazione *f*
ferroviaria

rain [reɪn] *n* pioggia ▷ *vi* piovere;
in the ~ sotto la pioggia; **it's ~ing**
piove; **rainbow** *n* arcobaleno;
raincoat *n* impermeabile *m;*
raindrop *n* goccia di pioggia; **rainfall**
n pioggia; (*measurement*) piovosità;
rainforest *n* foresta pluviale *or*
equatoriale; **rainy** *adj* piovoso/a

raise [reɪz] *n* aumento ▷ *vt*
(*lift*) alzare; sollevare; (*increase*)
aumentare; (*a protest, doubt,
question*) sollevare; (*cattle, family*)
allevare; (*crop*) coltivare; (*army, funds*)
raccogliere; (*loan*) ottenere; **to ~
one's voice** alzare la voce

raisin ['reɪzn] *n* uva secca

rake [reɪk] *n* (*tool*) rastrello ▷ *vt*
(*garden*) rastrellare

rally ['rælɪ] *n* (*Pol etc*) riunione *f;* (*Aut*)
rally *m inv;* (*Tennis*) scambio ▷ *vt*
riunire, radunare ▷ *vi* (*sick person,
Stock Exchange*) riprendersi

RAM [ræm] *n abbr* (*Comput:* = *random
access memory*) RAM *f*

ram [ræm] *n* montone *m,* ariete *m*
▷ *vt* conficcare; (*crash into*) cozzare,
sbattere contro; percuotere;
speronare

Ramadan [ræmə'dæn] *n* Ramadan
m inv

ramble ['ræmbl] *n* escursione *f* ▷ *vi*
(*pej: also:* **~ on**) divagare; **rambler**
n escursionista *m/f;* (*Bot*) rosa
rampicante; **rambling** *adj* (*speech*)
sconnesso/a; (*Bot*) rampicante;
(*house*) tutto/a a nicchie e corridoi

ramp [ræmp] *n* rampa; **on/off ~** (*US
Aut*) raccordo di entrata/uscita

rampage [ræm'peɪdʒ] *n:* **to go on
the ~** scatenarsi in modo violento

ran [ræn] *pt of* **run**

ranch [rɑːntʃ] *n* ranch *m inv*

random ['rændəm] *adj* fatto/a *or*
detto/a per caso; (*Comput, Math*)
casuale ▷ *n:* **at ~** a casaccio

rang [ræn] *pt of* **ring**

range [reɪndʒ] *n* (*of mountains*)
catena; (*of missile, voice*) portata;

(*of products*) gamma; (*Mil: also*: **shooting ~**) campo di tiro; (*also*: **kitchen ~**) fornello, cucina economica ▷ vt disporre ▷ vi: **to ~ over** coprire; **to ~ from ... to** andare da ... a

ranger ['reɪndʒə'] n guardia forestale

rank [ræŋk] n fila; (*status, Mil*) grado; (*BRIT: also*: **taxi ~**) posteggio di taxi ▷ vi: **to ~ among** essere tra ▷ adj puzzolente; (*hypocrisy, injustice*) vero/a e proprio/a; **the ~ and file** (*fig*) la gran massa

ransom ['rænsəm] n riscatto; **to hold sb to ~** (*fig*) esercitare pressione su qn

rant [rænt] vi vociare

rap [ræp] n (*music*) rap m inv ▷ vt dare dei colpetti a; bussare a

rape [reɪp] n violenza carnale, stupro; (*Bot*) ravizzone m ▷ vt violentare

rapid ['ræpɪd] adj rapido/a; **rapidly** adv rapidamente; **rapids** npl (*Geo*) rapida

rapist ['reɪpɪst] n violentatore m

rapport [ræ'pɔː'] n rapporto

rare [rɛə'] adj raro/a; (*Culin: steak*) al sangue; **rarely** ['rɛəlɪ] adv raramente

rash [ræʃ] adj imprudente, sconsiderato/a ▷ n (*Med*) eruzione f; (*of events etc*) scoppio

rasher ['ræʃə'] n fetta sottile (di lardo or prosciutto)

raspberry ['rɑːzbərɪ] n lampone m

rat [ræt] n ratto

rate [reɪt] n (*proportion*) tasso, percentuale f; (*speed*) velocità f inv; (*price*) tariffa ▷ vt valutare; stimare; **to ~ sb/sth as** valutare qn/qc come; **rates** npl (*BRIT: property tax*) imposte fpl comunali; (*fees*) tariffe fpl

rather ['rɑːðə'] adv piuttosto; **it's ~ expensive** è piuttosto caro; (*too much*) è un po' caro; **there's ~ a lot** ce n'è parecchio; **I would** or **I'd ~ go** preferirei andare

rating ['reɪtɪŋ] n (*assessment*) valutazione f; (*score*) punteggio di

merito; **ratings** npl (*Radio, TV*) indice m di ascolto

ratio ['reɪʃɪəu] n proporzione f; **in the ~ of 2 to 1** in rapporto di 2 a 1

ration ['ræʃən] n razione f ▷ vt razionare; **rations** npl razioni fpl

rational ['ræʃənl] adj razionale, ragionevole; (*solution, reasoning*) logico/a

rattle ['rætl] n tintinnio; (*louder*) rumore m di ferraglia; (*of baby*) sonaglino ▷ vi risuonare, tintinnare; fare un rumore di ferraglia ▷ vt

rave [reɪv] vi (*in anger*) infuriarsi; (*with enthusiasm*) andare in estasi; (*Med*) delirare ▷ n (*BRIT*): **a ~ (party)** un rave

raven ['reɪvən] n corvo

ravine [rə'viːn] n burrone m

raw [rɔː] adj (*uncooked*) crudo/a; (*not processed*) greggio/a; (*sore*) vivo/a; (*inexperienced*) inesperto/a; (*weather, day*) gelido/a

ray [reɪ] n raggio; **a ~ of hope** un barlume di speranza

razor ['reɪzə'] n rasoio; **razor blade** n lama di rasoio

Rd abbr = **road**

RE n abbr (*BRIT Mil: = Royal Engineers*) ≈ G.M.; (*BRIT*) = **religious education**

re [riː] prep con riferimento a

reach [riːtʃ] n portata; (*of river etc*) tratto ▷ vt raggiungere; arrivare a ▷ vi stendersi; **out of/within ~** fuori/a portata di mano; **within easy ~ (of)** vicino (a); **reach out** vt (*hand*) allungare ▷ vi: **to ~ out for** stendere la mano per prendere

react [riː'ækt] vi reagire; **reaction** [riː'ækʃən] n reazione f; **reactor** [riː'æktə'] n reattore m

read (*pt, pp* **read**) [riːd, rɛd] vi leggere ▷ vt leggere; (*understand*) intendere, interpretare; (*study*) studiare; **read out** vt leggere ad alta voce; **reader** n lettore/trice; (*BRIT: at university*) *professore con funzioni preminenti di ricerca*

r

readily ['rɛdɪlɪ] adv volentieri; (easily) facilmente; (quickly) prontamente

reading ['riːdɪŋ] n lettura; (understanding) interpretazione f; (on instrument) indicazione f

ready ['rɛdɪ] adj pronto/a; (willing) pronto/a, disposto/a; (available) disponibile ▷ n: **at the ~** (Mil) pronto a sparare ▷ vt preparare; **to get ~** vi prepararsi; **ready-made** adj prefabbricato/a; (clothes) confezionato/a

real [rɪəl] adj reale; vero/a; **in ~ terms** in realtà; **real ale** n birra ad effervescenza naturale; **real estate** n beni mpl immobili; **realistic** [rɪə'lɪstɪk] adj realistico/a; **reality** [riː'ælɪtɪ] n realtà f inv; **reality TV** n reality TV f

realization [rɪəlaɪ'zeɪʃən] n presa di coscienza; (of hopes, project etc) realizzazione f

realize ['rɪəlaɪz] vt (understand) rendersi conto di

really ['rɪəlɪ] adv veramente, davvero; **~!** (indicating annoyance) oh, insomma!

realm [rɛlm] n reame m, regno

Realtor® ['rɪəltɔːʳ] n (US) agente m immobiliare

reappear [riːə'pɪəʳ] vi ricomparire, riapparire

rear [rɪəʳ] adj di dietro; (Aut: wheel etc) posteriore ▷ n di dietro, parte f posteriore ▷ vt (cattle, family) allevare ▷ vi (also: ~ up: animal) impennarsi

rearrange [riːə'reɪndʒ] vt riordinare

rear: rear-view mirror ['rɪəvjuː-] n (Aut) specchio retrovisivo; **rear-wheel drive** n trazione fpl posteriore

reason ['riːzn] n ragione f; (cause, motive) ragione, motivo ▷ vi: **to ~ with sb** far ragionare qn; **it stands to ~ that** è ovvio che; **reasonable** adj ragionevole; (not bad) accettabile; **reasonably** adv ragionevolmente; **reasoning** n ragionamento

reassurance [riːə'ʃuərəns] n rassicurazione f

reassure [riːə'ʃuəʳ] vt rassicurare; **to ~ sb of** rassicurare qn di or su

rebate ['riːbeɪt] n (on tax etc) sgravio

rebel n ['rɛbl] ribelle m/f ▷ vi [rɪ'bɛl] ribellarsi; **rebellion** n ribellione f; **rebellious** adj ribelle

rebuild [riː'bɪld] vt (irreg) ricostruire

recall vt [rɪ'kɔːl] richiamare; (remember) ricordare, richiamare alla mente ▷ n ['riːkɔl] richiamo

recd. abbr = **received**

receipt [rɪ'siːt] n (document) ricevuta; (act of receiving) ricevimento; **receipts** npl (Comm) introiti mpl

receive [rɪ'siːv] vt ricevere; (guest) ricevere, accogliere; **receiver** [rɪ'siːvəʳ] n (Tel) ricevitore m; (Radio) apparecchio ricevente; (of stolen goods) ricettatore/trice; (Law, Comm) curatore m fallimentare

recent ['riːsnt] adj recente; **recently** adv recentemente

reception [rɪ'sɛpʃən] n ricevimento; (welcome) accoglienza; (TV etc) ricezione f; **reception desk** n (in hotel) reception f inv; (in hospital, at doctor's) accettazione f; (in large building, offices) portineria; **receptionist** n receptionist mf inv

recession [rɪ'sɛʃən] n recessione f; **recessionista** [rɪsɛʃə'nɪstə] n recessionista m/f

recharge [riː'tʃɑːdʒ] vt (battery) ricaricare

recipe ['rɛsɪpɪ] n ricetta

recipient [rɪ'sɪpɪənt] n beneficiario/a; (of letter) destinatario/a

recital [rɪ'saɪtl] n recital m inv

recite [rɪ'saɪt] vt (poem) recitare

reckless ['rɛkləs] adj (driver etc) spericolato/a; (spending) folle

reckon ['rɛkən] vt (count) calcolare; (think): **I ~ that ...** penso che ..

reclaim [rɪ'kleɪm] vt (land) bonificare; (demand back) richiedere, reclamare; (materials) recuperare

recline [rɪ'klaɪn] vi stare sdraiato/a
recognition [rɛkəg'nɪʃən] n
riconoscimento; **transformed
beyond ~** irriconoscibile
recognize ['rɛkəgnaɪz] vt: **to ~ (by/
as)** riconoscere (a or da/come)
recollection [rɛkə'lɛkʃən] n ricordo
recommend [rɛkə'mɛnd]
vt raccomandare; (advise)
consigliare; **recommendation**
[rɛkəmɛn'deɪʃən] n
raccomandazione f; consiglio
reconcile ['rɛkənsaɪl] vt (two people)
riconciliare; (two facts) conciliare,
quadrare; **to ~ o.s. to** rassegnarsi a
reconsider [ri:kən'sɪdər] vt
riconsiderare
reconstruct [ri:kən'strʌkt] vt
ricostruire
record n ['rɛkɔ:d] ricordo,
documento; (of meeting etc) nota,
verbale m; (register) registro; (file)
pratica, dossier m inv; (Comput)
record m inv; (also: **police ~**) fedina
penale sporca; (Mus: disc) disco;
(Sport) record m inv, primato
▷ vt ['rɛkɔ:d] (set down) prendere
nota di, registrare; (Comput, Mus:
song etc) registrare; **off the ~** adj
ufficioso/a; adv ufficiosamente; **in
~ time** a tempo di record; **recorded
delivery letter** n (BRIT Post) lettera
raccomandata; **recorder** n (Mus)
flauto diritto; (Mus)
registrazione f; **record player** n
giradischi m inv
recount [rɪ'kaunt] vt raccontare,
narrare
recover [rɪ'kʌvər] vt ricuperare
▷ vi: **to ~ (from)** riprendersi (da);
recovery [rɪ'kʌvərɪ] n ricupero;
ristabilimento; ripresa

> Be careful not to translate recover
> by the Italian word ricoverare.

recreate [ri:krɪ'eɪt] vt ricreare
recreation [rɛkrɪ'eɪʃən] n
ricreazione f; svago; **recreational
drug** [rɛkrɪ'eɪʃənl-] n droga usata

saltuariamente; **recreational vehicle**
n (US) camper m inv
recruit [rɪ'kru:t] n recluta; (in
company) nuovo/a assunto/a
▷ vt reclutare; **recruitment** n
reclutamento
rectangle ['rɛktæŋgl] n rettangolo;
rectangular [rɛk'tæŋgjulər] adj
rettangolare
rectify ['rɛktɪfaɪ] vt (error) rettificare;
(omission) riparare
rector ['rɛktər] n (Rel) parroco
(anglicano)
recur [rɪ'kə:r] vi riaccadere;
(symptoms) ripresentarsi; **recurring**
adj (Math) periodico/a
recyclable [ri:'saɪkləbl] adj riciclabile
recycle [ri:'saɪkl] vt riciclare
recycling [ri:'saɪklɪŋ] n riciclaggio
red [rɛd] n rosso; (Pol: pej) rosso/a
▷ adj rosso/a; **in the ~** (account)
scoperto; (business) in deficit; **Red
Cross** n Croce f Rossa; **redcurrant**
n ribes m inv
redeem [rɪ'di:m] vt (debt) riscattare;
(sth in pawn) ritirare; (fig, also Rel)
redimere
red: red-haired [-'hɛəd] adj dai capelli
rossi; **redhead** ['rɛdhɛd] n rosso/a;
red-hot adj arroventato/a; **red light**
n: **to go through a red light** (Aut)
passare col rosso; **red-light district**
[rɛd'laɪt-] n quartiere m a luci rosse;
red meat n carne f rossa
reduce [rɪ'dju:s] vt ridurre; (lower)
ridurre, abbassare; **"~ speed now"**
(Aut) "rallentare"; **at a ~d price**
scontato/a; **reduced** adj (decreased)
ridotto/a; **at a reduced price** a
prezzo ribassato or ridotto; **"greatly
reduced prices"** "grandi ribassi";
reduction [rɪ'dʌkʃən] n riduzione f;
(of price) ribasso; (discount) sconto
redundancy [rɪ'dʌndənsɪ] n;
licenziamento
redundant [rɪ'dʌndnt] adj
(worker) licenziato/a; (detail, object)
superfluo/a; **to be made ~** (BRIT)

r

essere licenziato (per eccesso di personale)

reed [riːd] n (Bot) canna; (Mus: of clarinet etc) ancia

reef [riːf] n (at sea) scogliera

reel [riːl] n bobina, rocchetto; (Fishing) mulinello; (Cine) rotolo; (dance) danza veloce scozzese ▷ vi (sway) barcollare

ref [rɛf] n abbr (col: = referee) arbitro

refectory [rɪˈfɛktərɪ] n refettorio

refer [rɪˈfəːʳ] vt: **to ~ sth to** (dispute, decision) deferire qc a; **to ~ sb to** (inquirer, Med: patient) indirizzare qn a; (reader: to text) rimandare qn a; **refer to** vt fus (allude to) accennare a; (consult) rivolgersi a

referee [rɛfəˈriː] n arbitro; (BRIT: for job application) referenza ▷ vt arbitrare

reference [ˈrɛfrəns] n riferimento; (mention) menzione f, allusione f; (for job application) referenza; **with ~ to** (Comm: in letter) in or con riferimento a; **reference number** n numero di riferimento

refill vt [riːˈfɪl] riempire di nuovo; (pen, lighter etc) ricaricare ▷ n [ˈriːfɪl] (for pen etc) ricambio

refine [rɪˈfaɪn] vt raffinare; **refined** adj (person, taste) raffinato/a; **refinery** n raffineria

reflect [rɪˈflɛkt] vt (light, image) riflettere; (fig) rispecchiare ▷ vi (think) riflettere, considerare; **it ~s badly/ well on him** si ripercuote su di lui in senso negativo/positivo; **reflection** [rɪˈflɛkʃən] n riflessione f; (image) riflesso; (criticism): **reflection on** giudizio su; attacco a; **on reflection** pensandoci sopra

reflex [ˈriːflɛks] adj riflesso/a ▷ n riflesso

reform [rɪˈfɔːm] n (of sinner etc) correzione f; (of law etc) riforma ▷ vt correggere; riformare

refrain [rɪˈfreɪn] vi: **to ~ from doing** trattenersi dal fare ▷ n ritornello

refresh [rɪˈfrɛʃ] vt rinfrescare; (food, sleep) ristorare; **refreshing** adj (drink) rinfrescante; (sleep) riposante, ristoratore/trice

refreshment n ristoro; **~(s)** rinfreschi mpl

refrigerator [rɪˈfrɪdʒəreɪtəʳ] n frigorifero

refuel [riːˈfjuəl] vi far rifornimento (di carburante)

refuge [ˈrɛfjuːdʒ] n rifugio; **to take ~ in** rifugiarsi in; **refugee** [rɛfjuˈdʒiː] n rifugiato/a, profugo/a

refund n [ˈriːfʌnd] rimborso ▷ vt [rɪˈfʌnd] rimborsare

refurbish [riːˈfəːbɪʃ] vt rimettere a nuovo

refusal [rɪˈfjuːzəl] n rifiuto; **to have first ~ on sth** avere il diritto d'opzione su qc

refuse¹ [ˈrɛfjuːs] n rifiuti mpl

refuse² [rɪˈfjuːz] vt, vi rifiutare; **to ~ to do sth** rifiutare or rifiutarsi di fare qc

regain [rɪˈɡeɪn] vt riguadagnare; riacquistare, ricuperare

regard [rɪˈɡaːd] n riguardo, stima ▷ vt considerare, stimare; **to give one's ~s to** porgere i suoi saluti a; **(kind) ~s** cordiali saluti; **regarding** prep riguardo a, per quanto riguarda; **regardless** adv lo stesso; **regardless of** a dispetto di, nonostante

regenerate [rɪˈdʒɛnəreɪt] vt rigenerare

reggae [ˈrɛɡeɪ] n reggae m

regiment n [ˈrɛdʒɪmənt] reggimento

region [ˈriːdʒən] n regione f; **in the ~ of** (fig) all'incirca di; **regional** adj regionale

register [ˈrɛdʒɪstəʳ] n registro; (also: **electoral ~**) lista elettorale ▷ vt registrare; (vehicle) immatricolare; (letter) assicurare; (instrument) segnare ▷ vi iscriversi; (at hotel) firmare il registro; (make impression) entrare in testa; **registered** adj (BRIT: letter) assicurato/a

registrar [ˈrɛdʒɪstrɑːʳ] n ufficiale m di stato civile; segretario

registration [rɛdʒɪsˈtreɪʃən] n (act) registrazione f; iscrizione f; (Aut: also: **~ number**) numero di targa

registry office n (BRIT) anagrafe f; **to get married in a ~** ≈ sposarsi in municipio

regret [rɪˈgrɛt] n rimpianto, rincrescimento ▷ vt rimpiangere; **regrettable** adj deplorevole

regular [ˈrɛgjuləʳ] adj regolare; (usual) abituale, normale; (soldier) dell'esercito regolare ▷ n (client etc) cliente m/f abituale; **regularly** adv regolarmente

regulate [ˈrɛgjuleɪt] vt regolare; **regulation** [rɛgjuˈleɪʃən] n (rule) regola, regolamento; (adjustment) regolazione f

rehabilitation [ˈriːəbɪlɪˈteɪʃən] n (of offender) riabilitazione f; (of disabled person) riadattamento

rehearsal [rɪˈhəːsəl] n prova

rehearse [rɪˈhəːs] vt provare

reign [reɪn] n regno ▷ vi regnare

reimburse [riːɪmˈbəːs] vt rimborsare

rein [reɪn] n (for horse) briglia

reincarnation [riːɪnkɑːˈneɪʃən] n reincarnazione f

reindeer [ˈreɪndɪəʳ] n (pl inv) renna

reinforce [riːɪnˈfɔːs] vt rinforzare

reinforcement n rinforzamento; **reinforcements** npl (Mil) rinforzi mpl

reinstate [riːɪnˈsteɪt] vt reintegrare

reject n [ˈriːdʒɛkt] (Comm) scarto ▷ vt [rɪˈdʒɛkt] rifiutare, respingere; (Comm: goods) scartare; **rejection** [rɪˈdʒɛkʃən] n rifiuto

rejoice [rɪˈdʒɔɪs] vi: **to ~ (at or over)** provare diletto (in)

relate [rɪˈleɪt] vt (tell) raccontare; (connect) collegare ▷ vi: **to ~ to** (refer to) riferirsi a; (get on with) stabilire un rapporto con; **relating to** che riguarda, rispetto a; **related** adj: **related to** imparentato/a con

relation [rɪˈleɪʃən] n (person) parente m/f; (link) rapporto, relazione f;

relations npl (relatives) parenti mpl; **relationship** n rapporto; (personal ties) rapporti mpl, relazioni fpl; (also: **family relationship**) legami mpl di parentela

relative [ˈrɛlətɪv] n parente m/f ▷ adj relativo/a; (respective) rispettivo/a; **relatively** adv relativamente; (fairly, rather) abbastanza

relax [rɪˈlæks] vi rilasciarsi; (person: unwind) rilassarsi ▷ vt rilasciare; (mind, person) rilassare; **relaxation** [riːlækˈseɪʃən] n rilasciamento; rilassamento; (entertainment) ricreazione f, svago; **relaxed** adj rilassato/a; **relaxing** adj rilassante

relay [ˈriːleɪ] n (Sport) corsa a staffetta ▷ vt (message) trasmettere

release [rɪˈliːs] n (from prison) rilascio; (from obligation) liberazione f; (of gas etc) emissione f; (of film etc) distribuzione f; (record) disco; (device) disinnesto ▷ vt (prisoner) rilasciare; (from obligation, wreckage etc) liberare; (book, film) fare uscire; (news) rendere pubblico/a; (gas etc) emettere; (Tech: catch, spring etc) disinnestare

relegate [ˈrɛləgeɪt] vt relegare; (BRIT Sport): **to be ~d** essere retrocesso/a

relent [rɪˈlɛnt] vi cedere; **relentless** adj implacabile

relevant [ˈrɛləvənt] adj pertinente; (chapter) in questione; **~ to** pertinente a

> Be careful not to translate *relevant* by the Italian word *rilevante*.

reliable [rɪˈlaɪəbl] adj (person, firm) fidato/a, che dà affidamento; (method) sicuro/a; (machine) affidabile

relic [ˈrɛlɪk] n (Rel) reliquia; (of the past) resto

relief [rɪˈliːf] n (from pain, anxiety) sollievo; (help, supplies) soccorsi mpl; (Art, Geo) rilievo

relieve [rɪˈliːv] vt (pain, patient) sollevare; (bring help) soccorrere; (take over from: gen) sostituire;

r

(: *guard*) rilevare; **to ~ sb of sth**
(*load*) alleggerire qn di qc; **to ~ o.s.**
fare i propri bisogni; **relieved** *adj*
sollevato/a; **to be relieved that ...**
essere sollevato/a (dal fatto) che ...;
I'm relieved to hear it mi hai tolto
un peso con questa notizia

religion [rɪ'lɪdʒən] *n* religione *f*

religious [rɪ'lɪdʒəs] *adj* religioso/a;
religious education *n* religione *f*

relish ['rɛlɪʃ] *n* (*Culin*) condimento;
(*enjoyment*) gran piacere *m* ▷ *vt* (*food
etc*) godere; **to ~ doing** adorare fare

relocate [ri:ləu'keɪt] *vt* trasferire
▷ *vi* trasferirsi

reluctance [rɪ'lʌktəns] *n* riluttanza

reluctant [rɪ'lʌktənt] *adj* riluttante,
mal disposto/a; **reluctantly** *adv* di
mala voglia, a malincuore

rely [rɪ'laɪ]: **to ~ on** *vt fus* contare su;
(*be dependent*) dipendere da

remain [rɪ'meɪn] *vi* restare,
rimanere; **remainder** *n* resto;
(*Comm*) rimanenza; **remaining** *adj*
che rimane; **remains** *npl* resti *mpl*

remand [rɪ'mɑ:nd] *n*: **on ~** in
detenzione preventiva ▷ *vt*: **to
~ in custody** rinviare in carcere,
trattenere a disposizione della legge

remark [rɪ'mɑ:k] *n* osservazione *f*
▷ *vt* osservare, dire; **remarkable** *adj*
notevole; eccezionale

remarry [ri:'mærɪ] *vi* risposarsi

remedy ['rɛmədɪ] *n*: **~ (for)** rimedio
(per) ▷ *vt* rimediare a

remember [rɪ'mɛmbəʳ] *vt* ricordare,
ricordarsi di; **~ me to your wife
and children!** saluti sua moglie e i
bambini da parte mia!

Remembrance Day (BRIT)
Remembrance Sunday *n* vedi
nota **"Remembrance Day"**

● **REMEMBRANCE DAY**
●
● Nel Regno Unito, la domenica
● più vicina all'11 di novembre, data
● in cui fu firmato l'armistizio con
● la Germania nel 1918, ricorre il
● *Remembrance Day* o *Remembrance
● Sunday*, giorno in cui vengono
● commemorati i caduti in guerra.
● In questa occasione molti portano
● un papavero di carta appuntato al
● petto in segno di rispetto.

remind [rɪ'maɪnd] *vt*: **to ~ sb of
sth** ricordare qc a qn; **to ~ sb to do**
ricordare a qn di fare; **reminder** *n*
richiamo; (*note etc*) promemoria
m inv

reminiscent [rɛmɪ'nɪsnt] *adj*: **~ of**
che fa pensare a, che richiama

remnant ['rɛmnənt] *n* resto, avanzo

remorse [rɪ'mɔ:s] *n* rimorso

remote [rɪ'məut] *adj* remoto/a,
lontano/a; (*person*) distaccato/a;
remote control *n* telecomando;
remotely *adv* remotamente;
(*slightly*) vagamente

removal [rɪ'mu:vəl] *n* (*taking
away*) rimozione *f*; soppressione
f; (BRIT: *from house*) trasloco; (*from
office: sacking*) destituzione *f*; (*Med*)
ablazione *f*; **removal man** *n* (*irreg:
BRIT*) addetto ai traslochi; **removal
van** *n* (BRIT) furgone *m* per traslochi

remove [rɪ'mu:v] *vt* togliere,
rimuovere; (*employee*) destituire;
(*stain*) far sparire; (*doubt, abuse*)
sopprimere, eliminare

Renaissance [rə'neɪsəns] *n*: **the ~** il
Rinascimento

rename [ri:'neɪm] *vt* ribattezzare

render ['rɛndəʳ] *vt* rendere

rendez-vous ['rɔndɪvu:] *n*
appuntamento; (*place*) luogo
d'incontro; (*meeting*) incontro

renew [rɪ'nju:] *vt* rinnovare;
(*negotiations*) riprendere; **renewable**
adj riutilizzabile; (*contract*)
rinnovabile; **renewable energy,
renewables** fonti *mpl* di energia
rinnovabile

renovate ['rɛnəveɪt] *vt* rinnovare;
(*art work*) restaurare

renowned [rɪ'naʊnd] *adj* rinomato/a

rent [rɛnt] *n* affitto ▷ *vt (take for rent)* prendere in affitto; *(also: ~ out)* dare in affitto; **rental** *n (cost: on TV, telephone)* abbonamento; *(: on car)* noleggio

reorganize [riː'ɔːɡənaɪz] *vt* riorganizzare

rep [rɛp] *n abbr (Comm: = representative)* rappresentante *m/f; (Theat: = repertory)* teatro di repertorio

repair [rɪ'pɛəʳ] *n* riparazione *f* ▷ *vt* riparare; **in good/bad ~** in buono/ cattivo stato; **repair kit** *n* kit *m inv* per riparazioni

repay [riː'peɪ] *vt (irreg: money, creditor)* rimborsare, ripagare; *(sb's efforts)* ricompensare; *(favour)* ricambiare; **repayment** *n* rimborso

repeat [rɪ'piːt] *n (Radio, TV)* replica ▷ *vt* ripetere; *(pattern)* riprodurre; *(promise, attack, also Comm: order)* rinnovare ▷ *vi* ripetere; **repeatedly** *adv* ripetutamente, spesso; **repeat prescription** *n (BRIT)* ricetta ripetibile

repellent [rɪ'pɛlənt] *adj* repellente ▷ *n*: **insect ~** prodotto *m* anti-insetti *inv*

repercussion [riːpə'kʌʃən] *n* ripercussione *f*

repetition [rɛpɪ'tɪʃən] *n* ripetizione *f*

repetitive [rɪ'pɛtɪtɪv] *adj (movement)* che si ripete; *(work)* monotono/a; *(speech)* pieno/a di ripetizioni

replace [rɪ'pleɪs] *vt (put back)* rimettere a posto; *(take the place of)* sostituire; **replacement** *n* rimessa; sostituzione *f; (person)* sostituto/a

replay ['riːpleɪ] *n (of match)* partita ripetuta; *(of tape, film)* replay *m inv*

replica ['rɛplɪkə] *n* replica, copia

reply [rɪ'plaɪ] *n* risposta ▷ *vi* rispondere

report [rɪ'pɔːt] *n* rapporto; *(Press etc)* cronaca; *(BRIT: also: **school ~**)* pagella; *(of gun)* sparo ▷ *vt* riportare; *(Press etc)* fare una cronaca su; *(bring to notice: occurrence)* segnalare; *(: person)* denunciare ▷ *vi (make a report)* fare un rapporto *(or* una cronaca); *(present o.s.)*: **to ~ (to sb)** presentarsi (a qn); **report card** *n (US, SCOTTISH)* pagella; **reportedly** *adv* stando a quanto si dice; **he reportedly told them to …** avrebbe detto loro di …; **reporter** *n* reporter *m inv*

represent [rɛprɪ'zɛnt] *vt* rappresentare; **representation** [rɛprɪzɛn'teɪʃən] *n* rappresentazione *f; (petition)* rappresentanza; **representative** *n* rappresentante *m* (di commercio); *(US Pol)* deputato/a ▷ *adj*: **representative (of)** rappresentativo/a (di)

repress [rɪ'prɛs] *vt* reprimere; **repression** [rɪ'prɛʃən] *n* repressione *f*

reprimand ['rɛprɪmɑːnd] *n* rimprovero ▷ *vt* rimproverare

reproduce [riːprə'djuːs] *vt* riprodurre ▷ *vi* riprodursi; **reproduction** [riːprə'dʌkʃən] *n* riproduzione *f*

reptile ['rɛptaɪl] *n* rettile *m*

republic [rɪ'pʌblɪk] *n* repubblica; **republican** *adj, n* repubblicano/a

reputable ['rɛpjutəbl] *adj* di buona reputazione; *(occupation)* rispettabile

reputation [rɛpju'teɪʃən] *n* reputazione *f*

request [rɪ'kwɛst] *n* domanda; *(formal)* richiesta ▷ *vt*: **to ~ (of** *or* **from sb)** chiedere (a qn); **request stop** *n (BRIT: for bus)* fermata facoltativa *or* a richiesta

require [rɪ'kwaɪəʳ] *vt (need: person)* aver bisogno di; *(: thing, situation)* richiedere; *(want)* volere; esigere; **to ~ sb to do sth/sth of sb** esigere che qn faccia qc/qc da qn; **requirement** *n* esigenza; bisogno; *(condition)* requisito

r

resat [ri:'sæt] *pt, pp of* **resit**
rescue ['rɛskjuː] *n* salvataggio; (*help*)
soccorso ▷ *vt* salvare
research [ri'səːtʃ] *n* ricerca, ricerche
fpl ▷ *vt* fare ricerche su
resemblance [ri'zɛmbləns] *n*
somiglianza
resemble [ri'zɛmbl] *vt* assomigliare a
resent [ri'zɛnt] *vt* risentirsi
di; **resentful** *adj* pieno/a di
risentimento; **resentment** *n*
risentimento
reservation [rɛzə'veɪʃən] *n* (*booking*)
prenotazione *f*; (*doubt*) dubbio;
(*protected area*) riserva; (*BRIT Aut:
also:* **central ~**) spartitraffico *m inv*;
reservation desk *n* (*US: in hotel*)
reception *f inv*
reserve [ri'zəːv] *n* riserva ▷ *vt* (*seats
etc*) prenotare; **reserved** *adj* (*shy*)
riservato/a
reservoir ['rɛzəvwɑːʳ] *n* serbatoio
residence ['rɛzɪdəns] *n* residenza;
residence permit *n* (*BRIT*) permesso
di soggiorno
resident ['rɛzɪdənt] *n* residente
m/f; (*in hotel*) cliente *m/f* fisso/a
▷ *adj* residente; (*doctor*) fisso/a;
(*course, college*) a tempo pieno
con pernottamento; **residential**
[rɛzɪ'dɛnʃəl] *adj* di residenza; (*area*)
residenziale
residue ['rɛzɪdjuː] *n* resto; (*Chem,
Physics*) residuo
resign [ri'zaɪn] *vt* (*one's post*)
dimettersi da ▷ *vi:* **to ~ (from)**
dimettersi (da); **to ~ o.s. to**
rassegnarsi a; **resignation**
[rɛzɪg'neɪʃən] *n* dimissioni *fpl*;
rassegnazione *f*
resin ['rɛzɪn] *n* resina
resist [ri'zɪst] *vt* resistere a;
resistance *n* resistenza
resit ['riːsɪt] (*pt, pp* **resat**) (*BRIT*) *vt*
(*exam*) ripresentarsi a; (*subject*) ridare
l'esame di ▷ *n:* **he's got his French
~ on Friday** deve ridare l'esame di
francese venerdì

resolution [rɛzə'luːʃən] *n*
risoluzione *f*
resolve [ri'zɔlv] *n* risoluzione *f* ▷ *vi*
(*decide*): **to ~ to do** decidere di fare
▷ *vt* (*problem*) risolvere
resort [ri'zɔːt] *n* (*town*) stazione *f*;
(*recourse*) ricorso ▷ *vi:* **to ~ to** far
ricorso a; **as a last ~** come ultima
risorsa
resource [ri'sɔːs] *n* risorsa;
resourceful *adj* pieno/a di risorse,
intraprendente
respect [ris'pɛkt] *n* rispetto
▷ *vt* rispettare; **respectable** *adj*
rispettabile; **respectful** *adj*
rispettoso/a; **respective** [ris'pɛktiv]
adj rispettivo/a; **respectively** *adv*
rispettivamente
respite ['rɛspaɪt] *n* respiro, tregua
respond [ris'pɔnd] *vi* rispondere;
response [ris'pɔns] *n* risposta
responsibility [rispɔnsi'biliti] *n*
responsabilità *f inv*
responsible [ris'pɔnsibl] *adj:* **~ (for)**
responsabile (di); (*trustworthy*)
fidato/a; (*job*) di (grande)
responsabilità; **responsibly** *adv*
responsabilmente
responsive [ris'pɔnsiv] *adj* che
reagisce
rest [rɛst] *n* riposo; (*stop*) sosta,
pausa; (*Mus*) pausa; (*support*)
appoggio, sostegno; (*remainder*)
resto, avanzi *mpl* ▷ *vi* riposarsi;
(*remain*) rimanere, restare; (*be
supported*): **to ~ on** appoggiarsi su
▷ *vt* (far) riposare; (*lean*): **to ~ sth
on/against** appoggiare qc su/
contro; **the ~ of them** gli altri; **it
~s with him to decide** sta a lui
decidere
restaurant ['rɛstərɔŋ] *n* ristorante
m; **restaurant car** *n* (*BRIT*) vagone
m ristorante
restless ['rɛstlis] *adj* agitato/a,
irrequieto/a
restoration [rɛstə'reɪʃən] *n*
restauro; restituzione *f*

restore [rɪ'stɔːʳ] vt (building) restaurare; (sth stolen) restituire; (peace, health) ristorare

restrain [rɪs'treɪn] vt (feeling) contenere, frenare; (person) **to ~ (from doing)** trattenere (dal fare); **restraint** n (restriction) limitazione f; (moderation) ritegno; (of style) contenutezza

restrict [rɪs'trɪkt] vt restringere, limitare; **restriction** [rɪs'trɪkʃən] n: **restriction (on)** restrizione f(di), limitazione f(di)

rest room n (US) toletta

restructure [riː'strʌktʃəʳ] vt ristrutturare

result [rɪ'zʌlt] n risultato ▷ vi: **to ~ in** avere per risultato; **as a ~ (of)** in di conseguenza (a), in seguito (a)

resume [rɪ'zjuːm] vt, vi (work, journey) riprendere

résumé ['reɪzjuːmeɪ] n riassunto; (US) curriculum vitae m inv

resuscitate [rɪ'sʌsɪteɪt] vt (Med) risuscitare

retail ['riːteɪl] cpd al minuto ▷ vt vendere al minuto; **retailer** n commerciante m/f al minuto, dettagliante m/f

retain [rɪ'teɪn] vt (keep) tenere, serbare

retaliation [rɪtælɪ'eɪʃən] n rappresaglie fpl

retarded [rɪ'tɑːdɪd] adj (Med: col!) ritardato/a

retire [rɪ'taɪəʳ] vi (give up work) andare in pensione; (withdraw) ritirarsi, andarsene; (go to bed) andare a letto, ritirarsi; **retired** adj (person) pensionato/a; **retirement** n pensione f; (act) pensionamento

retort [rɪ'tɔːt] vi rimbeccare

retreat [rɪ'triːt] n ritirata; (place) rifugio ▷ vi battere in ritirata

retrieve [rɪ'triːv] vt (sth lost) ricuperare, ritrovare; (situation, honour) salvare; (error, loss) rimediare a

retrospect ['retrəspekt] n: **in ~** guardando indietro; **retrospective** [retrə'spektɪv] adj retrospettivo/a; (law) retroattivo/a

return [rɪ'təːn] n (going or coming back) ritorno; (of sth stolen etc) restituzione f; (Comm: from land, shares) profitto, reddito; **in ~ (for)** in cambio (di) ▷ cpd (journey, match) di ritorno; (BRIT: ticket) di andata e ritorno ▷ vi tornare, ritornare ▷ vt rendere, restituire; (bring back) riportare; (send back) mandare indietro; (put back) rimettere; (Pol: candidate) eleggere; **returns** npl (Comm) incassi mpl; profitti mpl; **by ~ of post** a stretto giro di posta; **many happy ~s (of the day)!** cento di questi giorni!; **return ticket** n (esp BRIT) biglietto di andata e ritorno

retweet [riː'twiːt] vt (on Twitter) retwittare

reunion [riː'juːnɪən] n riunione f

reunite [riːjuː'naɪt] vt riunire

revamp ['riː'væmp] vt (firm) riorganizzare

reveal [rɪ'viːl] vt (make known) rivelare, svelare; (display) rivelare, mostrare; **revealing** adj rivelatore/trice; (dress) scollato/a

revel ['revl] vi: **to ~ in sth/in doing** dilettarsi di qc/a fare

revelation [revə'leɪʃən] n rivelazione f

revenge [rɪ'vendʒ] n vendetta ▷ vt vendicare; **to take ~ on** vendicarsi di

revenue ['revənjuː] n reddito

Reverend ['revərənd] adj (in titles) reverendo/a

reversal [rɪ'vəːsl] n capovolgimento

reverse [rɪ'vəːs] n contrario, opposto; (back) rovescio; (Aut: also: **~ gear**) marcia indietro ▷ adj (order) inverso/a; (direction) opposto/a ▷ vt (turn) invertire, rivoltare; (change) capovolgere, rovesciare; (Law: judgement) cassare; (car) fare marcia indietro con ▷ vi (BRIT Aut, person etc) fare marcia indietro; **reverse-charge call** [rɪ'vəːstʃɑːdʒ-] n (BRIT Tel) telefonata con addebito al ricevente;

reversing lights npl (BRIT Aut) luci fpl per la retromarcia

revert [rɪ'vəːt] vi: **to ~ to** tornare a

review [rɪ'vjuː] n rivista; (of book, film) recensione f; (of situation) esame m ▷ vt passare in rivista; fare la recensione di; fare il punto di

revise [rɪ'vaɪz] vt (manuscript) rivedere, correggere; (opinion) emendare, modificare; (study: subject, notes) ripassare; **revision** [rɪ'vɪʒən] n revisione f; ripasso

revival [rɪ'vaɪvəl] n ripresa; ristabilimento; (of faith) risveglio

revive [rɪ'vaɪv] vt (person) rianimare; (custom) far rivivere; (hope, courage, economy) ravvivare; (play, fashion) riesumare ▷ vi (person) rianimarsi; (hope) ravvivarsi; (activity) riprendersi

revolt [rɪ'vəult] n rivolta, ribellione f ▷ vi rivoltarsi, ribellarsi ▷ vt (far) rivoltare; **revolting** adj ripugnante

revolution [rɛvə'luːʃən] n rivoluzione f; (of wheel etc) rivoluzione, giro; **revolutionary** adj, n rivoluzionario/a

revolve [rɪ'vɔlv] vi girare

revolver [rɪ'vɔlvər] n rivoltella

reward [rɪ'wɔːd] n ricompensa, premio ▷ vt: **to ~ (for)** ricompensare (per); **rewarding** adj (fig) soddisfacente

rewind [riː'waɪnd] vt (irreg: watch) ricaricare; (ribbon etc) riavvolgere

rewritable [riː'raɪtəbl] adj (CD, DVD) riscrivibile

rewrite [riː'raɪt] vt (irreg) riscrivere

rheumatism ['ruːmətɪzəm] n reumatismo

rhinoceros [raɪ'nɔsərəs] n rinoceronte m

rhubarb ['ruːbɑːb] n rabarbaro

rhyme [raɪm] n rima; (verse) poesia

rhythm ['rɪðm] n ritmo

rib [rɪb] n (Anat) costola ▷ vt (tease) punzecchiare

ribbon ['rɪbən] n nastro; **in ~s** (torn) a brandelli

rice [raɪs] n riso; **rice pudding** n budino di riso

rich [rɪtʃ] adj ricco/a; (clothes) sontuoso/a; **to be ~ in sth** essere ricco di qc

rid (pt, pp **rid**) [rɪd] vt: **to ~ sb of** sbarazzare or liberare qn di; **to get ~ of** sbarazzarsi di

riddle ['rɪdl] n (puzzle) indovinello ▷ vt: **to be ~d with** (holes) essere crivellato/a di; (doubts) essere pieno/a di

ride (pt **rode**, pp **ridden**) [raɪd, rəud, 'rɪdn] n (on horse) cavalcata; (outing) passeggiata; (distance covered) cavalcata; corsa ▷ vi (as sport) cavalcare; (go somewhere: on horse, bicycle) andare a cavallo or in bicicletta etc); (journey: on bicycle, motorcycle, bus) andare, viaggiare ▷ vt (a horse) montare, cavalcare; **to ~ a horse/bicycle/camel** montare a cavallo/in bicicletta/in groppa a un cammello; **to take sb for a ~** (fig) prendere in giro qn; fregare qn; **rider** n cavalcatore/trice; (jockey) fantino; (on bicycle) ciclista m/f; (on motorcycle) motociclista m/f

ridge [rɪdʒ] n (of hill) cresta; (of roof) colmo; (on object) riga (in rilievo)

ridicule ['rɪdɪkjuːl] n ridicolo; scherno ▷ vt mettere in ridicolo; **ridiculous** [rɪ'dɪkjuləs] adj ridicolo/a

riding ['raɪdɪŋ] n equitazione f; **riding school** n scuola d'equitazione

rife [raɪf] adj diffuso/a; **to be ~ with** abbondare di

rifle ['raɪfl] n carabina ▷ vt vuotare

rift [rɪft] n fessura, crepatura; (fig: disagreement) incrinatura, disaccordo

rig [rɪg] n (also: **oil ~**: on land) derrick m inv; (: at sea) piattaforma di trivellazione ▷ vt (election etc) truccare

right [raɪt] adj giusto/a; (suitable) appropriato/a; (not left) destro/a ▷ n giusto; (title, claim) diritto;

(not left) destra ▷ adv (answer) correttamente; (not on the left) a destra ▷ adv (fig) riparare ▷ excl bene!; **to be ~** (person) aver ragione; (answer) essere giusto/aor corretto/a; **~ now** proprio adesso; subito; **~ away** subito; **by ~s** di diritto; **on the ~** a destra; **to be in the ~** aver ragione, essere nel giusto; **right angle** n angolo retto; **rightful** adj (heir) legittimo/a; **right-hand** adj: **right-hand drive** guida a destra; **the right-hand side** il lato destro; **right-handed** adj (person) che adopera la mano destra; **rightly** adv bene, correttamente; (with reason) a ragione; **right of way** n diritto di passaggio; (Aut) precedenza

right wing n (Pol) destra ▷ adj: **right-wing** (Pol) di destra

rigid ['rɪdʒɪd] adj rigido/a; (principle) rigoroso/a

rigorous ['rɪgərəs] adj rigoroso/a

rim [rɪm] n orlo; (of spectacles) montatura; (of wheel) cerchione m

rind [raɪnd] n (of bacon) cotenna; (of lemon etc) scorza

ring [rɪŋ] (pt **rang**, pp **rung**) n anello; (of people, objects) cerchio; (of spies) giro; (of smoke etc) spirale f; (arena) pista, arena; (for boxing) ring m inv; (sound of bell) scampanio ▷ vi (person, bell, telephone) suonare; (also: **~ out**: voice, words) risuonare; (Tel) telefonare; (ears) fischiare ▷ vt (BRIT Tel: also: **~ up**) telefonare a; (bell, doorbell) suonare; **to give sb a ~** (BRIT Tel) dare un colpo di telefono a qn; **ring back** vt, vi (Tel) richiamare; **ring off** vi (BRIT Tel) mettere giù, riattaccare; **ringing tone** n (BRIT Tel) segnale m di libero; **ringleader** n (of gang) capobanda m; **ring road** n (BRIT) raccordo anulare

ringtone n suoneria

rink [rɪŋk] n (also: **ice ~**) pista di pattinaggio

rinse [rɪns] n risciacquatura; (hair tint) cachet m inv ▷ vt sciacquare

riot ['raɪət] n sommossa, tumulto ▷ vi tumultuare; **a ~ of colours** un'orgia di colori; **to run ~** creare disordine

rip [rɪp] n strappo ▷ vt strappare ▷ vi strapparsi; **rip off** vt (col: cheat) fregare; **rip up** vt stracciare

ripe [raɪp] adj (fruit, grain) maturo/a; (cheese) stagionato/a

rip-off ['rɪpɔf] n (col): **it's a ~!** è un furto!

ripple ['rɪpl] n increspamento, ondulazione f; mormorio ▷ vi incresparsi

rise [raɪz] n (slope) salita, pendio; (hill) altura; (increase: in wages: BRIT) aumento; (: in prices, temperature) rialzo, aumento; (fig: to power etc) ascesa ▷ vi (pt **rose** [rəuz], pp **risen** ['rɪzn]) alzarsi, levarsi; (prices) aumentare; (waters, river) crescere; (sun, wind, person: from chair, bed) levarsi; (also: **~ up**) (building) ergersi; (rebel) insorgere; ribellarsi; (in rank) salire; **to give ~ to** provocare, dare origine a; **to ~ to the occasion** dimostrarsi all'altezza della situazione; **risen** ['rɪzn] pp of **rise**; **rising** adj (increasing: number) sempre crescente; (: prices) in aumento; (tide) montante; (sun, moon) nascente, che sorge

risk [rɪsk] n rischio; pericolo ▷ vt rischiare; **to take** or **run the ~ of doing** correre il rischio di fare; **at ~** in pericolo; **at one's own ~** a proprio rischio e pericolo; **risky** adj rischioso/a

rite [raɪt] n rito; **last ~s** l'estrema unzione

ritual ['rɪtjuəl] adj, n rituale (m)

rival ['raɪvl] n rivale m/f; (in business) concorrente m/f ▷ adj rivale; che fa concorrenza ▷ vt essere in concorrenza con; **to ~ sb/sth in** competere con qn/qc in; **rivalry** n rivalità; concorrenza

river ['rɪvə^r] n fiume m ▷ cpd (port, traffic) fluviale; **up/down ~** a monte/valle; **riverbank** n argine m

rivet ['rɪvɪt] n ribattino, rivetto ▷ vt (fig) concentrare, fissare

Riviera [rɪvɪ'ɛərə] n: **the (French) ~** la Costa Azzurra; **the Italian ~** la Riviera

road [rəud] n strada; (small) cammino; (in town) via ▷ cpd stradale; **major/minor ~** strada con/senza diritto di precedenza; **roadblock** n blocco stradale; **road map** n carta stradale; **road rage** n comportamento aggressivo al volante; **road safety** n sicurezza sulle strade; **roadside** n margine m della strada; **roadsign** n cartello stradale; **road tax** n (BRIT) tassa di circolazione; **roadworks** npl lavori mpl stradali

roam [rəum] vi errare, vagabondare

roar [rɔː^r] n ruggito; (of crowd) tumulto; (of thunder, storm) muggito; (of laughter) scoppio ▷ vi ruggire; tumultuare; muggire; **to ~ with laughter** scoppiare dalle risa; **to do a ~ing trade** fare affari d'oro

roast [rəust] n arrosto ▷ vt arrostire; (coffee) tostare, torrefare; **roast beef** n arrosto di manzo

rob [rɔb] vt (person) rubare; (bank) svaligiare; **to ~ sb of sth** derubare qn di qc; (fig: deprive) privare qn di qc; **robber** n ladro; (armed) rapinatore m; **robbery** n furto; rapina

robe [rəub] n (for ceremony etc) abito; (also: bath~) accappatoio; (US: also: lap ~) coperta

robin ['rɔbɪn] n pettirosso

robot ['rəubɔt] n robot m inv

robust [rəu'bʌst] adj robusto/a; (material, economy) solido/a

rock [rɔk] n (substance) roccia; (boulder) masso; roccia; (in sea) scoglio; (US: pebble) ciottolo; (BRIT: sweet) zucchero candito ▷ vt (swing gently: cradle) dondolare; (: child) cullare; (shake) scrollare, far tremare ▷ vi dondolarsi; oscillare; **on the ~s** (drink) col ghiaccio; (marriage etc) in crisi; **rock and roll** n rock and roll m; **rock climbing** n roccia

rocket ['rɔkɪt] n razzo

rocking chair n sedia a dondolo

rocky ['rɔkɪ] adj (hill) roccioso/a; (path) sassoso/a; (marriage etc) instabile

rod [rɔd] n (metallic, Tech) asta; (wooden) bacchetta; (also: fishing ~) canna da pesca

rode [rəud] pt of **ride**

rodent ['rəudnt] n roditore m

rogue [rəug] n mascalzone m

role [rəul] n ruolo; **role model** n modello (di comportamento)

roll [rəul] n rotolo; (of banknotes) mazzo; (also: bread ~) panino; (register) lista; (sound: of drums etc) rullo ▷ vt rotolare; (also: ~ up: string) aggomitolare; (: sleeves) rimboccare; (cigarettes) arrotolare; (eyes) roteare; (also: ~ out: pastry) stendere; (: lawn, road etc) spianare ▷ vi rotolare; (wheel) girare; (drum) rullare; (vehicle: also: ~ along) avanzare; (ship) rollare; **roll over** vi rivoltarsi; **roll up** vi (col: arrive) arrivare ▷ vt (carpet, cloth, map) arrotolare; **roller** n rullo; (wheel) rotella; (for hair) bigodino; **rollerblades®** ['rəuləbleɪdz] npl pattini mpl in linea; **roller coaster** [-'kəustə^r] n montagne fpl russe; **roller skates** npl pattini mpl a rotelle; **roller-skating** n pattinaggio a rotelle; **to go roller-skating** andare a pattinare (con i pattini a rotelle); **rolling pin** n matterello

ROM [rɔm] n abbr (Comput: = read-only memory) ROM f

Roman ['rəumən] adj, n romano/a; **Roman Catholic** adj, n cattolico/a

romance [rə'mæns] n storia (or avventura or film m inv) romantico/a; (charm) poesia; (love affair) idillio

Romania [rəu'meɪnɪə] n Romania

Romanian [rəʊ'meɪnɪən] *adj*
romeno/a ▷ *n* romeno/a; (*Ling*)
romeno
Roman numeral *n* numero romano
romantic [rə'mæntɪk] *adj*
romantico/a; sentimentale
Rome [rəʊm] *n* Roma
roof [ruːf] *n* tetto; (*of tunnel, cave*)
volta ▷ *vt* coprire (con un tetto); **~ of
the mouth** palato; **roof rack** *n* (*Aut*)
portabagagli *m inv*
rook [rʊk] *n* (*bird*) corvo nero; (*Chess*)
torre *f*
room [ruːm] *n* (*in house*) stanza;
(*bedroom, in hotel*) camera; (*in school
etc*) sala; (*space*) posto, spazio;
roommate *n* compagno/a di stanza;
room service *n* servizio da camera;
roomy *adj* spazioso/a; (*garment*)
ampio/a
rooster ['ruːstəʳ] *n* gallo
root [ruːt] *n* radice *f* ▷ *vi* (*plant, belief*)
attecchire
rope [rəʊp] *n* corda, fune *f*; (*Naut*)
cavo ▷ *vt* (*box*) legare; (*climbers*)
legare in cordata; **to ~ sb in** (*fig*)
coinvolgere qn; **to know the ~s** (*fig*)
conoscere i trucchi del mestiere
rort [rɔːt] *n* (*AUSTR, NZ col*) truffa ▷ *vt*
fregare
rose [rəʊz] *pt of* **rise** ▷ *n* rosa; (*also: ~
bush*) rosaio; (*on watering can*) rosetta
rosé ['rəʊzeɪ] *n* vino rosato
rosemary ['rəʊzmərɪ] *n* rosmarino
rosy ['rəʊzɪ] *adj* roseo/a
rot [rɔt] *n* (*decay*) putrefazione *f*; (*col:
nonsense*) stupidaggini *fpl* ▷ *vt, vi*
imputridire, marcire
rota ['rəʊtə] *n* tabella dei turni
rotate [rəʊ'teɪt] *vt* (*revolve*) far girare;
(*change round: jobs*) fare a turno ▷ *vi*
(*revolve*) girare
rotten ['rɔtn] *adj* (*decayed*) putrido/a,
marcio/a; (*dishonest*) corrotto/a; (*col:
bad*) brutto/a; (: *action*) vigliacco/a;
to feel ~ (*ill*) sentirsi a pezzi
rough [rʌf] *adj* (*skin, surface*) ruvido/a;
(*terrain, road*) accidentato/a;

(*voice*) rauco/a; (*person, manner:
coarse*) rozzo/a, aspro/a; (: *violent*)
brutale; (*district*) malfamato/a;
(*weather*) cattivo/a; (*sea*) mosso/a;
(*plan*) abbozzato/a; (*guess*)
approssimativo/a ▷ *n* (*Golf*) macchia;
to ~ it far vita dura; **to sleep ~** (*BRIT*)
dormire all'addiaccio; **roughly** *adv*
(*handle*) rudemente, brutalmente;
(*make*) grossolanamente; (*speak*)
bruscamente; (*approximately*)
approssimativamente
roulette [ruː'lɛt] *n* roulette *f*
round [raʊnd] *adj* rotondo/a ▷ *n*
(*BRIT: of toast*) fetta; (*of policeman,
milkman etc*) giro; (: *of doctor*) visite *fpl*;
(*game: of cards, golf, in competition*)
partita; (*Boxing*) round *m inv*; (*of talks*)
serie *f inv* ▷ *vt* (*corner*) girare; (*bend*)
prendere ▷ *prep* intorno a ▷ *adv*:
right ~, all ~ tutt'attorno; **the long
way ~** il giro più lungo; **all the year ~**
tutto l'anno; **in ~ figures** in cifra
tonda; **it's just ~ the corner** (*also fig*)
è dietro l'angolo; **to go ~ to sb's
(house)** andare da qn; **go ~ the back**
passi da dietro; **enough to go ~**
abbastanza per tutti; **~ the clock** 24
ore su 24; **~ of ammunition** cartuccia;
~ of applause applausi *mpl*; **~ of
drinks** giro di bibite; **~ of sandwiches**
sandwich *m inv*; **round off** *vt* (*speech
etc*) finire; **round up** *vt* radunare;
(*criminals*) fare una retata di; (*prices*)
arrotondare; **roundabout** *n* (*BRIT:
Aut*) rotatoria; (: *at fair*) giostra ▷ *adj*
(*route, means*) indiretto/a; **round trip**
n (viaggio di) andata e ritorno;
roundup *n* raduno; (*of criminals*) retata
rouse [raʊz] *vt* (*wake up*) svegliare;
(*stir up*) destare; provocare;
risvegliare
route [ruːt] *n* itinerario; (*of bus*)
percorso
router ['ruːtəʳ] *n* (*Comput*) router *m inv*
routine [ruː'tiːn] *adj* (*work*) corrente,
abituale; (*procedure*) solito/a ▷ *n* (*pej*)
routine *f*, tran tran *m*; (*Theat*) numero

r

row¹ [rəu] n (line) riga, fila; (Knitting) ferro; (behind one another: of cars, people) fila; (in boat) remata ▷ vi (in boat) remare; (as sport) vogare ▷ vt (boat) manovrare a remi; **in a ~** (fig) di fila

row² [rau] n (noise) baccano, chiasso; (dispute) lite f; (scolding) sgridata ▷ vi (argue) litigare

rowboat ['rəubəut] n (US) barca a remi

rowing ['rəuɪŋ] n canottaggio; **rowing boat** n (BRIT) barca a remi

royal ['rɔɪəl] adj reale; **royalty** ['rɔɪəltɪ] n (royal persons) (membri mpl della) famiglia reale; (payment: to author) diritti mpl d'autore

rpm abbr (= revolutions per minute) giri/min

RSVP abbr (= répondez s'il vous plaît) R.S.V.P.

Rt. Hon. abbr (BRIT: = Right Honourable) ≈ On.

rub [rʌb] n: **to give sth a ~** strofinare qc; (sore place) massaggiare qc ▷ vt strofinare; massaggiare; (hands: also: **~ together**) sfregarsi; **to ~ sb up** or (US) **~ sb the wrong way** lisciare qn contro pelo; **rub in** vt (ointment) far penetrare (massaggiando or frizionando); **rub off** vi andare via; **rub out** vt cancellare

rubber ['rʌbə'] n gomma; **rubber band** n elastico; **rubber gloves** npl guanti mpl di gomma

rubbish ['rʌbɪʃ] n (from household) immondizie fpl, rifiuti mpl; (fig, pej) cose fpl senza valore; robaccia; (nonsense) sciocchezze fpl; **rubbish bin** n (BRIT) pattumiera; **rubbish dump** n discarica

rubble ['rʌbl] n macerie fpl; (smaller) pietrisco

ruby ['ru:bɪ] n rubino

rucksack ['rʌksæk] n zaino

rudder ['rʌdə'] n timone m

rude [ru:d] adj (impolite: person) scortese, rozzo/a; (: word, manners) grossolano/a, rozzo/a; (shocking) indecente

ruffle ['rʌfl] vt (hair) scompigliare; (clothes, water) increspare; (fig: person) turbare

rug [rʌg] n tappeto; (BRIT: for knees) coperta

rugby ['rʌgbɪ] n (also: **~ football**) rugby m

rugged ['rʌgɪd] adj (landscape) aspro/a; (features, determination) duro/a; (character) brusco/a

ruin ['ru:ɪn] n rovina ▷ vt rovinare; **ruins** npl (of building, castle etc) rovine fpl, ruderi mpl

rule [ru:l] n regola; (regulation) regolamento, regola; (government) governo; (ruler) riga ▷ vt (country) governare; (person) dominare ▷ vi regnare; decidere; (Law) dichiarare; **as a ~** normalmente; **rule out** vt escludere; **ruler** n (sovereign) sovrano/a; (for measuring) regolo, riga; **ruling** adj (party) al potere; (class) dirigente ▷ n (Law) decisione f

rum [rʌm] n rum m

Rumania etc [ruː'meɪnɪə] = **Romania** etc

rumble ['rʌmbl] n rimbombo; brontolio ▷ vi rimbombare; (stomach, pipe) brontolare

rumour, (US) **rumor** ['ru:mə'] n voce f ▷ vt: **it is ~ed that** corre voce che

▌ Be careful not to translate rumour by the Italian word rumore.

rump steak [rʌmp-] n bistecca di girello

run [rʌn] (pt **ran**, pp **run**) n corsa; (outing) gita (in macchina); (distance travelled) percorso, tragitto; (series) serie f inv; (Theat) periodo di rappresentazione; (Ski) pista; (Cricket, Baseball) meta; (in tights, stockings) smagliatura ▷ vt (distance) correre; (operate: business) gestire, dirigere; (: competition, course) organizzare; (: hotel) gestire; (: house) governare; (Comput) eseguire; (water, bath) far

scorrere; (force through: rope, pipe):
to ~ sth through far passare qc
attraverso; (pass: hand, finger): **to
~ sth over** passare qc su; (Press:
feature) presentare ▷ vi correre; (flee)
scappare; (pass: road etc) passare;
(work: machine, factory) funzionare,
andare; (bus, train: operate) far
servizio; (: travel) circolare; (continue:
play, contract) durare; (slide: drawer:
flow: river, bath) scorrere; (colours,
washing) stemperarsi; (in election)
presentarsi come candidato; (nose)
colare; **to go for a ~** andare a correre;
(in car) fare un giro (in macchina); **to
break into a ~** mettersi a correre; **a
~ of luck** un periodo di fortuna; **to
have the ~ of sb's house** essere
libero di andare e venire in casa di
qn; **there was a ~ on ...** c'era una
corsa a ...; **in the long ~** a lungo
andare; **on the ~** in fuga; **to ~ a race**
partecipare ad una gara; **I'll ~ you to
the station** la porto alla stazione; **to
~ a risk** correre un rischio; **run after**
vt fus (to catch up) rincorrere; (chase)
correre dietro a; **run away** vi fuggire;
run down vi (clock) scaricarsi ▷ vt
(Aut) investire; (criticize) criticare;
(production) ridurre gradualmente;
(factory, shop) rallentare l'attività
di; **to be ~ down** (person) essere
spossato/a; **run into** vt fus (meet:
person) incontrare per caso; (: trouble)
incontrare, trovare; (collide with)
andare a sbattere contro; **run off**
vi fuggire ▷ vt (water) far defluire;
(copies) fare; **run out** vi (person)
uscire di corsa; (liquid) colare; (lease)
scadere; (money) esaurirsi; **run out
of** vt fus rimanere a corto di; **run
over** vt (Aut) investire, mettere sotto
▷ vt fus (revise) rivedere; **run through**
vt fus (instructions) dare una scorsa
a; (rehearse: play) riprovare, ripetere;
run up vt (debt) lasciar accumulare;
to ~ up against (difficulties)
incontrare; **runaway** adj (person)

fuggiasco/a; (horse) in libertà; (truck)
fuori controllo
rung [rʌŋ] pp of **ring** ▷ n (of ladder)
piolo
runner ['rʌnəʳ] n (in race) corridore
m; (: horse) partente m/f; (on sledge)
pattino; (for drawer etc) guida; **runner
bean** n (BRIT) fagiolino; **runner-up** n
secondo/a arrivato/a
running ['rʌnɪŋ] n corsa; direzione
f; organizzazione f; funzionamento
▷ adj (water) corrente; (commentary)
simultaneo/a; **6 days ~** 6 giorni di
seguito; **to be in/out of the ~ for
sth** essere/non essere più in lizza
per qc
runny ['rʌnɪ] adj che cola
run-up ['rʌnʌp] n (BRIT): **~ to sth**
(election etc) periodo che precede qc
runway ['rʌnweɪ] n (Aviat) pista (di
decollo)
rupture ['rʌptʃəʳ] n (Med) ernia
rural ['ruərl] adj rurale
rush [rʌʃ] n corsa precipitosa; (hurry)
furia, fretta; (of emotion) impeto;
(Bot) giunco; (sudden demand): **~ for**
corsa a; (current) flusso ▷ vt mandare
or spedire velocemente; (attack:
town etc) prendere d'assalto ▷ vi
precipitarsi; **rush hour** n ora di punta
Russia ['rʌʃə] n Russia; **Russian** adj
russo/a ▷ n russo/a; (Ling) russo
rust [rʌst] n ruggine f ▷ vi arrugginirsi
rusty ['rʌstɪ] adj arrugginito/a
ruthless ['ru:θlɪs] adj spietato/a
RV abbr (= revised version) versione
riveduta della Bibbia ▷ n abbr (US)
= **recreational vehicle**
rye [raɪ] n segale f

r

S

Sabbath ['sæbəθ] n (Jewish) sabato; (Christian) domenica

sabotage ['sæbətɑːʒ] n sabotaggio ▷ vt sabotare

saccharin(e) ['sækərɪn] n saccarina

sachet ['sæʃeɪ] n bustina

sack [sæk] n (bag) sacco ▷ vt (dismiss) licenziare, mandare a spasso; (plunder) saccheggiare; **to get the ~** essere mandato a spasso

sacred ['seɪkrɪd] adj sacro/a

sacrifice ['sækrɪfaɪs] n sacrificio ▷ vt sacrificare

sad [sæd] adj triste

saddle ['sædl] n sella ▷ vt (horse) sellare; **to be ~d with sth** (col) avere qc sulle spalle

sadistic [sə'dɪstɪk] adj sadico/a

sadly ['sædlɪ] adv tristemente; (regrettably) sfortunatamente; **~ lacking in** penosamente privo di

sadness ['sædnɪs] n tristezza

sae abbr (= stamped addressed envelope) busta affrancata e con indirizzo

safari [sə'fɑːrɪ] n safari m inv

safe [seɪf] adj sicuro/a; (out of danger) salvo/a, al sicuro; (cautious) prudente ▷ n cassaforte f; **~ from** al sicuro da; **~ and sound** sano/a e salvo/a; **(just) to be on the ~ side** per non correre rischi; **safely** adv sicuramente; sano/a e salvo/a; prudentemente; prudentemente; **safe sex** n sesso sicuro

safety ['seɪftɪ] n sicurezza; **safety belt** n cintura di sicurezza; **safety pin** n spilla di sicurezza

saffron ['sæfrən] n zafferano

sag [sæg] vi incurvarsi; afflosciarsi

sage [seɪdʒ] n (herb) salvia; (man) saggio

Sagittarius [sædʒɪ'tɛərɪəs] n Sagittario

Sahara [sə'hɑːrə] n: **the ~ Desert** il Deserto del Sahara

said [sɛd] pt, pp of **say**

sail [seɪl] n (on boat) vela; (trip): **to go for a ~** fare un giro in barca a vela ▷ vt (boat) condurre, governare ▷ vi (travel: ship) navigare; (: passenger) viaggiare per mare; (set off) salpare; (Sport) fare della vela; **they ~ed into Genoa** entrarono nel porto di Genova; **sailboat** ['seɪlbəut] n (us) barca a vela; **sailing** n (sport) vela; **to go sailing** fare della vela; **sailing boat** n barca a vela; **sailor** n marinaio

saint [seɪnt] n santo/a

sake [seɪk] n: **for the ~ of** per, per amore di

salad ['sæləd] n insalata; **salad cream** n (BRIT) (tipo di) maionese f; **salad dressing** n condimento per insalata

salami [sə'lɑːmɪ] n salame m

salary ['sælərɪ] n stipendio

sale [seɪl] n vendita; (at reduced prices) svendita, liquidazione f; (auction) vendita all'asta; **sales** npl (total

amount sold) vendite *fpl*; **"for ~"** "in
vendita"; **on ~** in vendita; **on ~ or
return** da vendere o rimandare;
sales assistant, (*US*) **sales clerk**
n commesso/a; **salesman** *n*
(*irreg*) commesso; (*representative*)
rappresentante *m*; **salesperson**
n (*irreg*) (*in shop*) /aommesso;
(*representative*) rappresentante
m/f di commercio; **sales rep** *n*
rappresentante *m/f* di commercio;
saleswoman *n* (*irreg*) commessa;
(*representative*) rappresentante *f*
saline ['seɪlaɪn] *adj* salino/a
saliva [sə'laɪvə] *n* saliva
salmon ['sæmən] *n* (*pl inv*) salmone *m*
salon ['sælɒn] *n* (*hairdressing salon*)
parrucchiere/a; (*beauty salon*) salone
m di bellezza
saloon [sə'lu:n] *n* (*US*) saloon *m inv*,
bar *m inv*; (*BRIT Aut*) berlina; (*ship's
lounge*) salone *m*
salt [sɔːlt] *n* sale *m* ▷ *vt* salare;
saltwater *adj* di mare; **salty** *adj*
salato/a
salute [sə'lu:t] *n* saluto ▷ *vt* salutare
salvage ['sælvɪdʒ] *n* (*saving*)
salvataggio; (*things saved*) beni *mpl*
salvati *or* recuperati ▷ *vt* salvare,
mettere in salvo
Salvation Army [sæl'veɪʃən-] *n*
Esercito della Salvezza
same [seɪm] *adj* stesso/a,
medesimo/a ▷ *pron*: **the ~** lo (la)
stesso/a, gli (le) stessi/e; **the ~ book
as** lo stesso libro di (*or* che); **at the
~ time** allo stesso tempo; **all** *or* **just
the ~** tuttavia; **to do the ~ as sb**
fare come qn; **and the ~ to you!**
altrettanto a lei!
sample ['sɑːmpl] *n* campione *m* ▷ *vt*
(*food*) assaggiare; (*wine*) degustare
sanction ['sæŋkʃən] *n* sanzione *f* ▷ *vt*
sancire, sanzionare; **sanctions** *npl*
(*Pol*) sanzioni *fpl*
sanctuary ['sæŋktjuərɪ] *n* (*holy
place*) santuario; (*refuge*) rifugio; (*for
wildlife*) riserva

sand [sænd] *n* sabbia ▷ *vt* (*also:
~ down*) cartavetrare
sandal ['sændl] *n* sandalo
sand: sandbox ['sændbɒks] *n* (*US: for
children*) buca di sabbia; **sandcastle**
['sændkɑːsl] *n* castello di sabbia;
sand dune *n* duna di sabbia;
sandpaper ['sændpeɪpər] *n* carta
vetrata; **sandpit** ['sændpɪt] *n* (*for
children*) buca di sabbia; **sands** *npl*
spiaggia; **sandstone** ['sændstəun]
n arenaria
sandwich ['sændwɪtʃ] *n*
tramezzino, panino, sandwich *m
inv* ▷ *vt*: **cheese/ham ~** sandwich
al formaggio/prosciutto; **to be ~ed
between** essere incastrato/a fra
sandy ['sændɪ] *adj* sabbioso/a;
(*colour*) color sabbia *inv*, biondo/a
rossiccio/a
sane [seɪn] *adj* (*person*) sano/a di
mente; (*outlook*) sensato/a
sang [sæŋ] *pt* of **sing**
sanitary towel ['sænɪtərɪ-], (*US*)
sanitary napkin *n* assorbente *m*
(igienico)
sanity ['sænɪtɪ] *n* sanità mentale;
(*common sense*) buon senso
sank [sæŋk] *pt* of **sink**
Santa Claus [sæntə'klɔːz] *n* Babbo
Natale
sap [sæp] *n* (*of plants*) linfa ▷ *vt*
(*strength*) fiaccare
sapphire ['sæfaɪər] *n* zaffiro
sarcasm ['sɑːkæzm] *n* sarcasmo
sarcastic [sɑː'kæstɪk] *adj*
sarcastico/a; **to be ~** fare del
sarcasmo
sardine [sɑː'diːn] *n* sardina
Sardinia [sɑː'dɪnɪə] *n* Sardegna
SASE *n abbr* (*US: = self-addressed
stamped envelope*) busta affrancata e
con indirizzo
sat [sæt] *pt, pp* of **sit**
Sat. *abbr* (= *Saturday*) sab.
satchel ['sætʃl] *n* cartella
satellite ['sætəlaɪt] *adj, n* satellite *m*;
satellite dish *n* antenna parabolica;

satellite television n televisione f via satellite

satin ['sætɪn] n raso ▷ adj di or in raso

satire ['sætaɪəʳ] n satira

satisfaction [sætɪs'fækʃən] n soddisfazione f

satisfactory [sætɪs'fæktərɪ] adj soddisfacente

satisfied ['sætɪsfaɪd] adj (customer) soddisfatto/a; **to be ~ (with sth)** essere soddisfatto/a (di qc)

satisfy ['sætɪsfaɪ] vt soddisfare; (convince) convincere

satnav ['sætnæv] n abbr (= satellite navigation) navigatore m satellitare

Saturday ['sætədɪ] n sabato

sauce [sɔːs] n salsa; (containing meat, fish) sugo; **saucepan** n casseruola

saucer ['sɔːsəʳ] n sottocoppa m, piattino

Saudi Arabia ['saʊdɪ-] n Arabia Saudita

sauna ['sɔːnə] n sauna

sausage ['sɔsɪdʒ] n salsiccia; **sausage roll** n rotolo di pasta sfoglia ripieno di salsiccia

sautéed ['səʊteɪd] adj saltato/a

savage ['sævɪdʒ] adj (cruel, fierce) selvaggio/a, feroce; (primitive) primitivo/a ▷ n selvaggio/a ▷ vt attaccare selvaggiamente

save [seɪv] vt (person, belongings, Comput) salvare; (money) risparmiare, mettere da parte; (time) risparmiare; (food) conservare; (avoid: trouble) evitare; (Sport) parare ▷ vi (also: ~ up) economizzare ▷ n (Sport) parata ▷ prep salvo, a eccezione di

saving ['seɪvɪŋ] n risparmio; **savings** npl risparmi mpl; **savings account** n libretto di risparmio; **savings and loan association** n (US) ≈ società di credito immobiliare

savoury, (US) **savory** ['seɪvərɪ] adj (dish: not sweet) salato/a

saw [sɔː] pt of **see** ▷ n (tool) sega ▷ vt (pt **sawed**, pp **sawed** or **sawn** [sɔːn]) segare; **sawdust** n segatura

sawn [sɔːn] pp of **saw**

saxophone ['sæksəfəʊn] n sassofono

say [seɪ] n: **to have one's ~** fare sentire il proprio parere; **to have a** or **some ~** avere voce in capitolo ▷ vt (pt, pp **said**) dire; **could you ~ that again?** potrebbe ripeterlo?; **that goes without ~ing** va da sé; **saying** n proverbio, detto

scab [skæb] n crosta; (pej) crumiro/a

scaffolding ['skæfəldɪŋ] n impalcatura

scald [skɔːld] n scottatura ▷ vt scottare

scale [skeɪl] n scala; (of fish) squama ▷ vt (mountain) scalare; **~ of charges** tariffa; **on a large ~** su vasta scala; **scales** npl (for weighing) bilancia

scallion ['skæljən] n cipolla; (US: shallot) scalogna; (: leek) porro

scallop ['skɔləp] n (Zool) pettine m; (Sewing) smerlo

scalp [skælp] n cuoio capelluto ▷ vt scotennare

scalpel ['skælpl] n bisturi m inv

scam [skæm] n (col) truffa

scampi ['skæmpɪ] npl scampi mpl

scan [skæn] vt scrutare; (glance at quickly) scorrere, dare un'occhiata a; (TV) analizzare; (Radar) esplorare ▷ n (Med) ecografia

scandal ['skændl] n scandalo; (gossip) pettegolezzi mpl

Scandinavia [skændɪ'neɪvɪə] n Scandinavia; **Scandinavian** adj, n scandinavo/a

scanner ['skænəʳ] n (Radar, Med) scanner m inv

scapegoat ['skeɪpgəʊt] n capro espiatorio

scar [skɑːʳ] n cicatrice f ▷ vt sfregiare

scarce [skɛəs] adj scarso/a; (copy, edition) raro/a; **to make o.s. ~** (col) squagliarsela; **scarcely** adv appena

scare [skɛəʳ] n spavento; panico ▷ vt spaventare, atterrire; **to ~ sb**

stiff spaventare a morte qn; **there was a bomb ~ at the bank** hanno evacuato la banca per paura di un attentato dinamitardo; **scarecrow** n spaventapasseri m inv; **scared** adj: **to be scared** aver paura

scarf (pl **scarves**) [skɑ:f, skɑ:vz] n (long) sciarpa; (square) fazzoletto da testa, foulard m inv

scarlet ['skɑ:lɪt] adj scarlatto/a

scarves [skɑ:vz] npl of **scarf**

scary ['skɛərɪ] adj (col) che fa paura

scatter ['skætər] vt spargere; (crowd) disperdere ▷ vi disperdersi

scenario [sɪ'nɑ:rɪəu] n (Theat, Cine) copione m; (fig) situazione f

scene [si:n] n (Theat, fig etc) scena; (of crime, accident) scena, luogo; (sight, view) vista, veduta; **scenery** n (Theat) scenario; (landscape) panorama m; **scenic** adj scenico/a; panoramico/a

scent [sɛnt] n profumo; (sense of smell) olfatto, odorato; (fig: track) pista

sceptical, (us) **skeptical** ['skɛptɪkl] adj scettico/a

schedule ['ʃɛdju:l, us 'skɛdju:l] n programma m, piano; (of trains) orario; (of prices etc) lista, tabella ▷ vt fissare; **on ~** in orario; **to be ahead of/behind ~** essere in anticipo/ritardo sul previsto; **scheduled flight** n volo di linea

scheme [ski:m] n piano, progetto; (method) sistema m; (dishonest plan, plot) intrigo, trama; (arrangement) disposizione f, sistemazione f; (pension scheme etc) programma m ▷ vi fare progetti; (intrigue) complottare

schizophrenic [skɪtsə'frɛnɪk] adj, n schizofrenico/a

scholar ['skɒlər] n studioso/a; **scholarship** ['skɒləʃɪp] n erudizione f; (grant) borsa di studio

school [sku:l] n (primary, secondary) scuola; (in university: us) scuola, facoltà f inv ▷ cpd scolare,

scolastico/a ▷ vt (animal) addestrare; **schoolbook** n libro scolastico; **schoolboy** n scolaro; **schoolchild** n (pl **-children**) scolaro/a; **schoolgirl** n scolara; **schooling** n istruzione f; **schoolteacher** n insegnante m/f, docente m/f; (primary) maestro/a

science ['saɪəns] n scienza; **science fiction** n fantascienza; **scientific** [saɪən'tɪfɪk] adj scientifico/a; **scientist** n scienziato/a

sci-fi ['saɪfaɪ] n abbr (col) = **science fiction**

scissors ['sɪzəz] npl forbici fpl

scold [skəuld] vt rimproverare

scone [skɒn] n focaccina da tè

scoop [sku:p] n mestolo; (for ice cream) cucchiaio dosatore; (Press) colpo giornalistico, notizia (in) esclusiva

scooter ['sku:tər] n (motorcycle) motoretta, scooter m inv; (toy) monopattino

scope [skəup] n (capacity: of plan, undertaking) portata; (: of person) capacità fpl; (opportunity) possibilità fpl

scorching ['skɔ:tʃɪŋ] adj cocente, scottante

score [skɔ:r] n punti mpl, punteggio; (Mus) partitura, spartito; (twenty): **a ~** venti ▷ vt (goal, point) segnare, fare; (success) ottenere ▷ vi segnare; (Football) fare un goal; (keep score) segnare i punti; **on that ~** a questo riguardo; **~s of people** (fig) un sacco di gente; **to ~ 6 out of 10** prendere 6 su 10; **score out** vt cancellare con un segno; **scoreboard** n tabellone m segnapunti; **scorer** n marcatore/trice; (keeping score) segnapunti m inv

scorn [skɔ:n] n disprezzo ▷ vt disprezzare

Scorpio ['skɔ:pɪəu] n Scorpione m

scorpion ['skɔ:pɪən] n scorpione m

Scot [skɒt] n scozzese m/f

Scotch tape® ['skɒtʃ-] n scotch® m

Scotland ['skɒtlənd] n Scozia

S

Scots [skɔts] *adj* scozzese; **Scotsman**
n (irreg) scozzese *m*; **Scotswoman**
n (irreg) scozzese *f*; **Scottish**
['skɔtɪʃ] *adj* scozzese; **the Scottish
Parliament** il Parlamento scozzese

scout [skaut] *n (Mil)* esploratore *m*;
(also: **boy ~**) giovane esploratore,
scout *m inv*

scowl [skaul] *vi* accigliarsi,
aggrottare le sopracciglia; **to ~ at**
guardare torvo

scramble ['skræmbl] *n* arrampicata
▷ *vi* inerpicarsi; **to ~ out** *etc* uscire
etc in fretta; **to ~ for** azzuffarsi
per; **scrambled eggs** *npl* uova *fpl*
strapazzate

scrap [skræp] *n* pezzo, pezzetto;
(fight) zuffa; *(also:* **~ iron**) rottami
mpl di ferro, ferraglia ▷ *vt* demolire;
(fig) scartare ▷ *vi*: **to ~ (with sb)** fare
a botte *(con qn)*; **scraps** *npl (waste)*
scarti *mpl*; **scrapbook** *n* album *m
inv* di ritagli

scrape [skreip] *vt, vi* raschiare,
grattare ▷ *n*: **to get into a ~** cacciarsi
in un guaio

scrap paper *n* cartaccia

scratch [skrætʃ] *n* graffio ▷ *cpd*: **~
team** squadra raccogliticcia ▷ *vt*
graffiare, rigare ▷ *vi* grattare; *(paint,
car)* graffiare; **to start from ~**
cominciare *or* partire da zero; **to be
up to ~** essere all'altezza; **scratch
card** *n (BRIT)* cartolina *f* gratta e vinci

scream [skriːm] *n* grido, urlo ▷ *vi*
urlare, gridare

screen [skriːn] *n* schermo; *(fig)* muro,
cortina, velo ▷ *vt* schermare, fare
schermo a; *(from the wind etc)* riparare;
(film) proiettare; *(book)* adattare per
lo schermo; *(candidates etc)* passare al
vaglio; **screening** *n (Med)* dépistage
m inv; **screenplay** *n* sceneggiatura;
screensaver *n (Comput)* screen saver
m inv; **screenshot** *n (Comput)*
screenshot *m inv*

screw [skruː] *n* vite *f* ▷ *vt* avvitare;
screw up *vt (paper, material)*

spiegazzare; *(col: ruin)* mandare a
monte; **to ~ up one's eyes** strizzare
gli occhi; **screwdriver** *n* cacciavite *m*

scribble ['skrɪbl] *n* scarabocchio ▷ *vt*
scribacchiare ▷ *vi* scarabocchiare

script [skrɪpt] *n (Cine etc)* copione *m*;
(in exam) elaborato *or* compito d'esame

scroll [skrəul] *n* rotolo di carta

scrub [skrʌb] *n (land)* boscaglia ▷ *vt*
pulire strofinando; *(reject)* annullare

scruffy ['skrʌfɪ] *adj* sciatto/a

scrum(mage) ['skrʌm(ɪdʒ)] *n*
mischia

scrutiny ['skruːtɪnɪ] *n* esame *m*
accurato

scuba diving ['skuːbə-] *n*
immersioni *fpl* subacquee

sculptor ['skʌlptəʳ] *n* scultore *m*

sculpture ['skʌlptʃəʳ] *n* scultura

scum [skʌm] *n* schiuma; *(pej: people)*
feccia

scurry ['skʌrɪ] *vi* sgambare,
affrettarsi

sea [siː] *n* mare *m* ▷ *cpd* marino/a,
del mare; *(ship, port, route, transport)*
marittimo/a; *(bird, fish)* di mare; **on
the ~** *(boat)* in mare; *(town)* di mare;
to go by ~ andare per mare; **out to ~**
al largo; **(out) at ~** in mare; **seafood**
n frutti *mpl* di mare; **sea front** *n*
lungomare *m*; **seagull** *n* gabbiano

seal [siːl] *n (animal)* foca; *(stamp)*
sigillo; *(impression)* impronta del
sigillo ▷ *vt* sigillare; **seal off** *vt (close)*
sigillare; *(forbid entry to)* bloccare
l'accesso a

sea level *n* livello del mare

seam [siːm] *n* cucitura; *(of coal)*
filone *m*

search [səːtʃ] *n* ricerca; *(Law: at sb's
home)* perquisizione *f* ▷ *vt* frugare
▷ *vi*: **to ~ for** ricercare; **in ~ of** alla
ricerca di; **search engine** *n (Comput)*
motore *m* di ricerca; **search party** *n*
squadra di soccorso

sea: seashore ['siːʃɔːʳ] *n* spiaggia;
seasick ['siːsɪk] *adj* che soffre il
mal di mare; **seaside** ['siːsaɪd] *n*

spiaggia; **seaside resort** n stazione f balneare

season ['si:zn] n stagione f ▷ vt condire, insaporire; **seasonal** adj stagionale; **seasoning** n condimento; **season ticket** n abbonamento

seat [si:t] n sedile m; (in bus, train: place) posto; (Parliament) seggio; (buttocks) didietro; (of trousers) fondo ▷ vt far sedere; (have room for) avere or essere fornito/a di posti a sedere per; **to be ~ed** essere seduto/a; **seat belt** n cintura di sicurezza; **seating** n posti mpl a sedere

sea: sea water n acqua di mare; **seaweed** ['si:wi:d] n alghe fpl

sec. abbr = **second**

secluded [sɪ'klu:dɪd] adj isolato/a, appartato/a

second ['sɛkənd] num secondo/a ▷ adv (in race etc) al secondo posto ▷ n (unit of time) secondo; (BRIT Scol: degree) laurea con punteggio discreto; (Aut: also: **~ gear**) seconda; (Comm: imperfect) scarto ▷ vt (motion) appoggiare; **~ thoughts** ripensamenti mpl; **on ~ thoughts** (BRIT) or **thought** (US) ripensandoci bene; **secondary** adj secondario/a; **secondary school** n scuola secondaria; **second-class** adj di seconda classe ▷ adv: **to travel second-class** viaggiare in seconda (classe); **second-hand** adj di seconda mano, usato/a; **secondly** adv in secondo luogo; **second-rate** adj scadente

secrecy ['si:krəsɪ] n segretezza

secret ['si:krɪt] adj segreto/a ▷ n segreto; **in ~** in segreto

secretary ['sɛkrətrɪ] n segretario/a; **S~ of State (for)** (BRIT Pol) ministro (di)

secretive ['si:krətɪv] adj riservato/a

secret service n servizi mpl segreti

sect [sɛkt] n setta

section ['sɛkʃən] n sezione f

sector ['sɛktər] n settore m

secular ['sɛkjulər] adj secolare

secure [sɪ'kjuər] adj sicuro/a; (firmly fixed) assicurato/a, ben fermato/a; (in safe place) al sicuro ▷ vt (fix) fissare, assicurare; (get) ottenere, assicurarsi

security [sɪ'kjuərɪtɪ] n sicurezza; (for loan) garanzia; **securities** npl (Stock Exchange) titoli mpl; **security guard** n guardia giurata

sedan [sə'dæn] n (US Aut) berlina

sedate [sɪ'deɪt] adj posato/a; calmo/a ▷ vt calmare

sedative ['sɛdɪtɪv] n sedativo, calmante m

seduce [sɪ'dju:s] vt sedurre; **seductive** [sɪ'dʌktɪv] adj seducente

see [si:] (pt **saw**, pp **seen**) vt vedere; (accompany): **to ~ sb to the door** accompagnare qn alla porta ▷ vi vedere; (understand) capire ▷ n sede f vescovile; **to ~ that** (ensure) badare che + sub, fare in modo che + sub; **~ you soon/later/tomorrow!** a presto/più tardi/domani!; **see off** vt salutare alla partenza; **see out** vt (take to the door) accompagnare alla porta; **see through** vt portare a termine ▷ vt fus non lasciarsi ingannare da; **see to** vt fus occuparsi di

seed [si:d] n seme m; (fig) germe m; (Tennis) testa di serie; **to go to ~** fare seme; (fig) scadere

seeing ['si:ɪŋ] conj: **~ (that)** visto che

seek [si:k] (pt, pp **sought**) vt cercare

seem [si:m] vi sembrare, parere; **there ~s to be ...** sembra che ci sia ...; **seemingly** adv apparentemente

seen [si:n] pp of **see**

seesaw ['si:sɔ:] n altalena a bilico

segment ['sɛgmənt] n segmento

segregate ['sɛgrɪgeɪt] vt segregare, isolare

seize [si:z] vt (grasp) afferrare; (take possession of) impadronirsi di; (Law) sequestrare

seizure ['si:ʒər] n (Med) attacco; (Law) confisca, sequestro

seldom ['sɛldəm] *adv* raramente
select [sɪ'lɛkt] *adj* scelto/a ▷ *vt* scegliere, selezionare; **selection** *n* selezione *f*, scelta; **selective** *adj* selettivo/a
self [sɛlf] *n*: **the ~** l'io *m* ▷ *prefix* auto…; **self-assured** *adj* sicuro/a di sé; **self-catering** *adj* (BRIT) in cui ci si cucina da sé; **self-centred**, (US) **self-centered** *adj* egocentrico/a; **self-confidence** *n* sicurezza di sé; **self-confident** *adj* sicuro/a di sé; **self-conscious** [sɛlf'kɔnʃəs] *adj* timido/a; **self-contained** *adj* (BRIT: *flat*) indipendente; **self-control** *n* autocontrollo; **self-defence**, (US) **self-defense** *n* autodifesa; (*Law*) legittima difesa; **self-drive** *adj* (BRIT: *rented car*) senza autista; **self-employed** *adj* che lavora in proprio; **self-esteem** *n* amor proprio *m*; **self-indulgent** *adj* indulgente verso se stesso/a; **self-interest** *n* interesse *m* personale; **selfish** *adj* egoista; **self-pity** *n* autocommiserazione *f*; **self-raising**, (US) **self-rising** *adj*: **self-raising flour** miscela di farina e lievito; **self-respect** *n* rispetto di sé, amor proprio; **self-service** *n* autoservizio, self-service *m*
selfie ['sɛlfɪ] *n* selfie *m inv*
sell (*pt*, *pp* **sold**) [sɛl, səuld] *vt* vendere ▷ *vi* vendersi; **to ~ at** *or* **for 100 euros** essere in vendita a 100 euro; **sell off** *vt* svendere, liquidare; **sell out** *vt* esaurire; **the tickets are all sold out** i biglietti sono esauriti; **sell-by date** ['sɛlbaɪ-] *n* data di scadenza; **seller** *n* venditore/trice
Sellotape® ['sɛləuteɪp] *n* (BRIT) nastro adesivo, scotch® *m*
selves [sɛlvz] *npl of* **self**
semester [sɪ'mɛstə'] *n* (US) semestre *m*
semi… ['sɛmɪ] *prefix* semi…; **semicircle** *n* semicerchio; **semidetached (house)** [sɛmɪdɪ'tætʃt-] *n* (BRIT) casa gemella; **semifinal** *n* semifinale *f*

seminar ['sɛmɪnɑː'] *n* seminario
semi-skimmed ['sɛmɪ'skɪmd] *adj* (*milk*) parzialmente scremato/a
senate ['sɛnɪt] *n* senato; **senator** *n* senatore/trice
send [sɛnd] (*pt*, *pp* **sent**) *vt* mandare; **send back** *vt* rimandare; **send for** *vt fus* mandare a chiamare, far venire; **send in** *vt* (*report, application, resignation*) presentare; **send off** *vt* (*goods*) spedire; (BRIT *Sport: player*) espellere; **send on** *vt* (BRIT: *letter*) inoltrare; (*luggage etc: in advance*) spedire in anticipo; **send out** *vt* (*invitation*) diramare; **send up** *vt* (*person, price*) far salire; (BRIT: *parody*) mettere in ridicolo; **sender** *n* mittente *m/f*; **send-off** *n*: **to give sb a good send-off** festeggiare la partenza di qn
senile ['siːnaɪl] *adj* senile
senior ['siːnɪə'] *adj* (*older*) più vecchio/a; (*of higher rank*) di grado più elevato; **senior citizen** *n* persona anziana; **senior high school** *n* (US) ≈ liceo
sensation [sɛn'seɪʃən] *n* sensazione *f*; **sensational** *adj* sensazionale; (*marvellous*) eccezionale
sense [sɛns] *n* senso; (*feeling*) sensazione *f*, senso; (*meaning*) senso, significato; (*wisdom*) buonsenso ▷ *vt* sentire, percepire; **it makes ~** ha senso; **~ of humour** (senso dell') umorismo; **senseless** *adj* sciocco/a; (*unconscious*) privo/a di sensi
sensible ['sɛnsɪbl] *adj* sensato/a, ragionevole

> Be careful not to translate *sensible* by the Italian word *sensibile*.

sensitive ['sɛnsɪtɪv] *adj* sensibile; (*skin, question*) delicato/a
sensual ['sɛnsjuəl] *adj* sensuale
sensuous ['sɛnsjuəs] *adj* sensuale
sent [sɛnt] *pt*, *pp of* **send**
sentence ['sɛntns] *n* (*Ling*) frase *f*; (*Law: judgement*) sentenza;

(: *punishment*) condanna ▷ *vt*: **to ~ sb to death/to 5 years** condannare qn a morte/a 5 anni

sentiment ['sɛntɪmənt] *n* sentimento; (*opinion*) opinione *f*; **sentimental** [sɛntɪ'mɛntl] *adj* sentimentale

Sep. *abbr* (= *September*) Sett.

separate *adj* ['sɛprɪt] separato/a ▷ *vt* ['sɛpəreɪt] separare ▷ *vi* ['sɛpəreɪt] separarsi; **separately** *adv* separatamente; **separates** *npl* (*clothes*) coordinati *mpl*; **separation** [sɛpə'reɪʃən] *n* separazione *f*

September [sɛp'tɛmbəʳ] *n* settembre *m*

septic ['sɛptɪk] *adj* settico/a; (*wound*) infettato/a; **septic tank** *n* fossa settica

sequel ['siːkwl] *n* conseguenza; (*of story*) seguito; (*of film*) sequenza

sequence ['siːkwəns] *n* (*series*) serie *f inv*; (*order*) ordine *m*

sequin ['siːkwɪn] *n* lustrino, paillette *f inv*

Serb [səːb] *adj, n* = **Serbian**

Serbia ['səːbɪə] *n* Serbia

Serbian ['səːbɪən] *adj* serbo/a ▷ *n* serbo/a; (*Ling*) serbo

sergeant ['sɑːdʒənt] *n* sergente *m*; (*Police*) brigadiere *m*

serial ['sɪərɪəl] *n* (*Press*) romanzo a puntate; (*Radio, TV*) trasmissione *f* a puntate, serial *m inv*; **serial killer** *n* serial killer *mf inv*; **serial number** *n* numero di serie

series ['sɪəriːz] *n* (*pl inv*) serie *f inv*; (*Publishing*) collana

serious ['sɪərɪəs] *adj* serio/a, grave; **seriously** *adv* seriamente

sermon ['səːmən] *n* sermone *m*

servant ['səːvənt] *n* domestico/a

serve [səːv] *vt* (*employer etc*) servire, essere a servizio di; (*purpose*) servire a; (*customer, food, meal*) servire; (*apprenticeship*) fare; (*prison term*) scontare ▷ *vi* (*also Tennis*) servire; (*be useful*): **to ~ as/for/to do** servire da/

per/per fare ▷ *n* (*Tennis*) servizio; **it ~s him right** ben gli sta, se l'è meritata; **server** *n* (*Comput*) server *m inv*

service ['səːvɪs] *n* servizio; (*Aut: maintenance*) assistenza, revisione *f* ▷ *vt* (*car, washing machine*) revisionare; **services** *npl* (*BRIT: on motorway*) stazione *f* di servizio; (*Mil*): **the S~s** le forze armate; **to be of ~ to sb** essere d'aiuto a qn; **~ included/not included** servizio compreso/escluso; **service area** *n* (*on motorway*) area di servizio; **service charge** *n* (*BRIT*) servizio; **serviceman** *n* (*irreg*) militare *m*; **service station** *n* stazione *f* di servizio

serviette [səːvɪ'ɛt] *n* (*BRIT*) tovagliolo

session ['sɛʃən] *n* (*sitting*) seduta, sessione *f*; (*Scol*) anno scolastico (*or* accademico)

set [sɛt] *n* serie *f inv*; (*of cutlery etc*) servizio; (*Radio, TV*) apparecchio; (*Tennis*) set *m inv*; (*group of people*) mondo, ambiente *m*; (*Cine*) scenario; (*Theat: stage*) scene *fpl*; (: *scenery*) scenario; (*Math*) insieme *m*; (*Hairdressing*) messa in piega ▷ *adj* (*fixed*) stabilito/a, determinato/a; (*ready*) pronto/a ▷ *vt* (*pt, pp* **set**) (*place*) posare, mettere; (*arrange*) sistemare; (*fix*) fissare; (*adjust*) regolare; (*decide: rules etc*) stabilire, fissare ▷ *vi* (*pt, pp* **set**) (*sun*) tramontare; (*jam, jelly*) rapprendersi; (*concrete*) fare presa; **to be ~ on doing** essere deciso a fare; **to ~ to music** mettere in musica; **to ~ on fire** dare fuoco a; **to ~ free** liberare; **to ~ sth going** mettere in moto qc; **to ~ sail** prendere il mare; **set aside** *vt* mettere da parte; **set down** *vt* (*bus, train*) lasciare; **set in** *vi* (*infection*) svilupparsi; (*complications*) intervenire; **the rain has ~ in for the day** ormai pioverà tutto il giorno; **set off** *vi* partire ▷ *vt* (*bomb*) far scoppiare; (*cause to*

S

start) mettere in moto; (*show up well*) dare risalto a; **set out** *vi* partire; **to ~ out to do** proporsi di fare ▷ *vt* (*arrange*) disporre; (*state*) esporre, presentare; **set up** *vt* (*organization*) fondare, costituire; **setback** *n* (*hitch*) contrattempo, inconveniente *m*; **set menu** *n* menù *m inv* fisso

settee [sɛ'tiː] *n* divano, sofà *m inv*

setting ['sɛtɪŋ] *n* (*background*) ambiente *m*; (*of controls*) posizione *f*; (*of sun*) tramonto; (*of jewel*) montatura

settle ['sɛtl] *vt* (*argument, matter*) appianare; (*bill, account*) regolare; (*Med: calm*) calmare ▷ *vi* (*bird, dust etc*) posarsi; (*sediment*) depositarsi; (*also: ~ down*) sistemarsi, stabilirsi; (*become calmer*) calmarsi; **to ~ for sth** accontentarsi di qc; **to ~ on sth** decidersi per qc; **settle in** *vi* sistemarsi; **settle up** *vi*: **to ~ up with sb** regolare i conti con qn; **settlement** *n* (*payment*) pagamento, saldo; (*agreement*) accordo; (*colony*) colonia; (*village etc*) villaggio, comunità *f inv*

setup ['sɛtʌp] *n* (*arrangement*) sistemazione *f*; (*situation*) situazione *f*

seven ['sɛvn] *num* sette; **seventeen** *num* diciassette; **seventeenth** [sɛvn'tiːnθ] *num* diciassettesimo/a; **seventh** *num* settimo/a; **seventieth** ['sɛvntɪɪθ] *num* settantesimo/a; **seventy** *num* settanta

sever ['sɛvəʳ] *vt* recidere, tagliare; (*relations*) troncare

several ['sɛvərl] *adj, pron* alcuni/e, diversi/e; **~ of us** alcuni di noi

severe [sɪ'vɪəʳ] *adj* severo/a; (*serious*) serio/a, grave; (*hard*) duro/a; (*plain*) semplice, sobrio/a

sew [səu] (*pt* **sewed**, *pp* **sewn**) *vt, vi* cucire

sewage ['suːɪdʒ] *n* acque *fpl* di scolo

sewer ['suːəʳ] *n* fogna

sewing ['səuɪŋ] *n* cucitura; cucito; **sewing machine** *n* macchina da cucire

sewn [səun] *pp of* **sew**

sex [sɛks] *n* sesso; **to have ~ with** avere rapporti sessuali con; **sexism** ['sɛksɪzəm] *n* sessismo; **sexist** *adj, n* sessista (*m/f*); **sexual** ['sɛksjuəl] *adj* sessuale; **sexual intercourse** rapporti *mpl* sessuali; **sexuality** [sɛksju'ælɪtɪ] *n* sessualità; **sexy** ['sɛksɪ] *adj* provocante, sexy *inv*

shabby ['ʃæbɪ] *adj* malandato/a; (*behaviour*) meschino/a

shack [ʃæk] *n* baracca, capanna

shade [ʃeɪd] *n* ombra; (*for lamp*) paralume *m*; (*of colour*) tonalità *f inv*; (*small quantity*): **a ~ (more/too large)** un po' (di più/troppo grande) ▷ *vt* ombreggiare, fare ombra a; **shades** *npl* (*us: sunglasses*) occhiali *mpl* da sole; **in the ~** all'ombra

shadow ['ʃædəu] *n* ombra ▷ *vt* (*follow*) pedinare; **shadow cabinet** *n* (*BRIT Pol*) governo *m* ombra *inv*

shady ['ʃeɪdɪ] *adj* ombroso/a; (*fig: dishonest*) losco/a, equivoco/a

shaft [ʃɑːft] *n* (*of arrow, spear*) asta; (*Aut, Tech*) albero; (*of mine*) pozzo; (*of lift*) tromba; (*of light*) raggio

shake [ʃeɪk] (*pt* **shook**, *pp* **shaken**) *vt* scuotere; (*bottle, cocktail*) agitare ▷ *vi* tremare; **to ~ one's head** (*in refusal, dismay*) scuotere la testa; **to ~ hands with sb** stringere *or* dare la mano a qn; **shake off** *vt* scrollare (via); (*fig*) sbarazzarsi di; **shake up** *vt* scuotere; **shaky** *adj* (*hand, voice*) tremante; (*building*) traballante

shall [ʃæl] *aux vb*: **I ~ go** andrò; **I open the door?** apro io la porta?; **I'll get some, ~ I?** ne prendo un po', va bene?

shallow ['ʃæləu] *adj* poco profondo/a; (*fig*) superficiale

sham [ʃæm] *n* finzione *f*, messinscena; (*jewellery, furniture*) imitazione *f*

shambles ['ʃæmblz] *n* confusione *f*, baraonda, scompiglio

shame [ʃeɪm] *n* vergogna ▷ *vt* far vergognare; **it is a ~ (that/to do)** è un peccato (che + *sub*/fare); **what a ~!** che peccato!; **shameful** *adj* vergognoso/a; **shameless** *adj* sfrontato/a; (*immodest*) spudorato/a

shampoo [ʃæm'puː] *n* shampoo *m inv* ▷ *vt* fare lo shampoo a

shandy ['ʃændɪ] *n* birra con gassosa

shan't [ʃɑːnt] = **shall not**

shape [ʃeɪp] *n* forma ▷ *vt* formare; (*statement*) formulare; (*sb's ideas*) condizionare; **to take ~** prendere forma

share [ʃɛəʳ] *n* (*thing received, contribution*) parte *f*; (*Comm*) azione *f* ▷ *vt* dividere; (*have in common*) condividere, avere in comune; **shareholder** *n* azionista *m/f*

shark [ʃɑːk] *n* squalo, pescecane *m*

sharp [ʃɑːp] *adj* (*razor, knife*) affilato/a; (*point*) acuto/a, acuminato/a; (*nose, chin*) aguzzo/a; (*outline*) netto/a; (*cold, pain*) pungente; (*voice*) stridulo/a; (*person: quick-witted*) sveglio/a; (: *unscrupulous*) disonesto/a; (*Mus*): **C ~** do diesis ▷ *n* (*Mus*) diesis *m inv* ▷ *adv*: **at 2 o'clock ~** alle due in punto; **sharpen** *vt* affilare; (*pencil*) fare la punta a; (*fig*) acuire; **sharpener** *n* (*also*: **pencil sharpener**) temperamatite *m inv*; **sharply** *adv* (*abruptly*) bruscamente; (*clearly*) nettamente; (*harshly*) duramente, aspramente

shatter ['ʃætəʳ] *vt* mandare in frantumi, frantumare; (*fig: upset*) distruggere; (: *ruin*) rovinare ▷ *vi* frantumarsi, andare in pezzi; **shattered** *adj* (*grief-stricken*) sconvolto/a; (*exhausted*) a pezzi, distrutto/a

shave [ʃeɪv] *vt* radere, rasare ▷ *vi* radersi, farsi la barba ▷ *n*: **to have a ~** farsi la barba; **shaver** *n* (*also*: **electric shaver**) rasoio elettrico

shaving cream *n* crema da barba

shaving foam *n* = **shaving cream**

shawl [ʃɔːl] *n* scialle *m*

she [ʃiː] *pron* ella, lei; **~-cat** gatta; **~-elephant** elefantessa

sheath [ʃiːθ] *n* fodero, guaina; (*contraceptive*) preservativo

shed [ʃed] *n* capannone *m* ▷ *vt* (*pt, pp* **shed**) (*leaves, fur etc*) perdere; (*tears, blood*) versare; (*workers*) liberarsi di

she'd [ʃiːd] = **she had; she would**

sheep [ʃiːp] *n* (*pl inv*) pecora; **sheepdog** *n* cane *m* da pastore; **sheepskin** *n* pelle *f* di pecora

sheer [ʃɪəʳ] *adj* (*utter*) vero/a (e proprio/a); (*steep*) a picco, perpendicolare; (*almost transparent*) sottile ▷ *adv* a picco

sheet [ʃiːt] *n* (*on bed*) lenzuolo; (*of paper*) foglio; (*of glass*) lastra; (*of metal*) foglio, lamina

sheik(h) [ʃeɪk] *n* sceicco

shelf (*pl* **shelves**) [ʃelf, ʃelvz] *n* scaffale *m*, mensola

shell [ʃel] *n* (*on beach*) conchiglia; (*of egg, nut etc*) guscio; (*explosive*) granata; (*of building*) scheletro ▷ *vt* (*peas*) sgranare; (*Mil*) bombardare

she'll [ʃiːl] = **she will; she shall**

shellfish ['ʃelfɪʃ] *n* (*pl inv*: **crab etc**) crostaceo; (*scallop etc*) mollusco; (*as food*) crostacei; molluschi

shelter ['ʃeltəʳ] *n* riparo, rifugio ▷ *vt* riparare, proteggere; (*give lodging to*) dare rifugio or asilo a ▷ *vi* ripararsi, mettersi al riparo; **sheltered** *adj* riparato/a

shelves [ʃelvz] *npl of* **shelf**

shelving ['ʃelvɪŋ] *n* scaffalature *fpl*

shepherd ['ʃepəd] *n* pastore *m* ▷ *vt* (*guide*) guidare; **shepherd's pie** (BRIT) *n* timballo di carne macinata e purè di patate

sheriff ['ʃerɪf] (US) *n* sceriffo

sherry ['ʃerɪ] *n* sherry *m inv*

she's [ʃiːz] = **she is; she has**

Shetland ['ʃetlənd] *n* (*also*: **the ~s, the ~ Isles**) le (isole) Shetland

shield [ʃiːld] *n* scudo; (*trophy*) scudetto; (*protection*) schermo ▷ *vt*: **to ~ (from)** riparare (da), proteggere (da *or* contro)

S

shift [ʃɪft] n (change) cambiamento; (of workers) turno ▷ vt spostare, muovere; (remove) rimuovere ▷ vi spostarsi, muoversi

shin [ʃɪn] n tibia

shine [ʃaɪn] (pt, pp **shone**) n splendore m, lucentezza ▷ vi (ri) splendere, brillare ▷ vt far brillare, far risplendere; (torch): **to ~ sth on** puntare qc verso

shingles ['ʃɪŋglz] n (Med) herpes zoster m

shiny ['ʃaɪnɪ] adj lucente, lucido/a

ship [ʃɪp] n nave f ▷ vt trasportare (via mare); (send) spedire (via mare); **shipment** n carico; **shipping** n (ships) naviglio; (traffic) navigazione f; **shipwreck** n relitto; (event) naufragio ▷ vt: **to be shipwrecked** naufragare, fare naufragio; **shipyard** n cantiere m navale

shirt [ʃəːt] n camicia; **in ~ sleeves** in maniche di camicia

shit [ʃɪt] excl (col!) merda (!)

shiver ['ʃɪvəʳ] n brivido ▷ vi rabbrividire, tremare

shock [ʃɔk] n (impact) urto, colpo; (Elec) scossa; (emotional) colpo, shock m inv; (Med) shock ▷ vt colpire, scioccare; scandalizzare; **shocking** adj scioccante, traumatizzante; (scandalous) scandaloso/a

shoe [ʃuː] n scarpa; (also: **horse~**) ferro di cavallo ▷ vt (pt, pp **shod** [ʃɔd]) (horse) ferrare; **shoelace** n stringa; **shoe polish** n lucido per scarpe; **shoeshop** n calzoleria

shone [ʃɔn] pt, pp of **shine**

shonky ['ʃɔŋkɪ] adj (AUST, NZ col: untrustworthy) sospetto/a

shook [ʃuk] pt of **shake**

shoot [ʃuːt] (pt, pp **shot**) n (on branch, seedling) germoglio ▷ vt (game) cacciare, andare a caccia di; (person) sparare a; (execute) fucilare; (film) girare ▷ vi (Football) sparare, tirare (forte); **to ~ (at)** (with gun) sparare (a), fare fuoco (su); (with bow)

tirare (su); **shoot down** vt (plane) abbattere; **shoot up** vi (fig) salire alle stelle; **shooting** n (shots) sparatoria; (Hunting) caccia

shop [ʃɔp] n negozio; (workshop) officina ▷ vi (also: **go ~ping**) fare spese; **shop assistant** n (BRIT) commesso/a; **shopkeeper** n negoziante m/f, bottegaio/a; **shoplifting** n taccheggio; **shopping** n (goods) spesa, acquisti mpl; **shopping bag** n borsa per la spesa; **shopping centre**, (US) **shopping center** n centro commerciale; **shopping mall** n centro commerciale; **shopping trolley** n (BRIT) carrello del supermercato; **shop window** n vetrina

shore [ʃɔːʳ] n (of sea) riva, spiaggia; (of lake) riva ▷ vt: **to ~ (up)** puntellare; **on ~** a riva

short [ʃɔːt] adj (not long) corto/a; (soon finished) breve; (person) basso/a; (curt) brusco/a, secco/a; (insufficient) insufficiente ▷ n (also: **~ film**) cortometraggio; **it is ~ for** è l'abbreviazione or il diminutivo di; **to be ~ of sth** essere a corto di or mancare di qc; **to run ~ of sth** rimanere senza qc; **in ~** in breve; **~ of doing** a meno che non si faccia; **everything ~ of** tutto fuorché; **to cut ~** (speech, visit) accorciare, abbreviare; **to fall ~ of** venire meno a; non soddisfare; **to stop ~** fermarsi di colpo; **to stop ~ of** non arrivare fino a; **shortage** n scarsezza, carenza; **shortbread** n biscotto di pasta frolla; **shortcoming** n difetto; **short(crust) pastry** n (BRIT) pasta frolla; **shortcut** n scorciatoia; **shorten** vt accorciare, ridurre; **shortfall** n deficit m inv; **shorthand** n stenografia; **short-lived** adj di breve durata; **shortly** adv fra poco; **shorts** npl (also: **a pair of shorts**) i calzoncini; **short-sighted** adj (BRIT) miope; **short-sleeved** ['ʃɔːtsliːvd] *adj* a maniche corte; **short story** *n* racconto, novella; **short-tempered** *adj* irascibile; **short-term** *adj* (*effect*) di *or* a breve durata; (*borrowing*) a breve scadenza

shot [ʃɔt] *pt, pp of* **shoot** ▷ *n* sparo, colpo; (*try*) prova; (*Football*) tiro; (*injection*) iniezione *f*; (*Phot*) foto *f inv*; **like a ~** come un razzo; (*very readily*) immediatamente; **shotgun** *n* fucile *m* da caccia

should [ʃud] *aux vb*: **I ~ go now** dovrei andare ora; **he ~ be there now** dovrebbe essere arrivato ora; **I ~ go if I were you** se fossi in lei andrei; **I ~ like to** mi piacerebbe

shoulder ['ʃəuldə'] *n* spalla; **hard ~** corsia d'emergenza ▷ *vt* (*fig*) addossarsi, prendere sulle proprie spalle; **shoulder blade** *n* scapola

shouldn't ['ʃudnt] = **should not**

shout [ʃaut] *n* urlo, grido ▷ *vt* gridare ▷ *vi* (*also*: **~ out**) urlare, gridare

shove [ʃʌv] *vt* spingere; (*col*: *put*): **to ~ sth in** ficcare qc in

shovel ['ʃʌvl] *n* pala ▷ *vt* spalare

show [ʃəu] (*pt* **showed**, *pp* **shown**) *n* (*of emotion*) dimostrazione *f*, manifestazione *f*; (*semblance*) apparenza; (*exhibition*) mostra, esposizione *f*; (*Theat, Cine*) spettacolo ▷ *vt* far vedere, mostrare; (*courage etc*) dimostrare, dar prova di; (*exhibit*) esporre ▷ *vi* vedersi, essere visibile; **to be on ~** essere esposto; **it's just for ~** è solo per far scena; **show in** *vt* (*person*) far entrare; **show off** *vi* (*pej*) esibirsi, mettersi in mostra ▷ *vt* (*display*) mettere in risalto; (*pej*) mettere in mostra; **show out** *vt* (*person*) accompagnare alla porta; **show up** *vi* (*stand out*) essere ben visibile; (*col*: *turn up*) farsi vedere ▷ *vt* mettere in risalto; **show business** *n* industria dello spettacolo

shower ['ʃauə'] *n* doccia; (*rain*) acquazzone *m*; (*of stones etc*) pioggia ▷ *vi* fare la doccia ▷ *vt*: **to ~ sb**

with (*gifts, abuse etc*) coprire qn di; (*missiles*) lanciare contro qn una pioggia di; **to have** *or* **take a ~** fare la doccia; **shower cap** *n* cuffia da doccia; **shower gel** *n* gel *m* doccia *inv*

showing ['ʃəuɪŋ] *n* (*of film*) proiezione *f*

show jumping *n* concorso ippico (di salto ad ostacoli)

shown [ʃəun] *pp of* **show**

show: show-off *n* (*col*: *person*) esibizionista *m/f*; **showroom** *n* sala d'esposizione

shrank [ʃræŋk] *pt of* **shrink**

shred [ʃrɛd] *n* (*gen pl*) brandello ▷ *vt* fare a brandelli; (*Culin*) sminuzzare, tagliuzzare

shrewd [ʃru:d] *adj* astuto/a, scaltro/a

shriek [ʃri:k] *n* strillo ▷ *vi* strillare

shrimp [ʃrɪmp] *n* gamberetto

shrine [ʃraɪn] *n* reliquario; (*place*) santuario

shrink [ʃrɪŋk] (*pt* **shrank**, *pp* **shrunk**) *vi* restringersi; (*fig*) ridursi; (*also*: **~ away**) ritrarsi ▷ *vt* (*wool*) far restringere ▷ *n* (*col, pej*) psicanalista *m/f*; **to ~ from doing sth** rifuggire dal fare qc

shrivel ['ʃrɪvl], **shrivel up** *vt* raggrinzare, avvizzire ▷ *vi* raggrinzirsi, avvizzire

shroud [ʃraud] *n* lenzuolo funebre ▷ *vt*: **~ed in mystery** avvolto/a nel mistero

Shrove Tuesday ['ʃrəuv-] *n* martedì *m* grasso

shrub [ʃrʌb] *n* arbusto

shrug [ʃrʌg] *n* scrollata di spalle ▷ *vt, vi*: **to ~ (one's shoulders)** alzare le spalle, fare spallucce; **shrug off** *vt* passare sopra a

shrunk [ʃrʌŋk] *pp of* **shrink**

shudder ['ʃʌdə'] *n* brivido ▷ *vi* rabbrividire

shuffle ['ʃʌfl] *vt* (*cards*) mescolare; **to ~ (one's feet)** strascicare i piedi

shun [ʃʌn] *vt* sfuggire, evitare

S

shut (pt, pp **shut**) [ʃʌt] vt chiudere ▷ vi
chiudersi, chiudere; **shut down** vt,
vi chiudere definitivamente; **shut up**
vi (col: keep quiet) stare zitto/a, fare
silenzio ▷ vt (close) chiudere; (silence)
far tacere; **shutter** n imposta, (Phot)
otturatore m
shuttle ['ʃʌtl] n spola, navetta; (space
shuttle) navetta (spaziale); (also:
~ service) servizio m navetta inv;
shuttlecock n volano
shy [ʃaɪ] adj timido/a
sibling ['sɪblɪŋ] n (formal) fratello/
sorella
Sicily ['sɪsɪlɪ] n Sicilia
sick [sɪk] adj (ill) malato/a; (humour)
macabro/a; **to be ~** (vomiting)
vomitare; **to feel ~** avere la nausea;
to be ~ of (fig) averne abbastanza
di; **sickening** adj (fig) disgustoso/a,
rivoltante; **sick leave** n congedo per
malattia; **sickly** adj malaticcio/a;
(causing nausea) nauseante; **sickness**
n malattia; (vomiting) vomito
side [saɪd] n lato; (of lake) riva; (team)
squadra ▷ cpd (door, entrance) laterale
▷ vi: **to ~ with sb** parteggiare per
qn, prendere le parti di qn; **by the
~ of** a fianco di; (road) sul ciglio di;
~ by ~ fianco a fianco; **to take ~s
(with)** schierarsi (con); **from ~ to ~**
da una parte all'altra; **sideboard** n
credenza; **sideboards** ['saɪdbɔ:dz],
(US) **sideburns** ['saɪdbə:nz] npl
(whiskers) basette fpl; **sidelight** n
(Aut) luce f di posizione; **sideline** n
(Sport) linea laterale; (fig) attività
secondaria; **side order** n contorno
(pietanza); **side road** n strada
secondaria; **side street** n traversa;
sidetrack vt (fig) distrarre; **sidewalk**
n (US) marciapiede m; **sideways** adv
(move) di lato, di fianco
siege [si:dʒ] n assedio
sieve [sɪv] n setaccio ▷ vt setacciare
sift [sɪft] vt passare al crivello; (fig)
vagliare
sigh [saɪ] n sospiro ▷ vi sospirare

sight [saɪt] n (faculty) vista; (spectacle)
spettacolo; (on gun) mira ▷ vt
avvistare; **in ~** in vista; **on ~** a vista;
out of ~ non visibile; **sightseeing**
n giro turistico; **to go sightseeing**
visitare una località
sign [saɪn] n segno; (with hand etc)
segno, gesto; (notice) insegna, cartello
▷ vt firmare; (player) ingaggiare; **as
a ~ of** in segno di; **it's a good/bad ~**
è buon/brutto segno; **to show ~s/
no ~ of doing sth** accennare/non
accennare a fare qc; **plus/minus
~** segno del più/meno; **to ~ one's
name** firmare, apporre la propria
firma; **sign for** vt fus (item) firmare per
l'accettazione di; **sign in** vi firmare il
registro (all'arrivo); **sign on** vi (Mil etc)
arruolarsi; (as unemployed) iscriversi
sulla lista (dell'ufficio di collocamento)
▷ vt (Mil) arruolare; (employee)
assumere; **sign up** (Mil) vt (player)
ingaggiare; (recruits) reclutare ▷ vi
arruolarsi; (for course) iscriversi
signal ['sɪgnl] n segnale m ▷ vt
(person) fare segno a; (message)
comunicare per mezzo di segnali ▷ vi
(Aut) segnalare, mettere la freccia; **to
~ to sb (to do sth)** far segno a qn (di
fare qc); **to ~ a left/right turn**
signature ['sɪgnətʃəʳ] n firma
significance [sɪg'nɪfɪkəns] n
significato; (of event) importanza
significant [sɪg'nɪfɪkənt] adj
significativo/a
signify ['sɪgnɪfaɪ] vt significare
sign language n linguaggio dei muti
signpost ['saɪnpəust] n cartello
indicatore
Sikh [si:k] adj, n sikh mf inv
silence ['saɪlns] n silenzio ▷ vt far
tacere, ridurre al silenzio
silent ['saɪlnt] adj silenzioso/a; (film)
muto/a; **to keep** or **remain ~** tacere,
stare zitto/a
silhouette [sɪlu:'ɛt] n silhouette f inv
silicon chip ['sɪlɪkən-] n chip m inv
(al silicio)

silk [sɪlk] n seta ▷ cpd di seta
silly ['sɪlɪ] adj stupido/a, sciocco/a
silver ['sɪlvəʳ] n argento; (money) monete da 5, 10, 20 o 50 pence; (also: ~ware) argenteria ▷ cpd d'argento; **silver-plated** adj argentato/a
SIM card ['sɪm-] n (Tel) SIM card f inv
similar ['sɪmɪləʳ] adj: ~ (to) simile (a); **similarity** [sɪmɪ'lærɪtɪ] n somiglianza, rassomiglianza; **similarly** adv allo stesso modo; (as is similar) così pure
simmer ['sɪməʳ] vi cuocere a fuoco lento
simple ['sɪmpl] adj semplice; **simplicity** [sɪm'plɪsɪtɪ] n semplicità; **simplify** vt semplificare; **simply** adv semplicemente
simulate ['sɪmjuleɪt] vt fingere, simulare
simultaneous [sɪməl'teɪnɪəs] adj simultaneo/a; **simultaneously** adv simultaneamente, contemporaneamente
sin [sɪn] n peccato ▷ vi peccare
since [sɪns] adv da allora ▷ prep da ▷ conj (time) da quando; (because) poiché, dato che; ~ **then, ever** ~ da allora
sincere [sɪn'sɪəʳ] adj sincero/a; **sincerely** adv: **Yours sincerely** distinti saluti
sing [sɪŋ] (pt **sang**, pp **sung**) vt, vi cantare
Singapore [sɪŋgə'pɔːʳ] n Singapore f
singer ['sɪŋəʳ] n cantante m/f
singing ['sɪŋɪŋ] n canto
single ['sɪŋgl] adj solo/a, unico/a; (unmarried: man) celibe; (: woman) nubile; (not double) semplice ▷ n (BRIT: also: ~ ticket) biglietto di (sola) andata; (record) 45 giri m inv; **single out** vt scegliere; (distinguish) distinguere; **single bed** n letto a una piazza; **single file** n: **in single file** in fila indiana; **single-handed** adv senza aiuto, da solo/a; **single-minded** adj tenace, risoluto/a;

single parent n ragazzo padre/ ragazza madre; genitore m separato; **single parent family** famiglia monoparentale; **single room** n camera singola; **singles** npl (Tennis) singolo
singular ['sɪŋgjuləʳ] adj singolare ▷ n (Ling) singolare m
sinister ['sɪnɪstəʳ] adj sinistro/a
sink [sɪŋk] (pt **sank**, pp **sunk**) n lavandino, acquaio ▷ vt (ship) (fare) affondare, colare a picco; (foundations) scavare; (piles etc): **to ~ sth into** conficcare qc in ▷ vi affondare, andare a fondo; (ground etc) cedere, avvallarsi; **my heart sank** mi sentii venir meno; **sink in** vi penetrare
sinus ['saɪnəs] n (Anat) seno
sip [sɪp] n sorso ▷ vt sorseggiare
sir [səʳ] n signore m; **S~ John Smith** Sir John Smith; **yes ~** sì, signore
siren ['saɪərn] n sirena
sirloin ['səːlɔɪn] n controfiletto
sister ['sɪstəʳ] n sorella; (nun) suora; (BRIT: nurse) infermiera f caposala inv; **sister-in-law** n cognata
sit [sɪt] (pt, pp **sat**) vi sedere, sedersi; (assembly) essere in seduta; (for painter) posare ▷ vt (exam) sostenere, dare; **sit back** vi (in seat) appoggiarsi allo schienale; **sit down** vi sedersi; **sit on** vt fus (jury, committee) far parte di; **sit up** vi tirarsi su a sedere; (not go to bed) stare alzato/a fino a tardi
sitcom ['sɪtkɔm] n abbr (TV: = situation comedy) sceneggiato a episodi (comico)
site [saɪt] n posto; (also: **building ~**) cantiere m ▷ vt situare
sitting ['sɪtɪŋ] n (of assembly etc) seduta; (in canteen) turno; **sitting room** n soggiorno
situated ['sɪtjueɪtɪd] adj situato/a
situation [sɪtjuˈeɪʃən] n situazione f; (job) lavoro; (location) posizione f; **"~s vacant/wanted"** (BRIT) "offerte/ domande di impiego"

six [sɪks] *num* sei; **sixteen** *num* sedici; **sixteenth** [sɪks'tiːnθ] *num* sedicesimo/a; **sixth** *num* sesto/a; **sixth form** *n* (BRIT) ultimo biennio delle scuole superiori; **sixth-form college** *n* istituto che offre corsi di preparazione all'esame di maturità per ragazzi dai 16 ai 18 anni; **sixtieth** ['sɪkstɪɪθ] *num* sessantesimo/a ▷ *pron* (in series) sessantesimo/a; (fraction) sessantesimo; **sixty** *num* sessanta

size [saɪz] *n* dimensioni *fpl*; (of clothing) taglia, misura; (of shoes) numero; (glue) colla; **sizeable** *adj* considerevole

sizzle ['sɪzl] *vi* sfrigolare

skate [skeɪt] *n* pattino; (fish: pl inv) razza ▷ *vi* pattinare; **skateboard** ['skeɪtbɔːd] *n* skateboard *m inv*; **skateboarding** *n* skateboard *m inv*; **skater** *n* pattinatore/trice; **skating** *n* pattinaggio; **skating rink** *n* pista da pattinaggio

skeleton ['skɛlɪtn] *n* scheletro

skeptical ['skɛptɪkl] (US) *adj* = **sceptical**

sketch [skɛtʃ] *n* (drawing) schizzo, abbozzo; (Theat etc) scenetta comica, sketch *m inv* ▷ *vt* abbozzare, schizzare

skewer ['skjuːəʳ] *n* spiedo

ski [skiː] *n* sci *m inv* ▷ *vi* sciare; **ski boot** *n* scarpone *m* da sci

skid [skɪd] *n* slittamento ▷ *vi* slittare

ski: skier ['skiːəʳ] *n* sciatore/trice; **skiing** ['skiːɪŋ] *n* sci *m*

skilful, (US) **skillful** ['skɪlful] *adj* abile

ski lift *n* sciovia

skill [skɪl] *n* abilità *f inv*, capacità *f inv*; **skilled** *adj* esperto/a; (worker) qualificato/a, specializzato/a

skim [skɪm] *vt* (milk) scremare; (glide over) sfiorare ▷ *vi*: **to ~ through** (fig) scorrere, dare una scorsa a; **skimmed milk**, (US) **skim milk** *n* latte *m* scremato

skin [skɪn] *n* pelle *f* ▷ *vt* (fruit etc) sbucciare; (animal) scuoiare, spellare;

skinhead *n* skinhead *mf inv*; **skinny** *adj* molto magro/a, pelle e ossa *inv*

skip [skɪp] *n* saltello; (BRIT) balzo; (container) benna ▷ *vi* saltare; (with rope) saltare la corda ▷ *vt* saltare

ski: ski pass *n* ski pass *m inv*; **ski pole** *n* racchetta (da sci)

skipper ['skɪpəʳ] *n* (Naut, Sport) capitano

skipping rope ['skɪpɪŋ-], (US) **skip rope** *n* corda per saltare

skirt [skəːt] *n* gonna, sottana ▷ *vt* fiancheggiare, costeggiare

skirting board *n* (BRIT) zoccolo

ski slope *n* pista da sci

ski suit *n* tuta da sci

skull [skʌl] *n* cranio, teschio

skunk [skʌŋk] *n* moffetta

sky [skaɪ] *n* cielo

Skype® [skaɪp] (Internet, Tel) Skype® *m* ▷ *vt*: **to s~ sb** chiamare qn con Skype

skyscraper *n* grattacielo

slab [slæb] *n* lastra; (of meat, cheese) fetta

slack [slæk] *adj* (loose) allentato/a; (slow) lento/a; (careless) negligente; **slacks** *npl* (trousers) pantaloni *mpl*

slain [sleɪn] *pp* of **slay**

slam [slæm] *vt* (door) sbattere; (throw) scaraventare; (criticize) stroncare ▷ *vi* sbattere

slander ['slɑːndəʳ] *n* calunnia; (Law) diffamazione *f*

slang [slæŋ] *n* gergo, slang *m*

slant [slɑːnt] *n* pendenza, inclinazione *f*; (fig) angolazione *f*, punto di vista

slap [slæp] *n* manata, pacca; (on face) schiaffo ▷ *vt* dare una manata a; schiaffeggiare ▷ *adv* (directly) in pieno; **~ a coat of paint on it** dagli una mano di vernice

slash [slæʃ] *vt* tagliare; (face) sfregiare; (fig: prices) ridurre drasticamente, tagliare

slate [sleɪt] *n* ardesia; (piece) lastra di ardesia ▷ *vt* (fig: criticize) stroncare, distruggere

slaughter ['slɔːtəʳ] n strage f, massacro ▷ vt (animal) macellare; (people) trucidare, massacrare; **slaughterhouse** n macello, mattatoio

Slav [slɑːv] adj, n slavo/a

slave [sleɪv] n schiavo/a ▷ vi (also: **~ away**) lavorare come uno schiavo; **slavery** n schiavitù f

slay (pt **slew**, pp **slain**) [sleɪ, sluː, sleɪn] vt (formal) uccidere

sleazy ['sliːzɪ] adj trasandato/a

sled [sled] (US) = **sledge**

sledge [sledʒ] n slitta

sleek [sliːk] adj (hair, fur) lucido/a, lucente; (car, boat) slanciato/a, affusolato/a

sleep [sliːp] n sonno ▷ vi (pt, pp **slept**) dormire; **to go to ~** addormentarsi; **sleep in** vi (oversleep) dormire fino a tardi; **sleep together** vi (have sex) andare a letto insieme; **sleeper** n (BRIT Rail: on track) traversina; (: train) treno di vagoni letto; **sleeping bag** n sacco a pelo; **sleeping car** n vagone m letto inv, carrozza f letto inv; **sleeping pill** n sonnifero; **sleepover** n il dormire a casa di amici, usato in riferimento a bambini; **sleepwalk** vi camminare nel sonno; (as a habit) essere sonnambulo/a; **sleepy** adj assonnato/a, sonnolento/a; (fig) addormentato/a

sleet [sliːt] n nevischio

sleeve [sliːv] n manica; (of record) copertina; **sleeveless** adj (garment) senza maniche

sleigh [sleɪ] n slitta

slender ['slɛndəʳ] adj snello/a, sottile; (not enough) scarso/a, esiguo/a

slept [slɛpt] pt, pp of **sleep**

slew [sluː] vi (BRIT: also: **~ round**) girare ▷ pt of **slay**

slice [slaɪs] n fetta ▷ vt affettare, tagliare a fette

slick [slɪk] adj (skilful) brillante ▷ n (also: **oil ~**) chiazza di petrolio

slide [slaɪd] n scivolone m; (in playground) scivolo; (Phot) diapositiva; (also: **hair ~**) fermaglio (per capelli) ▷ vt (pt, pp **slid** [slɪd]) far scivolare ▷ vi (pt, pp **slid** [slɪd]) scivolare; **sliding** adj (door) scorrevole

slight [slaɪt] adj (slim) snello/a, sottile; (frail) delicato/a, fragile; (trivial) insignificante; (small) piccolo/a ▷ n offesa, affronto; **not in the ~est** affatto, neppure per sogno; **slightly** adv lievemente, un po'

slim [slɪm] adj magro/a, snello/a ▷ vi dimagrire; fare or seguire) una dieta dimagrante; **slimming** ['slɪmɪŋ] adj (diet, pills) dimagrante; (food) ipocalorico/a

slimy ['slaɪmɪ] adj (also fig: person) viscido/a; (covered with mud) melmoso/a

sling [slɪŋ] n (Med) fascia al collo; (for baby) marsupio ▷ vt (pt, pp **slung** [slʌŋ]) lanciare, tirare

slip [slɪp] n scivolata, scivolone m; (mistake) errore m, sbaglio; (underskirt) sottoveste f; (paper) foglietto; tagliando, scontrino ▷ vt (slide) far scivolare ▷ vi (slide) scivolare; (decline) declinare; **to ~ into/out of** (move smoothly) scivolare in/fuori da; **to give sb the ~** sfuggire qn; **a ~ of paper** un foglietto; **a ~ of the tongue** un lapsus linguae; **slip up** vi sbagliarsi

slipper ['slɪpəʳ] n pantofola

slippery ['slɪpərɪ] adj scivoloso/a

slip road n (BRIT: to motorway) rampa di accesso

slit [slɪt] n fessura, fenditura; (cut) taglio ▷ vt (pt, pp **slit**) fendere; tagliare

slog [slɔg] (BRIT) n faticata ▷ vi lavorare con accanimento, sgobbare

slogan ['sləugən] n motto, slogan m inv

slope [sləup] n pendio; (side of mountain) versante m; (ski slope)

sloppy | 520

pista; (of roof) pendenza; (of floor) inclinazione f ▷ vi: **to ~ down** declinare; **to ~ up** essere in salita; **sloping** adj inclinato/a

sloppy ['slɔpɪ] adj (work) tirato/a via; (appearance) sciatto/a

slot [slɔt] n fessura ▷ vt: **to ~ into** infilare in; **slot machine** n (BRIT: vending machine) distributore m automatico; (for amusement) slot-machine f inv

Slovakia [sləu'vækɪə] n Slovacchia

Slovene ['sləuvi:n] adj sloveno/a ▷ n sloveno/a; (Ling) sloveno

Slovenia [sləu'vi:nɪə] n Slovenia; **Slovenian** adj, n = **Slovene**

slow [sləu] adj lento/a; (watch): **to be ~** essere indietro ▷ adv lentamente ▷ vt, vi (also: **~ down, ~ up**) rallentare; **"~"** (road sign) "rallentare"; **slowly** adv lentamente; **slow motion** n: **in slow motion** al rallentatore

slug [slʌg] n lumaca; (bullet) pallottola; **sluggish** adj lento/a; (business, market, sales) stagnante

slum [slʌm] n catapecchia

slump [slʌmp] n crollo, caduta; (economic) depressione f, crisi f inv ▷ vi crollare

slung [slʌŋ] pt, pp of **sling**

slur [sləː] n (smear): **~ (on)** macchia (su) ▷ vt pronunciare in modo indistinto

sly [slaɪ] adj (smile, remark) sornione/a; (person) furbo/a

smack [smæk] n (slap) pacca; (on face) schiaffo ▷ vt schiaffeggiare; (child) picchiare ▷ vi: **to ~ of** puzzare di

small [smɔːl] adj piccolo/a; **small ads** npl (BRIT) piccoli annunci mpl; **small change** n moneta, spiccioli mpl

smart [smɑːt] adj elegante; (fashionable) alla moda; (clever) intelligente; (quick) sveglio/a ▷ vi bruciare; **smartcard** n smartcard f inv, carta intelligente; **smartphone** n smartphone m inv

smash [smæʃ] n (also: **~-up**) scontro, collisione f; (smash hit) successone m ▷ vt frantumare, fracassare; (Sport: record) battere ▷ vi frantumarsi, andare in pezzi; **smashing** adj (col) favoloso/a, formidabile

smear [smɪə'] n macchia; (Med) striscio ▷ vt ungere; (make dirty) sporcare; (fig) denigrare, diffamare; **his hands were ~ed with oil/ink** aveva le mani sporche di olio/inchiostro; **smear test** n (BRIT Med) Pap-test m inv

smell (pt, pp **smelt** or **smelled**) [smɛl, smɛlt, smɛld] n odore m; (sense) olfatto, odorato ▷ vt sentire (l')odore di ▷ vi (food etc): **to ~ (of)** avere odore (di); (pej) puzzare, avere un cattivo odore; **smelly** adj puzzolente

smelt [smɛlt] pt, pp of **smell** ▷ vt (ore) fondere

smile [smaɪl] n sorriso ▷ vi sorridere

smirk [sməːk] n sorriso furbo; sorriso compiaciuto

smog [smɔg] n smog m

smoke [sməuk] n fumo ▷ vt, vi fumare; **smoke alarm** n rivelatore f di fumo; **smoked** adj (bacon, glass) affumicato/a; **smoker** n (person) fumatore/trice; (Rail) carrozza per fumatori; **smoking** n fumo; **"no smoking"** (sign) "vietato fumare"; **smoky** adj fumoso/a; (taste, surface) affumicato/a

smooth [smuːð] adj liscio/a; (sauce) omogeneo/a; (flavour, whisky) amabile; (movement) regolare; (person) mellifluo/a ▷ vt lisciare, spianare; (also: **~ out**) (difficulties) appianare

smother ['smʌðə'] vt soffocare

SMS n abbr (= short message service) SMS m; **SMS message** n SMS m inv, messaggino

smudge [smʌdʒ] n macchia; sbavatura ▷ vt imbrattare, sporcare

smug [smʌg] adj soddisfatto/a, compiaciuto/a

smuggle ['smʌgl] vt
contrabbandare; **smuggling** n
contrabbando

snack [snæk] n spuntino; **snack bar**
n tavola calda, snack bar m inv

snag [snæg] n intoppo, ostacolo
imprevisto

snail [sneɪl] n chiocciola

snake [sneɪk] n serpente m

snap [snæp] n (sound) schianto, colpo
secco; (photograph) istantanea ▷ adj
improvviso/a ▷ vt (far) schioccare;
(break) spezzare di netto ▷ vi spezzarsi
con un rumore secco; (fig: person)
crollare; **to ~ at sb** (dog) cercare di
mordere qn; **to ~ open/shut** aprirsi/
chiudersi di scatto; **snap up** vt
afferrare; **snapshot** n istantanea

snarl [snɑ:l] vi ringhiare

snatch [snætʃ] n (small amount): **~es
of** frammenti mpl di ▷ vt strappare
(con violenza); (steal) rubare

sneak [sni:k] ((us) pt **snuck**) vi:
to ~ in/out entrare/uscire di
nascosto ▷ n spione/a; **to ~ up on
sb** avvicinarsi quatto quatto a qn;
sneakers npl scarpe fpl da ginnastica

sneer [snɪər] vi sogghignare; **to ~ at
sb/sth** farsi beffe di qn/qc

sneeze [sni:z] n starnuto ▷ vi
starnutire

sniff [snɪf] n fiutata, annusata
▷ vi tirare su col naso ▷ vt fiutare,
annusare

snigger ['snɪgər] vi ridacchiare, ridere
sotto i baffi

snip [snɪp] n pezzetto; (bargain)
(buon) affare m, occasione f ▷ vt
tagliare

sniper ['snaɪpər] n (marksman) franco
tiratore m, cecchino

snob [snɔb] n snob mf inv

snooker ['snu:kər] n tipo di gioco
del biliardo

snoop [snu:p] vi: **to ~ about**
curiosare

snooze [snu:z] n sonnellino, pisolino
▷ vi fare un sonnellino

snore [snɔ:r] vi russare

snorkel ['snɔ:kl] n (of swimmer)
respiratore m a tubo

snort [snɔ:t] n sbuffo ▷ vi sbuffare

snow [snəu] n neve f ▷ vi nevicare;
snowball n palla di neve ▷ vi (fig)
crescere a vista d'occhio; **snowstorm**
n tormenta

snub [snʌb] vt snobbare ▷ n offesa,
affronto

snug [snʌg] adj comodo/a; (room,
house) accogliente, comodo/a

○ **KEYWORD**

so [səu] adv **1** (thus, likewise) così; **if
so** se è così, quand'è così; **I didn't
do it — you did so!** non l'ho fatto io
— sì che l'hai fatto!; **so do I, so am I**
anch'io; **it's 5 o'clock — so it is!** sono
le 5 — davvero!; **I hope so** lo spero; **I
think so** penso di sì; **so far** finora, fin
qui; (in past) fino ad allora
2 (in comparisons etc: to such a degree)
così; **so big (that)** così grande (che);
she's not as clever as her brother
lei non è (così) intelligente come
suo fratello
3: **so much** adj tanto/a; adv tanto;
I've got so much work/money ho
tanto lavoro/tanti soldi; **I love you so
much** ti amo tanto; **so many** tanti/e
4 (phrases): **10 or so** circa 10; **so long!**
(col) (goodbye) ciao!, ci vediamo!
▷ conj **1** (expressing purpose): **so as
to do** in modo or così da fare; **we
hurried so as not to be late** ci
affrettammo per non fare tardi; **so
(that)** affinché + sub, perché + sub
2 (expressing result): **he didn't arrive
so I left** non è venuto così me ne sono
andata; **so you see, I could have
gone** vedi, sarei potuto andare

soak [səuk] vt inzuppare; (clothes)
mettere a mollo ▷ vi (clothes) essere a
mollo; **soak up** vt assorbire; **soaking**
adj (also: **soaking wet**) fradicio/a

S

so-and-so ['səʊənsəʊ] n (somebody) un tale; **Mr/Mrs ~** signor/signora tal dei tali

soap [səʊp] n sapone m; **soap opera** n soap opera f inv; **soap powder** n detersivo

soar [sɔːʳ] vi volare in alto; (price, morale, spirits) salire alle stelle; (building) ergersi

sob [sɔb] n singhiozzo ▷ vi singhiozzare

sober ['səʊbəʳ] adj non ubriaco/a; (moderate) moderato/a; (colour, style) sobrio/a; **sober up** vt far passare la sbornia a ▷ vi farsi passare la sbornia

so-called ['səʊ'kɔːld] adj cosiddetto/a

soccer ['sɔkəʳ] n calcio

sociable ['səʊʃəbl] adj socievole

social ['səʊʃl] adj sociale ▷ n festa, serata; **socialism** n socialismo; **socialist** adj, n socialista m/f; **socialize** vi: **to socialize with** socializzare con; **social life** n vita sociale; **socially** adv socialmente, in società; **social media** npl social media mpl; **social network** n social network m inv; **social networking** n il comunicare tramite social network; **social networking site** n social network m; **social security** n previdenza sociale; **social services** npl servizi mpl sociali; **social work** n servizio sociale; **social worker** n assistente m/f sociale

society [sə'saɪətɪ] n società f inv; (club) società, associazione f; (also: **high ~**) alta società

sociology [səʊsɪ'ɒlədʒɪ] n sociologia

sock [sɔk] n calzino

socket ['sɔkɪt] n cavità f inv; (of eye) orbita; (BRIT Elec: also: **wall ~**) presa di corrente

soda ['səʊdə] n (Chem) soda; (also: **~ water**) acqua di seltz; (US: also: **~ pop**) gassosa

sodium ['səʊdɪəm] n sodio

sofa ['səʊfə] n sofà m inv; **sofa bed** n divano m letto inv

soft [sɔft] adj (not rough) morbido/a; (not hard) soffice; (not loud) sommesso/a; (not bright) tenue; (kind) gentile; **soft drink** n analcolico; **soft drugs** npl droghe fpl leggere; **soften** ['sɔfn] vt ammorbidire; addolcire; attenuare ▷ vi ammorbidirsi; addolcirsi; attenuarsi; **softly** adv dolcemente; morbidamente; **software** ['sɔftwɛəʳ] n (Comput) software m

soggy ['sɔgɪ] adj inzuppato/a

soil [sɔɪl] n terreno ▷ vt sporcare

solar ['səʊləʳ] adj solare; **solar power** n energia solare; **solar system** n sistema m solare

sold [səʊld] pt, pp of **sell**

soldier ['səʊldʒəʳ] n soldato, militare m

sold out adj (Comm) esaurito/a

sole [səʊl] n (of foot) pianta (del piede); (of shoe) suola; (fish: pl inv) sogliola ▷ adj solo/a, unico/a; **solely** adv solamente, unicamente; **I will hold you solely responsible** la considererò il solo responsabile

solemn ['sɔləm] adj solenne

solicitor [sə'lɪsɪtəʳ] n (BRIT: for wills etc) ≈ notaio; (in court) ≈ avvocato

solid ['sɔlɪd] adj (not hollow) pieno/a; (strong, sound, reliable, not liquid) solido/a; (meal) sostanzioso/a ▷ n solido

solitary ['sɔlɪtərɪ] adj solitario/a

solitude ['sɔlɪtjuːd] n solitudine f

solo ['səʊləʊ] n assolo; **soloist** n solista m/f

soluble ['sɔljubl] adj solubile

solution [sə'luːʃən] n soluzione f

solve [sɔlv] vt risolvere

solvent ['sɔlvənt] adj (Comm) solvibile ▷ n (Chem) solvente m

sombre, (US) **somber** ['sɔmbəʳ] adj scuro/a; (mood, person) triste

 KEYWORD

some [sʌm] adj 1 (a certain amount or number of): **some tea/water/cream**

del tè/dell'acqua/della panna; **some children/apples** dei bambini/ delle mele

2 (*certain: in contrasts*) certo/a; **some people say that ...** alcuni dicono che ..., certa gente dice che ...

3 (*unspecified*) un/a certo/a, qualche; **some woman was asking for you** una tale chiedeva di lei; **some day** un giorno; **some day next week** un giorno della prossima settimana

▶ *pron* **1** (*a certain number*) alcuni/e, certi/e; **I've got some** (*books etc*) ne ho alcuni; **some (of them) have been sold** alcuni sono stati venduti

2 (*a certain amount*) un po'; **I've got some** (*money, milk*) ne ho un po'; **I've read some of the book** ho letto parte del libro

▶ *adv*: **some 10 people** circa 10 persone

somebody ['sʌmbədɪ] *pron* qualcuno
somehow ['sʌmhaʊ] *adv* in un modo o nell'altro, in qualche modo; (*for some reason*) per qualche ragione
someone ['sʌmwʌn] *pron*
  = **somebody**
someplace ['sʌmpleɪs] *adv* (*us*)
  = **somewhere**
something ['sʌmθɪŋ] *pron* qualcosa, qualche cosa; **~ nice** qualcosa di bello; **~ to do** qualcosa da fare
sometime ['sʌmtaɪm] *adv* (*in future*) una volta o l'altra; (*in past*): **~ last month** durante il mese scorso; **sometimes** *adv* qualche volta
somewhat ['sʌmwɔt] *adv* piuttosto
somewhere ['sʌmwɛə'] *adv* in *or* da qualche parte
son [sʌn] *n* figlio
song [sɒŋ] *n* canzone *f*
son-in-law ['sʌnɪnlɔ:] *n* genero
soon [su:n] *adv* presto, fra poco; (*early*) presto; **~ afterwards** poco dopo; **as ~ as possible** prima possibile; **sooner** *adv* (*time*) prima; (*preference*): **I would sooner do**

preferirei fare; **sooner or later** prima o poi
soothe [su:ð] *vt* calmare
sophisticated [sə'fɪstɪkeɪtɪd] *adj* sofisticato/a; raffinato/a; complesso/a
sophomore ['sɒfəmɔ:'] *n* (*us*) studente/essa del secondo anno
soprano [sə'prɑ:nəʊ] *n* (*voice*) soprano *m*; (*singer*) soprano *m/f*
sorbet ['sɔ:beɪ] *n* sorbetto
sordid ['sɔ:dɪd] *adj* sordido/a
sore [sɔ:'] *adj* (*painful*) dolorante
  ▶ *n* piaga
sorrow ['sɒrəʊ] *n* dolore *m*
sorry ['sɒrɪ] *adj* spiacente; (*condition, excuse*) misero/a; **~!** scusa! (*or* scusi! *or* scusate!); **to feel ~ for sb** rincrescersi per qn
sort [sɔ:t] *n* specie *f*, genere *m* ▶ *vt* (*also: ~ **out***) (*papers*) classificare; ordinare; (*letters etc*) smistare; (*problems*) risolvere; (*Comput*) ordinare
SOS *n* S.O.S. *m inv*
so-so ['səʊsəʊ] *adv* così così
sought [sɔ:t] *pt, pp of* **seek**
soul [səʊl] *n* anima
sound [saʊnd] *adj* (*healthy*) sano/a; (*safe, not damaged*) solido/a, in buono stato; (*reliable, not superficial*) solido/a; (*sensible*) giudizioso/a, di buon senso ▶ *adv*: **~ asleep** profondamente addormentato ▶ *n* (*noise*) suono, rumore *m*; (*Geo*) stretto ▶ *vt* (*alarm*) suonare ▶ *vi* suonare; (*fig: seem*) sembrare; **to ~ like** rassomigliare a; **soundtrack** *n* (*of film*) colonna sonora
soup [su:p] *n* minestra; (*clear*) brodo; (*thick*) zuppa
sour ['saʊə'] *adj* aspro/a; (*fruit*) acerbo/a; (*milk*) acido/a; (*fig*) arcigno/a, acido/a; **it's ~ grapes** è soltanto invidia
source [sɔ:s] *n* fonte *f*, sorgente *f*; (*fig*) fonte
south [saʊθ] *n* sud *m*, meridione *m*, mezzogiorno ▶ *adj* del sud,

S

sud *inv*, meridionale ▷ *adv* verso sud; **South Africa** *n* Sudafrica *m*; **South African** *adj*, *n* sudafricano/a; **South America** *n* Sudamerica *m*, America del sud; **South American** *adj*, *n* sudamericano/a; **southbound** ['sauθbaund] *adj* (*gen*) diretto/a a sud; (*carriageway*) sud *inv*; **southeastern** [sauθ'i:stən] *adj* sudorientale; **southern** ['sʌðən] *adj* del sud, meridionale; (*wall*) esposto/a a sud; **South Korea** *n* Corea *f* del Sud; **South Pole** *n* Polo Sud; **southward(s)** *adv* verso sud; **southwest** *n* sud-ovest *m*; **southwestern** [sauθ'westən] *adj* sudoccidentale

souvenir [su:və'nɪər] *n* ricordo, souvenir *m inv*

sovereign ['sɔvrɪn] *adj*, *n* sovrano/a

sow¹ [sau] (*pt* **sowed**, *pp* **sown**) *vt* seminare

sow² [sau] *n* scrofa

soya ['sɔɪə], (*us*) **soy** *n*: **~ bean** seme *m* di soia; **~ sauce** salsa di soia

spa [spa:] *n* (*resort*) stazione *f* termale; (*us*: *also*: **health ~**) centro di cure estetiche

space [speɪs] *n* spazio; (*room*) posto; spazio; (*length of time*) intervallo ▷ *cpd* spaziale ▷ *vt* (*also*: **~ out**) distanziare; **spacecraft** *n* (*pl inv*) veicolo spaziale; **spaceship** *n* astronave *f*, navicella spaziale

spacious ['speɪʃəs] *adj* spazioso/a, ampio/a

spade [speɪd] *n* (*tool*) vanga; pala; (*child's*) paletta; **spades** *npl* (*Cards*) picche *fpl*

spaghetti [spə'gɛtɪ] *n* spaghetti *mpl*

Spain [speɪn] *n* Spagna

spam [spæm] (*Comput*) *n* spamming *m* ▷ *vt*: **to ~ sb** inviare a qn messaggi pubblicitari non richiesti via email

span [spæn] *n* (*of bird, plane*) apertura alare; (*of arch*) campata; (*in time*) periodo; durata ▷ *vt* attraversare; (*fig*) abbracciare

Spaniard ['spænjəd] *n* spagnolo/a

Spanish ['spænɪʃ] *adj* spagnolo/a ▷ *n* (*Ling*) spagnolo; **the ~** *n pl* gli Spagnoli

spank [spæŋk] *vt* sculacciare

spanner ['spænər] *n* (*BRIT*) chiave *f* inglese

spare [speər] *adj* di riserva, di scorta; (*surplus*) in più, d'avanzo ▷ *n* (*part*) pezzo di ricambio ▷ *vt* (*do without*) fare a meno di; (*afford to give*) concedere; (*refrain from hurting, using*) risparmiare; **to ~** (*surplus*) d'avanzo; **spare part** *n* pezzo di ricambio; **spare room** *n* stanza degli ospiti; **spare time** *n* tempo libero; **spare tyre**, (*us*) **spare tire** *n* (*Aut*) gomma di scorta; **spare wheel** *n* (*Aut*) ruota di scorta

spark [spa:k] *n* scintilla

sparkle ['spa:kl] *n* scintillio, sfavillio ▷ *vi* scintillare, sfavillare

Spark plug *n* candela

sparrow ['spærəu] *n* passero

sparse [spa:s] *adj* sparso/a, rado/a

spasm ['spæzəm] *n* (*Med*) spasmo; (*fig*) accesso, attacco

spat [spæt] *pt*, *pp* of **spit**

spate [speɪt] *n* (*fig*): **~ of** diluvio *or* fiume *m* di

spatula ['spætjulə] *n* spatola

speak (*pt* **spoke**, *pp* **spoken**) [spi:k, spəuk, 'spəukn] *vt* (*language*) parlare; (*truth*) dire ▷ *vi* parlare; **to ~ to sb/of** *or* **about sth** parlare a qn/ di qc; **~ up!** parli più forte!; **speaker** *n* (*in public*) oratore/trice; (*also*: **loudspeaker**) altoparlante *m*; (*Pol*): **the Speaker** il presidente della Camera dei Comuni *or* (*US*) dei Rappresentanti

spear [spɪər] *n* lancia ▷ *vt* infilzare

special ['spɛʃl] *adj* speciale; **special delivery** *n* (*Post*): **by special delivery** per espresso; **special effects** *npl* (*Cine*) effetti *mpl* speciali; **specialist** *n* specialista *m/f*; **speciality** [spɛʃɪ'ælɪtɪ] *n* specialità *f inv*; **specialize** *vi*: **to specialize (in)** specializzarsi (in); **specially** *adv* specialmente, particolarmente; **special needs** adj: **special needs children** bambini mpl con difficoltà di apprendimento; **special offer** n (Comm) offerta speciale; **special school** n (BRIT) scuola speciale (per portatori di handicap); **specialty** n (esp US) = **speciality**

species ['spi:ʃi:z] n (pl inv) specie f inv

specific [spə'sɪfɪk] adj specifico/a; preciso/a; **specifically** adv esplicitamente; (especially) appositamente

specify ['spɛsɪfaɪ] vt specificare, precisare; **unless otherwise specified** salvo indicazioni contrarie

specimen ['spɛsɪmən] n esemplare m, modello; (Med) campione m

speck [spɛk] n puntino, macchiolina; (particle) granello

spectacle ['spɛktəkl] n spettacolo; **spectacles** npl occhiali mpl; **spectacular** [spɛk'tækjulər] adj spettacolare

spectator [spɛk'teɪtər] n spettatore/trice

spectrum (pl **spectra**) ['spɛktrəm, -rə] n spettro

speculate ['spɛkjuleɪt] vi speculare; (try to guess): **to ~ about** fare ipotesi su

sped [spɛd] pt, pp of **speed**

speech [spi:tʃ] n (faculty) parola; (talk, Theat) discorso; (manner of speaking) parlata; (explain): **speechless** adj ammutolito/a, muto/a

speed [spi:d] n velocità f inv; (promptness) prontezza; **at full** or **top ~** a tutta velocità; **speed up** vi, vt accelerare; **speedboat** n motoscafo; **speeding** n (Aut) eccesso di velocità; **speed limit** n limite m di velocità; **speedometer** [spɪ'dɔmɪtər] n tachimetro; **speedy** adj veloce, rapido/a; (reply) pronto/a

spell [spɛl] n (also: **magic ~**) incantesimo; (period of time) (breve) periodo ▷ vt (pt, pp **spelt** or **spelled**)

(in writing) scrivere (lettera per lettera); (aloud) dire lettera per lettera; (fig) significare; (explain): **to ~ sth out for sb** spiegare qc a qn per filo e per segno; **spellchecker** ['spɛltʃekər] n correttore m ortografico; **spelling** n ortografia

spelt [spɛlt] pt, pp of **spell**

spend (pt, pp **spent**) [spɛnd, spɛnt] vt (money) spendere; (time, life) passare; **spending** ['spɛndɪŋ] n: **government spending** spesa pubblica

spent [spɛnt] pt, pp of **spend**

sperm [spə:m] n sperma m

sphere [sfɪər] n sfera

spice [spaɪs] n spezia ▷ vt aromatizzare

spicy ['spaɪsɪ] adj piccante

spider ['spaɪdər] n ragno

spike [spaɪk] n punta

spill (pt, pp **spilt** or **spilled**) [spɪl, -t, -d] vt versare, rovesciare ▷ vi versarsi, rovesciarsi

spin [spɪn] (pt, pp **spun**) n (revolution of wheel) rotazione f; (Aviat) avvitamento; (trip in car) giretto ▷ vt (wool etc) filare; (wheel) far girare ▷ vi girare

spinach ['spɪnɪtʃ] n spinacio; (as food) spinaci mpl

spinal ['spaɪnl] adj spinale

spin doctor n (col) esperto di comunicazioni responsabile dell'immagine di un partito politico

spin-dryer [spɪn'draɪər] n (BRIT) centrifuga

spine [spaɪn] n spina dorsale; (thorn) spina

spiral ['spaɪərl] n spirale f ▷ vi (prices) salire vertiginosamente

spire ['spaɪər] n guglia

spirit ['spɪrɪt] n spirito; (ghost) spirito, fantasma m; (mood) stato d'animo,

umore m; (courage) coraggio; **spirits**
npl (drink) alcolici mpl; **in good ~s** di
buon umore
spiritual ['spɪrɪtjuəl] adj spirituale
spit [spɪt] n (for roasting) spiedo;
(spittle) sputo; (saliva) saliva ▷ vi (pt,
pp **spat** [spæt]) sputare; (fire, fat)
scoppiettare
spite [spaɪt] n dispetto ▷ vt
contrariare, far dispetto a; **in ~ of**
nonostante, malgrado; **spiteful** adj
dispettoso/a
splash [splæʃ] n spruzzo; (sound)
tonfo; (of colour) schizzo ▷ vt
spruzzare ▷ vi (also: **~ about**)
sguazzare; **splash out** (col) vi (BRIT)
fare spese folli
splendid ['splɛndɪd] adj splendido/a,
magnifico/a
splinter ['splɪntəʳ] n scheggia ▷ vi
scheggiarsi
split [splɪt] (pt, pp **split**) n spaccatura;
(fig: division, quarrel) scissione f ▷ vt
spaccare; (party) dividere; (work,
profits) spartire, ripartire ▷ vi
(divide) dividersi; **split up** vi (couple)
separarsi, rompere; (meeting)
sciogliersi
spoil (pt, pp **spoilt** or **spoiled**) [spɔɪl,
-t, -d] vt (damage) rovinare, guastare;
(mar) sciupare; (child) viziare
spoilt [spɔɪlt] pt, pp of **spoil**
spoke [spəuk] pt of **speak** ▷ n raggio
spoken ['spəukn] pp of **speak**
spokesman ['spəuksmən] n (irreg)
portavoce m inv
spokesperson ['spəukspə:sn] n
portavoce m/f
spokeswoman ['spəukswumən] n
(irreg) portavoce f inv
sponge [spʌndʒ] n spugna; (also:
~ cake) pan m di Spagna ▷ vt
spugnare, pulire con una spugna ▷ vi:
to ~ on or **off** scroccare a; **sponge
bag** n (BRIT) nécessaire m inv
sponsor ['spɔnsəʳ] n (Radio, TV, Sport
etc) sponsor m inv; (of enterprise, bill)
promotore/trice ▷ vt sponsorizzare;

(bill) presentare; **sponsorship** n
sponsorizzazione f
spontaneous [spɔn'teɪnɪəs] adj
spontaneo/a
spooky ['spu:kɪ] adj (col) che fa
accapponare la pelle
spoon [spu:n] n cucchiaio; **spoonful**
n cucchiaiata
sport [spɔ:t] n sport m inv; (person)
persona di spirito ▷ vt sfoggiare;
sport jacket n (US) = **sports jacket**;
sports car n automobile f sportiva;
sports centre n (BRIT) centro
sportivo; **sports jacket** n (BRIT)
giacca sportiva; **sportsman** n (irreg)
sportivo; **sportswear** n abiti mpl
sportivi; **sportswoman** n (irreg)
sportiva; **sporty** adj sportivo/a
spot [spɔt] n punto; (mark) macchia;
(dot: on pattern) pallino; (pimple)
foruncolo; (place) posto; (Radio,
TV) spot m inv; (small amount):
a ~ of un po' di ▷ vt (notice)
individuare, distinguere; **on the
~** sul posto; **to do sth on the ~**
fare qc immediatamente or su
due piedi; **to put sb on the ~**
mettere qn in difficoltà; **spotless**
adj immacolato/a; **spotlight** n
proiettore m; (Aut) faro ausiliario
spouse [spauz] n sposo/a
sprain [spreɪn] n storta, distorsione
f ▷ vt: **to ~ one's ankle** storcersi
una caviglia
sprang [spræŋ] pt of **spring**
sprawl [sprɔ:l] vi sdraiarsi (in modo
scomposto); (place) estendersi
(disordinatamente)
spray [spreɪ] n spruzzo; (container)
nebulizzatore m, spray m inv; (of
flowers) mazzetto ▷ vt spruzzare;
(crops) irrorare
spread [sprɛd] (pt, pp **spread**) n
diffusione f; (distribution) distribuzione
f; (Culin) pasta (da spalmare); (col:
food) banchetto ▷ vt (cloth) stendere,
distendere; (butter etc) spalmare;
(disease, knowledge) propagare,

diffondere ▷ vi stenderi, distendersi; spalmarsi; propagarsi, diffondersi; **spread out** vi (move apart) separarsi; **spreadsheet** n foglio elettronico

spree [spriː] n: **to go on a ~** fare baldoria

spring [sprɪŋ] n (leap) salto, balzo; (coiled metal) molla; (season) primavera; (of water) sorgente f ▷ vi (pt **sprang**, pp **sprung**) saltare, balzare; **spring up** vi (problem) presentarsi; **spring onion** n (BRIT) cipollina

sprinkle ['sprɪŋkl] vt spruzzare; spargere; **to ~ water on, ~ with water** etc spruzzare dell'acqua etc su

sprint [sprɪnt] n scatto ▷ vi scattare

sprung [sprʌŋ] pp of **spring**

spun [spʌn] pt, pp of **spin**

spur [spəː] n sperone m; (fig) sprone m, incentivo ▷ vt (also: **~ on**) spronare; **on the ~ of the moment** lì per lì

spurt [spəːt] n (of water) getto; (of energy) esplosione f ▷ vi sgorgare

spy [spaɪ] n spia ▷ vi: **to ~ on** spiare ▷ vt (see) scorgere

sq. abbr = **square**

squabble ['skwɔbl] vi bisticciarsi

squad [skwɔd] n (Mil) plotone m; (Police) squadra

squadron ['skwɔdrn] n (Mil) squadrone m; (Aviat, Naut) squadriglia

squander ['skwɔndə] vt dissipare

square [skwɛə] n quadrato; (in town) piazza ▷ adj quadrato/a; (col: ideas, person) di vecchio stampo ▷ vt (arrange) regolare; (Math) elevare al quadrato; (reconcile) conciliare; **a ~ meal** un pasto abbondante; **2 metres ~** di 2 metri per 2; **1 ~ metre** 1 metro quadrato; **all ~** pari; **square root** n radice f quadrata

squash [skwɔʃ] n (vegetable) zucca; (Sport) squash m; **lemon/orange ~** (BRIT) sciroppo di limone/arancia ▷ vt schiacciare

squat [skwɔt] adj tarchiato/a, tozzo/a ▷ vi accovacciarsi; **squatter** n occupante m/f abusivo/a

squeak [skwiːk] vi squittire

squeal [skwiːl] vi strillare

squeeze [skwiːz] n pressione f; (also Econ) stretta ▷ vt premere; (hand, arm) stringere

squid [skwɪd] n calamaro

squint [skwɪnt] vi essere strabico/a ▷ n: **he has a ~** è strabico

squirm [skwəːm] vi contorcersi

squirrel ['skwɪrəl] n scoiattolo

squirt [skwəːt] vi schizzare; zampillare ▷ vt spruzzare

Sr abbr = **senior; sister**

Sri Lanka [srɪ'læŋkə] n Sri Lanka m

St abbr = **saint; street**

stab [stæb] n (with knife etc) pugnalata; (of pain) fitta; (col: try): **to have a ~ at (doing) sth** provare a fare qc ▷ vt pugnalare

stability [stə'bɪlɪtɪ] n stabilità

stable ['steɪbl] n (for horses) scuderia; (for cattle) stalla ▷ adj stabile

stack [stæk] n catasta, pila ▷ vt accatastare, ammucchiare

stadium ['steɪdɪəm] n stadio

staff [stɑːf] n (work force: gen) personale m; (: BRIT Scol) personale insegnante ▷ vt fornire di personale

stag [stæg] n cervo

stage [steɪdʒ] n (platform) palco; palcoscenico; **the ~** il teatro, la scena; (point) fase f, stadio ▷ vt (play) allestire, mettere in scena; (demonstration) organizzare; **in ~s** per gradi; a tappe

stagger ['stægə] vi barcollare ▷ vt (person) sbalordire; (hours, holidays) scaglionare; **staggering** adj (amazing) sbalorditivo/a

stagnant ['stægnənt] adj stagnante

stag night, stag party n festa di addio al celibato

stain [steɪn] n macchia; (colouring) colorante m ▷ vt macchiare; (wood) tingere; **stained glass**

S

[ˌsteɪnd'glɑːs] n vetro colorato;
stainless adj (steel) inossidabile

stair [steəʳ] n (step) gradino; **stairs** npl
(flight of stairs) scale fpl, scala

staircase ['steəkeɪs], **stairway**
['steəweɪ] n scale fpl, scala

stake [steɪk] n palo, piolo; (Comm)
interesse m; (Betting) puntata,
scommessa ▷ vt (bet) scommettere;
(risk) rischiare; **to be at ~** essere
in gioco

stale [steɪl] adj (bread) raffermo/a;
(food) stantio/a; (air) viziato/a; (beer)
svaporato/a; (smell) di chiuso

stalk [stɔːk] n gambo, stelo ▷ vt
inseguire

stall [stɔːl] n bancarella; (in stable) box
m inv di stalla ▷ vt (Aut) far spegnere;
(fig) bloccare ▷ vi (Aut) spegnersi,
fermarsi; (fig) temporeggiare

stamina ['stæmɪnə] n vigore m,
resistenza

stammer ['stæməʳ] n balbuzie f ▷ vi
balbettare

stamp [stæmp] n (postage stamp)
francobollo; (implement) timbro;
(mark, also fig) marchio, impronta;
(on document) bollo; timbro ▷ vi (also:
~ one's foot) battere il piede ▷ vt
battere; (letter) affrancare; (mark with
a stamp) timbrare; **~ed addressed
envelope** busta affrancata per
la risposta; **stamp out** vt (fire)
estinguere; (crime) eliminare;
(opposition) soffocare

> Be careful not to translate stamp
> by the Italian word stampa.

stampede [stæm'piːd] n fuggi
fuggi m inv

stance [stæns] n posizione f

stand [stænd] (pt, pp **stood**) n
(position) posizione f; (for taxis)
posteggio; (structure) supporto,
sostegno; (at exhibition) stand m
inv; (in shop) banco; (at market)
bancarella; (booth) chiosco; (Sport)
tribuna ▷ vi stare in piedi; (rise) alzarsi
in piedi; (be placed) trovarsi ▷ vt (place)

mettere, porre; (tolerate, withstand)
resistere, sopportare; **to make
a ~** prendere posizione; **to ~ for
parliament** (BRIT) presentarsi come
candidato (per il parlamento); **to ~
sb a drink/meal** offrire da bere/un
pranzo a qn; **stand back** vi prendere
le distanze; **stand by** vi (be ready)
tenersi pronto/a ▷ vt fus (opinion)
sostenere; **stand down** vi (withdraw)
ritirarsi; **stand for** vt fus (signify)
rappresentare, significare; (tolerate)
sopportare, tollerare; **stand in for**
vt fus sostituire; **stand out** vi (be
prominent) spiccare; **stand up** vi (rise)
alzarsi in piedi; **stand up for** vt fus
difendere; **stand up to** vt fus tener
testa a, resistere a

standard ['stændəd] n modello,
standard m inv; (level) livello; (flag)
stendardo ▷ adj (size etc) normale,
standard inv; **standards** npl (morals)
principi mpl, valori mpl; **~ of living**
livello di vita

stand-by ['stændbaɪ] n riserva,
sostituto; **to be on ~** (gen) tenersi
pronto/a; (doctor) essere di guardia;
stand-by ticket n (Aviat) biglietto
senza garanzia

standing ['stændɪŋ] adj diritto/a,
in piedi; (permanent) permanente
▷ n rango, condizione f, posizione
f: **of many years' ~** che esiste da
molti anni; **standing order** n (BRIT:
at bank) ordine m di pagamento
(permanente)

stand: standpoint ['stændpɔɪnt]
n punto di vista; **standstill**
['stændstɪl] n: **at a standstill**
fermo/a; (fig) a un punto morto;
to come to a standstill fermarsi;
giungere a un punto morto

stank [stæŋk] pt of **stink**

staple ['steɪpl] n (for papers) graffetta
▷ adj (food etc) di base ▷ vt cucire

star [stɑːʳ] n stella; (celebrity)
divo/a ▷ vi: **to ~ (in)** essere il (or la)
protagonista (di) ▷ vt (Cine) essere

interpretato/a da; **the stars** npl (Astrology) le stelle

starboard ['stɑːbəd] n dritta

starch [stɑːtʃ] n amido

stardom ['stɑːdəm] n celebrità

stare [steəʳ] n sguardo fisso ▷ vi: **to ~ at** fissare

stark [stɑːk] adj (bleak) desolato/a ▷ adv: **~ naked** completamente nudo/a

start [stɑːt] n inizio; (of race) partenza; (sudden movement) sobbalzo; (advantage) vantaggio ▷ vt cominciare, iniziare; (car) mettere in moto ▷ vi cominciare; (on journey) partire, mettersi in viaggio; (jump) sobbalzare; **to ~ doing sth** (in) cominciare a fare qc; **start off** vi cominciare; (leave) partire; **start out** vi (begin) cominciare; (set out) partire; **start up** vi cominciare; (car) avviarsi ▷ vt iniziare; (car) avviare; **starter** n (Aut) motorino d'avviamento; (Sport: official) starter m inv; (BRIT Culin) primo piatto; **starting point** n punto di partenza

startle ['stɑːtl] vt far trasalire; **startling** adj sorprendente

starvation [stɑːˈveɪʃən] n fame f, inedia

starve [stɑːv] vi morire di fame; soffrire la fame ▷ vt far morire di fame, affamare

state [steɪt] n stato ▷ vt dichiarare, affermare; annunciare; **to be in a ~** essere agitato/a; **statement** n dichiarazione f; **States** npl: **the States** (USA) gli Stati Uniti; **state school** n scuola statale; **statesman** n (irreg) statista m

static ['stætɪk] n (Radio) scariche fpl ▷ adj statico/a

station ['steɪʃən] n stazione f ▷ vt collocare, disporre

stationary ['steɪʃənərɪ] adj fermo/a, immobile

stationer ['steɪʃənəʳ] n cartolaio/a; **~'s shop** cartoleria

stationery ['steɪʃənərɪ] n articoli mpl di cancelleria

station wagon n (US) giardinetta

statistic [stəˈtɪstɪk] n statistica; **statistics** n (science) statistica

statue ['stætjuː] n statua

stature ['stætʃəʳ] n statura

status ['steɪtəs] n posizione f, condizione f sociale; (prestige) prestigio; (legal, marital) stato; **status quo** [-ˈkwəu] n: **the status quo** lo statu quo

statutory ['stætjutərɪ] adj stabilito/a dalla legge, statutario/a

staunch [stɔːntʃ] adj fidato/a, leale

stay [steɪ] n (period of time) soggiorno, permanenza ▷ vi rimanere; (reside) alloggiare, stare; (spend some time) trattenersi, soggiornare; **to ~ put** non muoversi; **to ~ the night** passare la notte; **stay away** vi (from person, building) stare lontano (from da) (from event) non andare (from a); **stay behind** vi restare indietro; **stay in** vi (at home) stare in casa; **stay on** vi restare, rimanere; **stay out** vi (of house) rimanere fuori (di casa); **stay up** vi (at night) rimanere alzato/a

steadily ['stedɪlɪ] adv (firmly) saldamente; (constantly) continuamente; (fixedly) fisso; (walk) con passo sicuro

steady ['stedɪ] adj (not wobbling) fermo/a; (regular) costante; (person, character) serio/a; (: calm) calmo/a, tranquillo/a ▷ vt stabilizzare; calmare

steak [steɪk] n (meat) bistecca; (fish) trancia

steal (pt **stole**, pp **stolen**) [stiːl, stəul, 'stəuln] vt rubare ▷ vi rubare; (move) muoversi furtivamente

steam [stiːm] n vapore m ▷ vt (Culin) cuocere a vapore ▷ vi fumare; **steam up** vi (window) appannarsi; **to get ~ed up about sth** (fig) andare in bestia per qc; **steamy** adj (room) pieno/a di vapore; (window) appannato/a

S

steel [sti:l] n acciaio ▷ cpd di acciaio
steep [sti:p] adj ripido/a, scosceso/a;
(price) eccessivo/a ▷ vt inzuppare;
(washing) mettere a mollo
steeple ['sti:pl] n campanile m
steer [stɪəʳ] vt guidare ▷ vi (Naut:
person) governare; (car) guidarsi;
steering n (Aut) sterzo; **steering
wheel** n volante m
stem [stɛm] n (of flower, plant) stelo;
(of tree) fusto; (of glass) gambo; (of
fruit, leaf) picciolo ▷ vt contenere,
arginare; **stem cell** n cellula
staminale
step [stɛp] n passo; (stair) gradino,
scalino; (action) mossa, azione f
▷ vi: **to ~ forward/back** fare un
passo avanti/indietro; **steps** npl
(BRIT) = **stepladder**; **to be in/
out of ~ with** stare/non stare
al passo con; **step down** vi (fig)
ritirarsi; **step in** vi fare il proprio
ingresso; **step up** vt aumentare;
intensificare; **stepbrother** n
fratellastro; **stepchild** n figliastro/a;
stepdaughter n figliastra;
stepfather n patrigno; **stepladder**
n scala a libretto; **stepmother** n
matrigna; **stepsister** n sorellastra;
stepson n figliastro
stereo ['stɛrɪəu] n (system) sistema
m stereofonico; (record player)
stereo m inv ▷ adj (also: **~phonic**)
stereofonico/a
stereotype ['stɪərɪətaɪp] n
stereotipo
sterile ['stɛraɪl] adj sterile; **sterilize**
['stɛrɪlaɪz] vt sterilizzare
sterling ['stə:lɪŋ] adj (gold, silver) di
buona lega ▷ n (Econ) (lira) sterlina; **a
pound ~** una lira sterlina
stern [stə:n] adj severo/a ▷ n (Naut)
poppa
steroid ['stɛrɔɪd] n steroide m
stew [stju:] n stufato ▷ vt cuocere
in umido
steward ['stju:əd] n (Aviat, Naut, Rail)
steward m inv; (in club etc) dispensiere

m; **stewardess** n assistente f di volo,
hostess f inv
stick [stɪk] (pt, pp **stuck**) n bastone m;
(of rhubarb, celery) gambo; (of dynamite)
candelotto ▷ vt (glue) attaccare;
(thrust): **to ~ sth into** conficcare or
piantare or infiggere qc in; (col: put)
ficcare; (: tolerate) sopportare ▷ vi
attaccarsi; (remain) restare, rimanere;
stick out vi sporgere, spuntare; **stick
up** vi sporgere, spuntare; **stick up for**
vt fus difendere; **sticker** n cartellino
adesivo; **sticking plaster** n cerotto
adesivo; **stick insect** n insetto m
stecco inv; **stick shift** n (US Aut)
cambio manuale
sticky ['stɪkɪ] adj attaccaticcio/a,
vischioso/a; (label) adesivo/a; (fig:
situation) difficile
stiff [stɪf] adj rigido/a, duro/a;
(muscle) legato/a, indolenzito/a;
(difficult) difficile, arduo/a; (cold)
freddo/a, formale; (strong) forte;
(high: price) molto alto/a ▷ adv:
bored ~ annoiato/a a morte
stifling ['staɪflɪŋ] adj (heat)
soffocante
stigma ['stɪgmə] n stigma m
stiletto [stɪ'lɛtəu] n (BRIT: also:
~ heel) tacco a spillo
still [stɪl] adj fermo/a; (quiet)
silenzioso/a ▷ adv (up to this time,
even) ancora; (nonetheless) tuttavia,
ciò nonostante
stimulate ['stɪmjuleɪt] vt stimolare
stimulus (pl **stimuli**) ['stɪmjuləs,
'stɪmjulaɪ] n stimolo
sting [stɪŋ] (pt, pp **stung**) n puntura;
(organ) pungiglione m ▷ vt pungere
stink [stɪŋk] n fetore m, puzzo ▷ vi (pt
stank, pp **stunk**) puzzare
stir [stə:ʳ] n agitazione f, clamore
m ▷ vt mescolare; (fig) risvegliare
▷ vi muoversi; **stir up** vt provocare,
suscitare; **stir-fry** vt saltare in
padella ▷ n pietanza al salto
stitch [stɪtʃ] n (Sewing) punto;
(Knitting) maglia; (Med) punto (di

sutura); (*pain*) fitta ▷ *vt* cucire, attaccare; suturare

stock [stɔk] *n* riserva, provvista; (*Comm*) giacenza, stock *m inv*; (*Agr*) bestiame *m*; (*Culin*) brodo; (*Finance*) titoli *mpl*, azioni *fpl*; (*descent, origin*) stirpe *f* ▷ *adj* (*fig: reply etc*) consueto/a, classico/a ▷ *vt* (*have in stock*) avere, vendere; **to have sth in ~** avere qc in magazzino; **out of ~** esaurito/a; **~s and shares** valori *mpl* di borsa; **stockbroker** ['stɔkbrəukə^r] *n* agente *m* di cambio; **stock cube** *n* (*BRIT*) dado; **stock exchange** *n* Borsa (valori); **stockholder** ['stɔkhəuldə^r] *n* (*Finance*) azionista *m/f*

stocking ['stɔkiŋ] *n* calza

stock market *n* Borsa, mercato finanziario

stole [stəul] *pt of* **steal** ▷ *n* stola

stolen ['stəuln] *pp of* **steal**

stomach ['stʌmək] *n* stomaco; (*belly*) pancia ▷ *vt* sopportare, digerire; **stomach ache** *n* mal *m* di stomaco

stone [stəun] *n* pietra; (*pebble*) sasso, ciottolo; (*in fruit*) nocciolo; (*Med*) calcolo; (*BRIT: weight*) 6.348 kg; 14 libbre ▷ *vt* lapidare; (*fruit*) togliere il nocciolo a

stood [stud] *pt, pp of* **stand**

stool [stu:l] *n* sgabello

stoop [stu:p] *vi* (*also*: **have a ~**) avere una curvatura; (*also*: **~ down**) chinarsi, curvarsi

stop [stɔp] *n* arresto; (*stopping place*) fermata; (*in punctuation*) punto ▷ *vt* arrestare, fermare; (*break off*) interrompere; (*also*: **put a ~ to**) porre fine a ▷ *vi* fermarsi; (*rain, noise etc*) cessare, finire; **to ~ doing sth** cessare *or* finire di fare qc; **to ~ dead** fermarsi di colpo; **stop by** *vi* passare, fare un salto; **stop off** *vi* sostare brevemente; **stopover** *n* breve sosta; (*Aviat*) scalo; **stoppage** ['stɔpidʒ] *n* arresto, fermata; (*of pay*) trattenuta; (*strike*) interruzione *f* del lavoro

storage ['stɔ:ridʒ] *n* immagazzinamento

store [stɔ:^r] *n* provvista, riserva; (*depot*) deposito; (*BRIT: department store*) grande magazzino; (*us: shop*) negozio ▷ *vt* immagazzinare; **in ~** di riserva; in serbo; **storekeeper** *n* (*us*) negoziante *m/f*

storey, (*us*) **story** ['stɔ:ri] *n* piano

storm [stɔ:m] *n* tempesta; temporale *m*, burrasca; uragano; (*fig*) infuriarsi ▷ *vt* prendere d'assalto; **stormy** *adj* tempestoso/a, burrascoso/a

story ['stɔ:ri] *n* storia; favola; racconto; (*us*) = **storey**

stout [staut] *adj* solido/a, robusto/a; (*supporter*) tenace; (*fat*) corpulento/a, grasso/a ▷ *n* birra scura

stove [stəuv] *n* (*for cooking*) fornello; (*: small*) fornelletto; (*for heating*) stufa

straight [streit] *adj* dritto/a; (*frank*) onesto/a, franco/a; (*plain, uncomplicated*) semplice ▷ *adv* diritto; (*drink*) liscio; **to put** *or* **get ~** mettere in ordine, mettere ordine in; **~ away, ~ off** (*at once*) immediatamente; **straighten** *vt* (*also*: **straighten out**) raddrizzare; **straighteners** ['streitnəz] *npl* (*for hair*) piastra *f* per capelli; **straightforward** *adj* semplice; (*frank*) onesto/a, franco/a

strain [strein] *n* (*Tech*) sollecitazione *f*; (*physical*) sforzo; (*mental*) tensione *f*; (*Med*) strappo; distorsione *f*; (*streak, trace*) tendenza; elemento ▷ *vt* tendere; (*muscle*) stirare; (*ankle*) slogar; (*resources*) pesare su; (*food*) colare; passare; **strained** *adj* (*muscle*) stirato/a; (*laugh etc*) forzato/a; (*relations*) teso/a; **strainer** *n* passino, colino

strait [streit] *n* (*Geo*) stretto; **straits** *npl*: **to be in dire ~s** (*fig*) essere nei guai

strand [strænd] *n* (*of thread*) filo; **stranded** *adj* nei guai; senza mezzi di trasporto

strange [streɪndʒ] adj (not known) sconosciuto/a; (odd) strano/a, bizzarro/a; **strangely** adv stranamente; **stranger** n sconosciuto/a; (from another place) estraneo/a

strangle ['stræŋgl] vt strangolare

strap [stræp] n cinghia; (of slip, dress) spallina, bretella

strategic [strə'tiːdʒɪk] adj strategico/a

strategy ['strætɪdʒɪ] n strategia

straw [strɔː] n paglia; (drinking straw) cannuccia; **that's the last ~!** è la goccia che fa traboccare il vaso!

strawberry ['strɔːbərɪ] n fragola

stray [streɪ] adj (animal) randagio/a; (bullet) vagante; (scattered) sparso/a ▷ vi perdersi

streak [striːk] n striscia; (of hair) mèche f inv ▷ vt striare, screziare ▷ vi: **to ~ past** passare come un fulmine

stream [striːm] n ruscello; corrente f; (of people, smoke etc) fiume m ▷ vt (Scol) dividere in livelli di rendimento ▷ vi scorrere; **to ~ in/out** entrare/ uscire a fiotti

street [striːt] n strada, via; **streetcar** n (US) tram m inv; **street light** n lampione m; **street map** n pianta (di una città); **street plan** n pianta (di una città)

strength [strɛŋθ] n forza; **strengthen** vt rinforzare; fortificare; (economy, currency) consolidare

strenuous ['strɛnjuəs] adj vigoroso/a, energico/a; (tiring) duro/a, pesante

stress [strɛs] n (force, pressure) pressione f; (mental strain) tensione f; (accent) accento ▷ vt insistere su, sottolineare; accentare; **stressed** adj (tense: person) stressato/a; (Ling, Poetry: syllable) accentato/a; **stressful** adj (job) difficile, stressante

stretch [strɛtʃ] n (of sand etc) distesa ▷ vi stirarsi; (extend): **to ~ to** or **as far as** estendersi fino a ▷ vt tendere, allungare; (spread) distendere; (fig) spingere (al massimo); **stretch out** vi allungarsi, estendersi ▷ vt (arm etc) allungare, tendere; (spread) distendere

stretcher ['strɛtʃəʳ] n barella, lettiga

strict [strɪkt] adj (severe) rigido/a, severo/a; (precise) preciso/a, stretto/a; **strictly** adv severamente; rigorosamente; strettamente

stride [straɪd] n passo lungo ▷ vi (pt **strode**, pp **stridden**) camminare a grandi passi

strike [straɪk] (pt, pp **struck**) n sciopero; (of oil etc) scoperta; (attack) attacco ▷ vt colpire; (oil etc) scoprire, trovare; (bargain) fare; (fig): **the thought** or **it ~s me that …** mi viene in mente che … ▷ vi scioperare; (attack) attaccare; (clock) suonare; **on ~** (workers) in sciopero; **to go on** or **come out on ~** mettersi in sciopero; **to ~ a match** accendere un fiammifero; **striker** n scioperante m/f; (Sport) attaccante m; **striking** adj impressionante

string [strɪŋ] n spago; (row) fila; sequenza; catena; (Mus) corda ▷ vt (pt, pp **strung**): **to ~ out** disporre di fianco; **to ~ together** (words, ideas) mettere insieme; **the strings** npl (Mus) gli archi; **to pull ~s for sb** (fig) raccomandare qn

strip [strɪp] n striscia ▷ vt spogliare; (paint) togliere; (also: **~ down**) (machine) smontare ▷ vi spogliarsi; **strip off** vt (paint etc) staccare ▷ vi (person) spogliarsi

stripe [straɪp] n striscia, riga; (Mil, Police) gallone m; **striped** adj a strisce or righe

stripper ['strɪpəʳ] n spogliarellista m/f

strip-search ['strɪpsəːtʃ] vt: **to ~ sb** perquisire qn facendolo/a spogliare ▷ n perquisizione f (facendo spogliare il perquisito)

strive (pt **strove**, pp **striven**) [straɪv, strəuv, 'strɪvn] vi: **to ~ to do** sforzarsi di fare

strode [strəud] *pt of* **stride**
stroke [strəuk] *n* colpo; (*Med*) colpo apoplettico; (*Swimming*) bracciata; (: *style*) stile *m* ▷ *vt* accarezzare; **at a ~** in un attimo
stroll [strəul] *n* giretto, passeggiatina ▷ *vi* andare a spasso; **stroller** *n* (*US*) passeggino
strong [strɔŋ] *adj* (*gen*) forte; (*sturdy: table, fabric etc*) robusto/a; **they are 50 ~** sono in 50; **stronghold** *n* (*also fig*) roccaforte *f*; **strongly** *adv* fortemente, con forza; energicamente
strove [strəuv] *pt of* **strive**
struck [strʌk] *pt, pp of* **strike**
structure ['strʌktʃəʳ] *n* struttura; (*building*) costruzione *f*, fabbricato
struggle ['strʌgl] *n* lotta ▷ *vi* lottare
strung [strʌŋ] *pt, pp of* **string**
stub [stʌb] *n* mozzicone *m*; (*of ticket etc*) matrice *f*, talloncino ▷ *vt*: **to ~ one's toe (on sth)** urtare *or* sbattere il dito del piede (contro qc); **stub out** *vt* schiacciare
stubble ['stʌbl] *n* stoppia; (*on chin*) barba ispida
stubborn ['stʌbən] *adj* testardo/a, ostinato/a
stuck [stʌk] *pt, pp of* **stick** ▷ *adj* (*jammed*) bloccato/a
stud [stʌd] *n* bottoncino; borchia; (*also: ~ earring*) orecchino a pressione (*of horses*) scuderia, allevamento di cavalli; (*also: ~ horse*) stallone *m* ▷ *vt* (*fig*): **~ded with** tempestato/a di
student ['stjuːdənt] *n* studente/essa ▷ *cpd* studentesco/a; universitario/a; degli studenti; **student driver** *n* (*US*) conducente *m/f* principiante; **students' union** *n* (*BRIT: association*) circolo universitario; (: *building*) sede *f* del circolo universitario
studio ['stjuːdɪəu] *n* studio; **studio flat**, (*US*) **studio apartment** *n* monolocale *m*
study ['stʌdɪ] *n* studio ▷ *vt* studiare; esaminare ▷ *vi* studiare

stuff [stʌf] *n* (*substance*) materiale *m*; (*belongings*) roba ▷ *vt* imbottire; (*animal: for exhibition*) impagliare; (*Culin*) farcire; (*col: push*) ficcare; **stuffing** *n* imbottitura; (*Culin*) ripieno; **stuffy** *adj* (*room*) mal ventilato/a, senz'aria; (*ideas*) antiquato/a
stumble ['stʌmbl] *vi* inciampare; **to ~ across** (*fig*) imbattersi in
stump [stʌmp] *n* ceppo; (*of limb*) moncone *m* ▷ *vt*: **to be ~ed** essere sconcertato/a
stun [stʌn] *vt* stordire; (*amaze*) sbalordire
stung [stʌŋ] *pt, pp of* **sting**
stunk [stʌŋk] *pp of* **stink**
stunned [stʌnd] *adj* (*from blow*) stordito/a; (*amazed, shocked*) sbalordito/a
stunning ['stʌnɪŋ] *adj* sbalorditivo/a; (*girl, dress*) stupendo/a
stunt [stʌnt] *n* bravata; trucco pubblicitario
stupid ['stjuːpɪd] *adj* stupido/a; **stupidity** [stjuː'pɪdɪtɪ] *n* stupidità *f inv*, stupidaggine *f*
sturdy ['stəːdɪ] *adj* robusto/a, vigoroso/a, solido/a
stutter ['stʌtəʳ] *n* balbuzie *f* ▷ *vi* balbettare
style [staɪl] *n* stile *m*; (*distinction*) eleganza, classe *f*; **stylish** *adj* elegante; **stylist** *n*: **hair stylist** parrucchiere/a
sub... [sʌb] *prefix* sub..., sotto...; **subconscious** *adj*, *n* subcosciente *m*
subdued [səb'djuːd] *adj* pacato/a; (*light*) attenuato/a
subject *n* ['sʌbdʒɪkt] soggetto; (*citizen etc*) cittadino/a; (*Scol*) materia ▷ *vt* [səb'dʒɛkt] **to ~ to** sottomettere a; esporre a; **to be ~ to** (*law*) essere sottomesso/a a; (*disease*) essere soggetto/a a; **subjective** [səb'dʒɛktɪv] *adj* soggettivo/a; **subject matter** *n* argomento; contenuto

S

subjunctive [səbˈdʒʌŋktɪv] *adj* congiuntivo/a ▷ *n* congiuntivo

submarine [sʌbməˈriːn] *n* sommergibile *m*

submission [səbˈmɪʃən] *n* sottomissione *f*; (*to committee etc*) richiesta

submit [səbˈmɪt] *vt* sottomettere ▷ *vi* sottomettersi

subordinate [səˈbɔːdɪnət] *adj, n* subordinato/a

subscribe [səbˈskraɪb] *vi* contribuire; **to ~ to** (*opinion*) approvare, condividere; (*fund*) sottoscrivere a; (*newspaper*) abbonarsi a; essere abbonato/a a

subscription [səbˈskrɪpʃən] *n* sottoscrizione *f*; abbonamento

subsequent [ˈsʌbsɪkwənt] *adj* successivo/a, seguente; conseguente; **subsequently** *adv* in seguito, successivamente

subside [səbˈsaɪd] *vi* cedere, abbassarsi; (*flood*) decrescere; (*wind*) calmarsi

subsidiary [səbˈsɪdɪərɪ] *adj* sussidiario/a; accessorio/a ▷ *n* filiale *f*

subsidize [ˈsʌbsɪdaɪz] *vt* sovvenzionare

subsidy [ˈsʌbsɪdɪ] *n* sovvenzione *f*

substance [ˈsʌbstəns] *n* sostanza

substantial [səbˈstænʃl] *adj* solido/a; (*amount, progress etc*) notevole; (*meal*) sostanzioso/a

substitute [ˈsʌbstɪtjuːt] *n* (*person*) sostituto/a; (*thing*) succedaneo, surrogato *m* ▷ *vt*: **to ~ sth/sb for** sostituire qc/qn a; **substitution** [sʌbstɪˈtjuːʃən] *n* sostituzione *f*

subtle [ˈsʌtl] *adj* sottile

subtract [səbˈtrækt] *vt* sottrarre

suburb [ˈsʌbəːb] *n* sobborgo; **the ~s** la periferia; **suburban** [səˈbəːbən] *adj* suburbano/a

subway [ˈsʌbweɪ] *n* (*US: underground*) metropolitana; (*BRIT: underpass*) sottopassaggio

succeed [səkˈsiːd] *vi* riuscire; avere successo ▷ *vt* succedere a; **to ~ in doing** riuscire a fare

success [səkˈses] *n* successo; **successful** *adj* (*venture*) coronato/a da successo, riuscito/a; **to be successful (in doing)** riuscire (a fare); **successfully** *adv* con successo

succession [səkˈseʃən] *n* successione *f*

successive [səkˈsesɪv] *adj* successivo/a; consecutivo/a

successor [səkˈsesər] *n* successore *m*

succumb [səˈkʌm] *vi* soccombere

such [sʌtʃ] *adj* tale; **~ books** tali libri, libri del genere; (*so much*): **~ courage** tanto coraggio; (*of that kind*): **~ a book** un tale libro, un libro del genere ▷ *adv* talmente, così; **~ a long trip** un viaggio così lungo; **~ a lot of** talmente *or* così tanto/a; **~ as** (*like*) come; **as ~** come *or* in quanto tale; **such-and-such** *adj* tale (*after noun*)

suck [sʌk] *vt* succhiare; (*baby*) poppare

Sudan [suːˈdɑːn] *n* Sudan *m*

sudden [ˈsʌdn] *adj* improvviso/a; **all of a ~** improvvisamente, all'improvviso; **suddenly** *adv* bruscamente, improvvisamente, di colpo

sudoku [suˈdəukuː] *n* sudoku *m inv*

sue [suː] *vt* citare in giudizio

suede [sweɪd] *n* pelle *f* scamosciata

suffer [ˈsʌfər] *vt* soffrire, patire; (*bear*) sopportare, tollerare ▷ *vi* soffrire; **to ~ from** soffrire di; **suffering** *n* sofferenza

suffice [səˈfaɪs] *vi* essere sufficiente, bastare

sufficient [səˈfɪʃənt] *adj* sufficiente; **~ money** abbastanza soldi

suffocate [ˈsʌfəkeɪt] *vi* (*have difficulty breathing*) soffocare; (*die through lack of air*) asfissiare

sugar [ˈʃugər] *n* zucchero ▷ *vt* zuccherare

suggest [sə'dʒɛst] vt proporre, suggerire; (indicate) indicare; **suggestion** [sə'dʒɛstʃən] n suggerimento, proposta; indicazione f

suicide ['suɪsaɪd] n (person) suicida m/f; (act) suicidio; **to commit ~** suicidarsi; **suicide bomber** n kamikaze mf inv, attentatore/ trice suicida; **suicide bombing** n attentato suicida

suit [su:t] n (man's) vestito; (woman's) completo, tailleur m inv; (lawsuit) causa; (Cards) seme m, colore m ▷ vt andar bene a or per; essere adatto/a a or per; (adapt): **to ~ sth to** adattare qc a; **well ~ed** (couple) ben assortito/a; **suitable** adj adatto/a; appropriato/a; **suitcase** ['su:tkeɪs] n valigia

suite [swi:t] n (of rooms) appartamento; (Mus) suite f inv; (furniture): **bedroom/dining room ~** arredo or mobilia per la camera da letto/sala da pranzo

sulfur etc ['sʌlfər] (US) = **sulphur** etc

sulk [sʌlk] vi fare il broncio

sulphur, (US) **sulfur** ['sʌlfər] n zolfo

sultana [sʌl'tɑ:nə] n (fruit) uva (secca) sultanina

sum [sʌm] n somma; (Scol etc) addizione f; **sum up** vt ▷ vi riassumere

summarize ['sʌməraɪz] vt riassumere, riepilogare

summary ['sʌməri] n riassunto

summer ['sʌmər] n estate f ▷ cpd d'estate, estivo/a; **summer holidays** npl vacanze fpl estive; **summertime** n (season) estate f

summit ['sʌmɪt] n cima, sommità; (Pol) vertice m

summon ['sʌmən] vt chiamare, convocare

sun [sʌn] n sole m

Sun. abbr (= Sunday) dom.

sun: sunbathe vi prendere un bagno di sole; **sunbed** n lettino solare; **sunblock** n crema solare a protezione totale; **sunburn** n

(painful) scottatura; **sunburnt** ['sʌnbə:nt], **sunburned** ['sʌnbə:nd] adj abbronzato/a; (painfully) scottato/a dal sole

Sunday ['sʌndɪ] n domenica

Sunday paper n giornale m della domenica

- **SUNDAY PAPERS**

- I *Sunday papers* sono i giornali
- che escono di domenica. Sono
- generalmente corredati da
- supplementi e riviste di argomento
- culturale, sportivo e di attualità ed
- hanno un'alta tiratura.

sunflower ['sʌnflauər] n girasole m

sung [sʌŋ] pp of **sing**

sunglasses ['sʌnglɑ:sɪz] npl occhiali mpl da sole

sunk [sʌŋk] pp of **sink**

sun: sunlight n (luce f del) sole m; **sun lounger** n sedia a sdraio; **sunny** adj assolato/a, soleggiato/a; (fig) allegro/a, felice; **sunrise** n levata del sole, alba; **sunroof** n (Aut) tetto apribile; **sunscreen** n (protective ingredient) filtro solare; (cream) crema solare protettiva; **sunset** n tramonto; **sunshade** n parasole m; **sunshine** n (luce f del) sole m; **sunstroke** n insolazione f, colpo di sole; **suntan** n abbronzatura; **suntan lotion** n lozione f solare; **suntan oil** n olio solare

super ['su:pər] adj (col) fantastico/a

superb [su:'pə:b] adj magnifico/a

superficial [su:pə'fɪʃəl] adj superficiale

superintendent [su:pərɪn'tɛndənt] n direttore/trice; (Police) ≈ commissario (capo)

superior [su'pɪərɪər] adj, n superiore m/f

superlative [su'pə:lətɪv] adj superlativo/a, supremo/a ▷ n (Ling) superlativo

S

supermarket ['su:pəmɑ:kɪt] n
supermercato

supernatural [su:pə'nætʃərəl] adj,
n soprannaturale m

superpower ['su:pəpauəʳ] n (Pol)
superpotenza

superstition [su:pə'stɪʃən] n
superstizione f

superstitious [su:pə'stɪʃəs] adj
superstizioso/a

superstore ['su:pəstɔːʳ] n (BRIT)
grande supermercato

supervise ['su:pəvaɪz] vt (person
etc) sorvegliare; (organization)
soprintendere a; **supervision**
[su:pə'vɪʒən] n sorveglianza;
supervisione f; **supervisor** n
sorvegliante m/f; soprintendente
m/f; (in shop) capocommesso/a

supper ['sʌpəʳ] n cena

supple ['sʌpl] adj flessibile; agile

supplement n ['sʌplɪmənt]
supplemento ▷ vt [sʌplɪ'mɛnt]
completare, integrare

supplier [sə'plaɪəʳ] n fornitore m

supply [sə'plaɪ] vt: **to ~ sth
(to sb)** (goods) fornire qc (a qn);
to ~ sth (with sth) (system,
machine) alimentare qc (con qc)
▷ n riserva, provvista; (supplying)
approvvigionamento; (Tech)
alimentazione f; **supplies** npl (food)
viveri mpl; (Mil) sussistenza

support [sə'pɔːt] n (moral, financial etc)
sostegno, appoggio; (Tech) supporto
▷ vt sostenere; (financially) mantenere;
(uphold) sostenere, difendere;
supporter n (Pol etc) sostenitore/
trice, fautore/trice; (Sport) tifoso/a

▌ Be careful not to translate
support by the Italian word
sopportare.

suppose [sə'pəuz] vt supporre;
immaginare; **to be ~d to do** essere
tenuto/a a fare; **supposedly**
[sə'pəuzɪdlɪ] adv presumibilmente;
supposing conj se, ammesso che
+ sub

suppress [sə'prɛs] vt reprimere;
sopprimere; occultare

supreme [su'pri:m] adj supremo/a

surcharge ['sə:tʃɑ:dʒ] n
supplemento

sure [ʃuəʳ] adj sicuro/a; (definite,
convinced) sicuro/a, certo/a; **~!** (of
course) senz'altro!, certo!; **~ enough**
infatti; **to make ~ of** assicurarsi
di; **surely** adv sicuramente;
certamente

surf [sə:f] n (waves) cavalloni mpl;
(foam) spuma

surface ['sə:fɪs] n superficie f ▷ vt
(road) asfaltare ▷ vi risalire alla
superficie; (fig: person, news, feeling)
venire a galla

surfboard ['sə:fbɔːd] n tavola per
surfing

surfer ['sə:fəʳ] n (in sea) surfista m/f;
(on the Internet) navigatore/trice

surfing ['sə:fɪŋ] n surfing m

surge [sə:dʒ] n (strong movement)
ondata; (of feeling) impeto ▷ vi
gonfiarsi; (people) riversarsi

surgeon ['sə:dʒən] n chirurgo

surgery ['sə:dʒərɪ] n chirurgia; (BRIT:
room) studio or gabinetto medico,
ambulatorio; (also: **~ hours**) orario
delle visite or di consultazione; **to
undergo ~** subire un intervento
chirurgico

surname ['sə:neɪm] n cognome m

surpass [sə:'pɑːs] vt superare

surplus ['sə:pləs] n eccedenza;
(Econ) surplus m inv ▷ adj eccedente,
d'avanzo

surprise [sə'praɪz] n sorpresa;
(astonishment) stupore m ▷ vt
sorprendere; stupire; **surprised**
[sə'praɪzd] adj (look, smile)
sorpreso/a; **to be surprised** essere
sorpreso, sorprendersi; **surprising**
adj sorprendente, stupefacente;
surprisingly adv (easy, helpful)
sorprendentemente

surrender [sə'rɛndəʳ] n resa,
capitolazione f ▷ vi arrendersi

surround [sə'raund] vt circondare; (Mil etc) accerchiare; **surrounding** adj circostante; **surroundings** npl dintorni mpl; (fig) ambiente m

surveillance [sə:'veɪləns] n sorveglianza, controllo

survey n ['sə:veɪ] quadro generale; (study) indagine f; (in housebuying etc) perizia; (of land) rilevamento, rilievo topografico ▷ vt [sə:'veɪ] osservare; esaminare; (building) fare una perizia di; (land) fare il rilevamento di; **surveyor** n perito; geometra m; (of land) agrimensore m

survival [sə'vaɪvl] n sopravvivenza; (relic) reliquia, vestigio

survive [sə'vaɪv] vi sopravvivere ▷ vt sopravvivere a; **survivor** n superstite m/f, sopravvissuto/a

suspect adj ['sʌspekt] sospetto/a ▷ n ['sʌspekt] persona sospetta ▷ vt [səs'pekt] sospettare; (think likely) supporre; (doubt) dubitare di

suspend [səs'pend] vt sospendere; **suspended sentence** n condanna con la condizionale; **suspenders** npl (BRIT) giarrettiere fpl; (US) bretelle fpl

suspense [səs'pens] n apprensione f; (in film etc) suspense m; **to keep sb in ~** tenere qn in sospeso

suspension [səs'penʃən] n (gen, Aut) sospensione f; (of driving licence) ritiro temporaneo; **suspension bridge** n ponte m sospeso

suspicion [səs'pɪʃən] n sospetto; **suspicious** [səs'pɪʃəs] adj (suspecting) sospettoso/a; (causing suspicion) sospetto/a

sustain [səs'teɪn] vt sostenere; sopportare; (Law: charge) confermare; (suffer) subire

SUV n abbr (= sports utility vehicle) SUV m inv

swallow ['swɔləu] n (bird) rondine f ▷ vt inghiottire; (fig: story) bere

swam [swæm] pt of **swim**

swamp [swɔmp] n palude f ▷ vt sommergere

swan [swɔn] n cigno

swap [swɔp] vt: **to ~ (for)** scambiare (con)

swarm [swɔ:m] n sciame m ▷ vi (bees) sciamare; (people) brulicare; (place): **to be ~ing with** brulicare di

sway [sweɪ] vi (tree) ondeggiare; (person) barcollare ▷ vt (influence) influenzare, dominare

swear [sweəʳ] (pt **swore**, pp **sworn**) vi (curse) bestemmiare, imprecare ▷ vt: **to ~ to sth** giurare qc; **swear in** vt prestare giuramento a; **swearword** n parolaccia

sweat [swet] n sudore m, traspirazione f ▷ vi sudare

sweater ['swetəʳ] n maglione m

sweatshirt ['swetʃə:t] n felpa f

sweaty ['sweti] adj sudato/a; bagnato/a di sudore

Swede [swi:d] n svedese m/f

swede [swi:d] n (BRIT) rapa svedese

Sweden ['swi:dn] n Svezia; **Swedish** ['swi:dɪʃ] adj svedese ▷ n (Ling) svedese m

sweep [swi:p] (pt, pp **swept**) n spazzata; (also: **chimney ~**) spazzacamino ▷ vt spazzare, scopare; (current) spazzare ▷ vi (hand) muoversi con gesto ampio; (wind) infuriare

sweet [swi:t] n (BRIT: pudding) dolce m; (candy) caramella ▷ adj dolce; (fresh) fresco/a; (fig) piacevole; delicato/a, grazioso/a; (kind) gentile; **sweetcorn** n granturco dolce; **sweetener** ['swi:tnəʳ] n (Culin) dolcificante m; **sweetheart** n innamorato/a; **sweetshop** n (BRIT) ≈ pasticceria

swell [swel] (pt **swelled**, pp **swollen** or **swelled**) n (of sea) mare m lungo ▷ adj (US col: excellent) favoloso/a ▷ vt gonfiare, ingrossare; (numbers, sales etc) aumentare ▷ vi gonfiarsi, ingrossarsi; (sound) crescere; (Med: also: **~ up**) gonfiarsi; **swelling** n (Med) tumefazione f, gonfiore m

S

swept [swɛpt] *pt, pp of* **sweep**
swerve [swə:v] *vi* deviare; *(driver)* sterzare; *(boxer)* scartare
swift [swɪft] *n (bird)* rondone *m* ⊳ *adj* rapido/a, veloce
swim [swɪm] *(pt* **swam**, *pp* **swum)** *n*: **to go for a ~** andare a fare una nuotata ⊳ *vi* nuotare; *(Sport)* fare del nuoto; *(head, room)* girare ⊳ *vt (river, channel)* attraversare *or* percorrere a nuoto; *(length)* nuotare; **swimmer** *n* nuotatore/trice; **swimming** *n* nuoto; **swimming costume** *n (BRIT)* costume *m* da bagno; **swimming pool** *n* piscina; **swimming trunks** *npl* costume *m* da bagno (da uomo); **swimsuit** *n* costume *m* da bagno
swine flu *n* influenza suina
swing [swɪŋ] *(pt, pp* **swung)** *n* altalena; *(movement)* oscillazione *f*; *(Mus)* ritmo; *(also: ~ music)* swing *m* ⊳ *vt* dondolare, far oscillare; *(also: ~ round)* far girare ⊳ *vi* oscillare, dondolare; *(also: ~ round) (object)* roteare; *(person)* girarsi, voltarsi; **to be in full ~** *(activity)* essere in piena attività; *(party etc)* essere nel pieno
swipe card *n* tessera magnetica
swirl [swə:l] *vi* turbinare, far mulinello
Swiss [swɪs] *adj, n (pl inv)* svizzero/a
switch [swɪtʃ] *n (for light, radio etc)* interruttore *m*; *(change)* cambiamento ⊳ *vt (also: ~ round, ~ over)* cambiare; scambiare; **switch off** *vt* spegnere; **switch on** *vt* accendere; *(engine, machine)* mettere in moto, avviare; **switchboard** *n (Tel)* centralino
Switzerland ['swɪtsələnd] *n* Svizzera
swivel ['swɪvl] *vi (also: ~ round)* girare
swollen ['swəulən] *pp of* **swell**
swoop [swu:p] *n* incursione *f* ⊳ *vi (also: ~ down)* scendere in picchiata, piombare
swop [swɔp] *n, vt =* **swap**

sword [sɔ:d] *n* spada; **swordfish** *n* pesce *m* spada *inv*
swore [swɔ:ʳ] *pt of* **swear**
sworn [swɔ:n] *pp of* **swear** ⊳ *adj* giurato/a
swum [swʌm] *pp of* **swim**
swung [swʌŋ] *pt, pp of* **swing**
syllable ['sɪləbl] *n* sillaba
syllabus ['sɪləbəs] *n* programma *m*
symbol ['sɪmbl] *n* simbolo
symbolic(al) [sɪm'bɔlɪk(l)] *adj* simbolico/a; **to be ~ of sth** simboleggiare qc
symmetrical [sɪ'mɛtrɪkl] *adj* simmetrico/a
symmetry ['sɪmɪtrɪ] *n* simmetria
sympathetic [sɪmpə'θɛtɪk] *adj* *(showing pity)* compassionevole; *(kind)* comprensivo/a; **~ towards** ben disposto/a verso

> Be careful not to translate *sympathetic* by the Italian word *simpatico*.

sympathize ['sɪmpəθaɪz] *vi*: **to ~ with sb** compatire qn; partecipare al dolore di qn; **to ~ with a cause** simpatizzare per una causa
sympathy ['sɪmpəθɪ] *n* compassione *f*
symphony ['sɪmfənɪ] *n* sinfonia
symptom ['sɪmptəm] *n* sintomo; indizio
synagogue ['sɪnəgɔg] *n* sinagoga
syndicate ['sɪndɪkɪt] *n* sindacato
syndrome ['sɪndrəum] *n* sindrome *f*
synonym ['sɪnənɪm] *n* sinonimo
synthetic [sɪn'θɛtɪk] *adj* sintetico/a
Syria ['sɪrɪə] *n* Siria
syringe [sɪ'rɪndʒ] *n* siringa
syrup ['sɪrəp] *n* sciroppo; *(also:* **golden ~)** melassa raffinata
system ['sɪstəm] *n* sistema *m*; *(order)* metodo; *(Anat)* apparato; **systematic** [sɪstə'mætɪk] *adj* sistematico/a; metodico/a; **systems analyst** *n* analista *m/f* di sistemi

t

ta [tɑː] *excl (BRIT col)* grazie!
tab [tæb] *n (loop: on coat etc)* laccetto; *(label)* etichetta; **to keep ~s on** *(fig)* tenere d'occhio
table ['teɪbl] *n* tavolo, tavola; *(Math, Chem etc)* tavola ▷ *vt (BRIT: motion etc)* presentare; **to lay** *or* **set the ~** apparecchiare *or* preparare la tavola; **tablecloth** *n* tovaglia; **table d'hôte** [tɑːbl'dəʊt] *adj (meal)* a prezzo fisso; **table lamp** *n* lampada da tavolo; **tablemat** *n* sottopiatto; **tablespoon** *n* cucchiaio da tavola; *(also:* **tablespoonful**: *as measurement)* cucchiaiata
tablet ['tæblɪt] *n (Med)* compressa; *(of stone)* targa; *(Comput)* tablet *m inv*
table tennis *n* tennis *m* da tavolo, ping-pong® *m*
tabloid ['tæblɔɪd] *n (newspaper)* tabloid *m inv (giornale illustrato di formato ridotto)*; **the ~s, the ~ press** i giornali popolari

taboo [tə'buː] *adj, n* tabù *m inv*
tack [tæk] *n (nail)* bulletta; *(fig)* approccio ▷ *vt* imbullettare; imbastire ▷ *vi* bordeggiare
tackle ['tækl] *n* attrezzatura, equipaggiamento; *(for lifting)* paranco; *(Rugby)* placcaggio; *(Football)* contrasto ▷ *vt (difficulty)* affrontare; *(Rugby)* placcare; *(Football)* contrastare
tacky ['tækɪ] *adj* appiccicaticcio/a; scadente
tact [tækt] *n* tatto; **tactful** *adj* delicato/a, discreto/a
tactics ['tæktɪks] *n, npl* tattica
tactless ['tæktlɪs] *adj* che manca di tatto
tadpole ['tædpəʊl] *n* girino
taffy ['tæfɪ] *n (US)* caramella *f* mou *inv*
tag [tæg] *n* etichetta
tail [teɪl] *n* coda; *(of shirt)* falda ▷ *vt (follow)* seguire, pedinare; **tails** *npl (formal suit)* frac *m inv*
tailor ['teɪlə*] *n* sarto
Taiwan [taɪ'wɑːn] *n* Taiwan *m*; **Taiwanese** [taɪwə'niːz] *adj, n* taiwanese
take [teɪk] *(pt* **took***, pp* **taken***) vt* prendere; *(gain: prize)* ottenere, vincere; *(require: effort, courage)* occorrere, volerci; *(tolerate)* accettare, sopportare; *(hold: passengers etc)* contenere; *(accompany)* accompagnare; *(bring, carry)* portare; *(exam)* sostenere, presentarsi a; **to ~ a photo/a shower** fare una fotografia/una doccia; **I ~ it that** suppongo che; **take after** *vt fus* assomigliare a; **take apart** *vt* smontare; **take away** *vt* portare via; togliere; **take back** *vt (return)* restituire; riportare; *(one's words)* ritirare; **take down** *vt (building)* demolire; *(letter etc)* scrivere; **take in** *vt (lodger)* prendere, ospitare; *(deceive)* imbrogliare, abbindolare; *(understand)* capire; *(include)* comprendere, includere;

t

take off vi (*Aviat*) decollare; (*go away*) andarsene ▷ vt (*remove*) togliere; **take on** vt (*work*) accettare, intraprendere; (*employee*) assumere; (*opponent*) sfidare, affrontare; **take out** vt portare fuori; (*remove*) togliere; (*licence*) prendere, ottenere; **to ~ sth out of** (*drawer, pocket etc*) tirare qc fuori da; estrarre qc da; **take over** vt (*business*) rilevare ▷ vi: **to ~ over from sb** prendere le consegne or il controllo da qn; **take up** vt (*dress*) accorciare; (*occupy: time, space*) occupare; (*engage in: hobby etc*) mettersi a; **to ~ sb up on sth** accettare qc da qn; **takeaway** ['teɪkəweɪ] (*BRIT*) n (*shop etc*) ≈ rosticceria; (*food*) pasto per asporto; **taken** pp of **take**; **takeoff** n (*Aviat*) decollo; **takeout** ['teɪkaut] adj, n (*US*) = **takeaway**; **takeover** n (*Comm*) assorbimento; **takings** ['teɪkɪŋz] npl (*Comm*) incasso

talc [tælk] n (*also*: **~um powder**) talco

tale [teɪl] n racconto, storia; **to tell ~s** (*fig: to teacher, parent etc*) fare la spia

talent ['tælənt] n talento; **talented** adj di talento

talk [tɔːk] n discorso; (*gossip*) chiacchiere fpl; (*conversation*) conversazione f; (*interview*) discussione f ▷ vi parlare; **talks** npl (*Pol etc*) colloqui mpl; **to ~ about** parlare di; **to ~ sb out of/into doing** dissuadere qn da/convincere qn a fare; **to ~ shop** parlare di lavoro or di affari; **talk show** n talk show m inv

tall [tɔːl] adj alto/a; **to be 6 feet ~** ≈ essere alto 1 metro e 80

tambourine [tæmbəˈriːn] n tamburello

tame [teɪm] adj addomesticato/a; (*fig: story, style*) insipido/a, scialbo/a

tamper ['tæmpəʳ] vi: **to ~ with** manomettere

tampon ['tæmpɔn] n tampone m

tan [tæn] n (*also*: **sun~**) abbronzatura ▷ vi abbronzarsi ▷ adj (*colour*) marrone rossiccio inv

tandem ['tændəm] n tandem m inv

tangerine [tændʒəˈriːn] n mandarino

tangle ['tæŋgl] n groviglio; **to get in(to) a ~** aggrovigliarsi; (*fig*) combinare un pasticcio

tank [tæŋk] n serbatoio; (*for fish*) acquario; (*Mil*) carro armato

tanker ['tæŋkəʳ] n (*ship*) nave f cisterna inv; (*truck*) autobotte f, autocisterna

tankini [tæn'kiːnɪ] n tankini m inv

tanned [tænd] adj abbronzato/a

tantrum ['tæntrəm] n accesso di collera

Tanzania [tænzə'nɪə] n Tanzania

tap [tæp] n (*on sink etc*) rubinetto; (*gentle blow*) colpetto ▷ vt dare un colpetto a; (*resources*) sfruttare, utilizzare; (*telephone*) mettere sotto controllo; **on ~** (*fig: resources*) a disposizione; **tap-dancing** n tip tap m

tape [teɪp] n nastro; (*also*: **magnetic ~**) nastro (magnetico); (*sticky tape*) nastro adesivo ▷ vt (*record*) registrare (su nastro); (*stick*) attaccare con nastro adesivo; **tape measure** n metro a nastro; **tape recorder** n registratore m (a nastro)

tapestry ['tæpɪstrɪ] n arazzo; tappezzeria

tar [tɑːʳ] n catrame m

target ['tɑːgɪt] n bersaglio; (*fig: objective*) obiettivo

tariff ['tærɪf] n tariffa

tarmac ['tɑːmæk] n (*BRIT: on road*) macadam m al catrame; (*Aviat*) pista di decollo

tarpaulin [tɑː'pɔːlɪn] n tela incatramata

tarragon ['tærəgən] n dragoncello

tart [tɑːt] n (*Culin*) crostata; (*BRIT col, pej: woman*) sgualdrina ▷ adj (*flavour*) aspro/a, agro/a

tartan ['tɑːtn] n tartan m inv
tartar(e) sauce n salsa tartara
task [tɑːsk] n compito; **to take to ~** rimproverare
taste [teɪst] n gusto; (flavour) sapore m, gusto; (sample) assaggio; (fig: glimpse, idea) idea ▷ vt gustare; (sample) assaggiare ▷ vi: **to ~ of** or **like** (fish etc) sapere di, avere sapore di; **in good/bad** di buon/cattivo gusto; **you can ~ the garlic (in it)** (ci) si sente il sapore dell'aglio; **can I have a ~?** posso assaggiarlo?; **tasteful** adj di buon gusto; **tasteless** adj (food) insipido/a; (remark) di cattivo gusto; **tasty** adj saporito/a, gustoso/a
tatters ['tætəz] npl: **in ~**; a brandelli
tattoo [tə'tuː] n tatuaggio; (spectacle) parata militare ▷ vt tatuare
taught [tɔːt] pt, pp of **teach**
taunt [tɔːnt] n scherno ▷ vt schernire
Taurus ['tɔːrəs] n Toro
taut [tɔːt] adj teso/a
tax [tæks] n (on goods) imposta; (on services) tassa; (on income) imposte fpl, tasse fpl ▷ vt tassare; (fig: strain: patience etc) mettere alla prova; **tax-free** adj esente da imposte
taxi ['tæksɪ] n taxi m inv ▷ vi (Aviat) rullare; **taxi driver** n tassista m/f; **taxi rank**, (US) **taxi stand** n posteggio dei taxi
tax payer n contribuente m/f
TB n abbr (= tuberculosis) TBC f
tea [tiː] n tè m inv; (BRIT: snack: for children) merenda; **high ~** (BRIT) cena leggera (presa nel tardo pomeriggio); **tea bag** n bustina di tè; **tea break** n (BRIT) intervallo per il tè
teach (pt, pp **taught**) [tiːtʃ, tɔːt] vt: **to ~ sb sth, ~ sth to sb** insegnare qc a qn ▷ vi insegnare; **teacher** n insegnante m/f; (in secondary school) professore/essa; (in primary school) maestro/a; **teaching** n insegnamento

tea: tea cloth n (for dishes) strofinaccio; (BRIT: for trolley) tovaglietta da tè; **teacup** ['tiːkʌp] n tazza da tè; **tea leaves** npl foglie fpl di tè
team [tiːm] n squadra; (of animals) tiro; **team up** vi: **to ~ up (with)** mettersi insieme (a)
teapot ['tiːpɔt] n teiera
tear¹ [tɪəʳ] n lacrima; **in ~s** in lacrime
tear² [tɛəʳ] (pt **tore**, pp **torn**) n strappo ▷ vt strappare ▷ vi strapparsi; **tear apart** vt (also fig) distruggere; **tear down** vt (building, statue) demolire; (poster, flag) tirare giù; **tear off** vt (sheet of paper etc) strappare; (one's clothes) togliersi di dosso; **tear up** vt (sheet of paper etc) strappare; **tearful** ['tɪəful] adj piangente, lacrimoso/a; **tear gas** n gas m lacrimogeno
tearoom ['tiːruːm] n sala da tè
tease [tiːz] vt canzonare; (unkindly) tormentare
tea: teaspoon n cucchiaino da tè; (also: **teaspoonful**) (as measurement) cucchiaino; **teatime** n ora del tè; **tea towel** n (BRIT) strofinaccio (per i piatti)
technical ['tɛknɪkl] adj tecnico/a
technician [tɛk'nɪʃən] n tecnico/a
technique [tɛk'niːk] n tecnica
technology [tɛk'nɔlədʒɪ] n tecnologia
teddy (bear) ['tɛdɪ-] n orsacchiotto
tedious ['tiːdɪəs] adj noioso/a, tedioso/a
tee [tiː] n (Golf) tee m inv
teen [tiːn] adj = **teenage** ▷ n (US) = **teenager**
teenage ['tiːneɪdʒ] adj (fashions etc) per giovani, per adolescenti; **teenager** n adolescente m/f
teens [tiːnz] npl: **to be in one's ~** essere adolescente
teeth [tiːθ] npl of **tooth**
teetotal ['tiː'təutl] adj astemio/a

t

telecommunications
['tɛlıkəmju:nı'keıfənz] n
telecomunicazioni fpl
telegram ['tɛlıgræm] n
telegramma m
telegraph pole n palo del telegrafo
telephone ['tɛlıfəun] n telefono
▷ vt (person) telefonare a; (message)
comunicare per telefono; **telephone
book** n elenco telefonico; **telephone
box**, (US) **telephone booth** n
cabina telefonica; **telephone call** n
telefonata; **telephone directory**
n elenco telefonico; **telephone
number** n numero di telefono
telesales ['tɛlıseılz] n vendita per
telefono
telescope ['tɛlıskəup] n telescopio
televise ['tɛlıvaız] vt teletrasmettere
television ['tɛlıvıʒən] n televisione f;
on ~ alla televisione; **television
programme** n programma m
televisivo
tell [tɛl] (pt, pp **told**) vt dire; (relate:
story) raccontare; (distinguish): **to
~ sth from** distinguere qc da ▷ vi
(talk): **to ~ (of)** parlare (di); (have
effect) farsi sentire, avere effetto; **to
~ sb to do** dire a qn di fare; **tell off** vt
rimproverare, sgridare; **teller** n (in
bank) cassiere/a
telly ['tɛlı] n abbr (BRIT) (col)
(= television) tivù f inv
temp [tɛmp] abbr (BRIT col);
= **temporary** ▷ n impiegato/a
interinale
temper ['tɛmpər] n (nature) carattere
m; (mood) umore m; (fit of anger)
collera ▷ vt (moderate) moderare; **to
be in a ~** essere in collera; **to lose
one's ~** andare in collera
temperament ['tɛmprəmənt]
n (nature) temperamento;
temperamental [tɛmprə'mɛntl]
adj capriccioso/a
temperature ['tɛmprətfər] n
temperatura; **to have** or **run a ~**
avere la febbre

temple ['tɛmpl] n (building) tempio;
(Anat) tempia
temporary ['tɛmpərərı] adj
temporaneo/a; (job, worker)
avventizio/a, temporaneo/a
tempt [tɛmpt] vt tentare; **to ~
sb into doing** indurre qn a fare;
temptation [tɛmp'teıfən] n
tentazione f; **tempting** adj allettante
ten [tɛn] num dieci
tenant ['tɛnənt] n inquilino/a
tend [tɛnd] vt badare a, occuparsi
di ▷ vi: **to ~ to do** tendere a fare;
tendency ['tɛndənsı] n tendenza
tender ['tɛndər] adj tenero/a; (sore)
dolorante ▷ n (Comm: offer) offerta;
(money): **legal ~** moneta in corso
legale ▷ vt offrire
tendon ['tɛndən] n tendine m
tenner ['tɛnər] n (BRIT col)
(banconota da) dieci sterline fpl
tennis ['tɛnıs] n tennis m; **tennis
ball** n palla da tennis; **tennis court**
n campo da tennis; **tennis match**
n partita di tennis; **tennis player**
n tennista m/f; **tennis racket** n
racchetta da tennis
tenor ['tɛnər] n (Mus) tenore m
tenpin bowling ['tɛnpın-] n
bowling m
tense [tɛns] adj teso/a ▷ n (Ling)
tempo
tension ['tɛnfən] n tensione f
tent [tɛnt] n tenda
tentative ['tɛntətıv] adj esitante,
incerto/a; (conclusion) provvisorio/a
tenth [tɛnθ] num decimo/a
tent: tent peg n picchetto da
tenda; **tent pole** n palo da tenda,
montante m
tepid ['tɛpıd] adj tiepido/a
term [tə:m] n termine m; (Scol)
trimestre m; (Law) sessione f ▷ vt
chiamare, definire; **terms** npl
(conditions) condizioni fpl; (Comm)
prezzi mpl, tariffe fpl; **in the short/
long ~** a breve/lunga scadenza; **to
be on good ~s with** essere in buoni

rapporti con; **to come to ~s with** (*problem*) affrontare

terminal ['tə:mɪnl] *adj* finale, terminale; (*disease*) terminale ▷ *n* (*Elec, Comput*) morsetto; (*Aviat, for oil, ore etc*) terminal *m inv*; (ʙʀɪᴛ: *also*: **coach ~**) capolinea *m*

terminate ['tə:mɪneɪt] *vt* mettere fine a

termini ['tə:mɪnaɪ] *npl of* **terminus**

terminology [tə:mɪ'nɔlədʒɪ] *n* terminologia

terminus (*pl* **termini**) ['tə:mɪnəs, 'tə:mɪnaɪ] *n* (*for buses*) capolinea *m*; (*for trains*) stazione *f* terminale

terrace ['tɛrəs] *n* terrazza; (ʙʀɪᴛ: *row of houses*) fila di case a schiera; **terraced** *adj* (*garden*) a terrazze

terrain [tɛ'reɪn] *n* terreno

terrestrial [tɪ'rɛstrɪəl] *adj* (*life*) terrestre; (ʙʀɪᴛ: *channel*) terrestre

terrible ['tɛrɪbl] *adj* terribile; **terribly** *adv* terribilmente; (*very badly*) malissimo

terrier ['tɛrɪəʳ] *n* terrier *m inv*

terrific [tə'rɪfɪk] *adj* incredibile, fantastico/a; (*wonderful*) formidabile, eccezionale

terrified ['tɛrɪfaɪd] *adj* atterrito/a

terrify ['tɛrɪfaɪ] *vt* terrorizzare; **terrifying** *adj* terrificante

territorial [tɛrɪ'tɔ:rɪəl] *adj* territoriale

territory ['tɛrɪtərɪ] *n* territorio

terror ['tɛrəʳ] *n* terrore *m*; **terrorism** *n* terrorismo; **terrorist** *n* terrorista *m/f*

test [tɛst] *n* (*trial, check: of courage etc*) prova; (*Med*) esame *m*; (*Chem*) analisi *f inv*; (*exam: of intelligence etc*) test *m inv*; (: *in school*) compito in classe; (*also*: **driving ~**) esame *m* di guida ▷ *vt* provare; esaminare; analizzare; sottoporre ad esame; **to ~ sb in history** esaminare qn in storia

testicle ['tɛstɪkl] *n* testicolo

testify ['tɛstɪfaɪ] *vi* (*Law*) testimoniare, deporre; **to ~ to**

sth (*Law*) testimoniare qc; (*gen*) comprovare *or* dimostrare qc

testimony ['tɛstɪmənɪ] *n* (*Law*) testimonianza, deposizione *f*

test: test match *n* (*Cricket, Rugby*) partita internazionale; **test tube** *n* provetta

tetanus ['tɛtənəs] *n* tetano

text [tɛkst] *n* testo; (*Tel*) sms *m inv*, messaggino ▷ *vi* messaggiarsi; **textbook** *n* libro di testo

textile ['tɛkstaɪl] *n* tessile *m*

text message *n* (*Tel*) sms *m inv*, messaggino

text messaging [-'mɛsɪdʒɪŋ] *n* il mandarsi sms

texture ['tɛkstʃəʳ] *n* tessitura; (*of skin, paper etc*) struttura

Thai [taɪ] *adj* tailandese ▷ *n* tailandese *m/f*; (*Ling*) tailandese *m*

Thailand ['taɪlænd] *n* Tailandia

Thames [tɛmz] *n*: **the ~** il Tamigi

than [ðæn, ðən] *conj* (*in comparisons*) che; (*with numerals, pronouns, proper names*) di; **more ~ 10/Maria/once** più di 10/Maria/una volta; **I have more/less ~ you** ne ho più/meno di te; **she has more apples ~ pears** ha più mele che pere; **she is older ~ you think** è più vecchia di quanto tu (non) pensi

thank [θæŋk] *vt* ringraziare; **~ you (very much)** grazie (tante); **thankfully** *adv* con riconoscenza; con sollievo; **thankfully there were few victims** grazie al cielo ci sono state poche vittime; **thanks** *npl* ringraziamenti *mpl*, grazie *fpl* ▷ *excl* grazie!; **thanks to** grazie a

Thanksgiving (Day) *n* giorno del ringraziamento

○ **THANKSGIVING (DAY)**

○

○ Negli Stati Uniti il quarto giovedì
○ di novembre ricorre il *Thanksgiving*

- (*Day*), festa nazionale in ricordo
- della celebrazione con cui i
- Padri Pellegrini, i puritani inglesi
- che fondarono la colonia di
- Plymouth nel Massachusetts,
- ringraziarono Dio del buon
- raccolto del 1621.

 KEYWORD

that [ðæt ʃ] (*pl* **those**) *adj*
(*demonstrative*) quel (quell', quello) *m*;
quella (quell') *f*; **that man/woman/
book** quell'uomo/quella donna/
quel libro; (*not "this"*) quell'uomo/
quella donna/quel libro là; **that one**
quello/a là
▶ *pron* **1** (*demonstrative*) ciò; (: *not "this
one"*) quello/a; **who's that?** chi è?;
what's that? cos'è quello?; **is that
you?** sei tu?; **I prefer this to that**
preferisco questo a quello; **that's
what he said** questo è ciò che ha
detto; **what happened after that?**
che è successo dopo?; **that is (to
say)** cioè
2 (*relative: direct*) che; (: *indirect*) cui;
the book (that) I read il libro che ho
letto; **the box (that) I put it in** la
scatola in cui l'ho messo; **the people
(that) I spoke to** le persone con cui
or con le quali ho parlato
3 (*relative: of time*) in cui; **the day
(that) he came** il giorno in cui è
venuto
▶ *conj* che; **he thought that I was ill**
pensava che io fossi malato
▶ *adv* (*demonstrative*) così; **I can't
work that much** non posso lavorare
(così) tanto; **that high** così alto; **the
wall's about that high and that
thick** il muro è alto circa così e spesso
circa così

thatched [θætʃt] *adj* (*roof*) di paglia
thaw [θɔ:] *n* disgelo ▶ *vi* (*ice*)
sciogliersi; (*food*) scongelarsi ▶ *vt*
(*food*) (fare) scongelare

 KEYWORD

the [ðiː, ðə] *def art* **1** (*gen*) il (lo, l') *m*; la
(l') *f*; l (gli) *mpl*; le *fpl*; **the boy/girl/
ink** il ragazzo/la ragazza/l'inchiostro;
the books/pencils i libri/le matite;
the history of the world la storia
del mondo; **give it to the postman**
dallo al postino; **I haven't the time/
money** non ho tempo/soldi; **the
rich and the poor** i ricchi e i poveri
2 (*in titles*): **Elizabeth the First**
Elisabetta prima; **Peter the Great**
Pietro il Grande
3 (*in comparisons*): **the more he
works, the more he earns** più
lavora più guadagna

theatre, (*us*) **theater** ['θɪətəʳ] *n*
teatro; (*also:* **lecture ~**) aula magna;
(*also:* **operating ~**) sala operatoria
theft [θɛft] *n* furto
their [ðɛəʳ] *adj* il (la) loro; (*pl*) i (le)
loro; **theirs** *pron* il (la) loro; (*pl*) i (le)
loro; *see also* **my; mine¹**
them [ðɛm, ðəm] *pron* (*direct*) li(le);
(*indirect*) gli, loro (*after vb*); (*stressed,
after prep: people*) loro; (: *people, things*)
essi/e; *see also* **me**
theme [θiːm] *n* tema *m*; **theme park**
n parco a tema
themselves [ðəm'sɛlvz] *pl pron*
(*reflexive*) si; (*emphatic*) loro stessi/e;
(*after prep*) se stessi/e
then [ðɛn] *adv* (*at that time*) allora;
(*next*) poi, dopo; (*and also*) e poi ▶ *conj*
(*therefore*) perciò, dunque, quindi ▶ *adj*:
the ~ president il presidente di allora;
by ~ allora; **from ~ on** da allora in poi
theology [θɪ'ɔlədʒɪ] *n* teologia
theory ['θɪərɪ] *n* teoria
therapist ['θɛrəpɪst] *n* terapista *m/f*
therapy ['θɛrəpɪ] *n* terapia

 KEYWORD

there [ðɛəʳ] *adv* **1**: **there is** c'è; **there
are** ci sono; **there are 3 of them**

(*people*) sono in 3; (*things*) ce ne sono 3; **there is no-one here** non c'è nessuno qui; **there has been an accident** c'è stato un incidente **2** (*referring to place*) là, lì; **up/in/down there** lassù/là dentro/laggiù; **he went there on Friday** ci è andato venerdì; **I want that book there** voglio quel libro lì *or* là; **there he is!** eccolo! **3: there, there** (*esp to child*) su, su; **thereabouts** ['ðɛərəbauts] *adv* (*place*) nei pressi, da quelle parti; (*amount*) giù di lì, all'incirca; **thereafter** [ðɛərˈɑːftəʳ] *adv* da allora in poi; **thereby** [ðɛəˈbaɪ] *adv* con ciò; **therefore** ['ðɛəfɔːʳ] *adv* perciò, quindi; **there's** [ðɛəz] = **there is**; **there has**

thermal ['θəːml] *adj* termico/a
thermometer [θəˈmɔmɪtəʳ] *n* termometro
thermostat ['θəːməstæt] *n* termostato
these [ðiːz] *pl pron, adj* questi/e
thesis (*pl* **theses**) ['θiːsɪs, 'θiːsiːz] *n* tesi *f inv*
they [ðeɪ] *pl pron* essi(esse); (*people only*) loro; **~ say that ...** (*it is said that*) si dice che ...; **they'd** [ðeɪd] = **they would; they had; they'll** [ðeɪl] = **they will; they shall; they're** [ðɛəʳ] = **they are; they've** = **they have**
thick [θɪk] *adj* spesso/a; (*crowd*) compatto/a; (*stupid*) ottuso/a, lento/a ▷ *n*: **in the ~ of** nel folto di; **it's 20 cm ~** ha uno spessore di 20 cm; **thicken** *vi* ispessire ▷ *vt* (*sauce etc*) ispessire, rendere più denso/a; **thickness** *n* spessore *m*
thief (*pl* **thieves**) [θiːf, θiːvz] *n* ladro/a
thigh [θaɪ] *n* coscia
thin [θɪn] *adj* sottile; (*person*) magro/a; (*soup*) poco denso/a ▷ *vt*: **to ~ (down)** (*sauce, paint*) diluire

thing [θɪŋ] *n* cosa; (*object*) oggetto; (*mania*): **to have a ~ about** essere fissato/a con; **things** *npl* (*belongings*) cose *fpl*; **the best ~ would be to** la cosa migliore sarebbe di; **poor ~** poveretto/a
think (*pt, pp* **thought**) [θɪŋk, θɔːt] *vi* pensare, riflettere ▷ *vt* pensare, credere; (*imagine*) immaginare; **to ~ of** pensare a; **what did you ~ of them?** cosa ne ha pensato?; **to ~ about sth/sb** pensare a qc/qn; **I'll ~ about it** ci penserò; **to ~ of doing** pensare di fare; **I ~ so/no** penso *or* credo di sì/no; **to ~ well of** avere una buona opinione di; **think over** *vt* riflettere su; **think up** *vt* ideare
third [θəːd] *n* terzo/a ▷ *n* terzo/a; (*fraction*) terzo, terza parte *f*; (*Aut*) terza; (BRIT *Scol: degree*) laurea col minimo dei voti; **thirdly** *adv* in terzo luogo; **third party insurance** *n* (BRIT) assicurazione *f* contro terzi; **Third World** *n*: **the Third World** il Terzo Mondo
thirst [θəːst] *n* sete *f*; **thirsty** *adj* (*person*) assetato/a, che ha sete
thirteen [θəːˈtiːn] *num* tredici; **thirteenth** [-ˈtiːnθ] *num* tredicesimo/a
thirtieth ['θəːtɪɪθ] *num* trentesimo/a
thirty ['θəːtɪ] *num* trenta

KEYWORD

this [ðɪs] (*pl* **these**) *adj* (*demonstrative*) questo/a; **this man/woman/book** quest'uomo/questa donna/questo libro; (*not "that"*) quest'uomo/questa donna/questo libro qui; **this one** questo/a qui ▷ *pron* (*demonstrative*) questo/a; (: *not "that one"*) questo/a qui; **who/what is this?** chi è/che cos'è questo?; **I prefer this to that** preferisco questo a quello; **this is where I live** io abito qui; **this is what he said** questo è ciò che ha detto; **this is Mr Brown**

(*in introductions, photo*) questo è il signor Brown; (*on telephone*) sono il signor Brown ▷ *adv* (*demonstrative*): **this high/long** *etc* alto/lungo *etc* così; **I didn't know things were this bad** non sapevo andasse così male

thistle ['θɪsl] *n* cardo
thorn [θɔːn] *n* spina
thorough ['θʌrə] *adj* (*search*) minuzioso/a; (*knowledge, research*) approfondito/a, profondo/a; (*person*) coscienzioso/a; (*cleaning*) a fondo; **thoroughly** *adv* (*search*) minuziosamente; (*wash, study*) a fondo; (*very*) assolutamente
those [ðəuz] *pl pron* quelli/e ▷ *pl adj* quei (quegli) *mpl*; quelle *fpl*
though [ðəu] *conj* benché, sebbene ▷ *adv* comunque
thought [θɔːt] *pt, pp of* **think** ▷ *n* pensiero; (*opinion*) opinione *f*; **thoughtful** *adj* pensieroso/a, pensoso/a; (*considerate*) premuroso/a; **thoughtless** *adj* sconsiderato/a; (*behaviour*) scortese
thousand ['θauzənd] *num* mille; **one ~** mille; **~s of** migliaia di; **thousandth** *num* millesimo/a
thrash [θræʃ] *vt* picchiare; (*defeat*) battere; **thrash about** *vi* dibattersi
thread [θrɛd] *n* filo; (*of screw*) filetto ▷ *vt* (*needle*) infilare
threat [θrɛt] *n* minaccia; **threaten** *vi* (*storm*) minacciare ▷ *vt*: **to threaten sb with sth/to do** minacciare qn con qc/di fare; **threatening** *adj* minaccioso/a
three [θriː] *num* tre; **three-dimensional** *adj* tridimensionale; (*film*) stereoscopico/a; **three-piece suite** *n* salotto comprendente un divano e due poltrone; **three-quarters** *npl* tre quarti *mpl*; **three-quarters full** pieno per tre quarti
threshold ['θrɛʃhəuld] *n* soglia

threw [θruː] *pt of* **throw**
thrill [θrɪl] *n* brivido ▷ *vt* (*audience*) elettrizzare; **to be ~ed** (*with gift etc*) essere elettrizzato/a; **thrilled** *adj*: **I was thrilled to get your letter** la tua lettera mi ha fatto veramente piacere; **thriller** *n* thriller *m inv*; **thrilling** *adj* (*book, play etc*) pieno/a di suspense; (*news, discovery*) elettrizzante
thriving ['θraɪvɪŋ] *adj* fiorente
throat [θrəut] *n* gola; **to have a sore ~** avere (un *or* il) mal di gola
throb [θrɔb] *vi* palpitare; (*engine*) vibrare; (*with pain*) pulsare
throne [θrəun] *n* trono
through [θruː] *prep* attraverso; (*time*) per, durante; (*by means of*) per mezzo di; (*owing to*) a causa di ▷ *adj* (*ticket, train, passage*) diretto/a ▷ *adv* attraverso; **to put sb ~ to sb** (*Tel*) passare qn a qn; **to be ~** (*Tel*) ottenere la comunicazione; (*have finished*) avere finito; **"no ~ road"** (*BRIT*) "strada senza sbocco"; **throughout** *prep* (*place*) dappertutto in; (*time*) per *or* durante tutto/a ▷ *adv* dappertutto; sempre
throw [θrəu] *n* tiro; (*Sport*) lancio ▷ *vt* (*pt* **threw**, *pp* **thrown**) tirare, gettare; (*Sport*) lanciare; (*rider*) disarcionare; (*fig*) confondere; **to ~ a party** dare una festa; **throw away** *vt* gettare *or* buttare via; **throw in** *vt* (*Sport: ball*) rimettere in gioco; (*include*) aggiungere; **throw off** *vt* sbarazzarsi di; **throw out** *vt* buttare fuori; (*reject*) respingere; **throw up** *vi* vomitare
thru [θruː] *prep, adj, adv* (*US*) = **through**
thrush [θrʌʃ] *n* tordo
thrust [θrʌst] *vt* (*pt, pp* **thrust**) spingere con forza; (*push in*) conficcare
thud [θʌd] *n* tonfo
thug [θʌg] *n* delinquente *m*

thumb [θʌm] n (Anat) pollice m; **to ~ a lift** fare l'autostop; **thumbtack** n (US) puntina da disegno

thump [θʌmp] n colpo forte; (sound) tonfo ▷ vt (person) picchiare; (object) battere su ▷ vi picchiare; battere

thunder ['θʌndər] n tuono ▷ vi tuonare; (train etc): **to ~ past** passare con un rombo; **thunderstorm** n temporale m

Thur(s). abbr (= Thursday) gio.

Thursday ['θəːzdɪ] n giovedì m inv

thus [ðʌs] adv così

thwart [θwɔːt] vt contrastare

thyme [taɪm] n timo

Tiber ['taɪbər] n: **the ~** il Tevere

Tibet [tɪ'bɛt] n Tibet m

tick [tɪk] n (sound, of clock) tic tac m inv; (mark) segno; spunta; (Zool) zecca; (BRIT col): **in a ~** in un attimo ▷ vi fare tic tac ▷ vt spuntare; **tick off** vt spuntare; (person) sgridare

ticket ['tɪkɪt] n biglietto; (in shop: on goods) etichetta; (for library) scheda; **to get a (parking) ~** (Aut) prendere una multa (per sosta vietata); **a single/return ~ to ...** un biglietto di sola andata/di andata e ritorno per...; **ticket barrier** n (BRIT Rail) cancelletto d'ingresso; **ticket collector** n bigliettaio; **ticket inspector** n controllore m; **ticket machine** n distributore m di biglietti; **ticket office** n biglietteria

tickle ['tɪkl] vt fare il solletico a ▷ vi: **it ~s** mi (or gli etc) fa il solletico; **ticklish** ['tɪklɪʃ] adj che soffre il solletico; (which tickles: blanket, cough) che provoca prurito; (problem) delicato/a

tide [taɪd] n marea; (fig: of events) corso; **high/low ~** alta/bassa marea

tidy ['taɪdɪ] adj (room) ordinato/a, lindo/a; (dress, work) curato/a, in ordine; (person) ordinato/a ▷ vt (also: **~ up**) riordinare, mettere in ordine

tie [taɪ] n (string etc) legaccio; (BRIT: also: **neck~**) cravatta; (fig: link) legame m; (Sport: draw) pareggio ▷ vt (parcel) legare; (ribbon) annodare ▷ vi (Sport) pareggiare; **to ~ sth in a bow** annodare qc; **to ~ a knot in sth** fare un nodo a qc; **tie down** vt legare, assicurare con una corda; **to ~ sb down to** (price etc) costringere qn ad accettare; **tie up** vt (parcel, dog) legare; (boat) ormeggiare; (arrangements) concludere; **to be ~d up** (busy) essere occupato or preso

tier [tɪər] n fila; (of cake) piano, strato

tiger ['taɪgər] n tigre f

tight [taɪt] adj (rope) teso/a, tirato/a; (money) poco/a; (clothes, budget, programme, bend) stretto/a; (control) severo/a, fermo/a; (col: drunk) sbronzo/a ▷ adv (squeeze) fortemente; (shut) ermeticamente; **tighten** vt (rope) tendere; (screw) stringere; (control) rinforzare ▷ vi tendersi; stringersi; **tightly** adv (grasp) bene, saldamente; **tights** npl (BRIT) collant m inv

tile [taɪl] n (on roof) tegola; (on floor, wall) mattonella, piastrella

till [tɪl] n registratore m di cassa ▷ vt (land) coltivare ▷ prep, conj = **until**

tilt [tɪlt] vt inclinare, far pendere ▷ vi inclinarsi, pendere

timber ['tɪmbər] n (material) legname m

time [taɪm] n tempo; (epoch: often pl) epoca, tempo; (by clock) ora; (moment) momento; (occasion) volta; (Mus) tempo ▷ vt cronometrare; (race) cronometrare; (programme) calcolare la durata di; (fix moment for) programmare; **a long ~** molto tempo; **for the ~ being** per il momento; **4 at a ~** 4 per o alla volta; **from ~ to ~** ogni tanto; **in ~** (soon enough) in tempo; (after some time) col tempo; (Mus) a tempo; **at ~s** a volte; **in a week's ~** fra una settimana; **in no ~** in un attimo; **any ~** in qualsiasi momento; **on ~** puntualmente; **5 ~s 5** 5 volte 5, 5 per 5; **what ~ is it?** che ora è?, che ore sono?; **to have a good ~** divertirsi; **time limit** n limite *m* di tempo; **timely** *adj* opportuno/a; **timer** *n* (*in kitchen*) contaminuti *m inv*; (*time switch*) temporizzatore *m*; **time-share** *adj*: **time-share apartment/villa** appartamento/villa in multiproprietà; **timetable** *n* orario; **time zone** *n* fuso orario

timid ['tɪmɪd] *adj* timido/a; (*easily scared*) pauroso/a

timing ['taɪmɪŋ] *n* (*fig*) scelta del momento opportuno; (*Sport*) cronometraggio

tin [tɪn] *n* stagno; (*also*: **~ plate**) latta; (*BRIT*: *can*) barattolo (di latta), lattina; (*container*) scatola; **tin foil** *n* stagnola

tingle ['tɪŋgl] *vi* pizzicare

tinker ['tɪŋkər]; **tinker with** *vt fus* armeggiare intorno a; cercare di riparare

tinned [tɪnd] *adj* (*BRIT*: *food*) in scatola

tin-opener ['tɪnəupnər] *n* (*BRIT*) apriscatole *m inv*

tint [tɪnt] *n* tinta; **tinted** *adj* (*hair*) tinto/a; (*spectacles, glass*) colorato/a

tiny ['taɪnɪ] *adj* minuscolo/a

tip [tɪp] *n* (*end*) punta; (*gratuity*) mancia; (*BRIT*: *for rubbish*) immondezzaio; (*advice*) suggerimento ▷ *vt* (*waiter*) dare la mancia a; (*tilt*) inclinare; (*overturn*: *also*: **~ over**) capovolgere; (*empty*: *also*: **~ out**) scaricare; **tip off** *vt* fare una soffiata a

tiptoe ['tɪptəu] *n*: **on ~** in punta di piedi

tire ['taɪər] *vt* stancare ▷ *vi* stancarsi ▷ *n* (*US*) = **tyre**; **tired** *adj* stanco/a; **to be tired of** essere stanco *or* stufo di; **tire pressure** *n* (*US*) = **tyre pressure**; **tiring** *adj* faticoso/a

tissue ['tɪʃuː] *n* tessuto; (*paper handkerchief*) fazzoletto di carta; **tissue paper** *n* carta velina

tit [tɪt] *n* (*bird*) cinciallegra; **to give ~ for tat** rendere pan per focaccia

title ['taɪtl] *n* titolo

T-junction [ˈtiːˈdʒʌŋkʃən] *n* incrocio a T

TM *n abbr* = **trademark**

 KEYWORD

to [tuː, tə] *prep* **1** (*direction*) a; **to go to France/London/school** andare in Francia/a Londra/a scuola; **to go to Paul's/the doctor's** andare da Paul/dal dottore; **the road to Edinburgh** la strada per Edimburgo; **to the left/right** a sinistra/destra

2 (*as far as*) (fino) a; **from here to London** da qui a Londra; **to count to 10** contare fino a 10; **from 40 to 50 people** da 40 a 50 persone

3 (*with expressions of time*): **a quarter to 5** le 5 meno un quarto; **it's twenty to 3** sono le 3 meno venti

4 (*for, of*): **the key to the front door** la chiave della porta d'ingresso; **a letter to his wife** una lettera per la moglie

5 (*expressing indirect object*) a; **to give sth to sb** dare qc a qn; **to talk to sb** parlare a qn; **to be a danger to sb/sth** rappresentare un pericolo per qn/qc

6 (*in relation to*) a; **3 goals to 2** 3 goal a 2; **30 miles to the gallon** ≈ 11 chilometri con un litro

7 (*purpose, result*): **to come to sb's aid** venire in aiuto a qn; **to sentence sb to death** condannare a morte qn; **to my surprise** con mia sorpresa

▶ *with vb* **1** (*simple infinitive*): **to go/eat** *etc* andare/mangiare *etc*

2 (*following another vb*): **to want/try/start to do** volere/cercare di/cominciare a fare

3 (*with vb omitted*): **I don't want to** non voglio (farlo); **you ought to** devi (farlo)

4 (*purpose, result*) per; **I did it to help you** l'ho fatto per aiutarti

5 (*equivalent to relative clause*): **I have things to do** ho da fare; **the**

main thing is to try la cosa più importante è provare
6 (*after adjective etc*): **ready to go** pronto/a a partire; **too old/young to …** troppo vecchio/a/giovane per …
▷ *adv*: **to push the door to** accostare la porta

toad [təud] *n* rospo; **toadstool** *n* fungo (velenoso)
toast [təust] *n* (*Culin*) pane *m* tostato; (*drink, speech*) brindisi *m inv* ▷ *vt* (*Culin*) tostare; (*drink to*) brindare a; **a piece** *or* **slice of** una fetta di pane tostato; **toaster** *n* tostapane *m inv*
tobacco [tə'bækəu] *n* tabacco
toboggan [tə'bɔgən] *n* toboga *m inv*
today [tə'deɪ] *adv, n* (*also fig*) oggi *m inv*
toddler ['tɔdlə*] *n* bambino/a che impara a camminare
toe [təu] *n* dito del piede; (*of shoe*) punta ▷ *vt*: **to ~ the line** (*fig*) stare in riga, conformarsi; **toenail** *n* unghia del piede
toffee ['tɔfɪ] *n* caramella
together [tə'gɛðə*] *adv* insieme; (*at same time*) allo stesso tempo; **~ with** insieme a
toilet ['tɔɪlət] *n* (*BRIT*: *lavatory*) gabinetto ▷ *cpd* (*soap etc*) da toletta; **toilet bag** *n* (*BRIT*) nécessaire *m inv* da toilette; **toilet paper** *n* carta igienica; **toiletries** *npl* articoli *mpl* da toletta; **toilet roll** *n* rotolo di carta igienica
token ['təukən] *n* (*sign*) segno ▷ *cpd* (*substitute coin*) gettone *m*; **book/record/gift ~** (*BRIT*) buono-libro/-disco/-regalo
Tokyo ['təukjəu] *n* Tokyo *f*
told [təuld] *pt, pp of* **tell**
tolerant ['tɔlərnt] *adj*: **~ (of)** tollerante (nei confronti di)
tolerate ['tɔləreɪt] *vt* sopportare; (*Med, Tech*) tollerare

toll [təul] *n* (*tax, charge*) pedaggio ▷ *vi* (*bell*) suonare; **the accident ~ on the roads** il numero delle vittime della strada; **toll call** *n* (*us Tel*) (telefonata) interurbana; **toll-free** (*us*) *adj* senza addebito, gratuito/a ▷ *adv* gratuitamente; **toll-free number** ≈ numero verde
tomato [tə'mɑːtəu] (*pl* **tomatoes**) *n* pomodoro; **tomato sauce** *n* salsa di pomodoro
tomb [tuːm] *n* tomba; **tombstone** ['tuːmstəun] *n* pietra tombale
tomorrow [tə'mɔrəu] *adv, n* (*also fig*) domani *m inv*; **the day after ~** dopodomani; **~ morning** domani mattina
ton [tʌn] *n* tonnellata (*Brit* = 1016 kg; 20 cwt; *US* = 907 kg; *metric* = 1000 kg); **~s of** (*col*) un mucchio *or* sacco di
tone [təun] *n* tono ▷ *vi* (*also*: **~ in**) intonarsi; **tone down** *vt* (*colour, criticism, sound*) attenuare
tongs [tɔŋz] *npl* tenaglie *fpl*; (*for coal*) molle *fpl*; (*for hair*) arricciacapelli *m inv*
tongue [tʌŋ] *n* lingua; **~ in cheek** (*say, speak*) ironicamente
tonic ['tɔnɪk] *n* (*Med*) ricostituente *m*; (*also*: **~ water**) acqua tonica
tonight [tə'naɪt] *adv* stanotte; (*this evening*) stasera ▷ *n* questa notte; questa sera
tonne [tʌn] *n* (*BRIT*: *metric ton*) tonnellata
tonsil ['tɔnsl] *n* tonsilla; **tonsillitis** [tɔnsɪ'laɪtɪs] *n* tonsillite *f*
too [tuː] *adv* (*excessively*) troppo; (*also*) anche; **~ much** *adv* troppo; *adj* troppo/a; **~ many** troppi/e
took [tuk] *pt of* **take**
tool [tuːl] *n* utensile *m*, attrezzo; **tool box** *n* cassetta *f* portautensili; **tool kit** *n* cassetta di attrezzi
tooth (*pl* **teeth**) [tuːθ, tiːθ] *n* (*Anat, Tech*) dente *m*; **toothache** *n* mal *m* di denti; **toothbrush** *n* spazzolino da denti; **toothpaste** *n* dentifricio; **toothpick** *n* stuzzicadenti *m inv*

top [tɒp] n (of mountain, page, ladder) cima; (of box, cupboard, table) sopra m inv, parte f superiore; (lid: of box, jar) coperchio; (: of bottle) tappo; (toy) trottola; (blouse etc) camicia (or maglietta etc) ▷ adj più alto/a; (in rank) primo/a, (best) migliore ▷ vt (exceed) superare; (be first in) essere in testa a; **on ~ of** sopra, in cima a; (in addition to) oltre a; **from ~ to bottom** da cima a fond; **top up**, (US) **top off** vt riempire; (salary) integrare; **top floor** n ultimo piano; **top hat** n cilindro

topic ['tɒpɪk] n argomento; **topical** adj d'attualità

topless ['tɒplɪs] adj (bather etc) col seno scoperto

topping ['tɒpɪŋ] n (Culin) guarnizione f

topple ['tɒpl] vt rovesciare, far cadere ▷ vi cadere; traballare

top-up ['tɒpʌp] n (for mobile phone: also: **~ card**) ricarica

torch [tɔːtʃ] n torcia; (BRIT: electric) lampadina tascabile

tore [tɔːr] pt of **tear²**

torment n ['tɔːmɛnt] tormento ▷ vt [tɔːˈmɛnt] tormentare

torn [tɔːn] pp of **tear²**

tornado [tɔːˈneɪdəu] (pl **tornadoes**) n tornado

torpedo [tɔːˈpiːdəu] (pl **torpedoes**) n siluro

torrent ['tɒrnt] n torrente m; **torrential** [tɔˈrɛnʃl] adj torrenziale

tortoise ['tɔːtəs] n tartaruga

torture ['tɔːtʃər] n tortura ▷ vt torturare

Tory ['tɔːrɪ] adj, n (BRIT Pol) tory mf inv, conservatore/trice

toss [tɒs] vt gettare, lanciare; (head) scuotere; **to ~ a coin** fare a testa o croce; **to ~ up for sth** fare a testa o croce per qc; **to ~ and turn** (in bed) girarsi e rigirarsi

total ['təutl] adj totale ▷ n totale m ▷ vt (add up) sommare; (amount to) ammontare a

totalitarian [təutælɪˈtɛərɪən] adj totalitario/a

totally ['təutəlɪ] adv completamente

touch [tʌtʃ] n tocco; (sense) tatto; (contact) contatto ▷ vt toccare; **a ~ of** (fig) un tocco di; un pizzico di; **to get in ~ with** mettersi in contatto con; **to lose ~** (friends) perdersi di vista; **touch down** vi (on land) atterrare; **touchdown** n atterraggio; (on sea) ammaraggio; (US Football) meta; **touched** adj commosso/a; **touching** adj commovente; **touchline** n (Sport) linea laterale; **touch screen** n (Tech) schermo touch screen; **touch-screen mobile** telefono touch screen; **touch-screen technology** tecnologia touch screen; **touch-sensitive** adj sensibile al tatto

tough [tʌf] adj duro/a; (resistant) resistente

tour [tuər] n viaggio; (also: **package ~**) viaggio organizzato or tutto compreso (of town, museum) visita; (by artist) tournée f inv ▷ vt visitare; **tour guide** n guida turistica

tourism ['tuərɪzəm] n turismo

tourist ['tuərɪst] n turista m/f ▷ adv (travel) in classe turistica ▷ cpd turistico/a; **tourist office** n pro loco f inv

tournament ['tuənəmənt] n torneo

tour operator n (BRIT) operatore m turistico

tow [təu] vt rimorchiare; **"on ~"**, (US) **"in ~"** (Aut) "veicolo rimorchiato"

toward(s) [təˈwɔːd(z)] prep verso; (of attitude) nei confronti di; (of purpose) per

towel ['tauəl] n asciugamano; (also: **tea ~**) strofinaccio; **towelling** n (fabric) spugna

tower ['tauər] n torre f; **tower block** n (BRIT) palazzone m

town [taun] n città f inv; **to go to ~** andare in città; (fig) mettercela tutta; **town centre** n centro (città); **town hall** n ≈ municipio

tow truck n (US) carro m attrezzi inv
toxic ['tɒksɪk] adj tossico/a; **toxic asset** n (Econ) titolo tossico; **toxic bank** n (Econ) banca cattiva (che investe in titoli tossici)
toy [tɔɪ] n giocattolo; **toy with** vt fus giocare con; (idea) accarezzare, trastullarsi con; **toyshop** n negozio di giocattoli
trace [treɪs] n traccia ▷ vt (draw) tracciare; (follow) seguire; (locate) rintracciare
track [træk] n (of person, animal) traccia; (on tape, Sport: gen) pista; (: of bullet etc) traiettoria; (: of suspect, animal) pista, tracce fpl; (Rail) binario, rotaie fpl ▷ vt seguire le tracce di; **to keep ~ of** seguire; **track down** vt (prey) scovare; snidare; (sth lost) rintracciare; **tracksuit** n tuta sportiva
tractor ['træktər] n trattore m
trade [treɪd] n commercio; (skill, job) mestiere m ▷ vi commerciare; **to ~ with/in** commerciare con/in ▷ vt: **to ~ sth (for sth)** barattare qc (con qc); **trade in** vt (old car etc) dare come pagamento parziale; **trademark** n marchio di fabbrica; **trader** n commerciante m/f; **tradesman** n (irreg) fornitore m; (shopkeeper) negoziante m; **trade union** n sindacato
trading ['treɪdɪŋ] n commercio
tradition [trə'dɪʃən] n tradizione f; **traditional** adj tradizionale
traffic ['træfɪk] n traffico ▷ vi: **to ~ in** (pej: liquor, drugs) trafficare in; **traffic circle** n (US) isola rotatoria; **traffic island** n salvagente m, isola f, spartitraffico inv; **traffic jam** n ingorgo (del traffico); **traffic lights** npl semaforo; **traffic warden** n addetto/a al controllo del traffico e del parcheggio
tragedy ['trædʒədɪ] n tragedia
tragic ['trædʒɪk] adj tragico/a

trail [treɪl] n (tracks) tracce fpl, pista; (path) sentiero; (of smoke etc) scia ▷ vt trascinare, strascicare; (follow) seguire ▷ vi essere al traino; (dress etc) strusciare; (plant) arrampicarsi; strusciare; (in game) essere in svantaggio; **trailer** n (Aut) rimorchio; (US) roulotte f inv; (Cine) prossimamente m inv
train [treɪn] n treno; (of dress) coda, strascico ▷ vt (apprentice, doctor etc) formare; (sportsman) allenare; (dog) addestrare; (memory) esercitare; (point: gun etc): **to ~ sth on** puntare qc contro ▷ vi formarsi; allenarsi; **one's ~ of thought** il filo dei propri pensieri; **trainee** [treɪ'niː] n (in trade) apprendista m/f; **trainer** n (Sport) allenatore/trice; (of dogs etc) addestratore/trice; **trainers** npl (shoes) scarpe fpl da ginnastica; **training** n formazione f; allenamento; addestramento; **in training** (Sport) in allenamento; **training course** n corso di formazione professionale; **training shoes** npl scarpe fpl da ginnastica
train wreck n (fig) persona distrutta; (: pej) rottame m; **he's a complete ~** è completamente distrutto, è un rottame
trait [treɪt] n tratto
traitor ['treɪtər] n traditore/trice
tram [træm] n (BRIT: also: **~car**) tram m inv
tramp [træmp] n (person) vagabondo/a; (col, pej: woman) sgualdrina
trample ['træmpl] vt: **to ~ (underfoot)** calpestare
trampoline ['træmpəliːn] n trampolino
tranquil ['træŋkwɪl] adj tranquillo/a; **tranquillizer**, (US) **tranquilizer** n (Med) tranquillante m
transaction [træn'zækʃən] n transazione f
transatlantic ['trænzət'læntɪk] adj transatlantico/a

t

transcript ['trænskrıpt] n
trascrizione f
transfer n ['trænsfə^r] (gen, also
Sport) trasferimento; (Pol: of
power) passaggio; (picture, design)
decalcomania; (: stick-on) autoadesivo
▷ vt [træns'fəː^r] trasferire; passare;
to ~ the charges (BRIT Tel) fare una
chiamata a carico del destinatario
transform [træns'fɔːm] vt
trasformare; **transformation** n
trasformazione f
transfusion [træns'fjuːʒən] n
trasfusione f
transit ['trænzıt] n: **in ~** in transito
transition [træn'zıʃən] n passaggio,
transizione f
transitive ['trænzıtıv] adj (Ling)
transitivo/a
translate [trænz'leıt] vt tradurre;
translation [trænz'leıʃən] n
traduzione f; **translator** n
traduttore/trice
transmission [trænz'mıʃən] n
trasmissione f
transmit [trænz'mıt] vt
trasmettere; **transmitter** n
trasmettitore m
transparent [træns'pærnt] adj
trasparente
transplant vt [træns'plɑːnt]
trapiantare ▷ n ['trænsplɑːnt] (Med)
trapianto
transport n ['trænspɔːt] trasporto
▷ vt [træns'pɔːt] trasportare;
transportation ['trænspɔː'teıʃən] n
(mezzo di) trasporto
transvestite [trænz'vɛstaıt] n
travestito/a
trap [træp] n (snare, trick) trappola;
(carriage) calesse m ▷ vt prendere in
trappola, intrappolare
trash [træʃ] n (col: goods) ciarpame m;
(: nonsense) sciocchezze fpl; **trash can**
n (US) secchio della spazzatura
trauma ['trɔːmə] n trauma m;
traumatic [trɔː'mætık] adj
traumatico/a

travel ['trævl] n viaggio; viaggi
mpl ▷ vi viaggiare ▷ vt (distance)
percorrere; **travel agency** n agenzia
(di) viaggi; **travel agent** n agente
m di viaggio; **travel insurance** n
assicurazione f di viaggio; **traveller**,
(US) **traveler** n viaggiatore/trice;
traveller's cheque, (US) **traveler's
check** n assegno turistico; **travelling**,
(US) **traveling** n viaggi mpl; **travel-
sick** adj: **to get travel-sick** (in vehicle)
soffrire di mal d'auto; (in aeroplane)
soffrire di mal d'aria; (in boat) soffrire di
mal di mare; **travel sickness** n mal m
d'auto (or di mare or d'aria)
tray [treı] n (for carrying) vassoio; (on
desk) vaschetta
treacherous ['trɛtʃərəs] adj infido/a
treacle ['triːkl] n melassa
tread [trɛd] n passo; (sound) rumore
m di passi; (of stairs) pedata; (of tyre)
battistrada m inv ▷ vi (pt **trod**, pp
trodden) camminare; **tread on** vt
fus calpestare
treasure ['trɛʒə^r] n tesoro ▷ vt (value)
tenere in gran conto, apprezzare
molto; (store) custodire gelosamente;
treasurer [trɛʒərə^r] n tesoriere/a
treasury ['trɛʒərı] n: **the T~**
(BRIT), **the T~ Department** (US) ≈ il
Ministero del Tesoro
treat [triːt] n regalo ▷ vt trattare;
(Med) curare; **to ~ sb to sth** offrire
qc a qn; **treatment** ['triːtmənt] n
trattamento
treaty ['triːtı] n patto, trattato
treble ['trɛbl] adj triplo/a, triplice ▷ vt
triplicare ▷ vi triplicarsi
tree [triː] n albero
trek [trɛk] n (hike) escursione
f a piedi; (in car) escursione f in
macchina; (tiring walk) camminata
sfiancante ▷ vi (as holiday) fare
dell'escursionismo
tremble ['trɛmbl] vi tremare
tremendous [trı'mɛndəs] adj
(enormous) enorme; (excellent)
meraviglioso/a, formidabile

Be careful not to translate *tremendous* by the Italian word *tremendo*.

trench [trɛntʃ] n trincea

trend [trɛnd] n (tendency) tendenza; (of events) corso; (fashion) moda; **trendy** adj (idea) di moda; (clothes) all'ultima moda

trespass ['trɛspəs] vi: **to ~ on** entrare abusivamente in; **"no ~ing"** "proprietà privata", "vietato l'accesso"

trial ['traɪəl] n (Law) processo; (test: of machine etc) collaudo; **to be on ~** (Law) essere sotto processo; **trial period** n periodo di prova

triangle ['traɪæŋgl] n (Math, Mus) triangolo

triangular [traɪ'æŋgjulər] adj triangolare

tribe [traɪb] n tribù f inv

tribunal [traɪ'bjuːnl] n tribunale m

tribute ['trɪbjuːt] n tributo, omaggio; **to pay ~ to** rendere omaggio a

trick [trɪk] n trucco; (joke) tiro; (Cards) presa ▷ vt imbrogliare, ingannare; **to play a ~ on sb** giocare un tiro a qn; **that should do the ~** vedrai che funziona

trickle ['trɪkl] n (of water etc) rivolo; gocciolio ▷ vi gocciolare

tricky ['trɪkɪ] adj difficile, delicato/a

tricycle ['traɪsɪkl] n triciclo

trifle ['traɪfl] n sciocchezza; (BRIT Culin) ≈ zuppa inglese ▷ adv: **a ~ long** un po' lungo

trigger ['trɪgər] n (of gun) grilletto

trim [trɪm] adj (house, garden) ben tenuto/a; (figure) snello/a ▷ n (haircut etc) spuntata, regolata; (embellishment) finiture fpl; (on car) guarnizioni fpl ▷ vt spuntare; (Naut: a sail) orientare; (decorate): **to ~ (with)** decorare (con)

trio ['triːəu] n trio

trip [trɪp] n viaggio; (excursion) gita, escursione f; (stumble) passo falso ▷ vi inciampare; (go lightly) camminare con passo leggero; **on a ~** in viaggio; **trip up** vi inciampare ▷ vt fare lo sgambetto a

triple ['trɪpl] adj triplo/a

triplets ['trɪplɪts] npl bambini/e trigemini/e

tripod ['traɪpɔd] n treppiede m

triumph ['traɪʌmf] n trionfo ▷ vi: **to ~ (over)** trionfare (su); **triumphant** [traɪ'ʌmfənt] adj trionfante

trivial ['trɪvɪəl] adj insignificante; (excuse, comment) banale

Be careful not to translate *trivial* by the Italian word *triviale*.

trod [trɔd] pt of **tread**

trodden ['trɔdn] pp of **tread**

trolley ['trɔlɪ] n carrello

trombone [trɔm'bəun] n trombone m

troop [truːp] n gruppo; (Mil) squadrone m; **troops** npl (Mil) truppe fpl

trophy ['trəufɪ] n trofeo

tropical ['trɔpɪkəl] adj tropicale

trot [trɔt] n trotto ▷ vi trottare; **on the ~** (BRIT fig) di fila, uno/a dopo l'altro/a

trouble ['trʌbl] n difficoltà f inv, problema m; (problems) difficoltà fpl, problemi mpl; (worry) preoccupazione f; (bother, effort) sforzo; (Pol) conflitti mpl, disordine m; (Med): **stomach etc ~** disturbi mpl gastrici etc ▷ vt disturbare; (worry) preoccupare ▷ vi: **to ~ to do** disturbarsi a fare; **troubles** npl (Pol etc) disordini mpl; **to be in ~** avere dei problemi; **it's no ~!** di niente!; **what's the ~?** cosa c'è che non va?; **troubled** adj (person) preoccupato/a, inquieto/a; (epoch, life) agitato/a, difficile; **troublemaker** n elemento disturbatore, agitatore/trice; (child) disloco/a; **troublesome** adj fastidioso/a, seccante

trough [trɔf] n (also: **drinking ~**) abbeveratoio; (also: **feeding ~**) trogolo, mangiatoia; (channel) canale m

t

trousers ['trauzəz] *npl* pantaloni *mpl*, calzoni *mpl*; **short ~** calzoncini *mpl*

trout [traut] *n* (*pl inv*) trota

trowel ['trauəl] *n* cazzuola

truant ['truənt] *n*: **to play ~** (*BRIT*) marinare la scuola

truce [tru:s] *n* tregua

truck [trʌk] *n* autocarro, camion *m inv*; (*Rail*) carro merci aperto; (*for luggage*) carrello *m* portabagagli *inv*; **truck driver** *n* camionista *m/f*

true [tru:] *adj* vero/a; (*accurate*) accurato/a, esatto/a; (*genuine*) reale; (*faithful*) fedele; **to come ~** avverarsi

truly ['tru:lɪ] *adv* veramente; (*truthfully*) sinceramente; **yours ~** (*in letter-writing*) distinti saluti

trumpet ['trʌmpɪt] *n* tromba

trunk [trʌŋk] *n* (*of tree, person*) tronco; (*of elephant*) proboscide *f*; (*case*) baule *m*; (*us Aut*) bagagliaio; **trunks** *npl* (*also*: **swimming trunks**) calzoncini *mpl* da bagno

trust [trʌst] *n* fiducia; (*Law*) amministrazione *f* fiduciaria; (*Comm*) trust *m inv* ▷ *vt* (*rely on*) contare su; (*entrust*): **to ~ sth to sb** affidare qc a qn; (*hope*): **to ~ (that)** sperare (che); **trusted** *adj* fidato/a; **trustworthy** *adj* fidato/a, degno/a di fiducia

truth (*pl* **truths**) [tru:θ, tru:ðz] *n* verità *f inv*; **truthful** *adj* (*person*) sincero/a; (*description*) veritiero/a, esatto/a

try [traɪ] *n* prova, tentativo; (*Rugby*) meta ▷ *vt* (*Law*) giudicare; (*test: also*: **~ out**) provare; (*strain*) mettere alla prova ▷ *vi* provare; **to have a ~** fare un tentativo; **to ~ to do** (*seek*) cercare di fare; **try on** *vt* (*clothes*) provare; **trying** *adj* (*day, experience*) logorante, pesante; (*child*) difficile, insopportabile

T-shirt ['ti:ʃə:t] *n* maglietta

tsunami [tsu'nɑ:mɪ] *n* tsunami *m inv*

tub [tʌb] *n* tinozza; mastello; (*bath*) bagno

tube [tju:b] *n* tubo; (*BRIT: underground*) metropolitana, metrò *m inv*; (*for tyre*) camera d'aria

tuberculosis [tjubə:kju'ləusɪs] *n* tubercolosi *f inv*

tube station *n* (*BRIT*) stazione *f* della metropolitana

tuck [tʌk] *n* piega ▷ *vt* (*put*) mettere; **tuck away** *vt* riporre; (*building*): **to be ~ed away** essere in un luogo isolato; **tuck in** *vt* mettere dentro; (*child*) rimboccare ▷ *vi* (*eat*) mangiare di buon appetito; abbuffarsi

tucker ['tʌkə'] *n* (*AUST, NZ col*) cibo

tuck shop *n* negozio di pasticceria (*in una scuola*)

Tue(s). *abbr* (= *Tuesday*) mar.

Tuesday ['tju:zdɪ] *n* martedì *m inv*

tug [tʌg] *n* (*ship*) rimorchiatore *m* ▷ *vt* tirare con forza

tuition [tju:'ɪʃən] *n* (*BRIT*) lezioni *fpl*; (: *private tuition*) lezioni *fpl* private; (*us: fees*) tasse *fpl* scolastiche (*or* universitarie)

tulip ['tju:lɪp] *n* tulipano

tumble ['tʌmbl] *n* (*fall*) capitombolo ▷ *vi* capitombolare, ruzzolare; **to ~ to sth** (*col*) realizzare qc; **tumble dryer** *n* (*BRIT*) asciugatrice *f*

tumbler ['tʌmblə'] *n* bicchiere *m* senza stelo

tummy ['tʌmɪ] *n* (*col*) pancia

tumour, (*us*) **tumor** ['tju:mə'] *n* tumore *m*

tuna ['tju:nə] *n* (*pl inv*: *also*: **~ fish**) tonno

tune [tju:n] *n* (*melody*) melodia, aria ▷ *vt* (*Mus*) accordare; (*Radio, TV, Aut*) regolare, mettere a punto; **to be in/out of ~** (*instrument*) essere accordato/a/scordato/a; (*singer*) essere intonato/a/stonato/a; **tune in** *vi* (*Radio, TV*): **to ~ in (to)** sintonizzarsi (su); **tune up** *vi* (*musician*) accordare lo strumento

tunic ['tju:nɪk] *n* tunica

Tunisia [tju:'nɪzɪə] *n* Tunisia

tunnel ['tʌnl] n galleria ▷ vi scavare una galleria

turbulence ['tə:bjuləns] n (Aviat) turbolenza

turf [tə:f] n terreno erboso; (clod) zolla ▷ vt coprire di zolle erbose

Turin [tjuə'rɪn] n Torino f

Turk [tə:k] n turco/a

Turkey ['tə:kɪ] n Turchia

turkey ['tə:kɪ] n tacchino

Turkish ['tə:kɪʃ] adj turco/a ▷ n (Ling) turco

turmoil ['tə:mɔɪl] n confusione f, tumulto

turn [tə:n] n giro; (change) cambiamento; (in road) curva; (tendency: of mind, events) tendenza; (performance) numero; (chance) turno; (Med) crisi f inv, attacco ▷ vt girare, voltare; (change): **to ~ sth into** trasformare qc in ▷ vi girare; (person: look back) girarsi, voltarsi; (reverse direction) girarsi indietro; (change) cambiare; (milk) andare a male; (become) diventare; **a good ~** un buon servizio; **it gave me quite a ~** mi ha fatto prendere un bello spavento; **"no left ~"** (Aut) "divieto di svolta a sinistra"; **it's your ~** tocca a lei; **in ~** a sua volta; a turno; **to take ~s (at sth)** fare (qc) a turno; **turn away** vi girarsi (dall'altra parte) ▷ vt mandar via; **turn back** vi ritornare, tornare indietro ▷ vt far tornare indietro; (clock) spostare indietro; **turn down** vt (refuse) rifiutare; (reduce) abbassare; (fold) ripiegare; **turn in** vi (col: go to bed) andare a letto ▷ vt (fold) voltare in dentro; **turn off** vi (from road) girare, voltare ▷ vt (light, radio, engine etc) spegnere; **turn on** vt (light, radio etc) accendere; **turn out** vt (light, gas) chiudere; spegnere ▷ vi (troops, doctor, voters etc) presentarsi; **to ~ out to be ...** rivelarsi ..., risultare ...; **turn over** vi (person) girarsi ▷ vt girare; **turn round** vi girare; (person) girarsi; **turn to** vt fus: **to ~ to sb** girarsi verso qn; **to ~ to sb for help** rivolgersi a qn per aiuto; **turn up** vi (person) arrivare, presentarsi; (lost object) saltar fuori ▷ vt (collar, sound, gas etc) alzare; **turning** n (in road) curva; **turning point** n (fig) svolta decisiva

turnip ['tə:nɪp] n rapa

turn: turnout ['tə:naut] n presenza, affluenza; **turnover** ['tə:nəuvə'] n (Comm) giro di affari; (Culin): **apple etc turnover** sfogliatella alle mele etc; **turnstile** ['tə:nstaɪl] n tornella; **turn-up** n (BRIT: on trousers) risvolto

turquoise [tə:kwɔɪz] n turchese m ▷ adj turchese

turtle ['tə:tl] n testuggine f; **turtleneck (sweater)** ['tə:tlnɛk-] n maglione m con il collo alto

Tuscany ['tʌskənɪ] n Toscana

tusk [tʌsk] n zanna

tutor ['tju:tə'] n (in college) docente m/f (responsabile di un gruppo di studenti); (private teacher) precettore m; **tutorial** [tju:'tɔ:rɪəl] n (Scol) lezione f con discussione (a un gruppo limitato)

tuxedo [tʌk'si:dəu] n (US) smoking m inv

TV [ti:'vi:] n abbr (= television) tivù f inv

tweed [twi:d] n tweed m inv

tweet [twi:t] n (on Twitter) post m su Twitter ▷ vt, vi (on Twitter) twittare

tweezers ['twi:zəz] npl pinzette fpl

twelfth [twɛlfθ] num dodicesimo/a

twelve [twɛlv] num dodici; **at ~** alle dodici, a mezzogiorno; (midnight) a mezzanotte

twentieth ['twɛntɪɪθ] num ventesimo/a

twenty ['twɛntɪ] num venti; **in ~ fourteen** nel duemilaquattordici

twice [twaɪs] adv due volte; **~ as much** due volte tanto; **~ a week** due volte alla settimana

twig [twɪg] n ramoscello ▷ vt, vi (col) capire

twilight ['twaɪlaɪt] n crepuscolo
twin [twɪn] adj, n gemello/a ▷ vt:
  to ~ one town with another fare il
  gemellaggio di una città con un'altra;
  twin-bedded room n stanza con
  letti gemelli; **twin beds** npl letti
  npl gemelli
twinkle ['twɪŋkl] vi scintillare; (eyes)
  brillare
twist [twɪst] n torsione f; (in wire, flex)
  piega; (in story) colpo di scena; (bend)
  svolta, piega; (in road) curva ▷ vt
  attorcigliare; (ankle) slogare; (weave)
  intrecciare; (roll around) arrotolare;
  (fig) distorcere ▷ vi (road) serpeggiare
twit [twɪt] n (col) cretino/a
twitch [twɪtʃ] n tiratina; (nervous) tic
  m inv ▷ vi contrarsi
Twitter® [twɪtəʳ] n Twitter® m
two [tuː] num due; **to put ~ and ~**
  together (fig) fare uno più uno
type [taɪp] n (category) genere m;
  (model) modello; (example) tipo;
  (Typ) tipo, carattere m ▷ vt (letter etc)
  battere (a macchina), dattilografare;
  typewriter n macchina da scrivere
typhoid ['taɪfɔɪd] n tifoidea
typhoon [taɪˈfuːn] n tifone m
typical ['tɪpɪkl] adj tipico/a;
  typically adv tipicamente;
  typically, he arrived late come al
  solito è arrivato tardi
typing ['taɪpɪŋ] n dattilografia
typist ['taɪpɪst] n dattilografo/a
tyre, (us) **tire** ['taɪəʳ] n pneumatico,
  gomma; **I've got a flat ~** ho una
  gomma a terra; **tyre pressure** n
  pressione f (delle gomme)

U

UFO ['juːfəu] n abbr (= unidentified
  flying object) UFO m inv
Uganda [juːˈgændə] n Uganda
ugly ['ʌglɪ] adj brutto/a
UHT adj abbr (= ultra heat treated) UHT
  inv, a lunga conservazione
UK n abbr = **United Kingdom**
ulcer ['ʌlsəʳ] n ulcera; **mouth ~**
  afta
ultimate ['ʌltɪmɪt] adj ultimo/a,
  finale; (authority) massimo/a,
  supremo/a; **ultimately** adv alla fine;
  in definitiva, in fin dei conti
ultimatum (pl **ultimatums** or
  ultimata) [ʌltɪˈmeɪtəm, -tə] n
  ultimatum m inv
ultrasound [ʌltrəˈsaund] n
  ultrasuono; (Med) ecografia
ultraviolet ['ʌltrəˈvaɪəlɪt] adj
  ultravioletto/a
umbrella [ʌmˈbrɛlə] n ombrello
umpire ['ʌmpaɪəʳ] n arbitro
UN n abbr (= United Nations) ONU f

unable [ʌn'eɪbl] *adj*: **to be ~ to** non potere, essere nell'impossibilità di; (*not to know how to*) essere incapace di

unacceptable [ʌnək'sɛptəbl] *adj* (*proposal, behaviour*) inaccettabile; (*price*) impossibile

unanimous [juː'nænɪməs] *adj* unanime

unarmed [ʌn'ɑːmd] *adj* (*person*) disarmato/a; (*combat*) senz'armi

unattended [ʌnə'tɛndɪd] *adj* (*car, child, luggage*) incustodito/a

unattractive [ʌnə'træktɪv] *adj* poco attraente

unavailable [ʌnə'veɪləbl] *adj* (*article, room, book*) non disponibile; (*person*) impegnato/a

unavoidable [ʌnə'vɔɪdəbl] *adj* inevitabile

unaware [ʌnə'wɛəʳ] *adj*: **to be ~ of** non sapere, ignorare; **unawares** *adv* di sorpresa, alla sprovvista

unbearable [ʌn'bɛərəbl] *adj* insopportabile

unbeatable [ʌn'biːtəbl] *adj* imbattibile

unbelievable [ʌnbɪ'liːvəbl] *adj* incredibile

unborn [ʌn'bɔːn] *adj* non ancora nato/a

unbutton [ʌn'bʌtn] *vt* sbottonare

uncalled-for [ʌn'kɔːldfɔːʳ] *adj* (*remark*) fuori luogo *inv*; (*action*) ingiustificato/a

uncanny [ʌn'kænɪ] *adj* misterioso/a, strano/a

uncertain [ʌn'səːtn] *adj* incerto/a; dubbio/a; **uncertainty** *n* incertezza

unchanged [ʌn'tʃeɪndʒd] *adj* immutato/a

uncle ['ʌŋkl] *n* zio

unclear [ʌn'klɪəʳ] *adj* non chiaro/a; **I'm still ~ about what I'm supposed to do** non ho ancora ben capito cosa dovrei fare

uncomfortable [ʌn'kʌmfətəbl] *adj* scomodo/a; (*uneasy*) a disagio, agitato/a; (*unpleasant*) fastidioso/a

uncommon [ʌn'kɔmən] *adj* raro/a, insolito/a, non comune

unconditional [ʌn'kən'dɪʃənl] *adj* incondizionato/a, senza condizioni

unconscious [ʌn'kɔnʃəs] *adj* privo/a di sensi, svenuto/a; (*unaware*) inconsapevole, inconscio/a ▷ *n*: **the ~** l'inconscio

uncontrollable [ʌnkən'trəuləbl] *adj* incontrollabile; indisciplinato/a

unconventional [ʌnkən'vɛnʃənl] *adj* poco convenzionale

uncover [ʌn'kʌvəʳ] *vt* scoprire

undecided [ʌndɪ'saɪdɪd] *adj* indeciso/a

undeniable [ʌndɪ'naɪəbl] *adj* innegabile, indiscutibile

under ['ʌndəʳ] *prep* sotto; (*less than*) meno di; al disotto di; (*according to*) secondo, in conformità a ▷ *adv* (al) disotto; **~ there** là sotto; **~ repair** in riparazione; **undercover** *adj* segreto/a, clandestino/a; **underdone** *adj* (*Culin*) al sangue; (*pej*) poco cotto/a; **underestimate** *vt* sottovalutare; **undergo** *vt* (*irreg*) subire; (*treatment*) sottoporsi a; **undergraduate** *n* studente/essa universitario/a; **underground** *n* (BRIT: *railway*) metropolitana; (*Pol*) movimento clandestino ▷ *adj* sotterraneo/a; (*fig*) clandestino/a ▷ *adv* sottoterra: **to go underground** (*fig*) darsi alla macchia; **undergrowth** *n* sottobosco; **underline** *vt* sottolineare; **undermine** *vt* minare; **underneath** [ʌndə'niːθ] *adv* sotto, disotto ▷ *prep* sotto, al di sotto di; **underpants** *npl* mutande *fpl*, slip *m inv*; **underpass** *n* (BRIT) sottopassaggio; **underprivileged** *adj* svantaggiato/a; **underscore** *vt* sottolineare; **undershirt** *n* (US) maglietta; **underskirt** (BRIT) *n* sottoveste *f*

understand [ʌndə'stænd] (*irreg: like* **stand**) *vt*, *vi* capire, comprendere;

u

I don't ~ non capisco; **I ~ that ...**
sento che ...; credo di capire che ...;
understandable adj comprensibile;
understanding adj comprensivo/a
▷ n comprensione f; (agreement)
accordo

understatement [ʌndə'steɪtmənt]
n: **that's an ~!** a dire poco!

understood [ʌndə'stud] pt, pp of
understand ▷ adj inteso/a; (implied)
sottinteso/a

undertake [ʌndə'teɪk] vt (irreg: like
take) intraprendere; **to ~ to do sth**
impegnarsi a fare qc

undertaker ['ʌndəteɪkəʳ] n
impresario di pompe funebri

undertaking [ʌndə'teɪkɪŋ] n
impresa; (promise) promessa

under: underwater [ʌndə'wɔːtəʳ]
adv sott'acqua ▷ adj subacqueo/a;
underway [ˌʌndə'weɪ] adj: **to
be underway** essere in corso;
underwear ['ʌndəwɛəʳ] n
biancheria (intima); **underwent**
[ʌndə'wɛnt] vb see **undergo**;
underworld ['ʌndəwə:ld] n (of
crime) malavita

undesirable [ʌndɪ'zaɪərəbl] adj
indesiderato/a

undisputed [ʌndɪs'pju:tɪd] adj
indiscusso/a

undo [ʌn'du:] vt (irreg) disfare

undone [ʌn'dʌn] pp of **undo**; **to
come ~** slacciarsi

undoubtedly [ʌn'dautɪdlɪ] adv
senza alcun dubbio

undress [ʌn'drɛs] vi spogliarsi

unearth [ʌn'ə:θ] vt dissotterrare;
(fig) scoprire

uneasy [ʌn'i:zɪ] adj a disagio;
(worried) preoccupato/a; (peace)
precario/a

unemployed [ʌnɪm'plɔɪd] adj
disoccupato/a ▷ npl: **the ~** i
disoccupati

unemployment [ʌnɪm'plɔɪmənt]
n disoccupazione f; **unemployment
benefit**, (US) **unemployment**

compensation n sussidio di
disoccupazione

unequal [ʌn'i:kwəl] adj (length,
objects) disuguale; (amounts)
diverso/a; (division of labour) ineguale

uneven [ʌn'i:vn] adj ineguale;
(heartbeat) irregolare

unexpected [ʌnɪk'spɛktɪd]
adj inatteso/a, imprevisto/a;
unexpectedly adv
inaspettatamente

unfair [ʌn'fɛəʳ] adj: **~ (to)** ingiusto/a
(nei confronti di)

unfaithful [ʌn'feɪθful] adj infedele

unfamiliar [ʌnfə'mɪlɪəʳ] adj
sconosciuto/a, strano/a; **to be ~
with sth** non avere familiarità con qc

unfashionable [ʌn'fæʃnəbl] adj
(clothes) fuori moda inv; (district) non
alla moda

unfasten [ʌn'fɑ:sn] vt slacciare;
sciogliere

unfavourable, (US) **unfavorable**
[ʌn'feɪvərəbl] adj sfavorevole

unfinished [ʌn'fɪnɪʃt] adj
incompiuto/a

unfit [ʌn'fɪt] adj (ill) non in forma;
(incompetent): **~ (for)** incompetente
(in); (work, Mil) inabile (a)

unfold [ʌn'fəuld] vt spiegare ▷ vi
(story) svelarsi

unforgettable [ʌnfə'gɛtəbl] adj
indimenticabile

unfortunate [ʌn'fɔ:tʃnɪt] adj
sfortunato/a; (event, remark)
infelice; **unfortunately** adv
sfortunatamente, purtroppo

unfriend [ʌn'frɛnd] vt (Internet)
cancellare dagli amici

unfriendly [ʌn'frɛndlɪ] adj poco
amichevole, freddo/a

unfurnished [ʌn'fə:nɪʃt] adj non
ammobiliato/a

unhappiness [ʌn'hæpɪnɪs] n
infelicità

unhappy [ʌn'hæpɪ] adj infelice;
~ about/with (arrangements etc)
insoddisfatto/a di

unhealthy [ʌnˈhɛlθɪ] adj (gen) malsano/a; (person) malaticcio/a

unheard-of [ʌnˈhəːdɔv] adj inaudito/a, senza precedenti

unhelpful [ʌnˈhɛlpful] adj poco disponibile

unhurt [ʌnˈhəːt] adj incolume, illeso/a

unidentified [ʌnaɪˈdɛntɪfaɪd] adj non identificato/a

uniform [ˈjuːnɪfɔːm] n uniforme f, divisa ▷ adj uniforme

unify [ˈjuːnɪfaɪ] vt unificare

unimportant [ʌnɪmˈpɔːtənt] adj senza importanza, di scarsa importanza

uninhabited [ʌnɪnˈhæbɪtɪd] adj disabitato/a

unintentional [ʌnɪnˈtɛnʃənəl] adj involontario/a

union [ˈjuːnjən] n unione f; (also: **trade ~**) sindacato ▷ cpd sindacale, dei sindacati; **Union Jack** n bandiera nazionale britannica

unique [juːˈniːk] adj unico/a

unisex [ˈjuːnɪsɛks] adj unisex inv

unit [ˈjuːnɪt] n unità f inv; (section: of furniture etc) elemento; (team, squad) reparto, squadra

unite [juːˈnaɪt] vt unire ▷ vi unirsi; **united** adj unito/a; unificato/a; (efforts) congiunto/a; **United Kingdom** n Regno Unito; **United Nations (Organization)** n (Organizzazione f delle) Nazioni Unite; **United States (of America)** n Stati mpl Uniti (d'America)

unity [ˈjuːnɪtɪ] n unità

universal [juːnɪˈvəːsl] adj universale

universe [ˈjuːnɪvəːs] n universo

university [juːnɪˈvəːsɪtɪ] n università f inv

unjust [ʌnˈdʒʌst] adj ingiusto/a

unkind [ʌnˈkaɪnd] adj poco gentile, scortese

unknown [ʌnˈnəun] adj sconosciuto/a

unlawful [ʌnˈlɔːful] adj illecito/a, illegale

unleaded [ˈʌnˈlɛdɪd] adj senza piombo; **~ petrol** benzina verde or senza piombo

unleash [ʌnˈliːʃ] vt (fig) scatenare

unless [ʌnˈlɛs] conj a meno che (non) + sub

unlike [ʌnˈlaɪk] adj diverso/a ▷ prep a differenza di, contrariamente a

unlikely [ʌnˈlaɪklɪ] adj improbabile

unlimited [ʌnˈlɪmɪtɪd] adj illimitato/a

unlisted [ʌnˈlɪstɪd] adj (us Tel): **to be ~** non essere sull'elenco

unload [ʌnˈləud] vt scaricare

unlock [ʌnˈlɔk] vt aprire

unlucky [ʌnˈlʌkɪ] adj sfortunato/a; (object, number) che porta sfortuna

unmarried [ʌnˈmærɪd] adj non sposato/a; (man only) scapolo, celibe; (woman only) nubile

unmistak(e)able [ʌnmɪsˈteɪkəbl] adj inconfondibile

unnatural [ʌnˈnætʃrəl] adj innaturale; contro natura

unnecessary [ʌnˈnɛsəsərɪ] adj inutile, superfluo/a

UNO [ˈjuːnəu] n abbr (= United Nations Organization) ONU f

unofficial [ʌnəˈfɪʃl] adj non ufficiale; (strike) non dichiarato/a dal sindacato

unpack [ʌnˈpæk] vi disfare la valigia (or le valige) ▷ vt disfare

unpaid [ʌnˈpeɪd] adj (holiday) non pagato/a; (work) non retribuito/a; (bill, debt) da pagare

unpleasant [ʌnˈplɛznt] adj spiacevole

unplug [ʌnˈplʌg] vt staccare

unpopular [ʌnˈpɔpjuləʳ] adj impopolare

unprecedented [ʌnˈprɛsɪdəntɪd] adj senza precedenti

unpredictable [ʌnprɪˈdɪktəbl] adj imprevedibile

unprotected [ˈʌnprəˈtɛktɪd] adj (sex) non protetto/a

u

unqualified [ʌnˈkwɔlɪfaɪd] *adj* (*in professions*) non abilitato/a; (*success*) assoluto/a, senza riserve

unravel [ʌnˈrævl] *vt* dipanare, districare

unreal [ʌnˈrɪəl] *adj* irreale

unrealistic [ʌnrɪəˈlɪstɪk] *adj* non realistico/a

unreasonable [ʌnˈriːznəbl] *adj* irragionevole

unrelated [ʌnrɪˈleɪtɪd] *adj*: ~ (to) senza rapporto (con); (*by family*) non imparentato/a (con)

unreliable [ʌnrɪˈlaɪəbl] *adj* (*person, machine*) che non dà affidamento; (*news, source of information*) inattendibile

unrest [ʌnˈrɛst] *n* agitazione *f*

unroll [ʌnˈrəʊl] *vt* srotolare

unruly [ʌnˈruːlɪ] *adj* indisciplinato/a

unsafe [ʌnˈseɪf] *adj* pericoloso/a, rischioso/a

unsatisfactory [ˈʌnsætɪsˈfæktərɪ] *adj* che lascia a desiderare, insufficiente

unscrew [ʌnˈskruː] *vt* svitare

unsettled [ʌnˈsɛtld] *adj* (*person, future*) incerto/a; indeciso/a; turbato/a; (*weather, market*) instabile

unsettling [ʌnˈsɛtlɪŋ] *adj* inquietante

unsightly [ʌnˈsaɪtlɪ] *adj* brutto/a, sgradevole a vedersi

unskilled [ʌnˈskɪld] *adj*: ~ **worker** operaio/a specializzato/a

unspoiled [ˈʌnˈspɔɪld], **unspoilt** [ˈʌnˈspɔɪlt] *adj* (*place*) non deturpato/a

unstable [ʌnˈsteɪbl] *adj* (*gen*) instabile; (*mentally*) squilibrato/a

unsteady [ʌnˈstɛdɪ] *adj* instabile, malsicuro/a

unsuccessful [ʌnsəkˈsɛsful] *adj* (*writer, proposal*) che non ha successo; (*marriage, attempt*) mal riuscito/a, fallito/a; **to be ~** (*in attempting sth*) non avere successo

unsuitable [ʌnˈsuːtəbl] *adj* inadatto/a; (*moment*) inopportuno/a; sconveniente

unsure [ʌnˈʃuər] *adj*: ~ (**of** or **about**) incerto/a (su); **to be ~ of o.s.** essere insicuro/a

untidy [ʌnˈtaɪdɪ] *adj* (*room*) in disordine; (*appearance, work*) trascurato/a; (*person, writing*) disordinato/a

untie [ʌnˈtaɪ] *vt* (*knot, parcel*) disfare; (*prisoner, dog*) slegare

until [ʌnˈtɪl] *prep* fino a; (*after negative*) prima di ▷ *conj* finché, fino a quando; (*in past, after negative*) prima che + *sub*, prima di + *infinitive*; ~ **he comes** finché or fino a quando non arriva; ~ **now** finora; ~ **then** fino ad allora

untrue [ʌnˈtruː] *adj* (*statement*) falso/a, non vero/a

unused [ʌnˈjuːzd] *adj* nuovo/a

unusual [ʌnˈjuːʒuəl] *adj* insolito/a, eccezionale raro/a; **unusually** *adv* insolitamente

unveil [ʌnˈveɪl] *vt* scoprire; svelare

unwanted [ʌnˈwɔntɪd] *adj* (*clothing*) smesso/a; (*child*) non desiderato/a

unwell [ʌnˈwɛl] *adj* indisposto/a; **to feel ~** non sentirsi bene

unwilling [ʌnˈwɪlɪŋ] *adj*: **to be ~ to do** non voler fare

unwind [ʌnˈwaɪnd] (*irreg: like* **wind²**) *like vt* svolgere, srotolare ▷ *vi* (*relax*) rilassarsi

unwise [ʌnˈwaɪz] *adj* poco saggio/a

unwittingly [ʌnˈwɪtɪŋlɪ] *adv* senza volerlo

unwrap [ʌnˈræp] *vt* disfare; (*present*) aprire

unzip [ʌnˈzɪp] *vt* aprire (la chiusura lampo di); (*Comput*) dezippare

KEYWORD

up [ʌp] *prep*: **he went up the stairs/ the hill** è salito su per le scale/sulla collina; **the cat was up a tree** il gatto era su un albero; **they live**

further up the street vivono un po' più su nella stessa strada
▶ adv **1** (*upwards, higher*) su, in alto; **up in the sky/the mountains** su nel cielo/in montagna; **up there** lassù; **up above** su in alto
2: **to be up** (*out of bed*) essere alzato/a; (*prices, level*) essere salito/a
3: **up to** (*as far as*) fino a; **up to now** finora
4: **to be up to** (*depending on*): **it's up to you** sta a lei, dipende da lei; (*equal to*): **he's not up to it** (*job, task etc*) non ne è all'altezza; (*be doing: col*): **what is he up to?** cosa sta combinando?
▶ n: **ups and downs** alti e bassi *mpl*

up-and-coming ['ʌpənd'kʌmɪŋ] *adj* pieno/a di promesse, promettente
upbringing ['ʌpbrɪŋɪŋ] *n* educazione *f*
update [ʌp'deɪt] *vt* aggiornare
upfront [ʌp'frʌnt] *adj* (*col*) franco/a, aperto/a ▶ adv (*pay*) subito
upgrade [ʌp'greɪd] *vt* (*job*) rivalutare; (*house*) rimodernare; (*employee*) avanzare di grado
upheaval [ʌp'hiːvl] *n* sconvolgimento; tumulto
uphill [ʌp'hɪl] *adj* in salita; (*fig: task*) difficile ▶ adv: **to go ~** andare in salita, salire
upholstery [ʌp'həulstərɪ] *n* tappezzeria
upload ['ʌpləud] *vt* caricare
up-market [ʌp'mɑːkɪt] *adj* (*product*) che si rivolge ad una fascia di mercato superiore
upon [ə'pɒn] *prep* su
upper ['ʌpə'] *adj* superiore ▶ n (*of shoe*) tomaia; **upper-class** *adj* dell'alta borghesia
upright ['ʌpraɪt] *adj* diritto/a; verticale; (*fig*) diritto/a, onesto/a
uprising ['ʌpraɪzɪŋ] *n* insurrezione *f*, rivolta

uproar ['ʌprɔː'] *n* tumulto, clamore *m*
upset *n* ['ʌpset] (*to plan etc*) contrattempo ▶ vt [ʌp'set] (*irreg: like* **set**) (*glass etc*) rovesciare; (*plan, stomach*) scombussolare; (*person: offend*) contrariare; (*: grieve*) addolorare; sconvolgere ▶ adj [ʌp'set] contrariato/a, addolorato/a; (*stomach*) scombussolato/a; **to have a stomach ~** avere lo stomaco in disordine *or* scombussolato
upside down ['ʌpsaɪd-] *adv* sottosopra
upstairs [ʌp'steəz] *adv, adj* di sopra, al piano superiore ▶ n piano di sopra
up-to-date ['ʌptə'deɪt] *adj* moderno/a; aggiornato/a
uptown ['ʌptaun] (*us*) *adv* verso i quartieri residenziali ▶ adj dei quartieri residenziali
upward ['ʌpwəd] *adj* ascendente; verso l'alto ▶ adv = **upwards**
uranium [juə'reɪnɪəm] *n* uranio
Uranus [juə'reɪnəs] *n* (*planet*) Urano
urban ['əːbən] *adj* urbano/a
urge [əːdʒ] *n* impulso; stimolo; forte desiderio ▶ vt: **to ~ sb to do** esortare qn a fare, spingere qn a fare; raccomandare a qn di fare
urgency ['əːdʒənsɪ] *n* urgenza; (*of tone*) insistenza
urgent ['əːdʒənt] *adj* urgente; (*tone, voice*) insistente
urinal ['juərɪnl] *n* (*BRIT: building*) vespasiano; (*: vessel*) orinale *m*, pappagallo
urinate ['juərɪneɪt] *vi* orinare
urine ['juərɪn] *n* orina
URL *n abbr* (= *uniform resource locator*) URL *m inv*
us [ʌs] *pron* ci; (*stressed, after prep*) noi; *see also* **me**
USA *n abbr* = **United States of America**
USB stick *n* pennetta USB
use *n* [juːs] uso; impiego, utilizzazione *f* ▶ vt [juːz] usare, utilizzare, servirsi di; **she ~d to do**

u

it lo faceva (una volta), era solita farlo; **in ~** in uso; **out of ~** fuori uso; **to be of ~** essere utile, servire; **it's no ~** non serve, è inutile; **to be ~d to** avere l'abitudine di; **use up** vt finire; (left-overs) consumare; **used** adj (car, object) usato/a; **useful** adj utile; **useless** adj inutile; (person) inetto/a; **user** n utente m/f; **user-friendly** adj (computer) di facile uso

username ['ju:zəneɪm] n (Comput) nome m utente

usual ['ju:ʒuəl] adj solito/a; **as ~** come al solito, come d'abitudine; **usually** adv di solito

ute [ju:t] n (AUST, NZ) pick-up m inv

utensil [ju:'tɛnsl] n utensile m; **kitchen ~s** utensili da cucina

utility [ju:'tɪlɪtɪ] n utilità; (also: **public ~**) servizio pubblico

utilize ['ju:tɪlaɪz] vt utilizzare; sfruttare

utmost ['ʌtməust] adj estremo/a ▷ n: **to do one's ~** fare il possibile or di tutto

utter ['ʌtə^r] adj assoluto/a, totale ▷ vt pronunciare, proferire; emettere; **utterly** adv completamente, del tutto

U-turn ['ju:tə:n] n inversione f a U

v abbr (= verse) v.; (= vide) v., vedi; (= volt) V.; (= versus) contro

vacancy ['veɪkənsɪ] n (job) posto libero; (room) stanza libera; **"no vacancies"** "completo"

> Be careful not to translate *vacancy* by the Italian word *vacanza*.

vacant ['veɪkənt] adj (job, seat etc) libero/a; (expression) assente

vacate [və'keɪt] vt lasciare libero/a

vacation [və'keɪʃən] n (esp US) vacanze fpl; **vacationer, vacationist** (US) n vacanziere/a

vaccination [væksɪ'neɪʃən] n vaccinazione f

vaccine ['væksi:n] n vaccino

vacuum ['vækjum] n vuoto; **vacuum cleaner** n aspirapolvere m inv

vagina [və'dʒaɪnə] n vagina

vague [veɪg] adj vago/a; (blurred: photo, memory) sfocato/a

vain [veɪn] *adj* (*useless*) inutile, vano/a; (*conceited*) vanitoso/a; **in ~** inutilmente, invano

Valentine's Day ['væləntaɪnzdeɪ] *n* San Valentino *m*

valid ['vælɪd] *adj* valido/a, valevole; (*excuse*) valido/a

valley ['vælɪ] *n* valle *f*

valuable ['væljuəbl] *adj* (*jewel*) di (grande) valore; (*time, help*) prezioso/a; **valuables** *npl* oggetti *mpl* di valore

value ['vælju:] *n* valore *m* ▷ *vt* (*fix price*) valutare, dare un prezzo a; (*cherish*) apprezzare, tenere a; **values** *npl* (*principles*) valori *mpl*

valve [vælv] *n* valvola

vampire ['væmpaɪə^r] *n* vampiro

van [væn] *n* (*Aut*) furgone *m*; (*BRIT Rail*) vagone *m*

vandal ['vændl] *n* vandalo/a; **vandalism** *n* vandalismo; **vandalize** *vt* vandalizzare

vanilla [və'nɪlə] *n* vaniglia ▷ *cpd* (*ice cream*) alla vaniglia

vanish ['vænɪʃ] *vi* svanire, scomparire

vanity ['vænɪtɪ] *n* vanità

vapour, (*US*) **vapor** ['veɪpə^r] *n* vapore *m*

variable ['veərɪəbl] *adj* variabile; (*mood*) mutevole

variant ['veərɪənt] *n* variante *f*

variation [veərɪ'eɪʃən] *n* variazione *f*; (*in opinion*) cambiamento

varied ['veərɪd] *adj* vario/a, diverso/a

variety [və'raɪətɪ] *n* varietà *f inv*; (*quantity*) quantità, numero

various ['veərɪəs] *adj* vario/a, diverso/a; (*several*) parecchi/e, molti/e

varnish ['vɑ:nɪʃ] *n* vernice *f*; (*nail varnish*) smalto ▷ *vt* verniciare; mettere lo smalto su

vary ['veərɪ] *vt, vi* variare, mutare

vase [vɑ:z] *n* vaso

Vaseline® ['væsɪli:n] *n* vaselina

vast [vɑ:st] *adj* vasto/a; (*amount, success*) enorme

VAT [væt] *n abbr* (*BRIT*: = *value added tax*) I.V.A. *f*

Vatican ['vætɪkən] *n*: **the ~** il Vaticano

vault [vɔ:lt] *n* (*of roof*) volta; (*tomb*) tomba; (*in bank*) camera blindata ▷ *vt* (*also*: **~ over**) saltare (d'un balzo)

VCR *n abbr* = **video cassette recorder**

VDU *n abbr* = **visual display unit**

veal [vi:l] *n* vitello

veer [vɪə^r] *vi* girare; virare

vegan ['vi:gən] *n* vegetaliano/a

vegetable ['vedʒtəbl] *n* verdura, ortaggio ▷ *adj* vegetale

vegetarian [vedʒɪ'teərɪən] *adj, n* vegetariano/a

vegetation [vedʒɪ'teɪʃən] *n* vegetazione *f*

vehicle ['vi:ɪkl] *n* veicolo

veil [veɪl] *n* velo

vein [veɪn] *n* vena; (*on leaf*) nervatura

Velcro® ['velkrəʊ] *n* velcro *m inv*

velvet ['velvɪt] *n* velluto ▷ *adj* di velluto

vending machine ['vendɪŋ-] *n* distributore *m* automatico

vendor ['vendə^r] *n* venditore/trice

vengeance ['vendʒəns] *n* vendetta; **with a ~** (*fig*) davvero; furiosamente

Venice ['venɪs] *n* Venezia

venison ['venɪsn] *n* carne *f* di cervo

venom ['venəm] *n* veleno

vent [vent] *n* foro, apertura; (*in dress, jacket*) spacco ▷ *vt* (*fig: one's feelings*) sfogare, dare sfogo a

ventilation [ventɪ'leɪʃən] *n* ventilazione *f*

venture ['ventʃə^r] *n* impresa (rischiosa) ▷ *vt* rischiare, azzardare ▷ *vi* arrischiarsi; **a business ~** un'iniziativa commerciale

venue ['venju:] *n* luogo (designato) per l'incontro

Venus ['vi:nəs] *n* (*planet*) Venere *m*

verb [və:b] *n* verbo; **verbal** *adj* verbale; (*translation*) orale

verdict ['və:dɪkt] *n* verdetto

V

verge [vəːdʒ] n bordo, orlo; **"soft ~s"** (BRIT) "banchina cedevole"; **on the ~ of doing** sul punto di fare

verify ['verifaɪ] vt verificare; (prove the truth of) confermare

versatile ['vəːsətaɪl] adj (person) versatile; (machine, tool etc) (che si presta) a molti usi

verse [vəːs] n (stanza) stanza, strofa; (in bible) versetto; (no pl: poetry) versi mpl

version ['vəːʃən] n versione f

versus ['vəːsəs] prep contro

vertical ['vəːtɪkl] adj, n verticale (m)

very ['verɪ] adv molto ▷ adj: **the ~ book which** proprio il libro che; **~ much** moltissimo; **the ~ last** proprio l'ultimo; **at the ~ least** almeno

vessel ['vesl] n (Anat) vaso; (Naut) nave f; (container) recipiente m

vest [vest] n (BRIT) maglia; (: sleeveless) canottiera; (US: waistcoat) gilè m inv

vet [vet] n abbr (BRIT: = veterinary surgeon) veterinario ▷ vt esaminare minuziosamente

veteran ['vetərn] n veterano; (also: **war ~**) veterano, reduce m

veterinary surgeon ['vetrɪnərɪ-], (US) **veterinarian** [vetrɪ'neərɪən] n veterinario

veto ['viːtəu] (pl **vetoes**) n veto ▷ vt opporre il veto a

via ['vaɪə] prep (by way of) via; (by means of) tramite

viable ['vaɪəbl] adj attuabile; vitale

vibrate [vaɪ'breɪt] vi: **to ~ (with)** vibrare (di); (resound) risonare (di)

vibration [vaɪ'breɪʃən] n vibrazione f

vicar ['vɪkər] n pastore m

vice [vaɪs] n (evil) vizio; (Tech) morsa; **vice-chairman** n (irreg) vicepresidente m

vice versa ['vaɪsɪ'vəːsə] adv viceversa

vicinity [vɪ'sɪnɪtɪ] n vicinanze fpl

vicious ['vɪʃəs] adj (remark) cattivo/a; (dog) cattivo/a; (blow) violento/a

victim ['vɪktɪm] n vittima

victor ['vɪktər] n vincitore m

Victorian [vɪk'tɔːrɪən] adj vittoriano/a

victorious [vɪk'tɔːrɪəs] adj vittorioso/a

victory ['vɪktərɪ] n vittoria

video ['vɪdɪəu] cpd video... ▷ n (video film) video m inv; (also: **~ cassette**) videocassetta; (also: **~ recorder**) videoregistratore m; **video call** n videochiamata; **video camera** n videocamera; **video game** n videogioco; **videophone** n videotelefono; **video shop** n videonoleggio; **video tape** n videotape m inv; **video wall** n schermo m multivideo inv

vie [vaɪ] vi: **to ~ with** competere con, rivaleggiare con

Vienna [vɪ'enə] n Vienna

Vietnam [vjet'næm] n Vietnam m; **Vietnamese** adj, n vietnamita m/f

view [vjuː] n vista, veduta; (opinion) opinione f ▷ vt (also fig: situation) considerare; (house) visitare; **on ~ (in museum etc)** esposto/a; **to be in** or **within ~ (of sth)** essere in vista (di qc); **in my ~** a mio parere; **in ~ of the fact that** considerato che; **viewer** n telespettatore/trice; **viewpoint** n punto di vista; (place) posizione f

vigilant ['vɪdʒɪlənt] adj vigile

vigorous ['vɪgərəs] adj vigoroso/a

vile [vaɪl] adj (action) vile; (smell) disgustoso/a, nauseante; (temper) pessimo/a

villa ['vɪlə] n villa

village ['vɪlɪdʒ] n villaggio; **villager** n abitante m/f di villaggio

villain ['vɪlən] n (scoundrel) canaglia; (BRIT: criminal) criminale m; (in novel etc) cattivo

vinaigrette [vɪneɪ'gret] n vinaigrette f inv

vine [vaɪn] n vite f; (climbing plant) rampicante m

vinegar ['vɪnɪgər] n aceto

vineyard ['vɪnjɑːd] n vigna, vigneto
vintage ['vɪntɪdʒ] n (year) annata, produzione f ▷ cpd d'annata
vinyl ['vaɪnl] n vinile m
viola [vɪ'əʊlə] n viola
violate ['vaɪəleɪt] vt violare
violation [vaɪə'leɪʃən] n violazione f; **in ~ of sth** violando qc
violence ['vaɪələns] n violenza
violent ['vaɪələnt] adj violento/a
violet ['vaɪələt] adj (colour) viola inv, violetto/a ▷ n (plant) violetta; (colour) violetto
violin [vaɪə'lɪn] n violino
VIP n abbr (= very important person) V.I.P. mf inv
viral ['vaɪərəl] adj (Comput) virale
virgin ['vəːdʒɪn] n vergine f ▷ adj vergine inv
Virgo ['vəːgəʊ] n (sign) Vergine f
virtual ['vəːtjʊəl] adj effettivo/a, vero/a; (Comput, Physics) virtuale; (in effect): **it's a ~ impossibility** è praticamente impossibile; **the ~ leader** il capo all'atto pratico; **virtually** ['vəːtjʊəlɪ] adv (almost) praticamente; **virtual reality** n (Comput) realtà f inv virtuale
virtue ['vəːtjuː] n virtù f inv; (advantage) pregio, vantaggio; **by ~ of** grazie a
virus ['vaɪərəs] n (also Comput) virus m inv
visa ['viːzə] n visto
vise [vaɪs] n (US Tech) = **vice**
visibility [vɪzɪ'bɪlɪtɪ] n visibilità
visible ['vɪzəbl] adj visibile
vision ['vɪʒən] n (sight) vista; (foresight, in dream) visione f
visit ['vɪzɪt] n visita; (stay) soggiorno ▷ vt (person: US: also: **~ with**) andare a trovare; (place) visitare; **visiting hours** npl (in hospital etc) orario delle visite; **visitor** n visitatore/trice; (guest) ospite m/f; **visitor centre**, (US) **visitor center** n centro informazioni per visitatori di museo, zoo, parco ecc

visual ['vɪzjuəl] adj visivo/a; visuale; ottico/a; **visualize** ['vɪzjuəlaɪz] vt immaginare, figurarsi; (foresee) prevedere
vital ['vaɪtl] adj vitale
vitality [vaɪ'tælɪtɪ] n vitalità
vitamin ['vɪtəmɪn] n vitamina
vivid ['vɪvɪd] adj vivido/a
V-neck ['viːnɛk] n maglione m con lo scollo a V
vocabulary [vəʊ'kæbjʊlərɪ] n vocabolario
vocal ['vəʊkl] adj (Mus) vocale; (communication) verbale
vocational [vəʊ'keɪʃənl] adj professionale
vodka ['vɒdkə] n vodka f inv
vogue [vəʊg] n moda; (popularity) popolarità, voga
voice [vɔɪs] n voce f ▷ vt (opinion) esprimere; **voice mail** n servizio di segreteria telefonica
void [vɔɪd] n vuoto ▷ adj (invalid) nullo/a; (empty): **~ of** privo/a di
volatile ['vɒlətaɪl] adj volatile; (fig) volubile
volcano [vɒl'keɪnəʊ] (pl **volcanoes**) n vulcano
volleyball ['vɒlɪbɔːl] n pallavolo f
volt [vəʊlt] n volt m inv; **voltage** n tensione f, voltaggio
volume ['vɒljuːm] n volume m
voluntarily ['vɒləntrɪlɪ] adv volontariamente; gratuitamente
voluntary ['vɒləntərɪ] adj volontario/a; (unpaid) gratuito/a, non retribuito/a
volunteer [vɒlən'tɪə'] n volontario/a ▷ vt offrire volontariamente ▷ vi (Mil) arruolarsi volontario; **to ~ to do** offrire (volontariamente) di fare
vomit ['vɒmɪt] n vomito ▷ vt, vi vomitare
vote [vəʊt] n voto, suffragio; (cast) voto; (franchise) diritto di voto ▷ vi votare ▷ vt (propose): **to ~ that** approvare la proposta che; **he**

V

was ~**d secretary** è stato eletto segretario; **~ of thanks** discorso di ringraziamento; **voter** n elettore/trice; **voting** n scrutinio

voucher ['vautʃə'] n (for meal, petrol) buono

vow [vau] n voto, promessa solenne ▷ vt: **to ~ to do/that** giurare di fare/che

vowel ['vauəl] n vocale f

voyage ['vɔɪɪdʒ] n viaggio per mare, traversata

vulgar ['vʌlgə'] adj volgare

vulnerable ['vʌlnərəbl] adj vulnerabile

vulture ['vʌltʃə'] n avvoltoio

waddle ['wɔdl] vi camminare come una papera

wade [weid] vi: **to ~ through** camminare a stento in; (fig: book) leggere con fatica

wafer ['weifə'] n (Culin) cialda

waffle ['wɔfl] n (Culin) cialda; (col) ciance fpl ▷ vi cianciare

wag [wæg] vt agitare, muovere ▷ vi agitarsi

wage [weidʒ] n (also: **~s**) salario, paga ▷ vt: **to ~ war** fare la guerra

wag(g)on ['wægən] n (horse-drawn) carro; (BRIT Rail) vagone m (merci)

wail [weil] n gemito; (of siren) urlo ▷ vi gemere; urlare

waist [weist] n vita, cintola; **waistcoat** n (BRIT) panciotto, gilè m inv

wait [weit] n attesa ▷ vi aspettare, attendere; **to ~ for** aspettare; **~ for me, please** aspettami, per favore; **I can't ~ to ...** (fig) non vedo l'ora di

...; **to lie in ~ for** stare in agguato a; **wait behind** vi rimanere (ad aspettare); **wait on** vt fus servire; **waiter** n cameriere m; **waiting list** n lista d'attesa; **waiting room** n sala d'aspetto or d'attesa; **waitress** n cameriera

waive [weɪv] vt rinunciare a, abbandonare

wake [weɪk] (pt **woke, waked**, pp **woken, waked**) vt (also: **~ up**) svegliare ▷ vi (also: **~ up**) svegliarsi ▷ n (for dead person) veglia funebre; (Naut) scia

Wales [weɪlz] n Galles m

walk [wɔːk] n passeggiata; (short) giretto; (gait) passo, andatura; (path) sentiero; (in park etc) sentiero, vialetto ▷ vi camminare; (for pleasure, exercise) passeggiare ▷ vt (distance) fare or percorrere a piedi; (dog) accompagnare, portare a passeggio; **10 minutes' ~ from** 10 minuti di cammino or a piedi da; **from all ~s of life** di tutte le condizioni sociali; **walk out** vi (audience) andarsene; (strike) scendere in sciopero; **walker** n (person) camminatore/trice; **walkie-talkie** ['wɔːkɪ'tɔːkɪ] n walkie-talkie m inv; **walking** n camminare m; **walking shoes** npl scarpe fpl da passeggio; **walking stick** n bastone m da passeggio; **Walkman®** ['wɔːkmən] n walkman® m inv; **walkway** n passaggio pedonale

wall [wɔːl] n muro; (internal, of tunnel, cave) parete f

wallet ['wɔlɪt] n portafoglio

wallpaper ['wɔːlpeɪpəʳ] n carta da parati ▷ vt (room) mettere la carta da parati in

walnut ['wɔːlnʌt] n noce f; (tree) noce m

walrus ['wɔːlrəs] (pl **walrus** or **walruses**) n tricheco

waltz [wɔːlts] n valzer m inv ▷ vi ballare il valzer

wand [wɔnd] n (also: **magic ~**) bacchetta (magica)

wander ['wɔndəʳ] vi (person) girare senza meta, girovagare; (thoughts) vagare ▷ vt girovagare per

want [wɔnt] vt volere; (need) aver bisogno di ▷ n: **for ~ of** per mancanza di; **wanted** adj (criminal) ricercato/a; **"wanted"** (in adverts) "cercasi"

war [wɔːʳ] n guerra; **to make ~ (on)** far guerra (a)

ward [wɔːd] n (in hospital: room) corsia; (: section) reparto; (Pol) circoscrizione f; (Law: child: also: **~ of court**) pupillo/a

warden ['wɔːdn] n (of institution) direttore/trice; (of park, game reserve) guardiano/a; (BRIT: also: **traffic ~**) addetto/a al controllo del traffico e del parcheggio

wardrobe ['wɔːdrəub] n (cupboard) guardaroba m inv, armadio; (clothes) guardaroba; (Theat) costumi mpl

warehouse ['wɛəhaus] n magazzino

warfare ['wɔːfɛəʳ] n guerra

warhead ['wɔːhɛd] n (Mil) testata

warm [wɔːm] adj caldo/a; (welcome, applause) caloroso/a; (person, greeting) cordiale; **it's ~** fa caldo; **I'm ~** ho caldo; **warm up** vi scaldarsi, riscaldarsi ▷ vt scaldare, riscaldare; (engine) far scaldare; **warmly** adv (applaud, welcome) calorosamente; (dress) con abiti pesanti; **warmth** n calore m

warn [wɔːn] vt: **to ~ sb not to do sth** or **against doing sth** avvertire or avvisare qn di non fare qc; **to ~ sb that** avvertire or avvisare qn che; **warning** n avvertimento; (notice) avviso; (signal) segnalazione f; **warning light** n spia luminosa

warrant ['wɔrnt] n (voucher) buono; (Law: to arrest) mandato di cattura; (: to search) mandato di perquisizione

warranty ['wɔrəntɪ] n garanzia

W

warrior ['wɒrɪəʳ] n guerriero/a

Warsaw ['wɔːsɔː] n Varsavia

warship ['wɔːʃɪp] n nave f da guerra

wart [wɔːt] n verruca

wartime ['wɔːtaɪm] n: **in ~** in tempo di guerra

wary ['wɛərɪ] adj prudente

was [wɒz] pt of **be**

wash [wɒʃ] vt lavare ▷ vi lavarsi; (sea): **to ~ over/against sth** infrangersi su/contro qc ▷ n lavaggio; (of ship) scia; **to give sth a ~** lavare qc, dare una lavata a qc; **to have a ~** lavarsi; **wash up** vi (BRIT) lavare i piatti; (US: have a wash) lavarsi; **washbasin**, (US) **washbowl** n lavabo; **washcloth** n (US) pezzuola (per lavarsi); **washer** n (Tech) rondella; **washing** n (linen etc) bucato; **washing line** n (BRIT) corda del bucato; **washing machine** n lavatrice f; **washing powder** n (BRIT) detersivo (in polvere)

Washington ['wɒʃɪŋtən] n Washington f

wash: washing-up n (dishes) piatti mpl sporchi; **washing-up liquid** n detersivo liquido (per stoviglie); **washroom** n gabinetto

wasn't ['wɒznt] = **was not**

wasp [wɒsp] n vespa

waste [weɪst] n spreco; (of time) perdita; (rubbish) rifiuti mpl; (also: **household ~**) immondizie fpl ▷ adj (material) di scarto; (food) avanzato/a; (land, ground) incolto/a ▷ vt sprecare; **waste ground** n (BRIT) terreno incolto or abbandonato; **wastepaper basket** ['weɪstpeɪpə-] n cestino per la carta straccia

watch [wɒtʃ] n (wristwatch) orologio (da polso); (act of watching, vigilance) sorveglianza; (guard: Mil, Naut) guardia; (Naut: spell of duty) quarto ▷ vt (look at) osservare; (: match, programme) guardare; (spy on, guard) sorvegliare, tenere d'occhio; (be careful of) fare attenzione a ▷ vi osservare, guardare; (keep guard) fare or montare la guardia; **watch out** vi fare attenzione; **watchdog** n cane m da guardia; **watch strap** n cinturino da orologio

water [wɔːtəʳ] n acqua ▷ vt (plant) annaffiare ▷ vi (eyes) lacrimare; **in British ~s** nelle acque territoriali britanniche; **to make sb's mouth ~** far venire l'acquolina in bocca a qn; **water down** vt (milk) diluire; (fig: story) edulcorare; **watercolour**, (US) **watercolor** n acquerello; **watercress** n crescione m; **waterfall** n cascata; **watering can** n annaffiatoio; **watermelon** n anguria, cocomero; **waterproof** adj impermeabile; **water-skiing** n sci m acquatico

watt [wɒt] n watt m inv

wave [weɪv] n onda; (of hand) gesto, segno; (in hair) ondulazione f; (fig: of enthusiasm, strikes etc) ondata ▷ vi fare un cenno con la mano; (branches, grass) ondeggiare; (flag) sventolare ▷ vt (hand) fare un gesto con; (handkerchief) sventolare; (stick) brandire; **wavelength** n lunghezza d'onda

waver ['weɪvəʳ] vi esitare; (voice) tremolare

wavy ['weɪvɪ] adj ondulato/a; ondeggiante

wax [wæks] n cera ▷ vt dare la cera a; (car) lucidare ▷ vi (moon) crescere

way [weɪ] n via, strada; (path, access) passaggio; (distance) distanza; (direction) parte f, direzione f; (manner) modo, stile m; (habit) abitudine f; **which ~? — this ~** da che parte or in quale direzione? — da questa parte or di qua; **on the ~** (en route) per strada; **to be on one's ~** essere in cammino or sulla strada; **to be in the ~** bloccare il passaggio; (fig) essere tra i piedi or d'impiccio; **to go out of one's ~ to do** (fig) mettercela tutta or fare di tutto per fare; **to**

be under ~ (work, project) essere in corso; **to lose one's ~** perdere la strada; **in a ~** in un certo senso; **in some ~s** sotto certi aspetti; **"~ in"** (BRIT) "entrata", "ingresso"; **"~ out"** (BRIT) "uscita"; **the ~ back** la via del ritorno; **"give ~"** (BRIT Aut) "dare la precedenza"; **no ~!** (col) neanche per idea!; **by the ~ ...** a proposito ...

WC n abbr (BRIT: = water closet) W.C. m inv, gabinetto

we [wiː] pl pron noi

weak [wiːk] adj debole; (health) precario/a; (beam etc) fragile; (tea, coffee) leggero/a; **weaken** vi indebolirsi ▷ vt indebolire; **weakness** n debolezza; (fault) punto debole, difetto; **to have a weakness for** avere un debole per

wealth [wɛlθ] n (money, resources) ricchezza, ricchezze fpl; (of details) abbondanza, profusione f; **wealthy** adj ricco/a

weapon ['wɛpən] n arma; **~s of mass destruction** armi di distruzione di massa

wear [wɛəʳ] (pt **wore**, pp **worn**) n (use) uso; (deterioration through use) logorio, usura; (clothing): **sports/baby ~** abbigliamento sportivo/per neonati ▷ vt (clothes) portare; (put on) mettersi; (damage: through use) consumare ▷ vi (last) durare; (rub etc through) consumarsi; **town/evening ~** abiti mpl or tenuta da città/sera; **wear off** vi sparire lentamente; **wear out** vt consumare; (person, strength) esaurire

weary ['wɪərɪ] adj stanco/a ▷ vi: **to ~ of** stancarsi di

weasel ['wiːzl] n (Zool) donnola

weather ['wɛðəʳ] n tempo ▷ vt (storm, crisis) superare; **what's the ~ like?** che tempo fa?; **under the ~** (fig: ill) poco bene; **weather forecast** n previsioni fpl del tempo, bollettino meteorologico

weave (pt **wove**, pp **woven**) [wiːv, wəuv, 'wəuvn] vt (cloth) tessere; (basket) intrecciare

web [wɛb] n (of spider) ragnatela; (on foot) palma; (fabric, also fig) tessuto; **the (World Wide) W~** la Rete; **web address** n indirizzo Internet; **webcam** n webcam f inv; **web page** n (Comput) pagina f web inv; **website** n (Comput) sito (Internet)

wed [wɛd] vt (pt, pp **wedded**) sposare ▷ vi sposarsi

Wed. abbr (= Wednesday) mer.

we'd [wiːd] = **we had**; = **we would**

wedding ['wɛdɪŋ] n matrimonio; **wedding anniversary** n anniversario di matrimonio; **wedding day** n giorno delle nozze or del matrimonio; **wedding dress** n abito nuziale; **wedding ring** n fede f

wedge [wɛdʒ] n (under door etc) zeppa; (of cake) fetta ▷ vt (fix) fissare con zeppe; (pack tightly) incastrare

Wednesday ['wɛdnzdɪ] n mercoledì m inv

wee [wiː] adj (SCOTTISH) piccolo/a

weed [wiːd] n erbaccia ▷ vt diserbare; **weed-killer** n diserbante m

week [wiːk] n settimana; **a ~ on Tuesday** martedì a otto; **a ~ today** oggi a otto; **weekday** n giorno feriale; (Comm) giornata lavorativa; **weekend** n fine settimana m inv or f inv, weekend m inv; **weekly** adv ogni settimana, settimanalmente ▷ adj, n settimanale (m)

weep (pt, pp **wept**) [wiːp, wɛpt] vi (person) piangere

weigh [weɪ] vt, vi pesare; **to ~ anchor** salpare or levare l'ancora; **weigh up** vt valutare

weight [weɪt] n peso; **to put on/lose ~** ingrassare/dimagrire; **weightlifting** n sollevamento pesi

weir [wɪəʳ] n diga

weird [wɪəd] adj strano/a, bizzarro/a; (eerie) soprannaturale

W

welcome ['wɛlkəm] adj benvenuto/a ▷ n accoglienza, benvenuto ▷ vt dare il benvenuto a; (be glad of) rallegrarsi di; **you're ~** (after thanks) prego

weld [wɛld] n saldatura ▷ vt saldare

welfare ['wɛlfɛəᵊ] n benessere m; **welfare state** n stato sociale

well [wɛl] n pozzo ▷ adv bene ▷ adj: **to be ~** (person) stare bene ▷ excl allora!; ma!; ebbene!; **~ done!** bravo/a!; **get ~ soon!** guarisci presto!; **to do ~** andare bene; **as ~** anche

we'll [wi:l] = **we will; we shall**

well: well-behaved adj ubbidiente; **well-built** adj (person) ben fatto/a; **well-dressed** adj ben vestito/a, vestito/a bene

wellies (col) ['wɛlɪz] npl (BRIT) stivali mpl di gomma

well: well-known adj noto/a, famoso/a; **well-off** adj benestante, danaroso/a; **well-paid** [wɛl'peɪd] adj ben pagato/a

Welsh [wɛlʃ] adj gallese ▷ n (Ling) gallese m; **Welshman** n (irreg) gallese m; **Welshwoman** n (irreg) gallese f

went [wɛnt] pt of **go**

wept [wɛpt] pt, pp of **weep**

were [wəːᵊ] pt of **be**

we're [wɪəᵊ] = **we are**

weren't [wəːnt] = **were not**

west [wɛst] n ovest m, occidente m, ponente m ▷ adj (a) ovest inv, occidentale ▷ adv verso ovest; **the W~** l'Occidente; **westbound** ['wɛstbaʊnd] adj (traffic) diretto/a a ovest; (carriageway) ovest inv; **western** adj occidentale, dell'ovest ▷ n (Cine) western m inv; **West Indian** adj delle Indie Occidentali ▷ n abitante m/f (or originario/a) delle Indie Occidentali; **West Indies** [-'ɪndɪz] npl: **the West Indies** le Indie Occidentali

wet [wɛt] adj umido/a, bagnato/a; (soaked) fradicio/a; (rainy) piovoso/a ▷ n (BRIT Pol) politico moderato; **to get ~** bagnarsi; **"~ paint"** "vernice fresca"; **wet suit** n tuta da sub

we've [wi:v] = **we have**

whack [wæk] vt picchiare, battere

whale [weɪl] n (Zool) balena

wharf (pl **wharves**) [wɔːf, wɔːvz] n banchina

 KEYWORD

what [wɔt] adj 1 (in direct/indirect questions) che; quale; **what size is it?** che taglia è?; **what colour is it?** di che colore è?; **what books do you want?** quali or che libri vuole?
2 (in exclamations) che; **what a mess!** che disordine!
▶ pron 1 (interrogative) che cosa, cosa, che; **what are you doing?** che or (che) cosa fai?; **what are you talking about?** di che cosa parli?; **what is it called?** come si chiama?; **what about me?** e io?; **what about doing ...?** e se facessimo ...?
2 (relative) ciò che, quello che; **I saw what you did** ho visto quello che hai fatto; **I saw what was on the table** ho visto cosa c'era sul tavolo
3 (indirect use) (che) cosa; **he asked me what she had said** mi ha chiesto che cosa avesse detto; **tell me what you're thinking about** dimmi a cosa stai pensando
▶ excl (disbelieving) cosa!, come!

whatever [wɔt'ɛvəᵊ] adj: **~ book** qualunque or qualsiasi libro + sub ▷ pron: **do ~ is necessary/you want** faccia qualunque or qualsiasi cosa sia necessaria/lei voglia; **~ happens** qualunque cosa accada; **no reason ~** or **whatsoever** nessuna ragione affatto or al mondo; **nothing ~** proprio niente

whatsoever [wɔtsəʊ'ɛvəᵊ] adj = **whatever**

wheat [wi:t] n grano, frumento

wheel [wi:l] n ruota; (Aut: also: **steering ~**) volante m; (Naut) (ruota del) timone m ▷ vt spingere ▷ vi (birds) roteare; (also: **~ round**) girare; **wheelbarrow** n carriola; **wheelchair** n sedia a rotelle; **wheel clamp** n (Aut) ganasce fpl (per vetture in sosta vietata)

wheeze [wi:z] vi ansimare

○ KEYWORD

when [wɛn] adv quando; **when did it happen?** quando è successo? ▷ conj 1 (at, during, after the time that) quando; **she was reading when I came in** quando sono entrato lei leggeva; **that was when I needed you** era allora che avevo bisogno di te 2 (on, at which): **on the day when I met him** il giorno in cui l'ho incontrato; **one day when it was raining** un giorno che pioveva 3 (whereas) quando, mentre; **you said I was wrong when in fact I was right** mi hai detto che avevo torto, quando in realtà avevo ragione

whenever [wɛnˈɛvəʳ] adv quando mai ▷ conj quando; (every time that) ogni volta che

where [wɛəʳ] adv, conj dove; **this is ~** è qui che; **whereabouts** adv dove ▷ n: **sb's whereabouts** luogo dove qn si trova; **whereas** conj mentre; **whereby** adv per cui; **wherever** [wɛəʳˈɛvəʳ] conj dovunque + sub; (interrogative) dove mai

whether ['wɛðəʳ] conj se; **I don't know ~ to accept or not** non so se accettare o no; **it's doubtful ~** è poco probabile che; **~ you go or not** che lei vada o no

○ KEYWORD

which [wɪtʃ] adj 1 (interrogative, direct, indirect) quale; **which picture do you want?** quale quadro vuole?; **which one?** quale?; **which one of you did it?** chi di voi lo ha fatto? 2: **in which case** nel qual caso ▷ pron 1 (interrogative) quale; **which (of these) are yours?** quali di questi sono suoi?; **which of you are coming?** chi di voi viene? 2 (relative) che; (: indirect) cui, il (la) quale; **the apple you ate/ which is on the table** la mela che hai mangiato/che è sul tavolo; **the chair on which you are sitting** la sedia sulla quale or su cui sei seduto; **he said he knew, which is true** ha detto che lo sapeva, il che è vero; **after which** dopo di che

whichever [wɪtʃˈɛvəʳ] adj: **take ~ book you prefer** prenda qualsiasi libro che preferisce; **~ book you take** qualsiasi libro prenda

while [waɪl] n momento ▷ conj mentre; (as long as) finché; (although) sebbene + sub; per quanto + sub; **for a ~** per un po'

whilst [waɪlst] conj = **while**

whim [wɪm] n capriccio

whine [waɪn] n gemito ▷ vi gemere; uggiolare; piagnucolare

whip [wɪp] n frusta; (for riding) frustino; (Pol: person) capogruppo (che sovrintende alla disciplina dei colleghi di partito) ▷ vt frustare; (Culin: cream, eggs etc) sbattere; **whipped cream** n panna montata

whirl [wə:l] vt (far) girare rapidamente; (far) turbinare ▷ vi (dancers) volteggiare; (leaves, water, dust) sollevarsi in un vortice

whisk [wɪsk] n (Culin) frusta; frullino ▷ vt sbattere, frullare; **to ~ sb away** or **off** portar via qn a tutta velocità

whiskers ['wɪskəz] npl (of animal) baffi mpl; (of man) favoriti mpl

whisky, (IRISH, US) **whiskey** ['wɪskɪ] n whisky m inv

whisper ['wɪspə^r] n sussurro ▷ vt, vi sussurrare

whistle ['wɪsl] n (sound) fischio; (object) fischietto ▷ vi fischiare

white [waɪt] adj bianco/a; (with fear) pallido/a ▷ n bianco; (person) bianco/a; **whiteboard** ['waɪtbɔːd] n lavagna bianca; **interactive whiteboard** lavagna interattiva; **White House** n: **the White House** la Casa Bianca; **whitewash** n (paint) bianco di calce ▷ vt imbiancare; (fig) coprire

whiting ['waɪtɪŋ] n (pl inv: fish) merlango

Whitsun ['wɪtsn] n Pentecoste f

whittle ['wɪtl] vt: **to ~ away** or **down** ridurre, tagliare

whizz [wɪz] vi: **to ~ past** or **by** passare sfrecciando

○ **KEYWORD**

who [huː] pron 1 (interrogative) chi; **who is it?, who's there?** chi è? 2 (relative) che; **the man who spoke to me** l'uomo che ha parlato con me; **those who can swim** quelli che sanno nuotare

whoever [huːˈɛvə^r] pron: **~ finds it** chiunque lo trovi; **ask ~ you like** lo chieda a chiunque vuole; **~ she marries** chiunque sposerà, non importa chi sposerà; **~ told you that?** chi mai gliel'ha detto?

whole [həul] adj (complete) tutto/a, completo/a; (not broken) intero/a, intatto/a ▷ n (all): **the ~ of** tutto/a il; (not broken) tutto; **the ~ lot (of it)** tutto; **the ~ of the town** tutta la città, la città intera; **on the ~, as a ~** nel complesso, nell'insieme; **wholefood(s)** n(pl) cibo integrale; **wholeheartedly** [həulˈhɑːtɪdlɪ] adv sentitamente, di tutto cuore; **wholemeal** ['həulmiːl] adj (BRIT: flour, bread) integrale; **wholesale** n commercio or vendita all'ingrosso ▷ adj all'ingrosso; (destruction) totale; **wholewheat** adj = **wholemeal**; **wholly** adv completamente, del tutto

○ **KEYWORD**

whom [huːm] pron 1 (interrogative) chi; **whom did you see?** chi hai visto?; **to whom did you give it?** a chi lo hai dato? 2 (relative) che, prep + il (la) quale; **the man whom I saw** l'uomo che ho visto; **the man to whom I spoke** l'uomo al or con il quale ho parlato

whore [hɔː^r] n (col, pej) puttana

○ **KEYWORD**

whose [huːz] adj 1 (possessive, interrogative) di chi; **whose book is this?, whose is this book?** di chi è questo libro?; **whose daughter are you?** di chi sei figlia? 2 (possessive, relative): **the man whose son you rescued** l'uomo il cui figlio hai salvato or a cui hai salvato il figlio; **the girl whose sister you were speaking to** la ragazza alla cui sorella stavi parlando ▷ pron di chi; **whose is this?** di chi è questo?; **I know whose it is** so di chi è

○ **KEYWORD**

why [waɪ] adv perché; **why not?** perché no?; **why not do it now?** perché non farlo adesso? ▷ conj perché; **I wonder why he said that** mi chiedo perché l'abbia detto; **that's not why I'm here** non è questo il motivo per cui sono qui; **the reason why** il motivo per cui ▷ excl (surprise) ma guarda un po'!; (remonstrating) ma (via)!; (explaining) ebbene!

wicked ['wɪkɪd] *adj* cattivo/a, malvagio/a; *(mischievous)* malizioso/a; *(terrible: prices, weather)* terribile

wicket ['wɪkɪt] *n (Cricket)* porta; area tra le due porte

wide [waɪd] *adj* largo/a; *(region, knowledge)* vasto/a; *(choice)* ampio/a ▷ *adv*: **to open ~** spalancare; **to shoot ~** tirare a vuoto *or* fuori bersaglio; **widely** *adv (different)* molto, completamente; *(believed)* generalmente; **widely spaced** molto distanziati/e; **widen** *vt* allargare, ampliare; **wide open** *adj* spalancato/a; **widescreen** *adj (television, TV)* a schermo panoramico; **widespread** *adj (belief etc)* molto *or* assai diffuso/a

widget ['wɪdʒɪt] *n (Comput)* widget *m inv*

widow ['wɪdəu] *n* vedova; **widower** *n* vedovo

width [wɪdθ] *n* larghezza

wield [wi:ld] *vt (sword)* maneggiare; *(power)* esercitare

wife *(pl* **wives)** [waɪf, waɪvz] *n* moglie *f*

Wi-Fi ['waɪfaɪ] *n* WiFi *m*

wig [wɪg] *n* parrucca

wild [waɪld] *adj* selvatico/a; *(countryside, appearance)* selvaggio/a; *(sea, weather)* tempestoso/a; *(idea, life)* folle; stravagante; *(applause)* frenetico/a; **wilderness** ['wɪldənɪs] *n* deserto; **wildlife** *n* natura; **wildly** *adv* selvaggiamente; *(applaud)* freneticamente; *(hit, guess)* a casaccio; *(happy)* follemente

 KEYWORD

will [wɪl] *aux vb* **1** *(forming future tense)*: **I will finish it tomorrow** lo finirò domani; **I will have finished it by tomorrow** lo finirò entro domani; **will you do it? — yes I will/no I won't** lo farai? — sì (lo farò)/

no (non lo farò)

2 *(in conjectures, predictions)*: **he will** *or* **he'll be there by now** a quest'ora dovrebbe essere arrivato; **that will be the postman** sarà il postino

3 *(in commands, requests, offers)*: **will you be quiet!** vuoi stare zitto?; **will you come?** vieni anche tu?; **will you help me?** mi aiuti?, mi puoi aiutare?; **will you have a cup of tea?** vorrebbe una tazza di tè?; **I won't put up with it!** non lo accetterò!

▷ *vt (pt, pp* **willed**): **to will sb to do** volere che qn faccia; **he willed himself to go on** continuò grazie a un grande sforzo di volontà

▷ *n* **1** volontà

2 *(Law)* testamento

willing ['wɪlɪŋ] *adj* volonteroso/a; **~ to do** disposto/a a fare; **willingly** *adv* volentieri

willow ['wɪləu] *n* salice *m*

willpower ['wɪlpauəʳ] *n* forza di volontà

wilt [wɪlt] *vi* appassire

win [wɪn] *(pt, pp* **won)** *n (in sports etc)* vittoria ▷ *vt (battle, prize, money)* vincere; *(popularity)* guadagnare ▷ *vi* vincere; **win over** *vt* convincere

wince [wɪns] *vi* trasalire

wind¹ [wɪnd] *n* vento; *(Med)* flatulenza; *(breath)* respiro, fiato ▷ *vt (take breath away)* far restare senza fiato

wind² *(pt, pp* **wound)** *vt* attorcigliare; *(wrap)* avvolgere; *(clock, toy)* caricare ▷ *vi (road, river)* serpeggiare; **wind down** *vt (car window)* abbassare; *(fig: production, business)* diminuire; **wind up** *vt (clock)* caricare; *(debate)* concludere

windfall ['wɪndfɔ:l] *n (money)* guadagno insperato

wind farm *n* centrale *f* eolica

winding ['waɪndɪŋ] *adj (road)* serpeggiante; *(staircase)* a chiocciola

W

windmill ['wɪndmɪl] n mulino a vento

window ['wɪndəʊ] n finestra; (in car, train, plane) finestrino; (in shop etc) vetrina; (also: **~ pane**) vetro; **window box** n cassetta da fiori; **window cleaner** n (person) pulitore m di finestre; **window pane** n vetro; **window seat** n posto finestrino; **windowsill** n davanzale m

wind: wind power n energia eolica; **windscreen** ['wɪndskriːn], (US) **windshield** n parabrezza m inv; **windscreen wiper**, (US) **windshield wiper** n tergicristallo; **windsurfing** ['wɪndsəːfɪŋ] n windsurf m inv; **wind turbine** ['wɪndtəːbaɪn] n pala eolica; **windy** ['wɪndɪ] adj ventoso/a; **it's windy** c'è vento

wine [waɪn] n vino; **wine bar** n enoteca (per degustazione); **wine glass** n bicchiere m da vino; **wine list** n lista dei vini; **wine tasting** n degustazione f dei vini

wing [wɪŋ] n ala; (Aut) fiancata; **wing mirror** n (BRIT) specchietto retrovisore esterno

wink [wɪŋk] n occhiolino ▷ vi ammiccare, fare l'occhiolino; (light) baluginare

winner ['wɪnəʳ] n vincitore/trice

winning ['wɪnɪŋ] adj (team) vincente; (goal) decisivo/a; (charming) affascinante

winter ['wɪntəʳ] n inverno; **winter sports** npl sport mpl invernali; **wintertime** n inverno, stagione f invernale

wipe [waɪp] n pulita, passata ▷ vt pulire (strofinando); (erase: tape) cancellare; **wipe out** vt (debt) pagare, liquidare; (memory) cancellare; (destroy) annientare; **wipe up** vt asciugare

wire ['waɪəʳ] n filo; (Elec) filo elettrico; (Tel) telegramma m ▷ vt (house) fare l'impianto elettrico di; (also:

~ up) collegare, allacciare; (person) telegrafare a

wireless ['waɪəlɪs] adj wireless inv, senza fili; **wireless technology** n tecnologia wireless

wiring ['waɪərɪŋ] n impianto elettrico

wisdom ['wɪzdəm] n saggezza; (of action) prudenza; **wisdom tooth** n dente m del giudizio

wise [waɪz] adj saggio/a; (advice, remark) prudente; giudizioso/a

wish [wɪʃ] n (desire) desiderio; (specific desire) richiesta ▷ vt desiderare, volere; **best ~es** (on birthday etc) i migliori auguri; **with best ~es** (in letter) cordiali saluti, con i migliori saluti; **to ~ sb goodbye** dire arrivederci a qn; **he ~ed me well** mi augurò di riuscire; **to ~ to do/sb to do** desiderare or volere fare/che qn faccia; **to ~ for** desiderare

wistful ['wɪstful] adj malinconico/a

wit [wɪt] n (gen pl) intelligenza; presenza di spirito; (wittiness) spirito, arguzia; (person) bello spirito

witch [wɪtʃ] n strega

KEYWORD

with [wɪð, wɪθ] prep **1** (in the company of) con; **I was with him** ero con lui; **we stayed with friends** siamo stati da amici; **I'll be with you in a minute** vengo subito
2 (descriptive) con; **a room with a view** una camera con vista (sul mare or sulle montagne etc); **the man with the grey hat/blue eyes** l'uomo con il cappello grigio/gli occhi blu
3 (indicating manner, means, cause): **with tears in her eyes** con le lacrime agli occhi; **red with anger** rosso/a dalla rabbia; **to shake with fear** tremare di paura
4: **I'm with you** (I understand) la seguo; **to be with it** (col: up-to-date)

essere alla moda; (: *alert*) essere
sveglio/a; **I'm not really with it
today** (*col*) oggi sono un po' fuori

withdraw (*irreg: like* **draw**) [wɪθ'drɔ:]
vt ritirare; (*money from bank*) ritirare;
prelevare ▷ *vi* ritirarsi; **withdrawal**
n ritiro, prelievo; (*of army*) ritirata;
withdrawal symptoms *npl* (*Med*)
crisi *f* di astinenza; **withdrawn** *adj*
(*person*) distaccato/a
withdrew [wɪθ'dru:] *pt of* **withdraw**
wither ['wɪðəʳ] *vi* appassire
withhold [wɪθ'həʊld] *vt* (*irreg:
like* **hold**) (*money*) trattenere;
(*permission*): **to ~ (from)** rifiutare (a);
(*information*) nascondere (a)
within [wɪð'ɪn] *prep* all'interno di; (*in
time, distances*) entro ▷ *adv* all'interno,
dentro; **~ reach (of)** alla portata
(di); **~ sight (of)** in vista (di); **~ a mile
of** entro un miglio da; **~ the week**
prima della fine della settimana
without [wɪð'aʊt] *prep* senza; **to go**
or **do ~ sth** fare a meno di qc
withstand [wɪθ'stænd] *vt* (*irreg: like*
stand) resistere a
witness ['wɪtnɪs] *n* (*person, also Law*)
testimone *m/f* ▷ *vt* (*event*) essere
testimone di; (*document*) attestare
l'autenticità di
witty ['wɪtɪ] *adj* spiritoso/a
wives [waɪvz] *npl of* **wife**
wizard ['wɪzəd] *n* mago
wk *abbr* = **week**
wobble ['wɔbl] *vi* tremare; (*chair*)
traballare
woe [wəʊ] *n* dolore *m*; disgrazia
woke [wəʊk] *pt of* **wake**
woken ['wəʊkn] *pp of* **wake**
wolf (*pl* **wolves**) [wʊlf, wʊlvz] *n* lupo
woman (*pl* **women**) ['wʊmən,
'wɪmɪn] *n* donna
womb [wu:m] *n* (*Anat*) utero
women ['wɪmɪn] *npl of* **woman**
won [wʌn] *pt, pp of* **win**
wonder ['wʌndəʳ] *n* meraviglia ▷ *vi*:
to ~ whether/why domandarsi se/

perché; **to ~ at** essere sorpreso/a
di; meravigliarsi di; **to ~ about**
domandarsi di; pensare a; **it's
no ~ that** c'è poco *or* non c'è da
meravigliarsi che + *sub*; **wonderful**
adj meraviglioso/a
won't [wəʊnt] = **will not**
wood [wʊd] *n* legno; (*timber*)
legname *m*; (*forest*) bosco;
wooden *adj* di legno; (*fig*) rigido/a;
inespressivo/a; **woodwind** *npl*
(*Mus*): **the woodwind** i legni;
woodwork *n* (*craft, subject*)
falegnameria
wool [wʊl] *n* lana; **to pull the ~ over
sb's eyes** (*fig*) gettare fumo negli
occhi a qn; **woollen**, (*us*) **woolen** *adj*
di lana; (*industry*) laniero/a; **woolly**,
(*us*) **wooly** *adj* di lana; (*fig: ideas*)
confuso/a
word [wə:d] *n* parola; (*news*) notizie
fpl ▷ *vt* esprimere, formulare; **in
other ~s** in altre parole; **to have
~s with sb** avere un diverbio con
qn; **to break/keep one's ~** non
mantenere/keep one's own
parola; **wording** *n* formulazione *f*;
word processing *n* word processing
m, elaborazione *f* testi; **word
processor** *n* word processor *m inv*
wore [wɔ:ʳ] *pt of* **wear**
work [wə:k] *n* lavoro; (*Art, Literature*)
opera ▷ *vi* lavorare; (*mechanism,
plan etc*) funzionare; (*medicine*)
essere efficace ▷ *vt* (*clay, wood
etc*) lavorare; (*mine etc*) sfruttare;
(*machine*) far funzionare; (*cause:
effect, miracle*) fare; **to be out of ~**
essere disoccupato/a; **how does
this ~?** come funziona?; **the TV isn't
~ing** la TV non funziona; **to ~ loose**
allentarsi; **work out** *vi* (*plans etc*)
riuscire, andare bene ▷ *vt* (*problem*)
risolvere; (*plan*) elaborare; **it ~s out
at £100** fa 100 sterline; **worker**
n lavoratore/trice; operaio/a;
work experience *n* (*previous jobs*)
esperienze *fpl* lavorative; (*student*

training placement) tirocinio; **work force** *n* forza lavoro; **working class** *n* classe f operaia *or* lavoratrice; **working week** *n* settimana lavorativa; **workman** *n* (*irreg*) operaio; **work of art** *n* opera d'arte; **workout** *n* (*Sport*) allenamento; **work permit** *n* permesso di lavoro; **workplace** *n* posto di lavoro; **works** *n* (BRIT: *factory*) fabbrica ▷ *npl* (*of clock, machine*) meccanismo; **workshop** *n* officina; (*practical session*) gruppo di lavoro; **work station** *n* stazione f di lavoro; **work surface** *n* piano di lavoro; **worktop** *n* piano di lavoro

world [wəːld] *n* mondo ▷ *cpd* (*tour, champion*) del mondo; (*record, power, war*) mondiale; **to think the ~ of sb** (*fig*) pensare un gran bene di qn; **World Cup** *n* (*Football*) Coppa del Mondo; **world-wide** *adj* universale; **World-Wide Web** *n* World Wide Web *m*

worm [wəːm] *n* (*also:* **earth~**) verme *m*

worn [wɔːn] *pp of* **wear** ▷ *adj* usato/a; **worn-out** *adj* (*object*) consumato/a, logoro/a; (*person*) sfinito/a

worried ['wʌrɪd] *adj* preoccupato/a

worry ['wʌrɪ] *n* preoccupazione f ▷ *vt* preoccupare ▷ *vi* preoccuparsi; **worrying** *adj* preoccupante

worse [wəːs] *adj* peggiore ▷ *adv*, *n* peggio; **a change for the ~** un peggioramento; **worsen** *vt*, *vi* peggiorare; **worse off** *adj* in condizioni (economiche) peggiori

worship ['wəːʃɪp] *n* culto ▷ *vt* (*God*) adorare, venerare; (*person*) adorare; **Your W~** (BRIT) (*to mayor*) signor sindaco; (*to judge*) signor giudice

worst [wəːst] *adj* il (la) peggiore ▷ *adv*, *n* peggio; **at ~** al peggio, per male che vada

worth [wəːθ] *n* valore *m* ▷ *adj*: **to be ~** valere; **it's ~ it** ne vale la pena; **it's not ~ the trouble** non ne vale la pena; **worthless** *adj* di nessun valore; **worthwhile** *adj* (*activity*) utile; (*cause*) lodevole

worthy ['wəːðɪ] *adj* (*person*) degno/a; (*motive*) lodevole; **~ of** degno di

would [wʊd] *aux vb* **1** (*conditional tense*): **if you asked him he would do it** se glielo chiedesse lo farebbe; **if you had asked him he would have done it** se glielo avesse chiesto lo avrebbe fatto
2 (*in offers, invitations, requests*): **would you like a biscuit?** vorrebbe *or* vuole un biscotto?; **would you ask him to come in?** lo faccia entrare, per cortesia; **would you open the window please?** apra la finestra, per favore
3 (*in indirect speech*): **I said I would do it** ho detto che l'avrei fatto
4 (*emphatic*): **it WOULD have to snow today!** doveva proprio nevicare oggi!
5 (*insistence*): **she wouldn't do it** non ha voluto farlo
6 (*conjecture*): **it would have been midnight** sarà stata mezzanotte; **it would seem so** sembrerebbe proprio di sì
7 (*indicating habit*): **he would go there on Mondays** andava lì ogni lunedì

wouldn't ['wʊdnt] = **would not**
wound¹ [wuːnd] *n* ferita ▷ *vt* ferire
wound² [waʊnd] *pt, pp of* **wind²**
wove [wəʊv] *pt of* **weave**
woven ['wəʊvn] *pp of* **weave**
wrap [ræp] *vt* (*also:* **~ up**) avvolgere; (*parcel*) incartare; **wrapper** *n* (*on chocolate*) carta; (BRIT: *of book*) copertina; **wrapping** ['ræpɪŋ] *n* carta; **wrapping paper** *n* carta da pacchi; (*for gift*) carta da regali
wreath (*pl* **wreaths**) [riːθ, riːðz] *n* corona

wreck [rɛk] n (sea disaster) naufragio; (ship) relitto; (pej: person) rottame m ▷ vt demolire; (ship) far naufragare; (fig) rovinare; **wreckage** n rottami mpl; (of building) macerie fpl; (of ship) relitti mpl

wren [rɛn] n (Zool) scricciolo

wrench [rɛntʃ] n (Tech) chiave f; (tug) torsione f brusca; (fig) strazio ▷ vt strappare; storcere; **to ~ sth from** strappare qc a o da

wrestle ['rɛsl] vi: **to ~ (with sb)** lottare (con qn); **wrestler** n lottatore/trice; **wrestling** n lotta

wretched ['rɛtʃɪd] adj disgraziato/a; (col: weather, holiday) orrendo/a, orribile; (: child, dog) pestifero/a

wriggle ['rɪgl] vi (also: **~ about**) dimenarsi; (snake, worm) serpeggiare, muoversi serpeggiando

wring (pt, pp **wrung**) [rɪŋ, rʌŋ] vt torcere; (wet clothes) strizzare; (fig): **to ~ sth out of** strappare qc a

wrinkle ['rɪŋkl] n (on skin) ruga; (on paper etc) grinza ▷ vt (nose) torcere; (forehead) corrugare ▷ vi (skin, paint) raggrinzirsi

wrist [rɪst] n polso

write (pt **wrote**, pp **written**) [raɪt, rəut, 'rɪtn] vt, vi scrivere; **write down** vt annotare; (put in writing) mettere per iscritto; **write off** vt (debt, plan) cancellare; **write out** vt mettere per iscritto; (cheque, receipt) scrivere; **write-off** n perdita completa; **writer** n autore/trice, scrittore/trice

writing ['raɪtɪŋ] n scrittura; (of author) scritto, opera; **in ~** per iscritto; **writing paper** n carta da lettere

written ['rɪtn] pp of **write**

wrong [rɔŋ] adj sbagliato/a; (not suitable) inadatto/a; (wicked) cattivo/a; (unfair) ingiusto/a ▷ adv in modo sbagliato, erroneamente ▷ n (injustice) torto ▷ vt fare torto a; **you are ~ to do it** ha torto a farlo; **you are ~ about that, you've got it ~** si sbaglia; **to be in the ~** avere torto; **what's ~?** cosa c'è che non va?; **to go ~** (person) sbagliarsi; (plan) fallire, non riuscire; (machine) guastarsi; **wrongly** adv (incorrectly, by mistake) in modo sbagliato; **wrong number** n: **you have the wrong number** (Tel) ha sbagliato numero

wrote [rəut] pt of **write**

wrung [rʌŋ] pt, pp of **wring**

WWW n abbr = **World Wide Web**; **the ~** la Rete

W

XL *abbr* = **extra large**
Xmas ['εksməs] *n abbr* = **Christmas**
X-ray ['εks'reɪ] *n* raggio X;
  (*photograph*) radiografia ▷ *vt*
  radiografare
xylophone ['zaɪləfəun] *n* xilofono

yacht [jɔt] *n* panfilo, yacht *m inv*;
  yachting *n* yachting *m*, sport *m*
  della vela
yard [jɑ:d] *n* (*of house etc*) cortile *m*;
  (*measure*) iarda (= 914 mm; 3 *feet*); **yard**
  sale (*US*) *n* vendita di oggetti usati nel
  cortile di una casa privata
yarn [jɑ:n] *n* filato; (*tale*) lunga storia
yawn [jɔ:n] *n* sbadiglio ▷ *vi*
  sbadigliare
yd. *abbr* = **yard**
yeah [jεə] *adv* (*col*) sì
year [jɪəʳ] *n* anno; (*referring to harvest,*
  wine etc) annata; **she's three ~s old**
  ha tre anni; **an eight-~-old child**
  un(a) bambino/a di otto anni; **yearly**
  adj annuale ▷ *adv* annualmente
yearn [jə:n] *vi*: **to ~ for sth/to do**
  desiderare ardentemente qc/di fare
yeast [ji:st] *n* lievito
yell [jεl] *n* urlo ▷ *vi* urlare
yellow ['jεləu] *adj* giallo/a; **Yellow**
  Pages® *npl* pagine *fpl* gialle

yes [jɛs] *adv, n* sì (*m inv*); **to say ~ (to)** dire di sì (a)

yesterday ['jɛstədɪ] *adv, n* ieri (*m inv*); **~ morning/evening** ieri mattina/sera; **all day ~** ieri per tutta la giornata

yet [jɛt] *adv* ancora; già ▷ *conj* ma, tuttavia; **it is not finished ~** non è ancora finito; **the best ~** finora il migliore finora; **as ~** finora

yew [ju:] *n* tasso (*albero*)

Yiddish ['jɪdɪʃ] *n* yiddish *m*

yield [ji:ld] *n* produzione *f*, resa; reddito ▷ *vt* produrre, rendere; (*surrender*) cedere ▷ *vi* cedere; (*US Aut*) dare la precedenza

yob(bo) ['jɔb(əu)] *n* (*BRIT col*) bullo

yoga ['jəugə] *n* yoga *m*

yog(h)urt ['jəugət] *n* iogurt *m inv*

yolk [jəuk] *n* tuorlo, rosso d'uovo

KEYWORD

you [ju:] *pron* **1** (*subject*) tu; (: *polite form*) lei; (: *pl*) voi; (: *formal*) loro; **you Italians enjoy your food** a voi italiani piace mangiare bene; **you and I will go** andiamo io e te (*or* lei ed io)
2 (*object: direct*) ti; la; vi; loro (*after vb*); (: *indirect*) ti; le; vi; loro (*after vb*); **I know you** ti (*or* la *or* vi) conosco; **I gave it to you** te l'ho dato; gliel'ho dato; ve l'ho dato; l'ho dato loro
3 (*stressed, after prep, in comparisons*) te; lei; voi; loro; **I told YOU to do it** ho detto a TE (*or* a LEI *etc*) di farlo; **she's younger than you** è più giovane di te (*or* lei *etc*)
4 (*impers: one*) si; **fresh air does you good** l'aria fresca fa bene; **you never know** non si sa mai

you'd [ju:d] = **you had; you would**
you'll [ju:l] = **you will; you shall**
young [jʌŋ] *adj* giovane ▷ *npl* (*of animal*) piccoli *mpl*; **the ~** i giovani, la gioventù; **youngster** *n*

giovanotto/a, ragazzo/a; (*child*) bambino/a

your [jɔ:ʳ] *adj* il (la) tuo/a; (*pl*) i (le) tuoi (tue); (*polite form*) il (la) suo/a; (*pl*) i (le) suoi (sue); (*pl*) il (la) vostro/a; (*pl*) i (le) vostri/e; (: *formal*) il (la) loro; (*pl*) i (le) loro

you're [juəʳ] = **you are**

yours [jɔ:z] *pron* il (la) tuo/a; (*pl*) i (le) tuoi (tue); (*polite form*) il (la) suo/a; (*pl*) i (le) suoi (sue); (*pl*) il (la) vostro/a; (*pl*) i (le) vostri/e; (: *formal*) il (la) loro; (*pl*) i (le) loro; **~ sincerely/faithfully** (*in letter*) cordiali/distinti saluti; *see also* **mine**[1]

yourself [jɔ:ˈsɛlf] *pron* (*reflexive*) ti; (: *polite form*) si; (*after prep*) te; sé; (*emphatic*) tu stesso/a; lei stesso/a; **yourselves** *pl pron* (*reflexive*) vi; (: *polite form*) si; (*after prep*) voi; loro; (*emphatic*) voi stessi/e; loro stessi/e; *see also* **oneself**

youth [ju:θ] *n* gioventù *f*; (*young man*) giovane *m*, ragazzo; **youth club** *n* centro giovanile; **youthful** *adj* giovane; da giovane; giovanile; **youth hostel** *n* ostello della gioventù

you've [ju:v] = **you have**

Yugoslavia [ju:gəuˈslɑ:vɪə] *n* (*formerly*) Jugoslavia

y

zoom [zuːm] *vi*: **to ~ past** sfrecciare; **zoom lens** *n* zoom *m inv*, obiettivo a focale variabile
zucchini [zuːˈkiːnɪ] *n* (*pl inv*: *US*) zucchina

Z

zeal [ziːl] *n* zelo; entusiasmo
zebra [ˈziːbrə] *n* zebra; **zebra crossing** *n* (*BRIT*) (passaggio pedonale a) strisce *fpl*, zebre *fpl*
zero [ˈzɪərəu] *n* zero
zest [zɛst] *n* gusto; (*Culin*) buccia
zigzag [ˈzɪgzæg] *n* zigzag *m inv* ▷ *vi* zigzagare
Zimbabwe [zɪmˈbɑːbwɪ] *n* Zimbabwe *m*
zinc [zɪŋk] *n* zinco
zip [zɪp] *n* (*also*: **~ fastener**) chiusura *f* or cerniera *f* lampo *inv* ▷ *vt* (*Comput*) zippare; (*also*: **~ up**) chiudere con una cerniera lampo; **zip code** *n* (*US*) codice *m* di avviamento postale; **zipper** (*US*) *n* cerniera *f* lampo *inv*
zit [zɪt] *n* brufolo
zodiac [ˈzəudɪæk] *n* zodiaco
zone [zəun] *n* (*also Mil*) zona
zoo [zuː] *n* zoo *m inv*
zoology [zuːˈɔlədʒɪ] *n* zoologia

VERB TABLES

Introduction

The **Verb Tables** in the following section contain 32 tables of the most common Italian verbs (some regular and some irregular) in alphabetical order. Each table shows you the following forms: **Present**, **Perfect**, **Imperfect**, **Future**, **Conditional**, **Present Subjunctive**, **Imperative** and the **Past Participle** and **Gerund**.

In order to help you use the verbs shown in Verb Tables correctly, there are also a number of example phrases at the bottom of each page to show the verb as it is used in context.

In Italian there are **regular** verbs (their forms follow the regular patterns of **-are**, **-ere** or **-ire** verbs), and **irregular** verbs (their forms do not follow the normal rules). Examples of regular verbs in these tables are:

> **parlare** (regular **-are** verb, Verb Table 16)
> **credere** (regular **-ere** verb, Verb Table 7)
> **capire** (regular **-ire** verb, Verb Table 6)

Some irregular verbs are irregular in most of their forms, while others may only have a couple of irregular forms.

▶ addormentarsi (to go to sleep)

PRESENT

(io)	mi addormento
(tu)	ti addormenti
(lui/lei) (lei/Lei)	si addormenta
(noi)	ci addormentiamo
(voi)	vi addormentate
(loro)	si addormentano

FUTURE

(io)	mi addormenterò
(tu)	ti addormenterai
(lui/lei) (lei/Lei)	si addormenterà
(noi)	ci addormenteremo
(voi)	vi addormenterete
(loro)	si addormenteranno

PERFECT

(io)	mi sono addormentato/a
(tu)	ti sei addormentato/a
(lui/lei) (lei/Lei)	si è addormentato/a
(noi)	ci siamo addormentati/e
(voi)	vi siete addormentati/e
(loro)	si sono addormentati/e

CONDITIONAL

(io)	mi addormenterei
(tu)	ti addormenteresti
(lui/lei) (lei/Lei)	si addormenterebbe
(noi)	ci addormenteremmo
(voi)	vi addormentereste
(loro)	si addormenterebbero

IMPERFECT

(io)	mi addormentavo
(tu)	ti addormentavi
(lui/lei) (lei/Lei)	si addormentava
(noi)	ci addormentavamo
(voi)	vi addormentavate
(loro)	si addormentavano

PRESENT SUBJUNCTIVE

(io)	mi addormenti
(tu)	ti addormenti
(lui/lei) (lei/Lei)	si addormenti
(noi)	ci addormentiamo
(voi)	vi addormentiate
(loro)	si addormentino

IMPERATIVE

addormentati
addormentiamoci
addormentatevi

PAST PARTICIPLE

addormentato

GERUND

addormentandosi

EXAMPLE PHRASES

Non voleva **addormentarsi**. *He didn't want to go to sleep.*
Mi si **è addormentato** un piede. *My foot has gone to sleep.*
Sono stanco: stasera **mi addormenterò** subito. *I'm tired: I'll go to sleep immediately tonight.*

▶ andare (to go)

PRESENT

(io)	vado
(tu)	vai
(lui/lei) (lei/Lei)	va
(noi)	andiamo
(voi)	andate
(loro)	vanno

PERFECT

(io)	sono andato/a
(tu)	sei andato/a
(lui/lei) (lei/Lei)	è andato/a
(noi)	siamo andati/e
(voi)	siete andati/e
(loro)	sono andati/e

IMPERFECT

(io)	andavo
(tu)	andavi
(lui/lei) (lei/Lei)	andava
(noi)	andavamo
(voi)	andavate
(loro)	and*a*vano

IMPERATIVE

vai
andiamo
andate

FUTURE

(io)	andrò
(tu)	andrai
(lui/lei) (lei/Lei)	andrà
(noi)	andremo
(voi)	andrete
(loro)	andranno

CONDITIONAL

(io)	andrei
(tu)	andresti
(lui/lei) (lei/Lei)	andrebbe
(noi)	andremmo
(voi)	andreste
(loro)	and*r*ebbero

PRESENT SUBJUNCTIVE

(io)	vada
(tu)	vada
(lui/lei) (lei/Lei)	vada
(noi)	andiamo
(voi)	andiate
(loro)	v*a*dano

PAST PARTICIPLE

andato

GERUND

andando

EXAMPLE PHRASES

Andremo in Grecia quest'estate. *We're going to Greece this summer.*
Su, **andiamo**! *Come on, let's go!*
Com'è **andata**? *How did it go?*
Come **va**? – bene, grazie! *How are you? – fine thanks!*
Stasera **andrei** volentieri al ristorante. *I'd like to go to a restaurant this evening.*

Italic letters in Italian words show where stress does not follow the usual rules.

▶ avere (to have)

PRESENT

(io)	ho
(tu)	hai
(lui/lei) (lei/Lei)	ha
(noi)	abbiamo
(voi)	avete
(loro)	hanno

FUTURE

(io)	avrò
(tu)	avrai
(lui/lei) (lei/Lei)	avrà
(noi)	avremo
(voi)	avrete
(loro)	avranno

PERFECT

(io)	ho avuto
(tu)	hai avuto
(lui/lei) (lei/Lei)	ha avuto
(noi)	abbiamo avuto
(voi)	avete avuto
(loro)	hanno avuto

CONDITIONAL

(io)	avrei
(tu)	avresti
(lui/lei) (lei/Lei)	avrebbe
(noi)	avremmo
(voi)	avreste
(loro)	avrebbero

IMPERFECT

(io)	avevo
(tu)	avevi
(lui/lei) (lei/Lei)	aveva
(noi)	avevamo
(voi)	avevate
(loro)	avevano

PRESENT SUBJUNCTIVE

(io)	abbia
(tu)	abbia
(lui/lei) (lei/Lei)	abbia
(noi)	abbiamo
(voi)	abbiate
(loro)	abbiano

IMPERATIVE

abbi
abbiamo
abbiate

PAST PARTICIPLE

avuto

GERUND

avendo

EXAMPLE PHRASES

All'inizio **ha avuto** un sacco di problemi. *He had a lot of problems at first.*
Ho già **mangiato**. *I've already eaten.*
Ha la macchina nuova. *She's got a new car.*
Aveva la mia età. *He was the same age as me.*
Quanti ne **abbiamo** oggi? *What's the date today?*

Remember that subject pronouns are not used very often in Italian.

▶ **bere** (to drink)

PRESENT

(io)	bevo
(tu)	bevi
(lui/lei) (lei/Lei)	beve
(noi)	beviamo
(voi)	bevete
(loro)	bevono

FUTURE

(io)	berrò
(tu)	berrai
(lui/lei) (lei/Lei)	berrà
(noi)	berremo
(voi)	berrete
(loro)	berranno

PERFECT

(io)	ho bevuto
(tu)	hai bevuto
(lui/lei) (lei/Lei)	ha bevuto
(noi)	abbiamo bevuto
(voi)	avete bevuto
(loro)	hanno bevuto

CONDITIONAL

(io)	berrei
(tu)	berresti
(lui/lei) (lei/Lei)	berrebbe
(noi)	berremmo
(voi)	berreste
(loro)	berrebbero

IMPERFECT

(io)	bevevo
(tu)	bevevi
(lui/lei) (lei/Lei)	beveva
(noi)	bevevamo
(voi)	bevevate
(loro)	bevevano

PRESENT SUBJUNCTIVE

(io)	beva
(tu)	beva
(lui/lei) (lei/Lei)	beva
(noi)	beviamo
(voi)	beviate
(loro)	bevano

IMPERATIVE

bevi
beviamo
bevete

PAST PARTICIPLE

bevuto

GERUND

bevendo

EXAMPLE PHRASES

Vuoi **bere** qualcosa? *Would you like something to drink?*
Berrei volentieri un bicchiere di vino bianco. *I'd love a glass of white wine.*
Beveva sei caffè al giorno, ma ora ha smesso. *He used to drink six cups of coffee a day, but he's stopped now.*

Italic letters in Italian words show where stress does not follow the usual rules.

▶ cadere (to fall)

PRESENT

(io)	cado
(tu)	cadi
(lui/lei) (lei/Lei)	cade
(noi)	cadiamo
(voi)	cadete
(loro)	cadono

FUTURE

(io)	cadrò
(tu)	cadrai
(lui/lei) (lei/Lei)	cadrà
(noi)	cadremo
(voi)	cadrete
(loro)	cadranno

PERFECT

(io)	sono caduto/a
(tu)	sei caduto/a
(lui/lei) (lei/Lei)	è caduto/a
(noi)	siamo caduti/e
(voi)	siete caduti/e
(loro)	sono caduti/e

CONDITIONAL

(io)	cadrei
(tu)	cadresti
(lui/lei) (lei/Lei)	cadrebbe
(noi)	cadremmo
(voi)	cadreste
(loro)	cadrebbero

IMPERFECT

(io)	cadevo
(tu)	cadevi
(lui/lei) (lei/Lei)	cadeva
(noi)	cadevamo
(voi)	cadevate
(loro)	cadevano

PRESENT SUBJUNCTIVE

(io)	cada
(tu)	cada
(lui/lei) (lei/Lei)	cada
(noi)	cadiamo
(voi)	cadiate
(loro)	cadano

IMPERATIVE

cadi
cadiamo
cadete

PAST PARTICIPLE

caduto

GERUND

cadendo

EXAMPLE PHRASES

Ho inciampato e **sono caduta**. *I tripped and fell.*
Il mio compleanno **cade** di lunedì. *My birthday is on a Monday.*
Ti **è caduta** la sciarpa. *You've dropped your scarf.*
Attento che fai **cadere** il bicchiere. *Mind you don't knock over your glass.*

Remember that subject pronouns are not used very often in Italian.

▶ capire (to understand)

PRESENT

(io)	capisco
(tu)	capisci
(lui/lei) (lei/Lei)	capisce
(noi)	capiamo
(voi)	capite
(loro)	capiscono

PERFECT

(io)	ho capito
(tu)	hai capito
(lui/lei) (lei/Lei)	ha capito
(noi)	abbiamo capito
(voi)	avete capito
(loro)	hanno capito

IMPERFECT

(io)	capivo
(tu)	capivi
(lui/lei) (lei/Lei)	capiva
(noi)	capivamo
(voi)	capivate
(loro)	capivano

IMPERATIVE

capisci
capiamo
capite

FUTURE

(io)	capirò
(tu)	capirai
(lui/lei) (lei/Lei)	capirà
(noi)	capiremo
(voi)	capirete
(loro)	capiranno

CONDITIONAL

(io)	capirei
(tu)	capiresti
(lui/lei) (lei/Lei)	capirebbe
(noi)	capiremmo
(voi)	capireste
(loro)	capirebbero

PRESENT SUBJUNCTIVE

(io)	capisca
(tu)	capisca
(lui/lei) (lei/Lei)	capisca
(noi)	capiamo
(voi)	capiate
(loro)	capiscano

PAST PARTICIPLE

capito

GERUND

capendo

EXAMPLE PHRASES

Va bene, **capisco**. *OK, I understand.*
Non **ho capito** una parola. *I didn't understand a word.*
Fammi **capire**... *Let me get this straight...*
Non ti **capirò** mai. *I'll never understand you.*

Italic letters in Italian words show where stress does not follow the usual rules.

▶ credere (to believe)

PRESENT

(io)	credo
(tu)	credi
(lui/lei) (lei/Lei)	crede
(noi)	crediamo
(voi)	credete
(loro)	credono

FUTURE

(io)	crederò
(tu)	crederai
(lui/lei) (lei/Lei)	crederà
(noi)	crederemo
(voi)	crederete
(loro)	crederanno

PERFECT

(io)	ho creduto
(tu)	hai creduto
(lui/lei) (lei/Lei)	ha creduto
(noi)	abbiamo creduto
(voi)	avete creduto
(loro)	hanno creduto

CONDITIONAL

(io)	crederei
(tu)	crederesti
(lui/lei) (lei/Lei)	crederebbe
(noi)	crederemmo
(voi)	credereste
(loro)	crederebbero

IMPERFECT

(io)	credevo
(tu)	credevi
(lui/lei) (lei/Lei)	credeva
(noi)	credevamo
(voi)	credevate
(loro)	credevano

PRESENT SUBJUNCTIVE

(io)	creda
(tu)	creda
(lui/lei) (lei/Lei)	creda
(noi)	crediamo
(voi)	crediate
(loro)	credano

IMPERATIVE

credi
crediamo
credete

PAST PARTICIPLE

creduto

GERUND

credendo

EXAMPLE PHRASES

Non dirmi che **credi** ai fantasmi! *Don't tell me you believe in ghosts!*
Non **credeva** ai suoi occhi. *She couldn't believe her eyes.*
Non ti **crederò** mai. *I'll never believe you.*

▶ **dare** (to give)

PRESENT

(io)	do
(tu)	dai
(lui/lei) (lei/Lei)	dà
(noi)	diamo
(voi)	date
(loro)	danno

FUTURE

(io)	darò
(tu)	darai
(lui/lei) (lei/Lei)	darà
(noi)	daremo
(voi)	darete
(loro)	daranno

PERFECT

(io)	ho dato
(tu)	hai dato
(lui/lei) (lei/Lei)	ha dato
(noi)	abbiamo dato
(voi)	avete dato
(loro)	hanno dato

CONDITIONAL

(io)	darei
(tu)	daresti
(lui/lei) (lei/Lei)	darebbe
(noi)	daremmo
(voi)	dareste
(loro)	darebbero

IMPERFECT

(io)	davo
(tu)	davi
(lui/lei) (lei/Lei)	dava
(noi)	davamo
(voi)	davate
(loro)	davano

PRESENT SUBJUNCTIVE

(io)	dia
(tu)	dia
(lui/lei) (lei/Lei)	dia
(noi)	diamo
(voi)	diate
(loro)	diano

IMPERATIVE

dai
diamo
date

PAST PARTICIPLE

dato

GERUND

dando

EXAMPLE PHRASES

Gli **ho dato** un libro. *I gave him a book.*
Dammelo. *Give it to me.*
La mia finestra **dà** sul giardino. *My window looks onto the garden.*
Domani sera **daranno** un bel film in tv. *There's a good film on TV tomorrow evening.*
Dandoti da fare, potresti ottenere molto di più. *If you exerted yourself you could achieve a lot more.*

Italic letters in Italian words show where stress does not follow the usual rules.

▶ **dire** (to say)

PRESENT

(io)	dico
(tu)	dici
(lui/lei) (lei/Lei)	dice
(noi)	diciamo
(voi)	dite
(loro)	dicono

PERFECT

(io)	ho detto
(tu)	hai detto
(lui/lei) (lei/Lei)	ha detto
(noi)	abbiamo detto
(voi)	avete detto
(loro)	hanno detto

IMPERFECT

(io)	dicevo
(tu)	dicevi
(lui/lei) (lei/Lei)	diceva
(noi)	dicevamo
(voi)	dicevate
(loro)	dicevano

IMPERATIVE

di'
diciamo
dite

FUTURE

(io)	dirò
(tu)	dirai
(lui/lei) (lei/Lei)	dirà
(noi)	diremo
(voi)	direte
(loro)	diranno

CONDITIONAL

(io)	direi
(tu)	diresti
(lui/lei) (lei/Lei)	direbbe
(noi)	diremmo
(voi)	direste
(loro)	direbbero

PRESENT SUBJUNCTIVE

(io)	dica
(tu)	dica
(lui/lei) (lei/Lei)	dica
(noi)	diciamo
(voi)	diciate
(loro)	dicano

PAST PARTICIPLE

detto

GERUND

dicendo

EXAMPLE PHRASES

Ha detto che verrà. *He said he'll come.*
Come si **dice** "quadro" in inglese? *How do you say "quadro" in English?*
Che ne **diresti** di andarcene? *Shall we leave?*
Ti **dirò** un segreto. *I'll tell you a secret.*
Dimmi dov'è. *Tell me where it is.*

Remember that subject pronouns are not used very often in Italian.

▶ dormire (to sleep)

PRESENT

(io)	dormo
(tu)	dormi
(lui/lei) (lei/Lei)	dorme
(noi)	dormiamo
(voi)	dormite
(loro)	dormono

PERFECT

(io)	ho dormito
(tu)	hai dormito
(lui/lei) (lei/Lei)	ha dormito
(noi)	abbiamo dormito
(voi)	avete dormito
(loro)	hanno dormito

IMPERFECT

(io)	dormivo
(tu)	dormivi
(lui/lei) (lei/Lei)	dormiva
(noi)	dormivamo
(voi)	dormivate
(loro)	dormivano

IMPERATIVE

dormi
dormiamo
dormite

FUTURE

(io)	dormirò
(tu)	dormirai
(lui/lei) (lei/Lei)	dormirà
(noi)	dormiremo
(voi)	dormirete
(loro)	dormiranno

CONDITIONAL

(io)	dormirei
(tu)	dormiresti
(lui/lei) (lei/Lei)	dormirebbe
(noi)	dormiremmo
(voi)	dormireste
(loro)	dormirebbero

PRESENT SUBJUNCTIVE

(io)	dorma
(tu)	dorma
(lui/lei) (lei/Lei)	dorma
(noi)	dormiamo
(voi)	dormiate
(loro)	dormano

PAST PARTICIPLE

dormito

GERUND

dormendo

EXAMPLE PHRASES

Sta dormendo. *She's sleeping.*
Vado a **dormire**. *I'm going to bed.*
Stanotte **dormirò** come un ghiro. *I'll sleep like a log tonight.*

Italic letters in Italian words show where stress does not follow the usual rules.

▶ **dovere** (to have to)

PRESENT		FUTURE	
(io)	devo	(io)	dovrò
(tu)	devi	(tu)	dovrai
(lui/lei) (lei/Lei)	deve	(lui/lei) (lei/Lei)	dovrà
(noi)	dobbiamo	(noi)	dovremo
(voi)	dovete	(voi)	dovrete
(loro)	devono	(loro)	dovranno

PERFECT		CONDITIONAL	
(io)	ho dovuto	(io)	dovrei
(tu)	hai dovuto	(tu)	dovresti
(lui/lei) (lei/Lei)	ha dovuto	(lui/lei) (lei/Lei)	dovrebbe
(noi)	abbiamo dovuto	(noi)	dovremmo
(voi)	avete dovuto	(voi)	dovreste
(loro)	hanno dovuto	(loro)	dovrebbero

IMPERFECT		PRESENT SUBJUNCTIVE	
(io)	dovevo	(io)	debba
(tu)	dovevi	(tu)	debba
(lui/lei) (lei/Lei)	doveva	(lui/lei) (lei/Lei)	debba
(noi)	dovevamo	(noi)	dobbiamo
(voi)	dovevate	(voi)	dobbiate
(loro)	dovevano	(loro)	debbano

IMPERATIVE
–

PAST PARTICIPLE
dovuto

GERUND
dovendo

EXAMPLE PHRASES

È **dovuto** partire. *He had to leave.*
Devi finire i compiti prima di uscire. *You must finish your homework before you go out.*
Dev'essere tardi. *It must be late.*
Dovrebbe arrivare alle dieci. *He should arrive at ten.*
Gli **dovevo** 30 euro e così l'ho invitato a cena. *I owed him 30 euros so I took him out to dinner.*

Remember that subject pronouns are not used very often in Italian.

▶ **essere** (to be)

PRESENT

(io)	sono
(tu)	sei
(lui/lei) (lei/Lei)	è
(noi)	siamo
(voi)	siete
(loro)	sono

FUTURE

(io)	sarò
(tu)	sarai
(lui/lei) (lei/Lei)	sarà
(noi)	saremo
(voi)	sarete
(loro)	saranno

PERFECT

(io)	sono stato/a
(tu)	sei stato/a
(lui/lei) (lei/Lei)	è stato/a
(noi)	siamo stati/e
(voi)	siete stati/e
(loro)	sono stati/e

CONDITIONAL

(io)	sarei
(tu)	saresti
(lui/lei) (lei/Lei)	sarebbe
(noi)	saremmo
(voi)	sareste
(loro)	sarebbero

IMPERFECT

(io)	ero
(tu)	eri
(lui/lei) (lei/Lei)	era
(noi)	eravamo
(voi)	eravate
(loro)	erano

PRESENT SUBJUNCTIVE

(io)	sia
(tu)	sia
(lui/lei) (lei/Lei)	sia
(noi)	siamo
(voi)	siate
(loro)	siano

IMPERATIVE

sii
siamo
siate

PAST PARTICIPLE

stato

GERUND

essendo

EXAMPLE PHRASES

Sono italiana. *I'm Italian.*
Mario **è** appena partito. *Mario has just left.*
Siete mai **stati** in Africa? *Have you ever been to Africa?*
Quando **è** arrivato erano le quattro in punto. *It was exactly four o'clock when he arrived.*
Alla festa ci **saranno** tutti i miei amici. *All my friends will be at the party.*

Italic letters in Italian words show where stress does not follow the usual rules.

▶ **fare** (to do; make)

PRESENT

(io)	faccio
(tu)	fai
(lui/lei)(lei/Lei)	fa
(noi)	facciamo
(voi)	fate
(loro)	fanno

FUTURE

(io)	farò
(tu)	farai
(lui/lei)(lei/Lei)	farò
(noi)	faremo
(voi)	farete
(loro)	faranno

PERFECT

(io)	ho fatto
(tu)	hai fatto
(lui/lei)(lei/Lei)	ha fatto
(noi)	abbiamo fatto
(voi)	avete fatto
(loro)	hanno fatto

CONDITIONAL

(io)	farei
(tu)	faresti
(lui/lei)(lei/Lei)	farebbe
(noi)	faremmo
(voi)	fareste
(loro)	farebbero

IMPERFECT

(io)	facevo
(tu)	facevi
(lui/lei)(lei/Lei)	faceva
(noi)	facevamo
(voi)	facevate
(loro)	facevano

PRESENT SUBJUNCTIVE

(io)	faccia
(tu)	faccia
(lui/lei)(lei/Lei)	faccia
(noi)	facciamo
(voi)	facciate
(loro)	facciano

IMPERATIVE

fai
facciamo
fate

PAST PARTICIPLE

fatto

GERUND

facendo

EXAMPLE PHRASES

Ho fatto un errore. *I made a mistake.*
Due più due **fa** quattro. *Two and two makes four.*
Cosa **stai facendo**? *What are you doing?*
Fa il medico. *He is a doctor.*
Fa caldo. *It's hot.*

Remember that subject pronouns are not used very often in Italian.

▶ **mettere** (to put)

PRESENT

(io)	metto
(tu)	metti
(lui/lei) (lei/Lei)	mette
(noi)	mettiamo
(voi)	mettete
(loro)	mettono

PERFECT

(io)	ho messo
(tu)	hai messo
(lui/lei) (lei/Lei)	ha messo
(noi)	abbiamo messo
(voi)	avete messo
(loro)	hanno messo

IMPERFECT

(io)	mettevo
(tu)	mettevi
(lui/lei) (lei/Lei)	metteva
(noi)	mettevamo
(voi)	mettevate
(loro)	mettevano

IMPERATIVE

metti
mettiamo
mettete

FUTURE

(io)	metterò
(tu)	metterai
(lui/lei) (lei/Lei)	metterà
(noi)	metteremo
(voi)	metterete
(loro)	metteranno

CONDITIONAL

(io)	metterei
(tu)	metteresti
(lui/lei) (lei/Lei)	metterebbe
(noi)	metteremmo
(voi)	mettereste
(loro)	metterebbero

PRESENT SUBJUNCTIVE

(io)	metta
(tu)	metta
(lui/lei) (lei/Lei)	metta
(noi)	mettiamo
(voi)	mettiate
(loro)	mettano

PAST PARTICIPLE

messo

GERUND

mettendo

EXAMPLE PHRASES

Hai messo i bambini a letto? *Have you put the children to bed?*
Metterò un annuncio sul giornale. *I'll put an advert in the paper.*
Mettiti là e aspetta. *Wait there.*
Quanto tempo ci **hai messo**? *How long did it take you?*
Non **metto** più quelle scarpe. *I don't wear those shoes any more.*

Italic letters in Italian words show where stress does not follow the usual rules.

▶ parere (to appear)

PRESENT

(io)	paio
(tu)	pari
(lui/lei) (lei/Lei)	pare
(noi)	pariamo
(voi)	parete
(loro)	paiono

PERFECT

(io)	sono parso/a
(tu)	sei parso/a
(lui/lei) (lei/Lei)	è parso/a
(noi)	siamo parsi/e
(voi)	siete parsi/e
(loro)	sono parsi/e

IMPERFECT

(io)	parevo
(tu)	parevi
(lui/lei) (lei/Lei)	pareva
(noi)	parevamo
(voi)	parevate
(loro)	parevano

IMPERATIVE

pari
pariamo
parete

FUTURE

(io)	parrò
(tu)	parrai
(lui/lei) (lei/Lei)	parrà
(noi)	parremo
(voi)	parrete
(loro)	parranno

CONDITIONAL

(io)	parrei
(tu)	parresti
(lui/lei) (lei/Lei)	parrebbe
(noi)	parremmo
(voi)	parreste
(loro)	parrebbero

PRESENT SUBJUNCTIVE

(io)	paia
(tu)	paia
(lui/lei) (lei/Lei)	paia
(noi)	paiamo
(voi)	paiate
(loro)	paiano

PAST PARTICIPLE

parso

GERUND

parendo

EXAMPLE PHRASES

Mi **pare** che sia già arrivato. *I think he's already here.*
Ci **è parso** che foste stanchi. *We thought you were tired.*
Faceva solo ciò che gli **pareva**. *He did just what he wanted.*

Remember that subject pronouns are not used very often in Italian.

▶ parlare (to speak)

PRESENT

(io)	parlo
(tu)	parli
(lui/lei) (lei/Lei)	parla
(noi)	parliamo
(voi)	parlate
(loro)	parlano

FUTURE

(io)	parlerò
(tu)	parlerai
(lui/lei) (lei/Lei)	parlerà
(noi)	parleremo
(voi)	parlerete
(loro)	parleranno

PERFECT

(io)	ho parlato
(tu)	hai parlato
(lui/lei) (lei/Lei)	ha parlato
(noi)	abbiamo parlato
(voi)	avete parlato
(loro)	hanno parlato

CONDITIONAL

(io)	parlerei
(tu)	parleresti
(lui/lei) (lei/Lei)	parlerebbe
(noi)	parleremmo
(voi)	parlereste
(loro)	parlerebbero

IMPERFECT

(io)	parlavo
(tu)	parlavi
(lui/lei) (lei/Lei)	parlava
(noi)	parlavamo
(voi)	parlavate
(loro)	parlavano

PRESENT SUBJUNCTIVE

(io)	parli
(tu)	parli
(lui/lei) (lei/Lei)	parli
(noi)	parliamo
(voi)	parliate
(loro)	parlino

IMPERATIVE

parla
parliamo
parlate

PAST PARTICIPLE

parlato

GERUND

parlando

EXAMPLE PHRASES

Pronto, chi **parla**? *Hello, who's speaking?*
Non **parliamone** più. *Let's just forget about it.*
Abbiamo parlato per ore. *We talked for hours.*
Gli **parlerò** di te. *I'll talk to him about you.*
Di cosa **parla** quel libro? *What is that book about?*

Italic letters in Italian words show where stress does not follow the usual rules.

▶ **piacere** (to be pleasing)

PRESENT

(io)	piaccio
(tu)	piaci
(lui/lei)(lei/Lei)	piace
(noi)	piacciamo
(voi)	piacete
(loro)	piacciono

PERFECT

(io)	sono piaciuto/a
(tu)	sei piaciuto/a
(lui/lei)(lei/Lei)	è piaciuto/a
(noi)	siamo piaciuti/e
(voi)	siete piaciuti/e
(loro)	sono piaciuti/e

IMPERFECT

(io)	piacevo
(tu)	piacevi
(lui/lei)(lei/Lei)	piaceva
(noi)	piacevamo
(voi)	piacevate
(loro)	piacevano

IMPERATIVE

piaci
piacciamo
piacciate

FUTURE

(io)	piacerò
(tu)	piacerai
(lui/lei)(lei/Lei)	piacerà
(noi)	piaceremo
(voi)	piacerete
(loro)	piaceranno

CONDITIONAL

(io)	piacerei
(tu)	piaceresti
(lui/lei)(lei/Lei)	piacerebbe
(noi)	piaceremmo
(voi)	piacereste
(loro)	piacerebbero

PRESENT SUBJUNCTIVE

(io)	piaccia
(tu)	piaccia
(lui/lei)(lei/Lei)	piaccia
(noi)	piacciamo
(voi)	piacciate
(loro)	piacciano

PAST PARTICIPLE

piaciuto

GERUND

piacendo

EXAMPLE PHRASES

Questa musica non **mi piace**. *I don't like this music.*
Cosa **ti piacerebbe** fare? *What would you like to do?*
Da piccola non **mi piacevano** i ragni. *When I was little I didn't like spiders.*

Remember that subject pronouns are not used very often in Italian.

▶ **potere** (to be able)

PRESENT

(io) posso
(tu) puoi
(lui/lei)
(lei/Lei) può
(noi) possiamo
(voi) potete
(loro) possono

PERFECT

(io) ho potuto
(tu) hai potuto
(lui/lei)
(lei/Lei) ha potuto
(noi) abbiamo potuto
(voi) avete potuto
(loro) hanno potuto

IMPERFECT

(io) potevo
(tu) potevi
(lui/lei)
(lei/Lei) poteva
(noi) potevamo
(voi) potevate
(loro) potevano

IMPERATIVE

–

FUTURE

(io) potrò
(tu) potrai
(lui/lei)
(lei/Lei) potrà
(noi) potremo
(voi) potrete
(loro) potranno

CONDITIONAL

(io) potrei
(tu) potresti
(lui/lei)
(lei/Lei) potrebbe
(noi) potremmo
(voi) potreste
(loro) potrebbero

PRESENT SUBJUNCTIVE

(io) possa
(tu) possa
(lui/lei)
(lei/Lei) possa
(noi) possiamo
(voi) possiate
(loro) possano

PAST PARTICIPLE

potuto

GERUND

potendo

EXAMPLE PHRASES

Si **può** visitare il castello tutti i giorni dell'anno. *You can visit the castle any day of the year.*
Non **è potuto** venire. *He couldn't come.*
Non **potrò** venire domani. *I won't be able to come tomorrow.*
Può aver avuto un incidente. *He may have had an accident.*
Potrebbe essere vero. *It could be true.*

Italic letters in Italian words show where stress does not follow the usual rules.

▶ prendere (to take)

PRESENT

(io)	prendo
(tu)	prendi
(lui/lei) (lei/Lei)	prende
(noi)	prendiamo
(voi)	prendete
(loro)	prendono

FUTURE

(io)	prenderò
(tu)	prenderai
(lui/lei) (lei/Lei)	prenderà
(noi)	prenderemo
(voi)	prenderete
(loro)	prenderanno

PERFECT

(io)	ho preso
(tu)	hai preso
(lui/lei) (lei/Lei)	ha preso
(noi)	abbiamo preso
(voi)	avete preso
(loro)	hanno preso

CONDITIONAL

(io)	prenderei
(tu)	prenderesti
(lui/lei) (lei/Lei)	prenderebbe
(noi)	prenderemmo
(voi)	prendereste
(loro)	prenderebbero

IMPERFECT

(io)	prendevo
(tu)	prendevi
(lui/lei) (lei/Lei)	prendeva
(noi)	prendevamo
(voi)	prendevate
(loro)	prendevano

PRESENT SUBJUNCTIVE

(io)	prenda
(tu)	prenda
(lui/lei) (lei/Lei)	prenda
(noi)	prendiamo
(voi)	prendiate
(loro)	prendano

IMPERATIVE

prendi
prendiamo
prendete

PAST PARTICIPLE

preso

GERUND

prendendo

EXAMPLE PHRASES

Prendi quella borsa. *Take that bag.*
Ho preso un bel voto. *I got a good mark.*
Prende qualcosa da bere? *Would you like something to drink?*
Per chi mi **prendi**? *Who do you think I am?*

Remember that subject pronouns are not used very often in Italian.

▶ rimanere (to stay)

PRESENT

(io)	rimango
(tu)	rimani
(lui/lei) (lei/Lei)	rimane
(noi)	rimaniamo
(voi)	rimanete
(loro)	rimangono

PERFECT

(io)	sono rimasto/a
(tu)	sei rimasto/a
(lui/lei) (lei/Lei)	è rimasto/a
(noi)	siamo rimasti/e
(voi)	siete rimasti/e
(loro)	sono rimasti/e

IMPERFECT

(io)	rimanevo
(tu)	rimanevi
(lui/lei) (lei/Lei)	rimaneva
(noi)	rimanevamo
(voi)	rimanevate
(loro)	rimanevano

IMPERATIVE

rimani
rimaniamo
rimanete

FUTURE

(io)	rimarrò
(tu)	rimarrai
(lui/lei) (lei/Lei)	rimarrà
(noi)	rimarremo
(voi)	rimarrete
(loro)	rimarranno

CONDITIONAL

(io)	rimarrei
(tu)	rimarresti
(lui/lei) (lei/Lei)	rimarrebbe
(noi)	rimarremmo
(voi)	rimarreste
(loro)	rimarrebbero

PRESENT SUBJUNCTIVE

(io)	rimanga
(tu)	rimanga
(lui/lei) (lei/Lei)	rimanga
(noi)	rimaniamo
(voi)	rimaniate
(loro)	rimangano

PAST PARTICIPLE

rimasto

GERUND

rimanendo

EXAMPLE PHRASES

Sono rimasto a casa tutto il giorno. *I stayed at home all day.*
Mi piacerebbe **rimanere** qualche altro giorno. *I'd like to stay a few more days.*
Ci **rimarrebbero** molto male. *They'd be very upset.*

Italic letters in Italian words show where stress does not follow the usual rules.

▶ **sapere** (to know)

PRESENT

(io)	so
(tu)	sai
(lui/lei) (lei/Lei)	sa
(noi)	sappiamo
(voi)	sapete
(loro)	sanno

FUTURE

(io)	saprò
(tu)	saprai
(lui/lei) (lei/Lei)	saprà
(noi)	sapremo
(voi)	saprete
(loro)	sapranno

PERFECT

(io)	ho saputo
(tu)	hai saputo
(lui/lei) (lei/Lei)	ha saputo
(noi)	abbiamo saputo
(voi)	avete saputo
(loro)	hanno saputo

CONDITIONAL

(io)	saprei
(tu)	sapresti
(lui/lei) (lei/Lei)	saprebbe
(noi)	sapremmo
(voi)	sapreste
(loro)	saprebbero

IMPERFECT

(io)	sapevo
(tu)	sapevi
(lui/lei) (lei/Lei)	sapeva
(noi)	sapevamo
(voi)	sapevate
(loro)	sapevano

PRESENT SUBJUNCTIVE

(io)	sappia
(tu)	sappia
(lui/lei) (lei/Lei)	sappia
(noi)	sappiamo
(voi)	sappiate
(loro)	sappiano

IMPERATIVE
sappi
sappiamo
sappiate

PAST PARTICIPLE
saputo

GERUND
sapendo

EXAMPLE PHRASES

Sai dove abita? *Do you know where he lives?*
Non **sapeva** andare in bicicletta. *He couldn't ride a bike.*
Sa di fragola. *It tastes of strawberries.*

Remember that subject pronouns are not used very often in Italian.

▶ **scegliere** (to choose)

PRESENT

(io)	scelgo
(tu)	scegli
(lui/lei) (lei/Lei)	sceglie
(noi)	scegliamo
(voi)	scegliete
(loro)	scelgono

PERFECT

(io)	ho scelto
(tu)	hai scelto
(lui/lei) (lei/Lei)	ha scelto
(noi)	abbiamo scelto
(voi)	avete scelto
(loro)	hanno scelto

IMPERFECT

(io)	sceglievo
(tu)	sceglievi
(lui/lei) (lei/Lei)	sceglieva
(noi)	sceglievamo
(voi)	sceglievate
(loro)	sceglievano

IMPERATIVE

scegli
scegliamo
scegliete

FUTURE

(io)	sceglierò
(tu)	sceglierai
(lui/lei) (lei/Lei)	sceglierà
(noi)	sceglieremo
(voi)	sceglierete
(loro)	sceglieranno

CONDITIONAL

(io)	sceglierei
(tu)	sceglieresti
(lui/lei) (lei/Lei)	sceglierebbe
(noi)	sceglieremmo
(voi)	scegliereste
(loro)	sceglierebbero

PRESENT SUBJUNCTIVE

(io)	scelga
(tu)	scelga
(lui/lei) (lei/Lei)	scelga
(noi)	scegliamo
(voi)	scegliate
(loro)	scelgano

PAST PARTICIPLE

scelto

GERUND

scegliendo

EXAMPLE PHRASES

Chi **sceglie** il vino? *Who's going to choose the wine?*
Hai scelto il regalo per lei? *Have you chosen her present?*
Sceglievano sempre il vino più costoso. *They always chose the most expensive wine.*
Scegli la pizza che vuoi. *Choose which pizza you want.*
Non sa ancora quale abito **sceglierà**. *She hasn't decided yet which dress she'll choose.*
Stavo **scegliendo** le pesche più mature. *I was choosing the ripest peaches.*

Italic letters in Italian words show where stress does not follow the usual rules.

▶ **sedere** (to sit)

PRESENT

(io)	siedo
(tu)	siedi
(lui/lei) (lei/Lei)	siede
(noi)	sediamo
(voi)	sedete
(loro)	siedono

PERFECT

(io)	sono seduto/a
(tu)	sei seduto/a
(lui/lei) (lei/Lei)	è seduto/a
(noi)	siamo seduti/e
(voi)	siete seduti/e
(loro)	sono seduti/e

IMPERFECT

(io)	sedevo
(tu)	sedevi
(lui/lei) (lei/Lei)	sedeva
(noi)	sedevamo
(voi)	sedevate
(loro)	sedevano

IMPERATIVE

siedi
sediamo
sedete

FUTURE

(io)	sederò
(tu)	sederai
(lui/lei) (lei/Lei)	sederà
(noi)	sederemo
(voi)	sederete
(loro)	sederanno

CONDITIONAL

(io)	sederei
(tu)	sederesti
(lui/lei) (lei/Lei)	sederebbe
(noi)	sederemmo
(voi)	sedereste
(loro)	sederebbero

PRESENT SUBJUNCTIVE

(io)	sieda
(tu)	sieda
(lui/lei) (lei/Lei)	sieda
(noi)	sediamo
(voi)	sediate
(loro)	siedano

PAST PARTICIPLE

seduto

GERUND

sedendo

EXAMPLE PHRASES

Era seduta accanto a me. *She was sitting beside me.*
Si **è seduto** per terra. *He sat on the floor.*
Siediti qui! *Sit here!*

Remember that subject pronouns are not used very often in Italian.

▶ spegnere (to put out)

PRESENT

(io)	spengo
(tu)	spegni
(lui/lei) (lei/Lei)	spegne
(noi)	spegniamo
(voi)	spegnete
(loro)	spengono

FUTURE

(io)	spegnerò
(tu)	spegnerai
(lui/lei) (lei/Lei)	spegnerà
(noi)	spegneremo
(voi)	spegnerete
(loro)	spegneranno

PERFECT

(io)	ho spento
(tu)	hai spento
(lui/lei) (lei/Lei)	ha spento
(noi)	abbiamo spento
(voi)	avete spento
(loro)	hanno spento

CONDITIONAL

(io)	spegnerei
(tu)	spegneresti
(lui/lei) (lei/Lei)	spegnerebbe
(noi)	spegneremmo
(voi)	spegnereste
(loro)	spegnerebbero

IMPERFECT

(io)	spegnevo
(tu)	spegnevi
(lui/lei) (lei/Lei)	spegneva
(noi)	spegnevamo
(voi)	spegnevate
(loro)	spegnevano

PRESENT SUBJUNCTIVE

(io)	spenga
(tu)	spenga
(lui/lei) (lei/Lei)	spenga
(noi)	spegniamo
(voi)	spegniate
(loro)	spengano

IMPERATIVE

spegni
spegniamo
spegnete

PAST PARTICIPLE

spento

GERUND

spegnendo

EXAMPLE PHRASES

Hai spento la sigaretta? *Have you put your cigarette out?*
Spegnete le luci che guardiamo il film. *Turn off the lights and we'll watch the film.*
La luce si **è spenta** all'improvviso. *The light went off suddenly.*

Italic letters in Italian words show where stress does not follow the usual rules.

▶ stare (to be)

PRESENT

(io)	sto
(tu)	stai
(lui/lei) (lei/Lei)	sta
(noi)	stiamo
(voi)	state
(loro)	stanno

PERFECT

(io)	sono stato/a
(tu)	sei stato/a
(lui/lei) (lei/Lei)	è stato/a
(noi)	siamo stati/e
(voi)	siete stati/e
(loro)	sono stati/e

IMPERFECT

(io)	stavo
(tu)	stavi
(lui/lei) (lei/Lei)	stava
(noi)	stavamo
(voi)	stavate
(loro)	stavano

IMPERATIVE

stai
stiamo
state

FUTURE

(io)	starò
(tu)	starai
(lui/lei) (lei/Lei)	starà
(noi)	staremo
(voi)	starete
(loro)	staranno

CONDITIONAL

(io)	starei
(tu)	staresti
(lui/lei) (lei/Lei)	starebbe
(noi)	staremmo
(voi)	stareste
(loro)	starebbero

PRESENT SUBJUNCTIVE

(io)	stia
(tu)	stia
(lui/lei) (lei/Lei)	stia
(noi)	stiamo
(voi)	stiate
(loro)	stiano

PAST PARTICIPLE

stato

GERUND

stando

EXAMPLE PHRASES

Sei mai **stato** in Francia? *Have you ever been to France?*
Come **stai**? *How are you?*
Stavo andando a casa. *I was going home.*
A Londra **starò** da amici. *I'll be staying with friends in London.*
Stavo per uscire quando ha squillato il telefono. *I was about to go out when the phone rang.*

Remember that subject pronouns are not used very often in Italian.

▶ tenere (to hold)

PRESENT

(io)	tengo
(tu)	tieni
(lui/lei) (lei/Lei)	tiene
(noi)	teniamo
(voi)	tenete
(loro)	tengono

FUTURE

(io)	terrò
(tu)	terrai
(lui/lei) (lei/Lei)	terrà
(noi)	terremo
(voi)	terrete
(loro)	terranno

PERFECT

(io)	ho tenuto
(tu)	hai tenuto
(lui/lei) (lei/Lei)	ha tenuto
(noi)	abbiamo tenuto
(voi)	avete tenuto
(loro)	hanno tenuto

CONDITIONAL

(io)	terrei
(tu)	terresti
(lui/lei) (lei/Lei)	terrebbe
(noi)	terremmo
(voi)	terreste
(loro)	terrebbero

IMPERFECT

(io)	tenevo
(tu)	tenevi
(lui/lei) (lei/Lei)	teneva
(noi)	tenevamo
(voi)	tenevate
(loro)	tenevano

PRESENT SUBJUNCTIVE

(io)	tenga
(tu)	tenga
(lui/lei) (lei/Lei)	tenga
(noi)	teniamo
(voi)	teniate
(loro)	tengano

IMPERATIVE

tieni
teniamo
tenete

PAST PARTICIPLE

tenuto

GERUND

tenendo

EXAMPLE PHRASES

Tiene la racchetta con la sinistra. *He holds the racket with his left hand.*
Tieniti forte! *Hold on tight!*
Si **tenevano** per mano. *They were holding hands.*
Tieniti pronta per le cinque. *Be ready by five.*
Tieni, questo è per te. *Here, this is for you*

Italic letters in Italian words show where stress does not follow the usual rules.

▶ **uscire** (to go out)

PRESENT

(io)	esco
(tu)	esci
(lui/lei) (lei/Lei)	esce
(noi)	usciamo
(voi)	uscite
(loro)	escono

FUTURE

(io)	uscirò
(tu)	uscirai
(lui/lei) (lei/Lei)	uscirà
(noi)	usciremo
(voi)	uscirete
(loro)	usciranno

PERFECT

(io)	sono uscito/a
(tu)	sei uscito/a
(lui/lei) (lei/Lei)	è uscito/a
(noi)	siamo usciti/e
(voi)	siete usciti/e
(loro)	sono usciti/e

CONDITIONAL

(io)	uscirei
(tu)	usciresti
(lui/lei) (lei/Lei)	uscirebbe
(noi)	usciremmo
(voi)	uscireste
(loro)	uscirebbero

IMPERFECT

(io)	uscivo
(tu)	uscivi
(lui/lei) (lei/Lei)	usciva
(noi)	uscivamo
(voi)	uscivate
(loro)	uscivano

PRESENT SUBJUNCTIVE

(io)	esca
(tu)	esca
(lui/lei) (lei/Lei)	esca
(noi)	usciamo
(voi)	usciate
(loro)	escano

IMPERATIVE

esci
usciamo
uscite

PAST PARTICIPLE

uscito

GERUND

uscendo

EXAMPLE PHRASES

È uscita a comprare il giornale. *She's gone out to buy a newspaper.*
Uscirà dall'ospedale domani. *He's coming out of hospital tomorrow.*
L'ho incontrata che **usciva** dalla farmacia. *I met her coming out of the chemist's.*
La rivista **esce** di lunedì. *The magazine comes out on Mondays.*

Remember that subject pronouns are not used very often in Italian.

▶ **valere** (to be worth)

PRESENT

(io)	valgo
(tu)	vali
(lui/lei) (lei/Lei)	vale
(noi)	valiamo
(voi)	valete
(loro)	valgono

FUTURE

(io)	varrò
(tu)	varrai
(lui/lei) (lei/Lei)	varrà
(noi)	varremo
(voi)	varrete
(loro)	varranno

PERFECT

(io)	sono valso/a
(tu)	sei valso/a
(lui/lei) (lei/Lei)	è valso/a
(noi)	siamo valsi/e
(voi)	siete valsi/e
(loro)	sono valsi/e

CONDITIONAL

(io)	varrei
(tu)	varresti
(lui/lei) (lei/Lei)	varrebbe
(noi)	varremmo
(voi)	varreste
(loro)	varrebbero

IMPERFECT

(io)	valevo
(tu)	valevi
(lui/lei) (lei/Lei)	valeva
(noi)	valevamo
(voi)	valevate
(loro)	valevano

PRESENT SUBJUNCTIVE

(io)	valga
(tu)	valga
(lui/lei) (lei/Lei)	valga
(noi)	valiamo
(voi)	valiate
(loro)	valgano

IMPERATIVE

vali
valiamo
valete

PAST PARTICIPLE

valso

GERUND

valendo

EXAMPLE PHRASES

L'auto **vale** tremila euro. *The car is worth three thousand euros.*
Non ne **vale** la pena. *It's not worth it.*
Senza il giardino, la casa non **varrebbe** niente. *Without the garden the house wouldn't be worth anything.*

Italic letters in Italian words show where stress does not follow the usual rules.

▶ vedere (to see)

PRESENT		FUTURE	
(io)	vedo	(io)	vedrò
(tu)	vedi	(tu)	vedrai
(lui/lei) (lei/Lei)	vede	(lui/lei) (lei/Lei)	vedrà
(noi)	vediamo	(noi)	vedremo
(voi)	vedete	(voi)	vedrete
(loro)	vedono	(loro)	vedranno

PERFECT		CONDITIONAL	
(io)	ho visto	(io)	vedrei
(tu)	hai visto	(tu)	vedresti
(lui/lei) (lei/Lei)	ha visto	(lui/lei) (lei/Lei)	vedrebbe
(noi)	abbiamo visto	(noi)	vedremmo
(voi)	avete visto	(voi)	vedreste
(loro)	hanno visto	(loro)	vedrebbero

IMPERFECT		PRESENT SUBJUNCTIVE	
(io)	vedevo	(io)	veda
(tu)	vedevi	(tu)	veda
(lui/lei) (lei/Lei)	vedeva	(lui/lei) (lei/Lei)	veda
(noi)	vedevamo	(noi)	vediamo
(voi)	vedevate	(voi)	vediate
(loro)	vedevano	(loro)	vedano

IMPERATIVE
vedi
vediamo
vedete

PAST PARTICIPLE
visto

GERUND
vedendo

EXAMPLE PHRASES

Non ci **vedo** senza occhiali. *I can't see without my glasses.*
Ci **vediamo** domani! *See you tomorrow!*
Non **vedevo** l'ora di conoscerlo. *I couldn't wait to meet him.*

Remember that subject pronouns are not used very often in Italian.

▶ venire (to come)

PRESENT

(io)	vengo
(tu)	vieni
(lui/lei) (lei/Lei)	viene
(noi)	veniamo
(voi)	venite
(loro)	vengono

PERFECT

(io)	sono venuto/a
(tu)	sei venuto/a
(lui/lei) (lei/Lei)	è venuto/a
(noi)	siamo venuti/e
(voi)	siete venuti/e
(loro)	sono venuti/e

IMPERFECT

(io)	venivo
(tu)	venivi
(lui/lei) (lei/Lei)	veniva
(noi)	venivamo
(voi)	venivate
(loro)	venivano

IMPERATIVE

vieni
veniamo
venite

FUTURE

(io)	verrò
(tu)	verrai
(lui/lei) (lei/Lei)	verrà
(noi)	verremo
(voi)	verrete
(loro)	verranno

CONDITIONAL

(io)	verrei
(tu)	verresti
(lui/lei) (lei/Lei)	verrebbe
(noi)	verremmo
(voi)	verreste
(loro)	verrebbero

PRESENT SUBJUNCTIVE

(io)	venga
(tu)	venga
(lui/lei) (lei/Lei)	venga
(noi)	veniamo
(voi)	veniate
(loro)	vengano

PAST PARTICIPLE

venuto

GERUND

venendo

EXAMPLE PHRASES

È venuto in macchina. *He came by car.*
Da dove **vieni**? *Where do you come from?*
Vieni a trovarci. *Come and see us!*
Quanto **viene**? *How much is it?*

Italic letters in Italian words show where stress does not follow the usual rules.

▶ volere (to want)

PRESENT

(io)	voglio
(tu)	vuoi
(lui/lei) (lei/Lei)	vuole
(noi)	vogliamo
(voi)	volete
(loro)	vogliono

FUTURE

(io)	vorrò
(tu)	vorrai
(lui/lei) (lei/Lei)	vorrà
(noi)	vorremo
(voi)	vorrete
(loro)	vorranno

PERFECT

(io)	ho voluto
(tu)	hai voluto
(lui/lei) (lei/Lei)	ha voluto
(noi)	abbiamo voluto
(voi)	avete voluto
(loro)	hanno voluto

CONDITIONAL

(io)	vorrei
(tu)	vorresti
(lui/lei) (lei/Lei)	vorrebbe
(noi)	vorremmo
(voi)	vorreste
(loro)	vorrebbero

IMPERFECT

(io)	volevo
(tu)	volevi
(lui/lei) (lei/Lei)	voleva
(noi)	volevamo
(voi)	volevate
(loro)	volevano

PRESENT SUBJUNCTIVE

(io)	voglia
(tu)	voglia
(lui/lei) (lei/Lei)	voglia
(noi)	vogliamo
(voi)	vogliate
(loro)	vogliano

IMPERATIVE

–

PAST PARTICIPLE

voluto

GERUND

volendo

EXAMPLE PHRASES

Voglio comprare una macchina nuova. *I want to buy a new car.*

Devo pagare subito o posso pagare domani? – Come **vuole**. *Do I have to pay now or can I pay tomorrow? – As you prefer.*

Quanto ci **vorrà** prima che finiate? *How long will it take you to finish?*

La campanella **voleva** dire che la lezione era finita. *The bell meant that the lesson was over.*

Anche **volendo** non posso invitarti: la festa è sua. *I'd like to, but I can't invite you: it's his party.*

Remember that subject pronouns are not used very often in Italian.

Collins

MORE THAN
TWO MILLION
EASY LEARNING
BOOKS SOLD

BESTSELLING
BILINGUAL
DICTIONARIES

easy learning Italian

Easy Learning Italian Dictionary
978-0-00-753093-9   £10.99

Easy Learning Italian Conversation
978-0-00-811199-1   £8.99

Easy Learning Italian Grammar
978-0-00-814202-5   £7.99

Easy Learning Italian Verbs
978-0-00-815844-6   £7.99

Easy Learning Italian Vocabulary
978-0-00-748394-5   £9.99

Easy Learning Complete Italian Grammar, Verbs and Vocabulary
(3 books in 1) 978-0-00-814175-2   £14.99

Easy Learning Italian Grammar & Practice
978-0-00-814166-0   £10.99

Available to buy from all good booksellers and online.
Many titles are also available as ebooks.
www.collins.co.uk/languagesupport

facebook.com/collinsdictionary

@collinsdict

Collins

easy learning French

Easy Learning French Dictionary
978-0-00-753096-0 £9.99

Easy Learning French Conversation
978-0-00-811198-4 £7.99

Easy Learning French Grammar
978-0-00-814199-8 £7.99

Easy Learning French Verbs
978-0-00-815841-5 £7.99

Easy Learning French Vocabulary
978-0-00-748391-4 £9.99

Easy Learning French Idioms
978-0-00-733735-4 £6.99

Easy Learning Complete French Grammar, Verbs and Vocabulary
(3 books in 1) 978-0-00-814172-1 £14.99

Easy Learning French Grammar & Practice
978-0-00-814163-9 £9.99

Easy Learning French Verbs & Practice
978-0-00-814208-7 £10.99

Available to buy from all good booksellers and online.
Many titles are also available as ebooks.
www.collins.co.uk/languagesupport

facebook.com/collinsdictionary

@collinsdict